Advanced
Language & Literature

For Honors and Pre-AP® English Courses

Advanced
Language & Literature

For Honors and Pre-AP® English Courses

Renée H. Shea
Bowie State University,
Maryland

John Golden
Cleveland High School,
Portland, Oregon

Lance Balla
Newport High School,
Bellevue, Washington

 bedford, freeman & worth
high school publishers

Boston | New York

Vice President, Editorial, Humanities: Edwin Hill
Publisher for High School: Ann Heath
Senior Sponsoring Editor: Nathan Odell
Senior Production Editor: Harold Chester
Media Editor: Kimberly Morté
Production Supervisor: Robert Cherry
Senior Marketing Manager: Lisa Erdely
Copy Editor: Diana Puglisi George
Senior Photo Editor: Martha Friedman
Photo Editor: Jennifer Atkins
Photo Researchers: Jennifer Atkins and Nick Ciani
Permissions Editor: Linda Winters
Director of Rights and Permissions: Hilary Newman
Senior Art Director: Anna Palchik
Text Design: Jerilyn Bockorick
Cover Design: William Boardman
Cover Image: photo © Orla/Shutterstock; art by Christian Mojallali
Composition: Cenveo Publisher Services
Printing and Binding: RR Donnelley and Sons

Manufactured in the United States of America.

2   3   4   5   6   21   20   19   18   17   16

For information, write: BFW Publishers, One New York Plaza, Suite 4500, New York, NY 10004   hsmarketing@bfwpub.com

ISBN 978-1-4576-5741-2

Acknowledgments

Text credits and copyrights appear at the back of the book on pages 1029–32, which constitute an extension of the copyright page. Art credits and copyrights appear on the same page as the art selections they cover. It is a violation of the law to reproduce these selections by any means whatsoever without the written permission of the copyright holder.

Pre-AP® is a trademark registered and/or owned by the College Board®, which was not involved in the production of, and does not endorse, this product.

To Rowan and Tobias Barnes,

Liam and Owen Shea,

Laura Lull and Eleanor Golden,

and Joan Balla

ABOUT THE AUTHORS

Renée H. Shea was professor of English and modern languages and director of freshman composition at Bowie State University in Maryland. A College Board® faculty consultant for more than thirty years in AP® Language, Literature, and Pre-AP® English, she has been a reader and question leader for both AP® English exams. Renée served as a member of the Development Committee for AP® Language and Composition and as a member of the English Academic Advisory Committee for the College Board® as well as the SAT® Critical Reading Test Development Committee. She is co-author of *The Language of Composition, Conversations in American Literature,* and *Literature & Composition*, as well as two volumes in the NCTE High School Literature series (on Amy Tan and Zora Neale Hurston).

Courtesy John Golden

John Golden is an English teacher and instructional specialist at Cleveland High School in Portland, Oregon, and is currently an advisor to the College Board®'s 6-12 English Language Arts Development Committee. An English teacher for over twenty years, John has developed curriculums and led workshops for the College Board's Pacesetter and SpringBoard® English programs. He is the author of *Reading in the Dark: Using Film as a Tool in the English Classroom* (NCTE, 2001) and *Reading in the Reel World: Teaching Documentaries and Other Nonfiction Texts* (NCTE, 2006), and the producer of *Teaching Ideas: A Video Resource for AP English* (Bedford/St. Martin's, 2008) and the NCTE Centennial Film: *Reading the Past, Writing the Future* (2010).

Courtesy Lance Balla

Lance Balla is former curriculum developer and current assistant principal in the Bellevue school district in Bellevue, Washington. He was an AP® teacher for almost twenty years, and a College Board® Faculty Consultant for over ten years, as well as being a reader and table leader for the AP® Literature Exam. Lance is a member of the College Board® English Academic Advisory Committee, has been a co-author on the College Board's Springboard® program and was a member of the SAT® Critical Reading Test Development Committee. His awards and recognitions include the White House Distinguished Teacher Award, the Teacher Recognition Award from the U.S. Department of Education, the Washington State Award for Professional Excellence, and the Woodring College of Education Award for Outstanding Teaching.

CONTENTS

3 THINKING ABOUT RHETORIC AND ARGUMENT   55

▼

4 THINKING ABOUT SYNTHESIS 87

5 IDENTITY AND SOCIETY 110

- What does "identity" mean?
- How is one's identity formed?
- How do personal experiences affect our identity?
- To what extent do institutions emphasize conformity at the expense of individuality?

▼

6 AMBITION AND RESTRAINT 250

- What drives individuals to succeed?
- What are the benefits and risks of ambition?
- What are some conditions that lead to rebellion against the status quo?
- When is violence ever justified?
- How can speeches inspire people to act for change?

7 ETHICS 410

- How do we tell "right" from "wrong"?
- Can there be a universal understanding of what is "right" or "wrong"?
- To what extent do age, culture, and other factors affect our ethical decisions?
- When making ethical decisions, whose needs should be most important? The individual's, other people's, the larger society's?
- What causes us to cheat? Is cheating always wrong? Who gets to define "cheating"?

▼
8 CULTURES IN CONFLICT 534

- What defines "culture"?
- What causes cultures to come into conflict with each other?
- Who gets to tell the story of a conflict?
- How do cultures respond to change and to outsiders?
- What is lost and gained by assimilating into a new culture?

9 (MIS)COMMUNICATION 664

- What role does language play in building relationships?
- What factors lead to effective or ineffective communication between people?
- How does our language shape our identity or culture as a whole?
- How can language be used to enhance or undermine social or political power?
- How do changes in technology affect how we communicate and relate to one another?

10 UTOPIA/DYSTOPIA 852

- What makes a perfect society?
- What can lead a utopia to become a dystopia?
- How do we define "happiness"?
- Will robots and artificial intelligence help us perfect ourselves and our world, or will they make humans obsolete?

Contents

GUIDE TO LANGUAGE AND MECHANICS 960

GUIDE TO SPEAKING AND LISTENING 994

GUIDE TO MLA DOCUMENTATION STYLE 1016

GLOSSARY 1020

CREDITS 1029

INDEX 1033

GUIDED TOUR OF
ADVANCED LANGUAGE & LITERATURE

> **"** Anyone who has ever taught AP® English Language or AP® English Literature knows that students' preparation for college-level coursework needs to start long before they set foot in an AP® classroom. We have developed this book to provide Honors and Pre-AP® English teachers with rigorous, high-interest literature, nonfiction, and visual texts, as well as engaging questions and activities designed to support and challenge developing young minds.
>
> Walking into their English classes at the beginning of the year, students may ask, "Why do I have to take English *again*? Didn't I do English already?" These are questions we, as authors of this book, have tried to anticipate and address. The answer we can give students is that this year they will have an opportunity to discuss compelling topics—some close to their own experience, others outside of their comfort zone—as they develop new skills and gain the knowledge they need to become college-ready readers, writers, and thinkers.
>
> —Renée Shea, John Golden, Lance Balla

Welcome to *Advanced Language & Literature*, a textbook designed specifically for Honors and Pre-AP® English courses. This Guided Tour of the book will introduce you to its structure and features.

STRUCTURE OF *ADVANCED LANGUAGE & LITERATURE*

Skill-Building Opening Chapters

1 Reading the World
2 Thinking about Literature
3 Thinking about Rhetoric and Argument
4 Thinking about Synthesis

◀ These opening chapters establish the core skills for college-level academic work: reading closely, thinking analytically, and writing persuasively. Each chapter uses brief and accessible texts to introduce key concepts, then provides multiple opportunities to practice those skills.

Thematic Readings Chapters

5 Identity and Society
6 Ambition and Restraint
7 Ethics
8 Cultures in Conflict
9 (Mis)Communication
10 Utopia/Dystopia

◀ Using readings that range from approachable to highly challenging, along with rigorous guided analysis tasks, these chapters allow students to hone and demonstrate their mastery of the skills built in the opening chapters.

Helpful Reference Section

Guide to Language and Mechanics
Guide to Speaking and Listening
Guide to MLA Documentation
Glossary

◀ These brief guides give students and teachers resources for developing presentation skills, problem-solving grammar issues, reinforcing documentation habits, and clarifying key terminology.

INSIDE THE OPENING CHAPTERS (Chs. 1–4)

The book begins with four opening chapters that are designed to introduce the key literary and rhetorical tools students will use in their reading and writing about imaginative literature and nonfiction texts. **Culminating Activities** at the end of each chapter can be used as formative assessments, and those in Chapters 2, 3, and 4 are designed to mimic the types of tasks required on the AP® Language and AP® Literature exams.

Chapter 1—Reading the World

In this chapter, we try to give students a bit of perspective on the **role of literacy** in the world, along with the **importance of analysis**—making observations, identifying patterns, and drawing conclusions—as the fundamental process humans use to make sense of the world around them, whether that means understanding a scientific principle or investigating a poem, graphic novel, or short story.

Chapter 2—Thinking about Literature

In this chapter, we introduce students to the skills of **literary analysis and close reading** required for success in the AP® Literature and Composition course. We begin by asking students to shift how they think from literal to metaphorical. We build on the familiar process of analyzing the elements of literature—setting, character, and so on—and move toward an analysis of theme: the meaning of the work as a whole. We then ask students to investigate how stylistic choices in prose and poetry help an author create specific effects and convey meaning.

Chapter 3—Thinking about Rhetoric and Argument

In this chapter, we introduce the skills of **rhetorical analysis, argument analysis, and persuasive writing** that are central to the AP® Language and Composition course and success in college. Through straightforward instruction based on brief examples, along with frequent skill-building activities, students move from understanding key concepts such as the rhetorical situation, ethos, logos, and pathos, to analyzing how authors use those rhetorical devices, and finally to how students can put those tools to work in their own writing.

Chapter 4—Thinking about Synthesis

This chapter introduces students to **synthesis**, a key concept in the AP® Language and Composition course, and likely unfamiliar to most students. This chapter builds on the familiar processes of drawing on a single source as evidence and using comparison and contrast, and then guides students through the process of considering multiple perspectives on an issue and integrating ideas from multiple sources into an evidence-based argument.

INSIDE THE THEMATIC READINGS CHAPTERS (Chs. 5–10)

Because we believe that big ideas are the heart and soul of every good English class, this portion of *Advanced Language & Literature* has been organized thematically to encourage students to ponder enduring questions, tackle cultural issues, and engage in current debates. This groundbreaking thematic anthology weds fiction with nonfiction, poetry with prose, and classic with global literary voices. The result draws students into the vibrant cultural conversations going on in the world around them.

Thematic Chapter Overview

Each thematic chapter shares the following key elements:

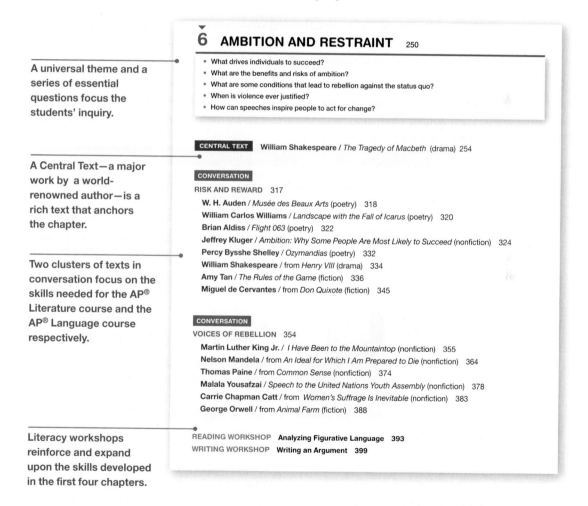

Readings—A Blend of Fresh and Familiar Selections

The drama, poetry, fiction, nonfiction, and visual texts in *Advanced Language & Literature* were designed to be both familiar and fresh, building on classic texts by Shakespeare and Martin Luther King Jr., but then departing from the usual fare by offering literature by authors from around the world such as Chimamanda Ngozi Adichie and Wisława Szymborska, as well as a wealth of new nonfiction voices.

The texts in *Advanced Language & Literature* range from the approachable to the challenging, and everything in between, to give students of various skill levels points of entry and opportunities to join the conversation.

Reading and Writing Workshops — Opportunities to Deepen Student Skills

Every thematic chapter ends with a Reading Workshop and a Writing Workshop. These brief skill-building workshops expand upon the skills introduced in the opening chapters and guide students through detailed instruction in analysis and writing.

- Each **Reading Workshop** begins with a quick skills refresher, and then asks students to work through analysis tasks using brief selections from readings in the chapter.
- Each **Writing Workshop** takes students step-by-step through the process of writing various types of academic essays.

	READING WORKSHOP	WRITING WORKSHOP
5	Analyzing Point of View	Writing a Personal Narrative
6	Analyzing Figurative Language	Writing an Argument
7	Argument by Analogy	Using Sources to Write a Synthesis Argument
8	Analyzing Character and Theme	Writing an Interpretation of Character and Theme
9	Understanding Irony	Writing a Close Analysis of Prose
10	Analyzing Diction and Tone	Writing a Rhetorical Analysis

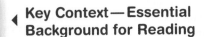

from An Ideal for Which I Am Prepared to Die

Nelson Mandela

Nobel Peace Prize recipient Nelson Mandela (1918–2013) was a South African political activist who eventually became the president of South Africa from 1994–1999. His actions as a political activist fighting for equality resulted in his spending 27 years in prison.

KEY CONTEXT   Long before he became the president of South Africa and a Nobel Prize winner, Nelson Mandela fought against a system known as apartheid, the racial segregation of people within South Africa. As a result, Mandela faced constant persecution from the ruling political party in South Africa at the time, the National Party. Mandela was arrested four times, in 1952, 1956, 1962, and then again in 1963, when he was tried along with ten other defendants in what is called the Rivonia Trial.

Mandela stood accused of four broad charges: (a) recruiting persons for training in the preparation and use of explosives and in guerrilla warfare for the purpose of violent revolution and committing acts of sabotage; (b) conspiring to commit these acts and to aid foreign military units when they [hypothetically] invaded the Republic; (c) acting in these ways to further the objectives of communism; and (d) soliciting and receiving money for these purposes from sympathizers outside South Africa. Due to a justice system that was beholden to the ruling National Party, Mandela was convicted and sentenced to life in prison.

When he was finally released after spending 27 years behind bars, Mandela had the political clout to help lead the charge to abolish apartheid, which was eventually terminated in 1993. He then went on to become the president of South Africa from 1994–1999. Under Mandela's presidency, South Africa began the long and arduous task of rebuilding the nation with a new vision of hope and equality.

What follows is a portion of Mandela's speech delivered in the courtroom at the opening of the defense case in the Rivonia Trial. Although he was eventually convicted of the charges,

◀ Key Context — Essential Background for Reading

Many of the readings in *Advanced Language & Literature* come from times, places, or disciplines that students might not be familiar with. To support these explorations, *Advanced Language & Literature* provides brief biographies, author images, and special Key Context notes to provide students with information on who is speaking, what the speaker's background is, and what social or historical context the student needs in order to engage with the text.

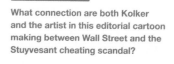

What connection are both Kolker and the artist in this editorial cartoon making between Wall Street and the Stuyvesant cheating scandal?

Bill Bramhall/NY Daily News via Getty Images

Visual Texts—Images with a Purpose

We believe that visual literacy is crucial to being able to understand and analyze our world, and that images in a textbook should not be mere decoration. We made it our goal in *Advanced Language & Literature* for every visual text to have a clear, authentic pedagogical purpose. Images were carefully selected to inform the reading of a print text, suggest new ideas, provide additional context, extend an understanding to the real world, or allow students to make interesting connections.

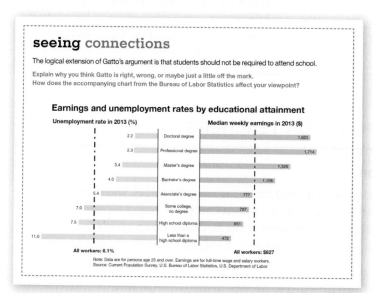

◀ Seeing Connections

The Seeing Connections boxes in *Advanced Language & Literature* give students the opportunity to ponder how the ideas of a piece connect with images, films, and outside texts. These boxes are departures from the text that ask students to explore the world of ideas and find new insights.

Probing Questions—Targeted Practice for Key Skills

Throughout the book are guided questions designed to support and challenge students as they engage with the texts.

QUESTIONS AFTER A READING	
Understanding and Interpreting	Laying the foundation for analysis, these questions guide students to an understanding of the content and move them toward an interpretation.
Analyzing Language, Style, and Structure	These questions ask students to look at craft—how the writer's choices create meaning.
Connecting, Arguing, and Extending	These writing prompts ask students to connect with the ideas of the text personally (connecting), respond to the issues in the text directly (arguing), or explore the ideas brought up by the text in the world as a whole (extending).
Topics for Composing	Found only after Central Texts, these extended essay and project ideas range from narrative and argumentative to research, creative writing, and even multimedia projects.

QUESTIONS AFTER A CONVERSATION SECTION	
Making Connections	By asking students to compare and contrast two texts in a Conversation, these questions lay the foundation for synthesis.
Synthesizing Sources	These are writing prompts that require the use of multiple sources to create original arguments and sometimes call for outside research.

WORLD-CLASS SUPPORT FOR TEACHERS

Teacher's Edition

The Teacher's Edition includes planning advice, assessment guides, and on-the-spot ideas from master teachers and seasoned professional development experts. Included are suggestions for building context, approaches for close reading, places to check for understanding, and teaching ideas designed to engage students and differentiate instruction.

Teacher's Resource Flash Drive

The Teacher's Resource Flash Drive includes responses to questions, text complexity information, classroom strategies, vocabulary support, and more.

YOUR E-BOOK SOLUTION

EDUCATIONAL ADAPTABLE TEXTBOOK
Powered by COPIA

Advanced Language & Literature is available in our new edaptext e-Book format. The edaptext e-Book offers the accessibility you want and the flexibility you need. The format features page fidelity that ensures the e-Book matches the print text, and allows each user to download and read the e-Book on multiple devices. Use it on a PC or Mac, an iPad or Android tablet. When you take notes on one device, the notes automatically sync via the cloud upon logging in. Communicate with your class, provide assignments or notes, or give quizzes to the entire class using the social media function of edaptext through the teacher dashboard.

The Ultimate Teacher's Resource

The Teacher's Edition of *Advanced Language & Literature* is also available in the edaptext e-Book format, putting all of the teacher support materials right where you need them.

ACKNOWLEDGMENTS

We would like to extend our sincerest thanks to all who inspired, advised, and supported us during the creation and development of this book.

From Renée: Once again, my husband Michael stood by during a long project with the love and encouragement that always keep me steady. Many thanks to the ladies who had my back: Heather, Meredith, Courtney, Kathleen, Elizabeth, Michele, Evelyn, Anne—and my wonderful Columbus book group. A special shout-out to the continuing inspiration of my original co-authors, Robin Aufses and Larry Scanlon. And, again, I salute my mother and dad, Dolores and Arthur Cunningham, for instilling in me the determination and confidence to keep going.

From John: Deepest thanks to Laura and Eleanor for your tremendous patience and support, and to Chris and Dick Golden, who never once doubted. My third-period English class at Cleveland High School in 2014–15 acted as willing, candid, and amazingly honest first responders to much of this material. Your suggestions—positive, and especially negative—helped to shape this book into its present form. Special thanks to Paul Cook and Tammy O'Neill for their leadership and support during my balancing act of teaching and writing, and to my teaching colleagues David Hillis, Alex Gordin, Therese Cooper, Santha Cassell, and Jamie Incorvia, from whom I have learned and stolen so much.

From Lance: Heartfelt and enduring thanks to Charise Hallberg for her unwavering support, love, and insightful feedback, to my sons Keir and Kellen for keeping me honest while making me the proudest dad on the planet, to my dad Victor for his guidance and love, to Brent Lawrence for his artistic influence, to Danny Lawrence for his mentorship in the AP® program, and to Mike Riley for showing me what it means to have courage and vision in the world of education.

To the team at Bedford, Freeman, and Worth: You are simply the best in the business. You care deeply about teachers and the work they do with students, and that makes all the difference. Nathan "Scissorhands" Odell is the kind of editor every English teacher should be lucky enough to have: creative, thoughtful, and brutally honest when needed. (And he can sing.) Our thanks to Ann Heath, who believed in this from the start and supported it in every way possible. But it took a village, so thanks also to Caitlin Kaufman, Corrina Santos, Kim Morté, Harold Chester, Diana George, Robert Cherry, Hilary Newman, Linda Winters, Margaret Gorenstein, and Jennifer Atkins on the editorial, production, and permissions teams. For sales and marketing, we thank the brilliant Lisa Erdely, Nicole Sheppard, Paul Altier, Nicole Desiato, Sabrina Van Glahn, and the A-team of sales reps. Finally, we are grateful to Daniel McDonough, who never, ever gave up on this project over its many years in the making. (And he can sing, too.)

To our gifted and committed colleagues: We are fortunate to have had the assistance of some amazing teachers at key times in this project, especially with the development of the Teacher's Edition. Our thanks to Carlos Escobar, Constance Green, David Hillis, Jamie Incorvia, Stephen Klinge, and Tracy Scholz.

Some of you reviewed early stages of this project while others participated in focus groups, but all of you shared with us your enthusiasm, expertise, and experience. This book changed substantially thanks to your insights and we are profoundly grateful. Our thanks to Eva Arce, Lisa Baker, Vinetta Bell, April

Ramsey Boyce, Claudette Brassil, Pam Cannon, Rebecca Chowske, Christian Cicoria, Patricia Conquest, Penny Crofford, Elizabeth Davis, Lisa Drance, Alex Gordin, Diana Halluska, Karen Hansen, Tamara Harrington, Stephen Heller, Joyce Herr, Amy Holthause, Ann Jackson, Carol Jago, Kristina Janeway, Elaine Jones, Yvonne Kaatz, Lynn Knowles, Joanne Krajeck, Jamie Mandel, Teri Marshall, Andie Martin, Debra McIntire, Lynn Meier, Chelsie Messenger, Jean Mullooly, Katherine Myers, Theresa Neman, Christine Palmer, Jo Palmore, Cheryl Petersohn, Rebecca Rogers, Ellen Ryan, Tracy Scholz, Pat Sherbert, Suzanne Skipper, Shannon Smith, Paul Stevenson, Violet Turner, Sarah Brown Wessling, and Robyn Westrem.

To any we have neglected to thank by name, rest assured that it is merely an error of the head and not of the heart. We appreciate you.

Advanced
Language & Literature

For Honors and Pre-AP® English Courses

1

Reading the World

▼

THINKING ABOUT LITERACY

Imagine that you were reading this textbook in Europe some time before the fifteenth century. First, you'd likely be reading it in Latin, since that was the language most commonly used by those who could read. Second, you'd probably be a priest or someone very, very rich because only those in specific professions and classes of society would have been taught to read. In fact, you'd probably be sharing this book with many other classmates, since books were copied by hand and thus very expensive to produce. And last, you almost certainly would not be female.

Very few people at the time would have been considered "literate" in the traditional sense of the word, meaning able to read and write. But consider this broader definition of "literacy":

Literacy is the ability to use available symbol systems [. . .] for the purposes of making and communicating meaning and knowledge.

—Patricia Stock, Professor, Michigan State University

While the majority of the population was not literate in the traditional sense, they had developed a variety of other types of literacies to compensate, what Professor Stock would call different "symbol systems." Farmers, for instance, could easily make do by communicating orally with nearby neighbors about the weather and crop prices and utilizing a system of accounting symbols to keep track of sales, livestock, and equipment.

The use of a printing press with movable type likely dates back to 1040 in China, but it was Johannes Gutenberg's discovery of this technology around 1450 that revolutionized reading and writing in the Western world. Gutenberg's press could produce thousands of pages of text per workday, greatly expanding the access that people had to books. Philosopher Francis Bacon, looking back on this invention in 1620, said it "changed the whole face and state of the world." Suddenly what it meant to be literate changed radically. The symbol systems once available only to the few were now accessible to the many.

During the Industrial Revolution in the eighteenth and nineteenth centuries, there was an even greater need for people to be able to read and write, as many jobs now required extensive expertise and training. Access to printed materials increased further as inexpensive newspapers and books became widely distributed. It became difficult to make and communicate information effectively in an industrialized society without using the printed word as a symbol system; the main function of schooling at this time was to make citizens literate by teaching them to read, write, and speak effectively.

The Gallery Collection/Corbis

How would the fact that books were copied by hand affect who had the opportunity to become literate?

▶

This engraving, *Arguing the Point* (1885), by Nathaniel Currier, depicts a scene on the American frontier in which a printed newspaper is being heatedly discussed.

What does this depiction suggest about literacy at this time?

Arguing the Point, engraved by Nathaniel Currier (1813–88) 1855 (litho), Tait, Arthur Fitzwilliam (1819–1905) (after)/© Museum of the City of New York, USA/ Bridgeman Images

▶

How is literacy represented differently in this photograph from a classroom in the early twentieth century and in the Currier engraving?

Lewis Wickes Hine/Library of Congress

Welcome to the Information Age

What defines literacy these days? The ability to read and write, for sure, but is that all? The "available symbol system" has expanded far beyond the printed word in our era, often referred to as the Information Age. We now have research, data, analysis, and opinion — in the forms of text, images, videos, and audio — all available digitally at the click of a button. As our definition of literacy has expanded in the Information Age, so has our definition of "text." That term used to refer exclusively to the printed word, but today it can refer to any cultural product — everything from advertisements to clothing to Internet memes.

@Johannberg
Johannes Gutenberg

Just invented new printing press with movable type. Is it working? #IHopeSo

15 minutes ago via Gutenberg Printing Press   ☆ Favorite ↻ Retweet ↩ Reply

Like the Gutenberg press, advances in technology throughout history have led to expansions in literacy.

To what extent do you think digital communication tools like Facebook, Twitter, and others are similar to the Gutenberg press in their effect on what it means to be "literate"?

With all of these changes to the ways that information is created and communicated, can people really be considered fully literate in our society if they cannot navigate the Internet, conduct online searches, tell good information from bad, and communicate through social media? These days, it's not enough to be able to read and write in print for school; people have to be fluent in all sorts of mediums for all sorts of audiences. Think about the kinds of "symbol systems" that you are likely to encounter in a typical week: textbooks for various classes, advertisements on TV and online, messages you read or send to friends through your phone or email, movies you've watched, and music you've listened to.

This photograph shows literacy in action in the twenty-first century.

What is similar and different between this image and the previous images of literacy you have seen in this chapter?

Richard Nowitz/National Geographic Creative/Corbis

Literacy Communities

In this era of human communication, as a user of the Internet you literally have access to the entire world. Thus, you need to possess multiple literacies and be able to create and communicate knowledge to people of different ages, interests, classes, genders, and backgrounds. These are the distinctions that define what are called "literacy communities," groups of people who not only share the same language but share the same slang, the same symbols, and the same points of reference. People tend to belong to a number of different literacy communities, and we often switch between these literacy communities effortlessly, though sometimes the switching can cause confusion.

For example, look at the following text message exchange between a mother and her daughter:

It is clear that the mother is not yet completely literate in texting, which causes confusion when she tries to share the same "symbol system" as her daughter. People tend to fall into various "literacy communities" based on age, interests, social class, gender, geography, and other factors. As much as the mother in the example above would like to be a part of her daughter's literacy community, she does not yet understand all of the language found within that community, perhaps because of her age or her lack of experience with texting.

ACTIVITY   THINKING ABOUT LITERACY COMMUNITIES

Describe the latest movie you saw, game you played, or song you listened to. Write one description directed to a close friend, one for a parent or grandparent, and one for your teacher who is going to grade you based on the level of detail you include in the description. Afterward, look back at the language choices you used and examine what is similar and different between the pieces. How do your language choices represent the differences among your literacy communities?

Let's look at another example of a literacy community, this section from the popular sports blog *Grantland*.

In this standard high pick-and-roll, you have Bargnani setting up at the top of the key by the 3-point line, setting a ball screen for Jose Calderon. Calderon does a good job of setting up the screen, coming off Bargnani, and using it effectively.

In terms of setting ball screens, versatility means the ability to do different things when the point guard comes off your screen. As a shooting 7-footer, Bargnani can either pop out or roll to the rim, and while he favors popping out, doing so close to 79 percent of the time, his size makes him a threat when rolling to the rim as well. So in this case, when JaVale McGee leaves him to hedge on this ball screen, Bargnani dives into the paint.

Now, unless you play or watch basketball regularly, there are a number of words and phrases that you probably recognize, but not in the way they are used here: *guard*, *paint*, *screen*, *hedge*, *key*, *pop*, *roll*, *dives*, and so on. These are terms that are familiar to those within this literacy community, but might confuse others outside of it. Someone with limited basketball knowledge might reasonably ask why a basketball player would suddenly dive into paint in the middle of a game.

It is also important to understand that literacy includes more than just being able to read and use words because many literacy communities utilize both verbal and nonverbal means to communicate information. Consider the following mathematical formula, which you are likely familiar with:

$$a^2 + b^2 = c^2$$

Those who are math-literate know that this formula is the Pythagorean theorem, and that it states — in nonverbal terms — that the square of the hypotenuse of a triangle is equal to the sum of the squares of the other two sides. The theorem can also be represented in this other nonverbal way:

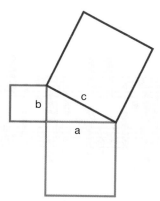

There are other types of nonverbal texts that we encounter and are expected to be able to understand, such as this pie chart:

Texting Car Accidents by Age

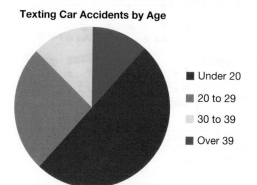

■ Under 20
■ 20 to 29
■ 30 to 39
■ Over 39

What conclusion are you expected to draw from this chart, and how does the design and format of the chart lead you to this conclusion?

ACTIVITY   RECOGNIZING DIFFERENT LITERACIES

a. Make a list of everything that you have read or written so far today. Consider all kinds of "texts," including videos, advertisements, text messages, cereal boxes, and so on. Then, try to categorize the texts you have encountered or created. What commonalities and patterns do you notice? How do these texts illustrate "literacy" in the twenty-first century?

b. Explain how each of the following texts demonstrates unique literacies and try to describe the symbol systems used to communicate the information. Are you or people you know "literate" within the communities that use these symbol systems? What can you understand and what can you not?

THE MOUNTAIN NYMPHS.

CAPRICE.

Mrs KATE ROBBINS.
AUSTIN TEXAS.

COPYRIGHT 1883 BY MRS KATE ROBBINS.

THURSDAY NIGHT PIZZA

THURSDAY
NOVEMBER 6

Fractalicious Pizza (with romanesco, olive pesto, and feta cheese)

Makes one 12-inch pizza

1/2 cup kalamata olives, pitted

1/2 cup green olives, pitted

1 garlic clove, chopped

1 heaping tablespoon fresh thyme leaves

1 heaping tablespoon fresh oregano leaves

1 heaping tablespoon chopped fresh basil

3 heaping tablespoons chopped fresh parsley

2 tablespoons pine nuts, toasted

1/3 to 2/3 cup extra-virgin olive oil

Freshly ground black pepper

1 medium (1-pound) head of Romanesca cauliflower

1 (14- to 16-ounce) ball Basic Pizza Dough (or pre-made dough)

2/3 cup crumbled feta cheese

 Seasonal   Vegetarian

To prep the toppings: In the bowl of a food processor, combine the olives, thyme, oregano, basil, parsley, and pine nuts. Pulse the mixture until the ingredients are all finely chopped

[read more]

ThursdayNightPizza.com

c. Write an explanation of your own literacies. You may want to consider one or more of the following questions to guide your response:

- Do the majority of your literacies tend to be part of unique literacy communities or are they literacies used by the general public?
- How are your literacies different from those of other people? What roles do age, gender, interests, and cultural background play?
- How have your literacies changed or grown over time? Why have they changed? What new literacies do you think you might add in the future?

▼
THINKING ABOUT ENGLISH CLASS

English is typically the only subject that is required for all four years of high school. Have you wondered why this is? Here is an actual conversation between two sophomores in the hallway at the beginning of the school year who were (probably unintentionally) wrestling with this question:

Student A: What English class are you in?

Student B: English 2.

Student A: What's that?

Student B: Don't know. Same as English 1, but one harder?

You might conclude that the two students really don't know much about why they've been studying English, but their conversation may also reflect your own feelings about English class: you do most of the same things each year (read books, write essays, give speeches), but the process just gets a little harder and you probably read different books.

So, what is English *for,* then?

And why is English so important that, if you have grown up in the United States, you have likely studied it every year for the past ten years? One easy answer is that it is essential that you learn to read, write, and speak effectively so that you can function as a literate citizen in society. You need to be able to fill out job applications, read and understand the key political issues in order to cast an informed vote in elections, and write a check to pay your taxes. Countries with high literacy rates among their citizens tend to be more productive and stable than countries with lower literacy rates. In other words, by studying English, you are able to practice the full definition of literacy from the beginning of this chapter: "the ability to use available symbol systems [. . .] for the purposes of making and communicating meaning and

> [I]t is vital to remember that information — in the sense of raw data — is not knowledge, that knowledge is not wisdom, and that wisdom is not foresight. But information is the first essential step to all of these.
>
> —Arthur C. Clarke

knowledge." An English class gives you lots of opportunities to make and communicate knowledge through particular symbol systems, including the written and spoken word, film, artwork, and other types of images. The study of English is a mental exercise for making meaning of the world around us and for sharing our ideas with others inside and outside of the classroom. It is also training in a specific academic literacy (the study of language and literature), but in the process you will be sharpening your mind so that picking up other literacies becomes increasingly easy.

ACTIVITY   **LITERACIES IN AND OUT OF ENGLISH CLASS**

Consider how the literacies that you use in English class are similar to and different from the literacies you use in other classes in school, as well as those you use outside of school, by drawing and filling in a Venn diagram with the following components:

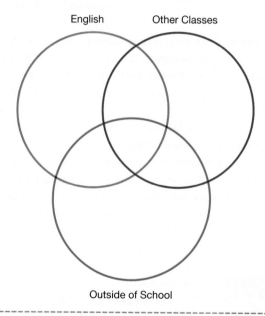

English   Other Classes

Outside of School

▼
THINKING ABOUT ANALYSIS

The true purpose of literacy is not to get an A in English or to ace the SATs, but to understand, analyze, and influence the world around you. And the process for this is a simple one, something you've been doing your whole life: you observe, you recognize patterns, and you draw conclusions. When you are driving down the street and you see an eight-sided red sign with white letters, you probably don't say to yourself, "Hey, that is a red sign with the letters *S*, *T*, *O*, and *P* on it." Hopefully, you just stop.

　　Let's examine that thought process a little more carefully. You <u>observed</u> the letters, color, and shape of the sign. You recognized a <u>pattern</u> in which other drivers (hopefully)

Scientific method is not just a method which it has been found profitable to pursue in this or that abstruse subject for purely technical reasons. It represents the only method of thinking that has proved fruitful in any subject — that is what we mean when we call it scientific. It is not a peculiar development of thinking for highly specialized ends; it *is* thinking.

—John Dewey

stop at the sign. You then <u>concluded</u> based on the word formed by the letters, the shape and color of the sign, and the actions of others around you that you probably ought to stop the car.

What you've just done is **analysis**. You used the literacies you've acquired to read those letters, symbols, and colors, as well as your ability to think about the world around you, in order to draw a conclusion and make something happen in the world: in this case, stop a car and avoid an accident.

This description of analysis might sound overly technical, but in practice it is both simple and common. Moreover it is useful, essential, even powerful. Observing, finding patterns, and drawing conclusions is something you've done in every science class you've ever taken. You have practiced this kind of analysis whenever your teacher has asked you to observe some kind of process, make a hypothesis about why it happens, and then draw a conclusion about the accuracy of your hypothesis.

Such conclusions can have far-reaching results. For example, in 1960, Jane Goodall, then a twenty-six-year old college student, went to Gombe Stream National Park in Tanzania in Africa to study chimpanzees. There she observed the chimpanzees hugging and patting each other on the back, and she began to recognize patterns of behavior in individual chimpanzees that demonstrated unique personalities and close relationships between family members. Goodall's observations enabled her to conclude that there are more similarities between humans and chimpanzees than anyone had suspected before. Her work on this subject eventually led to a greater

Bruce Coleman Inc./Alamy

awareness of the need for animal protection and conservation efforts.

Advances in business and technology also come about by observing, recognizing patterns, and drawing conclusions. The video rental and streaming company Netflix, for instance, was founded after Reed Hastings racked up $40 worth of late fees after renting a single movie. He observed his problem with late fees and reasoned that they likely were a problem for others as well. He then concluded (rightly, as it turned out) that customers would be eager to switch to a no-late-fee service.

It is important to understand that each of these examples required a **focused observation** to start off with. Jane Goodall didn't start off observing everything she could about chimpanzees; rather, she focused on what social behaviors they demonstrated with their family members. Netflix's founder focused his observations on customers' reactions to late fees, not on every possible customer behavior.

The world is full of examples of this approach that we're calling the analysis process. It is the fundamental process by which the human mind comes to understand the world, and it is the type of thinking that is being developed when you write an argument, interpret a poem, or analyze a story.

ACTIVITY   THE ANALYSIS PROCESS

Choose a topic that you know well or encounter often, such as a sports team you watch regularly, your boyfriend or girlfriend, your school, the weather in your hometown, your favorite singer or musician, or a video game you play often. Now, apply the analysis process to your topic, being sure to start off with a focused observation.

Observe. What do you notice about your subject? Pretend you are encountering your subject for the first time, and be sure to pick a focus for your observation.

Identify patterns. What aspects of your subject are repeated? What is different from what you expected or from similar subjects? What connections can you make?

Draw a conclusion. What conclusion or judgment can you make about your subject?

▼
THINKING ABOUT CONTEXT

It is important to understand the ways that background knowledge and context might influence how you observe, identify patterns, and draw conclusions about a subject. Imagine that you know nothing about the rules of football and you are attending a Super Bowl party with friends. You observe that when a player on a team kicks the ball through the goalposts, the team receives three points, but other times when a player does the same thing the team receives only one point. You notice this pattern repeated through the game, so you conclude that teams must get more points the farther away from the goalposts they kick. Then, you decide to act on your new knowledge by suggesting that the team ought to kick the ball from 70 yards away to earn lots of points. Hopefully, someone with background knowledge of the rules (context) will explain the difference between a field goal (3 points) and a point after touchdown (1 point), and you will adjust your conclusion, before you get kicked out of the party.

Look at the photograph on page 14 by Thomas Hoepker from September 11, 2001, the day of a major terrorist attack on the World Trade Center in New York City, which can be seen smoldering in the background of the photo.

Thomas Hoepker/Magnum

As you look closely at the picture, you might notice patterns of the relaxed postures of the people in direct contrast to the devastation of what is happening behind them. Then, you might conclude that the people in the photo are heartless or unconcerned about the tragedy of the day. *New York Times* commentator Frank Rich looked at this photo and drew the same conclusion:

> This is a country that likes to move on, and fast. The young people in Mr. Hoepker's photo aren't necessarily callous. They're just American. In the five years since the attacks, the ability of Americans to dust themselves off and keep going explains both what's gone right and what's gone wrong on our path to the divided and dispirited state the nation finds itself in today.

In response to Frank Rich, one of the people in the photograph wrote an email to the online magazine *Slate*. In his email, he wrote, "A snapshot can make mourners attending a funeral look like they're having a party." He went on to describe that, like most people who watched the Towers fall, they were in a "profound state of shock and disbelief," and that Thomas Hoepker did not ask permission to take the photograph and did not interview them to determine their state of mind. In his email to *Slate* magazine, he states, "Had Hoepker walked fifty feet over to introduce himself he would have discovered a bunch of New Yorkers in the middle of an animated discussion about what had just happened." Instead, Hoepker took the photograph without fully understanding the context of the situation.

Look back at the photograph now that you know more about the context. Do you see the scene differently now that you know more about the context of the photo? Would the writer Frank Rich and the photographer Thomas Hoepker have reached a different conclusion if they knew more about their subjects?

So, prior to making observations during the analysis process, try to keep in mind — or find out — the "who, what, where, when, and why" of your subject. This context can provide you with the framework necessary to make an accurate interpretation of the subject you observe. Context will play an important role in your work with the literature and nonfiction found in this book because much of it is either by or about people from different countries with different cultures and customs.

ACTIVITY CONSIDERING CONTEXT

Look at the painting reproduced below and try to describe the images to someone who has not seen the painting. Do **not** look at the context of the artist and the situation depicted in the painting. After you finish your description, look at the background information and re-describe the painting with that context in mind. Last, explain how knowing the context of the work affected your observation and what you tried to communicate.

Bridgeman Images/(c) 2015 Estate of Pablo Picasso/Artists Rights Society (ARS), New York

Pablo Picasso (1881–1973), *Guernica*, 1937. Oil on canvas, 137.4 inches by 305.5 inches. Museo Nacional Centro de Arte Reina Sofia, Madrid, Spain

Created in response to the bombing of Guernica, Spain by German and Italian forces during the Spanish Civil War, that resulted in nearly one thousand civilian deaths.

▼ A MODEL ANALYSIS

It's time to try your hand at this analysis process. Remember, whether it's analyzing a poem, teasing apart an argument, or thinking about an advertisement, the basic thought process remains the same:

1. Observe
2. Identify patterns
3. Draw conclusions

Let's try the analysis process with a photograph called *Life Goes On, Checa, Ecuador, 2011*.

Phil Douglis

1. For **observation**, you probably paid close attention to the pig and the cross. You likely also noticed that there is only a falling-down chain-link fence that separates the pig from the cemetery. Hopefully, you also considered the title of the photograph: *Life Goes On*.
2. In trying to recognize the **patterns**, you probably saw that the pig and the cross are set up as opposites — one represents death, the other is alive, and you might have been curious about why the photograph includes both a farm and a cemetery.
3. In drawing a **conclusion** about a text, you generally will ask yourself, "What meaning is the author/photographer/artist trying to communicate to the audience?" In analyzing this photograph, you might conclude something similar to what the photographer, Phil Douglis, says about his work: "The image symbolizes the fact that life continues to be lived, even in the constant presence of death itself." What's another conclusion you might draw from this image?

culminating activity

Read the following texts that are typical of the kinds of pieces you encounter in an English class, and respond to the questions that guide you through the analysis process. Before each text, you will see that some context has been provided for you, along with a focus for your initial observations.

Eating Poetry

Mark Strand

KEY CONTEXT Mark Strand (1934–2014) was born on Prince Edward Island in Canada and grew up in various cities across the United States. His first love was painting, and he originally hoped to become an artist. Strand has published nearly twenty collections of poetry, as well as children's stories and literary criticism, and has won numerous awards for his writing. This poem is part of a collection called *Reasons for Moving* that was published in 1968. One reviewer of Strand's work from this period wrote that his poems "show an uneasy preoccupation with self, and the vehicle used to express that preoccupation is often a dream state in which the speaker is divided between two worlds and can locate himself comfortably in neither."

Lawrence Schwartzwald/Splash News/Corbis

Focus for Your Observation

Think about the somewhat odd behaviors of the speaker ("I") in the poem.

Ink runs from the corners of my mouth.
There is no happiness like mine.
I have been eating poetry.

The librarian does not believe what she sees.
Her eyes are sad   5
and she walks with her hands in her dress.

The poems are gone.
The light is dim.
The dogs are on the basement stairs and coming up.

Their eyeballs roll,   10
their blond legs burn like brush.
The poor librarian begins to stamp her feet and weep.

She does not understand.
When I get on my knees and lick her hand,
she screams.   15

I am a new man.
I snarl at her and bark.
I romp with joy in the bookish dark.

1. **Observe:** What are the behaviors of the speaker that seem most unusual?
2. **Identify patterns:** What commonalities of the speaker's odd behavior do you notice? What is he behaving like?
3. **Draw conclusions:** Why does the poet have the speaker behave like he does? What evidence from the text supports your conclusion? What does this have to do with the title, "Eating Poetry"?

from The Shallows: What the Internet Is Doing to Our Brains

Nicholas Carr

John Todd/Sun Microsystems via Getty Images

KEY CONTEXT Nicholas Carr, a regular contributor to such publications as *Wired*, the *Atlantic*, and the *New York Times*, writes about technology and its influence on us and on our culture. One of his most famous articles is called "Is Google Making Us Stupid?"

In this excerpt from his 2010 book *The Shallows*, Carr starts with a reference to the science fiction film *2001*, in which a spaceship's computer, called HAL, malfunctions and tries to kill the astronauts onboard, until one, named Dave, is able to disconnect him. Carr also cites a famous twentieth-century researcher, Marshall McLuhan, who suggested that the means through which we receive information has more effect on us than the information itself. McLuhan famously said, "The medium is the message." In other words, we need to pay as much attention to how we receive information (television, newspapers, radio, Internet, Twitter) as to the information itself.

While sometimes tagged a "Luddite," a person who tends to resist technological advances, Carr would probably say that he simply questions the conventional thinking that technology will automatically make our lives better.

Focus for Your Observation

Think about the differences Carr identifies between reading books and reading online.

Dave, stop. Stop, will you? Stop, Dave. Will you stop?" So the supercomputer HAL pleads with the implacable astronaut Dave Bowman in a famous and weirdly poignant scene toward the end of Stanley Kubrick's *2001: A Space Odyssey*. Bowman, having nearly been sent to a deep-space death by the malfunctioning machine, is calmly, coldly, disconnecting the memory circuits that control its artificial brain. "Dave, my mind is going," HAL says, forlornly. "I can feel it. I can feel it."

I can feel it too. Over the last few years I've had an uncomfortable sense that someone, or something, has been tinkering with my brain, remapping the neural circuitry, reprogramming the memory. My mind isn't going — so far as I can tell — but it's changing. I'm not thinking the way I used to think. I feel it most strongly when I'm reading. I used to find it easy to immerse myself in a book or a lengthy article. My mind would get caught up in the twists of the narrative or the turns of the argument, and I'd spend hours strolling through long stretches of prose. That's rarely the case anymore. Now my concentration starts to drift after a page or two. I get fidgety, lose the thread, begin looking for something else to do. I feel like I'm always dragging my wayward brain back to the text. The deep reading that used to come naturally has become a struggle.

I think I know what's going on. For well over a decade now, I've been spending a lot of time online, searching and surfing and sometimes adding to the great databases of the Internet. The Web's been a godsend to me as a writer. Research that once required days in the stacks or periodical rooms of libraries can now be done in minutes. A few Google searches, some quick clicks on hyperlinks, and I've got the telltale fact or the pithy quote I was after. I couldn't begin to tally the hours or the gallons of gasoline the Net

has saved me. I do most of my banking and a lot of my shopping online. I use my browser to pay my bills, schedule my appointments, book flights and hotel rooms, renew my driver's license, send invitations and greeting cards. Even when I'm not working, I'm as likely as not to be foraging in the Web's data thickets — reading and writing e-mails, scanning headlines and blog posts, following Facebook updates, watching video streams, downloading music, or just tripping lightly from link to link to link.

The Net has become my all-purpose medium, the conduit for most of the information that flows through my eyes and ears and into my mind. The advantages of having immediate access to such an incredibly rich and easily searched store of data are many, and they've been widely described and duly applauded. "Google," says Heather Pringle, a writer with *Archaeology* magazine, "is an astonishing boon to humanity, gathering up and concentrating information and ideas that were once scattered so broadly around the world that hardly anyone could profit from them." Observes *Wired*'s Clive Thompson, "The perfect recall of silicon memory can be an enormous boon to thinking."

5   The boons are real. But they come at a price. As McLuhan suggested, media aren't just channels of information. They supply the stuff of thought, but they also shape the process of thought. And what the Net seems to be doing is chipping away my capacity for concentration and contemplation. Whether I'm online or not, my mind now expects to take in information the way the Net distributes it: in a swiftly moving stream of particles. Once I was a scuba diver in the sea of words. Now I zip along the surface like a guy on a Jet Ski.

Maybe I'm an aberration, an outlier. But it doesn't seem that way. When I mention my troubles with reading to friends, many say they're suffering from similar afflictions. The more they use the Web, the more they have to fight to stay focused on long pieces of writing. Some worry they're becoming chronic scatter-brains. Several of the bloggers I follow have also mentioned the phenomenon. Scott Karp, who used to work for a magazine and now writes a blog about online media, confesses that he has stopped reading books altogether. "I was a lit major in college, and used to be [a] voracious book reader," he writes. "What happened?" He speculates on the answer: "What if I do all my reading on the web not so much because the way I read has changed, i.e. I'm just seeking convenience, but because the way I THINK has changed?"

1. **Observe:** What are some of the significant differences Carr identifies between reading books and reading online?
2. **Identify patterns:** Make a list of the benefits and negative effects of the Internet that Carr identifies. On which "side" does Carr seem to provide more examples and supporting evidence?
3. **Draw conclusions:** What does Carr suggest about the effect the Internet is having on us? What evidence from the text supports your conclusion?

from Persepolis

Marjane Satrapi

KEY CONTEXT This excerpt is from *Persepolis*, an autobiography in the form of a graphic novel. *Persepolis* depicts Satrapi's early years growing up in Iran, just before and immediately after the Iranian Revolution of 1979. The revolution ousted the United States–backed Shah of Iran, who favored the aristocracy and was seen by the revolutionaries as corrupt. Satrapi's family, though wealthy by most Iranian standards, did not support the Shah, nor did they support the Islamic leaders who took power afterward and who are still in power in Iran today. Like many nations, Iran at the time of this story had significant differences between social classes, which would make a relationship between people of different economic levels difficult. When reading this selection — and graphic novels in general — you will want to take your time with each individual frame to consider how the narration (in rectangles at the top or bottom of the frame) works with the dialogue and the images.

Fabrizio Maltese/Contour by Getty Images

Consider the differences between social classes in Iran.

HER

THIS IS MEHRI.

SHE WAS EIGHT YEARS OLD WHEN SHE HAD TO LEAVE HER PARENTS' HOME TO COME TO WORK FOR US. JUST LIKE REZA, LEILA AND HASSAN.

WE HAVE TOO MANY CHILDREN, 14 OR 15 INCLUDING HER.

SHE WILL EAT WELL AT YOUR HOUSE.

WE WILL TAKE CARE OF HER.

SHE WAS JUST TEN YEARS OLD WHEN I WAS BORN...SHE TOOK CARE OF ME.

SHE PLAYED WITH ME.

AND SHE ALWAYS FINISHED MY FOOD.

SHE ALSO TOLD ME STORIES ABOUT JACKALS THAT SCARED ME.

AND IT CAME CLOSER! AND IT CAME CLOSER!

IN OTHER WORDS, WE GOT ALONG WELL.

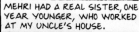

MEHRI HAD A REAL SISTER, ONE YEAR YOUNGER, WHO WORKED AT MY UNCLE'S HOUSE.

YOU KNOW, I HAVE A FIANCE.

OH REALLY, WHO?

IT'S HIM! IN FRONT OF THE TV. ISN'T HE HANDSOME?

NOT BAD!

AFTER A FEW VISITS, SHE FELL IN LOVE WITH HIM TOO.

HER JEALOUSY WAS MORE THAN SHE COULD BEAR AND SHE TOLD MEHRI'S STORY TO MY UNCLE, WHO TOLD IT TO MY GRANDMA, WHO TOLD IT TO MY MOM. THAT IS HOW THE STORY REACHED MY FATHER...

...WHO DECIDED TO CLARIFY THE SITUATION.

WHO'S THERE?

I AM YOUR NEIGHBOR. I WOULD LIKE TO HAVE A FEW WORDS WITH YOUR SON.

OK, I'LL GET STRAIGHT TO THE POINT: I KNOW THAT MEHRI PRETENDS SHE IS MY DAUGHTER. IN REALITY SHE IS MY MAID.

REAL-LY?

BEE GEES

Questions for Analysis

1. **Observe:** What are the differences that Satrapi identifies between the social classes?

2. **Identify patterns:** How are the maid, Mehri, and the narrator, Marji, similar? How are they different?

3. **Draw conclusions:** What is the author, Marjane Satrapi, suggesting about the nature of Iranian social classes in this excerpt? How does she demonstrate this point in the drawings and the text?

2 Thinking about Literature

Photo: Orla/Shutterstock, Art: Christian Mojallali

Humans tell stories.

It is how we communicate, it is how we entertain, and it is how we make sense of our world. In the words of writer Graham Swift: "Only animals live entirely in the Here and Now. Only nature knows neither memory nor history. But man—let me offer you a definition—is the storytelling animal."

Think about times that you get together with your family or friends. Much of your conversation is likely storytelling: telling them about something that happened to you, something you saw on the Internet, something that is going on in another person's life.

Storytelling seems to go as far back as humanity itself, even before the written word. The cave drawings in the Chauvet Cave in France (see p. 26) were created over forty thousand years ago. You can see the artists trying to communicate something about the animals around them and their relationships with them—perhaps documenting a hunt, or showing how to herd animals. It's a simple story, lacking all of the plot twists and drama we've come to appreciate, but it's a story nonetheless.

© Guillaume Horcajuelo/epa/Corbis

Why is storytelling so vital to our lives? When we listen to other's stories, we see ourselves in them—we identify with them; we empathize with them. Or, as Atticus Finch in *To Kill a Mockingbird* puts it, "You never really understand a person [. . .] until you climb into his skin and walk around in it."

Beyond hearing the stories of our close friends and relatives, we also encounter stories through films, plays, novels, short stories, and poetry. For shorthand, we will refer to all of these types of imaginative texts with the term "literature." Through literature, we can visit distant lands and meet people in cultures we might not otherwise encounter.

Literature is both an exploration of ourselves and of everything beyond ourselves. In fact, research by Ohio State University has "found that after reading literary fiction [. . .] people performed better on tests measuring empathy, social perception and emotional intelligence—skills that come in especially handy when you are trying to read someone's body language or gauge what they might be thinking." So, if telling stories makes us human, reading stories seems to put us in touch with our humanity.

▼ ANALYZING LITERATURE

While telling and hearing or reading stories is a fundamental part of the human experience, you still might wonder why we should *analyze* literature, and try to explain how it works, and, in the minds of some people, ruin it in the process. You may find yourself agreeing with Melinda from the young adult novel *Speak* by Laurie Halse Anderson, who in this excerpt describes how her teacher, "Hairwoman," teaches literature—in this case, the novel *The Scarlet Letter* by Nathaniel Hawthorne:

It's Nathaniel Hawthorne Month in English. Poor Nathaniel. Does he know what they've done to him? We are reading *The Scarlet Letter* one sentence at a time, tearing it up and chewing on its bones.

It's all about SYMBOLISM, says Hairwoman. Every word chosen by Nathaniel, every comma, every paragraph break—these were all done on purpose. To get a decent grade in her class, we have to figure out what he was really trying to say. Why couldn't he just say what he meant? Would they pin scarlet letters on his chest? B for blunt, S for straightforward?

Melinda raises two key issues about literature that you might agree or disagree with:

1. The study of literature is mostly about hunting for a bunch of hidden symbols and meanings in order to get a good grade.
2. Authors don't really mean to do whatever English teachers say they do. It's all made up.

What Melinda doesn't yet understand is something that we discussed in Chapter 1: the analytical process of making observations, finding patterns, and drawing conclusions is how we investigate most things in this world. So, why should literature be exempt? And what if we find a pattern that the author didn't intend to include? It still exists, right? It exists because it is in our nature to make meaning—to look at chaos and find a pattern.

Melinda, at this point, hasn't started thinking abstractly.

Literature loves the abstract. Authors work through implication, metaphor, symbol, and imagery to convey both literal and figurative meanings, concrete and abstract ideas. You'll need to be willing to think abstractly in order to understand and appreciate literature. When Romeo sees Juliet on the balcony, he says, "But, soft! What light through yonder window breaks? It is the east, and Juliet is the sun." Obviously, Romeo is saying not that Juliet is literally the sun, but rather that her beauty is like that of the sun, or maybe that seeing her is like the start of a brand-new day for him. Abstract language often leaves room for multiple possible interpretations. In this chapter, we're going to help you develop your abstract thinking skills, which are essential not only to understanding literature, but to understanding the myriad complexities of our world.

> Storytelling is ultimately a creative act of pattern recognition. Through characters, plot and setting, a writer creates places where previously invisible truths become visible. Or the storyteller posits a series of dots that the reader can connect.
>
> —Douglas Coupland

As for Melinda's second point—about whether authors intentionally mean to do what the English teachers say they do—she is probably half right. Language and storytelling are rich, complex things that even an author can't fully control. Sometimes the meaning we see in a piece of literature is just a happy accident, a pattern that readers found and the author neither noticed nor intended. But, nevertheless, it still exists. Joseph Heller, author of *Catch-22*, when asked whether readers sometimes found meaning in his work he had not intended, said, "This happens often, and in every case there is good reason for the inference; in many cases, I have been able to learn something about my own book, for readers have seen much in the book that is there, although I was not aware of it being there." Where Melinda is half wrong, however, is that there absolutely *are* times when authors intend to develop an idea abstractly—through implication, metaphor, or symbol—and that in doing so, they present the idea in a more interesting, powerful, or nuanced way than they would if they were "blunt" or "straightforward."

Consider the film *Edward Scissorhands* (1990), directed by Tim Burton. The film is about a mechanical man, played by Johnny Depp, whose creator died before he could finish building him, leaving him with scissors instead of hands. Circumstances cause Edward to leave his safe, solitary home and integrate into regular society. It's clear that the scissors are a metaphor. Burton could have chosen for Edward to have normal hands, or even, say, salad tongs for hands. So, to address Melinda's point, yes, Burton chose scissors on purpose because they work metaphorically: scissors can be both useful tools and dangerous weapons, which exactly mirrors the conflicting reactions Edward encounters as he tries to protect those he loves, often from himself.

Eventually Melinda from *Speak* begins thinking abstractly, and realizes something else too—writing that is completely literal wouldn't be all that interesting to read:

> I can't whine too much. Some of it is fun. It's like a code, breaking into his head and find-ing the key to his secrets. Like the whole guilt thing. Of course you know the minister feels guilty and Hester feels guilty, but Nathaniel wants us to know this is a big deal. If he kept repeating, "She felt guilty, she felt guilty, she felt guilty," it would be a boring book and no one would buy it.

▶
―――――――――
This is a promotional poster for *Edward Scissorhands* (1990).

How does this poster visually illustrate the conflict Edward faces? What are other films you know that ask their audiences to think metaphorically about the characters, subjects, settings, or situations?

ACTIVITY   **THINKING ABSTRACTLY**

Look at the painting by Salvador Dalí reproduced below, *The Persistence of Memory* (1931). As Burton does with the scissors in *Edward Scissorhands*, Dalí is treating the clocks metaphorically. After observing the clocks carefully and identifying any patterns in how Dalí represents the clocks, try to draw a conclusion about what he might be suggesting about time. What does the title tell you about Dalí's intended meaning in this piece? What is an alternate title for the painting that might reflect your conclusion?

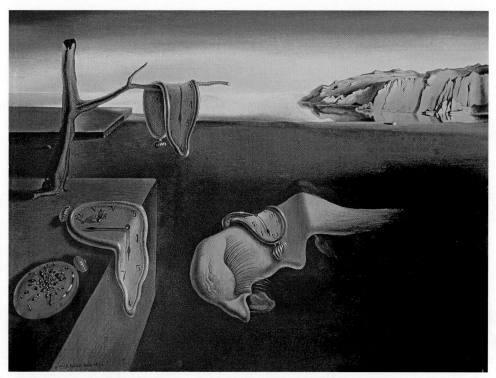

The Persistence of Memory, 1931 (oil on canvas), Dali, Salvador (1904–89)/Museum of Modern Art, New York, USA/Bridgeman Images. © Salvador Dalí, Fundació Gala-Salvador Dalí, Artists Rights Society (ARS), New York 2015.

THEME IN LITERATURE

When we analyze literature, what we are trying to do is understand what the work means and appreciate how that meaning was created. Sometimes one person finds a meaning that others didn't notice, but that's not because the author is trying to hide things from us; rather, it's because good literature is full of possibilities.

When we analyze literature, we also try to draw a conclusion about the meaning of the work as a whole, which is often called the **theme**.

Too often the term "theme" is misunderstood as the plot or topic of a work of literature. For example, some students who have read *Romeo and Juliet* might mistakenly identify the theme of the Shakespeare play as

The children of two feuding households fall in love with disastrous results.

That is a plot summary, not a theme. A possible theme could be better stated as

Romeo and Juliet suggests that love is a powerful force that, once unleashed, cannot be controlled.

The difference between the two statements is that the second identifies an *idea* in the piece that tells us something about life or the world we live in.

As a child, you may have heard Aesop's fable "The Tortoise and the Hare," in which the arrogant hare, thinking there's no way that the slow tortoise can beat him in a race, takes a nap in the middle of the competition. In the end, the moral is stated: "slow but steady wins the race." This example fits our definition of theme, since it identifies the idea of the text and reveals something about the real world outside of talking animals running races.

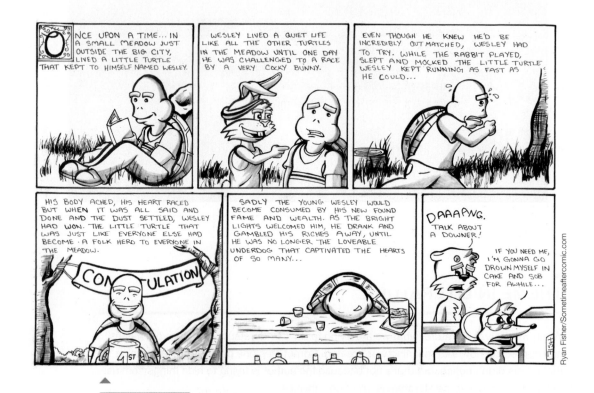

Read this version of "The Tortoise and the Hare" and identify the theme.

How is the theme of this version different from that of the original?

Sometimes the theme is clearly and explicitly stated in a text, as in the 2002 movie version of *Spider-Man*, when Uncle Ben tells Peter Parker, "With great power comes great responsibility," but more often the theme of a work is implied and established slowly through how the author tells a story or constructs the poem.

At this point, you might be thinking that the theme is just something you can make up, and that you can interpret literature any way you like because your interpretation is just based on your own personal opinion anyway. But while the answers in an English class are not always as concrete as they might be in a math class, there can, in fact, be right and wrong answers. Just because readers may differ in their interpretation of a piece of litera-ture, that does not mean that *any* interpretation is valid. As we said earlier, the act of inter-preting literature is about seeing how the details add up to a big idea; thus, the most important part of analyzing literature is that you build your interpretation using evidence from a careful observation of the text. So, for instance, it would be an incorrect interpreta-tion of *Romeo and Juliet* to say that young love has no value in the world and should just be dismissed as childish nonsense. Upon examining
the text, we would find too many patterns that would show that this is simply not what the text is saying.

ACTIVITY IDENTIFYING THEME

Choose one text from the following list of fairy tales, fables, and films that you may have heard, read, or seen, or choose one of your own. Briefly summarize the *plot* of the text, identity the *theme*, or central idea of the work, and provide *evidence that you remember from the text* that supports your statement of theme. Remember, the theme may be explicitly stated, but it is more likely to be implied throughout the work.

1. Cinderella
2. The Wizard of Oz
3. The Three Little Pigs
4. Star Wars series
5. Little Red Riding Hood
6. The Ant and the Grasshopper
7. The Harry Potter series

Analyzing Theme

When you are asked to analyze literature, especially a long piece like a novel or a play, it can be overwhelming to know what to look for. It is certainly tempting and a whole lot easier to just Google, "What is the theme of _____?" But any information you gather in that way is secondhand. Moreover, you miss the opportunity to engage with a text on your own terms, finding the patterns that you find interesting and that can lead to an original interpretation of the work. Writer Francine Prose describes her own experience reading for theme in high school English:

> When I was a high school junior, our English teacher assigned a term paper on the theme of blindness in *Oedipus Rex* and *King Lear*. We were supposed to go through the two tragedies and circle every reference to eyes, light, darkness, and vision, then draw some conclusion on which we would base our final essay. [. . .]
>
> Tracing those patterns and making those connections was fun. Like cracking a code that the playwright had embedded in the text, a riddle that existed just for me to decipher. I felt as if I were engaged in some intimate communication with the writer, as if the ghosts of Sophocles and Shakespeare had been waiting patiently all those centuries for a bookish sixteen-year-old to come along and find them.
>
> I believed that I was learning to read in a whole new way.

What Prose outlines here is the analytical process: she observes the text closely for references to blindness, she sees patterns relating to which characters are literally blind and which ones just act blindly, and, while Prose does not, in this excerpt, reveal exactly what she discovered, she implies that she drew an interesting conclusion about the works in the term paper she was assigned.

So, determining theme starts with careful observation and looking for patterns, but what exactly should you be looking for? Here are some things you might look for that will help you turn your observations into conclusions:

- **Curiosities.** Things you find puzzling, intriguing, or ambiguous. This is where you try to think metaphorically, as described on page 28.
- **Repetitions.** Repeated images, words, phrases, settings, structures, rhymes, and so on.
- **Opposites.** Contrasts like light/dark, good/evil, or characters or settings that seem to be in opposition.
- **Links.** Connections or references in the text to something else outside the text, often called *allusions* — references to people, places, or things the writer expects the reader to know.

Look carefully at *The Third of May 1808*, (p. 33) a painting by Francisco Goya that depicts the Spanish resistance to the army of Napoleon, who had conquered Spain. The topic of the painting is "war," but what is Goya suggesting about war in this painting? We can apply the four ideas above to answer this question and determine a possible theme.

Curiosities. You might find it curious that despite what looks to be his imminent death, the man in the center has thrown his arms wide in defiance — or is it submission? You might find it curious that the people in the background seem to blend into the earth in the background.

Repetitions. You might notice that each soldier on the right has a hood on, and that you can't see these soldiers' faces.

Francisco Goya (1746–1828), *The Shootings of May Third 1808*, 1814. Oil on canvas, 106 inches x 137 inches. Museo del Prado, Madrid, Spain.

Album/Art Resource, NY

Opposites. You probably notice right away the opposites in the painting; the man about to be executed is in bright light, while his executioners are in dark. Additionally, you can see opposites in the straight, formal line of soldiers contrasting with the chaotic alignment of the civilians.

Links. As the central character in this painting is wearing white and holding his arms out, Goya might be suggesting a Christlike pose and indicating the righteousness of his sacrifice. The hooded soldiers might be a reference to the Grim Reaper.

From these observations and patterns, you could probably draw a reasonable conclusion that Goya is commenting on the heroism and sacrifice of average citizens who face death in the fight for their country's freedom.

ACTIVITY ANALYZING THEME

As you read the poem "Famous" by Naomi Shihab Nye, look for curiosities, opposites, repetitions, and links in order to make a reasonable interpretation about what Nye might be suggesting about what being famous really means. Be sure to include specific references to the poem to support your interpretation.

Famous / Naomi Shihab Nye

The river is famous to the fish.

The loud voice is famous to silence,
which knew it would inherit the earth
before anybody said so.

5 The cat sleeping on the fence is famous to the birds
watching him from the birdhouse.

The tear is famous, briefly, to the cheek.

The idea you carry close to your bosom
is famous to your bosom.

10 The boot is famous to the earth,

more famous than the dress shoe,
which is famous only to floors.

The bent photograph is famous to the one who carries it
and not at all famous to the one who is pictured.

15 I want to be famous to shuffling men

who smile while crossing streets,
sticky children in grocery lines,
famous as the one who smiled back.

I want to be famous in the way a pulley is famous,
20 or a buttonhole, not because it did anything spectacular,
but because it never forgot what it could do.

▼

LITERARY ELEMENTS

You are probably familiar with the standard elements of storytelling—point of view, characterization, plot and conflict, setting, and symbol—but have you ever really wondered why English teachers are so insistent that they are important? The reason is that each one of those elements is a tool that authors use to build their story, and therefore these are the details they use to help convey their ideas—the themes of their work. In this next section, you will have an opportunity to refresh your memory of these elements (because you likely know them from previous English classes), but even more important, you'll consider how to use them to help you draw plausible and supported conclusions about the theme of a piece of literature.

Point of View

One of the very first, and most significant, decisions a writer makes is from whose perspective the story will be told. In general, the choices of point of view in a novel or short story are the following:

First person: uses "I," and is a character who is often, but not always, the main character in the story.

Third person: uses "he," "she," "they," and so on, and a narrator who is usually not a character within the story. There are a few different types of third person narration:

- An *omniscient* narrator is one who knows what every character is thinking and can move easily through time.
- A *limited omniscient* narrator is one who knows the thoughts of only one character.
- An *objective narrator* is one who reports the actions and dialogue of the characters and describes the setting, but does not move into the thoughts of any of the characters.

Second person: While it is used very rarely, some authors choose a second person narration, which uses the pronoun "you" to address the reader directly, essentially making the reader like a character within the story.

KEY QUESTIONS

When connecting point of view to theme, two key questions to ask are:

- How does the perspective from which the story or poem is told affect what the reader learns about the text?
- What does the perspective reveal and what does it hide?

Characterization

One of the most significant ways to determine a central idea, or theme, of a work is to closely examine the characters of the work, since the characters are often the focus of the action in a text. When Harry Potter decides to sacrifice himself in order to save others from Lord Voldemort at the very end of the series, this reveals the idea that the evil of the world will only be conquered by remembering the importance of community, family, and friendship.

As you probably know, the two main characters in a piece of literature are the **protagonist** (main character) and the **antagonist** (who opposes the main character). It is important to remember that the protagonist is not necessarily good and the antagonist is not necessarily bad. Some of Edgar Allan Poe's short stories, for instance, feature protagonists who are murderers and antagonists who are potential victims or the police.

The way an author brings a character to life is called **characterization**, and there are two basic techniques:

Direct characterization is when a writer explicitly comments on or describes a character. For instance, when the narrator directly states that a character is tall, short, mean, or friendly.

Indirect characterization is when the author develops the character through things the character does or says, or what others say about the character, rather than through direct statements. The reader is expected to infer certain aspects of the character through this type of characterization. If the narrator states, "The young woman got up and offered her seat on the bus to the old woman," the reader might conclude that the young woman is kind and polite, without the author's saying it.

The essential components that authors tend to include for characterization are

- physical descriptions
- actions, gestures, movements
- dialogue
- what other characters say or think about a character, or how they behave toward him or her
- character motivations
- character internal thoughts

KEY QUESTION

When focusing on how character relates to theme, focus on how the characters function within the work and what roles they play.

- What do the characters' actions, inactions, traits, and motivations reveal about the meaning of the work as a whole?

Plot and Conflict

You are probably used to thinking of the words "story" and "plot" as interchangeable, but it is important to distinguish between these terms. The story in a literary text is what happens, while the **plot** is how the author chooses to structure that story. The story of *The Odyssey*, for example, is that of a general in the Greek army who wins a war against Troy and spends the next ten years trying to get home to Ithaca, experiencing many adventures along the way, including a battle with the Cyclops. The plot of *The Odyssey*, however, is far more complex. It begins when a council of the Greek gods determines the fate of Odysseus, who is already many years into his journey home; from there, the reader meets

Odysseus's nearly grown son and we see what life is like in Ithaca without Odysseus. Only then do we get the stories, told in flashback, of Odysseus's adventures. The story is not told chronologically or linearly. When analyzing literature, remember that authors can present a story in any manner they wish, and you always ask yourself why the events of the story unfold the way that they do. In the case of *The Odyssey*, you might draw the conclusion that beginning with the council of the gods demonstrates the primary role the gods played in Greek culture and illustrates their overwhelming power over mortal lives.

The key to every plot is **conflict.** This conflict is generally summarized as a struggle between a protagonist and an antagonist, but it doesn't have to be limited to a conflict between two characters. The main types of conflicts are:

- *Character vs. Another Character*: Harry Potter against Voldemort; Dorothy against the Wicked Witch.
- *Character vs. Society*: Katniss going up against the Capitol; Atticus Finch battling the racism of the American South in the 1930s.
- *Character vs. Nature*: Odysseus against the winds of the Mediterranean; Frodo against the snowstorm on the mountainside.
- *Character vs. Self:* Hazel Grace against her fears of seeing a friend die; Odysseus against his own arrogance.

KEY QUESTIONS

When thinking about plot, the main questions to ask are:

- Why is the story told in the chosen order?
- What are the significant conflicts and how are they resolved—or not?

Setting

Setting gives a piece of literature context. It establishes the location, the time period, and the cultural background, and it creates a specific atmosphere that provokes an emotional response in the audience. Think about a horror film or mystery you may have seen. Many scenes probably took place at night, with lots of shadows, maybe in creepy abandoned houses. Obviously these settings create feelings of suspense and unease. Like all of these literary elements, however, setting is also used as a tool by authors to illustrate meaning in their work. For instance, because *To Kill a Mockingbird* is set in the American South during the Jim Crow era, it's a pretty good bet that the author has chosen that setting because she has something to say about race in American society.

KEY QUESTION

When thinking about the setting of a piece of literature, ask yourself:

- What details of time and place create a specific feeling that leads to an understanding of the work as a whole?

Symbol

Earlier in this chapter, you saw how the scissors in the film *Edward Scissorhands* were used metaphorically; they are also an example of a **symbol**, which is a literary element that has both literal and metaphorical uses in the work. A symbol may be an object, a person, a situation, or events or actions. In *Edward Scissorhands*, the character literally has scissors for hands, but the scissors metaphorically represent his difficulty in connecting with other people. Our stories are filled with symbols: Cinderella's glass slipper; the poison in *Romeo and Juliet*; the dawning of a new day at the end of a horror film. They all have meanings beyond their literal use in the work. In Edgar Allan Poe's poem "The Raven," the black bird is literally sitting in the room with the narrator but is also metaphorically representing the narrator's feelings of loss and depression. In the movie *Citizen Kane*, the main character has had his childhood taken away from him, symbolized by a sled left behind. You can often recognize symbols in a piece of literature by noting their repeated use and links to ideas outside of the text.

KEY QUESTIONS

When thinking about symbols in a piece of literature, you should always ask yourself:

- What larger significance do the objects, situations, or events have?
- How do they help to illustrate a larger meaning of the work?

Literary Elements in Other Genres

The elements you've just thought about are all aspects of storytelling, but they're not necessarily limited to fiction. They might, however, be presented slightly differently in other literary genres.

Drama. A primary difference between fiction and drama is that in drama the story is told mainly through dialogue. Setting and any direct characterization are handled via stage directions, and point of view is unlikely to be a factor in your literary analysis. It is also important to note that all drama has a performance aspect, so one performance might use a different setting than another, and different actors will most certainly bring their own interpretation to the performance of a character.

Poetry. The presence of the literary elements of point of view, characterization, plot, setting, and symbol in poetry depends on the type of poem. Some poems are mostly descriptive and do not incorporate many storytelling elements, while some poems are narrative in structure and may incorporate all of these elements. The primary difference is that in analyzing poetry we tend to call the main voice of the piece the "speaker" rather than the "narrator."

▼
ANALYZING LITERARY ELEMENTS AND THEME

In the previous section, we reviewed the five main literary elements—point of view, characterization, plot and conflict, setting, and symbol. Now we will look to see how all of these elements can work together as building blocks to support the analysis of the overall meaning of a piece of literature.

Make Observations

We're investigating the building blocks of a work:

- Point of View (p. 35)
- Characterization (p. 35)
- Plot and Conflict (p. 36)
- Setting (p. 37)
- Symbol (p. 38)

Identify Patterns

Some things to look for among your observations are:

- Curiosities (p. 32)
- Repetitions (p. 32)
- Opposites (p. 32)
- Links (p. 32)

You will not see all of these things in every part of a literary work, but you should keep them in mind as you read.

Draw Conclusions

What is a theme and how did the author develop it?

A Model Analysis

Read the very short story "Popular Mechanics," by Raymond Carver, and then look at some ways that you can analyze each of the literary elements for the purpose of drawing a conclusion about the possible themes of the work.

Popular Mechanics / Raymond Carver

Early that day the weather turned and the snow was melting into dirty water. Streaks of it ran down from the little shoulder-high window that faced the backyard. Cars slushed by on the street outside, where it was getting dark. But it was getting dark on the inside too.

He was in the bedroom pushing clothes into a suitcase when she came to the door.

I'm glad you're leaving! I'm glad you're leaving! she said. Do you hear?

He kept on putting his things into the suitcase.

5 Son of a bitch! I'm so glad you're leaving! She began to cry. You can't even look me in the face, can you?

Then she noticed the baby's picture on the bed and picked it up.

He looked at her and she wiped her eyes and stared at him before turning and going back to the living room.

Bring that back, he said.

Just get your things and get out, she said.

10 He did not answer. He fastened the suitcase, put on his coat, looked around the bedroom before turning off the light. Then he went out to the living room.

She stood in the doorway of the little kitchen, holding the baby.

I want the baby, he said.

Are you crazy?

No, but I want the baby. I'll get someone to come by for his things.

15 You're not touching this baby, she said.

The baby had begun to cry and she uncovered the blanket from around his head.

Oh, oh, she said, looking at the baby.

He moved toward her.

For God's sake! she said. She took a step back into the kitchen.

20 I want the baby.

Get out of here!

She turned and tried to hold the baby over in a corner behind the stove.

But he came up. He reached across the stove and tightened his hands on the baby.

Let go of him, he said.

25 Get away, get away! she cried.

The baby was red-faced and screaming. In the scuffle they knocked down a flowerpot that hung behind the stove.

He crowded her into the wall then, trying to break her grip. He held on to the baby and pushed with all his weight.

Let go of him, he said.

Don't, she said. You're hurting the baby, she said.

30 I'm not hurting the baby, he said.

The kitchen window gave no light. In the near-dark he worked on her fisted fingers with one hand and with the other hand he gripped the screaming baby up under an arm near the shoulder.

She felt her fingers being forced open. She felt the baby going from her.

No! she screamed just as her hands came loose.

She would have it, this baby. She grabbed for the baby's other arm. She caught the baby around the wrist and leaned back.

35 But he would not let go. He felt the baby slipping out of his hands and he pulled back very hard.

In this manner, the issue was decided.

Point of View. Carver chooses to use a third person limited narrator for this story, which prevents the reader from knowing exactly what is going on in the characters' thoughts. The reader can only watch the story unfold and guess at why it is happening. The reader is intentionally kept at a distance from the characters.

Characters. It is probably curious to you that the characters are not named and that the author provides only minimal physical descriptions of them. Note, however, the repeated actions and dialogue of each character. The man is always the aggressor ("He moved toward her" and "He crowded her"). The woman is always shouting, evidenced by the exclamation points. She also often retreats from him. They are clearly set up as opposites.

Plot/Conflict. Carver's choice of when to begin the story — dropping the reader right into the middle of a fight—and where to end it must be among the most significant curiosities of the story. Carver only hints at the nature of the conflict between the characters; the reader knows the man is leaving but is forced to infer the reasons from the repeated lines like "I'm glad you're leaving" and dialogue like "You can't even look me in the face, can you?" The vagueness of the ending ("In this manner, the issue was decided") leaves the reader wondering exactly what happens to the baby and the parents. The characters certainly know how the conflict between them is resolved, but the reader can only speculate.

Setting. Notice how the first paragraph sets up a dark setting even as it moves from outside to inside the house: "But it was getting dark on the inside too." That ominous atmosphere echoes throughout the piece. The man turns off the light as he leaves the bedroom, and the kitchen window "[gives] no light." You might also be curious about the house itself, especially its size. Everything, — the kitchen, the bedroom, the living room, and the hallway — feels very tight and confined.

Symbol. There are several things that you might be curious about that could be acting as symbols here. In the very first line, the snow, something that is often thought of as white and pure, is "melting into dirty water," suggesting that things are turning bad. Then there is the light inside the house, which keeps getting darker and darker, like the outside. In addition, a flowerpot, one of the only objects described in the house, falls down. Most especially, there is the baby himself, who seems to be both literally and figuratively torn apart by his parents. This is also a link to the biblical story of King Solomon, who ordered a baby to be split in half to determine which of the two women who claimed him loved the baby the most (1 Kings).

Possible Themes. Carver is certainly making a point about the dreadful repercussions that can occur in a relationship without communication. The man and woman never really talk (which is why we never find out what the source of the conflict is), only shout or ignore one another's statements. The relationship they had built together, as symbolized by the house, the flowerpot, and the baby, is being destroyed by their inability or unwillingness to communicate. What was once beautiful, like the snow outside, is now dirty and corrupted.

ACTIVITY LITERARY ELEMENTS AND THEME IN FICTION

Carefully read the following excerpt from *The Scarlet Letter*, the novel by Nathaniel Hawthorne that Melinda, the narrator from *Speak*, was complaining about.

For your focused observation, be sure to consider how Hawthorne uses point of view, characterization, plot and conflict, setting, and symbol.

To recognize patterns, be sure to look for curiosities, repetitions, opposites, and links.

Lastly, draw a conclusion about what Hawthorne might be suggesting about guilt and punishment in this excerpt.

from **The Scarlet Letter** / Nathaniel Hawthorne

This novel, published in 1850, focuses on life in Massachusetts during the Puritan era of the 1640s. Puritans were a group of religious dissidents from England who left their parent country to establish a religious utopia in the New World. They led a strict and pious way of life, valued chastity and frugality, and banned nonreligious entertainment, games, and even the celebration of holidays.

The main character in this story is a young woman, Hester Prynne, whose husband is presumed to be lost at sea; she is convicted of adultery after giving birth to a child, Pearl. In addition to being imprisoned for what the Puritans considered to be a crime, Hester was ordered to embroider a scarlet *A*, and to wear it on the outside of her clothes. In this excerpt, Hester is released from prison and the townspeople, all strict Puritans, see her, Pearl, and the *A* Hester has made for the first time since her conviction. She is ordered to stand on a scaffold for three hours for everyone to see her.

When the young woman — the mother of this child — stood fully revealed before the crowd, it seemed to be her first impulse to clasp the infant closely to her bosom; not so much by an impulse of motherly affection, as that she might thereby conceal a certain token, which was wrought or fastened into her dress. In a moment, however, wisely judging that one token of her shame would but poorly serve to hide another, she took the baby on her arm, and with a burning blush, and yet a haughty smile, and a glance that would not be abashed, looked around at her townspeople and neighbours. On the breast of her gown, in fine red cloth, surrounded with an elaborate embroidery and fantastic flourishes of gold thread, appeared the letter A. It was so artistically done, and with so much fertility and gorgeous luxuriance of fancy, that it had all the effect of a last and fitting decoration to the apparel which she wore, and which was of a splendour in accordance with the taste of the age, but greatly beyond what was allowed by the sumptuary regulations of the colony.

The young woman was tall, with a figure of perfect elegance, on a large scale. She had dark and abundant hair, so glossy that it threw off the sunshine with a gleam, and a face which, besides being beautiful from regularity of feature and richness of complexion, had the impressiveness belonging to a marked brow and deep black eyes. She was lady-like, too, after the manner of the feminine gentility of those days; characterized by a certain state and dignity, rather than by the delicate, evanescent, and indescribable grace, which is now recognized as its indication. And never had Hester Prynne appeared more lady-like, in the antique interpretation of the term, than as she issued from the prison. Those who had before known her, and had expected to behold her dimmed and obscured by a disastrous cloud, were astonished, and even startled, to perceive how her beauty shone out, and made a halo of the misfortune and ignominy in which she was enveloped. It may be true, that, to a sensitive observer, there was something exquisitely painful in it. Her attire, which, indeed, she had wrought for the occasion, in prison, and had modelled much after her own fancy, seemed to express the attitude of her spirit, the desperate recklessness of her mood, by its wild and picturesque peculiarity. But the point which drew all eyes, and, as it were, transfigured the wearer, — so that both men and women, who had been familiarly acquainted with Hester Prynne, were now impressed as if they beheld her for the first time, — was that SCARLET LETTER, so fantastically embroidered and illuminated upon her bosom. It had the effect of a spell, taking her out of the ordinary relations with humanity, and inclosing her in a sphere by herself.

ACTIVITY **LITERARY ELEMENTS AND THEME IN DRAMA**

Carefully read the following excerpt from *A Raisin in the Sun*, by Lorraine Hansberry.

For your focused observation, be sure to consider how Hansberry uses characterization, plot and conflict, setting, and symbol. To identify patterns, be sure to look for curiosities, repetitions, opposites, and links. Last, draw a conclusion about what Hansberry might be suggesting about money in this excerpt.

from **A Raisin in the Sun** / Lorraine Hansberry

The play takes place in Chicago in the 1950s. The Younger family has been having money difficulties, but recently Mama has received an insurance settlement after the death of her husband. Her son, Walter, wants to use the money for a risky business investment.

WALTER Why do women always think there's a woman somewhere when a man gets restless. (*picks up the check*) Do you know what this money means to me? Do you know what this money can do for us? (*puts it back*) Mama — Mama — I want so many things . . .

MAMA Yes, son —

WALTER I want so many things that they are driving me kind of crazy . . . Mama — look at me.

MAMA I'm looking at you. You a good-looking boy. You got a job, a nice wife, a fine boy and —

5 **WALTER** A job. (*looks at her*) Mama, a job? I open and close car doors all day long. I drive a man around in his limousine and I say, "Yes, sir; no, sir; very good, sir; shall I take the Drive, sir?" Mama, that ain't no kind of job . . . that ain't nothing at all. (*very quietly*) Mama, I don't know if I can make you understand.

MAMA Understand what, baby?

WALTER (*quietly*) Sometimes it's like I can see the future stretched out in front of me — just plain as day. The future, Mama. Hanging over there at the edge of my days. Just waiting for me — a big, looming blank space — full of *nothing*. Just waiting for *me*. But it don't have to be. (*Pause. Kneeling beside her chair.*) Mama — sometimes when I'm downtown and I pass them cool, quiet-looking restaurants where them white boys are sitting back and talking 'bout things . . . sitting there turning deals worth millions of dollars . . . sometimes I see guys don't look much older than me —

MAMA Son — how come you talk so much 'bout money?

WALTER (*with immense passion*) Because it is life, Mama!

10 **MAMA** (*quietly*) Oh — (*very quietly*) So now it's life. Money is life, Once upon a time freedom used to be life — now it's money. I guess the world really do change . . .

WALTER No — it was always money, Mama. We just didn't know about it.

MAMA No . . . something has changed. (*She looks at him.*) You something new, boy. In my time we was worried about not being lynched and getting to the North if we could and how to stay alive and still have a pinch of dignity too . . . Now here come you and Beneatha — talking 'bout things we never even thought about hardly, me and your daddy. You ain't satisfied or proud of nothing we done. I mean that you had a home; that we kept you out of trouble till you was grown; that you don't have to ride to work on the back of nobody's streetcar — You my children — but how different we done become.

WALTER (*A long beat. He pats her hand and gets up*) You just don't understand, Mama, you just don't understand.

LANGUAGE AND STYLE

In this chapter, so far, you have been thinking about and practicing the various ways to read literary texts by looking at the building blocks of storytelling—point of view, characterization, plot and conflict, setting and symbol—that writers use to convey their ideas. Now it's time to think about even more detailed analysis and begin asking how the building blocks themselves are constructed. Think back to setting, for instance. When we say that a setting creates a "dreary" atmosphere, how exactly does the author create that dreariness? Or, think back to characterization. How exactly does the reader get the impression that the main character is an arrogant jerk? The answer is: with **style**. Style is the term we use to discuss all of the language decisions authors make as they write.

Notice in this short passage from *A Tale of Two Cities* how Charles Dickens uses language to build his setting and create a very specific feeling. (We have underlined some words for emphasis.)

> There was a steaming mist in all the hollows, and it had roamed in its forlornness up the hill, like an evil spirit, seeking rest and finding none. A clammy and intensely cold mist, it made its slow way through the air in ripples that visibly followed and overspread one another, as the waves of an unwholesome sea might do. It was dense enough to shut out everything from the light of the coach-lamps but these its own workings, and a few yards of road; and the reek of the labouring horses steamed into it, as if they had made it all.

The stylistic choices of "reek," "clammy," "unwholesome," and "evil" create a setting so dismal and depressing that it almost seems hopeless.

While style is important in fiction and drama, it is *vital* to poetry. In poetry, style is often employed for its own sake, to make something that sounds beautiful, or to convey a surprising idea or powerful image. Look, for instance, at this section from a poem called "America" by Claude McKay, and notice how the language choices—the style—bring the ideas to life and fill them with power:

> Although she feeds me bread of bitterness,
> And sinks into my throat her tiger's tooth,
> Stealing my breath of life, I will confess
> I love this cultured hell that tests my youth.
> Her vigor flows like tides into my blood,
> Giving me strength erect against her hate,
> Her bigness sweeps my being like a flood.

Thinking about how an author's style affects the meaning of a work of literature is what we call close reading, or close analysis. Close reading is not about labeling stylistic devices with fancy terms. It is about looking closely at the author's craft and seeing how each small choice contributes to the piece.

So far, we've been talking about style as a broad term to describe an author's language choices. Next, we'll look at four specific components that contribute to an author's style:

- Diction
- Syntax
- Figurative Language
- Imagery

Each of these components builds on and supports the others. These small but essential language choices allow writers to create the settings, characters, conflicts, and other literary elements described earlier in this chapter.

Diction

Like an artist who paints in watercolor, pastel, or oil, a writer works in words. **Diction** is the technical term for "word choice." There are literally thousands and thousands of words available for a writer to use, so most authors make very careful choices about the words they include.

Denotation and Connotation. To fully understand the idea of diction, we have to recognize the differences between two essential terms:

> **Denotation** is the literal meaning of a word, free from any associated meanings.
>
> **Connotation** is the cultural or emotional associations attached to a word.

An easy way to understand the difference between the two is to think about the word *home*. The denotation is simply "the place where one resides," but think about the connotative meanings associated with the word: "comfort," "safety," "warmth." You can see this even more clearly when you contrast *home* to another word the writer might have chosen—*house*, which has a more impersonal connotation to it than *home*.

Formal and Informal. In addition to creating a variety of associations for the reader, diction choices can also can create a certain level of formality through the use of very proper words or technical jargon, or casualness through the intentional use of slang.

Look, for example, at these two short passages from the novel *Pride and Prejudice* by Jane Austen. Both describe the same character, Lydia, but notice how the diction in each passage is different and can lead to contradictory feelings toward Lydia:

1. Lydia was a stout, well-grown girl of fifteen, with a fine complexion and good-humoured countenance; a favourite with her mother, whose affection had brought her into public at an early age. She had high animal spirits, and a sort of natural self-consequence, which the attentions of the officers, to whom her uncle's good dinners and her own easy manners recommended her, had increased into assurance.

2. At the mention of his youngest daughter's name, Mr. Bennet shook his head. Although quite pretty, Lydia was a lively headstrong girl prone to a breathiness of speech. [. . .] He despaired of Lydia and for any man who would eventually take her as a wife.

Syntax

Another stylistic choice that an author makes is **syntax**, which is simply word order—how an author strings words together to make phrases, clauses, and sentences.

To some extent, grammar dictates how writers can construct their sentences, but there are often a number of different choices, including intentionally reversing the normal word order sequencing for emphasis, such as "Quit my job I cannot," instead of the more typical "I cannot quit my job."

Length of Sentences. Syntax often gives a text a particular rhythm. Short sentences, for example, can create a choppy rhythm or a sense of urgency, whereas longer sentences can feel smooth and flowing. If you are familiar with musical dynamics, you might think of short sentences as being staccato, while long sentences are legato. Often, writers will use changes in sentence length or sentence types to create rhythmic effects. The most common is to follow a series of long sentences with a short one to create impact, but the pattern can work the other way as well.

Types of Sentences. There are a number of sentence types a writer can use. The most common is the declarative sentence, but writers can also use sentence fragments, interrogative sentences (questions), and exclamatory sentences (with exclamation points at the end).

Punctuation. How (or whether) a writer uses punctuation is also a matter of syntax. William Faulker, for instance, regularly includes run-on sentences to reflect the rambling stream-of-consciousness thoughts of his characters. Punctuation is especially important in poetry because it is optional, so the punctuation the author uses is there for a specific effect, not just for grammatical correctness.

How does the actual syntax of this cartoon illustrate the definition of *syntax*?

Syntax can be tricky to analyze, but the thing to be on the lookout for are times when *form follows function,* meaning when the syntax somehow emphasizes a point the author is making.

For example, read the following passage from a classic detective novel, *The Maltese Falcon,* by Dashiell Hammett, and notice how the detective, Sam Spade, uses short, simple, declarative sentences that reveal his no-nonsense approach to his job:

> When a man's partner is killed he's supposed to do something about it. It doesn't make any difference what you thought of him. He was your partner and you're supposed to do something about it. Then it happens we were in the detective business. Well, when one of your organization gets killed it's bad business to let the killer get away with it. It's bad all around—bad for that one organization, bad for every detective everywhere.

Figurative Language

Authors use **figurative language** when they choose words or phrases that are not meant to be taken literally, just as you do when you say something like "I'm so hungry that I could eat a horse." You are not literally going to eat a horse, but you are using figurative language (hyperbole, in this case) to communicate just how hungry you are. Some of the most common elements of figurative language are

- *metaphor*: a direct comparison between unlike things, without the word "like" or "as"
- *simile*: a comparison between unlike things using "like" or "as"
- *hyperbole*: a deliberate exaggeration or overstatement (often for the sake of humor)
- *personification*: giving human qualities to inanimate objects
- *allusion*: a reference to something well known—a piece of literature, art, a historical event, and so on

Imagery

Another element of style that writers have at their disposal is **imagery**, a term that refers to the ways that writers try to appeal to the reader's senses by evoking sights, sounds, smells, tastes, and touch. Keep in mind that imagery can be both literal and figurative.

literal imagery: The wind shook the trees.

figurative imagery: The trees danced with the wind.

Writers communicate the worlds they create through imagery; they want their readers to feel as if they are right there in the middle of the worlds, not just reading about them.

Look at the opening lines of the poem "Winter Place" by Genny Lim, and notice how Lim uses both figurative language, allusions in particular, and imagery to describe a setting that is dismal and depressing:

> I live in this foghorn moon of a fishhole alley
> Every night there's a derelict dog, mangy with a cataract stare
> Lickin' the wounds of old North Beach
> Leftovers, fish 'n chips, upchucked cheesesteak, antipasti

Blasted against the antiseptic glare of trendy restaurants,
glossy Gelatos
Where MTV couples glide frozenly by
Catching in the corners of their ray-banned eyes
Their store-bought reflections

Analyzing Style and Tone

As you've looked at all of these elements of style, you may have noticed that they share something. Because they are ways that an author presents his or her ideas, a reader can use them to see what the author's or narrator's feelings are toward the subject. This is what we call **tone**. In your study of literature, you will often be asked to analyze the author's tone, and to do this, you will focus on the author's stylistic choices.

You've probably heard the term *tone* before in the expression "tone of voice." With your tone of voice, you can make what you say sound angry, happy, sarcastic, and so on. You use your tone of voice to indicate your attitude toward what you are saying. In writing, tone works very similarly. By looking carefully at language choices (style), we can pick up on the attitude that an author or a narrator takes toward his or her subject.

There are many possible ways to describe the author's or narrator's tone in a piece of literature. Here are just a few:

Positive Tone	Negative Tone
sentimental, light, fanciful, sympathetic, benevolent, vibrant, joyful, complimentary	angry, sharp, cold, condescending, detached, sarcastic

A Model Analysis

Look at this famous opening paragraph from *The Catcher in the Rye* by J. D. Salinger.

If you really want to hear about it, the first thing you'll probably want to know is where I was born, and what my lousy childhood was like, and how my parents were occupied and all before they had me, and all that David Copperfield kind of crap, but I don't feel like going into it, if you want to know the truth. In the first place, that stuff bores me, and in the second place, my parents would have about two hemorrhages apiece if I told anything pretty personal about them. They're quite touchy about anything like that, especially my father. They're nice and all. I'm not saying that—but they're also touchy as hell. Besides, I'm not going to tell you my whole goddam autobiography or anything. I'll just tell you about this madman stuff that happened to me around last Christmas just before I got pretty run-down and had to come out here and take it easy.

Let's consider the elements of style here that create narrator Holden Caulfield's sarcastic and even condescending tone.

Diction. His use of the words "lousy," "crap," and "goddam" show that Holden doesn't care if he offends someone with his slang or profanity.

Syntax. The first sentence is one long rush, like a sudden outpouring of thoughts, but then the narrator switches to shorter sentences when he makes it clear that he is not going to reveal much, especially about his parents.

Figurative Language. Holden uses hyperbole when he says that his parents would have "two hemorrhages apiece." This reveals his sarcastic tone and his willingness to exaggerate to make a point.

A literary work rarely maintains a single tone throughout the text; even Holden's softens, especially toward his sister later in the novel. A piece may begin with one tone and switch to another to illustrate a particular point. A doctor in a story, for instance, might start off with a very clinical and detached tone toward her patient with an illness, but then move to a more sympathetic tone to reflect her compassion and growing engagement in the lives of her patients.

ACTIVITY   STYLE AND TONE

Read this poem by Emily Dickinson and analyze how the diction, syntax, figurative language, and imagery help to create the speaker's tone.

My river runs to thee / Emily Dickinson

My river runs to thee:
Blue sea, wilt welcome me?

My river waits reply.
Oh sea, look graciously!

5 I'll fetch thee brooks
From spotted nooks,—

Say, sea,
Take me!

▼
ANALYZING STYLE AND THEME

While sometimes the goal of analyzing style is to pick up on the speaker's or narrator's tone and figure out how that tone is created, other times we want to look at how these stylistic moves help create the meaning of the work as a whole: the theme. You can use the analysis process to guide your close reading:

1. Make observations
   - Diction (pp. 45–46)
   - Syntax (pp. 46–47)
   - Figurative Language (p. 47)
   - Imagery (pp. 47–48)

2. Identify patterns
   - **Curiosities.** Places where the author uses an interesting word or phrase, or uses words in an unusual or unexpected way
   - **Repetitions.** Places where the same words or phrases are used several times, or an image is repeated often throughout the work
   - **Opposites.** Places in a work where the words or phrases intentionally contrast with each other; perhaps the syntax puts sentences in conflict with each other
   - **Links.** Connections in the text to something else outside of the text

3. Draw conclusions about the work as a whole
   - Theme (pp. 29–34)

A Model Analysis

Read the poem "Slam, Dunk, & Hook" by Yusef Komunyakaa, and then look at some ways that you can analyze each stylistic element and draw a conclusion about how it supports the themes of the work.

Slam, Dunk, & Hook / Yusef Komunyakaa

Fast breaks. Lay ups. With Mercury's
Insignia on our sneakers,
We outmaneuvered the footwork
Of bad angels. Nothing but a hot
5 Swish of strings like silk
Ten feet out. In the roundhouse
Labyrinth our bodies
Created, we could almost
Last forever, poised in midair
10 Like storybook sea monsters.
A high note hung there
A long second. Off
The rim. We'd corkscrew
Up & dunk balls that exploded
15 The skullcap of hope & good
Intention. Bug-eyed, lanky,
All hands & feet . . . sprung rhythm.
We were metaphysical when girls
Cheered on the sidelines.

20 Tangled up in a falling,
   Muscles were a bright motor
   Double-flashing to the metal hoop
   Nailed to our oak.
   When Sonny Boy's mama died
25 He played nonstop all day, so hard
   Our backboard splintered.
   Glistening with sweat, we jibed
   & rolled the ball off our
   Fingertips. Trouble
30 Was there slapping a blackjack
   Against an open palm.
   Dribble, drive to the inside, feint,
   & glide like a sparrow hawk.
   Lay ups. Fast breaks.
35 We had moves we didn't know
   We had. Our bodies spun
   On swivels of bone & faith,
   Through a lyric slipknot
   Of joy, & we knew we were
40 Beautiful & dangerous.

Diction. Notice how often the speaker in the poem sets up his word choice as opposites, such as "bad angels," "On swivels of bone & faith," "slipknot / Of joy," and "we were / Beautiful & dangerous." These opposites may set up the idea that things, like a game of basketball, are not quite so simple as you might originally think. The speaker repeats a lot of words that refer to violence or the potential for it: "monsters," "exploded," "falling," "splintered," "slapping a blackjack," and "dangerous." The basketball game, constrained by the rules of the court, keeps this violence under control, especially when Sonny Boy takes out his grief on the backboard, not on anyone or anything else. Some of the diction probably piqued your curiosity, such as why do the balls explode "The skullcap of hope & good / Intention" or why the hoop is "Nailed to our oak"—and what is a "slipknot of joy," anyway? The game and the players, through the diction, seem powerful, but also some-what unknowable, at least to outsiders.

Syntax. There are a number of short sentences, even sentence fragments, such as "Fast breaks. Lay ups." and "Off / The rim." You might find it curious that the first two sentences are repeated in line 34, but the order of them is reversed. Notice too the repeated syntacti-cal use of the ampersand (&) that connects two nouns that do not automatically relate to each other, such as "bone & faith" and "Beautiful & dangerous." Much of the syntax of this poem creates a sense of urgency and speed, appropriate for a poem celebrating the power and beauty of the game.

Figurative Language. This poem includes a lot of links to mythology, such as "Mercury's / Insignia," "storybook sea monsters," and "roundhouse / Labyrinth," which together give the players an almost heroic status. In addition to these allusions are similes, such as "Dribble, drive to the inside, feint, / & glide like a sparrow hawk" and "Swish of strings like silk," which elevate the components of basketball beyond the court to the larger world. The metaphor of "Muscles were a bright motor" gives the players an inhuman speed and strength. Adding to the otherworldly feeling of the game, the speaker uses hyperbole ("balls that exploded / The skullcap") and personification ("Trouble / Was there slapping a blackjack / Against an open palm").

Imagery. Sensory details are repeated throughout this poem. Sounds, such as "hot / Swish," "high note hung," "exploded," "Cheered on the sidelines," "slapping a blackjack," work to give the reader a feeling of being right there in the midst of the game. There are powerful visual images as well of the players that seem to be opposites, such as when they are "poised in midair," but also in constant motion, for instance, "Tangled up in a fall- ing" and "Double-flashing to the metal hoop." Or, when they are described as "Bug-eyed, lanky, / All hands & feet" but this physical awkwardness doesn't prevent them from being able to "corkscrew / Up & dunk" and "[outmaneuver] the footwork / Of bad angels." These opposites in imagery show the conflicts the players face in their opponents as well as in themselves.

Possible Themes. Because of all of the allusions to mythology and the otherworldliness of some of the imagery, Komunyakaa could be suggesting that basketball allows the play- ers to go beyond themselves and to escape from everyday, ordinary realities.

ACTIVITY   STYLE AND THEME

Earlier in this chapter, you read the short story "Popular Mechanics" by Raymond Carver (p. 39), and you looked specifically at the ways the literary elements, such as setting and characterization, led to an interpretation of the theme of the story. Reread the story, this time focusing on how Carver uses diction, syntax, figurative language, and imagery to illustrate theme. If you need help recognizing stylistic patterns, try looking for curiosities, repetitions, opposites, and links.

culminating activity

1. The following poem is by the eighteenth-century English poet William Blake. Read the poem carefully. Then write a response in which you analyze how the tone of the speaker is developed through such devices as diction, syntax, figurative language, and imagery.

The Tyger / William Blake

Tyger Tyger, burning bright,
In the forests of the night;
What immortal hand or eye,
Could frame thy fearful symmetry?

5 In what distant deeps or skies
Burnt the fire of thine eyes?
On what wings dare he aspire?
What the hand, dare seize the fire?

And what shoulder, & what art,
10 Could twist the sinews of thy heart?
And when thy heart began to beat,
What dread hand? & what dread feet?

What the hammer? what the chain,
In what furnace was thy brain?
15 What the anvil? what dread grasp,
Dare its deadly terrors clasp!

When the stars threw down their spears
And water'd heaven with their tears:
Did he smile his work to see?
20 Did he who made the Lamb make thee?

Tyger Tyger burning bright,
In the forests of the night:
What immortal hand or eye,
Dare frame thy fearful symmetry?

2. The following passage is from the short story "The Tell-Tale Heart," by Edgar Allan Poe. Read the passage carefully. Then, in a well-organized response, analyze how the author reveals the character of the unnamed narrator. In your analysis, you will want to explain how the characterization can support a conclusion about the meaning of the passage as a whole.

from **The Tell-Tale Heart** / Edgar Allan Poe

In this scene, the narrator has just murdered an old man, who lived in a room in the narrator's house, for no stated reason other than that the old man's vulture-like eye disturbed him. Just as he finishes burying the old man beneath the floorboards, the police knock on the narrator's door.

As the bell sounded the hour, there came a knocking at the street door. I went down to open it with a light heart, — for what had I now to fear? There entered three men, who introduced themselves, with perfect suavity, as officers of the police. A shriek had been heard by a neighbor during the night; suspicion of foul play had been aroused; information had been lodged at the police office, and they (the officers) had been deputed to search the premises.

I smiled, — for what had I to fear? I bade the gentlemen welcome. The shriek, I said, was my own in a dream. The old man, I mentioned, was absent in the country. I took my visitors all over the house. I bade them search — search well. I led them, at length, to his chamber. I showed them his treasures, secure, undisturbed. In the enthusiasm of my confidence, I brought chairs into the room, and desired them here to rest from their fatigues, while I myself, in the wild audacity of my perfect triumph, placed my own seat upon the very spot beneath which reposed the corpse of the victim.

The officers were satisfied. My manner had convinced them. I was singularly at ease. They sat, and while I answered cheerily, they chatted of familiar things. But, ere long, I felt myself getting pale and wished them gone. My head ached, and I fancied a ringing in my ears: but still they sat and still they chatted. The ringing became more distinct: — it continued and became more distinct: I talked more freely to get rid of the feeling: but it continued and gained definiteness — until, at length, I found that the noise was not within my ears.

3. A coming-of-age story often tells about the social and ethical moral development of its protagonist as he or she begins to reach adulthood and starts to identify his or her place in the world. Select an important moment in the development of the protagonist of a coming-of-age story — perhaps the climax of the story — and write a response that explains how that single moment affects the character's development and shapes the meaning of the work as a whole. Choose a novel or a film that you know well, and be sure to support your response with relevant details from the story.

Photo: Orla/Shutterstock, Art: Christian Mojallali

3
Thinking about Rhetoric and Argument

I t may seem odd that this book includes a chapter about something that most people try to avoid. Arguing with friends often leads to hurt feelings, and arguing with teachers or parents may lead to punishments. But there is another, more positive meaning of the term *argument*: using language, reason, and evidence to influence the thoughts and behavior of others, and that is the kind of **argument** that will be the focus of this chapter.

You have heard and even likely used the word *argument* in this sense. You may, for example, have said something like, "Yeah, Eva made a good argument. I think I might take Mandarin Chinese." You and your friend did not have a disagreement that involved anything unpleasant; she was simply trying to convince you to do something, in this case, learn a particular language.

Let's flip the scenario. If you wanted to convince your friend to take Mandarin with you, what argument would you make? Would you beg and plead because you didn't know anyone else in that class? Would you remind her of how great it would look on a college application? Would you entice her with an adventuresome tale of backpacking the Great

Truth springs from
argument among friends.

—David Hume

Wall of China? It would depend on your audience: what your friend is like and what's important to her. These choices, the *how* of an argument, are what we call **rhetoric**.

Simply put, rhetoric refers to the strategies we use to make an argument persuasive — to achieve its purpose. Rhetoric, which had its beginnings in ancient Greece, also gives us a vocabulary to analyze the effectiveness of arguments, whether written, spoken, or visual. It reminds us, too, that argument is not a matter of winning, losing, or wearing an opponent down: it's a matter of strategy and persuasion.

▼ CHANGING MINDS, CHANGING THE WORLD

Argument and rhetoric are not just for English class or for silver-tongued politicians. They are how ideas get shared, how minds get changed, how movements begin. Argument and rhetoric can change the world. The philosopher Plato said that "rhetoric is the art of ruling the minds of men." The way he says it may sound a bit manipulative, but rhetoric and argument can also be about improving the world and changing minds for the better.

In the early seventeenth century, Galileo Galilei presented evidence supporting Nicolaus Copernicus's theory that the earth revolved around the sun, despite the claim of most scientists and religious leaders at the time that the earth was the center of the universe. While he was arrested and imprisoned for arguing his position, eventually the ban on his work was lifted, and his ideas prevailed because of the compelling evidence he had presented.

In 1852, Harriet Beecher Stowe published the novel *Uncle Tom's Cabin*, which became the best-selling book—after the Bible—of the nineteenth century. The book's fictional depictions of the cruel realities of slavery in the United States before the Civil War have been credited with greatly expanding the support for the antislavery movement of the time.

▶

How does this painting visually represent the challenges that Galileo faced?

Joseph-Nicolas Robert-Fleury, *Galileo before the Holy Office*, 1847. Oil on canvas. Louvre, Paris, France.

© RMN-Grand Palais/Art Resource, NY

This statue of Harriet Beecher Stowe and Abraham Lincoln stands in front of the Lincoln Financial building in Hartford, Connecticut, where Stowe lived.

In what ways do the figures' gestures, clothing, and positions illustrate the importance that the artist gives to Stowe?

Ann Rosow-Lucchesi

Upon meeting Stowe, President Abraham Lincoln reportedly said, "So this is the little lady who started this great war." Whether he actually said this to her is doubted by some, but few historians discount the impact Stowe's argument against slavery had on the country.

The American biologist Rachel Carson published *Silent Spring* in 1962, arguing that widespread use of DDT and other synthetic pesticides would have a disastrous impact on our environment. She claimed that these pesticides not only killed insects but also made

Rachel Carson testifying before Congress in 1963 on the environmental hazards of pesticides and other chemicals.

Science is expected to be based solely on facts and evidence, but why does it sometimes take persuasion and rhetoric for a scientific idea to be accepted by the wider community?

AP Photo

their way up the food chain to threaten bird and fish populations and that they could eventually sicken humans. At a congressional hearing on pesticides, one senator described *Silent Spring*, which eventually sold more than 2 million copies, as a book that "substantially altered the course of history."

Even more recently, Malala Yousafzai began blogging in 2009 about the Taliban, which had taken control of her town in Pakistan and banned girls from attending school. Despite the threats of violence, the preteen continued posting to her blog to express her point of view, and on October 9, 2012, a Taliban fighter boarded her school bus, asked for her by name, and shot her three times. Yousafzai recovered fully and has since continued to advocate for education for girls, leading Pakistan to pass its very first Right to Education bill—and she was honored with the Nobel Peace Prize in 2014.

As you can see, making strong arguments is important because it gives us an opportunity to influence the world around us, whether the change we create is globally dramatic or personally significant.

Just as important as developing our own arguments, however, is the ability to critically examine the arguments that others present to us. We are bombarded daily by arguments that people, governments, corporations, and others are making in order to influence us in one way or another. Companies try to get us to buy their products, politicians try to get our votes, researchers present evidence to convince us of their findings and conclusions, and artists challenge our point of view. We have to be careful consumers, voters, readers, viewers, and listeners, so that we can make informed choices in all areas of our lives, and not be manipulated by faulty arguments.

Pat Bagley/Cagle Cartoons

This political cartoon by artist Pat Bagley is from 2012, soon after Yousafzai was shot by the Taliban.

How does Bagley make his argument about the power of Malala's message?

The process of thinking carefully about the rhetoric around us, and of analyzing how rhetoric is used as a tool of persuasion, is the same analysis process that we introduced in Chapter 1.

- make observations
- identify patterns
- draw conclusions

In analyzing rhetoric, you carefully observe what writers or speakers say and how they say it. You look for patterns in their language, evidence, or reasoning, and you draw conclusions about whether their use of rhetoric is effective, manipulative, flawed, masterful, or somewhere in between.

KEY QUESTIONS

When you think about rhetoric, the key questions to ask are:

- What strategies does the writer or speaker use to reach (or persuade) his or her audience?
- What goal (or purpose) does the writer or speaker have in mind?

▼

EFFECTIVE ARGUMENTATIVE CLAIMS

Central to every argument is a **claim**. This is the position taken by the person making the argument. This is what he or she is hoping to prove, to persuade the audience to believe. The claims for the examples we just discussed could be summarized as:

Galileo: The earth revolves around the sun.

Stowe: Slavery is inhumane and should be eliminated.

Carson: DDT has dangerous, long-term effects on humans and the natural world.

Yousafzai: Education should be available to everyone, regardless of gender.

If you think carefully about these claims, you'll notice something a bit odd: at this point in time, the claims put forth by Galileo, Stowe, and Carson seem indisputable. It is a verifiable scientific truth that the earth revolves around the sun. Slavery is absolutely inhumane and was long ago outlawed in the United States. The use of DDT was banned in the United States in 1972. It's a testament to the power of these arguments that these issues are no longer subject to debate.

However, what made all of these arguments effective was that at one point each of these claims *was* controversial and the subject of debate. In the case of Yousafzai's claim that education should be available to everyone regardless of gender, the matter might seem indisputable to you, but in her homeland it is still a matter of ongoing debate. And that's what makes her stance so powerful.

So, the first step in crafting a strong argument is developing an arguable claim. After all, what's the point of trying to persuade someone of something that's already a proven fact? Finding an arguable claim is also about more than just personal preference. "I like popcorn better than pretzels" is a statement of preference about snack foods, but it's not arguable if the speaker of the statement is merely stating his viewpoint. What is there to prove? And accusations are generally counterproductive: "Anybody who prefers pretzels to popcorn has bad taste" might sum up how you feel when the buttery aroma of popcorn hits your nose in the movie theater, but framing the argument as an attack on people who disagree ignores the issue at hand, which is to weigh the benefits of popcorn versus pretzels. However, if you changed these opinions and judgments to something like "Popcorn is a more nutritious snack than pretzels," now there's a claim that you can support, and that can serve as the basis of an argument. You would consider what "nutritious" means in terms of calories, fat, vitamins, or various other measures. Does nutritious mean healthful, or simply providing a lot of nutrition (calories)? It's an arguable claim.

KEY QUESTION

When writing or analyzing a claim, be sure to ask yourself:

- Is the claim arguable to begin with?

ACTIVITY IDENTIFYING ARGUABLE CLAIMS

Identify which of the following statements are arguable claims.

1. World War I occurred before World War II.

2. World War I caused World War II.

3. The novel *To Kill a Mockingbird* is an influential study of racism in America.

4. Anyone who does not appreciate the importance of *To Kill a Mockingbird* is either not very smart or downright prejudiced.

5. *To Kill a Mockingbird* should be required reading for every student in public schools in America.

6. Many schools have policies on what constitutes plagiarism and what the consequences are for anyone found guilty of plagiarism.

7. All high schools should have clear policies on what constitutes plagiarism and what the consequences are for anyone found guilty of plagiarism.

8. Plagiarism is cheating, pure and simple.

ACTIVITY FINDING THE CLAIM

Identify the claim in the following arguments.

from On Being a Cripple / Nancy Mairs

First, the matter of semantics. I am a cripple. I choose this word to name me. I choose from among several possibilities, the most common of which are "handicapped" and "disabled." I made the choice a number of years ago, without thinking, unaware of my motives for doing so. Even now, I'm not sure what those motives are, but I recognize that they are complex and not entirely flattering. People—crippled or not—wince at the word "cripple," as they do not at "handicapped" or "disabled." Perhaps I want them to wince. I want them to see me as a tough customer, one to whom the fates/gods/viruses have not been kind, but who can face the brutal truth of her existence squarely. As a cripple, I swagger.

from Last Child in the Woods / Richard Louv

Researchers at the State University of New York at Buffalo are experimenting with a genetic technology through which they can choose the colors that appear on butterfly wings. The announcement of this in 2002 led writer Matt Richtel to conjure a brave new advertising medium: "There are countless possibilities for moving ads out of the virtual world and into the real one. Sponsorship-wise, it's time for nature to carry its weight." Advertisers already stamp their messages into the wet sands of public beaches. Cashstrapped municipalities hope corporations agree to affix their company logo on parks in exchange for dollars to keep the public spaces maintained. "The sheer popularity" of simulating nature or using nature as ad space "demands that we acknowledge, even respect, their cultural importance," suggests Richtel. Culturally important, yes. But the logical extension of synthetic nature is the irrelevance of "true" nature — the certainty that it's not even worth looking at.

The Case for a Higher Minimum Wage / *New York Times* Editorial Board

The political posturing over raising the minimum wage sometimes obscures the huge and growing number of low-wage workers it would affect. An estimated 27.8 million people would earn more money under the Democratic proposal to lift the hourly minimum from $7.25 today to $10.10 by 2016. And most of them do not fit the low-wage stereotype of a teenager with a summer job. Their average age is 35; most work full time; more than one-fourth are parents; and, on average, they earn half of their families' total income.

None of that, however, has softened the hearts of opponents, including congressional Republicans and low-wage employers, notably restaurant owners and executives.

This is not a new debate. The minimum wage is a battlefield in a larger political fight between Democrats and Republicans — dating back to the New Deal legislation that instituted the first minimum wage in 1938 — over government's role in the economy, over raw versus regulated capitalism, over corporate power versus public needs.

But the results of the wage debate are clear. Decades of research, facts and evidence show that increasing the minimum wage is vital to the economic security of tens of millions of Americans, and would be good for the weak economy.

THE RHETORICAL SITUATION OF AN ARGUMENT

Imagine that you are making the argument to your parents or guardians that you ought to have a later curfew. Your claim might be something like: *because I am mature and respon-sible, I should be able to stay out until midnight*. Now, let's consider how the *context* can affect the argument. What if you were nine years old when you made this argument? Would it be received differently than if you made it when you were fifteen or sixteen or even eigh-teen? What if you had just made the honor roll at school? What about the audience of your argument? Would your parents react differently if they had recently read a newspaper story about a child being abducted? If you knew that one of your parents was having a difficult time at work, would you try to ease into your argument slowly and carefully?

The point here is that all arguments exist within a context, which directly influences not only *what* is presented but also *how* it is presented. We call this the **rhetorical situation**.

When thinking about context, remember to take into account the **occasion:** the time and place, and what circumstances gave rise to the argument. You should also think about the **purpose:** whether the speaker intends to entertain, educate, explain, respond to an accusation, bring about an action, or change a behavior.

The Rhetorical Triangle

The easiest way to examine the choices we make when building an argument is to consider three key elements, represented in the accompanying diagram, which is often referred to as the **rhetorical triangle**:

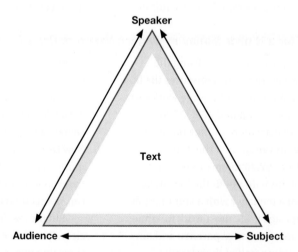

When we develop arguments, we're looking at the interaction between and among the three key elements—**speaker (writer)**, **subject**, and **audience**—and how those three elements determine the form and content of the argument. Think about changing just one of them. If, for instance, you're asked to persuade a group of fourth graders about the importance of reading both widely and often, how would you approach them? Would you consider research studies and all sorts of statistical data? Not likely. You might if you were asked to make a formal presentation to a group of your peers, but what would get the fourth graders' attention? A personal story? Maybe a video clip of celebrities or famous athletes talking about what reading means to them?

SOAPS

Another way to remember all of these elements is the acronym **SOAPS**: Subject, Occasion, Audience, Purpose, and Speaker. SOAPS is a useful start as a way to organize your ideas, whether you're analyzing someone else's argument or planning one of your own.

Subject. What is the speaker or writer's general topic or content? Harriet Beecher Stowe's subject was slavery in the United States. Carson's was DDT specifically, pesticides in general. Remember that the subject can be stated in a few words or a phrase, while the claim is the speaker's position on the subject. Part of your analysis of subject is determining if the writer has chosen a fairly narrow subject or a much larger one, and whether that subject is sufficiently developed.

Occasion. What circumstances give rise to the argument? Is there a controversy already in play? Is the speaker or writer responding to an accusation or an existing or urgent situation? When Rachel Carson published *Silent Spring*, there was emerging evidence that DDT softened the shells of bird eggs (particularly those of bald eagles and peregrine falcons), resulting in a dramatic drop in the birds' population. This finding and others led Carson to sound the alarm and argue for action to preserve the environment.

Audience. While there are often multiple audiences for any argument, usually the speaker or writer has a primary audience in mind for his or her claim and will tailor the argument depending on the expectations, prejudices, anticipated objections, and interests of that audience. As Galileo was proposing his theories about our solar system, his greatest opponent was the Roman Catholic Church, so, in making his argument, he tried to be careful not to offend religious leaders.

Purpose. What is the speaker or writer's intention? What does he or she want the audience to do? In many cases, a speaker wants action: vote, buy, stop, start, do something. But a speaker may want the audience simply to consider a different perspective or a new angle on an idea. In some cases, there is more than one purpose, an immediate and specific one and then a larger issue. For example, Malala Yousafzai wrote her blog primarily to call attention to what she believed was an unfair situation — limitations on the educational opportunities available to women in her culture — but she also intended to criticize the regime that created such oppression.

Speaker. Who is putting forward the claim? The speaker or writer is often a person, but it also could be a corporation, a political party, or a group of individuals. What do you know about the speaker? What is his or her age, gender, race, socioeconomic status, and so on? What are the speaker's interests, biases, or political leanings? We know, for example, that Harriet Beecher Stowe was a committed abolitionist, and we also know that she was a devout Christian. Both aspects of her background greatly influenced how she presented her argument in *Uncle Tom's Cabin*.

ACTIVITY   IDENTIFYING RHETORICAL CONTEXT

Use SOAPS to determine the full rhetorical situation for the speech below.

Challenger Speech / Ronald Reagan

This speech was delivered the evening of January 28, 1986, after the space shuttle *Challenger* exploded during liftoff earlier that day. All seven crew members, including Christa McAuliffe, a high school teacher, perished. President Reagan was scheduled to deliver the State of the Union address to Congress that evening, but given the tragedy he gave this speech from the Oval Office instead. Analyze each of the components: that is, subject, occasion, audience, purpose, and speaker.

Ladies and Gentlemen, I'd planned to speak to you tonight to report on the state of the Union, but the events of earlier today have led me to change those plans. Today is a day for mourning and remembering. Nancy and I are pained to the core by the tragedy of the shuttle *Challenger*. We know we share this pain with all of the people of our country. This is truly a national loss.

Nineteen years ago, almost to the day, we lost three astronauts in a terrible accident on the ground. But, we've never lost an astronaut in flight; we've never had a tragedy like this. And perhaps we've forgotten the courage it took for the crew of the shuttle; but they, the *Challenger* Seven, were aware of the dangers, but overcame them and did their jobs brilliantly. We mourn seven heroes: Michael Smith, Dick Scobee, Judith Resnik, Ronald McNair, Ellison Onizuka, Gregory Jarvis, and Christa McAuliffe. We mourn their loss as a nation together.

For the families of the seven, we cannot bear, as you do, the full impact of this tragedy.

But we feel the loss, and we're thinking about you so very much. Your loved ones were daring and brave, and they had that special grace, that special spirit that says, "Give me a challenge and I'll meet it with joy." They had a hunger to explore the universe and discover its truths. They wished to serve, and they did. They served all of us. We've grown used to wonders in this century. It's hard to dazzle us. But for twenty-five years the United States space program has been doing just that. We've grown used to the idea of space, and perhaps we forget that we've only just begun. We're still pioneers. They, the members of the *Challenger* crew, were pioneers.

And I want to say something to the schoolchildren of America who were watching the live coverage of the shuttle's takeoff. I know it is hard to understand, but sometimes painful things like this happen. It's all part of the process of exploration and discovery. It's all part of taking a chance and expanding man's horizons. The future doesn't belong to the fainthearted; it belongs to the brave. The

Challenger crew was pulling us into the future, and we'll continue to follow them.

5 I've always had great faith in and respect for our space program, and what happened today does nothing to diminish it. We don't hide our space program. We don't keep secrets and cover things up. We do it all up front and in public. That's the way freedom is, and we wouldn't change it for a minute. We'll continue our quest in space. There will be more shuttle flights and more shuttle crews and, yes, more volunteers, more civilians, more teachers in space. Nothing ends here; our hopes and our journeys continue. I want to add that I wish I could talk to every man and woman who works for NASA or who worked on this mission and tell them: "Your dedication and professionalism have moved and impressed us for decades. And we know of your anguish. We share it."

There's a coincidence today. On this day 390 years ago, the great explorer Sir Francis Drake died aboard ship off the coast of Panama. In his lifetime the great frontiers were the oceans, and a historian later said, "He lived by the sea, died on it, and was buried in it." Well, today we can say of the *Challenger* crew: Their dedication was, like Drake's, complete.

The crew of the space shuttle *Challenger* honored us by the manner in which they lived their lives. We will never forget them, nor the last time we saw them, this morning, as they prepared for the journey and waved goodbye and "slipped the surly bonds of earth" to "touch the face of God." ■

ACTIVITY   SHIFTING THE RHETORICAL SITUATION

Another way to understand how the rhetorical situation affects an argument is to practice writing short arguments that ask you to take on different roles as a speaker for different audiences on various topics. Look over the following situations, and write a few sentences of the argument you might write, taking into account your role as the speaker, the occasion, the audience, your purpose, and your subject. Afterward, reflect on what changed in each argument as a result of the changed context.

1. You get caught defacing a statue of your rival school's mascot.

    Scenario 1: You need to explain to a college you have applied to why the incident is on your school disciplinary record, and why it should admit you anyway.

    Scenario 2: You need to apologize to the rival school's student body and prevent any retaliation against your mascot or school.

2. A student is caught plagiarizing an essay, which results in failing the course:

    Scenario 1: You are a senior in high school with a full scholarship to college next year, and you are talking to the teacher who caught you plagiarizing.

    Scenario 2: You are the teacher in a meeting with the student's parents and their lawyer, who are contesting the failing grade.

    What changed when the rhetorical situation changed?

3. A rhetorical situation of your own choosing:

   Scenario 1: _____

   Scenario 2: _____

   What changed when the rhetorical situation changed?

KEY QUESTION

When thinking about the rhetorical situation, the key question to ask is:

- How do the speaker, occasion, audience, purpose, and subject influence the way the argument is expressed?

▼

RHETORICAL APPEALS

Once a speaker has a claim and understands the rhetorical situation, it's time to make some choices about how to make the argument persuasive. The Greek philosopher Aristotle broke down persuasion into three basic ways of appealing to an audience:

- reason **(logos)**
- emotion **(pathos)**
- credibility **(ethos)**

While we discuss each of these individually, keep in mind that an effective argument takes all three into account.

Logos

The appeal to logic can be very powerful in our data-driven society. Arguments based on logos rely primarily on statistical data, expert testimony, research, historical fact, clear reasoning, and an objective tone. An argument about the need for increased security in schools, for instance, might appeal to logos by examining data about the relationship between increased security and decreased violence in school settings.

Don't raise your voice; improve your argument.

—Bishop Desmond Tutu

There are many ways to make an appeal based on logic. Columnist Charles Blow uses several of them as he argues against the death penalty in the following excerpt from the 2014 article "Eye-for-an-Eye Incivility."

from **Eye-for-an-Eye Incivility** / Charles Blow

When President Obama was asked on Friday about the Oklahoma execution, he repeated his belief that capital punishment should be an option in some cases but pointed out:

> The application of the death penalty in this country, we have seen significant problems — racial bias, uneven application of the death penalty, you know, situations in which there were individuals on death row who later on were discovered to have been innocent because of exculpatory evidence. And all these, I think, do raise significant questions about how the death penalty is being applied. [...]

And not only are there application and misapplication issues, the death penalty is also a tremendous drain on resources.

Prof. Jeffrey A. Fagan of Columbia Law School has argued that "even in states where prosecutors infrequently seek the death penalty, the price of obtaining convictions and executions ranges from $2.5 million to $5 million per case (in current dollars), compared to less than $1 million for each killer sentenced to life without parole."

Our continued use of the death penalty does not put us in good company. According to a 2014 report from Amnesty International, "only nine countries have continuously executed in each of the past five years — Bangladesh, China, Iran, Iraq, North Korea, Saudi Arabia, Sudan, U.S.A. and Yemen." ■

To support his first reason against the death penalty, which he sums up as "application and misapplication issues," Blow begins by citing President Barack Obama, who was trained as a constitutional lawyer. Then Blow quotes a law school professor to present a second practical reason, which is the financial cost of execution versus life in prison. Then, Blow offers a third reason against the death penalty by naming the other countries that use capital punishment—most of which are not exemplary democracies. Although the death penalty is a very emotionally charged issue, in this section of his article Blow approaches it with calm authority—by appealing to reason.

How does this *Dilbert* cartoon poke fun at the appeal to logos?

KEY QUESTION

> When thinking about the appeal to logos, ask yourself:
>
> - How does the writer use evidence and logic to appeal to the audience's intellect?

Pathos

The appeal to emotion can be evoked by descriptive and vivid language, or even a visual image. Let's return to the speech given by former president Ronald Reagan after the space shuttle *Challenger* disaster (p. 64). Notice the appeals to pathos in this paragraph:

> But we feel the loss, and we're thinking about you so very much. Your loved ones were daring and brave, and they had that special grace, that special spirit that says, "Give me a challenge and I'll meet it with joy." They had a hunger to explore the universe and discover its truths. They wished to serve, and they did. They served all of us.

The very language is filled with emotion that underscores the tragedy of the loss: those who died "were daring and brave," with a "special grace [. . .] special spirit." They "had a hunger to explore" and "wished to serve." Every word strikes a note of admiration and affirmation that honors the sacrifice this crew made.

Sometimes a writer appeals to pathos with a personal story or anecdote. When the basketball player LeBron James returned to his hometown of Cleveland in 2014 after having angered many of his fans a few years before when he joined the Miami Heat, he wrote a letter published in *Sports Illustrated* with the purpose of regaining his hometown fan base.

> I always believed that I'd return to Cleveland and finish my career there. I just didn't know when. After the season, free agency wasn't even a thought. But I have two boys and my wife, Savannah, is pregnant with a girl. I started thinking about what it would be like to raise my family in my hometown. I looked at other teams, but I wasn't going to leave Miami for anywhere except Cleveland. The more time passed, the more it felt right. This is what makes me happy.

Who could resist that scenario of a hometown hero returning to his roots to raise his growing family? If LeBron is arguing for his audience—his fans—to give him another chance, he's making a heartfelt case.

But be careful. While pathos can be a powerful strategy, pathos alone results in a weak argument. Once the emotional response wears off and logic kicks in, your audience will assess your argument with a more critical eye.

KEY QUESTIONS

> When thinking about pathos, ask yourself:
>
> - How does the writer appeal to the audience's emotions?
> - Are these effective strategies to gain sympathy, or do they go overboard to become overly sentimental, dramatic, or manipulative?

Ethos

The Greek philosopher and godfather of rhetoric, Aristotle, believed that **ethos**, an appeal to the credibility and authority of the speaker, was the most important of the three appeals. If the speaker is not seen as trustworthy or knowledgeable on the subject, then all the logic and emotion in the world is unlikely to sway an audience. There are two primary ways to appeal to ethos:

- demonstrate authority
- demonstrate shared values

Some speakers have a certain amount of ethos because of who they are, such as a well-respected scientist who presents an argument on the effects of caffeine. But what if that scientist wanted to talk to the school board about increasing security at her son's school? Does being a well-respected chemist help? A bit, sure, but it's not really relevant to the issue at hand. At that point the scientist would have to establish her ethos as a parent who shared the values and concerns of other parents in the room.

> You persuade a man only insofar as you can talk his language by speech, gesture, tonality, order, image, attitude, idea, identifying your ways with his.
>
> —Kenneth Burke

Here's the opening to a letter to the editor of the *Columbus Dispatch* newspaper written by high school senior Owen Dirkse in response to a proposal to put police officers in his high school in Columbus, Ohio. As a young person, Dirkse realizes that some readers might dismiss his argument; he therefore is careful to firmly establish his ethos as an insider with knowledge of the situation, as well as a person who values his school and community:

> As a senior at Upper Arlington High School, I am extremely proud of both my school and community. Except for two years in private education, I have spent my entire life in the Upper Arlington School District and know firsthand what an amazing system it is. We have a reputation as one of the best school districts in the state, and others look at our productive, safe learning environments with admiration.
>
> Unfortunately, the high school made a major misstep recently by employing a school resource officer. [. . .]
>
> Like most people, I feel that school safety is a top priority, but involving law enforcement in our day-to-day routine is neither the best nor most cost-effective means to keep our students safe.

Dirkse opens with what amounts to his credentials: he is not a psychologist or a law enforcement expert (though later on, he cites a relevant study by the Justice Policy Institute) but simply a concerned student. He recognizes that his audience is less likely to be his peers than the adults who read a print copy of the local newspaper; thus, he continues in the next few lines with the statement, "Like most people, I feel that school safety is a top priority," assuring readers that he shares their concern and understands the legitimate motivation that might lead to a decision to put law enforcement officers in the schools. Dirkse wants his adult readers to respond positively to the case he is making—so he emphasizes various ways that he, a student of good character, respects their shared values. In fact, he uses those values to argue that putting police in the schools increases the risk that students may come into conflict with them.

KEY QUESTIONS

When thinking about ethos, ask yourself:

- What values or concerns does the speaker share with the audience?
- How does the speaker establish his or her good character?

ACTIVITY   ANALYZING APPEALS

Discuss the appeals to ethos, pathos, and logos in the following public service advertisement sponsored by the American Academy of Pediatrics. Keep in mind that this ad
would most likely appear in magazines that are available in doctors' waiting rooms,
particularly children's clinics and the offices of pediatricians. Do you think it would be
an effective argument for parents or guardians considering vaccinations? Why or why
not? Does the ad rely too heavily on one of the appeals and neglect others, or is it
evenhanded in its approach? Cite specific elements of the ad—both written text and
visual images—in your analysis.

If you're concerned about the possible
side effects of immunizations,

consider the possible effects of not getting them.

As a parent, the side effects of immunizations can be unsettling. They may include
redness, swelling and fever.

But, the effects of not getting your child immunized can be worse. The same diseases
that have plagued children for generations still exist today. But now, you can do
something about them.

For more information about immunizations, ask your pediatrician.

American Academy of Pediatrics
DEDICATED TO THE HEALTH OF ALL CHILDREN™
Visit healthychildren.org

┌ - - - - - - - - - - - - -

ACTIVITY   USING APPEALS

Look over the following scenarios. Discuss how you might employ all three major appeals—ethos, pathos, and logos—and when it might be appropriate to emphasize one over the others.

1. You are the spokesperson for a student group hoping to convince your school's administration that your school day ought to start one hour later.
2. You are speaking to your town's governing council about an issue in which you have an interest, such as building a new park, ending a curfew, or supporting more school funding.
3. You are trying to persuade a group of teenagers who are angry about the verdict in a controversial court case to make their protest in an orderly, peaceful manner.
4. You are the president of the United States hoping to convince Congress and the public to support (or oppose) a military action against another country.

▼

USING EVIDENCE

You have probably witnessed or participated in an exchange like this at some point in your life:

Child: I don't want to. Why do I have to?

Parent: Because I said so.

Child: But that's not fair!

The parent may have "won" this argument, but it's clear that the child is far from convinced. That's understandable because the parent offers no evidence to support his or her position. Successful arguments—those that influence the intended audience—require evidence to support the claim. Evidence is the heart of an argument: without effective evidence, you're basically just reasserting your claim. Learning how to use evidence effectively is therefore very important. If you recall the rhetorical triangle, one of the key components of writing and analyzing an argument is to understand the intended audience of the argument, and to think about what might be convincing to members of that audience. Effective writers know how to appeal to their audiences by including types of evidence that their readers will find appealing.

Keep in mind too that you can cite evidence either to support your argument directly or to show your understanding of a counter position.

Just as a good argument shouldn't be based entirely on one type of appeal, a good argument shouldn't be based on just one type of evidence. Solid evidence appeals strongly to reason (logos) and builds the speaker's credibility (ethos). A shocking statistic or anecdote might appeal to emotion (pathos). It's important to use a variety of evidence and use it strategically to make your point.

Let's look at a few common types of evidence.

Personal Experience and Anecdote

A story about personal experience can be used as effective evidence if it has clear relevance to the claim. Or, a writer might provide an anecdote about the experience of others as a way to support a claim. This sort of evidence often can be used to make an argument less detached and more personal, building a connection with the reader (ethos) and possibly stirring up emotions (pathos).

Facts

It's true that often you need to do research in order to find factual information, and if that's the case, you need to indicate where you got those facts. But you also have many facts at your fingertips because of your reading and general knowledge. Depending upon your topic and your background, you might know historical facts or facts from current events on a local or global scale. If you're writing an argument that's a movie review, for instance, your knowledge of that movie can serve as evidence to make your point.

Scholarly Research and Expert Opinion

Using evidence from those who have specialized knowledge strengthens your argument in two ways. For one, you're showing that you're not basing your argument solely on personal opinion, which boosts your credibility. Second, you cite the actual work, often words, of those who have made it their career to study a topic in great depth and therefore can provide reliable information. So, if you're writing an argument for requiring vaccinations for entrance to college, then evidence from physicians who have researched the topic or someone who works at the U.S. Centers for Disease Control and Prevention could be very effective. In the same way, if you're writing about national security, providing the viewpoint of someone who serves or has served as secretary of state would add authority to your argument.

Data and Statistics

In today's world of "data-driven decisions," quantitative data can be very compelling either in paragraph form or as a chart or table. At the same time, you have to be careful about where your statistics come from. Data can be manipulated or framed in a way that serves a biased agenda. As the saying goes, "There are three kinds of lies: lies, damn lies, and statistics."

ACTIVITY **ANALYZING EVIDENCE**

In "What's Fair?," an opinion piece published in the conservative political blog *Town Hall* in 2015, commentator John Stossel argues against government intervention to address income inequality. Analyze the evidence that Stossel presents. What is his chief claim? Identify at least three types of evidence he uses. How does that evidence support his claim?

What's Fair? / John Stossel

Donald Trump's kids and Paris Hilton's siblings were born rich. That gave them a big advantage in life. Unfair!

Inequality in wealth has grown. Today the richest 1 percent of Americans own a third of the assets. That's not fair!

But wherever people are free, that's what happens.

Some people are luckier, smarter or just better at making money. Often they marry other wealthy, well-connected people. Over time, these advantages compound. Globalization increases the effect. This month's issue of *Forbes* says the world now has 1,826 billionaires, and some struggle to find enough parking places for their jets.

5   President Obama calls inequality "the defining issue of our time." Really? Not our unsustainable debt? Not ISIS? The president also said, "No challenge poses a greater threat to future generations than climate change!"

Politicians constantly find crises they will solve by increasing government power. But why is inequality a crisis?

Alexis Goldstein, of a group called The Other 98 percent, complains that corporations got richer but workers' wages "are lower than they've been in 65 years."

That's a common refrain, but it's wrong. Over the past 30 years, CBO data shows that the average income of the poorest fifth of Americans is *up* by 49 percent. That doesn't include all the innovations that have dramatically improved everyone's life. Today even the poorest Americans have comforts and lifespans that kings didn't have a century ago.

George Mason University economist Garett Jones says, "If I was going to be in the bottom fifth in the America of today versus the bottom fifth of America in 1970 or 1960, it's hard to imagine that anybody would take that time machine into the past."

10   And despite America's lousy government schools and regulations that make it tough to start a business, there is still economic *mobility*. Poor people don't have to stay poor. Sixty-four percent of those born in the poorest fifth of the U.S. population move out of that quintile. Eleven percent of them rise all the way to the top, according to economists at Harvard and Berkeley. Most of the billionaires atop the *Forbes* richest list weren't rich. They got rich by innovating.

Rich people aren't guaranteed their place at the top, either. Sixty-six percent fell from the top quintile, and eight percent fell all the way to the bottom.

That mobility is a reason most of us are better off than we would have been in a more rigid society, controlled by central economic planners.

Life will always be unfair. I want to play pro basketball. It's unfair that LeBron James is bigger and more talented! It's also unfair that George Clooney is better looking! It's unfair that my brother is smarter than me.

Jones points out, "I was born with an advantage, too. Being born in the United States . . . totally unfair." He also has two married parents — another huge advantage.

15   The question is not whether people start out life in homogeneous circumstances, he adds. "The question is whether government policies that try to fix this actually make things better or worse." ∎

▼
COUNTERARGUMENTS

An important element of effective argument is acknowledging the **counterargument**—that is, an opposing viewpoint. Ignoring or dismissing any position not in agreement with yours demonstrates bias, while addressing one or more counterarguments demonstrates that you are reasonable. For instance, if you were arguing in favor of increased school security, you might cite the counterargument that security guards are detrimental to the learning environment because they make students feel like criminals and act accordingly, but then refute that argument by pointing out that violence is much more disruptive to the school environment and that any feelings of being treated like a criminal are no more than inconveniences in comparison. In this way, you indicate that you have recognized and considered a position counter to your own as part of the process of developing your viewpoint. The result is that you not only appeal to logos by sounding reasonable but also establish your ethos as a fair-minded person.

When you work with counterargument, an effective strategy is called **concession** and refutation (or "concede and refute"). You start out by agreeing with the opposition (conceding) to show that you respect the views of others, even those you disagree with. Then—and here's the trick—you refute the argument by pointing out how the opposition either doesn't account for important issues or is outweighed by other considerations.

For instance, in an article about the downside to police officers' wearing body cameras, *New York Times* writer David Brooks opens by acknowledging the reasons one might argue in favor of body cams:

> First, there have been too many cases in which police officers have abused their authority and then covered it up. Second, it seems probable that cops would be less likely to abuse their authority if they were being tracked. Third, human memory is an unreliable faculty. We might be able to reduce the number of wrongful convictions and acquittals if we have cameras recording more events.

▶

What does this cartoon have to say about the importance of acknowledging counterarguments?

"WHILE DOING THE RESEARCH, KEEP IN MIND THERE ARE ONLY TWO KINDS OF FACTS... THOSE THAT SUPPORT MY POSITION... AND INCONCLUSIVE."

Edgar Argo/www.cartoonstock.com

Does Brooks undermine his own argument? Not at all. By starting with objections right up front, he avoids sounding confrontational. In fact, he sounds downright agreeable. This encourages his readers, even those who disagree, to be receptive to what he has to say. In the article, Brooks goes on to appeal to readers' emotions, evoking cases of controversial police behavior that occurred in 2015, within a few months of his article's publication. He counters the argument in support of body cams *not by saying that people who advocate them are entirely wrong*, but by arguing that they do not take other critical issues into account—problems that, in his opinion, outweigh the advantages:

> Cop-cams strike a blow for truth, but they strike a blow against relationships. Society will be more open and transparent, but less humane and trusting.

▼

PITFALLS AND VULNERABILITIES

Whether analyzing arguments, or writing your own, it's important to be on the lookout for pitfalls and vulnerabilities that weaken the argument, or seem manipulative. Detecting these vulnerabilities takes careful reading and critical thinking.

Detecting Bias

Bias refers to a speaker or writer's having an identifiable preference for—or a prejudice against—one particular side or viewpoint on an issue. True objectivity is impossible, especially when someone is advocating one view over another; nevertheless, it is important to understand what influences a speaker or writer might bring to a subject. For example, a person's religious or political affiliation might play a part in the position she takes on a particular issue. That's unavoidable, but it's essential that we understand *how* it influences her viewpoint.

Similarly, place and time have an impact on a speaker's or writer's perspective. If the mayor of a major city argues that a Fortune 500 company should build its headquarters in his city, we would expect his viewpoint to be biased toward the best interests of his city and his legacy. His view can't be entirely dismissed, but it does reflect some self-interest.

The key is to understand what potential sources of bias might be—ethnicity, politics, religion, age, position/job, geographical region, socioeconomic status—and scrutinize if and how that bias affects the argument.

The trouble comes, however, when a bias toward one side leads to a willful deception or omission of facts in order to "win" the argument.

KEY QUESTIONS

As you scrutinize an argument for bias, keep the following questions in mind:

- What facts or perspectives has the speaker left out?
- Is the speaker affiliated with a company, political party, cultural movement, or other group that might suggest a hidden agenda?
- Does the author at least acknowledge, rather than dismiss, other perspectives by addressing a counterargument or different ways to consider the issue at hand?
- Does the author's choice of words seem reasonable, or is it deliberately intended to stir up fear or anger?

Logical Fallacies

When you're examining an argument, including your own, you want to be on the lookout for gaps in logic, called **logical fallacies**. In some cases, a speaker or writer may deliberately try to manipulate an audience through a logical fallacy. In other instances, however, a logical fallacy may be the result of unclear thinking. There are many types of fallacies, but here are five very common ones to put on your rhetorical radar.

Ad Hominem. Latin for "to the man," this fallacy takes place when a speaker or writer attacks the character of his or her opponent rather than the opponent's ideas. This is a way to shift attention from the issue to the person. For instance, in an argument in favor of the construction of a new school building, someone might point out that a person holding an opposing view was recently fined for speeding or texting while driving. That fact may not be admirable, but it's unlikely to have any connection to the person's credibility when it comes to new school construction.

Bandwagon Appeal. Go with the crowd! That's essentially the fallacy that occurs when an argument is based on the logic that because a number of people believe something, it must be true or right. So, for instance, you might argue that because millions have used the latest herbal diet supplement, then it must be both safe and effective. Advertisers often use bandwagon appeals in an attempt to persuade consumers that large sales translate into proof of excellence or—perhaps with even faultier logic—that because a celebrity endorses a product, so should you.

Either-Or Fallacy. This fallacy (also known as "false dilemma") occurs when a speaker or writer makes a veiled threat by reducing a complex issue to two options: either you see it my way or this bad thing will happen. "You're either with us or you're with the terrorists" exemplifies the either-or fallacy. Such thinking cuts off the possibility of middle ground or compromise. In addition, this fallacy can artificially limit choices to direct opposites, such as "Either everyone should be allowed to carry a gun or no one should."

Hasty Generalization. This fallacy occurs when an inference or conclusion is drawn on the basis of insufficient evidence. For instance, if you make an argument that a company is guilty of ageism because your grandfather applied for a job and was not hired, you risk making a hasty generalization. If there is, indeed, a pattern of failing to hire people over a certain age, then you might have a case—but not hiring one person is not a pattern. Note that stereotypes are often formed as a result of hasty generalizations: for example, women are bad drivers; men won't ask for directions, Midwesterners are overly friendly.

Slippery Slope. This fallacy relies on fear. Also known as the "floodgates fallacy," the slippery slope occurs when someone argues that if you allow X to occur, Y will surely follow. So, for instance, if you argue that convicted felons should be allowed to vote after they have served their sentences, someone might respond that soon criminals will be running the country. In other words, by doing one thing, you're on a slippery slope to a far worse and (usually exaggerated) situation.

ACTIVITY   IDENTIFYING LOGICAL FALLACIES

Explain the logical fallacy in each of the following statements.

1. Unless you can close your eyes to abuse, write a check to save this puppy.
2. Both of my parents smoked all their lives, and they lived into their eighties, so cigarettes can't really be that bad for you.
3. Don't ever gamble! Once you start, you won't be able to stop, and you'll end up bankrupt.
4. People from big cities are not as friendly as those from small towns.
5. He can't be a great athlete; he cheated on his wife.
6. If you're not part of the solution, then you're part of the problem.

ACTIVITY **ANALYZING BIAS**

What potential bias or logical fallacies do you find in the following argument opposing granting voting rights (called *suffrage*) to women?

Argument against Senate Constitutional Amendment No. 8 / J. B. Sanford

This argument from 1911 was written by California state senator J. B. Sanford for a voter information flyer.

Suffrage is not a right. It is a privilege that may or may not be granted. Politics is no place for a woman consequently the privilege should not be granted to her.

The mother's influence is needed in the home. She can do little good by gadding[1] the streets and neglecting her children. Let her teach her daughters that modesty, patience, and gentleness are the charms of a woman. Let her teach her sons that an honest conscience is every man's first political law; that no splendor can rob him nor no force justify the surrender of the simplest right of a free and independent citizen. The mothers of this country can shape the destinies of the nation by keeping in their places and attending to those duties that God Almighty intended for them. The kindly, gentle influence of the mother in the home and the dignified influence of the teacher in the school will far outweigh all the influence of all the mannish female politicians on earth.

The courageous, chivalrous, and manly men and the womanly women, the real mothers and home builders of the country, are opposed to this innovation in American political life. There was a bill (the Sanford bill) before the last legislature which proposed to leave the equal suffrage question to women to decide first before the men should vote on it. This bill was defeated by the suffragettes because they knew that the women would vote down the amendment by a vote of ten to one.

The men are able to run the government and take care of the women. Do women have to vote in order to receive the protection of man? Why, men have gone to war, endured every privation and death itself in defense of woman. To man, woman is the dearest creature on earth, and there is no extreme to which he would not go for his mother or sister. By keeping woman in her exalted position man can be induced to do more for her than he could by having her mix up in affairs that will cause him to lose respect and regard for her. Woman does not have to vote to secure her rights. Man will go to any extreme to protect and elevate her now. As long as woman is woman and keeps her place she will get more protection and more consideration than man gets. When she abdicates her throne she throws down the scepter of her power and loses her influence.

5   Woman suffrage has been proven a failure in states that have tried it. It is wrong. California should profit by the mistakes of other states. Not one reform has equal suffrage effected. On the contrary, statistics go to show that in most equal suffrage states, Colorado particularly, that divorces have greatly increased since the adoption of the equal suffrage amendment, showing that it has been a home destroyer. Crime has also increased due to lack of the mothers in the home.

Woman is woman. She can not unsex herself or change her sphere. Let her be

---

[1] gadding: going places idly, or in the pursuit of pleasure or excitement. —Eds.

content with her lot and perform those high duties intended for her by the Great Creator, and she will accomplish far more in governmental affairs that she can ever accomplish by mixing up in the dirty pool of politics. Keep the home pure and all will be well with the Republic. Let not the sanctity of the home be invaded by every little politician that may be running up and down the highway for office. Let the manly men and the womanly women defeat this amendment and keep woman where she belongs in order that she may retain the respect of all mankind. ∎

LANGUAGE AND STYLE

The language of an argument is more than just icing on the argumentative cake. A writer's stylistic choices can make an argument both memorable and persuasive. Not everyone has the stylistic genius of Abraham Lincoln or Martin Luther King Jr., but you can study their brilliant arguments, along with others, to learn to make effective stylistic choices in your own writing.

Connotative Language

Connotative language adds impact to an argument by stirring emotions or by painting a visual picture. Let's look at how Jay Griffiths uses connotative language to set the stage for an argument about privacy rights. This excerpt is from Griffiths's essay "The Tips of Your Fingers," which appeared in a 2010 issue of the magazine *Orion*:

> In the woods near the border checkpoint from France to Britain, several people sit around a fire, pushing iron bars deeper into the flames until the metal is red hot. Taking out the iron, with searing pain they burn their own fingertips, trying to erase their identification.
>
> The fingertips are a border checkpoint of the human body, and through them the self reaches out to touch the world. Fingertips are diviners, lovers, poets of the perhaps, emissaries of empathy. They are feelingful, exquisitely sensitive to metal, dough, moss or splinter. They are also one of the body's places of greatest idiosyncrasy: a fingerprint is the body's signature.

The language draws readers in. We're at the border checkpoint, we see the flames and the "red hot" metal, and we feel the "searing pain." Even the description of what a fingertip is—"exquisitely sensitive to metal, dough, moss or splinter"—adds emotional intensity as we begin reading this essay. Such skillful use of language is intended to make us more receptive to an argument about the dangers of particular kinds of surveillance. Griffiths turns to various kinds of evidence as she develops her argument, but her stylistic choices in this opening get our attention first.

Figurative Language

You're probably used to thinking about metaphors and similes as poetic tools, but, like other kinds of **figurative language**, they can serve as a rhetorical strategy to give an idea more impact. Figurative language appeals to our emotions and helps us to understand a different perspective. In the opening to her essay "On Seeing England for the First Time," Jamaica Kincaid uses figurative language to help us understand the feelings of a young girl in the Caribbean toward the "mother country" of England.

> When I was in school for the first time, I was a child in school sitting at a desk. The England I was looking at was laid out on a map gently, beautifully, delicately, a very special jewel; it lay on a bed of sky blue—the background of the map—its yellow form mysterious, because though it looked like a leg of mutton, it could not really look like anything so familiar as a leg of mutton because it was England—with shadings of pink and green, unlike any shad-ings of pink and green I had seen before, squiggly veins of red running in every direction. England was a special jewel all right, and only special people got to wear it.

By comparing England to a jewel, then a leg of mutton (sheep), and then again a jewel, Kincaid gives us a sense of her mixed emotions. As she lets us in on her thought process of why England "could not really look like anything so familiar as a leg of mutton," we also begin to hear the sarcasm in her attitude toward the place.

Not all figurative language has to be as lyrical as in Kincaid's example, however. Note that in his speech on the evening of September 11, 2001, President George W. Bush— known for his practical and straightforward language — used one brief but effective figure of speech. He warned the enemies of the United States: "Terrorist attacks can shake the foundations of our biggest buildings, but they cannot touch the foundation of America. These acts shatter steel, but they cannot dent the steel of American resolve."

Allusion

In fiction and poetry, an allusion is usually used to refer to a cultural touchstone—a myth, a famous painting. In argument that still can hold true, but speakers and writers need to choose allusions not only for their broad cultural relevance, but also for their appeal to a specific audience. Thus, a historical allusion might resonate with one community, while a sports allusion might be effective for another audience, and a pop culture reference might work where a historical allusion would otherwise fall flat.

Understanding his audience well, President Abraham Lincoln used a series of biblical allusions in his second inaugural address to urge unity between the North and South at the end of the Civil War:

> Both read the same Bible and pray to the same God, and each invokes His aid against the other. It may seem strange that any men should dare to ask a just God's assistance in wringing their bread from the sweat of other men's faces, but let us judge not, that we be not judged. The prayers of both could not be answered. That of neither has been answered fully. The Almighty has His own purposes. "Woe unto the world because of offenses; for it must needs be that offenses come, but woe to that man by whom the offense cometh."

Given that citizens of both sides revered the Bible and worshipped the Christian God, Lincoln's allusions emphasized the need for Americans to seek similar beliefs that outweighed differences.

Parallel Structure

Parallelism means using similar grammatical structures to emphasize related ideas. Parallel structure may involve a single word, a phrase, a clause, a full sentence, or even a series of paragraphs.

In his speech to mark the fiftieth anniversary of the civil rights march in Selma, Alabama, President Barack Obama uses parallel structure to stress the unity of a diverse nation. Toward the end of his speech, he exhorts, "Look at our history." He then goes through various people that mark our nation's history:

> We are Lewis and Clark and Sacajawea, pioneers who braved the unfamiliar, followed by a stampede of farmers and miners, and entrepreneurs and hucksters. [. . .]
>
> We are Sojourner Truth and Fannie Lou Hamer. [. . .]
>
> We're the immigrants who stowed away on ships to reach these shores, the huddled masses yearning to breathe free—Holocaust survivors, Soviet defectors, the Lost Boys of Sudan. [. . .]
>
> We're the slaves who built the White House. [. . .] We're the ranch hands and cowboys. [. . .]
>
> We're the fresh-faced GIs who fought to liberate a continent. And we're the Tuskegee Airmen, and the Navajo code-talkers, and the Japanese Americans who fought for this country even as their own liberty had been denied.
>
> We're the firefighters who rushed into those buildings on 9/11, the volunteers who signed up to fight in Afghanistan and Iraq. [. . .]
>
> We are storytellers, writers, poets, artists who abhor unfairness, and despise hypocrisy, and give voice to the voiceless, and tell truths that need to be told.
>
> We're the inventors of gospel and jazz and blues, bluegrass and country, and hip-hop and rock and roll, and our very own sound with all the sweet sorrow and reckless joy of freedom.

After this catalog of all the different people and voices who make up this country, Obama concludes, "That's what America is." The similar structure at the beginning of each sentence, along with the different endings, allows for differences while stressing the likenesses that Obama claims are the hallmark of the United States.

Rhetorical Questions

A rhetorical question is a question asked to encourage your audience to reflect on an issue but not to elicit a direct response. Thus, in "Letter from Birmingham Jail," Martin Luther King Jr. writes, "One may well ask, 'How can you advocate breaking some laws and obeying others?'" He does not intend for his audience to answer but instead uses the rhetorical question to lead to his explanation of the difference between just and unjust laws. Rhetorical questions allow you to frame the issue, engage your readers, and offer a transition from one idea or issue to the next.

ACTIVITY ANALYZING LANGUAGE AND STYLE

Following are the opening paragraphs from Elie Wiesel's acceptance speech when he was awarded the Nobel Peace Prize in 1986. How do Wiesel's stylistic choices convey his challenge to take action, rather than remain silent, in the face of injustice?

from **Nobel Prize Speech** / Elie Wiesel

It is with a profound sense of humility that I accept the honor you have chosen to bestow upon me. I know: your choice transcends me. This both frightens and pleases me.

It frightens me because I wonder: do I have the right to represent the multitudes who have perished? Do I have the right to accept this great honor on their behalf? [. . .] I do not. That would be presumptuous. No one may speak for the dead, no one may interpret their mutilated dreams and visions.

It pleases me because I may say that this honor belongs to all the survivors and their children, and through us, to the Jewish people with whose destiny I have always identified.

I remember: it happened yesterday or eternities ago. A young Jewish boy discovered the kingdom of night. I remember his bewilderment, I remember his anguish. It all happened so fast. The ghetto. The deportation. The sealed cattle car. The fiery altar upon which the history of our people and the future of mankind were meant to be sacrificed.

5   I remember: he asked his father: "Can this be true?" This is the twentieth century, not the Middle Ages. Who would allow such crimes to be committed? How could the world remain silent?

And now the boy is turning to me: "Tell me," he asks. "What have you done with my future? What have you done with your life?"

And I tell him that I have tried. That I have tried to keep memory alive, that I have tried to fight those who would forget. Because if we forget, we are guilty, we are accomplices.

And then I explained to him how naive we were, that the world did know and remain silent. And that is why I swore never to be silent whenever and wherever human beings endure suffering and humiliation. ∎

▼ A MODEL ANALYSIS

Let's examine a two-page advertisement for Whole Foods Market. Before you start analyzing it, take a moment to brainstorm what you know about Whole Foods. Why would the store take out such an extensive ad in a magazine like the *Atlantic*? What might be the company's purpose? Who is the audience?

Let's start by looking at appeals to ethos, pathos, and logos. Pathos is the easiest to consider in this ad: the image of the fairly young man with a little boy, likely father and son (note that the man is wearing a ring that looks like a wedding band), evokes feelings of a

VALUES MATTER

WE BELIEVE THAT HEALTHY FOOD CAN IMPROVE PEOPLE'S LIVES IN ALL KINDS OF WAYS. THAT'S WHY WE'RE HELPING MORE PEOPLE GET IT, GROW IT, AND UNDERSTAND IT.

Our **Whole Kids Foundation®** has improved children's nutrition by providing grants for salad bars in 3,551 schools, and gardens in 2,116 schools, throughout the U.S., U.K., and Canada.

Our **Whole Cities Foundation™** supports efforts to improve community health through collaborative partnerships, education, and access to nutritious food in underserved communities. We are currently focused on projects in New Orleans, Chicago, Jackson, MS, and Newark, NJ.

Our **Whole Planet Foundation®** currently supports the businesses of over 700,000 women entrepreneurs in 60 countries, including the U.S., with microcredit loans and the chance to lift themselves and their families out of poverty.

Our community giving exceeds 5% of our total net profits each year.

WFM.COM/VALUESMATTER

America's Healthiest Grocery Store®

happy home life. On the second page, we see lots of green, which is the color of Whole Foods Market's logo, the color of plants, and a color associated with growth and environmental movements. The font is casual and even a bit whimsical. All of these things are calculated to make you feel positive toward Whole Foods, and to subtly suggest that shopping there will help both children and the environment.

Advertisements usually rely primarily on appeals to pathos, but this one makes a concerted effort to appeal to logos. Look at the descriptions of the three foundations being featured and note the evidence being provided to support the claim that Whole Foods "does good"—as in good works. Opinions of experts are invoked in this ad in several ways. The Whole Cities Foundation, we are told, has developed "collaborative partnerships" that include educational efforts. The Whole Planet Foundation advises women entrepreneurs about microcredit loans, likely through experts in economics.

As you read the advertisement, note the "we" and "our" statements, which establish a corporate ethos positioning Whole Foods as concerned about more than just profits: "Our community giving exceeds 5% of our total net profits each year." But, even more striking is the emphasis on "values"—shared values, which are the heart of ethos: "Values Matter" is a banner headline, suggesting both that Whole Foods has high values and that the corporation shares its customers' values.

Notice also that this Whole Foods ad often makes more than one appeal with the same evidence. For instance, the Whole Planet Foundation appeals to logos with hard data ("700,000 women entrepreneurs in 60 countries") and appeals to pathos by using positive language, such as "supports," and "chance to lift themselves." In fact, we see connotative language at work throughout the ad with the use (and repetition) of words that carry positive associations, such as "healthy," "improve," "support," and "community." The verbs are strong and active: "improve," "helping," "providing," "supports," "focused." The sentence in large print on the second page—"That's why we're helping more people get it, grow it, and understand it"—features a string of verbs—"get," "grow," "understand"— which is not only easy to read but also suggestive of a clear march of positive activity.

culminating activity

The following is a newspaper article by Lenore Skenazy that was originally published in 2008 in the *New York Sun* and was subsequently reprinted in newspapers throughout the United States. A syndicated columnist and National Public Radio commentator, Skenazy received so much feedback on her article, both positive and negative, that she expanded her ideas into a book titled *Free-Range Kids: Giving Our Children the Freedom We Had without Going Nuts with Worry* (2010).

First, analyze the rhetorical appeals and strategies Skenazy employs to achieve her purpose in this article. How persuasive do you think her argument is? Second, write your own brief essay arguing whether you believe a nine-year-old in your community should be allowed to travel (on a subway, bus, bicycle) without adult supervision, and if so, to what extent.

Why I Let My 9-Year-Old Ride the Subway Alone / Lenore Skenazy

I left my 9-year-old at Bloomingdale's (the original one) a couple weeks ago. Last seen, he was in first floor handbags as I sashayed out the door.

Bye-bye! Have fun!

And he did. He came home on the subway and bus by himself.

Was I worried? Yes, a tinge. But it didn't strike me as that daring, either. Isn't New York as safe now as it was in 1963? It's not like we're living in downtown Baghdad.

5 Anyway, for weeks my boy had been begging for me to please leave him somewhere, anywhere, and let him try to figure out how to get home on his own. So on that sunny Sunday I gave him a subway map, a MetroCard, a $20 bill, and several quarters, just in case he had to make a call.

No, I did not give him a cell phone. Didn't want to lose it. And no, I didn't trail him, like a mommy private eye. I trusted him to figure out that he should take the Lexington Avenue subway down, and the 34th Street crosstown bus home. If he couldn't do that, I trusted him to ask a stranger. And then I even trusted that stranger not to think, "Gee, I was about to catch my train home, but now I think I'll abduct this adorable child instead."

Long story short: My son got home, ecstatic with independence.

Long story longer, and analyzed, to boot: Half the people I've told this episode to now want to turn me in for child abuse. As if keeping kids under lock and key and helmet and cell phone and nanny and surveillance is the right way to rear kids. It's not. It's debilitating — for us and for them.

And yet —

10 "How would you have felt if he didn't come home?" a New Jersey mom of four, Vicki Garfinkle, asked.

Guess what, Ms. Garfinkle: I'd have been devastated. But would that just prove that no mom should ever let her child ride the subway alone?

No. It would just be one more awful but extremely rare example of random violence, the kind that hyper parents cite as proof that every day in every way our children are more and more vulnerable.

"Carlie Brucia — I don't know if you're familiar with that case or not, but she was in Florida and she did a cut-through about a mile from her house . . . and midday, at 11 in the morning, she was abducted by a guy who violated her several times, killed her, and left her behind a church."

That's the story that the head of safetynet4kids.com, Katharine Francis, immediately told me when I asked her what she thought of my son getting around on his own. She runs a company that makes wallet-sized copies of a child's photo and fingerprints, just in case.

15 Well of course I know the story of Carlie Brucia. That's the problem. We all know that

story — and the one about the Mormon girl in Utah and the one about the little girl in Spain — and because we do, we all run those tapes in our heads when we think of leaving our kids on their own. We even run a tape of how we'd look on Larry King.

"I do not want to be the one on TV explaining my daughter's disappearance," a father, Garth Chouteau, said when we were talking about the subway issue.

These days, when a kid dies, the world — i.e., cable TV — blames the parents. It's simple as that. And yet, Trevor Butterworth, a spokesman for the research center STATS.org, said, "The statistics show that this is an incredibly rare event, and you can't protect people from very rare events. It would be like trying to create a shield against being struck by lightning."

Justice Department data actually show the number of children abducted by strangers has been going down over the years. So why not let your kids get home from school by themselves?

"Parents are in the grip of anxiety and when you're anxious, you're totally warped," the author of *A Nation of Wimps*, Hara Estroff Marano, said. We become so bent out of shape over something as simple as letting your children out of sight on the playground that it starts seeming on par with letting them play on the railroad tracks at night. In the rain. In dark non-reflective coats.

20 The problem with this everything-is-dangerous outlook is that over-protectiveness is a danger in and of itself. A child who thinks he can't do anything on his own eventually can't.

Meantime, my son wants his next trip to be from Queens. In my day, I doubt that would have struck anyone as particularly brave. Now it seems like hitchhiking through Yemen.

Here's your MetroCard, kid. Go.

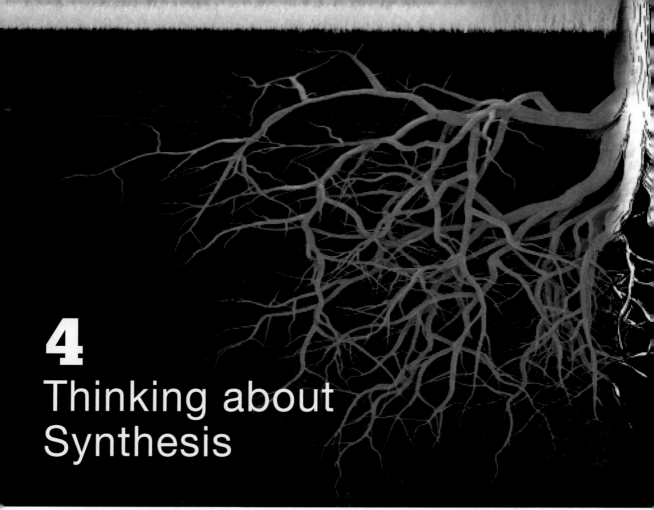

Photo: Orla/Shutterstock, Art: Christian Mojallali

4
Thinking about Synthesis

One of the myths about writing is that it's all about loneliness and isolation: the writer toils all alone, usually after midnight, rarely talking to anyone or at least not talking about what she's writing. But today's reality is far from this image. While it's true that when we actually sit down to write, we need some time by ourselves to focus and draft our ideas, the thinking process that prepares us to write is often collaborative: you have an idea that you bounce off of someone; you read online or in print what somebody else has to say about an issue; you respond via a blog post; or maybe you just talk with one or two people. You have a conversation. And that's what you're going to do in this chapter: learn how to enter a conversation.

We are using the metaphor of conversation, which is common in rhetoric, as we discuss how to use sources to write a synthesis essay — that is, an argument based on multiple pieces of evidence. In order to develop an opinion on an unfamiliar subject or to deepen your view of a familiar one, you start by listening. Instead of reacting right away, you listen to what others are writing or saying. You may have heard someone comment! "She says whatever pops into her mind." It's not meant as a compliment! It's a reminder that our first opinions are not always smart opinions. So, part of the process we will be discussing in this chapter is reflection: what are some strategies we can use to take a moment to engage with a range of viewpoints, even those that initially we might want to dismiss?

As you explore an issue, it is also important to take stock of the rhetorical context: are you reading a series of blog posts or comments on social media? reading an article in a well-regarded print publication (such as the *Atlantic* magazine or the *New York Times*)? researching professional journals in a specific discipline, such as biology or history? watching a TedTalk given by an expert on a particular subject? listening to a political speech? Once you have a sense of the context of a conversation—especially who the audience is—and you've listened and considered what's being said, you're ready to join in.

▼
WORKING WITH A SINGLE SOURCE

All good thinkers and writers go through a process of finding and using sources to inform their thinking.

For instance, author Jane McGonigal writes about video games and how we can use them to solve serious problems in the real world. One of the things video games do very well is urge us to play more, and in her book *Reality Is Broken: Why Games Make Us Better and How They Can Change the World*, McGonigal explores how we might harness that power. The question is, how do video games motivate us? To answer that, McGonigal considered the work of several psychologists, including research that Sonja Lyubomirsky reported in her book *The How of Happiness*. Here's a passage from that book; as you read it, think about how Lyubomirsky's ideas might apply to the realm of video games.

> If I have seen further than others, it is by standing upon the shoulders of giants.
>
> —Isaac Newton

> The media are constantly telling us about the latest newfangled strategy shown to "really" work in boosting health and well-being. These strategies keep changing, each one evidently bested by the next, such that every new pronouncement becomes harder to believe. If the new kind of yoga or meditation or marital therapy technique were as effective as the reports claim, then wouldn't everyone be doing it and benefiting from it? Well, no. Any major life-changing endeavor must be accompanied by considerable sustained effort, and I would speculate that the majority of people do not or cannot continue putting out that kind of effort. What's more, all new happiness-enhancing or health-boosting strategies have something in common; each one bestows on the person a specific *goal*, something to do and to look forward. Moreover, as I explain later on, having goals in and of themselves is strongly associated with happiness and life satisfaction. That's why — at least for a time — any new happiness strategy does work!

Now, let's examine how McGonigal draws on Lyubomirsky's ideas and uses them to inform her argument about video games, specifically *World of Warcraft (WoW)*:

> When you're on a *WoW* quest, there's never any doubt about what you're supposed to do or where or how. It's not a game that emphasizes puzzle solving or trial-and-error investigation. You simply have to get the job done, and then you will collect your reward.

Why do we crave this kind of guaranteed productivity? In *The How of Happiness*, Sonja Lyubomirsky writes that the fastest way to improve someone's everyday quality of life is to "bestow on the person a specific goal, something to do and to look forward." When a clear goal is attached to a specific task, she explains, it gives us an energizing push, a sense of purpose. That's why receiving more quests every time we complete one in *World of Warcraft* is more of a reward than the experience points and the gold we've earned. Each quest is another clear goal with actionable steps.

Lyubomirsky may not be writing about video games per se, but her research on the relationship between goals and personal satisfaction lends authority to McGonigal's analysis of how video games motivate players. Could McGonigal have made her point without citing this source? Certainly, but bringing in an expert adds credibility and shows that McGonigal is an active participant in a scholarly and ongoing conversation on her topic.

Notice *how* McGonigal uses this source—she doesn't just drop in a quote. She begins with a summary of Lyubormirsky's larger ideas, and places the quote in that context. McGonigal introduces the quote by acknowledging the source, and finds a way to incorporate the quote smoothly into her own sentence. Then McGonigal follows up with an explanation of how that quote and idea apply to the point she's making about video games, and *WoW* in particular. This commentary ensures that McGonigal's ideas remain central and that the quotation is serving the purpose she wants it to serve. What we've just described are the primary steps to integrating quotations:

- provide context and acknowledge the source
- incorporate smoothly into a sentence
- add commentary

ACTIVITY DRAWING ON A SOURCE

Following are two passages, each one preceded by a question. Develop a response to one of those questions — even if it's a simple yes or no. Then, read the source that follows and select two quotes that support, challenge, or expand on your response. Finally, write a paragraph response that draws on those quotes, using the three steps to integrating a quotation described above. Pay special attention to how the source might challenge your initial response.

1. Should the Washington Redskins football team change its name?

Redskins and Reason / Charles Krauthammer

This article appeared in the *Washington Post* in 2013.

I wouldn't want to use a word that defines a people — living or dead, offended or not — in a most demeaning way. It's a question not of who or how many had their feelings hurt, but of whether you want to associate yourself with a word that, for whatever historical reason having nothing to do with you, carries inherently derogatory connotations.

Years ago, the word "retarded" emerged as the enlightened substitute for such cruel terms as "feeble-minded" or "mongoloid." Today, however, it is considered a form of denigration, having been replaced by the clumsy but now conventional "developmentally disabled." There is no particular logic to this evolution. But it's a social fact. Unless you're looking to give gratuitous offense, you don't call someone "retarded."

Let's recognize that there are many people of good will for whom "Washington Redskins" contains sentimental and historical attachment — and not an ounce of intended animus. So let's turn down the temperature. What's at issue is not high principle but adaptation to a change in linguistic nuance. A close call, though I personally would err on the side of not using the word if others are available. ■

2. Do today's commercial films and television go beyond stereotypes in their depiction of women and girls?

Sugar, Spice and Guts / A. O. Scott and Manohla Dargis

This article appeared in the *New York Times* in 2014

American mainstream cinema, a timid enterprise dependent on formulas and genres, can be mind-blowingly retrograde when it comes to women and girls. And while an occasional woman or girl rules the box office, too many of their on-screen sisters are sidelined or just left out of the picture.

Characters like Katniss Everdeen are changing girlhood and challenging tired stereotypes by not waiting for some guy to save the day: They're saving themselves and their worlds, too. Yet Katniss, her screen sisters and the industry have a very long way to go. In one study the Geena Davis Institute on Gender in Media looked at 5,554 "distinct speaking characters" in 122 family movies rated G, PG or PG-13 that were released between 2006 and 2009. The institute discovered that only 29.2 percent of those roles were female, while a whopping 70.8 percent were male. In other words, there were 2.42

male characters for every female one. Put another way, there was Harry and Ron and then there was Hermione, the smartest girl in the class. Hermione ruled, but not nearly enough.

In the past, some actresses had a measure of power or at least staying power in Hollywood, but too many more were typecast as bratty sisters, dutiful daughters or sexpots, and then cast aside. And some of their most memorable characters were, like their adult counterparts, defined by hypersexuality or asexuality. [. . .] What has changed in the years since? Quite a lot off screen, if not nearly enough on: Nymphets and tomboys still show up, as do brainy, funny, scary and tough girls. The picture of girlhood at the movies has become an increasingly diverse, sometimes contradictory array of identities, including bold revisions of age-old archetypes and brave new heroines. ■

WORKING WITH MULTIPLE SOURCES

Up to this point, we have been looking at how a single source can be used to inform an argument. But it is never wise to base our ideas on only one viewpoint, even if it's from a credible source. If your goal is to develop an argument that is balanced and demonstrates your understanding of key issues involved, then you'll consult a number of sources — probably several more than you actually use and cite in your argument. To think critically and argue persuasively, we need to learn everything we can about the issue, and listen to what others who are knowledgeable have to say, *especially* those who disagree with us or have an idea that's never occurred to us. We call this process of analyzing multiple sources in order to develop a new viewpoint **synthesis.**

DILBERT   *BY SCOTT ADAMS*

What is the difference between an *opinion* and an *informed opinion?* Think about a time when you changed your opinion. What caused the change? Was it reading another viewpoint, listening to someone whose opinion differed from yours, or maybe experiencing something that changed your perspective?

To practice this process, let's look at a series of sources — a Conversation — on one subject, probably one you already have an opinion about: high school sports.

Using the following group of texts, we'll examine this issue and develop an opinion that goes beyond a simple pro-or-con stance. Very often, you might start with an agree-or-disagree response to a controversial issue, just as you did in the previous Activity. But once you start listening to what others have said, your response is likely to be less black-and-white and more gray.

Each text you'll read in this Conversation introduces ideas or issues you might not have considered. And in the process, your thinking about the issue will become more informed, nuanced, and sophisticated. Eventually, you will get a chance to share your view on the subject, and show readers which ideas from these readings shaped the way you think about this issue. Thus, you'll be formulating an **evidence-based argument** or **synthesis essay,** an argument driven by your ideas but supported by the insights, research, and reasoning of others.

ACTIVITY   FORMING AN INITIAL OPINION

Brainstorm for a few minutes by talking or writing about your initial reactions to these two questions:

> What exactly is the value of having school-sponsored sports programs in high schools?
>
> Are the costs — in money and time — worth those benefits?

Now, ask yourself how much of your reaction is how you *feel* about the issue rather than what you *think* or *know* about it. If you play high school sports, how does that experience influence your viewpoint? Do you know if countries other than the United States have sports as part of their high school culture? What are some of the issues you'd like to know more about before you take a stand on whether sports should be part of high school?

Now let's take a look at the readings on this topic. Note that the first article, by Amanda Ripley, is a bit longer than the others. It anchors our discussion on this issue because it was very controversial when it was published and stirred up a lot of reactions. In fact, two of the texts included here are direct responses that take issue with Ripley's argument. The last two texts, both published earlier than Ripley's essay, are relevant to the topic, though obviously neither is a direct response to her argument.

The synthesis process begins with careful reading and analysis—making observations, finding patterns, and drawing conclusions. As you read and analyze, you want to do two things that at first might sound contradictory: keep an open mind and approach the source skeptically. On the one hand, you want to put yourself in the writer's position and try to understand the case he or she's making, but on the other hand you want to keep a critical eye on what the writer's purpose is and what biases he or she might have.

Keeping those things in mind, let's move on to examine the sources before we enter the Conversation on the role of sports in high schools.

High School Sports and Academic Achievement: Collaboration or Competition?

SOURCES

Amanda Ripley / *from* The Case against High School Sports

Kai Sato / *from* The Case for High School Sports

Daniel Bowen and Collin Hitt / *from* High School Sports Aren't Killing Academics

Mark Edmundson / *from* Do Sports Build Character or Damage It?

Organization for Economic Cooperation and Development / Comparative Test Scores (table)

from **The Case against High School Sports** / Amanda Ripley

The following is a selection from an article that appeared in the *Atlantic* magazine.
Amanda Ripley is an investigative journalist for *Time* magazine and a senior fellow at the
New American Foundation, a nonpartisan research think tank based in Washington, D.C.
She is the author of *The Smartest Kids in the World — and How They Got That Way* (2013).

Every year, thousands of teenagers move to the United States from all over the world, for all kinds of reasons. They observe everything in their new country with fresh eyes, including basic features of American life that most of us never stop to consider.

One element of our education system consistently surprises them: "Sports are a big deal here," says Jenny, who moved to America from South Korea with her family in 2011. Shawnee High, her public school in southern New Jersey, fields teams in 18 sports over the course of the school year, including golf and bowling. Its campus has lush grass fields, six tennis courts, and an athletic Hall of Fame. "They have days when teams dress up in Hawaiian clothes or pajamas just because — 'We're the soccer team!'" Jenny says. (To protect the privacy of Jenny and other students in this story, only their first names are used.)

By contrast, in South Korea, whose 15-year-olds rank fourth in the world (behind Shanghai, Singapore, and Hong Kong) on a test of critical thinking in math, Jenny's classmates played pickup soccer on a dirt field at lunchtime. They brought badminton rackets from home and pretended there was a net. If they made it into the newspaper, it was usually for their academic accomplishments.

Sports are embedded in American schools in a way they are not almost anywhere else. Yet this difference hardly ever comes up in domestic debates about America's international mediocrity in education. (The U.S. ranks 31st on the same international math test.) The challenges we do talk about are real ones, from under-trained teachers to entrenched poverty. But what to make of this other glaring reality, and the signal it sends to children, parents, and teachers about the very purpose of school?

5   When I surveyed about 200 former exchange students last year, in cooperation with an international exchange organization called AFS, nine out of 10 foreign students who had lived in the U.S. said that kids here cared more about sports than their peers back home did. A majority of Americans who'd studied abroad agreed.

Even in eighth grade, American kids spend more than twice the time Korean kids spend playing sports, according to a 2010 study published in the *Journal of Advanced Academics*. In countries with more-holistic, less hard-driving education systems than Korea's, like Finland and Germany, many kids play club sports in their local towns — outside of school. Most schools do not staff, manage, transport, insure, or glorify sports teams, because, well, why would they?

When I was growing up in New Jersey, not far from where Jenny now lives, I played soccer from age 7 to 17. I was relieved to find a place where girls were not expected to sit quietly or look pretty, and I still love the game. Like most other Americans, I can rattle off the many benefits of high-school sports: exercise, lessons in sportsmanship and perseverance, school spirit, and just plain fun. All of those things matter, and Jenny finds it refreshing to attend a school that is about so much more than academics. But as I've traveled around the world visiting places that do things differently — and get better results — I've started to wonder about the trade-offs we make.

Nearly all of Jenny's classmates at Shawnee are white, and 95 percent come from middle- or upper-income homes. But in 2012, only 17 percent of the school's juniors and seniors took at least one Advanced Placement test — compared with the 50 percent of students who played school sports.

As states and districts continue to slash education budgets, as more kids play on traveling teams outside of school, and as the globalized economy demands that children learn higher-order skills so they can compete down the line, it's worth reevaluating the American sporting tradition. If sports were not *central* to the mission of American high schools, then what would be? [. . .]

10   In many schools, sports are so entrenched that no one — not even the people in charge — realizes their actual cost. When Marguerite Roza, the author of *Educational Economics*, analyzed the finances of one public high school in the Pacific Northwest, she and her colleagues found that the school was spending $328 a student for math instruction and more than four times that much for cheerleading — $1,348 a cheerleader. "And it is not even a school in a district that prioritizes cheerleading," Roza wrote. "In fact, this district's 'strategic plan' has for the past three years claimed that *math* was the primary focus."

Many sports and other electives tend to have lower student-to-teacher ratios than math and reading classes, which drives up the cost. And contrary to what most people think, ticket and concession sales do not begin to cover the cost of sports in the vast majority of high schools (or colleges).

Football is, far and away, the most expensive high-school sport. Many football teams have half a dozen or more coaches, all of whom typically receive a stipend. Some schools hire professional coaches at full salaries, or designate a teacher as the full-time athletic director. New bleachers can cost half a million dollars, about the same as artificial turf. Even maintaining a grass field can cost more than $20,000 a year. Reconditioning helmets, a ritual that many teams pay for every year, can cost more than $1,500 for a large team. Some communities collect private donations or levy a special tax to fund new school-sports facilities. [. . .]

Over the past few years, budget cuts have forced more school districts, from Florida to Illinois, to scale back on sports programs. But in most of these places, even modest cuts to athletics are viewed as temporary — and tragic — sacrifices, not as necessary adaptations to a new reality. Many schools have shifted more of the cost of athletics to parents rather than downsize programs. Others have cut basic academic costs to keep their sports programs intact. Officials in Pasco County, Florida, have considered squeezing athletic budgets for each of the past six years. They've so far agreed to cut about 700 education jobs, and they extended winter break in 2011, but sports have been left mostly untouched.

In these communities, the dominant argument is usually that sports lure students into school and keep them out of trouble — the same argument American educators have made for more than a century. And it remains relevant, without a doubt, for some small portion of students.

15   But at this moment in history, now that more than 20 countries are pulling off better high-school-graduation rates than we are, with mostly nominal athletic offerings, using sports to tempt kids into getting an education feels dangerously old-fashioned. America has not found a way to dramatically improve its children's academic performance over the past 50 years, but other countries have — and they are starting to reap the economic benefits.

Andreas Schleicher, a German education scientist at the Organization for Economic Cooperation and Development, has visited schools all over the world and is an authority on different regional approaches to education. (I profiled Schleicher for this magazine in 2011.) He is wary of the theory that sports can encourage sustained classroom engagement. "Our analysis suggests that the most engaging environment you can offer students is one of cognitive challenge combined with individualised pedagogical support," he told me in an e-mail. "If you offer boring and poor math instruction and try to compensate that with interesting sport activities, you may get students interested in sports but I doubt it will do much good to their engagement with school." [. . .]

Imagine, for a moment, if Americans transferred our obsessive intensity about high-school sports — the rankings, the trophies, the ceremonies, the pride — to high-school academics. We would look not so different from South Korea, or Japan, or any of a handful of Asian countries whose hypercompetitive, pressure-cooker approach to academics in many ways mirrors the American approach to sports. Both approaches can be dysfunctional; both set kids up for stress and disappointment. The difference is that 93 percent of South Korean students graduate from high school, compared with just 77 percent of American students — only about 2 percent of whom receive athletic scholarships to college.

Basis public charter schools, located in Arizona, Texas, and Washington, D.C., are modeled on rigorous international standards. They do not offer tackle football; the founders deemed it too expensive and all-consuming. Still, Basis schools offer other, cheaper sports, including basketball and soccer. Anyone who wants to play can play; no one has to try out. Arizona's mainstream league is costly to join, so Basis Tucson North belongs to an alternative league that costs less and requires no long-distance travel, meaning students rarely miss class for games. Athletes who want to play at an elite level do so on their own, through club teams — not through school.

Basis teachers channel the enthusiasm usually found on football fields into academic conquests. On the day of Advanced Placement exams, students at Basis Tucson North file into the classroom to "Eye of the Tiger," the *Rocky III* theme song. In 2012, 15-year-olds at two Arizona Basis schools took a new test designed to compare individual schools' performance with that of schools from around the world. The average Basis student not only outperformed the typical American student by nearly three years in reading and science and by four years in math, but outscored the average student in Finland, Korea, and Poland as well. The Basis kid did better even than the average student from Shanghai, China, the region that ranks No. 1 in the world.

20 "I actually believe that sports are extremely important," Olga Block, a Basis co-founder, told me. "The problem is that once sports become important to the school, they start colliding with academics." ■

Since Ripley's essay is central to this Conversation on the role of organized sports in high schools, the first step is critical: analyze what her argument is. Whether you *end up* agreeing, disagreeing, or a little bit of both, you have to *start* by understanding what Ripley has to say. And — this is the tricky part — you want to "understand" the author on her own terms rather than standing ready to react at every point. Resist the impulse to insert your opinion, particularly when it differs from the author's. Be mindful of separating these two steps.

ACTIVITY UNDERSTANDING RIPLEY'S ARGUMENT

Analyze the overall argument Ripley is making by completing these sentence templates. These templates take you step-by-step through the thought process of understanding and analyzing the source.

Understand. In "The Case against High School Sports," Amanda Ripley makes the

central claim that _____.

Assess Evidence. One way she supports her position is _____. Another point she raises as evidence for her argument is _____.

Identify Counterarguments. She addresses several counterarguments, including these two: _____.

Form an Opinion. I agree with Ripley that _____. For example, in my experience, _____. On the other hand, I have doubts/reservations about another of her beliefs. Specifically, _____.

---

from **The Case for High School Sports** / Kai Sato

The following is a portion of an article posted on HuffingtonPost.com in response to Amanda Ripley's essay in the *Atlantic*. Kai Sato is the cofounder and chief operating officer of FieldLevel, Inc., a social network that, according to its website, "makes it easy for recruiting coaches and pro scouts to find players who fit their needs." He enters the Conversation with Ripley by drawing on his personal experience and disagreeing with some of her assumptions.

While it's imperative that we constantly strive to improve the educational experience for America's youth, the article's representation of high school sports in our country is short-sighted. It suggests that high schools should not subsidize sports teams, stating, "(in other countries) most schools do not staff, manage, transport, insure, or glorify sports teams, because, well, why would they?"

Here are a few reasons, well, why they would.

The goal of high school is to educate our young people so that they may become productive citizens, not to simply score well on the "international math test" to which the article makes several references.

The benefits of sports as part of the education process are abundant and sometimes beyond quantification, but the article merely brushes them off with only a slight acknowledgment. Today's employers, however, recognize those benefits in evaluating potential employees.

5 "We try to recruit people that can work in a team environment, are competitive and driven, and it is not a pre-requisite, but many times athletes have those traits," says Ken Marschner, Executive Director of UBS.

"In my 30 years in the business world, I have found that what an athlete brings to the workplace is discipline, teamwork, a drive for success, the desire to be held accountable and a willingness to have their performance measured," says Steve Reinemund, former Chairman & CEO, of PepsiCo. [. . .]

In 2002, a study by mutual fund company Oppenheimer revealed that a shocking 82% of women in executive-level jobs had played organized sports in middle, high or post-secondary school. Moreover, nearly half of women earning over $75,000 identified themselves as 'athletic.'

There is a long list of proven leaders that can attribute part of their development to sports like Jeffrey Immelt (General Electric), Meg Whitman (Hewlett Packard), and even President George H. W. Bush.

The article states that sports are overly emphasized in American high schools, commanding significant budgetary dollars. Yes, sports are a big deal in America, and it affords Americans the freedom of choice. In other countries, sports and academics are often mutually exclusive. In China, for example, a girl who wants to pursue competitive gymnastics must be identified at a young age, may then be removed from her family, and thrust into rigorous habitual training. Academics become secondary. The same happens around the world in soccer, as Lionel Messi, now one the world's best players, was plucked at a young age and placed into a soccer academy.

10   Thanks to high school sports, American children can be both students and athletes. ■

One of the moves in developing an informed argument, as we discussed in Chapter 3, is to consider a range of perspectives. In this case, Kai Sato takes issue with Ripley on several counts. Note, too, that he draws on a few other sources of information; that is, he enlarges the conversation beyond Ripley. Once you have established that one of your sources challenges or disagrees with another, the next step is to determine where you stand. You might agree or disagree entirely with the challenging author, or you might concede one point but refute another.

ACTIVITY   **COMPARING SOURCES**

Analyze the challenge Sato makes to Ripley's position by completing the following sentence templates. Note that your analysis includes not only what Sato argues but also your opinion of the strength of his position.

Compare and Contrast. One reason Kai Sato disagrees with Amanda Ripley is that he believes athletes develop traits that are attractive to employers. He points out that _____. Another reason he disagrees with her argument is _____.

Interpret. In my view, the main strength of Sato's case for high school sports is _____.

Assess Evidence. He cites as evidence _____. However, I question _____.

Detect Bias. It seems that he might be biased in that _____.

High School Sports Aren't Killing Academics / Daniel Bowen and Collin Hitt

This response to Amanda Ripley's essay also appeared in the *Atlantic* in 2013. Daniel Bowen is with Rice University's Houston Education Research Consortium; Collin Hitt works with the University of Arkansas's Department of Education Reform.

The need to build trust and social capital[1] is even more essential when schools are serving disadvantaged and at-risk students. Perhaps the most promising empirical evidence on this point comes from a Chicago program called Becoming A Man — Sports Edition. In this program, at-risk male students are assigned for a year to counselors and athletic coaches who double as male role models. In this partnership between Chicago Public Schools, Youth Guidance, and World Sport Chicago, sports are used to form bonds between the boys and their mentors and to teach self-control. The usual ball and basket sports are

---

[1] social capital: A sociological term for the value found in the community and relationships that surround a person. —Eds.

sometimes played, but participants are also trained in violent sports like boxing at school. [. . .]

According to a 2013 evaluation conducted by the Crime Lab at the University of Chicago, Becoming a Man—Sports Edition creates lasting improvements in the boys' study habits and grade point averages. During the first year of the program, students were found to be less likely to transfer schools or be engaged in violent crime. A year after the program, participants were less likely to have had an encounter with the juvenile justice system.

If school-sponsored sports were completely eliminated tomorrow, many American students would still have opportunities to participate in organized athletics elsewhere, much like they do

in countries such as Finland, Germany, and South Korea. The same is not certain when it comes to students from more disadvantaged back-grounds. In an overview of the research on non-school based after-school programs, Gardner, Roth, and Brooks-Gunn find that disadvantaged children participate in these programs at signifi-cantly lower rates. They find that low-income students have less access due to challenges with regard to transportation, non-nominal fees, and off-campus safety. Therefore, reducing or elimi-nating these opportunities would most likely deprive disadvantaged students of the benefits from athletic participation, not least of which is the opportunity to interact with positive role models outside of regular school hours. ■

While Bowen and Hitt also disagree with Ripley, they do not directly challenge her; instead, they object by raising a new issue, one that they believe she has not adequately addressed — that is, the impact of participating in sports on "disadvantaged and at-risk students." Notice that this move strengthens their argument because they've not abso-lutely or categorically disagreed with Ripley so much as they've broken her argument down and noted issues they believe she has failed to adequately consider.

ACTIVITY COMPARING SOURCES

Analyze the contribution Bowen and Hitt make to the Conversation by completing the following sentence templates. Note that you are also being asked to consider how Ripley might respond to their objection.

Understand. Daniel Bowen and Collin Hitt raise another issue regarding the role of sports in high schools. That is, they discuss _____.

Interpret. The research they cite to support their case indicates _____.

Compare and Contrast. Ripley would likely concede that _____, yet she might point out _____.

Do Sports Build Character or Damage It? / Mark Edmundson

This essay appeared on January 15, 2012, in the *Chronicle of Higher Education*, a newspaper and website that presents news and information relevant to college faculty and staff. Edmundson is an English professor at the University of Virginia. Following is an excerpt from the opening section of the essay, where he discusses the positive elements of participating in sports.

The first year I played high-school football, the coaches were united in their belief that drinking water on the practice field was dangerous. It made you cramp up, they told us. It made you sick to your stomach, they said. So at practice, which went on for two and a half hours, twice a day, during a roaring New England summer, we got no water.

The coaches didn't cut anyone from the squad that year. Kids cut themselves. Guys with what appeared to be spectacular athletic talent would, after four days of double-session drills, walk hangdog into the coaches' locker room and hand over their pads. When I asked one of them why he quit, he said simply, "I couldn't take it."

Could I? There was no reason going in to think that I would be able to. Compared with those of my fellow ballplayers, my physical gifts were meager. What I had was a will that was anything but weak. It was a surprise to me, and to everyone who knew me, how ferociously I wanted to stay with the game.

I liked the transforming aspect of the game: I came to the field one thing — a diffident guy with a slack body — and worked like a dog and so became something else — a guy with some physical prowess and more faith in himself. Mostly, I liked the whole process because it was so damned hard. I didn't think I could make it, and no one I knew did either. My parents were ready to console me if I came home bruised and dead weary and said that I was quitting. In time, one of the coaches confessed to me that he was sure I'd be gone in a few days. I had not succeeded in anything for a long time: I was a crappy student; socially I was close to a wash; my part-time job was scrubbing pans in a hospital kitchen; the first girl I liked in high school didn't like me; the second and the third followed her lead. But football was something I could do, though I was never going to be anything like a star. It was hard, it took some strength of will, and — clumsily, passionately — I could do it.

5   No one really noticed my improvements, least of all the coaches. But I did, and I took great pleasure in them. Football became a prototype for every endeavor in later life that required lonely, painstaking work and that was genuinely demanding. Through the game, I learned to care more about how I myself judged this or that performance of mine and less about how the world did. ■

Although Edmundson, whose essay was published prior to Ripley's, is not directly responding to her article in the *Atlantic*, his ideas have a more general connection. Basing his argument on his own experience, Edmundson focuses on the behaviors and habits of mind that participating in sports in high school fostered in him, suggesting that these effects might apply to others as well.

ACTIVITY   COMPARING SOURCES

Use the sentence templates below to analyze how Edmundson's position supports or challenges Ripley's ideas.

Understand. Mark Edmundson, a professor at the University of Virginia, cites his own experience to argue that _____.

Compare and Contrast. His experience relates to Ripley's argument because

_____.

Interpret. I think that Edmundson is/is not effective in raising questions about the strength of Ripley's argument in that _____.

Comparative Test Scores / Organization for Economic Cooperation and Development

The following bar graph compares rankings of students from the United States to their international counterparts. It summarizes data from 2012 gathered by the Organization for Economic Cooperation and Development, an international group whose mission is stated on its website as "to promote policies that will improve the economic and social well-being of people around the world."

U.S. students lag behind international peers

In tests of reading, math and science, U.S. 15-year-olds were outperformed by many of their counterparts in Asia and Europe — in some cases placing below the international average.

READING	Avg. 496	MATH	Avg. 494	SCIENCE	Avg. 501
1. Shanghai (China)	570	1. Shanghai (China)	613	1. Shanghai (China)	580
2. Hong Kong (China)	545	2. Singapore	573	2. Hong Kong (China)	555
3. Singapore	542	3. Hong Kong (China)	561	3. Singapore	551
4. Japan	538	4. Taiwan	560	4. Japan	547
5. S. Korea	536	5. S. Korea	554	5. Finland	545
6. Finland	524	6. Macao (China)	538	6. Estonia	541
7. Ireland	523	7. Japan	536	7. S. Korea	538
8. Taiwan	523	8. Liechtenstein	535	8. Vietnam	528
9. Canada	523	9. Switzerland	531	9. Poland	526
10. Poland	518	10. Netherlands	523	10. Canada	525
24. U.S.	498	36. U.S.	481	28. U.S.	497

NOTE: Scores were on a 1,000-point scale.

Much of Amanda Ripley's case against high school sports is based on concern for how the United States compares with the rest of the world on international tests. What does this graph actually tell us about the reasons for the lower test scores of U.S. fifteen-year-olds?

ACTIVITY   **COMPARING SOURCES**

Use the sentence templates below to analyze how the data from the Organization for Economic Cooperation and Development supports or challenges Ripley's ideas.

Understand. This graph emphasizes that, when viewed globally, students in the United States _____.

Interpret. Although the graph does not make any claims about what caused such comparatively low scores, it does demonstrate _____.

Compare and Contrast. Ripley would interpret this graph as proof of _____, but her opponents might argue that _____.

ACTIVITY ROLE PLAYING

Now that you have examined the ideas of each author individually and begun to make connections, it's time to really get inside their heads! Take on the role of one of the authors you have just read, and respond to one of the following questions *as if you were that author. Speak as "I" rather than saying, for instance, "Ripley would say"* or *"Edmundson believes."*

1. To what extent are participation in high school sports and the pursuit of academic excellence incompatible activities?
2. Should high schools severely cut back their sports programs? Why or why not?

▼
ENTERING THE CONVERSATION

At this point, you've read a lot of different ideas on the issue of whether high school sports are a distraction from academics. Now it's time to formulate your own response and enter the Conversation. As you might recall from Chapter 3, an argument begins with a claim.

Staking a Claim

On page 92 you did some brainstorming and thought about your opinion on this issue. Now, take a minute to think about how the different texts influenced your view. Have the ideas in these sources, either individually or as a group, changed your mind entirely? Modified your ideas a bit? Confirmed your initial opinion? Do you have a deeper under-standing of what the issues are? Did any of the sources challenge you to reconsider your position? Which one(s) validated your ideas?

ACTIVITY WRITING A CLAIM

After considering the questions above, write a claim — a working thesis — that clearly states your viewpoint.

Organizing Evidence

Once you have a claim, the next step in the synthesis process is to put your thoughts into writing and call on sources to support your ideas. Remember that you aren't just looking for evidence to support your claim; it's just as important to gather counterarguments that might help make your argument civil and nuanced.

ACTIVITY   CONNECTING CLAIM AND EVIDENCE

Use the graphic organizer to begin to think about how your claim relates to each source, and what use that source might be, whether to support your claim, to qualify your claim, or to serve as a counterargument that you can concede and refute. Of course, you probably won't use all five sources in your essay, but this exercise will help you decide which ones are more and less useful in reinforcing your ideas.

Source	Main Point	How I Might Use the Source in My Argument
Ripley		
Sato		
Bowen and Hitt		
Edmundson		
Comparative Test Scores		

The key thing to remember when you start to gather sources is that your own ideas need to remain central in your synthesis essay. You don't want outside sources to replace your argument: you want them to inform it.

We've been thinking of synthesis as a conversation. If you're talking with three other people, would you just repeat back what they've already said? Or would you contribute to the conversation by *connecting* to what they've said? So, instead of joining in by saying,

> "Mark Edmundson participated in sports in high school even though he never became a star athlete. He describes how he went to practice and put forth effort so that he improved, slowly and steadily. He was proud of that accomplishment. Thus, he developed strong character traits such as discipline and perseverance, . . ." etc., etc.,

it is more effective to use wording that connects Edmundson's argument to your own view. For instance, you might say,

> "We shouldn't underestimate the value of participating in sports to those who don't become star athletes. As Edmundson reminds us with his own experience, just participating can instill positive lifelong characteristics such as perseverance and discipline."

Evaluating Sources

Thus far, you've participated in a ready-made Conversation in which all the sources have been provided for you. Now it's your turn to move beyond these and come up with at least one other source on your own.

As you look for another source, be choosy. Is it a convincing source, or a weak one? You should especially be on the lookout for bias. "Check your sources" is the first rule of journalism, and it might also be the first rule of argument. Choosing untrustworthy sources can result in weak assertions and unconvincing support. Maybe even worse, using sources that lack credibility can give the impression that you are trying to manipulate your audience.

> I have yet to see a piece of writing, political or non-political, that does not have a slant. All writing slants the way a writer leans, and no man is born perpendicular.
>
> —E. B. White

When considering whether a source is credible or not, you need to figure out biases. This can be difficult at times, and some biases are more obvious than others, but there are a few basic questions that should help:

Questions to Detect Bias

1. Where did the source appear? Was it a respected publication (online or print)?
2. Does the writer or publication represent a specific political group, community, or corporation? (Follow the money.)
3. Is the source written by a person well respected in his or her field? Or is the source a lesser-known figure offering a personal experience?

ACTIVITY   FINDING AND EVALUATING SOURCES

Find an additional source that is relevant to the topic of the value of high school sports. You might look for a viewpoint that is directly relevant by searching for responses to Amanda Ripley via Google or a database that you have access to through your school or public library. Or you might research more broadly, considering the impact of sports on character, for instance, or the correlation between academic achievement and participation in sports. Or you might interview an "expert" — not necessarily someone who has published extensive scholarly studies but someone with first-hand experience, such as a coach, another student, or a community member who supports your school. Add that source to the graphic organizer you have been developing.

Using Literary Texts as Sources

Although literary texts — poems, plays, short stories, and novels — may not have the persuasive heft of research studies with data presented in tables and charts or the weight that the expert testimony of scholars carries, they certainly can add to your argument by providing vivid examples or reminding your readers of a story or character they are likely to know (such Gatsby or Hamlet). The key is not to support your argument entirely or exclusively with a literary text. Let's look at a poem by John Updike and consider its possible connections to the topic of high school sports that we've been discussing.

Ex-Basketball Player / John Updike

Pearl Avenue runs past the high-school lot,
Bends with the trolley tracks, and stops, cut off
Before it has a chance to go two blocks,
At Colonel McComsky Plaza. Berth's Garage
5 Is on the corner facing west, and there,
Most days, you'll find Flick Webb, who helps Berth out.

Flick stands tall among the idiot pumps —
Five on a side, the old bubble-head style,
Their rubber elbows hanging loose and low.
10 One's nostrils are two S's, and his eyes
An E and O. And one is squat, without
A head at all — more of a football type.

Once Flick played for the high-school team, the Wizards.
He was good: in fact, the best. In '46
15 He bucketed three hundred ninety points,
A county record still. The ball loved Flick.
I saw him rack up thirty-eight or forty
In one home game. His hands were like wild birds.

He never learned a trade, he just sells gas,
20 Checks oil, and changes flats. Once in a while,
As a gag, he dribbles an inner tube,
But most of us remember anyway.
His hands are fine and nervous on the lug wrench.
It makes no difference to the lug wrench, though.

25 Off work, he hangs around Mae's Luncheonette.
Grease-gray and kind of coiled, he plays pinball,
Smokes those thin cigars, nurses lemon phosphates.
Flick seldom says a word to Mae, just nods
Beyond her face toward bright applauding tiers
30 Of Necco Wafers, Nibs, and Juju Beads.

How might this poem support Ripley's argument that we should reassess the emphasis on sports in the American high school? We might interpret the poem as a description of an athletic star who fails to develop intellectually or even emotionally. Updike depicts Flick Webb as the quintessential case of arrested development. Content to be the basketball hero, he neglects learning a trade or developing skills that would lead to a bigger life beyond high school. We can presume that Flick lacked a school environment that prized academic achievement, and can see his sad life as the result of not being encouraged to prepare himself for life off the court.

But think, too, of ways that this poem might not support an argument about high school sports. If you relied too heavily on this depiction of Flick Webb for your support, you would be vulnerable on several counts. Most obvious, this is one example in a poem — not even real life. Another possible objection would be that the poem was written in the 1950s, a time when high school students' expectations for college and career were different from now. Still another potential criticism would be that we know so little about Flick; maybe without those glory days, his life would be worse.

So, if you use a literary work as evidence, make sure you incorporate it as a vivid example, possibly using some of the distinctive language to appeal to pathos, but placing it within or alongside other evidence that strengthens your overall position.

As you read more essays by professional writers, you'll start to notice that they tend to use literary texts to either open or close a piece. Imagine an introduction to an argument against high school sports that opens with the imagery of Flick Webb, who has gone from being a star athlete whose "hands were like wild birds" to an adult gas station attendant "stand[ing] tall among the idiot pumps." That striking contrast might be just what you need to get your audience's attention and lead into your claim.

ACTIVITY   DRAFTING A SYNTHESIS ESSAY

You've done a good part of the heavy lifting of thinking, analyzing, connecting, and evaluating these sources on the role of sports in high school. Now it's time to put it all together. Write a draft of an evidence-based synthesis essay explaining your view on whether the role of sports in American high schools should be re-evaluated.

---

culminating activity

Following are several texts on the ethics and economics of eating meat. After reading and analyzing them as you have done with the texts on sports, explain your position on the ethics of eating meat. Reference at least three of the sources in your argument.

TEXTS

Wendell Berry / *from* The Pleasures of Eating

Barbara Kingsolver / *from* Animal, Vegetable, Miracle

Michael Pollan / *from* An Animal's Place

Jonathan Safran Foer / *from* Let Them Eat Dog: A Modest Proposal for Tossing Fido in the Oven

Humane Research Council / Vegetarianism in the United States (infographic)

from **The Pleasures of Eating** / Wendell Berry

In this excerpt from a 1990 essay, author and environmentalist Wendell Berry asks the reader
to no longer be a "passive consumer of food."

The industrial eater is, in fact, one who does not know that eating is an agricultural act, who no longer knows or imagines the connections between eating and the land, and who is therefore necessarily passive and uncritical — in short, a victim. When food, in the minds of eaters, is no longer associated with farming and with the land, then the eaters are suffering a kind of cultural amnesia that is misleading and dangerous. The current version of the "dream home" of the future involves "effortless" shopping from a list of available goods on a television monitor and heating precooked food by remote control. Of course, this implies and depends on a perfect ignorance of the history of the food that is consumed. It requires that the citizenry should give up their hereditary and sensible aversion to buying a pig in a poke.[1] It wishes to make the selling of pigs in pokes an honorable and glamorous activity. The dreams in this dream home will perforce know nothing about the kind or quality of this food, or where it came from, or how it was produced and prepared, or what ingredients, additives, and residues it contains — unless, that is, the dreamer undertakes a close and constant study of the food industry, in which case he or she might as well wake up and play an active and responsible part in the economy of food.

There is, then, a politics of food that, like any politics, involves our freedom. We still (sometimes) remember that we cannot be free if our minds and voices are controlled by someone else. But we have neglected to understand that we cannot be free if our food and its sources are controlled by someone else. The condition of the passive consumer of food is not a democratic condition. One reason to eat responsibly is to live free. [. . .]

The pleasure of eating should be an extensive pleasure, not that of the mere gourmet. People who know the garden in which their vegetables have grown and know that the garden is healthy will remember the beauty of the growing plants, perhaps in the dewy first light of morning when gardens are at their best. Such a memory involves itself with the food and is one of the pleasures of eating. The knowledge of the good health of the garden relieves and frees and comforts the eater. The same goes for eating meat. The thought of the good pasture and of the calf contentedly grazing flavors the steak. Some, I know, will think of it as bloodthirsty or worse to eat a fellow creature you have known all its life. On the contrary, I think it means that you eat with understanding and with gratitude. A significant part of the pleasure of eating is in one's accurate consciousness of the lives and the world from which food comes. The pleasure of eating, then, may be the best available standard of our health. And this pleasure, I think, is pretty fully available to the urban consumer who will make the necessary effort.

---

[1] pig in a poke: A poke is an archaic word for *bag*, so this phrase
means buying something sight unseen, or without really knowing
what it is. —Eds.

from **Animal, Vegetable, Miracle** / Barbara Kingsolver

Barbara Kingsolver (b. 1955) is an award-winning novelist and essayist. Her fiction
includes *The Bean Trees* (1988), *Animal Dreams* (1990), and *The Poisonwood Bible* (1998).
The following excerpt is from *Animal, Vegetable, Miracle* (2007), her account of her family's
effort to eat only locally grown food for an entire year.

The blunt biological truth is that we animals can only remain alive by eating other life. Plants are inherently more blameless, having been born with the talent of whipping up their own food, peacefully and without noise, out of sunshine, water, and the odd mineral ingredient sucked up through their toes. Strangely enough, it's the animals to which we've assigned some rights, while the saintly plants we maim and behead with moral impunity. Who thinks to beg forgiveness while mowing the lawn?

The moral rules of destroying our fellow biota get even more tangled, the deeper we go. If we draw the okay-to-kill line between "animal" and "plant," and thus exclude meat, fowl, and fish from our diet on moral grounds, we still must live with the fact that every sack of flour and every soybean-based block of tofu came from a field where countless winged and furry lives were extinguished in the plowing, cultivating, and harvest. An estimated 67 million birds die each year from pesticide exposure on U.S. farms. Butterflies, too, are universally killed on contact in larval form by the genetically modified pollen contained in most U.S. corn. Foxes, rabbits, and bobolinks are starved out of their homes or dismembered by the sickle mower. [. . .]

I find myself fundamentally allied with a vegetarian position in every way except one: however selectively, I eat meat. I'm unimpressed by arguments that condemn animal harvest while ignoring, wholesale, the animal killing that underwrites vegetal foods. Uncountable deaths by pesticide and habitat removal — the beetles and bunnies that die collaterally for our bread and veggie-burgers — are lives plumb wasted. Animal harvest is at least not gratuitous, as part of a plan involving labor and recompense. We raise these creatures for a reason. Such premeditation may be presumed unkind, but without it our gentle domestic beasts in their picturesque shapes, colors, and finely tuned purposes would never have had the distinction of existing.

---

from **An Animal's Place** / Michael Pollan

The following selection has been taken from a 2002 article in the *New York Times* by journalist and food writer Michael Pollan.

Before you swear off meat entirely, let me describe a very different sort of animal farm. It is typical of nothing, and yet its very existence puts the whole moral question of animal agriculture in a different light. Polyface Farm occupies 550 acres of rolling grassland and forest in the Shenandoah Valley of Virginia. Here, Joel Salatin and his family raise six different food animals — cattle, pigs, chickens, rabbits, turkeys and sheep — in an intricate dance of symbiosis designed to allow each species, in Salatin's words, "to fully express its physiological distinctiveness."

What this means in practice is that Salatin's chickens live like chickens; his cows, like cows; [pig]s, pigs. As in nature, where birds tend to follow herbivores, once Salatin's cows have finished grazing a pasture, he moves them out and tows in his "eggmobile," a portable chicken coop that houses several hundred laying hens — roughly the natural size of a flock. The hens fan out over the pasture, eating the short grass and picking insect larvae out of the cowpats — all the while spreading the cow manure and eliminating the farm's parasite problem. A diet of grubs and grass makes for exceptionally tasty eggs and contented chickens, and their nitrogenous manure feeds the pasture. A few weeks later, the chickens move out, and the sheep come in, dining on the lush new growth, as well as on the weed species (nettles, nightshade) that the cattle and chickens won't touch.

I thought a lot about vegetarianism and animal rights during the day I spent on Joel Salatin's extraordinary farm. So much of what I'd read, so much of what I'd accepted, looked very different from here. To many animal rightists, even Polyface Farm is a death camp. But to look at these animals is to see this for the sentimental conceit it is. In the same way that we can probably recognize animal suffering when we see it, animal happiness is unmistakable, too, and here I was seeing it in abundance.

For any animal, happiness seems to consist in the opportunity to express its creaturely character — its essential pigness or wolfness or chickenness. Aristotle speaks of each creature's "characteristic form of life." For domesticated species, the good life, if we can call it that, cannot be achieved apart from humans — apart from our farms and, therefore, our meat eating. This, it seems to me, is where animal rightists betray a profound ignorance about the workings of nature. To think of domestication as a form of enslavement or even exploitation is to misconstrue the whole relationship, to project a human idea of power onto what is, in fact, an instance of mutualism between species. Domestication is an evolutionary, rather than a political, development. It is certainly not a regime humans imposed on animals some 10,000 years ago.

from Let Them Eat Dog: A Modest Proposal for Tossing Fido in the Oven / Jonathan Safran Foer

Following is an excerpt from novelist Jonathan Safran Foer's controversial article "Let Them Eat Dog," which appeared in the *Wall Street Journal* in 2009.

Despite the fact that it's perfectly legal in 44 states, eating "man's best friend" is as taboo as a man eating his best friend. Even the most enthusiastic carnivores won't eat dogs. TV guy and sometimes cooker Gordon Ramsay can get pretty macho with lambs and piglets when doing publicity for something he's selling, but you'll never see a puppy peeking out of one of his pots. And though he once said he'd electrocute his children if they became vegetarian, one can't help but wonder what his response would be if they poached the family pooch.

Dogs are wonderful, and in many ways unique. But they are remarkably unremarkable in their intellectual and experiential capacities. Pigs are every bit as intelligent and feeling, by any sensible definition of the words. They can't hop into the back of a Volvo, but they can fetch, run and play, be mischievous and reciprocate affection. So why don't they get to curl up by the fire? Why can't they at least be spared being tossed on the fire? Our taboo against dog eating says something about dogs and a great deal about us.

The French, who love their dogs, sometimes eat their horses.

The Spanish, who love their horses, sometimes eat their cows.

5 The Indians, who love their cows, sometimes eat their dogs.

While written in a much different context, George Orwell's words (from *Animal Farm*) apply here: "All animals are equal, but some animals are more equal than others."

This infographic comes from HumaneSpot.org, the website of the Humane Research Council, which claims to be "the world's most comprehensive resource for public opinion and behavior research about animal protection issues."

5

Identity and Society

- What does "identity" mean?
- How is one's identity formed?
- How do personal experiences affect our identity?
- To what extent do institutions emphasize conformity at the expense of individuality?

irror, mirror on the wall, who is the fairest of them all?

It's a line that most everyone has heard from childhood: the Evil Queen from *Snow White* asking her magic mirror if she's the prettiest in the kingdom. For years, the mirror replies exactly as she hoped—"You, my queen, are fairest of all." When, however, Snow White begins to eclipse the queen in beauty, the magic mirror tells her so.

Think about this idea for a minute. Where does the Queen look for confirmation of her own beauty? Not to a regular mirror that would reveal her own true reflection, but rather to a magic mirror that doesn't reflect her own image at all, but only compares the Queen's image to other people's beauty. The Queen's identity is not tied to her self, but to others, whom she tries — unsuccessfully — to control.

Look at another mirror. This one is from a poem by Sylvia Plath, a brilliant but troubled poet who took her own life at the age of thirty-one.

Mirror / Sylvia Plath

© Everett Collection Inc/Alamy

I am silver and exact. I have no preconceptions.
Whatever I see I swallow immediately
Just as it is, unmisted by love or dislike.
I am not cruel, only truthful —
The eye of a little god, four-cornered.   5
Most of the time I meditate on the opposite wall.
It is pink, with speckles. I have looked at it so long
I think it is a part of my heart. But it flickers.
Faces and darkness separate us over and over.

Now I am a lake. A woman bends over me,   10
Searching my reaches for what she really is.
Then she turns to those liars, the candles or the moon.
I see her back, and reflect it faithfully.
She rewards me with tears and an agitation of hands.
I am important to her. She comes and goes.   15
Each morning it is her face that replaces the darkness.
In me she has drowned a young girl, and in me an old woman
Rises toward her day after day, like a terrible fish.

Unlike the Evil Queen's magic mirror, notice how the mirror in the first stanza, as well as the lake in the second, claim that they are not cruel, but truthful, and reflect the image of the woman faithfully. The woman reflected in this mirror may not be happy with what she sees ("tears and an agitation of hands," l. 14), but at least she has the truth. So, these are two contrasting ways of trying to define one's identity: the Evil Queen looks outward to others, while the woman in the poem looks at herself by using a mirror that is "silver and exact" (l. 1).

OPENING ACTIVITY

One way to define *identity* is to ask yourself, "How do I view myself and how do others view me?" Explain how each of the following factors affects how you view yourself and how you think others view you:

- your gender
- your age
- your race, culture, and/or religion
- your socioeconomic status

To begin considering the essential questions of this chapter, make a list of personal attributes or experiences that you have had that you feel make you unique—as many as you'd like. Then categorize each item in a chart with the following headings (feel free to add other categories):

Physical Traits	Clothing/ Jewelry/Etc.	Interests	Experiences	Family/Friends

Now, choose one item from your list that has been mostly affected by looking outside of yourself (as the Evil Queen was affected by looking into her magic mirror) and one item that has been mostly affected by looking at yourself (like the narrator in Plath's poem was affected). Write a paragraph that explains how the chosen items reflect your identity and explore the inner and outer forces that have shaped that identity. Focus especially on the role that society (including your school, city, geographical area, religion, and so on) has played in shaping your identity.

Shooting an Elephant

George Orwell

George Orwell, the author of several well-known novels and essays, including *Animal Farm*, *1984*, and *Down and Out in Paris and London*, was born Eric Blair in 1903 in India. The son of a British government official, Orwell went to school and lived in England until his early twenties, when he joined the Indian Imperial Police in Burma (now known as Myanmar), a country in Southeast Asia that was under British control at the time. Orwell became disenchanted with imperialism and resigned after a short period of time. He then turned to writing full-time. This classic essay, published in 1936, recounts a situation Orwell faced as a member of the Indian Imperial Police force.

Popperfoto/Getty Images

KEY CONTEXT   The term "imperialism," especially British imperialism, is an important one to understand for this piece. From the late sixteenth century through World War I, at the beginning of the twentieth century, England had history's largest empire. At various times throughout this time period, England had colonies in areas now known as the United States, Canada, Australia, Asia, Africa, and South America; a popular and true saying at the time was "The sun never sets on the British Empire."

The British government in the Indian subcontinent — which includes what is now India, as well as Pakistan, Myanmar/Burma, Bangladesh, and other countries — was called the Raj, a Hindi word for "rule." While England regularly conquered its colonies through military strength, it ruled them by forcing its educational, judicial, economic, and governmental structures onto the colonized people with the goal of making the world British. But, starting with the American Revolution in the late eighteenth century, most of the former colonies, often through war, were able to gain their independence. Burma (now Myanmar), where this piece is set, became independent from England in 1948, only about twenty years after Orwell worked there.

In Moulmein, in Lower Burma, I was hated by large numbers of people — the only time in my life that I have been important enough for this to happen to me. I was sub-divisional police officer of the town, and in an aimless, petty kind of way anti-European feeling was very bitter. No one had the guts to raise a riot, but if a European woman went through the bazaars alone somebody would probably spit betel juice over her dress. As a police officer I was an obvious target and was baited whenever it seemed safe to do so. When a nimble Burman tripped me up on

Burma Provincial Police
Training School, Mandalay, 1923.
Eric Blair (George Orwell)
standing third from left.

**How does this photograph of
Orwell as a young man
illustrate the separation he
likely felt from the Burmese
natives?**

the football field and the referee (another Burman) looked the other way, the crowd yelled with hideous laughter. This happened more than once. In the end the sneering yellow faces of young men that met me everywhere, the insults hooted after me when I was at a safe distance, got badly on my nerves. The young Buddhist priests were the worst of all. There were several thousands of them in the town and none of them seemed to have anything to do except stand on street corners and jeer at Europeans.

All this was perplexing and upsetting. For at that time I had already made up my mind that imperialism was an evil thing and the sooner I chucked up my job and got out of it the better. Theoretically — and secretly, of course — I was all for the Burmese and all against their oppressors, the British. As for the job I was doing, I hated it more bitterly than I can perhaps make clear. In a job like that you see the dirty work of Empire at close quarters. The wretched prisoners huddling in the stinking cages of the lock-ups, the grey, cowed faces of the long-term convicts, the scarred buttocks of the men who

had been flogged with bamboos — all these oppressed me with an intolerable sense of guilt. But I could get nothing into perspective. I was young and ill-educated and I had had to think out my problems in the utter silence that is imposed on every Englishman in the East. I did not even know that the British Empire is dying, still less did I know that it is a great deal better than the younger empires that are going to supplant it. All I knew was that I was stuck between my hatred of the empire I served and my rage against the evil-spirited little beasts who tried to make my job impossible. With one part of my mind I thought of the British Raj as an unbreakable tyranny, as something clamped down, *in saecula saeculorum*[1] upon the will of prostrate peoples; with another part I thought that the greatest joy in the world would be to drive a bayonet into a Buddhist priest's guts. Feelings like these are the normal by-products of imperialism; ask any Anglo-Indian official, if you can catch him off duty.

---

[1] *in saecula saeclorum*: Latin for "a century of centuries," a figurative way of saying "forever" or "for eternity" —Eds.

▶

Elephants in colonial Burma were largely industrial animals, primarily used in the lumber industry. Their drivers were called "mahouts."

What evidence from paragraph 6 supports the idea that shooting a working elephant in Burma was a significant event.

NGS Image Collection/The Art Archive at Art Resource, NY

One day something happened which in a roundabout way was enlightening. It was a tiny incident in itself, but it gave me a better glimpse than I had had before of the real nature of imperialism — the real motives for which despotic governments act. Early one morning the sub-inspector at a police station the other end of the town rang me up on the phone and said that an elephant was ravaging the bazaar. Would I please come and do something about it? I did not know what I could do, but I wanted to see what was happening and I got on to a pony and started out. I took my rifle, an old .44 Winchester and much too small to kill an elephant, but I thought the noise might be useful *in terrorem*.[2] Various Burmans stopped me on the way and told me about the elephant's doings. It was not, of course, a wild elephant, but a tame one which had gone "must."[3] It had been chained up, as tame elephants always are when their attack of "must" is due, but on the previous night it had broken its

chain and escaped. Its mahout, the only person who could manage it when it was in that state, had set out in pursuit, but had taken the wrong direction and was now twelve hours' journey away, and in the morning the elephant had suddenly reappeared in the town. The Burmese population had no weapons and were quite helpless against it. It had already destroyed somebody's bamboo hut, killed a cow and raided some fruit-stalls and devoured the stock; also it had met the municipal rubbish van and, when the driver jumped out and took to his heels, had turned the van over and inflicted violences upon it.

The Burmese sub-inspector and some Indian constables were waiting for me in the quarter where the elephant had been seen. It was a very poor quarter, a labyrinth of squalid bamboo huts, thatched with palm-leaf, winding all over a steep hillside. I remember that it was a cloudy, stuffy morning at the beginning of the rains. We began questioning the people as to where the elephant had gone and, as usual, failed to get any definite information. That is invariably the case in the East; a story always sounds clear enough at a distance, but the nearer you get to the scene of events the vaguer

---

[2] *in terrorem*: A legal term meaning "to scare a person into complying with terms." —Eds.

[3] must: A temporary condition occurring in male elephants; their testosterone level increases dramatically and they can become violent and unpredictable. —Eds.

it becomes. Some of the people said that the elephant had gone in one direction, some said that he had gone in another, some professed not even to have heard of any elephant. I had almost made up my mind that the whole story was a pack of lies, when we heard yells a little distance away. There was a loud, scandalized cry of "Go away, child! Go away this instant!" and an old woman with a switch in her hand came round the corner of a hut, violently shooing away a crowd of naked children. Some more women followed, clicking their tongues and exclaiming; evidently there was something that the children ought not to have seen. I rounded the hut and saw a man's dead body sprawling in the mud. He was an Indian, a black Dravidian coolie,[4] almost naked, and he could not have been dead many minutes. The people said that the elephant had come suddenly upon him round the corner of the hut, caught him with its trunk, put its foot on his back and ground him into the earth. This was the rainy season and the ground was soft, and his face had scored a trench a foot deep and a couple of yards long. He was lying on his belly with arms crucified and head sharply twisted to one side. His face was coated with mud, the eyes wide open, the teeth bared and grinning with an expression of unendurable agony. (Never tell me, by the way, that the dead look peaceful. Most of the corpses I have seen looked devilish.) The friction of the great beast's foot had stripped the skin from his back as neatly as one skins a rabbit. As soon as I saw the dead man I sent an orderly to a friend's house nearby to borrow an elephant rifle. I had already sent back the pony, not wanting it to go mad with fright and throw me if it smelt the elephant.

5   The orderly came back in a few minutes with a rifle and five cartridges, and meanwhile some Burmans had arrived and told us that the elephant was in the paddy fields below, only a few hundred yards away. As I started forward practically the whole population of the quarter flocked out of the houses and followed me. They had seen the rifle and were all shouting excitedly that I was going to shoot the elephant. They had not shown much interest in the elephant when he was merely ravaging their homes, but it was different now that he was going to be shot. It was a bit of fun to them, as it would be to an English crowd; besides they wanted the meat. It made me vaguely uneasy. I had no intention of shooting the elephant — I had merely sent for the rifle to defend myself if necessary — and it is always unnerving to have a crowd following you. I marched down the hill, looking and feeling a fool, with the rifle over my shoulder and an ever-growing army of people jostling at my heels. At the bottom, when you got away from the huts, there was a metalled road and beyond that a miry waste of paddy fields a thousand yards across, not yet ploughed but soggy from the first rains and dotted with coarse grass. The elephant was standing eight yards from the road, his left side towards us. He took not the slightest notice of the crowd's approach. He was tearing up bunches of grass, beating them against his knees to clean them and stuffing them into his mouth.

I had halted on the road. As soon as I saw the elephant I knew with perfect certainty that I ought not to shoot him. It is a serious matter to shoot a working elephant — it is comparable to destroying a huge and costly piece of machinery — and obviously one ought not to do it if it can possibly be avoided. And at that distance, peacefully eating, the elephant looked no more dangerous than a cow. I thought then and I think now that his attack of "must" was already passing off; in which case he would merely wander harmlessly about until the mahout came back and caught him. Moreover, I did not in the least want to shoot him. I decided

---

[4]Dravidian coolie: Dravidians are an ethnic group from Southern India. "Coolie" is a term that was used in Orwell's time for laborers of Asian descent; it is now considered derogatory. —Eds.

that I would watch him for a little while to make sure that he did not turn savage again, and then go home.

But at that moment I glanced round at the crowd that had followed me. It was an immense crowd, two thousand at the least and growing every minute. It blocked the road for a long distance on either side. I looked at the sea of yellow faces above the garish clothes — faces all happy and excited over this bit of fun, all certain that the elephant was going to be shot. They were watching me as they would watch a conjurer about to perform a trick. They did not like me, but with the magical rifle in my hands I was momentarily worth watching. And suddenly I realized that I should have to shoot the elephant after all. The people expected it of me and I had got to do it; I could feel their two thousand wills pressing me forward, irresistibly. And it was at this moment, as I stood there with the rifle in my hands, that I first grasped the hollowness, the futility of the white man's dominion in the East. Here was I, the white man with his gun, standing in front of the unarmed native crowd — seemingly the leading actor of the piece; but in reality I was only an absurd puppet pushed to and fro by the will of those yellow faces behind. I perceived in this moment that when the white man turns tyrant it is his own freedom that he destroys. He becomes a sort of hollow, posing dummy, the conventionalized figure of a sahib.[5] For it is the condition of his rule that he shall spend his life in trying to impress the "natives," and so in every crisis he has got to do what the "natives" expect of him. He wears a mask, and his face grows to fit it. I had got to shoot the elephant. I had committed myself to doing it when I sent for the rifle. A sahib has got to act like a sahib; he has got to appear resolute, to

know his own mind and do definite things. To come all that way, rifle in hand, with two thousand people marching at my heels, and then to trail feebly away, having done nothing — no, that was impossible. The crowd would laugh at me. And my whole life, every white man's life in the East, was one long struggle not to be laughed at.

But I did not want to shoot the elephant. I watched him beating his bunch of grass against his knees, with that preoccupied grandmotherly air that elephants have. It seemed to me that it would be murder to shoot him. At that age I was not squeamish about killing animals, but I had never shot an elephant and never wanted to. (Somehow it always seems worse to kill a *large* animal.) Besides, there was the beast's owner to be considered. Alive, the elephant was worth at least a hundred pounds; dead, he would only be worth the value of his tusks, five pounds, possibly. But I had got to act quickly. I turned to some experienced-looking Burmans who had been there when we arrived, and asked them how the elephant had been behaving. They all said the same thing: he took no notice of you if you left him alone, but he might charge if you went too close to him.

It was perfectly clear to me what I ought to do. I ought to walk up to within, say, twenty-five yards of the elephant and test his behavior. If he charged, I could shoot; if he took no notice of me, it would be safe to leave him until the mahout came back. But also I knew that I was going to do no such thing. I was a poor shot with a rifle and the ground was soft mud into which one would sink at every step. If the elephant charged and I missed him, I should have about as much chance as a toad under a steam roller. But even then I was not thinking particularly of my own skin, only of the watchful yellow faces behind. For at that moment, with the crowd watching me, I was not afraid in the ordinary sense, as I would have been if I had been alone. A white man mustn't be frightened in front of "natives"; and so, in general, he isn't frightened.

---

[5]sahib: While in Arabic the term means "friend," during the British Raj the term was used as a form of address to a person of authority similar to how we might use "Mister" to a person of authority today. —Eds.

seeing connections

Library of Congress Prints and Photographs Division, LC-USZ62-131443

▲

Teddy Roosevelt was arguably the most aggressive imperialist in American history, annexing numerous ports and territories, including the Philippines, Puerto Rico, Cuba, Panama, Alaska, and Hawaii, during his time in office as either president or vice president. Roosevelt was also an avid big-game hunter; he shot eleven elephants during a one-year-long hunting trip in Africa just after his presidency.

Based on what you already know or can quickly learn through research about Teddy Roosevelt's expansionist policies and love of hunting, consider what ideas may link his imperialism and his love of hunting. How could they be related? How do those ideas help you understand more about "Shooting an Elephant"?

The sole thought in my mind was that if anything went wrong those two thousand Burmans would see me pursued, caught, trampled on and reduced to a grinning corpse like that Indian up the hill. And if that happened it was quite probable that some of them would laugh. That would never do. There was only one alternative. I shoved the cartridges into the magazine and lay down on the road to get a better aim.

10   The crowd grew very still, and a deep, low, happy sigh, as of people who see the theatre curtain go up at last, breathed from innumerable throats. They were going to have their bit of fun after all. The rifle was a beautiful German thing with cross-hair sights. I did not then know that

in shooting an elephant one would shoot to cut an imaginary bar running from ear-hole to ear-hole. I ought, therefore, as the elephant was sideways on, to have aimed straight at his ear-hole; actually I aimed several inches in front of this, thinking the brain would be further forward.

When I pulled the trigger I did not hear the bang or feel the kick — one never does when a shot goes home — but I heard the devilish roar of glee that went up from the crowd. In that instant, in too short a time, one would have thought, even for the bullet to get there, a mysterious, terrible change had come over the elephant. He neither stirred nor fell, but every line of his body had altered. He looked suddenly stricken, shrunken, immensely old, as though the frightful impact of the bullet had paralysed him without knocking him down. At last, after what seemed a long time — it might have been five seconds, I dare say — he sagged flabbily to his knees. His mouth slobbered. An enormous senility seemed to have settled upon him. One could have imagined him thousands of years old. I fired again into the same spot. At the second shot he did not collapse but climbed with desperate slowness to his feet and stood weakly upright, with legs sagging and head drooping. I fired a third time. That was the shot that did for him. You could see the agony of it jolt his whole body and knock the last remnant of strength from his legs. But in falling he seemed for a moment to rise, for as his hind legs collapsed beneath him he seemed to tower upward like a huge rock toppling, his trunk reaching skywards like a tree. He trumpeted, for the first and only time. And then down he came, his belly towards me, with a crash that seemed to shake the ground even where I lay.

I got up. The Burmans were already racing past me across the mud. It was obvious that the elephant would never rise again, but he was not dead. He was breathing very rhythmically with

Orwell with a Burmese dah.

In what ways does this photo capture the cultural conflict in this essay?

long rattling gasps, his great mound of a side painfully rising and falling. His mouth was wide open — I could see far down into caverns of pale pink throat. I waited a long time for him to die, but his breathing did not weaken. Finally I fired my two remaining shots into the spot where I thought his heart must be. The thick blood welled out of him like red velvet, but still he did not die. His body did not even jerk when the shots hit him, the tortured breathing continued without a pause. He was dying, very slowly and in great agony, but in some world remote from me where not even a bullet could damage him further. I felt that I had got to put an end to that dreadful noise. It seemed dreadful to see the great beast lying there, powerless to move and yet powerless to die, and not even to be able to finish him. I sent back for my small rifle and poured shot after shot into his heart and down his throat. They seemed to make no impression. The tortured gasps continued as steadily as the ticking of a clock.

In the end I could not stand it any longer and went away. I heard later that it took him half an hour to die. Burmans were bringing dahs[6] and baskets even before I left, and I was told they had stripped his body almost to the bones by the afternoon.

Afterwards, of course, there were endless discussions about the shooting of the elephant. The owner was furious, but he was only an

Indian and could do nothing. Besides, legally I had done the right thing, for a mad elephant has to be killed, like a mad dog, if its owner fails to control it. Among the Europeans opinion was divided. The older men said I was right, the younger men said it was a damn shame to shoot an elephant for killing a coolie, because an elephant was worth more than any damn Coringhee[7] coolie. And afterwards I was very glad that the coolie had been killed; it put me legally in the right and it gave me a sufficient pretext for shooting the elephant. I often wondered whether any of the others grasped that I had done it solely to avoid looking a fool.

---

[6]dah: Burmese knife, often long enough to be considered a sword. —Eds.

[7]Coringhee: a Southern Indian ethnicity. —Eds.

Understanding and Interpreting

1 George Orwell was stationed in Burma and left the police force soon after his time there. What specific evidence from the text can you find that might suggest why he left the police force?

2 Identify the speaker's attitude toward the inhabitants of Burma at the following three places in the text:
- **a.** the first paragraph
- **b.** the paragraphs just before he shoots the elephant (pars. 9–10)
- **c.** the last paragraph

Then, explain his overall feelings toward the Burmese.

3 In paragraph 3, the speaker says that this incident gave him "a better glimpse than I had had before of the real nature of imperialism—the real motives for which despotic governments act." Look back at the following statements from paragraph 7 and explain what each statement reveals about the speaker's view of the nature of imperialism:
- **a.** "Here was I, the white man with his gun, standing in front of the unarmed native crowd—seemingly the leading actor of the piece; but in reality I was only an absurd puppet pushed to and fro by the will of those yellow faces behind."
- **b.** "I perceived in this moment that when the white man turns tyrant it is his own freedom that he destroys."
- **c.** "He becomes a sort of hollow, posing dummy, the conventionalized figure of a sahib. For it is the condition of his rule that he shall spend his life in trying to impress the 'natives,' and so in every crisis he has got to do what the 'natives' expect of him. He wears a mask, and his face grows to fit it."
- **d.** "The crowd would laugh at me. And my whole life, every white man's life in the East, was one long struggle not to be laughed at."

4 While this essay is specifically about a time when Orwell shot an elephant, it continues to be widely read and studied in classes because it has meaning and application beyond 1920s Burma. What is the central idea that Orwell is presenting in this essay about identity? Use direct evidence from the text to support your response.

Analyzing Language, Style, and Structure

1 Reread the second paragraph of the piece, where the speaker provides some of his feelings about imperialism. Identify the contrasting and often contradictory choices of words as he describes the Burmese and the British. What do the contradictions reveal about the speaker's attitude toward imperialism?

2 This essay is told as a narrative with the speaker looking back on a significant event in his life. How does the older Orwell view his younger self, and what specific language choices reflect this tone?

3 Reread paragraph 11, where the speaker first shoots the elephant. What are some of the words and phrases that are used to humanize the elephant's death and how do these details help to illustrate Orwell's point about imperialism?

4 You are reading this piece in a textbook almost eighty years after it was originally published. Who do you think was Orwell's intended audience in 1936, and what do you think he was trying to communicate to them? How successful do you think he might have been in communicating his message? Why?

5 Below is the last paragraph of the essay with some words underlined. Reread this paragraph, looking closely at the underlined words and the synonyms that follow in parentheses. Discuss how changing Orwell's word choice to one of the words in parentheses would affect the meaning of the sentences containing these words and the passage as a whole.

Afterwards, of course, there were <u>endless</u> (interminable/incessant) discussions about the shooting of the elephant. The owner was furious, but he was only an Indian and could do nothing. Besides, <u>legally</u> (justly/legitimately) I had done the right thing, for a mad elephant has to be <u>killed</u> (executed/put down/slaughtered), like a mad dog, if its owner fails to control it. Among the Europeans opinion was divided. The older men said I was right, the younger men said it was a damn shame to shoot an elephant for killing a coolie, because an elephant was worth more than any damn Coringhee coolie. And afterwards I was very <u>glad</u> (cheerful/content/pleased) that the coolie had been killed; it put me legally in the right and it gave me a <u>sufficient</u> (ample/acceptable) <u>pretext</u> (alibi/excuse/pretense) for shooting the elephant. I often wondered whether any of the others grasped that I had done it solely to avoid looking a <u>fool</u> (buffoon/idiot/bonehead).

Topics for Composing

1 **Exposition**
Many of the reasons that the speaker gives for shooting the elephant are implied rather than directly stated. In an essay, identify and explain the most significant reasons for the shooting, and conclude with an evaluation of which one was likely the primary motivation.

2 **Exposition**
How aware is the speaker of his own role in the worst elements of colonialism? Write an essay in which you respond to that question by drawing solely on the evidence that Orwell presents within the text.

3 **Argument**
At the end of the piece, Orwell writes, "The owner was furious, but he was only an Indian and could do nothing." Write two letters about this situation:

- The first letter should be from the point of view of the elephant's owner, trying to convince the district administrator of Burma to compensate you for the loss of your elephant. Imagine that upon receiving this letter, the district administrator demands an explanation from Orwell.

- The second letter should be written as if you were Orwell responding to the district administrator. Be sure to explain why the shooting of the elephant was justified, and address the points contained within the letter from the elephant's owner. Your letters should be limited only to the events presented in the piece, but you should use whatever persuasive techniques you think would be useful in convincing your audience.

4 Research

How can psychological principles help us understand the factors that may have contributed to Orwell's decision to shoot the elephant, even though he did not want to? Research a relevant psychological study or psychological perspective, explain the experiment and its findings to your readers, and then describe how the findings help explain the psychological factors at work in "Shooting an Elephant." You might begin by looking into the Stanford Prison Experiment (Philip Zimbardo), the Asch Conformity Experiments (Solomon Asch), the Good Samaritan Study (John Darley and C. Daniel Batson), the Milgram Experiment (Stanley Milgram), or the Bystander Effect (John Darley and Bibb Latané). Feel free to uncover additional studies that interest you.

5 Research

While the speaker in Orwell's piece regularly uses the word "imperialism" to describe the British activities in Burma because it refers to the expansion of an "empire," another related and more general term is "colonialism," which applies to any country's conquering and exploiting the resources of another country. Research present-day Myanmar, or another country that was colonized, and identify the effects colonialism had.

6 Narrative

At the moment the speaker decides to shoot the elephant, he states, "[I]t is the condition of his rule that [the white man] shall spend his life in trying to impress the 'natives,' and so in every crisis he has got to do what the 'natives' expect of him. He wears a mask, and his face grows to fit it" (par. 7). Write a story about a time when you had to wear a metaphorical mask (do something that someone expected you to do). What caused you to wear the mask? Did your face "grow to fit it," as the speaker of "Shooting an Elephant" suggests, or were you able to take the mask off and become yourself again?

7 Multimodal

Make a short film—or draw a storyboard of scenes—in which you reenact paragraph 7 from "Shooting an Elephant." Then, write a brief explanation about why you chose to film or draw it the way you did. How did the music, camera angles, lighting, acting choices, and so on that you used relate to the specific words that Orwell used?

8 Discussion or performance

Hold a mock trial to debate the speaker's actions. There should be a prosecutor who is trying to convict the speaker of property damage, a defense attorney who is trying to justify the speaker's actions, a judge, and a jury to determine guilt or innocence. Be sure that all of the evidence you consider comes directly from the text itself and any relevant research you conduct on the time period and location.

9 Creative

George Orwell is not a hero in this piece. He doesn't take a principled stand and refuse to shoot the elephant, nor does he rebel against an imperial system that he seems to disapprove of and yet participates in. Write a new ending for the essay in which Orwell decides *not* to shoot the elephant. Continue to use the first person narration, try to mimic Orwell's style as closely as possible, and include the reasoning behind his decision. Be sure to consider how the last paragraph would change significantly as a result of this different decision. Include a reflection that explains what changed and why.

CONVERSATION

CHANGES AND TRANSFORMATIONS

This chapter is about identity and the fact that identities change. You are probably not exactly the same as you were in elementary school. You might not even be exactly the same as you were last month. Why do our identities change? What factors lead to those changes? Certain aspects of our identities may change frequently, like hairstyles, clothes, and interests, perhaps as a result of growing older, moving to a new town, or getting a different group of friends.

Other aspects of identity, such as race, gender, and ethnicity, are seemingly more fixed, although society's and one's own perception of these aspects certainly do change. Remember that in the United States, women were not allowed to vote as recently as 1920, and racial segregation was legal in schools until 1954. So in some of these cases, identities can change due to new laws, historical events, and social trends.

David Bowie, a pop singer who began his career in the late 1960s and made a habit of changing his identity with almost every album he released, wrote a song in 1971 called "Changes." Take a look at a portion of the lyrics on the next page:

Bowie in '68

Bowie in the early '70s

Bowie in '83

In the photos of David Bowie at various times in his career, what portions of his identity change, and what seems to remain constant? What do you think Bowie means in the lyric, "But I've never caught a glimpse / Of how the others must see the faker"?

So I turned myself to face me
But I've never caught a glimpse
Of how the others must see the faker
I'm much too fast to take that test

While the speaker in the Bowie song seems to embrace the changes that are a natural part of life, the protagonists in this Conversation of texts are not necessarily as accepting of the changes they face. Among others, you will read about a young man who leaves all his material goods behind to live in the wilds of Alaska, a young woman who considers leaving her native Ireland to travel to South America, and a middle school student who faces the challenge of keeping an old friend while making new ones. At the end of this section, you will have an opportunity to enter this Conversation on Changes and Transformations, identifying similarities and differences among the various texts and adding your own voice to the discussion of how identities change and transform.

TEXTS

Jon Krakauer / The Devils Thumb (nonfiction)
Caitlin Horrocks / Zolaria (fiction)
Sharon Olds / My Son the Man *and* The Possessive (poetry)
William Shakespeare / The Seven Ages of Man (drama)
James Joyce / Eveline (fiction)
from Souvenir of the Carlisle Indian School (photographs)

The Devils Thumb

Jon Krakauer

John Storey/The LIFE Images Collection/Getty Images

Writer **Jon Krakauer** (b. 1954) has been a risk taker and adventurer most of his life. The author of the highly acclaimed account of a disastrous attempt to climb Mount Everest, *Into Thin Air*, Krakauer spent much of his own youth climbing various mountains around the world, the accounts of which were collected in *Eiger Dreams: Ventures among Men and Mountains*, from which this narrative is taken. Krakauer is also the author of *Into the Wild*, the true story of the life and death of Chris McCandless, a young man who tried to live on his own in the backcountry of Alaska, and died as a result. Rather than simply celebrating the accomplishments of adventurers, Krakauer examines the risks and contradictions of trying to find yourself by going toe-to-toe with nature, concluding in *Into the Wild* that "mountains make poor receptacles for dreams."

By the time I reached the interstate I was having trouble keeping my eyes open. I'd been okay on the twisting two-lane blacktop between Fort Collins and Laramie, but when the Pontiac eased onto the smooth, unswerving pavement of I-80, the soporific hiss of the tires began to gnaw at my wakefulness like ants in a dead tree.

That afternoon, after nine hours of humping 2 X 10s and pounding recalcitrant nails, I'd told my boss I was quitting: "No, not in a couple of weeks, Steve; right now was more like what I had in mind." It took me three more hours to clear my tools and other belongings out of the rust-stained construction trailer that had served as my home in Boulder. I loaded everything into the car, drove up Pearl Street to Tom's Tavern, and downed a ceremonial beer. Then I was gone.

At 1 a.m., thirty miles east of Rawlins, the strain of the day caught up to me. The euphoria that had flowed so freely in the wake of my quick escape gave way to overpowering fatigue; suddenly I felt tired to the bone. The highway stretched straight and empty to the horizon and beyond. Outside the car the night air was cold, and the stark Wyoming plains glowed in the moonlight like Rousseau's painting of the sleeping gypsy. I wanted very badly just then to be that gypsy, conked out on my back beneath the stars. I shut my eyes — just for a second, but it was a second of bliss. It seemed to revive me, if only briefly. The Pontiac, a sturdy behemoth from the Eisenhower years, floated down the road on its long-gone shocks like a raft on an ocean swell. The lights of an oil rig twinkled reassuringly in the distance. I closed my eyes a second time, and kept them closed a few moments longer. The sensation was sweeter than sex.

A few minutes later I let my eyelids fall again. I'm not sure how long I nodded off this time — it might have been for five seconds, it might have been for thirty — but when I awoke it was to the rude sensation of the Pontiac bucking violently along the dirt shoulder at seventy miles per hour. By all rights, the car should have sailed off into the rabbitbrush and rolled. The rear wheels fishtailed wildly six or seven times, but I eventually managed to guide the unruly machine back onto the pavement without so much as blowing a tire, and let it coast gradually to a stop. I loosened my death grip on the wheel, took several deep breaths to quiet the pounding in my chest, then slipped the shifter back into drive and continued down the highway.

5   Pulling over to sleep would have been the sensible thing to do, but I was on my way to Alaska to change my life, and patience was a concept well beyond my twenty-three-year-old ken.

Sixteen months earlier I'd graduated from college with little distinction and even less in the way of marketable skills. In the interim an off-again, on-again four-year relationship — the first serious romance of my life — had come to a messy, long-overdue end; nearly a year later, my love life was still zip. To support myself I worked on a house-framing crew, grunting under crippling loads of plywood, counting the minutes until the next coffee break, scratching in vain at the sawdust stuck *in perpetuum* to the sweat on the back of my neck. Somehow, blighting the Colorado landscape with condominiums and tract houses for three-fifty an hour wasn't the sort of career I'd dreamed of as a boy.

Late one evening I was mulling all this over on a barstool at Tom's, picking unhappily at my existential scabs, when an idea came to me, a scheme for righting what was wrong in my life. It was wonderfully uncomplicated, and the more I thought about it, the better the plan sounded. By the bottom of the pitcher its merits seemed unassailable. The plan consisted, in its entirety, of climbing a mountain in Alaska called the Devils Thumb.

The Devils Thumb is a prong of exfoliated diorite that presents an imposing profile from any

Henri Rousseau, *The Sleeping Gypsy*, 1897. Oil on canvas.

Why do you think Krakauer refers to this particular painting in his narrative?

Digital Image © The Museum of Modern Art/Licensed by SCALA/ Art Resource, NY

point of the compass, but especially so from the north: its great north wall, which had never been climbed, rises sheer and clean for six thousand vertical feet from the glacier at its base. Twice the height of Yosemite's El Capitan, the north face of the Thumb is one of the biggest granitic walls on the continent; it may well be one of the biggest in the world. I would go to Alaska, ski across the Stikine Icecap to the Devils Thumb, and make the first ascent of its notorious nordwand. It seemed, midway through the second pitcher, like a particularly good idea to do all of this solo.

Writing these words more than a dozen years later, it's no longer entirely clear just *how* I thought soloing the Devils Thumb would transform my life. It had something to do with the fact that climbing was the first and only thing I'd ever been good at. My reasoning, such as it was, was fueled by the scattershot passions of youth, and a literary diet overly rich in the works of Nietzsche, Kerouac, and John Menlove Edwards — the latter a deeply troubled writer/psychiatrist who, before putting an end to his life with a cyanide capsule in 1958, had been one of the preeminent British rock climbers of the day.

10   Dr. Edwards regarded climbing as a "psycho-neurotic tendency" rather than sport; he climbed not for fun but to find refuge from the inner torment that characterized his existence. I remember, that spring of 1977, being especially taken by a passage from an Edwards short story titled "Letter From a Man":

> So, as you would imagine, I grew up exuberant in body but with a nervy, craving mind: It was wanting something more, something tangible. It sought for reality intensely, always if it were not there . . .
>
> But you see at once what I do. I climb.

To one enamored of this sort of prose, the Thumb beckoned like a beacon. My belief in the plan became unshakeable. I was dimly aware that I might be getting in over my head, but if I could somehow get to the top of the Devils Thumb, I was convinced, everything that followed would turn out all right. And thus did I push the accelerator a little closer to the floor and, buoyed by the jolt of adrenaline that followed the Pontiac's brush with destruction, speed west into the night.

. . .

You can't actually get very close to the Devils Thumb by car. The peak stands in the Boundary Ranges on the Alaska–British Columbia border, not far from the fishing village of Petersburg, a place accessible only by boat or plane. There is regular jet service to Petersburg, but the sum of my liquid assets amounted to the Pontiac and two hundred dollars in cash, not even enough for one-way airfare, so I took the car as far as Gig Harbor, Washington, then hitched a ride on a north-bound seine boat that was short on crew. Five days out, when the *Ocean Queen* pulled into Petersburg to take on fuel and water, I jumped ship, shouldered my backpack, and walked down the dock in a steady Alaskan rain.

Back in Boulder, without exception, every person with whom I'd shared my plans about the Thumb had been blunt and to the point: I'd been smoking too much pot, they said; it was a monumentally bad idea. I was grossly over-estimating my abilities as a climber, I'd never be able to hack a month completely by myself, I would fall into a crevasse and die.

The residents of Petersburg reacted differently. Being Alaskans, they were accus-tomed to people with screwball ideas; a sizeable percentage of the state's population, after all, was sitting on half-baked schemes to mine uranium in the Brooks Range, or sell icebergs to the Japanese, or market mail-order moose drop-pings. Most of the Alaskans I met, if they reacted at all, simply asked how much money there was in climbing a mountain like the Devils Thumb.

15   In any case, one of the appealing things about climbing the Thumb — and one of the appealing things about the sport of mountain climbing in general — was that it didn't matter a rat's ass what anyone else thought. Getting the scheme off the ground didn't hinge on winning the approval of some personnel director, admis-sions committee, licensing board, or panel of stern-faced judges; if I felt like taking a shot at some unclimbed alpine wall, all I had to do was get myself to the foot of the mountain and start swinging my ice axes.

Petersburg sits on an island, the Devils Thumb rises from the mainland. To get myself to the foot of the Thumb it was first necessary to cross twenty-five miles of salt water. For most of a day I walked the docks, trying without success to hire a boat to ferry me across Frederick Sound. Then I bumped into Bart and Benjamin.

Bart and Benjamin were ponytailed consti-tuents of a Woodstock Nation tree-planting collective called the Hodads. We struck up a conversation. I mentioned that I, too, had once worked as a tree planter. The Hodads allowed that they had chartered a floatplane to fly them to their camp on the mainland the next morn-ing. "It's your lucky day, kid," Bart told me. "For twenty bucks you can ride over with us. Get you to your [. . .] mountain in style." On May 3, a day and a half after arriving in Petersburg, I stepped off the Hodads' Cessna, waded onto the tidal flats at the head of Thomas Bay, and began the long trudge inland.

The Devils Thumb pokes up out of the Stikine Icecap, an immense, labyrinthine network of glaciers that hugs the crest of the Alaskan panhandle like an octopus, with myriad tenta-cles that snake down, down to the sea from the craggy uplands along the Canadian frontier. In putting ashore at Thomas Bay I was gambling that one of these frozen arms, the Baird Glacier, would lead me safely to the bottom of the Thumb, thirty miles distant.

An hour of gravel beach led to the tortured blue tongue of the Baird. A logger in Petersburg had suggested I keep an eye out for grizzlies along this stretch of shore. "Them bears over there is just waking up this time of year," he smiled. "Tend to be kinda cantankerous after not eatin' all winter. But you keep your gun handy, you shouldn't have no problem." Problem was, I didn't have a gun. As it turned out, my only encounter with hostile wildlife involved a flock of gulls who dive-bombed my head with Hitchcockian fury. Between the avian assault and my ursine anxiety, it was with no small amount of relief that I turned my back to the beach, donned crampons, and scrambled up onto the glacier's broad, lifeless snout.

20   After three or four miles I came to the snow-line, where I exchanged crampons for skis. Putting the boards on my feet cut fifteen pounds from the awful load on my back and made the going much faster besides. But now that the ice was covered with snow, many of the glacier's crevasses were hidden, making solitary travel extremely dangerous.

In Seattle, anticipating this hazard, I'd stopped at a hardware store and purchased a pair of stout aluminum curtain rods, each ten feet long. Upon reaching the snowline, I lashed the rods together at right angles, then strapped the arrangement to the hip belt on my backpack so the poles extended horizontally over the snow. Staggering slowly up the glacier with my over-loaded backpack, bearing the queer tin cross, I felt like some kind of strange *Penitente*. Were I to break through the veneer of snow over a hidden crevasse, though, the curtain rods would — I hoped mightily — span the slot and keep me from dropping into the chilly bowels or the Baird.

The first climbers to venture onto the Stikine Icecap were Bestor Robinson and Fritz Wiessner, the legendary German-American alpinist, who spent a stormy month in the Boundary Ranges in 1937 but failed to reach any major summits. Wiessner returned in 1946 with Donald Brown and Fred Beckey to attempt the Devils Thumb, the nastiest looking peak in the Stikine. On that trip Fritz mangled a knee during a fall on the hike in and limped home in disgust, but Beckey went back that same summer with Bob Craig and Cliff Schmidtke. On August 25, after several aborted tries and some exceedingly hairy climb-ing on the peak's east ridge, Beckey and company sat on the Thumb's wafer-thin summit

tower in a tired, giddy daze. It was far and away the most technical ascent ever done in Alaska, an important milestone in the history of American mountaineering.

In the ensuing decades three other teams also made it to the top of the Thumb, but all steered clear of the big north face. Reading accounts of these expeditions, I had wondered why none of them had approached the peak by what appeared, from the map at least, to be the easiest and most logical route, the Baird. I wondered a little less after coming across an article by Beckey in which the distinguished mountaineer cautioned, "Long, steep icefalls block the route from the Baird Glacier to the icecap near Devils Thumb," but after studying aerial photographs I decided that Beckey was mistaken, that the icefalls weren't so big or so bad. The Baird, I was certain, really was the best way to reach the mountain.

For two days I slogged steadily up the glacier without incident, congratulating myself for discovering such a clever path to the Thumb. On the third day, I arrived beneath the Stikine Icecap proper, where the long arm of the Baird joins the main body of ice. Here, the glacier spills abruptly over the edge of a high plateau, dropping seaward through the gap between two peaks in a phantasmagoria of shattered ice. Seeing the icefall in the flesh left a different impression than the photos had. As I stared at the tumult from a mile away, for the first time since leaving Colorado the thought crossed my mind that maybe this Devils Thumb trip wasn't the best idea I'd ever had.

25   The icefall was a maze of crevasses and teetering seracs[1]. From afar it brought to mind a bad train wreck, as if scores of ghostly white boxcars had derailed at the lip of the icecap and tumbled down the slope willy-nilly. The closer I got, the more unpleasant it looked. My ten-foot

---

[1]seracs: Large columns of ice, usually found in the cracks of glaciers, and prone to toppling over, making it especially dangerous for climbers. —Eds.

curtain rods seemed a poor defense against crevasses that were forty feet across and two hundred fifty feet deep. Before I could finish figuring out a course through the icefall, the wind came up and snow began to slant hard out of the clouds, stinging my face and reducing visibility to almost nothing.

In my impetuosity, I decided to carry on anyway. For the better part of the day I groped blindly through the labyrinth in the whiteout, retracing my steps from one dead end to another. Time after time I'd think I'd found a way out, only to wind up in a deep blue cul de sac, or stranded atop a detached pillar of ice. My efforts were lent a sense of urgency by the noises emanating underfoot. A madrigal of cracks and sharp reports — the sort of protests a large fir limb makes when it's slowly bent to the breaking point — served as a reminder that it is the nature of glaciers to move, the habit of seracs to topple.

As much as I feared being flattened by a wall of collapsing ice, I was even more afraid of falling into a crevasse, a fear that intensified when I put a foot through a snow bridge over a slot so deep I couldn't see the bottom of it. A little later I broke through another bridge to my waist; the poles kept me out of the hundred-foot hole, but after I extricated myself I was bent double with dry heaves thinking about what it would be like to be lying in a pile at the bottom of the crevasse, waiting for death to come, with nobody even aware of how or where I'd met my end.

Night had nearly fallen by the time I emerged from the top of the serac slope onto the empty, wind-scoured expanse of the high glacial plateau. In shock and chilled to the core, I skied far enough past the icefall to put its rumblings out of earshot, pitched the tent, crawled into my sleeping bag, and shivered myself to a fitful sleep.

Although my plan to climb the Devils Thumb wasn't fully hatched until the spring of 1977, the mountain had been lurking in the recesses of my mind for about fifteen years — since April 12, 1962, to be exact. The occasion was my eighth birthday. When it came time to open birthday presents, my parents announced that they were offering me a choice of gifts: According to my wishes, they would either escort me to the new Seattle World's Fair to ride the Monorail and see the Space Needle, or give me an introductory taste of mountain climbing by taking me up the third highest peak in Oregon, a long-dormant volcano called the South Sister that, on clear days, was visible from my bedroom window. It was a tough call. I thought the matter over at length, then settled on the climb.

30   To prepare me for the rigors of the ascent, my father handed over a copy of *Mountaineering: The Freedom of the Hills*, the leading how-to manual of the day, a thick tome that weighed only slightly less than a bowling ball. Thenceforth I spent most of my waking hours poring over its pages, memorizing the intricacies of pitoncraft and bolt placement, the shoulder stand and the tension traverse. None of which, as it happened, was of any use on my inaugural ascent, for the South Sister turned out to be a decidedly less than extreme climb that demanded nothing more in the way of technical skill than energetic walking, and was in fact ascended by hundreds of farmers, house pets, and small children every summer.

Which is not to suggest that my parents and I conquered the mighty volcano: From the pages and pages of perilous situations depicted in *Mountaineering: The Freedom of the Hills*, I had concluded that climbing was a life-and-death matter, always. Halfway up the South Sister I suddenly remembered this. In the middle of a twenty-degree snow slope that would be impossible to fall from if you tried, I decided that I was in mortal jeopardy and burst into tears, bringing the ascent to a halt.

Perversely, after the South Sister debacle my interest in climbing only intensified. I resumed my obsessive studies of *Mountaineering*. There was something about the scariness of the activities portrayed in those pages that just wouldn't leave me alone. In addition to the scores of line drawings — most of them cartoons of a little man in a jaunty Tyrolean cap — employed to illustrate arcana like the boot-axe belay and the Bilgeri rescue, the book contained sixteen black-and-white plates of notable peaks in the Pacific Northwest and Alaska. All the photographs were striking, but the one on page 147 was much, much more than that: it made my skin crawl. An aerial photo by glaciologist Maynard Miller, it showed a singularly sinister tower of ice-plastered black rock. There wasn't a place on the entire mountain that looked safe or secure; I couldn't imagine anyone climbing it. At the bottom of the page the mountain was identified as the Devils Thumb.

From the first time I saw it, the picture — a portrait of the Thumb's north wall — held an almost pornographic fascination for me. On hundreds — no, make that thousands — of occasions over the decade and a half that followed I took my copy of *Mountaineering* down from the shelf, opened it to page 147, and quietly stared. How would it feel, I wondered over and over, to be on that thumbnail-thin summit ridge, worrying over the storm clouds building on the horizon, hunched against the wind and dunning cold , contemplating the horrible drop on either side? How could anyone keep it together? Would I, if I found myself high on the north wall, clinging to that frozen rock, even attempt to keep it together? Or would I simply decide to surrender to the inevitable straight away, and jump?

I had planned on spending between three weeks and a month on the Stikine Icecap. Not relishing the prospect of carrying a four-week load of food, heavy winter camping gear, and a small mountain of climbing hardware all the way up the Baird on my back, before leaving Petersburg I paid a bush pilot a hundred and

John Scurlock

A view of the still-unclimbed northwest face of the Devils Thumb. Krakauer ascended from the left side, the eastern ascent. The sharp, slightly shorter peak just to the right of the Devils Thumb is called the Cat Ear Spire.

How does the language Krakauer uses to describe this mountain compare with this picture of it?

fifty dollars — the last of my cash — to have six cardboard cartons of supplies dropped from an airplane when I reached the foot of the Thumb. I showed the pilot exactly where, on his map, I intended to be, and told him to give me three days to get there; he promised to fly over and make the drop as soon thereafter as the weather permitted.

35   On May 6 I set up a base camp on the Icecap just northeast of the Thumb and waited for the airdrop. For the next four days it snowed, nixing any chance for a flight. Too terrified of crevasses

to wander far from camp, I occasionally went out for a short ski to kill time, but mostly I lay silently in the tent — the ceiling was too low to sit upright — with my thoughts, fighting a rising chorus of doubts.

As the days passed, I grew increasingly anxious. I had no radio, nor any other means of communicating with the outside world. It had been many years since anyone had visited this part of the Stikine Icecap, and many more would likely pass before anyone did so again. I was nearly out of stove fuel, and down to a single chunk of cheese, my last package of ramen noodles, and half a box of Cocoa Puffs. This, I figured, could sustain me for three or four more days if need be, but then what would I do? It would only take two days to ski back down the Baird to Thomas Bay, but then a week or more might easily pass before a fisherman happened by who could give me a lift back to Petersburg (the Hodads with whom I'd ridden over were camped fifteen miles down the impassable, headland-studded coast, and could be reached only by boat or plane).

When I went to bed on the evening of May 10 it was still snowing and blowing hard. I was going back and forth on whether to head for the coast in the morning or stick it out on the icecap, gambling that the pilot would show before I starved or died of thirst, when, just for a moment, I heard a faint whine, like a mosquito. I tore open the tent door. Most of the clouds had lifted, but there was no airplane in sight. The whine returned, louder this time. Then I saw it: a tiny red-and-white speck, high in the western sky, droning my way.

A few minutes later the plane passed directly overhead. The pilot, however, was unaccustomed to glacier flying and he'd badly misjudged the scale of the terrain. Worried about winding up too low and getting nailed by unexpected turbulence, he flew a good thousand feet above me — believing all the while he was just off the

deck — and never saw my tent in the flat evening light. My waving and screaming were to no avail; from that altitude I was indistinguishable from a pile of rocks. For the next hour he circled the icecap, scanning its barren contours without success. But the pilot, to his credit, appreciated the gravity of my predicament and didn't give up. Frantic, I tied my sleeping bag to the end of one of the crevasse poles and waved it for all I was worth. When the plane banked sharply and began to fly straight at me, I felt tears of joy well in my eyes.

The pilot buzzed my tent three times in quick succession, dropping two boxes on each pass, then the airplane disappeared over a ridge and I was alone. As silence again settled over the glacier I felt abandoned, vulnerable, lost. I realized that I was sobbing. Embarrassed, I halted the blubbering by screaming obscenities until I grew hoarse.

40   I awoke early on May 11 to clear skies and the relatively warm temperature of twenty degrees Fahrenheit. Startled by the good weather, mentally unprepared to commence the actual climb, I hurriedly packed up a rucksack nonetheless, and began skiing toward the base of the Thumb. Two previous Alaskan expeditions had taught me that, ready or not, you simply can't afford to waste a day of perfect weather if you expect to get up anything.

A small hanging glacier extends out from the lip of the icecap, leading up and across the north face of the Thumb like a catwalk. My plan was to follow this catwalk to a prominent rock prow in the center of the wall, and thereby execute an end run around the ugly, avalanche-swept lower half of the face.

The catwalk turned out to be a series of fifty-degree ice fields blanketed with knee-deep powder snow and riddled with crevasses. The depth of the snow made the going slow and exhausting; by the time I front-pointed up the overhanging wall of the uppermost *bergschrund,*[2] some three or four hours after leaving camp, I was whipped. And I hadn't even gotten to the "real" climbing yet. That would begin immediately above, where the hanging glacier gave way to vertical rock.

The rock, exhibiting a dearth of holds and coated with six inches of crumbly rime, did not look promising, but just left of the main prow was an inside corner — what climbers call an open book — glazed with frozen melt water. This ribbon of ice led straight up for two or three hundred feet, and if the ice proved substantial enough to support the picks of my ice axes, the line might go. I hacked out a small platform in the snow slope, the last flat ground I expected to feel underfoot for some time, and stopped to eat a candy bar and collect my thoughts. Fifteen minutes later I shouldered my pack and inched over to the bottom of the corner. Gingerly, I swung my right axe into the two-inch-thick ice. It was solid, plastic — a little thinner than I would have liked but otherwise perfect. I was on my way.

The climbing was steep and spectacular, so exposed it made my head spin. Beneath my boot soles, the wall fell away for three thousand feet to the dirty, avalanche-scarred cirque of the Witches Cauldron Glacier. Above, the prow soared with authority toward the summit ridge, a vertical half-mile above. Each time I planted one of my ice axes, that distance shrank by another twenty inches.

45   The higher I climbed, the more comfortable I became. All that held me to the mountainside, all that held me to the world, were six thin spikes of chrome-molybdenum stuck half an inch into a smear of frozen water, yet I began to feel invincible, weightless, like those lizards that live on the ceilings of cheap Mexican hotels. Early on a difficult climb, especially a difficult solo climb,

[2] *bergschrund*: German. Literally, "mountain crevice." A large horizontal crack in a slope, especially one caused by the lower part of an ice sheet sliding away from the upper part. —Eds.

you're hyperaware of the abyss pulling at your back. You constantly feel its call, its immense hunger. To resist takes a tremendous conscious effort; you don't dare let your guard down for an instant. The siren song of the void puts you on edge, it makes your movements tentative, clumsy, herky-jerky. But as the climb goes on, you grow accustomed to the exposure, you get used to rubbing shoulders with doom, you come to believe in the reliability of your hands and feet and head. You learn to trust your self-control.

By and by, your attention becomes so intensely focused that you no longer notice the raw knuckles, the cramping thighs, the strain of maintaining nonstop concentration. A trance-like state settles over your efforts, the climb becomes a clear-eyed dream. Hours slide by like minutes. The accrued guilt and clutter of day-to-day existence — the lapses of conscience, the unpaid bills, the bungled opportunities, the dust under the couch, the festering familial sores, the inescapable prison of your genes — all of it is temporarily forgotten, crowded from your thoughts by an overpowering clarity of purpose, and by the seriousness of the task at hand.

At such moments, something like happiness actually stirs in your chest, but it isn't the sort of emotion you want to lean on very hard. In solo climbing, the whole enterprise is held together with little more than chutzpa, not the most reliable adhesive. Late in the day on the north face of the Thumb, I felt the glue disintegrate with a single swing of an ice axe.

I'd gained nearly seven hundred feet of altitude since stepping off the hanging glacier, all of it on crampon front-points and the picks of my axes. The ribbon of frozen melt water had ended three hundred feet up, and was followed by a crumbly armor of frost feathers. Though just barely substantial enough to support body weight, the rime was plastered over the rock to a thickness of two or three feet, so I kept plugging upward. The wall, however, had been growing imperceptibly steeper, and as it did so the frost feathers became thinner. I'd fallen into a slow, hypnotic rhythm — swing, swing; kick, kick; swing, swing; kick, kick — when my left ice axe slammed into a slab of diorite a few inches beneath the rime.

I tried left, then right, but kept striking rock. The frost feathers holding me up, it became apparent, were maybe five inches thick and had the structural integrity of stale cornbread. Below was thirty-seven hundred feet of air, and I was balanced atop a house of cards. Waves of panic rose in my throat. My eyesight blurred, I began to hyperventilate, my calves started to vibrate. I shuffled a few feet farther to the right, hoping to find thicker ice, but managed only to bend an ice axe on the rock.

50   Awkwardly, stiff with fear, I started working my way back down. The rime gradually thickened, and after descending about eighty feet I got back on reasonably solid ground. I stopped for a long time to let my nerves settle, then leaned back from my tools and stared up at the face above, searching for a hint of solid ice, for some variation in the underlying rock strata, for anything that would allow passage over the frosted slabs. I looked until my neck ached, but nothing appeared. The climb was over. The only place to go was down.

Heavy snow and incessant winds kept me inside the tent for most of the next three days. The hours passed slowly. In the attempt to hurry them along I chain-smoked for as long as my supply of cigarettes held out, and read. I'd made a number of bad decisions on the trip, there was no getting around it, and one of them concerned the reading matter I'd chosen to pack along: three back issues of *The Village Voice*, and Joan Didion's latest novel, *A Book of Common Prayer*. The *Voice* was amusing enough — there on the icecap, the subject matter took on an edge, a certain sense of the absurd, from which the

paper (through no fault of its own) benefited greatly — but in that tent, under those circumstances, Didion's necrotic take on the world hit a little too close to home.

Near the end of *Common Prayer*, one of Didion's characters says to another, "You don't get any real points for staying here, Charlotte." Charlotte replies, "I can't seem to tell what you do get real points for, so I guess I'll stick around here for awhile."

When I ran out of things to read, I was reduced to studying the ripstop pattern woven into the tent ceiling. This I did for hours on end, flat on my back, while engaging in an extended and very heated self-debate: Should I leave for the coast as soon as the weather broke, or stay put long enough to make another attempt on the mountain? In truth, my little escapade on the north face had left me badly shaken, and I didn't want to go up on the Thumb again at all. On the other hand, the thought of returning to Boulder in defeat — of parking the Pontiac behind the trailer, buckling on my tool belt, and going back to the same brain-dead drill I'd so triumphantly walked away from just a month before — that wasn't very appealing, either. Most of all, I couldn't stomach the thought of having to endure the smug expressions of condolence from all the chumps and nimrods who were certain I'd fail right from the get-go.

By the third afternoon of the storm I couldn't stand it any longer: the lumps of frozen snow poking me in the back, the clammy nylon walls brushing against my face, the incredible smell drifting up from the depths of my sleeping bag. I pawed through the mess at my feet until I located a small green stuff sack, in which there was a metal film can containing the makings of what I'd hoped would be a sort of victory cigar. I'd intended to save it for my return from the summit, but what the hey, it wasn't looking like I'd be visiting the top any time soon. I poured most of the can's contents into a leaf of cigarette paper, rolled it into a crooked, sorry looking joint, and promptly smoked it down to the roach.

55   The reefer, of course, only made the tent seem even more cramped, more suffocating, more impossible to bear. It also made me terribly hungry. I decided a little oatmeal would put things right. Making it, however, was a long, ridiculously involved process: a potful of snow had to be gathered outside in the tempest, the stove assembled and lit, the oatmeal and sugar located, the remnants of yesterday's dinner scraped from my bowl. I'd gotten the stove going and was melting the snow when I smelled something burning. A thorough check of the stove and its environs revealed nothing. Mystified, I was ready to chalk it up to my chemically enhanced imagination when I heard something crackle directly behind me.

    I whirled around in time to see a bag of garbage, into which I'd tossed the match I'd used to light the stove, flare up into a conflagration. Beating on the fire with my hands, I had it out in a few seconds, but not before a large section of the tent's inner wall vaporized before my eyes. The tent's built-in rainfly escaped the flames, so the shelter was still more or less weatherproof; now, however, it was approximately thirty degrees cooler inside. My left palm began to sting. Examining it, I noticed the pink welt of a burn. What troubled me most, though, was that the tent wasn't even mine — I'd borrowed the shelter from my father. An expensive Early Winters Omnipo Tent, it had been brand new before my trip — the hang-tags were still attached — and had been loaned reluctantly. For several minutes I sat dumbstruck, staring at the wreckage of the shelter's once-graceful form amid the acrid scent of singed hair and melted nylon. You had to hand it to me, I thought: I had a real knack for living up to the old man's worst expectations.

    The fire sent me into a funk that no drug known to man could have alleviated. By the time I'd finished cooking the oatmeal my mind was made up: the moment the storm was over, I was breaking camp and booking for Thomas Bay.

Twenty-four hours later, I was huddled inside a bivouac sack under the lip of the *bergschrund* on the Thumb's north face. The weather was as bad as I'd seen it. It was snowing hard, probably an inch every hour. Spindrift avalanches hissed down from the wall above and washed over me like surf, completely burying the sack every twenty minutes.

    The day had begun well enough. When I emerged from the tent, clouds still clung to the ridge tops but the wind was down and the icecap was speckled with sunbreaks. A patch of sunlight, almost blinding in its brilliance, slid lazily over the camp. I put down a foam sleeping mat and sprawled on the glacier in my long johns. Wallowing in the radiant heat, I felt the gratitude of a prisoner whose sentence has just been commuted.

60   As I lay there, a narrow chimney that curved up the east half of the Thumb's north face, well to the left of the route I'd tried before the storm, caught my eye. I twisted a telephoto lens onto my camera. Through it I could make out a smear of shiny grey ice — solid, trustworthy, hard-frozen ice — plastered to the back of the cleft. The alignment of the chimney made it impossible to discern if the ice continued in an unbroken line from top to bottom. If it did, the chimney might well provide passage over the rime-covered slabs that had foiled my first attempt. Lying there in the sun, I began to think about how much I'd hate myself a month hence if I threw in the towel after a single try, if I scrapped the whole expedition on account of a little bad weather. Within the hour I had assembled my gear and was skiing toward the base of the wall.

    The ice in the chimney did in fact prove to be continuous, but it was very, very thin — just a gossamer film of verglas. Additionally, the cleft was a natural funnel for any debris that happened to slough off the wall; as I scratched my way up the chimney I was hosed by a continuous stream of powder snow, ice chips, and small stones. One hundred twenty feet up the groove the last remnants of my composure flaked away like old plaster, and I turned around.

Instead of descending all the way to base camp, I decided to spend the night in the 'schrund beneath the chimney, on the off chance that my head would be more together the next morning. The fair skies that had ushered in the day, however, turned out to be but a momentary lull in a five-day gale. By midafternoon the storm was back in all its glory, and my bivouac site became a less than pleasant place to hang around. The ledge on which I couched was continually swept by small spindrift avalanches. Five times my bivvy sack — a thin nylon envelope, shaped exactly like a Baggies brand sandwich bag, only bigger — was buried up to the level of the breathing slit. After digging myself out the fifth time, I decided I'd had enough. I threw all my gear in my pack and made a break for base camp.

The descent was terrifying. Between the clouds, the ground blizzard, and the flat, fading light, I couldn't tell snow from sky, nor whether a slope went up or down. I worried, with ample reason, that I might step blindly off the top of a serac and end up at the bottom of the Witches Cauldron, a half-mile below. When I finally arrived on the frozen plain of the icecap, I found that my tracks had long since drifted over. I didn't have a clue how to locate the tent on the featureless glacial plateau. I skied in circles for an hour or so, hoping I'd get lucky and stumble across camp, until I put a foot into a small crevasse and realized I was acting like an idiot — that I should hunker down right where I was and wait out the storm.

I dug a shallow hole, wrapped myself in the bivvy bag, and sat on my pack in the swirling snow. Drifts piled up around me. My feet became numb. A damp chill crept down my chest from the base of my neck, where spindrift

had gotten inside my parka and soaked my shirt. If only I had a cigarette, I thought, a single cigarette, l could summon the strength of character to put a good face on this [messed]-up situation, on the whole [messed]-up trip. "If we had some ham, we could have ham and eggs, if we had some eggs." I remembered my friend Nate uttering that line in a similar storm, two years before, high on another Alaskan peak, the Mooses Tooth. It had struck me as hilarious at the time; I'd actually laughed out loud. Recalling the line now, it no longer seemed funny. I pulled the bivvy sack tighter around my shoulders. The wind ripped at my back. Beyond shame, I cradled my head in my arms and embarked on an orgy of self-pity.

65 I knew that people sometimes died climbing mountains. But at the age of twenty-three personal mortality — the idea of my own death — was still largely outside my conceptual grasp; it was as abstract a notion as non-Euclidian geometry or marriage. When I decamped from Boulder in April, 1977, my head swimming with visions of glory and redemption on the Devils Thumb, it didn't occur to me that I might be bound by the same cause-effect relationships that governed the actions of others. I'd never heard of hubris. Because I wanted to climb the mountain so badly, because l had thought about the Thumb so intensely for so long, it seemed beyond the realm of possibility that some minor obstacle like the weather or crevasses or rime-covered rock might ultimately thwart my will.

At sunset the wind died and the ceiling lifted a hundred fifty feet off the glacier, enabling me to locate base camp. I made it back to the tent intact, but it was no longer possible to ignore the fact that the Thumb had made hash of my plans. I was forced to acknowledge that volition alone, however powerful, was not going to get me up the north wall. I saw, finally, that nothing was.

There still existed an opportunity for salvaging the expedition, however. A week earlier I'd

A view of the eastern route up the Devils Thumb, the route that Krakauer ultimately took.

Comparing this to the north face of the mountain, would you ultimately call Krakauer's trip a success or a failure?

Matthias Breiter/Getty Images

skied over to the southeast side of the mountain to take a look at the route Fred Beckey had pioneered in 1946 — the route by which I'd intended to descend the peak after climbing the north wall. During that reconnaissance I'd noticed an obvious unclimbed line to the left of the Beckey route — a patchy network of ice angling across the southeast face — that struck me as a relatively easy way to achieve the summit. At the time, I'd considered this route unworthy of my attentions. Now, on the rebound from my calamitous entanglement with the nordwand, I was prepared to lower my sights.

On the afternoon of May 15, when the blizzard finally petered out, I returned to the southeast face and climbed to the top of a slender ridge that abutted the upper peak like a flying buttress on a gothic cathedral. I decided to spend the night there, on the airy, knife-edged ridge crest, sixteen hundred feet below the summit. The evening sky was cold and cloudless. I could see all the way to tidewater and beyond. At dusk I watched, transfixed, as the house lights of Petersburg blinked on in the west. The closest thing I'd had to human contact since the airdrop, the distant lights set off a flood of emotion that caught me completely off guard.

I imagined people watching the Red Sox on the tube, eating fried chicken in brightly lit kitchens, drinking beer, making love. When I lay down to sleep I was overcome by a soul-wrenching loneliness. I'd never felt so alone, ever.

That night I had troubled dreams, of cops and vampires and a gangland-style execution. I heard someone whisper, "He's in there. As soon as he comes out, waste him." I sat bolt upright and opened my eyes. The sun was about to rise. The entire sky was scarlet. It was still clear, but wisps of high cirrus were streaming in from the southwest, and a dark line was visible just above the horizon. I pulled on my boots and hurriedly strapped on my crampons. Five minutes after waking up, I was front-pointing away from the bivouac.

70   I carried no rope, no tent or bivouac gear, no hardware save my ice axes. My plan was to go ultralight and ultrafast, to hit the summit and make it back down before the weather turned. Pushing myself, continually out of breath, I scurried up and to the left across small snowfields linked by narrow runnels of verglas and short rock bands. The climbing was almost fun — the rock was covered with large, in-cut holds, and the ice, though thin, never got steep enough to

seeing connections

In 1993, Krakauer wrote an article for *Outside* magazine about Chris McCandless, a twenty-four-year old who made headlines when he tried to live off the land by himself in the backcountry of Alaska and died in the attempt. Many people suggested that the young man was suicidal. Krakauer's article was later expanded into the book *Into the Wild*, which was then made into a movie of the same name directed by Sean Penn. In the original *Outside* magazine article, Krakauer draws a connection between McCandless and himself and reflects on the similarities and differences in their motivations for going to Alaska, saying,

> In 1977, when I was 23—a year younger than McCandless at the time of his death—I [. . .] set off alone into the backcountry to attempt an ascent of a malevolent stone digit called the Devils Thumb. [. . .] By choice I had no radio, no way of summoning help, no safety net of any kind.
>
> When I decided to go to Alaska that April, I was an angst-ridden youth who read too much

Nietzsche, mistook passion for insight, and functioned according to an obscure gap-ridden logic. I thought climbing the Devils Thumb would fix all that was wrong with my life. In the end it changed almost nothing, of course. I came to appreciate, however, that mountains make poor receptacles for dreams. And I lived to tell my tale.

As a young man, I was unlike Chris McCandless in many important respects—most notably I lacked his intellect and his altruistic leanings—but I suspect we had a similar intensity, a similar heedlessness, a similar agitation of the soul.

The fact that I survived my Alaskan adventure and McCandless did not survive his was largely a matter of chance; had I died on the Stikine Icecap in 1977 people would have been quick to say of me, as they now say of him, that I had a death wish. Fifteen years after the event, I now recognize that I suffered from hubris, perhaps, and a monstrous innocence, certainly, but I wasn't suicidal.

Read the excerpt below from the screenplay of *Into the Wild*, and comment on whether McCandless and Krakauer do in fact share a similar "agitation of the soul." Compare Krakauer's motivations with those ascribed to McCandless in the following scene from the movie, in which he talks about his trip to Alaska with his friend Wayne Westberg.

CHRIS

I'm thinking about going to Alaska.

WAYNE

Alaska, Alaska? Or city Alaska? The city Alaska does have markets.

CHRIS
(with a drunken, excited energy)
No, Alaska, Alaska. I want to be all the way out there. On my own. No map. No watch. No axe.

Just out there. Big mountains, rivers, sky. Game. Just be out there in it. In the wild.

WAYNE

In the wild.

CHRIS
Yeah. Maybe write a book about my travels. About getting out of this sick society.

WAYNE
(coughing)
Society, right.

CHRIS
Because you know what I don't understand? I don't understand why, why people are so bad to each other, so often. It just doesn't make any sense to me. Judgment. Control. All that.

WAYNE
Who "people" we talking about?

CHRIS
You know, parents and hypocrites. Politicians and [jerks].

▲ A frame from the movie *Into the Wild* showing Chris McCandless leaving the road behind and entering the Alaskan wilderness.

How is this setting and situation similar to that of Krakauer in Alaska? What effect is created by the overhead point of view of this shot?

▲ A frame from the movie *Into the Wild* showing Chris McCandless burning his wallet and heading out into the Arizona desert. In the movie, Chris's sister comments: "Chris began to see 'careers' as a diseased invention of the twentieth century and to resent money and the useless priority people made of it in their lives."

Do you think a young Krakauer would have agreed with this sentiment?

feel extreme — but I was anxious about the bands of clouds racing in from the Pacific, covering the sky.

In what seemed like no time (I didn't have a watch on the trip) I was on the distinctive final ice field. By now the sky was completely overcast. It looked easier to keep angling to the left, but quicker to go straight for the top. Paranoid about being caught by a storm high on the peak without any kind of shelter, I opted for the direct route. The ice steepened, then steepened some more, and as it did so it grew thin. I swung my left ice axe and struck rock. I aimed for another spot, and once again it glanced off unyielding diorite with a dull, sickening clank. And again, and again: It was a reprise of my first attempt on the north face. Looking between my legs, I stole a glance at the glacier, more than two thousand feet below. My stomach churned. I felt my poise slipping way like smoke in the wind.

Forty-five feet above the wall eased back onto the sloping summit shoulder. Forty-five more feet, half the distance between third base and home plate, and the mountain would be mine. I clung stiffly to my axes, unmoving, paralyzed with fear and indecision. I looked down at the dizzying drop to the glacier again, then up, then scraped away the film of ice above my head. I hooked the pick of my left axe on a nickel-thin lip of rock, and weighted it. It held. I pulled my right axe from the ice, reached up, and twisted the pick into a crooked half-inch crack until it jammed. Barely breathing now, I moved my feet up, scrabbling my crampon points across the verglas. Reaching as high as I could with my left arm, I swung the axe gently at the shiny, opaque surface, not knowing what I'd hit beneath it. The pick went in with a heartening *THUNK!* A few minutes later I was standing on a broad, rounded ledge. The summit proper, a series of slender fins sprouting a grotesque meringue of atmospheric ice, stood twenty feet directly above.

The insubstantial frost feathers ensured that those last twenty feet remained hard, scary, onerous. But then, suddenly, there was no place higher to go. It wasn't possible, I couldn't believe it. I felt my cracked lips stretch into a huge, painful grin. I was on top of the Devils Thumb.

Fittingly, the summit was a surreal, malevolent place, an improbably slender fan of rock and rime no wider than a filing cabinet. It did not encourage loitering. As I straddled the highest point, the north face fell away beneath my left boot for six thousand feet; beneath my right boot the south face dropped off for twenty-five hundred. I took some pictures to prove I'd been there, and spent a few minutes trying to straighten a bent pick. Then I stood up, carefully turned around, and headed for home.

75 Five days later I was camped in the rain beside the sea, marveling at the sight of moss, willows, mosquitoes. Two days after that, a small skiff motored into Thomas Bay and pulled up on the beach not far from my tent. The man driving the boat introduced himself as Jim Freeman, a timber faller from Petersburg. It was his day off, he said, and he'd made the trip to show his family the glacier, and to look for bears. He asked me if I'd "been huntin', or what?"

"No," I replied sheepishly. "Actually, I just climbed the Devils Thumb. I've been over here twenty days."

Freeman kept fiddling with a cleat on the boat, and didn't say anything for a while. Then he looked at me real hard and spat, "You wouldn't be givin' me double talk now, wouldja, friend?" Taken aback, I stammered out a denial. Freeman, it was obvious, didn't believe me for a minute. Nor did he seem wild about my snarled shoulder-length hair or the way I smelled. When I asked if he could give me a lift back to town, however, he offered a grudging, "I don't see why not."

The water was choppy, and the ride across Frederick Sound took two hours. The more we

▶
Taking the western route, climber Mikey Schaefer ascends the Cat Ear Spire on his way to the top of the Devils Thumb.

How does this image change your perspective of Krakauer's ascent?

Colin Haley

talked, the more Freeman warmed up. He still didn't believe I'd climbed the Thumb, but by the time he steered the skiff into Wrangell Narrows he pretended to. When we got off the boat, he insisted on buying me a cheeseburger. That night he even let me sleep in a derelict step-van parked in his backyard.

I lay down in the rear of the old truck for a while but couldn't sleep, so I got up and walked to a bar called Kito's Kave. The euphoria, the over-whelming sense of relief, that had initially accompanied my return to Petersburg faded, and an unexpected melancholy took its place. The people I chatted with in Kito's didn't seem to doubt that I'd been to the top of the Thumb, they just didn't much care. As the night wore on the place emptied except for me and an Indian at a back table. I drank alone, putting quarters in the jukebox, playing the same five songs over and over, until the barmaid yelled angrily, "Hey! Give it a [. . .] rest, kid! If I hear 'Fifty Ways to Lose Your Lover' one more time, *I'm* gonna be the one who loses it." I mumbled an apology, quickly headed for the door, and lurched back to Freeman's

step-van. There, surrounded by the sweet scent of old motor oil, I lay down on the floorboards next to a gutted transmission and passed out.

80   It is easy, when you are young, to believe that what you desire is no less than what you deserve, to assume that if you want something badly enough it is your God-given right to have it. Less than a month after sitting on the summit of the Thumb I was back in Boulder, nailing up siding on the Spruce Street Townhouses, the same condos I'd been framing when I left for Alaska. I got a raise, to four dollars an hour, and at the end of the summer moved out of the job-site trailer to a studio apartment on West Pearl, but little else in my life seemed to change. Somehow, it didn't add up to the glorious trans-formation I'd imagined in April.

Climbing the Devils Thumb, however, had nudged me a little further away from the obdu-rate innocence of childhood. It taught me something about what mountains can and can't do, about the limits of dreams. I didn't recog-nize that at the time, of course, but I'm grateful for it now.

Understanding and Interpreting

1 Much of Krakauer's motivation to successfully climb the mountain seems to come from his need to impress others. Locate at least two places in the text where this appears to be true and explain how those passages illustrate this aspect of Krakauer.

2 There are several places in the narrative in which Krakauer demonstrates an appalling lack of planning or forethought, and there are others where he does successfully make plans. Identify examples of both and explain which trait is more prevalent in the narrative.

3 Make an argumentative claim about Krakauer's decision-making and reasoning skills. Then, support that claim with direct evidence from the text.

4 Trace the numerous setbacks Krakauer faces in trying to scale the Devils Thumb. Select one setback, and explain what his response to that setback reveals about his character.

5 What purpose does the history lesson about the previous climbs and attempts on the Devils Thumb (pars. 22 and 23) serve in the narrative? Why does Krakauer include it?

6 What role has the Devils Thumb played in Krakauer's imagination since he started looking at it in the book he received when he was eight? How does this role influence his later decisions?

7 Reread paragraph 46. What effect does the physical act of climbing have on Krakauer?

8 What is the connection that the reader is expected to draw between Krakauer and the character in the Joan Didion novel (par. 52)?

9 In terms of Krakauer's own personal development, there is probably no other passage from the narrative that is as important as his statement, "At the time, I'd considered this route unworthy of my attentions. Now . . . I was prepared to lower my sights" (par. 67). In what way does this revelation signal a significant change in Krakauer?

10 To what extent is Krakauer satisfied or disappointed with his climb? What evidence from the text supports your position?

11 Krakauer writes at the end that climbing the Devils Thumb taught him "something about what mountains can and can't do, about the limits of dreams" (par. 81). What is this "something" that he learned?

Analyzing Language, Structure, and Style

1 What is the effect that Krakauer achieves by starting his narrative with his drive up to Alaska?

2 Krakauer includes two flashbacks in his narrative— in paragraphs 6–7 and then paragraphs 29–33. Analyze those two structural choices, examining why each flashback is placed where it is, and what effect it has on the reader's knowledge about and impressions of Krakauer.

3 It is clear that Krakauer is writing this narrative as an older man looking back on an event that happened to him when he was younger ("Writing these words more than a dozen years later. . . ." [par. 9]). How would you describe the tone Krakauer takes toward his younger self? What specific words or phrases communicate this tone? How does this tone help Krakauer to create a theme of the narrative?

4 In paragraphs 13 and 14, Krakauer constructs a contrast between Coloradans and Alaskans in their attitudes toward his plans to climb the Devils Thumb. What is the purpose of this contrast?

5 Reread paragraph 18, paying attention to the imagery Krakauer uses. How does it help illustrate the conflict Krakauer is facing?

6 Reread the following lines from the essay and explain what the word choice reveals about Krakauer:

   a. "I'd never heard of hubris" (par. 65).
   b. "and the mountain would be mine" (par. 72)
   c. "my head swimming with visions of glory and redemption" (par. 65)

Connecting, Arguing, and Extending

1 In the last paragraph, Krakauer says that this experience moved him "a little further away from the obdurate innocence of childhood." The word "obdurate" means "stubborn," and it often has a negative connotation. Tell a story about a time when you, perhaps unwillingly, had to give up some of the innocence of your own childhood. In what ways was your childhood innocence "obdurate" like Krakauer's?

2 You may recall reading about the Evil Queen from the *Snow White* story at the beginning of this chapter, and about the two different ways that people define their identities: as they see themselves, and as others see them. In this narrative, does Krakauer seem more concerned about how other people view him and his climb or how he views himself? Use direct evidence from the text to support your argument.

3 There are many places where Krakauer faces serious peril in his climb. Should he have stopped or gone forward? What evidence from the text, and your own reasoning, can you use to support your argument?

4 Krakauer writes, "Because I wanted to climb the mountain so badly, because I had thought about the Thumb so intensely for so long, it seemed beyond the realm of possibility that some minor obstacle like the weather or crevasses or rime-covered rock might ultimately thwart my will" (par. 65). In other words, because he thought about it so much, his success should automatically happen. This is an example of what is often referred to as "magical thinking," belief that thinking about something can make it happen. A common example of magical thinking is when viewers of a sporting event think they can influence the outcome of the game by what they wear or the foods they eat during a game. Research the topic of magical thinking, identify and explain other instances in the narrative where Krakauer engages in this process, and connect one of these instances to another example from outside the text, perhaps even from your own life.

5 In paragraph 65, Krakauer admits, "I knew that people sometimes died climbing mountains. But at the age of twenty-three personal mortality — the idea of my own death — was still largely out of my conceptual grasp. . . ." Here, Krakauer addresses a significant concern that has been the subject of a lot of research: adolescents often take part in risky behaviors that can lead to injury and death because of a number of factors. Research one or more factors — including brain development — that can lead adolescents to be unconcerned about "personal mortality" and apply that factor to Krakauer's actions in this narrative.

6 Look over these famous lines from Ralph Waldo Emerson, an American writer who popularized what was called the Transcendentalist Movement during the middle of the nineteenth century. Transcendentalists believed in the beauty of nature, the power of the individual, and the importance of freedom. Based upon your reading of his narrative, explain why Krakauer might agree or disagree with each and describe your own thoughts about the lines.

a. "Do not be too timid and squeamish about your actions. All life is an experiment. The more experiments you make the better."

b. "There is a time in every man's education when he arrives at the conviction that envy is ignorance; that imitation is suicide; that he must take himself for better for worse as his portion."

c. "Trust thyself: every heart vibrates to that iron string. Accept the place the divine providence has found for you, the society of your contemporaries, the connection of events. Great men have always done so."

d. "Whoso would be a man must be a nonconformist."

Zolaria

Caitlin Horrocks

Caitlin Horrocks (b. 1980) is an assistant professor of writing at Grand Valley State University in Allendale, Michigan. Her first story collection, *This Is Not Your City*, from which this story is taken, was published to widespread acclaim in 2011. This story is about two friends who invent a magical world called Zolaria, a place that becomes more difficult to sustain as they get older.

Courtesy Caitlin Horrocks

It is July and we are a miraculous age. We have been sprung from our backyards, from the neighborhood park, from the invisible borders that rationed all our other summers. We are old enough to have earned a larger country, and young enough to make it larger still. The woods between Miller and Arborview become haunted. Basilisks patrol the Dairy Queen. We are so beset by dangers we make ourselves rulers over them, and by July we are the princesses of an undiscovered kingdom. We make maps with colored pencils. Here be Dragons, I write across the square of Wellington Park, at the end of our street. Here be Brothers, Hanna writes across her own backyard, and we avoid them both. We are too old for these games, too big for this much imagination, but we are so unpopular that summer that there is no one to care. We have finished the fifth grade alive and we consider that an accomplishment. We have earned this summer.

The neighborhood has been emptying of children. There are bigger houses being built past Wagner, past the edge of the western edge of town. The houses here, one story, one bathroom, have become a place to live after children or a place to move away from when they come. This year Hanna-Khoury-eight-houses-down and I are best friends, a thing I haven't had before and won't have again until I'm married,

both of us twenty-four, an age my family will say is too young and I will be proud years later of proving them wrong.

That summer we pick blackberries in the Miller woods and take them to Hanna's house where her mother rinses them in a plastic colander. Hanna's parents still live together and their house feels friendlier than mine. When Mr. Khoury visited our fifth-grade class our teacher introduced him as a man there to talk about his "troubled homeland." He was a man from somewhere else, a troubled country people left and then called home, a country defined only by its perpetual unhappiness. Mr. Khoury told us that we were lucky, lucky boys and lucky girls, lucky American children, and Hanna rolled her eyes, embarrassed. Mr. Khoury has a Lebanese flag on the wall of his study and I think it must be a kinder sort of country that puts a tree on its flag. This is one of many things I do not understand that summer.

The gas station at the corner of Miller and Maple closes and there is a sign in the windows announcing upcoming construction, Project Managers Ogan/Veen. We don't know that the construction will never happen, that nothing will ever be built there, because the gasoline has leached into the earth 100, 200, 300 feet down, some impossible depth that no one will own up to and that can't be cleaned. That summer we ride our bikes around and around the empty gas station and look in all the windows. Hanna says Ogan/Veen looks like the name of a monster, and from then on he haunts our summer in a friendly sort of way, a goblin who lives in an empty Shell station and wanders the neighborhood at sundown. If we are lucky, he will encounter only the children who have spent the past year tormenting us, and he will grind their bones for bread.

5 "Ogan Veen, Ogan Veen,
  His farts all smell like gasoline,
  His stomach's full of children's spleens,
  Ogan Veen, Ogan Veen," we sing. There are other verses but this one's my favorite because I've come up with "spleen" all by myself. Hanna doesn't know what it means and I'm not so clear either, but it rhymes and my mother's said it's a part of someone that can be eaten.

  "If you're a cannibal, I guess," she said, and I said *perfect*.

10 On one of my dad's weekends, I ask him to take us to Dolph Park, too far to bike to. The hiking path circles two lakes, Little Sister Lake and Big Sister Lake, and since I am an only child and Hanna has two brothers, we decide to split the lakes between us. We fight over who gets which. We are the same age and nearly the same size, although Hanna's arms and legs are gangly and seem destined for great height. In seventh grade, the year Hanna will slip a note between the vents of my locker that reads "I Hate You" over and over, filling an entire notebook page, I will be 5'2" and as tall as I will ever grow. My father is 6'1" and will call me "Midget." When I briefly register with an online dating site after college I will call myself "petite." Hanna will never grow tall, either, and because we can't know these things, we ask my father to flip a coin over Big Sister Lake. I can see him peek and scuttle the coin when I call heads, a move too quick for Hanna to notice. She cedes the lake to me, accepts the smaller for her kingdom, and I try to tell my father that night over carryout

Chinese what I am only beginning to understand myself, that the way in which he loves me is not quite the way I wish he would.

In fifth grade Hanna and I doomed ourselves. On the second day of school we took out our folders, our pencil cases, organized our desks, and Hanna had space dolphins and I had pink unicorns. Two years ago all the girls had school supplies like this, and I don't understand why they have abandoned the things they loved. Hanna and I were startled but not stupid, and if no one had noticed us that day we would both have begged our mothers to take us to K-Mart that night and exchange them. But it was too late. We were the girls with the wrong school supplies, and everything we did after that, even the things that were just like everyone else, were the wrong things to do. I will never tell Hanna that space dolphins aren't really as bad as pink unicorns, and that she wasn't really doomed until I made her my friend.

The Little and Big Sister Lakes are the eastern edge of what we name Zolaria that summer, simply for the sound of it, the exotic "Z" and the trailing vowels like a movie star's name. The northwestern border is the Barton Dam. It takes us most of the summer to get there, sneaking closer and closer, up Newport Road and through the grounds of what will be our junior high school. One day there is a door propped open by the tennis courts and we decide to explore. There is a sticker beside the door: No Shirt, No Shoes, No Service. I am barefoot and we are so timid this sticker foils our plan until Hanna takes off her left shoe and gives it to me. Now we are within the law, and follow a chlorine smell as far as the locker rooms, the labyrinth of showers, the locked door to the pool. We hear footsteps and run, directionless, past the library, the main office, the Cafetorium, past the music room where I'll play flute for three shrill years. Hanna will have quit band by then;

Hanna has only so much energy, her mother will tell mine on the phone, and doesn't want to waste it on the trombone. We run past the glass trophy cases in the foyer and finally we find the open door, the patch of blue sky and red and green tennis courts. In the homestretch Hanna's shoe flies off my foot and she yells, "Forget it! Don't stop!" but I go back and we make it out anyway.

The next day we bike through the junior high parking lot and across the freeway overpass just north, where we yank our arms up and down until three trucks have honked their horns. We take our bikes into the nature preserve and ride them until the hills get so steep they rattle our teeth. We ride bikes like girls, throw like girls, we know it, and there is no one around that summer to make us ashamed. We walk our bikes through the forest, the sound of the freeway to our right and a creek to our left, a symmetrical hum. Eventually there is a fence and a gate and a dirt road that leads to the Barton Dam. We ride to the huge gray wall of it, the rush of water at the base, the scum scudding across the surface of the river like soap suds. There is a dead animal floating at the base of the dam, bloated and spongy and colorless. Its fur is breaking off in hanks, drifting in the patches of foam. It is a cloudy day and we are alone on the river path. A man comes out of the pump station at the top of the dam and walks out along the wall. He leans against the safety railing and shades his eyes with a hand and looks down at us. We know we are in the borderlands, where our kingdom meets a stranger's, where Ogan Veen wanders in daylight, and where we should not linger.

Thirteen years later, Cal and I will announce our engagement on Christmas morning over crumpled wrapping paper and freshly squeezed orange juice. It will be the coldest morning of any year of my life so far, the paper's lead headline the temperature, 26 below, but as we unwrap presents we will see one of the Khoury boys outside walking their dog. My mother will call me into the kitchen to tell me I am young. "You're young," she'll say. "You're still so young."

15   "Not that young," I will tell her.

"Yes, that young. You barely know each other."

"I know him."

"You don't know yourself," she'll say. "That's what I worry about. How can you get married when you don't know yourself yet?"

"I know myself plenty," I'll say. "I think I know all I want to."

20 One night in July, Hanna and I have a sleepover and dream almost the same dream, in which Ogan Veen is chasing us, gnashing his long, stinking teeth. Zolaria is not his to haunt, so we build traps in the woods, stretch fishing line between trees, scatter tacks in the dirt and make piles of throwing-rocks in places with good cover. In my backyard is a half-dug decorative fishpond, a project my father started and abandoned, and we lattice the top with long sticks, camouflage it with leaves and cut grass. Every day I wait for Hanna to come up the street so we can check it together. I do not want to face our quarry alone. We bow branches, harp them with yarn, notch twigs and practice our archery. We strip the leaves from long tendrils of weeping willow and crack the whips in the air. We run shouting through the woods brandishing foam swords from a Nerf fencing set. We are girded for battle, but the enemy will not show himself. We catch nothing, but we have made ourselves afraid. It seems unfair, that a kingdom we invented should have its own mysteries, its unvanquishable foes. By September, we are almost eager for school to begin. We are tired of checking a dry fishpond for ogres every morning. But as princesses of Zolaria, we cannot say such a thing out loud. We have certain duties to our kingdom, to our adoring

subjects. We must give the appearance of keeping them safe.

My father will take me once more to Dolph Park, when I am in high school, for old times' sake. The lakes are in the middle of an algae bloom, the weather hot and the water full of nitrogen and phosphorus. I will explain this to my father, nitrogen, phosphorus, when he grimaces at the damp mat of green over the pond, looking solid enough to walk on. My high school will have implemented an experimental science curriculum the year I enter tenth grade and I will know a great deal about eutrophication and very little about anything else. We will pretend to skip rocks but will really just be throwing things, stones and sticks and clods of dirt, watching them break apart the algae and sink out of sight. We will throw until our arms are tired and I will talk about the environmental benchmarks of healthy aquatic environments. We will get milkshakes at the Dairy Queen on Stadium Boulevard and two weeks later my father will move to San Diego.

In sixth grade Hanna and I will still be in the same Girl Scout troop. We will sing Christmas carols for the old people at Hillside Terrace nursing home, and in the spring we will sell cookies. I will sell enough to earn a stuffed giraffe, while Hanna sells only enough for a patch to be sewn on her vest. She will already be sick and I will have no idea. She will miss the whole last month of sixth grade, and four Girl Scout meetings, but it will be summer before my mother takes me to visit her. The hospital will remind me of a shopping mall, places to buy medicine and gifts and food, departments for having babies and looking after babies and looking after children and fixing all the different things that can go wrong with them. It is a weighty place but exciting, the way my mother asks the front desk for Pediatric Oncology and I press the button in the elevator.

Hanna's mother and mine will go for coffee, leaving us alone. Hanna will be wearing a violet-colored bandanna. She will say she is a gangster, and I say she would make the worst gangster in the world, which is true. She says a highwayman, then, which feels a little closer, and when I suggest pirate, we're off. We go once more to Zolaria, the bed rails marking the deck of our ship, and Hanna says climb on, that I won't hurt her, and our kingdom acquires an ocean, high seas. Aweigh anchor, we say, trim the sails, cast off, fore-and-aft, and we are all right for a time. We will be eleven, almost twelve; we will keep looking at the door, hoping no one comes in and sees us. After half an hour Hanna will throw up twice in a plastic tub beside the bed. She will say she leaned over to take a sounding, that the sea is a thousand fathoms deep where we are, that if we don't make it back to port we'll drown for sure. I will ask her if she wants some water. She won't say anything, but I'll fill a plastic cup from the jug on the nightstand.

"I had a dream the other night that Ogan Veen was back," I will say. "It was in the woods and he was chasing us and when we went out the fence we were saying, 'I don't hear him, I think we made it,' but then he was right there in front of us smiling and then I woke up." Hanna will look at me and her eyes will be dark and flat and I will know it was a terrible idea, to tell her this dream. She will sip her water and I will watch her sip it and we will wait for our mothers to come back and when they do we will be glad.

I will be unprepared for how long this sickness takes, for how long Hanna will be neither cured nor desperate. I will visit her once more at the hospital, twice more while she's at home. I will realize I am waiting for her to be either well or dead. She will feel very far away. I will start junior high alone, and when Hanna comes for her first day, in late November, I will be startled to see her. Our morning classes must all be different because I recognize her for the first time at lunch, sitting by herself. I will already be sitting in the middle of a long table by the time I see her, my lunch unpacked in front of me. I will be pressed tight on either side by people who, if asked, would probably say I am their friend. Hanna will be wearing an awful wig, stiff and styled like an old woman's perm. The hair will be dark brown, not black, and will no longer match her eyes. She will be pale and her face swollen and she will not seem like someone I can afford to know.

The summer we are ten we sketch maps of our kingdom and outline its Constitution, its Declaration of Independence, its City Charter. In the end they all become zoological surveys. The Haisley woods harbor griffins, borometz, simurghs. There are dragons on Linwood Street, basilisks on Duncan who turn children to stone. We understand that we have no sway over basilisks and dragons; we understand that they are the minions of Ogan Veen. He has servants now, he has armies, and despite all our efforts Zolaria is not as safe as it was.

We make other lists, too, of "People Who, In Zolaria, Would Be Imprisoned In The Dungeon FOREVER." Hanna keeps adding her brothers' names to the list and then erasing them until the paper is ready to tear and I tell her to leave them off, if she's going to feel so guilty about it. We make a list of "Animals That Can Be Ridden: Pegasus, Centaur, Griffins, and Space Dolphins." We decide this is too charitable, and amend it to "Animals That Can Be Ridden By Us." We decide to hire young men to look after our stable of space dolphins, and when we deem ourselves a little older, and ready for love, we will notice the groomsmen and swoon. We prepare speeches of protest, in which we declare our unwillingness to marry foreign princes, our determination to follow our hearts, until we are disappointed to remember that in our kingdom we have no parents, and may marry whomever we choose.

. . .

Fourteen years later, when I marry Cal at a Unitarian church that four months later will be sold and remodeled into a bed and breakfast, Hanna Khoury's parents will still be living down the street. My father will fly in from San Diego for the wedding, and he and my mother will agree to pose for photographs together: them, them and me, them and me and Cal, them and me and Cal and Cal's parents, the symmetry of happy marriages. The Khourys won't be at the wedding because I won't have invited them. I won't have invited them because I'm scared of what Hanna might have told them. Not about the way I never sat with her at lunch or talked to her in band, or the way I didn't ever claim, precisely, not to know her, or the way I never said I did. Not even the way her life got worse and worse and I did nothing to make it better. Or the way when I saw how bad things got for her in school I was glad we weren't still friends. The day I will worry she's told them about will be a Monday in February during sixth period, Phys Ed, one of our two classes together. Hanna will be excused from almost everything except changing. She won't have to run or throw or dribble or swim, but she will have to put on gym clothes. She'll try to get her sweater off and T-shirt on without disturbing her wig, but it will almost always catch, tip, slide to one side. Sometimes it will fall limp onto the bench between the lockers. One day Barbara Zabrodska will steal it and send it flying. Marti Orringer will catch it, and throw it to Naomi Sullivan, who will throw it to Elizabeth Dugan, who will throw it to Jamie Piakowski, who will throw it to Carla Deleon, who will throw it to Mary-Alice, who will throw it to Roberta, who will throw it to me. And instead of giving it back I will throw it to Andrea, who will throw it to Aisha, who will throw it to a girl whose name I don't remember, and another, and another, and another, because there will be thirty girls in sixth-period gym and I can't remember them all.

seeing connections

▶

In the film *Heavenly Creatures* (1994) directed by Peter Jackson, two young girls invent a rich imaginary world for themselves.

In what ways do these images reflect or diverge from the imaginary world of "Zolaria"? What words or phrases from the short story support your response?

Then Leah Campo will throw it to Kendra Danielson, who will throw it to Jasmine, who will throw it finally, accidentally, to Mrs. Pendall the gym teacher, who will have heard Hanna crying and come in the back way, through the showers. Mrs. Pendall will give Hanna back her wig and will send all twenty-nine of us to detention, where we fill the room and are sent out into the hall, along the wall like a tornado drill. The detention supervisor will make us crouch the rest of the period, tornado-style, on our knees with our foreheads almost touching the wall, our hands curled around the backs of our necks to protect our spines from flying shards of glass. My knees will hurt and I will think that if a tornado really did sever my spine and paralyze me for life, I wouldn't have to worry anymore about not doing the right things. I will think that the feel of her wig in my hand was like a gutted animal, empty and dry and bristling.

Hanna will be in remission by the next fall, but her parents will already have taken her out of Forsythe Junior High and placed her in a private school. I will not know when the cancer comes back. I will have discovered how easy it is to never see someone, even an eight-houses-down-someone, if you do not wish to see each other. When she passes away, my mother will find out from a newspaper obituary. She will come up to my bedroom, will still be deciding whether to tell me herself or just show me the paper. She will hand it to me and say, "There's bad news, honey."

30   It will be my first funeral, and my mother and I will go shopping for black clothing together. As we leave the mall I will thank her for paying, like she's bought me birthday gifts or new back-to-school clothes, and then to fill the silence I will say something about JV field hockey, and then my mother will drop the shopping bags in the middle of the parking lot and hold me tighter than she ever has or ever will again. At the funeral I will be so worried about avoiding Mr. and Mrs. Khoury and their sons that I won't have time to cry.

At the wedding Cal's mother will squint at me and ask if I'm really Unitarian, or just needed a cheap place for the wedding. I will tell her that I'm pagan, that I make burnt offerings to forest demons in the Bird Hills Nature Preserve. She won't laugh. Cal and I will go to Toronto for the honeymoon and three and a half years later the doctor will tell us to get ready for twins, girls. I will be terrified. It seems like a sign. It seems like a coin has already been flipped, and we will spend years waiting for it to fall. I will stare at my daughters in matching pajamas and wonder

which one Ogan Veen will ask for. Which one he'll try to take. If he will give them ten years, if he will come calling sooner.

One winter the twins, bored, will unearth old photos in the basement: their baby pictures, our wedding, school portraits of Cal and snapshots of my elementary school birthday parties. The year I turned ten there was no one I wanted to invite except Hanna, no one I thought would come if I asked. In the picture there is a cake with ten candles and only two girls grinning above it — they look as if they should be lonely but are somehow perfectly happy. Madison will ask me who the dark-haired girl is, and I will get a look on my face that will make Sophie elbow her sister into silence. She is the perceptive one, I will think, the one who reads people. And then I will think, please no, not her. And then I will think, please no, I didn't mean the other one.

On a July morning the summer before the girls begin kindergarten I will ask them to get dressed in their swimsuits, pull old shorts and T-shirts on over. I will pack a bag with beach towels and dry clothes, and they will ask which city pool we're going to. Wait and see, I will say, and we will all climb into the car. I will drive down the township road that skirts the edge of Bird Hills Nature Preserve; it will be lined with condos but still unpaved. I will park at the lot downriver from the Barton Dam, and we will climb the wooden steps up to the calm pond above the pump station. We will leave the trail to slide down the embankment toward the water. The shore is reedy, the ground spongy with black, rank mud. We will stand ankle deep in the water, and Sophie will yelp when her feet start to sink. I will suggest a short swim, and the girls will look at me with horror. The water will smell warm and spongy and tattered curtains of algae will stroke our toes. Madison will hold her nose, and in the end, I have to push them in. It will be only a moment, I promise, a slice of a second, that I hold them under. And then I will be tugging at their hair and the backs of their T-shirts and wrestling us all into a heap on the grass above the reeds, and a woman on a bicycle will be standing on the embankment trail shouting at me that the pond is no place for swimming. The water isn't clean, she yells. She talks about nitrogen, phosphorus. I'm sorry, I will say. I didn't realize. It's such a hot day, the girls were so hot. They asked to go wading and slipped. My daughters will not contradict me, and the bicycle woman will leave, and I will bundle them into towels, warm and dry. At home we will all stand under the shower, all of us crowded together, and then eat ice cream in the backyard. I will ask Madison if she heard anything underwater, a gnashing of teeth, a creature with eyes like an oil slick and incisors like bread knives, long and serrated. I will tell Sophie that Ogan Veen has a laugh like I-94 and a stink like algae. I will tell her that I have introduced them now, the three of them, Madison and Sophie and Mr. Veen, and if they ever meet him they must run away. They must tell him that they are princesses, that they are mine, that I will protect them in the only ways I know how.

Cal will get home from work and while I cook dinner the girls will tell him what I did and Cal will shout and I will try to explain myself and Cal will misunderstand and talk to his parents about having the girls baptized at First Methodist. I won't know how to tell him

that that won't help, that it isn't what I meant. I won't know how to tell him that I am still bracing for a day when Sophie complains of a headache that turns out to be something more, when Madison reels dizzily in gym class and the teacher sends her home with a concerned note. When a doctor has something to tell me he asks me to sit down to hear. I will be trying not to think about the possibility of a day when I will drive to the dam again, climb the stairs to Barton Pond and wade in. I will walk until I can hear the pressing silence of the water, the rushing, vacuous weight of it. I will say, "Mr. Veen, do you remember me?" I will say, "Mr. Veen, I once ruled a kingdom and left traps for you in the woods. Don't you want your revenge?" I will say, "Mr. Veen, you are an ogre and a thief and the patron saint of Julys, of summer Sundays, of miracles." I will say, "Mr. Veen, do not take my children."

35   And if he asks, and if I think it will help, and if I think it is truly what I have to do, we will be swimming and it will be July and we are a miraculous age. We are in Zolaria, we are children, our bodies are honest children's bodies. We are narrow and quick and we still fit in all our hiding places, the sun-wet hollows and the flowers in pink and purple and turquoise, all the damp colors of girlhood. We are riding our space dolphins, and either we can breathe the water of Zolaria or we are no longer breathing and it is July and we are a miraculous age and we are ten.

Understanding and Interpreting

1 After completing the story, you can probably think back on it and see how often Hanna's death was foreshadowed. Locate as many places as you can and explain why there are so many instances of foreshadowing.

2 In fifth grade, Hanna and the narrator "doomed" themselves because they showed up with school supplies decorated with space dolphins and unicorns, styles that the other girls had stopped using. The narrator then says, "I don't understand why they have abandoned the things they loved" (par. 11). How does this statement seem to reflect one of the themes of this story?

3 When the narrator announces her engagement, her mother says that she is too young and that she doesn't even know herself yet. The narrator responds, "I know myself plenty. . . . I think I know all I want to." (par. 19) What does her response reveal about her? How does it relate to what we know about her when she was a child?

4 In less than two years, the narrator goes from being Hanna's co-princess of Zolaria to being one of her tormentors in the locker room. What changes between Hanna and the narrator? How do Hanna and the narrator deal with the changes between them?

5 Zolaria means different things to the narrator as the story progresses. What does it seem to represent at the following stages?

  a. during that first summer when she is ten (pars. 1–13)
  b. when Hanna becomes sick (pars. 22–25)
  c. when the narrator is an adult and has children of her own (pars. 33–35)

6 What is the narrator hoping to accomplish by pushing her children into the pond (par. 33)? How successful is she?

7 Read this excerpt from an interview with Caitlin Horrocks, which was published on a website called *The Rumpus*. What do you think of the interviewer's, and Horrocks's, assessment of the narrator as being too self-aware?

> **The Rumpus:** "I know myself plenty," the main character in "Zolaria" says to her mother. "I think I know all I want to." And in fact she and the other protagonists [. . .] know a great deal about themselves, maybe too much to be happy. Have you worked with characters who don't understand themselves?

> **Horrocks:** Self-awareness is usually thought of as an unmitigated good thing—how can someone be happy or stable or fit company without it? But the main character in "Zolaria" is so convinced of her own cowardice she'd be willing to die to make amends, to save her own children. Her idea of herself doesn't bring her any comfort. But now I'm just agreeing with what you already said.

8 Reread the opening paragraph and the closing paragraph of the story. They both take place in Zolaria and are both written in the present tense, but what is the difference between them?

Analyzing Language, Style, and Structure

1 Look back through the story and notice the places where the narrator uses "we" and then shifts to "I." Why do you think she switches and what is the effect of those shifts?

2 Notice the interesting shifts in the tense the narrator uses. For example, the story begins in the present tense with the line, "It is July and we are a miraculous age," but at various times, she switches to the future tense, as in "My father will take me once more to Dolph Park, when I am in high school" (par. 21). Looking back through the story, when does the narrator use the present tense and when does she use the future tense? What is the effect of these shifts?

3 If the narrator had decided to tell this story in chronological order, she would have started when she and Hanna were in the fifth grade, continued through their one summer together, described Hanna's illness and death, and wrapped up with her own marriage and parenthood. But instead, she shifts back and forth in time throughout the story. Look back through the story and identify one significant time shift.

Why do you think Horrocks structured this portion of the story in this way? What is the effect of the time shift?

4 Reread the descriptions of Zolaria, the world the narrator and Hanna create when they are ten (pars. 1, 12–13, 20, and 26–27). What specific language choices give it the feeling of both magic and danger?

5 One of the saddest parts of this story is when the narrator's relationship with Hanna changes after she becomes sick. Reread the following sentences and explain the effect of the underlined words. What do they reveal about the narrator?

   a. "She will be pale and her face swollen and she will not seem <u>like someone I can afford to know</u>" (par. 25).

   b. "I will think that the feel of her wig in my hand was <u>like a gutted animal, empty and dry and bristling</u>" (par. 28).

   c. "I will have discovered how easy it is to never see someone, even an <u>eight-houses-down-someone</u>, if you do not wish to see each other" (par. 29).

Connecting, Arguing, and Extending

1 It is very likely that you have had an experience similar to the narrator's, in which you and a friend have changed to such a degree that you are no longer as close as you once were. What factors caused this change? Is this growing apart an inevitable part of growing up or can it be avoided? Why?

2 The narrator clearly fails in her opportunity to stand up for Hanna when she is being bullied in the locker room in junior high school; in fact, she even participates in the bullying of her friend (par. 28). Conduct a brief search on the social forces that contribute to bullying in school, focusing on the most recent research by scholars such as Jaana Juvonen from UCLA, Ken Rigby from the University of South Australia, and others. Using the findings from your research, explain the actions of the narrator toward Hanna.

3 It is apparent that even years after the events the narrator has still not forgiven herself for her actions (and inactions) toward Hanna. Is the narrator truly responsible for her actions, or should she be excused

because of her youth and other factors? Support your response with direct evidence from the story.

4 Look over these two differing views about childhood and its relationship to adulthood. Explain what each is suggesting about childhood and explain how they each compare to "Zolaria."

   a. "When I was a child, I spoke like a child, I thought like a child, I reasoned like a child. When I became a man, I gave up childish ways." —1 Corinthians 13:11, English Standard Version

   b. My heart leaps up when I behold
   A rainbow in the sky:
   So was it when my life began;
   So is it now I am a man;
   So be it when I shall grow old,
       Or let me die!
   The Child is father of the Man;
       I could wish my days to be
   Bound each to each by natural piety.

   —William Wordsworth

My Son the Man *and* The Possessive

Sharon Olds

Born in San Francisco in 1942, Sharon Olds has become one of America's most well-known and critically praised poets. She has published numerous collections of poetry, including *The Dead and the Living* (1984), which received the National Book Critics Circle Award. Considered a "confessional poet," Olds typically writes about her own life, as she does in these two poems about her children growing up and the effect it has on her as a mother.

© Bruce Davidson/Magnum Photos

Olds   My Son the Man

Suddenly his shoulders get a lot wider,
the way Houdini would expand his body
while people were putting him in chains. It seems
no time since I would help him put on his sleeper,
5   guide his calves into the shadowy interior,
zip him up and toss him up and
catch his weight. I cannot imagine him
no longer a child, and I know I must get ready,
get over my fear of men now my son
10   is going to be one. This was not
what I had in mind when he pressed up through me like a
sealed trunk through the ice of the Hudson,
snapped the padlock, unsnaked the chains,
appeared in my arms. Now he looks at me
15   the way Houdini studied a box
to learn the way out, then smiled and let himself be manacled.

▶
─────────────

This is Harry Houdini, the magician, just before he is sealed into a trunk and dumped into the Hudson River, in a famous illusion that becomes an extended metaphor in "My Son the Man."

Why do you think Olds found this particular Houdini illusion such a compelling metaphor for watching her son grow up?

FPG/Getty Images

Understanding and Interpreting

1 Describe the speaker of this poem. What concerns her? What scares her? Be sure to use evidence from the text to support your response.

2 This poem makes use of a literary device known as a "conceit" or an "extended metaphor," in which an author repeats a comparison multiple times throughout a text. In this case, the speaker makes three separate comparisons between her son and the famous magician Harry Houdini. For each of the following lines from the poem, explain how the reference to Houdini reveals a different aspect of the relationship between the speaker and her son:

a. "his shoulders get a lot wider / the way Houdini would expand his body / while people were putting him in chains. . . ." (ll. 1–3)

b. "when he pressed up through me like a / sealed trunk through the ice of the Hudson, / snapped the padlock, unsnaked the chains, / appeared in my arms. . . ." (ll. 11–14)

c. "he looks at me / the way Houdini studied a box / to learn the way out. . . ." (ll. 14–16)

Now that you have explored the individual parts of the extended Houdini metaphor, explain the overall purpose of the comparison. What is Sharon Olds saying about the relationships between mothers and sons by using the multiple comparisons to Houdini?

3 The speaker admits that "[t]his was not what she had in mind" when confronted by the inevitable maturation of her son into a man. In what ways is the speaker's concern specifically about gender, and in what ways is it about watching a child grow up?

4 The final lines of the poem bring the situation into the present, as the son looks at his mother and smiles like Houdini does before he lets "himself be manacled" (l. 16). From the point of view of the speaker, is this a sinister or a playful smile, or something else?

Analyzing Language, Style, and Structure

1 The poem begins with the word "suddenly" in describing how the speaker's son's shoulders seem to expand quickly. How does the use of this opening signal the way that time will be presented in this poem? Explain the possible implications of the speaker's sense of time.

2 Explain how the imagery in lines 3–7 establishes the relationship between the mother and her son.

3 The speaker claims that she must get over her "fear of men" (l. 9). How does she communicate this fear throughout this poem?

4 In lines 7–8, the speaker admits, "I cannot imagine him / no longer a child." Discuss how this description, which contrasts with the title of the poem, reveals a central struggle that the speaker is experiencing.

Connecting, Arguing, and Extending

1 How much different would this poem be if the speaker were a father instead of a mother? What would the father likely focus on that the mother does not? Why? Think of an extended metaphor that could be used by the father to illustrate the fear he might have in watching his son grow up and explain why you think this would be an effective comparison.

2 In what ways has your relationship to a parent, guardian, or older friend or sibling been similar to or different from the relationship Olds describes in this poem? What do you think that the older person has struggled with as you have grown older yourself?

3 One reviewer for the *New York Times* said of Sharon Olds, "She has made the minutiae of a woman's everyday life as valid a subject for poetry as the grand abstract themes that have preoccupied other poets." Do you agree or disagree with the reviewer, and why?

My daughter — as if I
owned her — that girl with the
hair wispy as a frayed bellpull

has been to the barber, that knife grinder,
5 and had the edge of her hair sharpened.

Each strand now cuts
both ways. The blade of new bangs
hangs over her red-brown eyes
like carbon steel.

10   All the little
spliced ropes are sliced. The curtain of
dark paper-cuts veils the face that
started from next to nothing in my body —

My body. My daughter. I'll have to find
15 another word. In her bright helmet
she looks at me as if across a
great distance. Distant fires can be
glimpsed in the resin lights of her eyes:

the watch fires of an enemy, a while before
20 the war starts.

seeing connections

These photographs are part of a collection called *A Girl and Her Room* by photographer Rania Matar. In her project statement, Matar says, "As a mother of teenage daughters I watch their passage from girlhood into adulthood, fascinated with the transformation taking place, the adult personality taking shape and a gradual self-consciousness replacing the carefree world they had known and lived in so far."

How do the images reflect this transformation, and how might the images relate to Olds's poem "The Possessive"?

Dima, Beirut, Lebanon, 2010

Krystal, Brookline, Massachusetts, 2009

Brianna, Winchester, Massachusetts, 2009

Understanding and Interpreting

1 The "possessive" is a grammatical term indicating ownership. How is the idea of ownership that is introduced in the title developed further in the poem?

2 On a literal level, the speaker is describing her daughter's visit to the barber where she gets a significantly different hairstyle. But, what does the haircut represent metaphorically? And what effect is this change having on the speaker?

3 In the fifth stanza, the speaker decides that "daughter" is no longer an adequate description and she will have to find "another word" (l. 15). What has led her to decide she needs a different word? What words do you think the speaker might choose to express her new understanding of her relationship with her daughter?

4 By the final stanza, according to the speaker, the daughter has become an "enemy" who awaits a "war" (ll. 19–20). In what way is the haircut part of the preparation for this war?

Analyzing Language, Style, and Structure

1 The speaker begins the poem by considering the phrase "my daughter," and then dismisses it because it implies ownership. What effect does the speaker's dismissal of the phrase have on our understanding of her attitude toward her daughter?

2 In the opening stanza, the speaker reveals that her daughter has just been to the barber for a haircut. She also describes the barber as a "knife grinder," who sharpens the "edge" of her daughter's hair (ll. 4–5). In what ways does this description set up different possible ways of understanding the significance of this event?

3 The phrase "cuts both ways" means that something has two different effects simultaneously, usually one positive and the other negative. What are two possible effects that may be occurring as a result of the daughter's haircut?

4 The speaker sees "[d]istant fires" in the "resin lights" (ll. 17–18) of her daughter's eyes, continuing the warlike imagery. Describe the tone that these phrases, along with those in the previous stanza, create in the poem as a whole. In your description, try using two adjectives to express the complexity of the speaker's position.

Connecting, Arguing, and Extending

1 For a variety of reasons, adolescence is often a difficult time for the relationship between parents and their children. This poem uses extensive imagery of weapons and warfare to describe the changing relationship between the mother and daughter. Explain the ways in which the conflict between parents and children is like warfare and the ways it can be seen in less adversarial terms.

2 Consider the gender issues raised in this poem and the previous poem, "My Son the Man." Both are by the same poet, but the speaker response to each child is quite different, in part because of gender differences. Write a comparison analyzing how gender affects the parent-child relationships in these two poems.

3 In "The Possessive," the speaker focuses specifically on her relationship with her daughter and possible conflicts with her daughter in the future. However, researcher Karen Fingerman, PhD, who interviewed adult women about their relationships with their elderly mothers, found that despite conflicts and complicated emotions, the mother-daughter bond is so strong that 80 percent to 90 percent of women at midlife report good relationships with their mothers—though they wish those relationships were even better. What do you think creates this strong bond between mothers and daughters, even if they experience some conflict earlier in life? Is there something inevitable about conflict between mothers and daughters earlier in life that is then resolved later in life? If so, what are some possible reasons for the changed relationships?

Donna Ward/Getty Images Entertainment/Getty Images

4 Emma Watson, the actress who played Hermione in the Harry Potter films, cut her hair immediately after the end of filming the last installment. The haircut became a major media event, and marked a clear departure between the old Emma and the new Emma.

> "I have to [grow my hair out] for roles. But if I had it my way, I would have just kept it short forever. Of course, men like long hair. There's no two ways about it. The majority of the boys around me were like, 'Why did you do that? That's such an error.' And I was like, 'Well, honestly, I don't really care what you think!' I've never felt so confident as I did with short hair—I felt really good in my own skin."
> —*Glamour* Magazine

Similarly, Sharon Olds has taken a simple haircut and elevated its importance in this poem. Is getting a new hairstyle really that significant? Do you think that there are different standards for males and females when it comes to the significance of hair?

The Seven Ages of Man

William Shakespeare

William Shakespeare (1564–1616) is considered one of the greatest playwrights in history. His plays *Romeo and Juliet*, *Macbeth*, *Hamlet*, *Julius Caesar*, *Othello*, and many others are among the most widely read and performed plays in the English language. While many of Shakespeare's best-known works are classified as tragedies, he also wrote a number of very successful comedies, including *A Midsummer Night's Dream*, *The Taming of the Shrew*, *Much Ado about Nothing*, and *As You Like It*.

Portrait of William Shakespeare (1564–1616) c. 1610 (oil on canvas), Taylor, John (d. 1651)

(attr. to)/National Portrait Gallery, London, UK/Bridgeman Images

KEY CONTEXT   The excerpt that follows is from the comedy *As You Like It* (1603), which is about a group of exiled noblemen and women who find love amid mistaken identities in a forest in rural France. The speech below, one of Shakespeare's most famous, is delivered as a monologue by the often-gloomy Jaques, one of the exiled lords. In it, Jaques describes what he sees as the life cycle of mankind, from childhood to old age, with five "ages" in between.

All the world's a stage,
And all the men and women merely players.
They have their exits and their entrances,
And one man in his time plays many parts,

5 His acts being seven ages. At first the infant,
Mewling and puking in the nurse's arms.
Then the whining schoolboy, with his satchel
And shining morning face, creeping like snail
Unwillingly to school. And then the lover,
10 Sighing like furnace, with a woeful ballad
Made to his mistress' eyebrow. Then a soldier,
Full of strange oaths, and bearded like the pard,[1]
Jealous in honor, sudden, and quick in quarrel,
Seeking the bubble reputation
15 Even in the cannon's mouth. And then the justice,
In fair round belly with good capon[2] lined,
With eyes severe and beard of formal cut,
Full of wise saws and modern instances;
And so he plays his part. The sixth age shifts
20 Into the lean and slippered pantaloon,[3]
With spectacles on nose and pouch on side,
His youthful hose, well saved, a world too wide
For his shrunk shank;[4] and his big manly voice,
Turning again toward childish treble, pipes
25 And whistles in his sound. Last scene of all,
That ends this strange eventful history,
Is second childishness and mere oblivion,
Sans teeth, sans eyes, sans taste, sans everything.

---

[1]pard: Leopard. —Eds.

[2]capon: Rooster intended for eating. —Eds.

[3]pantaloon: A stock character in the Italian commedia dell'arte, the pantaloon is an absurd doddering old man. —Eds.

[4]shank: Calf. —Eds.

seeing connections

▶

In a reading room at the Folger Shakespeare Library in Washington, D.C., there is a large stained glass by artist Nicola d'Ascenzo that represents each of the seven ages of man.

Examine each section of the stained glass shown here and explain which words or phrases from Jaques's speech you think likely contributed to d'Ascenzo's interpretation.

Understanding and Interpreting

1 Paraphrase the seven ages in seven sentences.

2 Explain William Shakespeare's opening metaphor: "All the world's a stage, / And all the men and women merely players." How is life like being an actor onstage? What aspects of life are not accounted for in this metaphor?

3 Clearly these seven ages of man have been selected intentionally to represent a fairly gloomy outlook on life. What ages of man are missing and how would their inclusion change the meaning of the monologue?

Analyzing Language, Style, and Structure

1 After the opening line, Shakespeare writes "the men and women <u>merely</u> players." What is the effect of the word "merely" in the second line? How would the tone be different if that word was not included?

2 Shakespeare uses a number of similes to describe the stages men and women go through in life. Paraphrase each of the following similes and explain how each contributes to the overall tone:

   a. "creeping like snail" (l. 8)
   b. "Sighing like furnace" (l. 10)
   c. "bearded like the pard" (l. 12)

3 In addition to using similes, Shakespeare also uses imagery to describe many of the stages of life. Paraphrase each of the following lines and explain how each contributes to the overall theme:

   a. "Mewling and puking in the nurse's arms" (l. 6)
   b. "Seeking the bubble reputation / Even in the cannon's mouth" (ll. 14–15)
   c. "In fair round belly with good capon lined" (l. 16)
   d. "big manly voice, / Turning again toward childish treble, pipes / And whistles in his sound" (ll. 23–25)

4 There are a number of places where Shakespeare seems to be mocking the representations of man. Identify one of these lines and explain the specific words that he uses for humor.

5 What is the effect of the repetition of the word "sans" in the last line?

6 Each of the stages does not receive the same number of lines: some are longer and some are shorter. Look back through the speech to identify the "ages" with the fewest and most number of lines. What significance can you place on these choices?

7 What is Shakespeare's tone toward each of the stages of life? How does this tone change or shift as the speech progresses? Rewrite one or more of the ages with different words that change the tone.

Connecting, Arguing, and Extending

1 In the opening lines of the speech, Jaques implies that both men and women are included in these ages of "man." How would his monologue be different if it were specifically about the seven ages of "woman"? Write a line or two that would reflect one or more of these ages.

2 Jaques, the character from the play who speaks these lines, presents humankind as pretty foolish throughout all seven stages of life. Write a piece in which you argue that Jaques's representation of our foolishness is either accurate or not. Be sure to use your own experiences and other real-life events along with lines from the play to support your response.

3 *As You Like It* was first performed in 1603. Think about how this excerpt from the play would be similar or different if it were written today. Consider differences such as changes in available professions, medical care, life expectancy, technology, transportation, and so on. Then, in poetry or prose, write the "Seven Ages of Twenty-First-Century Man (or Woman)" to reflect today's stages of life. Or, using magazine cutouts or your own drawings, construct a contemporary "Seven Ages of Man" collage.

Eveline

James Joyce

James Joyce (1882–1941) is considered one of the most influential writers of the twentieth century. His masterpiece, *Ulysses*, takes the myth of the *Odyssey* and updates it to contemporary Ireland. While often recognized for his novels, Joyce was also a highly acclaimed short-story writer. This story is taken from his collection *Dubliners*, which he finished writing in 1904 at the age of twenty-two but was not able to publish until 1914. The story focuses on the difficult choices faced by Eveline, a young Irish woman: should she stay with her family and the only home she has known, or leave with a young man for the promise of something new?

She sat at the window watching the evening invade the avenue. Her head was leaned against the window curtains and in her nostrils was the odour of dusty cretonne.[1] She was tired.

Few people passed. The man out of the last house passed on his way home; she heard his footsteps clacking along the concrete pavement and afterwards crunching on the cinder path before the new red houses. One time there used to be a field there in which they used to play every evening with other people's children. Then a man from Belfast bought the field and built houses in it — not like their little brown houses but bright brick houses with shining roofs. The children of the avenue used to play together in that field — the Devines, the Waters, the Dunns, little Keogh the cripple, she and her brothers and sisters. Ernest, however, never played: he was too grown up. Her father used often to hunt them in out of the field with his blackthorn stick; but usually little Keogh used to keep nix[2] and call out when he saw her father coming. Still they seemed to have been rather happy then. Her father was not so bad then; and besides, her mother was alive. That was a long time ago; she and her brothers and sisters were all grown up her mother was dead. Tizzie Dunn was dead, too, and the Waters had gone back to England. Everything changes. Now she was going to go away like the others, to leave her home.

Home! She looked round the room, reviewing all its familiar objects which she had dusted once a week for so many years, wondering where on earth all the dust came from. Perhaps she would never see again those familiar objects from which she had never dreamed of being divided. And yet during all those years she had never found out the name of the priest whose yellowing photograph hung on the wall above the broken harmonium[3] beside the coloured print of the promises made to Blessed Margaret Mary Alacoque. He had been a school friend of her father. Whenever he showed the photograph to a visitor her father used to pass it with a casual word:

"He is in Melbourne now."

5   She had consented to go away, to leave her home. Was that wise? She tried to weigh each side of the question. In her home anyway she

---

[1]cretonne: Heavy cotton fabric used for upholstery. —Eds.
[2]keep nix: Keep watch. —Eds.

[3]harmonium: A small organ powered by a foot-operated bellows. —Eds.

had shelter and food; she had those whom she had known all her life about her. Of course she had to work hard, both in the house and at business. What would they say of her in the Stores when they found out that she had run away with a fellow? Say she was a fool, perhaps; and her place would be filled up by advertisement. Miss Gavan would be glad. She had always had an edge on her, especially whenever there were people listening.

"Miss Hill, don't you see these ladies are waiting?"

"Look lively, Miss Hill, please."

She would not cry many tears at leaving the Stores.

But in her new home, in a distant unknown country, it would not be like that. Then she would be married — she, Eveline. People would treat her with respect then. She would not be treated as her mother had been. Even now, though she was over nineteen, she sometimes felt herself in danger of her father's violence. She knew it was that that had given her the palpitations. When they were growing up he had never gone for her like he used to go for Harry and Ernest, because she was a girl but latterly he had begun to threaten her and say what he would do to her only for her dead mother's sake. And no she had nobody to protect her. Ernest was dead and Harry, who was in the church decorating business, was nearly always down somewhere in the country. Besides, the invariable squabble for money on Saturday nights had begun to weary her unspeakably. She always gave her entire

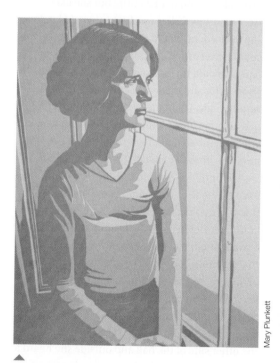

Mary Plunkett is an Irish artist, graphic designer, and printmaker who specializes in letterpress. She created these images based on the story "Eveline."

Look carefully at each image, identifying a specific phrase or sentence that likely inspired Plunkett, and explain Plunkett's interpretation of Joyce's words.

wages — seven shillings — and Harry always sent up what he could but the trouble was to get any money from her father. He said she used to squander the money, that she had no head, that he wasn't going to give her his hard-earned money to throw about the streets, and much more, for he was usually fairly bad on Saturday night. In the end he would give her the money and ask her had she any intention of buying Sunday's dinner. Then she had to rush out as quickly as she could and do her marketing, holding her black leather purse tightly in her hand as she elbowed her way through the crowds and returning home late under her load of provisions. She had hard work to keep the house together and to see that the two young children who had been left to her charge went to school regularly and got their meals regularly. It was hard work — a hard life — but now that she was about to leave it she did not find it a wholly undesirable life.

10   She was about to explore another life with Frank. Frank was very kind, manly, open-hearted. She was to go away with him by the night-boat to be his wife and to live with him in Buenos Ayres where he had a home waiting for her. How well she remembered the first time she had seen him; he was lodging in a house on the main road where she used to visit. It seemed a few weeks ago. He was standing at the gate, his peaked cap pushed back on his head and his hair tumbled forward over a face of bronze. Then they had come to know each other. He used to meet her outside the Stores every evening and see her home. He took her to see *The Bohemian Girl* and she felt elated as she sat in an unaccustomed part of the theatre with him. He was awfully fond of music and sang a little. People knew that they were courting and, when he sang about the lass that loves a sailor, she always felt pleasantly confused. He used to call her Poppens out of fun. First of all it had been an excitement for her to have a fellow and

then she had begun to like him. He had tales of distant countries. He had started as a deck boy at a pound a month on a ship of the Allan Line going out to Canada. He told her the names of the ships he had been on and the names of the different services. He had sailed through the Straits of Magellan and he told her stories of the terrible Patagonians. He had fallen on his feet in Buenos Ayres, he said, and had come over to the old country just for a holiday. Of course, her father had found out the affair and had forbidden her to have anything to say to him.

"I know these sailor chaps," he said.

One day he had quarrelled with Frank and after that she had to meet her lover secretly.

The evening deepened in the avenue. The white of two letters in her lap grew indistinct. One was to Harry; the other was to her father. Ernest had been her favourite but she liked Harry too. Her father was becoming old lately, she noticed; he would miss her. Sometimes he could be very nice. Not long before, when she had been laid up for a day, he had read her out a ghost story and made toast for her at the fire. Another day, when their mother was alive, they had all gone for a picnic to the Hill of Howth. She remembered her father putting on her mother's bonnet to make the children laugh.

Her time was running out but she continued to sit by the window, leaning her head against the window curtain, inhaling the odour of dusty cretonne. Down far in the avenue she could hear a street organ playing. She knew the air. Strange that it should come that very night to remind her of the promise to her mother, her promise to keep the home together as long as she could. She remembered the last night of her mother's illness; she was again in the close dark room at the other side of the hall and outside she heard a melancholy air of Italy. The organ-player had been ordered to go away and given sixpence. She remembered her father strutting back into the sickroom saying:

15   "Damned Italians! coming over here!"

As she mused the pitiful vision of her mother's life laid its spell on the very quick of her being — that life of commonplace sacrifices closing in final craziness. She trembled as she heard again her mother's voice saying constantly with foolish insistence:

"Derevaun Seraun! Derevaun Seraun![4]"

She stood up in a sudden impulse of terror. Escape! She must escape! Frank would save her. He would give her life, perhaps love, too. But she wanted to live. Why should she be unhappy? She had a right to happiness. Frank would take her in his arms, fold her in his arms. He would save her.

She stood among the swaying crowd in the station at the North Wall. He held her hand and she knew that he was speaking to her, saying something about the passage over and over again. The station was full of soldiers with brown baggages. Through the wide doors of the sheds she caught a glimpse of the black mass of the boat, lying in beside the quay[5] wall, with illumined portholes. She answered nothing. She felt her cheek pale and cold and, out of a maze of distress, she prayed to God to direct her, to show her what was her duty. The boat blew a long mournful whistle into the mist. If she went, tomorrow she would be on the sea with Frank, steaming towards Buenos Ayres. Their passage had been booked. Could she still draw back after all he had done for her? Her distress awoke a nausea in her body and she kept moving her lips in silent fervent prayer.

20   A bell clanged upon her heart. She felt him seize her hand:

"Come!"

Erich Lessing/Art Resource, NY

▲

Look at this painting, *Girl at a Window Reading a Letter*, by Jan Vermeer. It was created around 1659, over two hundred years before this short story was written.

What elements found in the painting would apply to the character of Eveline and her situation, and what elements would not?

All the seas of the world tumbled about her heart. He was drawing her into them: he would drown her. She gripped with both hands at the iron railing.

"Come!"

No! No! No! It was impossible. Her hands clutched the iron in frenzy. Amid the seas she sent a cry of anguish.

25   "Eveline! Evvy!"

He rushed beyond the barrier and called to her to follow. He was shouted at to go on but he still called to her. She set her white face to him, passive, like a helpless animal. Her eyes gave him no sign of love or farewell or recognition.

---

[4]Gaelic for "The end of pleasure is pain." —Eds.

[5]quay: Concrete walkway along or extending out over a body of water used as a loading area for ships. Similar to a pier, or jetty. —Eds.

Understanding and Interpreting

1 "Eveline" focuses on the central character's decision-making process. What are the conflicting forces pulling Eveline in different directions? Identify and discuss at least three.

2 What is the nature of the relationship Eveline has with her father? In what ways has it changed over time?

3 Eveline thinks of Frank in fairly general terms: he is "very kind, manly, open-hearted" (par. 10). What more specific information does James Joyce give us? What is it about Frank that appeals to Eveline?

4 Joyce characterizes the existence of Eveline's mother as "that life of commonplace sacrifices closing in final craziness" (par. 16). In what ways is Eveline influenced by her mother's life? How does her perception of her mother's experience affect the way Eveline thinks of marriage?

5 Is Eveline a victim of her time and place—when opportunities for women were limited primarily to the domestic realm—or is she a victim of her own indecisive character? Or is she a combination of both? Support your response with reference to specific passages in the story as well as your knowledge of the time period.

6 Critics of "Eveline" disagree on their interpretations of the ending. Many conclude that Eveline's inability to strike out with Frank is essentially accepting a life sentence as a housekeeper, even a servant, to her family. Others argue that in choosing to stay with her father, she defies Frank and thus shows at least the promise of becoming an independent woman. Which interpretation do you find most plausible? Support your response with references and specific passages from the story.

Analyzing Language, Style, and Structure

1 What is the feeling Joyce conveys in the opening paragraph? What specific words and images contribute to that feeling? What is the effect of this paragraph's being a third person observation while the rest of the story is told from Eveline's perspective?

2 Much of "Eveline" centers on Eveline's home life, both before and after her mother's death. Joyce ends paragraph 2 with the sentence, "Now she was going to go away like the others, to leave her home." He opens the next paragraph with the one word, "Home!" What does this repetition suggest about the meaning(s) of home to Eveline?

3 What symbolic value does Buenos Aires have in this story?

4 The last few paragraphs of the story takes place at the dock. Water is both literal (for example, the sea) and metaphoric (for example, "All the seas of the world tumbled about her heart"). How do these images contribute to our understanding of Eveline's decision not to go with Frank?

5 Joyce explores the difficulty characters have in making important life decisions in several stories in *Dubliners*. In what ways does he demonstrate that Eveline is paralyzed or unable to take action? Pay attention to concrete descriptive details, connotative language, and imagery.

6 In this brief story, Joyce gives us glimpses of the past and the (imagined) future as well as the present. How do the past and future inform Eveline's present thinking?

Connecting, Arguing, and Extending

1 Joyce writes that as "the evening deepened in the avenue" (par. 13), Eveline sits with two letters in her lap, one to her father, the other to her brother Harry. What do you imagine she has written in those letters? Try writing one and explain what in the story leads you to believe would be in the letter.

2 The photo below shows Dublin at about the time "Eveline" was set. How does the mood in this contemporary image of Dublin compare to the mood that Joyce creates in "Eveline"? What creates the mood in "Eveline" and in this photograph?

© Bettmann/Corbis

3 One of the themes Joyce explores in "Eveline" is the tension between responsibility (to family, to community) and the desire for individual freedom. To what extent do you find the way that tension plays out in today's society similar to the way Eveline experienced it? In what ways have you experienced something similar to the choice that Eveline has to face?

4 Suppose that Eveline goes to Buenos Aires with Frank. Write a letter in her voice — a year later — describing her new life to her brother Harry. Think about how her audience would influence what she would say and how she would say it.

from Souvenir of the Carlisle Indian School

The following images come from a pamphlet called *Souvenir of the Carlisle Indian School*, published in 1902.

KEY CONTEXT By the end of the nineteenth century, American westward expansion had driven much of the native population of American Indians onto reservations. As part of the policy of the day, many American Indian children were compelled to attend public schools, either day or boarding schools. The first off-reservation boarding school was the Carlisle Indian Industrial School in Pennsylvania, founded in 1879 by Richard Henry Pratt, who was a general in the army with over nine years' experience fighting the American Indians of the Great Plains. The school's motto at Carlisle, often ascribed to Pratt, was "To civilize the Indian, get him into civilization. To keep him civilized, let him stay." To that end, children at Indian schools were often forbidden to speak their native language, and they were required to dress in the manner of white students and leave behind the cultural and religious practices they had grown up with. What you will see in many of these photographs are "before" and "after" shots: how the students looked upon arrival at the Carlisle school and how they looked after they had been there a while.

Eskimo Group

From John N. Choate's Souvenir of the Carlisle Indian School (Carlisle, PA: J. N. Choate, 1902)/Archives & Special Collections at Dickinson College

As they entered Carlisle in 1897.

From John N. Choate's Souvenir of the Carlisle Indian School (Carlisle, PA: J. N. Choate, 1902)/Archives & Special Collections at Dickinson College

As they appear in school dress.

Tom Torlino–Navajo

John N. Choate, Carlisle, PA, National Archives and Records Administration

John N. Choate, Carlisle, PA, National Archives and Records Administration

As he entered the school in 1882.

As he appeared three years later.

Wounded Yellow Robe, Henry Standing Bear, Chauncy Yellow Robe

From John N. Choate's Souvenir of the Carlisle Indian School (Carlisle, PA: J. N. Choate, 1902)/Archives & Special Collections at Dickinson College

From John N. Choate's Souvenir of the Carlisle Indian School (Carlisle, PA: J. N. Choate, 1902)/Archives & Special Collections at Dickinson College

Sioux boys as they entered the school in 1883.

Three years later.

Group of Pueblo Girls

From John N. Choate's Souvenir of the Carlisle Indian School (Carlisle, PA: J. N. Choate, 1902)/Archives & Special Collections at Dickinson College

Entered Carlisle in 1884.

seeing connections

The following excerpt is from *The School Days of an Indian Girl*, a memoir by Zitkala-Sa (1876–1938). Zitkala-Sa taught music at the Carlisle School from 1899 to 1901 but was fired after publishing this memoir, which is critical of her own school experience and the overall philosophy of forcing American Indians to adopt the cultural identities of white Americans.

In this section of her memoir, Zitkala-Sa describes having her hair cut against her will, in a short style called "shingling" that you can see in the image above.

from **The School Days of an Indian Girl**

Late in the morning, my friend Judéwin gave me a terrible warning. Judéwin knew a few words of English, and she had overheard the paleface woman talk about cutting our long, heavy hair. Our mothers had taught us that only unskilled warriors who were captured had their hair shingled by the enemy. Among our people, short hair was worn by mourners, and shingled hair by cowards!

We discussed our fate some moments, and when Judéwin said, "We have to submit, because they are strong," I rebelled.

"No, I will not submit! I will struggle first!" I answered.

I watched my chance, and when no one noticed I disappeared. I crept up the stairs as quietly as I could in my squeaking shoes — my moccasins had been exchanged for shoes. Along the hall I passed, without knowing whither I was going. Turning aside to an open door, I found a large room with three white beds in it. The windows were covered with dark green curtains, which made the room very dim. Thankful that no one was there, I directed my steps toward the corner farthest from the door. On my hands and knees I crawled under the bed, and cuddled myself in the dark corner.

5   From my hiding place I peered out, shuddering with fear whenever I heard footsteps nearby. Though in the hall loud voices were calling my name, and I knew that even Judéwin was searching for me, I did not open my mouth to answer. Then the steps were quickened and the voices became excited. The sounds came nearer and nearer. Women and girls entered the room. I held my breath, and watched them open closet doors and peep behind large trunks. Some one threw up the curtains, and the room was filled with sudden light. What caused them to stoop and look under the bed I do not know. I remember being dragged out, though I resisted by kicking and scratching wildly. In spite of myself, I was carried downstairs and tied fast in a chair.

How do the ideas in this diary entry affect your reading of the photos from the Carlisle Indian School?

Gertrude Kasebier, Division of Culture & the Arts, National Museum of American History, Smithsonian Institution

I cried aloud, shaking my head all the while until I felt the cold blades of the scissors against my neck, and heard them gnaw off one of my thick braids. Then I lost my spirit. Since the day I was taken from my mother I had suffered extreme indignities. People had stared at me. I had been tossed about in the air like a wooden puppet. And now my long hair was shingled like a coward's! In my anguish I moaned for my mother, but no one came to comfort me. Not a soul reasoned quietly with me, as my own mother used to do; for now I was only one of many little animals driven by a herder.

Understanding and Interpreting

1 Several of the images document children on their arrival at Carlisle School and then sometime later after they have been at the school for a while. What are the significant differences between each "before" and "after" shot? How do these images connect to the school's motto identified in the Key Context note on page 167?

2 *Juxtaposition* is the placement of two or more things near each other for the purpose of comparison or contrast. The "before" and "after" photographs here have been deliberately juxtaposed. Explain the effect of this juxtaposition by considering how the meaning would have been different had you only seen the "after" images.

3 These images that you are looking at in the early twenty-first century were taken near the turn of the twentieth century. How might your interpretation of these images differ from that of someone looking at them one hundred years ago? Why do you think this is? What has changed in our society and culture?

4 To what extent do the photographs prove that the school was successful in achieving its motto: "To civilize the Indian, get him into civilization. To keep him civilized, let him stay"?

Analyzing Language, Style, and Structure

1 Look back through the images carefully to see if there are differences in the way the individuals are positioned in the "before" and "after" photographs. How do the children relate to one another physically (for example, in the placement of their arms and legs, in relative proximity)? What inferences can you draw about the intended effect of the differences between the "before" and "after" pictures?

2 Look back more closely at the pictures of Tom Torlino, which are a fairly well-known pair of images. If you look at the "after" picture, it appears that

Torlino's skin color is significantly lighter than it was when he first arrived. Some historians have suggested this was an intentional choice by the photographer. If this is true, why do you think the photographer would do this?

3 Look back once more at the pictures of Tom Torlino. What is the most striking difference apart from the clothing? How does the first photo contrast with traditional Western notions of masculinity? Is the first or second image more threatening? What details contribute to your response to this last question?

Connecting, Arguing, and Extending

1 Look back through pictures of yourself, a friend, or a family member, and try to locate a pair of pictures that show a significant change in appearance over time. What were the internal and external forces that led to these changes? In what ways do the changes reflect pressures similar to the ones that the Native Americans at the Carlisle School faced?

2 Based only on the brief context you were provided at the start of this text and on the images you examined, write a diary entry from the perspective of a young American Indian on the day of his or her arrival at the Carlisle School, and then another entry a few months later. Try to focus your entries by addressing one or more of the essential questions about identity you have been thinking about throughout this chapter.

3 An organization called the Boarding School Healing Project has been working to raise awareness of the lasting effects of schools such as Carlisle, and pushing for reparations, which is a legal term for paying money to or otherwise compensating a group of people who have been wronged or their descendants. The Healing Project claims that the students at schools like Carlisle were subjected to human rights violations, including malnutrition, cultural and religious repression, inadequate medical care, and physical abuse. Do you agree or disagree with the payment of reparations to these students or their descendants? Why?

ENTERING THE CONVERSATION
CHANGES AND TRANSFORMATIONS

Making Connections

1 Reread the "Seven Ages of Man" speech from Shakespeare's *As You Like It* (p. 159), and apply the stages Jaques describes to the characters—major or minor—from two or more texts from this Conversation. In other words, where do the characters fall in his definitions, and why do you say this?

2 Jon Krakauer (p. 125) and Eveline from the story by James Joyce (p. 162) face the difficult decision of leaving behind the known and setting off into the unknown. Compare and contrast their circumstances and motivations. Then explain why Krakauer chose the unknown while Eveline did not.

3 "Zolaria" (p. 144) and "Eveline" (p. 162) are both considered to be "coming of age" stories, in which the protagonists learn to face the world more as adults than as children. What do the protagonists of "Zolaria" and "Eveline" each learn about the world and themselves? How are their coming of age experiences similar or different?

4 The photographs from the Carlisle Indian School (pp. 168–69) and the excerpt from *The School Days of an Indian Girl* (pp. 170–71) show the effects of change or transformation that is forced on someone rather than chosen by the individual. Compare the powerlessness of the American Indians in these texts with the powerlessness that the speakers in the two Sharon Olds poems feel in the face of their children's changes.

Synthesizing Sources

1 One of the key factors in shaping our identities is the role that parents, guardians, teachers, and other adults play in our lives. Write an essay in which you examine the influence — good or bad — that parents, guardians, or other adults have in the development of the identities of young people. Refer to two or more texts in this Conversation.

2 Do you think that you would be the same person you are today if you lived in a different part of the country or the world, a different time period, or even went to a different school? In other words, how much does the environment around us affect our identities? Respond by considering both your own experiences and those described in two or more texts in this Conversation.

3 Characters in stories, like people in real life, make choices that can lead to positive or negative outcomes. Choose two protagonists from the texts in this Conversation that make difficult decisions. Write a letter or email from one character to the other, offering suggestions on the appropriate choices to make. Then, write a letter or email in response to that character's

suggestion. In both cases, be sure to maintain the voice and attitude of the protagonists in the texts.

4 What is the most significant factor in determining one's identity? Culture, family, friends, or something else? Refer to your own experiences, as well as at least two texts in the Conversation.

5 Is it better to take risks like Jon Krakauer, or play it safe like Eveline? At what point is too much change too risky, and at what point does too little change become stagnation? Refer to your own experiences, as well as at least two texts in the Conversation.

6 A number of the texts in this Conversation address the transition from innocence to experience. Think of at least two protagonists from the texts in this Conversation. Compare or contrast a transition that you are facing to that confronted by two or more protagonists from the texts in this Conversation.

CONVERSATION

THE INDIVIDUAL IN SCHOOL

At this point in your life, you have spent nearly ten years in school, which translates into roughly ten thousand hours. On most days, you spend more time doing school-related work than you do at any other activity other than sleeping. Kurt Vonnegut wrote that high school "is closer to the core of the American experience than anything else I can think of." Clearly, school must be seen as one of the most significant influences on your life and your identity. The question is what kind of influence it has on you.

▶

The top image, which was produced in 1910 in France, imagines what school might be like in the year 2000. The bottom image shows an actual twenty-first-century classroom.

What is the implicit message about education in the top image, and how does this prediction compare to the bottom image?

Thomas Trutschel/Phototek/Getty Images

There are some who believe that in addition to teaching students the skills and knowledge they need to be successful later in life, school is supposed to indoctrinate students to become model citizens by teaching them the behaviors, attitudes, and beliefs of the dominant social and political culture. Consider the following statement about the purpose of school from Henry Ward Beecher, a popular clergyman of the mid-nineteenth century who sought to abolish slavery:

> The common schools are the stomachs of the country in which all people that come to us are assimilated within a generation. When a lion eats an ox, the lion does not become an ox but the ox becomes a lion.

In other words, a main purpose of school is to assimilate those who are different so that everyone becomes the same "lion." Contrast Beecher with this passage from *Democracy and Education*, written by education reformer John Dewey in 1916:

> How one person's abilities compare in quantity with those of another is none of the teacher's business. It is irrelevant to his work. What is required is that every individual shall have opportunities to employ his own powers in activities that have meaning. Mind, individual method, originality (these are convertible terms) signify the *quality* of purposive or directed action.

It is clear from this passage that Dewey does not think that school should be about assimilation, but rather about individuals having the opportunity to develop their own skills and knowledge as determined by their unique needs and interests.

In this Conversation, you will have an opportunity to think about the role of an individual's identity within the larger community of school. You will read mostly nonfiction pieces about the pressures of popularity in high school, the positive and negative effects that teachers have, and the arguments for and against public schooling. And, having logged so many hours as a part of the school community yourself, at the end of the Conversation, you will have an opportunity to add your own expert voice to the debate.

TEXTS

Alexandra Robbins / *from* The Geeks Shall Inherit the Earth (nonfiction)
Faith Erin Hicks / *from* Friends with Boys (graphic novel)
John Taylor Gatto / Against School (nonfiction)
Horace Mann / *from* The Common School Journal (nonfiction)
Theodore Sizer / *from* Horace's School: Redesigning the American High School (nonfiction)
Maya Angelou / *from* I Know Why the Caged Bird Sings (memoir)

from The Geeks Shall Inherit the Earth

Alexandra Robbins

Reporter and lecturer Alexandra Robbins is a graduate of Yale University and the author of *Pledged* (2004), which describes the secretive world of college sororities, and *The Overachievers* (2006), which documents the overwhelming academic pressures that today's high school students face. For *The Geeks Shall Inherit the Earth* (2011), Robbins followed seven high school students from private, public, suburban, and inner city schools from all over the country for a year, all of whom, she says in the introduction, have "more in common than they know."

Courtesy Alexandra Robbins

KEY CONTEXT   In the prologue to her book, Robbins writes:

> Early 2011. Bullying in school has recently driven several teenagers to suicide. Exclusion and clique warfare are so rampant that the media declares bullying an epidemic and rallies for the public to view the tragedies as a national wake-up call.
>
> Throngs of students who are not outright bullied are disheartened because it is getting increasingly more difficult to become an "insider," to fit into a group, to be accepted as "normal." Students feel trapped, despairing that in today's educational landscape, they either have to conform to the popular crowd's arbitrary standards — forcing them to hide their true selves — or face dismissive treatment that batters relentlessly at their souls.
>
> Schools struggle to come up with solutions. Even the most beloved parents are met with disbelief when they insist, "This too shall pass." Adults tell students that it gets better, that the world changes after school, that being "different" will pay off sometime after graduation.
>
> But no one explains to them why.
>
> Enter quirk theory.

In the excerpt that follows, you will read about the social and biological pressures to conform that students face and the difficulty students have in maintaining their individuality in the larger environment of high school. Throughout the book, Robbins profiles several students, following and interviewing them throughout a school year. This section focuses on Whitney, called the "popular bitch," who tries to have friendships outside the popular clique, of which she is a member.

Introduction

CAFETERIA FRINGE: People who are not part of or who are excluded from a school's or society's in crowd.

In the decade I've spent examining various microcosms of life in U.S. schools — from the multitude of students pressured to succeed in school and sports to the twentysomething products of this educational Rube Goldberg machine — a disturbing pattern has emerged. Young people are trying frantically to force themselves into an unbending mold of expectations, convinced that they live in a two-tiered system in which they are either a resounding success or they have already failed. And the more they try to squeeze themselves into that shrinking, allegedly normative space, the faster the walls close in.

The students outside these walls are the kids who typically are not considered part of the in crowd, the ones who are excluded, blatantly or subtly, from the premier table in the lunchroom. I refer to them as "cafeteria fringe." Whether alone or in groups, these geeks, loners, punks, floaters, nerds, freaks, dorks, gamers, bandies, art kids, theater geeks, choir kids, Goths, weirdos, indies, scenes, emos, skaters, and various types of racial and other minorities are often relegated to subordinate social status simply because they are, or seem to be, even the slightest bit different.

Students alone did not create these boundaries. The No Child Left Behind law, a disproportionate emphasis on SATs, APs, and other standardized tests, and a suffocating homogenization of the U.S. education system have all contributed to a rabidly conformist atmosphere that stifles unique people, ideas, and expression. The methods that schools and government officials claimed would improve America's "progress" are the same methods that hold back the students who are most likely to further that progress.

In precisely the years that we should be embracing differences among students, urging them to pursue their divergent interests at full throttle, we're instead forcing them into a skyline of sameness, muffling their voices, grounding their dreams. The result? As a Midwestern senior told me for my book *The Overachievers,* high schoolers view life as "a conveyor belt," making monotonous scheduled stops at high school, college, graduate school, and a series of jobs until death. Middle schools in North America have been called "the Bermuda triangle of education." Only 22 percent of U.S. youth socialize with people of another race. U.S. students have some of the highest rates of emotional problems and the most negative views of peer culture among countries surveyed by the World Health Organization. [. . .]

QUIRK THEORY: Many of the differences that cause a student to be excluded in school are the same traits or real-world skills that others will value, love, respect, or find compelling about that person in adulthood and outside of the school setting.

5   Quirk theory suggests that popularity in school is not a key to success and satisfaction in adulthood. Conventional notions of popularity are wrong. What if popularity is not the same thing as social success? What if students who are considered outsiders aren't really socially inadequate at all? Being an outsider doesn't necessarily indicate any sort of social failing. We do not view a tuba player as musically challenged if he cannot play the violin. He's just a different kind of musician. A sprinter is still considered an athlete even if she can't play basketball. She's a different kind of athlete. Rather than view the cafeteria fringe as less socially successful than the popular crowd, we could simply accept that they are a different kind of social.

. . .

To investigate the cause and consequence of the gut-wrenching social landscape that characterizes too many schools, I followed seven "main characters" — real people — for a year and interviewed hundreds of other students, teachers, and counselors individually and in groups. I talked with students from public schools, private schools, technical schools, schools for the arts, boarding schools, college prep academies, inner city schools, small rural schools, and suburban schools. They have more in common than they know. [. . .]

Whitney, New York | The Popular Bitch

Before leaving home for her last first day of high school, Whitney glanced at herself in all of her mirrors for the seventeenth time: the large mirror above her dresser, the small one by her TV for scrutinizing hair and makeup, and the full-length one behind her door. She had spent two hours getting ready this morning. Her white-blonde hair, highlighted from a summer of lifeguarding, cascaded to her shoulders in meticulously crafted, loose, bouncy curls behind a funky knit headband that she wore so she'd have an excuse to brag that members of a famous rock group had complimented her on it. Several bracelets dangled from her wrist, still tan from cheerleading camp the week before. Her makeup was flawless, accentuated by a smattering of glitter above her eyes; it looked good now, but she knew she would check her makeup again in the school bathroom three or four times that day, hunting for imperfections and correcting them with her Sephora-only arsenal.

People told Whitney all the time that she was pretty, as in beauty pageant pretty or talk show host pretty. Whitney thought this was because of her smile. In her opinion, her straight white teeth slightly made up for her body, which dissatisfied her when she compared it to her

friends'. When they went to the local diner together, the girls did not eat; they only sat and watched the guys stuff their faces. If the girls were really hungry, the most they would order in front of the group was lemon water.

Whitney checked her makeup again in the kitchen mirror, forced herself to guzzle a Slim-Fast shake to jump-start her metabolism, grabbed her Coach purse, lacrosse bag, and book bag, and ran out the door, pausing briefly at the mirror in the foyer. She drove too quickly into the school parking lot, unapologetically cutting off people on her way, and parked her SUV crookedly, taking up two spots, but leaving it there anyway because she could. She met up with Giselle, her best friend until recently. Giselle, who had been the schoolwide Homecoming Queen as a sophomore, had become popular through cheerleading and by dating a popular senior — when she was in the eighth grade. "Well, this is it!" Giselle said, and they stepped into the building.

10   Riverland Academy, located in a small town in upstate New York, catered to a mostly white, Christian community. Its four hundred students crowded into the gym, standing in small groups or lining the bleachers. Amidst the chaos, the girls easily spotted their group, which other students called the "preps" or the "populars," in the center of the gym. Bianca, the queen bee, thin and tan, stood with Kendra, a senior; Peyton, a junior; and Madison, Bianca's best friend. Chelsea, the only brunette standing among the populars, had worked her way up from "being a loser," according to Whitney, by "sucking up to Bianca like crazy and giving her information about people." The preps tolerated Chelsea, but didn't include her as a stalwart member of the group. This meant they didn't allow her in their Homecoming limo, but they did invite her to take pictures with them.

A few of the prep boys orbited the girls: Chip and Spencer, hot high-society seniors; Bobby,

seeing connections

Read the following summary of a research experiment that ran in *Scientific American*. The study investigated how peer pressure influences teenagers' tastes in music.

The researchers chose to study adolescents between the ages of 12 and 17, a cohort thought to be highly susceptible to social influence, and known to buy at least one third of albums in the United States. Each participant heard a short clip of a song downloaded from the social-networking website Myspace. Following the clip they were asked to make two ratings, one indicating how familiar they were with the clip (which was always the hook or chorus of the chosen song) and one indicating how much they liked the clip on a five point scale. The clip was then played a second time, and they were again asked to rate how much they liked the song. However, in two thirds of these second trials the teens were shown a popularity rating that was estimated based on the number of times the song was downloaded.

When no information about the popularity of a song was displayed, teens changed their likability rating of the song 12 percent of the time. Not surprisingly, after being shown the popularity of a song, teens changed their ratings more frequently, on average 22 percent of the time. This difference was highly significant, and it is worth noting that among those who changed their likability ratings, 79 percent of the time teens changed their ratings in the direction of the popularity rating—they followed the crowd.

Explain how you see—or don't see—similar types of influence in other areas of teenagers' lives.

a chubby, boisterous football star; and Seth, an overachieving junior. The preps were each on two or more sports teams, partied with college students, and in Whitney's words, "just own[ed] the school."

The girls appraised the surrounding students and whispered to each other, standing as they typically did, one hand on a hip, one knee bent, in what the cheerleading coach referred to as "the hooker's pose." [. . .]

The group caught up briefly before resuming the assessment of the students swarming around them. "Oh my God. Who is that?!" Peyton sniffed, nodding her head toward a band girl.

"That's Shay," Chelsea answered.

15   "Dude, I didn't even recognize her," Peyton said. "Did she gain like fifteen pounds over the summer?! Why did her hair get so big and frizzy?" This led to a discussion about how there were too many skanks and trailer trash kids at Riverland.

The preps took stock of the new freshmen, as they did at the beginning of every year, to decide who was going to be cool and to whom they were going to be mean. They automatically deemed one girl cool because her older sister was dating a prep. The freshman cheerleaders were acceptable. If freshman girls didn't already have something going for them when they got to Riverland — an older boyfriend, a popular sibling, a varsity sport, money, or a parent with connections — they were out of luck. "If we don't know them already by some other affiliation," Whitney said, "they aren't worth getting to know" — and they were automatically labeled skanks. [. . .]

Students gathered together in the bleachers, group by group. The "badasses," allegedly bullies who liked to destroy property, were tossing basketballs in the air. The FFAs, or members of the Future Farmers of America club — the preps called them hicks and rednecks — sat at the end of the bleachers. The wannabes, dressed like their role models but discernible by their whiff of uncertainty, stood at a far corner of the room. Those were the kids who fed the preps' egos. Whitney would walk down the hall like royalty, while the wannabes would gush, "Whitney, you look so pretty today!" or "Whitney, you did such a good job cheering last night!" If a prep girl showed up at school with a shaved head, Whitney was sure the wannabes would visit the salon that night to do the same. It was the fact that they tried so hard that doomed them.

Whitney looked at the punks, who wore tight pants and band shirts. They could scream every word of the music they listened to. They were unafraid to strike up conversations with other groups, but they usually clashed with the preps. As Whitney saw it, the cliques were just too different. Whitney was certain that the punk girls thought the populars were loud and snobby. Besides, she mused, odds were that she and her friends probably had been mean to the punk girls before.

The popular guys referred to the punks as "weird" and "useless." They called Dirk, the punks' alpha male, a scumbag within his earshot. Whitney was as friendly with Dirk as her group allowed, which meant in hallways their communication was limited to awkward eye contact and brief exchanges. She was attracted to Dirk, a funny and talented drummer, but she didn't tell anyone, because a popular cheerleader dating a punk would cause "crazy scandalous controversy" and further escalate the

tension between the groups. She was having enough trouble with the preps as it was.

20   After the welcome-back hug, the preps hardly acknowledged Whitney, though she stood next to them. The group brought up inside jokes and memories from the summer that didn't include her. Whitney recognized this weapon because she had used it before. The preps enjoyed purposely making someone feel bad for not being at an event. If you weren't at a party one weekend, the group wouldn't stop talking about it in front of you until the next party.

Whitney loved the power and perks of popularity. When the teachers began handing out senior schedules at the back of the gym, Whitney's group pushed to the front of the line en masse, as students parted without protest. The teachers didn't bat an eye at the line cut, instead complimenting the girls on their hair and their tans. *We haven't been in school for more than ten minutes and already our egos have grown*, Whitney thought. Her group got away with everything. For example, students who were late to class four times automatically received detention. Not Giselle. She regularly escaped detention because of cheerleading practice, and no one dared complain. [. . .]

Schedules in hand, the preps left the gym before they were dismissed, and strutted toward "their" hallway. Other students walked by the Prep Hall quickly, so as not to attract attention in the area where the preps heckled the "weird kids." By the end of junior year, one such student was so fed up with the preps' rude comments that when they made fun of him for drawing a robot, he lashed out: "You're going to be sorry when I come to school with a gun and kill all of you." The preps didn't say another word to him.

"Ugh," Bianca shouted. "I hate when stupid freshmen don't know how to walk in the hall! You walk on the *right* side of the hallway! Goddamn!"

seeing connections

CADY (V.O.)

Having lunch with the Plastics was like leaving
the actual world and entering "Girl World." And
Girl World had a lot of rules.

GRETCHEN

We only wear jeans or track pants on Friday.
You can't wear a tank top two days in a row.
You can only wear your hair in a ponytail once
a week. So, I guess, you picked today. And if you
break any of these rules you can't sit with us at
lunch. I mean, not just you, any of us. Like, if I
was wearing jeans today, I would be sitting over
there with the art freaks.

▲

This is a film still and a section from the script
of the movie *Mean Girls* (2004).

**How are the rules of the fictional Plastics, and
especially the consequences for violating them,
similar to the pressures that Whitney faces in this
excerpt?**

As the halls filled up, crowds parted for the
preps. Some students said hello, but Whitney
and her friends gave them the "what's-up-but-
I-won't-really-acknowledge-you" head nod.

When Whitney walked into advertising class
with Peyton, she spotted Dirk. "Hey, Whitney!"
he yelled across the room.

"I'm not sitting with Dirk," Peyton whispered
to Whitney. "I don't see why you like those
people. They scare me."

Whitney shrugged and grinned at Dirk as
she sat next to him anyway.

At lunch, the preps cut to the front of the
line, as usual, and sat at "their" lunch table in
the center of the cafeteria. Whitney hadn't
waited in the lunch line since she was a freshman. In the past, when students told the preps
to stop cutting, Whitney's group either ignored
them or shot nasty glares. When the protestors
walked off, the preps would follow them and
make loud comments, such as, "Wow, fat-asses
need their food quickly, don't they?! I mean, do
you really think they *need* that much food? They
look like they could do without lunch once in a
while . . . " Nobody complained anymore.
Because they favored the preps, the teachers in
the room looked the other way.

Before cheer practice that afternoon,
Whitney and Giselle claimed their gym lockers.
It hardly mattered that they always took the
lockers in the back corner of the last row.
When the prep cheerleaders changed their
clothes, the younger athletes waited until the
preps were dressed and gone before going to
their own lockers. Once, an underclassman
tried to squeeze by and accidentally stepped
on Whitney's Ugg boot. "Jesus Christ!
Seriously?!" Whitney yelled. The girl looked
mortified, blurted out a meek "I'm sorry!", and
ran away.

30   As much as she loved being popular, Whitney wished other students understood that it wasn't so easy. Preps were stereotyped like everyone else, she said. "A prep talks like a Valley Girl, thinks she's better than everyone, is obsessed with looks, sleeps around, is usually a cheerleader, doesn't eat, parties all the time, and gets away with murder. Basically, emos want us dead."

Whitney insisted that the prep description didn't fit the "real" Whitney. "I'm not snobby," she said. "I have to be this way because it's what my friends do. If I wasn't like this, I wouldn't have any friends." She loathed the immediate judgments students made about her. She was a cheerleader; therefore she was a slut. She was a class officer; therefore she was stuck up. She wore expensive clothes; therefore she was spoiled. She said "like" too often; therefore she was flaky. She was a prep; therefore she was a bitch.

The funny thing was that if Whitney could have chosen any group at school to belong to, she wouldn't have chosen the clique that intimidated other students with cruelty. She would have chosen to be in what she considered the most nonjudgmental, down-to-earth crew at school: the punks. But it didn't matter. There was no changing groups. Once you were in a group, you were stuck there until graduation, no matter what. That was just the way high school was, Whitney was sure. So she didn't tell a soul.

The Courage of Nonconformists

If there is one trait that most cafeteria fringe share, it is courage. No matter how awkward, timid, or insecure he or she might seem, any teenager who resists blending in with the crowd is brave.

A closer look at this age group's psychology reveals that the deck is stacked against singularity from early on. Studies have shown that children are psychologically drawn to peers who are similar and more likely to end friendships with kids who are different. From the age of five, students increasingly exclude peers who don't conform to group norms. Children learn this lesson quickly. A popular Indiana eighth grader told me, "I have to be the same as everybody else, or people won't like me anymore."

35   Numerous studies show that students in the same social circle tend to have similar levels of academics, leadership, aggression, and cooperation. The most influential kids are also typically the same ones who insist most stridently on conformity; researchers have found that even in late adolescence, popular cliques are more conformist than other groups. Given that many children often try to copy populars' behavior, it makes sense that conformity trickles down the social hierarchy.

But conformity is not an admirable trait. Conformity is a cop-out. It threatens self-awareness. It can lead groups to enforce rigid and arbitrary rules. Adolescent groups with high levels of conformity experience more negative behavior — with group members and outsiders — than do groups with lower levels of conformity. Conformity can become dangerous, leading to unhealthy behaviors, and it goes against a teenager's innate desire to form a unique identity. Why, then, is conformity so common?

In the mid-twentieth century, psychologists discovered that when asked to judge an ambiguous test, such as an optical illusion, individuals usually parroted the opinions of the other people in the room. In the 1950s, social psychologist Solomon Asch decided to gauge levels of conformity when the test answers were absolutely clear. Asch assumed that people wouldn't bother to conform to an incorrect group opinion when the answer was obvious.

Asch was wrong — and his results stunned academia. For the experiment, he brought college students, one by one, into a room with six to eight other participants. He showed the room a picture of one line and a separate picture containing three lines labeled 1, 2, and 3. One of the three lines was the same length as the line in the first picture, while the other two differed by as much as several inches. Asch then had each volunteer call out the number of the line he believed to be the same length as the first. Unbeknownst to the college student, who was the last to be called on, the other participants were in on the experiment. Asch had instructed them to call out the wrong number on twelve out of eighteen trials. At least once, even when the answer was plain to see, nearly three-quarters of the students repeated the group's wrong answer.

Sixty years later, scientists are discovering that there are deeper factors at work than even Asch could have imagined. New research using brain imaging studies suggests that there is a biological explanation for the variation in people's ability to resist the temptation to conform. Neuroscientists monitoring brain images during conformity experiments similar to Asch's have found that participants are not necessarily imitating the majority merely to fit in. Instead, participants' visual perception seems to change to align with the answers of the rest of the group.

40   To understand how this change could take place, it's helpful to know that the brain is an efficient organ that likes to cheat. In order to conserve energy, it takes shortcuts whenever possible, such as the reliance on labels explained earlier. Another shortcut is a concept known as the Law of Large Numbers, a probability theorem according to which, "the more measurements you make of something,

the more accurate the average of these measurements becomes." When the students in Asch's experiment conformed to group opinion, their brains were taking the Law of Large Numbers shortcut, assuming that the opinion of the group was more statistically accurate than any individual's. In 2005, neuroscientist Gregory Berns conducted a similar experiment, this time using MRIs to measure participants' brain activity. Berns observed that deferring to the group took some of the pressure off the decision-making part of the brain.

Berns also noticed something else, as he wrote in his intriguing book *Iconoclast*: "We observed the fear system kicking in, almost like a fail-safe when the individual went against the group. These are powerful biological mechanisms that make it extremely difficult to think like an iconoclast."

Berns saw increased activity in the amygdala when his test subjects did not conform to group opinion. Amygdala activity can lead to a rise in blood pressure and heart rate, sweating, and rapid breathing. "Its activation during non-conformity underscored the unpleasant nature of standing alone — even when the individual had no recollection of it," Berns wrote. "In many people, the brain would rather avoid activating the fear system and just change perception to conform with the social norm." [. . .]

Nonconformists, therefore, aren't just going against the grain; they're going against the *brain*. Either their brains aren't taking the easy way out to begin with, or in standing apart from their peers, these students are standing up to their biology.

Understanding and Interpreting

1 What internal and external conflicts does Whitney face in school as a member of the popular clique? Focus on the pressures she experiences. Find examples of those conflicts to support your point.

2 Alexandra Robbins includes lengthy descriptions of students from the popular clique, including what they are wearing, how they talk, and how they behave. What does the inclusion of these descriptions reveal about Robbins's attitude toward this group? What purpose do these descriptions serve in her argument about nonconformists?

3 What is the reader expected to conclude from the last line of the section about Whitney: "So she didn't tell a soul" (par. 32)?

4 Perhaps unsurprisingly in a book about kids in high school, there are only a few references to adults in this excerpt. Skim back through the first part of the excerpt and identify places where Robbins mentions adults. How do the adults behave? How do they either perpetuate or fight against the social structures she describes? How do you think Robbins feels about the adults' roles in high school?

5 Explain what connections the reader is expected to make between individuality in high school and the Asch experiments (pars. 37–38), and the Berns experiments (pars. 40–42). When have you witnessed similar outcomes in your own day-to-day experience in high school?

6 Summarize the position Robbins takes at the end of the selection about the nonconformists, those whom she refers to as the "cafeteria fringe."

7 Based only upon the information provided in this excerpt, create a simile for popularity as Robbins describes it in this excerpt: Popularity is like _____ because _____. Again, based only on the text, complete the following: Nonconformity is like _____ because _____.

Language, Style, and Structure

1 Robbins invents a concept she calls "quirk theory," likely a play on the physics term "quark theory." Reread the definition following paragraph 4 and explain the effect of Robbins's word choice and why you think she introduces the term where she does.

2 While this excerpt is taken from a book that is considered to be nonfiction, Robbins at times uses a writing style and narrative elements that are much more common in fiction than in most nonfiction books. Look back through the section about Whitney and identify some techniques that you are used to seeing in novels or short stories and explain the effect of Robbins's choices.

3 Reread the section on Whitney (pars. 7–32), looking specifically at the dialogue that Robbins includes. What impression is Robbins trying to create about the popular crowd through this dialogue?

4 What is Robbins's attitude or tone toward Whitney? What specific lines from the text lead you to this conclusion?

5 This excerpt includes sections from two different places in Robbins's book. How are the tones Robbins takes in each section similar to or different from one other? What specific language choices create these tones?

6 List some possible audiences for Robbins's book. Which audience is most likely the audience she had in mind while writing it? What specific language choices, descriptions, and definitions lead you to this conclusion?

7 In this selection, Robbins summarizes the results of several scholarly research experiments. Through her language and structural choices, how does she try to keep her piece interesting to a nonacademic audience? Offer specific examples to support your answer.

Connecting, Arguing, and Extending

1 Robbins presents a school environment with very strict social groupings that have inflexible rules for membership. How is the social situation she describes similar to or different from your own school? You might want to make a diagram of your own school's cafeteria or other public spaces and identify the spots where the various groups of your school gather. How much of this space is exclusive to one group and how much is shared space? Why do you think it is like this?

2 Write an argument in which you agree or disagree with the following conclusion that Robbins draws about high school: "In precisely the years that we should be embracing differences among students, urging them to pursue their divergent interests at full throttle, we're instead forcing them into a skyline of sameness, muffling their voices, grounding their dreams" (par. 4).

3 At the end of her book (not included here), Robbins lists "31 Tips for Students, Parents, Teachers, and Schools." Use the Robbins piece above, as well as your own research and experiences, to write an argument for one step that you think your school, your teachers, or your peers should take in order to help all students feel welcome and accepted by everyone at your school.

4 To what extent is the institution of school itself responsible for the influence that popularity has on students? How do schools use the pressures of conformity that Robbins describes to maintain order and control?

---

from Friends with Boys

Faith Erin Hicks

Faith Erin Hicks is an artist, writer, and animator who lives in Nova Scotia, Canada. She is most well-known for her long-running web comic called *Demonology 101*, which tells the story of a teenage demon named Raven as she struggles to live a normal life in the human world.

Photo by Nathan Boone; Courtesy Faith Erin Hicks

KEY CONTEXT   This excerpt from Hicks's graphic novel *Friends with Boys* focuses on Maggie's first days in a public school after being homeschooled for her whole life.
   Characters in the comic include:

Maggie

Her brother Daniel

Her other brother, Zander

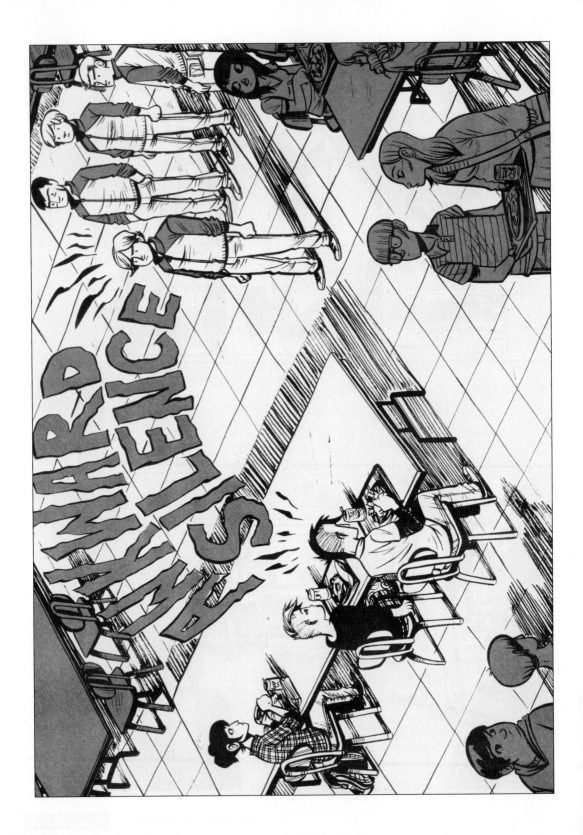

WHATEVER

REMEMBER, TWO WEEKS, CITIZENS! BE A PART OF HISTORY!

SO ARE YOU FRIENDS WITH DANIEL? I SAW YOU WITH HIM BEFORE CLASS—

HE'S MY BROTHER

OH... ARE WE LEAVING?

YEP.

SORRY, GOTTA GO!

NICE MEETING YOU!

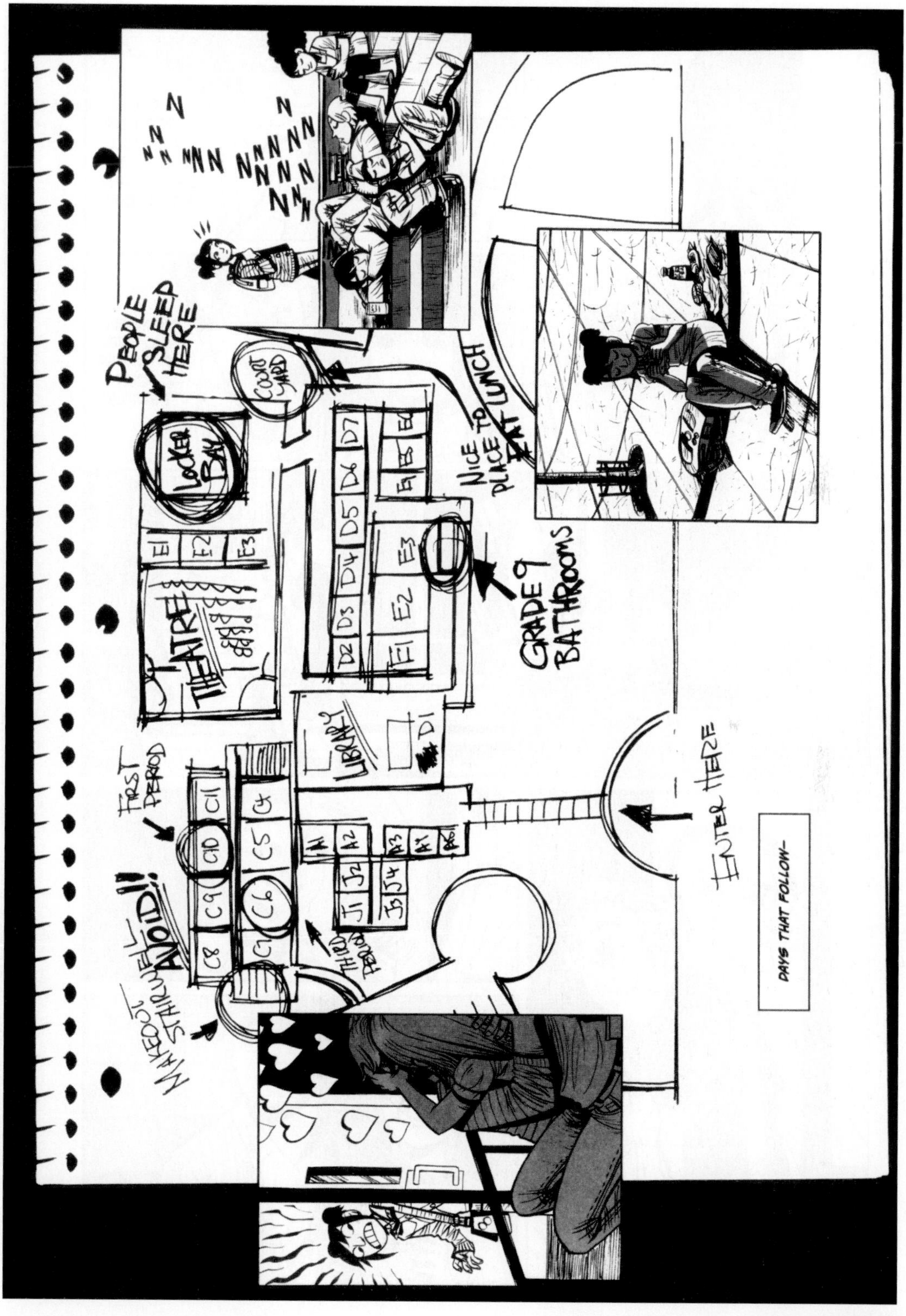
DAYS THAT FOLLOW-
ENTER HERE
MAKEOUT STAIRWELL
AVOID!!
FIRST PERIOD
THIRD PERIOD
LIBRARY?
THEATRE
LOCKER BAY
COURT YARD
PEOPLE SLEEP HERE
NICE PLACE TO EAT LUNCH
GRADE 9 BATHROOMS

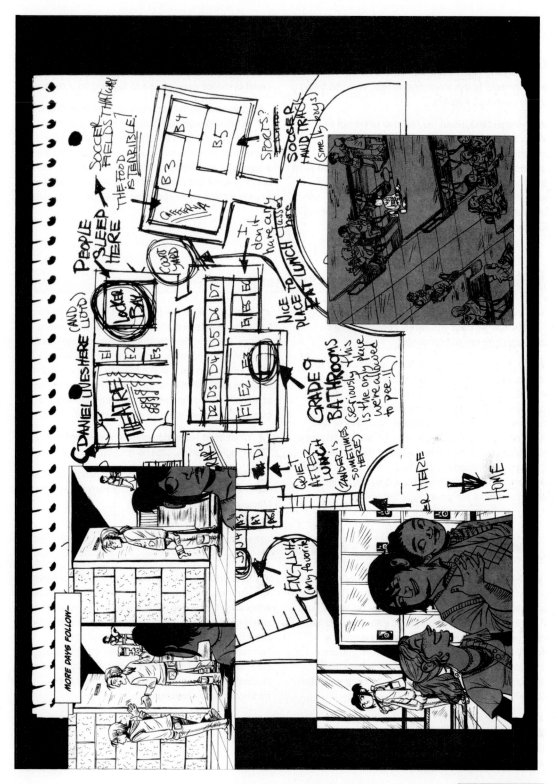

Understanding and Interpreting

1 What seems to be Maggie's biggest fear about attending high school outside her home environment? Is this a reasonable fear, or is she being overly cautious? Explain.

2 Maggie talks about her first day of school as a "rite of passage" (p. 193), an event which is normally considered to be a transition between significant stages in one's life. Looking carefully at all of the panels after she is first on her own, describe at least three rites of passage that Maggie faces on her first day. Does she overcome these challenges or not? Explain.

3 How would you characterize the relationship that Maggie has with her brothers? What textual and visual evidence can you use to support your response?

4 Look back at the two maps that Maggie draws to help her navigate both the building and the social environment of the school. First, what do the places that she chooses to identify reveal about her as a character and her attempts to understand school? Second, what does she add to the second map and what does this show about her development at school?

Analyzing Language, Style, and Structure

1 The first four pages of this piece have no dialogue at all. What does this reveal about Maggie's character and her surroundings?

2 Throughout the excerpt, there are a number of panels in which there is no dialogue and author Faith Erin Hicks relies on the expressions of the characters to suggest specific ideas about school. Select one panel in which there is no dialogue, and write dialogue that would be appropriate for the scene. The dialogue can be either the thoughts of a single character or a discussion between characters. Explain why you chose that dialogue and how the added dialogue affects the meaning of the scene.

3 Look closely at the panels that show the two boys in the cafeteria (pp. 199–201). The author does not provide much context for the conflict: we don't really know who the boys are or why they are fighting. In other words, we are just like Maggie, who is watching from the side. What strategies does Hicks use—lines, shading, framing, angles, text, or other tools of the comic book artist—to portray this conflict?

4 What does Hicks do artistically to establish Maggie as an outcast on her first day of school?

5 How does the author distinguish flashbacks from the present? What do the flashbacks reveal about Maggie?

Connecting, Arguing, and Extending

1 Select a panel in which you can closely identify with what a character is experiencing. This can be any character in the selection. Discuss the visual cues Faith Erin Hicks uses to bring that experience to life, and then compare and contrast your experience to what the character is going through. If you were to draw a panel of a similar experience from your life, what visual cues might you use to bring your story to life?

2 Look back at the two maps that Maggie draws to help her navigate her school. Create your own map for a section of your school and include labels and drawings relevant to your experiences.

3 Maggie's experience shows a lot of the positives and negatives of both homeschooling and public schooling. Which one is more effective at educating students? Locate a research article or two about the benefits and challenges of homeschooling as compared to education in the public schools. How does each group of students perform? Why do some students and parents choose homeschool over traditional school settings?

Against School

John Taylor Gatto

A three-time Teacher of the Year in New York State, John Taylor Gatto (b. 1935) has become one of public schooling's fiercest critics; in fact, he resigned his teaching job in a 1991 editorial in the *Wall Street Journal*, stating "I can't teach this way any longer. If you hear of a job where I don't have to hurt kids to make a living, let me know." The title of one of Gatto's books, *Dumbing Us Down: The Hidden Curriculum of Compulsory Schooling* (2002), reveals his attitude toward the public school system. Gatto notes that it forces attendance and promotes standardization and conformity. In this essay, which was published in the September 2003 issue of *Harper's*, Gatto wonders whether children even need school at all anymore.

John Gatto

I taught for thirty years in some of the worst schools in Manhattan, and in some of the best, and during that time I became an expert in boredom. Boredom was everywhere in my world, and if you asked the kids, as I often did, *why* they felt so bored, they always gave the same answers: They said the work was stupid, that it made no sense, that they already knew it. They said they wanted to be doing something real, not just sitting around. They said teachers didn't seem to know much about their subjects and clearly weren't interested in learning more. And the kids were right: their teachers were every bit as bored as they were.

Boredom is the common condition of schoolteachers, and anyone who has spent time in a teachers' lounge can vouch for the low energy, the whining, the dispirited attitudes, to be found there. When asked why *they* feel bored, the teachers tend to blame the kids, as you might expect. Who wouldn't get bored teaching students who are rude and interested only in grades? If even that. Of course, teachers are themselves products of the same twelve-year compulsory school programs that so thoroughly bore their students, and as school personnel they are trapped inside structures even more rigid than those imposed upon the children. Who, then, is to blame?

We all are. My grandfather taught me that. One afternoon when I was seven I complained to him of boredom, and he batted me hard on the head. He told me that I was never to use that term in his presence again, that if I was bored it was my fault and no one else's. The obligation to amuse and instruct myself was entirely my own, and people who didn't know that were childish people, to be avoided if possible. Certainly not to be trusted. That episode cured me of boredom forever, and here and there over the years I was able to pass on the lesson to some remarkable student. For the most part, however, I found it futile to challenge the official notion that boredom and childishness were the natural state of affairs in the classroom. Often I had to defy custom, and even bend the law, to help kids break out of this trap.

The empire struck back, of course; childish adults regularly conflate opposition with disloyalty. I once returned from a medical leave to discover that all evidence of my having been granted the leave had been purposely destroyed, that my job had been terminated, and that I no longer possessed even a teaching license. After nine months of tormented effort I was able to retrieve the license when a school secretary testified to witnessing the plot unfold. In the meantime my family suffered more than I care to remember. By the time I finally retired in 1991, I had more than enough reason to think of our schools — with their long-term, cell-block-style, forced confinement of both students and teachers — as virtual factories of childishness. Yet I honestly could not see why they had to be that way. My own experience had revealed to me what many other teachers must learn along the way, too, yet keep to themselves for fear of reprisal: if we wanted to we could easily and inexpensively jettison the old, stupid structures and help kids take an education rather than merely receive a schooling. We could encourage the best qualities of youthfulness — curiosity, adventure, resilience, the capacity for surprising insight — simply by being more flexible about time, texts, and tests, by introducing kids to truly competent adults, and by giving each student what autonomy he or she needs in order to take a risk every now and then.

5   But we don't do that. And the more I asked why not, and persisted in thinking about the "problem" of schooling as an engineer might, the more I missed the point: What if there is no "problem" with our schools? What if they are the way they are, so expensively flying in the face of common sense and long experience in how children learn things, not because they are doing something wrong but because they are doing something right? Is it possible that George W. Bush accidentally spoke the truth when he said we would "leave no child behind"? Could it be that our schools are designed to make sure not one of them ever really grows up?

Do we really need school? I don't mean education, just forced schooling: six classes a day, five days a week, nine months a year, for twelve years. Is this deadly routine really necessary? And if so, for what? Don't hide behind reading, writing, and arithmetic as a rationale, because 2 million happy homeschoolers have surely put that banal justification to rest. Even if they hadn't, a considerable number of

Identify a piece of evidence from Gatto's article that would support this character's claim about school.

" I DON'T THINK OF IT AS GOING BACK TO SCHOOL. I THINK OF IT AS A MANDATORY MINIMUM SENTENCE! "

well-known Americans never went through the twelve-year wringer our kids currently go through, and they turned out all right. George Washington, Benjamin Franklin, Thomas Jefferson, Abraham Lincoln? Someone taught them, to be sure, but they were not products of a school system, and not one of them was ever "graduated" from a secondary school.

Throughout most of American history, kids generally didn't go to high school, yet the unschooled rose to be admirals, like Farragut; inventors, like Edison; captains of industry, like Carnegie and Rockefeller; writers, like Melville and Twain and Conrad; and even scholars, like Margaret Mead. In fact, until pretty recently people who reached the age of thirteen weren't looked upon as children at all. Ariel Durant, who co-wrote an enormous, and very good, multi-volume history of the world with her husband, Will, was happily married at fifteen, and who could reasonably claim that Ariel Durant was an uneducated person? Unschooled, perhaps, but not uneducated.

We have been taught (that is, schooled) in this country to think of "success" as synonymous with, or at least dependent upon, "schooling," but historically that isn't true in either an intellectual or a financial sense. And plenty of people throughout the world today find a way to educate themselves without resorting to a system of compulsory secondary schools that all too often resemble prisons. Why, then, do Americans confuse education with just such a system? What exactly is the purpose of our public schools?

Mass schooling of a compulsory nature really got its teeth into the United States between 1905 and 1915, though it was conceived of much earlier and pushed for throughout most of the nineteenth century. The reason given for this enormous upheaval of family life and cultural traditions was, roughly speaking, threefold: 1) To make good people. 2) To make good citizens. 3) To make each person his or her personal best.

10   These goals are still trotted out today on a regular basis, and most of us accept them in one form or another as a decent definition of public education's mission, however short schools actually fall in achieving them. But we are dead wrong. Compounding our error is the fact that the national literature holds numerous and surprisingly consistent statements of compulsory schooling's true purpose. We have, for example, the great H. L. Mencken, who wrote in *The American Mercury* for April 1924 that the aim of public education is not

> to fill the young of the species with knowledge and awaken their intelligence. . . . Nothing could be further from the truth. The aim is simply to reduce as many individuals as possible to the same safe level, to breed and train a standardized citizenry, to put down dissent and originality. That is its aim in the United States . . . and that is its aim everywhere else.

There you have it. Now you know. We don't need Karl Marx's conception of a grand warfare between the classes to see that it is in the interest of complex management, economic or political, to dumb people down, to demoralize them, to divide them from one another, and to discard them if they don't conform. Class may frame the proposition, as when Woodrow Wilson, then president of Princeton University, said the following to the New York City School Teachers Association in 1909: "We want one class of persons to have a liberal education, and we want another class of persons, a very much larger class, of necessity, in every society, to forgo the privileges of a liberal education and fit themselves to perform specific difficult manual tasks." But the motives behind the disgusting decisions that bring about these ends need not be class-based at all. They can stem purely from fear, or from the by now familiar belief that "efficiency" is the paramount virtue, rather than love, liberty, laughter, or hope. Above all, they can stem from simple greed.

seeing connections

The logical extension of Gatto's argument is that students should not be required to attend school.

**Explain why you think Gatto is right, wrong, or maybe just a little off the mark.
How does the accompanying chart from the Bureau of Labor Statistics affect your viewpoint?**

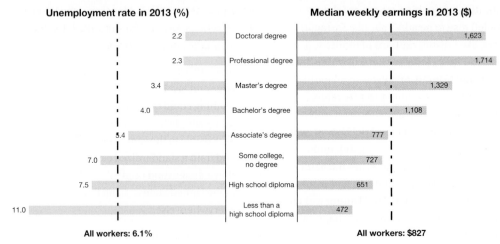

Earnings and unemployment rates by educational attainment

Unemployment rate in 2013 (%)		Median weekly earnings in 2013 ($)
2.2	Doctoral degree	1,623
2.3	Professional degree	1,714
3.4	Master's degree	1,329
4.0	Bachelor's degree	1,108
5.4	Associate's degree	777
7.0	Some college, no degree	727
7.5	High school diploma	651
11.0	Less than a high school diploma	472

All workers: 6.1%   **All workers: $827**

Note: Data are for persons age 25 and over. Earnings are for full-time wage and salary workers.
Source: Current Population Survey, U.S. Bureau of Labor Statistics, U.S. Department of Labor

There were vast fortunes to be made, after all, in an economy based on mass production and organized to favor the large corporation rather than the small business or the family farm. But mass production required mass consumption, and at the turn of the twentieth century most Americans considered it both unnatural and unwise to buy things they didn't actually need. Mandatory schooling was a godsend on that count. School didn't have to train kids in any direct sense to think they should consume nonstop, because it did something even better: it encouraged them not to think at all. And that left them sitting ducks for another great invention of the modern era — marketing.

We buy televisions, and then we buy the things we see on the television. We buy computers, and then we buy the things we see on the computer. We buy $150 sneakers whether we need them or not, and when they fall apart too soon we buy another pair. We drive SUVs and believe the lie that they constitute a kind of life insurance, even when we're upside-down in them. And, worst of all, we don't bat an eye when Ari Fleischer tells us to "be careful what you say," even if we remember having been told somewhere back in school that America is the land of the free. We simply buy that one too. Our schooling, as intended, has seen to it.

Now for the good news. Once you understand the logic behind modern schooling, its tricks and traps are fairly easy to avoid. School trains children to be employees and consumers; teach your own to be leaders and adventurers.

School trains children to obey reflexively; teach your own to think critically and independently. Well-schooled kids have a low threshold for boredom; help your own to develop an inner life so that they'll never be bored. Urge them to take on the serious material, the *grown-up* material, in history, literature, philosophy, music, art, economics, theology — all the stuff schoolteachers know well enough to avoid. Challenge your kids with plenty of solitude so that they can learn to enjoy their own company, to conduct inner dialogues. Well-schooled people are conditioned to dread being alone, and they seek constant companionship through the TV, the computer, the cell phone, and through shallow friendships quickly acquired and quickly abandoned. Your children should have a more meaningful life, and they can.

15 First, though, we must wake up to what our schools really are: laboratories of experimentation on young minds, drill centers for the habits and attitudes that corporate society demands. Mandatory education serves children only incidentally; its real purpose is to turn them into servants. Don't let your own have their childhoods extended, not even for a day. If David Farragut could take command of a captured British warship as a preteen, if Thomas Edison could publish a broadsheet at the age of twelve, if Ben Franklin could apprentice himself to a printer at the same age (then put himself through a course of study that would choke a Yale senior today), there's no telling what your own kids could do. After a long life, and thirty years in the public school trenches, I've concluded that genius is as common as dirt. We suppress our genius only because we haven't yet figured out how to manage a population of educated men and women. The solution, I think, is simple and glorious. Let them manage themselves.

Understanding and Interpreting

1 What is the main claim that John Taylor Gatto makes? Find one sentence that states his claim.

2 Gatto begins his essay with an examination of boredom. What does he say causes this boredom and what is the result?

3 Gatto says that the purpose of mandatory education offered by society is "1) To make good people. 2) To make good citizens. 3) To make each person his or her personal best" (par. 9), and then he attacks these ideas by quoting H. L. Mencken and Woodrow Wilson. Summarize what conclusions Gatto expects his readers to draw from these sources.

4 How does Gatto link consumerism with the habits of mind taught in public schools? Do you agree or disagree with Gatto's claim that a significant purpose of school is to create consumers?

5 According to Gatto, who is most responsible for the problems in American education? Is it the teachers? School administrators? Parents? Students? Politicians? What evidence can you cite to support your response?

6 Reread the paragraph that begins with "Now for the good news" (par. 14). What are the solutions that Gatto suggests for how parents can fight back and encourage their children's education without school? Are these solutions that could work within the school system? Why or why not?

Analyzing Language, Style, and Structure

1 John Taylor Gatto begins by describing his own experience, a discouraging one, as a teacher. What effect does the inclusion of his personal experience have on his argument? How does the biographical information that precedes the article, as well as the biographical information Gatto chooses to include, help to establish his ethos?

2 Gatto cites examples of presidents, inventors, writers, and wealthy businesspersons to make his case that compulsory schooling is not necessary for success (par. 7). He returns to this list at the end of the essay (par. 15). Explain why you do or do not find such examples persuasive.

3 Gatto lists three reasons for mandatory public schooling, as it was conceived in the United States — and then asserts that they are not truly the principles that govern education today. What evidence (including examples) does he cite to support this assertion?

4 What vulnerabilities do you find in Gatto's argument? Look back through the piece and identify a place where you think that Gatto does not effectively support a claim he is making, or where his logic seems faulty. Why do you think his writing is not effective in this section?

5 Gatto's language moves between informal expressions (such as "The empire struck back") and quite elevated language ("Class may frame the proposition"). Do you find such movement an effective rhetorical strategy, or does it seem inconsistent? Support your response by referring to specific passages.

6 This essay first appeared in 2003 in *Harper's* magazine, a monthly publication appealing to an educated, fairly liberal readership. What are some of the ways Gatto specifically appeals to this demographic?

Connecting, Arguing, and Extending

1 Choose one of the following assertions that John Taylor Gatto or one of the sources he cites makes and discuss how your own experience confirms or challenges it:

  a. "[O]ur schools [. . .] [are] virtual factories of child-ishness" (par. 4).

  b. "[S]econdary schools [. . .] all too often resemble prisons" (par. 8).

  c. "[T]he aim of public education is [. . .] 'to reduce as many individuals as possible to the same safe level, to breed and train a standardized citizenry, to put down dissent and originality'" (par. 10, quoting H. L. Mencken).

  d. "Mandatory education serves children only incidentally; its real purpose is to turn them into servants" (par. 15).

  e. "[W]e must wake up to what our schools really are: laboratories of experimentation on young minds, drill centers for the habits and attitudes that corporate society demands" (par. 15).

2 Toward the end of the essay, Gatto calls on parents to teach their own children to be "leaders and adventurers," to think "critically and independently," and to "develop an inner life so that they'll never be bored" (par. 14). Write a proposal for a school that would serve these purposes or that you think has the promise of achieving some of them. What would be its main guiding principles and characteristics?

3 According to some studies, schools in countries like Finland, Singapore, and Japan, among others, regularly outperform the United States, and could be judged as more successful education systems. Research an educational system in another country or culture. Discuss what values it tries to develop in its students and, based on your research and experience, develop a position about whether you think that system is more or less effective than the United States system. Also consider how Gatto would likely evaluate that system.

from The Common School Journal

Horace Mann

Horace Mann (1796–1859) is often called the "father of American Public Education," because of his strong support for publicly funded schools. He was the first secretary of the Massachusetts Board of Education, a position from 1837 to 1848. Mann is particularly noted for his contributions to the *Common School Journal*, which he founded and edited, and from which this excerpt is taken. In addition to holding the post of secretary of the Board of Education, Mann was at different times in his life a tutor, college librarian, lawyer, and state legislator.

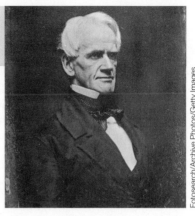

Fotosearch/Archive Photos/Getty Images

KEY CONTEXT   Mann once said, "Be ashamed to die until you have won some victory for humanity," which is now the motto of Antioch College, of which Mann was the first president. As you read, keep in mind that this excerpt is from 1842, and the United States was still a newly formed, largely rural and agrarian country. There was not yet widespread agreement on the need for education for all citizens, especially for children of lower socioeconomic status. It was not until the 1920s that more than half of the teenage population even attended high school. The question that Mann tries to answer here is: why is school important to the individual as well as society?

Mankind are rapidly passing through a transition state. The idea and feeling that the world was made, and life given, for the happiness of all, and not for the ambition, or pride, or luxury, of one, or of a few, are pouring in, like a resistless tide, upon the minds of men, and are effecting a universal revolution in human affairs. Governments, laws, social usages, are rapidly dissolving, and recombining in new forms. The axiom which holds the highest welfare of all the recipients of human existence to be the end and aim of that existence, is the theoretical foundation of all the governments of this Union; it has already modified all the old despotisms of Europe, and has obtained a foothold on the hitherto inaccessible shores of Asia and Africa, and the islands of the sea. A new phrase, — the people, — is becoming incorporated into all languages and laws; and the correlative idea of human rights is evolving, and casting off old institutions and customs, as the expanding body bursts and casts away the narrow and worn-out garments of childhood.

In all the towns in our Common wealth, — in the small and obscure, and perhaps still more in cities and in other populous places, — there are many children, — orphans, or those who, in the curse of vicious parentage, suffer a worse evil than orphanage, — children doomed to incessant drudgery, and who, from the straitened circumstances of the household, from awkwardness of manners, or indigence in dress, never emerge from their solitude and obscurity, and therefore necessarily grow up with all the coarseness, narrowness, prejudices, and bad manners, almost inseparable from spending the years of non-age in entire seclusion from the world. This is a true picture of the condition of

seeing connections

Horace Mann argues in this piece for the importance of universal education.

Look at this chart and, first, make a claim about the trends in the graduation rate in the United States. Then, based upon what you have read in the Mann piece, explain what you believe might have caused these trends.

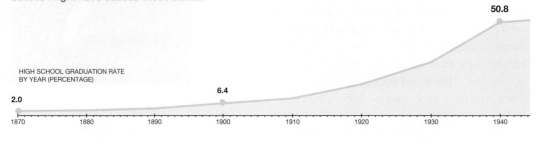

HIGH SCHOOL GRADUATION RATE
BY YEAR (PERCENTAGE)

2.0

6.4

50.8

1870   1880   1890   1900   1910   1920   1930   1940

many children in every town in the State. Although there may be a few exceptions, in regard to *sons*, as to the effects which these misfortunes of birth and parentage tend to produce, yet there are scarcely any such exceptions in regard to *daughters*. At the age of sixteen or eighteen, a vigorous-minded boy may break away from the dark hovel where his eyes first saw the light, and go abroad in quest of better fortunes; but there is hardly any such option in regard to girls. As a general rule, they will remain at home, until, perhaps, the relation of marriage is entered into with some individual of fortunes similar to their own, when it will become their turn to rear up children after the model which was furnished in their own degraded and degrading birthplace.

Now, in the common course of events, and without the instrumentality of schools, this class of children, during the whole period of their minority, would never be brought into communication or acquaintance with a single educated, intelligent, benevolent individual, — with one who loves children with a wise and forecasting love, — with one whose manners are refined, whose tastes and

sentiments are pure and elevating, — who can display the beauty and excellence of knowledge, and win others to obtain what they cannot fail to admire. The most which this class of children would be likely to see of any educated men, would be when the clergyman should make his brief annual parochial call, or when the physician should be summoned to administer to diseases brought on by ignorance or improper indulgences, or when they should be carried before the courts to answer for offences which their untaught and unchastened passions had prompted them to commit. But let a company of well-educated, well-trained, devoted teachers be sent into the school districts of the Commonwealth, to hold intercourse and communion with these children, week after week and month after month, — let their qualities of knowledge, dignity, kindness, purity, and refinement, be brought to act upon the ignorance, vulgarity, squalidness, and obscenity, of these neglected and perverted beings, — and how inexpressibly beautiful it would be to see the latter gradually enlightened, purified, and humanized, by the benignant influences of the former, — to see them casting

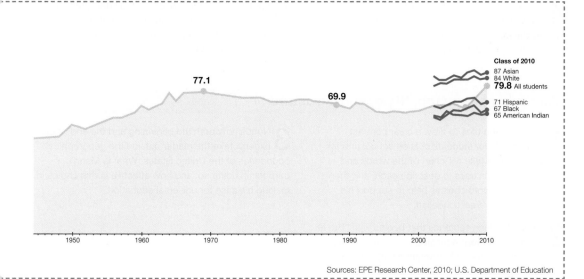

Class of 2010
87 Asian
84 White
79.8 All students

71 Hispanic
67 Black
65 American Indian

77.1

69.9

1950   1960   1970   1980   1990   2000   2010

Sources: EPE Research Center, 2010; U.S. Department of Education

off not only the foul *exuviae*[1] of the surface, but the deeper impurities of the soul! By wise precepts, by patterns and examples of what is good and great in human character, how many of them may be led to admire, to reverence, and then to imitate! O, how beautiful and divine the work by which the jungles of a society that calls itself civilized, can be cleared from the harpies, the wild beasts, and the foul creeping things which now dwell therein! This is the work of

[1]exuviae: Skin shed by an animal, usually referring to the molting of an insect larva. —Eds.

civilization and Christianity; and it is time that those who call upon us to send our wealth to other lands should bestow a thought upon the barbarism and heathenism around their own doors. It is time that the current of public senti-ment should be changed on another point, and that the honor and glory of a people should be held to consist in the *general prevalence* of virtue and intelligence, rather than in the production of a few splendid examples of genius and knowledge. In the great march of society, it is rather our duty to bring up the rear than to push forward the van.

Understanding and Interpreting

1 Summarize the "transition state" that Horace Mann suggests mankind is passing through (par. 1), and explain how this historical movement relates to the idea of universal education.

2 According to Mann, what is the effect of the widespread use of the new phrase "the people" (par. 1)?

3 Despite the fact that at the time he was writing women were unable to vote in the United States, Mann takes the time to describe the unique circumstances of young women who are not educated. Explain how the plight of women at the time that he describes helps to make his case for universal education.

4 Reread the first part of paragraph 3, which begins "Now, in the common course of events," and identify the main goal that Mann believes schools should attempt to achieve.

5 Explain what Mann means in the final sentence of the excerpt: "In the great march of society, it is rather our duty to bring up the rear than to push forward the van" (par. 3).

Analyzing Language, Style, and Structure

1 Horace Mann tries to draw a clear contrast between life for students *outside* school and for students *inside*. Make a T-chart of the words and phrases that Mann uses to describe each, and then explain how his word choices help to support his argument for universal schooling.

2 Reread the long sentence that begins with "But let a company of well-educated . . ." (par. 3). How do the language choices in this sentence attempt to convince the reader of the value of education?

3 Notice how both the beginning and the end of the excerpt take the reader outside the geographical boundaries of the United States. What is Mann's purpose in doing so, and how effective is this choice in making his case for universal education?

Connecting, Arguing, and Extending

1 One of the arguments that Mann makes about universal education is the effect that it can have on women and society as a whole. Look at the following chart and conduct additional research in order to explain the effect that educating women in developing countries today can have on a society.

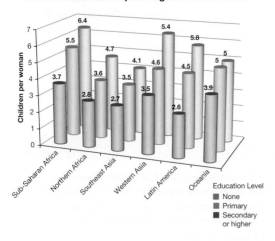

Total Fertility Rates by Women's Education Level in Less-Developed Regions of the World

Children per woman

Sub-Saharan Africa: 3.7, 5.5, 6.4
Northern Africa: 2.8, 4.7, 3.6
Southeast Asia: 2.7, 3.5, 4.1
Western Asia: 3.5, 4.6, 5.4
Latin America: 2.6, 4.5, 5.8
Oceania: 3.9, 5, 5

Education Level
■ None
■ Primary
■ Secondary or higher

2 Near the end of this excerpt, Mann says that education is the work of civilization and of Christianity. And yet today, Mann is known for being a secularist in education, meaning that he felt that religion did not have a place in the public schools. Additionally, the concept of the separation of church and state appears in the First Amendment to the U.S. Constitution, adopted in 1791, which says, in part, "Congress shall make no law respecting an establishment of religion, or prohibiting the free exercise thereof." There are many examples of how the conflict between secularism and someone's right to practice his or her religion openly plays out in schools. In your opinion, what is the proper place for religion in school, and what evidence can you provide to support your position?

3 Mann describes school as a place where young people should be in the company of "well-educated, well-trained, devoted teachers" who share "their qualities of knowledge, dignity, kindness, purity, and refinement" with their students. To what extent has this been your experience with teachers throughout your experience, from elementary school into high school? Be sure *not* to identify specific teachers by name in your response.

from Horace's School: Redesigning the American High School

Theodore Sizer

Theodore Sizer (1932–2009) was one of the leading figures in the American school reform movement of the 1980s and 1990s, pushing schools to be more effective places for students to learn. A former high school teacher, professor, and college dean, Sizer is probably most well-known for his work in founding the Coalition of Essential Schools, which is an organization designed to support school leaders who are undertaking the kinds of reform Sizer promoted. Specifically, the Coalition focuses on what Sizer called the Common Principles, which include learning to use one's mind well, "less is more," depth over coverage, and personalization.

Brown University Archives

KEY CONTEXT This excerpt is taken from Sizer's book *Horace's School: Redesigning the American High School* (1997), which is the middle volume of a trilogy examining the state of American high schools and making suggestions for their improvement. In all three of the books, Sizer utilizes an unusual storytelling device that he calls "nonfiction fiction." Sizer invents the character of Horace Smith, a teacher and school leader (and likely named as homage to Horace Mann) at a fictional school called Franklin High, which he says is a composite of a number of schools he visited. This excerpt begins with Sizer's own personal account of a real classroom he visited, but ends with a fictionalized scene of Horace leading a faculty meeting. In his introduction, Sizer suggests that this device "carries its own sort of authenticity."

When seeing schools as a visitor, I often ask to take a class. Sometimes teachers let me, though rarely with the brisk assent I received in a northeastern city high school when, on a moment's notice, I was handed a ninth-grade humanities group for a period of an hour and a half. I inherited the topic under study — crafting an essay — and plunged into questioning the kids on their topics. Each essay was to center on an incident involving a close family member and was to include, in one graceful way or another, a portrait of that person, the narrative of the incident, and a description of the writer's deeper or differing sense of his relative on the basis of that incident. It was a demanding topic for fourteen-year-olds.

However, not every kid presented the essence of fourteenness. Of the twenty or so youngsters eyeing me doubtfully, there were little and big ones, the bearded man and the childish boy, the women-girls looking like mothers or children, sometimes both. They were surely a tough lot, on the whole; they had probably seen much of life, much that was foreign to my own experience. The class was predominantly black and brown; there were no Asian-Americans or Asians.

Some talked easily about their work; most did not. Two large girls stumbled badly in English; their whispers to each other were in rapid, easy Portuguese. The most vocal student was a stringy, slouched boy wearing a black

T-shirt emblazoned with the face of a recent film character and a Chicago Bulls cap with the visor turned to the back. He had a quick retort for everything, usually spoken into thin air, not to me or even to his classmates. These comments were usually apt, always funny, clever, bordering on but never crossing the line of insolence. He was utterly unignorable. He was intensely watched by a virtually mute bigger boy, a particular friend, obviously, who grinned and nodded assent from time to time.

In one corner, leaning against the wall, the tablet of her desk teetering, was a slight white girl, apart from the rest of the group but attending with care. She wore studiously unkempt clothes, jeans well ripped at the knees. She took her time to talk, but when she did her language was standard English, her references from a different part of town. Her language separated her even more than her race, but the others ignored her. She seemed oblivious of her isolation. By contrast, the group's central figure was an older-looking tall boy, whose talk was carefully phrased, melodious with Caribbean intonations, and as precise as it was predictable. He seemed the class's leader, an Eagle Scout in deportment, an ad for a college admissions brochure.

5   My impressions of these kids and my conversation with them immediately evoked stereotypes. I guessed from their appearances alone who they were. I knew that this mental sorting-out was happening; it happens to us all: we try to make sense of strangers, the quicker the better. Although one tries to rein in one's judgments, one still makes them.

After a time, the students set to work on their essays, I traveled among them, peering over shoulders, reading the starts of their work. Different people — different stereotypes — emerged. Some could barely write simple prose but could whisper to me rich ideas they were struggling to put to paper. Others, like the isolated white girl, could write easily but could not tell me clearly what they wanted to express. This student of the kneeless jeans presented a tangle of notions. Whatever her technical writing skills, she lacked a coherent story to tell. She was childish, not so much naïve as living in a world of flat simplicities.

Some had no idea of what a narrative was. Others created tales about their brothers that would have dazzled Steven Spielberg. Some loved writing, seemingly losing themselves in concentration. Chicago Bulls whipped off a pageant of paragraphs, his bon mots[1] of the earlier discussion now finding their way to paper. His work was sloppy but wonderful. Others slouched, pencils relentlessly tapping, gazing around, a few words put down, not even a sentence, utterly unengaged. Only the Caribbean-American proved true to form. He whispered and wrote as he had talked publicly. He exuded assurance.

As their attention waned, I shifted the activity to a discussion of a historical incident that once raised and still raises some enduring issues of fundamental justice. As I go among schools, I like to use this particular exercise, because it gives consistency to my class watching. The merchant vessel *Emily*, out of Salem, Massachusetts, in 1819, dropped anchor in the harbor of Canton, China, to sell and buy goods. While the captain carried out the major transactions, several Chinese entrepreneurs tied their junks up to the ship and noisily hawked their wares to the men on board. One of the seamen, named Terranova, was swabbing the deck near the tethered boat of an especially persistent woman peddler. Somehow a large pottery jug on deck was loosened and fell onto the hawker's junk. The peddler fell overboard and drowned. The Cantonese authorities

---

[1]bon mots: Witty remarks. —Eds.

demanded that the captain turn Terranova over for trial by a Chinese magistrate. The justice of Canton harbor was balanced, the captain knew, on different scales from those of Massachusetts. The question to the students: If you were the captain, would you turn Terranova over?

The case can elicit all sorts of responses: fact gathering, weighing of alternatives, separation of the immediate situation from principle, empathy for a different cultural position, the need to understand trade, Salem, and Canton in the first part of the nineteenth century. And more. The kids jumped in, at first tentatively, then more vociferously. I served as a human encyclopedia, a fact giver; I expressed no opinion. The Cape Verdean girls took positions of principle; Chicago Bulls looked for a quick way out. Just pull anchor and sail away, he argued. Others protested. What about the *Emily*'s trade next year? What about the rights of the family of the drowned woman? And more. Some refused to make a decision, paralyzed. Again, patterns of response were different; now different stereotypes emerged. The quick portraits I had twice formed disappeared again. Eagle Scout, for example, was silent. He could not make a decision. What might be right for him was not only unclear but unfathomable. I was unfair to push for a decision. He and a few others angrily resented my final call for each student to put on a slip of paper his or her "answer" to the authorities about Terranova's release to Cantonese law.

10   The complexity of young people was displayed in a ninety-minute spread in the restricted world of a high school classroom, even to a stranger who had had no briefing about these kids and who had his hands full simply maintaining order, no less being amateur ethnographer. My impressions changed several times. One "cut" at establishing what each youngster could or could not do, even with a test, carefully crafted, was not the answer. What

kind of day was each student having? Where was his mind this morning? Could she understand what I was saying? Did a word I used mean something different to him from what I intended? Did my "style" smother one but provoke another to do what he was "unsupposed" to do? Beautifully complicated these students were, and to pretend otherwise would be to deny humanity.

How can teachers know the students, know them well enough to understand how their minds work, know where they come from, what pressures buffet them, what they are and are not disposed to do? A teacher cannot stimulate a child to learn without knowing that child's mind any more than a physician can guide an ill patient to health without knowing that patient's physical condition. Tendencies, patterns, likelihoods exist, but the course of action necessary for an individual requires an understanding of the particulars.

And so, what to do? Remedies are actually obvious. They promise, however, to challenge a clutch of traditional educational practices.

First, the number of students per teacher must be limited. Teachers, even the most experienced, can know well only a finite number of individual students, surely not more than eighty and in many situations probably fewer. The typical secondary school teacher today is assigned anywhere from 100 to over 180, coming at him, rapid fire, in groups of twenty to forty. Horace Smith daily sees five groups of some twenty-four students each for three quarters of an hour. Can he really know well how each youngster thinks, how each one is progressing and why, what each one cares about?

People, adolescents included, are complicated and changeable, and knowing them well is not something one can easily attain or hold on to forever. Kids seem different to different adults; they respond in different ways to different

seeing connections

Throughout *Horace's School*, Sizer describes a series of Exhibitions, which are long-term projects that students complete, and which he also includes in the book to demonstrate the principles he is promoting. Look at the Exhibition included here and explain how it connects to one or more of the significant ideas Sizer raises in this excerpt. Additionally, compare this Exhibition to some of the assignments you are asked to complete in school. In what ways are the principles Sizer values present—or not—in the work you are asked to do?

An Exhibition: Form 1040

Your group of five classmates is to complete accurately the federal Internal Revenue Service Form 1040 for each of five families. Each member of your group will prepare the 1040 for one of the families. You may work in concert, helping one another. "Your" particular family's form must be completed by you personally, however.

Attached are complete financial records for the family assigned to you, including the return filed by that family last year. In addition, you will find a blank copy of the current 1040, including related schedules, and explanatory material provided by the Internal Revenue Service.

You will have a month to complete this work. Your result will be "audited" by an outside expert and one of your classmates after you turn it in. You will have to explain the financial situation of "your" family and to defend the 1040 return for it which you have presented.

Each of you will serve as a "co-auditor" on the return filed by a student from another group. You will be asked to comment on that return.

Good luck. Getting your tax amount wrong—or the tax for any of the five families in your group—could end you in legal soup!

. . .

situations or when studying different disciplines. Few students open up to older people they do not know or trust; to know a youngster in order to teach her well means knowing her first as a person. Moreover, there are no perfect tests one can administer to get a permanent fix on a child, no matter how educators struggle to create such devices and to believe in them. Current research on learning and adolescent development is full of speculation, of conflicting findings and incomplete results, and it gives no simple answer to the nature of learning or growing up. In sum, teachers (like parents) are very much on their own, drawing on a mixture of signals from research, from experience, and from common sense as the basis for their decisions.

15 Accordingly, and reflecting the ambiguous nature of each student's progress or lack thereof, wise teachers, knowing that they must be diagnosticians of the youngster's progress, take counsel regularly with their colleagues about the student, sharing impressions, hunches, and suggestions. Teachers confer with parents. And teachers make time to confer with the student himself, privately — formally or more likely informally — not only in the rush of class time. [. . .]

All this personalization can be taken too far, or worse yet can be bureaucratized with solemn Meetings called on a Schedule to examine Each Student's Brain and Navel. Compromises and common sense and flexibility are always needed in schools, just as they are in good families.

Here is another educational target.

It is authentic, painfully so. The importance of the 1040 is self-evident. Knowing how not to be intimidated by the process of filing is obviously worthwhile.

It will appeal to students. It deals with two issues paramount in most of their lives: money and fairness (the latter particularly if the families selected come from radically different walks of life).

Taught intelligently, it opens the door wide, and for many students in a compelling way, to a cluster of important disciplines such as microeconomics, politics, ethics, and political history. It can thereby be the springboard for sustained serious study in several directions. For example, it raises provocative questions about equality, about what "tax breaks" are and who gets them and why. It is an example of government at work, with its use of financial incentives. In all these respects, it spurs teaching, animates it — this is a quality of a good Exhibition.

It teaches the importance of accurate, consistent records, the necessity to read closely, the nature of the tax system, and who and what it favors. It also calls for a demonstration of arithmetic, logical, and analytic skills.

It is organized so that students can work together, helping one another. Some may promptly race out and consult a tax expert or call the IRS, asking for help. While this is not recommended, it is tolerable: the costs of such outside help are minimized by the necessity to withstand and explain an audit. Indeed, the act of getting such help may serve as a powerful teacher. Further, the necessity to be another person's co-auditor requires the display of useful knowledge.

It allows a teacher to vary the difficulty of material among the students involved, giving a financially simpler family to a struggling student and a more complex set of issues to the class tax whiz. The students will, of course, help one another, and they all must stand behind all five returns.

Adjustments must be made quickly and thoughtfully. The key ingredients here are time during the school day for people to meet, schedules that allow the teachers of particular youngsters to gather together, teachers committed to such gatherings, and a school program flexible enough to respond to adjustments recommended for each student. Schools should do no less for students than effective hospitals do for patients. Good hospitals allow time for staff consultations. They expect collaboration in the diagnosis of problems and the selection of remedies. Good hospitals consult patients carefully. Schools are not hospitals and school kids are not "sick," yet the analogies in this case hold.

Finally, the mores of the school — the ways it goes about its business — must implicitly show respect for individual students, for the expectation that each can succeed, and for the belief that each deserves success. It is in this context that schools' "dirty little secrets," incendiary issues like race, can be addressed. A school faculty that knows its students has taken each beyond his or her race, has accepted each as a person. This is not to say that race or gender or ethnicity is not of consequence; it means only that other matters, such as a kid's personality, his hopes, his friends, his passions, his family, his idiosyncrasies, count more. It is one thing to say, "Those three black kids and those two white kids over there are . . ."; it is better to say, "Bill,

Amanda, Susan, Roger, and Ernest . . ." The person emerging from the caricature can help to dissolve the stereotype. A stereotype is one of the roots of prejudice, one readily confronted in good schools. The "dirty little secrets" will never be eliminated or go away: America's prejudices run too deep for that. The tensions and wranglings they incite will always be with us, and schools must accept them — but always in the context of the reality that no two people, young or old, are ever quite alike, nor should they ever be treated precisely alike.

A thoughtful school "culture" cannot be readily codified or structured. An advisory period merely offers the possibility of "advice" given and taken. What happens within that opportunity is the nub of it. Fuzzy but fundamental qualities of caring and honesty, attentiveness both to the immediate and to a young person's future, empathy, patience, knowing when to draw the line, the expression of disappointment or anger or forgiveness when such is deserved — indeed, those qualities which characterize us as humans rather than programmed robots — mark the essence of a school that is at once compassionate, respectful, and efficient.

How do such schools come to be? Through the leadership of their adults, people who set and reset the standards, people who stay around a school long enough to give it a heart as well as a program, people who are ready to build a community that extends beyond any one classroom, people who know the potentials and limitations of technical expertise and of humane judgment. One does not "design" such schools.

20   Such schools, rather, grow, usually slowly and almost always painfully, as tough issues are met.

Horace's committee seemed stumped about how to respect the differences among students and yet meet the need for some absolute academic standards. Comparisons to athletics were tried, but what kept cropping up was tracking — with academic varsities, junior varsities, and the rest.

The problem, committee members knew, was that the game of life was all played at the varsity level. In the use of their minds, if not their passing arms and kicking feet, all the young people had to be made as competitive as possible.

"Take your taxes," Margaret suggested. "Everybody has to do his taxes. Taxophobes are not let off. Everyone must be able to play that game."

There was laughter. "The Form 1040 is the test we all must pass . . ." More embarrassed laughter.

25   "Not everyone will be able to make sense of all that IRS gobbledygook."

"Why not?" Margaret persisted. "It isn't all that hard. It takes time, persistence, careful reading, good records, patience galore. Why can't we set those ends as a standard for any Franklin graduate?"

"In the real world, lots of people do their taxes with others. In our house it's a collective late March hassle. And if we don't understand, we ask for help."

"So, isn't that OK?" Margaret again. "We can't teach every student the tax code forever and ever, but we should be able to expect everyone of them to do some sort of tax return. If in collaboration, so much the better. It will give each young person the confidence that with help as needed he can complete the 1040."

"Can we expect the same of the faculty?" More laughter. The committee was learning to like itself.

30   Green: "The 1040 is the Real World. Why isn't that a good Exhibition?"

Again someone protested: "It will be too hard for some of the kids!"

Coach: "It can't be. They have to be able to do it."

Understanding and Interpreting

1 At the beginning of this selection, Theodore Sizer describes several of his students in simplistic, stereotypical terms, but by paragraph 10, he concludes, "Beautifully complicated these students were." What changes for Sizer, and what is the reader expected to conclude from his changed perceptions?

2 What is Sizer's intention in asking the students about the story of the merchant ship *Emily*? What is he hoping to learn? What conclusion is the reader expected to draw from the inclusion of the students' responses?

3 Sizer concludes, probably unsurprisingly, that in order to personalize instruction, teachers have to know their students. In addition to large class sizes, to what other factors does Sizer attribute the difficulty of teachers' knowing their students well?

4 Sizer compares an effective school to an effective hospital. While he identifies the effective practices that occur in a hospital, he does not explicitly identify how these practices would look in a school. Finish the comparison for Sizer by explaining what the effective school practices might be.

5 Sizer suggests that the most important step a school can take to ensure that all students are receiving individualized attention is to look closely at "the mores of the school" (par. 17). According to Sizer, what is an effective school culture?

6 In the last section of this excerpt (pars. 21–32), Sizer switches to the "nonfiction fiction" approach and describes the fictional faculty meeting that Horace leads. How does the teachers' dialogue illustrate the points that Sizer makes in the preceding paragraphs?

Analyzing Language, Style, and Structure

1 This excerpt is taken from a chapter called "Kids Differ." In what ways does Sizer illustrate the meaning of the chapter title through his word choice in the first four paragraphs, where he describes the kids in the class he is teaching?

2 Select one of the students whom Sizer observes while teaching the class at the beginning of the excerpt. How does Sizer describe that student upon first encountering him or her, and how do his descriptions change later on? How does this changing language illustrate a point that Sizer is making about the individual in school?

3 Ultimately, this piece is an argument, making a point about the need for individualized knowledge of students. Why does Sizer start with a narrative? How does the story he tells support his argument?

4 After the narrative opening about the classroom he visited, Sizer switches to an expository mode of address. Does his attitude toward his topic shift or remain the same? Point to specific language choices in each part of the selection to support your conclusion.

Connecting, Arguing, and Extending

1 Sizer spends considerable time identifying the qualities of an effective school culture. Compare your own school's culture to the ideal one that Sizer describes.

2 Reread the scenario of the merchant ship *Emily* (par. 8). What is your opinion on the case? What might your response reveal about you?

from I Know Why the Caged Bird Sings

Maya Angelou

One of America's most well-known and celebrated writers, Maya Angelou (1928–2014) was born Marguerite Johnson in St. Louis, Missouri. Throughout her career, she published numerous volumes of poetry, several plays and screenplays, and six autobiographies that traced her life from birth all the way to 1968. Her most famous autobiography is her first, *I Know Why the Caged Bird Sings*, which recounts her early childhood up to about age seventeen.

KEY CONTEXT   Very controversial when it was released — and still challenged by some groups even today — *I Know Why the Caged Bird Sings* tells the story of the often-brutal racism that Angelou (then called "Marguerite") faced growing up with her brother (Bailey) and her grandmother (Momma) in Stamps, Arkansas, a rural community about two hours from Little Rock. Angelou speaks frankly of the sexual abuse she suffered as a child, her five-year self-imposed muteness, and the salvation she found in books and writing. In this excerpt, the excitement and pride Marguerite feels in her accomplishments are severely tested by "the ancient tragedy" of racism during her eighth-grade graduation.

In the Store I was the person of the moment. The birthday girl. The center. Bailey had graduated the year before, although to do so he had had to forfeit all pleasures to make up for his time lost in Baton Rouge.

My class was wearing butter-yellow piqué dresses, and Momma launched out on mine. She smocked the yoke into tiny crisscrossing puckers, then slurred the rest of the bodice. Her dark fingers ducked in and out of the lemony cloth as she embroidered raised daisies around the hem. Before she considered herself finished she had added a crocheted cuff on the puff sleeves, and a pointy crocheted collar.

I was going to be lovely. A walking model of all the various styles of fine hand sewing and it didn't worry me that I was only twelve years old and merely graduating from the eighth grade. Besides, many teachers in Arkansas Negro schools had only that diploma and were licensed to impart wisdom.

The days had become longer and more noticeable. The faded beige of former times had been replaced with strong and sure colors. I began to see my classmates' clothes, their skin tones, and the dust that waved off pussy willows. Clouds that lazed across the sky were objects of great concern to me. Their shiftier shapes might have held a message that in my new happiness and with a little bit of time I'd soon decipher. During that period I looked at the arch of heaven so religiously my neck kept a steady ache. I had taken to smiling more often, and my jaws hurt from the unaccustomed activity. Between the two physical sore spots, I suppose I could have been uncomfortable, but that was not the case. As a member of the winning team (the graduating class of 1940) I had outdistanced unpleasant sensations by miles. I was headed for the freedom of open fields.

5   Youth and social approval allied themselves with me and we trammeled memories of slights and insults. The wind of our swift passage remodeled my features. Lost tears were pounded to mud and then to dust. Years of withdrawal were brushed aside and left behind, as hanging ropes of parasitic moss.

My work alone had awarded me a top place and I was going to be one of the first called in the graduating ceremonies. On the classroom blackboard, as well as on the bulletin board in the auditorium, there were blue stars and white stars and red stars. No absences, no tardinesses, and my academic work was among the best of the year. I could say the preamble to the Constitution even faster than Bailey. We timed ourselves often: "WethepeopleoftheUnitedStates-inordertoformamoreperfectunion . . ." I had memorized the Presidents of the United States from Washington to Roosevelt in chronological as well as alphabetical order.

My hair pleased me too. Gradually the black mass had lengthened and thickened, so that it kept at last to its braided pattern, and I didn't have to yank my scalp off when I tried to comb it.

Louise and I had rehearsed the exercises until we tired out ourselves. Henry Reed was class valedictorian. He was a small, very black boy with hooded eyes, a long, broad nose and an oddly shaped head. I had admired him for years because each term he and I vied for the best grades in our class. Most often he bested me, but instead of being disappointed I was pleased that we shared top places between us. Like many Southern Black children, he lived with his grandmother, who was as strict as Momma and as kind as she knew how to be. He was courteous, respectful and soft-spoken to elders, but on the playground he chose to play the roughest games. I admired him. Anyone, I reckoned, sufficiently afraid or sufficiently dull could be polite.

But to be able to operate at a top level with both adults and children was admirable.

His valedictory speech was entitled "To Be or Not to Be." The rigid tenth-grade teacher had helped him write it. He'd been working on the dramatic stresses for months.

10   The weeks until graduation were filled with heady activities. A group of small children were to be presented in a play about buttercups and daisies and bunny rabbits. They could be heard throughout the building practicing their hops and their little songs that sounded like silver bells. The older girls (nongraduates, of course) were assigned the task of making refreshments for the night's festivities. A tangy scent of ginger, cinnamon, nutmeg and chocolate wafted around the home economics building as the budding cooks made samples for themselves and their teachers.

In every corner of the workshop, axes and saws split fresh timber as the woodshop boys made sets and stage scenery. Only the graduates were left out of the general bustle. We were free to sit in the library at the back of the building or look in quite detachedly, naturally, on the measures being taken for our event.

Even the minister preached on graduation the Sunday before. His subject was, "Let your light so shine that men will see your good works and praise your Father, Who is in Heaven." Although the sermon was purported to be addressed to us, he used the occasion to speak to backsliders, gamblers and general ne'er-do-wells. But since he had called our names at the beginning of the service we were mollified.

Among Negroes the tradition was to give presents to children going only from one grade to another. How much more important this was when the person was graduating at the top of the class. Uncle Willie and Momma had sent away for a Mickey Mouse watch like Bailey's. Louise gave me four embroidered handkerchiefs. (I gave her three crocheted doilies.) Mrs. Sneed, the minister's wife, made me an underskirt to wear for graduation, and nearly every customer gave me a nickel or maybe even a dime with the instruction "Keep on moving to higher ground," or some such encouragement.

Amazingly the great day finally dawned and I was out of bed before I knew it. I threw open the back door to see it more clearly, but Momma said, "Sister, come away from that door and put your robe on."

15   I hoped the memory of that morning would never leave me. Sunlight was itself still young, and the day had none of the insistence maturity would bring it in a few hours. In my robe and barefoot in the backyard, under cover of going to see about my new beans, I gave myself up to the gentle warmth and thanked God that no matter what evil I had done in my life He had allowed me to live to see this day. Somewhere in my fatalism I had expected to die, accidentally, and never have the chance to walk up the stairs in the auditorium and gracefully receive my hard-earned diploma. Out of God's merciful bosom I had won reprieve.

Bailey came out in his robe and gave me a box wrapped in Christmas paper. He said he had saved his money for months to pay for it. It felt like a box of chocolates, but I knew Bailey wouldn't save money to buy candy when we had all we could want under our noses.

He was as proud of the gift as I. It was a soft-leather-bound copy of a collection of poems by Edgar Allan Poe, or, as Bailey and I called him, "Eap." I turned to "Annabel Lee" and we walked up and down the garden rows, the cool dirt between our toes, reciting the beautifully sad lines.

Momma made a Sunday breakfast although it was only Friday. After we finished the blessing, I opened my eyes to find the watch on my plate. It was a dream of a day. Everything went smoothly and to my credit. I didn't have to be reminded or scolded for anything. Near evening

I was too jittery to attend to chores, so Bailey volunteered to do all before his bath.

Days before, we had made a sign for the Store, and as we turned out the lights Momma hung the cardboard over the doorknob. It read clearly: CLOSED. GRADUATION.

20   My dress fitted perfectly and everyone said that I looked like a sunbeam in it. On the hill, going toward the school, Bailey walked behind with Uncle Willie, who muttered, "Go on, Ju." He wanted him to walk ahead with us because it embarrassed him to have to walk so slowly. Bailey said he'd let the ladies walk together, and the men would bring up the rear. We all laughed, nicely.

Little children dashed by out of the dark like fireflies. Their crepe-paper dresses and butterfly wings were not made for running and we heard more than one rip, dryly, and the regretful "uh uh" that followed.

The school blazed without gaiety. The windows seemed cold and unfriendly from the lower hill. A sense of ill-fated timing crept over me, and if Momma hadn't reached for my hand I would have drifted back to Bailey and Uncle Willie, and possibly beyond. She made a few slow jokes about my feet getting cold, and tugged me along to the now-strange building.

Around the front steps, assurance came back. There were my fellow "greats," the graduating class. Hair brushed back, legs oiled, new dresses and pressed pleats, fresh pocket handkerchiefs and little handbags, all homesewn. Oh, we were up to snuff, all right. I joined my comrades and didn't even see my family go in to find seats in the crowded auditorium.

The school band struck up a march and all classes filed in as had been rehearsed. We stood in front of our seats, as assigned, and on a signal from the choir director, we sat. No sooner had this been accomplished than the band started to play the national anthem. We rose again and sang the song, after which we recited the pledge of allegiance. We remained standing for a brief minute before the choir director and the principal signaled to us, rather desperately I thought, to take our seats. The command was so unusual that our carefully rehearsed and smooth-running machine was thrown off. For a full minute we fumbled for our chairs and bumped into each other awkwardly. Habits change or solidify under pressure, so in our state of nervous tension we had been ready to follow our usual assembly pattern: the American national anthem, then the pledge of allegiance, then the song every Black person I knew called the Negro National Anthem. All done in the same key, with the same passion and most often standing on the same foot.

25   Finding my seat at last, I was overcome with a presentiment of worse things to come. Something unrehearsed, unplanned, was going to happen, and we were going to be made to look bad. I distinctly remember being explicit in the choice of pronoun. It was "we," the graduating class, the unit, that concerned me then.

The principal welcomed "parents and friends" and asked the Baptist minister to lead us in prayer. His invocation was brief and punchy, and for a second I thought we were getting back on the high road to right action. When the principal came back to the dais, however, his voice had changed. Sounds always affected me profoundly and the principal's voice was one of my favorites. During assembly it melted and lowed weakly into the audience. It had not been in my plan to listen to him, but my curiosity was piqued and I straightened up to give him my attention.

He was talking about Booker T. Washington, our "late great leader," who said we can be as close as the fingers on the hand, etc. . . . Then he said a few vague things about friendship and the friendship of kindly people to those less fortunate than themselves. With that his voice nearly faded, thin, away. Like a river diminishing to a

stream and then to a trickle. But he cleared his throat and said, "Our speaker tonight, who is also our friend, came from Texarkana to deliver the commencement address, but due to the irregularity of the train schedule, he's going to, as they say, 'speak and run.'" He said that we understood and wanted the man to know that we were most grateful for the time he was able to give us and then something about how we were willing always to adjust to another's program, and without more ado — "I give you Mr. Edward Donleavy."

Not one but two white men came through the door offstage. The shorter one walked to the speaker's platform, and the tall one moved over to the center seat and sat down. But that was our principal's seat, and already occupied. The dislodged gentleman bounced around for a long breath or two before the Baptist minister gave him his chair, then with more dignity than the situation deserved, the minister walked off the stage.

Donleavy looked at the audience once (on reflection, I'm sure that he wanted only to reassure himself that we were really there), adjusted his glasses and began to read from a sheaf of papers.

30   He was glad "to be here and to see the work going on just as it was in the other schools."

At the first "Amen" from the audience I willed the offender to immediate death by choking on the word. But Amens and Yes, sir's began to fall around the room like rain through a ragged umbrella.

He told us of the wonderful changes we children in Stamps had in store. The Central School (naturally, the white school was Central) had already been granted improvements that would be in use in the fall. A well-known artist was coming from Little Rock to teach art to them. They were going to have the newest microscopes and chemistry equipment for their laboratory. Mr. Donleavy didn't leave us long in the dark over who made these improvements available to Central High. Nor were we to be ignored in the general betterment scheme he had in mind.

He said that he had pointed out to people at a very high level that one of the first-line football tacklers at Arkansas Agricultural and Mechanical College had graduated from good old Lafayette County Training School. Here fewer Amen's were heard. Those few that did break through lay dully in the air with the heaviness of habit.

He went on to praise us. He went on to say how he had bragged that "one of the best basket-ball players at Fisk sank his first ball right here at Lafayette County Training School."

35 The white kids were going to have a chance to become Galileos and Madame Curies and Edisons and Gauguins, and our boys (the girls weren't even in on it) would try to be Jesse Owenses and Joe Louises.

Owens and the Brown Bomber were great heroes in our world, but what school official in the white-goddom of Little Rock had the right to decide that those two men must be our only heroes? Who decided that for Henry Reed to become a scientist he had to work like George Washington Carver, as a bootblack, to buy a lousy microscope? Bailey was obviously always going to be too small to be an athlete, so which concrete angel glued to what country seat had decided that if my brother wanted to become a lawyer he had to first pay penance for his skin by picking cotton and hoeing corn and studying correspondence books at night for twenty years?

The man's dead words fell like bricks around the auditorium and too many settled in my belly. Constrained by hard-learned manners I couldn't look behind me, but to my left and right the proud graduating class of 1940 had dropped their heads. Every girl in my row had found something new to do with her handker-chief. Some folded the tiny squares into love knots, some into triangles, but most were wadding them, then pressing them flat on their yellow laps.

On the dais, the ancient tragedy was being replayed. Professor Parsons sat, a sculptor's reject, rigid. His large, heavy body seemed devoid of will or willingness, and his eyes said he was no longer with us. The other teachers exam-ined the flag (which was draped stage right) or

The events Angelou describes in her autobiography take place about fifteen years before the court-ordered integration of Little Rock's Central High School in 1957. In this photo, National Guard troops protect a girl arriving to attend school.

What perspective on this historic event, and this scene in particular, does Angelou's memoir give you?

© Bettmann/Corbis

their notes, or the windows which opened on our now-famous playing diamond.

Graduation, the hush-hush magic time of frills and gifts and congratulations and diplomas, was finished for me before my name was called. The accomplishment was nothing. The meticulous maps, drawn in three colors of ink, learning and spelling decasyllabic words, memorizing the whole of *The Rape of Lucrece* — it was for nothing. Donleavy had exposed us.

40 We were maids and farmers, handymen and washerwomen, and anything higher that we aspired to was farcical and presumptuous.

Then I wished that Gabriel Prosser and Nat Turner had killed all whitefolks in their beds and that Abraham Lincoln had been assassinated before the signing of the Emancipation Proclamation, and that Harriet Tubman had been killed by that blow on her head and Christopher Columbus had drowned in the *Santa María*.

It was awful to be Negro and have no control over my life. It was brutal to be young and already trained to sit quietly and listen to charges brought against my color with no chance of defense. We should all be dead. I thought I should like to see us all dead, one on top of the other. A pyramid of flesh with the whitefolks on the bottom, as the broad base, then the Indians with their silly tomahawks and teepees and wigwams and treaties, the Negroes with their mops and recipes and cotton sacks and spirituals sticking out of their mouths. The Dutch children should all stumble in their wooden shoes and break their necks. The French should choke to death on the Louisiana Purchase (1803) while silkworms ate all the Chinese with their stupid pigtails. As a species, we were an abomination. All of us.

Donleavy was running for election, and assured our parents that if he won we could count on having the only colored paved playing field in that part of Arkansas. Also — he never looked up to acknowledge the grunts of acceptance — also, we were bound to get some new equipment for the home economics building and the workshop.

He finished, and since there was no need to give any more than the most perfunctory thank-you's, he nodded to the men on the stage, and the tall white man who was never introduced joined him at the door. They left with the attitude that now they were off to something really important. (The graduation ceremonies at Lafayette County Training School had been a mere preliminary.)

45 The ugliness they left was palpable. An uninvited guest who wouldn't leave. The choir was summoned and sang a modern arrangement of "Onward, Christian Soldiers," with new words pertaining to graduates seeking their place in the world. But it didn't work. Elouise, the daughter of the Baptist minister, recited "Invictus," and I could have cried at the impertinence of "I am the master of my fate, I am the captain of my soul."

My name had lost its ring of familiarity and I had to be nudged to go and receive my diploma. All my preparations had fled. I neither marched up to the stage like a conquering Amazon, nor did I look in the audience for Bailey's nod of approval. Marguerite Johnson, I heard the name again, my honors were read, there were noises in the audience of appreciation, and I took my place on the stage as rehearsed.

I thought about colors I hated: ecru, puce, lavender, beige and black.

There was shuffling and rustling around me, then Henry Reed was giving his valedictory address, "To Be or Not to Be." Hadn't he heard the whitefolks? We couldn't *be*, so the question was a waste of time. Henry's voice came out clear and strong. I feared to look at him. Hadn't he got the message? There was no "nobler in the mind" for Negroes because the world didn't think we had minds, and they let us know it. "Outrageous fortune"? Now, that was a joke.

When the ceremony was over I had to tell Henry Reed some things. That is, if I still cared. Not "rub," Henry, "erase." "Ah, there's the erase." Us.

Henry had been a good student in elocution. His voice rose on tides of promise and fell on waves of warnings. The English teacher had helped him to create a sermon winging through Hamlet's soliloquy. To be a man, a doer, a builder, a leader, or to be a tool, an unfunny joke, a crusher of funky toadstools. I marveled that Henry could go through with the speech as if we had a choice.

50   I had been listening and silently rebutting each sentence with my eyes closed; then there was a hush, which in an audience warns that something unplanned is happening. I looked up and saw Henry Reed, the conservative, the proper, the A student, turn his back to the audience and turn to us (the proud graduating class of 1940) and sing, nearly speaking,

> "Lift ev'ry voice and sing
> Till earth and heaven ring
> Ring with the harmonies of Liberty . . ."

It was the poem written by James Weldon Johnson. It was the music composed by J. Rosamond Johnson. It was the Negro national anthem. Out of habit we were singing it.

Our mothers and fathers stood in the dark hall and joined the hymn of encouragement. A kindergarten teacher led the small children onto the stage and the buttercups and daisies and bunny rabbits marked time and tried to follow:

> "Stony the road we trod
> Bitter the chastening rod
> Felt in the days when hope, unborn, had
>   died.
> Yet with a steady beat
> Have not our weary feet
> Come to the place for which our fathers
>   sighed?"

Every child I knew had learned that song with his ABC's and along with "Jesus Loves Me This I Know." But I personally had never heard it before. Never heard the words, despite the thousands of times I had sung them. Never thought they had anything to do with me.

On the other hand, the words of Patrick Henry had made such an impression on me that I had been able to stretch myself tall and trembling and say, "I know not what course others may take, but as for me, give me liberty or give me death."

And now I heard, really for the first time:

> "We have come over a way that with tears has
>   been watered,
> We have come, treading our path through the
>   blood of the slaughtered."

55   While echoes of the song shivered in the air, Henry Reed bowed his head, said "Thank you," and returned to his place in the line. The tears that slipped down many faces were not wiped away in shame.

We were on top again. As always, again. We survived. The depths had been icy and dark, but now a bright sun spoke to our souls. I was no longer simply a member of the proud graduating class of 1940; I was a proud member of the wonderful, beautiful Negro race.

Oh, Black known and unknown poets, how often have your auctioned pains sustained us? Who will compute the lonely nights made less lonely by your songs, or by the empty pots made less tragic by your tales?

If we were a people much given to revealing secrets, we might raise monuments and sacrifice to the memories of our poets, but slavery cured us of that weakness. It may be enough, however, to have it said that we survive in exact relationship to the dedication of our poets (include preachers, musicians and blues singers).

Understanding and Interpreting

1 Trace Marguerite's changing attitude toward her own accomplishments in school at the following points in the narrative. Be sure to identify a passage from the text that supports your response:

   a. before the ceremony (pars. 6–15)

   b. during and immediately after Mr. Donleavy's speech (pars. 24–44)

   c. after Henry Reed begins to sing (pars. 50–56)

2 What are some of the differences between Marguerite's school, Lafayette County Training School, and Central High School, the white school in the same town? How does Marguerite feel about these differences?

3 Look back closely at the speech that Mr. Donleavy delivers. What is the content of his speech and how is his message received by his audience? Why does the audience receive the message this way?

4 A "coming of age" story typically features a protagonist who learns a lesson about the world that requires him or her to put childhood aside and start becoming an adult. With this definition in mind, consider ways in which this excerpt from *I Know Why the Caged Bird Sings* can be considered a "coming of age" story.

5 This excerpt is from about two-thirds through *I Know Why the Caged Bird Sings*. Make an inference about how Marguerite's thoughts about racism and her own sense of self might evolve in the remainder of the autobiography. Point to specific passages from the text to support your response.

Analyzing Language, Style, and Structure

1 There are a number of allusions to specific texts in this excerpt, including the "To be or not to be" speech from *Hamlet*, and "Lift Every Voice and Sing," referred to in this piece as the "Negro National Anthem." Explain how each of these texts helps to illustrate Marguerite's inner conflicts with the effects of racism.

2 Before Mr. Donleavy's speech, Maya Angelou uses a strikingly different tone to describe the graduation ceremony than she does after the speech. Choose two short passages, one from each section, identify the tone, and explain how Angelou uses diction to create it.

3 Look back at paragraphs 43–44 and explain how Angelou uses style to reveal the obvious indifference and racism of the two white men.

4 Reread paragraph 42. The imagery is brutal and shocking, compared to the rest of the excerpt, as the narrator imagines a pile of dead people of all races. What are the objects she imagines that the people from each race have with them and how does the language she chooses illustrate Marguerite's attitude toward racism? What might this paragraph be like if Marguerite had a more optimistic view of the world? Rewrite the paragraph with this more optimistic tone.

Connecting, Arguing, and Extending

1 In this excerpt, Marguerite has her expectations of a wonderful day dampened — at least temporarily — by someone else's actions, actions that are beyond her control. Write about a time in your life when you have experienced a similar event. Be sure, as Angelou does, to include a reflection on what caused this disappointment.

2 Leading up to the graduation ceremony, we learn that there are two schools in Stamps, Arkansas: one for whites and one for African Americans. About twenty years later, in 1954, the Supreme Court, in *Brown v. Board of Education*, ruled this type of segregation illegal, and schools throughout the country began to integrate. And yet, according to Jonathan Kozol, an education researcher, today's schools may be just as segregated by race as they were during Angelou's childhood. In an interview about one of his books called *The Shame of the Nation: The Restoration of Apartheid Schooling in America*, Kozol said,

> It goes to the question of whether we are going to be one society or two, whether our children will grow up to know one another as friends or view each other eternally as strangers, and especially as fearful strangers. But it also speaks directly to academic issues, because overwhelmingly segregated schools in the United States are the schools that have the lowest scores, the highest class sizes, the least experienced teachers, and the most devastating dropout rates. And of course these are the schools that always receive the least amount of money. Segregated schools, despite occasional exceptions, are almost always funded at far lower levels than the schools that serve white and middle-class children. Nationally, on average, a school serving primarily black and Latino students gets $1,000 less per pupil than an overwhelmingly white school. That's a lot of money when you realize that kids aren't educated individually but in a class of 25–30 kids — that's a difference of $25,000–$30,000 every year for every class.

What is the racial and socioeconomic background of the school populations in your area? Does this cause any disparities that you can see? Write an essay that proposes specific solutions to the issues of segregation and funding that Kozol raises and Angelou demonstrates.

3 Angelou has said that she took the title of her autobiography from the poem "Sympathy" by Paul Laurence Dunbar. Read the third stanza from the poem and explain how the poem's speaker faces a situation similar to that of Marguerite in this excerpt. How is the message of the poem similar to or different from that of Angelou's autobiography?

> I know why the caged bird sings, ah me,
> When his wing is bruised and his bosom sore,
> When he beats his bars and would be free;
> It is not a carol of joy or glee,
> But a prayer that he sends from his heart's deep core,
> But a plea, that upward to Heaven he flings—
> I know why the caged bird sings.

ENTERING THE CONVERSATION
THE INDIVIDUAL IN SCHOOL

Making Connections

1 Read or reread the section from the Central Text of this chapter, "Shooting an Elephant" (p. 114), in which the narrator is standing in front of the crowd of Burmese who silently urge him to shoot the animal, even though he states clearly that he does not want to. Compare the social forces at work in that passage with those Alexandra Robbins describes in her piece. Are there any research studies that she cites that would be applicable to the actions of the narrator in "Shooting an Elephant"?

2 In the excerpt from *The Geeks Shall Inherit the Earth*, Robbins describes the biological and social factors that often force high school students to conform. What visual and textual evidence shows these factors at work in the excerpt from *Friends with Boys*?

3 While Horace Mann clearly values universal education (p. 213), John Taylor Gatto suggests that compulsory education turns citizens into "servants" (p. 211, par. 15). How would Mann respond to Gatto's arguments, and which position do you support? Why?

4 What is a problematic aspect of school on which Theodore Sizer and John Taylor Gatto might agree? What are the differences in their proposed solutions to the problem?

5 Based on your reading of Theodore Sizer's *Horace's School*, what would Sizer likely identify as being the strengths and weaknesses with the districtwide and specific-school culture described in Maya Angelou's *I Know Why the Caged Bird Sings*? What solutions would Sizer probably suggest to address these concerns?

Synthesizing Sources

1 John Taylor Gatto, the author of "Against School" (p. 207), wonders if we really even need school anymore. With so much of the world's knowledge accessible with a quick Google search, what is the purpose of school in the twenty-first century? Be sure to support your own ideas with those of the authors in this Conversation.

2 The great majority of American high school students are educated in a traditional learning environment: a group of a few hundred to a few thousand students move from class to class in one main building, studying subjects like English, math, science, and so on; they are taught by teachers who take attendance, give tests, grade papers, and assign homework. While there are students who are homeschooled or take high school classes online, the traditional learning structure has not significantly changed since the invention of the American high school in the nineteenth century. Propose a new model for high school that meets the needs of today's learners, referring to at least two texts in this Conversation as support for your proposal.

3 Many of the texts in this Conversation include descriptions of both supportive and hostile school environments. Considering at least two of these texts along with your own personal experiences, what would you say are the most important qualities that make a supportive learning environment? Write your response in the form of a letter to your principal to inform him or her about the attributes that he or she should consider when making changes to the school.

4 One attribute that seems to run through many of these texts is the power that school—peers, teachers, the institution itself—has to enforce conformity among students. While we often think of "conformity" in a negative way, some of the texts point out that inculcating students with certain values and skills that society thinks are important can be a positive outcome of the educational process. A case could be made, however, that schools have no business indoctrinating their students and that students should resist all pressures to conform to a school's or society's intended outcomes. Referring to two or more texts in this Conversation, explain what role conformity ought to play in the educational process.

5 Imagine that an incoming ninth grader asked you for advice on how to handle high school. What suggestions would you offer? Why? What advice would one or more of the authors of texts in this Conversation offer?

▼
ANALYZING POINT OF VIEW

Imagine that three of your friends got into an argument when you were not around, and then two of them tell you their sides of the story, separately. Their stories are very different from each other. Which friend do you believe? How do you know the truth? And what about that third friend who never got to tell her side? Where's her story? Now imagine that you have to tell someone else what happened. Think about how your perspective as someone who did not even witness the conflict would shape the events even further.

The point is: perspective matters. Your friends have their own points of view, you have a point of view, and inevitably those perspectives will shade the story slightly, even subconsciously; each individual comes across better in his or her own version of the story.

ACTIVITY

Look at the following pair of images of the Taj Mahal in India. How does the photographer's perspective affect how we view the subject? What is included and excluded in the frame, and for what purpose?

Marvin Bartels/500px

Pankaj Nangia/Bloomberg via Getty Images

The Effect of Point of View in Narrative

Just as perspective matters in real life—whether with friends or photographs—it also matters in storytelling, whether the narrative is nonfiction or fiction.

As you likely remember from Chapter 2, writers tend to choose from the following points of view:

First Person Narration: uses "I," and is a character in the story (often, but not always the protagonist).

Third Person Narration: uses "he," "she," "they," and so on, and is not a character within the story. There are a few different types of third person narration:

- Omniscient narrators are ones who know the thoughts and feelings of every character and can move easily through time.
- Limited omniscient narrators are ones who know the thoughts of just one character.
- Objective narrators are ones who report actions and dialogue and describe the setting, but do not know the thoughts and feelings of any of the characters.

But more than simply being able to identify the type of narration an author chooses to use, the goal of analyzing a text for its point of view is to consider the *effects* of that choice. Each point of view creates a unique relationship with the reader based upon what the narrator is able to reveal or not; for instance:

Intimacy: how close or removed does the reader feel to or from the characters and events in the story?

Reliability: to what extent does the reader believe or trust the narrator's perspective on the events in the story?

Depth and breadth of knowledge: how much or how little information does the reader receive about events and characters in the story?

Treatment of time periods: does the reader learn about the past or future of the characters in the story, or is what he or she learns limited to events in the present?

Multiplicity of viewpoints: does the reader see different perspectives on the events and characters within a story?

ACTIVITY

Look at the following images. The photo on the left is taken from the visual equivalent of the first person, while the one on the right is taken from a third person point of view. What is the effect of each point of view, especially on the audience of the photographs? What do we see or not see? What is lost or gained in the choice of each point of view?

lechatnoir/Getty Images

lechatnoir/Getty Images

A Model Analysis

Below is an excerpt from *I Know Why the Caged Bird Sings* by Maya Angelou about her eighth-grade graduation ceremony at an all–African American school in the 1940s. She and all of her classmates are excited about the ceremony until a white politician speaks, praising the graduates solely for their athletic accomplishments, while talking about the academic accomplishments and facilities at the nearby all-white school. In this section, the narrator has stopped recounting what the white man said and we hear what she's thinking.

> We were maids and farmers, handymen and washerwomen, and anything higher that we aspired to was farcical and presumptuous. [. . .]
>
> It was awful to be Negro and have no control over my life. It was brutal to be young and already trained to sit quietly and listen to charges brought against my color with no chance of defense. We should all be dead. I thought I should like to see us all dead, one on top of the other. A pyramid of flesh with the whitefolks on the bottom, as the broad base, then the Indians with their silly tomahawks and teepees and wigwams and treaties, the Negroes with their mops and recipes and cotton sacks and spirituals sticking out of their mouths. The Dutch children should all stumble in their wooden shoes and break their necks. The French should choke to death on the Louisiana Purchase (1803) while silkworms ate all the Chinese with their stupid pigtails. As a species, we were an abomination. All of us. (pars. 40–42)

In this case, the first person narration allows Angelou to paint a very intimate portrait of her pain. A third person point of view could never capture her absolute frustration when she says that she has "no control over [her] life" or that she has been "trained to sit quietly." Those words belong to the narrator directly, and describe her own anger. Through this intimate first person perspective, we too feel her anger. Angelou's narrator then takes the audience deep into her own tortured imagination, picturing a "pyramid of flesh." The reader is likely to be horrified at her fantasy here, but it gives us a picture of the lasting effects of racism.

ACTIVITY

1. Look at this excerpt from George Orwell's "Shooting an Elephant." Refer to the list of effects on page 235 and identify which Orwell creates through his choice of a first person point of view. Consider especially Orwell's level of intimacy and relationship with the reader.

   As for the job I was doing, I hated it more bitterly than I can perhaps make clear. In a job like that you see the dirty work of Empire at close quarters. The wretched prisoners huddling in the stinking cages of the lock-ups, the grey, cowed faces of the long-term convicts, the scarred buttocks of the men who had been flogged with bamboos — all these oppressed me with an intolerable sense of guilt. But I could get nothing into perspective. I was young and ill-educated and I had had to think out my problems in the utter silence that is imposed on every Englishman in the East. I did not even know that the British Empire is dying, still less did I know that it is a great deal better than the younger empires that are going to supplant it. All I knew was that I was stuck between my hatred of the empire I served and my rage against the evil-spirited little beasts who tried to make my job impossible. (par. 2)

2. Read this excerpt from "Shooting an Elephant," by George Orwell, in which the narrator describes being a young British police officer stationed in Burma in the 1930s. Like the authors of most personal narratives, Orwell uses the first person point of view. Using the list of on page 235, as a reference, consider the effects Orwell's choice of narration creates, especially in terms of his reliability and the viewpoint the reader receives.

As a police officer I was an obvious target and was baited whenever it seemed safe to do so. When a nimble Burman tripped me up on the football field and the referee (another Burman) looked the other way, the crowd yelled with hideous laughter. This happened more than once. In the end the sneering yellow faces of young men that met me everywhere, the insults hooted after me when I was at a safe distance, got badly on my nerves. The young Buddhist priests were the worst of all. There were several thousands of them in the town and none of them seemed to have anything to do except stand on street corners and jeer at Europeans. (par. 1)

3. Now read the following version of the passage, which has been written from a third person limited point of view. Using the list of possible effects mentioned above, what is the effect of this change in point of view?

As for the job he was doing, he hated it more bitterly than he can perhaps make clear. In a job like that you see the dirty work of Empire at close quarters. The wretched prisoners huddling in the stinking cages of the lock-ups, the grey, cowed faces of the long-term convicts, the scarred buttocks of the men who had been flogged with bamboos — all these oppressed him with an intolerable sense of guilt. But he could get nothing into perspective. He was young and ill-educated and he had had to think out his problems in the utter silence that is imposed on every Englishman in the East. He did not even know that the British Empire is dying, still less did he know that it is a great deal better than the younger empires that are going to supplant it. All he knew was that he was stuck between his hatred of the empire he served and his rage against the evil-spirited little beasts who tried to make his job impossible.

Connecting Point of View and Theme

Ultimately, the purpose of looking at a text for point of view and thinking about the effects of certain perspectives is to connect the author's choice of point of view to a theme he or she is trying to create in the story. There are many tools that authors use to establish theme, including characterization, conflict, symbols, and so on, and point of view is an often-overlooked device.

A Model Analysis

Look at the ending of the short story "Eveline," by James Joyce. In this excerpt, Eveline is trying to decide whether she should leave home and travel with her boyfriend, Frank, to Argentina. Joyce has chosen to use a third person limited narration, in which the reader receives the inside thoughts of Eveline, but we are excluded from the inside thoughts of Frank.

> She stood among the swaying crowd in the station at the North Wall. He held her hand and she knew that he was speaking to her, saying something about the passage over and over again. The station was full of soldiers with brown baggages. Through the wide doors of the sheds she caught a glimpse of the black mass of the boat, lying in beside the quay wall, with illumined portholes. She answered nothing. She felt her cheek pale and cold and, out of a maze of distress, she prayed to God to direct her, to show her what was her duty. The boat blew a long mournful whistle into the mist. If she went, tomorrow she would be on the sea with Frank, steaming towards Buenos Ayres. Their passage had been booked. Could she still draw back after all he had done for her? Her distress awoke a nausea in her body and she kept moving her lips in silent fervent prayer.
>
> A bell clanged upon her heart. She felt him seize her hand:
>
> "Come!"
>
> All the seas of the world tumbled about her heart. He was drawing her into them: he would drown her. She gripped with both hands at the iron railing.
>
> "Come!"
>
> No! No! No! It was impossible. Her hands clutched the iron in frenzy. Amid the seas she sent a cry of anguish.
>
> "Eveline! Evvy!"
>
> He rushed beyond the barrier and called to her to follow. He was shouted at to go on but he still called to her. She set her white face to him, passive, like a helpless animal. Her eyes gave him no sign of love or farewell or recognition. (pars. 19–26)

Notice how the reader receives only Eveline's perspective but is also held at some remove because of the third person point of view; it is not quite as intimate or personal as a first person perspective. Joyce keeps us focused on Eveline's difficult decision, but we also get the whole scene of the water and the crowds that surround Eveline, as if we were watching a film. If Joyce had employed a third person omniscient narration, the reader would have also had Frank's inside thoughts, which might have influenced the reader's opinion of Eveline's decision. As it stands, only one voice matters in this scene; only one decision is important. This is not an easy choice that Eveline has to make, and because Joyce limits us only to Eveline's perspective, we could argue that he suggests life's difficult decisions are ultimately all faced alone.

ACTIVITY

Look at this excerpt from "Zolaria," by Caitlin Horrocks, which recounts the day that the unnamed narrator and Hanna became friends. As you read, be sure to consider what level of intimacy and reliability the reader feels because of the first person narration.

> In fifth grade Hanna and I doomed ourselves. On the second day of school we took out our folders, our pencil cases, organized our desks, and Hanna had space dolphins and I had pink unicorns. Two years ago all the girls had school supplies like these, and I don't understand why they have abandoned the things they loved. Hanna and I were startled but not stupid, and if no one had noticed us that day we would both have begged our mothers to take us to K-Mart that night and exchange them. But it was too late. We were the girls with the wrong school supplies, and everything we did after that, even the things that were just like everyone else, were the wrong things to do. I will never tell Hanna that space dolphins aren't really as bad as pink unicorns, and that she wasn't really doomed until I made her my friend. (par. 11)

Read the following excerpt from later in the story, after Hanna has become sick. How does the first person narration assist Horrocks in making a point about the nature of friendship?

> I will be unprepared for how long this sickness takes, for how long Hanna will be neither cured nor desperate. I will visit her once more at the hospital, twice more while she's at home. I will realize I am waiting for her to be either well or dead. She will feel very far away. I will start junior high alone, and when Hanna comes for her first day, in late November, I will be startled to see her. Our morning classes must all be different because I recognize her for the first time at lunch, sitting by herself. I will already be sitting in the middle of a long table by the time I see her, my lunch unpacked in front of me. I will be pressed tight on either side by people who, if asked, would probably say I am their friend. Hanna will be wearing an awful wig, stiff and styled like an old woman's perm. The hair will be dark brown, not black, and will no longer match her eyes. She will be pale and her face swollen and she will not seem like someone I can afford to know. (par. 25)

ACTIVITY

Practice analyzing point of view with the following excerpt from *The School Days of an Indian Girl* by Zitkala-Sa. Write an analytical paragraph about the effect of the first person point of view of the piece and how that choice of point of view helps Zitkala-Sa develop her theme.

from **The School Days of an Indian Girl** / **Zitkala-Sa**

Late in the morning, my friend Judéwin gave me a terrible warning. Judéwin knew a few words of English, and she had overheard the paleface woman talk about cutting our long, heavy hair. Our mothers had taught us that only unskilled warriors who were captured had their hair shingled by the enemy. Among our people, short hair was worn by mourners, and shingled hair by cowards!

We discussed our fate some moments, and when Judéwin said, "We have to submit, because they are strong," I rebelled.

"No, I will not submit! I will struggle first!" I answered.

I watched my chance, and when no one noticed I disappeared. I crept up the stairs as quietly as I could in my squeaking shoes, — my moccasins had been exchanged for shoes. Along the hall I passed, without knowing whither I was going. Turning aside to an open door, I found a large room with three white beds in it. The windows were covered with dark green curtains, which made the room very dim. Thankful that no one was there, I directed my steps toward the corner farthest from the door. On my hands and knees I crawled under the bed, and cuddled myself in the dark corner.

From my hiding place I peered out, shuddering with fear whenever I heard footsteps near by. Though in the hall loud voices were calling my name, and I knew that even Judéwin

was searching for me, I did not open my mouth to answer. Then the steps were quickened and the voices became excited. The sounds came nearer and nearer. Women and girls entered the room. I held my breath, and watched them open closet doors and peep behind large trunks. Some one threw up the curtains, and the room was filled with sudden light. What caused them to stoop and look under the bed I do not know. I remember being dragged out, though I resisted by kicking and scratching wildly. In spite of myself, I was carried downstairs and tied fast in a chair.

I cried aloud, shaking my head all the while until I felt the cold blades of the scissors against my neck, and heard them gnaw off one of my thick braids. Then I lost my spirit. Since the day I was taken from my mother I had suffered extreme indignities. People had stared at me. I had been tossed about in the air like a wooden puppet. And now my long hair was shingled like a coward's! In my anguish I moaned for my mother, but no one came to comfort me. Not a soul reasoned quietly with me, as my own mother used to do; for now I was only one of many little animals driven by a herder. ■

WRITING A PERSONAL NARRATIVE

Writing an Effective Narrative

A narrative is a story, usually told from a first person point of view, that is intended to reveal something significant about the narrator to the reader. Effective narratives must have a reason for existence beyond being a classroom assignment. They should not be the "what I did last summer" stories you wrote in elementary school, but rather, "What I did last summer, and *why it matters.*"

The goal of writing an effective narrative is to communicate a meaningful experience to an audience in an interesting way. Writing an effective narrative requires two essential components: you have to have something to say, and you need to say it well. While the purpose of this Workshop is to improve your narrative writing skills, at several points you will read or reread professional models of effective narrative elements before having an opportunity to practice each one for yourself.

ACTIVITY

Besides being a common classroom assignment, stories actually do matter. Our own stories matter to us, and to others. Look over the following quotes about storytelling, and think about the value of storytelling to the writer and to society:

- "There is no greater agony than bearing an untold story inside you."—Maya Angelou
- "People become the stories they hear and the stories they tell."—Elie Wiesel
- "Without our stories, how will we know it's us? Without the stories of others, how will we know who they are?"—Dudley Cocke
- "Stories simultaneously celebrate what is unique about us and provide bridges to what is common among us."—The Storyweavers, Lucinda Flodin and Dennis Frederick

Step 1: Finding a Topic

One of the most important—and most challenging—steps in writing a narrative is the first one, when you have to ask yourself, "What should I write about?" While sometimes the narrative prompts are very straightforward, such as "write about the time you were most happy" or "write about your favorite vacation," oftentimes the prompt will be much more open-ended, so you will have to decide on your topic. Remember that the story you tell needs to have significance to you, and hope that it will be meaningful to your reader as well. That said, this does not mean that your story needs to be about a huge or earthshaking event in your life, like the time you saved a child from drowning or traveled to some faraway country. In fact, the best narratives are often smaller stories that have gained greater significance to you upon reflection. Early in his narrative "Shooting an Elephant,"

George Orwell writes, "One day something happened which in a roundabout way was enlightening. It was a tiny incident in itself, but it gave me a better glimpse than I had had before of the real nature of imperialism—the real motives for which despotic governments act" (par. 3). So, when you are thinking of topics, focus on the "tiny incidents" that may have given you a glimpse into something enlightening about yourself or others.

ACTIVITY

Brainstorm for possible stories using the following categories to help you generate ideas:

- **Firsts**, such as the first time you won a class spelling bee
- **New**, such as the time when you were the new person in class
- **Conflicts**, such as the time you got into a disagreement with a teacher about the grading policy
- **Realizations**, such as the time you realized that you are really good at art

---

Step 2: Determining What You Want to Reveal about Yourself

Before you finalize a topic, be sure that the story you tell will reveal something about yourself in the telling. Look at another section from Orwell's "Shooting an Elephant" to see how the author reveals details of himself in the story: "I was young and ill-educated and I had had to think out my problems in the utter silence that is imposed on every Englishman in the East. I did not even know that the British Empire is dying, still less did I know that it is a great deal better than the younger empires that are going to supplant it. All I knew was that I was stuck between my hatred of the empire I served and my rage against the evil-spirited little beasts who tried to make my job impossible" (par. 2). He is brutally honest about his own ignorance and the frustration he feels in his situation. Because most narratives are written in the first person point of view, readers will expect you to use that form of narration to get the reader to feel and learn something about you.

ACTIVITY

Return to the list of possible topics you brainstormed in Step 1. Choose a few of them and write a line or two about what you would be likely to reveal about yourself in the story. The topic that gives you the most to say about yourself is likely to be the best one for your narrative, especially if you can also remember or re-create a lot of details relating to the story.

Step 3: Organizing and Starting Your Narrative

Remember that two of the essential components of writing an effective narrative are having a story worth telling and telling it well. So far, you have been working mostly on the first component. The next few steps will focus on how you can make your narrative interesting and engaging for the reader.

By far, the majority of personal narratives are written in chronological order, meaning that they recount the details of an event in the order in which they occurred, perhaps adding relevant background when necessary. You can certainly experiment with other organizational structures, including a variety of flashbacks for particular effects, but know that the reader, in general, expects a story to unfold in chronological order. If you vary that structure, be prepared to assist the reader in following your narrative by using effective and clear time transitions, such as "earlier that month . . ." or "long before this happened . . ."

Now, just because your narrative will likely be told in chronological order, this does not mean that you need to begin at the beginning. In fact, one of the most ineffective ways to begin a narrative is "It all started when . . ." or "I remember a time when I . . ." Just as in any other piece of writing, you will want to hook your readers immediately with something that will draw them into your story.

Here are a few openings from texts in this Conversation:

- "Shooting an Elephant": "In Moulmein, in Lower Burma, I was hated by large numbers of people." Starting with being hated is engaging because readers want to find out exactly why the narrator was hated, especially by so many people.
- "Zolaria": "It is July and we are a miraculous age. We have been sprung from our backyards, from the neighborhood park, from the invisible borders that rationed all our other summers." This opening raises many questions. What is this age, who are "we," and what will we do with this new freedom?
- "Against School": "I taught for thirty years in some of the worst schools in Manhattan, and in some of the best, and during that time I became an expert in boredom." It is surprising that the commonality that the narrator identifies between good and bad schools is "boredom." Readers wants to learn more about what has made him an "expert" in boredom.

ACTIVITY

Think about one of the topics that you brainstormed earlier. Write a sentence or two of an engaging opening for that topic. Consider using an interesting piece of dialogue or a specific detail from the event, or even drop the reader right in the middle of a situation that you will describe in greater detail later in your narrative.

Now, write an entirely different opening for the same narrative, using a different approach. Which one is more effective at capturing your reader's attention? Which one feels most natural to your style?

Step 4: Using Details

Another way to engage your reader is through your use of details and description. If the main goal of a narrative is to communicate an experience to a reader, then a writer needs to do everything in his or her power to convey the specific details that will clearly describe the characters, settings, and feelings you had. Remember that your audience is unfamiliar with the people, places, and objects in the story. You may know everything about your grandma: what she looks like and acts like, and what her house smells like, but your reader does not. You have to bring these details to life through your description.

Look at this excerpt from *I Know Why the Caged Bird Sings*. Identify the details that Maya Angelou uses, especially words and phrases that communicate the feeling of being right there at her graduation as the white men address the crowd of African Americans:

> The man's dead words fell like bricks around the auditorium and too many settled in my belly. Constrained by hard-learned manners I couldn't look behind me, but to my left and right the proud graduating class of 1940 had dropped their heads. Every girl in my row had found something new to do with her handkerchief. Some folded the tiny squares into love knots, some into triangles, but most were wadding them, then pressing them flat on their yellow laps.
>
> On the dais, the ancient tragedy was being replayed. Professor Parsons sat, a sculptor's reject, rigid. His large, heavy body seemed devoid of will or willingness, and his eyes said he was no longer with us. The other teachers examined the flag (which was draped stage right) or their notes, or the windows which opened on our now-famous playing diamond. (pars. 37–38)

ACTIVITY

Close your eyes and imagine that you are at the beach, in the woods, in a busy city, or in another location that you know well. Write down *ten* things that you could see, hear, smell, taste, and so on if you were actually there. Write a brief (three- to five-sentence) narrative about being in that location, using at least five of the details you imagined.

ACTIVITY

Think about someone who will likely appear in the narrative that you brainstormed and wrote the opening for earlier. Then, write a paragraph about this person using details that will make the person come alive for a reader who does not know him or her.

   a. **Physical descriptions:** age, height, weight, and so on
   b. **Background information:** race, career, education, marital status, and so on
   c. **Emotional description:** his or her overall personality and characteristic emotions
   d. **Main desires:** what does he or she want out of life?
   e. **Unique features:** what makes this person different from others? Does he or she have an accent? Like to curse or use a lot of slang?

ACTIVITY

Look at the following paintings, and write a paragraph from the point of view of one of the figures in the painting that describes the surroundings. Be sure to use a lot of vivid details, especially those that appeal to the five senses.

Andrew Wyeth, *Christina's World*, 1948. Tempera on panel, $32\frac{1}{4}$ inches x $47\frac{3}{4}$ inches. The Museum of Modern Art, New York.

Christina's World, 1948 tempera © Andrew Wyeth. Digital Image © The Museum of Modern Art/Licensed by SCALA/Art Resource, NY

Palmer Hayden, *Midsummer Night in Harlem*, 1930. Oil on canvas, 25 inches x 30 inches. The Museum of African American Art, Los Angeles.

Painting by Palmer C. Hayden (1890–1973) National Archives and Records Administration

Step 5: Using Dialogue

Another key component of writing an effective narrative is the inclusion of dialogue. When you include what people say during a story, it has the effect of bringing your reader into your narrative. Dialogue makes the story feel more immediate and can be a very effective way of revealing something about yourself or others in a narrative.

Look, for example, at this exchange between the narrator of "Zolaria" and her mother. Notice how the dialogue quickly shows the reasons for the conflict between mother and daughter, as well as hinting at the fact that the narrator is probably unwilling to reflect too much on her own self:

Thirteen years later, Cal and I will announce our engagement on Christmas morning over crumpled wrapping paper and freshly squeezed orange juice. It will be the coldest morning of any year of my life so far, the paper's lead headline the temperature, 26 below, but as we unwrap presents we will see one of the Khoury boys outside walking their dog. My mother will call me into the kitchen to tell me I am young. "You're young," she'll say. "You're still so young."

"Not that young," I will tell her.

"Yes, that young. You barely know each other."

"I know him."

"You don't know yourself," she'll say. "That's what I worry about. How can you get married when you don't know yourself yet?"

"I know myself plenty," I'll say. "I think I know all I want to." (pars. 14–19)

In general, the dialogue in a narrative typically follows a very specific format. Here are some of the most common rules and a few suggestions for writing dialogue:

- Use a separate paragraph every time the speaker changes. See how the author of "Zolaria" uses a new paragraph for the mother and for the daughter.
- Continue in the same paragraph if the speaker continues, but change if you return to narration.
- Place punctuation inside quotation marks.
- Avoid too much dialogue. Not everything needs to be in dialogue.
- Make it sound real. Feel free to use slang or even improper grammar if it helps the reader to understand something about the character who is speaking.

ACTIVITY

Look over the following two versions of a story. The first does not use dialogue and the second does. What does the dialogue add to the story? What is revealed through the dialogue that is not apparent in the first version?

Version A

One day my friend Tim and I decided that we wanted a new video game, but neither of us had any money to buy one at the store. We debated who should steal it, and stupidly, we each decided to steal one. We almost made it out the door, but Tim got caught, and I ran away.

Version B

As soon as we got inside the store, the question immediately came up.

"Who's gonna do it?" I asked.

"I'm not doing it," Tim replied quickly. "We're gonna play it on my console, so I think that you oughta do it."

The store was suddenly too quiet and I thought everyone was listening to us. I really didn't want to do it, but I was scared.

"No way," I whispered. "I don't steal."

"Fine, but I'm not doing it!"

We went around and around like this for a while until we decided that it would only be fair if we each stole a game. We each had one in our hands when someone grabbed us from behind.

"Hey!" the store manager yelled at us. "What are y'all doing?"

"We didn't steal anything," my not-too-bright friend said. "Maybe we were gonna pay for them!"

I didn't wait to hear the rest; I just ran.

ACTIVITY

Now return to the narrative that you have been working with throughout this Workshop. Identify a place in your story where you could include a dialogue exchange. Using the format and suggestions on pages 244–45, write a few pieces of dialogue and think about how the dialogue makes your narrative more effective.

Step 6: Using Blocking

Another key component of effective narrative that is often underused in student writing is "blocking," which essentially is the stage directions for the characters in the narrative. Blocking describes what the characters are doing while they are talking, Like dialogue, it helps to put the reader right into the action of your story. If a character in your narrative is "leaning against the wall" as she speaks, this might reveal something about her easygoing nature; if he constantly brushes his hair back from his face, he might be nervous about something.

Look at this example from *The Geeks Shall Inherit the Earth,* a nonfiction book about social cliques in high school. Notice how the details of blocking—especially the body language, gestures, and movements—establish and reinforce the exclusionary nature of the popular clique.

As the halls filled up, crowds parted for the preps. Some students said hello, but Whitney and her friends gave them the "what's-up-but-I-won't-really-acknowledge-you" head nod.

When Whitney walked into advertising class with Peyton, she spotted Dirk. "Hey, Whitney!" he yelled across the room.

"I'm not sitting with Dirk," Peyton whispered to Whitney. "I don't see why you like those people. They scare me."

Whitney shrugged and grinned at Dirk as she sat next to him anyway.

At lunch, the preps cut to the front of the line, as usual, and sat at "their" lunch table in the center of the cafeteria. Whitney hadn't waited in the lunch line since she was a freshman. In the past, when students told the preps to stop cutting, Whitney's group either ignored them or shot nasty glares.

"That's Shay," Chelsea answered.

"Dude, I didn't even recognize her," Peyton said. Did she gain like fifteen pounds over the summer? Why did her hair get so big and frizzy?" This led to a discussion about how there were too many skanks and trailer trash kids at Riverland.

ACTIVITY

Imagine that you were writing a narrative from the point of view of the character Maggie (who has her back to the reader in the first frame on p. 187) in Faith Erin Hicks's graphic novel *Friends with Boys.* Write a few sentences about Maggie's first day attending a public school after years of being homeschooled. Be sure to focus on the blocking of the other students as well as Maggie.

ACTIVITY

Return to the dialogue exchange that you wrote for your own narrative earlier, and include blocking for the characters involved in the conversation that reveals some aspect of their personalities or feelings.

Step 7: Reflecting on the Significance

One of the features that makes narrative writing distinct from other modes of writing is that it often includes some type of reflection, or a summary of the value of the experience that the writer wants to pass on to the reader. In less sophisticated narratives, this might take the form of a concluding statement such as, "What I learned from this was . . . ," but in more complex narratives, the reflection, which may or may not even be placed at the end of the story, is closer to a statement of the theme the writer wants to communicate. It is entirely possible that this reflection will be not explicitly stated, but rather implied indirectly. What's essential is that the reader ought to be able discern from your narrative some significant point you are hoping to communicate.

Look back at this section from the middle of "Shooting an Elephant." While he does not directly state it, what is George Orwell hoping the reader can infer about what caused him to shoot the elephant despite his reluctance to do so?

> Here was I, the white man with his gun, standing in front of the unarmed native crowd—seemingly the leading actor of the piece; but in reality I was only an absurd puppet pushed to and fro by the will of those yellow faces behind. I perceived in this moment that when the white man turns tyrant it is his own freedom that he destroys. He becomes a sort of hollow, posing dummy, the conventionalized figure of a sahib. For it is the condition of his rule that he shall spend his life in trying to impress the "natives," and so in every crisis he has got to do what the "natives" expect of him. He wears a mask, and his face grows to fit it. (par. 7)

ACTIVITY

Return to the narrative that you have been working on throughout this Workshop and write a few sentences that reflect on the significance of this event. Ideally, this reflection will reveal something about you, but also have some kind of application to others.

6
Ambition and Restraint

- What drives individuals to succeed?
- What are the benefits and risks of ambition?
- What are some conditions that lead to rebellion against the status quo?
- When is violence ever justified?
- How can speeches inspire people to act for change?

In many ways, ambition is the force behind humankind's greatest achievements. Whether it is exploring the universe, pushing technology forward, campaigning for equality, fighting against oppression, or just trying to make a better life for yourself and others, ambition is the fuel that drives us forward.

And yet, ambition has a dark side. Left unchecked, ambition can lead to greed, corruption, and violence. The ambition to unlock the secrets of the atom, for instance, led to the development of the most destructive weapons ever created.

Photo: majeczka/Shutterstock Art: Christian Mojallali

Where is the line at which bravery becomes foolishness? At what point does failing to take a risk become cowardice? Do you agree with Theodore Roosevelt, who said, "Far better is it to dare mighty things, to win glorious triumphs, even though checkered by failure, than to rank with those poor spirits who neither enjoy nor suffer much, because they live in a gray twilight that knows not victory nor defeat." It seems daring and inspirational to agree, but not everybody wants to live the outrageous sort of life that Teddy Roosevelt did.

In the movie *Wall Street*, the character Gordon Gekko is a stockbroker who becomes an American symbol of blind ambition. At a critical moment in the movie, he shares his philosophy with a group of stockholders:

> The point is, ladies and gentleman, that greed — for lack of a better word — is good.
>> Greed is right.
>> Greed works.
>> Greed clarifies, cuts through, and captures the essence of the evolutionary spirit.
>> Greed, in all of its forms — greed for life, for money, for love, knowledge — has marked the upward surge of mankind.

What makes Gordon Gekko's character so compelling is that his ideas hold a kernel of truth, and yet he has also become a cautionary tale in American culture—a person destroyed by his own ambition.

It seems clear that ambition must be held in check by some kind of restraint, which could be external like laws or other people, or internal like emotions or personal beliefs. But where is the line?

In this chapter, we'll ponder these two forces—ambition and restraint—to identify an appropriate and reasonable balance between them.

What aspects of this scene from *Wall Street* capture Gordon Gekko's power and ambition?

OPENING ACTIVITY 1

Consider Gekko's statements regarding greed. Then, summarize each of his ideas and provide an example from history, current events, or personal experience that supports each of his ideas:

- How is greed "good" and in what ways does it "work"?
- What is the "evolutionary spirit" and in what ways does greed capture its essence?
- What is the "upward surge of mankind" and how has it been influenced or "marked" by greed?

Now imagine you are interviewing Gekko for a story in a magazine. Write three questions you would ask him that would challenge his ideas and three questions that would support his assertions. After you have written your questions, select one and then write a response from Gekko's perspective.

OPENING ACTIVITY 2

Consider your own ambitions at this point in your life. What do you wish to achieve this year? What do you wish to achieve in the next five years? When you are much older and perhaps getting ready to retire, what accomplishments would you hope to have by that point in your life?

After considering your own ambitions, discuss what lengths you are prepared to go to in order to achieve your ambitions and what limitations or constraints you will place on yourself as you work to achieve your aspirations.

The Tragedy of Macbeth

William Shakespeare

William Shakespeare (1564–1616) was an English poet, actor, and playwright who is considered to be one of the greatest writers in the English language and the world's preeminent dramatist and is credited with 38 plays, 154 sonnets, and two long narrative poems. Little is known of his life aside from the fact that he married Anne Hathaway when he was eighteen, worked as an actor-playwright in London, and retired in 1613. His plays fall into four principal categories: early comedies (1585–1594); more sophisticated comedies and histories (1595–1599); the great tragedies (1599–1607); and the final phase (1608–1613). His most accomplished works—including *Hamlet* (1601), *Othello* (1603), *King Lear* (1605), and *Macbeth* (1606)—belong to the third period.

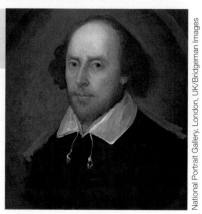

National Portrait Gallery, London, UK/Bridgeman Images

KEY CONTEXT   Written around 1606, *Macbeth* is loosely based on the life of the historical king Mac Bethed who reigned in Scotland from 1040 to 1057. The real Macbeth killed his predecessor Duncan I, and was in turn killed by Duncan's son Malcolm III. Events such as these were not uncommon in the feudal Scotland of the eleventh century; of the fourteen kings who reigned between 943 and 1097, ten were murdered. However, the Scottish king bears very little resemblance to the character in Shakespeare's play. Shakespeare was a playwright, after all, and driven by very different goals than a historian.

One of those goals was writing a play that Shakespeare's patron, the newly crowned King James I, would enjoy. King James I had ascended to the throne in England in 1603, and Shakespeare began writing *Macbeth* soon after. King James I came from the same families who led to the real Macbeth's downfall, and Shakespeare's play acknowledges this fact and even flatters the man who had recently become the king of England. It was also well known that King James I was fascinated with witchcraft, even writing a book on demonology, which is probably why witches play a mysterious and important role in this play.

Dramatis Personae

DUNCAN *King of Scotland*

MALCOLM
DONALBAIN ⎤ *his sons*

MACBETH *Thane of Glamis, later of Cawdor, later King of Scotland*

LADY MACBETH

BANQUO *a thane of Scotland*

FLEANCE *his son*

MACDUFF *Thane of Fife*

LADY MACDUFF

SON *of Macduff and Lady Macduff*

LENNOX
ROSS
MENTEITH ⎤ *thanes and noblemen of Scotland*
ANGUS
CAITHNESS ⎦
SIWARD *Earl of Northumberland*
YOUNG SIWARD *his son*
SEYTON *an officer attending Macbeth*
Another LORD
ENGLISH DOCTOR
SCOTTISH DOCTOR
GENTLEWOMAN *attending Lady Macbeth*
CAPTAIN *serving Duncan*

PORTER
OLD MAN
Three MURDERERS *of Banquo*
FIRST MURDERER *at Macduff's castle*
MESSENGER *to Lady Macbeth*
MESSENGER *to Lady Macduff*
SERVANT *to Macbeth*
SERVANT *to Lady Macbeth*
Three WITCHES *or* WEIRD SISTERS
HECATE
Three APPARITIONS

Lords, Gentlemen, Officers, Soldiers, Murderers, and Attendants

Act 1 Macbeth

SCENE Scotland; England

Scene 1°

Thunder and lightning. Enter three Witches.

FIRST WITCH When shall we three meet again?
  In thunder, lightning, or in rain?
SECOND WITCH When the hurlyburly's° done,
  When the battle's lost and won.
5 THIRD WITCH That will be ere the set of sun.
FIRST WITCH Where the place?
SECOND WITCH   Upon the heath.
THIRD WITCH There to meet with Macbeth.
FIRST WITCH I come, Grimalkin!°
SECOND WITCH Paddock° calls.
10 THIRD WITCH Anon.°
  ALL Fair is foul, and foul is fair.
    Hover through the fog and filthy air.

                              Exeunt. 10

Scene 2°

*Alarum° within. Enter King [Duncan], Malcolm,
Donalbain, Lennox, with attendants, meeting a
bleeding Captain.*

DUNCAN What bloody man is that? He can
    report,
  As seemeth by his plight, of the revolt
  The newest state.°
MALCOLM   This is the sergeant°
  Who like a good and hardy soldier fought
5 'Gainst my captivity. Hail, brave friend!
  Say to the King the knowledge of the broil°
  As thou didst leave it.
CAPTAIN   Doubtful it stood,
  As two spent° swimmers that do cling together
  And choke their art.° The merciless
    Macdonwald—
10 Worthy to be a rebel, for to that°
  The multiplying villainies of nature
  Do swarm upon him°—from the Western Isles°
  Of kerns° and gallowglasses° is supplied;

Act 1, Scene 1. Location: An open place.   3. **hurlyburly:** tumult.   8. **Grimalkin:** i.e., gray cat, name of the witch's familiar — a demon or evil spirit supposed to answer a witch's call and to allow him or her to perform black magic.   9. **Paddock:** toad; also a familiar.   10. **Anon:** at once, right away.   **Act 1, Scene 2. Location:** A camp near Forres.   s.d. *Alarum:* trumpet call to arms.   3. **newest state:** latest news.   **sergeant:** i.e., staff officer. (There may be no inconsistency with his rank of "captain" in the stage direction and speech prefixes in the Folio.)   6. **broil:** battle.
8. **spent:** tired out.   9. **choke their art:** render their skill in swimming useless.   10. **to that:** as if to that end or purpose.   11–12. **The multiplying . . . him:** ever increasing numbers of villainous rebels (or perhaps villainous qualities) swarm about him like vermin.   12. **Western Isles:** islands to the west of Scotland — the Hebrides and perhaps Ireland.   13. **Of kerns:** with light-armed Irish foot soldiers.   **gallowglasses:** horsemen armed with axes.

seeing connections

Macbeth is often reimagined in a modern context, and the witches have taken several different forms in these modern versions. Consider these two examples. The first is from a 2010 adaptation of the play to Stalinist Russia, and the witches are nurses in the combat hospital. The second is from a 2005 BBC production in which Macbeth runs a fancy restaurant and the witches are sanitation workers.

What is the effect of reimagining the witches in these ways? If you were directing a modern version, what choice would you make when deciding how to present the witches?

	And Fortune, on his damnèd quarrel° smiling,
15	Showed° like a rebel's whore. But all's too weak;
	For brave Macbeth — well he deserves that name°—
	Disdaining Fortune, with his brandished steel,
	Which smoked with bloody execution,
	Like valor's minion° carved out his passage
20	Till he faced the slave,°
	Which° ne'er shook hands nor bade farewell to him°
	Till he unseamed him from the nave° to th' chops,°

And fixed his head upon our battlements.

DUNCAN O valiant cousin,° worthy gentleman!

25 **CAPTAIN** As whence° the sun 'gins his reflection°
Shipwrecking storms and direful thunders break,
So from that spring whence comfort seemed to come
Discomfort swells. Mark, King of Scotland, mark.
No sooner justice had, with valor armed,
30 Compelled these skipping° kerns to trust their heels
But the Norweyan lord, surveying vantage,°

---

14. **quarrel:** cause.   15. **Showed:** appeared.   16. **name:** i.e., "brave."   19. **minion:** darling.   20. **the slave:** i.e., Macdonwald.   21. **Which:** who, i.e., Macbeth.   **ne'er . . . to him:** proffered no polite salutation or farewell, acted without ceremony.   22. **nave:** navel.   **chops:** jaws.   24. **cousin:** kinsman.   25. **As whence:** just as from the place where.   **'gins his reflection:** begins its turning back (from its southward progression during winter).   30. **skipping:** (1) lightly armed, quick at maneuvering (2) skittish.   31. **surveying vantage:** seeing an opportunity.

With furbished arms and new supplies of men,
Began a fresh assault.

DUNCAN Dismayed not this our captains,
Macbeth and Banquo?

35 **CAPTAIN** Yes, as sparrows eagles, or the hare the
lion.
If I say sooth,° I must report they were
As cannons overcharged with double cracks,°
So they doubly redoubled strokes upon the foe.
Except° they meant to bathe in reeking wounds
40 Or memorize° another Golgotha,°
I cannot tell.
But I am faint. My gashes cry for help.

DUNCAN So well thy words become thee as thy
wounds;
They smack of honor both. — Go get him
surgeons.

[*Exit Captain, attended.*]

Enter Ross and Angus.

45 Who comes here?

MALCOLM The worthy Thane° of Ross.

LENNOX What a haste looks through his eyes!
So should he look that seems to° speak things
strange.

ROSS God save the King!

DUNCAN Whence cam'st thou, worthy thane?

50 **ROSS** From Fife, great King,
Where the Norweyan banners flout° the sky
And fan our people cold.°
Norway° himself, with terrible numbers,°
Assisted by that most disloyal traitor,
55 The Thane of Cawdor, began a dismal° conflict,
Till that Bellona's bridegroom, lapped in proof,°
Confronted him° with self-comparisons,°
Point against point, rebellious arm 'gainst arm,
Curbing his lavish spirit; and to conclude,
The victory fell on us.

60 **DUNCAN** Great happiness!

ROSS That now
Sweno, the Norways'° king, craves composition;°
Nor would we deign him burial of his men
Till he disbursèd at Saint Colme's Inch°
65 Ten thousand dollars° to our general use.

DUNCAN No more that Thane of Cawdor shall
deceive
Our° bosom° interest. Go pronounce his
present° death,
And with his former title greet Macbeth.

ROSS I'll see it done.

70 **DUNCAN** What he hath lost noble Macbeth hath
won. *Exeunt.*

Scene 3°

Thunder. Enter the three Witches.

FIRST WITCH Where hast thou been, sister?

SECOND WITCH Killing swine.

THIRD WITCH Sister, where thou?

FIRST WITCH A sailor's wife had chestnuts in
her lap,
5 And munched, and munched, and munched.
"Give me," quoth I.
"Aroint thee,° witch!" the rump-fed° runnion°
cries.
Her husband's to Aleppo gone, master o' the
Tiger;°
But in a sieve I'll thither sail,
And like a rat without a tail
10 I'll do,° I'll do, and I'll do.°

SECOND WITCH I'll give thee a wind.

FIRST WITCH Thou'rt kind.

THIRD WITCH And I another.

FIRST WITCH I myself have all the other,°
15 And the very ports they blow,°
All the quarters that they know

---

36. **say sooth:** tell the truth. 37. **cracks:** charges of explosive. 39. **Except:** unless. 40. **memorize:** make memorable or famous. **Golgotha:** "place of a skull," where Christ was crucified (Mark 15:22). 45. **Thane:** Scottish title of honor, roughly equivalent to "Earl." 47. **seems to:** seems about to. 51. **flout:** mock, insult. 52. **fan . . . cold:** fan cold fear into our troops. 53. **Norway:** the King of Norway. **terrible numbers:** terrifying numbers of troops. 55. **dismal:** ominous. 56. **Till . . . proof:** i.e., until Macbeth, clad in well-tested armor. (Bellona was the Roman goddess of war.) 57. **him:** i.e., the King of Norway. **self-comparisons:** i.e., matching counterthrusts. 62. **Norways':** Norwegians'. **composition:** agreement, treaty of peace. 64. **Saint Colme's Inch:** Inchcolm, the Isle of St. Columba in the Firth of Forth. 65. **dollars:** Spanish or Dutch coins. 67. **Our:** (The royal "we.") **bosom:** close and affectionate. **present:** immediate. **Act 1, Scene 3.** Location: a heath near Forres. 6. **Aroint thee:** begone. **rump-fed:** fed on refuse, or fat-rumped. **runnion:** mangy creature, scabby woman. 7. *Tiger:* (A ship's name.) 9–10. **like . . . do:** (Suggestive of the witches' deformity and sexual insatiability. Witches were thought to seduce men sexually.) 10. **do:** (1) act (2) perform sexually. 14. **other:** others. 15. **And . . . blow:** (The witches can prevent a ship from entering port by causing the winds to blow from land.)

I' the shipman's card°
I'll drain him dry as hay.
Sleep shall neither night nor day
20 Hang upon his penthouse lid.°
He shall live a man forbid.°

25 Weary sev'nnights° nine times nine
Shall he dwindle, peak,° and pine.
Though his bark cannot be lost,
Yet it shall be tempest-tossed.
Look what I have.

---

17. **shipman's card:** compass card.   20. **penthouse lid:** i.e., eyelid (which projects out over the eye like a *penthouse* or slope-roofed structure).
21. **forbid:** accursed.   22. **sev'nnights:** weeks.   23. **peak:** grow peaked or thin.

seeing connections

Here are two paintings depicting Macbeth and Banquo's meeting with the Weird Sisters. Notice the vast difference in how the witches are depicted.

Based on evidence from the text, which depiction do you prefer, either because it is most faithful to the text, or because it presents a compelling interpretation?

Samuel John Egbert Jones, *"Macbeth,"* *Act 1, Scene 3, the Weird Sisters,* c. 1820s. Oil on canvas. Royal Shakespeare Company Collection, Stratford-upon-Avon, United Kingdom.

Royal Shakespeare Company Collection, Stratford-upon-Avon, Warwickshire/ Bridgeman Images

Francesco Zuccarelli, "*Macbeth,*" *Act 1, Scene 3, Macbeth, Banquo and the Witches,* c. 1760. Oil on canvas. Royal Shakespeare Company Collection, Stratford-upon-Avon, United Kingdom.

Royal Shakespeare Company Collection, Stratford-upon-Avon, Warwickshire/Bridgeman Images

SECOND WITCH Show me, show me.

FIRST WITCH Here I have a pilot's thumb,
Wrecked as homeward he did come.

Drum within.

30 **THIRD WITCH** A drum, a drum!
Macbeth doth come.

ALL [*dancing in a circle*] The Weird Sisters,° hand
in hand,
Posters of° the sea and land,
Thus do go about, about,

35 Thrice to thine, and thrice to mine,
And thrice again, to make up nine.
Peace! The charm's wound up.

Enter Macbeth and Banquo

MACBETH So foul and fair a day I have not seen.

BANQUO How far is 't called° to Forres? — What
are these,

40 So withered and so wild in their attire,
That look not like th' inhabitants o' th' earth
And yet are on 't? — Live you? Or are you aught
That man may question? You seem to
understand me
By each at once her chappy° finger laying

45 Upon her skinny lips. You should be women,
And yet your beards forbid me to interpret
That you are so.

MACBETH Speak, if you can. What are you?

FIRST WITCH All hail, Macbeth! Hail to thee,
Thane of Glamis!

SECOND WITCH All hail, Macbeth! Hail to thee,
Thane of Cawdor!

50 **THIRD WITCH** All hail, Macbeth, that shalt be
king hereafter!

BANQUO Good sir, why do you start and seem to
fear
Things that do sound so fair? — I' the name of
truth,
Are ye fantastical° or that indeed
Which outwardly ye show?° My noble partner

55 You greet with present grace° and great
prediction

Of noble having and of royal hope,
That he seems rapt withal.° To me you speak
not.
If you can look into the seeds of time
And say which grain will grow and which will
not,

60 Speak then to me, who neither beg nor fear
Your favors nor your hate.°

FIRST WITCH Hail!

SECOND WITCH Hail!

THIRD WITCH Hail!

65 **FIRST WITCH** Lesser than Macbeth, and greater.

SECOND WITCH Not so happy,° yet much happier.

THIRD WITCH Thou shalt get° kings, though thou
be none.
So all hail, Macbeth and Banquo!

FIRST WITCH Banquo and Macbeth, all hail!

70 **MACBETH** Stay, you imperfect° speakers, tell me
more!
By Sinel's° death I know I am Thane of Glamis,
But how of Cawdor? The Thane of Cawdor
lives
A prosperous gentleman; and to be king
Stands not within the prospect of belief,

75 No more than to be Cawdor. Say from whence
You owe this strange intelligence,° or why
Upon this blasted° heath you stop our way
With such prophetic greeting? Speak, I charge
you. *Witches vanish.*

BANQUO The earth hath bubbles, as the water
has,

80 And these are of them. Whither are they
vanished?

MACBETH Into the air; and what seemed
corporal° melted,
As breath into the wind. Would they had
stayed!

BANQUO Were such things here as we do speak
about?
Or have we eaten on° the insane root°

85 That takes the reason prisoner?

MACBETH Your children shall be kings.

---

32. **Weird Sisters:** women connected with fate or destiny; also women having a mysterious or unearthly, uncanny appearance.   33. **Posters of:** swift travelers over.   39. **is't called:** is it said to be.   44. **chappy:** chapped.   53. **fantastical:** creatures of fantasy or imagination.   54. **show:** appear.   55. **grace:** honor.   57. **rapt withal:** carried out of himself, distracted by these predictions.   **withal:** with it, by it.   60–61. **beg . . . hate:** beg your favors nor fear your hate.   66. **happy:** fortunate.   67. **get:** beget.   70. **imperfect:** cryptic.   71. **Sinel's:** (Sinel was Macbeth's father.) 75–76. **Say . . . intelligence:** say from what source you have this unusual information.   77. **blasted:** blighted.   81. **corporal:** bodily.   84. **on:** of. **insane root:** root causing insanity; variously identified.

BANQUO   You shall be king.

MACBETH And Thane of Cawdor too. Went it not
　　so?

BANQUO To th' selfsame tune and words.
　　—Who's here?

Enter Ross and Angus.

ROSS The King hath happily received, Macbeth,
90　　The news of thy success; and when he reads°
　　Thy personal venture in the rebels' fight,°
　　His wonders and his praises do contend
　　Which should be thine or his. Silenced with
　　　that,°
　　In viewing o'er the rest o' the selfsame day
95　　He finds thee in the stout Norweyan ranks,
　　Nothing° afeard of what thyself didst make,
　　Strange images of death. As thick as tale
　　Came post with post,° and every one did bear
　　Thy praises in his kingdom's great defense,
　　And poured them down before him.

ANGUS   We are sent
100
　　To give thee from our royal master thanks,
　　Only to herald thee into his sight,
　　Not pay thee.

ROSS And, for an earnest° of a greater honor,
105　　He bade me, from him, call thee Thane of
　　　Cawdor;
　　In which addition,° hail, most worthy thane,
　　For it is thine.

BANQUO   What, can the devil speak true?

MACBETH The Thane of Cawdor lives. Why do
　　you dress me
　　In borrowed robes?

ANGUS   Who° was the thane lives yet,
110　　But under heavy judgment bears that life
　　Which he deserves to lose. Whether he was
　　　combined°
　　With those of Norway, or did line° the rebel°
　　With hidden help and vantage, or that with both
　　He labored in his country's wrack,° I know not;

115　　But treasons capital,° confessed and proved,
　　Have overthrown him.

MACBETH [*aside*]   Glamis, and Thane of
　　Cawdor!
　　The greatest is behind.° [*To Ross and Angus*].
　　　Thanks for your pains.
　　[*Aside to Banquo.*] Do you not hope your chil-
　　　dren shall be kings
　　When those that gave the Thane of Cawdor to me
　　Promised no less to them?

120 BANQUO [*to Macbeth*]   That, trusted home,°
　　Might yet enkindle you unto the crown,
　　Besides the Thane of Cawdor. But 'tis strange;
　　And oftentimes to win us to our harm
　　The instruments of darkness° tell us truths,
125　　Win us with honest trifles, to betray 's
　　In deepest consequence.° —
　　Cousins,° a word, I pray you.
　　　　[*He converses apart with Ross and Angus*].

MACBETH [*aside*] Two truths are told,
　　As happy prologues to the swelling act°
130　　Of the imperial theme. — I thank you, gentlemen.
　　[*Aside.*] This supernatural soliciting°
　　Cannot be ill, cannot be good. If ill,
　　Why hath it given me earnest of success
　　Commencing in a truth? I am Thane of Cawdor.
135　　If good, why do I yield to that suggestion
　　Whose horrid° image doth unfix my hair
　　And make my seated heart knock at my ribs,
　　Against the use° of nature? Present fears°
　　Are less than horrible imaginings.
140　　My thought, whose° murder yet is but
　　　fantastical,°
　　Shakes so my single state of man°
　　That function° is smothered in surmise,°
　　And nothing is but what is not.°

BANQUO Look how our partner's rapt.

145 MACBETH [*aside*] If chance will have me king,
　　why, chance may crown me
　　Without my stir.°

---

90. **reads:** i.e., considers.   91. **Thy . . . fight:** your endangering yourself in fighting the rebels; or (reading *fight* as *sight*) your endangering yourself before the very eyes of the rebels.   92–93. **His . . . that:** i.e., your wondrous deeds so outdo any praise he could offer that he is silenced.   96. **Nothing:** not at all.   97–98. **As . . . with post:** as fast as could be told, i.e., counted, came messenger after messenger (unless the text should be amended to "As thick as hail").   104. **earnest:** token payment.   106. **addition:** title.   109. **Who:** he who.   111. **combined:** confederate.   112. **line:** reinforce.   **the rebel:** i.e., Macdonwald   114. **in . . . wrack:** to bring about his country's ruin.   115. **capital:** deserving death.   117. **behind:** to come.   120. **home:** all the way.   124. **darkness:** (Indicates the demonic beyond the witches.)   126. **In deepest consequence:** in the profoundly important sequel.   127. **Cousins:** i.e., fellow lords.   129. **swelling act:** stately drama.   131. **soliciting:** tempting.   136. **horrid:** literally, "bristling," like Macbeth's hair.   138. **use:** custom. **fears:** things feared.   140. **whose:** in which.   **but fantastical:** merely imagined.   141. **single . . . man:** weak human condition.   142. **function:** normal power of action.   **surmise:** speculation, imaginings.   143. **nothing . . . not:** only unreal imaginings have (for me) any reality.   146. **stir:** bestirring (myself).

BANQUO   New honors come° upon him,
Like our strange garments, cleave not to their mold
    But with the aid of use.°
MACBETH [*aside*]   Come what come may,
Time and the hour runs through the roughest day.°

150 **BANQUO** Worthy Macbeth, we stay° upon your leisure.

MACBETH Give me your favor.° My dull brain was wrought°
With things forgotten. Kind gentlemen, your pains
Are registered° where every day I turn
The leaf to read them. Let us toward the King.

155 [*Aside to Banquo.*] Think upon what hath chanced, and at more time,°
The interim having weighed it, let us speak
Our free hearts° each to other.

BANQUO [*to Macbeth*] Very gladly.

MACBETH [*to Banquo*] Till then, enough.—Come, friends.

Exeunt.

Scene 4°

Flourish. Enter King [Duncan], Lennox, Malcolm, Donalbain, and attendants.

DUNCAN Is execution done on Cawdor? Are not
Those in commission° yet returned?

MALCOLM   My liege,
They are not yet come back. But I have spoke
With one that saw him die, who did report

5 That very frankly he confessed his treasons,
Implored Your Highness' pardon, and set forth
A deep repentance. Nothing in his life
Became him like the leaving it. He died
As one that had been studied° in his death

10 To throw away the dearest thing he owed°
As 'twere a careless° trifle.

DUNCAN   There's no art
To find the mind's construction in the face.
He was a gentleman on whom I built
An absolute trust.

Enter Macbeth, Banquo, Ross, and Angus.

        O worthiest cousin!
15 The sin of my ingratitude even now
Was heavy on me. Thou art so far before°
That swiftest wing of recompense is slow
To overtake thee. Would thou hadst less deserved,
That the proportion both of thanks and payment

20 Might have been mine!° Only I have left to say,
More is thy due than more than all can pay.

MACBETH The service and the loyalty I owe,
In doing it, pays itself. Your Highness' part
Is to receive our duties; and our duties

25 Are to your throne and state children and servants,°
Which do but what they should by doing everything
Safe toward your love and honor.°

DUNCAN   Welcome hither!
I have begun to plant thee, and will labor
To make thee full of growing. Noble Banquo,

30 That hast no less deserved, nor must be known
No less to have done so, let me infold thee
And hold thee to my heart.

BANQUO   There if I grow,
The harvest is your own.

DUNCAN   My plenteous joys,
Wanton° in fullness, seek to hide themselves

35 In drops of sorrow.—Sons, kinsmen, thanes,
And you whose places are the nearest, know
We° will establish our estate° upon
Our eldest, Malcolm, whom we name hereafter

---

146. **come:** i.e., which have come.   147–148. **cleave . . . use:** do not take the shape of the wearer until often worn. (Macbeth is often connected in the text with clothes that don't really fit him.)   149. **Time . . . day:** i.e., what must happen will happen one way or another.   150. **stay:** wait.   151. **favor: pardon. wrought:** shaped, preoccupied.   153. **registered:** recorded (in my memory).   155. **at more time:** at a time of greater leisure.   157. **Our free hearts:** our hearts freely.   **Act 1, Scene 4. Location:** Forres. The palace.   2. **in commission:** having warrant (to see to the execution of Cawdor).   9. **been studied:** made it his study.   10. **owed:** owned.   11. **careless:** uncared for.   16. **before:** ahead (in deserving).   19–20. **That . . . mine:** that I might have thanked and rewarded you in ample proportion to your worth.   25. **Are . . . servants:** are like children and servants in relation to your throne and dignity, existing only to serve you.   27. **Safe . . . honor:** to safeguard you whom we love and honor.   34. **Wanton:** unrestrained.   37. **We:** (The royal "we.")   **establish our estate:** fix the succession of our state.

The Prince of Cumberland;° which honor must
40 Not unaccompanied invest him only,°
But signs of nobleness, like stars, shall shine
On all deservers. — From hence to Inverness,°
And bind us further to you.°

MACBETH The rest is labor which is not used for
you.°
45 I'll be myself the harbinger° and make joyful
The hearing of my wife with your approach;
So humbly take my leave.

DUNCAN   My worthy Cawdor!

MACBETH [*aside*] The Prince of Cumberland!
That is a step
On which I must fall down or else o'erleap,
50 For in my way it lies.° Stars, hide your fires;
Let not light see my black and deep desires.
The eye wink at the hand;° yet let that be°
Which the eye fears, when it is done, to see.
                                                        Exit.

DUNCAN True, worthy Banquo. He is full so valiant,°
55 And in his commendations° I am fed;
It is a banquet to me. Let's after him,
Whose care is gone before to bid us welcome.
It is a peerless kinsman.   *Flourish. Exeunt.*

Scene 5°

Enter Macbeth's Wife, alone, with a letter.

LADY MACBETH [*reads*] "They met me in the day
of success; and I have learned by the
perfect'st° report they have more in them
than mortal knowledge. When I burnt in
5   desire to question them further, they made
themselves air, into which they vanished.
Whiles I stood rapt in the wonder of it
came missives° from the King, who all-
hailed me 'Thane of Cawdor,' by which

10 title, before, these Weird Sisters saluted
me, and referred me to the coming on of
time with 'Hail, king that shalt be!' This
have I thought good to deliver thee,° my
dearest partner of greatness, that thou
15 mightst not lose the dues of rejoicing by
being ignorant of what greatness is promised thee. Lay it to thy heart, and farewell."
Glamis thou art, and Cawdor, and shalt be
What thou art promised. Yet do I fear° thy
nature;
20 It is too full o' the milk of human kindness
To catch the nearest way. Thou wouldst be great,
Art not without ambition, but without
The illness° should attend it. What thou
wouldst highly,°
That wouldst thou holily; wouldst not play false,
25 And yet wouldst wrongly win. Thou'dst have,
great Glamis,
That which cries "Thus thou must do," if thou
have° it,
And that which rather thou dost fear to do
Than wishest should be undone.° Hie° thee
hither,
That I may pour my spirits in thine ear
30 And chastise with the valor of my tongue
All that impedes thee from the golden round°
Which fate and metaphysical° aid doth seem
To have thee crowned withal.°

Enter [a servant as] Messenger.

                                      What is your tidings?

MESSENGER The King comes here tonight.

LADY MACBETH   Thou'rt mad to say it!
35 Is not thy master with him, who, were 't so,
Would have informed for preparation?°

MESSENGER So please you, it is true. Our thane is
coming.

---

39. **Prince of Cumberland:** title of the heir apparent to the Scottish throne.   40. **Not . . . only:** not be bestowed on Malcolm alone; other deserving nobles are to share honors.   42. **Inverness:** the seat or location of Macbeth's castle, Dunsinane.   43. **bind . . . you:** put me further in your (Macbeth's) obligation by your hospitality.   44. **The . . . you:** inactivity, not being devoted to your service, becomes tedious and wearisome. 45. **harbinger:** forerunner, messenger to arrange royal lodging.   50. **in my way it lies:** (The monarchy was not hereditary, and Macbeth had a right to believe that he himself might be chosen as Duncan's successor; he here questions whether he will interfere with the course of events.)   52. **wink . . . hand:** blind itself to the hand's deed.   **let that be:** may that thing come to pass.   54. **full so valiant:** fully as valiant as you say. (Apparently, Duncan and Banquo have been conversing privately on this subject during Macbeth's soliloquy.)   55. **his commendations:** the praises given to him. **Act 1, Scene 5. Location:** Inverness. Macbeth's castle.   3. **perfect'st:** most accurate.   8. **missives:** messengers.   13. **deliver thee:** inform you of. 19. **do I fear:** I am anxious about, mistrust.   23. **illness:** evil (that).   **highly:** greatly.   26. **have:** are to have, want to have.   27–28. **And that . . . undone:** i.e., and the thing you ambitiously crave frightens you more in terms of the means needed to achieve it than in the idea of having it; if you could have it without those means, you certainly wouldn't wish it undone.   28. **Hie:** hasten.   31. **round:** crown.   32. **metaphysical:** supernatural.   33. **withal:** with.   36. **informed for preparation:** i.e., sent me word so that I might get things ready.

One of my fellows had the speed of° him,
Who, almost dead for breath, had scarcely more
40 Than would make up his message.

LADY MACBETH   Give him
        tending;°
He brings great news.   *Exit Messenger.*

                                        The raven himself is hoarse
That croaks the fatal entrance of Duncan
Under my battlements. Come, you spirits
That tend on mortal thoughts,° unsex me here
45 And fill me from the crown to the toe top-full
Of direst cruelty! Make thick my blood;

---

38. **had . . . of:** outstripped.   40. **tending:** attendance.   44. **tend . . . thoughts:** attend on, act as the instruments of, deadly or murderous thoughts.

seeing connections

The 1958 film *Throne of Blood* by legendary Japanese filmmaker Akira Kurosawa is an adaptation of *Macbeth* staged with distinct elements of traditional Japanese Noh theater.

Look at this scene, in which one of the witches gives the Macbeth character advice, saying, "If you choose ambition, lord . . . then choose it honestly, with cruelty."

How is this advice similar to or different from Lady Macbeth's observations in the soliloquy in Scene 5?

CENTRAL TEXT   263

Stop up th' access and passage to remorse,°
That no compunctious visitings of nature°
Shake my fell° purpose, nor keep peace° between
50   Th' effect and it!° Come to my woman's breasts
And take my milk for gall,° you murdering
     ministers,°
Wherever in your sightless° substances
You wait on° nature's mischief!° Come, thick
     night,
And pall° thee in the dunnest° smoke of hell,
55   That my keen knife see not the wound it makes,
Nor heaven peep through the blanket of the dark
To cry "Hold, hold!"

Enter Macbeth.

              Great Glamis! Worthy Cawdor!
Greater than both by the all-hail hereafter!
Thy letters have° transported me beyond
60   This ignorant present, and I feel now
The future in the instant.

MACBETH   My dearest love,
Duncan comes here tonight.

LADY MACBETH   And when goes
     hence?

MACBETH   Tomorrow, as he purposes.

LADY MACBETH   O, never
     Shall sun that morrow see!
65   Your face, my thane, is as a book where men
May read strange matters. To beguile the time,°
Look like the time;° bear welcome in your eye,
Your hand, your tongue. Look like th' innocent
     flower
But be the serpent under 't. He that's coming
70   Must be provided for; and you shall put
This night's great business into my dispatch,°
Which shall to all our nights and days to come
Give solely sovereign sway and masterdom.

MACBETH   We will speak further.

LADY MACBETH   Only look up
     clear.°
75   To alter favor ever is to fear.°
Leave all the rest to me.   *Exeunt.*

Scene 6°

*Hautboys° and torches. Enter King [Duncan],
Malcolm, Donalbain, Banquo, Lennox, Macduff,
Ross, Angus, and attendants.*

DUNCAN   This castle hath a pleasant seat.° The
     air
Nimbly and sweetly recommends itself
Unto our gentle° senses.

BANQUO   This guest of summer,
The temple-haunting° martlet,° does approve°
5   By his loved mansionry° that the heaven's
     breath
Smells wooingly here. No jutty,° frieze,
Buttress, nor coign of vantage° but this bird
Hath made his pendent bed and procreant°
     cradle.
Where they most breed and haunt, I have
     observed
The air is delicate.

Enter Lady [Macbeth].

10   DUNCAN   See, see, our honored
     hostess!
The love that follows us sometimes is our
     trouble,
Which still we thank as love.° Herein I teach
     you
How you shall bid God 'ild° us for your pains,°
And thank us for your trouble.

LADY MACBETH   All our service
15   In every point twice done, and then done
     double,

47. **remorse:** pity.   48. **nature:** natural feelings.   49. **fell:** fierce, cruel.   **keep peace:** intervene.   50. **Th' effect and it:** i.e., my *fell purpose* and its accomplishment.   51. **for gall:** in exchange for gall, or perhaps *as* gall, with the milk itself being the gall.   **ministers:** agents.   52. **sightless:** invisible.   53. **wait on:** attend, assist.   **nature's mischief:** the kind of evil to which human nature is prone.   54. **pall:** envelop.   **dunnest:** darkest.   59. **letters have:** i.e., letter has.   66. **beguile the time:** i.e., deceive all observers.   67. **Look like the time:** look the way people expect you to look.   71. **dispatch:** management.   74. **look up clear:** give the appearance of being untroubled.   75. **To . . . fear:** i.e., to show a troubled countenance is to arouse suspicion.   **Act 1, Scene 6. Location:** Before Macbeth's castle.   **s.d.** *Hautboys:* oboelike instruments.   1. **seat:** site.   3. **gentle:** (1) noble (2) refined (by the delicate air).   4. **temple-haunting:** nesting in churches.   **martlet:** house martin.   **approve:** prove.   5. **mansionry:** nest building.   6. **jutty:** projection of wall or building.   7. **coign of vantage:** convenient corner, i.e., for nesting.   8. **procreant:** for breeding.   11–12. **The love . . . love:** the love that sometimes forces itself inconveniently upon us we still appreciate, since it is meant as love. (Duncan is graciously suggesting that his visit is a bother, but, he hopes, a welcome one.)   13. **bid . . . pains:** ask God to reward me for the trouble I'm giving you. (This is said in the same gently jocose spirit as lines 11–12.)   **'ild:** yield, repay.

Were poor and single° business to contend
Against° those honors deep and broad wherewith
Your Majesty loads our house. For those of old,°
And the late° dignities heaped up to° them,
We rest° your hermits.°

20 **DUNCAN**   Where's the Thane of Cawdor?
We coursed° him at the heels, and had a purpose
To be his purveyor;° but he rides well,
And his great love, sharp as his spur, hath holp° him
To his home before us. Fair and noble hostess,
We are your guest tonight.

25 **LADY MACBETH**   Your servants ever
Have theirs, themselves, and what is theirs in compt
To make their audit at Your Highness' pleasure,
Still to return your own.°

DUNCAN   Give me your hand.
Conduct me to mine host. We° love him highly,
30 And shall continue our graces towards him.
By your leave, hostess.   *Exeunt.*

Scene 7°

*Hautboys. Torches. Enter a sewer,° and divers
servants with dishes and service, [and pass] over
the stage. Then enter Macbeth.*

MACBETH If it were done when 'tis done, then 'twere well
It were done quickly. If th' assassination
Could trammel up the consequence,° and catch

With his surcease° success° — that but° this blow
5 Might be the be-all and the end-all! — here,°
But here, upon this bank and shoal of time,
We'd jump° the life to come. But in these cases
We still have judgment° here, that° we but teach
Bloody instructions,° which, being taught, return
10 To plague th' inventor. This evenhanded justice
Commends° th' ingredience° of our poisoned chalice
To our own lips. He's here in double trust:
First, as I am his kinsman and his subject,
Strong both against the deed; then, as his host,
15 Who should against his murderer shut the door,
Not bear the knife myself. Besides, this Duncan
Hath borne his faculties° so meek, hath been
So clear° in his great office, that his virtues
Will plead like angels, trumpet-tongued, against
20 The deep damnation of his taking-off;°
And Pity, like a naked newborn babe
Striding° the blast,° or heaven's cherubin, horsed
Upon the sightless couriers° of the air,
Shall blow the horrid deed in every eye,
25 That tears shall drown the wind.° I have no spur
To prick the sides of my intent, but only
Vaulting ambition, which o'erleaps itself
And falls on th' other° —

---

16. **single:** small, inconsiderable.   16–17. **contend Against:** vie with.   18. **those of old:** i.e., honors formerly bestowed on us.   19. **late:** recent. **to:** besides, in addition to.   20. **rest:** remain.   **hermits:** i.e., those who will pray for you like hermits or beadsmen.   21. **coursed:** followed (as in a hunt).   22. **purveyor:** an officer sent ahead to provide for entertainment; here, forerunner.   23. **holp:** helped.   25–28. **Your . . . own:** those who serve you hold their own servants, themselves, and all their possessions in trust from you, and can render an account whenever you wish, ready always to render back to you what is yours. (A feudal concept of obligation.)   29. **We:** (The royal "we.")   **Act 1, Scene 7.** Location: Macbeth's castle; an inner courtyard.   **s.d. *sewer:*** chief waiter, butler.   3. **trammel . . . consequence:** entangle as in a net and prevent the consequences that follow any action.   4. **his surcease:** cessation (of the assassination and of Duncan's life).   **success:** what succeeds, follows. (If only the assassination itself were the end of the matter.)   **that but:** so that only.   5. **here:** in this world.   7. **jump:** risk. (But imaging the physical act is characteristic of Macbeth; compare this with line 27.)   8. **still have judgment:** are invariably punished.   **that:** in that.   9. **instructions:** lessons.   11. **Commends:** presents.   **ingredience:** contents of a mixture.   17. **faculties:** powers of office.   18. **clear:** free of taint.   20. **taking-off:** murder.   22. **Striding:** bestriding.   **blast:** tempest (of compassionate horror).   23. **sightless couriers:** invisible steeds or runners, i.e., the winds.   25. **shall drown the wind:** i.e., will be as heavy as a downpour of rain and thereby still the wind.   28. **other:** other side. (The image is of a horseman vaulting into his saddle and ignominiously falling on the opposite side.)

Enter Lady [Macbeth].

How now, what news?

30 **LADY MACBETH** He has almost supped. Why have
you left the chamber?

MACBETH Hath he asked for me?

LADY MACBETH   Know you not
he has?

MACBETH We will proceed no further in this
business.

He hath honored me of late, and I have bought°
Golden opinions from all sorts of people,

35 Which would° be worn now in their newest
gloss,

Not cast aside so soon.

LADY MACBETH   Was the hope drunk
Wherein you dressed yourself? Hath it slept
since?

And wakes it now, to look so green° and pale
At what it did so freely? From this time

40 Such I account thy love. Art thou afeard
To be the same in thine own act and valor
As thou art in desire? Wouldst thou have that
Which thou esteem'st the ornament of life,°
And live a coward in thine own esteem,

45 Letting "I dare not" wait upon° "I would,"
Like the poor cat i' th' adage?°

MACBETH   Prithee, peace!
I dare do all that may become a man;
Who dares do more is none.

LADY MACBETH   What beast was 't, then,
That made you break° this enterprise to me?

50 When you durst do it, then you were a man;
And, to be more than what you were, you would
Be so much more the man. Nor time nor place
Did then adhere,° and yet you would° make
both.

They have made themselves, and that their
fitness° now

55 Does unmake you. I have given suck, and know

How tender 'tis to love the babe that milks me;
I would, while it was smiling in my face,
Have plucked my nipple from his boneless gums
And dashed the brains out, had I so sworn as
you

60 Have done to this.

MACBETH   If we should fail?

LADY MACBETH   We fail?
But° screw your courage to the sticking place°
And we'll not fail. When Duncan is asleep —
Whereto the rather shall his day's hard journey
Soundly invite him — his two chamberlains°

65 Will I with wine and wassail° so convince°
That memory, the warder of the brain,
Shall be a fume, and the receipt° of reason
A limbeck° only.° When in swinish sleep
Their drenchèd natures lies as in a death,

70 What cannot you and I perform upon
Th' unguarded Duncan? What not put upon
His spongy° officers, who shall bear the guilt
Of our great quell?°

MACBETH   Bring forth men-children
only!

For thy undaunted mettle° should compose

75 Nothing but males. Will it not be received,°
When we have marked with blood those
sleepy two

Of his own chamber and used their very
daggers,

That they have done 't?

LADY MACBETH   Who dares receive it
other,°

As° we shall make our griefs and clamor roar
Upon his death?

80 **MACBETH**   I am settled, and bend up
Each corporal agent° to this terrible feat.
Away, and mock° the time with fairest show.
False face must hide what the false heart doth
know.   *Exeunt.*

---

33. **bought:** acquired (by bravery in battle).   35. **would:** ought to, should.   38. **green:** sickly.   43. **the ornament of life:** i.e., the crown.   45. **wait upon:** accompany, always follow.   46. **adage:** (i.e., "The cat would eat fish but she will not wet her feet.")   49. **break:** broach.   53. **adhere:** agree, suit.   **would:** wanted to.   54. **that their fitness:** that very suitability of time and place.   61. **But:** only.   **the sticking place:** the notch into which is fitted the string of a crossbow cranked taut for shooting.   64. **chamberlains:** attendants on the bedchamber.   65. **wassail:** carousal, drink. **convince:** overpower.   66–68. **warder . . . only:** (The brain was thought to be divided into three ventricles: imagination in front, memory at the back, and between them the seat of reason. The fumes of wine, arising from the stomach, would deaden memory and judgment.)   67. **receipt:** receptacle, ventricle.   68. **limbeck:** device for distilling liquids.   72. **spongy:** soaked, drunken.   73. **quell:** murder.   74. **mettle:** (The same word as *metal.*) substance, temperament.   75. **received:** i.e., as truth.   78. **other:** otherwise.   79. **As:** inasmuch as.   80–81. **bend . . . agent:** strain every muscle.   82. **mock:** deceive.

seeing connections

The 1990 film *Men of Respect* is an adaptation of *Macbeth* in which the protagonist, Mike Battaglia, is an Italian mobster trying to seize control of a crime family from the current "Padrino," or Godfather, Charlie DeMico.

Read this bit of dialogue, in which Mike Battaglia's wife, Ruthie, urges her husband to take action. What remains consistent with Macbeth, and what has changed?

Mike Battaglia: This is Padrino DeMico here. Alright? Now we have respect.

Ruthie Battaglia: Charlie respects the fat end of a bat. The sharp end of a stick.

Charlie respects what he fears. And that ain't you.

Mike: You just wait and see what he has in mind.

Ruthie: All Charlie cares about is number one. Him and his. That's why Charlie is Charlie, and you are not.

Why you have to wait for other people to give you?

Why does everything always have to pass through somebody else's hands? Show a little ambition.

Mike: Stop it alright!? I'm as ambitious as the next guy.

More! Alright?

My time comes; I'll know it. And I'll know what to do.

Ruthie: This is the time. And you better know it now. This is it staring you in the face.

Don't close your eyes.

Mike: You don't know what you're asking.

Ruthie: Tell me. Tell me you don't want it.

If I was the man, I'd know what to do.

Mike: There's no guarantee, if Charlie's out of the picture, we'll be any better off.

Ruthie: In this life Michael, there's no safe standing still.

◀ What does this image from the movie suggest about the power relationship between husband and wife? Is it similar to that of Macbeth and Lady Macbeth? What details helped you draw your conclusion?

Understanding and Interpreting

1 Right after the witches affirm that they are about to meet Macbeth, they declare, "Fair is foul, and foul is fair" (Scene 1, l. 11). Explain what this inversion of the natural order might foreshadow.

2 In Scene 2, the injured Captain is asked to explain to King Duncan the outcome of a battle he has just witnessed. Using direct quotes from the text, explain what we learn about Macbeth as a soldier.

3 *"Thane"* was a Scottish term for a nobleman whose position was dependent upon loyalty and service to the king. Disloyalty to the king was considered not only the highest dishonor, but also grounds for execution. In Scene 2, lines 66–68, the current Thane of Cawdor is pronounced a traitor and sentenced to death, and his title is given to Macbeth. What does this immediate transfer of power suggest about the nature of a monarch's authority during these times? What does it suggest about the nature of a thane's authority?

4 In Scene 3, the witches speak in ambiguous riddles. For example, they declare that Banquo will be "[l]esser than Macbeth, and greater" (l. 65). How does Macbeth react to this ambiguity, and what does that suggest about his character? How does Banquo's reaction differ from Macbeth's, and what does that suggest about his character?

5 Right after the witches disappear, Ross and Angus arrive to share the news that Macbeth is now the Thane of Cawdor, just as the witches had foretold (Scene 3, ll. 104–107). Describe Macbeth and Banquo's reaction. Are they excited about the news? Are they concerned? Or does each character have a unique reaction? Explain, using text from their conversation.

6 In Scene 4, Macbeth starts to show two different sides now that he has been promoted. He declares publicly to Duncan that "[t]he service and the loyalty that I owe, / In doing it, pays itself" (ll. 22–23). Yet, a few lines later he refers to the Prince of Cumberland, Duncan's son, as a "step" he must "o'erleap" (ll. 48–49). How do these contrasting sides of Macbeth begin to shape his character and increase the complexity of the play at this point?

7 In contrast to Duncan's earlier assertion that "There's no art / To find the mind's construction in the face" (Scene 4, ll. 11–12), in Scene 5 Lady Macbeth tells her husband that his face is "as a book where men / May read strange matters" (ll. 65–66). What does her contrasting opinion suggest about her character and her attitudes toward others?

8 Shakespearean tragedies often feature a main character who possesses a fatal flaw. A *fatal flaw* is the primary personality trait responsible for a character's downfall. At the end of his soliloquy in Scene 7, Macbeth refers to his "[v]aulting ambition" (l. 27), which is a phrase that many believe captures his fatal flaw. In what ways has Macbeth already shown his ambition, and to what degree has his ambition controlled the events in the play so far?

9 Lady Macbeth challenges Macbeth when she believes he may be wavering in his resolve to kill Duncan (Scene 7, ll. 48–73). In making this response to Macbeth, does she intend to motivate him to follow through with the murder, or is she just telling him what he wants to hear? Explain.

10 Explain how Lady Macbeth plans to kill Duncan without Macbeth's getting blamed for the murder (Scene 7, ll. 62–73).

Analyzing Language, Style, and Structure

1 The concept of Fortune, or Fate, was central to the worldview of this era as people considered it to be a central controlling force in life. In Scene 2, lines 16–20, the Captain describes Macbeth as one who fought while "[d]isdaining Fortune." In what ways does this description of Macbeth serve both as a compliment and as a hint as to what Macbeth's character is like?

2 In his extended description of the battle in Scene 2, the Captain employs several similes (ll. 7–23). Identify one of the similes and discuss how it helps characterize the nature of the battle.

3 Before the bleeding Captain is taken away to have his injuries treated, Duncan tells him that his "words become thee as thy wounds; / They smack of honor both" (Scene 2, ll. 43–44). What does this statement reveal about the men's attitude toward warfare?

4 In Scene 3, after Angus and Ross tell of Macbeth's promotion to Thane of Cawdor, Banquo suggests to Macbeth that sometimes "instruments of darkness tell us truths" to "win us to our harm" (ll. 123–124). Explain what he means by this as well as why these words of caution might be significant at this point in the play.

5 Macbeth is troubled by the prophecy of the witches, asserting that it "[c]annot be ill, cannot be good" (Scene 3, l. 132). This antithesis (two opposing ideas) is followed by two more antitheses. Identify those antitheses and explain what they reveal about Macbeth's state of mind at this point.

6 When Banquo recognizes that Macbeth is struggling to understand his promotion to Thane of Cawdor, he concludes that the new "honors" bestowed on Macbeth are like "strange garments" that "cleave not to their mold / But with the aid of use" (Scene 3, ll. 146–148). Discuss why this simile is an effective way to describe Macbeth's current attitude toward his promotion.

7 Duncan muses that the recently executed Cawdor was "a gentleman on whom I built / An absolute trust" (Scene 4, ll. 13–14). Just after Duncan says these words, Macbeth enters. How does timing Macbeth's entrance right after Duncan's comment affect the play at this point?

8 Scene 7 opens with Macbeth's first major soliloquy (ll. 1–28). Soliloquies offer characters a chance to reveal their private thoughts and inner turmoil. Taking all of Macbeth's soliloquy into account, do you think he is ready to kill Duncan? Or does he still have doubts? Use evidence from the text to explain your reasoning.

9 Lady Macbeth uses particularly violent imagery related to a baby when she confronts Macbeth about "[breaking] this enterprise" and not following through with the murder (Scene 7, ll. 49–60). In what ways does the imagery emphasize Lady Macbeth's resolve, and what does it suggest about her character?

Connecting, Arguing, and Extending

1 Letters written from the battlefield have long been a part of how civilians at home learn about the events that soldiers experience in war. Imagine you were at the battle that Macbeth just fought. Using details from the Captain's description in Scene 2, write a letter to someone at home about what you witnessed.

2 The witches are described in some detail by Banquo when he and Macbeth encounter them on the heath (Scene 3, ll. 39–47). There are many imaginative works that include witches, including many children's stories. Taking Banquo's description into account, as well as popular images of witches, explain how these witches might be staged today. What features should be emphasized to create particularly fearsome characters? If you like, you may use images or video to help your audience visualize your version of this scene.

3 A *self-fulfilling prophecy* is a prediction that leads to behavior that causes the prediction to come true. For example, imagine that a player at a basketball game hears someone in the stands say, "That kid will never make varsity." The player thinks the comment is directed at her. She gets discouraged, stops practicing, and doesn't make varsity. That original comment becomes a self-fulfilling prophecy. What if the person in the stands was actually talking about someone else? What if the player responded to the comment by working even harder? Do a bit of research on the psychology behind how self-fulfilling prophecies work, and then write an expository essay in which you investigate the role that a self-fulfilling prophecy played in a current day example.

4 It is clear that Macbeth desires to be king, but he is also a loyal soldier who understands that killing the current king would be an act of treason. This struggle between ambition and restraint is central to the action of the play.

Consider other pieces you have read, in this book or elsewhere, that involved a significant choice a character had to make. Identify the context of the decision, summarize the decision, and discuss how the motivation behind that decision compares to or contrasts with Macbeth's motivation.

5 A traditional proverb says that the eyes are the window to the soul. In Scene 4, lines 11–12, Duncan suggests that you cannot tell what's really going on inside someone's mind just by looking at that person's face. Do some research into facial expressions or law enforcement lie-detecting techniques, and then write an argument in which you contend either that Duncan or the traditional proverb is closer to the truth.

6 *Macbeth* offers specific ideas about gender. Look back through Act 1 and find as many references as you can to gender roles or the nature of men and women. Then, do some research about the Jacobean period, the time the play was written, and write a response discussing how the historical accounts of gender roles compare to or contrast with the gender roles you find in *Macbeth*.

7 Act 1 offers a number of different settings and significant actions in each place. Write seven different headlines, one for each scene. Then, using either original images or images from the Internet, design and create a picture that would be appropriate for each headline.

6

Ambition and Restraint

Scene 1°

Enter Banquo, and Fleance, with a torch° before him.

BANQUO How goes the night, boy?

FLEANCE The moon is down. I have not heard the clock.

BANQUO And she goes down at twelve.

FLEANCE   I take 't 'tis later, sir.

BANQUO Hold, take my sword. [*He gives him his sword.*] There's husbandry° in heaven;
Their candles are all out. Take thee that too.

5   [*He gives him his belt and dagger.*]
A heavy summons° lies like lead upon me,
And yet I would not° sleep. Merciful powers,°
Restrain in me the cursèd thoughts that nature
Gives way to in repose!

Enter Macbeth, and a Servant with a torch.

Give me my sword. Who's there?

10   [*He takes his sword.*]

MACBETH A friend.

BANQUO What, sir, not yet at rest? The King's abed.
He hath been in unusual pleasure,
And sent forth great largess° to your offices.°

15   This diamond he greets your wife withal,
By the name of most kind hostess, and shut up
In° measureless content.

                              [*He gives a diamond.*]

MACBETH   Being unprepared,
Our will became the servant to defect,°
Which else should free° have wrought.

20 **BANQUO** All's well.
I dreamt last night of the three Weird Sisters.
To you they have showed some truth.

MACBETH   I think
not of them.
Yet, when we can entreat an hour to serve,
We would spend it in some words upon that business,
If you would grant the time.

25 **BANQUO**   At your kind'st leisure.

MACBETH If you shall cleave to my consent when 'tis,°
It shall make honor for you.

BANQUO   So° I lose none
In seeking to augment it, but still keep
My bosom franchised° and allegiance clear,°
I shall be counseled.°

30 **MACBETH**   Good repose the while!

BANQUO Thanks, sir. The like to you.

                    Exit Banquo [with Fleance].

MACBETH [*to Servant*]
Go bid thy mistress, when my drink° is ready,
She strike upon the bell. Get thee to bed.

                              Exit [Servant].
Is this a dagger which I see before me,

35   The handle toward my hand? Come, let me clutch thee.
I have thee not, and yet I see thee still.
Art thou not, fatal° vision, sensible°
To feeling as to sight? Or art thou but
A dagger of the mind, a false creation,

40   Proceeding from the heat-oppressèd° brain?
I see thee yet, in form as palpable
As this which now I draw.

                    [*He draws a dagger.*]
Thou marshall'st me the way that I was going,°
And such an instrument I was to use.

Act 2, Scene 1. **Location:** Inner courtyard of Macbeth's castle. Time is virtually continuous from the previous scene.   **s.d. *torch:*** (This may mean "torchbearer," although it does not at line 9 s.d.)   **4. husbandry:** economy.   **6. summons:** i.e., to sleep.   **7. would not:** am reluctant to (owing to my uneasy fears).   **powers:** order of angels deputed by God to resist demons.   **14. largess:** gifts, gratuities.   **offices:** quarters used for the household work.   **16–17. shut up/In:** concluded what he had to say with expressions of, or, perhaps, he professes himself enclosed in.   **18. Our . . . defect:** our good will (to entertain the King handsomely) was limited by our meager means (at such short notice).   **19. free:** freely, unrestrainedly.   **26. cleave . . . 'tis:** give me your support, adhere to my view, when the time comes.   **27. So:** provided.   **29. franchised:** free (from guilt).   **clear:** unstained.   **30. counseled:** receptive to suggestion.   **32. drink:** i.e., posset or bedtime drink of hot spiced milk curdled with ale or wine, as also in 2.2.6.   **37. fatal:** ominous.   **sensible:** perceivable by the senses.   **40. heat-oppressèd:** fevered.   **43. Thou . . . going:** you seem to guide me toward the destiny I intended, toward Duncan's chambers.

45 Mine eyes are made the fools o' th' other senses,
Or else worth all the rest.° I see thee still,
And on thy blade and dudgeon° gouts° of
   blood,
Which was not so before. There's no such thing.

It is the bloody business which informs°
50 Thus to mine eyes. Now o'er the one half
   world
Nature seems dead, and wicked dreams abuse°
The curtained° sleep. Witchcraft celebrates

45–46. **Mine . . . rest:** i.e., either this is a fantasy, deceiving me with what my eyes seem to see, or else it is a true vision expressing something that is beyond ordinary sensory experience.   47. **dudgeon:** hilt of a dagger.   **gouts:** drops.   49. **informs:** creates forms or impressions.   51. **abuse:** deceive.   52. **curtained:** (1) veiled by bed curtains (2) screened from rationality and consciousness.

seeing connections

When staging *Macbeth*, filmmakers must make the choice of either showing Macbeth's phantom dagger, or leaving it to our imagination. Below are two different takes on the subject. The first is from director Rupert Goold's 2010 adaptation starring Patrick Stewart. The second is from Roman Polanski's 1971 film.

Which approach do you think is more effective? How would you shoot this scene? Why?

Pale Hecate's offerings,° and withered Murder,
Alarumed° by his sentinel, the wolf,
55 Whose howl's his watch,° thus with his
    stealthy pace,
With Tarquin's° ravishing strides, towards his
    design
Moves like a ghost. Thou sure and firm-set earth,
Hear not my steps which way they walk, for fear
Thy very stones prate of my whereabouts
60 And take the present horror from the time
Which now suits with it.° Whiles I threat, he
    lives;
Words to the heat of deeds too cold breath
    gives.°   *A bell rings.*
I go, and it is done. The bell invites me.
Hear it not, Duncan, for it is a knell
65 That summons thee to heaven or to hell.

                                         Exit.

Scene 2°

Enter Lady [Macbeth].

LADY MACBETH That which hath made them
    drunk hath made me bold;
What hath quenched them hath given me fire.
    Hark! Peace!
It was the owl that shrieked, the fatal
    bellman,°
Which gives the stern'st good-night.° He is
    about it.
5 The doors are open; and the surfeited grooms°
Do mock their charge° with snores. I have
    drugged their possets,°
That death and nature do contend about them
Whether they live or die.

MACBETH [*within*]   Who's there? What, ho!

LADY MACBETH Alack, I am afraid they have
    awaked,

10 And 'tis not done. Th' attempt and not the deed
Confounds° us. Hark! I laid their daggers ready;
He could not miss 'em. Had he not resembled
My father as he slept, I had done't.

Enter Macbeth [bearing bloody daggers].

My husband!
15 **MACBETH** I have done the deed. Didst thou not
    hear a noise?

LADY MACBETH I heard the owl scream and the
    crickets° cry.
Did not you speak?

MACBETH When?

LADY MACBETH Now.

20 **MACBETH** As I descended?

LADY MACBETH Ay.

MACBETH Hark! Who lies i' the second chamber?

LADY MACBETH Donalbain.

MACBETH [*looking at his hands*]
This is a sorry sight.

25 **LADY MACBETH** A foolish thought, to say a sorry
    sight.

MACBETH There's one did laugh in 's sleep, and
    one cried "Murder!"
That they did wake each other. I stood and
    heard them.
But they did say their prayers, and addressed
    them°
Again to sleep.

LADY MACBETH There are two° lodged together.

30 **MACBETH** One cried "God bless us!" and "Amen!"
    the other,
As° they had seen me with these hangman's
    hands.°
List'ning their fear, I could not say "Amen"
When they did say "God bless us!"

LADY MACBETH Consider it not so deeply.

35 **MACBETH** But wherefore could not I pronounce
    "Amen"?

---

53. **Pale Hecate's offerings:** sacrificial offerings to Hecate, the goddess of night and witchcraft. (She is *pale* because she is identified with the pale moon.) 54. **Alarumed:** given the signal to action. 55. **watch:** watchword, or cry like the hourly call of the night watchman. 56. **Tarquin's:** (Tarquin was a Roman tyrant who ravished Lucrece.) 60–61. **And take . . . with it:** and thus echo and augment the horror which is so suited to this evil hour, or, usurp the present horror by breaking the silence. 62. **Words . . . gives:** words give only lifeless expression to live deeds, are no substitute for deeds. **Act 2, Scene 2. Location:** Scene continues. 3. **bellman:** one who rings a bell to announce a death or to mark the hours of the night. 4. **stern'st good-night:** i.e., notice to condemned criminals that they are to be executed in the morning. 5. **grooms:** servants. 6. **mock their charge:** make a mockery of their guard duty. **possets:** hot bedtime drinks (as in 2.1.32). 11. **Confounds:** ruins. 16. **owl, crickets:** (The sounds of both could be ominous and prophetic of death.) 28. **addressed them:** settled themselves. 29. **two:** i.e., Malcolm and Donalbain. 31. **As:** as if. **hangman's hands:** bloody hands (because the hangman would draw and quarter the condemned, and also executed with an ax).

I had most need of blessing, and "Amen"
Stuck in my throat.

LADY MACBETH   These deeds must not be
    thought°
After these ways; so,° it will make us mad.

MACBETH Methought I heard a voice cry "Sleep
    no more!
40 Macbeth does murder sleep," the innocent sleep,
Sleep that knits up the raveled sleave° of care,
The death of each day's life, sore labor's bath,°
Balm of hurt minds, great nature's second
    course,°
Chief nourisher in life's feast —

LADY MACBETH   What do you
    mean?

45 **MACBETH** Still it cried "Sleep no more!" to all the
    house;
"Glamis hath murdered sleep, and therefore
    Cawdor
Shall sleep no more; Macbeth shall sleep no
    more."

LADY MACBETH Who was it that thus cried? Why,
    worthy thane,
You do unbend° your noble strength to think

50 So brainsickly of things. Go get some water
And wash this filthy witness° from your hand.
Why did you bring these daggers from the place?
They must lie there. Go, carry them and smear
The sleepy grooms with blood.

MACBETH   I'll go no more.
55 I am afraid to think what I have done;
Look on 't again I dare not.

LADY MACBETH   Infirm of purpose!
Give me the daggers. The sleeping and the
    dead
Are but as pictures. 'Tis the eye of childhood
That fears a painted devil. If he do bleed,
60 I'll gild° the faces of the grooms withal,
For it must seem their guilt.

    [*She takes the daggers, and*] *exit. Knock within.*

MACBETH   Whence is that
    knocking?
How is 't with me, when every noise appalls me?
What hands are here? Ha! They pluck out
    mine eyes.
Will all great Neptune's ocean wash this blood
65 Clean from my hand? No, this my hand will
    rather

▶
——————————

This painting depicts Lady Macbeth
seizing the daggers from Macbeth.

Note the details of this painting, and
explain what you believe the artist
reveals about these two characters in
this moment.

Johann Heinrich Fuseli, *Lady Macbeth
Seizing the Daggers*, 1812. Oil on canvas,
40″ x 50″. Tate Gallery, London.

———————

37. **thought:** thought about.   38. **so:** if we do so.   41. **raveled sleave:** tangled skein.   42. **bath:** i.e., to relieve the soreness.   43. **second course:**
(Ordinary feasts had two courses, of which the second was the *chief nourisher*; here, sleep is seen as following eating in a restorative process.)
49. **unbend:** slacken (as one would a bow; contrast with "bend up" in 1.7.80).   51. **witness:** evidence.   60. **gild:** smear, coat, as if with a thin layer of
gold. (Gold was ordinarily spoken of as red.)

The multitudinous° seas incarnadine,°
Making the green one red.°

Enter Lady [*Macbeth*].

LADY MACBETH My hands are of your color, but I shame
To wear a heart so white. (*Knock.*) I hear a knocking
70   At the south entry. Retire we to our chamber.
A little water clears us of this deed.
How easy is it, then! Your constancy
Hath left you unattended.° (*Knock.*) Hark! More knocking.
Get on your nightgown,° lest occasion call us
75   And show us to be watchers.° Be not lost
So poorly° in your thoughts.
MACBETH To know my deed, 'twere best not know myself.°   *Knock.*
Wake Duncan with thy knocking! I would thou couldst!   *Exeunt.*

Scene 3°

Knocking within. Enter a Porter.

PORTER Here's a knocking indeed! If a
man were porter of hell gate, he should
have old° turning the key. (*Knock.*)
Knock, knock, knock! Who's there, i' the
5   name of Beelzebub?° Here's a farmer that
hanged himself on th' expectation of
plenty.° Come in time!° Have napkins°
enough about you; here you'll sweat for 't
(*Knock.*) Knock, knock! Who's there, in

10   th' other devil's name? Faith, here's an
equivocator,° that could swear in both
the scales against either scale, who
committed treason enough for God's
sake, yet could not equivocate to heaven.
15   O, come in, equivocator. (*Knock.*) Knock,
knock, knock! Who's there? Faith, here's
an English tailor come hither for stealing
out of a French hose.° Come in, tailor.
Here you may roast your goose.° (*Knock.*)
20   Knock, knock! Never at quiet! What are
you? But this place is too cold for hell. I'll
devil-porter it no further. I had thought
to have let in some of all professions that
go the primrose way to th' everlasting
25   bonfire. (*Knock*). Anon, anon! [*He opens
the gate.*] I pray you, remember the porter.

Enter Macduff and Lennox.

MACDUFF Was it so late, friend, ere you went to bed,
That you do lie so late?
PORTER Faith, sir, we were carousing till the
30   second cock;° and drink, sir, is a great
provoker of three things.
MACDUFF What three things does drink especially provoke?
PORTER Marry,° sir, nose-painting,° sleep, and
urine. Lechery, sir, it provokes and un-
35   provokes: it provokes the desire but it takes
away the performance. Therefore much
drink may be said to be an equivocator
with lechery: it makes him and it mars
him; it sets him on and it takes him off; it

---

66. **multitudinous:** both multiform and teeming.   **incarnadine:** make red.   67. **one red:** one all-pervading red.   72–73. **Your . . . unattended:** your firmness has deserted you.   74 . **nightgown:** dressing gown.   75. **watchers:** those who have remained awake.   76. **poorly:** dejectedly.   77. **To . . . myself:** i.e., it were better to be lost in my thoughts than to have consciousness of my deed; if I am to live with myself, I will have to shut this out or be no longer the person I was.   **Act 2, Scene 3. Location:** Scene continues. The knocking at the door has already been heard in 2.2. It is not necessary to assume literally, however, that Macbeth and Lady Macbeth have been talking near the *south entry* (2.2.70) where the knocking is heard.   3. **old:** plenty of.   5. **Beelzebub:** a devil.   5–7. **Here's . . . plenty:** i.e., here's a farmer who has hoarded in anticipation of a scarcity and will be justly punished by a crop surplus and low prices.   7. **Come in time:** i.e., you have come in good time.   **napkins:** handkerchiefs (to mop up the sweat).   11. **equivocator:** (This is regarded by many editors as an allusion to the trial of the Jesuit Henry Garnet for treason in the spring of 1606 and to the doctrine of equivocation said to have been presented in his defense; according to this doctrine, a lie was not a lie if the utterer had in his mind a different meaning in which the utterance was true.)   18. **French hose:** very narrow breeches of the sort that would easily reveal the tailor's attempt to skimp on the cloth supplied him for their manufacture — as he evidently had done with impunity when the French style ran to loose-fitting breeches.   19. **roast your goose:** heat your tailor's smoothing iron (with an obvious pun on the sense, "cook your goose").   30. **second cock:** i.e., 3 A.M., when the cock was thought to crow a second time.   33. **Marry:** (Originally an oath, "by the Virgin Mary.")   **nose-painting:** i.e., reddening of the nose through drink.

40 persuades him and disheartens him,
makes him stand to and not stand to°; in
conclusion, equivocates him in a sleep°
and, giving him the lie,° leaves him.°

MACDUFF I believe drink gave thee the lie° last
night.

45 **PORTER** That it did, sir, i' the very throat on me.°
But I requited him for his lie, and, I think,
being too strong for him, though he took
up my legs° sometimes, yet I made a shift°
to cast° him.

50 **MACDUFF** Is thy master stirring?

Enter Macbeth.

Our knocking has awaked him. Here he comes.
[*Exit Porter.*]

LENNOX Good morrow, noble sir.

MACBETH Good morrow,
both.

MACDUFF Is the King stirring, worthy thane?

MACBETH Not
yet.

MACDUFF He did command me to call timely°
on him.
I have almost slipped° the hour.

55 **MACBETH** I'll bring you
to him.

MACDUFF I know this is a joyful trouble to you,
But yet 'tis one.

MACBETH The labor we delight in physics pain.°
This is the door.

MACDUFF I'll make so bold to call,

60 For 'tis my limited° service. *Exit Macduff.*

LENNOX Goes the King hence today?

MACBETH He does; he did appoint so.

LENNOX The night has been unruly. Where we lay,
Our chimneys were blown down, and, as they
say,

65 Lamentings heard i' th' air, strange screams of
death,
And prophesying with accents terrible°
Of dire combustion° and confused events
New hatched to the woeful time.° The obscure
bird°
Clamored the livelong night. Some say the earth

70 Was feverous and did shake.

MACBETH 'Twas a rough
night.

LENNOX My young remembrance cannot parallel
A fellow to it.

Enter Macduff.

MACDUFF O, horror, horror, horror!
Tongue nor heart cannot conceive nor name
thee!

MACBETH AND LENNOX What's the matter?

75 **MACDUFF** Confusion° now hath made his
masterpiece!
Most sacrilegious murder hath broke ope
The Lord's anointed temple and stole thence
The life o' the building!

MACBETH What is 't you say? The life?

80 **LENNOX** Mean you His Majesty?

MACDUFF Approach the chamber and destroy
your sight
With a new Gorgon.° Do not bid me speak;
See, and then speak yourselves.

Exeunt Macbeth and Lennox.
Awake, awake!
Ring the alarum bell. Murder and treason!

85 Banquo and Donalbain, Malcolm, awake!
Shake off this downy sleep, death's counterfeit,
And look on death itself! Up, up, and see
The great doom's image!° Malcolm, Banquo,
As from your graves rise up° and walk like
sprites°

---

41. **makes . . . stand to:** stimulates him sexually but without sexual capability.   42. **equivocates . . . sleep:** (1) lulls him asleep (2) gives him an erotic experience in dream only.   43. **giving him the lie:** (1) deceiving him (2) laying him out flat.   **leaves him:** (1) dissipates as intoxication (2) is passed off as urine.   44. **gave thee the lie:** (1) called you a liar (2) made you unable to stand and put you to sleep.   45. **i' the . . . me:** i.e., insulting me with a deliberate lie that requires a duel (with a pun on the literal sense).   **on:** of.   47–48. **took up my legs:** lifted me as a wrestler would (with a suggestion of the drunkard's unsteadiness on his legs and perhaps also of lifting the leg as a dog might to urinate).   48. **made a shift:** managed.   49. **cast:** (1) throw, as in wrestling (2) vomit.   54. **timely:** betimes, early.   55. **slipped:** let slip.   58. **physics pain:** i.e., cures that labor of its troublesome aspect.   60. **limited:** appointed.   66. **accents terrible:** terrifying utterances.   67. **combustion:** tumult.   68. **New . . . time:** newly born to accompany the woeful nature of the time.   **obscure bird:** owl, the bird of darkness.   75. **Confusion:** destruction.   82. **Gorgon:** one of three monsters with hideous faces (Medusa was a Gorgon), whose look turned the beholders to stone.   88. **great doom's image:** replica of Doomsday.   89. **As . . . rise up:** (At the Last Judgment, the dead will rise from their graves to be judged.)   **sprites:** souls, ghosts.

90   To countenance° this horror! Ring the bell.

                                    Bell rings.

     Enter Lady [Macbeth].

LADY MACBETH   What's the business,
     That such a hideous trumpet° calls to parley
     The sleepers of the house? Speak, speak!
MACDUFF   O gentle lady,
95   'Tis not for you to hear what I can speak.
     The repetition° in a woman's ear
     Would murder as it fell.

     Enter Banquo.

                         O Banquo, Banquo,
     Our royal master's murdered!
LADY MACBETH   Woe, alas!
     What, in our house?
BANQUO   Too cruel anywhere.
100 Dear Duff, I prithee, contradict thyself
     And say it is not so.

     Enter Macbeth, Lennox, and Ross.

MACBETH   Had I but died an hour before this
           chance°
     I had lived a blessèd time; for from this instant
     There's nothing serious in mortality.°
105 All is but toys.° Renown and grace is dead;
     The wine of life is drawn, and the mere lees°
     Is left this vault° to brag of.

     Enter Malcolm and Donalbain.

DONALBAIN   What is amiss?
MACBETH   You are, and do not
           know 't.
     The spring, the head, the fountain of your
           blood
110 Is stopped, the very source of it is stopped.
MACDUFF   Your royal father's murdered.
MALCOLM   O, by
           whom?
LENNOX   Those of his chamber, as it seemed, had
           done 't.

Their hands and faces were all badged° with
     blood;
So were their daggers, which unwiped we
     found
115 Upon their pillows. They stared and were
           distracted;
     No man's life was to be trusted with them.
MACBETH   O, yet I do repent me of my fury,
     That I did kill them.
MACDUFF   Wherefore did you so?
MACBETH   Who can be wise, amazed,° temp'rate
           and furious,
120 Loyal and neutral, in a moment? No man.
     Th' expedition° of my violent love
     Outran the pauser, reason. Here lay Duncan,
     His silver skin laced with his golden° blood,
     And his gashed stabs looked like a breach in
           nature°
125 For ruin's wasteful° entrance; there the
           murderers,
     Steeped in the colors of their trade, their
           daggers
     Unmannerly breeched with gore.° Who could
           refrain
     That had a heart to love, and in that heart
     Courage to make 's love known?°
LADY MACBETH   [*fainting*]   Help me
           hence, ho!
MACDUFF   Look to the lady.
MALCOLM   [*aside to Donalbain*]
130   Why do we hold our tongues,
     That most may claim this argument° for ours?
DONALBAIN   [*aside to Malcolm*]   What should be
           spoken here, where our fate,
     Hid in an auger hole,° may rush and seize us?
     Let's away. Our tears are not yet brewed.
135 MALCOLM   [*aside to Donalbain*]   Nor our strong
           sorrow upon the foot of motion.°
BANQUO   Look to the lady.

                         [*Lady Macbeth is helped out.*]

---

90. **countenance:** (1) be in keeping with (2) behold.   92. **trumpet:** (Another metaphorical suggestion of the Last Judgment; the *trumpet* here is the shouting and the bell.)   96. **repetition:** recital, report.   102. **chance:** occurrence (the murder of Duncan).   104. **serious in mortality:** worthwhile in mortal life.   105. **toys:** trifles.   106. **lees:** dregs.   107. **vault:** (1) wine-vault (2) earth, with its vaulted sky.   113. **badged:** marked, as with a badge or emblem.   119. **amazed:** bewildered.   121. **expedition:** haste.   123. **golden:** (See the note for 2.2.60.)   124. **breach in nature:** gap in the defenses of life. (A metaphor of military siege.)   125. **wasteful:** destructive.   127. **breeched with gore:** covered (as with breeches) to the hilts with gore.   129. **make 's love known:** make manifest his love.   131. **argument:** topic, business.   133. **in an auger hole:** i.e., in some hiding place, in ambush.   135. **upon . . . motion:** yet in motion, ready to act.

And when we have our naked frailties hid,°
That suffer in exposure, let us meet
And question° this most bloody piece of work
140 To know it further. Fears and scruples° shake us.
In the great hand of God I stand, and thence
Against the undivulged pretense° I fight
Of treasonous malice.°

MACDUFF   And so do I.

ALL   So all.

MACBETH Let's briefly° put on manly readiness°
And meet i' the hall together.

145 **ALL**   Well contented.

Exeunt [all but Malcolm and Donalbain].

MALCOLM What will you do? Let's not consort°
with them.
To show an unfelt sorrow is an office
Which the false man does easy.° I'll to England.

DONALBAIN To Ireland, I. Our separated fortune
150 Shall keep us both the safer. Where we are,
There's daggers in men's smiles; the nea'er in
blood,
The nearer bloody.°

MALCOLM   This murderous shaft
that's shot
Hath not yet lighted,° and our safest way
Is to avoid the aim. Therefore to horse,
155 And let us not be dainty of° leave-taking,
But shift away.° There's warrant° in that theft
Which steals itself when there's no mercy left.

Exeunt.

Scene 4°

Enter Ross with an Old Man.

OLD MAN Threescore and ten I can remember well,
Within the volume of which time I have seen
Hours dreadful and things strange, but this
sore° night
Hath trifled former knowings.°

ROSS   Ha, good
father,°
5 Thou seest the heavens,° as troubled with
man's act,°
Threatens his bloody stage.° By th' clock 'tis
day,
And yet dark night strangles the traveling lamp.°
Is 't night's predominance° or the day's shame
That darkness does the face of earth entomb
When living light should kiss it?

10 **OLD MAN**   'Tis unnatural,
Even like the deed that's done. On Tuesday
last
A falcon, towering° in her pride of place,°
Was by a mousing° owl hawked at and killed.

ROSS And Duncan's horses — a thing most
strange and certain —
15 Beauteous and swift, the minions° of their
race,
Turned wild in nature, broke their stalls, flung
out,
Contending 'gainst obedience, as° they would
Make war with mankind.

OLD MAN   'Tis said they eat°
each other.

ROSS They did so, to th' amazement of mine eyes
That looked upon 't.

Enter Macduff.

20   Here comes the good
Macduff —
How goes the world, sir, now?

MACDUFF   Why, see you not?

ROSS Is 't known who did this more than bloody
deed?

MACDUFF Those that Macbeth hath slain.

ROSS   Alas the
day,
What good could they pretend?°

---

137. **our naked frailties hid:** clothed our poor, shivering bodies (which remind us of our human frailty).   139. **question:** discuss.   140. **scruples:** doubts, suspicions.   141–43. **thence . . . malice:** with God's help, I will fight against the as-yet-unknown purpose that prompted this treason. 142. **pretense:** design.   143. **malice:** enmity.   144. **briefly:** quickly.   **manly readiness:** men's clothing and resolute purpose.   146. **consort:** keep company, associate.   148. **easy:** easily.   151–52. **the nea'er . . . bloody:** the closer the kinship, the greater the danger of being murdered. 153. **lighted:** alighted, descended.   155. **dainty of:** particular about.   156. **shift away:** disappear by stealth.   **warrant:** justification.   **Act 2, Scene 4. Location:** Outside Macbeth's castle of Inverness.   3. **sore:** dreadful, grievous.   4. **trifled former knowings:** made trivial all former experiences.   **father:** old man.   5–6. **heavens, act, stage:** (A theatrical metaphor; the *heavens* refer to the decorated roof over the *stage*.) 7. **traveling lamp:** i.e., sun.   8. **predominance:** ascendancy, superior influence (as of a heavenly body).   12. **towering:** circling higher and higher. (A term in falconry.)   **place:** pitch, highest point in the falcon's flight.   13. **mousing:** i.e., ordinarily preying on mice.   15. **minions:** darlings. 17. **as:** as if.   18. **eat:** ate. (Pronounced "et.")   24. **What . . . pretend:** i.e., what could they hope to gain by it?   **pretend:** intend.

MACDUFF   They were
     suborned.°
25   Malcolm and Donalbain, the King's two sons,
     Are stol'n away and fled, which puts upon
          them
     Suspicion of the deed.
     ROSS   'Gainst nature still!
     Thriftless° ambition, that will ravin up°
     Thine own life's means! Then 'tis most like°
30   The sovereignty will fall upon Macbeth.
     MACDUFF He is already named° and gone to
          Scone°
     To be invested.
     ROSS   Where is Duncan's body?
     MACDUFF Carried to Colmekill,°

The sacred storehouse of his predecessors
And guardian of their bones.
35   **ROSS**   Will you to Scone?
     MACDUFF No, cousin, I'll to Fife.°
     ROSS   Well, I will
          thither.
     MACDUFF Well, may you see things well done
          there. Adieu,
     Lest our old robes sit easier than our new!
     ROSS Farewell, father.
40   **OLD MAN** God's benison° go with you, and with
          those
     That would make good of bad, and friends of
          foes!   *Exeunt omnes.*

---

24. **suborned:** bribed, hired.   28. **Thriftless:** wasteful.   **ravin up:** devour ravenously.   29. **like:** likely.   31. **named:** chosen. (See the note for 1.4.50.)
Scone: ancient royal city of Scotland near Perth.   33. **Colmekill:** Icolmkill, i.e., Cell of St. Columba, the barren islet of Iona in the Western Islands, a
sacred spot where the kings were buried; here, called a *storehouse.*   36. **Fife:** (Of which Macduff is Thane.)   40. **benison:** blessing.

Understanding and Interpreting

1 This act opens with Banquo talking with his son Fleance. What is Banquo concerned about at this point, and what effect does Shakespeare create by beginning with this brief conversation between father and son?

2 In Scene 1, Banquo tells Macbeth that the king is pleased with the hospitality the Macbeths have shown him, saying that the king "hath been in unusual pleasure" (l. 13), and even passing along a diamond as a thank-you from the king to Lady Macbeth. What is the effect of this short exchange's taking place right after Lady Macbeth and Macbeth have discussed at length their plan to murder Duncan?

3 After Banquo exits, Macbeth sees a dagger floating in front of him (Scene 1, l. 34). Explain whether you think the dagger is real or imagined—a "dagger of the mind" (l. 39), perhaps a vision sent by supernatural forces. What are the implications of both possibilities? Why do you think Macbeth calls the dagger a "fatal vision" (l. 37)? How does the dagger's being real or imagined affect your interpretation of Macbeth's psychological state at this point in the play?

4 Compare and contrast how Macbeth and Lady Macbeth respond to the murder in Scene 2. What do their differing responses suggest about their characters at this point?

5 After killing Duncan, Macbeth cannot bear returning to the scene of the murder to plant the bloody knives, but Lady Macbeth is willing to do it, saying, "The sleeping and the dead / Are but as pictures" (Scene 3, ll. 57–58). What does this suggest about the role Lady Macbeth will play in Macbeth's future attempts to gain greater power?

6 After the king's murder is discovered, Macbeth and Lady Macbeth must be careful in their response. In what ways are they successful in hiding their guilt, and in what ways might they arouse the suspicions of other characters?

7 Summarize the events in Scene 3, lines 112–129, in which Lennox and Macbeth describe the scene in Duncan's chamber.

8 Banquo proposes that the men "question this most bloody piece of work / To know it further" (Scene 3, ll. 139–140). He then declares that he stands in the "great hand of God" and will fight "treasonous malice" (ll. 141–143). Do you think these lines indicate that Banquo may be suspicious of Macbeth in particular or that he just wants to know more about the circumstances surrounding Duncan's murder? Explain your reasoning.

9 In Scene 4, Macduff states that the hasty departure of Malcolm and Donalbain "puts upon them / Suspicion of the deed" (ll. 25–27), even though they are Duncan's sons. Historically, sons of kings sometimes did kill their fathers in order to gain the power of the throne. Summarize the reasons Malcolm and Donalbain provide for fleeing to England and Ireland (Scene 3, ll. 146–157).

Analyzing Language, Style, and Structure

1 In literature, a *foil* is a character who, by his or her contrast with the main character, accentuates the main character's distinctive characteristics. In *Macbeth*, Banquo serves as a foil to Macbeth. Read the lines between Banquo and Macbeth at the opening of Scene 1, and focus on how these lines accentuate the characteristics of both Banquo and Macbeth. Then, create a list of characteristics for each man, using text to support your observations about the two characters.

2 In Scene 1, lines 51–60, Macbeth makes numerous references to witchcraft and evil omens. Identify these references and analyze what these references indicate about Macbeth's state of mind.

3 When Macbeth enters in Scene 2, he is carrying two bloody daggers. Characterize Lady Macbeth's response to her husband's appearance and explain how their exchange heightens the tension of the moment.

4 Macbeth seems inconsolable after he kills the two men (Scene 2, ll. 62–67). Using text to support your response, discuss how Shakespeare uses water imagery to emphasize the different reactions of Lady Macbeth and Macbeth to the murder.

5 Macbeth claims that he heard someone cry "Glamis hath murdered sleep [. . .] Macbeth shall sleep no more" (Scene 2, ll. 46–47). What other references to sleep does Macbeth make and what purpose do his descriptions of sleep serve within the scene?

6 After Macduff and Lennox ask Macbeth about the king, Lennox goes on to describe the tumultuous weather of the night before (Scene 3, ll. 63–70). Summarize Lennox's description of the night and explain the effect it has at this moment in the play.

7 At the beginning of Scene 3, the porter says, "Faith, here's an equivocator, that could swear in both the scales against either scale" (ll. 10–12). *Equivocation* was a Catholic doctrine during Shakespeare's time that stated that using words with vague or double meanings in order to avoid persecution or even death at the hands of the Protestants who were in power at the time was not truly lying, and therefore not actually a sin. In other words, it was a way of lying under oath without facing judgment from God.

As the porter makes his way to open the door he references equivocation several times. How is this concept of equivocation connected to the murder that has just been committed?

8 A *double entendre* is a word or expression that can be understood in two different ways, with one of the ways often involving a sexual or risqué reference. In his brief conversation with Macduff (Scene 3, ll. 29–49), the porter employs the literary device of double entendre several times for a humorous effect. Read the porter's lines closely and identify at least one double entendre. Discuss why these lines can be considered comical.

9 Analyze how Macbeth uses imagery and hyperbole to describe his reaction to Duncan's death in Scene 3, lines 102–107. What effect does he intend his language choices to have on the other characters present?

10 Examine Scene 3 lines 119–143, in which the men discuss what next steps they should take. Focus on language related to masculinity. What do their comments indicate concerning how men should respond to tragedy?

Connecting, Arguing, and Extending

1 Throughout the first two acts of *Macbeth*, there are numerous references to witchcraft, spells, and omens. These references would have been immediately recognized by a Jacobean audience, but are no longer common knowledge in the twenty-first century. Research a belief or superstition that is referenced in the play and prepare a short presentation on the background of that belief and how it may have influenced Shakespeare when he wrote *Macbeth*.

CENTRAL TEXT

2 The porter at the opening of Scene 3 seems to serve no function in terms of the plot of the play, even though he has a significant number of lines. While some productions of *Macbeth* omit the porter altogether, many keep him in, perhaps as a form of comic relief to help provide an emotional outlet and change of pace for the audience or to help create a contrast that emphasizes the seriousness of the work. If you were the director of the play, explain whether or not you would keep the porter in the production and why.

3 Macbeth's succession to the throne at the end of the act may seem sudden. However, at the time, Scottish kings were elected by the thanes, who would have acted quickly to make sure that there was someone elected king as soon as possible after the death of a current ruler.

Because this play is loosely based on actual events in Scotland, it is possible to connect the characters in the play with the actual historical figures on which they were based. Research the kings of Scotland and create a family

tree based on the information you find. Also research the actual order of succession, and look up any history related to the battles these thanes and kings fought. Prepare the historical account in a visually interesting manner, and include quotes from the play that seem most related to each of the historical figures you research.

4 Macbeth is king by the end of Act 2. Thus, Macbeth's family coat of arms would be featured prominently in his court.

Do some online research about traditional designs for a coat of arms, including the elements that go into making one, and then create two symbolic coats of arms for the newly kinged Macbeth. For the first one, create a coat of arms that represents what the public knows about Macbeth, including his bravery on the battlefield. For the second one, create a coat of arms that represents the true Macbeth, who was willing to kill his king in order to gain power. Under each coat of arms, provide an explanation of what the different images symbolize about Macbeth's character.

Scene 1°

Enter Banquo.

BANQUO Thou hast it now — King, Cawdor, Glamis, all
As the weird women promised, and I fear
Thou played'st most foully for 't. Yet it was said
It should not stand° in thy posterity,
5 But that myself should be the root and father
Of many kings. If there come truth from them —
As upon thee, Macbeth, their speeches shine° —
Why, by the verities on thee made good,
May they not be my oracles as well
10 And set me up in hope? But hush, no more.

Sennet° sounded. Enter Macbeth as King, Lady [Macbeth], Lennox, Ross, lords, and attendants.

MACBETH Here's our chief guest.

LADY MACBETH If he had been forgotten,

It had been as a gap in our great feast
And all-thing° unbecoming.

MACBETH Tonight we hold a solemn° supper, sir,
And I'll request your presence.

15 **BANQUO** Let Your Highness
Command° upon me, to the which my duties
Are with a most indissoluble tie
Forever knit.

MACBETH Ride you this afternoon?

20 **BANQUO** Ay, my good lord.

MACBETH We should have else desired your good advice,
Which still° hath been both grave° and prosperous,°
In this day's council; but we'll take tomorrow.
Is 't far you ride?

25 **BANQUO** As far, my lord, as will fill up the time
Twixt this and supper. Go not my horse the better,°

Act 3, Scene 1. Location: Forres. The palace. **4. stand:** stay, remain. **7. shine:** are brilliantly manifest. **s.d.** *Sennet:* trumpet call. **13. all-thing:** in every way. **14. solemn:** ceremonious. **16. Command:** lay your command. **22. still:** always. **grave:** weighty. **prosperous:** profitable. **26. Go . . . better:** unless my horse makes better time than I expect.

I must become a borrower of the night
For a dark hour or twain.
MACBETH Fail not our feast.
30 BANQUO My lord, I will not.
MACBETH We hear our bloody cousins are
    bestowed°
  In England and in Ireland, not confessing
  Their cruel parricide, filling their hearers
  With strange invention.° But of that tomorrow,
35 When therewithal° we shall have cause of
    state
  Craving us jointly.° Hie you to horse. Adieu,
  Till you return at night. Goes Fleance with
    you?
BANQUO Ay, my good lord. Our time does call
    upon 's.
MACBETH I wish your horses swift and sure of
    foot,
40 And so I do commend° you to their backs.
  Farewell.   *Exit Banquo.*
  Let every man be master of his time
  Till seven at night. To make society
  The sweeter welcome, we will keep ourself°
45 Till suppertime alone. While° then, God be
    with you!
  Exeunt Lords [and all but Macbeth and a Servant].
  Sirrah,° a word with you. Attend those men
  Our pleasure?
SERVANT They are, my lord, without the palace
    gate.
MACBETH Bring them before us.   *Exit Servant.*
                   To be thus° is
    nothing,
50 But° to be safely thus. — Our fears in° Banquo
  Stick deep, and in his royalty of nature°
  Reigns that which would be° feared. 'Tis much
    he dares;
  And to° that dauntless temper of his mind
  He hath a wisdom that doth guide his valor

55 To act in safety. There is none but he
  Whose being I do fear; and under him
  My genius is rebuked,° as it is said
  Mark Antony's was by Caesar.° He chid the
    sisters
  When first they put the name of king upon
    me,
60 And bade them speak to him. Then,
    prophetlike,
  They hailed him father to a line of kings.
  Upon my head they placed a fruitless crown
  And put a barren scepter in my grip,
  Thence to be wrenched with° an unlineal°
    hand,
65 No son of mine succeeding. If 't be so,
  For Banquo's issue have I filed° my mind;
  For them the gracious Duncan have I
    murdered,
  Put rancors° in the vessel of my peace
  Only for them, and mine eternal jewel°
70 Given to the common enemy of man°
  To make them kings, the seeds of Banquo
    kings.
  Rather than so, come fate into the list,°
  And champion me° to th' utterance!° — Who's
    there?

  Enter Servant and two Murderers.

  Now go to the door, and stay there till we call.
                   Exit Servant.
75 Was it not yesterday we spoke together?
MURDERERS It was, so please Your Highness.
MACBETH   Well
    then, now
  Have you considered of my speeches? Know
  That it was he in the times past which held
    you
  So under fortune,° which you thought had
    been
80 Our innocent self. This I made good to you

---

31. bestowed: lodged.   **34. invention:** falsehood (i.e., that Macbeth was the murderer).   **35. therewithal:** besides that.   **35–36. cause . . . jointly:** questions of state occupying our joint attention.   **40. commend:** commit, entrust.   **44. we . . . ourself:** I will keep to myself.   **45. While:** till.   **46. Sirrah:** (A form of address to a social inferior.)   **49. thus:** i.e., king.   **50. But:** unless.   **in:** concerning.   **51. royalty of nature:** natural kingly bearing.   **52. would be:** deserves to be.   **53. to:** added to.   **57. My genius is rebuked:** my guardian spirit is daunted or abashed.   **58. Caesar:** Octavius Caesar.   **64. with:** by.   **unlineal:** not of lineal descent from me.   **66. filed:** defiled.   **68. rancors:** malignant enemies (here visualized as a poison added to a vessel full of wholesome drink).   **69. eternal jewel:** i.e., soul.   **70. common . . . man:** i.e., devil.   **72. list:** lists, place of combat.   **73. champion me:** fight with me in single combat.   **to th' utterance:** to the last extremity (French, *à l'outrance*).   **79. under fortune:** down in your fortunes.

In our last conference, passed in probation°
　　with you
How you were borne in hand,° how crossed,°
　　the instruments,°
Who wrought with them, and all things else
　　that might
To half a soul° and to a notion° crazed
Say, "Thus did Banquo."

85 **FIRST MURDERER**　　　　　You made it known
　　to us.

MACBETH　I did so, and went further, which is
　　now
Our point of second meeting. Do you find
Your patience so predominant in your nature
That you can let this go? Are you so gospeled°

90 To pray for this good man and for his issue,
Whose heavy hand hath bowed you to the grave
And beggared yours° forever?

FIRST MURDERER　　　　　We are men, my
　　liege.

MACBETH　Ay, in the catalogue ye go for° men,
As hounds and greyhounds, mongrels,
　　spaniels, curs,

95 Shoughs,° water-rugs,° and demi-wolves° are
　　clept°
All by the name of dogs. The valued file°
Distinguishes the swift, the slow, the subtle,
The housekeeper,° the hunter, every one
According to the gift which bounteous nature

100 Hath in him closed,° whereby he does receive
Particular addition from the bill
That writes them all alike;° and so of men.
Now, if you have a station in the file,°
Not i' the worst rank of manhood, say 't,

105 And I will put that business in your bosoms
Whose execution° takes your enemy off,
Grapples you to the heart and love of us,

Who wear our health but sickly in his life,°
Which in his death were perfect.

SECOND MURDERER　　　　　I am one, my
　　liege,

110 Whom the vile blows and buffets of the world
Hath so incensed that I am reckless what
I do to spite the world.

FIRST MURDERER　　　　And I another,
So weary with disasters, tugged with° fortune,
That I would set° my life on any chance
To mend it or be rid on 't.

115 **MACBETH**　　　　　Both of you
Know Banquo was your enemy.

BOTH MURDERERS　　　　　True, my lord.

MACBETH　So is he mine, and in such bloody
　　distance°
That every minute of his being thrusts°
Against my near'st of life.° And though I could

120 With barefaced power° sweep him from my
　　sight
And bid my will avouch it,° yet I must not,
For° certain friends that are both his and
　　mine,
Whose loves I may not drop, but wail° his fall
Who° I myself struck down. And thence it is

125 That I to your assistance do make love,°
Masking the business from the common eye
For sundry weighty reasons.

SECOND MURDERER　　　　　We shall, my lord,
Perform what you command us.

FIRST MURDERER　　　　　Though our
　　lives —

MACBETH　Your spirits shine through you.°
　　Within this hour at most

130 I will advise° you where to plant yourselves,
Acquaint you with the perfect spy° o' the time,
The moment on 't,° for 't must be done tonight,

---

81. **passed in probation:** went over the proof.　82. **borne in hand:** deceived by false promises.　**crossed:** thwarted.　**instruments:** agents.　84. **To half a soul:** even to a half-wit.　**notion:** mind.　89. **gospeled:** imbued with the gospel spirit.　92. **yours:** your family.　93. **go for:** pass for, are entered for.　95. **Shoughs:** a kind of shaggy dog.　**water-rugs:** long-haired water dogs.　**demi-wolves:** a crossbreed with the wolf.　**clept:** called.　96. **valued file:** list classified according to value.　98. **housekeeper:** watchdog.　100. **in him closed:** enclosed in him, set in him like a jewel.　101–02. **Particular . . . alike:** particular qualification apart from the catalog that lists them all indiscriminately.　103. **file:** military row, as in "rank and file"; see *rank* in line 104.　106. **Whose execution:** the doing of which.　108. **in his life:** while he lives.　113. **tugged with:** pulled about by (as in wrestling).　114. **set:** risk, stake.　117. **distance:** (1) hostility, enmity (2) interval of distance between fencers.　118. **thrusts:** (As in fencing.)　119. **near'st of life:** most vital part, the heart.　120. **With barefaced power:** by open use of my supreme royal authority.　121. **And . . . avouch it:** and use my mere wish as my justification.　122. **For:** because of, for the sake of.　123. **wail:** i.e., I must lament.　124. **Who:** whom.　125. **to . . . make love:** woo your aid.　129. **Your . . . you:** i.e., enough; I can see your determination in your faces.　130. **advise:** instruct.　131–32. **with . . . on 't:** with full and precise instructions as to when it is to be done.　**spy:** espial, observation.

And something from° the palace; always thought°
That I require a clearness.° And with him —
135   To leave no rubs° nor botches in the work —
Fleance his son, that keeps him company,
Whose absence is no less material to me
Than is his father's, must embrace the fate
Of that dark hour. Resolve yourselves apart;°
I'll come to you anon.
140 **BOTH MURDERERS**   We are resolved, my lord.
MACBETH I'll call upon you straight. Abide
    within.   *Exeunt* [*Murderers*].
It is concluded. Banquo, thy soul's flight,
If it find heaven, must find it out tonight.
                            [*Exit.*]

Scene 2°

Enter Macbeth's Lady and a Servant.

LADY MACBETH Is Banquo gone from court?
SERVANT Ay, madam, but returns again tonight.
LADY MACBETH Say to the King I would attend
    his leisure
For a few words.
5 **SERVANT** Madam, I will.   *Exit.*
LADY MACBETH Naught's had, all's spent,
Where our desire is got without content.°
'Tis safer to be that which we destroy
Than by destruction dwell in doubtful joy.°

Enter Macbeth.

10 How now, my lord? Why do you keep alone,
Of sorriest° fancies your companions making,
Using° those thoughts which should indeed
    have died
With them they think on? Things without° all
    remedy

Should be without regard.° What's done is
    done.
15 **MACBETH** We have scorched° the snake, not
    killed it.
She'll close° and be herself, whilst our poor
    malice°
Remains in danger of her former tooth.°
But let the frame of things disjoint, both the
    worlds suffer,°
Ere we will eat our meal in fear and sleep
20 In the affliction of these terrible dreams
That shake us nightly. Better be with the dead,
Whom we, to gain our peace, have sent to
    peace,°
Than on the torture° of the mind to lie
In restless ecstasy.° Duncan is in his grave;
25 After life's fitful fever he sleeps well.
Treason has done his worst; nor steel,° nor
    poison,
Malice domestic,° foreign levy,° nothing
Can touch him further.
  LADY MACBETH Come on,
30 Gentle my lord, sleek o'er your rugged looks.°
Be bright and jovial among your guests
    tonight.
MACBETH So shall I, love, and so, I pray, be you.
Let your remembrance apply° to Banquo;
Present him eminence,° both with eye and
    tongue —
35 Unsafe the while, that we
Must lave our honors in these flattering
    streams°
And make our faces vizards° to our hearts,
Disguising what they are.
LADY MACBETH   You must leave this.
MACBETH O, full of scorpions is my mind, dear
    wife!

---

133. **something from:** some distance removed from.   **thought:** being borne in mind.   134. **clearness:** freedom from suspicion.   135. **rubs:** defects, rough spots.   139. **Resolve yourselves apart:** make up your minds in private conference.   **Act 3, Scene 2. Location:** The palace.
7. **content:** contentedness.   9. **Than . . . joy:** than by destroying achieve only an apprehensive joy.   11. **sorriest:** most despicable or wretched.
12. **Using:** keeping company with, entertaining.   13. **without:** beyond.   14. **without regard:** not pondered upon.   15. **scorched:** slashed, cut.
16. **close:** heal, close up again.   **poor malice:** feeble hostility.   17. **her former tooth:** her fang, just as before.   18. **let . . . suffer:** let the universe itself fall apart, both heaven and earth perish.   22. **to gain . . . to peace:** to gain contentedness through satisfied ambition, have sent to eternal rest.
23. **torture:** rack.   24. **ecstasy:** frenzy.   26. **nor steel:** neither steel.   27. **Malice domestic:** civil war.   **foreign levy:** the levying of troops abroad (against Scotland).   30. **Gentle . . . looks:** my noble lord, smooth over your rough looks.   33. **Let . . . apply:** remember to pay special attention.
34. **eminence:** favor.   35–36. **Unsafe . . . streams:** i.e., we are unsafe at present and so must put on a show of flattering cordiality to make our reputation look clean, or, we are unsafe so long as we must flatter thus. (*Lave* means "wash.")   37. **vizards:** masks.

40   Thou know'st that Banquo and his Fleance
          lives.

LADY MACBETH But in them nature's copy's° not
          eterne.°

MACBETH There's° comfort yet; they are assailable.
      Then be thou jocund. Ere the bat hath flown
      His cloistered° flight, ere to black Hecate's°
          summons

45   The shard-borne° beetle with his drowsy hums
      Hath rung night's yawning° peal, there shall
          be done
      A deed of dreadful note.

LADY MACBETH   What's to be done?

MACBETH Be innocent of the knowledge, dearest
          chuck,°
      Till thou applaud the deed. Come, seeling°
          night,

50   Scarf up° the tender eye of pitiful° day,
      And with thy bloody and invisible hand
      Cancel and tear to pieces that great bond°
      Which keeps me pale!° Light thickens,°
      And the crow° makes wing to th' rooky° wood;

55   Good things of day begin to droop and
          drowse,
      Whiles night's black agents to their preys do
          rouse.°
      Thou marvel'st at my words, but hold thee
          still.
      Things bad begun make strong themselves by ill.
      So, prithee, go with me.   *Exeunt.*

Scene 3°

Enter three Murderers.

FIRST MURDERER But who did bid thee join
          with us?

THIRD MURDERER   Macbeth.

SECOND MURDERER [*to the First Murderer*]
      He needs not our mistrust, since he delivers
      Our offices° and what we have to do
      To° the direction just.°

FIRST MURDERER   Then stand with us.

5   The west yet glimmers with some streaks of
          day.
      Now spurs the lated° traveler apace
      To gain the timely° inn, and near approaches
      The subject of our watch.

THIRD MURDERER Hark, I hear horses.

10 **BANQUO** (*within*) Give us a light there, ho!

SECOND MURDERER Then 'tis he. The rest
      That are within the note of expectation°
      Already are i' the court.

FIRST MURDERER His horses go about.°

15 **THIRD MURDERER** Almost a mile; but he does
          usually —
      So all men do — from hence to th' palace gate
      Make it their walk.

      Enter Banquo and Fleance, with a torch.

SECOND MURDERER A light, a light!

THIRD MURDERER 'Tis he.

20 **FIRST MURDERER** Stand to 't.

BANQUO It will be rain tonight.

FIRST MURDERER Let it come down!
                    [*They attack Banquo.*]

BANQUO O, treachery! Fly, good Fleance, fly, fly,
          fly!
      Thou mayst revenge. — O slave!
                    [*He dies. Fleance escapes.*]

THIRD MURDERER Who did strike out the light?

25 **FIRST MURDERER**   Was 't
          not the way?°

THIRD MURDERER There's but one down; the son
          is fled.

---

41. **nature's copy:** lease of life (i.e., by copyhold or lease subject to cancellation); also, the individual human being made from nature's mold. **eterne:** perpetual. 42. **There's:** i.e., in that thought there is. 44. **cloistered:** i.e., in and among buildings. **Hecate:** goddess of night and witchcraft, as in 2.1.53. 45. **shard-borne:** borne on shards, or horny wing cases, or, *shard-born*, bred in cow-droppings (shards). 46. **yawning:** drowsy. 48. **chuck:** (A term of endearment.) 49. **seeling:** eye-closing. (Night is pictured here as a falconer sewing up the eyes of day lest it should struggle against the deed that is to be done.) 50. **Scarf up:** blindfold. **pitiful:** compassionate. 52. **bond:** i.e., bond by which Banquo and Fleance hold their lives from nature, or moral law against murder, or bond of prophecy. 53. **pale:** pallid from fear (with a suggestion perhaps of *paled*, "fenced in"). **thickens:** grows opaque and dim. 54. **crow:** rook. **rooky:** full of rooks. 56. **to . . . rouse:** bestir themselves to hunt their prey.
Act 3, Scene 3. Location: A park near the palace. 2-3. **He . . . offices:** we need not mistrust this man, since he states exactly our duties (as told us by Macbeth). 4. **To:** according to. **just:** exactly. (That is, one can tell he comes from Macbeth, since he has instructions identical to ours.) 6. **lated:** belated. 7. **timely:** arrived in good time. 12. **within . . . expectation:** in the list of those expected. 14. **go about:** i.e., can be heard as servants take them to the stables (while Banquo and Fleance, provided with a torch, walk from the palace gate to the castle). 25. **way:** i.e., thing to do.

SECOND MURDERER We have lost best half of our
  affair.

FIRST MURDERER Well, let's away and say how
  much is done.   *Exeunt.*°

Scene 4°

*Banquet prepared. Enter Macbeth, Lady
[Macbeth], Ross, Lennox, Lords, and attendants.*

MACBETH You know your own degrees;° sit
  down. At first
  And last,° the hearty welcome.   [*They sit.*]

LORDS   Thanks to Your Majesty.

MACBETH Ourself will mingle with society°
  And play the humble host.

5 Our hostess keeps her state,° but in best time°
  We will require her welcome.°

LADY MACBETH Pronounce it for me, sir, to all
  our friends,
  For my heart speaks they are welcome.

Enter First Murderer [to the door].

MACBETH See, they encounter° thee with their
  hearts' thanks.

10 Both sides are even.° Here I'll sit i' the midst.
  Be large° in mirth; anon we'll drink a
  measure°
  The table round. [*He goes to the Murderer.*]
  There's blood upon thy face.

MURDERER 'Tis Banquo's, then.

MACBETH 'Tis better thee without than he
  within.°

15 Is he dispatched?

MURDERER My lord, his throat is cut. That I did
  for him.

MACBETH Thou art the best o' the cutthroats.
  Yet he's good that did the like for Fleance;
  If thou didst it, thou art the nonpareil.°

20 **MURDERER** Most royal sir, Fleance is scaped.

MACBETH Then comes my fit again. I had else
  been perfect,
  Whole as the marble, founded° as the rock,
  As broad and general° as the casing° air.
  But now I am cabined, cribbed,° confined,
  bound in

25 To saucy° doubts and fears. But Banquo's
  safe?

MURDERER Ay, my good lord. Safe in a ditch he
  abides,
  With twenty trenchèd gashes on his head,
  The least a death to nature.

MACBETH   Thanks for that.
  There the grown serpent lies; the worm° that's
  fled

30 Hath nature that in time will venom breed,
  No teeth for th' present. Get thee gone.
  Tomorrow
  We'll hear ourselves° again.   *Exit Murderer.*

LADY MACBETH   My royal lord,
  You do not give the cheer.° The feast is sold
  That is not often vouched, while 'tis a-making,

35 'Tis given with welcome.° To feed were best at
  home;°
  From thence,° the sauce to meat° is
  ceremony;
  Meeting were bare° without it.

*Enter the Ghost of Banquo, and sits in
Macbeth's place.*

MACBETH   Sweet
  remembrancer!
  Now, good digestion wait on° appetite,
  And health on both!

LENNOX   May 't please Your
  Highness sit?

40 **MACBETH** Here had we now our country's honor
  roofed°

---

s.d. *Exeunt:* (Presumably, the murderers drag the body of Banquo offstage as they go.)   **Act 3, Scene 4. Location:** A room of state in the palace.
1. degrees: ranks (as a determinant of seating).   **1–2. At . . . last:** once for all.   **3. mingle with society:** i.e., leave the chair of state and circulate among the guests.   **5. keeps her state:** remains in her canopied chair of state.   **in best time:** when it is most appropriate.   **6. require her welcome:** call upon her to give the welcome.   **9. encounter:** respond to.   **10. even:** full, with equal numbers on both sides.   **11. large:** liberal, free.   **measure:** i.e., cup filled to the brim for a toast.   **14. 'Tis . . . within:** it is better for you to have his blood on you than for him to have it within him.   **19. the nonpareil:** without equal.   **22. founded:** firmly established.   **23. broad and general:** unconfined.   **casing:** encasing, enveloping.   **24. cribbed:** shut in.   **25. saucy:** sharp, impudent, importunate.   **29. worm:** small serpent.   **32. hear ourselves:** confer.   **33. give the cheer:** welcome your guests.   **33–35. is sold . . . welcome:** seems grudgingly given, as if in return for money, unless it is often accompanied with assurances of welcome while it is in progress.   **35. To feed . . . home:** mere eating is best done at home.   **36. From thence:** away from home, dining in company.   **meat:** food.   **37. Meeting were bare:** gatherings of friends would be unadorned.   **38. wait on:** attend.   **40. roofed:** under one roof.

Were the graced person of our Banquo present,
Who may I° rather challenge for° unkindness
Than pity for mischance.

ROSS   His absence, sir,
Lays blame upon his promise. Please 't Your
     Highness

45 To grace us with your royal company?

MACBETH [*seeing his place occupied*]
The table's full.

LENNOX   Here is a place reserved, sir.

MACBETH Where?

LENNOX Here, my good lord. What is 't that
     moves Your Highness?

MACBETH Which of you have done this?

LORDS   What, my
     good lord?

50 MACBETH Thou canst not say I did it. Never
     shake
Thy gory locks at me.

ROSS Gentlemen, rise. His Highness is not well.
                              [*They start to rise.*]

LADY MACBETH Sit, worthy friends. My lord is
     often thus,
And hath been from his youth. Pray you, keep
     seat.

55 The fit is momentary; upon a thought°
He will again be well. If much you note him
You shall offend him° and extend° his
     passion.
Feed, and regard him not. — [*She confers apart
     with Macbeth.*] Are you a man?

MACBETH Ay, and a bold one, that dare look on
     that
Which might appall the devil.

60 LADY MACBETH   O, proper stuff!°
This is the very painting of your fear.
This is the air-drawn° dagger which, you said,
Led you to Duncan. O, these flaws° and starts,
Impostors to° true fear, would well become°
65 A woman's story at a winter's fire,
Authorized by° her grandam. Shame itself!
Why do you make such faces? When all's
     done,
You look but on a stool.

MACBETH   Prithee, see there!
Behold, look! Lo, how say you?
70 Why, what care I? If thou canst nod, speak too.
If charnel houses° and our graves must send
Those that we bury back, our monuments
Shall be the maws of kites.°   [*Exit Ghost.*]

> Look carefully at this painting depicting the scene in which Banquo's ghost shows up at Macbeth's banquet.
>
> **What specific details does the artist include that reflect the chaos of the moment?**

The Garrick Club/The Art Archive at Art Resource, NY

---

42. **Who may I:** whom I hope I may. **challenge for:** reprove for.   55. **upon a thought:** in a moment.   57. **offend him:** make him worse.   **extend:** prolong.   60. **O, proper stuff!** O, nonsense!   62. **air-drawn:** made of thin air, or floating disembodied in space.   63. **flaws:** gusts, outbursts. 64. **to:** compared with.   **become:** befit.   66. **Authorized by:** told on the authority of.   71. **charnel houses:** depositories for bones or bodies. 72–73. **our . . . kites:** i.e., we will have to leave the unburied bodies to scavenging birds of prey.

LADY MACBETH What, quite unmanned in folly?

MACBETH If I stand here, I saw him.

75 **LADY MACBETH** Fie, for
shame!

MACBETH Blood hath been shed ere now, i' th'
olden time,
Ere humane° statute purged the gentle weal;°
Ay, and since too, murders have been
performed
Too terrible for the ear. The time has been

80 That, when the brains were out, the man
would die,
And there an end; but now they rise again
With twenty mortal murders° on their crowns,°
And push us from our stools.° This is more
strange
Than such a murder is.

LADY MACBETH My worthy lord,
Your noble friends do lack you.

85 **MACBETH** I do forget.
Do not muse at me, my most worthy friends;
I have a strange infirmity, which is nothing
To those that know me. Come, love and health
to all!
Then I'll sit down. Give me some wine. Fill full.

[He is given wine.]

Enter Ghost.

90 I drink to the general joy o' th' whole table,
And to our dear friend Banquo, whom we miss.
Would he were here! To all, and him, we thirst,°
And all to all.°

LORDS Our duties and the pledge.°

[They drink.]

MACBETH *[seeing the Ghost]*
Avaunt, and quit my sight! Let the earth hide
thee!

95 Thy bones are marrowless, thy blood is cold;

Thou hast no speculation° in those eyes
Which thou dost glare with!

LADY MACBETH Think of this, good
peers,
But as a thing of custom. 'Tis no other;
Only it spoils the pleasure of the time.

100 **MACBETH** What man dare, I dare.
Approach thou like the rugged Russian bear,
The armed° rhinoceros, or th' Hyrcan° tiger;
Take any shape but that, and my firm nerves°
Shall never tremble. Or be alive again

105 And dare me to the desert° with thy sword.
If trembling I inhabit then,° protest° me
The baby of a girl.° Hence, horrible shadow!
Unreal mockery, hence! [*Exit Ghost.*] Why, so;
being gone,
I am a man again. Pray you, sit still.

110 **LADY MACBETH** You have displaced the mirth,
broke the good meeting
With most admired° disorder.°

MACBETH Can such things be,
And overcome° us like a summer's cloud,
Without our special wonder? You make me
strange
Even to the disposition that I owe,°

115 When now I think you can behold such sights
And keep the natural ruby of your cheeks
When mine is blanched with fear.

ROSS What sights, my lord?

LADY MACBETH I pray you, speak not. He grows
worse and worse;
Question° enrages him. At once,° good night.

120 Stand not upon the order of your going,°
But go at once.°

LENNOX Good night, and better health
Attend His Majesty!

LADY MACBETH A kind good night to all!

Exeunt Lords [and attendants].

---

77. **Ere . . . weal:** before the institution of law cleansed the commonwealth of violence and made it gentle. **humane:** (This spelling, interchangeable with *human*, carries both meanings: "appertaining to humankind" and "befitting humanity.") 82. **mortal murders:** deadly wounds. **crowns:** heads. 83. **push . . . stools:** usurp our places at feasts (with a suggestion of usurpation of the throne). 92. **thirst:** desire to drink. 93. **all to all:** all good wishes to all, or, let all drink to everyone else. **Our . . . pledge:** in drinking the toast you just proposed, we offer our homage. 96. **speculation:** power of sight. 102. **armed:** armor-plated. **Hyrcan:** of Hyrcania, in ancient times a region near the Caspian Sea. 103. **nerves:** sinews. 105. **the desert:** some solitary place. 106. **If . . . then:** i.e., if then I tremble. **protest:** proclaim. 107. **The baby of a girl:** a baby girl, or, girl's doll. 111. **admired:** wondered at. **disorder:** lack of self-control. 112. **overcome:** come over. 113–14. **You make . . . owe:** you cause me to feel I do not know my own nature (which I had presumed to be that of a brave man). 119. **Question:** talk. **At once:** to you all; now. 120. **Stand . . . going:** i.e., do not take the time to leave in ceremonious order of rank, as you entered. 121. **at once:** all together and now.

seeing connections

Compare these two movie versions of *Macbeth*, one with a modern setting and the other with a traditional setting.

How do the directors use similar techniques to effectively project Macbeth's strange behavior and the guests' response? In what ways do these directors make choices that indicate slightly different interpretations of the same scene, other than the different time period in which each one is set?

—You make me strange
even to that disposition that I owe

MACBETH It will have blood, they say; blood will
   have blood.
   Stones have been known to move, and trees to
      speak;°
125 Augurs° and understood relations° have
   By maggotpies and choughs° and rooks
      brought forth°
   The secret'st man of blood.° What is the night?°
LADY MACBETH Almost at odds with morning,
   which is which.

MACBETH How sayst thou,° that Macduff denies
   his person
   At our great bidding?
130 **LADY MACBETH**   Did you send to him, sir?
MACBETH I hear it by the way;° but I will send.
   There's not a one of them but in his house
   I keep a servant fee'd.° I will tomorrow —
   And betimes° I will — to the Weird Sisters.
135 More shall they speak, for now I am bent° to
   know

---

124. **Stones ... speak:** i.e., even inanimate nature speaks in such a way as to reveal the unnatural act of murder.   125. **Augurs:** prophecies.
understood relations: reports able to be interpreted or understood, or the hidden ties that link the parts of nature to one another.   126. **By ...**
choughs: by means of magpies and jackdaws.   **brought forth:** revealed.   127. **man of blood:** murderer.   **the night:** i.e., the time of night.
129. **How sayst thou:** what do you say to the fact.   131. **by the way:** indirectly.   133. **fee'd:** i.e., paid to spy.   134. **betimes:** (1) early (2) while there
is still time.   135. **bent:** determined.

By the worst means the worst. For mine own
good

All causes° shall give way. I am in blood

Stepped in so far that, should I wade no more,°

Returning were° as tedious as go° o'er.

140 Strange things I have in head, that will to hand,

Which must be acted ere they may be
scanned.°

LADY MACBETH You lack the season° of all
natures, sleep.

MACBETH Come, we'll to sleep. My strange and
self-abuse°

Is the initiate fear° that wants hard use.°

145 We are yet but young in deed.   *Exeunt.*

Scene 5°

Thunder. Enter the three Witches, meeting Hecate.

FIRST WITCH Why, how now, Hecate? You look
angerly.°

HECATE Have I not reason, beldams° as you are?

Saucy and overbold, how did you dare

To trade and traffic with Macbeth

5 In riddles and affairs of death,

And I, the mistress of your charms,

The close° contriver of all harms,

Was never called to bear my part

Or show the glory of our art?

10 And, which is worse, all you have done

Hath been but for a wayward son,

Spiteful and wrathful, who, as others do,

Loves for his own ends, not for you.

But make amends now. Get you gone,

15 And at the pit of Acheron°

Meet me i' the morning. Thither he

Will come to know his destiny.

Your vessels and your spells provide,

Your charms and everything beside.

20 I am for th' air. This night I'll spend

Unto a dismal° and a fatal end.

Great business must be wrought ere noon.

Upon the corner of the moon

There hangs a vaporous drop profound;°

25 I'll catch it ere it come to ground,

And that, distilled by magic sleights,

Shall raise such artificial sprites°

As by the strength of their illusion

Shall draw him on to his confusion.°

30 He shall spurn fate, scorn death, and bear

His hopes 'bove wisdom, grace, and fear.

And you all know, security°

Is mortals' chiefest enemy.   *Music and a song.*

Hark! I am called. My little spirit, see,

35 Sits in a foggy cloud and stays for me.   [*Exit.*]

Sing within, "Come away, come away,"° *etc.*

FIRST WITCH Come, let's make haste. She'll soon
be back again.   *Exeunt.*

Scene 6°

Enter Lennox and another Lord.

LENNOX My former speeches have but hit your
thoughts,

Which can interpret farther.° Only I say

Things have been strangely borne.° The
gracious Duncan

Was pitied of Macbeth; marry, he was dead.°

5 And the right valiant Banquo walked too late,

Whom you may say, if 't please you, Fleance
killed,

For Fleance fled. Men must not walk too late.

Who cannot want the thought° how monstrous

---

137. **All causes:** all other considerations.   138. **should . . . more:** even if I were to wade no farther.   139. **were:** would be.   **go:** going.   141. **acted . . . scanned:** put into performance even before there is time to scrutinize them.   142. **season:** preservative.   143. **strange and self-abuse:** strange self-delusion.   144. **initiate fear:** fear experienced by a novice.   **wants hard use:** lacks toughening experience.   **Act 3, Scene 5. Location:** A heath. (This scene is probably by another author.)   1. **angerly:** angrily, angry.   2. **beldams:** hags.   7. **close:** secret.   15. **Acheron:** the river of sorrows in Hades; here, hell itself.   21. **dismal:** disastrous, ill-omened.   24. **profound:** i.e., heavily pendent, ready to drop off.   27. **artificial sprites:** spirits produced by magical arts.   29. **confusion:** ruin.   32. **security:** overconfidence.   **s.d. Come away etc.:** (The song occurs in Thomas Middleton's *The Witch.*)   **Act 3, Scene 6. Location:** Somewhere in Scotland.   1–2. **My . . . farther:** what I 've just said has coincided with your own thought. I needn't say more; you can surmise the rest.   3. **borne:** carried on.   4. **of:** by.   **marry . . . dead:** i.e., to be sure, this pity occurred after Duncan died, not before.   8. **cannot . . . thought:** can help thinking.

It was for Malcolm and for Donalbain

10 To kill their gracious father? Damnèd fact!°
How it did grieve Macbeth! Did he not straight°
In pious° rage the two delinquents tear
That were the slaves of drink and thralls° of
    sleep?
Was not that nobly done? Ay, and wisely too;

15 For 'twould have angered any heart alive
To hear the men deny 't. So that I say
He has borne all things well;° and I do think
That had he Duncan's sons under his key —
As, an 't° please heaven, he shall not — they
    should° find

20 What 'twere to kill a father. So should Fleance.
But peace! For from broad words,° and 'cause
    he failed
His presence° at the tyrant's feast, I hear
Macduff lives in disgrace. Sir, can you tell
Where he bestows himself?°

LORD   The son of Duncan,

25 From whom this tyrant holds the due of birth,°
Lives in the English court, and is received
Of° the most pious Edward° with such grace
That the malevolence of fortune nothing
Takes from his high respect.° Thither Macduff

30 Is gone to pray the holy king, upon his aid,°
To wake Northumberland° and warlike Siward,
That by the help of these — with Him above
To ratify the work — we may again
Give to our tables meat,° sleep to our nights,

35 Free from our feasts and banquets° bloody
    knives,
Do faithful homage, and receive free° honors —
All which we pine for now. And this report
Hath so exasperate the King° that he
Prepares for some attempt of war.

40 **LENNOX** Sent he to Macduff?

LORD He did; and with an absolute "Sir, not I,"°
The cloudy° messenger turns me° his back
And hums, as who should say,° "You'll rue the
    time
That clogs° me with this answer."

LENNOX   And that well might

45 Advise him to a caution, t' hold what distance
His wisdom can provide.° Some holy angel
Fly to the court of England and unfold
His message ere he come, that a swift blessing
May soon return to this our suffering country

50 Under° a hand accursed!

LORD I'll send my prayers with him.   *Exeunt.*

---

10. **fact:** deed, crime. 11. **straight:** straightway, at once. 12. **pious:** holy, loyal, sonlike. 13. **thralls:** slaves. 17. **borne all things well:** managed everything cleverly. 19. **an 't:** if it. **should:** would be sure to. 21. **from broad words:** on account of plain speech. 22. **His presence:** i.e., to be present. 24. **bestows himself:** is quartered, has taken refuge. 25. **holds . . . birth:** withholds the birthright (i.e., the Scottish crown). 27. **Of:** by. **Edward:** Edward the Confessor, King of England. 29. **his high respect:** the high respect paid to him. (Being out of fortune has not lessened the dignity with which Malcolm is received in England.) 30. **upon his aid:** in aid of Malcolm. 31. **wake Northumberland:** rouse the people of Northumberland. 34. **meat:** food. 35. **Free . . . banquets:** free our feasts and banquets from. 36. **free:** freely bestowed, or, pertaining to freemen. 38. **exasperate the King:** exasperated Macbeth. 41. **with . . . I:** i.e., when Macduff answered the messenger curtly with a refusal. 42. **cloudy:** louring, scowling. **turns me:** i.e., turns. (*Me* is used colloquially for emphasis.) 43. **hums . . . say:** says "umph!" as if to say. 44. **clogs:** encumbers, loads. 45–46. **Advise . . . provide:** warn him (Macduff) to keep what safe distance he can (from Macbeth). 49–50. **suffering country Under:** country suffering under.

Understanding and Interpreting

1 Banquo opens the first scene in Act 3 with a brief soliloquy expressing his fear that Macbeth played "most foully" (l. 3) in order to gain the throne. What is keeping him from revealing his suspicions to others at this point?

2 After Macbeth is alone, he states, "To be thus is nothing, / But to be safely thus" (Scene 1, ll. 49–50). What does this statement indicate about Macbeth's beliefs about the nature of power?

3 Taking all of Macbeth's speech into account (Scene 1, ll. 49–73), what is his attitude toward the murder at this point, as well as toward Banquo?

4 In Scene 2, Macbeth does not tell Lady Macbeth about the plan to kill Banquo and Fleance, even though she has known of all of his other deeds so far. Why does he keep this information to himself at this point?

5 As the murderers attack in Scene 3, Banquo's final act is to tell his son Fleance to run away (l. 23). He tells Fleance that he "mayst revenge" (l. 24), but does not mention that Macbeth is the guilty party. Why do you think that is?

6 In the feast scene (Scene 4), Macbeth is the host, but he is preoccupied with Banquo's murder and Lady Macbeth admonishes him for not giving "cheer" to the party (l. 33). Why is Macbeth's failure to provide the "sauce" (l. 36) to the ceremony an important issue for Lady Macbeth?

7 Macbeth is willing to do anything to avoid blame for Banquo's murder. He even tells Banquo's ghost, "Thou canst not say I did it" (Scene 4, l. 50). Explain what it suggests about Macbeth's character that he would attempt to deny his guilt even to his victim's ghost.

8 After Lady Macbeth chides Macbeth for responding to a ghost that only he can see (Scene 4, ll. 73 and 75), Macbeth seems to suddenly lose his fear of the mute ghostly visitor. Does he truly recover his nerve, or does Lady Macbeth shame him into pretending he has regained his composure? Explain your reasoning.

9 During Macbeth's outbursts at the feast in Scene 4, do you think the guests are convinced by the explanations for his "infirmity" or still suspicious of Macbeth?

10 Even after all the guests have left, Macbeth expresses concern that Macduff didn't attend the feast (Scene 4, ll. 129–130). Why is Macbeth concerned about Macduff's absence?

11 Explain what the Lord reveals in Scene 6 about Macduff's current situation and how he is attempting to respond to Macbeth's reign in Scotland.

Analyzing Language, Style, and Structure

1 In Scene 1, Macbeth openly expresses his fear of Banquo (ll. 50–73) in a speech that features numerous literary devices. Using specific examples of literary devices such as imagery and allusion from Macbeth's speech, explain what qualities give him cause for concern.

2 Evaluate the persuasive strategies Macbeth uses to convince the murderers to kill Banquo (Scene 1, ll. 77–92). Why are they effective? Are they similar to the strategies Lady Macbeth used to convince Macbeth to kill Duncan (Act 1, Scene 7, ll. 37–60)? Explain.

3 Shakespeare ends Scene 1 with this rhyming couplet:

> It is concluded. Banquo, thy soul's flight,
> If it find heaven, must find it out tonight.

Compare that with the couplet that concludes Act 2, Scene 1, just before Macbeth kills Duncan:

> Hear it not [the bell tolling], Duncan, for it is a knell
> That summons thee to heaven or to hell.

What does the contrast between these two couplets suggest about Macbeth's attitude toward each of these men?

4 In Scene 2, lines 49–56, Macbeth provides an elaborate description of nightfall. Analyze how he uses language to connect day and night with good and evil.

5 When Lady Macbeth addresses Macbeth directly after she has tried to calm the guests, she demands, "Are you a man?" (Scene 4, l. 58). How does this reinforce attitudes expressed so far in the play about the nature of men and women?

6 Lady Macbeth calls Macbeth's vision a "painting of [his] fear" (Scene 4, l. 61). How accurately does this metaphor reflect what is going on psychologically with Macbeth at this point in the play?

7 Toward the end of Scene 4, Macbeth tells his wife:

> I am in blood
> Stepped in so far that, should I wade no more,
> Returning were as tedious as go o'er. (ll. 137–139)

What does he mean by this, and what does his statement suggest about his attitude toward the consequences of his future actions?

8 In Scene 5, Hecate calls Macbeth a "wayward son" (l. 11), and then provides a list of his personal qualities. What qualities does she ascribe to Macbeth, and how do those qualities make him easily manipulated by the witches' predictions?

9 In Scene 6, we get the sense that Lennox cannot speak his mind freely with the Lord about his feelings toward Macbeth. Look carefully at his lines and identify the ways in which he reveals his true feelings indirectly. Then, discuss how his guarded response reflects the general atmosphere in Scotland.

Connecting, Arguing, and Extending

1 The first comprehensive classification of nature was attempted by the Greek philosopher Aristotle in his book *History of Animals*. In it, he arranged the world (and beyond) into a "Great Chain of Being" with God at the top, followed by angelic beings, humans, animals, plants, and finally, minerals. Within these categories were further categories; for instance, animals were arranged according to the food chain, and humans were arranged with kings at the top, then nobles, then peasants. Attempts to change one's position in the Great Chain of Being (for example, for a man to become an animal or for prey to become a predator) were considered the definition of chaos and would result in severe repercussions from Fate until order was restored. This idea of the Great Chain of Being continued to be incredibly influential all the way through Shakespeare's time, and Shakespeare in particular found the idea compelling. Notice how, after the murder of Duncan in *Macbeth*, the Old Man and Ross report chaos in the Great Chain of Being:

OLD MAN   'Tis unnatural,
  Even like the deed that's done. On Tuesday last
  A falcon, towering in her pride of place,
  Was by a mousing owl hawked at and killed.
ROSS And Duncan's horses — a thing most strange
      and certain —
  Beauteous and swift, the minions of their race,
  Turned wild in nature, broke their stalls, flung
      out,
  Contending 'gainst obedience, as they would
  Make war with mankind. (2.4.10–18)

Given this background, it is puzzling that Macbeth would believe it was Fate that he be crowned king, even though his assassination of the king was a direct violation of the Great Chain of Being. Prepare a presentation that explains the reasoning behind Macbeth's belief that Fate will secure his rule as king. In other words, create an argument that Macbeth would offer if he were asked to explain his apparently contradictory belief in and defiance of the Great Chain of Being.

2 Macbeth and Lady Macbeth both have a public and private identity. In their private lives they are murderers willing to do anything for power, while publicly they pretend to be loyal subjects who are horrified by the murders of Duncan and others. This split identity means that much of what Macbeth and Lady Macbeth say in the play is understood one way by the characters in the play, and another way by the audience who is aware of their crimes. This is called *dramatic irony*, and it is a device often employed by Shakespeare.

It is not only in plays but in real life that it is sometimes discovered that someone who is thought to be an upstanding person is in fact guilty of an unthinkable act. Research a recent or current example of a case in which a person who was held in high regard is found to have committed a terrible crime. Then, write a short scene that incorporates a bit of dramatic irony.

3 The murder of Banquo in Scene 3 happens very quickly, and the scene has five actors. Think about how you would stage this scene to produce the most stunning and dramatic effect. How would you design the physical space in which the action occurs, and how would you use the actors in that space to produce the effects? You may compose your response in writing, as an illustration, as a stage production, or even as a video.

4 Ghosts in Shakespeare's plays are frequently visible only to a single character (as in *Macbeth*), leading to great confusion on the part of the other characters. When directors stage these hallucinatory ghost scenes, they must choose whether to actually have an actor on stage playing the part of the ghost or not.

How would you stage the scene with Banquo's ghost (Act 3, Scene 4)? Write up your version of how this scene should be played. Consider all of the elements, including costuming, where the actors are standing, and the set. Then explain why you chose either to include or exclude the ghost, and how you intend that decision to affect how an audience experiences or interprets the scene.

Scene 1°

[*A cauldron.*] *Thunder. Enter the three Witches.*

FIRST WITCH Thrice the brinded° cat hath
    mewed.

SECOND WITCH Thrice, and once the hedgepig°
    whined.

THIRD WITCH Harpier° cries.° 'Tis time, 'tis time!

FIRST WITCH Round about the cauldron go;

5   In the poisoned entrails throw.
    Toad, that under cold stone
    Days and nights has thirty-one
    Sweltered venom, sleeping got,°
    Boil thou first i' the charmèd pot.

ALL [*as they dance round the cauldron*]

10   Double, double, toil and trouble;
    Fire burn, and cauldron bubble.

SECOND WITCH Fillet° of a fenny° snake,
    In the cauldron boil and bake;
    Eye of newt and toe of frog,

15   Wool of bat and tongue of dog,
    Adder's fork° and blindworm's° sting,
    Lizard's leg and owlet's wing,
    For a charm of powerful trouble,
    Like a hell-broth boil and bubble.

20 **ALL** Double, double, toil and trouble;
    Fire burn, and cauldron bubble.

THIRD WITCH Scale of dragon, tooth of wolf,
    Witches' mummy,° maw and gulf°
    Of the ravined° salt-sea shark,

25   Root of hemlock digged i' the dark,
    Liver of blaspheming Jew,
    Gall° of goat, and slips° of yew°
    Slivered° in the moon's eclipse,
    Nose of Turk and Tartar's lips,

30   Finger of birth-strangled babe
    Ditch-delivered by a drab,°
    Make the gruel thick and slab.°

Add thereto a tiger's chaudron°
For th' ingredience° of our cauldron.

35 **ALL** Double, double, toil and trouble;
    Fire burn, and cauldron bubble.

SECOND WITCH Cool it with a baboon's blood,

This painting by English artist Michael Ayrton was created as part of the costume design for the witches in the 1942 rendition of *Macbeth*, produced by the famous Shakespearean actor John Gielgud at the Piccadilly Theatre in London.

What effect do you think Ayrton is going for in this design, and how would it affect the telling of this tale?

Act 4, Scene 1. **Location:** A cavern (see 3.5.15). In the middle, a boiling cauldron (provided presumably by means of the trapdoor, see 4.1.106. The trapdoor must also be used in this scene for the apparitions).   1. **brinded:** marked by streaks (as by fire), brindled.   2. **hedgepig.** hedgehog.   3. **Harpier:** (The name of a familiar spirit; probably derived from *harpy*.)   **cries:** i.e., gives the signal to begin.   7–8. **Days . . . got:** for thirty-one days and nights has exuded venom formed during sleep.   12. **Fillet:** slice.   **fenny:** inhabiting fens or swamps.   16. **fork:** forked tongue. **blindworm:** slowworm, a harmless burrowing lizard.   23. **mummy:** mummified flesh made into a magical potion.   **maw and gulf:** gullet and stomach.   24. **ravined:** ravenous, or glutted with prey.   27. **Gall:** the secretion of the liver, bile.   **slips:** cuttings for grafting or planting. **yew:** (A tree often planted in churchyards and associated with mourning.)   28. **Slivered:** broken off (as a branch).   31. **Ditch . . . drab:** born in a ditch of a harlot.   32. **slab:** viscous.   33. **chaudron:** entrails.   34. **ingredience:** contents of a mixture.

CENTRAL TEXT   293

Then the charm is firm and good.

Enter Hecate to the other° three Witches.

HECATE O, well done! I commend your pains,
40   And everyone shall share i' the gains.
      And now about the cauldron sing
      Like elves and fairies in a ring,
      Enchanting all that you put in.°
              Music and a song: "Black spirits,"° etc.
                              [*Exit Hecate.*]
SECOND WITCH By the pricking of my thumbs,
45   Something wicked this way comes.
          Open, locks,
          Whoever knocks!

Enter Macbeth.

MACBETH How how, you secret, black,° and
          midnight hags?
      What is 't you do?
ALL   A deed without a name.
50 MACBETH I conjure you, by that which you profess,
      Howe'er you come to know it, answer me.
      Though you untie the winds and let them fight
      Against the churches, though the yeasty° waves
      Confound° and swallow navigation up,
55   Though bladed corn° be lodged° and trees
          blown down,
      Though castles topple on their warders' heads,
      Though palaces and pyramids do slope°
      Their heads to their foundations, though the
          treasure
      Of nature's germens° tumble all together,
60   Even till destruction sicken,° answer me
      To what I ask you.
FIRST WITCH   Speak.
SECOND WITCH   Demand.
THIRD WITCH   We'll answer.
FIRST WITCH Say if thou'dst rather hear it from
          our mouths
      Or from our masters?

MACBETH   Call 'em. Let me see 'em.
FIRST WITCH Pour in sow's blood, that hath eaten
65   Her nine farrow;° grease that's sweaten°
      From the murderer's gibbet° throw
      Into the flame.
ALL   Come high or low,°
      Thyself and office° deftly show!

Thunder. First Apparition, an armed Head.°

MACBETH Tell me, thou unknown power —
FIRST WITCH   He knows
          thy thought.
70   Hear his speech, but say thou naught.
FIRST APPARITION Macbeth! Macbeth! Macbeth!
          Beware Macduff,
      Beware the Thane of Fife. Dismiss me.
          Enough.
                              He descends.°
MACBETH Whate'er thou art, for thy good
          caution, thanks;
      Thou hast harped° my fear aright. But one
          word more —
75 FIRST WITCH He will not be commanded. Here's
          another,
      More potent than the first.

Thunder. Second Apparition, a bloody Child.°

SECOND APPARITION Macbeth! Macbeth!
          Macbeth!
MACBETH Had I three ears, I'd hear thee.
SECOND APPARITION Be bloody, bold, and reso-
          lute; laugh to scorn
80   The power of man, for none of woman born
      Shall harm Macbeth.   *Descends.*
MACBETH Then live, Macduff; what need I fear of
          thee?
      But yet I'll make assurance double sure,
      And take a bond of° fate. Thou shalt not live,
85   That I may tell pale-hearted fear it lies,
      And sleep in spite of thunder.

s.d. *other*: (Said because Hecate is a witch, too, not because more witches enter.)   39–43. **O . . . in:** (These lines are universally regarded as non-Shakespearean.)   s.d. **Black spirits etc.:** (This song is found in Middleton's *The Witch.*)   48. **black:** i.e., dealing in black magic.   53. **yeasty:** foamy.   54. **Confound:** destroy.   55. **bladed corn:** grain that is enclosed in the blade, not yet in full ear.   **lodged:** thrown down, laid flat.   57. **slope:** bend.   59. **nature's germens:** seed or elements from which all nature operates.   60. **sicken:** be surfeited, grow faint with horror and nausea at its own excess.   65. **nine farrow:** litter of nine.   **sweaten:** sweated.   66. **gibbet:** gallows.   67. **high or low:** of the upper or lower air, from under the earth or in hell; or, of whatever rank.   68. **office:** function.   s.d. *armed Head:* (Perhaps symbolizes the head of Macbeth cut off by Macduff and presented by him to Malcolm, or else the head of Macduff, armed in rebellion against Macbeth.)   s.d. *He descends:* (i.e., by means of the trapdoor.)   74. **harped:** hit, touched (as in touching a harp to make it sound.)   s.d. *bloody Child:* (Symbolizes Macduff untimely ripped from his mother's womb; see 5.8.15–16.)   84. **take a bond of:** get a guarantee from (i.e., by killing Macduff, to make doubly sure he can do no harm).

Set design depicting witches' cave, watercolor for performance of *Macbeth*, 1847, opera by Giuseppe Verdi (1813–1901).

De Agostini Picture Library/G. Cigolini/Bridgeman Images

This painting depicts one of the most fantastical and imaginative scenes in the entire play. As in the opening scenes of the play, Macbeth is offered several prophecies and must decide how to interpret them. This scene has some historical significance as well, as many of the ghostly descendants that the witches reveal are rooted in actual royal figures contemporary to Shakespeare.

Examine the painting carefully, noting all of the details that the artist included. Then, explain how the details work together to capture the moment.

Thunder. Third Apparition, a Child crowned, with a tree in his hand.°

What is this
That rises like° the issue of a king
And wears upon his baby brow the round
And top° of sovereignty?

ALL   Listen, but speak not to 't.

90 **THIRD APPARITION** Be lion-mettled, proud, and take no care
Who chafes, who frets, or where conspirers are.
Macbeth shall never vanquished be until
Great Birnam Wood to high Dunsinane Hill
Shall come against him.   *Descends.*

MACBETH   That will never be.
95   Who can impress° the forest, bid the tree
Unfix his earthbound root? Sweet bode-
        ments,° good!
Rebellious dead,° rise never till the wood
Of Birnam rise, and our high-placed Macbeth
Shall live the lease of nature,° pay his breath
100   To time and mortal custom.° Yet my heart
Throbs to know one thing. Tell me, if your art
Can tell so much: shall Banquo's issue ever
Reign in this kingdom?

ALL   Seek to know no more.

MACBETH I will be satisfied. Deny me this,
105   And an eternal curse fall on you! Let me know.

---

s.d. Child . . . hand: (Symbolizes Malcolm, the royal child; the tree anticipates the cutting of boughs in Birnam Wood, 5.4.)   87. **like:** in the likeness of.   88–89. **round And top:** crown.   95. **impress:** press into service, like soldiers.   96. **bodements:** prophecies.   97. **Rebellious dead:** i.e., Banquo and his lineage.   99. **lease of nature:** natural period, full life span.   100. **mortal custom:** death, the common lot of humanity.

[*The cauldron descends*]. *Hautboys.*
Why sinks that cauldron? And what noise° is this?

FIRST WITCH Show!

SECOND WITCH Show!

THIRD WITCH Show!

110 **ALL** Show his eyes, and grieve his heart;
Come like shadows, so depart!
*A show of eight Kings° and Banquo last, [the eighth
King] with a glass° in his hand.*

MACBETH Thou art too like the spirit of Banquo.
Down!
Thy crown does sear mine eyeballs. And thy
hair,
Thou other° gold-bound brow, is like the first.

115 A third is like the former. Filthy hags,
Why do you show me this? A fourth? Start,° eyes!
What, will the line stretch out to th' crack of
doom?°
Another yet? A seventh? I'll see no more.
And yet the eighth appears, who bears a glass

120 Which shows me many more; and some I see
That twofold balls° and treble scepters° carry.
Horrible sight! Now I see 'tis true,
For the blood-boltered° Banquo smiles upon me
And points at them for his.° [*The apparitions
vanish.*] What, is this so?

125 **FIRST WITCH** Ay, sir, all this is so. But why
Stands Macbeth thus amazedly?°
Come, sisters, cheer we up his sprites°
And show the best of our delights.
I'll charm the air to give a sound,

130 While you perform your antic round,°
That this great king may kindly say
Our duties did his welcome pay.°
Music. The Witches dance, and vanish.

MACBETH Where are they? Gone? Let this pernicious hour

Stand aye accursèd in the calendar!
Come in, without there!

Enter Lennox.

135 **LENNOX** What's Your Grace's will?

MACBETH Saw you the Weird Sisters?

LENNOX No, my lord.

MACBETH Came they not by you?

LENNOX No, indeed,
my lord.

MACBETH Infected be the air whereon they ride,
And damned all those that trust them! I did
hear

140 The galloping of horse.° Who was 't came by?

LENNOX 'Tis two or three, my lord, that bring you
word
Macduff is fled to England.

MACBETH Fled to England!

LENNOX Ay, my good lord.

MACBETH [*aside*]
Time, thou anticipat'st° my dread exploits.

145 The flighty° purpose never is o'ertook
Unless the deed go with it.° From this
moment
The very firstlings of my heart shall be
The firstlings of my hand.° And even now,
To crown my thoughts with acts, be it thought
and done:

150 The castle of Macduff I will surprise,°
Seize upon Fife, give to th' edge o' the sword
His wife, his babes, and all unfortunate souls
That trace him in his line.° No boasting like a
fool;
This deed I'll do before this purpose cool.

155 But no more sights! — Where are these
gentlemen?
Come, bring me where they are. *Exeunt.*

---

106. **noise:** music.   **s.d.** *eight Kings:* (Banquo was the supposed ancestor of the Stuart dynasty, ending in King James VI of Scotland and James I of England, the *eighth King* here.)   **glass:** (magic) mirror (also in line 119).   114. **other:** i.e., second.   116. **Start:** bulge from their sockets.   117. **th' crack of doom:** the thunder-peal of Doomsday at the end of time.   121. **twofold balls:** (A probable reference to the double coronation of James at Scone and Westminster, as King of England and Scotland.)   **treble scepters:** (Probably refers to James's assumed title as King of Great Britain, France, and Ireland.)   123. **blood-boltered:** having his hair matted with blood.   124. **for his:** as his descendants.   125–32. **Ay . . . pay:** (These lines are assumed to have been written by someone other than Shakespeare.)   126. **amazedly:** stunned.   127. **sprites:** spirits.   130. **antic round:** grotesque dance in a circle.   132. **pay:** repay.   140. **horse:** horses.   144. **thou anticipat'st:** you forestall (since, by allowing time to pass without my acting, I have lost an opportunity).   145. **flighty:** fleeting.   146. **Unless . . . it:** unless the execution of the deed accompanies the conception of it immediately.   147–48. **The very . . . hand:** the first-born promptings of my heart will be the purposes I will first act upon.   150. **surprise:** seize without warning.   153. **trace . . . line:** follow him in the line of inheritance.

Scene 2°

Enter Macduff's Wife, her Son, and Ross.

LADY MACDUFF What had he done to make him
    fly the land?

ROSS You must have patience, madam.

LADY MACDUFF   He had
    none.
    His flight was madness. When our actions do not,
    Our fears do make us traitors.°

ROSS   You know not
5   Whether it was his wisdom or his fear.

LADY MACDUFF Wisdom? To leave his wife, to
    leave his babes,
    His mansion, and his titles° in a place
    From whence himself does fly? He loves us
    not,
    He wants the natural touch;° for the poor wren,
10   The most diminutive of birds, will fight,
    Her young ones in her nest,° against the owl.
    All is the fear and nothing is the love,
    As little is the wisdom, where the flight
    So runs against all reason.

ROSS   My dearest coz,°
15   I pray you, school° yourself. But, for° your
    husband,
    He is noble, wise, judicious, and best knows
    The fits o' the season.° I dare not speak much
    further,
    But cruel are the times when we are traitors
    And do not know ourselves,° when we hold
    rumor
20   From what we fear,° yet know not what we fear,
    But float upon a wild and violent sea
    Each way and none.° I take my leave of you;
    Shall° not be long but° I'll be here again.
    Things at the worst will cease, or else climb
    upward

25   To what they were before. — My pretty cousin,
    Blessing upon you!

LADY MACDUFF Fathered he is, and yet he's
    fatherless.

ROSS I am so much a fool, should I stay longer
    It would be my disgrace and your discomfort.°
30   I take my leave at once.   *Exit Ross.*

LADY MACDUFF Sirrah,° your father's dead;
    And what will you do now? How will you live?

SON As birds do, Mother.

LADY MACDUFF   What, with worms and
    flies?

SON With what I get, I mean; and so do they.

35 **LADY MACDUFF** Poor bird! Thou'dst never fear
    The net nor lime,° the pitfall nor the gin.°

SON Why should I, Mother? Poor birds they are
    not set for.°
    My father is not dead, for all your saying.

LADY MACDUFF Yes, he is dead. How wilt thou do
    for a father?

40 **SON** Nay, how will you do for a husband?

LADY MACDUFF Why, I can buy me twenty at any
    market.

SON Then you'll buy 'em to sell again.

LADY MACDUFF Thou speak'st with all thy wit,
    And yet, i' faith, with wit enough for thee.

45 **SON** Was my father a traitor, Mother?

LADY MACDUFF Ay, that he was.

SON What is a traitor?

LADY MACDUFF Why, one that swears and lies.°

SON And be all traitors that do so?

50 **LADY MACDUFF** Every one that does so is a
    traitor,
    And must be hanged.

SON And must they all be hanged that swear and
    lie?

LADY MACDUFF Every one.

Act 4, Scene 2. Location: Fife. Macduff's castle.   **3–4. When . . . traitors:** even when we have committed no treasonous act, our fearful responses make us look guilty (since fleeing to the English court is in itself treasonous).   **7. titles:** possessions to which he has title.   **9. wants . . . touch:** lacks the natural instinct (to protect one's family).   **11. Her . . . nest:** when her young ones are in the nest.   **14. coz:** kinswoman.   **15. school:** control. **for:** as for.   **17. fits o' the season:** violent convulsions of the time.   **18–19. are traitors . . . ourselves:** are accused of treason without recognizing ourselves as such, or are alienated from one another by a climate of fear and suspected treason.   **19–20. hold . . . From what we fear:** believe every fearful rumor on the basis of what we fear might be.   **22. Each . . . none:** being tossed this way and that without any real progress.   **23. Shall:** it shall. **but:** before.   **29. It . . . discomfort:** I should disgrace my manhood by weeping and cause you distress.   **31. Sirrah:** (Here, an affectionate form of address to a child.)   **36. lime:** birdlime (a sticky substance put on branches to snare birds). **gin:** snare.   **37. Poor . . . for:** i.e., traps are not set for *poor* birds, as you call me.   **48. swears and lies:** swears an oath and breaks it (though the boy may understand *swears* to mean "uses profanity").

SON Who must hang them?

55 **LADY MACDUFF** Why, the honest men.

SON Then the liars and swearers are fools, for
there are liars and swearers enough to beat
the honest men and hang up them.

LADY MACDUFF Now, God help thee, poor
60   monkey! But how wilt thou do for a father?

SON If he were dead, you'd weep for him; if you
would not, it were a good sign that I should
quickly have a new father.

LADY MACDUFF Poor prattler, how thou talk'st!

Enter a Messenger.

65 **MESSENGER** Bless you, fair dame! I am not to you
     known,
Though in your state of honor° I am perfect.°
I doubt° some danger does approach you
     nearly.
If you will take a homely° man's advice,
Be not found here. Hence with your little ones!
70 To fright you thus, methinks, I am too savage;
To do worse° to you were fell° cruelty,
Which is too nigh your person.° Heaven
     preserve you!
I dare abide no longer.   *Exit Messenger.*

LADY MACDUFF   Whither should I fly?
I have done no harm. But I remember now
75 I am in this earthly world, where to do harm
Is often laudable, to do good sometimes
Accounted dangerous folly. Why then, alas,
Do I put up that womanly defense
To say I have done no harm?

Enter Murderers.

               What are these
     faces?

80 **FIRST MURDERER** Where is your husband?

LADY MACDUFF I hope in no place so
     unsanctified
Where such as thou mayst find him.

FIRST MURDERER   He's a
     traitor.

SON Thou liest, thou shag-haired villain!

FIRST MURDERER   What,
     you egg?   *[He stabs him.]*
Young fry° of treachery!

SON   He has killed me,
     Mother.
85 Run away, I pray you!   *[He dies.]*
     Exit [Lady Macduff] crying "Murder!"
     [followed by the Murderers with the Son's body].

Scene 3°

Enter Malcolm and Macduff.

MALCOLM Let us seek out some desolate shade,
     and there
Weep our sad bosoms empty.

MACDUFF   Let us rather
Hold fast the mortal° sword, and like good
     men
Bestride° our downfall'n birthdom.° Each new
     morn
5 New widows howl, new orphans cry, new
     sorrows
Strike heaven on the face, that it resounds°
As if it felt with Scotland and yelled out
Like syllable of dolor.°

MALCOLM   What I believe, I'll wail;
What know, believe;° and what I can redress,
10 As I shall find the time to friend,° I will.
What you have spoke it may be so,
     perchance.
This tyrant, whose sole° name blisters our
     tongues,
Was once thought honest. You have loved him
     well;
He hath not touched you yet.° I am young;°
     but something

---

66. **in . . . honor:** with your honorable state.   **perfect:** perfectly acquainted.   67. **doubt:** fear.   68. **homely:** plain.   71. **To do worse:** i.e., actually to harm you.   **fell:** savage.   72. **Which . . . person:** i.e., which savage cruelty is all too near at hand.   84. **fry:** spawn, progeny.   **Act 4, Scene 3. Location:** England. Before King Edward the Confessor's palace.   3. **mortal:** deadly.   4. **Bestride:** stand over in defense.   **birthdom:** native land.   6. **that it resounds:** so that it echoes.   7–8. **As . . . dolor:** as if heaven, feeling itself the blow delivered to Scotland, cried out with a similar cry of pain. 8–9. **What . . . believe:** i.e., what I believe to be amiss in Scotland I will grieve for, and anything I am certain to be true I will believe. (But one must be cautious in these duplicitous times.)   10. **to friend:** opportune, congenial.   12. **sole:** mere.   14. **He . . . yet:** i.e., the fact that Macbeth hasn't hurt you yet makes me suspicious of your loyalties.   **young:** i.e., inexperienced.

15   You may deserve of him through me,° and
           wisdom°
      To offer up a weak, poor, innocent lamb
      T' appease an angry god.

MACDUFF I am not treacherous.

MALCOLM But Macbeth is.

20   A good and virtuous nature may recoil°
      In an imperial charge.° But I shall crave your
           pardon.
      That which you are my thoughts cannot
           transpose;°
      Angels are bright still, though the brightest°
           fell.
      Though all things foul would wear the brows
           of grace,
      Yet grace must still look so.°

25 **MACDUFF**   I have lost my
           hopes.°

MALCOLM Perchance even there° where I did
           find my doubts.°
      Why in that rawness° left you wife and child,
      Those precious motives,° those strong knots of
           love,
      Without leave-taking? I pray you,
30   Let not my jealousies be your dishonors,
      But mine own safeties.° You may be rightly
           just,
      Whatever I shall think.

MACDUFF   Bleed, bleed, poor
           country!
      Great tyranny, lay thou thy basis° sure,
      For goodness dare not check° thee; wear thou
           thy wrongs,°
35   The title is affeered!° Fare thee well, lord.

      I would not be the villain that thou think'st
      For the whole space that's in the tyrant's
           grasp,
      And the rich East to boot.°

MALCOLM   Be not offended.
      I speak not as in absolute fear° of you.
40   I think our country sinks beneath the yoke;
      It weeps, it bleeds, and each new day a gash
      Is added to her wounds. I think withal°
      There would be hands uplifted in my right;°
      And here from gracious England° have I offer
45   Of goodly thousands. But, for all this,
      When I shall tread upon the tyrant's head,
      Or wear it on my sword, yet my poor country
      Shall have more vices than it had before,
      More suffer, and more sundry° ways than ever,
      By him that shall succeed.

50 **MACDUFF**   What should he be?°

MALCOLM It is myself I mean, in whom I know
      All the particulars of vice so grafted°
      That, when they shall be opened,° black
           Macbeth
      Will seem as pure as snow, and the poor state
55   Esteem him as a lamb, being compared
      With my confineless harms.°

MACDUFF   Not in the legions
      Of horrid hell can come a devil more damned
      In evils to top° Macbeth.

MALCOLM   I grant him bloody,
      Luxurious,° avaricious, false, deceitful,
60   Sudden,° malicious, smacking of every sin
      That has a name. But there's no bottom, none,
      In my voluptuousness. Your wives, your
           daughters,

14–15. **something . . . me:** i.e., you may win favor with Macbeth by delivering me to him.   15. **wisdom:** i.e., it would be worldly-wise.   20. **recoil:** give way, fall back (as in the firing of a gun).   21. **In . . . charge:** under pressure from royal command. (*Charge* puns on the idea of a quantity of powder and shot for a gun, as in *recoil*.)   22. **That . . . transpose:** my suspicious thoughts cannot change you from what you are, cannot make you evil.   23. **the brightest:** i.e., Lucifer.   24–25. **Though . . . so:** even though evil puts on the appearance of good so often as to cast that appearance into deep suspicion, yet goodness must go on looking and acting like itself.   25. **hopes:** i.e., hopes of persuading Malcolm to lead the cause against Macbeth.   26. **Perchance even there:** i.e., perhaps in that same mistrustful frame of mind.   **doubts:** i.e., fears such as that Macduff may covertly be on Macbeth's side.   27. **rawness:** unprotected condition. (Malcolm suggests that Macduff's leaving his family unprotected could be construed as more evidence of his not having anything to fear from Macbeth.)   28. **motives:** persons inspiring you to cherish and protect them; incentives to offer strong protection.   30–31. **Let . . . safeties:** may it be true that my suspicions of your lack of honor are founded only in my own wariness.   33. **basis:** foundation.   34. **check:** rebuke, call to account.   **wear . . . wrongs:** continue to enjoy your wrongfully gained powers.   35. **affeered:** confirmed, certified.   38. **to boot:** in addition.   39. **absolute fear:** complete mistrust.   42. **withal:** in addition.   43. **right:** cause.   44. **England:** i.e., the King of England.   49. **more sundry:** in more various.   50. **What . . . be?:** whom could you possibly mean?   52. **grafted:** (1) engrafted, indissolubly mixed (2) grafted like a plant that will then *open* or unfold.   53. **opened:** unfolded (like a bud).   56. **my confineless harms:** the boundless injuries I shall inflict.   58. **top:** surpass.   59. **Luxurious:** lecherous.   60. **Sudden:** violent, passionate.

Your matrons, and your maids could not fill up
The cistern of my lust, and my desire
65   All continent° impediments would o'erbear
That did oppose my will.° Better Macbeth
Than such an one to reign.

MACDUFF   Boundless intemperance
In nature° is a tyranny; it hath been
Th' untimely emptying of the happy throne
70   And fall of many kings. But fear not yet°
To take upon you what is yours. You may
Convey° your pleasures in a spacious plenty,
And yet seem cold;° the time you may so hoodwink.°
We have willing dames enough. There cannot be
75   That vulture in you to devour so many
As will to greatness dedicate themselves,
Finding it so inclined.

MALCOLM   With this there grows
In my most ill-composed affection° such
A stanchless° avarice that, were I king,
80   I should cut off the nobles for their lands,
Desire his° jewels and this other's° house,
And my more-having would be as a sauce
To make me hunger more, that° I should forge
Quarrels unjust against the good and loyal,
Destroying them for wealth.

85 **MACDUFF**   This avarice
Sticks deeper, grows with more pernicious root
Than summer-seeming° lust, and it hath been
The sword° of our slain kings. Yet do not fear;
Scotland hath foisons° to fill up your will
90   Of your mere own.° All these are portable,°
With other graces weighed.°

MALCOLM   But I have none. The king-becoming graces,
As justice, verity, temperance, stableness,
Bounty, perseverance, mercy, lowliness,°
95   Devotion, patience, courage, fortitude,
I have no relish° of them, but abound
In the division° of each several° crime,
Acting it many ways. Nay, had I power, I should
Pour the sweet milk of concord into hell,
100   Uproar° the universal peace, confound
All unity on earth.

MACDUFF   O Scotland, Scotland!

MALCOLM   If such a one be fit to govern, speak.
I am as I have spoken.

MACDUFF   Fit to govern?
No, not to live. O nation miserable,
105   With an untitled° tyrant bloody-sceptered,
When shalt thou see thy wholesome days again,
Since that the truest issue of thy throne
By his own interdiction° stands accurst
And does blaspheme his breed?° Thy royal father
110   Was a most sainted king; the queen that bore thee,
Oft'ner upon her knees than on her feet,
Died every day she lived.° Fare thee well.
These evils thou repeat'st upon thyself
Hath banished me from Scotland. O my breast,°
Thy hope ends here!

115 **MALCOLM**   Macduff, this noble passion,
Child of integrity,° hath from my soul
Wiped the black scruples, reconciled my thoughts
To thy good truth and honor. Devilish Macbeth
By many of these trains° hath sought to win me
120   Into his power, and modest wisdom plucks me°
From over credulous haste. But God above
Deal between thee and me! For even now
I put myself to thy direction and

---

65. **continent:** (1) chaste (2) restraining, containing.   66. **will:** lust (also in line 89).   68. **nature:** human nature.   70. **yet:** nevertheless.   72. **Convey:** manage with secrecy.   73. **cold:** chaste.   **the time . . . hoodwink:** you may thus deceive the age.   **hoodwink:** blindfold.   78. **ill-composed affection:** evil disposition.   79. **stanchless:** insatiable.   81. **his:** one man's.   **this other's:** another's.   83. **that:** so that.   87. **summer-seeming:** appropriate to youth (and lessening in later years).   88. **sword:** i.e., cause of overthrow.   89. **foisons:** resources, plenty.   90. **Of . . . own:** out of your own royal estates alone.   **portable:** bearable.   91. **weighed:** counterbalanced.   94. **lowliness:** humility.   96. **relish:** flavor or trace. 97. **division:** subdivisions, various possible forms.   **several:** separate.   100. **Uproar:** throw into an uproar.   105. **untitled:** lacking rightful title, usurping.   108. **interdiction:** debarring of self.   109. **does blaspheme his breed:** defames his breeding, i.e., is a disgrace to his royal lineage. 112. **Died . . . lived:** lived a life of daily mortification.   114. **breast:** heart.   116. **Child of integrity:** a product of your integrity of spirit.   119. **trains:** plots, artifices.   120. **modest . . . me:** wise prudence holds me back.

Unspeak my own detraction,° here abjure
125 The taints and blames I laid upon myself
For° strangers to my nature. I am yet
Unknown to woman,° never was forsworn,
Scarcely have coveted what was mine own,
At no time broke my faith, would not betray
130 The devil to his fellow, and delight
No less in truth than life. My first false speaking
Was this upon° myself. What I am truly
Is thine and my poor country's to command —
Whither indeed, before thy here-approach,
135 Old Siward with ten thousand warlike men,
Already at a point,° was setting forth.
Now we'll together; and the chance of goodness
Be like our warranted quarrel!° — Why are you
silent?

MACDUFF Such welcome and unwelcome things
at once
140 'Tis hard to reconcile.

Enter a Doctor.

MALCOLM Well, more anon. — Comes the King
forth, I pray you?

DOCTOR Ay, sir. There are a crew of wretched souls
That stay° his cure. Their malady convinces°
The great essay of art;° but at his touch —
145 Such sanctity hath heaven given his hand —
They presently° amend.

MALCOLM   I thank you, Doctor.
Exit [Doctor].

MACDUFF What's the disease he means?

MALCOLM   'Tis called the evil.°
A most miraculous work in this good king,
Which often, since my here-remain° in England,
150 I have seen him do. How he solicits° heaven
Himself best knows; but strangely-visited°
people,
All swoll'n and ulcerous, pitiful to the eye,
The mere° despair of surgery, he cures,

Hanging a golden stamp° about their necks
155 Put on with holy prayers; and 'tis spoken,
To the succeeding royalty he leaves
The healing benediction.° With this strange
virtue°
He hath a heavenly gift of prophecy,
And sundry blessings hang about his throne
That speak him full of grace.

Enter Ross.

160 MACDUFF   See who comes here.

MALCOLM My countryman,° but yet I know° him
not.

MACDUFF My ever-gentle° cousin, welcome
hither.

MALCOLM I know him now. Good God betimes°
remove
The means that makes us strangers!

ROSS   Sir, amen.

MACDUFF Stands Scotland where it did?

165 ROSS   Alas,
poor country
Almost afraid to know itself. It cannot
Be called our mother, but our grave; where
nothing
But who° knows nothing is once° seen to smile;
Where sighs and groans and shrieks that rend
the air
170 Are made, not marked;° where violent sorrow
seems
A modern ecstasy.° The dead man's knell
Is there scarce asked for who, and good men's
lives
Expire before the flowers° in their caps,
Dying or ere they sicken.°

MACDUFF   O, relation°
Too nice,° and yet too true!

175 MALCOLM   What's the newest
grief?

---

124. **mine own detraction:** my detraction of myself.   126. **For:** as.   127. **Unknown to woman:** a virgin.   132. **upon:** against.   136. **at a point:** prepared.   137–38. **the chance . . . quarrel:** may the chance of success be proportionate to the justice of our cause.   143. **stay:** wait for. **convinces:** conquers.   144. **essay of art:** efforts of medical skill.   146. **presently:** immediately.   147. **evil:** i.e., scrofula, supposedly cured by the royal touch; James I claimed this power.   149. **here-remain:** stay.   150. **solicits:** prevails by prayer with.   151. **strangely-visited:** afflicted by strange diseases.   153. **mere:** utter.   154. **stamp:** minted coin.   156–57. **To . . . benediction:** to his royal successors he bequeathes this healing blessedness.   157. **virtue:** healing power.   161. **My countryman:** (So identified by his dress.)   **know:** recognize.   162. **gentle:** noble. 163. **betimes:** speedily.   167–68. **nothing But who:** nobody except a person who.   168. **once:** ever.   170. **marked:** noticed (because they are so common).   171. **modern ecstasy:** commonplace emotion.   173. **flowers:** (Often worn in Elizabethan caps.)   174. **or ere they sicken:** before they have had time to fall ill.   **relation:** report.   175. **nice:** minutely accurate, elaborately phrased.

ROSS That of an hour's age doth hiss° the speaker;
Each minute teems° a new one.

MACDUFF   How does my
wife?

ROSS Why, well.°

MACDUFF   And all my children?

ROSS   Well too.

MACDUFF The tyrant has not battered at their
peace?

180 **ROSS** No, they were well at peace when I did
leave 'em.

MACDUFF Be not niggard of your speech. How
goes 't?

ROSS When I came hither to transport the tidings
Which I have heavily° borne, there ran a rumor
Of many worthy fellows that were out,°
185 Which was to my belief witnessed the rather°
For that° I saw the tyrant's power° afoot.
Now is the time of help. [*To Malcolm.*] Your
eye in Scotland
Would create soldiers, make our women fight,
To doff ° their dire distresses.

MALCOLM   Be 't their comfort
190 We are coming thither. Gracious England° hath
Lent us good Siward and ten thousand men;
An older and a better soldier none°
That Christendom gives out.°

ROSS   Would I could
answer
This comfort with the like! But I have words
195 That would° be howled out in the desert air,
Where hearing should not latch° them.

MACDUFF   What
concern they?
The general cause? Or is it a fee-grief °
Due to° some single breast?

ROSS   No mind that's
honest

But in it shares some woe, though the main part
Pertains to you alone.

200 **MACDUFF**   If it be mine,
Keep it not from me; quickly let me have it.

ROSS Let not your ears despise my tongue forever,
Which shall possess them with° the heaviest
sound
That ever yet they heard.

MACDUFF   Hum! I guess at it.

205 **ROSS** Your castle is surprised, your wife and babes
Savagely slaughtered. To relate the manner
Were, on the quarry° of these murdered deer,
To add the death of you.

MALCOLM   Merciful heaven!
What, man, ne'er pull your hat° upon your
brows;
210 Give sorrow words. The grief that does not speak
Whispers° the o'erfraught° heart and bids it
break.

MACDUFF My children too?

ROSS   Wife, children,
servants, all
That could be found.

MACDUFF   And I must° be from
thence!
My wife killed too?

ROSS   I have said.

MALCOLM   Be comforted.
215 Let's make us medicines of our great revenge
To cure this deadly grief.

MACDUFF He has no children.° All my pretty ones?
Did you say all? O hell-kite! All?
What, all my pretty chickens and their dam
220 At one fell swoop?°

MALCOLM Dispute it° like a man.

MACDUFF I shall do so;
But I must also feel it as a man.
I cannot but remember such things were,

---

176. **hiss:** cause to be hissed (for repeating stale news).   177. **teems:** teems with, yields.   178. **well:** (Ross quibbles, in his reluctance to tell the bad news, on the saying that "the dead are well," i.e., at rest.)   183. **heavily:** sadly.   184. **Of . . . out:** i.e., that many worthy Scots had taken up arms in rebellion against tyranny.   185. **witnessed the rather:** made the more believable.   186. **For that:** because, in that.   **power:** army.   189. **doff:** put off, get rid of.   190. **Gracious England:** i.e., Edward the Confessor.   192. **none:** there is none.   193. **gives out:** tells of, proclaims.   195. **would:** should.   196. **latch:** catch (the sound of).   197. **fee-grief:** a grief with an individual owner, having absolute ownership.   198. **Due to:** i.e., owned by.   203. **possess them with:** put them in possession of.   207. **quarry:** heap of slaughtered deer at a hunt (with a pun on *dear, deer*).   209. **pull your hat:** (A conventional gesture of grief.)   211. **Whispers:** whispers to.   **o'erfraught:** overburdened.   213. **must:** had to.   217. **He has no children:** (Referring either to Macbeth, who must not be a father if he can do such a thing, or, to Malcolm, who speaks comfortingly without knowing what such a loss feels like to a father.)   220. **fell swoop:** cruel swoop of the *hell-kite*, bird of prey from hell (with a suggestion too of swoopstake, sweepstake).   221. **Dispute it:** struggle against.

225 That were most precious to me. Did heaven
     look on
And would not take their part? Sinful Macduff,
They were all struck for thee!° Naught° that I am,
Not for their own demerits, but for mine,
Fell slaughter on their souls. Heaven rest them
     now!
230 **MALCOLM** Be this the whetstone of your sword.
     Let grief
Convert° to anger; blunt not the heart, enrage it.
MACDUFF O, I could play the woman with mine
     eyes
And braggart with my tongue! But, gentle
     heavens,

Cut short all intermission.° Front to front°
235 Bring thou this fiend of Scotland and myself;
Within my sword's length set him. If he scape,
Heaven forgive him too!°
MALCOLM   This tune goes manly.
Come, go we to the King. Our power° is ready;
Our lack is nothing but our leave.° Macbeth
240 Is ripe for shaking, and the powers above
Put on their instruments.° Receive what cheer
     you may.
The night is long that never finds the day.
                                         Exeunt.

227. **for thee:** i.e., as divine punishment for your sins. **Naught:** wicked. 231. **Convert:** change. 234. **intermission:** delay, interval. **Front to front:** face to face. 236–37. **If . . . too:** if I let him escape, may he find forgiveness not only from me but from Heaven itself! (This is a condition that Macduff will not allow to happen.) 238. **power:** army. 239. **Our . . . leave:** we need only to take our leave (of the English King). 241. **Put . . . instruments:** Set us on as their agents, or, arm themselves.

Understanding and Interpreting

1 What does Macbeth demand to know from the witches in the first scene, and why is he so determined to get this information?

2 Each of the apparitions that appear in Scene 1 share a different prophecy with Macbeth, all of which are both specific and ambiguous. Based on your understanding of the play and the characters at this point, predict what each of the prophecies means and how each one will influence Macbeth.

3 After the witches leave in Scene 1, Macbeth is disturbed to find out that Lennox did not see them. Macbeth then declares that "all those who trust" the witches should be "damned" (l. 139). Does this indicate that Macbeth himself does not trust them, or is he trying to deal with his own fears that the witches may be telling the truth? Explain.

4 Macbeth is deeply concerned when Lennox reports that Macduff has fled to England at the end of Scene 1. What about the witches' prophecy can still come true if Macduff is alive?

5 In Scene 2, Ross will not tell Lady Macduff why her husband has fled to England, leaving her alone.

Instead, he describes why the times are "cruel" (ll. 17–26). Using text from his response, describe the current state of affairs in Scotland.

6 At the end of Scene 2, Macduff's wife and young son are murdered by a killer hired by Macbeth. Unlike the murder of King Duncan, this one happens onstage. What is the effect of including this particular scene onstage in the play?

7 Summarize the qualities Malcolm ascribes to Macbeth (Scene 3, ll. 58–61) and discuss how those qualities have been revealed through Macbeth's actions so far in the play.

8 Malcolm lies about himself to Macduff, suggesting "black Macbeth / [would] seem as pure as snow" when compared to Malcolm's "confineless harms" (Scene 3, ll. 53–56). In what line does Malcolm admit that he was not telling the truth when he was describing his character flaws, and what reason does he give for lying to Macduff?

9 Ross shares news of Scotland with Malcolm and Macduff (Scene 3, ll. 165–174). What is the current state of affairs, according to Ross?

Analyzing Language, Style, and Structure

1 In the first scene of this act, the witches stir a cauldron and utter one of their most famous and often quoted lines: "Double, double, toil and trouble" (l. 10). The witches' lines are intended to evoke terror, yet the sing-song rhyming may not produce the effect that was intended when originally performed.

Directors will often cut lines or even entire scenes from Shakespeare's plays in order to appeal to a contemporary audience. Looking back over Act 4, Scene 1, identify five lines or phrases that you think would still evoke fear in a modern audience and explain why those lines should not be cut from the scene.

2 During the procession of the eight ghostly kings in Scene 1 (ll. 112–124), Macbeth makes numerous references to sight and seeing. Identify these references, and discuss how they highlight Macbeth's current mental state.

3 Right before she is murdered, Lady Macduff declares that "in this earthly world [. . .] to do harm / Is often laudable, to do good sometimes / Accounted dangerous folly" (Scene 2, ll. 75–77). How does her ironic statement reflect the current state of affairs in Scotland?

4 In discussing his attitude toward Macbeth, Malcolm says, "Angels are bright still, though the brightest fell" (Scene 3, l. 23). Explain the meaning behind this allusion to Lucifer.

5 Malcolm finally tells Ross and Macduff that he plans to take up arms against Macbeth in Scotland (Scene 3, ll. 132–136). What is the effect of his waiting until this point to reveal this important information, and why does he not reveal his plan sooner?

6 Ross must deliver the terrible news to Macduff that his entire family has been murdered by Macbeth. Though he knows Macduff is grief-stricken over the news, Malcolm uses this moment in Scene 3 as an opportunity to recruit Macduff and tells him to "dispute it [his feelings about his loss] like a man" (l. 221). He later commends Macduff's willingness to fight Macbeth as a "tune [that] goes manly" (l. 237). How do these statements further develop a theme in the play about the nature of men and women?

7 There are many different revelations and events in Scene 3. Analyze the effect of Shakespeare's choices regarding the order in which he introduces the different events in this scene.

Connecting, Arguing, and Extending

1 The appearance of the witches, Hecate, and three different apparitions at the beginning of Act 4 are among the most visually interesting and terrifying moments in the play. Historians believe that the reason Shakespeare included witches in the play was that King James I, who was the king of England at the time *Macbeth* was written, was fascinated by witches and witchcraft.

Witches have long been present in plays, television shows, and movies. Find images of witches in various productions throughout the years, and then select images that you believe most match your idea of what the witches and apparitions in *Macbeth* should look like. Provide a brief explanation as to why your selected images are most appropriate for a production of this play.

2 In Scene 3, Malcolm lists the qualities he believes contribute to someone's being a great king. First, make a list in which you provide examples of each of

the qualities that Malcolm lists. Then, write an argument in which you discuss whether or not those qualities are still a part of being a great leader, or if they are irrelevant to the modern age. Use specific examples of current leaders to support your claims.

3 Consider the type of headlines that you read whenever you visit a news website. These headlines attempt to capture the "big idea" behind the story, such as "Brave Boy Breaks Leg While Attempting to Rescue Cat from Tree." The headline provides the general idea and invites you to read on for the details. For each of the events in this Act, create a headline that captures the essence or main idea of the event. Once you have a headline for each event, draw (or describe) a picture that would logically accompany the headline. For example, with the cat headline above, you might expect a picture of the boy proudly displaying his cast.

Scene 1°

Enter a Doctor of Physic and a waiting-Gentlewoman.

DOCTOR I have two nights watched with you, but can perceive no truth in your report. When was it she last walked?

GENTLEWOMAN Since His Majesty went into the
5   field, I have seen her rise from her bed,
throw her nightgown upon her, unlock her
closet,° take forth paper, fold it, write
upon 't, read it, afterwards seal it, and
again return to bed; yet all this while in a
10   most fast sleep.

DOCTOR A great perturbation in nature, to
receive at once the benefit of sleep and do
the effects of watching!° In this slumbery
agitation,° besides her walking and other
15   actual performances, what, at any time,
have you heard her say?

GENTLEWOMAN That, sir, which I will not report
after her.

DOCTOR You may to me, and 'tis most meet° you
20   should.

GENTLEWOMAN Neither to you nor anyone,
having no witness to confirm
my speech.

Enter Lady [Macbeth], with a taper.

Lo you, here she comes! This is her very
25   guise, and, upon my life, fast asleep.
Observe her. Stand close.°

[*They stand aside*.]

DOCTOR How came she by that light?

GENTLEWOMAN Why, it stood by her. She has
light by her continually. 'Tis her command.

30 **DOCTOR** You see her eyes are open.

GENTLEWOMAN Ay, but their sense are shut.

DOCTOR What is it she does now? Look how she
rubs her hands.

GENTLEWOMAN It is an accustomed action with
35   her to seem thus washing her hands. I have
known her continue in this a quarter of an
hour.

Johann Heinrich Fuseli, *The Sleepwalking Lady Macbeth*, c. 1781. Oil on canvas, 87″ x 63″. Louvre Museum, Paris, France.

Although she is sleepwalking, Lady Macbeth still appears quite animated in this image depicting the scene.

What ideas about Lady Macbeth's mental state does the artist offer in this painting and what details about both Lady Macbeth and the onlookers serve to convey those ideas?

LADY MACBETH Yet here's a spot.

DOCTOR Hark, she speaks. I will set down what
40   comes from her, to satisfy° my
remembrance the more strongly.

LADY MACBETH Out, damned spot! Out, I say!
One — two — why then, 'tis time to do 't.
Hell is murky. — Fie, my lord, fie, a soldier,
45   and afeard? What need we fear who knows
it, when none can call our power to

Act 5, Scene 1. Location: Dunsinane. Macbeth's castle.   **7. closet:** chest or desk.   **13. effects of watching:** deeds characteristic of waking.
14. agitation: activity.   **19. meet:** suitable.   **26. close:** concealed.   **40. satisfy:** confirm, support.

account? Yet who would have thought the old man to have had so much blood in him?

50 **DOCTOR** Do you mark that?

LADY MACBETH The Thane of Fife had a wife. Where is she now? — What, will these hands ne'er be clean? — No more o' that, my lord, no more o' that; you mar all with
55 this starting.°

DOCTOR Go to,° go to. You have known what you should not.

GENTLEWOMAN She has spoke what she should not, I am sure of that. Heaven knows what
60 she has known.

LADY MACBETH Here's the smell of the blood still. All the perfumes of Arabia will not sweeten this little hand. O, o, o!

DOCTOR What a sigh is there! The heart is sorely
65 charged.°

GENTLEWOMAN I would not have such a heart in my bosom for the dignity° of the whole body.

DOCTOR Well, well, well.

GENTLEWOMAN Pray God it be, sir.°

70 **DOCTOR** This disease is beyond my practice. Yet I have known those which have walked in their sleep who have died holily in their beds.

LADY MACBETH Wash your hands, put on your nightgown; look not so pale! I tell you yet
75 again, Banquo's buried. He cannot come out on 's° grave.

DOCTOR Even so?

LADY MACBETH To bed, to bed! There's knocking at the gate. Come, come, come, come, give
80 me your hand. What's done cannot be undone. To bed, to bed, to bed!

Exit Lady.

DOCTOR Will she go now to bed?

GENTLEWOMAN Directly.

DOCTOR Foul whisperings are abroad. Unnatural deeds

85 Do breed unnatural troubles. Infected minds To their deaf pillows will discharge their secrets.
More needs she the divine than the physician. God, God forgive us all! Look after her; Remove from her the means of all annoyance,°
90 And still° keep eyes upon her. So, good night. My mind she has mated,° and amazed my sight.
I think, but dare not speak.

GENTLEWOMAN   Good night, good Doctor.   *Exeunt.*

Scene 2°

Drum and colors. Enter Menteith, Caithness, Angus, Lennox, [and] soldiers.

MENTEITH The English power is near, led on by Malcolm,
His uncle Siward, and the good Macduff. Revenges burn in them, for their dear causes Would to the bleeding and the grim alarm Excite the mortified man.°

5 **ANGUS**   Near Birnam Wood Shall we well° meet them; that way are they coming.

CAITHNESS Who knows if Donalbain be with his brother?

LENNOX For certain, sir, he is not. I have a file° Of all the gentry. There is Siward's son,
10 And many unrough° youths that even now Protest° their first of manhood.

MENTEITH   What does the tyrant?

CAITHNESS Great Dunsinane he strongly fortifies. Some say he's mad, others that lesser hate him Do call it valiant fury; but for certain
15 He cannot unbuckle his distempered° cause Within the belt of rule.

ANGUS   Now does he feel His secret murders sticking on his hands;

---

55. **this starting:** these startled movements.   56. **Go to:** (An exclamation of reproof, directed at Lady Macbeth.)   64–65. **sorely charged:** heavily burdened.   67. **dignity:** worth, value.   69. **Pray . . . sir:** pray God it will turn out well, as you say, sir (playing on the Doctor's "*Well, well,*" i.e., "dear, dear").   76. **on 's:** of his.   89. **annoyance:** i.e., harming herself.   90. **still:** constantly.   91. **mated:** bewildered, stupefied.   **Act 5, Scene 2. Location:** The country near Dunsinane.   3–5. **their . . . man:** their grievous wrongs would awaken even the dead to answer the bloody and grim call to battle.   6. **well:** no doubt.   8. **file:** list, roster.   10. **unrough:** beardless.   11. **Protest:** assert publicly.   15. **distempered:** disease-swollen, dropsical.

seeing connections

Just as the scene in which Macbeth imagines a dagger floating in the air reflects a central psychological struggle for him, this scene in which Lady Macbeth tries to scrub non-existent blood from her hands reflects the deep psychological struggle her character faces.

Compare these images from four different versions of this scene, and explain how each actress has made specific choices that represent Lady Macbeth's struggle.

This still is from a 1983 BBC television version of *Macbeth* directed by Jack Gold. Lady Macbeth is played by Jane Lapotaire.

A scene from Trevor Nunn's stage version of *Macbeth*, filmed in 1978, with Dame Judi Dench as Lady Macbeth.

This still is from the 1971 film directed by Roman Polanski. Francesca Annis plays Lady Macbeth.

This still is from the 2008 version of *Macbeth* directed by Rupert Goold, with Kate Fleetwood as Lady Macbeth.

Now minutely° revolts upbraid° his
    faith-breach.°
Those he commands move only in command,°
20 Nothing in love. Now does he feel his title
Hang loose about him, like a giant's robe
Upon a dwarfish thief.

MENTEITH   Who then shall blame
His pestered° senses to recoil and start,
When all that is within him does condemn
Itself for being there?

25 CAITHNESS   Well, march we on
To give obedience where 'tis truly owed.
Meet we the med'cine of the sickly weal,°
And with him pour we in our country's purge
Each drop of us.°

LENNOX   Or so much as it needs
30 To dew° the sovereign° flower and drown the
    weeds.
Make we our march towards Birnam.

Exeunt, marching.

Scene 3°

Enter Macbeth, Doctor, and attendants.

MACBETH Bring me no more reports. Let them°
    fly° all!
Till Birnam Wood remove to Dunsinane,
I cannot taint with° fear. What's the boy
    Malcolm?
Was he not born of woman? The spirits that
    know
5 All mortal consequences° have pronounced
    me thus:
"Fear not, Macbeth. No man that's born of
    woman
Shall e'er have power upon thee." Then fly,
    false thanes,
And mingle with the English epicures!°

The mind I sway° by and the heart I bear
10 Shall never sag with doubt nor shake with fear.

Enter Servant.

The devil damn thee black, thou cream-faced
    loon!°
Where gott'st thou that goose look?

SERVANT There is ten thousand —

MACBETH   Geese, villain?

SERVANT   Soldiers, sir.

MACBETH Go prick thy face and over-red thy fear,°
15 Thou lily-livered boy. What soldiers, patch?°
Death of thy° soul! Those linen cheeks of thine
Are counselors to fear.° What soldiers,
    whey-face?

SERVANT The English force, so please you.

MACBETH Take thy face hence. [*Exit Servant.*]
    Seyton! — I am sick at heart
20 When I behold° — Seyton, I say! — This push°
Will cheer° me ever, or disseat° me now.
I have lived long enough. My way° of life
Is fall'n into the sere,° the yellow leaf,
And that which should accompany old age,
25 As° honor, love, obedience, troops of friends,
I must not look to have, but in their stead
Curses, not loud but deep, mouth-honor, breath
Which the poor heart would fain deny and
    dare not.
Seyton!

Enter Seyton.

SEYTON What's your gracious pleasure?
30 MACBETH   What
    news more?

SEYTON All is confirmed, my lord, which was
    reported.

MACBETH I'll fight till from my bones my flesh be
    hacked.
Give me my armor.

---

18. **minutely:** every minute.   **upbraid:** censure.   **faith-breach:** violation of all trust and sacred vows.   19. **in command:** under orders.   23. **pestered:** troubled, tormented.   27. **Meet we . . . weal:** i.e., let us join forces with Malcolm, the physician of our sick land.   28–29. **pour . . . of us:** i.e., let us shed all our blood as a bloodletting or purge of our country.   30. **dew:** bedew, water.   **sovereign:** (1) royal (2) medically efficacious.   **Act 5, Scene 3. Location:** Dunsinane. Macbeth's castle.   1. **them:** i.e., the thanes.   **fly:** desert.   3. **taint with:** become imbued or infected with, weakened by.   5. **mortal consequences:** what befalls humanity.   8. **English epicures:** luxury-loving Englishmen (as seen from the Scottish point of view).   9. **sway:** rule myself.   11. **loon:** stupid fellow.   14. **Go prick . . . fear:** i.e., go prick or pinch your pale cheeks to bring some color into them. (The servant's blood has all retired into his lower abdomen on account of his fear, so that he is very pale and there is no blood in his liver, where his courage should have resided — hence, *lily-livered*, line 15.)   15. **patch:** domestic fool.   16. **of thy:** on your.   17. **Are . . . fear:** i.e., teach others to fear.   20. **behold:** (Macbeth does not finish this thought.)   **push:** effort, crisis.   21. **cheer:** (With a suggestion of "chair.")   **disseat:** dethrone.   22. **way:** course.   23. **sere:** dry and withered.   25. **As:** such as.

SEYTON 'Tis not needed yet.

35 **MACBETH** I'll put it on.

Send out more horses. Skirr° the country round.
Hang those that talk of fear. Give me mine armor.
How does your patient, Doctor?

DOCTOR Not so sick, my lord,

40 As she is troubled with thick-coming fancies
That keep her from her rest.

MACBETH Cure her of that.
Canst thou not minister to a mind diseased,
Pluck from the memory a rooted sorrow,
Raze° out the written troubles of° the brain,

45 And with some sweet oblivious° antidote
Cleanse the stuffed bosom of that perilous stuff
Which weighs upon the heart?

DOCTOR Therein the patient
Must minister to himself.

MACBETH Throw physic° to the dogs! I'll none of it.

50 Come, put mine armor on. Give me my staff.°

[*Attendants arm him.*]

Seyton, send out. Doctor, the thanes fly
from me. —
Come, sir, dispatch.° — If thou couldst, Doctor, cast
The water° of my land, find her disease,
And purge it to a sound and pristine health,

55 I would applaud thee to the very echo,
That should applaud again. — Pull 't off,°
I say. —
What rhubarb, senna,° or what purgative drug
Would scour° these English hence? Hear'st
thou of them?

DOCTOR Ay, my good lord. Your royal preparation
Makes us hear something.

60 **MACBETH** Bring it° after me. —
I will not be afraid of death and bane,

Till Birnam Forest comes to Dunsinane.

Exeunt [all but the Doctor].

DOCTOR Were I from Dunsinane away and clear,
Profit again should hardly draw me here.

[*Exit.*]

Scene 4°

Drum and colors. Enter Malcolm, Siward, Macduff, Siward's Son, Menteith, Caithness, Angus, [Lennox, Ross,] and soldiers, marching.

MALCOLM Cousins, I hope the days are near at hand
That chambers will be safe.°

MENTEITH We doubt it nothing.°

SIWARD What wood is this before us?

MENTEITH The wood of Birnam.

MALCOLM Let every soldier hew him down a bough

5 And bear 't before him. Thereby shall we shadow
The numbers of our host and make discovery°
Err in report of us.

SOLDIERS It shall be done.

SIWARD We learn no other but° the confident tyrant
Keeps° still in Dunsinane and will endure°
Our setting down before° 't.

10 **MALCOLM** 'Tis his main hope;
For where there is advantage° to be given,
Both more and less° have given him the revolt,
And none serve with him but constrainèd things
Whose hearts are absent too.

---

36. **Skirr:** scour.   44. **Raze:** (Suggesting also *race*, "erase, obliterate.")   **written troubles of:** troubles written on.   45. **oblivious:** causing forgetfulness.   49. **physic:** medicine.   50. **staff:** lance or baton of office.   52. **dispatch:** hurry.   52–53. **cast The water:** diagnose disease by the inspection of urine.   56. **Pull 't off:** (Refers to some part of the armor not properly put on.)   57. **senna:** a purgative drug.   58. **scour:** purge, cleanse, rid.   60. **it:** i.e., the armor not yet put on Macbeth.   **Act 5, Scene 4. Location:** Country near Birnam Wood.   2. **chambers . . . safe:** i.e., we may sleep safely in our bedchambers.   **nothing:** not at all.   6. **discovery:** scouting reports.   8. **no other but:** no other news but that.   9. **Keeps:** remains.   **endure:** allow, not attempt to prevent.   10. **setting down before:** laying siege to.   11. **advantage:** opportunity (i.e., in military operations outside Macbeth's castle in which it is possible for would-be deserters to slip away; in a siege, his forces will be more confined to the castle and under his watchful eye).   12. **more and less:** high and low.

MACDUFF   Let our just censures

15   Attend the true event,° and put we on
       Industrious soldiership.

SIWARD   The time approaches
       That will with due decision make us know
       What we shall say we have and what we owe.°
       Thoughts speculative their unsure hopes relate,

20   But certain issue strokes must arbitrate° —
       Towards which advance the war.°

                              Exeunt, marching.

Scene 5°

Enter Macbeth, Seyton, and soldiers, with drum and colors.

MACBETH Hang out our banners on the outward
                      walls.
       The cry is still, "They come!"Our castle's
                      strength
       Will laugh a siege to scorn. Here let them lie
       Till famine and the ague eat them up.

5   Were they not forced° with those that should
                      be ours,
       We might have met them dareful,° beard to
                      beard,
       And beat them backward home.

                      A cry within of women.
                                    What is that
       noise?

SEYTON It is the cry of women, my good lord.
                      [*He goes to the door.*]

MACBETH I have almost forgot the taste of fears.

10   The time has been my senses would have
                      cooled°
       To hear a night-shriek, and my fell of hair°
       Would at a dismal treatise° rouse and stir
       As° life were in 't. I have supped full with
                      horrors;

Direness, familiar to my slaughterous thoughts,
Cannot once start me.°

[*Seyton returns.*]

                              Wherefore was that cry?

15 SEYTON The Queen, my lord, is dead.

MACBETH She should have died hereafter;°
       There would have been a time for such a word.
       Tomorrow, and tomorrow, and tomorrow

20   Creeps in this° petty pace from day to day
       To the last syllable of recorded time,
       And all our yesterdays have lighted° fools
       The way to dusty° death. Out, out, brief candle!
       Life's but a walking shadow, a poor player

25   That struts and frets his hour upon the stage
       And then is heard no more. It is a tale
       Told by an idiot, full of sound and fury,
       Signifying nothing.°

Enter a Messenger.

       Thou com'st to use thy tongue; thy story
                      quickly.

30 MESSENGER Gracious my lord,
       I should report that which I say I saw,
       But know not how to do 't.

MACBETH   Well, say, sir.

MESSENGER As I did stand my watch upon the hill,
       I looked toward Birnam, and anon,
                      methought,
       The wood began to move.

35 MACBETH   Liar and slave!

MESSENGER Let me endure your wrath if 't be not
                      so.
       Within this three mile may you see it coming;
       I say, a moving grove.

MACBETH   If thou speak'st false,
       Upon the next tree shalt thou hang alive

40   Till famine cling° thee. If thy speech be sooth,°
       I care not if thou dost for me as much.

14–15. **Let . . . event:** let us postpone judgment about these uncertain matters until we've achieved our goal.   18. **What . . . owe:** what we only claim to have, as distinguished from what we actually have (or perhaps what we *owe* as duty).   **owe:** own.   19–20. **Thoughts . . . arbitrate:** speculating can only convey our sense of hope; blows must decide the actual outcome.   21. **war:** army.   **Act 5, Scene 5. Location:** Dunsinane. Macbeth's castle.   5. **forced:** reinforced.   6. **dareful:** boldly, in open battle.   10. **cooled:** felt the chill of terror.   11. **my fell of hair:** the hair of my scalp.   12. **dismal treatise:** sinister story.   13. **As:** as if.   15. **start me:** make me start.   17. **She . . . hereafter:** she would have died someday, or, she should have died at some more appropriate time, freed from the relentless pressures of the moment.   19–28. **Tomorrow . . . nothing:** (For biblical echoes in this speech, see Psalms 18:28, 22:15, 90:9; Job 8:9, 14:1–2, 18:6.)   20. **this:** at this.   22. **lighted:** (The metaphor is of a candle used to light one to bed, just as life is a brief transit for wretched mortals to their deathbeds.)   23. **dusty:** (Since life, made out of dust, returns to dust.)   40. **cling:** cause to shrivel.   **sooth:** truth.

I pull in resolution,° and begin
To doubt th' equivocation of the fiend
That lies like truth. "Fear not, till Birnam Wood
45 Do come to Dunsinane," and now a wood
Comes toward Dunsinane. Arm, arm, and out!
If this which he avouches does appear,
There is nor flying hence nor tarrying here.
I 'gin to be aweary of the sun,
50 And wish th' estate° o' the world were now
   undone.
Ring the alarum bell! Blow wind, come wrack,°
At least we'll die with harness° on our back.

                              Exeunt.

Scene 6°

Drum and colors. Enter Malcolm, Siward,
Macduff, and their army, with boughs.

MALCOLM   Now near enough. Your leafy screens
   throw down,
And show° like those you are. You, worthy uncle,°
Shall with my cousin, your right noble son,
Lead our first battle.° Worthy Macduff and we
5 Shall take upon 's what else remains to do,
According to our order.°
SIWARD   Fare you well.
Do we° but find the tyrant's power° tonight,
Let us be beaten, if we cannot fight.
MACDUFF   Make all our trumpets speak! Give
   them all breath,
10 Those clamorous harbingers° of blood and
   death.
                    Exeunt. Alarums continued.

Scene 7°

Enter Macbeth.

MACBETH   They have tied me to a stake. I cannot
   fly,

But bearlike I must fight the course.° What's he
That was not born of woman? Such a one
Am I to fear, or none.

   Enter young Siward.

5 YOUNG SIWARD   What is thy name?
   MACBETH   Thou'lt be afraid to hear it.
   YOUNG SIWARD   No, though thou call'st thyself a
      hotter name
   Than any is in hell.
   MACBETH   My name's Macbeth.
   YOUNG SIWARD   The devil himself could not
      pronounce a title
   More hateful to mine ear.
10 MACBETH   No, nor more fearful.
   YOUNG SIWARD   Thou liest, abhorrèd tyrant! With
      my sword
   I'll prove the lie thou speak'st.
                    Fight, and young Siward slain.°
   MACBETH   Thou wast born
      of woman.
   But swords I smile at, weapons laugh to scorn,
   Brandished by man that's of a woman born.
                                        Exit.

   Alarums. Enter Macduff.

15 MACDUFF   That way the noise is. Tyrant, show thy
      face!
   If thou be'st slain, and with no stroke of mine,
   My wife and children's ghosts will haunt me
      still.
   I cannot strike at wretched kerns,° whose arms
   Are hired to bear their staves.° Either thou,°
      Macbeth,
20 Or else my sword with an unbattered edge
   I sheathe again undeeded.° There thou
      shouldst be;°
   By this great clatter one of greatest note
   Seems bruited.° Let me find him, Fortune,

---

42. **pull in resolution:** can no longer give free rein to my self-confident determination.   50. **estate:** settled order.   51. **wrack:** ruin.   52. **harness:** armor.
Act 5, Scene 6. Location: Dunsinane. Before Macbeth's castle.   2. **show:** appear.   **uncle:** i.e., Siward.   4. **battle:** battalion.   6. **order:** plan of
battle.   7. **Do we:** if we do.   **power:** army.   10. **harbingers:** forerunners.   **Act 5, Scene 7. Location:** Before Macbeth's castle; the battle action is
continuous here.   2. **course:** bout or round of bearbaiting, in which the bear was tied to a stake and dogs were set upon him.   s.d. **young Siward**
slain: (In some unspecified way, young Siward's body must be removed from the stage; his own father enters at line 24 and perceives nothing amiss,
and in 5.8.38 young Siward is reported *missing* in action. Perhaps Macbeth drags off the body, or perhaps it is removed by soldiers during the
alarums.)   18. **kerns:** (Properly, Irish foot soldiers; here, applied contemptuously to the rank and file.)   19. **staves:** spears.   **Either thou:** i.e.,
either I find you.   21. **undeeded:** having seen no action.   **shouldst be:** ought to be (judging by the noise).   23. **bruited:** announced

And more I beg not.   *Exit. Alarums.*

Enter Malcolm and Siward.

25 SIWARD This way, my lord. The castle's gently
    rendered:°
    The tyrant's people on both sides do fight,
    The noble thanes do bravely in the war,
    The day almost itself professes° yours,
    And little is to do.
MALCOLM   We have met with foes
    That strike beside us.°
30 SIWARD   Enter, sir, the castle.
                                    Exeunt. Alarum.

Scene 8°

Enter Macbeth.

MACBETH Why should I play the Roman fool°
    and die
    On mine own sword? Whiles I see lives,° the
    gashes
    Do better upon them.

Enter Macduff.

MACDUFF   Turn, hellhound, turn!
MACBETH Of all men else I have avoided thee.
5   But get thee back! My soul is too much
    charged
    With blood of thine already.
MACDUFF   I have no words;
    My voice is in my sword, thou bloodier villain
    Than terms can give thee out!° *Fight. Alarum.*
MACBETH   Thou losest
    labor.
    As easy mayst thou the intrenchant° air
10   With thy keen sword impress° as make me
    bleed.
    Let fall thy blade on vulnerable crests;
    I bear a charmèd life, which must not yield

To one of woman born.
MACDUFF   Despair° thy charm,
    And let the angel° whom thou still° hast
    served
15   Tell thee, Macduff was from his mother's womb
    Untimely° ripped.
MACBETH Accursèd be that tongue that tells me
    so,
    For it hath cowed my better part of man!°
    And be these juggling° fiends no more
    believed
20   That palter with us in a double sense,°
    That keep the word of promise to our ear
    And break it to our hope. I'll not fight with
    thee.
MACDUFF Then yield thee, coward,
    And live to be the show and gaze o' the time!°
25   We'll have thee, as our rarer monsters are,
    Painted upon a pole,° and underwrit,
    "Here may you see the tyrant."
MACBETH   I will not yield
    To kiss the ground before young Malcolm's
    feet
    And to be baited with the rabble's curse.
30   Though Birnam Wood be come to Dunsinane,
    And thou opposed, being of no woman born,
    Yet I will try the last.° Before my body
    I throw my warlike shield. Lay on, Macduff,
    And damned be him that first cries, "Hold,
    enough!"
                        Exeunt, fighting. Alarums.

*Enter fighting, and Macbeth slain. [Exit
Macduff with Macbeth's body.] Retreat,° and
flourish. Enter, with drum and colors,°
Malcolm, Siward, Ross, thanes, and soldiers.*

35 MALCOLM I would the friends we miss were safe
    arrived.

---

25. **gently rendered:** surrendered without fighting.   28. **professes:** declares itself.   30. **strike beside us:** fight on our side, or miss us deliberately.
Act 5, Scene 8. Location: Before Macbeth's castle, as the battle continues; after line 34, within the castle.   1. **Roman fool:** i.e., suicide, like Brutus,
Mark Antony, and others.   2. **Whiles . . . lives:** i.e., as long as I see any enemy living.   8. **give thee out:** name you, describe you.   9. **intrenchant:**
that cannot be cut, indivisible.   10. **impress:** make an impression on.   13. **Despair:** despair of.   14. **angel:** evil angel, Macbeth's genius.   **still:**
always.   16. **Untimely:** prematurely, i. e., by caesarean delivery.   18. **better . . . man:** i. e., courage.   19. **juggling:** deceiving.   20. **palter . . . sense:**
equivocate with us.   24. **gaze o' the time:** spectacle or sideshow of the age.   26. **Painted . . . pole:** i. e., painted on a board or cloth and suspended
on a pole.   32. **the last:** i. e., my last resort; my own strength and resolution.   **s.d. Retreat:** a trumpet call ordering an end to the fighting.   *Enter,*
***with drum and colors,* etc.:** (The remainder of the play is perhaps imagined as taking place in Macbeth's castle and could be marked as a separate
scene. In Shakespeare's theater, however, the shift is so nonrepresentational and without scenic alteration that the action is virtually continuous.)

SIWARD Some must go off;° and yet, by these° I see
So great a day as this is cheaply bought.

MALCOLM Macduff is missing, and your noble son.

ROSS Your son, my lord, has paid a soldier's debt.

40   He only lived but till he was a man,
The which no sooner had his prowess confirmed
In the unshrinking station° where he fought,
But like a man he died.

SIWARD   Then he is dead?

ROSS Ay, and brought off the field. Your cause of sorrow

45   Must not be measured by his worth, for then
It hath no end.

SIWARD   Had he his hurts before?

ROSS Ay, on the front.

SIWARD   Why then, God's soldier be he!
Had I as many sons as I have hairs
I would not wish them to a fairer death.
And so, his knell is knolled.

50 **MALCOLM**   He's worth more sorrow,
And that I'll spend for him.

SIWARD   He's worth no more.
They say he parted° well and paid his score,°
And so, God be with him! Here comes newer comfort.

Enter Macduff, with Macbeth's head.

MACDUFF Hail, King! For so thou art. Behold where stands°

55   Th' usurper's cursèd head. The time is free.°
I see thee compassed with thy kingdom's pearl,°
That speak my salutation in their minds,
Whose voices I desire aloud with mine:
Hail, King of Scotland!

60 **ALL** Hail, King of Scotland!   *Flourish.*

MALCOLM We shall not spend a large expense of time
Before we reckon° with your several° loves
And make us even with you.° My thanes and kinsmen,
Henceforth be earls, the first that ever Scotland

65   In such an honor named. What's more to do
Which would be planted newly with the time,°
As calling home our exiled friends abroad
That fled the snares of watchful tyranny,
Producing forth° the cruel ministers°

70   Of this dead butcher and his fiendlike queen —
Who, as 'tis thought, by self and violent° hands
Took off her life — this, and what needful else
That calls upon us, by the grace of Grace
We will perform in measure, time, and place.

75   So, thanks to all at once and to each one,
Whom we invite to see us crowned at Scone.

Flourish. Exeunt omnes.

---

36. **go off:** die. **by these:** to judge by these (assembled).   42. **unshrinking station:** post from which he did not shrink.   52. **score:** reckoning.   54. **stands:** i.e., on a pole.   55. **free:** released from tyranny.   56. **compassed . . . pearl:** surrounded by the nobles of your kingdom (literally, the pearls encircling a crown).   62. **reckon:** come to a reckoning.   **several:** individual.   63. **make . . . you:** i.e., repay your worthiness.   66. **would . . . time:** should be established at the commencement of this new era.   69. **Producing forth:** bringing forward to trial. **ministers:** agents.   71. **self and violent:** her own violent.

Understanding and Interpreting

1 As she is sleepwalking, Lady Macbeth mentions her desire to clean her hands several times, but is unable to do so (Scene 1, ll. 42, 52–53). Using evidence from the text to support your interpretation, explain what the cleaning of hands might represent for Lady Macbeth.

2 In Scene 2, the four thanes provide an account of the current state of affairs in Scotland. Summarize the information they provide and explain the growing difficulties that Macbeth faces.

3 In Scene 4, Malcolm states that "none serve [Macbeth] but constrained things" (l. 13). What does he mean by this and why does this give him greater confidence in victory?

4 Even after Macbeth has seen the first prophecy fail to protect him, he continues to believe he will not be harmed when facing Macduff in the final scene, telling him that he "bear[s] a charmèd life" (Scene 8, l. 12). Why is Macbeth still unwilling to admit that he may not be invincible given what he has seen transpire so far?

5 What does Macduff mean when he says that he "was from his mother's womb / Untimely ripp'd" (Scene 8, ll. 15–16), and what is Macbeth's response to this information?

6 Macduff tells Macbeth that once he is dead, his corpse will be displayed publicly with a sign saying "Here may you see the tyrant" (Scene 8, ll. 23–27). What purpose would this public display serve?

Analyzing Language, Style, and Structure

1 Although Lady Macbeth's comments and actions in Scene 1 seem random and inexplicable to the Doctor and the Gentlewoman, knowledge of her actions in the past provides insight into her "slumbery agitation" (ll. 13–14). Find several examples where Lady Macbeth says something that has no clear meaning for the Doctor and Gentlewoman, but in fact reveals her secrets.

2 In Act 2, Scene 2, shortly after he has killed Duncan, Macbeth hears a voice telling him that "Macbeth does murder sleep" (l. 40). In what ways do Lady Macbeth's actions in Act 5 reinforce that earlier proclamation heard by Macbeth?

3 Angus compares Macbeth's title as king to something that "Hang[s] loose about him, like a giant's robe / Upon a dwarfish thief" (Scene 2, ll. 21–22). His statement echoes an earlier remark when, shortly after hearing of his appointment as the Thane of Cawdor, Macbeth responds by asking Angus and Ross why they dress him in "borrowed robes" (Act 1, Scene 3, l. 109). Explain how this imagery relates to Macbeth's kingship.

4 Macbeth's response to the news of Lady Macbeth's death is complex (Scene 5, ll. 17–28).

Using specific text examples, describe the tone of his response and then explain possible reasons for his attitude.

5 Macbeth concludes his response to news of Lady Macbeth's death with perhaps the most famous soliloquy in all of Shakespeare's plays (Scene 5, ll. 17–28). Analyze that speech, paying close attention to how Shakespeare uses resources of language to reinforce the ideas of the speech.

6 Look carefully at Macbeth's final lines (Scene 8, ll. 27–34) and analyze how Macbeth uses language to reveal his attitude toward his impending death.

7 In one of the most dramatic and intense moments in any of Shakespeare's plays, Macduff enters holding a spear on which he has mounted Macbeth's head (Scene 8, ll. 54–59). What is the effect of ending the play in this manner rather than having Macduff merely tell all of the other men that he has killed Macbeth?

8 Analyze Malcolm's final speech, paying attention to the order in which he addresses the issues that the country must now face and the language he uses to demonstrate his readiness to lead as the new king (Scene 8, ll. 61–76).

Connecting, Arguing, and Extending

1 At one of the most poignant moments in the play, Macbeth asserts that "Life [. . .] is a tale / Told by an idiot, full of sound and fury, / Signifying nothing" (Act 5, Scene 5, ll. 24–28). Write an essay in which you argue whether Macbeth suggests that life is truly meaningless, or whether the play ultimately does demonstrate that there is purpose or meaning to life.

2 When the Doctor tells Macbeth that he cannot cure mental disorders, Macbeth decries the limitations of medicine. Conduct research into mental disorders that might be affecting Macbeth and Lady Macbeth. Then, based on your research and evidence taken from the play, offer a diagnosis for both Lady Macbeth and Macbeth.

3 First, contrast Macbeth's leadership approach in Scene 3 with Malcolm's approach in Scene 4 and consider how these two characters view what it means to be a leader, what the differences suggest about each man and his attitude toward the coming battle, and what the contrasts suggest about the nature of true leadership. Then, using current examples from American culture, explain which approach to leadership is most effective when facing the challenges of the twenty-first century.

4 Staging Act 5 is a particular challenge because of the number of scenes and the numerous battles and fights. Imagine you are a director who has to create a single set in which all eight scenes must take place. Create a visual design of your set and be prepared to explain how you would stage each of the eight scenes in that single set.

Topics for Composing

1 Exposition/Analysis
Macbeth is a play that addresses many themes. Select one that you find compelling and, using evidence from the play, write an essay in which you explore how that theme is revealed over the course of the play.

2 Exposition/Analysis
Imagery is central to *Macbeth*. Using evidence from the play, write an essay in which you analyze how Shakespeare uses imagery in *Macbeth* to develop a central theme.

3 Argument
Although Banquo is murdered long before the end of *Macbeth*, some literary scholars argue that he is as important to the play after he has died as when he is still alive. Using evidence from the play, write an argument that either supports or refutes this claim.

4 Argument
English poet Samuel Taylor Coleridge once said that the witches in *Macbeth* "have the power of tempting those, who have been tempters themselves." Write an essay in which you analyze and evaluate Coleridge's comments using evidence from the play.

5 Exposition/Analysis
Consider Macbeth's attitude toward Lady Macbeth after the murder of Duncan. Is it true that he does not need her anymore? What impact does her death have on him? Write an essay in which you analyze Macbeth's attitude toward his wife and how that attitude illuminates a theme in the play as a whole.

6 Synthesis
In the sonnets "Mezzo Cammin" by Henry Wadsworth Longfellow and "When I Have Fears" by John Keats, both poets express similar ideas about the necessity of achieving one's goals and aspirations. Find the poems online and examine those ideas in light of Macbeth's goals and aspirations, and decide how Longfellow and Keats might respond to Macbeth's behavior in the play. Write a paragraph of advice to Macbeth by each poet, expressing concern and advice regarding Macbeth's situation.

7 Exposition/Research
Macbeth has been adapted to film numerous times. Research the film adaptations and select one that you find especially interesting. Then, write a review in which you evaluate how well the adaption captures the major ideas and themes in the original play.

8 Argument
Many critics over the years have suggested that Lady Macbeth was the real motivation behind Macbeth's violent rise to power. Examine the play for lines that these critics may have selected to support the claim that Macbeth would not have killed for power without the urging of Lady Macbeth, and then defend or challenge this claim. Read Lady Macbeth's lines carefully, and then discuss what qualities she exhibits that may have led these critics to see her as the source of Macbeth's ambition.

9 Multimodal
Macbeth has been produced for stage and screen countless times over the years. Using the five-act structure of the play, create a storyboard by selecting images of the most important scenes or ideas in the play overall. The images you select should represent the most interesting depictions of each scene or idea that you can find. Provide captions for all of your images, making sure to include direct quotes from the play.

10 Narrative/Multimodal

Written over five hundred years ago, *Macbeth* continues to be regularly produced for stage and screen, although many directors choose to set the play in different time periods and locations. For example, Akira Kurosawa's famous film *Throne of Blood* is an adaptation of *Macbeth* set in feudal Japan. Another adaptation was set in the Zulu culture of the early nineteenth century, prompting Nelson Mandela to remark that "[t]he similarities between Shakespeare's Macbeth and our own Shaka become a glaring reminder that the world is, philosophically, a very small place."

Prepare to pitch an original adaptation of *Macbeth* to a hypothetical theater or movie producer. To do so, you will need to write a screenplay for one scene, and using your screenplay as guide, you will need to explain the concept, time period, and location for your adaptation. While your pitch will not necessarily involve costumes or memorizing lines, it is still a performance. You will be taking your instructor and classmates through your scene, positioning the actors, explaining the camera angles, and discussing the stage directions; in other words, you are going to help them "see" your film.

11 Creative

Create a newspaper that details what you believe are the most significant events in *Macbeth*. You should include at least five articles that reflect events in the play, as well as accompanying graphics. Include the various sections you would find in a modern newspaper, such as the front section, containing major news; a sports page; an op-ed page; a dining or food section; and so on. Your final newspaper should provide a broad overview of the events and major themes in the play.

12 Multimodal

There are a number of classic music compositions inspired by the play *Macbeth*. These include everything from operas to symphonies. Find an example of a musical composition inspired by the play, and then provide a short presentation with audio examples, making sure to demonstrate the connection between the composition and the play.

CONVERSATION

RISK AND REWARD

The ancient Greek myth of Icarus has cautioned us about the risks of *hubris*, or unchecked pride, for thousands of years. In the myth, the master craftsman Daedalus angers King Minos and is imprisoned, with his son Icarus, within the Labyrinth that he himself built for the king. Too clever to be trapped for long, Daedalus fashions two sets of wings, one for himself and one for his son. Before taking flight, he warns his son not to fly too high and not to fly too low. Overcome with the thrill of flying, however, Icarus flies too high and the heat of the sun melts the wax holding his wings together.

While the myth itself is a cautionary tale warning us not to "fly to close to the sun," and to keep our ambition in check, the figure of Icarus has become an inspiration of sorts. After all, before his fall, he was *flying*. He has come to represent the type of boundless optimism and breathtaking bravery that put a man on the moon—and that is responsible for countless dreams that have come true against all odds. The risks of taking flight like Icarus may be high, but so might the rewards.

In this Conversation, you will explore literature and art that is directly inspired by the myth of Icarus, as well as other pieces that consider both the highs and lows of ambition. You'll look at leaders brought low and empires turned to dust, as well as inspirational people who have dared to do great things.

TEXTS

W. H. Auden / Musée des Beaux Arts (poetry)
William Carlos Williams / Landscape with the Fall of Icarus (poetry)
Brian Aldiss / Flight 063 (poetry)
Jeffrey Kluger / *from* Ambition: Why Some People Are Most Likely to Succeed (nonfiction)
Percy Bysshe Shelley / Ozymandias (poetry)
William Shakespeare / *from* Henry VIII (drama)
Amy Tan / The Rules of the Game (fiction)
Miguel de Cervantes / *from* Don Quixote (fiction)

Musée des Beaux Arts

W. H. Auden

Wystan Hugh (W. H.) Auden (1907–1973) was a virtuoso poet and essayist who wrote in almost every traditional poetic form. Born in England, Auden studied English literature at Christ's Church, Oxford. He found success as a poet in England but decided to immigrate to the United States and eventually became a citizen. In this poem, Auden responds directly to Bruegel's *Landscape with the Fall of Icarus*. As you are reading, note the details in the painting that he references directly, as well as his conclusions about the main idea he believes is offered in the painting.

About suffering they were never wrong,
The Old Masters: how well they understood
Its human position; how it takes place
While someone else is eating or opening a window or just walking dully along;
5　How, when the aged are reverently, passionately waiting
For the miraculous birth, there always must be
Children who did not specially want it to happen, skating
On a pond at the edge of the wood:
They never forgot
10　That even the dreadful martyrdom must run its course
Anyhow in a corner, some untidy spot
Where the dogs go on with their doggy life and the torturer's horse
Scratches its innocent behind on a tree.

In Brueghel's *Icarus*, for instance: how everything turns away
15　Quite leisurely from the disaster; the ploughman may
Have heard the splash, the forsaken cry,
But for him it was not an important failure; the sun shone
As it had to on the white legs disappearing into the green
Water; and the expensive delicate ship that must have seen
20　Something amazing, a boy falling out of the sky,
Had somewhere to get to and sailed calmly on.

seeing connections

Auden's poem refers to this painting, *Landscape with the Fall of Icarus*, by Pieter Bruegel "The Elder" (1525–1569). Unlike Italian Renaissance painters who used high style and mastery to depict grand biblical tableaus or paint opulent portraits of royalty, Flemish artists like Bruegel tended to use a grand style to depict landscapes and scenes of everyday life.

The title of this painting, *Landscape with the Fall of Icarus*, suggests that the focus of the painting is more on the landscape than on the myth. The fallen Icarus is reduced to a small pair of bare legs splashing down in the bottom right corner.

What point is Bruegel making through this artistic choice? What perspective on this painting does Auden's poem add?

Pieter Bruegel the Elder, *Landscape with the Fall of Icarus*, c. 1558. Oil on canvas, 28.9″ × 44.1″. Musée d'Art Ancien, Musées Royaux des Beaux-Arts, Brussels, Belgium.

Scala/Art Resource, NY

Understanding and Interpreting

1 This poem is a direct response to Bruegel's *Landscape with the Fall of Icarus* (above). After taking a moment to review the painting that inspired this poem, discuss whether or not you think Auden's understanding of the painting is accurate. Explain.

2 In the second stanza, the characters in the painting are described as turning "away / Quite leisurely from the disaster" (ll. 14–15), which suggests that everyone in the scene is intentionally ignoring Icarus's fall. How does the difference between the figures ignoring Icarus's fall, as opposed just being unaware of it, affect your reading of both the poem and the painting?

3 The Icarus story comes from Greek mythology, and Icarus's fall is considered to be tragic in the classic sense (refer to the Glossary if you are unsure what constitutes a classic tragedy). In what ways does Auden's poem bring into question the importance of these and other stories?

Analyzing Language, Style, and Structure

1 In his poem, Auden begins with an assertion in the first stanza and then provides an example that supports that assertion in the second stanza. Identify the assertion he makes and then discuss whether or not his example supports that assertion.

2 Auden goes back and forth between using elevated diction such as *reverently*, *miraculous*, and *martyrdom*, and more common language, such as *untidy*, *doggy*, and *behind*. What is the effect of his using both types of diction on the poem as a whole?

3 Auden juxtaposes general observations regarding the Old Masters' understanding of suffering with the specific illustration of the myth in Bruegel's painting. What is the purpose of this juxtaposition in terms of the overall meaning of the poem?

Connecting, Arguing, and Extending

1 Auden's poem suggests that sometimes an event that is particularly important to a certain group of people will be entirely insignificant to another group. Think of a time that something important happened to you or someone you knew. Describe the event and then imagine that no one else expressed any interest in that event. How would you respond to people's lack of interest?

2 Auden offers his interpretation of Bruegel's painting in this poem. However, his interpretation was informed by his own knowledge and experience, and not by any "official" interpretation offered by

Bruegel. Write a response either supporting or challenging Auden's interpretation of Bruegel's painting using details from the painting as well as Auden's poem.

3 What challenges do expressing ideas through visual art rather than the written word pose? Are there certain kinds of ideas that are better expressed through visual mediums? Do some ideas lend themselves better to writing? Explain, using the Icarus poems and paintings presented here (pp. 318-323) as part of your evidence.

Landscape with the Fall of Icarus

William Carlos Williams

William Carlos Williams (1883–1963) was an American novelist and essayist and a poet associated closely with the modernist movement. A prolific writer, Williams won the National Book Award as well as the Pulitzer Prize. Williams's experimental style pushed the boundaries of modern poetry and his focus on the everyday separated him from those poets whom he felt were simply extending European culture and tradition rather than challenging outdated ideas. This poem was directly inspired by Bruegel's painting *Landscape with the Fall of Icarus*. As you read the poem, take note of how Williams offers a specific interpretation of the painting and then turns that into a poetic reflection.

According to Brueghel
when Icarus fell
it was spring

a farmer was ploughing
5   his field
the whole pageantry

of the year was
awake tingling
near

10   the edge of the sea
concerned
with itself

sweating in the sun
that melted
15   the wings' wax

unsignificantly
off the coast
there was

a splash quite unnoticed
20   this was
Icarus drowning

---

seeing connections

Here is a second painting of the Icarus myth, created by Dutch painter Ferdinand Bol almost one hundred years after Bruegel's painting.

Compare and contrast this depiction of the Icarus myth to Bruegel's (p. 319). How does each painting reflect a different interpretation of the significance of that myth? Base your response on the details you observe. If Auden and Williams wrote poems about this painting, how would their poems have to change?

Scala/Art Resource, NY

Ferdinand Bol, *Fall of Icarus*, c. 16th century. Oil on canvas. Museum Mayer van den Bergh, Antwerp, Belgium.

Understanding and Interpreting

1 The poem describes the scene as taking place in the spring. What effect does placing Icarus's death in spring have on the ideas in the poem as a whole?

2 In mythology, Icarus's drowning is a tragic and significant event. However, in this poem, Icarus's death is reduced to a "splash quite unnoticed" (l. 19). What ideas about mythology as a whole does Williams offer by minimizing the significance of this event?

3 What is the speaker's conclusion about Bruegel's interpretation of the fall of Icarus?

Analyzing Language, Style, and Structure

1 Each line in this poem is composed of no more than four words, with a couple of lines made up of only a single word. How does this brevity contribute to the ideas in the poem?

2 Even though there are line breaks, the ideas often are carried from one stanza to the next. What effect does this stylistic choice have on the poem as a whole?

3 In line 16, the speaker uses the word "unsignificantly." How does this word vary in meaning from "insignificantly," and what is the effect of using this invented word?

Connecting, Arguing, and Extending

1 The inspiration for this poem was Bruegel's painting of the same name, shown on page 319. The myth dates back to around 800 B.C., and the painting was completed in 1558, separating these two pieces by over two thousand years. Williams's poem presents a specific interpretation of that more recent painting, rather than focusing on the ancient myth. How might the poet's choice to focus on the painting itself rather than the myth make it more relevant to a modern audience? In what ways might he be adding his artistic voice to an ongoing conversation between artists by focusing on the painting?

2 Using details from the poem and your understanding of the myth of Icarus, write a response in which you identify the argument Williams is making regarding Bruegel's painting. Then explain whether or not you agree with Williams's assertion and why.

3 This poem is a direct response to a painting. Think of a painting with which you are familiar, or go online and find a painting that interests you. Write a poem about the painting you have selected. Then, write a commentary about what interested you about the piece, what your poem tried to capture about the painting, and what you learned from the process.

Flight 063

Brian Aldiss

Brian Aldiss (b. 1925) is a lecturer, a critic, a poet, and an essayist who is also well known for his science fiction novels, which gained him entry into the Science Fiction Hall of Fame in 2004. His short story "Super Toys Last All Summer Long" was the basis for the Steven Spielberg film *A.I. Artificial Intelligence*. In this poem, which is not a work of science fiction, the speaker contemplates while flying in a large Boeing plane how flight, once considered impossible, is now commonplace.

Rob Monk/SFX Magazine via Getty Images

Why always speak of Icarus' fall?—
That legendary plunge
Amid a shower of tallow
And feathers and the poor lad's
5 Sweat? And that little splash
Which caught the eye of Brueghel
While the sun remained
Aloof within its private zone?

That fall remains
10 Suspended in the corporate mind.
Yet as our Boeing flies
High above the Arctic Circle
Into the sun's eye, think—
Before the fall the flight was.
15 (So with Adam—just before
The Edenic Fall, he had
That first taste of Eve.)

Dinner is served aboard Flight 063.
We eat from plastic trays, oblivious
20 To the stratosphere.
But Icarus—his cliff-top jump,
The leap of heart, the blue air scaled—
His glorious sense of life
Imperiled. Time
25 Fell far below, the everyday
Was lost in his ascent.

Up, up, he sailed, unheeding
Such silly limitations as
The melting point of wax.

This 1870 engraving is from the book *Wonderful Balloon Ascents or the Conquest of the Skies*, created eighty-seven years after the first time a human took flight in a hot air balloon.

What does the image tell you about our fascination with flight?

Private Collection/Ken Welsh/Bridgeman Images

Understanding and Interpreting

1 The speaker puts the story of Icarus's fall into a modern context—flying in a passenger jet "High above the Arctic Circle / Into the sun's eye" (ll. 12–13). Thus, he or she places all of the passengers in the plane in a situation similar to that of Icarus, who flew close to the sun as well. How does this juxtaposition between the ancient Icarus and modern passengers on a commercial flight contribute to the overall meaning of the poem?

2 How do the "oblivious" passengers (l. 19) on the plane support the speaker's main assertions about the significance of Icarus's flight?

3 The speaker claims that Icarus had a "glorious sense of life" (l. 23). In what ways is that attitude toward Icarus reflected in the ideas offered within the poem as a whole?

Analyzing Language, Style, and Structure

1 The speaker begins with a rhetorical question. What is the purpose of directing our attention to an aspect of the myth that is often ignored?

2 How does the inverted syntax in lines 11–14 refocus the emphasis concerning the outcome of Icarus's flight?

3 The poem ends with Icarus still ascending. How does this choice reinforce the rhetorical question in line 1?

4 How do the connotations of the word "silly" (l. 28) contribute to the speaker's attitude toward Icarus's fall?

Connecting, Arguing, and Extending

1 The speaker in the poem uses Icarus's failed flight to comment on our current response to flying in an airplane. Once considered nothing but a fantasy, flying is now a common occurrence — in the United States alone, an average of 1.8 million people fly every day, according to the Transportation Security Administration. The ability to fly has not only provided people with a chance to go places they would otherwise never visit but changed the course of history. What technology do you use regularly that once was considered impossible? In what significant ways has this technology changed the world?

2 The poem raises the idea that terrible consequences sometimes befall individuals who push the limits of technology. For example, even though Icarus did fly, he paid for that flight with his life. Pilots also risk their lives when testing new airplanes and many have perished during test flights. However, it is also true that technological failures provide an opportunity for people to figure out what went wrong and correct the problems. Those who fail can ultimately inspire others to try even harder to achieve what previously was deemed impossible. What do you think drives individuals to risk their lives attempting to push the limits of technology?

3 A quick search for "extreme sports" on YouTube will call up thousands of videos of people taking incredible risks and filming their attempts. Some of the videos show people taking incredible risks and succeeding, while many others catalog spectacular failures. These risk takers are not generally trying to advance technology in any way but seem to be interested simply in the thrill of the attempt. Explain what you believe to be the motivation for this risk taking and argue whether it serves a larger purpose or is just an interesting distraction.

Ambition: Why Some People Are Most Likely to Succeed

Jeffrey Kluger

Jeffrey Kluger (b. 1954) is a senior editor of science and technology reporting at *Time* magazine. He has written several books, including *Splendid Solution* (2006) and *Simplexity: Why Simple Things Become Complex* (2008), and coauthored *Lost Moon: The Perilous Journey of Apollo 13,* the book that was the basis for the movie *Apollo 13,* released in 1995. In his essay "Ambition: Why Some People Are Most Likely to Succeed," written for *Time* in 2005, Kluger explores possible reasons why some individuals are able to find great success in life while others struggle to get ahead.

Camera Press/Guillem Lopez/Redux

You don't get as successful as Gregg and Drew Shipp by accident. Shake hands with the 36-year-old fraternal twins who co-own the sprawling Hi Fi Personal Fitness club in Chicago, and it's clear you're in the presence of people who thrive on their drive. But that wasn't always the case. The twins' father founded the Jovan perfume company, a glamorous business that spun off the kinds of glamorous profits that made it possible for the Shipps to amble through high school, coast into college and never much worry about getting the rent paid or keeping the fridge filled. But before they graduated, their sense of drift began to trouble them. At about the same time, their father sold off the company, and with it went the cozy billets in adult life that had always served as an emotional backstop for the boys.

That did it. By the time they got out of school, both Shipps had entirely transformed themselves, changing from boys who might have grown up to live off the family's wealth to men consumed with going out and creating their own. "At this point," says Gregg, "I consider myself to be almost maniacally ambitious."

It shows. In 1998 the brothers went into the gym trade. They spotted a modest health club doing a modest business, bought out the owner and transformed the place into a luxury facility where private trainers could reserve space for top-dollar clients. In the years since, the company has outgrown one building, then another, and the brothers are about to move a third time. Gregg, a communications major at college, manages the club's clients, while Drew, a business major, oversees the more hardheaded chore of finance and expansion. "We're not sitting still," Drew says. "Even now that we're doing twice the business we did at our old place, there's a thirst that needs to be quenched."

Why is that? Why are some people born with a fire in the belly, while others — like the Shipps — need something to get their pilot light lit? And why do others never get the flame of ambition going? Is there a family anywhere that doesn't have its overachievers and underachievers — its Jimmy Carters and Billy Carters, its Jeb Bushes and Neil Bushes — and find itself wondering how they all could have come splashing out of exactly the same gene pool?

5   Of all the impulses in humanity's behavioral portfolio, ambition — that need to grab an ever bigger piece of the resource pie before someone else gets it — ought to be one of the most democratically distributed. Nature is a zero-sum game, after all. Every buffalo you kill for your family is one less for somebody else's; every acre of land you occupy elbows out somebody else. Given that, the need to get ahead ought to be hard-wired into all of us equally.

And yet it's not. For every person consumed with the need to achieve, there's someone content to accept whatever life brings. For everyone who chooses the 80-hour workweek, there's someone punching out at 5. Men and women — so it's said — express ambition differently; so do Americans and Europeans, baby boomers and Gen Xers, the middle class and the well-to-do. Even among the manifestly motivated, there are degrees of ambition. Steve Wozniak co-founded Apple Computer and then left the company in 1985 as a 34-year-old multimillionaire. His partner, Steve Jobs, is still innovating at Apple and moonlighting at his second blockbuster company, Pixar Animation Studios.

Not only do we struggle to understand why some people seem to have more ambition than others, but we can't even agree on just what ambition is. "Ambition is an evolutionary product," says anthropologist Edward Lowe at Soka University of America, in Aliso Viejo, Calif. "No matter how social status is defined, there are certain people in every community who aggressively pursue it and others who aren't so aggressive."

Dean Simonton, a psychologist at the University of California, Davis, who studies genius, creativity and eccentricity, believes it's more complicated than that. "Ambition is energy and determination," he says. "But it calls for goals too. People with goals but no energy are the ones who wind up sitting on the couch saying 'One day I'm going to build a better mousetrap.' People with energy but no clear goals just dissipate themselves in one desultory project after the next."

Assuming you've got drive, dreams and skill, is all ambition equal? Is the overworked lawyer on the partner track any more ambitious than the overworked parent on the mommy track? Is the successful musician to whom melody comes naturally more driven than the unsuccessful one who sweats out every note? We may listen to Mozart, but should we applaud Salieri?[1]

---

[1] Antonio Salieri (1750–1825) was an Italian composer whose career, though impressive, has been overshadowed historically by that of Mozart. Their supposed rivalry was famously chronicled, and to an extent fictionalized, in the Oscar-winning film *Amadeus*. —Eds.

10   Most troubling of all, what about when enough ambition becomes way too much? Grand dreams unmoored from morals are the stuff of tyrants — or at least of Enron. The 16-hour workday filled with high stress and at-the-desk meals is the stuff of burnout and heart attacks. Even among kids, too much ambition quickly starts to do real harm. In a just completed study, anthropologist Peter Demerath of Ohio State University surveyed 600 students at a high-achieving high school where most of the kids are triple-booked with advanced-placement courses, sports and after-school jobs. About 70% of them reported that they were starting to feel stress some or all of the time. "I asked one boy how his parents react to his workload, and he answered, 'I don't really

---

The *Wall Street Journal* asked Gene Luen Yang, the author of the graphic novel *American Born Chinese*, to offer his cartoon response to *Battle Hymn of the Tiger Mother*, a book written by Amy Chua.

In what ways does Yang's comic connect to Kluger's account of stressed-out high school students at a high-performing school?

ADVENTURES IN CHINESE PARENTING by Gene Luen Yang

get home that often,' " says Demerath. "Then he handed me his business card from the video store where he works."

Anthropologists, psychologists and others have begun looking more closely at these issues, seeking the roots of ambition in family, culture, gender, genes and more. They have by no means thrown the curtain all the way back, but they have begun to part it. "It's fundamentally human to be prestige conscious," says Soka's Lowe. "It's not enough just to be fed and housed. People want more."

If humans are an ambitious species, it's clear we're not the only one. Many animals are known to signal their ambitious tendencies almost from birth. Even before wolf pups are weaned, they begin sorting themselves out into alphas and all the others. The alphas are quicker, more curious, greedier for space, milk, Mom — and they stay that way for life. Alpha wolves wander widely, breed annually and may live to a geriatric 10 or 11 years old. Lower-ranking wolves enjoy none of these benefits — staying close to home, breeding rarely and usually dying before they're 4.

Humans often report the same kind of temperamental determinism. Families are full of stories of the inexhaustible infant who grew up to be an entrepreneur, the phlegmatic child who never really showed much go. But if it's genes that run the show, what accounts for the Shipps, who didn't bestir themselves until the cusp of adulthood? And what, more tellingly, explains identical twins — precise genetic templates of each other who ought to be temperamentally identical but often exhibit profound differences in the octane of their ambition?

Ongoing studies of identical twins have measured achievement motivation — lab language for ambition — in identical siblings separated at birth, and found that each twin's profile overlaps 30% to 50% of the other's. In genetic terms, that's an awful lot — "a benchmark for heritability," says geneticist Dean Hamer of the National Cancer Institute. But that still leaves a great deal that can be determined by experiences in infancy, subsequent upbringing and countless other imponderables.

15 Some of those variables may be found by studying the function of the brain. At Washington University, researchers have been conducting brain imaging to investigate a trait they call persistence — the ability to stay focused on a task until it's completed just so — which they consider one of the critical engines driving ambition.

The researchers recruited a sample group of students and gave each a questionnaire designed to measure persistence level. Then they presented the students with a task — identifying sets of pictures as either pleasant or unpleasant and taken either indoors or outdoors — while conducting magnetic resonance imaging of their brains. The nature of the task was unimportant, but how strongly the subjects felt about performing it well — and where in the brain that feeling was processed — could say a lot. In general, the researchers found that students who scored highest in persistence had the greatest activity in the limbic region, the area of the brain related to emotions and habits. "The correlation was .8 [or 80%]," says professor of psychiatry Robert Cloninger, one of the investigators. "That's as good as you can get."

It's impossible to say whether innate differences in the brain were driving the ambitious behavior or whether learned behavior was causing the limbic to light up. But a number of researchers believe it's possible for the non-ambitious to jump-start their drive, provided the right jolt comes along. "Energy level may be genetic," says psychologist Simonton, "but a lot of times it's just finding the right thing to be ambitious about." Simonton and others often cite the case of Franklin D. Roosevelt, who might not have been the same President he became — or even become President at all — had his disabling polio not taught him valuable lessons about patience and tenacity.

Is such an epiphany possible for all of us, or are some people immune to this kind of lightning?

Are there individuals or whole groups for whom the amplitude of ambition is simply lower than it is for others? It's a question — sometimes a charge — that hangs at the edges of all discussions about gender and work, about whether women really have the meat-eating temperament to survive in the professional world. Both research findings and everyday experience suggest that women's ambitions express themselves differently from men's. The meaning of that difference is the hinge on which the arguments turn.

Economists Lise Vesterlund of the University of Pittsburgh and Muriel Niederle of Stanford University conducted a study in which they assembled 40 men and 40 women, gave them five minutes to add up as many two-digit numbers as they could, and paid them 50¢ for each correct answer. The subjects were not competing against one another but simply playing against the house. Later, the game was changed to a tournament in which the subjects were divided into teams of two men or two women each. Winning teams got $2 per computation; losers got nothing. Men and women performed equally in both tests, but on the third round, when asked to choose which of the two ways they wanted to play, only 35% of the women opted for the tournament format; 75% of the men did.

20 "Men and women just differ in their appetite for competition," says Vesterlund. "There seems to be a dislike for it among women and a preference among men."

To old-line employers of the old-boy school, this sounds like just one more reason to keep the glass ceiling polished. But other behavioral experts think Vesterlund's conclusions go too far. They say it's not that women aren't ambitious enough to compete for what they want; it's that they're more selective about when they engage in competition; they're willing to get ahead at high cost but not at any cost. "Primate-wide, males are more directly competitive than females, and that makes sense," says Sarah Blaffer Hardy, emeritus professor of anthropology at the University of California, Davis. "But that's not the same as saying women aren't innately competitive too."

As with so much viewed through the lens of anthropology, the roots of these differences lie in animal and human mating strategies. Males are built to go for quick, competitive reproductive hits and move on. Women are built for the it-takes-a-village life, in which they provide long-term care to a very few young and must sail them safely into an often hostile world. Among some of our evolutionary kin — baboons, macaques and other old-world monkeys — this can be especially tricky since young females inherit their mother's social rank. The mothers must thus operate the levers of society deftly so as to raise both their own position and, eventually, their daughters. If you think that kind of ambition-by-proxy doesn't translate to humans, Hardy argues, think again. "Just read an Edith Wharton novel about women in old New York competing for marriage potential for their daughters," she says.

Import such tendencies into the 21st century workplace, and you get women who are plenty able to compete ferociously but are inclined to do it in teams and to split the difference if they don't get everything they want. And mothers who appear to be unwilling to strive and quit the workplace altogether to go raise their kids? Hardy believes they're competing for the most enduring stakes of all, putting aside their near-term goals to ensure the long-term success of their line. Robin Parker, 46, a campaign organizer who in 1980 was already on the presidential stump with Senator Edward Kennedy, was precisely the kind of lifetime pol who one day finds herself in the West Wing. But in 1992, at the very moment a President of her party was returning to the White House and she might have snagged a plum Washington job, she decamped from the capital, moved to Boston with her family and became a full-time mom to her two sons.

"Being out in the world became a lot less important to me," she says. "I used to worry about getting Presidents elected, and I'm still an incredibly ambitious person. But what I want to succeed at now is managing my family, raising my boys, helping my husband and the community. In 10 years, when the boys are launched, who knows what I'll be doing? But for now, I have my world."

25 But even if something as primal as the reproductive impulse wires you one way, it's possible for other things to rewire you completely. Two of the biggest influences on your level of ambition are the family that produced you and the culture that produced your family.

There are no hard rules for the kinds of families that turn out the highest achievers. Most psychologists agree that parents who set tough but realistic challenges, applaud successes and go easy on failures produce kids with the greatest self-confidence.

What's harder for parents to control but has perhaps as great an effect is the level of privilege into which their kids are born. Just how wealth or poverty influences drive is difficult to predict. Grow up in a rich family, and you can inherit either the tools to achieve (think both Presidents Bush) or the indolence of the aristocrat. Grow up poor, and you can come away with either the motivation to strive (think Bill Clinton) or the inertia of the hopeless. On the whole, studies suggest it's the upper middle class that produces the greatest proportion of ambitious people — mostly because it also produces the greatest proportion of anxious people.

When measuring ambition, anthropologists divide families into four categories: poor, struggling but getting by, upper middle class, and rich. For members of the first two groups, who are fighting just to keep the electricity on and the phone bill paid, ambition is often a luxury. For the rich, it's often unnecessary. It's members of the upper middle class, reasonably safe economically but not so safe that a bad break couldn't spell catastrophe, who are most driven to improve their lot. "It's called status anxiety," says anthropologist Lowe, "and whether you're born to be concerned about it or not, you do develop it."

But some societies make you more anxious than others. The U.S. has always been a me-first culture, as befits a nation that grew from a scattering of people on a fat saddle of continent where land was often given away. That have-it-all ethos persists today, even though the resource freebies are long since gone. Other countries — where the acreage is smaller and the pickings are slimmer — came of age differently, with the need to cooperate getting etched into the cultural DNA. The American model has produced wealth, but it has come at a price — with ambition sometimes turning back on the ambitious and consuming them whole.

30 The study of high-achieving high school students conducted by Ohio State's Demerath was noteworthy for more than the stress he found the students were suffering. It also revealed the lengths to which the kids and their parents were willing to go to gain an advantage over other suffering students. Cheating was common, and most students shrugged it off as only a minor problem. A number of parents — some of whose children carried a 4.0 average — sought to have their kids classified as special-education students, which would entitle them to extra time on standardized tests. "Kids develop their own moral code," says Demerath. "They have a keen sense of competing with others and are developing identities geared to that."

Demerath got very different results when he conducted research in a very different place — Papua, New Guinea.

In the mid-1990s, he spent a year in a small village there, observing how the children learned. Usually, he found, they saw school as a noncompetitive place where it was important to succeed collectively and then move on. Succeeding at the expense of others was seen as a form of vanity that the New Guineans call "acting extra." Says Demerath: "This is an odd thing for them."

That makes tactical sense. In a country based on farming and fishing, you need to know that if you get sick and can't work your field or cast your net, someone else will do it for you. Putting on airs in the classroom is not the way to ensure that will happen.

Of course, once a collectivist not always a collectivist. Marcelo Suárez-Orozco, a professor of globalization and education at New York University, has been following 400 families that immigrated to the U.S. from Asia, Latin America and the Caribbean. Many hailed from villages where the American culture of competition is alien, but once they got here, they changed fast.

35 As a group, the immigrant children in his study are outperforming their U.S.-born peers. What's more, the adults are dramatically out-performing the immigrant families that came before them. "One hundred years ago, it took people two to three generations to achieve a middle-class standard of living," says Suárez-Orozco. "Today they're getting there within a generation."

So this is a good thing, right? Striving people come here to succeed — and do. While there are plenty of benefits that undeniably come with learning the ways of ambition, there are plenty of perils too — many a lot uglier than high school students cheating on the trig final.

Human history has always been writ in the blood of broken alliances, palace purges and strong people or nations beating up on weak ones — all in the service of someone's hunger for power or resources. "There's a point at which you find an interesting kind of nerve circuitry between optimism and hubris," says Warren Bennis, a professor of business administration at the University of Southern California and the author of three books on leadership. "It becomes an arro-gance or conceit, an inability to live without power."

While most ambitious people keep their secret Caesar tucked safely away, it can emerge surprisingly, even suddenly. Says Frans de Waal, a primatologist at the Yerkes Primate Center in Atlanta and the author of a new book, *Our Inner Ape*: "You can have a male chimp that is the most laid-back character, but one day he sees the chance to overthrow the leader and becomes a totally different male. I would say 90% of people would behave this way too. On an island with three people, they might become a little dictator."

But a yearning for supremacy can create its own set of problems. Heart attacks, ulcers and other stress-related ills are more common among high achievers — and that includes nonhuman achievers. The blood of alpha wolves routinely shows elevated levels of cortisol, the same stress hormone that is found in anxious humans. Alpha chimps even suffer ulcers and occasional heart attacks.

40 For these reasons, people and animals who have an appetite for becoming an alpha often settle contentedly into life as a beta. "The desire to be in a high position is universal," says de Waal. "But that trait has co-evolved with another skill — the skill to make the best of lower positions."

Humans not only make peace with their beta roles but they also make money from them. Among corporations, an increasingly well-rewarded portion of the workforce is made up of B players, managers and professionals some-where below the top tier. They don't do the power lunching and ribbon cutting but instead perform the highly skilled, everyday work of making the company run. As skeptical shareholders look ever more askance at overpaid corporate A-listers, the B players are becoming more highly valued. It's an adaptation that serves the needs of both the corporation and the culture around it. "Everyone has ambition," says Lowe. "Societies have to provide alternative ways for people to achieve."

Ultimately, it's that very flexibility — that multi-plicity of possible rewards — that makes dreaming big dreams and pursuing big goals worth all the bother. Ambition is an expensive impulse, one that requires an enormous investment of emotional capital. Like any investment, it can pay off in countless different kinds of coin. The trick, as any good speculator will tell you, is recognizing the riches when they come your way.

Understanding and Interpreting

1 Kluger cites a study led by economists from the University of Pittsburgh and Stanford University that looked at the difference in appetite for competition between males and females (par. 19). What connection does Kluger make between competition and ambition, and how does that connection support the goals of his essay?

2 Kluger addresses the issue of the level of financial privilege into which an individual is born. What are the advantages and disadvantages of being born into privilege? In what ways does this discussion about privilege support Kluger's goals in his argument?

3 While there are many benefits to being ambitious, there are also a number of drawbacks. According to Kluger, what are some of the possible problems associated with ambition? Do these problems outweigh the benefits in some cases? Explain.

4 Taking the entire essay into account, discuss how Kluger structures his argument. What is the order in which he makes his points, how does he develop them, and what connections does he draw between his different points?

Analyzing Language, Style, and Structure

1 Using evidence from the text, explain how Kluger develops his definition of ambition over the course of the essay. Pay specific attention to the types of evidence he uses to support his claims.

2 Throughout the essay, Kluger uses examples from the animal kingdom to make points about the roots of human ambition. To what degree are these examples helpful in reinforcing his argument, and in what ways does introducing these examples lead to possible objections?

3 Kluger begins his essay with an anecdote about two brothers who entirely transform themselves after finishing college. In what ways is this example an effective way to begin an essay about the nature of ambition?

4 In paragraph 5, Kluger asserts that ambition as a quality seems like it should be "democratically distributed," yet it isn't. What specific rebuttals does he give to refute the notion of equal distribution of ambition? Do you agree with his rebuttals, or do you think there is something he is not considering?

5 Kluger not only discusses the benefits of ambition but also raises the possibility that ambition can go too far. The examples he uses include the immoral choices that executives at Enron made in their pursuit of success (par. 10), as well as students who are "triple-booked with advanced-placement courses, sports and after-school jobs" and reportedly feeling under stress some or all of the time (par. 10). What effect do these negative examples of ambition have on his overall discussion of ambition?

6 Kluger cites a number of different findings from various research studies over the course of his essay. What do the types of research studies he cites have in common? Try to identify a pattern in the way he uses research to support his main assertions.

7 In his essay, Kluger sometimes makes an assertion about ambition based on selected evidence and then contradicts that evidence in the following paragraph. In what ways is this an effective approach to making his argument and in what ways might it undermine his purpose?

8 Kluger introduces the idea of "status anxiety" (par. 28) when discussing the influence of family and culture on ambition. How does he use this concept to further his overall argument?

Connecting, Arguing, and Extending

1 Do you consider yourself to be an ambitious person, as outlined in Kluger's essay? Do you think that ambition is of primary importance, or is it more important just to be happy—whether that means being ambitious or not?

2 Kluger begins his essay with the story of two ambitious brothers who have found considerable success in the fitness industry. These two men, according to Kluger, only became ambitious after completing their college education, when they needed to figure out how to become successful without simply inheriting the family business. In other words, they were motivated by external forces. In your personal experience, what motivates you to take action? Are you an individual who is intrinsically motivated and naturally works hard? Or do you need some kind of external motivation in order to take specific action? Cite a specific example from Kluger's article that may help explain why you believe you are extrinsically or intrinsically motivated.

3 Kluger identifies self-confidence and privilege as two driving factors that determine how ambitious a person will be. According to psychologists, self-confidence can be fostered by parents who "set tough but realistic challenges, applaud successes and go easy on failures" (par. 26). Discuss this balance that psychologists describe. Do you think these three factors are important to developing self-confident

children, and, if so, how important do you think the relationship is between self-confidence and ambition? If you don't agree with the psychologists' theories about the development of self-confidence, what do you think they are failing to recognize about human nature?

4 Kluger takes into account the experiences of students in a high-performing school who report feeling stressed or overwhelmed by the amount of work they do both in and outside of school. Create a survey for your classmates that either confirms or refutes this example in your school. In creating your survey, consider what questions you can ask that will best reveal how your peers feel about their ability to balance success in school with their ability to also enjoy their lives. Once you have created your questions and given the survey to a number of your peers, evaluate the results to see if they support the original study's conclusions or if the situation is significantly different in your school.

5 Kluger cites a study that concludes that men and women have different appetites for competition. In your experience both in and outside of school, do you see this difference between males and females? Use your personal experience to argue whether or not this difference exists, and cite specific examples that lead you to your conclusions.

Ozymandias

Percy Bysshe Shelley

Percy Bysshe Shelley (1792–1822) is considered one of the most important poets of the romantic school. Shelley's work was often controversial and led him to be rejected by his family as well as British society. Undaunted by those who claimed his work was inappropriate, Shelley continued to write prolifically until his death just before his thirtieth birthday. He drowned in a storm while attempting to sail from Leghorn, Italy, to La Spezia in his schooner, the *Don Juan*.

Keats-Shelley Memorial House, Rome, Italy/Bridgeman Images

KEY CONTEXT   In this poem, the speaker relates the account of a traveler who is walking through a vast desert when he encounters the ruins of Ozymandias, almost entirely buried in the sand. Ozymandias, more commonly known as Ramses II, was an Egyptian pharaoh of the Nineteenth Dynasty.

I met a traveller from an antique land
Who said: "Two vast and trunkless legs of stone
Stand in the desert. Near them, on the sand,
Half sunk, a shattered visage lies, whose frown,
5   And wrinkled lip, and sneer of cold command,
Tell that its sculptor well those passions read
Which yet survive, stamped on these lifeless things,
The hand that mocked them and the heart that fed.
And on the pedestal these words appear —
10   'My name is Ozymandias, king of kings:
Look on my works, ye Mighty, and despair!'
Nothing beside remains. Round the decay
Of that colossal wreck, boundless and bare
The lone and level sands stretch far away."

© BnF, Dist. RMN-Grand Palais/Art Resource, NY

Consider this photograph of the actual archaeological dig that unearthed the statue of Ramses II referred to in this poem.

How does this image reinforce ideas offered in Shelley's poem? What additional ideas does the photo offer that Shelley did not address in his poem?

Understanding and Interpreting

1 Based on the description of Ozymandias's expression, as well as the inscription on the pedestal, what kind of ruler was Ozymandias?

2 The inscription on the pedestal exhorts those who read it to look on Ozymandias's works and "despair" (l. 11). However, all that remains of the "works" are a decaying "colossal wreck" (l. 13) in the desert. In what ways is this an ironic commentary on the nature of human power?

Analyzing Language, Style, and Structure

1 The first line of the poem begins with the word "I," but then introduces a "traveller from an antique land" who then completes the remaining lines. What is the effect of this narrative structure, and how does it help convey the meaning of the poem?

2 The traveler describes the "frown, / And wrinkled lip, and sneer of cold command" (ll. 4–5) that the sculptor "mocked" (l. 8). "Mocked" can mean "described" as well as the more modern definition of "imitated in an unflattering manner." How do these two definitions of the same word create different ways of interpreting the sculptor's original goal?

Connecting, Arguing, and Extending

1 Unchecked pride, or *hubris*, is the subject of many works of literature. Choose something you have read in the past, or a movie you have seen, in which hubris plays a significant role. Discuss the role of hubris in your selected example, specifically explaining how it influenced the story.

2 If Ozymandias were able to see his own statue wearing down to nothing in the desert, do you think he would elect to change the inscription, or would he retain the original wording? Explain.

from Henry VIII

William Shakespeare

William Shakespeare (1564–1616) is considered one of the greatest playwrights in history. His plays *Romeo and Juliet*, *Macbeth*, *Hamlet*, *Julius Caesar*, *Othello*, and many others are among the most widely read and performed plays in the English language. While many of his well-known works are tragedies, Shakespeare also wrote a number of plays, such as *Henry VIII*, that focus on English history, specifically the many wars fought for the English throne.

National Portrait Gallery, London, UK/Bridgeman Images

KEY CONTEXT This excerpt comes from Shakespeare's *Henry VIII*, a history play about the mercurial king of England from 1509 to 1547. In this soliloquy from Act 3, Scene 2, the speaker, Cardinal Wolsey, has just been dismissed as an advisor to the king. As the advisor, Wolsey had power, authority, and the king's favor. Now he has lost everything — "goods, lands, tenements, / Castles, and whatsoever" — and is even in jeopardy of losing his life. Right before Wolsey speaks, the duke who announces Wolsey's fate says, "So fare you well, my little good lord cardinal," and leaves the stage.

CARDINAL WOLSEY So farewell — to the little
    good you bear me.
Farewell! a long farewell to all my greatness!
This is the state of man: to-day he puts forth
The tender leaves of hopes, to-morrow blossoms,
5 And bears his blushing honours thick upon him;
The third day comes a frost, a killing frost,
And when he thinks, good easy man, full surely
His greatness is a-ripening, nips his root,
And then he falls as I do. I have ventur'd,
10 Like little wanton boys that swim on bladders,
This many summers in a sea of glory,

But far beyond my depth. My high-blown pride
At length broke under me, and now has left me,
Weary and old with service, to the mercy
15 Of a rude stream that must for ever hide me.
Vain pomp and glory of this world, I hate ye!
I feel my heart new open'd. O how wretched
Is that poor man that hangs on princes' favors!
There is, betwixt that smile we would aspire to,
20 That sweet aspect of princes, and their ruin,
More pangs and fears than wars or women have;
And when he falls, he falls like Lucifer,
Never to hope again.

▶

Consider this painting depicting Wolsey's dismissal, with Wolsey on the far left while the Duke of Norfolk bows to take his leave and the Duke of Suffolk, Early of Surrey, and the Lord Chamberlain look on.

Contrast Wolsey with the other men in the scene. In what ways does Wolsey's expression and physical position relative to the other men sum up the moment for Wolsey? What is the significance of the king's absence from this dismissal of the man who was once his top advisor?

John Pettie, *The Disgrace of Cardinal Wolsey*, 1869. Oil on canvas, 100 cm x 155 cm. Sheffield Galleries, UK.

Understanding and Interpreting

1 Trace Wolsey's complex response to the sudden news of his dismissal by the king.

2 Consider Wolsey's assertion that "There is, betwixt that smile we would aspire to, / That sweet aspect of princes, and their ruin, / More pangs and fears than wars or women have" (ll. 19–21). Explain what Wolsey means by this statement.

Analyzing Language, Style, and Structure

1 In lines 3–9, Wolsey describes what he believes to be the condition or state of the human experience. Paraphrase his description, and then discuss how it sets up the rest of the speech.

2 In lines 9–15, Wolsey compares his current situation with that of boys who have swum too far in the ocean, where they risk drowning, and are kept afloat by air-filled sacs. Instead of air, what has carried Wolsey out of his depth? How does this simile effectively support his main assertion concerning his current situation?

3 In line 16, Wolsey denounces the "vain pomp and glory of this world" and declares "I hate ye!" How does this declaration set up the conclusion of the speech and how does his allusion to Lucifer support that conclusion?

Connecting, Arguing, and Extending

1 Do some research about how people respond to losing their jobs and the possible reasons for their responses. Then write an essay in which you explain why the loss of a job causes great anxiety beyond the mere loss of income.

2 The sudden loss of power by people in high-ranking positions is something that continues to occur in modern politics. When an individual is forced to resign from his or her position, the resignation will often be accompanied by a very public statement in which the person who is resigning expresses his or her feelings about the situation. Select an example of a recent politician who has been disgraced and forced to resign from power. Then, examine how the public speech the politician offers either attempts to explain how he or she will make up for various transgressions or attempts to explain why the dismissal is unfair. Identify the speaker's goal, and analyze how the speaker uses language to accomplish that goal.

The Rules of the Game

Amy Tan

Susan Watts/NY Daily News Archive via Getty Images

Amy Tan (b. 1952) grew up in California, has a Master of Arts in linguistics, and has written several best-selling novels, including the recent *The Valley of Amazement* (2013). Tan draws on her Chinese heritage to depict the clash of traditional Chinese culture with modern-day American customs. This short story, "The Rules of the Game," became the basis for her critically acclaimed and popular novel *The Joy Luck Club* (1989).

I was six when my mother taught me the art of invisible strength. It was a strategy for winning arguments, respect from others, and eventually, though neither of us knew it at the time, chess games.

"Bite back your tongue," scolded my mother when I cried loudly, yanking her hand toward the store that sold bags of salted plums. At home, she said, "Wise guy, he not go against wind. In Chinese we say, Come from South, blow with wind — poom! — North will follow. Strongest wind cannot be seen."

The next week I bit back my tongue as we entered the store with the forbidden candies. When my mother finished her shopping, she quietly plucked a small bag of plums from the rack and put it on the counter with the rest of the items.

My mother imparted her daily truths so she could help my older brothers and me rise above our circumstances. We lived in San Francisco's Chinatown. Like most of the other Chinese children who played in the back alleys of restaurants and curio shops, I didn't think we were poor. My bowl was always full, three five-course meals every day, beginning with a soup of mysterious things I didn't want to know the names of.

5 We lived on Waverly Place, in a warm, clean, two-bedroom flat that sat above a small Chinese bakery specializing in steamed pastries and dim sum. In the early morning, when the alley was still quiet, I could smell fragrant red beans as

they were cooked down to a pasty sweetness. By daybreak, our flat was heavy with the odor of fried sesame balls and sweet curried chicken crescents. From my bed, I would listen as my father got ready for work, then locked the door behind him, one-two-three clicks.

At the end of our two-block alley was a small sandlot playground with swings and slides well-shined down the middle with use. The play area was bordered by wood-slat benches where old-country people sat cracking roasted watermelon seeds with their golden teeth and scattering the husks to an impatient gathering of gurgling pigeons. The best playground, however, was the dark alley itself. It was crammed with daily mysteries and adventures. My brothers and I would peer into the medicinal herb shop, watching old Li dole out onto a stiff sheet of white paper the right amount of insect shells, saffron-colored seeds, and pungent leaves for his ailing customers. It was said that he once cured a woman dying of an ancestral curse that had eluded the best of American doctors. Next to the pharmacy was a printer who specialized in gold-embossed wedding invitations and festive red banners.

Farther down the street was Ping Yuen Fish Market. The front window displayed a tank crowded with doomed fish and turtles struggling to gain footing on the slimy green-tiled sides. A hand-written sign informed tourists, "Within this store, is all for food, not for pet." Inside, the butchers with their bloodstained white smocks deftly gutted the fish while customers cried out their orders and shouted, "Give me your freshest," to which the butchers always protested, "All are freshest." On less crowded market days, we would inspect the crates of live frogs and crabs which we were warned not to poke, boxes of dried cuttlefish, and row upon row of iced prawns, squid, and slippery fish. The sanddabs made me shiver each time; their eyes lay on one flattened side and reminded me of my mother's story of a careless girl who ran into a crowded street and was crushed by a cab. "Was smash flat," reported my mother.

At the corner of the alley was Hong Sing's, a four-table cafe with a recessed stairwell in front that led to a door marked "Tradesmen." My brothers and I believed the bad people emerged from this door at night. Tourists never went to Hong Sing's, since the menu was printed only in Chinese. A Caucasian man with a big camera once posed me and my playmates in front of the restaurant. He had us move to the side of the picture window so the photo would capture the roasted duck with its head dangling from a juice-covered rope. After he took the picture, I told him he should go into Hong Sing's and eat dinner. When he smiled and asked me what they served, I shouted, "Guts and duck's feet and octopus gizzards!" Then I ran off with my friends, shrieking with laughter as we scampered across the alley and hid in the entryway grotto of the China Gem Company, my heart pounding with hope that he would chase us.

My mother named me after the street that we lived on: Waverly Place Jong, my official name for important American documents. But my family called me Meimei, "Little Sister." I was the youngest, the only daughter. Each morning before school, my mother would twist and yank on my thick black hair until she had formed two tightly wound pigtails. One day, as she struggled to weave a hard-toothed comb through my disobedient hair, I had a sly thought.

10   I asked her, "Ma, what is Chinese torture?" My mother shook her head. A bobby pin was wedged between her lips. She wetted her palm and smoothed the hair above my ear, then pushed the pin in so that it nicked sharply against my scalp.

"Who say this word?" she asked without a trace of knowing how wicked I was being. I shrugged my shoulders and said, "Some boy in my class said Chinese people do Chinese torture."

What does this picture, taken in San Francisco's Chinatown, suggest about how the cultural traditions of China have been translated in an American setting?

"Chinese people do many things," she said simply. "Chinese people do business, do medicine, do painting. Not lazy like American people. We do torture. Best torture."

My older brother Vincent was the one who actually got the chess set. We had gone to the annual Christmas party held at the First Chinese Baptist Church at the end of the alley. The missionary ladies had put together a Santa bag of gifts donated by members of another church. None of the gifts had names on them. There were separate sacks for boys and girls of different ages. One of the Chinese parishioners had donned a Santa Claus costume and a stiff paper beard with cotton balls glued to it. I think the only children who thought he was the real thing were too young to know that Santa Claus was not Chinese. When my turn came up, the Santa man asked me how old I was. I thought it was a trick question; I was seven according to the American formula and eight by the Chinese calendar. I said I was born on March 17, 1951. That seemed to satisfy him. He then solemnly asked if I had been a very, very good girl this year and did I believe in Jesus Christ and obey my parents. I knew the only answer to that. I nodded back with equal solemnity.

Having watched the older children opening their gifts, I already knew that the big gifts were not necessarily the nicest ones. One girl my age got a large coloring book of biblical characters, while a less greedy girl who selected a smaller box received a glass vial of lavender toilet water. The sound of the box was also important. A ten-year-old boy had chosen a box that jangled when he shook it. It was a tin globe of the world with a slit for inserting money. He must have thought it was full of dimes and nickels, because when he saw that it had just ten pennies, his face fell with such undisguised disappointment that his mother slapped the side of his head and led him out of the church hall, apologizing to the crowd for her son who had such bad manners he couldn't appreciate such a fine gift.

15   As I peered into the sack, I quickly fingered the remaining presents, testing their weight, imagining what they contained. I chose a heavy, compact one that was wrapped in shiny silver foil and a red satin ribbon. It was a twelve-pack of Life Savers and I spent the rest of the party

arranging and rearranging the candy tubes in the order of my favorites. My brother Winston chose wisely as well. His present turned out to be a box of intricate plastic parts; the instructions on the box proclaimed that when they were properly assembled he would have an authentic miniature replica of a World War II submarine.

Vincent got the chess set, which would have been a very decent present to get at a church Christmas party, except it was obviously used and, as we discovered later, it was missing a black pawn and a white knight. My mother graciously thanked the unknown benefactor, saying, "Too good. Cost too much." At which point, an old lady with fine white, wispy hair nodded toward our family and said with a whistling whisper, "Merry, merry Christmas."

When we got home, my mother told Vincent to throw the chess set away. "She not want it. We not want it," she said, tossing her head stiffly to the side with a tight, proud smile. My brothers had deaf ears. They were already lining up the chess pieces and reading from the dog-eared instruction book. I watched Vincent and Winston play during Christmas week. The chessboard seemed to hold elaborate secrets waiting to be untangled. The chessmen were more powerful than old Li's magic herbs that cured ancestral curses. And my brothers wore such serious faces that I was sure something was at stake that was greater than avoiding the tradesmen's door to Hong Sing's.

"Let me! Let me!" I begged between games when one brother or the other would sit back with a deep sigh of relief and victory, the other annoyed, unable to let go of the outcome. Vincent at first refused to let me play, but when I offered my Life Savers as replacements for the buttons that filled in for the missing pieces, he relented. He chose the flavors: wild cherry for the black pawn and peppermint for the white knight. Winner could eat both.

As our mother sprinkled flour and rolled out small doughy circles for the steamed dumplings that would be our dinner that night, Vincent explained the rules, pointing to each piece. "You have sixteen pieces and so do I. One king and queen, two bishops, two knights, two castles, and eight pawns. The pawns can only move forward one step, except on the first move. Then they can move two. But they can only take men by moving crossways like this, except in the beginning, when you can move ahead and take another pawn."

20   "Why?" I asked as I moved my pawn. "Why can't they move more steps?" "Because they're pawns," he said.

"But why do they go crossways to take other men? Why aren't there any women and children?"

"Why is the sky blue? Why must you always ask stupid questions?" asked Vincent. "This is a game. These are the rules. I didn't make them up. See. Here in the book." He jabbed a page with a pawn in his hand. "Pawn. P-A-W-N. Pawn. Read it yourself."

My mother patted the flour off her hands. "Let me see book," she said quietly. She scanned the pages quickly, not reading the foreign English symbols, seeming to search deliberately for nothing in particular.

"This American rules," she concluded at last. "Every time people come out from foreign country, must know rules. You not know, judge say, Too bad, go back. They not telling you why so you can use their way go forward. They say, Don't know why, you find out yourself. But they knowing all the time. Better you take it, find out why yourself." She tossed her head back with a satisfied smile.

25   I found out about all the whys later. I read the rules and looked up all the big words in a dictionary. I borrowed books from the Chinatown library. I studied each chess piece, trying to absorb the power each contained.

I learned about opening moves and why it's important to control the center early on; the shortest distance between two points is straight down the middle. I learned about the middle game and why tactics between two adversaries are like clashing ideas; the one who plays better has the clearest plans for both attacking and getting out of traps. I learned why it is essential in the endgame to have foresight, a mathematical understanding of all possible moves, and patience; all weaknesses and advantages become evident to a strong adversary and are obscured to a tiring opponent. I discovered that for the whole game one must gather invisible strengths and see the endgame before the game begins.

I also found out why I should never reveal "why" to others. A little knowledge withheld is a great advantage one should store for future use. That is the power of chess. It is a game of secrets in which one must show and never tell.

I loved the secrets I found within the sixty-four black and white squares. I carefully drew a handmade chessboard and pinned it to the wall next to my bed, where I would stare for hours at imaginary battles. Soon I no longer lost any games or Life Savers, but I lost my adversaries. Winston and Vincent decided they were more interested in roaming the streets after school in their Hopalong Cassidy cowboy hats.

On a cold spring afternoon, while walking home from school, I detoured through the playground at the end of our alley. I saw a group of old men, two seated across a folding table playing a game of chess, others smoking pipes, eating peanuts, and watching. I ran home and grabbed Vincent's chess set, which was bound in a cardboard box with rubber bands. I also carefully selected two prized rolls of Life Savers. I came back to the park and approached a man who was observing the game.

30 "Want to play?" I asked him. His face widened with surprise and he grinned as he looked at the box under my arm.

"Little sister, been a long time since I play with dolls," he said, smiling benevolently. I quickly put the box down next to him on the bench and displayed my retort.

Lau Po, as he allowed me to call him, turned out to be a much better player than my brothers. I lost many games and many Life Savers. But over the weeks, with each diminishing roll of candies, I added new secrets. Lau Po gave me the names. The Double Attack from the East and West Shores. Throwing Stones on the Drowning Man. The Sudden Meeting of the Clan. The Surprise from the Sleeping Guard. The Humble Servant Who Kills the King. Sand in the Eyes of Advancing Forces. A Double Killing Without Blood.

There were also the fine points of chess etiquette. Keep captured men in neat rows, as well-tended prisoners. Never announce "Check" with vanity, lest someone with an unseen sword slit your throat. Never hurl pieces into the sandbox after you have lost a game, because then you must find them again, by yourself, after apologizing to all around you. By the end of the summer, Lau Po had taught me all he knew, and I had become a better chess player.

A small weekend crowd of Chinese people and tourists would gather as I played and defeated my opponents one by one. My mother would join the crowds during these outdoor exhibition games. She sat proudly on the bench, telling my admirers with proper Chinese humility, "Is luck."

35 A man who watched me play in the park suggested that my mother allow me to play in local chess tournaments. My mother smiled graciously, an answer that meant nothing. I desperately wanted to go, but I bit back my tongue. I knew she would not let me play among strangers. So as we walked home I said in a small voice that I didn't want to play in the local tournament. They would have American rules. If I lost, I would bring shame on my family.

"Is shame you fall down nobody push you," said my mother.

During my first tournament, my mother sat with me in the front row as I waited for my turn. I frequently bounced my legs to unstick them from the cold metal seat of the folding chair. When my name was called, I leapt up. My mother unwrapped something in her lap. It was her chang, a small tablet of red jade which held the sun's fire. "Is luck," she whispered, and tucked it into my dress pocket. I turned to my opponent, a fifteen-year-old boy from Oakland. He looked at me, wrinkling his nose.

As I began to play, the boy disappeared, the color ran out of the room, and I saw only my white pieces and his black ones waiting on the other side. A light wind began blowing past my ears. It whispered secrets only I could hear.

"Blow from the South," it murmured. "The wind leaves no trail." I saw a clear path, the traps to avoid. The crowd rustled. "Shhh! Shhh!" said the corners of the room. The wind blew stronger. "Throw sand from the East to distract him." The knight came forward ready for the sacrifice. The wind hissed, louder and louder. "Blow, blow, blow. He cannot see. He is blind now. Make him lean away from the wind so he is easier to knock down."

40 "Check," I said, as the wind roared with laughter. The wind died down to little puffs, my own breath.

My mother placed my first trophy next to a new plastic chess set that the neighborhood Tao society had given to me. As she wiped each piece with a soft cloth, she said, "Next time win more, lose less."

"Ma, it's not how many pieces you lose," I said. "Sometimes you need to lose pieces to get ahead."

"Better to lose less, see if you really need."

At the next tournament, I won again, but it was my mother who wore the triumphant grin.

45 "Lost eight piece this time. Last time was eleven. What I tell you? Better off lose less!" I was annoyed, but I couldn't say anything.

I attended more tournaments, each one farther away from home. I won all games, in all divisions. The Chinese bakery downstairs from our flat displayed my growing collection of trophies in its window, amidst the dust-covered cakes that were never picked up. The day after I won an important regional tournament, the window encased a fresh sheet cake with whipped-cream frosting and red script saying "Congratulations, Waverly Jong, Chinatown Chess Champion." Soon after that, a flower shop, headstone engraver, and funeral parlor offered to sponsor me in national tournaments. That's when my mother decided I no longer had to do the dishes. Winston and Vincent had to do my chores.

"Why does she get to play and we do all the work," complained Vincent. "Is new American rules," said my mother. "Meimei play, squeeze all her brains out for win chess. You play, worth squeeze towel."

By my ninth birthday, I was a national chess champion. I was still some 429 points away from grand-master status, but I was touted as the Great American Hope, a child prodigy and a girl to boot. They ran a photo of me in *Life* magazine next to a quote in which Bobby Fischer said, "There will never be a woman grand master." "Your move, Bobby," said the caption.

The day they took the magazine picture I wore neatly plaited braids clipped with plastic barrettes trimmed with rhinestones. I was playing in a large high school auditorium that echoed with phlegmy coughs and the squeaky rubber knobs of chair legs sliding across freshly waxed wooden floors. Seated across from me was an American man, about the same age as Lau Po, maybe fifty. I remember that his sweaty brow seemed to weep at my every move. He wore a dark, malodorous suit. One of his pockets was stuffed with a great white kerchief on which he wiped his palm before sweeping his hand over the chosen chess piece with great flourish.

50 In my crisp pink-and-white dress with scratchy lace at the neck, one of two my mother had sewn for these special occasions, I would clasp my hands under my chin, the delicate points of my elbows poised lightly on the table in the manner my mother had shown me for posing for the press. I would swing my patent leather shoes back and forth like an impatient child riding on a school bus. Then I would pause, suck in my lips, twirl my chosen piece in midair as if undecided, and then firmly plant it in its new threatening place, with a triumphant smile thrown back at my opponent for good measure.

I no longer played in the alley of Waverly Place. I never visited the playground where the pigeons and old men gathered. I went to school, then directly home to learn new chess secrets, cleverly concealed advantages, more escape routes.

But I found it difficult to concentrate at home. My mother had a habit of standing over me while I plotted out my games. I think she thought of herself as my protective ally. Her lips would be sealed tight, and after each move I made, a soft "Hmmmmph" would escape from her nose.

"Ma, I can't practice when you stand there like that," I said one day. She retreated to the kitchen and made loud noises with the pots and pans. When the crashing stopped, I could see out of the corner of my eye that she was standing in the doorway. "Hmmmmph!" Only this one came out of her tight throat.

My parents made many concessions to allow me to practice. One time I complained that the bedroom I shared was so noisy that I couldn't think. Thereafter, my brothers slept in a bed in the living room facing the street. I said I couldn't finish my rice; my head didn't work right when my stomach was too full. I left the table with half-finished bowls and nobody complained. But there was one duty I couldn't avoid. I had to accompany my mother on Saturday market days when I had no tournament to play. My mother would proudly walk with me, visiting many shops, buying very little. "This my daughter Wave-ly Jong," she said to whoever looked her way.

55 One day after we left a shop I said under my breath, "I wish you wouldn't do that, telling everybody I'm your daughter." My mother stopped walking.

Crowds of people with heavy bags pushed past us on the sidewalk, bumping into first one shoulder, than another.

"Aii-ya. So shame be with mother?" She grasped my hand even tighter as she glared at me.

I looked down. "It's not that, it's just so obvious. It's just so embarrassing." "Embarrass you be my daughter?" Her voice was cracking with anger. "That's not what I meant. That's not what I said."

"What you say?"

60 I knew it was a mistake to say anything more, but I heard my voice speaking, "Why do you have to use me to show off? If you want to show off, then why don't you learn to play chess?"

My mother's eyes turned into dangerous black slits. She had no words for me, just sharp silence.

I felt the wind rushing around my hot ears. I jerked my hand out of my mother's tight grasp and spun around, knocking into an old woman. Her bag of groceries spilled to the ground.

"Aii-ya! Stupid girl!" my mother and the woman cried. Oranges and tin cans careened down the sidewalk. As my mother stooped to help the old woman pick up the escaping food, I took off.

I raced down the street, dashing between people, not looking back as my mother screamed shrilly, "Meimei! Meimei!" I fled down an alley, past dark, curtained shops and merchants washing the grime off their windows. I sped into the sunlight, into a large street crowded with tourists examining trinkets and souvenirs. I ducked into another dark alley, down another street, up another alley. I ran until it hurt and I realized I had nowhere to go, that I was not running from anything. The alleys contained no escape routes.

65   My breath came out like angry smoke. It was cold. I sat down on an upturned plastic pail next to a stack of empty boxes, cupping my chin with my hands, thinking hard. I imagined my mother, first walking briskly down one street or another looking for me, then giving up and returning home to await my arrival. After two hours, I stood up on creaking legs and slowly walked home. The alley was quiet and I could see the yellow lights shining from our flat like two tiger's eyes in the night. I climbed the sixteen steps to the door, advancing quietly up each so as not to make any warning sounds. I turned the knob; the door was locked. I heard a chair moving, quick steps, the locks turning — click! click! click! — and then the door opened.

"About time you got home," said Vincent. "Boy, are you in trouble."

He slid back to the dinner table. On a platter were the remains of a large fish, its fleshy head still connected to bones swimming upstream in vain escape. Standing there waiting for my punishment, I heard my mother speak in a dry voice.

"We not concerning this girl. This girl not have concerning for us." Nobody looked at me. Bone chopsticks clinked against the inside of bowls being emptied into hungry mouths.

I walked into my room, closed the door, and lay down on my bed. The room was dark, the ceiling filled with shadows from the dinnertime lights of neighboring flats.

70   In my head, I saw a chessboard with sixty-four black and white squares. Opposite me was my opponent, two angry black slits. She wore a triumphant smile. "Strongest wind cannot be seen," she said.

Her black men advanced across the plane, slowly marching to each successive level as a single unit. My white pieces screamed as they scurried and fell off the board one by one. As her men drew closer to my edge, I felt myself growing light. I rose up into the air and flew out the window. Higher and higher, above the alley, over the tops of tiled roofs, where I was gathered up by the wind and pushed up toward the night sky until everything below me disappeared and I was alone.

I closed my eyes and pondered my next move.

Understanding and Interpreting

1 The first nine paragraphs of the story are devoted to a detailed description of Waverly's neighborhood, which is located in San Francisco's Chinatown. What are some of the challenges that Waverly must face growing up in a non-Western community, while at the same time striving to become fully accepted in the surrounding Western culture?

2 Waverly asks her mother to explain what Chinese torture is after a classmate tells her that "Chinese people do Chinese torture" (par. 11). Her mother responds by explaining that Chinese people do many things well, including torture. Torturing well is generally not something to be proud of, so what message is Waverly's mother trying to convey?

3 The giving and receiving of gifts often involves a complex set of social or cultural rules. When Waverly and her brothers go to the annual Christmas party held at the First Chinese Baptist Church, she describes the subtle rules that the children must follow while the gifts are being distributed (par. 13). What are the rules that Waverly details? In what ways do they match general rules around Christmas gift giving and receiving familiar in Western culture, and in what ways are the rules specifically related to Waverly's culture?

4 When Waverly first begins to play chess with her brothers, she becomes frustrated with rules that do not make any sense to her. Her brother Vincent suggests that her questions are stupid and that she just needs to accept that "[t]his is a game. These are the rules" (par. 22). Her mother responds to Waverly's question by saying, "This American rules. [. . .] Every time people come out from foreign country, must know rules" (par. 25). In what ways do these responses from Vincent and her mother reflect a central theme in the story as a whole?

5 As Waverly progresses as a chess player, she explains that she "loved the secrets [she] found within the sixty-four black and white squares" (par. 28). Lau Po, an old man who further mentors Waverly, teaches her even more secrets. These secrets were not written down into chess instructions that she read, but they were crucial to her success as a chess player. Discuss the connection between the unwritten secrets that lead to her success in chess and the unwritten secrets of life that Waverly must learn.

6 When Waverly begins winning many chess matches and her reputation begins to grow, her mother sits "proudly" and watches her, yet when asked why her daughter is doing so well, she explains that it is luck that allows Waverly to win. Is this a dismissive statement or is there another reason that Waverly's mother responds in this manner? Does this example of "proper Chinese humility" (par. 34) serve to diminish Waverly's confidence in herself? Explain.

7 As Waverly becomes a national chess champion and is touted as the Great American Hope, her family dynamic begins to change. How does her newfound success change her relationship with her brothers and her mother?

8 Waverly eventually becomes embarrassed by the fact that her mother proudly tells everyone that Waverly is her daughter. This deeply upsets her mother and leads to an argument. The story concludes with Waverly imagining her mother as an opponent in a chess match and saying, "I closed my eyes and pondered my next move." Explain the meaning of this statement in the context of the story as a whole.

Analyzing Language, Style, and Structure

1 The first sentence in the short story references the "art of invisible strength," which establishes that there is an invisible force under the surface from the beginning of the story. Find four or five examples within the first five paragraphs that reinforce this idea that there is something more going on than what is on the surface, and connect those examples to the larger discussion of the cultural forces Waverly must contend with as she develops a greater understanding of the interaction between Chinese and American culture.

2 In paragraphs 5–9, Waverly provides detailed descriptions of the playground, the medicinal herb shop, the fish market, and a neighborhood café. Citing specific examples from the text, explain how she conveys the specific qualities of her neighborhood in terms of the strong influence of Chinese culture.

3 Whenever Waverly recounts conversations with her mother, she re-creates the dialogue accurately, without correcting her mother's grammatical errors. What is the effect of presenting these conversations in this way, rather than changing her mother's responses to standard English?

4 Tan begins her story by having Waverly describe her neighborhood, and then moves into detailed explanation of Waverly's first exposure to chess and her initial learning process. Suddenly, Waverly explains that she has become a national chess competitor (par. 48). What is the effect of Tan's spending considerable narrative time describing the backstory and very little time describing how Waverly moved up the ranks to become a competitor on the national level?

5 The story is framed by a quote from Waverly's mother, "Strongest wind cannot be seen" (pars. 2 and 70). In what ways does this quote serve as an appropriate opening, as well as conclusion, to Waverly's narrative?

Connecting, Arguing, and Extending

1 At one point in the story the late chess grand master Bobby Fischer is quoted as saying, "There will never be a woman grand master." Others have asserted that chess is a game more suited to males than females. However, studies have shown that the reason there are more male chess grand masters than female ones is simply that far more males play chess. In what ways does Waverly combat stereotypical images of young girls and in what ways does her personality lend itself to the game of chess?

2 Rules play a major role in this story; most of the important rules, however, seem to be unwritten. Think about your experience in school. What are some of the unwritten rules when it comes to successfully operating within the different classes you attend each day? What are some of the unwritten rules when it

comes to spending time with your peers? Waverly's family has specific unwritten rules as well, and the same is probably true of your family. What are the unwritten rules within your home?

After thinking about these rules in your classrooms, with your peers, and in your home, discuss how you learned all of these rules considering they were never explicitly written down in a guidebook.

3 America has long been a country to which people from many different cultures have brought their own traditions and at the same time learned how to operate within a distinctly American culture. Write an argument in which you defend the value of living in a country that embraces multiple cultural influences in spite of the challenges this creates.

---

from Don Quixote

Miguel de Cervantes

Real Academia de la Historia, Madrid, Spain/Index/Bridgeman Images

Translated by Samuel Putnam

Miguel de Cervantes (1547–1616) was a Spanish poet, playwright, and novelist. His masterpiece, *Don Quixote* (1605), had significant influence on Western literature and established Cervantes as one of the most important Spanish writers of all time. He is held in the same high regard in the Spanish literary tradition as Shakespeare is in the English tradition. Cervantes joined the Spanish military and eventually became a soldier known for his bravery on the battlefield, receiving grievous wounds while fighting against the Ottoman Empire. Even with two serious chest wounds and a left hand that was completely maimed, Cervantes remained undaunted and continued to fight until he was captured and imprisoned for five years. He returned to his homeland after a ransom secured his release. Cervantes went on to write plays but did not find success as a playwright. His greatest literary achievement, *Don Quixote*, is widely regarded as the first modern novel. Translated into over sixty languages, it eventually became a global best seller

KEY CONTEXT   Fully titled *The Ingenious Gentleman Don Quixote of La Mancha, Don Quixote* (pronounced Kee-*ho*-tay) was originally intended to satirize the chivalric romantic fiction of Cervantes's time — grand adventures that focused on quests by heroic knights. The novel's protagonist, Don Quixote, is an elderly knight who has read many of these chivalric romances and decides that he too will seek adventure. He sets out with his squire, Sancho Panza, and the result is a series of comic encounters that poke fun at the overblown adventures described in the popular romances.

In the following selection, which includes one of the most famous scenes from the novel, Sancho and Don Quixote encounter a set of windmills that Don Quixote believes are great giants that he must vanquish. He believes that a magician named Frestón, who actually is a figment of his own imagination, has stolen his books and enchanted the windmills. That scene is followed by an encounter with a group of friars from the Order of St. Benedict, who Don Quixote believes are "enchanters" he must engage in battle.

Of the Good Fortune Which the Valorous Don Quixote Had in the Terrifying and Never-Before-Imagined Adventure of the Windmills, along with Other Events That Deserve to Be Suitably Recorded

At this point they caught sight of thirty or forty windmills which were standing on the plain there, and no sooner had Don Quixote laid eyes upon them than he turned to his squire and said, "Fortune is guiding our affairs better than we could have wished; for you see there before you, friend Sancho Panza, some thirty or more lawless giants with whom I mean to do battle. I shall deprive them of their lives, and with the spoils from this encounter we shall begin to enrich ourselves; for this is righteous warfare, and it is a great service to God to remove so accursed a breed from the face of the earth."

"What giants?" said Sancho Panza.

"Those that you see there," replied his master, "those with the long arms some of which are as much as two leagues in length."

"But look, your Grace, those are not giants but windmills; and what appear to be arms are their wings which, when whirled in the breeze, cause the millstone to go."

5   "It is plain to be seen," said Don Quixote, "that you have had little experience in this matter of adventures. If you are afraid, go off to one side and say your prayers while I am engaging them in fierce, unequal combat."

Saying this, he gave spurs to his steed Rocinante, without paying any heed to Sancho's warning that these were truly windmills and not giants that he was riding forth to attack. Nor even when he was close upon them did he perceive what they really were, but shouted at the top of his lungs, "Do not seek to flee, cowards and vile creatures that you are, for it is but a single knight with whom you have to deal!"

At that moment a little wind came up and the big wings began turning.

"Though you flourish as many arms as did the giant Briareus," said Don Quixote when he perceived this, "you still shall have to answer to me."

He thereupon commended himself with all his heart to his lady Dulcinea, beseeching her to succor him in this peril; and, being well covered with his shield and with his lance at rest, he bore down upon them at a full gallop and fell upon the first mill that stood in his way, giving a thrust at the wing, which was whirling at such a speed that his lance was broken into bits and both horse and horseman went rolling over the plain, very much battered indeed. Sancho upon his donkey came hurrying to his master's assistance as fast as he could, but when he reached the spot, the knight was unable to move, so great was the shock with which he and Rocinante had hit the ground.

10   "God help us!" exclaimed Sancho, "did I not tell your Grace to look well, that those were nothing but windmills, a fact which no one could fail to see unless he had other mills of the same sort in his head?"

"Be quiet, friend Sancho," said Don Quixote. "Such are the fortunes of war, which more than any other are subject to constant change. What is more, when I come to think of it, I am sure that this must be the work of that magician Frestón, the one who robbed me of my study and my books, and who has thus changed the giants into windmills in order to deprive me of the glory of overcoming them, so great is the enmity that he bears me; but in the end his evil arts shall not prevail against this trusty sword of mine."

"May God's will be done," was Sancho Panza's response. And with the aid of his squire the knight was once more mounted on Rocinante, who stood there with one shoulder half out of joint. And so, speaking of the adventure that had just befallen them, they continued along the Puerto Lápice highway; for there, Don Quixote said, they could not fail to find many and varied adventures, this being a much traveled thoroughfare. The only thing was, the knight was exceedingly downcast over the loss of his lance.

"I remember," he said to his squire, "having read of a Spanish knight by the name of Diego Pérez de Vargas, who, having broken his sword in battle, tore from an oak a heavy bough or branch and with it did such feats of valor that day, and pounded so many Moors, that he came to be known as Machuca, and he and his descendants from that day forth have been called Vargas y Machuca. I tell you this because I too intend to provide myself with just such a bough as the one he wielded, and with it I propose to do such exploits that you shall deem yourself fortunate to have been found worthy to come with me and behold and witness things that are almost beyond belief."

"God's will be done," said Sancho. "I believe everything that your Grace says; but straighten yourself up in the saddle a little, for you seem to be slipping down on one side, owing, no doubt, to the shaking-up that you received in your fall."

15   "Ah, that is the truth," replied Don Quixote, "and if I do not speak of my sufferings, it is for the reason that it is not permitted knights-errant to complain of any wound whatsoever, even though their bowels may be dropping out."

"If that is the way it is," said Sancho, "I have nothing more to say; but, God knows, it would suit me better if your Grace did complain when something hurts him. I can assure you that I mean to do so, over the least little thing that ails me — that is, unless the same rule applies to squires as well."

Don Quixote laughed long and heartily over Sancho's simplicity, telling him that he might complain as much as he liked and where and when he liked, whether he had good cause or not; for he had read nothing to the contrary in the ordinances of chivalry. Sancho then called his master's attention to the fact that it was time to eat. The knight replied that he himself had no need of food at the moment, but his squire might eat whenever he chose. Having been granted this permission, Sancho seated himself as best he could upon his beast, and, taking out from his saddlebags the provisions that he had stored there, he rode along leisurely behind his master, munching his victuals and taking a good, hearty swig now and then at the leather flask in a manner that might well have caused the biggest-bellied tavernkeeper of Málaga to envy him. Between draughts he gave not so much as a thought to any promise that his master might have made him, nor did he look upon it as any hardship, but rather as good sport, to go in quest of adventures however hazardous they might be.

The short of the matter is, they spent the night under some trees, from one of which Don Quixote tore off a withered bough to serve him as a lance, placing it in the lance head from which he had removed the broken one. He did not sleep all night long for thinking of his lady Dulcinea; for this was in accordance with what he had read in his books, of men of arms in the forest or desert places who kept a wakeful vigil, sustained by the memory of their ladies fair. Not so with Sancho, whose stomach was full, and not with chicory water. He fell into a dreamless slumber, and had not his master called him, he would not have been awakened either by the rays of the sun

▶

Consider the artist's rendering of Don Quixote's imaginary world and the reality that Sancho Panza sees.

In what ways does this painting illustrate the "disconnect" between Don Quixote's perception of the world and reality?

Charles-Antoine Coypel, *Don Quixote Being Led by Folly*, 1714–1734. Oil on canvas, 48.5″ x 48.5″. Chateau, Compiègne, France.

in his face or by the many birds who greeted the coming of the new day with their merry song.

Upon arising, he had another go at the flask, finding it somewhat more flaccid than it had been the night before, a circumstance which grieved his heart, for he could not see that they were on the way to remedying the deficiency within any very short space of time. Don Quixote did not wish any breakfast; for, as has been said, he was in the habit of nourishing himself on savorous memories. They then set out once more along the road to Puerto Lápice, and around there in the afternoon they came in sight of the pass that bears that name.

20   "There," said Don Quixote as his eyes fell upon it, "we may plunge our arms up to the elbow in what are known as adventures. But I must warn you that even though you see me in the greatest peril in the world, you are not to lay hand upon your sword to defend me, unless it be that those who attack me are rabble and men of low degree, in which case you may very well

come to my aid; but if they be gentlemen, it is in no wise permitted by the laws of chivalry that you should assist me until you yourself shall have been dubbed a knight."

"Most certainly, sir," replied Sancho, "your Grace shall be very well obeyed in this; all the more so for the reason that I myself am of a peaceful disposition and not fond of meddling in the quarrels and feuds of others. However, when it comes to protecting my own person, I shall not take account of those laws of which you speak, seeing that all laws, human and divine, permit each one to defend himself whenever he is attacked."

"I am willing to grant you that," assented Don Quixote, "but in this matter of defending me against gentlemen you must restrain your natural impulses."

"I promise you I shall do so," said Sancho. "I will observe this precept as I would the Sabbath day."

As they were conversing in this manner, there appeared in the road in front of them two friars of the Order of St. Benedict, mounted upon drom-edaries—for the she-mules they rode were certainly no smaller than that. The friars wore travelers' spectacles and carried sunshades, and behind them came a coach accompanied by four or five men on horseback and a couple of mule-teers on foot. In the coach, as was afterwards learned, was a lady of Biscay, on her way to Seville to bid farewell to her husband, who had been appointed to some high post in the Indies. The religious were not of her company although they were going by the same road.

25   The instant Don Quixote laid eyes upon them he turned to his squire. "Either I am mistaken or this is going to be the most famous adventure that ever was seen; for those black-clad figures that you behold must be, and with-out any doubt are, certain enchanters who are bearing with them a captive princess in that coach, and I must do all I can to right this wrong."

"It will be worse than the windmills," declared Sancho. "Look you, sir, those are Benedictine friars and the coach must be that of some travelers. Mark well what I say and what you do, lest the devil lead you astray."

"I have already told you, Sancho," replied Don Quixote, "that you know little where the subject of adventures is concerned. What I am saying to you is the truth, as you shall now see."

With this, he rode forward and took up a position in the middle of the road along which the friars were coming, and as soon as they appeared to be within earshot he cried out to them in a loud voice, "O devilish and monstrous beings, set free at once the highborn princesses whom you bear captive in that coach, or else prepare at once to meet your death as the just punishment of your evil deeds."

The friars drew rein and sat there in aston-ishment, marveling as much at Don Quixote's appearance as at the words he spoke. "Sir Knight," they answered him, "we are neither devilish nor monstrous but religious of the Order of St. Benedict who are merely going our way. We know nothing of those who are in that coach, nor of any captive princesses either."

30   "Soft words," said Don Quixote, "have no effect on me. I know you for what you are, lying rabble!" And without waiting for any further parley he gave spur to Rocinante and, with lowered lance, bore down upon the first friar with such fury and intrepidity that, had not the fellow tumbled from his mule of his own accord, he would have been hurled to the ground and either killed or badly wounded. The second religious, seeing how his companion had been treated, dug his legs into his she-mule's flanks and scurried away over the countryside faster than the wind.

Seeing the friar upon the ground, Sancho Panza slipped lightly from his mount and, falling upon him, began stripping him of his habit. The two mule drivers accompanying the religious thereupon came running up and asked Sancho why he was doing this. The latter replied that the friar's garments belonged to him as legitimate spoils of the battle that his master Don Quixote had just won. The muleteers, however, were lads with no sense of humor, nor did they know what all this talk of spoils and battles was about; but, perceiving that Don Quixote had ridden off to one side to converse with those inside the coach, they pounced upon Sancho, threw him to the ground, and proceeded to pull out the hair of his beard and kick him to a pulp, after which they went off and left him stretched out there, bereft at once of breath and sense.

Without losing any time, they then assisted the friar to remount. The good brother was trem-bling all over from fright, and there was not a speck of color in his face, but when he found himself in the saddle once more, he quickly spurred his beast to where his companion, at some little distance, sat watching and waiting to see what the result of the encounter would be. Having no curiosity as to the final outcome of the fray, the two of them now resumed their journey, making more signs of the cross than the devil would be able to carry upon his back.

Meanwhile Don Quixote, as we have said, was speaking to the lady in the coach.

"Your beauty, my lady, may now dispose of your person as best may please you, for the arrogance of your abductors lies upon the ground, overthrown by this good arm of mine; and in order that you may not pine to know the name of your liberator, I may inform you that I am Don Quixote de la Mancha, knight-errant and adventurer and captive of the peerless and beauteous Doña Dulcinea del Toboso. In payment of the favor which you have received from me, I ask nothing other than that you return to El Toboso and on my behalf pay your respects to this lady, telling her that it was I who set you free."

35 One of the squires accompanying those in the coach, a Biscayan, was listening to Don Quixote's words, and when he saw that the knight did not propose to let the coach proceed upon its way but was bent upon having it turn back to El Toboso, he promptly went up to him, seized his lance, and said to him in bad Castilian and worse Biscayan, "Go, *caballero*, and bad luck go with you; for by the God that created me, if you do not let this coach pass, me kill you or me no Biscayan."

Don Quixote heard him attentively enough and answered him very mildly, "If you were a *caballero*, which you are not, I should already have chastised you, wretched creature, for your foolhardiness and your impudence."

"Me no *caballero*?" cried the Biscayan. "Me swear to God, you lie like a Christian. If you will but lay aside your lance and unsheath your sword, you will soon see that you are carrying water to the cat! Biscayan on land, gentleman at sea, but a gentleman in spite of the devil, and you lie if you say otherwise."

" ' "You shall see as to that presently," said Agrajes,' " Don Quixote quoted. He cast his lance to the earth, drew his sword, and, taking his buckler on his arm, attacked the Biscayan with intent to slay him. The latter, when he saw his adversary approaching, would have liked to dismount from his mule, for she was one of the worthless sort that are let for hire and he had no confidence in her; but there was no time for this, and so he had no choice but to draw his own sword in turn and make the best of it. However, he was near enough to the coach to be able to snatch a cushion from it to serve him as a shield; and then they fell upon each other as though they were mortal enemies. The rest of those present sought to make peace between them but did not succeed, for the Biscayan with his disjointed phrases kept muttering that if they did not let him finish the battle then he himself would have to kill his mistress and anyone else who tried to stop him.

The lady inside the carriage, amazed by it all and trembling at what she saw, directed her coachman to drive on a little way; and there from a distance she watched the deadly combat, in the course of which the Biscayan came down with a great blow on Don Quixote's shoulder, over the top of the latter's shield, and had not the knight been clad in armor, it would have split him to the waist.

40 Feeling the weight of this blow, Don Quixote cried out, "O lady of my soul, Dulcinea, flower of beauty, succor this your champion who out of gratitude for your many favors finds himself in so perilous a plight!" To utter these words, lay hold of his sword, cover himself with his buckler, and attack the Biscayan was but the work of a moment; for he was now resolved to risk everything upon a single stroke.

As he saw Don Quixote approaching with so dauntless a bearing, the Biscayan was well aware of his adversary's courage and forthwith determined to imitate the example thus set him. He kept himself protected with his cushion, but he was unable to get his she-mule to budge to one side or the other, for the beast, out of sheer exhaustion and being, moreover, unused to such childish play, was incapable of taking a single step. And so, then, as has been stated, Don Quixote was approaching the wary Biscayan, his sword raised on high and with the firm resolve of cleaving his enemy in two; and the Biscayan was awaiting the knight in the same posture, cushion in front of him and with uplifted sword. All the bystanders were trembling with suspense at what would happen as a result of the terrible blows that were threatened, and the lady in the coach and her maids were making a thousand vows and offerings to all the images and shrines in Spain, praying that God would save them all and the lady's squire from this great peril that confronted them.

But the unfortunate part of the matter is that at this very point the author of the history breaks off and leaves the battle pending, excusing himself upon the ground that he has been unable to find anything else in writing concerning the exploits of Don Quixote beyond those already set forth. It is true, on the other hand, that the second author of this work could not bring himself to believe that so unusual a chronicle would have been consigned to oblivion, nor that the learned ones of La Mancha were possessed of so little curiosity as not to be able to discover in their archives or registry offices certain papers that have to do with this famous knight. Being convinced of this, he did not despair of coming upon the end of this pleasing story, and Heaven favoring him, he did find it, as shall be related in the second part.

Understanding and Interpreting

1 After realizing that the windmills are not giants, Don Quixote explains his mistake to Sancho by claiming that it was a trick that turned them from giants into windmills (par. 11). This is the first of a number of examples in which Don Quixote bends reality to fit his delusions rather than admitting that he was mistaken. How do Don Quixote's repeated failures to see the world as it really is rather than as he wishes to see it develop a theme over the course of the chapter as a whole?

2 Don Quixote acts "in accordance with what he had read in his books" (par. 18) during his adventure. Based on the choices that Don Quixote makes, what are the ideals that he is trying to uphold? In what ways do these ideals lead him to consistently misunderstand the situations in which he finds himself?

3 Don Quixote takes this quest very seriously and often references the importance of the journey. Sancho Panza is loyal to Don Quixote but seems to have a slightly different attitude concerning their quest. Describe Sancho's attitude using specific examples from the text.

4 Sancho claims that "all laws, human and divine, permit each one to defend himself whenever he is attacked" (par. 21). Explain Sancho's reasoning and discuss how it might conflict with Don Quixote's high ideals.

5 Before he challenges the friars of St. Benedict, Don Quixote dismisses Sancho's attempt to explain the reality of the situation (par. 27). How does Don Quixote's continued insistence that he is right and Sancho is deluded contribute to the point that Cervantes is making?

6 Describe the encounter with the friars of the Order of St. Benedict. What is Don Quixote's perception and how does that contrast with the reality?

7 Cervantes uses humor to develop serious ideas. What is one of his main ideas and why is humor an effective way to communicate this idea?

Analyzing Language, Style, and Structure

1 This chapter from *Don Quixote* exemplifies the humor in Cervantes's satire. Discuss the ways in which Don Quixote's language exaggerates the battles he is involved in and lends humor to the scenes.

2 After his lance is broken during his encounter with the windmills, Don Quixote makes a new lance using the branch of a tree (par. 18). In what ways does his new "weapon" further emphasize the ridiculousness of Don Quixote's quest, and how does Cervantes's continued use of hyperbole make a larger point?

3 Even though Sancho knows that Don Quixote has mistaken the friars for knights, he attempts to take a gown from one of the friars who has been knocked off of his mule (par. 31). What purpose does Cervantes's use of understatement to describe Sancho's treatment by the mule drivers serve at this point in the story?

4 This chapter concludes with a detailed description of the fight between Don Quixote and a Biscayan. Which details create a scene of a fierce battle and which details create a more comic scene?

5 The story of Don Quixote's encounter with the Biscayan abruptly ends without divulging the outcome of the fight. What effect does Cervantes achieve by ending the chapter in this way?

Connecting, Arguing, and Extending

1 In *Don Quixote*, Cervantes uses humor to address serious ideas. Although it can sometimes be challenging to explain why something is humorous, consider other pieces you have read that you found funny and speculate about the reasons why you found those pieces humorous. In general, do you think that using humor is an effective way to make more serious points or do you find that humor conflicts with the goal of raising important questions?

2 Comedies like *The Simpsons*, a show that has been running for more than twenty-five years, will often use satire to comment on some aspect of American culture. Choose an example of television satire that you have seen lately. Discuss how the satire raises serious cultural questions or concerns.

3 Choose a shortcoming in education that you believe needs to change and discuss how you could use satire to point out that shortcoming to others. First think about the specific problem, and then decide which audience could most directly address the problem you have identified. In what ways could you humorously bring up the problems that you believe need to be addressed to that specific audience?

4 In *Don Quixote,* Cervantes wishes to call important aspects of contemporary culture into question. Mark Twain's novel *Huckleberry Finn* is another example of a novel that challenged notions that were held at the time by certain groups of people. Both novels use humor to address serious concerns. Write an argument in which you discuss how using humor to critique a serious problem can be a particularly effective approach. You may use *Don Quixote* or another satirical novel of literary merit as the source for your argument.

ENTERING THE CONVERSATION
RISK AND REWARD

Making Connections

1 Both W. H. Auden in his poem "Musée des Beaux Arts" (p. 318) and William Carlos Williams in his poem "Landscape with the Fall of Icarus" (p. 320) refer directly to Bruegel's painting *Landscape with the Fall of Icarus* (p. 319). Revisit each poem and compare and contrast their interpretations of Bruegel's work.

2 Percy Bysshe Shelley's poem "Ozymandias" (p. 332) and the excerpt from Shakespeare's *Henry VIII* (p. 334) feature individuals who once had power and then lost it. In Shelley's poem, the individual is the once-great "king of kings" Ozymandias, and in the speech from *Henry VIII* it is the once-powerful advisor to the king, Cardinal Wolsey. Compare and contrast the fundamental causes of Ozymandias's and Cardinal Wolsey's loss of power and the extent to which each was responsible for his own downfall. Use evidence from the texts to support your analysis.

3 In his essay "Ambition" (p. 324), Jeffrey Kluger explores some of the science behind ambition and the drive to win. In the short story "The Rules of the Game" (p. 336), Amy Tan's protagonist, Waverly, is an individual who exhibits a strong will to win as she learns how to play chess and navigate two distinct cultures. Explain how the ideas in Kluger's piece are either illustrated or contradicted by Waverly's actions. Use evidence from each text to support your analysis.

4 In Brian Aldiss's poem "Flight 063" (p. 322), the speaker asks why the focus is on the fall of Icarus rather than the flight, pointing out that "[b]efore the fall, the flight was" achieved. The traveler in Shelley's poem "Ozymandias" (p. 332) discovers the remains of a statue that, when it was constructed, glorified a once-mighty king but now stands as a monument to his downfall. Using these two texts as your sources, pair up with a peer and prepare a debate in which you argue whether ambition is its own reward, or if it is better to play it safe and not risk the dire consequences of experiencing a great downfall.

5 Culturally, what are the legacies of the character Don Quixote and the character Icarus? Are both admired? Pitied? What lessons have we learned from these stories, and how do those lessons compare?

Synthesizing Sources

1 In this Conversation, you have explored both the concept of ambition and the need to balance a will to succeed with restraint. The mythological Icarus was an inspiration for many of the texts. Synthesize evidence from at least three of the texts in this Conversation, as well as your personal experience and observations, and incorporate this evidence into a coherent, well-developed argument for your own position on whether Icarus should be considered a hero or a failure. Your argument should be the focus of your essay. Avoid merely summarizing the sources.

2 For some people, ambition is by its very definition negative. To those who hold this view, being ambitious suggests a drive that is inherently aggressive and self-serving. Other people view ambition as a positive force that pushes individuals to achievements previously thought impossible, such as sending astronauts to the moon. Referring to at least three texts in this Conversation, discuss at what point ambition goes from being a positive quality to becoming a negative trait.

3 Is ambition more often the subject for cautionary tales warning us of hubris, or for inspirational messages urging us on to greatness? Base your response on at least three texts from this Conversation, as well as any novels or films that you may be familiar with.

4 Icarus stands as a testament to the will to succeed in the face of impossible odds. There are many examples from history that illustrate the same ambition that led Icarus to his doom. Explorers died trying to reach places previously unknown to them. Test pilots have died attempting to stretch the limits of aviation. Mountain climbers have died attempting to summit previously unreached heights. Do some research and select a person from history whose ambition led to greatness, but at a great cost. In your research, determine what drove this historical figure to achieve and how his or her accomplishments contributed to history. Refer to at least two sources from this Conversation as you present your findings.

CONVERSATION

VOICES OF REBELLION

Sadly, injustice is all around us. Sometimes it might be in a faraway country where political prisoners are being held by an oppressive government, and sometimes it's closer to home where individuals are being discriminated against because of their race, ethnicity, gender, religious affiliation, or sexual orientation. What do we do when we see, read about, or even directly face an injustice? Too often, people change the channel or look away, but some people speak out, reaching out to broad audiences and leading them to act.

It takes an astonishing amount of ambition to look at the world around you and decide that your voice will be the one to reshape it. And yet that's exactly what the writers in this Conversation did. Through the power of their rhetoric they fought oppression, and through their words and deeds, they changed the world.

It has been said that the pen is mightier than the sword, but is that always true? Should the American Founding Fathers, for instance, have relied only on the pen to free the colonies from British rule? Is there a time when words fail and action is required? Is violence a necessary strategy in seeking justice, and if so, at what point does it become necessary? At what point is restraint called for? Is nonviolent resistance more effective than violent resistance?

In this Conversation, you'll hear from people who have different views on the issue of restraint, some who chose violence, like Thomas Paine and Nelson Mandela, and some who chose nonviolence, who relied unreservedly on the power of language as their weapon, like Martin Luther King Jr. and Malala Yousafzai.

TEXTS

Martin Luther King Jr. / I Have Been to the Mountaintop (nonfiction)

Nelson Mandela / *from* An Ideal for Which I am Prepared to Die (nonfiction)

Thomas Paine / *from* Common Sense (nonfiction)

Malala Yousafzai / Speech to the United Nations Youth Assembly (nonfiction)

Carrie Chapman Catt / *from* Women's Suffrage Is Inevitable (nonfiction)

George Orwell / *from* Animal Farm (fiction)

I Have Been to the Mountaintop

Martin Luther King Jr.

© Marvin Koner/Corbis

Dr. Martin Luther King Jr. (1929–1968) was a Baptist minister and civil rights leader whose contributions improved race relations in America in the twentieth century. Through his political activism, King played a vital role in ending the legal segregation that was widespread in the South at the time. King's leadership was instrumental in the creation of the Civil Rights Act of 1964 and the Voting Rights Act of 1965, two significant legislative acts of the twentieth century that expanded equality for African American citizens. King also helped to organize the 1963 March on Washington, where he delivered his legendary "I Have a Dream" speech. For his work in civil rights, King was awarded the Nobel Peace Prize in 1964.

KEY CONTEXT In March of 1968, Martin Luther King traveled to Memphis, Tennessee, to lend his support and inspiration to the black sanitation and public works employees who were on strike for better wages and fair treatment. Violence between police and protestors had broken out at the rally on March 28. This speech, "I Have Been to the Mountaintop," was delivered to an audience of supporters on April 3, 1968, and responds to that violence of a few days before.

Tragically, this speech was King's last, as he was assassinated the following day by a southerner who saw King's ideas as a threat to the racist ideas held by many in the South at that time.

Thank you very kindly, my friends. As I listened to Ralph Abernathy and his eloquent and generous introduction and then thought about myself, I wondered who he was talking about. It's always good to have your closest friend and associate to say something good about you. And Ralph Abernathy is the best friend that I have in the world. I'm delighted to see each of you here tonight in spite of a storm warning. You reveal that you are determined to go on anyhow.

Something is happening in Memphis; something is happening in our world. And you know, if I were standing at the beginning of time, with the possibility of taking a kind of general and panoramic view of the whole of human history up to now, and the Almighty said to me, "Martin Luther King, which age would you like to live in?" I would take my mental flight by Egypt and I would watch God's children in their magnificent trek from the dark dungeons of Egypt through, or rather across the Red Sea, through the wilderness on toward the promised land. And in spite of its magnificence, I wouldn't stop there.

I would move on by Greece and take my mind to Mount Olympus. And I would see Plato, Aristotle, Socrates, Euripides and Aristophanes assembled around the Parthenon. And I would watch them around the Parthenon as they discussed the great and eternal issues of reality. But I wouldn't stop there.

I would go on, even to the great heyday of the Roman Empire. And I would see developments around there, through various emperors and leaders. But I wouldn't stop there.

I would even come up to the day of the Renaissance, and get a quick picture of all that the Renaissance did for the cultural and aesthetic life of man. But I wouldn't stop there.

I would even go by the way that the man for whom I am named had his habitat. And I would watch Martin Luther as he tacked his ninety-five theses on the door at the church of Wittenberg. But I wouldn't stop there.

I would come on up even to 1863, and watch a vacillating President by the name of Abraham Lincoln finally come to the conclusion that he had to sign the Emancipation Proclamation. But I wouldn't stop there.

I would even come up to the early thirties, and see a man grappling with the problems of the bankruptcy of his nation. And come with an eloquent cry that we have nothing to fear but "fear itself." But I wouldn't stop there.

Strangely enough, I would turn to the Almighty, and say, "If you allow me to live just a few years in the second half of the twentieth century, I will be happy."

Now that's a strange statement to make, because the world is all messed up. The nation is sick. Trouble is in the land; confusion all around. That's a strange statement. But I know, some-how, that only when it is dark enough can you see the stars. And I see God working in this period of the twentieth century in a way that men, in some strange way, are responding.

Something is happening in our world. The masses of people are rising up. And wherever they are assembled today, whether they are in Johannesburg, South Africa; Nairobi, Kenya; Accra, Ghana; New York City; Atlanta, Georgia; Jackson, Mississippi; or Memphis, Tennessee — the cry is always the same: "We want to be free."

And another reason that I'm happy to live in this period is that we have been forced to a point where we are going to have to grapple with the problems that men have been trying to grapple with through history, but the demands didn't force them to do it. Survival demands that we grapple with them. Men, for years now, have been talking about war and peace. But now, no longer can they just talk about it. It is no longer a choice between violence and nonviolence in this world; it's nonviolence or nonexistence. That is where we are today.

And also in the human rights revolution, if something isn't done, and done in a hurry, to bring the colored peoples of the world out of their long years of poverty, their long years of hurt and neglect, the whole world is doomed. Now, I'm just happy that God has allowed me to live in this period to see what is unfolding. And I'm happy that He's allowed me to be in Memphis.

I can remember — I can remember when Negroes were just going around as Ralph has said, so often, scratching where they didn't itch, and laughing when they were not tickled. But that day is all over. We mean business now, and we are determined to gain our rightful place in God's world.

And that's all this whole thing is about. We aren't engaged in any negative protest and in any negative arguments with anybody. We are saying that we are determined to be men. We are determined to be people. We are saying — We are saying that we are God's children. And that we are God's children, we don't have to live like we are forced to live.

Now, what does all of this mean in this great period of history? It means that we've got to stay together. We've got to stay together and main-tain unity. You know, whenever Pharaoh wanted to prolong the period of slavery in Egypt, he had a favorite, favorite formula for doing it. What was that? He kept the slaves fighting among them-selves. But whenever the slaves get together, something happens in Pharaoh's court, and he cannot hold the slaves in slavery. When the slaves get together, that's the beginning of getting out of slavery. Now let us maintain unity.

Secondly, let us keep the issues where they are. The issue is injustice. The issue is the refusal of Memphis to be fair and honest in its dealings with its public servants, who happen to be sanitation workers. Now, we've got to keep attention on that. That's always the problem with a little violence. You know what happened the other day, and the press dealt only with the window-breaking. I read the articles. They very seldom got around to mentioning the fact that one thousand, three hundred sanitation workers are on strike, and that Memphis is not being fair to them, and that Mayor Loeb is in dire need of a doctor. They didn't get around to that.

Now we're going to march again, and we've got to march again, in order to put the issue where it is supposed to be — and force everybody to see that there are thirteen hundred of God's children here suffering, sometimes going hungry, going through dark and dreary nights wondering how this thing is going to come out. That's the issue. And we've got to say to the nation: We know how it's coming out. For when people get caught up with that which is right and they are willing to sacrifice for it, there is no stopping point short of victory.

We aren't going to let any mace stop us. We are masters in our nonviolent movement in disarming police forces; they don't know what to do. I've seen them so often. I remember in Birmingham, Alabama, when we were in that majestic struggle there, we would move out of the 16th Street Baptist Church day after day; by the hundreds we would move out. And Bull Connor would tell them to send the dogs forth, and they did come; but we just went before the dogs singing, "Ain't gonna let nobody turn me around."

20   Bull Connor next would say, "Turn the fire hoses on." And as I said to you the other night, Bull Connor didn't know history. He knew a kind of physics that somehow didn't relate to the transphysics that we knew about. And that was the fact that there was a certain kind of fire that no water could put out. And we went before the fire hoses; we had known water. If we were Baptist or some other denominations, we had been immersed. If we were Methodist, and some others, we had been sprinkled, but we knew water. That couldn't stop us.

And we just went on before the dogs and we would look at them; and we'd go on before the water hoses and we would look at it, and we'd just go on singing "Over my head I see freedom in the air." And then we would be thrown in the paddy wagons, and sometimes we were stacked in there like sardines in a can. And they would throw us in, and old Bull would say, "Take 'em off," and they did; and we would just go in the paddy wagon singing, "We Shall Overcome." And every now and then we'd get in jail, and we'd see the jailers looking through the windows being moved by our prayers, and being moved by our words and our songs. And there was a power there which Bull Connor couldn't adjust to; and so we ended up transforming Bull into a steer, and we won our struggle in Birmingham. Now we've got to go on in Memphis just like that. I call upon you to be with us when we go out Monday.

Now about injunctions: We have an injunction and we're going into court tomorrow morning to fight this illegal, unconstitutional injunction. All we say to America is, "Be true to what you said on paper." If I lived in China or even Russia, or any totalitarian country, maybe I could understand some of these illegal injunctions. Maybe I could understand the denial of certain basic First Amendment privileges, because they hadn't committed themselves to that over there. But somewhere I read of the freedom of assembly. Somewhere I read of the freedom of speech. Somewhere I read of the freedom of press. Somewhere I read that the greatness of America is the right to protest for right. And so just as I say, we aren't going to let dogs or water hoses turn us around, we aren't going to let any injunction turn us around. We are going on.

We need all of you. And you know what's beautiful to me is to see all of these ministers of the Gospel. It's a marvelous picture. Who is it that is supposed to articulate the longings and aspirations of the people more than the preacher? Somehow the preacher must have a kind of fire shut up in his bones. And whenever injustice is around he tell it. Somehow the preacher must be an Amos, and saith, "When God speaks who can but prophesy?" Again with Amos, "Let justice roll down like waters and righteousness like a mighty stream." Somehow the preacher must say with Jesus, "The Spirit of the Lord is upon me, because he hath anointed me, and he's anointed me to deal with the problems of the poor."

And I want to commend the preachers, under the leadership of these noble men: James Lawson, one who has been in this struggle for many years; he's been to jail for struggling; he's been kicked out of Vanderbilt University for this struggle, but he's still going on, fighting for the rights of his people. Reverend Ralph Jackson, Billy Kiles; I could just go right on down the list, but time will not permit. But I want to thank all of them. And I want you to thank them, because so often, preachers aren't concerned about anything but themselves. And I'm always happy to see a relevant ministry.

25   It's all right to talk about "long white robes over yonder," in all of its symbolism. But ultimately people want some suits and dresses and shoes to wear down here! It's all right to talk about "streets flowing with milk and honey," but God has commanded us to be concerned about the slums down here, and his children who can't eat three square meals a day. It's all right to talk about the new Jerusalem, but one day, God's preacher must talk about the new New York, the new Atlanta, the new Philadelphia, the new Los Angeles, the new Memphis, Tennessee. This is what we have to do.

This political cartoon by Joe Heller of the *Green Bay Press-Gazette* depicts the *Stone of Hope* statue at the Martin Luther King Jr. Memorial in Washington, D.C., along with one of King's quotes.

Choose a quote from this speech that would be a suitable replacement for the one in this cartoon. Explain why you chose the quote you did, and how it works with the image in the cartoon to capture King's legacy.

Now the other thing we'll have to do is this: Always anchor our external direct action with the power of economic withdrawal. Now, we are poor people. Individually, we are poor when you compare us with white society in America. We are poor. Never stop and forget that collectively — that means all of us together — collectively we are richer than all the nations in the world, with the exception of nine. Did you ever think about that? After you leave the United States, Soviet Russia, Great Britain, West Germany, France, and I could name the others, the American Negro collectively is richer than most nations of the world. We have an annual income of more than thirty billion dollars a year, which is more than all of the exports of the United States, and more than the national budget of Canada. Did you know that? That's power right there, if we know how to pool it.

We don't have to argue with anybody. We don't have to curse and go around acting bad with our words. We don't need any bricks and bottles. We don't need any Molotov cocktails. We just need to go around to these stores, and to these massive industries in our country, and say, "God sent us by here, to say to you that you're not treating his children right. And we've come by here to ask you to make the first item on your agenda fair treatment, where God's children are concerned. Now, if you are not prepared to do that, we do have an agenda that we must follow. And our agenda calls for withdrawing economic support from you."

And so, as a result of this, we are asking you tonight, to go out and tell your neighbors not to buy Coca-Cola in Memphis. Go by and tell them not to buy Sealtest milk. Tell them not to buy — what is the other bread? — Wonder Bread. And what is the other bread company, Jesse? Tell them not to buy Hart's bread. As Jesse Jackson has said, up to now, only the garbage men have been feeling pain; now we must kind of re-distribute the pain. We are choosing these

companies because they haven't been fair in their hiring policies; and we are choosing them because they can begin the process of saying they are going to support the needs and the rights of these men who are on strike. And then they can move on downtown and tell Mayor Loeb to do what is right.

But not only that, we've got to strengthen black institutions. I call upon you to take your money out of the banks downtown and deposit your money in Tri-State Bank. We want a "bank-in" movement in Memphis. Go by the savings and loan association. I'm not asking you something that we don't do ourselves at SCLC. Judge Hooks and others will tell you that we have an account here in the savings and loan association from the Southern Christian Leadership Conference. We are telling you to follow what we are doing. Put your money there. You have six or seven black insurance companies here in the city of Memphis. Take out your insurance there. We want to have an "insurance-in."

30   Now these are some practical things that we can do. We begin the process of building a greater economic base. And at the same time, we are putting pressure where it really hurts. I ask you to follow through here.

Now, let me say as I move to my conclusion that we've got to give ourselves to this struggle until the end. Nothing would be more tragic than to stop at this point in Memphis. We've got to see it through. And when we have our march, you need to be there. If it means leaving work, if it means leaving school — be there. Be concerned about your brother. You may not be on strike. But either we go up together, or we go down together.

Let us develop a kind of dangerous un-selfishness. One day a man came to Jesus, and he wanted to raise some questions about some vital matters of life. At points he wanted to trick Jesus, and show him that he knew a little more than Jesus knew and throw him off base. . . .

Now that question could have easily ended up in a philosophical and theological debate. But Jesus immediately pulled that question from mid-air, and placed it on a dangerous curve between Jerusalem and Jericho. And he talked about a certain man, who fell among thieves. You remember that a Levite and a priest passed by on the other side. They didn't stop to help him. And finally a man of another race came by. He got down from his beast, decided not to be compassionate by proxy. But he got down with him, administered first aid, and helped the man in need. Jesus ended up saying, this was the good man, this was the great man, because he had the capacity to project the "I" into the "thou," and to be concerned about his brother.

Now you know, we use our imagination a great deal to try to determine why the priest and the Levite didn't stop. At times we say they were busy going to a church meeting, an ecclesiastical gathering, and they had to get on down to Jerusalem so they wouldn't be late for their meeting. At other times we would speculate that there was a religious law that "One who was engaged in religious ceremonials was not to touch a human body twenty-four hours before the ceremony." And every now and then we begin to wonder whether maybe they were not going down to Jerusalem — or down to Jericho, rather to organize a "Jericho Road Improvement Association." That's a possibility. Maybe they felt that it was better to deal with the problem from the causal root, rather than to get bogged down with an individual effect.

35   But I'm going to tell you what my imagination tells me. It's possible that those men were afraid. You see, the Jericho road is a dangerous road. I remember when Mrs. King and I were first in Jerusalem. We rented a car and drove from Jerusalem down to Jericho. And as soon as we got on that road, I said to my wife, "I can see why Jesus used this as the setting for his parable." It's a winding, meandering road. It's really

conducive for ambushing. You start out in Jerusalem, which is about 1200 miles — or rather 1200 feet above sea level. And by the time you get down to Jericho, fifteen or twenty minutes later, you're about 2200 feet below sea level. That's a dangerous road. In the days of Jesus it came to be known as the "Bloody Pass." And you know, it's possible that the priest and the Levite looked over that man on the ground and wondered if the robbers were still around. Or it's possible that they felt that the man on the ground was merely faking. And he was acting like he had been robbed and hurt, in order to seize them over there, lure them there for quick and easy seizure. And so the first question that the priest asked — the first question that the Levite asked was, "If I stop to help this man, what will happen to me?" But then the Good Samaritan came by. And he reversed the question: "If I do not stop to help this man, what will happen to him?"

That's the question before you tonight. Not, "If I stop to help the sanitation workers, what will happen to my job?" Not, "If I stop to help the sanitation workers what will happen to all of the hours that I usually spend in my office every day and every week as a pastor?" The question is not, "If I stop to help this man in need, what will happen to me?" The question is, "If I do not stop to help the sanitation workers, what will happen to them?" That's the question.

Let us rise up tonight with a greater readiness. Let us stand with a greater determination. And let us move on in these powerful days, these days of challenge to make America what it ought to be. We have an opportunity to make America a better nation. And I want to thank God, once more, for allowing me to be here with you.

You know, several years ago, I was in New York City autographing the first book that I had written. And while sitting there autographing books, a demented black woman came up. The only question I heard from her was, "Are you Martin Luther

HAPPY BIRTHDAY, DR KING...

...AND THANKS FOR EVERYTHING

AFRICAN AMERICAN JUDGES, MAYORS, CEO's, SHERIFFS, BANK-MANAGERS, PROFESSORS, DOCTORS, COACHES, POLICE OFFICERS, T.V. ANCHORS, MEMBERS OF CONGRESS, SENATORS, CABINET MEMBERS, AND PRESIDENT OF THE USA

MACLEOD
FACEBOOK.COM/MACLEODCARTOONS

▶

Martin Luther King's ideas concerning civil rights and equality were not just for his generation.

Explain how this political cartoon attempts to express the full influence of King as his ideas continue to shape modern American culture.

King?" And I was looking down writing, and I said, "Yes." And the next minute I felt something beating on my chest. Before I knew it I had been stabbed by this demented woman. I was rushed to Harlem Hospital. It was a dark Saturday afternoon. And that blade had gone through, and the X-rays revealed that the tip of the blade was on the edge of my aorta, the main artery. And once that's punctured, you're drowned in your own blood—that's the end of you.

It came out in the *New York Times* the next morning, that if I had merely sneezed, I would have died. Well, about four days later, they allowed me, after the operation, after my chest had been opened, and the blade had been taken out, to move around in the wheel chair in the hospital. They allowed me to read some of the mail that came in, and from all over the states and the world, kind letters came in. I read a few, but one of them I will never forget. I had received one from the President and the Vice-President. I've forgotten what those telegrams said. I'd received a visit and a letter from the Governor of New York, but I've forgotten what that letter said. But there was another letter that came from a little girl, a young girl who was a student at the White Plains High School. And I looked at that letter, and I'll never forget it. It said simply,

Dear Dr. King,

I am a ninth-grade student at the White Plains High School.

And she said,

While it should not matter, I would like to mention that I'm a white girl. I read in the paper of your misfortune, and of your suffering. And I read that if you had sneezed, you would have died. And I'm simply writing you to say that I'm so happy that you didn't sneeze.

40   And I want to say tonight—I want to say tonight that I too am happy that I didn't sneeze. Because if I had sneezed, I wouldn't have been around here in 1960, when students all over the South started sitting-in at lunch counters. And I knew that as they were sitting-in, they were really standing up for the best in the American dream, and taking the whole nation back to those great wells of democracy which were dug deep by the Founding Fathers in the Declaration of Independence and the Constitution.

If I had sneezed, I wouldn't have been around here in 1961, when we decided to take a ride for freedom and ended segregation in interstate travel.

If I had sneezed, I wouldn't have been around here in 1962, when Negroes in Albany,

Georgia, decided to straighten their backs up. And whenever men and women straighten their backs up, they are going somewhere, because a man can't ride your back unless it is bent.

If I had sneezed — If I had sneezed I wouldn't have been here in 1963, when the black people of Birmingham, Alabama, aroused the conscience of this nation, and brought into being the Civil Rights Bill.

If I had sneezed, I wouldn't have had a chance later that year, in August, to try to tell America about a dream that I had had.

45   If I had sneezed, I wouldn't have been down in Selma, Alabama, to see the great Movement there.

If I had sneezed, I wouldn't have been in Memphis to see a community rally around those brothers and sisters who are suffering.

I'm so happy that I didn't sneeze.

And they were telling me —. Now, it doesn't matter, now. It really doesn't matter what happens now. I left Atlanta this morning, and as we got started on the plane, there were six of us. The pilot said over the public address system, "We are sorry for the delay, but we have Dr. Martin Luther King on the plane. And to be sure that all of the bags were checked, and to be sure that nothing would be wrong with on the plane, we had to check out everything carefully. And we've had the plane protected and guarded all night."

And then I got into Memphis. And some began to say the threats, or talk about the threats that were out. What would happen to me from some of our sick white brothers?

50   Well, I don't know what will happen now. We've got some difficult days ahead. But it really doesn't matter with me now, because I've been to the mountaintop.

And I don't mind.

Like anybody, I would like to live a long life. Longevity has its place. But I'm not concerned about that now. I just want to do God's will. And He's allowed me to go up to the mountain. And I've looked over. And I've seen the Promised Land. I may not get there with you. But I want you to know tonight, that we, as a people, will get to the promised land!

And so I'm happy, tonight.

I'm not worried about anything.

55   I'm not fearing any man!

Mine eyes have seen the glory of the coming of the Lord!!

Understanding and Interpreting

1 At the opening of this 1968 speech, Martin Luther King Jr. references several historical points, including the crossing of the Red Sea, Greek philosophers assembled around the Parthenon, the heyday of the Roman Empire, the Renaissance, the signing of the Emancipation Proclamation, and the Great Depression. To varying degrees all of these references have to do with the question of individual rights within the larger system. In what ways do King's comments regarding the situation in Memphis have to do with individual rights — both the individual rights of the sanitation workers, specifically, and civil rights for African Americans in general?

2 King claims that were he given the choice to live in any time period, he would choose the second half of the twentieth century even though the world is "all messed up" (par. 10). Explain King's reasoning.

3 King argues for nonviolent solutions to the problems he outlines. What are some examples of nonviolent solutions that King offers in his speech, and how do those solutions support his overall argument?

4 In Birmingham, Alabama, civil rights protestors were abused by the authorities. Specifically, Bull Connor, the Commissioner of Public Safety for the city, ordered that protestors be sprayed with high-powered

fire hoses. King asserts that the water coming out of those fire hoses could not stop the protestors because, as baptized Christians, they "knew water" (par. 20). How does King's example of overcoming abuse in Birmingham support his argument regarding the protests in Memphis, Tennessee?

5 King tells the audience that "either we go up together, or we go down together" (par. 31). How is this message of unity reinforced in other parts of King's speech and why is it so important to the overall themes in the speech?

6 The speech includes a letter King received from a young white girl after he had been stabbed and almost killed at a book signing in New York City. While recovering in the hospital, King learned that the attack had come so close to the largest artery in his body, that if he had sneezed after the attack he would have bled to death. In the letter the girl expresses how happy she is that King "didn't sneeze." Discuss how King uses this letter, and specifically the phrase "didn't sneeze," in his speech.

7 When King references the Promised Land (par. 52), he is talking about the land where, according to the Old Testament, the Jewish people would finally be able to live in peace and freedom after years of captivity in Egypt. What is the promised land that King is assuring the members of his audience they all will one day find?

8 This speech would be King's last, as he was shot to death by an assassin on April 4, 1968, just one day after this speech. Some people believe that his closing comments indicate that he knew that his life was in danger. Citing specific examples from the speech, explain how people may come to this conclusion.

Analyzing Language, Style, and Structure

1 King begins his speech with a hypothetical situation in which he could choose to live in any time. What specific historical times does he reference, and what is the effect of his putting the speech he is about to give in Memphis, Tennessee, within a broader historical context?

2 When King alludes to Abraham Lincoln (par. 7), he describes the former president as "vacillating" and indicates that Lincoln "had to sign the Emancipation Proclamation." What do these specific choices indicate about how King views Lincoln's role in freeing the slaves?

3 King argues that the Egyptian pharaohs maintained their power by keeping the "slaves fighting among themselves" (par. 16). How does this analogy connect to the situation in the United States in the 1960s, and to the situation in Memphis specifically?

4 Explain why King brings up China (par. 22), Russia (par. 22), and other totalitarian countries during a speech that focuses on events in Memphis, Tennessee.

5 An ordained Baptist minister himself, King references other religious leaders, as well as the Bible, frequently. What is the effect of King's integrating the idea of faith in general, and religion specifically, into his argument?

6 King turns his attention to the economic power of the community. What is the advantage of focusing on the kinds of goods people purchase? Why does he focus on what people are buying when the larger issue is one of justice?

7 Explain what King means when he talks about a "dangerous unselfishness," and how does his example about Jesus in paragraphs 32 and 33 reinforce King's meaning?

8 King alludes to a trip that he and his wife took to Jericho. How does King's recounting of this trip reinforce one of his main ideas?

9 Explain the effect of the repetition of the introductory phrase "If I had sneezed" in the series of statements in paragraphs 41–46.

Connecting, Arguing, and Extending

1 One of the hallmarks of the speeches of Martin Luther King is their inspirational quality. His speeches were memorable not only for their eloquence but for spurring people to action. Think of a particularly memorable speech that you have heard or watched on video. What is it about that speech that makes it memorable? When you first heard it, in what ways did it motivate you—did you take some kind of action or change the way that you thought about something? In general, what makes speeches inspirational or memorable? Are there certain features that need to be present in every inspirational speech, or does the level of the speech's success have more to do with the subject of the speech than the delivery? Explain your thinking.

2 Martin Luther King is a central figure in American culture who symbolizes the difficult struggle toward attaining basic human rights for all people regardless of race, creed, economic standing, or gender. While this particular speech may be unfamiliar to many people, King's "I Have a Dream" speech, in which he asserts the fundamental equality of all people, is familiar to most Americans. In that speech King utters one of his most famous lines, declaring, "I have a dream that my four little children will one day live in a nation where they will not be judged by the color of their skin but by the content of their character." In what ways do the ideas offered in "I Have Been to the Mountaintop" reflect this basic principle?

3 King preached nonviolent protest as the best way to achieve the goals of the civil rights movement. To this day, there are current events that illustrate the fact that complete equality for all has not yet been achieved. Write an argument in which you support or challenge the position that Martin Luther King's approach to social and political change has been effective. Use specific examples from current events in support of your argument.

4 Not all civil rights leaders agreed with Dr. King's nonviolent approach to gaining equality. Research other strategies used during the civil rights era and discuss to what extent they were effective, or counterproductive, in bringing about change.

from An Ideal for Which I Am Prepared to Die

Nelson Mandela

Nobel Peace Prize recipient Nelson Mandela (1918–2013) was a South African political activist who eventually became the president of South Africa from 1994 to 1999. His actions as a political activist fighting for equality resulted in his spending twenty-seven years in prison.

© David Brauchli/Sygma/Corbis

KEY CONTEXT Long before he became the president of South Africa and a Nobel Prize winner, Nelson Mandela fought against a system known as apartheid, the racial segregation of people within South Africa. As a result, Mandela faced constant persecution from the ruling political party in South Africa at the time, the National Party. Mandela was arrested four times, in 1952, 1956, 1962, and then again in 1963, when he was tried along with ten other defendants in what is called the Rivonia Trial.

Mandela stood accused of four broad charges: "(a) recruiting persons for training in the preparation and use of explosives and in guerrilla warfare for the purpose of violent revolution and committing acts of sabotage; (b) conspiring to commit these acts and to aid foreign military units when they [hypothetically] invaded the Republic; (c) acting in these ways to further the objectives of communism; and (d) soliciting and receiving money for these purposes from sympathizers outside South Africa." Due to a justice system that was beholden to the ruling National Party, Mandela was convicted and sentenced to life in prison.

When he was finally released after spending twenty-seven years behind bars, Mandela had the political clout to help lead the charge to abolish apartheid, which was eventually terminated in 1993. He then went on to become the president of South Africa from 1994 to 1999. Under Mandela's presidency, South Africa began the long and arduous task of rebuilding the nation with a new vision of hope and equality.

What follows is a portion of Mandela's speech delivered in the courtroom at the opening of the defense case in the Rivonia Trial. Although he was eventually convicted of the charges, the speech became a rallying point for opposition leaders and is considered to be one of the most compelling and important speeches made by Mandela in his illustrious career.

I am the first accused. I hold a bachelor's degree in arts and practised as an attorney in Johannesburg for a number of years in partnership with Oliver Tambo. I am a convicted prisoner serving five years for leaving the country without a permit and for inciting people to go on strike at the end of May 1961.

At the outset, I want to say that the suggestion made by the state in its opening that the struggle in South Africa is under the influence of foreigners or communists is wholly incorrect. I have done whatever I did, both as an individual and as a leader of my people, because of my experience in South Africa and my own proudly felt African background, and not because of what any outsider might have said.

In my youth in the Transkei[1] I listened to the elders of my tribe telling stories of the old days. Amongst the tales they related to me were those of wars fought by our ancestors in defence of the fatherland. The names of Dingane and Bambata, Hintsa and Makana, Squngthi and Dalasile, Moshoeshoe and Sekhukhuni,[2] were praised as the glory of the entire African nation. I hoped then that life might offer me the opportunity to serve my people and make my own humble contribution to their freedom struggle. This is what has motivated me in all that I have done in relation to the charges made against me in this case.

Having said this, I must deal immediately and at some length with the question of violence. Some of the things so far told to the court are true and some are untrue. I do not, however, deny that I planned sabotage. I did not plan it in a spirit of recklessness, nor because I have any love of violence. I planned it as a result of a calm and sober assessment of the political situation that had arisen after many years of tyranny, exploitation, and oppression of my people by the whites.

5   I admit immediately that I was one of the persons who helped to form Umkhonto we Sizwe,[3] and that I played a prominent role in its affairs until I was arrested in August 1962. [. . .]

---

[1] Transkei was a "Bantustan" in South Africa, meaning an area set aside for blacks of certain ethnicities. —Eds.

[2] Names of African kings and chiefs. Revered leaders of various African ethnic groups. —Eds.

[3] The military wing of the African National Congress, translated as "Spear of the Nation." —Eds.

I, and the others who started the organisation, did so for two reasons. Firstly, we believed that as a result of Government policy, violence by the African people had become inevitable, and that unless responsible leadership was given to canalise and control the feelings of our people, there would be outbreaks of terrorism which would produce an intensity of bitterness and hostility between the various races of this country which is not produced even by war. Secondly, we felt that without violence there would be no way open to the African people to succeed in their struggle against the principle of white supremacy. All lawful modes of expressing opposition to this principle had been closed by legislation, and we were placed in a position in which we had either to accept a permanent state of inferiority, or to defy the government. We chose to defy the law. We first broke the law in a way which avoided any recourse to violence; when this form was legislated against, and then the government resorted to a show of force to crush opposition to its policies, only then did we decide to answer violence with violence.

But the violence which we chose to adopt was not terrorism. We who formed Umkhonto were all members of the African National Congress, and had behind us the ANC tradition of non-violence and negotiation as a means of solving political disputes. We believe that South Africa belongs to all the people who live in it, and not to one group, be it black or white. We did not want an interracial war, and tried to avoid it to the last minute. [. . .]

In the words of my leader, Chief Lutuli, who became President of the ANC in 1952, and who was later awarded the Nobel Peace Prize:

> Who will deny that thirty years of my life have been spent knocking in vain, patiently, moderately, and modestly at a closed and barred door? What have been the fruits of moderation? The past thirty years have seen the greatest number of laws restricting our rights and progress, until today we have reached a stage where we have almost no rights at all.

[. . .] What were we, the leaders of our people, to do? Were we to give in to the show of force and the implied threat against future action, or were we to fight it and, if so, how?

Consider this political cartoon in response to Mandela's passing in 2013.

In what ways does this capture the essence of Mandela's rebellion against apartheid?

NELSON MANDELA
1918 – 2013

10   We had no doubt that we had to continue the fight. Anything else would have been abject surrender. Our problem was not whether to fight, but was how to continue the fight. We of the ANC had always stood for a non-racial democracy, and we shrank from any action which might drive the races further apart than they already were. But the hard facts were that fifty years of non-violence had brought the African people nothing but more and more repressive legislation, and fewer and fewer rights. It may not be easy for this court to understand, but it is a fact that for a long time the people had been talking of violence — of the day when they would fight the white man and win back their country — and we, the leaders of the ANC, had nevertheless always prevailed upon them to avoid violence and to pursue peaceful methods. When some of us discussed this in May and June of 1961, it could not be denied that our policy to achieve a non-racial state by non-violence had achieved nothing, and that our followers were beginning to lose confidence in this policy and were developing disturbing ideas of terrorism. [. . .]

    At the beginning of June 1961, after a long and anxious assessment of the South African situation, I, and some colleagues, came to the conclusion that as violence in this country was inevitable, it would be unrealistic and wrong for African leaders to continue preaching peace and non-violence at a time when the government met our peaceful demands with force.

    This conclusion was not easily arrived at. It was only when all else had failed, when all channels of peaceful protest had been barred to us, that the decision was made to embark on violent forms of political struggle, and to form Umkhonto we Sizwe. We did so not because we desired such a course, but solely because the government had left us with no other choice. In the Manifesto of Umkhonto published on 16 December 1961, which is exhibit AD, we said:

    The time comes in the life of any nation when there remain only two choices — submit or fight. That time has now come to South Africa. We shall not submit and we have no choice but to hit back by all means in our power in defence of our people, our future, and our freedom.

    [. . .] When we took this decision, and subsequently formulated our plans, the ANC heritage of non-violence and racial harmony was very much with us. We felt that the country was drifting towards a civil war in which blacks and whites would fight each other. We viewed the situation with alarm. Civil war could mean the destruction of what the ANC stood for; with civil war, racial peace would be more difficult than ever to achieve. We already have examples in South African history of the results of war. It has taken more than fifty years for the scars of the South African War to disappear. How much longer would it take to eradicate the scars of inter-racial civil war, which could not be fought without a great loss of life on both sides?

    The avoidance of civil war had dominated our thinking for many years, but when we decided to adopt violence as part of our policy, we realised that we might one day have to face the prospect of such a war. This had to be taken into account in formulating our plans. We required a plan which was flexible and which permitted us to act in accordance with the needs of the times; above all, the plan had to be one which recognised civil war as the last resort, and left the decision on this question to the future. We did not want to be committed to civil war, but we wanted to be ready if it became inevitable.

15   Four forms of violence were possible. There is sabotage, there is guerrilla warfare, there is terrorism, and there is open revolution. We chose to adopt the first method and to exhaust it before taking any other decision.

    In the light of our political background the choice was a logical one. Sabotage did not involve loss of life, and it offered the best hope for future race relations. Bitterness would be kept to a minimum and, if the policy bore fruit, democratic government could become a reality. This is what we felt at the time, and this is what we said in our manifesto (exhibit AD):

> We of Umkhonto we Sizwe have always sought to achieve liberation without blood-shed and civil clash. We hope, even at this late hour, that our first actions will awaken every-one to a realisation of the disastrous situation to which the nationalist policy is leading. We hope that we will bring the government and its supporters to their senses before it is too late, so that both the government and its poli-cies can be changed before matters reach the desperate state of civil war.

The initial plan was based on a careful analysis of the political and economic situation of our country. We believed that South Africa depended to a large extent on foreign capital and foreign trade. We felt that planned destruc-tion of power plants, and interference with rail and telephone communications, would tend to scare away capital from the country, make it more difficult for goods from the industrial areas to reach the seaports on schedule, and would in the long run be a heavy drain on the economic life of the country, thus compelling the voters of the country to reconsider their position.

Attacks on the economic life-lines of the country were to be linked with sabotage on government buildings and other symbols of apartheid. These attacks would serve as a source of inspiration to our people. In addition, they would provide an outlet for those people who were urging the adoption of violent methods and would enable us to give concrete proof to our followers that we had adopted a stronger line and were fighting back against government violence.

In addition, if mass action were successfully organised, and mass reprisals taken, we felt that sympathy for our cause would be roused in other countries, and that greater pressure would be brought to bear on the South African government.

20   This then was the plan. Umkhonto was to perform sabotage, and strict instructions were given to its members right from the start, that on no account were they to injure or kill people in planning or carrying out operations. [. . .]

Umkhonto had its first operation on 16 December 1961, when Government buildings in Johannesburg, Port Elizabeth and Durban were attacked. The selection of targets is proof of the policy to which I have referred. Had we intended to attack life we would have selected targets where people congregated and not empty buildings and power stations. [. . .]

The Manifesto of Umkhonto was issued on the day that operations commenced. The response to our actions and manifesto among the white population was characteristically violent. The government threatened to take strong action, and called upon its supporters to stand firm and to ignore the demands of the Africans. The whites failed to respond by suggesting change; they responded to our call by suggesting the laager.[4]

In contrast, the response of the Africans was one of encouragement. Suddenly there was hope again. Things were happening. People in the townships became eager for political news. A great deal of enthusiasm was generated by the initial successes, and people began to speculate on how soon freedom would be obtained. But we in Umkhonto weighed up the white response with anxiety. The lines were being drawn. The whites and blacks were moving into separate camps, and the prospects of avoiding a civil war were made less. The white newspapers carried reports that sabotage would be punished by death. If this was so, how could we continue to keep Africans away from terrorism? [. . .]

---

[4] The literal definition of *laager* is an encampment protected by a circle of tanks or armored vehicles. A more general definition is a defensive position, policy, or attitude. —Eds.

▶ How do these images from the media coverage of the trial reflect the racial division that Mandela was fighting against? Do you think the newspaper was expressing support for Mandela's cause in its selection of these images? Explain.

Rivonia Trial pictures
THOSE WHO WAITED AS "TIME EXPIRED"
Pictures by James Soullier

● The changing moods of the crowd and the police outside the Palace of Justice, Pretoria, on Friday reflected all the tension and drama when the Rivonia sabotage trial accused were jailed for life by the Judge President, Mr. Justice De Wet.

ABOVE: Clutching her mother-in-law's hand, Mrs. Winnie Mandela (centre) and a relative walk past police guards at the Pretoria Palace of Justice after sentence was passed on her husband.

"Time expired" says the parking meter and African women spectators look anxious as the cry echoes through the crowd: "Life for all." The woman on the right wore the green and black uniform of the multi-racial Federation of South African Women.

★

LEFT: Crowds scatter as a police dog walks menacingly in their direction.

He wanted to deliver post . . .
She wanted to see father

GALVANISED ROOFING
From 10c per square ft.

● Modern Appearance.
● Stormproof.
● Leakproof.
● Easy Fixing.
● Economical.
● Stronger.

© Radu Sigheti/Reuters/Corbis

Our fight is against real, and not imaginary, hardships or, to use the language of the state prosecutor, "so-called hardships." Basically, we fight against two features which are the hall-marks of African life in South Africa and which are entrenched by legislation which we seek to have repealed. These features are poverty and lack of human dignity, and we do not need communists or so-called "agitators" to teach us about these things.

25   South Africa is the richest country in Africa, and could be one of the richest countries in the world. But it is a land of extremes and remarkable contrasts. The whites enjoy what may well be the highest standard of living in the world, whilst Africans live in poverty and misery. Forty per cent of the Africans live in hopelessly overcrowded and, in some cases, drought-stricken reserves, where soil erosion and the overworking of the soil makes it impossible for them to live properly off the land. Thirty per cent are labourers, labour tenants, and squatters on white farms and work and live under conditions similar to those of the serfs of the Middle Ages. The other 30 per cent live in towns where they have developed economic and social habits which bring them closer in many respects to white standards. Yet most Africans, even in this group, are impoverished by low incomes and high cost of living. [. . .]

Poverty goes hand in hand with malnutrition and disease. The incidence of malnutrition and deficiency diseases is very high amongst Africans. Tuberculosis, pellagra, kwashiorkor, gastro-enteritis, and scurvy bring death and destruction of health. The incidence of infant mortality is one of the highest in the world. According to the medical officer of health for Pretoria, tuberculosis kills forty people a day (almost all Africans), and in 1961 there were 58,491 new cases reported. These diseases not only destroy the vital organs of the body, but they result in retarded mental conditions and lack of initiative, and reduce powers of concentration. The secondary results of such conditions affect the whole community and the standard of work performed by African labourers.

The complaint of Africans, however, is not only that they are poor and the whites are rich, but that the laws which are made by the whites are designed to preserve this situation. There are two ways to break out of poverty. The first is by formal education, and the second is by the worker acquiring a greater skill at his work and thus higher wages. As far as Africans are concerned, both these avenues of advancement are deliberately curtailed by legislation.

The present government has always sought to hamper Africans in their search for education. One of their early acts, after coming into power, was to stop subsidies for African school feeding. Many African children who attended schools depended on this supplement to their diet. This was a cruel act.

There is compulsory education for all white children at virtually no cost to their parents, be they rich or poor. Similar facilities are not provided for the African children, though there are some who receive such assistance. African children, however, generally have to pay more for their schooling than whites. According to figures quoted by the South African Institute of Race Relations in its 1963 journal, approximately 40 per cent of African children in the age group between seven to fourteen do not attend school. [. . .]

30   The quality of education is also different. According to the *Bantu Educational Journal*, only 5,660 African children in the whole of South Africa passed their junior certificate in 1962, and in that year only 362 passed matric.[5] This is presumably consistent with the policy of Bantu education about which the present Prime Minister said, during the debate on the Bantu Education Bill in 1953:

> When I have control of native education I will reform it so that natives will be taught from childhood to realise that equality with Europeans is not for them . . . People who believe in equality are not desirable teachers for natives. When my Department controls native education it will know for what class of higher education a native is fitted, and whether he will have a chance in life to use his knowledge.

---

[5]matric: Short for *matriculation*, which is a formal term for entering college. In this context, it refers to passing an exam that serves as both a graduation requirement for high school and qualification for entering a college. —Eds.

Examine this 1989 poster in support of Nelson Mandela's release from prison. The small print reads: "These brave compatriots have been imprisoned because they fought for our freedom and rights[.] We demand the release of Nelson Mandela and all our leaders Amandla Ngawethu! Their prolonged imprisonment is a sign of the inability of the apartheid regime to crush the fighting spirit of the oppressed[.]"

In what ways does the message of this poster echo the themes in Mandela's speech to the court?

Graeme Williams/akg-images

The other main obstacle to the economic advancement of the African is the industrial colour-bar under which all the better jobs of industry are reserved for whites only. Moreover, Africans who do obtain employment in the unskilled and semi-skilled occupations which are open to them are not allowed to form trade unions which have recognition under the industrial conciliation act. This means that strikes of African workers are illegal, and that they are denied the right of collective bargaining which is permitted to the better-paid white workers. The discrimination in the policy of successive South African governments towards African workers is demonstrated by the so-called "civilised labour policy" under which sheltered, unskilled government jobs are found for those white workers who cannot make the grade in industry, at wages which far exceed the earnings of the average African employee in industry.

The government often answers its critics by saying that Africans in South Africa are economically better off than the inhabitants of the other countries in Africa. I do not know whether this statement is true and doubt whether any comparison can be made without having regard to the cost-of-living index in such countries. But even if it is true, as far as the African people are concerned it is irrelevant. Our complaint is not that we are poor by comparison with people in other countries, but that we are poor by comparison with the white people in our own country, and that we are prevented by legislation from altering this imbalance.

The lack of human dignity experienced by Africans is the direct result of the policy of white supremacy. White supremacy implies black inferiority. Legislation designed to preserve white supremacy entrenches this notion. Menial tasks in South Africa are invariably performed by

Africans. When anything has to be carried or cleaned the white man will look around for an African to do it for him, whether the African is employed by him or not. Because of this sort of attitude, whites tend to regard Africans as a separate breed. They do not look upon them as people with families of their own; they do not realise that they have emotions — that they fall in love like white people do; that they want to be with their wives and children like white people want to be with theirs; that they want to earn enough money to support their families properly, to feed and clothe them and send them to school. And what "house-boy" or "garden-boy" or labourer can ever hope to do this?

Poverty and the breakdown of family life have secondary effects. Children wander about the streets of the townships because they have no schools to go to, or no money to enable them to go to school, or no parents at home to see that they go to school, because both parents (if there be two) have to work to keep the family alive. This leads to a breakdown in moral standards, to an alarming rise in illegitimacy, and to growing violence which erupts not only politically, but everywhere. Life in the townships is dangerous. There is not a day that goes by without somebody being stabbed or assaulted. And violence is carried out of the townships in to the white living areas. People are afraid to walk alone in the streets after dark. Housebreakings and robberies are increasing, despite the fact that the death sentence can now be imposed for such offences. Death sentences cannot cure the festering sore. [. . .]

35 Africans want to be paid a living wage. Africans want to perform work which they are capable of doing, and not work which the government declares them to be capable of. Africans want to be allowed to live where they obtain work, and not be endorsed out of an area because they were not born there. Africans want to be allowed to own land in places where they work, and not to be obliged to live in rented houses which they can never call their own.

Africans want to be part of the general population, and not confined to living in their own ghettoes. African men want to have their wives and children to live with them where they work, and not be forced into an unnatural existence in men's hostels. African women want to be with their menfolk and not be left permanently widowed in the Reserves. Africans want to be allowed out after eleven o'clock at night and not to be confined to their rooms like little children. Africans want to be allowed to travel in their own country and to seek work where they want to and not where the labour bureau tells them to. Africans want a just share in the whole of South Africa; they want security and a stake in society.

Above all, we want equal political rights, because without them our disabilities will be permanent. I know this sounds revolutionary to the whites in this country, because the majority of voters will be Africans. This makes the white man fear democracy.

But this fear cannot be allowed to stand in the way of the only solution which will guarantee racial harmony and freedom for all. It is not true that the enfranchisement of all will result in racial domination. Political division, based on colour, is entirely artificial and, when it disappears, so will the domination of one colour group by another. [. . .]

This then is what the ANC is fighting. Their struggle is a truly national one. It is a struggle of the African people, inspired by their own suffering and their own experience. It is a struggle for the right to live.

During my lifetime I have dedicated myself to this struggle of the African people. I have fought against white domination, and I have fought against black domination. I have cherished the ideal of a democratic and free society in which all persons live together in harmony and with equal opportunities. It is an ideal which I hope to live for and to achieve. But if needs be, it is an ideal for which I am prepared to die.

Understanding and Interpreting

1 Look back at the Key Context section before this piece, and think about the charges that Mandela stands trial for. What does the nature of those charges tell you about the political context of this speech?

2 What distinction does Mandela make between "violence" and "terrorism" (par. 7), and what purpose does this distinction serve?

3 Explain the concept of a "non-racial democracy" (par. 10) and why this is of central concern to Mandela and the ANC.

4 How does Mandela justify abandoning nonviolent protest and how does he make the case for sabotage as his preferred alternative? How does this reasoning support his overall argument in this speech?

5 Mandela says that the "complaint of Africans, however, is not only that they are poor and the whites are rich, but that the laws which are made by the whites are designed to preserve this situation" (par. 27). Explain the distinction he is making and why it is important in terms of his overall justification for violent resistance.

6 Mandela addresses the state of education in South Africa at the time. What are the main points he raises, and how do the issues he discusses perpetuate the inequalities of apartheid?

7 Mandela references the "industrial colour-bar" (par. 31) when discussing economic advancement. To what is he referring and what evidence does he cite in support of his use of this term?

8 What large social problems does Mandela link to the "policy of white supremacy" (par. 33) and what logic does he use to make this connection?

Analyzing Language, Style, and Structure

1 How does opening with a counterargument help Mandela establish his overall purpose?

2 Mandela provides two reasons for establishing the resistance group Umkhonto. How effectively do these reasons justify the organization's actions?

3 What purpose does quoting Chief Lutuli serve in Mandela's argument (par. 8)? In your response, consider both the quote itself as well as the speaker.

4 In what ways does Mandela use the prospect of civil war in South Africa to explain the choice to adopt a more violent approach?

5 Mandela states that the "whites failed to respond [to the Manifesto of Umkhonto] by suggesting change; they responded to our call by suggesting the laager" (par. 22). *Laager* is an Afrikaans (South African Dutch) word, so it is closely associated with the white National Party that was largely responsible for the imprisonment of political activists such as Mandela. Its original meaning was a camp formed by a circle of wagons. It later came to mean an entrenched position or viewpoint that is defended against opponents. How might the choice of the term *laager* reinforce Mandela's justification for the use of violent opposition to the government?

6 Notice the repeated use of the phrase "so-called" in paragraph 24. Explain how Mandela uses that phrase as a rhetorical tool in that paragraph.

7 Mandela discusses education and economic opportunities, which lead to his assertion that "[w]hite supremacy implies black inferiority" and that "[l]egislation designed to preserve white supremacy entrenches this notion" (par. 33). Discuss how the order of his evidence and the specific examples he uses build to this assertion.

8 Explain how Mandela's statement that "[p]olitical division, based on colour, is entirely artificial and, when it disappears, so will the domination of one colour group by another" (par. 37) is linked to his argument as a whole.

Connecting, Arguing, and Extending

1 Mandela gave numerous speeches during his career as a political activist. Research other speeches he made, and then select one that you find inspiring. Then, create a PowerPoint presentation using words from the speech you select and images (from various sources) that capture the tone of the speech.

2 Mandela was imprisoned for standing up against a white supremacist government whose primary purpose was to ensure white privilege and institutionalize inferiority for nonwhite South Africans. As he indicates in his speech, he changed his stance from one of passive, nonviolent resistance to one that embraced the need to engage in violent opposition. Write an argument in which you address the following questions: Was Nelson Mandela justified in the use of violence to overthrow apartheid? What does it mean that he was awarded the Nobel Peace Prize in spite of his call for violent opposition?

3 Find Martin Luther King's "Letter from a Birmingham Jail" online and consider the similarities between this speech and Mandela's. Specifically consider the ways in which both King and Mandela use the circumstances of their imprisonment to advance their individual causes.

4 Mandela put his life on the line, and ultimately sacrificed his freedom in pursuit of his cause. Consider a current political, social, or economic issue that you consider to be of great importance. Then, write a persuasive speech in which you explain the issue, why you believe it's important, why you believe others should agree with your position, and what you would be willing to do in order to support your position. This can be an issue related to your school, your local community, the entire nation, or even the global community.

5 Mandela was called a rebel and ultimately imprisoned for his political views as he strove for justice. In spite of his long imprisonment, he inspired lasting change in his country and around the world. Research other leaders who have also been imprisoned for their activism and were nonetheless able to motivate powerful and lasting change, selecting one whom you find particularly compelling. Then prepare a presentation in which you share the ways in which the leader you selected influenced or changed the world.

from **Common Sense**

Thomas Paine

Thomas Paine (1737–1809) was born in England and worked as a rope maker and tax collector. Paine met Benjamin Franklin in England and moved to Philadelphia in 1774 on his recommendation. Paine eventually became an editor for *Pennsylvania* magazine, and the primary propagandist for the Revolutionary cause.

KEY CONTEXT Paine arrived in Philadelphia just as the conflict between the colonies and England was becoming especially intense, as many colonists were calling for independence from England. The initial revolt against England focused on the colonists' anger over taxation from the king, but after the first battles of the Revolutionary War, Paine argued that the colonists should not merely resist taxation but rather fight for complete independence from England. He explained his ideas concerning the necessity of independence in a fifty-page pamphlet titled *Common Sense*. This pamphlet, published in 1776, was well received by the colonists and became wildly popular, often read aloud in busy taverns and town meeting halls. "Without the pen of the author of *Common Sense*, the sword of Washington would have been raised in vain," John Adams said. In the following excerpt, Paine provides an argument detailing the reasons why the colonists should seek independence from England. Although he calls for rebellion, it is important to also note how he uses reason as a form of restraint.

Thoughts of the Present State of American Affairs

In the following pages I offer nothing more than simple facts, plain arguments, and common sense; and have no other preliminaries to settle with the reader, than that he will divest himself of prejudice and prepossession, and suffer his reason and his feelings to determine for themselves; that he will put on, or rather that he will not put off the true character of a man, and generously enlarge his views beyond the present day.

Volumes have been written on the subject of the struggle between England and America. Men of all ranks have embarked in the controversy, from different motives, and with various designs; but all have been ineffectual, and the period of debate is closed. Arms, as the last resource, decide the contest; the appeal[1] was the choice of the king, and the continent hath accepted the challenge.

It hath been reported of the late Mr. Pelham[2] (who tho' an able minister was not without his faults) that on his being attacked in the house of commons, on the score, that his measures were only of a temporary kind, replied, "they will last my time." Should a thought so fatal and unmanly possess the colonies in the present contest, the name of ancestors will be remembered by future generations with detestation.

The sun never shined on a cause of greater worth. 'Tis not the affair of a city, a country, a province, or a kingdom, but of a continent — of at least one eighth part of the habitable globe. 'Tis not the concern of a day, a year, or an age; posterity are virtually involved in the contest, and will be more or less affected, even to the end of time, by the proceedings now. Now is the seed time of continental union, faith and honor. The least fracture now will be like a name engraved with the point of a pin on the tender rind of a young oak; the wound will enlarge with the tree, and posterity read it in full grown characters.

5 By referring the matter from argument to arms, a new area for politics is struck; a new method of thinking hath arisen. All plans, proposals, &c. prior to the nineteenth of April, i.e., to the commencement of hostilities, are like the almanacs of the last year; which, though proper then, are superseded and useless now. Whatever was advanced by the advocates on either side of the question then, terminated in one and the same point, viz., a union with Great Britain; the only difference between the parties was the method of effecting it; the one proposing force, the other friendship; but it hath so far happened that the first hath failed, and the second hath withdrawn her influence.

As much hath been said of the advantages of reconciliation, which, like an agreeable dream, hath passed away and left us as we were, it is but right, that we should examine the contrary side of the argument, and inquire into some of the many material injuries which these colonies sustain, and always will sustain, by being connected with, and dependant on Great Britain. To examine that connection and dependance, on the principles of nature and common sense, to see what we have to trust to, if separated, and what we are to expect, if dependant.

I have heard it asserted by some, that as America hath flourished under her former connection with Great Britain, that the same connection is necessary towards her future happiness, and will always have the same effect. Nothing can be more fallacious than this kind of

[1] Paine is referring to the appeal to arms, meaning the decision to go to war. —Eds.
[2] Henry Pelham (1694–1754), former British prime minister. —Eds.

This is a political cartoon created by Ben Franklin and published in his *Pennsylvania Gazette* on May 9, 1754. The sections of the "snake" represent different colonies.

In what way does Franklin's political cartoon either reinforce or reject the ideas offered by Paine in *Common Sense*? Find a direct quote that supports your response.

argument. We may as well assert, that because a child has thrived upon milk, that it is never to have meat; or that the first twenty years of our lives is to become a precedent for the next twenty. But even this is admitting more than is true, for I answer roundly, that America would have flourished as much, and probably much more, had no European power had anything to do with her. The commerce by which she hath enriched herself are the necessaries of life, and will always have a market while eating is the custom of Europe.

But she has protected us, say some. That she hath engrossed us is true, and defended the continent at our expense as well as her own is admitted, and she would have defended Turkey from the same motive, viz., the sake of trade and dominion.

Alas, we have been long led away by ancient prejudices and made large sacrifices to superstition. We have boasted the protection of Great Britain, without considering, that her motive was interest not attachment; that she did not protect us from our enemies on our account, but from her enemies on her own account, from those who had no quarrel with us on any other account, and who will always be our enemies on the same account. Let Britain wave her pretensions to the continent, or the continent throw off

the dependance, and we should be at peace with France and Spain were they at war with Britain. The miseries of Hanover last war ought to warn us against connections.

10   It hath lately been asserted in parliament, that the colonies have no relation to each other but through the parent country, i.e., that Pennsylvania and the Jerseys, and so on for the rest, are sister colonies by the way of England; this is certainly a very roundabout way of proving relationship, but it is the nearest and only true way of proving enemyship, if I may so call it. France and Spain never were, nor perhaps ever will be our enemies as Americans, but as our being the subjects of Great Britain.

But Britain is the parent country, say some. Then the more shame upon her conduct. Even brutes do not devour their young; nor savages make war upon their families; wherefore the assertion, if true, turns to her reproach; but it happens not to be true, or only partly so, and the phrase parent or mother country hath been jesuitically adopted by the king and his parasites, with a low papistical design of gaining an unfair bias on the credulous weakness of our minds. Europe, and not England, is the parent country of America. This new world hath been the asylum for the persecuted lovers of civil and religious liberty from every Part of Europe. Hither have they fled, not from the tender embraces of the mother, but from the cruelty of the monster; and it is so far true of England, that the same tyranny which drove the first emigrants from home pursues their descendants still.

Understanding and Interpreting

1 Paine states that he has no other "preliminaries," or conditions, for the reader other than that the reader divest himself of "prejudice and prepossession" (par. 1) before reading the text. What is Paine asking of the reader, and why is it important at this point?

2 In paragraph 3, Paine refers to a statement made by "the late Mr. Pelham" that measures put in place would "last [his] time." Why does Paine consider this statement "fatal and unmanly" with respect to the situation the colonies face?

3 Paine discusses several advantages that have been offered as reasons for reconciling with England. Identify each of the so-called advantages that Paine mentions and then explain how he refutes each one.

4 Explain what Paine means by "enemyship" (par. 10), and why, according to Paine, that term explains the relationship between the colonies and other countries that are in conflict with Great Britain.

5 Paine claims that "Europe, and not England, is the parent country of America" (par. 11). Explain the reasoning behind his assertion.

Analyzing Language, Style, and Structure

1 Consider the first sentence of the passage. How do the connotations of the adjectives "simple," "plain," and "common" help Paine establish the tone of his argument?

2 At the end of the second paragraph, Paine indicates that the "continent," meaning the colonies, accepted the challenge of battle. What is the effect of beginning his argument with an acknowledgment that an armed conflict seems inevitable?

3 Explain how the simile regarding the "name engraved" on the "tender rind of a young oak" (par. 4) illustrates the significance of the cause that Paine is discussing.

4 In paragraph 5, Paine refers to the "commencement of hostilities" on the "nineteenth of April," a reference to the battle of Lexington and Concord, which marked the beginning of armed conflict between the colonies and Great Britain. Explain how the simile the "almanacs of the last year" advances how Paine wishes the reader to understand the current situation.

5 Paine asserts that the protection of England was motivated by "interest not attachment" (par. 9). How do the connotations of these words serve to advance his argument while at the same time acknowledging the practical nature of the relationship between the colonies and England?

6 Paine advances a complex argument that encompasses several points. Explain how the structure of his argument, specifically the order in which he introduces his points, is effective in achieving his rhetorical purpose for his intended audience.

Connecting, Arguing, and Extending

1 Paine's *Common Sense* is considered one of the primary founding documents in American history. Research the background of Paine and his influence on the American Revolution and Declaration of Independence. and prepare a presentation that argues what his impact was in shaping modern America.

2 Paine was a common target of British propaganda during the Revolutionary War. One coin used in British camps read "End of Pain" and showed Thomas Paine hanged from the gallows. Research other examples in which Paine was used by Britain as war propaganda and provide a written or oral presentation analyzing one example of how Paine was used to motivate British soldiers to fight against the Continental Army.

Speech to the United Nations Youth Assembly

Malala Yousafzai

Odd Andersen/AFP/Getty Images

Nobel Peace Prize winner Malala Yousafzai (b. 1997) is a Pakistani girl who has become a symbol for social justice, human rights, and resistance to Taliban rule.

KEY CONTEXT Using a pseudonym, at the age of eleven Malala Yousafzai began writing a blog about the hardships of her life under Taliban rule, specifically addressing the Taliban's ban on education for girls. It soon became widely read and eventually led to appearances on television, where Yousafzai spoke out for education rights for girls around the world. On October 9, 2012, the Taliban made an attempt to assassinate Yousafzai while she was riding a bus home from school. She was shot in the head but survived the attack.

On July 12, 2013, young people were given control of the United Nations for the first time in the sixty-eight-year history of the organization. More than one hundred organizations came together along with hundreds of young education advocates from around the world, including Malala Yousafzai, who made her first public speech since recovering from the Taliban's assassination attempt. Below is the speech she gave on that celebrated day.

In the name of God, The Most Beneficent, The Most Merciful.
Honorable UN Secretary General Mr. Ban Ki-moon,
Respected President General Assembly Vuk Jeremic,
Honorable UN envoy for Global education Mr. Gordon Brown,
Respected elders and my dear brothers and sisters;

Today, it is an honor for me to be speaking again after a long time. Being here with such honorable people is a great moment in my life.

I don't know where to begin my speech. I don't know what people would be expecting me to say. But first of all, thank you to God for whom we all are equal and thank you to every person who has prayed for my fast recovery and a new life. I cannot believe how much love people have shown me. I have received thousands of good wish cards and gifts from all over the world. Thank you to all of them. Thank you to the children whose innocent words encouraged me. Thank you to my elders whose prayers strengthened me.

I would like to thank my nurses, doctors and all of the staff of the hospitals in Pakistan and the UK and the UAE government who have helped me get better and recover my strength. I fully support Mr. Ban Ki-moon the Secretary-General in his Global Education First Initiative and the work of the UN Special Envoy Mr. Gordon Brown. And I thank them both for the leadership they continue to give. They continue to inspire all of us to action.

Dear brothers and sisters, do remember one thing. Malala Day is not my day. Today is the day of every woman, every boy and every girl who have raised their voice for their rights. There are hundreds of human rights activists and social

Education advocates from around the world attend the first Youth Takeover of the United Nations. Youth Takeover Day at the UN provided young people an opportunity to bring their perspective on top global issues.

What in particular do you think these youth offer that adults either ignore or are unaware of altogether?

Courtesy Theirworld

workers who are not only speaking for human rights, but who are struggling to achieve their goals of education, peace and equality. Thousands of people have been killed by the terrorists and millions have been injured. I am just one of them.

5   So here I stand . . . one girl among many.

I speak — not for myself, but for all girls and boys.

I raise up my voice — not so that I can shout, but so that those without a voice can be heard.

Those who have fought for their rights:

Their right to live in peace.

10   Their right to be treated with dignity.

Their right to equality of opportunity.

Their right to be educated.

Dear Friends, on the 9th of October 2012, the Taliban shot me on the left side of my forehead. They shot my friends too. They thought that the bullets would silence us. But they failed. And then, out of that silence came thousands of voices. The terrorists thought that they would change our aims and stop our ambitions but nothing changed in my life except this: Weakness, fear and hopelessness died. Strength, power and courage was born. I am the same Malala. My ambitions are the same. My hopes are the same. My dreams are the same.

Dear sisters and brothers, I am not against anyone. Neither am I here to speak in terms of personal revenge against the Taliban or any other terrorists group. I am here to speak up for the right of education of every child. I want education for the sons and the daughters of all the extremists especially the Taliban.

15   I do not even hate the Talib who shot me. Even if there is a gun in my hand and he stands in front of me. I would not shoot him. This is the compassion that I have learnt from Muhammad — the prophet of mercy, Jesus Christ and Lord Buddha. This is the legacy of change that I have inherited from Martin Luther King, Nelson Mandela and Muhammad Ali Jinnah. This is the philosophy of non-violence that I have learnt from Gandhi Jee, Bacha Khan and Mother Teresa. And this is the forgiveness that I have learnt from my mother and father. This is what my soul is telling me, be peaceful and love everyone.

Dear sisters and brothers, we realize the importance of light when we see darkness. We realize the importance of our voice when we are silenced. In the same way, when we were in Swat, the north of Pakistan, we realized the importance of pens and books when we saw the guns.

The wise saying, "The pen is mightier than sword" was true. The extremists are afraid of books and pens. The power of education frightens them. They are afraid of women. The power of the voice of women frightens them. And that is why they killed 14 innocent medical students in the recent attack in Quetta. And that is why they killed many female teachers and polio workers in Khyber Pukhtoon Khwa and FATA. That is why they are blasting schools every day. Because they were and they are afraid of change, afraid of the equality that we will bring into our society.

I remember that there was a boy in our school who was asked by a journalist, "Why are the Taliban against education?" He answered very simply. By pointing to his book he said, "A Talib doesn't know what is written inside this book." They think that God is a tiny, little conservative being who would send girls to the hell just because of going to school. The terrorists are misusing the name of Islam and Pashtun society for their own personal benefits. Pakistan is peace-loving democratic country. Pashtuns want education for their daughters and sons. And Islam is a religion of peace, humanity and brotherhood. Islam says that it is not only each child's right to get education, rather it is their duty and responsibility.

Honorable Secretary General, peace is necessary for education. In many parts of the world especially Pakistan and Afghanistan; terrorism, wars and conflicts stop children to go to their schools. We are really tired of these wars. Women and children are suffering in many parts

of the world in many ways. In India, innocent and poor children are victims of child labor. Many schools have been destroyed in Nigeria. People in Afghanistan have been affected by the hurdles of extremism for decades. Young girls have to do domestic child labor and are forced to get married at early age. Poverty, ignorance, injustice, racism and the deprivation of basic rights are the main problems faced by both men and women.

20 Dear fellows, today I am focusing on women's rights and girls' education because they are suffering the most. There was a time when women social activists asked men to stand up for their rights. But, this time, we will do it by ourselves. I am not telling men to step away from speaking for women's rights rather I am focusing on women to be independent to fight for themselves.

Dear sisters and brothers, now it's time to speak up.

So today, we call upon the world leaders to change their strategic policies in favor of peace and prosperity.

We call upon the world leaders that all the peace deals must protect women and children's rights. A deal that goes against the dignity of women and their rights is unacceptable.

This political cartoon by Ann Telnaes satirizes the Taliban, the group behind the shooting of Malala Yousafzai.

Look carefully at the details of the cartoon and explain how its elements comment on the shortcomings of the Taliban. How do you think Malala Yousafzai would respond to this cartoon?

We call upon all governments to ensure free compulsory education for every child all over the world.

25 We call upon all governments to fight against terrorism and violence, to protect children from brutality and harm.

We call upon the developed nations to support the expansion of educational opportunities for girls in the developing world.

We call upon all communities to be tolerant — to reject prejudice based on cast[e], creed, sect, religion or gender. To ensure freedom and equality for women so that they can flourish. We cannot all succeed when half of us are held back.

We call upon our sisters around the world to be brave — to embrace the strength within themselves and realize their full potential.

Dear brothers and sisters, we want schools and education for every child's bright future. We will continue our journey to our destination of peace and education for everyone. No one can stop us. We will speak for our rights and we will bring change through our voice. We must believe in the power and the strength of our words. Our words can change the world.

30 Because we are all together, united for the cause of education. And if we want to achieve our goal, then let us empower ourselves with the weapon of knowledge and let us shield ourselves with unity and togetherness.

Dear brothers and sisters, we must not forget that millions of people are suffering from poverty, injustice and ignorance. We must not forget that millions of children are out of schools. We must not forget that our sisters and brothers are waiting for a bright peaceful future.

So let us wage a global struggle against illiteracy, poverty and terrorism and let us pick up our books and pens. They are our most powerful weapons.

One child, one teacher, one pen and one book can change the world.

Education is the only solution. Education First.

Understanding and Interpreting

1 In recounting her traumatic experience, Malala Yousafzai states, "I do not even hate the Talib who shot me. Even if there is a gun in my hand and he stands in front of me. I would not shoot him" (par. 15). What rationale does she offer for this attitude? Why does she include this commentary?

2 Yousafzai says that while in Swat, she and others realized that "[t]he wise saying, 'The pen is mightier than sword' was true" (par. 17). What is the meaning of this proverb, and what is the significance of her claim that it is "true"?

3 Yousafzai stresses the importance of "unity and togetherness" (par. 30) in approaching the issues surrounding women's rights and girls' education. Why is a unified approach so important to achieving the goals Yousafzai sets forth? What calls to action does she declare to specific groups within that unified front?

4 The closing lines of the speech declare, "Education is the only solution. Education First." However, Yousafzai acknowledges that other rights must be secured before education can be provided effectively. What problems, according to Yousafzai, must be addressed before efforts to provide and improve education in a community can be fruitful?

Analyzing Language, Style, and Structure

1 In the opening paragraphs of the speech, Yousafzai establishes her persona as a simple spokesperson for a much greater cause. She states, "Malala Day is not my day" (par. 4) and goes on to explain that she is just one of many who have suffered oppression and violence. What does this approach add to her message and how does it build her ethos?

2 In recounting her harrowing experience, Yousafzai explores her perspective on the motivations and goals of the Taliban in carrying out such violence, stating that it failed to achieve its intentions. In what ways did the Taliban fail? What is Yosafzai's rhetorical purpose in presenting this perspective?

3 Consider the tone with which Yousafzai discusses the actions of those who would eliminate educational opportunities. What attitude does she express toward these efforts, and what connotative words provide evidence of this attitude?

4 Yousafzai's speech includes two significant uses of anaphora—repetition of words at the beginning of successive clauses, sentences, or paragraphs. She repeatedly opens paragraphs with "Dear brothers and sisters" and later phrases her calls to action with the opening "We call upon." What is the specific effect of each of these examples of anaphora? What important element do they have in common?

5 In many ways throughout the speech, Yousafzai suggests that peace will encourage education and that education will encourage peace. How does she establish this symbiotic relationship, and how does it aid her rhetorical purpose?

6 Toward the end of her speech, Yousafzai states, "And if we want to achieve our goal, then let us empower ourselves with the weapon of knowledge and let us shield ourselves with unity and togetherness" (par. 30). Why are these metaphors particularly appropriate for the content of her speech and the specifics of her experience?

Connecting, Arguing, and Extending

1 To clarify her declaration that she would not retaliate in violence against her shooter, Yousafzai explains, "This is the compassion that I have learnt from Muhammad—the prophet of mercy, Jesus Christ and Lord Buddha. This is the legacy of change that I have inherited from Martin Luther King, Nelson Mandela and Muhammad Ali Jinnah. This is the philosophy of non-violence that I have learnt from Gandhi Jee, Bacha Khan and Mother Teresa. And this is the forgiveness that I have learnt from my mother and father. This is what my soul is telling me, be peaceful and love everyone" (par. 15).

Yousafzai values compassion, nonviolence, forgiveness, and positive change. Consider what you value, and to what sources of inspiration and education you would attribute these values. Then create a composition in which you explain a few of your strongest values and the inspirational sources to which you would credit the development of these values in you.

2 Martin Luther King once said, "Darkness cannot drive out darkness; only light can do that. Hate cannot drive out hate; only love can do that." This sentiment is embraced by Yousafzai's speech as well. Some critics argue that Yousafzai's (and King's) position is unrealistically optimistic; that peaceful and loving answers to violent and oppressive problems are not forceful enough to bring about change. Consider whether you agree with Yousafzai or her critics, and why. Then, in a well-organized argument, take a position that defends, challenges, or qualifies King's assertion.

from Women's Suffrage Is Inevitable

Carrie Chapman Catt

Carrie Chapman Catt (1859–1947) was an activist who worked tirelessly for the right for women to vote in the United States. The founder of the League of Women Voters, Catt was a leader of the suffrage movement and eventually succeeded Susan B. Anthony as the president of the National American Suffrage Association. Catt was a founder and president of the International Woman Suffrage Association, serving from 1904 to 1923 and until her death as honorary president. Her leadership was crucial in the eventual passage in 1920 of the Nineteenth Amendment to the United Sates Constitution, which gave American women at last the right to vote. Catt delivered the speech below before an all-male Congress in 1917 in the final years of her campaign to secure voting rights for women.

Woman suffrage is inevitable. Suffragists knew it before November 4, 1917; opponents afterward. Three distinct causes made it inevitable.

History of Democracy

First, the history of our country. Ours is a nation born of revolution, of rebellion against a system of government so securely entrenched in the customs and traditions of human society that in 1776 it seemed impregnable. From the beginning of things, nations had been ruled by kings and for kings, while the people served and paid the cost. The American Revolutionists boldly proclaimed the heresies: "Taxation without representation is tyranny." "Governments derive their just powers from the consent of the governed." The colonists won, and the nation which was established as a result of their victory has held unfailingly that these two fundamental principles of democratic government are not only the spiritual source of our national existence but have been our chief historic pride and at all times the sheet anchor of our liberties.

Eighty years after the Revolution, Abraham Lincoln welded those two maxims into a new

one: "Ours is a government of the people, by the people, and for the people." Fifty years more passed and the president of the United States, Woodrow Wilson, in a mighty crisis of the nation, proclaimed to the world: "We are fighting for the things which we have always carried nearest to our hearts: for democracy, for the right of those who submit to authority to have a voice in their own government."

All the way between these immortal aphorisms political leaders have declared unabated faith in their truth. Not one American has arisen to question their logic in the 141 years of our national existence. However stupidly our country may have evaded the logical application at times, it has never swerved from its devotion to the theory of democracy as expressed by those two axioms. [. . .]

5   With such a history behind it, how can our nation escape the logic it has never failed to follow, when its last unenfranchised class calls for the vote? Behold our Uncle Sam floating the banner with one hand, "Taxation without representation is tyranny," and with the other seizing the billions of dollars paid in taxes by women to whom he refuses "representation." Behold him

again, welcoming the boys of twenty-one and the newly made immigrant citizen to "a voice in their own government" while he denies that fundamental right of democracy to thousands of women public school teachers from whom many of these men learn all they know of citizenship and patriotism, to women college presidents, to women who preach in our pulpits, interpret law in our courts, preside over our hospitals, write books and magazines, and serve in every uplifting moral and social enterprise. Is there a single man who can justify such inequality of treatment, such outrageous discrimination? Not one. [. . .]

Suffrage Already Established in Some States

Second, the suffrage for women already established in the United States makes women suffrage for the nation inevitable. When Elihu Root, as president of the American Society of

International Law, at the eleventh annual meeting in Washington, April 26, 1917, said, "The world cannot be half democratic and half autocratic. It must be all democratic or all Prussian. There can be no compromise," he voiced a general truth. Precisely the same intuition has already taught the blindest and most hostile foe of woman suffrage that our nation cannot long continue a condition under which government in half its territory rests upon the consent of half of the people and in the other half upon the consent of all the people; a condition which grants representation to the taxed in half of its territory and denies it in the other half; a condition which permits women in some states to share in the election of the president, senators, and representatives and denies them that privilege in others. It is too obvious to require demonstration that woman suffrage, now covering half our territory,

Museum of London/Heritage Images/Getty Images

In what ways does this 1912 political cartoon effectively make its point about woman's suffrage? Who do you think the audience was for a piece like this, and why would it appeal to that audience?

will eventually be ordained in all the nation. No one will deny it. The only question left is when and how will it be completely established.

Fundamental American Principle

Third, the leadership of the United States in world democracy compels the enfranchisement of its own women. The maxims of the Declaration were once called "fundamental principles of government." They are now called "American principles" or even "Americanisms." They have become the slogans of every movement toward political liberty the world around, of every effort to widen the suffrage for men or women in any land. Not a people, race, or class striving for freedom is there anywhere in the world that has not made our axioms the chief weapon of the struggle. More, all men and women the world around, with farsighted vision into the verities of things, know that the world tragedy of our day is not now being waged over the assassination of an archduke, nor commercial competition, nor national ambitions, nor the freedom of the seas. It is a death grapple between the forces which deny and those which uphold the truths of the Declaration of Independence. [...]

Do You Realize?

Do you realize that in no other country in the world with democratic tendencies is suffrage so completely denied as in a considerable number of our own states? There are thirteen black states where no suffrage for women exists, and fourteen others where suffrage for women is more limited than in many foreign countries.

Do you realize that when you ask women to take their cause to state referendum you compel them to do this: that you drive women of education, refinement, achievement, to beg men who cannot read for their political freedom?

10 Do you realize that such anomalies as a college president asking her janitor to give her a vote are overstraining the patience and driving women to desperation?

Do you realize that women in increasing numbers indignantly resent the long delay in their enfranchisement?

Woman Suffrage and the Parties

Your party platforms have pledged women suffrage. Then why not be honest, frank friends of our cause, adopt it in reality as your own, make it a party program, and "fight with us"? As a party measure — a measure of all parties — why not put the amendment through Congress and the legislatures? We shall all be better friends, we shall have a happier nation, we women will be free to support loyally the party of our choice, and we shall be far prouder of our history.

"There is one thing mightier than kings and armies" — aye, than Congresses and political parties — "the power of an idea when its time has come to move." The time for woman suffrage has come. The woman's hour has struck. If parties prefer to postpone action longer and thus do battle with this idea, they challenge the inevitable. The idea will not perish; the party which opposes it may. Every delay, every trick, every political dishonesty from now on will antagonize the women of the land more and more, and when the party or parties which have so delayed woman suffrage finally let it come, their sincerity will be doubted and their appeal to the new voters will be met with suspicion. This is the psychology of the situation. Can you afford the risk? Think it over.

The Opposition

We know you will meet opposition. There are a few "women haters" left, a few "old males of the tribe," as Vance Thompson calls them, whose duty they believe it to be to keep women in the places they have carefully picked out for them. Treitschke, made world famous by war literature, said some years ago, "Germany, which knows all about Germany and France, knows far better what is good for Alsace-Lorraine than that miserable people can possibly know." A few

American Treitschkes we have who know better than women what is good for them. There are women, too, with "slave souls" and "clinging vines" for backbones. There are female dolls and male dandies. But the world does not wait for such as these, nor does liberty pause to heed the plaint of men and women with a grouch. She does not wait for those who have a special interest to serve, nor a selfish reason for depriving other people of freedom. Holding her torch aloft, liberty is pointing the way onward and upward and saying to America, "Come."

To Congress

15 To you and the supporters of our cause in Senate and House, and the number is large, the suffragists of the nation express their grateful thanks. This address is not meant for you. We are more truly appreciative of all you have done than any words can express. We ask you to make a last, hard fight for the amendment during the present session. Since last we asked a vote on this amendment, your position has been fortified by the addition to suffrage territory of Great Britain, Canada, and New York.

Some of you have been too indifferent to give more than casual attention to this question. It is worthy of your immediate consideration. A question big enough to engage the attention of our allies in wartime is too big a question for you to neglect.

Some of you have grown old in party service. Are you willing that those who take your places by and by shall blame you for having failed to keep pace with the world and thus having lost for them a party advantage? Is there any real gain for you, for your party, for your nation by delay? Do you want to drive the progressive men and women out of your party?

Some of you hold to the doctrine of states' rights as applying to woman suffrage. Adherence to that theory will keep the United States far behind all other democratic nations upon this question. A theory which prevents a nation from keeping up with the trend of world progress cannot be justified.

Gentlemen, we hereby petition you, our only designated representatives, to redress our grievances by the immediate passage of the Federal Suffrage Amendment and to use your influence to secure its ratification in your own state, in order that the women of our nation may be endowed with political freedom before the next presidential election, and that our nation may resume its world leadership in democracy.

20 Woman suffrage is coming — you know it. Will you, Honorable Senators and Members of the House of Representatives, help or hinder it?

Understanding and Interpreting

1 Catt states, "However stupidly our country may have evaded the logical application at times, it has never swerved from its devotion to the theory of democracy as expressed by those two axioms" (par. 4). Explain Catt's meaning, and how this language might affect her audience.

2 Catt illustrates the current situation for women who desire to vote with a series of examples in the form of rhetorical questions that begin with "Do you realize [. . .] ?" (par. 8). Summarize the claims behind the examples, and what Catt is hoping to illuminate with each.

3 In discussing the opposition the audience will face, Catt uses loaded diction to characterize those who would contest suffrage. What does she suggest about the types of people who are not in favor of suffrage, and how are these suggestions intended to influence the audience?

4 Review the reasons that Catt offers to her audience to fulfill her petition that they advocate suffrage for women. Summarize her prominent claims regarding how suffrage is best for the country and the political parties currently in office.

Analyzing Language, Style, and Structure

1 Examine Catt's references to "heresies" and "maxims" in the opening paragraphs of her speech. How do these sentiments build her ethos and the validity of her cause? What effect is Catt hoping to have by opening with these ideas?

2 Revisit the imagery of Uncle Sam in the last paragraph under "History of Democracy" (par. 5). What hypocrisy does Catt illustrate with the description of what Uncle Sam is doing with each hand? What loaded language in this paragraph aids Catt in her assertiveness? How is this image a strong appeal to logos?

3 Examine the overall structure of the paragraph under "Suffrage Already Established in Some States" (par. 6). Note how Catt uses the quote from Elihu Root to establish a "general truth" and then provides a specific application of that general truth. Explain how Catt uses this structure to strengthen her argument that suffrage is inevitable.

4 Consider Catt's repeated use of rhetorical questions beginning with "Do you realize [. . .] ?" What tone does this diction contribute to the content? How does Catt's choice of questioning, rather than declaring, change the impact of the examples? What does Catt imply by phrasing her questions in this manner?

5 Consider the extremely methodical approach that Catt takes in her speech. Write a response in which you analyze the ways in which she carefully structures her argument so that the audience can clearly follow her line of reasoning.

6 Nearing the conclusion of her speech, Catt addresses her audience directly with a series of rhetorical questions, including "Some of you have grown old in party service. Are you willing that those who take your places by and by shall blame you for having failed to keep pace with the world and thus having lost for them a party advantage? Is there any real gain for you, for your party, for your nation by delay? Do you want to drive the progressive men and women out of your party?" (par. 17). Explain what Catt implies with her questions, and how she uses the competitive relationship between the political parties to her advantage.

Connecting, Arguing, and Extending

1 The suffrage movement in the United States worked for decades to get the Nineteenth Amendment passed. During that time, suffragists faced a long list of opposing arguments and were lambasted in political cartoons, pamphlets, and other anti-suffrage propaganda. Explore the rhetorical materials of organizations opposed to suffrage. What claims do they promote? How are suffragists depicted? What appeals are employed, and to what effect? Can you identify and articulate any recognizable fallacies behind these claims?

2 Catt asserts that our nation "has never swerved from its devotion to the theory of democracy" but it has "stupidly [. . .] evaded [its] logical application at times" (par. 4). Consider your perspective on this viewpoint. Then, in a well-organized argument, take a position that defends, challenges, or qualifies Catt's assertion that there is sometimes a disconnect between what our nation values in theory and what actions it takes in reality.

3 While they didn't agree on specifics, both suffragists and anti-suffragists anticipated that the right to vote for women would impact the future of politics and culture in the United States. What, in truth, was the significance of the Nineteenth Amendment? Research the effects of this amendment on political platforms, policies, and laws. How dramatically did the Nineteenth Amendment change the face of politics and culture in our country?

from Animal Farm

George Orwell

George Orwell (1903–1950) was an English political critic, essayist, and novelist whose most famous work is *1984*, a dystopian novel about government control. Orwell was the son of a British civil servant stationed in the British-controlled nation of India. Raised in England, he returned to Asia to join the Indian Imperial Police in Burma in his midtwenties, but resigned shortly thereafter after becoming disenchanted with imperialism.

Popperfoto/Getty Images

KEY CONTEXT   Written at the end of World War II, *Animal Farm* (1945) is an anti-Soviet satire set on a farm in which the animals rebel against the farmer. In the excerpt below, Old Major, who represents the ideas of Karl Marx and Vladimir Lenin, offers reasons why the animals in the farm should rebel against the often-drunk owner of the farm, Mr. Jones.

Comrades, you have heard already about the strange dream that I had last night. But I will come to the dream later. I have something else to say first. I do not think, comrades, that I shall be with you for many months longer, and before I die, I feel it my duty to pass on to you such wisdom as I have acquired. I have had a long life, I have had much time for thought as I lay alone in my stall, and I think I may say that I understand the nature of life on this earth as well as any animal now living. It is about this that I wish to speak to you.

"Now, comrades, what is the nature of this life of ours? Let us face it: our lives are miserable, laborious, and short. We are born, we are given just so much food as will keep the breath in our bodies, and those of us who are capable of it are forced to work to the last atom of our strength; and the very instant that our usefulness has come to an end we are slaughtered with hideous cruelty. No animal in England knows the meaning of happiness or leisure after he is a year old. No animal in England is free. The life of an animal is misery and slavery: that is the plain truth.

"But is this simply part of the order of nature? Is it because this land of ours is so poor that it cannot afford a decent life to those who dwell upon it? No, comrades, a thousand times no! The soil of England is fertile, its climate is good, it is capable of affording food in abundance to an enormously greater number of animals than now inhabit it. This single farm of ours would support a dozen horses, twenty cows, hundreds of sheep — and all of them living in a comfort and a dignity that are now almost beyond our imagining. Why then do we continue in this miserable condition? Because nearly the whole of the produce of our labour is stolen from us by human beings. There, comrades, is the answer to all our problems. It is summed up in a single word — Man. Man is the only real enemy we have. Remove Man from the scene, and the root cause of hunger and overwork is abolished for ever.

"Man is the only creature that consumes without producing. He does not give milk, he does not lay eggs, he is too weak to pull the plough, he cannot run fast enough to catch rabbits. Yet he is lord of all the animals. He sets them to work, he gives back to them the bare minimum that will prevent them from starving, and the rest he keeps for himself. Our labour tills the soil, our dung fertilises it, and yet there is not one of us that owns more than his bare skin. You cows that I see before me, how many thousands of gallons of milk have you given during this last year? And what has happened to that milk which should have been breeding up sturdy calves? Every drop of it has gone down the throats of our enemies. And you hens, how many eggs have you laid in this last year, and how many of those eggs ever hatched into chickens? The rest have all gone to market to bring in money for Jones and his men. And you, Clover, where are those four foals you bore, who should have been the support and pleasure of your old age? Each was sold at a year old — you will never see one of them again. In return for your four confinements and all your labour in the fields, what have you ever had except your bare rations and a stall?

5   "And even the miserable lives we lead are not allowed to reach their natural span. For myself I do not grumble, for I am one of the lucky ones. I am twelve years old and have had over four hundred children. Such is the natural life of a pig. But no animal escapes the cruel knife in the end. You young porkers who are sitting in front of me, every one of you will scream your lives out at the block within a year. To that horror we all must come — cows, pigs, hens, sheep, everyone. Even the horses and the dogs have no better fate. You, Boxer, the very day that those great muscles of yours lose their power, Jones will sell you to the knacker, who will cut your throat and boil you down for the foxhounds. As for the dogs, when they grow old and toothless, Jones ties a brick round their necks and drowns them in the nearest pond.

"Is it not crystal clear, then, comrades, that all the evils of this life of ours spring from the tyranny of human beings? Only get rid of Man,

FOUR LEGS GOOD TWO LEGS BAD

Brandon Schaefer, seekandspeak.com

During the time that Orwell wrote this novel, the Soviet Union made effective use of propaganda, including posters with simple slogans and images. **Examine this contemporary Soviet-style poster, created in response to *Animal Farm*, and discuss the ways in which this poster might, or might not, be an effective propaganda tool in support of the animals' rebellion against Mr. Jones.**

and the produce of our labour would be our own. Almost overnight we could become rich and free. What then must we do? Why, work night and day, body and soul, for the overthrow of the human race! That is my message to you, comrades: Rebellion! I do not know when that Rebellion will come, it might be in a week or in a hundred years, but I know, as surely as I see this straw beneath my feet, that sooner or later justice will be done. Fix your eyes on that, comrades, throughout the short remainder of your lives! And above all, pass on this message of mine to those who come after you, so that future generations shall carry on the struggle until it is victorious.

"And remember, comrades, your resolution must never falter. No argument must lead you astray. Never listen when they tell you that Man and the animals have a common interest, that the prosperity of the one is the prosperity of the others. It is all lies. Man serves the interests of no creature except himself. And among us animals let there be perfect unity, perfect comradeship in the struggle. All men are enemies. All animals are comrades."

At this moment there was a tremendous uproar. While Major was speaking four large rats had crept out of their holes and were sitting on their hindquarters, listening to him. The dogs had suddenly caught sight of them, and it was only by a swift dash for their holes that the rats saved their lives. Major raised his trotter for silence.

"Comrades," he said, "here is a point that must be settled. The wild creatures, such as rats and rabbits — are they our friends or our enemies? Let us put it to the vote. I propose this question to the meeting: Are rats comrades?"

10   The vote was taken at once, and it was agreed by an overwhelming majority that rats were comrades. There were only four dissentients, the three dogs and the cat, who was afterwards discovered to have voted on both sides. Major continued:

"I have little more to say. I merely repeat, remember always your duty of enmity towards Man and all his ways. Whatever goes upon two legs is an enemy. Whatever goes upon four legs, or has wings, is a friend. And remember also that in fighting against Man, we must not come to resemble him. Even when you have conquered him, do not adopt his vices. No animal must ever live in a house, or sleep in a bed, or wear clothes, or drink alcohol, or smoke tobacco, or touch money, or engage in trade. All the habits of Man are evil. And, above all, no animal must ever tyrannise over his own kind. Weak or strong, clever or simple, we are all brothers. No animal must ever kill any other animal. All animals are equal."

Understanding and Interpreting

1 According to Old Major, what is the fate of every animal and why is it unjust?

2 Old Major acknowledges that a rebellion may not happen for one hundred years, long after the lives of the animals he is speaking to have ended (par. 6). What does he suggest that the animals do in order to overcome this obstacle and keep the hope of rebellion alive?

3 Why does the cat vote on both sides of the issue regarding whether or not wild creatures are comrades?

4 Old Major makes a distinction between the farm animals and the "wild creatures" such as rats and rabbits, and then calls for a vote to determine if these wild creatures are comrades (pars. 9–10). What is Old Major's purpose in asking the farm animals to take this vote?

5 What are the "habits of Man" (par. 11), according to Old Major, and why does he admonish the animals to never take on these habits themselves?

Analyzing Language, Style, and Structure

1 In the second paragraph, how do the adjectives serve to establish the "plain truth" about the life of animals for Old Major's argument?

2 What function does Old Major's rhetorical question in the second paragraph serve in the structure of his overall argument?

3 What evidence does Old Major use to support his ultimate claim that Man is "the only real enemy" (par. 3) that the animals have?

4 What rhetorical strategies does Old Major rely on in presenting his argument? Do you find them effective?

5 How does Old Major's assertion "All men are enemies. All animals are comrades" (par. 7) effectively promote his call for rebellion?

6 Old Major concludes his call for rebellion with the statement that "[a]ll animals are equal." How does this declaration ultimately support his purpose?

Connecting, Arguing, and Extending

1 Orwell's *Animal Farm* is an allegory. In Old Major's speech, the farm animals represent the workers, and the humans represent the capitalists who profit from their labor. What might *Animal Farm* be an allegory for in contemporary times? What would Old Major rebel against today?

2 There are many movements that fight for animal rights, specifically farm animal rights. Research some organizations working for this cause, and compare the rhetoric in their messaging. Do they echo Old Major's speech in any way?

3 The novel *Animal Farm* was written in the 1940s, a time when there were fears about the rise of communism in general, and the Soviet Union and Stalin in particular. Was *Animal Farm* effective as anti-communist literature? Read the novel yourself, then research how the story is read and taught in schools, and research what its cultural legacy seems to be. Based on that, determine if it was ultimately effective at its rhetorical purpose.

ENTERING THE CONVERSATION
VOICES OF REBELLION

Making Connections

1 Both Martin Luther King (p. 355) and Nelson Mandela (p. 364) worked to change not just unjust laws but the belief systems that allowed those laws to exist. In other words, they had to leverage pathos to change hearts, and logos to change laws. Revisit the speeches by King and Mandela, and discuss whether one speaker relies more on one appeal than the other speaker, and how audiences may have contributed to these rhetorical choices.

2 Both Thomas Paine (p. 374) and Nelson Mandela (p. 364) recognize that the political changes they are calling for will likely require violence. Revisit both of their texts, and then compare and contrast the degree and magnitude of the changes that Paine and Mandela seem to be suggesting are necessary in order to achieve their political ends.

3 Like Mandela in his statements before his trial, Paine (p. 374) offers reasons why taking arms against the ruling political power is not only justified, but necessary.

Select two significant moments from both the Paine and Mandela arguments, and discuss the ways in which the attitude of each speaker shows ambition as well as restraint. Use textual evidence from each passage in your response.

4 The pieces by Carrie Chapman Catt (p. 383) and Malala Yousafzai (p. 378) both call for women's rights, in one case to vote, in the other to education. Revisit these speeches and analyze how each speaker challenges the men in her audience to change their positions, without alienating them. What rhetorical strategies do Catt and Yousafzai employ to maintain this crucial balance? In what ways are their strategies different and in what ways are they similar?

5 Both Nelson Mandela (p. 364) and Old Major, from Orwell's *Animal Farm* (p. 388) call for the use of force to overcome oppression. Revisit each text, and compare the ways each speaker justifies the use of violence as a response to oppression.

Synthesizing Sources

1 All of the texts in this Conversation are in response to very specific circumstances, yet they all include ideas that transcend the particular issue they are addressing. Revisit the speeches and identify a universal theme that at least three speakers address. Then, in a well-organized essay, explain how each of the speakers addresses the theme you identified. Also identify the rhetorical strategies each speaker uses to effectively argue his or her point.

2 Many of the texts in this Conversation contain references to religion or faith, even though most of the speakers are not religious leaders. Select three of the texts in this Conversation, identify the references to faith or religion in each of the texts, and write an essay in which you analyze how these references are used to advocate political change.

3 What rhetorical moves do these calls for change share? What makes an effective voice of rebellion? What, in your mind, makes some of the texts in this Conversation more effective than others?

4 You have read pieces by leaders calling for change through peaceful means and by force. In a well-reasoned response, argue whether a peaceful approach to change is effective in the long run, or whether lasting change must ultimately involve violence. Use specific examples from the texts in this Conversation to support your argument.

5 In this Conversation, we hear only the voices of the oppressed calling for justice. What sort of rhetoric do the powerful use? Choose one or two of the texts in this Conversation and research speeches or responses from those on the other side of the issue. What characterizes their rhetoric, and how does it differ from the voice of rebellion?

6 Each of the texts in this Conversation advocates for significant political and social changes. Without referencing the specific speaker, create a political poster using images and a slogan that capture a main argument in each of the speeches. Share the posters with your peers and ask them to decide which poster accompanies each of the speeches, justifying their reasons for pairing each poster with the speech with which they think it belongs.

ANALYZING FIGURATIVE LANGUAGE

As you may have read in Chapter 2, **figurative language** refers to nonliteral uses of language, such as when your teachers say they have told your class to pay attention "a million times." They probably have not really said so one million times but are using figurative language (hyperbole, in this case) to communicate just how frustrated they are.

Some of the most common figures of speech are:

- *Metaphor:* a direct comparison between unlike things
- *Simile:* a comparison between unlike things using "like" or "as"
- *Hyperbole:* a deliberate exaggeration or overstatement
- *Personification:* giving human qualities to inanimate objects
- *Allusion:* a reference to something well known—a work of literature or art, a historical event, and so on

Figurative language is one tool among many that writers use to convey their ideas—some writers employ figurative language regularly; others rarely do. In your study of literature, or on standardized tests, you sometimes will be asked to identify examples of figurative language. That's an essential place to start, but you can't stop there. Analyzing figurative language is not a treasure hunt to find as many literary devices as possible, nor is it a contest to see how many fancy terms you can memorize. It is much more important to be able to describe how an author uses figurative language to create meaning, to add emotion, to give a piece power. Analyzing figurative language is about *effect*.

In this Workshop, you will begin by identifying examples of figurative language from texts in this chapter. You will then have an opportunity to practice creating your own figures of speech before looking at how the choices of figurative language affect meaning in this chapter's Central Text, *Macbeth*. Finally, you will apply this knowledge to an analysis of another piece from the chapter.

Identifying Figurative Language

Read or reread the first two stanzas of "Flight 063" by Brian Aldiss, in which the speaker of the poem, a passenger on a plane, thinks about the Greek myth of Icarus, which tells of a boy who flew too close to the sun, melting the wax of his homemade wings.

> Why always speak of Icarus' fall? —
> That legendary plunge
> Amid a shower of tallow
> And feathers and the poor lad's
> Sweat? And that little splash
> Which caught the eye of Brueghel
> While the sun remained
> Aloof within its private zone?

That fall remains
Suspended in the corporate mind.
Yet as our Boeing flies
High above the Arctic Circle
Into the sun's eye, think —
Before the fall the flight was.
(So with Adam — just before
The Edenic Fall, he had
That first taste of Eve.)

Notice how many different elements of figurative language Aldiss employs:

- **Allusions:** the myth of Icarus, the painter Bruegel, the airplane manufacturer Boeing, and the biblical story of Adam, Eve, and Eden
- **Personification:** "the sun remained / Aloof"; "Suspended in the corporate mind"; "Into the sun's eye"
- **Metaphor:** "a shower of tallow"

ACTIVITY

Too often figurative language is thought of as something only found in poetry, but it is also common in fiction and nonfiction. Look at this excerpt from *Common Sense* by Thomas Paine, which was written in 1776 in an effort to convince Americans to support the Revolutionary War. Identify as many examples of figurative language as you can.

> The sun never shined on a cause of greater worth. 'Tis not the affair of a city, a country, a province, or a kingdom, but of a continent — of at least one eighth part of the habitable globe. 'Tis not the concern of a day, a year, or an age; posterity are virtually involved in the contest, and will be more or less affected, even to the end of time, by the proceedings now. Now is the seed time of continental union, faith and honor. The least fracture now will be like a name engraved with the point of a pin on the tender rind of a young oak; the wound will enlarge with the tree, and posterity read it in full grown characters.

Effect of Figurative Language

Identifying examples of figurative language is a good first step, but it is far more important to consider *how* the figurative language contributes to the overall meaning of the work. In other words, you need to understand its effect.

Often the goal of using figurative language is to create strong images in the mind of the reader, usually by comparing one thing to another. Comparisons help convey images because they give the reader a frame of reference to understand what the writer is trying to communicate. A sportswriter trying to convey the sheer size of a boxer, for instance, might call him "Herculean," making an allusion to the familiar Greek hero.

A famous example of figurative language can be found near the end of Shakespeare's *Macbeth*, the Central Text in this chapter, when Macbeth learns of his wife's suicide (5.5.24–26):

> Life's but a walking shadow, a poor player
> That struts and frets his hour upon the stage
> And then is heard no more.

This metaphor, which compares life to a minor actor, is more than just imagery. The audience learns about Macbeth's perspective—at this point in the play—about the value and importance he is putting on ambition: perhaps it just doesn't matter since it's all just a show anyway. Or perhaps he is lamenting how he was manipulated by fate and the Weird Sisters, until his life no longer feels like it is under his control. He is just an actor playing a role in a play he didn't write. Metaphors, and all figurative language, often allow for multiple readings. Embrace that ambiguity. It's what gives depth to literature.

Look at this excerpt from "Landscape with the Fall of Icarus" by William Carlos Williams and notice the personification:

> the whole pageantry
>
> of the year was
> awake tingling
> near
>
> the edge of the sea
> concerned
> with itself
>
> sweating in the sun

While the personification of the "pageantry" being "awake" and "tingling" and the sea being "concerned" and "sweating" certainly adds to the imagery of the poem, it also relates to the central meaning, showing how the fall of Icarus, a man-made disaster, was insignificant to nature, which continued along, unaware of the boy's fall.

ACTIVITY

Look carefully at this photo of a tent camped beneath the aurora borealis, or northern lights. Describe the scene by using three or more different examples of figurative language. Try using comparisons to create images in the mind of a reader who cannot see the photograph. Then, explain the intended effect of your figurative language choices.

Piriya Photography/Getty Images

Analyzing Figurative Language

It is important that when you are reading a text closely for figurative language you remember that each instance is the result of a specific *choice* that a writer has made. In other words, if he or she had made a different choice, the effect would have been different. For example, when at the very beginning of his speech "I Have Been to the Mountaintop," Martin Luther King Jr. imagines being asked what time period in all of human history he would like to see, he chooses to respond with an allusion:

> I would take my mental flight by Egypt and I would watch God's children in their magnificent trek from the dark dungeons of Egypt through, or rather across the Red Sea, through the wilderness on toward the promised land.

The biblical allusion to ancient Egypt is not random: it is a direct comparison between the slaves escaping the pharaoh and the fight for civil rights that King has been championing. If he had, for instance, begun with a more recent allusion, say, to the signing of the Emancipation Proclamation, he would have lost the chance to tap into a quest for freedom with roots deep in the Judeo-Christian tradition, a tradition shared by both his audience and his oppressors. The fight for freedom, he suggests with his allusion, is a righteous cause, and those who oppose it are going against their own Christian values. It's a clever two-pronged approach.

Look at this chart of examples of figurative language from *Macbeth* and notice how the specific choices Shakespeare makes not only create images through comparison but also reveal something significant about Macbeth's character or the theme of the play.

	Example	**Analysis of Effect**
Metaphor	As Macbeth is surrounded by the invading troops, he says: They have tied me to a stake. (5.7.1)	Macbeth is not literally tied to a stake awaiting execution, but the implied comparison allows him to communicate how powerless he feels.
Simile	Preparing to kill Duncan, but having second thoughts, Macbeth says: And Pity, like a naked newborn babe [. . .] Shall blow the horrid deed in every eye, That tears shall drown the wind. (1.721–25)	Everyone will know the pity of this murder, but he compares pity to a naked, newborn babe, which is ultimately weak and powerless in the face of his ambition. Bad things happen to good people all throughout this play; weakness and innocence will not keep anyone from being hurt.

	Example	Analysis of Effect
Personification	When the invading troops are approaching his stronghold, Macbeth says: Our castle's strength Will laugh a siege to scorn. (5.5.2–3)	By giving his castle a human quality—the ability to laugh at the invaders—he demonstrates not only his confidence, but also how much he and his castle are connected. He will survive only as it does.
Allusion	As the invading forces are overwhelming his own, Macbeth asks: Why should I play the Roman fool and die On mine own sword? (5.8.1–2)	The Roman fool is a reference to historical characters featured in another Shakespearean play, *Julius Caesar*, in which Brutus and Cassius kill themselves instead of being captured or dying in battle. Macbeth sees no honor in this and vows to fight to the very end.

Hyperbole	Just after Macbeth has killed Duncan, he looks at the blood on his hands and says:
	
	Will all great Neptune's ocean wash this
	    blood
	Clean from my hand? No, this my hand will
	    rather
	The multitudinous seas incarnadine,
	Making the green one red. (2.2.64–67)
		The blood on his hands certainly can be washed off, but Macbeth claims that there is so much blood that it would actually turn the ocean red, which demonstrates just how deep his sense of guilt is.

ACTIVITY

Read or reread this excerpt from *Henry VIII* by William Shakespeare, in which Cardinal Wolsey considers his sudden downfall from his position as advisor to the king. Spokesmen for the king have just left Wolsey alone on stage to think about "the state of man." Make a chart similar to the one above by analyzing the figurative language used in Cardinal Wolsey's speech. Note that not every figure of speech listed above may be present in the selection. After analyzing the individual examples of figurative language and their effects, discuss any patterns that emerge, and explain how Shakespeare's use of figurative language supports the message of a once-proud man losing everything.

CARDINAL WOLSEY So farewell — to the little good you bear me.
    Farewell! a long farewell, to all my greatness!
    This is the state of man: to-day he puts forth
    The tender leaves of hopes; to-morrow blossoms,
    And bears his blushing honours thick upon him;

The third day comes a frost, a killing frost,
And when he thinks, good easy man, full surely
His greatness is a-ripening, nips his root,
And then he falls, as I do. I have ventur'd,
Like little wanton boys that swim on bladders,
This many summers in a sea of glory,
But far beyond my depth. My high-blown pride
At length broke under me, and now has left me,
Weary and old with service, to the mercy
Of a rude stream that must for ever hide me. [. . .]
And when he falls, he falls like Lucifer,
Never to hope again.

ACTIVITY

Read the following selection from "The Rules of the Game," by Amy Tan, in which the narrator, a young Chinese American girl, is competing in her first chess tournament, which her very competitive mother encourages her to win. Identify and explain how the use of figurative language contributes to the meaning of the passage.

from The Rules of the Game / Amy Tan

During my first tournament, my mother sat with me in the front row as I waited for my turn. I frequently bounced my legs to unstick them from the cold metal seat of the folding chair. When my name was called, I leapt up. My mother unwrapped something in her lap. It was her chang, a small tablet of red jade which held the sun's fire. "Is luck," she whispered, and tucked it into my dress pocket. I turned to my opponent, a fifteen-year-old boy from Oakland. He looked at me, wrinkling his nose.

As I began to play, the boy disappeared, the color ran out of the room, and I saw only my white pieces and his black ones waiting on the other side. A light wind began blowing past my ears. It whispered secrets only I could hear.

"Blow from the South," it murmured. "The wind leaves no trail." I saw a clear path, the traps to avoid. The crowd rustled. "Shhh! Shhh!" said the corners of the room. The wind blew stronger. "Throw sand from the East to distract him." The knight came forward ready for the sacrifice. The wind hissed, louder and louder. "Blow, blow, blow. He cannot see. He is blind now. Make him lean away from the wind so he is easier to knock down."

"Check," I said, as the wind roared with laughter. The wind died down to little puffs, my own breath.

WRITING AN ARGUMENT

Why Write an Argument?

Few skills are more valuable than the ability to make an effective argument. The ability to present your reasoned point of view clearly and to convince others that your ideas are correct will be useful in every area of your life, both today and in the future. Do you need to convince a teacher that you deserve a different grade? Make a good argument. Do you need to persuade your parents to let you stay out later this weekend? Is there a political policy that you believe unfairly targets certain individuals based on race, gender, or sexual orientation? Do you need to convince a potential employer you're the best fit for a job? Make a good argument.

Earlier in this chapter, you may have read some of the speeches in the Voices of Rebellion Conversation and saw the impact an effective argument can have on the world. Martin Luther King Jr. made the case for nonviolent economic boycotts to improve conditions for workers in Memphis; Malala Yousafzai presented her argument for universal education in the face of religious extremism before an international audience; and Thomas Paine penned words that some historians credit with convincing the colonists to support the American Revolution. Real arguments matter in the real world.

Step 1: Find a Topic

One of the first difficulties we face when assigned to write an argumentative essay is finding something to write about. Malala Yousafzai wasn't assigned to write a persuasive speech; she had an important idea that she wanted to communicate to others. So, the key thing is to be sure that you are writing about something that you are genuinely interested in. This will make your writing much more authentic.

It is also important to think about *questions* you have, rather than *topics* you might write about. Although you might be tempted to jump right to the point you want to make, it is better to take some time and ask as many questions as you can about the topic first. For instance, if you are interested in sports, you might ask questions such as:

- Why are players paid so much?
- Is it ethical to watch football, knowing the risk of concussions for the players?
- Are there acceptable uses of performance-enhancing drugs in sports, and if so, what are they?
- What are the differences between the support that female athletes receive and the support received by male athletes?

Focusing on questions such as these will allow you to begin narrowing down your broad topic (sports) into more specific ones (such as safety, or salaries), while at the same time keeping your options open to a lot of argumentative possibilities within your topic.

Ambition and Restraint

ACTIVITY

Look over the list of topics below and write two or three questions that you have about the topics. Avoid questions that can be answered with yes or no or with a single statement. Also avoid questions that have obvious pro/con sides to them, such as "should cell phones be banned in schools?" Try writing provocative questions that reasonable people might have different opinions about. Eventually, you will select one question that you will use throughout the rest of this Workshop.

1. Education
2. Sports
3. Entertainment (such as movies, video games, music)
4. Local or national politics
5. Interactions between the United States and other countries
6. Technology
7. Topics of your own

Step 2: Gather Information

Once you've decided on a particular question that you have a genuine interest in, your next step is to begin gathering information and developing an informed opinion on the subject.

Start with What You Know

While you will certainly want to consult a wide variety of sources, including research studies, statistics, and articles by experts, it's often a good idea to start with what you know. Draw on your experiences, as well as those of others around you, to begin informing your view on the subject.

Look at this excerpt from the speech that Malala Yousafzai delivered at the United Nations and notice how she incorporates an anecdote about a classmate's experience into her argument:

> I remember that there was a boy in our school who was asked by a journalist, "Why are the Taliban against education?" He answered very simply. By pointing to his book he said, "A Talib doesn't know what is written inside this book." They think that God is a tiny, little conservative being who would send girls to the hell just because of going to school. The terrorists are misusing the name of Islam and Pashtun society for their own personal benefits.

When you have a genuine interest in the argument you plan to write, there is likely some kind of personal experience that you (or people you know) have had with your topic. If, for instance, your question is "Why do some school districts receive more funding than others?" you can think about the facilities and class sizes at your own school, and you can ask your family members or friends about the schools they attended.

ACTIVITY

Choose one of the questions that you wrote for the Activity above and write three to five examples from your own experiences, or those of people you know, that could give you information about your question. While eventually, this might be used as evidence, at this point, you are still at the information-gathering stage. Feel free to ask friends, classmates, and relatives, or to even conduct surveys (either online or offline) to learn more about their feelings or experiences with the question you selected. If you cannot identify personal examples that might illustrate elements of your question, consider choosing a different topic because this one might not be authentic or relevant to your interests.

Investigate the Issue

Personal experience is a good place to start an argument. It gets you invested in the issue. Nevertheless, personal experience is not enough to give you the complete picture. You need to encounter multiple perspectives on the issue, look into the details of the situation, and investigate every angle possible. You need to go from having an opinion to having an *informed* opinion.

Begin by seeking answers to your questions. Who might have expertise on the issue you've chosen to write about? Scientists? Psychologists? Politicians?

In his piece "Ambition: Why Some People Are Most Likely to Succeed," Jeffrey Kluger asks this question:

> Why are some people born with a fire in the belly, while others [. . .] need something to get their pilot light lit? And why do others never get the flame of ambition going?

To answer this question, Kluger consults the Shipp brothers—two very successful businessmen who were unmotivated until their late twenties, when they started their first business—for information about their personal experience, but then he moves on to consider a variety of disciplines to inform his opinion on the question:

- Biology: "Even before wolf pups are weaned, they begin sorting themselves out into alphas and all the others."
- Business: "Steve Wozniak co-founded Apple Computer and then left the company. [. . .]"
- Anthropology: " 'Ambition is an evolutionary product,' says anthropologist Edward Lowe. [. . .]"
- Psychology: "Dean Simonton, a psychologist [. . .], believes it's more complicated than that. 'Ambition is energy and determination,' he says."
- History: "We may listen to Mozart, but should we applaud Salieri?"
- Genetics: "Ongoing studies of identical twins have measured achievement motivation. [. . .]"
- Economics: "Economists [. . .] gave them five minutes to add up as many two-digit numbers as they could, and paid them 50¢ for each correct answer."

Although you do not necessarily need to consult sources from this many disciplines, we hope that Kluger's examples give you some sense of what it means to develop an informed opinion. So, as you develop your topic and the questions that will guide your investigation, ask yourself which different fields of study might hold some answers.

It's likely that your investigation will uncover just as many new questions as it does answers. Learn to embrace that complexity. Understanding that every issue is complicated and that issues almost never have a clear answer will prevent you from writing an argument that is closed-minded, unreasonable, and not persuasive to anyone who doesn't already agree with you.

ACTIVITY

Returning to your question, begin conducting research in order to identify the following:

1. Who are three to five experts in the fields that your question relates to? These will be the names of people who are referenced in many articles or in the bibliographies of multiple Wikipedia pages.
2. What are the most controversial parts to your question? Why is there controversy?
3. What are two or three of the most interesting or surprising facts or results of research studies that relate to your question?

If you cannot find a wide range of information or controversy about your question, consider choosing a different topic. It is far better to switch topics at this point than to continue forward with one that might not work well.

Step 3: Make a Claim

So far in this Workshop, you have not been asked to write about your own position on the question you have been exploring. This is intentional; too often writers go into a topic already knowing their position, which can blind them to the complexity of the issue. But now, after conducting research and thinking about your own personal experiences with the topic, it is time for you to begin thinking about how you would answer the question you've been thinking about. You cannot have a successful argument if you do not have a **claim**, which is what you are hoping to prove, or convince your audience to believe. All strong arguments have a claim that the reader can identify and debate.

In the speech during his trial for supporting and planning terrorist attacks against the South African government during the apartheid period, a time of forced separation of whites and blacks, Nelson Mandela stated this claim:

> I must deal immediately and at some length with the question of violence. [. . .]
>
> We first broke the law in a way which avoided any recourse to violence; when this form was legislated against, and then the government resorted to a show of force to crush opposition to its policies, only then did we decide to answer violence with violence.

But the violence which we chose to adopt was not terrorism. We who formed Umkhonto were all members of the African National Congress, and had behind us the ANC tradition of non-violence and negotiation as a means of solving political disputes. We believe that South Africa belongs to all the people who live in it, and not to one group, be it black or white. We did not want an interracial war, and tried to avoid it to the last minute.

You can see that Mandela, while admitting that he participated in and planned violence, claims that this violence was not terrorism because it was the only means left to him to oppose the oppression of his people.

It's important to remember that an argument's claim must be debatable. Without a debate, there is nothing to prove. So, when making a claim, be sure that it is something that people are able to disagree with. You should also avoid simply stating a preference ("chocolate is better than vanilla"). There is no way to prove a claim like that using hard evidence. In addition, you should avoid a claim that just states a fact that is easily proved or disproved ("teenagers require more sleep than adults"). If it's a proven fact, it's not debatable. Mandela's claim might seem undeniable because it has the force of history behind it, but a reasonable person might argue that violence is never justified, no matter what oppression and atrocities are committed upon you. The South African government at the time certainly disputed his claim: they sentenced him to life in prison.

ACTIVITY

Consider the question you have been using throughout this Workshop, and write a claim that stakes out your own position on the question. Your claim should answer the question and state your main reasons for believing what you do or include a call for an action that ought to be taken (or both). Try including a "because _____" phrase in your claim to help explain not just what you will argue, but why. Be sure that the claim is a debatable one as in the example above.

Avoid including the phrases "I think," "I believe," or "in my opinion." The purpose of an argument is to say what you think or believe, so these phrases are redundant.

Step 4: Select Your Evidence

In Step 2, when you were gathering information about your question, it was for the purpose of learning as much as possible about your topic before coming to an informed position in the form of your claim or thesis. Now it is time to begin making your case—by turning the information you gained into evidence that you can use to support your claim. A good argument includes a wide range and variety of evidence. Also, as we will see in Step 6, you will need to identify the opposition to your claim, and the evidence that your opponents might use (the **counterargument**), before you begin actually writing your argument.

One way of selecting your evidence is to sort the information you have gathered by *viewpoint, appeal, and strength*. For instance, imagine that you have been researching whether whaling should be banned globally. In your research, you probably found a lot of different information about the current whale population and current laws that have been put in place to protect them, as well as the role that whaling plays in various cultures, including Japan. From this research, imagine that you made a claim that because the whale population has not increased enough, all commercial hunting of whales should be banned worldwide. As you start to plan your essay, you will need to focus. You can't talk about everything, and you can't use every scrap of information you've gathered, so you need to pick the strongest pieces that are the most relevant to your claim. How do you decide which are the strongest? Some potential evidence might be strong because it appeals to logos: the quote perfectly expresses your idea with some facts or statistics. Some might be strong because of ethos: the credentials of the source add weight to your argument. Some might be strong because it appeals to pathos: the information lends a strong emotional aspect to your argument.

- You could then make a chart like the following to help you organize and select your information:

Information	Viewpoint	Appeal	Strength
Historical information about international bans on the practice of whaling	Supports	Logos	Very strong evidence
An interview about the cultural significance of whales in Japan	Opposes	Pathos	Strong for opposition
Facts about endangered status of whales	Supports	Logos	Extremely strong
Reports questioning the science behind the endangered status	Opposes	Logos	Moderately strong
Information about how wasteful whaling practices are	Supports	Logos/pathos	Not very strong
Testimonials about the special place that whales have in our hearts	Supports	Pathos	Not very strong

You can see that through this ongoing process of sorting information and selecting evidence, a possible organizational structure has emerged. This essay on Japan's whaling might start with the endangered status of whales while addressing the concerns of the flaws in the science, then move on to the international bans in place, and finally address the counterargument by discussing the cultural significance of whales in Japan and other places.

Step 5: Write Your Opening

One of the most difficult parts of writing any piece is how to start. Think of your opening as having three parts:

1. The hook
2. Context
3. Your claim or thesis

The Hook

Regardless of who the members of your audience are, they have a lot of demands on their time and a lot of options for what to read. You have to make them want to read *your* piece. So, begin your argument by "hooking" your readers with some kind of attention grabber. This might be a shocking fact, a startling statistic, a profound personal story, or any number of other things. Whatever it takes to draw your readers in. If you think back to the rhetorical appeals discussed in Chapter 3, you can see that a successful hook often relies on an appeal to pathos—emotion. Pathos is the spice of an argument. It makes it interesting, gives it flavor, but should be used sparingly. The hook is a great place to use it.

Take a look at how Martin Luther King Jr. uses pathos to establish both the danger and the epic historical nature of an important moment in Memphis:

> Something is happening in Memphis; something is happening in our world. And you know, if I were standing at the beginning of time, with the possibility of taking a kind of general and panoramic view of the whole of human history up to now, and the Almighty said to me, "Martin Luther King, which age would you like to live in?" I would take my mental flight by Egypt and I would watch God's children in their magnificent trek from the dark dungeons of Egypt through, or rather across the Red Sea, through the wilderness on toward the promised land. And in spite of its magnificence, I wouldn't stop there.

The Context

Another thing to think about when starting your argument is how much background you need to provide for your audience. If you are making an argument, for example, that a Mac computer is a better choice than a PC for gamers because of the graphics and processing speed, you will have to ask yourself whether your audience has enough technological knowledge to understand a sentence like: "The MacBook Pro has a 2.2GHz quad-core Intel Core i7 processor (Turbo Boost up to 3.4GHz) with 6MB shared L3 cache." If the members of your audience do not have some technological knowledge, you may need to explain some of these terms and the effect they have on the gaming experience. If your audience does not understand the context of your argument, you have little chance of persuading it of your claim. The amount of context you will need to include will vary based on the complexity of the issue or the specificity of the evidence you will likely use.

When Yousafzai spoke at the United Nations in 2013, her story was well known to all or most of her audience, but she still offered some context for her argument by saying, "Dear Friends, on the 9th of October 2012, the Taliban shot me on the left side of my forehead. They shot my friends too." This information is key to understanding her argument.

ACTIVITY

Write a draft of your introductory paragraph by putting together the following components:

1. Your hook (ethos, logos, or pathos)
2. Appropriate and necessary context—the background information your audience will need to understand what follows
3. Your claim

Step 6: Write Your Body Paragraphs

At some point in your education, you may have heard that an essay is supposed to have five paragraphs: an introduction, three body paragraphs, and a conclusion. Your argumentative essay might, in fact, have five paragraphs, but it also might have four or fourteen, or any other number in between or beyond, depending on the complexity of your argument, and the scope of the project you have been given. Nelson Mandela's speech, "An Ideal for Which I Am Prepared to Die," for instance, reportedly went on for over two hours, while Malala Yousafzai's address at the U.N. took about twenty minutes. The point is that your argument should be as long as it needs to be to convince your audience of your claim. This is not to say that there are no guidelines at all for how you make your argument. In general, you should have an introduction and a conclusion, and include body paragraphs that provide a variety of evidence that is fully explained and connected to your claim. You should also address the significant counterarguments to your claim.

Structuring a Paragraph

Just like the "five-paragraph essay" can be a useful template that you can adapt to suit your purpose, paragraphs in academic papers also tend to have a consistent pattern that can give you a good model to follow. Essentially, each of your body paragraphs will have a topic sentence that identifies a component of your claim, evidence that supports it, and your own commentary about how that evidence supports that part of your claim. You will include as much or as little evidence as you need to make your point, though it is always important to follow every piece of evidence with your commentary. In this way, you will be sure to "connect the dots" for your reader.

Again, this structure is not intended as a formula but is suggested as a guide for you to use as it fits for you and your argument. You can see how elements of this structure are in place in some of the paragraphs in this excerpt from "Ambition: Why Some People Are Most Likely to Succeed," by Jeffrey Kluger:

Topic sentence — If humans are an ambitious species, it's clear we're not the only one. Many animals are known to signal their ambitious tendencies — Clarification/context almost from birth. Even before wolf pups are weaned, they begin sorting themselves out into alphas and all the others. The alphas are quicker, more curious, greedier for space, milk, Mom—and they stay that way for life. Alpha wolves wander widely, breed annually and may live to a geriatric 10 or 11 years old. Lower-ranking wolves enjoy none of these benefits—staying close to home, breeding rarely and usually dying before they're 4. — Evidence

Topic sentence — Humans often report the same kind of temperamental determinism. Families are full of stories of the inexhaustible infant who grew up to be an entrepreneur, the phlegmatic child who never really showed much go. But if it's genes that run the show, what accounts for the Shipps, who didn't bestir themselves until the cusp of adulthood? And what, more tellingly, explains identical twins—precise genetic templates of each other who ought to be temperamentally identical but often exhibit profound differences in the octane of their ambition? — Commentary comparing human behavior to wolf behavior from the previous paragraph

Notice that Kluger spreads the evidence and commentary over two paragraphs. Again, the structure suggested above is not a rigid formula. The point here is that evidence should never stand on its own. It should be accompanied by commentary from you, the writer. In an argumentative essay, telling your audience what the evidence proves, and why it is relevant to your overall argument, is an important part of your job.

ACTIVITY

Write a draft of one or more body paragraphs of your argument, starting with the strongest reason that supports your claim. Be sure to use and explain the evidence. Use the format and the models above to guide you.

Addressing the Counterargument

An essential part of making your argument is to address the counterargument, the ideas that differ from the one you are using as your claim. These ideas are not necessarily against your entire position, but they might represent a different course of action, or might go beyond what you are willing to propose.

Some writers address the counterarguments immediately, at the beginning of their piece, acknowledging and quickly dismissing their opponents' points. Other writers may wait until later in their argument, after they have made their strongest points. In Old Major's speech in *Animal Farm*, he addresses the counterargument near the beginning, in order to remove the objection right away:

> "No animal in England is free. The life of an animal is misery and slavery: that is the plain truth.
>
> "But is this simply part of the order of nature? Is it because this land of ours is so poor that it cannot afford a decent life to those who dwell upon it? No, comrades, a thousand times no! The soil of England is fertile, its climate is good, it is capable of affording food in abundance to an enormously greater number of animals than now inhabit it."

Given Old Major's firebrand style, the refutation of the counterargument is a bit harsher than what we might expect in an academic paper, but note that Old Major supports his strident rejection with solid logical evidence.

The basic approach of addressing the counterarguments is to acknowledge and concede any valid points your opponents might make, and then refute the main thrust of their arguments. Unaddressed counterarguments linger in the minds of thoughtful readers who say, "Yeah, but what about _____?" Your job as a successful writer of arguments includes anticipating all reasonable objections to your claim and presenting evidence that your point of view is the most reasonable.

It may be tempting to use a phrase such as "Some people say . . . ," but this only prompts readers to question: "Who?" Try, instead, to fully understand and describe the opposition's position, and respectfully identify any noteworthy experts who hold that view.

Be careful to avoid the **straw man** logical fallacy in which you misrepresent the opposition or present an opponent's view in an incomplete or exaggerated way just to make it easy to refute. Here is a straw man from President Obama's second inaugural address: "We reject the belief that America must choose between caring for the generation that built this country and investing in the generation that will build its future."

Whose belief is Obama referring to? Was anyone really suggesting that we shouldn't care for the previous generations *and* invest in the future? Even people who opposed

Obama's fiscal policies likely never believed something so extreme. A straw man fallacy sets up the opposition's weakest argument or misrepresents it for the sole purpose of refuting it. You build your own ethos by addressing opponents' objections ethically and fully.

ACTIVITY

Write a draft of a body paragraph in which you address one of the strongest counter-arguments to your claim. Describe it fully and ethically and be sure to refute it with evidence and reasoning. Also, consider where in your essay this paragraph will appear. Near the beginning or at the end? Or paired with a particular point you want to make? Why?

Step 7: Wrap Up the Argument

Just as pathos is frequently an effective hook to introduce your essay, it is, more often than not, the most powerful approach to concluding it. Writers often want to get their readers to feel something before they ask for them to take some kind of action. Look at the conclusion of Yousafzai's speech, which is filled with appeals to emotion:

> Dear brothers and sisters, we must not forget that millions of people are suffering from poverty, injustice and ignorance. We must not forget that millions of children are out of schools. We must not forget that our sisters and brothers are waiting for a bright peaceful future.
>
> So let us wage a global struggle against illiteracy, poverty and terrorism and let us pick up our books and pens. They are our most powerful weapons.
>
> One child, one teacher, one pen and one book can change the world.
>
> Education is the only solution. Education First.

Notice, too, that Yousafzai's conclusion includes a call to action—"So let us wage a global struggle against illiteracy. [. . .]" In addition to pathos, a good conclusion to an argument usually includes a "So what?" statement that tells readers what you want them to think about, or do. What reforms should take place? What studies should be conducted? What viewpoint should be re-evalutated? What programs should be funded? This is a final opportunity for you to connect directly with your readers.

ACTIVITY

Write a conclusion to your argumentative essay that includes a final appeal to emotion and a call to action.

7
Ethics

- How do we tell "right" from "wrong"?
- Can there be a universal understanding of what is "right" or "wrong"?
- To what extent do age, culture, and other factors affect our ethical decisions?
- When making ethical decisions, whose needs should be most important? The individual's, other people's, the larger society's?
- What causes us to cheat? Is cheating always wrong? Who gets to define "cheating"?

Imagine that you are the operator of a train that has suddenly lost its brakes. Ahead of you on the tracks are *five* railroad workers who are unaware that you are moments away from slamming into them at a speed that will likely kill them all. But then, you notice that there is a split up ahead, which would allow you to switch to a different track, at the end of which is only *one* railroad worker. Your choice: keep on the first track and kill five, or switch tracks and kill only one. Do you kill the one to save the five? Why or why not?

This is a classic ethical dilemma that Michael Sandel, the author of the Central Text in this chapter, offers students in his justice course at Harvard University in order to illustrate the complexity of ethical choices. Philosopher Judith Jarvis Thomson complicates the dilemma even further by asking you to imagine that you were no longer the operator, but instead a bystander on a bridge watching the train heading toward the five workers, and next to you on the bridge—leaning far over—is a rather large man. You could very easily

Photo: Shutterstock. Art: Christian Mojallali.

push the man off the bridge in front of the train, which would stop its progress, thereby saving the five at the end of the track. Would you push the man, killing one to save the five? Why or why not? What's similar and different between this scenario and the previous one? What if you knew for certain that the large man on the bridge was a murderer who had gotten away with his crime?

Obviously, these are situations that do not occur too frequently, but they can help us to clarify what we mean by "ethics." As a branch of philosophy, ethics tries to articulate the reasons that some actions are considered "right" and others "wrong." Just about everyone will say that killing is wrong, and yet, in scenarios such as the ones above, could killing sometimes be justified? Most people will say that stealing is wrong—yet could stealing be acceptable if you couldn't afford the medicine that was needed to save your dying child? Is it OK to cheat on a test that everyone else is cheating on, especially since you might be competing with them for acceptance into a good college?

We know that different cultures, religions, and nations have different customs, laws, and practices, but do they also have different ethical codes? Philosopher Bertrand Russell wrote, "I cannot see how to refute the arguments for the subjectivity of ethical values, but I find myself incapable of believing that all that is wrong with wanton cruelty is that I don't like it." In other words, he expects that there should be some things that all people— regardless of culture—ought to be able to agree are right or wrong, in at least some situations.

▶

What essential ethical conflict does this cartoon rely on to make its point? Think of an example of this conflict from your own life.

OPENING ACTIVITY 1

Working with a partner or a small group, look through the follow[...]
actions as either "very bad," "kind of bad," or "not so bad." Be [...]
reasoning for why you put each where you did:

- robbing a bank
- taking money from a parent without asking
- cheating on a husband or wife
- cheating on a girlfriend or boyfriend
- copying answers during a test
- copying homework
- lying to your friends about why you didn't meet up with them
- lying to a friend about whether the terrible haircut he or she got looks good
- illegally downloading a song from the Internet
- stealing a CD from a music store
- overcharging an insurance company if you are a doctor
- overcharging a patient if you are a doctor
- stealing a book from a bookstore
- taking a library book without checking it out
- going 15 miles per hour over the speed limit
- texting while driving
- driving while intoxicated

OPENING ACTIVITY 2

Read through the following scenarios and determine what you would do in each situation and why:

1. It is May of your senior year and your best friend has been accepted to Harvard on a full scholarship. Unfortunately, her mother has become very sick, and your friend has had to take care of her younger siblings, which has made it difficult for her to stay on top of her schoolwork and maintain the GPA required for her scholarship. She calls you one night in a panic because she has forgotten to do a major assignment due the following day and her teacher never accepts late work. You have completed the identical assignment for a different teacher. You go to a very big school and it is unlikely that either of the two teachers will ever see the other's assignments, so if you let your friend copy your work, the chances of your being caught are not high. Nevertheless, your school has a zero tolerance policy for cheating, and if you are caught, both of you could be subject to severe punishments, including an automatic F in the class. Do you email your friend your assignment so that she can turn it in as her own work? Why or why not?

2. You are a parent of an eighteen-year-old boy, and you, he, and your spouse are traveling to Singapore, a country with extremely strict drug laws. At the airport in Singapore, the security officials, using drug-sniffing dogs, begin looking closely at

your son's bag. You have suspected in the past that your son may have smoked marijuana, but you never knew for sure or confronted him about it. As the security officials move closer to the bag, you look at your son's face, and you know for sure that he has brought marijuana with him. At the same time, you realize your spouse knows this as well and is preparing to take the blame for your son, which would likely lead to his or her serving many years in prison. When the security officials ask, "Whose bag is this?" what do you do? Why?

3. Imagine that you are working for a government intelligence agency. You captured a confirmed terrorist whom you suspect might have information about an imminent terrorist attack that you believe would result in the deaths of thousands of citizens. The terrorist is not offering the information willingly. Would you authorize torture on the terrorist if you thought it gave you a reasonable chance of preventing the attack? Why or why not?

4. The following scenario is a real-life example from a famous court case in England called *The Queen v. Dudley and Stephens.* In 1884, four British men survived a shipwreck and floated for three weeks in a lifeboat in the Atlantic. When they ran out of food and water, the captain decided that they should draw straws to determine who would be killed and eaten in order to save the remaining three. The others refused. Eventually, the cabin boy became sick. When he was near death, the captain decided to kill him. The captain and the other two survivors ate his body, which kept them alive until they were rescued four days later. Upon returning to England, the captain was charged with murder. If you were on the jury, would you vote to convict the captain? Why or why not?

5. The following scenario is a classic fictional ethical situation called "The Heinz Dilemma": Imagine that you had a wife dying from a rare disease. A drug that might save her was available from a pharmacist in town, but he was charging $200,000, a sum that you could never pay and was ten times what the pharmacy paid for the drug wholesale. You borrowed all the money you could and went to the pharmacist with half the amount needed and asked him to sell the drug cheaper. When he refused, you became desperate and broke into the pharmacy to steal the drug. Should you have done that? More important, why or why not?

from The Case against Perfection

Michael Sandel

Political philosopher and Harvard professor Michael Sandel (b. 1953) is best known for the extremely popular course on ethics and justice that he has taught for the past twenty years. His class often needs to be held in a large lecture hall to accommodate the thousand or more students who enroll each semester. The selection you are about to read comes from an article published in the *Atlantic* in April 2004; five years later, Sandel expanded his argument into a book with the same title.

© Rick Friedman/Corbis

KEY CONTEXT   In this essay, Sandel explores the ethics of genetic engineering in order to enhance the physical, intellectual, or emotional characteristics of a child. Although such procedures are not yet approved in the United States, the Food and Drug Administration has begun explorations into radical biological procedures that, if successful, would produce genetically modified human beings. At this point, the techniques being considered involve manipulation of DNA to prevent inheritance of devastating diseases that result from genetic abnormalities.

Part 1   **The Case against Perfection**

Breakthroughs in genetics present us with a promise and a predicament. The promise is that we may soon be able to treat and prevent a host of debilitating diseases. The predicament is that our newfound genetic knowledge may also enable us to manipulate our own nature — to enhance our muscles, memories, and moods; to choose the sex, height, and other genetic traits of our children; to make ourselves "better than well." When science moves faster than moral understanding, as it does today, men and women struggle to articulate their unease. In liberal societies they reach first for the language of autonomy, fairness, and individual rights. But this part of our moral vocabulary is ill equipped to address the hardest questions posed by genetic engineering. The genomic revolution has induced a kind of moral vertigo.

Consider cloning. The birth of Dolly the cloned sheep, in 1997, brought a torrent of concern about the prospect of cloned human beings. There are good medical reasons to worry. Most scientists agree that cloning is unsafe, likely to produce offspring with serious abnormalities. (Dolly recently died a premature death.) But suppose technology improved to the point where clones were at no greater risk than naturally conceived offspring. Would human cloning still be objectionable? Should our hesitation be moral as well as medical? What, exactly, is wrong with creating a child who is a genetic twin of one parent, or of an older sibling who has tragically died — or, for that matter, of an admired scientist, sports star, or celebrity?

Some say cloning is wrong because it violates the right to autonomy: by choosing a child's genetic makeup in advance, parents deny the child's right to an open future. A similar objection can be raised against any form of bioengineering that allows parents to select or reject genetic characteristics. According to this argument, genetic enhancements for musical talent, say, or athletic prowess, would point children toward particular choices, and so designer children would never be fully free.

At first glance the autonomy argument seems to capture what is troubling about human cloning and other forms of genetic engineering. It is not persuasive, for two reasons. First, it wrongly implies that absent a designing parent, children are free to choose their characteristics for themselves. But none of us chooses his genetic inheritance. The alternative to a cloned or genetically enhanced child is not one whose future is unbound by particular talents but one at the mercy of the genetic lottery.

5   Second, even if a concern for autonomy explains some of our worries about made-to-order children, it cannot explain our moral hesitation about people who seek genetic remedies or enhancements for themselves. Gene therapy on somatic (that is, nonreproductive) cells, such as muscle cells and brain cells, repairs or replaces defective genes. The moral quandary arises when people use such therapy not to cure a disease but to reach beyond health, to enhance their physical or cognitive capacities, to lift themselves above the norm.

Like cosmetic surgery, genetic enhancement employs medical means for nonmedical ends — ends unrelated to curing or preventing disease or repairing injury. But unlike cosmetic surgery, genetic enhancement is more than skin-deep. If

we are ambivalent about surgery or Botox injections for sagging chins and furrowed brows, we are all the more troubled by genetic engineering for stronger bodies, sharper memories, greater intelligence, and happier moods. The question is whether we are right to be troubled, and if so, on what grounds.

In order to grapple with the ethics of enhancement, we need to confront questions largely lost from view — questions about the moral status of nature, and about the proper stance of human beings toward the given world. Since these questions verge on theology, modern philosophers and political theorists tend to shrink from them. But our new powers of biotechnology make them unavoidable.

Muscles. Everyone would welcome a gene therapy to alleviate muscular dystrophy and to reverse the debilitating muscle loss that comes with old age. But what if the same therapy were used to improve athletic performance? Researchers have developed a synthetic gene that, when injected into the muscle cells of mice, prevents and even reverses natural muscle deterioration. The gene not only repairs wasted or injured muscles but also strengthens healthy ones. This success bodes well for human applications. H. Lee Sweeney, of the University of Pennsylvania, who leads the research, hopes his discovery will cure the immobility that afflicts the elderly. But Sweeney's bulked-up mice have already attracted the attention of athletes seeking a competitive edge. Although the therapy is not yet approved for human use, the prospect of genetically enhanced weight lifters, home-run sluggers, linebackers, and sprinters is easy to imagine. The widespread use of steroids and other performance-improving drugs in professional sports suggests that many athletes will be eager to avail themselves of genetic enhancement.

Suppose for the sake of argument that muscle-enhancing gene therapy, unlike steroids, turned out to be safe — or at least no riskier than a rigorous weight-training regimen. Would there be a reason to ban its use in sports? There is something unsettling about the image of genetically altered athletes lifting SUVs or hitting 650-foot home runs or running a three-minute mile. But what, exactly, is troubling about it? Is it simply that we find such superhuman spectacles too bizarre to contemplate? Or does our unease point to something of ethical significance?

10   It might be argued that a genetically enhanced athlete, like a drug-enhanced athlete, would have an unfair advantage over his unenhanced competitors. But the fairness argument against enhancement has a fatal flaw: it has always been the case that some athletes are better endowed genetically than others, and yet we do not consider this to undermine the fairness of competitive sports. From the standpoint of fairness, enhanced genetic differences would be no worse than natural ones, assuming they were safe and made available to all. If genetic enhancement in sports is morally objectionable, it must be for reasons other than fairness.

Sex selection. Perhaps the most inevitable nonmedical use of bioengineering is sex selection. For centuries parents have been trying to choose the sex of their children. Today biotech succeeds where folk remedies failed.

One technique for sex selection arose with prenatal tests using amniocentesis and ultrasound. These medical technologies were developed to detect genetic abnormalities such as spina bifida and Down syndrome. But they can also reveal the sex of the fetus — allowing for the abortion of a fetus of an undesired sex. Even among those who favor abortion rights, few advocate abortion simply because the parents do not want a girl. Nevertheless, in traditional societies with a powerful cultural preference for boys, this practice has become widespread.

Sex selection need not involve abortion, however. For couples undergoing *in vitro* fertilization (IVF), it is possible to choose the sex of the child before the fertilized egg is implanted in the womb. One method makes use of preimplantation genetic diagnosis (PGD), a procedure developed to screen for genetic diseases. Several eggs are fertilized in a petri dish and grown to the eight-cell stage (about three days). At that point the embryos are tested to determine their sex. Those of the desired sex are implanted; the others are typically discarded. Although few couples are likely to undergo the difficulty and expense of IVF simply to choose the sex of their child, embryo screening is a highly reliable means of sex selection. And as our genetic knowledge increases, it may be possible to use PGD to cull embryos carrying undesired genes, such as those associated with obesity, height, and skin color. The science-fiction movie *Gattaca* depicts a future in which parents routinely screen embryos for sex, height, immunity to disease, and even IQ. There is something troubling about the *Gattaca* scenario, but it is not easy to identify what exactly is wrong with screening embryos to choose the sex of our children.

One line of objection draws on arguments familiar from the abortion debate. Those who believe that an embryo is a person reject embryo screening for the same reasons they reject abortion. If an eight-cell embryo growing in a petri dish is morally equivalent to a fully developed human being, then discarding it is no better than aborting a fetus, and both practices are equivalent to infanticide. Whatever its merits, however, this "pro-life" objection is not an argument against sex selection as such.

15   The latest technology poses the question of sex selection unclouded by the matter of an embryo's moral status. The Genetics & IVF Institute, a for-profit infertility clinic in Fairfax, Virginia, now offers a sperm-sorting technique that makes it possible to choose the sex of one's child before it is conceived. X-bearing sperm,

seeing connections

In a survey of 999 people who sought genetic counseling, most were eager for a wider spectrum of prenatal genetic tests—as long as they were for disease, according to Feighanne Hathaway, MS, of New York University Langone Medical Center, and colleagues.

Only a handful said they'd be interested in genetic tests for such traits as intelligence or height, the researchers said online in the *Journal of Genetic Counseling*.

"Although the media portrays a desire for 'designer babies,' this does not appear to be true among consumers of genetic testing services," Hathaway said in a statement.

The findings come from a questionnaire given to 2,246 people who came to the NYU Human Genetics Program for prenatal genetic counseling from July 2006 to February 2007.

Almost half of them—999, or 45 percent—agreed to answer the ten-question survey, the researchers said.

A majority of respondents said they would screen for mental retardation (75 percent), blindness (56 percent), deafness (54 percent), heart disease (52 percent), and cancer (51 percent).

The volunteers were also asked whether they'd test for diseases that caused death within a defined period of time after birth. Almost half— 49.3 percent—said they'd elect prenatal testing for a condition that resulted in death by the age of five.

But the proportion who would seek testing fell as the hypothetical lifespan increased: 41.1 percent would choose testing for a disease that caused death by the age of twenty, 24.9 percent if the age of death was forty, and 19 percent if it was fifty.

Only a minority of respondents said they'd want genetic testing for enhancements, including athletic ability (10 percent), superior intelligence (12.6 percent), height (10.4 percent), and longevity (9.2 percent).

On the other hand, a majority of the volunteers (52.2 percent) would not rule out any form of genetic testing.

The questionnaire did not ask about sex selection using genetic testing, but five respondents who added comments said they thought testing for sex was never merited.

Based on this data, what conclusions can you draw about the attitude of the general public toward genetic engineering as a means of predicting and enhancing the well-being of human offspring?

which produce girls, carry more DNA than Y-bearing sperm, which produce boys; a device called a flow cytometer can separate them. The process, called MicroSort, has a high rate of success.

If sex selection by sperm sorting is objectionable, it must be for reasons that go beyond the debate about the moral status of the embryo. One such reason is that sex selection is an instrument of sex discrimination — typically against girls, as illustrated by the chilling sex

ratios in India and China. Some speculate that societies with substantially more men than women will be less stable, more violent, and more prone to crime or war. These are legitimate worries — but the sperm-sorting company has a clever way of addressing them. It offers MicroSort only to couples who want to choose the sex of a child for purposes of "family balancing." Those with more sons than daughters may choose a girl, and vice versa. But customers may not use the technology to stock up on children of the same sex, or even to choose the sex of their firstborn child. (So far the majority of MicroSort clients have chosen girls.) Under restrictions of this kind, do any ethical issues remain that should give us pause?

The case of MicroSort helps us isolate the moral objections that would persist if muscle-enhancement, memory-enhancement, and height-enhancement technologies were safe and available to all.

It is commonly said that genetic enhancements undermine our humanity by threatening our capacity to act freely, to succeed by our own efforts, and to consider ourselves responsible — worthy of praise or blame — for the things we do and for the way we are. It is one thing to hit seventy home runs as the result of disciplined training and effort, and something else, something less, to hit them with the help of steroids or genetically enhanced muscles. Of course, the roles of effort and enhancement will be a matter of degree. But as the role of enhancement increases, our admiration for the achievement fades — or, rather, our admiration for the achievement shifts from the player to his pharmacist. This suggests that our moral response to enhancement is a response to the diminished agency of the person whose achievement is enhanced.

Though there is much to be said for this argument, I do not think the main problem with enhancement and genetic engineering is that they undermine effort and erode human agency. The deeper danger is that they represent a kind of hyperagency — a Promethean aspiration to remake nature, including human nature, to serve our purposes and satisfy our desires. The problem is not the drift to mechanism but the drive to mastery. And what the drive to mastery misses and may even destroy is an appreciation of the gifted character of human powers and achievements.

20 To acknowledge the giftedness of life is to recognize that our talents and powers are not wholly our own doing, despite the effort we expend to develop and to exercise them. It is also to recognize that not everything in the world is open to whatever use we may desire or devise. Appreciating the gifted quality of life constrains the Promethean project and conduces to a certain humility. It is in part a religious sensibility. But its resonance reaches beyond religion.

It is difficult to account for what we admire about human activity and achievement without drawing upon some version of this idea. Consider two types of athletic achievement. We appreciate players like Pete Rose, who are not blessed with great natural gifts but who manage, through striving, grit, and determination, to excel in their sport. But we also admire players like Joe DiMaggio, who display natural gifts with grace and effortlessness. Now, suppose we learned that both players took performance-enhancing drugs. Whose turn to drugs would we find more deeply disillusioning? Which aspect of the athletic ideal — effort or gift — would be more deeply offended?

Some might say effort: the problem with drugs is that they provide a shortcut, a way to win without striving. But striving is not the point of sports; excellence is. And excellence consists at least partly in the display of natural talents and gifts that are no doing of the athlete who possesses them. This is an uncomfortable fact for democratic societies. We want to believe that success, in sports and in life, is something we earn, not something we inherit. Natural gifts, and the admiration they inspire, embarrass the meritocratic faith; they cast doubt on the conviction that praise and rewards flow from effort alone. In the face of this embarrassment we inflate the moral significance of striving, and depreciate giftedness. This distortion can be seen, for example, in network-television coverage of the Olympics, which focuses less on the feats the athletes perform than on heartrending stories of the hardships they have overcome and the struggles they have waged to triumph over an injury or a difficult upbringing or political turmoil in their native land.

But effort isn't everything. No one believes that a mediocre basketball player who works and trains even harder than Michael Jordan deserves greater acclaim or a bigger contract. The real problem with genetically altered athletes is that they corrupt athletic competition as a human activity that honors the cultivation and display of natural talents. From this standpoint, enhancement can be seen as the ultimate expression of the ethic of effort and willfulness — a kind of high-tech striving. The ethic of willfulness and the biotechnological powers it now enlists are arrayed against the claims of giftedness.

Understanding and Interpreting

1 In the opening paragraph, Michael Sandel asserts that recent "breakthroughs in genetics present us with a promise and a predicament" that have caused "a kind of moral vertigo." Why? What is his explanation of how these breakthroughs affect our moral and ethical beliefs?

2 Sandel states that "breakthroughs in genetics" challenge our basic notions of "autonomy, fairness, and individual rights" (par. 1). According to Sandel, what is the basis for each of these three moral objections to genetic manipulation, and what is his assessment of each argument?

3 Sandel argues that "questions about the moral status of nature, and about the proper status of human beings toward the given world" make many people uncomfortable, yet "our new powers of biotechnology make them unavoidable" (par. 7). Why does he believe that we cannot avoid addressing these questions?

4 Why does Sandel believe that the fairness argument against genetic enhancement of muscles "has a fatal flaw" (par. 10)? Explain how you would support or challenge his reasoning in this instance.

5 Why does the process called "MicroSort," according to Sandel, "isolate the moral objections that would persist" if various genetic enhancement technologies "were safe and available to all" (par. 17)? Pay attention to why many view MicroSort as a more acceptable alternative to other methods of genetically engineered sex selection.

6 Explain what Sandel means in this statement: "The problem is not the drift to mechanism but the drive to mastery" (par. 19). How does this "drive to mastery" relate to what Sandel characterizes as "the gifted character of human powers and achievements"?

Analyzing Language, Style, and Structure

1 Sandel makes a provocative statement at the beginning of this essay: "The genomic revolution has induced a kind of moral vertigo" (par. 1). What is the impact of the figure of speech "moral vertigo"? Do you find it appropriate? Do you think it serves the author's purpose in the introduction to his argument? Explain why or why not.

2 In paragraphs 2 and 3, Sandel discusses cloning, a technique that had not, at the time of the article's publication, proved successful. How does this issue lay a foundation for the argument he is building?

3 Sandel draws a comparison between cosmetic surgery and genetic enhancement (par. 6), then points out that the comparison is limited, even faulty. What is the effect of his drawing the comparison and then dismissing it so quickly?

4 At the end of paragraph 2, Sandel asks a series of rhetorical questions, a strategy he uses throughout the essay. To what extent is it effective in this instance?

5 In his discussion of gene therapy for muscle enhancement (par. 8), Sandel cites the work of researcher H. Lee Sweeney, not a household name to most readers of the *Atlantic*. What is Sandel's purpose in including this specific reference rather than merely explaining that research into application of muscle enhancement therapy is in progress?

6 Sandel's explanation of sex selection is quite detailed, with considerable scientific information about several biotechnologies. Why does Sandel go to such lengths in an article published in a magazine appealing to a fairly general, although educated, audience?

7 Is Sandel's allusion to the mythical Prometheus (pars. 19 and 20) rhetorically appropriate to his topic and position, or does it strike you as hyperbole? Support your response with specifics from the essay.

8 Sandel supports one of his points using two baseball players, Joe DiMaggio and Pete Rose, as examples (par. 21). What is his purpose in choosing this example? Are these athletes likely to be familiar to his audience? Why do you think the example works or does not work to support his point?

Connecting, Arguing, and Extending

1 Sandel asserts that the "moral quandary arises when people use such [gene] therapy not to cure a disease but to reach beyond health, to enhance their physical or cognitive capacities, to lift themselves above the norm" (par. 5). To what extent do you believe it is morally wrong to use gene therapy for purposes other than prevention or cure of disease? Where do you draw the line between what is morally acceptable and unacceptable?

2 Sandel points out that one of the arguments against bioengineering sex selection is that it is "an instrument of sex discrimination" (par. 16). Explain why you agree or disagree with this viewpoint.

3 Some philosophers have criticized Sandel for being guilty of the slippery-slope fallacy. That is, they believe that his contention that "science moves faster than moral understanding" (par. 1) suggests that allowing certain forms of genetic engineering will pave the way for any and all types of enhancement. To what extent do you think that Sandel's argument is weakened by a slippery-slope line of reasoning?

4 Sandel asserts that "striving is not the point of sports; excellence is" (par. 22). Develop your own argument—not necessarily discussing genetic enhancement—to support, challenge, or qualify Sandel's claim.

5 Some ethicists argue that somatic cell gene therapy, which affects only people who are already alive, is acceptable, but any genetic engineering that affects future generations is not. Explain why you do or do not agree with this distinction, and include specific examples in your explanation.

Part 2 **The Case against Perfection**

The ethic of giftedness, under siege in sports, persists in the practice of parenting. But here, too, bioengineering and genetic enhancement threaten to dislodge it. To appreciate children as gifts is to accept them as they come, not as objects of our design or products of our will or instruments of our ambition. Parental love is not contingent on the talents and attributes a child happens to have. We choose our friends and spouses at least partly on the basis of qualities we find attractive. But we do not choose our children. Their qualities are unpredictable, and even the most conscientious parents cannot be held wholly responsible for the kind of children they have. That is why parenthood, more than other human relationships, teaches what the theologian William F. May calls an "openness to the unbidden."

25   May's resonant phrase helps us see that the deepest moral objection to enhancement lies less in the perfection it seeks than in the human disposition it expresses and promotes. The problem is not that parents usurp the autonomy of a child they design. The problem lies in the hubris of the designing parents, in their drive to master the mystery of birth. Even if this disposition did not make parents tyrants to their children, it would disfigure the relation between parent and child, and deprive the parent of the humility and enlarged human sympathies that an openness to the unbidden can cultivate.

To appreciate children as gifts or blessings is not, of course, to be passive in the face of illness or disease. Medical intervention to cure or prevent illness or restore the injured to health does not desecrate nature but honors it. Healing sickness or injury does not override a child's natural capacities but permits them to flourish.

Nor does the sense of life as a gift mean that parents must shrink from shaping and directing the development of their child. Just as athletes and artists have an obligation to cultivate their talents, so parents have an obligation to cultivate their children, to help them discover and develop their talents and gifts. As May points out, parents give their children two kinds of love: accepting love and transforming love. Accepting love affirms the being of the child, whereas transforming love seeks the well-being of the child. Each aspect corrects the excesses of the other, he writes: "Attachment becomes too quietistic if it slackens into mere acceptance of the child as he is." Parents have a duty to promote their children's excellence.

These days, however, overly ambitious parents are prone to get carried away with transforming love — promoting and demanding all manner of accomplishments from their children, seeking perfection. "Parents find it difficult to maintain an equilibrium between the two sides of love," May observes. "Accepting love, without transforming love, slides into indulgence and finally neglect. Transforming love, without accepting love, badgers and finally rejects." May finds in these competing impulses a parallel with modern science: it, too, engages

▶
————————

This political cartoon by Tom Toles appeared in 1999.

To what extent is the argument Toles makes similar to that of Sandel in "The Case against Perfection"?

us in beholding the given world, studying and savoring it, and also in molding the world, transforming and perfecting it.

The mandate to mold our children, to cultivate and improve them, complicates the case against enhancement. We usually admire parents who seek the best for their children, who spare no effort to help them achieve happiness and success. Some parents confer advantages on their children by enrolling them in expensive schools, hiring private tutors, sending them to tennis camp, providing them with piano lessons, ballet lessons, swimming lessons, SAT-prep courses, and so on. If it is permissible and even admirable for parents to help their children in these ways, why isn't it equally admirable for parents to use whatever genetic technologies may emerge (provided they are safe) to enhance their children's intelligence, musical ability, or athletic prowess?

30   The problem with genetic engineering is that [it] represent[s] the one-sided triumph of willfulness over giftedness, of dominion over reverence, of molding over beholding. Why, we may wonder, should we worry about this triumph? Why not shake off our unease about genetic enhancement as so much superstition? What would be lost if biotechnology dissolved our sense of giftedness?

From a religious standpoint the answer is clear: To believe that our talents and powers are wholly our own doing is to misunderstand our place in creation, to confuse our role with God's. Religion is not the only source of reasons to care about giftedness, however. The moral stakes can also be described in secular terms. If bioengineering made the myth of the "self-made man" come true, it would be difficult to view our talents as gifts for which we are indebted, rather than as achievements for which we are responsible. This would transform three key features of our moral landscape: humility, responsibility, and solidarity.

In a social world that prizes mastery and control, parenthood is a school for humility. That we care deeply about our children and yet cannot choose the kind we want teaches parents to be open to the unbidden. Such openness is a disposition worth affirming, not only within families but in the wider world as well. It invites us to abide the unexpected, to live with dissonance, to rein in the impulse to control. A *Gattaca*-like world in which parents became accustomed to specifying the sex and genetic traits of their children would be a world inhospitable to the unbidden, a gated community writ large. The awareness that our talents and abilities are not wholly our own doing restrains our tendency toward hubris.

Though some maintain that genetic enhancement erodes human agency by overriding effort, the real problem is the explosion, not the erosion, of responsibility. As humility gives way, responsibility expands to daunting proportions. We attribute less to chance and more to choice. Parents become responsible for choosing, or failing to choose, the right traits for their children. Athletes become responsible for acquiring, or failing to acquire, the talents that will help their teams win.

A lively sense of the contingency of our gifts — a consciousness that none of us is wholly responsible for his or her success — saves a meritocratic society from sliding into the smug assumption that the rich are rich because they are more deserving than the poor. Without this, the successful would become even more likely than they are now to view themselves as self-made and self-sufficient, and hence wholly responsible for their success. Those at the bottom of society would be viewed not as disadvantaged, and thus worthy of a measure of compensation, but as simply unfit, and thus worthy of eugenic repair. The meritocracy, less chastened by chance, would become harder, less forgiving.

35   There is something appealing, even intoxicating, about a vision of human freedom unfettered by the given. It may even be the case that the allure of that vision played a part in summoning the genomic age into being. It is often assumed that the powers of enhancement we now possess arose as an inadvertent by-product of biomedical progress — the genetic revolution came, so to speak, to cure disease, and stayed to tempt us with the prospect of enhancing our performance, designing our children, and perfecting our nature. That may have the story backwards. It is more plausible to view genetic engineering as the ultimate expression of our resolve to see ourselves astride the world, the masters of our nature. But that promise of mastery is flawed. It threatens to banish our appreciation of life as a gift, and to leave us with nothing to affirm or behold outside our own will.

Understanding and Interpreting

1 In this final section, what is Sandel's view of how bioengineering and genetic enhancement "threaten to dislodge" the "ethic of giftedness" in parenting (par. 24)?

2 Sandel explains William F. May's distinction between the "accepting love" and "transforming love" (par. 27) that parents give their children. Which of these types of love does Sandel believe is most jeopardized by genetic enhancement?

3 What does Sandel mean by "the hubris of the designing parents" (par. 25)? To what extent do you think Sandel is imposing a value judgment on parents who would consider genetically engineering their children?

4 Sandel raises the issue of parents who endeavor to help their children become successful by providing SAT tutors or private coaching in sports and asks whether these efforts are different from genetic enhancement (pars. 29–32). How does he answer that question? Do you agree or disagree?

5 How does Sandel answer the question he asks in paragraph 30: "What would be lost if biotechnology dissolved our sense of giftedness?" Consider the language he uses to frame his response, including "moral stakes" and "secular terms" (par. 31).

6 What does Sandel mean when he asserts that the "real problem" with genetic enhancement "is the explosion, not the erosion, of responsibility" (par. 33)?

7 Why does Sandel question the impact of genetic engineering on a "meritocratic' society" (par. 34)? Why is this specific context relevant to his viewpoint?

8 What is Sandel's final conclusion about genetic enhancement? Does he qualify his earlier position or reassert it?

Analyzing Language, Style, and Structure

1 As Sandel explores the concept of "giftedness," he alludes to the theologian William F. May's phrase "openness to the unbidden" (pars. 24 and 25). To what extent does using May as a source strengthen or weaken the argument Sandel is in the process of developing?

2 What counterarguments does Sandel cite in this section? How effective is he in refuting them? Comment on at least two examples of counterarguments.

3 What is the logic that Sandel uses to develop his point that genetically engineering children would undermine or "transform" our sense of "humility" and "solidarity" (par. 31)? Does he move from a series of examples to a general conclusion or the reverse: that is, from a general statement to a series of examples that support it?

4 In this section, Sandel refers to "a religious standpoint," and in the previous section he refers to the "pro-life" position on abortion (par. 14). Issues of

religion and abortion can sometimes be volatile and evoke strong reactions. How does he maintain a balanced perspective on these issues? Consider both his language and organization.

5 When Sandel argues against "a world inhospitable to the unbidden," he uses the metaphor that our world would risk becoming "a gated community writ large" (par. 32). What does that figure of speech suggest? To what extent do you think it is an effective strategy to promote his argument?

6 In paragraph 34, Sandel moves to a more political discussion of income inequity. Do you think he connects that issue clearly to the larger topic, or does it seem tangential or forced? Explain in terms of the argument he is developing.

7 How would you describe the tone of the conclusion to this essay? Is Sandel optimistic or pessimistic? Is he guarded or emphatic? Cite specific language choices to support your response.

Connecting, Arguing, and Extending

1 Consider the analogy Sandel draws between parents' efforts to ensure the best for their children—that is, sending them to expensive schools, hiring private tutors, providing music and other artistic enrichment—and the possibility of their choosing to genetically enhance their children's intellectual ability, athletic ability, and physical appearance. Where would you draw the line between what is acceptable and what is not? And why?

2 Bonnie Steinbock, PhD, is a professor of philosophy at the University at Albany, State University of New York, with a specialty in bioethics. In an October 2008 article in the *Lancet*, a well-regarded British medical journal, she argues that "it's far from obvious that such interventions [as genetic engineering] would be wrong" and concludes as follows:

> Genetic enhancement of embryos is, for the present, science fiction. Its opponents think that we need to ban it now, before it ever becomes a reality. What they have not provided are clear reasons to agree. Their real opposition is not to a particular means of shaping children, but rather to a certain style of parenting. Rather than fetishising

the technology, the discussion should focus on which parental attitudes and modes of parenting help children to flourish. It may be that giving children "genetic edges" of certain kinds would not constrain their lives and choices, but actually make them better. That possibility should not be dismissed out of hand.

Are you more in agreement with Sandel in "The Case against Perfection" or with Steinbock? Explain with specific references to Sandel's essay.

3 Much of Sandel's argument in this section pivots on the distinction between accepting and transforming love. Psychologists tell us that accepting love is essential for healthy emotional development of a child. To what extent do you think that permitting all types of genetic enhancement might eliminate the very concept of accepting love?

4 What would you do? Imagine that ten years from now you want to have a child and technology that would enable you to deliberately choose specific mental or physical characteristics of the child is available. Would you use the technology or take your chances on a throw of the genetic dice?

Topics for Composing

1 Argument
Ultimately, how does Sandel challenge the case for perfection? Do you believe that striving for perfection is a worthy goal? A dangerous pursuit? A futile effort? Where do you draw the ethical line between what is acceptable and what is not? Is there truth in the saying that "perfect is the enemy of the good"? Explain your response with examples from your own experience and reading as well as reference to Sandel.

2 Research/Exposition

After researching the topic of genetically engineering children, explain what you believe are the most compelling ethical concerns. Consider "The Case against Perfection" in your response. You might also read other works by Sandel, listen to one or more of his lectures, or explore additional works on your own. You might also consult two U.S. government websites: the Human Genome Project and the Presidential Commission for the Study of Bioethical Issues.

3 Research/Exposition

Read "The Birthmark" by Nathaniel Hawthorne, a short story about a scientist's obsession to remove his wife's birthmark. What does this story have to say about the pursuit of perfection?

4 Research/Argument

In a review of Sandel's book that is an expansion of this essay, *The Case against Perfection*, critic William Saletan questions whether the ideas are outdated. He points out that in an earlier era, having a coach was believed to violate the spirit of sportsmanlike competition. He then asks: "Once gene therapy becomes routine, the case against genetic engineering will sound as quaint as the case against [. . .] coaches. If the genetic lottery were better than the self-made man, we might prefer the old truth to the new one. But Sandel's egalitarian fatalism already feels a bit 20th-century." Explain why you agree or disagree with Saletan's assessment.

5 Speech/Argument

Sandel's argument pivots on his definition of what it means to be a parent in the early twenty-first century. Write a speech that you would deliver to an audience of parents from your community explaining why you agree or disagree with Sandel's viewpoint.

6 Exposition

The 1997 sci-fi film *Gattaca* explores the consequences of genetic engineering. After viewing the film, explain what position the filmmakers take on the subject.

7 Research/Exposition

Broadly speaking, "The Case against Perfection" focuses on the complex ethical issues created by a new technology. Choose another example of technology and discuss the moral or ethical issues that it raises. You might choose a current technology, a technological development from the past, or a new emerging technology.

8 Multimodal/Argument

Choose one point or statement that Sandel makes and challenge or support it with your own observations, experience, or knowledge. Make your argument using only images (still, moving, or a combination) and sound but no words (neither voice-over narration nor written text).

CONVERSATION

DO THE RIGHT THING

Everyday life presents us with choices. Most times we make the right choice, sometimes we make the wrong choice, and just about every time, we wonder what would have happened had we made the other one. While it's unlikely that you have yet to face the ethical situation of "designing" your own baby as presented in the Central Text, you certainly have faced, and will face, difficult situations in which it will be hard to figure out the right thing to do. It might be something simple, such as a cashier's giving you too much change—do you really need to give it back? Or it could be a more difficult experience, such as seeing someone you don't know—or even someone you know and dislike—getting bullied at school. Do you intervene? All of those anti-bullying presentations say that you should, but do you? Why or why not?

Here's another scenario: imagine that you are walking down the street and you find an envelope filled with cash and no identification about who owns it. You know that you're *supposed* to take it to the police or put up signs in an effort to find the owner, and yet . . . in reality, most people would consider themselves lucky to find such a "gift," and keep it for themselves. Is that the right thing to do in that situation? Perhaps you could justify the act of keeping the money by giving some to charity or by paying off your grandparent's medical

In Homer's *Odyssey*, Odysseus is told by the sorceress Circe that in order to make it home, he must sail between Scylla and Charybdis—Scylla being a six-headed sea monster that jutted out from a rock to devour one sailor per head, and Charybdis being a monstrous whirlpool that engulfed entire ships. The dilemma is that if Odysseus sails too close to Charybdis, his entire ship will be destroyed and all his crew will be killed, while if he sails too close to Scylla, six of his men will be killed and eaten. Odysseus chose to sail closer to Scylla, choosing to save the many and sacrifice the few.

What does this story have to tell us about the challenges of making ethical decisions?

Erich Lessing/Art Resource, NY

bills, but really, you just want to keep the money. . . . Everyone tells stories to himself or herself to put the best spin on any situation, but when we can isolate a single ethical choice, as in the scenarios above, we can begin to recognize the parameters of the ethical dilemmas we face and, more important, to determine the best ways to make those choices.

In this Conversation, you will read short stories, nonfiction, and poetry that take place in a variety of settings, including a jail cell in Nigeria, a supermarket too far from the beach for bikinis, the side of a deserted road at night, and an unnamed village overrun with crabs. In each text, the protagonists wrestle with doing the right thing. The answers rarely come easily for them, and often they come at significant costs.

TEXTS

Gabriel García Márquez / A Very Old Man with Enormous Wings (fiction)
Chimamanda Ngozi Adichie / Cell One (fiction)
Nathan Englander / Free Fruit for Young Widows (fiction)
John Updike / A & P (fiction)
William Stafford / Traveling through the Dark (poetry)
Wisława Szymborska / A Contribution to Statistics (poetry)
Annie Dillard / An American Childhood (memoir)
Sam Harris / Lying (nonfiction)

A Very Old Man with Enormous Wings: A Tale for Children

Gabriel García Márquez

Translated by Gregory Rabassa

Colombian writer Gabriel García Márquez (1928–2014) was considered to be one of the most important literary figures of the twentieth century. Winner of the Nobel Prize for Literature in 1982, García Márquez wrote such famous novels as *One Hundred Years of Solitude*, *Love in the Time of Cholera*, and *Autumn of the Patriarch*. The story included here is from his collection *Leaf Storm and Other Stories*, which was published in English in 1972.

Ulf Andersen/Hulton Archive/Getty Images

KEY CONTEXT Even though he began his career as a journalist, García Márquez popularized what is often called "magical realism," in which elements of fantasy are inserted into situations that might otherwise seem ordinary. For instance, a character in *One Hundred Years of Solitude* who is considered to be too beautiful for this world ascends to heaven while in the middle of hanging the laundry. García Márquez's magical realism can also be seen in this story, in which a character named Pelayo finds an angel face down in the mud.

On the third day of rain they had killed so many crabs inside the house that Pelayo had to cross his drenched courtyard and throw them into the sea, because the newborn child had a temperature all night and they thought it was due to the stench. The world had been sad since Tuesday. Sea and sky were a single ash-gray thing and the sands of the beach, which on March nights glimmered like powdered light, had become a stew of mud and rotten shellfish. The light was so weak at noon that when Pelayo was coming back to the house after throwing away the crabs, it was hard for him to see what it was that was moving and groaning in the rear of the courtyard. He had to go very close to see that it was an old man, lying face down in the mud, who, in spite of his tremendous efforts, couldn't get up, impeded by his enormous wings.

Frightened by that nightmare, Pelayo ran to get Elisenda, his wife, who was putting compresses on the sick child, and he took her to the rear of the courtyard. They both looked at the fallen body with mute stupor. He was dressed like a ragpicker. There were only a few faded hairs left on his bald skull and very few teeth in his mouth, and his pitiful condition of a drenched great-grandfather had taken away any sense of grandeur he might have had. His huge buzzard wings, dirty and half-plucked, were forever entangled in the mud. They looked at him so long and so closely that Pelayo and Elisenda very soon overcame their surprise and in the end found him familiar. Then they dared speak to him, and he answered in an incomprehensible dialect with a strong sailor's voice. That was how they skipped over the inconvenience of the wings and quite intelligently concluded that he was a lonely castaway from some foreign ship wrecked by the storm. And yet, they called in a neighbor woman who knew everything about life and death to see him, and all she needed was one look to show them their mistake.

"He's an angel," she told them. "He must have been coming for the child, but the poor fellow is so old that the rain knocked him down."

On the following day everyone knew that a flesh-and-blood angel was held captive in Pelayo's house. Against the judgment of the wise neighbor woman, for whom angels in those times were the fugitive survivors of a celestial conspiracy, they did not have the heart to club him to death. Pelayo watched over him all afternoon from the kitchen, armed with his bailiff's club, and before going to bed he dragged him out of the mud and locked him up with the hens in the wire chicken coop. In the middle of the night, when the rain stopped, Pelayo and Elisenda were still killing crabs. A short time afterward the child woke up without a fever and with a desire to eat. Then they felt magnanimous and decided to put the angel on a raft with fresh water and provisions for three days and leave him to his fate on the high seas. But when they went out into the courtyard with the first light of dawn, they found the whole neighborhood in front of the chicken coop having fun with the angel, without the slightest reverence, tossing him things to eat through the openings in the wire as if he weren't a supernatural creature but a circus animal.

5   Father Gonzaga arrived before seven o'clock, alarmed at the strange news. By that time onlookers less frivolous than those at dawn had already arrived and they were making all kinds of conjectures concerning the captive's future. The simplest among them thought that he should be named mayor of the world. Others of sterner mind felt that he should be promoted to the rank of five-star general in order to win all wars. Some visionaries hoped that he could be put to stud in order to implant on earth a race of winged wise men who could take charge of the universe. But Father Gonzaga, before becoming a priest, had been a robust woodcutter. Standing by the wire, he reviewed his catechism in an instant and asked them to open the door so that

seeing connections

Erich Lessing/Art Resource, NY

The Good Samaritan, c.1550–70 (oil on canvas), Bassano, Jacopo (Jacopo da Ponte) (1510–92)/National Gallery, London, UK/Bridgeman Images

▲

This sixteenth-century painting by Charles Le Brun, *The Fall of the Rebel Angels*, depicts the angels who rebelled against God being sent out of heaven down to hell.

In what way is García Márquez using the biblical story of the fallen angels being cast out of heaven as an allusion in this short story? What is similar and different between the two?

▲

In the Bible, Jesus tells a parable about the Good Samaritan, a man who helped a stranger who was beaten and robbed, while several other people passed by without helping. The lesson is supposed to be "Love your neighbor as yourself," and everyone should be considered your neighbor.

What is the Samaritan doing in this sixteenth-century painting by Jacopo Bassano that the characters in the short story do or do not do? What point is García Márquez making about the townspeople by making an allusion to this parable?

he could take a close look at that pitiful man who looked more like a huge decrepit hen among the fascinated chickens. He was lying in a corner drying his open wings in the sunlight among the fruit peels and breakfast leftovers that the early risers had thrown him. Alien to the impertinences of the world, he only lifted his

antiquarian eyes and murmured something in his dialect when Father Gonzaga went into the chicken coop and said good morning to him in Latin. The parish priest had his first suspicion of an imposter when he saw that he did not understand the language of God or know how to greet His ministers. Then he noticed that seen close up he was much too human: he had an unbearable smell of the outdoors, the back side of his wings was strewn with parasites and his main feathers had been mistreated by terrestrial winds, and nothing about him measured up to the proud dignity of angels. Then he came out of the chicken coop and in a brief sermon warned the curious against the risks of being ingenuous. He reminded them that the devil had the bad habit of making use of carnival tricks in order to confuse the unwary. He argued that if wings were not the essential element in determining the difference between a hawk and an airplane, they were even less so in the recognition of angels. Nevertheless, he promised to write a letter to his bishop so that the latter would write to his primate[1] so that the latter would write to the Supreme Pontiff in order to get the final verdict from the highest courts.

His prudence fell on sterile hearts. The news of the captive angel spread with such rapidity that after a few hours the courtyard had the bustle of a marketplace and they had to call in troops with fixed bayonets to disperse the mob that was about to knock the house down. Elisenda, her spine all twisted from sweeping up so much marketplace trash, then got the idea of fencing in the yard and charging five cents admission to see the angel.

The curious came from far away. A traveling carnival arrived with a flying acrobat who buzzed over the crowd several times, but no one paid any attention to him because his wings were not those of an angel but, rather, those of a sidereal bat. The most unfortunate invalids on earth came in search of health: a poor woman who since childhood had been counting her heartbeats and had run out of numbers; a Portuguese man who couldn't sleep because the noise of the stars disturbed him; a sleepwalker who got up at night to undo the things he had done while awake; and many others with less serious

ailments. In the midst of that shipwreck disorder that made the earth tremble, Pelayo and Elisenda were happy with fatigue, for in less than a week they had crammed their rooms with money and the line of pilgrims waiting their turn to enter still reached beyond the horizon.

The angel was the only one who took no part in his own act. He spent his time trying to get comfortable in his borrowed nest, befuddled by the hellish heat of the oil lamps and sacramental candles that had been placed along the wire. At first they tried to make him eat some mothballs, which, according to the wisdom of the wise neighbor woman, were the food prescribed for angels. But he turned them down, just as he turned down the papal lunches that the penitents brought him, and they never found out whether it was because he was an angel or because he was an old man that in the end he ate nothing but eggplant mush. His only supernatural virtue seemed to be patience. Especially during the first days, when the hens pecked at him, searching for the stellar parasites that proliferated in his wings, and the cripples pulled out feathers to touch their defective parts with, and even the most merciful threw stones at him, trying to get him to rise so they could see him standing. The only time they succeeded in arousing him was when they burned his side with an iron for branding steers, for he had been motionless for so many hours that they thought he was dead. He awoke with a start, ranting in his hermetic language and with tears in his eyes, and he flapped his wings a couple of times, which brought on a whirlwind of chicken dung and lunar dust and a gale of panic that did not seem to be of this world. Although many thought that his reaction had been one not of rage but of pain, from then on they were careful not to annoy him, because the majority understood that his passivity was not that of a hero taking his ease but that of a cataclysm in repose.

Father Gonzaga held back the crowd's frivolity with formulas of maidservant inspiration

---

[1] primate: The chief bishop or archbishop of a province. —Eds.

while awaiting the arrival of a final judgment on the nature of the captive. But the mail from Rome showed no sense of urgency. They spent their time finding out if the prisoner had a navel, if his dialect had any connection with Aramaic, how many times he could fit on the head of a pin,[2] or whether he wasn't just a Norwegian with wings. Those meager letters might have come and gone until the end of time if a providential event had not put an end to the priest's tribulations.

10   It so happened that during those days, among so many other carnival attractions, there arrived in town the traveling show of the woman who had been changed into a spider for having disobeyed her parents. The admission to see her was not only less than the admission to see the angel, but people were permitted to ask her all manner of questions about her absurd state and to examine her up and down so that no one would ever doubt the truth of her horror. She was a frightful tarantula the size of a ram and with the head of a sad maiden. What was most heartrending, however, was not her outlandish shape but the sincere affliction with which she recounted the details of her misfortune. While still practically a child she had sneaked out of her parents' house to go to a dance, and while she was coming back through the woods after having danced all night without permission, a fearful thunderclap rent the sky in two and through the crack came the lightning bolt of brimstone that changed her into a spider. Her only nourishment came from the meatballs that charitable souls chose to toss into her mouth. A spectacle like that, full of so much human truth and with such a fearful lesson, was bound to defeat without even trying that of a haughty angel who scarcely deigned to look at mortals. Besides, the few miracles attributed to the angel showed a certain mental disorder, like the blind

man who didn't recover his sight but grew three new teeth, or the paralytic who didn't get to walk but almost won the lottery, and the leper whose sores sprouted sunflowers. Those consolation miracles, which were more like mocking fun, had already ruined the angel's reputation when the woman who had been changed into a spider finally crushed him completely. That was how Father Gonzaga was cured forever of his insomnia and Pelayo's courtyard went back to being as empty as during the time it had rained for three days and crabs walked through the bedrooms.

The owners of the house had no reason to lament. With the money they saved they built a two-story mansion with balconies and gardens and high netting so that crabs wouldn't get in during the winter, and with iron bars on the windows so that angels wouldn't get in. Pelayo also set up a rabbit warren close to town and gave up his job as bailiff for good, and Elisenda bought some satin pumps with high heels and many dresses of iridescent silk, the kind worn on Sunday by the most desirable women in those times. The chicken coop was the only thing that didn't receive any attention. If they washed it down with creolin[3] and burned tears of myrrh inside it every so often, it was not in homage to the angel but to drive away the dungheap stench that still hung everywhere like a ghost and was turning the new house into an old one. At first, when the child learned to walk, they were careful that he did not get too close to the chicken coop. But then they began to lose their fears and got used to the smell, and before the child got his second teeth he'd gone inside the chicken coop to play, where the wires were falling apart. The angel was no less standoffish with him than with other mortals, but he tolerated the most ingenious infamies with the patience of a dog who had no illusions. They both came down with chicken-pox at the same time. The doctor

---

[2] The common expression, "How many angels can dance on the head of a pin?" comes from an arcane theological debate over how much space an angel occupies. It has come to mean any frivolous question that is impossible to answer. —Eds.

[3] creolin: Thick black coal tar used as an antiseptic, germicide, or deodorant. —Eds.

who took care of the child couldn't resist the temptation to listen to the angel's heart, and he found so much whistling in the heart and so many sounds in his kidneys that it seemed impossible for him to be alive. What surprised him most, however, was the logic of his wings. They seemed so natural on that completely human organism that he couldn't understand why other men didn't have them too.

When the child began school it had been some time since the sun and rain had caused the collapse of the chicken coop. The angel went dragging himself about here and there like a stray dying man. They would drive him out of the bedroom with a broom and a moment later find him in the kitchen. He seemed to be in so many places at the same time that they grew to think that he'd been duplicated, that he was reproducing himself all through the house, and the exasperated and unhinged Elisenda shouted that it was awful living in that hell full of angels. He could scarcely eat and his antiquarian eyes had also become so foggy that he went about bumping into posts. All he had left were the bare cannulae of his last feathers. Pelayo threw a blanket over him and extended him the charity of letting him sleep in the shed, and only then did they notice that he had a temperature at night, and was delirious with the tongue twisters of an old Norwegian. That was one of the few times they became alarmed, for they thought he was going to die and not even the wise neighbor woman had been able to tell them what to do with dead angels.

And yet he not only survived his worst winter, but seemed improved with the first sunny days. He remained motionless for several days in the farthest corner of the courtyard, where no one would see him, and at the beginning of December some large, stiff feathers began to grow on his wings, the feathers of a scarecrow, which looked more like another misfortune of decrepitude. But he must have known the reason for those changes, for he was quite careful that no one should notice them, that no one should hear the sea chanteys that he sometimes sang under the stars. One morning Elisenda was cutting some bunches of onions for lunch when a wind that seemed to come from the high seas blew into the kitchen. Then she went to the window and caught the angel in his first attempts at flight. They were so clumsy that his fingernails opened a furrow in the vegetable patch and he was on the point of knocking the shed down with the ungainly flapping that slipped on the light and couldn't get a grip on the air. But he did manage to gain altitude. Elisenda let out a sigh of relief, for herself and for him, when she saw him pass over the last houses, holding himself up in some way with the risky flapping of a senile vulture. She kept watching him even when she was through cutting the onions and she kept on watching until it was no longer possible for her to see him, because then he was no longer an annoyance in her life but an imaginary dot on the horizon of the sea.

Understanding and Interpreting

1 Trace the townspeople's, including Pelayo's and Elisenda's, changing treatment of the old man through the course of the story. What conclusions could we draw about the theme of the story from this treatment?

2 What is the tone the narrator takes toward Father Gonzaga, and for what purpose?

3 How is "spider girl" different from the old man? Why is she a better attraction for the people? What point is García Márquez trying to make by contrasting her with the old man?

4 García Márquez gave this story a subtitle: "A Tale for Children." In what way can this be considered a children's story, and in what ways is it not one?

5 How do the last two lines, as Elisenda watches the old man fly away, illustrate the theme of the story?

Analyzing Language, Style, and Structure

1 Magical realism often includes paired contrasts; for instance, the otherworldliness of the man's wings is contrasted with the ordinariness of the few faded hairs on his bald head. Identify similar contrasts in the story and explain how they create the sense of magical realism.

2 Compare these two sentences identifying the old man, and explain the effect of the townspeople's conflicting conclusions:

   a. "That was how they skipped over the inconvenience of the wings and quite intelligently concluded that he was a lonely castaway from some foreign ship wrecked by the storm" (par. 2).
   b. "On the following day everyone knew that a flesh-and-blood angel was held captive in Pelayo's house" (par. 4).

3 Reread the following statement: "Pelayo threw a blanket over him and extended him the charity of letting him sleep in the shed, and only then did they notice that he had a temperature at night" (par. 12). Using this sentence and others that you identify, how would you characterize the narrator of this story? What is the narrator's tone toward the old man and toward the townspeople?

4 This piece contains many examples of figurative language intended to create an exaggerated, somewhat unreal feeling for the town, such as "The world had been sad since Tuesday." Identify other examples of figurative language and explain how they create this exaggerated effect.

Connecting, Arguing, and Extending

1 Evaluate the ethical choices that Pelayo and Elisenda make. Do they do "the right thing" or not? Who is harmed and who benefits the most from their choices? What are the most significant factors that cause them to make the choices they do?

2 Read a short story, novel, or poem classified as "magical realism." In addition to García Márquez, some of the most well-known authors of magical realism are Isabel Allende, Laura Esquivel, Jorge Luis Borges, Salman Rushdie, Toni Morrison, and Rudolfo Anaya. How is this author's use of magical realism similar to or different from García Márquez's use?

3 Throughout the story, the old man tries to speak, but in a language or dialect that no one, including the narrator, can understand. Identify a place in the story where the old man is unable to communicate effectively. Now, imagine that he is capable of making himself understood, and write a few lines of dialogue that he might say. How would the townspeople react to his speech?

4 Read the following excerpt from García Márquez's 1982 Nobel Prize speech, in which he responds to William Faulkner's 1950 Nobel speech warning of the dangers of nuclear war. After reading the excerpt, explain how García Márquez's tone toward humanity is reflected—or not—in "A Very Old Man with Enormous Wings":

> On a day like today, my master William Faulkner said, "I decline to accept the end of man." I would fall unworthy of standing in this place that was his, if I were not fully aware that the colossal tragedy he refused to recognize thirty-two years ago is now, for the first time since the beginning of humanity, nothing more than a simple scientific possibility. Faced with this awesome reality that must have seemed a mere utopia through all of human time, we, the inventors of tales, who will believe anything, feel entitled to believe that it is not yet too late to engage in the creation of the opposite utopia. A new and sweeping utopia of life, where no one will be able to decide for others how they die, where love will prove true and happiness be possible, and where the races condemned to one hundred years of solitude will have, at last and forever, a second opportunity on earth.

Cell One

Chimamanda Ngozi Adichie

Chimamanda Ngozi Adichie [chi-mah-*man*-dah nn-*go*-zee ah-*dee*-chee] was born in Nigeria in 1977. Her father was Nigeria's first professor of statistics, and later became deputy vice-chancellor of the University of Nigeria, where her mother became the first female registrar. Adichie moved to the United States when she was nineteen to attend college. She is the author of the novels *Americanah* (2013), *Half of a Yellow Sun* (2006), and *Purple Hibiscus* (2003), as well as a collection of short stories titled *The Thing around Your Neck* (2009), from which this story is taken.

KEY CONTEXT   "Cell One" takes place in Nigeria and focuses on the narrator's brother, a college student and part-time criminal who finds himself at the mercy of the Nigerian justice system. Nigeria is the most populous country in Africa. Like many African nations, it was colonized by England and other Western countries in the nineteenth and twentieth centuries, an experience from which it is still trying to recover. Because of its colonial past, Nigeria's official language is English. Nevertheless, many Nigerians, especially those in more rural areas, speak one or more of nearly three hundred ethnic languages, including Yoruba, Hausa, and Igbo. Of Nigeria's colonial past, Adichie has said, "Not only was colonialism an awful thing, it also created conditions where the Africans who took over became colonialists themselves. They were copying what they had seen." Transparency International, a group that tries to identify worldwide corruption, ranks Nigeria as one of the most politically corrupt countries in the world, ranked 136th out of 175 countries in terms of fairness and transparency.

▶

An aerial shot of Lagos, Nigeria. In an interview, Adichie has commented that "if you followed the media you'd think that everybody in Africa was starving to death, and that's not the case; so it's important to engage with the other Africa."

Compare this scene with your mental image of Africa.

The first time our house was robbed, it was our neighbor Osita who climbed in through the dining-room window and stole our TV and VCR, and the "Purple Rain" and "Thriller" videotapes that my father had brought back from America. The second time our house was robbed, it was my brother Nnamabia, who faked a break-in and stole my mother's jewelry. It happened on a Sunday. My parents had travelled to their home town to visit our grandparents, so Nnamabia and I went to church alone. He drove my mother's green Peugeot 504. We sat together in church as we usually did, but we did not have time to nudge each other and stifle giggles about somebody's ugly hat or threadbare caftan, because Nnamabia left without a word after ten minutes. He came back just before the priest said, "The Mass is ended, go in peace." I was a little piqued. I imagined that he had gone off to smoke or to see some girl, since he had the car to himself for once; but he could at least have told me. We drove home in silence, and when he parked in our long driveway I stayed back to pick some ixora flowers while Nnamabia unlocked the front door. I went inside to find him standing in the middle of the parlor.

"We've been robbed!" he said.

It took me a moment to take in the room. Even then, I felt that there was a theatrical quality to the way the drawers had been flung open. Or perhaps it was simply that I knew my brother too well. Later, when my parents had come home and neighbors began to troop in to say *ndo* — sorry — and to snap their fingers and heave their shoulders up and down, I sat alone in my room upstairs and realized what the queasiness in my gut was: Nnamabia had done it, I knew. My father knew, too. He pointed out that the window louvres had been slipped out from the inside, rather than from the outside (Nnamabia was usually smarter than that — perhaps he had been in a hurry to get

back to church before Mass ended), and that the robber knew exactly where my mother's jewelry was: in the back left corner of her metal trunk. Nnamabia stared at my father with wounded eyes and said that he may have done horrible things in the past, things that had caused my parents pain, but that he had done nothing in this case. He walked out the back door and did not come home that night. Or the next night. Or the night after. Two weeks later, he came home gaunt, smelling of beer, crying, saying he was sorry, that he had pawned the jewelry to the Hausa traders in Enugu, and that all the money was gone.

"How much did they give you for my gold?" our mother asked him. And when he told her she placed both hands on her head and cried, "Oh! Oh! *Chi m egbuo m!* My God has killed me!" I wanted to slap her. My father asked Nnamabia to write a report: how he had pawned the jewelry, what he had spent the money on, with whom he had spent it. I didn't think that Nnamabia would tell the truth, and I don't think that my father thought he would, but he liked reports, my professor father, he liked to have things written down and nicely documented. Besides, Nnamabia was seventeen, with a carefully tended beard. He was already between secondary school and university, and was too old for caning. What else could my father have done? After Nnamabia had written the report, my father filed it in the steel cabinet in his study where he kept our school papers.

5   "That he could hurt his mother like that!" was the last thing my father said on the subject.

But Nnamabia hadn't set out to hurt her. He had done it because my mother's jewelry was the only thing of any value in the house: a lifetime's accumulation of solid-gold pieces. He had done it, too, because other sons of professors were doing it. This was the season of thefts on our serene campus. Boys who had grown up watching *Sesame Street*, reading Enid Blyton,[1] eating cornflakes for breakfast, and attending the university staff primary school in polished brown sandals were now cutting through the mosquito netting of their neighbors' windows, sliding out glass louvres, and climbing in to steal TVs and VCRs. We knew the thieves. Still, when the professors saw one another at the staff club or at church or at a faculty meeting, they were careful to moan about the riffraff from town coming onto their sacred campus to steal.

The thieving boys were the popular ones. They drove their parents' cars in the evening, their seats pushed back and their arms stretched out to reach the steering wheel. Osita, our neighbor who had stolen our TV only weeks before Nnamabia's theft, was lithe and handsome in a brooding sort of way, and walked with the grace of a cat. His shirts were always crisply ironed, and I used to watch him across the hedge, then close my eyes and imagine that he was walking toward me, coming to claim me as his. He never noticed me. When he stole from us, my parents did not go over to Professor Ebube's house to ask for our things back. But they knew it was Osita. Osita was two years older than Nnamabia; most of the thieving boys were a little older than Nnamabia, and maybe that was why Nnamabia had not stolen from another person's house. Perhaps he did not feel old enough, qualified enough, for anything more serious than my mother's jewelry.

Nnamabia looked just like my mother — he had her fair complexion and large eyes, and a generous mouth that curved perfectly. When my mother took us to the market, traders would call

out, "Hey! Madam, why did you waste your fair skin on a boy and leave the girl so dark? What is a boy doing with all this beauty?" And my mother would chuckle, as though she took a mischievous and joyful responsibility for Nnamabia's looks. When, at eleven, Nnamabia broke the window of his classroom with a stone, my mother gave him the money to replace it and didn't tell my father. When, a few years later, he took the key to my father's car and pressed it into a bar of soap that my father found before Nnamabia could take it to a locksmith, she made vague sounds about how he was just experimenting and it didn't mean anything. When he stole the exam questions from the study and sold them to my father's students, she yelled at him, but then told my father that Nnamabia was sixteen, after all, and really should be given more pocket money.

I don't know whether Nnamabia felt remorse for stealing her jewelry. I could not always tell from my brother's gracious, smiling face what he really felt. He and I did not talk about it, and neither did my parents. Even though my mother's sisters sent her their gold earrings, even though she bought a new gold chain from Mrs. Mozie — the glamorous woman who imported gold from Italy — and began to drive to Mrs. Mozie's house once a month to pay in installments, we never talked about what had happened to her jewelry. It was as if by pretending that Nnamabia had not done the things he had done we could give him the opportunity to start afresh. The robbery might never have been mentioned again if Nnamabia had not been arrested two years later, in his second year of university.

10   By then, it was the season of cults on the Nsukka campus, when signs all over the university read in bold letters, "say no to cults." The Black Axe, the Buccaneers, and the Pirates were the best known. They had once been benign

---

[1] Enid Blyton: A prolific English children's author whose work was most popular in the 1950s. Adichie may even be alluding to Blyton's book *The Mystery That Never Was*, which features a group of thieves as its main antagonists. One critic wrote that there was "a faint but unattractive touch of old-fashioned xenophobia in the author's attitude to the thieves," who were "foreign' [. . .] and this seem[ed] to be sufficient to explain their criminality."—Eds.

fraternities, but they had evolved, and now eighteen-year-olds who had mastered the swagger of American rap videos were undergoing secret initiations that sometimes left one or two of them dead on Odim Hill. Guns and tortured loyalties became common. A boy would leer at a girl who turned out to be the girlfriend of the Capone of the Black Axe, and that boy, as he walked to a kiosk later to buy a cigarette, would be stabbed in the thigh. He would turn out to be a Buccaneer, and so one of his fellow-Buccaneers would go to a beer parlor and shoot the nearest Black Axe in the leg, and then the next day another Buccaneer would be shot dead in the refectory, his body falling onto aluminum plates of *garri*,[2] and that evening a Black Axe — a professor's son — would be hacked to death in his room, his CD player splattered with blood. It was inane. It was so abnormal that it quickly became normal. Girls stayed in their rooms after classes, and lecturers quivered, and when a fly buzzed too loudly people jumped. So the police were called in. They sped across campus in their rickety blue Peugeot 505 and glowered at the students, their rusty guns poking out of the car windows. Nnamabia came home from his lectures laughing. He thought that the police would have to do better than that; everyone knew the cult boys had newer guns.

My parents watched Nnamabia with silent concern, and I knew that they, too, were wondering if he was in a cult. Cult boys were popular, and Nnamabia was very popular. Boys yelled out his nickname — "The Funk!" — and shook his hand whenever he passed by, and girls, especially the popular ones, hugged him for too long when they said hello. He went to all the parties, the tame ones on campus and the wilder ones in town, and he was the kind of ladies' man who was also a guy's guy, the kind

who smoked a packet of Rothmans a day and was reputed to be able to finish a case of Star beer in a single sitting. But it seemed more his style to befriend all the cult boys and yet not be one himself. And I was not entirely sure, either, that my brother had whatever it took — guts or diffidence — to join a cult.

The only time I asked him if he was in a cult, he looked at me with surprise, as if I should have known better than to ask, before replying, "Of course not." I believed him. My dad believed him, too, when he asked. But our believing him made little difference, because he had already been arrested for belonging to a cult.

This is how it happened. On a humid Monday, four cult members waited at the campus gate and waylaid a professor driving a red Mercedes. They pressed a gun to her head, shoved her out of the car, and drove it to the Faculty of Engineering, where they shot three boys who were coming out of the building. It was noon. I was in a class nearby, and when we heard the shots our lecturer was the first to run out the door. There was loud screaming, and suddenly the stairwells were packed with scrambling students unsure where to run. Outside, the bodies lay on the lawn. The Mercedes had already screeched away. Many students hastily packed their bags, and okada drivers charged twice the usual fare to take them to the motor park to get on a bus. The vice-chancellor announced that all evening classes would be cancelled and everyone had to stay indoors after 9 P.M. This did not make much sense to me, since the shooting had happened in sparkling daylight, and perhaps it did not make sense to Nnamabia, either, because the first night of the curfew he didn't come home. I assumed that he had spent the night at a friend's; he did not always come home anyway. But the next morning a security man came to tell my parents that Nnamabia had been arrested at a bar with some cult boys and was at the police station. My

---

[2] *garri*: A West African dish made from cassava tubers. — Eds.

mother screamed, "*Ekwuzikwana!* Don't say that!" My father calmly thanked the security man. We drove to the police station in town, and there a constable chewing on the tip of a dirty pen said, "You mean those cult boys arrested last night? They have been taken to Enugu. Very serious case! We must stop this cult business once and for all!"

We got back into the car, and a new fear gripped us all. Nsukka, which was made up of our slow, insular campus and the slower, more insular town, was manageable; my father knew the police superintendent. But Enugu was anonymous. There the police could do what they were famous for doing when under pressure to produce results: kill people.

15   The Enugu police station was in a sprawling, sandy compound. My mother bribed the policemen at the desk with money, and with jollof rice and meat, and they allowed Nnamabia to come out of his cell and sit on a bench under a mango tree with us. Nobody asked why he had stayed out the night before. Nobody said that the police were wrong to walk into a bar and arrest all the boys drinking there, including the barman. Instead, we listened to Nnamabia talk.

"If we ran Nigeria like this cell," he said, "we would have no problems. Things are so organized. Our cell has a chief and he has a second-in-command, and when you come in you are expected to give them some money. If you don't, you're in trouble."

"And did you have any money?" my mother asked.

Nnamabia smiled, his face more beautiful than ever, despite the new pimple-like insect bite on his forehead, and said that he had slipped his money into his anus shortly after the arrest. He knew the policemen would take it if he didn't hide it, and he knew that he would need it to buy his peace in the cell. My parents said nothing for a while. I imagined Nnamabia rolling hundred-naira notes into a

thin cigarette shape and then reaching into the back of his trousers to slip them into himself. Later, as we drove back to Nsukka, my father said, "This is what I should have done when he stole your jewelry. I should have had him locked up in a cell."

My mother stared out the window.

20   "Why?" I asked.

"Because this has shaken him. Couldn't you see?" my father asked with a smile. I couldn't see it. Nnamabia had seemed fine to me, slipping his money into his anus and all.

Nnamabia's first shock was seeing a Buccaneer sobbing. The boy was tall and tough, rumored to have carried out one of the killings and likely to become Capone next semester, and yet there he was in the cell, cowering and sobbing after the chief gave him a light slap on the back of the head. Nnamabia told me this in a voice lined with both disgust and disappointment; it was as if he had suddenly been made to see that the Incredible Hulk was really just painted green. His second shock was learning about the cell farthest away from his, Cell One. He had never seen it, but every day two policemen carried a dead man out of Cell One, stopping by Nnamabia's cell to make sure that the corpse was seen by all.

Those in the cell who could afford to buy old plastic paint cans of water bathed every other morning. When they were let out into the yard, the policemen watched them and often shouted, "Stop that or you are going to Cell One now!" Nnamabia could not imagine a place worse than his cell, which was so crowded that he often stood pressed against the wall. The wall had cracks where tiny *kwalikwata*[3] lived; their bites were fierce and sharp, and when he yelped his cellmates mocked him. The biting was worse during the night, when they all slept on their sides, head to foot, to make room for one

---

[3] *kwalikwata:* Bedbugs. —Eds.

another, except the chief, who slept with his whole back lavishly on the floor.

It was also the chief who divided up the two plates of rice that were pushed into the cell every day. Each person got two mouthfuls.

25   Nnamabia told us this during the first week. As he spoke, I wondered if the bugs in the wall had bitten his face or if the bumps spreading across his forehead were due to an infection. Some of them were tipped with cream-colored pus. Once in a while, he scratched at them. I wanted him to stop talking. He seemed to enjoy his new role as the sufferer of indignities, and he did not understand how lucky he was that the policemen allowed him to come out and eat our food, or how stupid he'd been to stay out drinking that night, and how uncertain his chances were of being released.

We visited him every day for the first week. We took my father's old Volvo, because my mother's Peugeot was unsafe for trips outside Nsukka. By the end of the week, I noticed that my parents were acting differently — subtly so, but differently. My father no longer gave a monologue, as soon as we were waved through the police checkpoints, on how illiterate and corrupt the police were. He did not bring up the day when they had delayed us for an hour because he'd refused to bribe them, or how they had stopped a bus in which my beautiful cousin Ogechi was travelling and singled her out and called her a whore because she had two cell phones, and asked her for so much money that she had knelt on the ground in the rain begging them to let her go. My mother did not mumble that the policemen were symptoms of a larger malaise. Instead, my parents remained silent. It was as if by refusing to criticize the police they would somehow make Nnamabia's freedom more likely. "Delicate" was the word the superintendent at Nsukka had used. To get Nnamabia out anytime soon would be delicate, especially with the police commissioner in Enugu giving gloating, preening interviews about the arrest of the cultists. The cult problem was serious. Big Men in Abuja were following events. Everybody wanted to seem as if he were doing something.

The second week, I told my parents that we were not going to visit Nnamabia. We did not know how long this would last, and petrol was too expensive for us to drive three hours every day. Besides, it would not hurt Nnamabia to fend for himself for one day.

My mother said that nobody was begging me to come — I could sit there and do nothing while my innocent brother suffered. She started walking toward the car, and I ran after her. When I got outside, I was not sure what to do, so I picked up a stone near the ixora bush and hurled it at the windshield of the Volvo. I heard the brittle sound and saw the tiny lines spreading like rays on the glass before I turned and dashed upstairs and locked myself in my room. I heard my mother shouting. I heard my father's voice. Finally, there was silence. Nobody went to see Nnamabia that day. It surprised me, this little victory.

We visited him the next day. We said nothing about the windshield, although the cracks had spread out like ripples on a frozen stream. The policeman at the desk, the pleasant dark-skinned one, asked why we had not come the day before — he had missed my mother's jollof rice. I expected Nnamabia to ask, too, even to be upset, but he looked oddly sober. He did not eat all of his rice.

30   "What is wrong?" my mother said, and Nnamabia began to speak almost immediately, as if he had been waiting to be asked. An old man had been pushed into his cell the day before — a man perhaps in his mid-seventies, white-haired, skin finely wrinkled, with an old-fashioned dignity about him. His son was wanted for armed robbery, and when the police had not been able to find his son they had decided to lock up the father.

"The man did nothing," Nnamabia said.

"But you did nothing, either," my mother said.

Nnamabia shook his head as if our mother did not understand. The following days, he was more subdued. He spoke less, and mostly about the old man: how he could not afford bathing water, how the others made fun of him or accused him of hiding his son, how the chief ignored him, how he looked frightened and so terribly small.

"Does he know where his son is?" my mother asked.

35 "He has not seen his son in four months," Nnamabia said.

"Of course it is wrong," my mother said. "But this is what the police do all the time. If they do not find the person they are looking for, they lock up his relative."

"The man is ill," Nnamabia said. "His hands shake, even when he's asleep."

He closed the container of rice and turned to my father. "I want to give him some of this, but if I bring it into the cell the chief will take it."

My father went over and asked the policeman at the desk if we could be allowed to see the old man in Nnamabia's cell for a few minutes. The policeman was the light-skinned acerbic one who never said thank you when my mother handed over the rice-and-money bribe, and now he sneered in my father's face and said that he could well lose his job for letting even Nnamabia out and yet now we were asking for another person? Did we think this was visiting day at a boarding school? My father came back and sat down with a sigh, and Nnamabia silently scratched at his bumpy face.

40 The next day, Nnamabia barely touched his rice. He said that the policemen had splashed soapy water on the floor and walls of the cell, as they usually did, and that the old man, who had not bathed in a week, had yanked his shirt off and rubbed his frail back against the wet floor.

The policemen started to laugh when they saw him do this, and then they asked him to take all his clothes off and parade in the corridor outside the cell; as he did, they laughed louder and asked whether his son the thief knew that Papa's buttocks were so shrivelled. Nnamabia was staring at his yellow-orange rice as he spoke, and when he looked up his eyes were filled with tears, my worldly brother, and I felt a tenderness for him that I would not have been able to describe if I had been asked to.

There was another attack on campus — a boy hacked another boy with an axe — two days later.

"This is good," my mother said. "Now they cannot say that they have arrested all the cult boys." We did not go to Enugu that day; instead my parents went to see the local police superintendent, and they came back with good news. Nnamabia and the barman were to be released immediately. One of the cult boys, under questioning, had insisted that Nnamabia was not a member. The next day, we left earlier than usual, without jollof rice. My mother was always nervous when we drove, saying to my father, "*Nekwa ya!* Watch out!," as if he could not see the cars making dangerous turns in the other lane, but this time she did it so often that my father pulled over before we got to Ninth Mile and snapped, "Just who is driving this car?"

Two policemen were flogging a man with *koboko* as we drove into the police station. At first, I thought it was Nnamabia, and then I thought it was the old man from his cell. It was neither. I knew the boy on the ground, who was writhing and shouting with each lash. He was called Aboy and had the grave ugly face of a hound; he drove a Lexus around campus and was said to be a Buccaneer. I tried not to look at him as we walked inside. The policeman on duty, the one with tribal marks on his cheeks who always said "God bless you" when he took his bribe, looked away when he saw us, and I knew that something was wrong. My parents gave him the note from the superintendent. The policeman did not even glance at it. He knew about the release order, he told my father; the barman had already been released, but there was a complication with the boy. My mother began to shout, "What do you mean? Where is my son?"

The policeman got up. "I will call my senior to explain to you."

45 My mother rushed at him and pulled on his shirt. "Where is my son? Where is my son?" My father pried her away, and the policeman brushed at his chest, as if she had left some dirt there, before he turned to walk away.

"Where is our son?" my father asked in a voice so quiet, so steely, that the policeman stopped.

"They took him away, sir," he said.

"They took him away? What are you saying?" my mother was yelling. "Have you killed my son? Have you killed my son?"

"Where is our son?" my father asked again.

50 "My senior said I should call him when you came," the policeman said, and this time he hurried through a door.

It was after he left that I felt suddenly chilled by fear; I wanted to run after him and, like my mother, pull at his shirt until he produced Nnamabia. The senior policeman came out, and I searched his blank face for clues.

"Good day, sir," he said to my father.

"Where is our son?" my father asked. My mother breathed noisily.

"No problem, sir. It is just that we transferred him. I will take you there right away." There was something nervous about the policeman; his face remained blank, but he did not meet my father's eyes.

55 "Transferred him?"

"We got the order this morning. I would have sent somebody for him, but we don't have petrol, so I was waiting for you to come so that we could go together."

"Why was he transferred?"

"I was not here, sir. They said that he misbehaved yesterday and they took him to Cell One, and then yesterday evening there was a transfer of all the people in Cell One to another site."

"He misbehaved? What do you mean?"

60 "I was not here, sir."

My mother spoke in a broken voice: "Take me to my son! Take me to my son right now!"

I sat in the back with the policeman, who smelled of the kind of old camphor that seemed

Image courtesy Amnesty International, © Chijioke Ugwu Clement

This drawing is an artist's depiction of overcrowded prison conditions in Nigeria in 2014. The artwork was commissioned by Amnesty International for its Stop Torture Campaign. The artwork is the artist's creative interpretation of torture techniques based on information and testimony supplied to the artist by Amnesty International.

What similarities do you see between this drawing and the prison where Nnamabia was held in this story?

to last forever in my mother's trunk. No one spoke except for the policeman when he gave my father directions. We arrived about fifteen minutes later, my father driving inordinately fast. The small, walled compound looked neglected, with patches of overgrown grass strewn with old bottles and plastic bags. The policeman hardly waited for my father to stop the car before he opened the door and hurried out, and again I felt chilled. We were in a god-forsaken part of town, and there was no sign that said "Police Station." There was a strange deserted feeling in the air. But the policeman soon emerged with Nnamabia. There he was, my handsome brother, walking toward us, seemingly unchanged, until he came close enough for my mother to hug him, and I saw him wince and back away — his arm was covered in soft-looking welts. There was dried blood around his nose.

"Why did they beat you like this?" my mother asked him. She turned to the policeman. "Why did you people do this to my son? Why?"

The man shrugged. There was a new insolence to his demeanor; it was as if he had been uncertain about Nnamabia's well-being but now, reassured, could let himself talk. "You cannot raise your children properly — all of you people who feel important because you work at the university — and when your children misbehave you think they should not be punished. You are lucky they released him."

65 My father said, "Let's go."

He opened the door and Nnamabia climbed in, and we drove home. My father did not stop at any of the police checkpoints on the road, and, once, a policeman gestured threateningly with his gun as we sped past. The only time my mother opened her mouth on the drive home was to ask Nnamabia if he wanted us to stop and buy some *okpa*.[4] Nnamabia said no. We had arrived in Nsukka before he finally spoke.

"Yesterday, the policemen asked the old man if he wanted a free half bucket of water. He said yes. So they told him to take his clothes off and parade the corridor. Most of my cellmates were laughing. Some of them said it was wrong to treat an old man like that." Nnamabia paused. "I shouted at the policeman. I told him the old man was innocent and ill, and if they kept him here it wouldn't help them find his son, because the man did not even know where his son was. They said that I should shut up immediately, that they would take me to Cell One. I didn't care. I didn't shut up. So they pulled me out and slapped me and took me to Cell One."

Nnamabia stopped there, and we asked him nothing else. Instead, I imagined him calling the policeman a stupid idiot, a spineless coward, a sadist, a bastard, and I imagined the shock of the policemen — the chief staring openmouthed, the other cellmates stunned at the audacity of the boy from the university. And I imagined the old man himself looking on with surprised pride and quietly refusing to undress. Nnamabia did not say what had happened to him in Cell One, or what happened at the new site. It would have been so easy for him, my charming brother, to make a sleek drama of his story, but he did not.

---

[4] okpa: A Nigerian dish made with the flour from crushed Bambara groundnuts (also known as Bambara-beans), which are grown in West Africa and resemble peanuts. —Eds.

Understanding and Interpreting

1 Trace Nnamabia's transformation throughout this story. What are the significant stages in his growing self-awareness?

2 Why does the narrator throw a stone and break the windshield of the family's Volvo (par. 28)? What does she mean by describing her action as "this little victory" (par. 28)?

3 Though she is a character in the story, the narrator, whose name we never learn, seems extremely passive. Other than throwing the rock through the car window, she does not do much other than report on her brother's actions. How does Adichie's choice of narrator affect the characterization of Nnamabia?

4 Compare the differences in the ways that at least two of the following characters view Nnamabia: his sister, his father, his mother, or the jailers. Provide evidence to support your response.

5 Evaluate the variety of ethical choices that the characters in this story face, including Nnamabia, his sister, his parents, and the jailers. Which people do the right thing in this story, and how do their choices help to illustrate a theme of "Cell One"?

6 Reread the last paragraph in the story. Notice that Nnamabia does not say anything further about his ordeal, but instead the narrator says, "Instead, I imagined him. [. . .]" What does Nnamabia's refusal to speak and his sister's imagining his actions reveal about both of the characters?

Analyzing Language, Style, and Structure

1 Because she is focused so much on her brother, Nnamabia, we learn very little about the narrator, not even her name. Look back at the following excerpts and explain what each reveals about the narrator:

   a. Osita, our neighbor who had stolen our TV only weeks before Nnamabia's theft, was lithe and handsome in a brooding sort of way, and walked with the grace of a cat. His shirts were always crisply ironed, and I used to watch him across the hedge, then close my eyes and imagine that he was walking toward me, coming to claim me as his. He never noticed me. (par. 7)

   b. "How much did they give you for my gold?" our mother asked him. And when he told her she placed both hands on her head and cried, "Oh! Oh! *Chi m egbuo m!* My God has killed me!" I wanted to slap her. (par. 4)

   c. The second week, I told my parents that we were not going to visit Nnamabia. We did not know how long this would last, and petrol was too expensive for us to drive three hours every day. Besides, it would not hurt Nnamabia to fend for himself for one day. (par. 27)

2 While English is the official language of Nigeria and most of the educated class in the urban areas of the country speak it, Adichie also includes several non-English words as well. Sometimes they are translated for the reader and sometimes they are not. Locate examples of non-English words and explain their role within the story.

3 Though the story is called "Cell One," Adichie gives the actual cell only the most limited description. What is the effect of this absence of description?

4 There is a great deal of suspense at the end of the story as the family learns that Nnamabia has been transferred. Look back at this final scene and explain how Adichie creates the suspense.

5 How would you describe the author's attitude toward Nigeria and its criminal justice system in particular? Cite specific passages to support your response.

Connecting, Arguing, and Extending

1 Write a narrative about watching a sibling, friend, or loved one doing things that you knew at the time were wrong, dangerous, or harmful, as the narrator of this story did. Did the person you know have a transformative experience similar to Nnamabia's? Why or why not?

2 What were your perceptions of Africa before reading this story? What were those notions based on? Did this story confirm or contradict what you thought Africa was like?

3 Look back through the story and identify places where the characters seem to be influenced by American popular culture. What point is Adichie making about cross-cultural influence, or even the lingering effects of colonialism? You may need to conduct additional research on the topic of colonialism to help you answer this question.

4 The Nigerian criminal justice system, as described in this story, does not come across in a positive way. Locate a magazine or newspaper article about an event that has occurred in the United States that shows its system to be similarly flawed. Compare the real-life event from the United States with the fictionalized one from Nigeria. What conclusions can you draw about the similarities and differences between the two justice systems?

5 In "Cell One," the parents responded to the theft in their home first by denying that it was actually occurring, and then by blaming others. Is this response typical of parents? And is it better for parents to show faith in their children rather than being suspicious of them? Explain why you believe that the actions of the parents in this story do or do not seem believable or appropriate.

Free Fruit for Young Widows

Nathan Englander

Nathan Englander (b. 1970) is an American writer who wrote the novel *The Ministry of Special Cases* (2007) and two short-story collections, including *What We Talk about When We Talk about Anne Frank* (2012), which was a finalist for the Pulitzer Prize and from which this story is taken. Englander grew up in an Orthodox Jewish community in New York, and as an adult, lived in Israel for five years.

Basso Cannarsa/LUZphoto/Redux

KEY CONTEXT This story, told mostly in flashbacks, focuses on the ethical choices that a character named Professor Tendler, a Holocaust survivor, faces immediately after World War II. The Holocaust — also called "the Shoah," which means "the catastrophe" in Hebrew, the official language of Israel — refers to the systematic genocide by Adolf Hitler and the German Nazi regime of approximately 6 million Jewish people, as well as millions of other religious or ethnic minorities, homosexuals, and mentally or physically disabled people during the war.

After World War II, the modern state of Israel was formed in the traditional Middle Eastern homeland of the Jewish people. The land, which had become a British territory after the fall of the Ottoman Empire in World War I, was also the home of many Palestinians, who resented being displaced. This led to a series of wars between Israel and its neighboring countries, including a 1956 conflict between Israel and Egypt over control of the Suez Canal that is referred to in the beginning of this story.

When the Egyptian president Gamal Abdel Nasser took control of the Suez Canal, threatening Western access to that vital route, an agitated France shifted allegiances, joining forces with Britain and Israel against Egypt. This is a fact neither here nor there, except that during the 1956 Sinai Campaign there were soldiers in the Israeli Army and soldiers in the Egyptian Army who ended up wearing identical French-supplied uniforms to battle.

Not long into the fighting, an Israeli platoon came to rest at a captured Egyptian camp to the east of Bir Gafgafa, in the Sinai Desert. There Private Shimmy Gezer (formerly Shimon Bibberblat, of Warsaw, Poland) sat down to eat at a makeshift outdoor mess. Four armed commandos sat down with him. He grunted. They grunted. Shimmy dug into his lunch.

A squad mate of Shimmy's came over to join them. Professor Tendler (who was then only Private Tendler, not yet a professor, and not yet even in possession of a high school degree) placed the tin cup that he was carrying on the edge of the table, taking care not to spill his tea. Then he took up his gun and shot each of the commandos in the head.

They fell quite neatly. The first two, who had been facing Professor Tendler, tipped back off the bench into the sand. The second pair, who had their backs to the professor and were still staring open-mouthed at their dead friends, fell face down, the sound of their skulls hitting the table somehow more violent than the report of the gun.

5 Shocked by the murder of four fellow soldiers, Shimmy Gezer tackled his friend. To Professor Tendler, who was much bigger than Shimmy, the attack was more startling than threatening. Tendler grabbed hold of Shimmy's hands while screaming, "Egyptians! Egyptians!" in Hebrew. He was using the same word about the same people in the same desert that had been used thousands of years before. The main difference, if the old stories are to be believed,

was that God no longer raised his own fist in the fight.

Professor Tendler quickly managed to contain Shimmy in a bear hug. "Egyptian commandos — confused," Tendler said, switching to Yiddish. "The enemy. The enemy joined you for lunch."

Shimmy listened. Shimmy calmed down.

Professor Tendler, thinking the matter was settled, let Shimmy go. As soon as he did, Shimmy swung wildly. He continued attacking, because who cared who those four men were? They were people. They were human beings who had sat down at the wrong table for lunch. They were dead people who had not had to die.

"You could have taken them prisoner," Shimmy yelled. "Halt!" he screamed in German. "That's all — halt!" Then, with tears streaming and fists flying, Shimmy said, "You didn't have to shoot."

10 By then Professor Tendler had had enough. He proceeded to beat Shimmy Gezer. He didn't just defend himself. He didn't subdue his friend. He flipped Shimmy over, straddled his body, and pounded it down until it was level with the sand. He beat his friend until his friend couldn't take any more beating, and then he beat him some more. Finally he climbed off his friend, looked up into the hot sun, and pushed through the crowd of soldiers who had assembled in the minutes since the Egyptians sat down to their fate. Tendler went off to have a smoke.

For those who had come running at the sound of gunfire to find five bodies in the sand, it was the consensus that a pummeled Shimmy Gezer looked to be in the worst condition of the bunch.

At the fruit-and-vegetable stand that Shimmy Gezer eventually opened in Jerusalem's Mahane Yehuda Market, his son, little Etgar, asked about the story of Professor Tendler again and again. From the time he was six, Etgar had worked the *duchan* at his father's side whenever he wasn't in school. At that age, knowing only a child's version of the story — that Tendler had done something in one of the wars that upset Etgar's father, and Etgar's father had jumped on the man, and the man had (his father never hesitated to admit) beat him up very badly — Etgar couldn't understand why his father was so nice to the professor now. Reared, as he was, on the laws of the small family business, Etgar couldn't grasp why he was forbidden to accept a single lira[1] from Tendler. The professor got his vegetables free.

After Etgar weighed the tomatoes and the cucumbers, his father would take up the bag, stick in a nice fat eggplant, unasked, and pass it over to Professor Tendler.

"*Kach*,"[2] his father would say. "Take it. And wish your wife well."

15　As Etgar turned nine and ten and eleven, the story began to fill out. He was told about the commandos and the uniforms, about shipping routes and the Suez, and the Americans and the British and the French. He learned about the shots to the head. He learned about all the wars his father had fought in — '73, '67, '56, '48 — though Shimmy Gezer still stopped short of the one he'd first been swept up in, the war that ran from 1939 to 1945.

Etgar's father explained the hazy morality of combat, the split-second decisions, the assessment of threat and response, the nature of percentages and absolutes. Shimmy did his best to make clear to his son that Israelis — in their nation of unfinished borders and unwritten constitution — were trapped in a gray space that was called real life.

In this gray space, he explained, even absolutes could maintain more than one position, reflect more than one truth. "You too," he said to his son, "may someday face a decision such as Professor Tendler's — may you never know from it." He pointed at the bloody stall across from

theirs, pointed at a fish below the mallet, flopping on the block. "God forbid you should have to live with the consequences of decisions, permanent, eternal, that will chase you in your head, turning from this side to that, tossing between wrong and right."

But Etgar still couldn't comprehend how his father saw the story to be that of a fish flip-flopping, when it was, in his eyes, only ever about that mallet coming down.

Etgar wasn't one for the gray. He was a tiny, thoughtful, buck-toothed boy of certainties. And every Friday when Tendler came by the stand, Etgar would pack up the man's produce and then run through the story again, searching for black-and-white.

20　This man had saved his father's life, but maybe he hadn't. He'd done what was necessary, but maybe he could have done it another way. And even if the basic schoolyard rule applied in adult life — that a beating delivered earns a beating in return — did it ever justify one as fierce as the beating his father had described? A pummeling so severe that Shimmy, while telling the story, would run Etgar's fingers along his left cheek, to show him where Professor Tendler had flattened the bone.

Even if the violence had been justified, even if his father didn't always say, "You must risk your friend's life, your family's, your own, you must be willing to die — even to save the life of your enemy — if ever, of two deeds, the humane one may be done," it was not his father's act of forgiveness but his kindness that baffled Etgar.

Shimmy would send him running across Agrippas Street to bring back two cups of coffee or two glasses of tea to welcome Professor Tendler, telling Etgar to snatch a good-sized handful of pistachios from Eizenberg's cart along the way. This treatment his father reserved only for his oldest friends.

And absolutely no one but the war widows got their produce free. Quietly and with dignity,

---

[1] lira: The currency in Israel from 1948 to 1980. It was then replaced with the shekel. — Eds.

[2] Kach: Hebrew for "thus" or "so." — Eds.

so as to cause these women no shame, Etgar's father would send them off with fresh fruit and big bags of vegetables, sometimes for years after their losses. He always took care of the young widows. When they protested, he'd say, "You sacrifice, I sacrifice. All in all, what's a bag of apples?"

"It's all for one country," he'd say.

25   When it came to Professor Tendler, so clear an answer never came.

When Etgar was twelve, his father acknowledged the complexities of Tendler's tale.

"Do you want to know why I can care for a man who once beat me? Because to a story there is context. There is always context in life."

"That's it?" Etgar asked.

"That's it."

30   At thirteen, he was told a different story. Because at thirteen Etgar was a man.

"You know I was in the war," Shimmy said to his son. The way he said it Etgar knew that he didn't mean '48 or '56, '67 or '73. He did not mean the Jewish wars, in all of which he had fought. He meant the big one. The war that no one in his family but Shimmy had survived, which was also the case for Etgar's mother. This was why they had taken a new name, Shimmy explained. In the whole world, the Gezers were three.

"Yes," Etgar said. "I know."

"Professor Tendler was also in that war," Shimmy said.

"Yes," Etgar said.

35   "It was hard on him," Shimmy said. "And that is why, why I am always nice."

Etgar thought. Etgar spoke.

"But you were there too. You've had the same life as him. And you'd never have shot four men, even the enemy, if you could have taken them prisoner, if you could have spared a life. Even if you were in danger, you'd risk —" Etgar's father smiled, and stopped him.

"*Kodem kol,*"[3] he said, "a similar life is not a same life. There is a difference." Here Shimmy's face turned serious, the lightness gone. "In that first war, in that big war, I was the lucky one," he said. "In the Shoah, I survived."

"But he's here," Etgar said. "He survived, just the same as you."

40   "No," Etgar's father said. "He made it through the camps. He walks, he breathes, and he was very close to making it out of Europe alive. But they killed him. After the war, we still lost people. They killed what was left of him in the end."

For the first time, without Professor Tendler there, without one of Shimmy's friends from the ghetto who stopped by to talk in Yiddish, without one of the soldier buddies from his unit in the reserves, or one of the *kibbutzniks*[4] from whom he bought his fruits and his vegetables, Etgar's father sent Etgar across Agrippas Street to get two glasses of tea. One for Etgar and one for him.

"Hurry," Shimmy said, sending Etgar off with a slap on his behind. Before Etgar had taken a step, his father grabbed his collar and popped open the register, handing him a brand-new ten-shekel bill. "And buy us a nice big bag of seeds from Eizenberg. Tell him to keep the change. You and I, we are going to sit awhile."

Shimmy took out the second folding chair from behind the register. It would also be the first time that father and son had ever sat down in the store together. Another rule of good business: a customer should always find you standing. Always there's something you can be doing — sweeping, stacking, polishing apples. The customers will come to a place where there is pride.

This is why Professor Tendler got his tomatoes free, why the sight of the man who beat Shimmy made his gaze go soft with kindness in the way

---
[3] Kodem kol: Hebrew for "first of all." — Eds.
[4] kibbutzniks: Members of a kibbutz, a collective community in Israel. — Eds.

that it did when one of the *miskenot*[5] came by — why it took on what Etgar called his father's free-fruit-for-young-widows eyes. This is the story that Shimmy told Etgar when he felt that his boy was a man:

45   The first thing Professor Tendler saw when his death camp was liberated was two big, tough American soldiers fainting dead away. The pair (presumably war-hardened) stood before the immense, heretofore unimaginable brutality of modern extermination, frozen, slack-jawed before a mountain of putrid, naked corpses, a hill of men.

And from this pile of broken bodies that had been — prior to the American invasion — set to be burned, a rickety skeletal Tendler stared back. Professor Tendler stared and studied, and when he was sure that those soldiers were not Nazi soldiers he crawled out from his hiding place among the corpses, pushing and shoving those balsa-wood arms and legs aside.

It was this hill of bodies that had protected Tendler day after day. The poor Sonderkommandos who dumped the bodies, as well as those who came to cart them to the ovens, knew that the boy was inside. They brought him the crumbs of their crumbs to keep him going. And though it was certain death for these prisoners to protect him, it allowed them a sliver of humanity in their inhuman jobs. This was what Shimmy was trying to explain to his son — that these palest shadows of kindness were enough to keep a dead man alive.

When Tendler finally got to his feet, straightening his body out, when the corpse that was Professor Tendler at age thirteen — "your age" — came crawling from that nightmare, he looked at the two Yankee soldiers, who looked at him and then hit the ground with a thud.

Professor Tendler had already seen so much in life that this was not worth even a pause, and so he walked on. He walked on naked through the gates of the camp, walked on until he got some food and some clothes, walked on until he had shoes and then a coat. He walked on until he had a little bread and a potato in his pocket — a surplus.

50   Soon there was also in that pocket a cigarette and then a second; a coin and then a second. Surviving in this way, Tendler walked across borders until he was able to stand straight and tall, until he showed up in his childhood town in a matching suit of clothes, with a few bills in his pocket and, in his waistband, a six-shooter with five bullets chambered, in order to protect himself during the nights that he slept by the side of the road.

Professor Tendler was expecting no surprises, no reunions. He'd seen his mother killed in front of him, his father, his three sisters, his grandparents, and, after some months in the camp, the two boys that he knew from back home.

But home — that was the thing he held on to. Maybe his house was still there, and his bed. Maybe the cow was still giving milk, and the goats still chewing garbage, and his dog still barking at the chickens as before. And maybe his other family — the nurse at whose breast he had become strong (before weakened), her husband who had farmed his father's field, and their son (his age), and another (two years younger), boys with whom he had played like a brother — maybe this family was still there waiting. Waiting for him to come home.

Tendler could make a new family in that house. He could call every child he might one day have by his dead loved ones' names.

The town looked as it had when he'd left. The streets were his streets, the linden trees in the square taller but laid out as before. And when Tendler turned down the dirt road that led to his gate, he fought to keep himself from running, and he fought to keep himself from crying, because, after what he had seen, he knew that to survive in this world he must always act like a man.

---

[5] miskenot: Plural of *misken*, meaning unfortunate person; victim of circumstance. — Eds.

▲

This Holocaust memorial sculpture by Kenneth Treister, titled *The Sculpture of Love and Anguish*, can be found in Miami, Florida.

How does this Holocaust memorial reflect the images of the concentration camp that Englander uses in this short story?

55 So Tendler buttoned his coat and walked quietly toward the fence, wishing that he had a hat to take off as he passed through the gate — just the way the man of the house would when coming home to what was his.

But when he saw her in the yard — when he saw Fanushka his nurse, their maid — the tears came anyway. Tendler popped a precious button from his coat as he ran to her and threw himself into her arms, and he cried for the first time since the trains.

With her husband at her side, Fanushka said to him, "Welcome home, son," and "Welcome home, child," and "We prayed," "We lit candles," "We dreamed of your return."

When they asked, "Are your parents also coming? Are your sisters and your grandparents far behind?," when they asked after all the old neighbors, house by house, Tendler answered, not by metaphor, and not by insinuation. When he knew the fate, he stated it as it was: beaten or starved, shot, cut in half, the front of the head caved in. All this he related without feeling — matters, each, of fact. All this he shared before venturing a step through his front door.

Looking through that open door, Tendler decided that he would live with these people as family until he had a family of his own. He would grow old in this house. Free to be free, he would gate himself up again. But it would be his gate, his lock, his world.

60 A hand on his hand pulled him from his reverie. It was Fanushka talking, a sad smile on her face. "Time to fatten you up," she said. "A feast for first dinner." And she grabbed the chicken at her feet and twisted its neck right there in the yard. "Come in," she said, while the animal twitched. "The master of the house has returned.

"Just as you left it," she said. "Only a few of our things."

Tendler stepped inside.

It was exactly as he remembered it: the table, the chairs, except that all that was personal was gone.

Fanushka's two sons came in, and Tendler understood what time had done. These boys, fed and housed, warmed and loved, were fully twice his size. He felt, then, something he had never known in the camps, a civilized emotion that would have served no use. Tendler felt ashamed. He turned red, clenched his jaw tight, and felt his gums bleeding into his mouth.

65 "You have to understand," Etgar's father said to his son. "These boys, his brothers, they were now twice his size and strangers to him."

The boys, prodded, shook hands with Tendler. They did not know him anymore.

. . .

"Still, it is a nice story," Etgar said. "Sad. But also happy. He makes it home to a home. It's what you always say. Survival, that's what matters. Surviving to start again."

Etgar's father held up a sunflower seed, thinking about this. He cracked it between his front teeth.

"So they are all making a dinner for Professor Tendler," he said. "And he is sitting on the kitchen floor, legs crossed, as he did when he was a boy, and he is watching. Watching happily, drinking a glass of goat's milk, still warm. And then the father goes out to slaughter that goat. 'A feast for dinner,' he says. 'A chicken's not enough.' Professor Tendler, who has not had meat in years, looks at him, and the father, running a nail along his knife, says, 'I remember the kosher way.'"

70   Tendler was so happy that he could not bear it. So happy and so sad. And, with the cup of warm milk and the warm feeling, Tendler had to pee. But he didn't want to move now that he was there with his other mother and, resting on her shoulder, a baby sister. A year and a half old and one curl on the head. A little girl, fat and happy. Fat in the ankle, fat in the wrist.

Professor Tendler rushed out at the last second, out of the warm kitchen, out from under his roof. Professor Tendler, a man whom other men had tried to turn into an animal, did not race to the outhouse. It didn't cross his mind. He stood right under the kitchen window to smell the kitchen smells, to stay close. And he took a piss. Over the sound of the stream, he heard his nurse lamenting.

He knew what she must be lamenting — the Tendler family destroyed.

He listened to what she was saying. And he heard.

"He will take everything," is what she said. "He will take it all from us — our house, our field. He'll snatch away all we've built and protected, everything that has been — for so long — ours."

75   There outside the window, pissing and listening, and also "disassociating," as Professor Tendler would call it (though he did not then have the word), he knew only that he was watching himself from above, that he could see himself feeling all the disappointment as he felt it, until he was keenly and wildly aware that he had felt nothing all those years, felt nothing when his father and mother were shot, felt nothing while in the camps, nothing, in fact, from the moment he was driven from his home to the moment he returned.

In that instant, Tendler's guilt was sharper than any sensation he had ever known.

And here, in response to his precocious son, Shimmy said, "Yes, yes, of course it was about survival — Tendler's way of coping. Of course he'd been feeling all along." But Tendler — a boy who had stepped over his mother's body and kept walking — had, for those peasants, opened up.

It was right then, Professor Tendler later told Shimmy, that he became a philosopher.

"He will steal it all away," Fanushka said. "Everything. He has come for our lives."

80   And her son, whom Tendler had considered a brother, said, "No." And Tendler's other almost-brother said, "No."

"We will eat," Fanushka said. "We will celebrate. And when he sleeps we will kill him." To one of the sons she said, "Go. Tell your father to keep that knife sharp." To the other she said, "You get to sleep early, and you get up early, and before you grab the first tit on that cow I want his throat slit. Ours. Ours, not to be taken away."

Tendler ran. Not toward the street but back toward the outhouse in time to turn around as the kitchen door flew open, in time to smile at the younger brother on his way to find his father, in time for Tendler to be heading back the right way.

"Do you want to hear what was shared at such a dinner?" Shimmy asked his son. "The memories roused and oaths sworn? There was wine, I know. 'Drink, drink,' the mother said.

There was the chicken and a pot of goat stew. And, in a time of great deprivation, there was also sugar for the tea.'' At this, Shimmy pointed at the bounty of their stand. "And, as if nothing, next to the baby's basket on the kitchen floor sat a basket of apples. Tendler hadn't had an apple in who knows how long."

Tendler brought the basket to the table. The family laughed as he peeled the apples with a knife, first eating the peels, then the flesh, and savoring even the seeds and the cores. It was a celebration, a joyous night. So much so that Professor Tendler could not by its end, belly distended, eyes crossed with drink, believe what he knew to have been said.

85 There were hugs and there were kisses, and Tendler — the master of the house — was given his parents' bedroom upstairs, the two boys across the hall, and below, in the kitchen ("It will be warmest"), slept the mother and the father and the fat-ankled girl.

"Sleep well," Fanushka said. "Welcome home, my son." And, sweetly, she kissed Tendler on both eyes.

Tendler climbed the stairs. He took off his suit and went to bed. And that was where he was when Fanushka popped through the door and asked him if he was warm enough, if he needed a lamp by which to read.

"No, thank you," he said.

"So formal? No thanks necessary," Fanushka said. "Only 'Yes, Mother,' or 'No, Mother,' my poor reclaimed orphan son."

90 "No light, Mother," Tendler said, and Fanushka closed the door.

Tendler got out of bed. He put on his suit. Once again without any shame to his actions, Tendler searched the room for anything of value, robbing his own home.

Then he waited. He waited until the house had settled into itself, the last creak slipping from the floorboards as the walls pushed back against the wind. He waited until his mother, his Fanushka, must surely sleep, until a brother

intent on staying up for the night — a brother who had never once fought for his life — convinced himself that it would be all right to close his eyes.

Tendler waited until he too had to sleep, and that's when he tied the laces of his shoes together and hung them over his shoulder. That's when he took his pillow with one hand and, with the other, quietly cocked his gun.

Then, with goose feathers flying, Tendler moved through the house. A bullet for each brother, one for the father and one for the mother. Tendler fired until he found himself standing in the warmth of the kitchen, one bullet left to protect him on the nights when he would sleep by the side of the road.

95 That last bullet Tendler left in the fat baby girl, because he did not know from mercy, and did not need to leave another of that family to grow to kill him at some future time.

"He murdered them," Etgar said. "A murderer."

"No," his father told him. "There was no such notion at the time."

"Even so, it is murder," Etgar said.

"If it is, then it's only fair. They killed him first. It was his right."

100 "But you always say — "

"Context."

"But the baby. The girl."

"The baby is hardest, I admit. But these are questions for the philosopher. These are the theoretical instances put into flesh and blood."

"But it's not a question. These people, they are not the ones who murdered his family."

105 "They were coming for him that night."

"He could have escaped. He could have run for the gate when he overheard. He didn't need to race back toward the outhouse, race to face the brother as he came the other way."

"Maybe there was no more running in him. Anyway, do you understand 'an eye for an eye'? Can you imagine a broader meaning of *self-defense*?"

"You always forgive him," Etgar said. "You suffered the same things — but you aren't that way. You would not have done what he did."

"It is hard to know what a person would and wouldn't do in any specific instance. And you, spoiled child, apply the rules of civilization to a boy who had seen only its opposite. Maybe the fault for those deaths lies in a system designed for the killing of Tendlers that failed to do its job. An error, a slip that allowed a Tendler, no longer fit, back loose in the world."

110   "Is that what you think?"

"It's what I ask. And I ask you, my Etgar, what you would have done if you were Tendler that night?"

"Not kill."

"Then you die."

"Only the grownups."

115   "But it was a boy who was sent to cut Tendler's throat."

"How about killing only those who would do harm?"

"Still it's murder. Still it is killing people who have yet to act, murdering them in their sleep."

"I guess," Etgar said. "I can see how they deserved it, the four. How I might, if I were him, have killed them."

Shimmy shook his head, looking sad.

120   "And whoever are we, my son, to decide who should die?"

It was on that day that Etgar Gezer became a philosopher himself. Not in the manner of

Professor Tendler, who taught theories up at the university on the mountain, but, like his father, practical and concrete. Etgar would not finish high school or go to college, and except for his three years in the army, he would spend his life — happily — working the stand in the *shuk*.[6] He'd stack the fruit into pyramids and contemplate weighty questions with a seriousness of thought. And when there were answers Etgar would try employing them to make for himself and others, in whatever small way, a better life.

It was on that day too that Etgar decided Professor Tendler was both a murderer and, at the same time, a *misken*. He believed he understood how and why Professor Tendler had come to kill that peasant family, and how men sent to battle in uniform — even in the same uniform — would find no mercy at his hand. Etgar also came to see how Tendler's story could just as easily have ended for the professor that first night, back in his parents' room, in his parents' bed, a gun with four bullets held in a suicide's hand — how the first bullet Tendler ever fired might have been into his own head.

Still, every Friday Etgar packed up Tendler's fruit and vegetables. And in that bag Etgar would add, when he had them, a pineapple or a few fat mangos dripping honey. Handing it to Tendler, Etgar would say, "*Kach*, Professor. Take it." This, even after his father had died.

---

[6] shuk: Market. — Eds.

Understanding and Interpreting

1 The story of Professor Tendler shooting the Egyptian commandos at the beginning is one that the narrator returns to multiple times throughout the story. Summarize Tendler's actions and explain the different choices that Shimmy, and later Etgar, think Tendler could have made.

2 As much as Etgar, the "buck-toothed boy of certainties" (par. 19), wants to believe in black-and-white ethical choices, like killing, his father tries to teach him that Israelis, in particular, "were trapped in a gray space that was called real life" (par. 16), and he tells his son, "There is always context in life" (par. 27). What role does context play in the ethical decision making of the characters in this story?

3 When Professor Tendler tells the family living in his childhood home about what happened to his parents and sisters during the Holocaust, the narrator says that Tendler answered "not by metaphor, and not by insinuation. When he knew the fate, he stated it as it was" (par. 58). What does this reveal about Tendler and how he views life after the Holocaust?

4 Authors often develop their characters by describing their physical actions. Skim back through the story and focus on Shimmy's actions, especially those toward the young widows, his son, and Professor Tendler in the marketplace. What do these actions reveal about Shimmy, and how do they relate to the theme of this story?

5 Reread paragraphs 96–120 where Etgar and his father debate Professor Tendler's killing of the family. Summarize Etgar's and Shimmy's arguments, and explain what changes Etgar's mind.

6 Both Etgar and Professor Tendler, the narrator says, "became a philosopher" (pars. 78 and 121). What does this mean, and how does each character come to this moment differently?

Analyzing Language, Style, and Structure

1 Several times in this story Professor Tendler is referred to as dead; for instance in paragraph 48, the narrator says, "[T]he corpse that was Professor Tendler [...] came crawling from that nightmare." What does Englander's use of death imagery illustrate about Tendler's character?

2 The shooting of the Egyptian soldiers is shocking and brutal, especially since it occurs within the first three paragraphs of the story. What effect is created with this opening? How does Englander's choice to begin in this fashion lead to other structural choices he makes in the story?

3 Reread paragraphs 48–55, in which Professor Tendler walks away from the camp back to his home. How does Englander use imagery to describe his transformation and for what effect?

4 Look back at the section where Professor Tendler learns the family living in his old house is planning on killing him (pars. 78–91). How are the words "mother," "brother," and "son" used in this section, and how do these language choices illustrate aspects of Tendler's character?

5 Englander uses the phrases "a bullet for each brother" and "[t]hat last bullet Tendler left in the fat baby girl" (pars. 93–94) instead of directly stating that Tendler shot each of them. What is the effect of this phrasing, and how does it relate to the central question of the ethics of Tendler's actions?

Connecting, Arguing, and Extending

1 Were Professor Tendler's actions justified? Were they the right thing to do? Is there a difference between his actions against the Egyptian soldiers and his actions against the family? Use evidence from the text as well as your own knowledge or research to support your position.

2 Research the psychological effects that the Holocaust had on its survivors, specifically "disassociating," which Professor Tendler was experiencing outside his house listening to the family plotting to kill him. What are the implications of disassociation in people's lives? And how might

this disassociation have led to Professor Tendler's actions?

3 In trying to determine a universal approach to ethics, German philosopher Immanuel Kant (1724–1804) developed the concept he called the "categorical imperative," which describes laws that must be followed by all people at all times and in all circumstances. Conduct brief research about the categorical imperative and apply its approach to Professor Tendler's actions in this story. Was he justified or not, according to Kant?

4 At the end of the story, Etgar determines that Professor Tendler is both a murderer and a *misken*, which is a Hebrew word with no simple English translation. Read through the following description of the word by Rabbi Yaacov Yisroel Bar-Chaiim and explain how you think its usage relates to the theme of the story.

> One very common but profoundly misunderstood Hebrew word is Misken. It's usually translated as Pitiful, Poor, Miserable, Pathetic. [. . .]
>
> The problem is that all these connote condescension. Something is wrong—with that individual. He has failed at something and is now stuck in a place, at best, where we never hope to be.
>
> If you've ever heard the term being used with spontaneous Jewish compassion, however, you know it means something very different. "Oy, Misken!" conveys a piercing overlap of spirit; an abiding kinship; a mutual commiseration that leaves each feeling a little lighter, a little holier.

5 Read the following excerpt from the classic Holocaust memoir *Night* by Elie Wiesel. Explain how this passage is similar to and different from the attitude that Professor Tendler had after being released from the camp.

> Never shall I forget that night, the first night in camp, which has turned my life into one long night, seven times cursed and seven times sealed. Never shall I forget the smoke. Never shall I forget the little faces of the children whose bodies I saw turned into wreaths of smoke beneath a silent blue sky.
>
> Never shall I forget those flames which consumed my faith forever.
>
> Never shall I forget that nocturnal silence which deprived me, for all eternity, of the desire to live. Never shall I forget those moments which murdered my God and my soul and turned my dreams to dust.
>
> Never shall I forget these things, even if I am condemned to live as long as God Himself. Never.

A & P

John Updike

American writer John Updike (1932–2009) is best known for a series of books featuring Harry "Rabbit" Angstrom, whose fictional life Updike traced from young adulthood to old age. Averaging nearly one novel or short-story collection every year between 1960 and 2009, he is one of only three writers to win the Pulitzer Prize for literature twice. In his novels and short stories, many of which were first published in the *New Yorker* magazine, Updike often reflects the religious, economic, societal, and marital conflicts faced by middle-class white men.

Hulton Archive/Getty Images

In this, one of his most famous short stories, published in 1961, the narrator, Sammy, recounts what seems to be a typical day in the A & P grocery store where he works, but it quickly turns into a situation in which Sammy faces an ethical choice that has significant consequences for him.

In walks these three girls in nothing but bathing suits. I'm in the third checkout slot, with my back to the door, so I don't see them until they're over by the bread. The one that caught my eye first was the one in the plaid green two-piece. She was a chunky kid, with a good tan and a sweet broad soft-looking can with those two crescents of white just under it, where the sun never seems to hit, at the top of the backs of her legs. I stood there with my hand on a box of HiHo crackers trying to remember if I rang it up or not. I ring it up again and the customer starts giving me hell. She's one of these cash-register-watchers, a witch about fifty with rouge on her cheekbones and no eyebrows, and I know it made her day to trip me up. She'd been watching cash registers for fifty years and probably never seen a mistake before.

By the time I got her feathers smoothed and her goodies into a bag — she gives me a little snort in passing, if she'd been born at the right time they would have burned her over in Salem — by the time I get her on her way the girls had circled around the bread and were coming back, without a pushcart, back my way along the counters, in the aisle between the checkouts and the Special bins. They didn't even have shoes on. There was this chunky one, with the two-piece — it was bright green and the seams on the bra were still sharp and her belly was still pretty pale so I guessed she just got it (the suit) — there was this one, with one of those chubby berry-faces, the lips all bunched together under her nose, this one, and a tall one, with black hair that hadn't quite frizzed right, and one of these sunburns right across under the eyes, and a chin that was too long — you know, the kind of girl other girls think is very "striking" and "attractive" but never quite makes it, as they very well know, which is why they like her so much — and then the third one, that wasn't quite so tall. She was the queen. She kind of led them, the other two peeking around and making their shoulders round. She didn't look around, not this queen, she just walked straight on slowly, on these long white prima-donna legs. She came down a little hard on her heels, as if she didn't walk in her bare feet that much, putting down her heels and then letting the weight move along to her toes as if she was testing the floor with every step, putting a little deliberate extra action into it. You never know for sure how girls' minds work (do you really think it's a mind in there or just a little buzz like a bee in a glass jar?) but you got the idea she had talked the other two into coming in here with her, and now she was showing them how to do it, walk slow and hold yourself straight.

She had on a kind of dirty-pink — beige maybe, I don't know — bathing suit with a little nubble all over it and, what got me, the straps were down. They were off her shoulders looped loose around the cool tops of her arms, and I guess as a result the suit had slipped a little on her, so all around the top of the cloth there was this shining rim. If it hadn't been there you wouldn't have known there could have been anything whiter than those shoulders. With the straps pushed off, there was nothing between the top of the suit and the top of her head except just *her*, this clean bare plane of the top of her chest down from the shoulder bones like a dented sheet of metal tilted in the light. I mean, it was more than pretty.

She had sort of oaky hair that the sun and salt had bleached, done up in a bun that was unraveling, and a kind of prim face. Walking into the A & P with your straps down, I suppose it's the only kind of face you *can* have. She held her head so high her neck, coming up out of those white shoulders, looked kind of stretched, but I didn't mind. The longer her neck was, the more of her there was.

5 She must have felt in the corner of her eye me and over my shoulder Stokesie in the second

slot watching, but she didn't tip. Not this queen. She kept her eyes moving across the racks, and stopped, and turned so slow it made my stomach rub the inside of my apron, and buzzed to the other two, who kind of huddled against her for relief, and then they all three of them went up the cat-and-dog-food-breakfast-cereal-macaroni-rice-raisins-seasonings-spreads-spaghetti-soft-drinks-crackers-and-cookies aisle. From the third slot I look straight up this aisle to the meat counter, and I watched them all the way. The fat one with the tan sort of fumbled with the cookies, but on second thought she put the package back. The sheep pushing their carts down the aisle — the girls were walking against the usual traffic (not that we have one-way signs or anything) — were pretty hilarious. You could see them, when Queenie's white shoulders dawned on them, kind of jerk, or hop, or hiccup, but their eyes snapped back to their own baskets and on they pushed. I bet you could set off dynamite in an A & P and the people would by and large keep reaching and checking oatmeal off their lists and muttering "Let me see, there was a third thing, began with A, asparagus, no, ah, yes, applesauce!" or whatever it is they do mutter. But there was no doubt, this jiggled them. A few houseslaves in pin curlers even looked around after pushing their carts past to make sure what they had seen was correct.

You know, it's one thing to have a girl in a bathing suit down on the beach, where what with the glare nobody can look at each other much anyway, and another thing in the cool of the A & P, under the fluorescent lights, against all those stacked packages, with her feet paddling along naked over our checkerboard green-and-cream rubber-tile floor.

"Oh Daddy," Stokesie said beside me. "I feel so faint."

"Darling," I said. "Hold me tight." Stokesie's married, with two babies chalked up on his fuselage already, but as far as I can tell that's the only difference. He's twenty-two, and I was nineteen this April.

"Is it done?" he asks, the responsible married man finding his voice. I forgot to say he thinks he's going to be manager some sunny day, maybe in 1990 when it's called the Great Alexandrov and Petrooshki Tea Company or something.

10   What he meant was, our town is five miles from a beach, with a big summer colony out on the Point, but we're right in the middle of town, and the women generally put on a shirt or shorts or something before they get out of the car into the street. And anyway these are usually women with six children and varicose veins mapping their legs and nobody, including them, could care less. As I say, we're right in the middle of town, and if you stand at our front doors you can see two banks and the Congregational church and the newspaper store and three real-estate offices and about twenty-seven old freeloaders tearing up Central Street because the sewer broke again. It's not as if we're on the Cape; we're north of Boston and there's people in this town haven't seen the ocean for twenty years.

The girls had reached the meat counter and were asking McMahon something. He pointed, they pointed, and they shuffled out of sight behind a pyramid of Diet Delight peaches. All that was left for us to see was old McMahon patting his mouth and looking after them sizing up their joints. Poor kids, I began to feel sorry for them, they couldn't help it.

Now here comes the sad part of the story, at least my family says it's sad, but I don't think it's so sad myself. The store's pretty empty, it being Thursday afternoon, so there was nothing much to do except lean on the register and wait for the girls to show up again. The whole store was like a pinball machine and I didn't know which tunnel they'd come out of. After a while they come around out of the far aisle, around the light bulbs, records at discount of the Carib-bean Six or Tony Martin Sings or some such gunk you wonder they waste the wax on, sixpacks of candy bars, and plastic toys done up in cellophane that fall apart when a kid looks at them anyway. Around they come, Queenie still leading the way, and holding a little gray jar in her hand. Slots Three through Seven are unmanned and I could see her wondering between Stokes and me, but Stokesie with his usual luck draws an old party in baggy gray pants who stumbles up with four giant cans of pineapple juice (what do these bums *do* with all that pineapple juice? I've often asked myself) so the girls come to me. Queenie puts down the jar and I take it into my fingers icy cold. King-fish Fancy Herring Snacks in Pure Sour Cream: 49¢. Now her hands are empty, not a ring or a bracelet, bare as God made them, and I wonder where the money's coming from. Still with that prim look she lifts a folded dollar bill out of the hollow at the center of her nubbled pink top. The jar went heavy in my hand. Really, I thought that was so cute.

Then everybody's luck begins to run out. Lengel comes in from haggling with a truck full of cabbages on the lot and is about to scuttle into that door marked MANAGER behind which he hides all day when the girls touch his eye. Lengel's pretty dreary, teaches Sunday school and the rest, but he doesn't miss that much. He comes over and says, "Girls, this isn't the beach."

Queenie blushes, though maybe it's just a brush of sunburn I was noticing for the first time, now that she was so close. "My mother asked me to pick up a jar of herring snacks." Her voice kind of startled me, the way voices do when you see the people first, coming out so flat and dumb yet kind of tony, too, the way it ticked over "pick up" and "snacks." All of a sudden I slid right down her voice into the living room. Her father and the other men were standing around in ice-cream coats and bow ties and the

women were in sandals picking up herring snacks on toothpicks off a big glass plate and they were all holding drinks the color of water with olives and sprigs of mint in them. When my parents have somebody over they get lemonade and if it's a real racy affair Schlitz in tall glasses with "They'll Do It Every Time" cartoons sten-cilled on.

15   "That's all right," Lengel said. "But this isn't the beach." His repeating this struck me as funny, as if it had just occurred to him, and he had been thinking all these years the A & P was a great big dune and he was the head lifeguard. He didn't like my smiling — as I say he doesn't miss much — but he concentrates on giving the girls that sad Sunday-school-superintendent stare.

Queenie's blush is no sunburn now, and the plump one in plaid, that I liked better from the back — a really sweet can — pipes up, "We weren't doing any shopping. We just came in for the one thing."

"That makes no difference," Lengel tells her, and I could see from the way his eyes went that he hadn't noticed she was wearing a two-piece before. "We want you decently dressed when you come in here."

"We *are* decent," Queenie says suddenly, her lower lip pushing, getting sore now that she remembers her place, a place from which the crowd that runs the A & P must look pretty crummy. Fancy Herring Snacks flashed in her very blue eyes.

"Girls, I don't want to argue with you. After this come in here with your shoulders covered. It's our policy." He turns his back. That's policy for you. Policy is what the kingpins want. What the others want is juvenile delinquency.

20   All this while, the customers had been show-ing up with their carts but, you know, sheep, seeing a scene, they had all bunched up on Stokesie, who shook open a paper bag as gently as peeling a peach, not wanting to miss a word. I could feel in the silence everybody getting

nervous, most of all Lengel, who asks me, "Sammy, have you rung up their purchase?"

I thought and said "No" but it wasn't about that I was thinking. I go through the punches, 4, 9, GROC, TOT — it's more complicated than you think, and after you do it often enough, it begins to make a little song, that you hear words to, in my case "Hello (*bing*) there, you (*gung*) hap-py *pee*-pul (*splat*)!" — the *splat* being the drawer flying out. I uncrease the bill, tenderly as you may imagine, it just having come from between the two smoothest scoops of vanilla I had ever known were there, and pass a half and a penny into her narrow pink palm, and nestle the herrings in a bag and twist its neck and hand it over, all the time thinking.

The girls, and who'd blame them, are in a hurry to get out, so I say "I quit" to Lengel quick enough for them to hear, hoping they'll stop and watch me, their unsuspected hero. They keep right on going, into the electric eye; the door flies open and they flicker across the lot to their car, Queenie and Plaid and Big Tall Goony-Goony (not that as raw material she was so bad), leaving me with Lengel and a kink in his eyebrow.

"Did you say something, Sammy?"

"I said I quit."

25   "I thought you did."

"You didn't have to embarrass them."

"It was they who were embarrassing us."

I started to say something that came out "Fiddle-de-doo." It's a saying of my grandmother's, and I know she would have been pleased.

"I don't think you know what you're saying," Lengel said.

30   "I know you don't," I said. "But I do." I pull the bow at the back of my apron and start shrugging it off my shoulders. A couple customers that had been heading for my slot begin to knock against each other, like scared pigs in a chute.

Lengel sighs and begins to look very patient and old and gray. He's been a friend of my parents for years. "Sammy, you don't want to do this to your Mom and Dad," he tells me. It's true, I don't. But it seems to me that once you begin a gesture it's fatal not to go through with it. I fold the apron, "Sammy" stitched in red on the pocket, and put it on the counter, and drop the bow tie on top of it. The bow tie is theirs, if you've ever wondered. "You'll feel this for the rest of your life," Lengel says, and I know that's true, too, but remembering how he made the pretty girl blush makes me so scrunchy inside I punch the No Sale tab and the machine whirs "pee-pul" and the drawer splats out. One advantage to this scene taking place in summer, I can follow this up with a clean exit, there's no fumbling around getting your coat and galoshes, I just saunter into the electric eye in my white shirt that my mother ironed the night before, and the door heaves itself open, and outside the sunshine is skating around on the asphalt.

I look around for my girls, but they're gone, of course. There wasn't anybody but some young married screaming with her children about some candy they didn't get by the door of a powder-blue Falcon station wagon. Looking back in the big windows, over the bags of peat moss and aluminum lawn furniture stacked on the pavement, I could see Lengel in my place in the slot, checking the sheep through. His face was dark gray and his back stiff, as if he'd just had an injection of iron, and my stomach kind of fell as I felt how hard the world was going to be to me hereafter.

seeing connections

Katie and the Dock Workers by Rob Gage

▲

If the girls in Updike's story were on the beach and not in a grocery store, no one would even notice they were in their bathing suits.

Look at this image by Rob Gage. What is the point he is trying to make by showing a ballerina out of the context of the ballet? What is the effect of the juxtaposition between the dancer and the dock workers? How is this juxtaposition similar to or different from the one in the story "A & P"?

Understanding and Interpreting

1 All of the characterization of the girls comes directly from Sammy's point of view. Skim back through the story and locate a place where the narrator directly describes the girls. What does this description reveal about the girls, and, more important, what does it reveal about Sammy?

2 In literature, a "foil" is a character whose purpose in the story is intended to draw a contrast to the protagonist, revealing some aspect of the protagonist's character that might not have been otherwise revealed. Stokesie acts as a foil to Sammy in this story. Explain what Stokesie's actions and traits reveal about Sammy.

3 While there can be little doubt that Sammy is physically attracted to the girls, he also seems to be attracted to the way that they do not conform to the expectations of the A & P. Identify sections of the story where Sammy is attracted to the girls in this way, and explain why he might find this nonconformity attractive.

4 There are two settings in this story: the A & P store and the town in which the store sits. Explain Sammy's attitude toward both of these settings and explain the role that both play in Sammy's final decision.

5 Reread the sentence in paragraph 14: "All of a sudden I slid right down her voice into the living room." What is the contrast that Sammy draws between what he imagines about Queenie's life and his own? How might this contrast lead to Sammy's act at the end of the story?

6 Why does Sammy quit? What motivates his decision? Does he regret it? Is Sammy really an "unsuspected hero" (par. 22)?

Analyzing Language, Style, and Structure

1 Notice that Updike chooses to use the present tense, with only a few exceptions, throughout the story. What is the effect of a narrative being told in this manner? How might the effect have been different if it were in the past tense?

2 Look back through the story and identify Updike's use of parenthetical asides. What do these asides have in common? What purpose do they serve?

3 What does the repetition of the phrase "not this queen" (pars. 2 and 5) reveal both about Queenie and Sammy?

4 How do the metaphors that Updike uses to describe the customers in the store help to illustrate the theme of this story?

5 At almost exactly the halfway point, the narrator breaks the flow, and especially the time sequence, of the story when he says, "Now here comes the sad part of the story, at least my family says it's sad, but I don't think it's so sad myself" (par. 12). What is the effect of this interruption in the story at this particular point?

6 Reread the exchange between Sammy and Lengel. How does Updike create humor in this dialogue, and why does he play this scene somewhat lightly?

7 The last sentence includes a description of Lengel, who has taken Sammy's place at the checkout slot, which leads Sammy to feel "how hard the world was going to be to [him] hereafter." How does the contrast with Lengel lead to this realization? How is this line different in tone from the rest of the story?

Connecting, Arguing, and Extending

1 Is Sammy's quitting really the right thing to do? What effect does it have? Are there options that Sammy could have taken that would have been more effective? Be sure to use support from the story to support your position.

2 Even if he is less than successful, Sammy does take a stand, protesting the treatment of the girls by the manager. Describe a time when you or someone you know stood up for someone like Sammy did, or a time when someone stood up for you. What was the outcome? What was the ethical choice that was faced?

3 As much as we would all like to believe that we are willing to sacrifice something important for our philosophical beliefs, the truth is that few of do so on a regular basis. For instance, we might recognize that brain injuries are a serious risk for professional football players, but millions of us still tune in to the Super Bowl every year. Identify a philosophical belief that you hold about a topic (the environment, education, discrimination, and so on) and explain what sacrifices you personally make—or do not make—for your beliefs. What keeps you from making the sacrifices, or why do you make them?

4 What happens to Sammy afterward? Imagine him at least ten years in the future, and write a story about another ethical choice that he faces. Does he still do the right thing, or has he changed his ethical behavior?

Traveling through the Dark

William Stafford

American poet William Stafford (1914–1993) grew up in Kansas during the Depression, working odd jobs to help his family and pay his way through college at the University of Kansas. A conscientious objector who refused to serve in the military during World War II, Stafford wrote extensively in journals throughout his life but did not publish his first collection of poems until he was almost fifty. This poem, about an encounter with a deer on the edge of the road, is typical of Stafford's narrative approach to poetry.

Traveling through the dark I found a deer
dead on the edge of the Wilson River road.
It is usually best to roll them into the canyon:
that road is narrow; to swerve might make more dead.

5 By glow of the tail-light I stumbled back of the car
and stood by the heap, a doe, a recent killing;
she had stiffened already, almost cold.
I dragged her off; she was large in the belly.

My fingers touching her side brought me the reason —
10 her side was warm; her fawn lay there waiting,
alive, still, never to be born.
Beside that mountain road I hesitated.

The car aimed ahead its lowered parking lights;
under the hood purred the steady engine.
15 I stood in the glare of the warm exhaust turning red;
around our group I could hear the wilderness listen.

I thought hard for us all — my only swerving —,
then pushed her over the edge into the river.

Understanding and Interpreting

1 Trace the speaker's changing position on the issue of pushing the deer off the side of the road, from the first look at the deer, to the discovery of the fawn, to the final choice. Was it such a difficult choice after all, since the speaker ended up doing what he or she thought about doing at first?

2 In the last stanza, the speaker says, "I thought hard for us all" (l. 17). Who does the speaker mean by "us"? What conclusion does he or she arrive at, and why? Be sure to support your response with examples from the text.

3 Where does the poem shift in terms of theme, tone, or subject matter? What is the effect created by this shift?

4 There is a clear contrast drawn in this poem between the world of man and the world of nature. Identify how Stafford draws this contrast and for what purpose.

5 The title of the poem can be taken literally: the speaker is traveling in the dark. What are metaphorical interpretations of the title?

Analyzing Language, Style, and Structure

1 Stafford uses a form of the word "swerve" in both the first and last stanzas. Explain the similarities and contrasts in the usage in the two parts of the poem. Is Stafford referring to the same type of swerving?

2 Reread the descriptions of the fawn "waiting, / alive, still, never to be born" (ll. 10–11). Explain how the word choice here emphasizes the difficulty that the speaker faces.

3 Explain the effects of Stafford's changing use of pronouns throughout the poem: *I*, *she*, *our*, and *us*.

4 Although the poem is called "Traveling through the Dark," there are several descriptions of the light. Identify the various sources of light in the poem and explain how they contribute to the conflict the speaker is facing.

5 What is the effect of the personification in the line "I could hear the wilderness listen" (l. 16)?

6 Because of its use of commonplace words, Stafford's poetry is sometimes mistakenly considered to be simplistic. Examine Stafford's use of the following simple words, and explain how the figurative meaning of each supports the poem's theme: *narrow*, *cold*, *warm*, *dead*, *alive*, *still*, *swerving*, *road*, *river*.

Connecting, Arguing, and Extending

1 At the end of the poem, the speaker decides to push the deer off the road. Is this the right thing to do in this situation? What alternatives could the speaker have considered?

2 How do we know what the right thing to do is? Philosophers John Stuart Mill and Immanuel Kant struggled with that question and came up with very different answers. Mill promoted the idea of utilitarianism, which means that we must make the choice that is likely to lead to the greatest happiness for the greatest number of people, while Kant proposed the idea of the categorical imperative, which

determines the morality of an act by asking whether it would still be right if everyone did this act, all of the time, in all situations. Conduct research on these two approaches and explain which philosopher would likely agree with the speaker's actions in this poem and why.

3 Even though the speaker did not cause the situation, he or she feels a responsibility to act. Write a narrative about a time in your own life when you felt that you had a responsibility to do something. What were the circumstances that led up to the situation, what did you do, and why?

/ Stanisław Barańczak and Claire Cavanagh

...ymborska [vis-*wah*-vah shim-*bawrs*-kah]
...2) was born in western Poland and lived there all her
...ing being deported by the Nazis during World War II
by working as a railroad operator throughout the war. After the
war, she began writing her poetry but often found her work
censored by the ruling Polish Socialist Party, from which she
slowly began distancing herself. She published her first poem,
"I Am Looking for a World," in 1945 and her first book, *Dłatego
Żyjemy* (*That's What We Live For*), in 1952. Although she had published eighteen
volumes of poetry, which had been translated into more than a dozen languages,
she was not well known in the English-speaking world until she was awarded the
Nobel Prize for Literature in 1996 "for poetry that with ironic precision allows the
historical and biological context to come to light in fragments of human reality."

Alberto Cristofari A3/Contrasto/Redux

Out of a hundred people

those who always know better
— fifty-two,

doubting every step
5 — nearly all the rest,

glad to lend a hand
if it doesn't take too long
— as high as forty-nine,

always good
10 because they can't be otherwise
— four, well maybe five,

able to admire without envy
— eighteen,

suffering illusions
15 induced by fleeting youth
— sixty, give or take a few,

not to be taken lightly
— forty and four,

living in constant fear
20 of someone or something
— seventy-seven,

capable of happiness
— twenty-something tops,

harmless singly,
25 savage in crowds
— half at least,

cruel
when forced by circumstances
— better not to know
30 even ballpark figures,

wise after the fact
— just a couple more
than wise before it,

taking only things from life
35 — thirty
(I wish I were wrong),

hunched in pain,
no flashlight in the dark
— eighty-three
40 sooner or later,

righteous
— thirty-five, which is a lot,

righteous
and understanding
45 — three,

worthy of compassion
— ninety-nine,

mortal
— a hundred out of a hundred.
50 Thus far this figure still remains unchanged.

Understanding and Interpreting

1 Which human behaviors receive the highest percentages in the poem? Which ones receive the lowest? Overall, what does the speaker wish to communicate about how people behave from these percentages?

2 What are the aspects of humanity that the speaker chooses to focus on? How do these choices support the theme about people's behavior to one other?

3 The way that people act, according to the speaker, is situational. Explain how the context of the situation affects people's behavior as presented in this poem.

Analyzing Language, Style, and Structure

1 Notice how often Szymborska uses modifiers or qualifiers with the numbers. For instance, she writes "twenty-something tops" (l. 23) instead of just "twenty." What is the effect of these modifiers?

2 The author does not present the topics she chooses in random order, and often groups the statistics in pairs or clusters of ideas. Choose one or more groups of statistics and explain how they connect to or reply to each other.

3 Some of the numbers the speaker provides are very specific, but others are vague. Why do you think he or she does so?

4 Reread the final stanza of the poem, beginning with "mortal." How does this stanza serve as a conclusion for the rest of the poem?

5 Overall, is the tone pessimistic or optimistic? What language choices create this tone?

Connecting, Arguing, and Extending

1 Polish jazz trumpet player Tomasz Stanko, with his New York Quartet, recorded an album dedicated to Szymborska. Songs from the album, which is called *Wisława*, are available on YouTube and iTunes. Listen to one or more of the songs and explain how the music compares to the tone of "A Contribution to Statistics" or other Szymborska poems you have read.

2 Rewrite the numbers for the lines with which you disagree, and write an argument in which you explain why you made the numbers higher or lower than Szymborska did.

3 Write a new poem called "A Contribution to Statistics in High School" that focuses on the teachers, students, administrators, community members, and parents involved in your school. Analyze the tone of your own poem. How similar to or different from the original is the tone of your poem?

from An American Childhood

Annie Dillard

While Annie Dillard (b. 1945) writes poetry and has published
two novels, she is most widely known for what she calls
nonfiction narrative writing, which tends to include observational
essays about travel, nature, and the life of being a writer.
One of her most famous books, *Pilgrim at Tinker Creek* (1974),
is typical of her topics and approach: it is a collection of essays
about the natural world around her house in Virginia, with titles
such as "Spring," "Flood," and "The Waters of Separation."
In this excerpt from her memoir *An American Childhood* (1987),
Dillard recounts events from when she was seven years old, hanging out on
a neighboring street "where the boys grew up dark and furious, grew
up skinny, knowing, and skilled."

Some boys taught me to play football. This
was fine sport. You thought up a new strategy for every play and whispered it to the others.
You went out for a pass, fooling everyone. Best,
you got to throw yourself mightily at someone's
running legs. Either you brought him down or
you hit the ground flat out on your chin, with
your arms empty before you. It was all or
nothing. If you hesitated in fear, you would miss
and get hurt: you would take a hard fall while
the kid got away, or you would get kicked in the
face while the kid got away. But if you flung
yourself wholeheartedly at the back of his
knees — if you gathered and joined body and
soul and pointed them diving fearlessly — then
you likely wouldn't get hurt, and you'd stop the
ball. Your fate, and your team's score, depended
on your concentration and courage. Nothing
girls did could compare with it.

Boys welcomed me at baseball, too, for I
had, through enthusiastic practice, what was
weirdly known as a boy's arm. In winter, in the
snow, there was neither baseball nor football, so
the boys and I threw snowballs at passing cars.
I got in trouble throwing snowballs, and have
seldom been happier since.

. . .

On one weekday morning after Christmas, six
inches of new snow had just fallen. We were
standing up to our boot tops in snow on a front
yard on trafficked Reynolds Street, waiting for
cars. The cars traveled Reynolds Street slowly
and evenly; they were targets all but wrapped in
red ribbons, cream puffs. We couldn't miss.

I was seven; the boys were eight, nine, and
ten. The oldest two Fahey boys were there —
Mikey and Peter — polite blond boys who lived
near me on Lloyd Street, and who already had
four brothers and sisters. My parents approved
Mikey and Peter Fahey. Chickie McBride was
there, a tough kid, and Billy Paul and Mackie
Kean too, from across Reynolds, where the boys
grew up dark and furious, grew up skinny, knowing, and skilled. We had all drifted from our
houses that morning looking for action, and had
found it here on Reynolds Street.

5   It was cloudy but cold. The cars' tires laid
behind them on the snowy street a complex trail
of beige chunks like crenellated castle walls.
I had stepped on some earlier; they squeaked.
We could not have wished for more traffic. When
a car came, we all popped it one. In the intervals

between cars we reverted to the natural solitude of children.

I started making an iceball — a perfect iceball, from perfectly white snow, perfectly spherical, and squeezed perfectly translucent so no snow remained all the way through. (The Fahey boys and I considered it unfair actually to throw an iceball at somebody, but it had been known to happen.)

I had just embarked on the iceball project when we heard tire chains come clanking from afar. A black Buick was moving toward us down the street. We all spread out, banged together some regular snowballs, took aim, and, when the Buick drew nigh, fired.

A soft snowball hit the driver's windshield right before the driver's face. It made a smashed star with a hump in the middle.

Often, of course, we hit our target, but this time, the only time in all of life, the car pulled over and stopped. Its wide black door opened; a man got out of it, running. He didn't even close the car door.

10   He ran after us, and we ran away from him, up the snowy Reynolds sidewalk. At the corner, I looked back; incredibly, he was still after us. He was in city clothes: a suit and tie, street shoes. Any normal adult would have quit, having sprung us into flight and made his point. This man was gaining on us. He was a thin man, all action. All of a sudden, we were running for our lives.

Wordless, we split up. We were on our turf; we could lose ourselves in the neighborhood backyards, everyone for himself. I paused and considered. Everyone had vanished except Mikey Fahey, who was just rounding the corner of a yellow brick house. Poor Mikey, I trailed him. The driver of the Buick sensibly picked the two of us to follow. The man apparently had all day.

He chased Mikey and me around the yellow house and up a backyard path we knew by heart: under a low tree, up a bank, through a hedge, down some snowy steps, and across the grocery store's delivery driveway. We smashed through a gap in another hedge, entered a scruffy backyard and ran around its back porch and tight between houses to Edgerton Avenue; we ran across Edgerton to an alley and up our own sliding woodpile to the Halls' front yard; he kept coming. We ran up Lloyd Street and wound through mazy backyards toward the steep hill-top at Willard and Lang.

He chased us silently, block after block. He chased us silently over picket fences, through thorny hedges, between houses, around garbage cans, and across streets. Every time I glanced back, choking for breath, I expected he would have quit. He must have been as breathless as we were. His jacket strained over his body. It was an immense discovery, pounding into my hot head with every sliding, joyous step, that this ordinary adult evidently knew what I thought only chil-dren who trained at football knew: that you have to fling yourself at what you're doing, you have to point yourself, forget yourself, aim, dive.

Mikey and I had nowhere to go, in our own neighborhood or out of it, but away from this man who was chasing us. He impelled us forward; we compelled him to follow our route. The air was cold; every breath tore my throat. We kept running, block after block; we kept impro-vising, backyard after backyard, running a frantic course and choosing it simultaneously, failing always to find small places or hard places to slow him down, and discovering always, exhilarated, dismayed, that only bare speed could save us — for he would never give up, this man — and we were losing speed.

15   He chased us through the backyard laby-rinths of ten blocks before he caught us by our jackets. He caught us and we all stopped.

We three stood staggering, half blinded, coughing, in an obscure hilltop backyard: a man in his twenties, a boy, and a girl. He had released our jackets, our pursuer, our captor, our hero: he knew we weren't going anywhere. We all played by the rules. Mikey and I unzipped our jackets. I pulled off my sopping mittens. Our tracks multiplied in the backyard's new snow. We had been breaking new snow all morning. We didn't look at each other. I was cherishing my excitement. The man's lower pants legs were wet; his cuffs were full of snow, and there was a prow of snow beneath them on his shoes and socks. Some trees bordered the little flat backyard, some messy winter trees. There was no one around: a clearing in a grove, and we the only players.

It was a long time before he could speak. I had some difficulty at first recalling why we were there. My lips felt swollen; I couldn't see out of the sides of my eyes; I kept coughing.

"You stupid kids," he began perfunctorily.

We listened perfunctorily indeed, if we listened at all, for the chewing out was redundant, a mere formality, and beside the point. The point was that he had chased us passionately without giving up, and so he had caught us. Now he came down to earth. I wanted the glory to last forever.

20   But how could the glory have lasted forever? We could have run through every backyard in North America until we got to Panama. But when he trapped us at the lip of the Panama Canal, what precisely could he have done to prolong the drama of the chase and cap its glory? I brooded about this for the next few years. He could only have fried Mikey Fahey and me in boiling oil, say, or dismembered us piecemeal, or staked us to anthills. None of which I really wanted, and none of which any adult was likely to do, even in the spirit of fun. He could only chew us out there in the Panamanian jungle, after months or years of exalting pursuit. He could only begin, "You stupid kids," and continue in his ordinary Pittsburgh accent with his normal righteous anger and the usual common sense.

If in that snowy backyard the driver of the black Buick had cut off our heads, Mikey's and mine, I would have died happy, for nothing has required so much of me since as being chased all over Pittsburgh in the middle of winter — running terrified, exhausted — by this sainted, skinny, furious redheaded man who wished to have a word with us. I don't know how he found his way back to his car.

Understanding and Interpreting

1 Reread the first paragraph. What elements of the narrator's character are revealed by her description of playing football?

2 There are a lot of rules in this narrative. Identify Dillard's rules for the following and explain how they are similar to or different from the expected rules for such an activity:

  a. football
  b. iceball throwing
  c. chasing after kids who threw a snowball

3 What is the purpose of the scene in paragraph 20, in which Dillard metaphorically takes the reader to the Panama Canal? How does this illustrate a theme of this piece?

4 What is "the glory" the narrator mentions in paragraph 19? How does this "glory" relate to the overall theme that Dillard develops in this narrative?

5 Explain what Dillard means when she says "If in that snowy backyard the driver of the black Buick had cut off our heads [. . .] I would have died happy" (par. 21).

6 Is the man playing the same game as the narrator? How do you know?

7 How does Dillard use setting to reflect the theme of the piece?

Analyzing Language, Style, and Structure

1 What does the sentence "This was fine sport" (par. 1) reveal about Dillard as a child?

2 How is the effect of the last sentence of the second paragraph—"I got in trouble throwing snowballs, and have seldom been happier since"— different when you read it again knowing the ending of the story?

3 What does Dillard mean in these contrasting descriptions of the man?
   a. "our pursuer, our captor, our hero" (par. 16)
   b. "this sainted, skinny, furious redheaded man" (par. 21)

4 Dillard describes her pursuer's "ordinary Pittsburgh accent with his normal righteous anger and the usual common sense" (par. 20). How do her word choices reflect the lessons she learns from this incident?

5 Writing a narrative about a time in childhood can be difficult because a writer often tries to re-create a child's voice while maintaining the voice of an adult looking backward at the event. Describe the narrative voice in this story. When is the voice childlike and when is it more adult? What words and phrases does Dillard use to capture these distinct voices?

Connecting, Arguing, and Extending

1 Write about a time in your life when you learned one of the following lessons that Dillard communicates in this narrative:
   a. "[Y]ou have to fling yourself" (par. 13).
   b. "But how could the glory have lasted forever?" (par. 20).
   c. "I would have died happy, for nothing has required so much of me since" (par. 21).

2 Nostalgia is a sentimental yearning for the past. Would you characterize this piece by Dillard as nostalgic? Why or why not?

3 This could be read as a "carpe diem" piece, which is Latin for "seize the day." Write an argument about the dangers and benefits of "carpe diem" as a guiding philosophy in life.

4 At several points in this narrative, Dillard describes various rules for situations that are not usually thought of as having rules, such as chasing kids who throw snowballs. Choose a situation that does not have explicitly stated rules and describe five or ten rules that, in your opinion, should govern the actions in that situation.

5 In this piece, Dillard makes an implicit argument for the value of physical activity in teaching a child about life. Begin by examining Dillard's argument, and introduce research into childhood development that either supports, qualifies, or challenges the argument implicit in her narrative.

from Lying

Sam Harris

Sam Harris (b. 1967) is an American author and neuroscientist who has written a number of books examining ethics and morality from a scientific and philosophical perspective, including *Waking Up: A Guide to Spirituality without Religion* (2014), *The Moral Landscape: How Science Can Determine Values* (2010), *Letter to a Christian Nation* (2006), and *The End of Faith* (2004). Harris is a self-described secularist and a critic of organized religions. This excerpt from *Lying*, a long essay published in 2011, advocates always telling the truth regardless of the circumstances.

Charles Ommanney/Getty Images

Among the many paradoxes of human life, this is perhaps the most peculiar and consequential: *We often behave in ways that are guaranteed to make us unhappy.* Many of us spend our lives marching with open eyes toward remorse, regret, guilt, and disappointment. And nowhere do our injuries seem more casually self-inflicted, or the suffering we create more disproportionate to the needs of the moment, than in the lies we tell to other human beings. Lying is the royal road to chaos.

As an undergraduate at Stanford, I took a seminar that profoundly changed my life. It was called "The Ethical Analyst," and it was conducted in the form of a Socratic dialogue by an extraordinarily gifted professor, Ronald A. Howard.[1] Our discussion focused on a single question of practical ethics:

> *Is it wrong to lie?*

At first glance, this may seem a scant foundation for an entire college course. After all, most people already believe that lying is generally wrong—and they also know that some situations seem to warrant it. What was so fascinating about this seminar, however, was how difficult it

was to find examples of virtuous lies that could withstand Professor Howard's scrutiny. Whatever the circumstances, even in cases where most good people would lie without a qualm, Howard nearly always found truths worth telling.

5   I do not remember what I thought about lying before I took "The Ethical Analyst," but the course accomplished as close to a firmware upgrade of my brain as I have ever experienced. I came away convinced that lying, even about the smallest matters, needlessly damages personal relationships and public trust.

It would be hard to exaggerate what a relief it was to realize this. It's not that I had been in the habit of lying before taking Howard's course — but I now knew that endless forms of suffering and embarrassment could be easily avoided by *simply telling the truth*. And, as though for the first time, I saw all around me the consequences of others' failure to live by this principle.

That experience remains one of the clearest examples in my life of the power of philosophical reflection. "The Ethical Analyst" affected me in ways that college courses seldom do: It made me a better person.

What Is a Lie?

Deception can take many forms, but not all acts of deception are lies. Even the most ethical among us regularly struggle to keep appearances and reality apart. By wearing cosmetics, a woman seeks to seem younger or more beautiful than she otherwise would. But honesty does not require that she issue continual disclaimers — "I see that you are looking at my face: Please be aware that I do not look this good first thing in the morning . . ." A person in a hurry might pretend not to notice an acquaintance passing by on the street. A polite host might not acknowledge that one of her guests has said something so stupid as to slow the rotation of the earth. When asked "How are you?" most of us reflexively say that we are well, understanding the question to be merely a greeting, rather than an invitation to discuss our career disappointments, our marital troubles, or the condition of our bowels. Elisions of this kind can be forms of deception, but they are not quite lies. We may skirt the truth at such moments, but we do not deliberately manufacture falsehood or conceal important facts to the detriment of others.

The boundary between lying and deception is often vague. It is even possible to deceive with the truth. I could, for instance, stand on the sidewalk in front of the White House and call the headquarters of Facebook on my cell phone: "Hello, this is Sam Harris. I'm calling from the White House, and I'd like to speak to Mark Zuckerberg." My words would, in a narrow sense, be true — but the statement seems calculated to deceive. Would I be lying? Close enough.

10   To lie is to intentionally mislead others when they expect honest communication.[2] This leaves stage magicians, poker players, and other harmless dissemblers off the book, while illuminating a psychological and social landscape whose general shape is very easy to recognize. People lie so that others will form beliefs that are not true.

The more consequential the beliefs — that is, the more a person's well-being demands a correct understanding of the world or of other people's opinions — the more consequential the lie.

As the philosopher Sissela Bok observed, however, we cannot get far on this topic without first distinguishing between truth and truthfulness — for a person may be impeccably truthful while being mistaken.[3] To speak truthfully is to accurately represent one's beliefs. But candor offers no assurance that one's beliefs about the world are true. Nor does truthfulness require that one speak the *whole* truth, because communicating every fact on a given topic is almost never useful or even possible. Of course, if one is not sure whether or not something is true, representing one's degree of uncertainty is a form of honesty.

Leaving these ambiguities aside, communicating what one believes to be both true and useful is surely different from concealing or distorting that belief. The *intent* to communicate honestly is the measure of truthfulness. And most of us do not require a degree in philosophy to distinguish this attitude from its counterfeits.

People tell lies for many reasons. They lie to avoid embarrassment, to exaggerate their accomplishments, and to disguise wrongdoing. They make promises they do not intend to keep. They conceal defects in their products or services. They mislead competitors to gain advantage. Many of us lie to our friends and family members to spare their feelings.

Whatever our purpose in telling them, lies can be gross or subtle. Some entail elaborate ruses or forged documents. Others consist merely of euphemisms or tactical silences. But it is in believing one thing while intending to communicate another that every lie is born.

15 We have all stood on both sides of the divide between what someone believes and what he intends others to understand — and the gap generally looks quite different depending on

whether one is the liar or the dupe. The liar often imagines that he does no harm so long as his lies go undetected. But the one lied to rarely shares this view. The moment we consider our dishonesty from the perspective of those we lie to, we recognize that we would feel betrayed if the roles were reversed.

A friend of mine, Sita, was once going to visit the home of another friend and wanted to take her a small gift. Unfortunately, she was traveling with her young son and hadn't found time to go shopping. As they were getting ready to leave their hotel, however, Sita noticed that the bath products supplied in their room were unusually nice. So she put some soaps, shampoos, and body lotions into a bag, tied it with a ribbon she got at the front desk, and set off.

When Sita presented this gift, her friend was delighted.

"Where did you get them?" she asked.

Surprised by the question, and by a lurching sense of impropriety, Sita sought to regain her footing with a lie: "Oh, we just bought them in the hotel gift shop."

20 The next words came from her innocent son: "No, Mommy, you got them in the bathroom!"

Imagine the faces of these women, briefly frozen in embarrassment and then yielding to smiles of apology and forgiveness. This may seem the most trivial of lies — and it was — but it surely did nothing to increase the level of trust between two friends. Funny or not, the story reveals something distasteful about Sita: She will lie when it suits her needs.

The opportunity to deceive others is ever present and often tempting, and each instance of deception casts us onto some of the steepest ethical terrain we ever cross. Few of us are murderers or thieves, but we have all been liars. And many of us will be unable to get into our beds tonight without having told several lies over the course of the day.

What does this say about us and about the life we are making with one another?

The Mirror of Honesty

At least one study suggests that 10 percent of communication between spouses is deceptive.[4] Another found that 38 percent of encounters among college students contain lies.[5] Lying is ubiquitous, and yet even liars rate their deceptive interactions as less pleasant than truthful ones. This is not terribly surprising: We know that trust is deeply rewarding and that deception and suspicion are two sides of the same coin. Research suggests that all forms of lying — including white lies meant to spare the feelings of others — are associated with less satisfying relationships.[6]

25 Once one commits to telling the truth, one begins to notice how unusual it is to meet someone who shares this commitment. Honest people are a refuge: You know they mean what they say; you know they will not say one thing to your face and another behind your back; you know they will tell you when they think you have failed — and for this reason their praise cannot be mistaken for mere flattery.

Honesty is a gift we can give to others. It is also a source of power and an engine of simplicity. Knowing that we will attempt to tell the truth, whatever the circumstances, leaves us with little to prepare for. Knowing that we told the truth in the past leaves us with nothing to keep track of. We can simply be ourselves in every moment.

In committing to being honest with everyone, we commit to avoiding a wide range of long-term problems, but at the cost of occasional short-term discomfort. However, the discomfort should not be exaggerated: You can be honest and kind, because your purpose in telling the truth is not to offend people. You simply want them to have the information you have and would want to have if you were in their shoes.

But it may take practice to feel comfortable with this way of being in the world — to cancel plans, decline invitations, negotiate contracts, critique others' work, all while being honest about what one is thinking and feeling. To do this is also to hold a mirror up to one's life — because a commitment to telling the truth requires that one pay attention to what the truth is in every moment. What sort of person are you? How judgmental, self-interested, or petty have you become?

You might discover that some of your friendships are not really that — perhaps you habitually lie to avoid making plans, or fail to express your true opinions for fear of conflict. Whom, exactly, are you helping by living this way? You might find that certain relationships cannot be honestly maintained. Of course, we all have associations that must persist in some form, whether we enjoy them or not — with family, in-laws, colleagues, employers, and so forth. I'm not denying that tact can play a role in minimizing conflict. Holding one's tongue, or steering a conversation toward topics of relative safety, is not the same as lying (nor does it require that one deny the truth in the future).

30   Honesty can force any dysfunction in your life to the surface. Are you in an abusive relationship? A refusal to lie to others — How did you get that bruise? — would oblige you to come to grips with this situation very quickly. Do you have a problem with drugs or alcohol? Lying is the lifeblood of addiction. If we have no recourse to lies, our lives can unravel only so far without others' noticing.

Telling the truth can also reveal ways in which we want to grow but haven't. I remember learning that I had been selected as the class valedictorian at my high school. I declined the honor, saying that I felt that someone who had been at the school longer should give the graduation speech. But that was a lie. The truth was that I was terrified of public speaking and would do almost anything to avoid it. Apparently, I wasn't ready to confront this fact about myself — and my willingness to lie at that moment allowed me to avoid doing so for many years. Had I been forced to tell my high school

principal the truth, he might have begun a conversation with me that would have been well worth having. [. . .]

White Lies

Have you ever received a truly awful gift? The time it took to tear away the wrapping paper should have allowed you to steel yourself — but suddenly there it was:

"Wow . . ."

"Do you like it?"

35   "That's amazing. Where did you get it?"

"Bangkok. Do you like it?"

"When were you in Bangkok?"

"Christmas. Do you like it?"

"Yes . . . Definitely. Where else did you go in Thailand?"

40   I have now broken into a cold sweat. I am not cut out for this. Generally speaking, I have learned to be honest even when ambushed. I don't always communicate the truth in the way that I want to — but one of the strengths of telling the truth is that it remains open for elaboration. If what you say in the heat of the moment isn't quite right, you can amend it. I have learned that I would rather be maladroit, or even rude, than dishonest.

What could I have said in the above situation?

"Wow . . . Does one wear it or hang it on the wall?"

"You wear it. It's very warm. Do you like it?"

"You know, I'm really touched you thought of me. But there's no way I can pull this off. My style is somewhere between boring and very boring."

45   This is getting much closer to the sort of response I'm comfortable with. Some euphemism is creeping in, perhaps, but the basic communication is truthful. I have given my friend fair warning that she is unlikely to see me wearing her gift the next time we meet. I have also given her an opportunity to keep it for herself or perhaps bestow it on another friend who might actually like it.

Some readers may now worry that I am recommending a regression to the social ineptitude of early childhood. After all, children do not learn to tell white lies until about the age of four, once they have achieved a hard-won awareness of the mental states of others.[7] But we have no reason to believe that the social conventions that happen to stabilize in primates like ourselves at about the age of eleven will lead to optimal human relationships. In fact, there are many reasons to believe that lying is precisely the sort of behavior we need to outgrow in order to build a better world.

What could be wrong with truly "white" lies? First, they are still lies. And in telling them, we incur all the problems of being less than straightforward in our dealings with other people. Sincerity, authenticity, integrity, mutual understanding — these and other sources of moral wealth are destroyed the moment we deliberately misrepresent our beliefs, whether or not our lies are ever discovered.

And although we imagine that we tell certain lies out of compassion for others, it is rarely difficult to spot the damage we do in the process. By lying, we deny our friends access to reality[8] — and their resulting ignorance often harms them in ways we did not anticipate. Our friends may act on our falsehoods, or fail to solve problems that could have been solved only on the basis of good information. Rather often, to lie is to infringe on the freedom of those we care about.

A primal instance:

50 "Do I look fat in this dress?"

Most people insist that the correct answer to this question is always "No." In fact, many believe that it's not a question at all: The woman is simply saying, "Tell me I look good." If she's your wife or girlfriend, she might even be saying, "Tell me you love me." If you sincerely believe that this is the situation you are in — that the text is a distraction and the subtext conveys the

entire message — then so be it. Responding honestly to the subtext would not be lying.

But this is an edge case for a reason: It crystallizes what is tempting about white lies. Why not simply reassure someone with a tiny lie and send her out into the world feeling more confident? Unless one commits to telling the truth in situations like this, however, one finds that the edges creep inward, and exceptions to the principle of honesty begin to multiply. Very soon, you may find yourself behaving as most people do quite effortlessly: shading the truth, or even lying outright, without thinking about it. The price is too high.

A friend of mine recently asked me whether I thought he was overweight. In fact he probably was just asking for reassurance: It was the beginning of summer, and we were sitting with our wives by the side of his pool. However, I'm more comfortable relying on the words that actually come out of a person's mouth, rather than on my powers of telepathy. So I answered my friend's question very directly: "No one would ever call you 'fat,' but if I were you, I'd want to lose twenty-five pounds." That was two months ago, and he is now fifteen pounds lighter.[9] Neither of us knew that he was ready to go on a diet until I declined the opportunity to lie about how he looked in a bathing suit.

Back to our friend in the dress: What is the truth? Perhaps she does look fat in that dress but it's the fault of the dress. Telling her the truth will allow her to find a more flattering outfit.

55 But let's imagine the truth is harder to tell: Your friend looks fat in that dress, or any dress, because she *is* fat. Let's say she is also thirty-five years old and single, and you know that her greatest desire is to get married and start a family. You also believe that many men would be disinclined to date her at her current weight. And, marriage aside, you are confident that she would be happier and healthier, and would feel better about herself, if she got in shape.

A white lie is simply a denial of these realities. It is a refusal to offer honest guidance in a storm. Even on so touchy a subject, lying seems a clear failure of friendship. By reassuring your friend about her appearance, you are not helping her to do what you think she should do to get what she wants out of life.[10]

In many circumstances in life, false encouragement can be very costly to another person. Imagine that you have a friend who has spent years striving unsuccessfully to build a career as an actor. Many fine actors struggle in this way, of course, but in your friend's case the reason seems self-evident: He is a terrible actor. In fact, you know that his other friends — and even his parents — share this opinion but cannot bring themselves to express it. What do you say the next time he complains about his stalled career? Do you encourage him to "just keep at it"? False encouragement is a kind of theft: It steals time, energy, and motivation that a person could put toward some other purpose.

This is not to say that we are always correct in our judgments of other people. And honesty demands that we communicate any uncertainty we may feel about the relevance of our own opinions. But if we are convinced that a friend has taken a wrong turn in life, it is no sign of friendship to simply smile and wave him onward.

If the truth itself is painful to tell, often background truths are not — and these can be communicated as well, deepening the friendship. In the examples above, the more basic truth is that you love your friends and want them to be happy, and they could make changes in their lives that might lead to greater fulfillment. In lying to them, you are not only declining to help them — you are denying them useful information and setting them up for future disappointment. Yet the temptation to lie in these circumstances can be overwhelming.

60 When we presume to lie for the benefit of others, we have decided that *we* are the best judges of how much they should understand about their own lives—about how they appear, their reputations, or their prospects in the world. This is an extraordinary stance to adopt toward other human beings, and it requires justification. Unless someone is suicidal or otherwise on the brink, deciding how much he should know about himself seems the quintessence of arrogance. What attitude could be more disrespectful of those we care about?

Notes

1 Howard has put much of his material in book form: R. A. Howard and C. D. Korver, *Ethics for the Real World: Creating a Personal Code to Guide Decisions in Work and Life* (Cambridge: Harvard Business School Press, 2008). While I do not entirely agree with how the authors separate ethics from the rest of human values, I believe readers will find this a very useful book.

2 Some have argued that evolution must have selected for an ability to deceive oneself, thereby making it easier to mislead others [see William von Hippel and Robert Trivers, "The Evolution and Psychology of Self-Deception," *The Behavioral and Brain Sciences* 34, no. 1 (2011): 1–16; discussion 16–56]. But whether a form of self-deception exists that is really tantamount to "lying to oneself" is still a matter of controversy. There is no question that we can be blind to facts about ourselves or about the world that we really *should* see — and the research on cognitive bias is fascinating — but the question remains whether we see the truth and unconsciously convince ourselves otherwise, or simply do not see the truth in the first place. In any case, truly believing one's own falsehoods when in dialogue with others is tantamount to honesty. Thus, it seems that we need not worry about self-deception for the time being.

3 S. Bok, *Lying: Moral Choice in Public and Private Life* (New York: Vintage, 1999).

4 B. M. DePaulo and D. A. Kashy, "Everyday Lies in Close and Casual Relationships," *Journal of Personality and Social Psychology* 74, no. 1 (Jan. 1998): 63–79.

5 B. M. DePaulo, et al., "Lying in Everyday Life," *Journal of Personality and Social Psychology* 70, no. 5 (1996): 979–995.

6 P. J. Kalbfleisch, "Deceptive Message Intent and Relational Quality," *Journal of Language and Social Psychology* 20, nos. 1–2 (2001): 214–230; T. Cole, "Lying to the One You Love: The Use of Deception in

Romantic Relationships," *Journal of Social and Personal Relationships* 18, no. 1 (2001): 107–129.

7 K. A. Broomfield, E. J. Robinson, and W. P. Robinson, "Children's Understanding about White Lies," *British Journal of Developmental Psychology* 20, no. 1 (2002): 47–65.

8 At the very least, we deny them access to reality *as we see it*. Of course, when it is a matter of our *opinions* — whether we like a person's work, his new haircut, and so forth — there is no difference between the reality in question and our view of it.

9 He eventually lost twenty pounds. It has now been two years, and he has kept the weight off.

10 Many readers have pushed back strongly on this point — and some have come up with scenarios where the consequences of telling the truth are so grave, and the benefits so obscure, that the virtue of a white lie seems undeniable. For instance:

Imagine that you are with your daughter on her wedding day and are now seeing her wedding dress for the first time. Should she look fat in it, there is no way for her to put your candor to good use. You are about to walk her down the aisle; delivering anything but pure reassurance at this point seems a failure of love. This is one of the most important days in your daughter's life. You have a choice between (selfishly) maintaining your unblemished record of honesty and protecting her from feeling terrible about herself at the precise moment when she can least afford it. What do you do? Here's a hint: A good father would not say, "Yes, you look fat in that dress," and then offer advice on diet and exercise as he led his daughter down the aisle.

I agree. I suspect, however, that honest reassurance would still be possible even here. Given a father's love for his daughter, "You look beautiful" — a statement that focuses on the daughter rather than the particulars of her dress — seems like a more important truth that can be easily told. But I am not dogmatically adhering to the principle of honesty at any cost. If the parameters of the situation are tuned so that there is really no conceivable benefit to telling the truth, and the harm seems obvious, then the lie seems genuinely "white."

Understanding and Interpreting

1 Reread the section headed "What Is a Lie?" What distinction does Harris draw between the following, and why are these distinctions important to his argument?

   a. certain forms of deception (like makeup) and lying
   b. truth and truthfulness

2 According to Harris, what is the definition of a lie? How does he use evidence to support his definition?

3 Look back through the section called "The Mirror of Honesty." It is clear that Harris is arguing, at least in part, that we should all avoid lying. What does he claim are some of the most significant benefits of telling the truth? What counterarguments does Harris *not* include in this section about the potential harm that can result from always telling the truth?

4 Probably most people agree that lying is wrong, but most people are also likely to think that telling "white lies" is OK in certain circumstances. What are the main reasons that Harris offers to support his claim that even white lies should be avoided?

5 Reread the final two paragraphs of the piece. Harris is claiming that when we lie, we are being arrogant. What evidence or explanation does he offer as support? To what extent do you think Harris proves his claim?

6 Reread paragraphs 55–56, which end with note 10. Read that note and explain what Harris seems to suggest is the one possible definition of a truly harmless white lie. What is achieved by putting this exception in the notes section, not in the body of his essay?

Analyzing Language, Style, and Structure

1 The opening paragraph of this essay states an assumption about human behavior. What tone is created through this assumption, and how does this tone assist Harris in making his argument?

2 How does the story about the course that Harris took at Stanford as an undergraduate help to establish his ethos at the very beginning of the essay?

3 Throughout this piece, Harris uses specific examples from his own life as well as made-up scenarios to support his argument. Locate one such example, explain its purpose within Harris's argument, and evaluate its effectiveness.

4 Reread paragraph 24 following the heading "The Mirror of Honesty," and then look at Harris's notes 4, 5, and 6. How does Harris illustrate his credibility and support his claim through his choice of sources?

5 Evaluate Harris's logical reasoning in the section in paragraph 52 where he discusses how white lies lead to other lies.

6 Harris is particularly good at explaining complex topics, such as ethics, to a general audience. Identify examples of this accessible writing style and explain how it assists him in making his argument. Or, identify places where you feel Harris's style is not accessible and keeps his audience from understanding his position.

Connecting, Arguing, and Extending

1 Harris talks a lot about the value of honesty in friendship, but after reading this excerpt, would you want him as a friend? Why or why not? Use specific evidence from the text to support your response.

2 Make a list of things that you have said to people in the past week that Harris might consider to be lies. Why would Harris classify them as lies? Be sure to use direct evidence from this piece as support. Then, in retrospect, explain what you might have said instead, according to Harris, and explain your reasoning.

3 Write a piece in which you argue in favor of "white lies." Be sure to counter at least one direct quote from Harris on the subject.

4 Write a piece in which you try to define a lie, as Harris has tried to do. What would constitute a lie to you and what would not?

5 Most of what Harris talks about in this selection are the lies that happen between individuals, specifically the erosion of trust that happens between friends who lie. What about the lies that governments, corporations, or other institutions tell the public? Choose a significant lie or deception that has been told to a large number of people and, after conducting brief research, explain the effect that the lie had.

ENTERING THE CONVERSATION
DO THE RIGHT THING

Making Connections

1 Choose one line or a cluster of related lines from the poem "A Contribution to Statistics" and explain why those lines accurately describe the actions of a character, speaker, or narrator from one of the other texts in the Conversation.

2 Questions of ethics often come down to power. In several of the texts in this Conversation, whoever has more power gets to decide what the right thing is. Choose two texts from the Conversation, compare the ways that power leads to decisions, and examine the results of those decisions.

3 Part of doing the right thing is being able to empathize with other people, to understand their situation and act in a way that account for their feelings. Choose two characters from the Conversation and compare the ways that they empathize—or do not empathize—with others. What are the similarities and differences in the results of their actions?

4 What would Sam Harris, the author of *Lying*, have to say about the actions of a narrator, character, or speaker from one of the other works in the Conversation? Use evidence from both texts to support your response.

5 Look back at Opening Activity 2 from the beginning of this chapter, which presents a series of ethical dilemmas. Choose two characters, speakers, or narrators from two different texts in the Conversation and explain how they would each respond to the dilemma. Be sure to use evidence from each text to support your position.

Synthesizing Sources

1 Throughout the Conversation you have been reading about people wrestling with what it means to do the right thing. Based on these readings, what values, actions, or attitudes seem to define "the right thing"? Refer to at least two texts in the Conversation in your response, as well as examples from your own experience.

2 In *The Republic*, Plato tells a story about a man who finds a magical ring that lets him become invisible, and begins to steal anything he wants. Plato uses the story to wonder whether human beings only do the right thing because they fear being caught. Write a piece in which you consider the following: Do people do the right thing only when other people are watching? Is an act still a moral one if you do it for selfish reasons, such as feeling good about yourself or being thought of as a good person? Be sure to refer to at least two texts from the Conversation, as well as your own ideas, to help illustrate your position.

3 Most of the texts in this Conversation focus on how poorly or well people treat each other. How much should the idea of "generosity" determine the right way to act toward someone else? Is generosity a virtue demonstrated only by the most ethical, or is it a characteristic of everyone within a society? Write an expository piece in which you examine the role of generosity in your experience, making sure to refer to at least two texts in this Conversation.

4 With the exception of "Cell One," the stories and poems in this Conversation explore dilemmas that characters experience outside any organized justice system. In an expository piece, explain the appropriate role that government and a formalized justice system should play in ethical issues. Should the courts and government become involved in issues typically considered to be ethical, not criminal? You can use your own knowledge and experience, in addition to texts from this Conversation, to illustrate your points.

5 Imagine that a character, narrator, or speaker from one text in the Conversation had to face the ethical situation of another character, narrator, or speaker. What would Professor Tendler do, for example, if he were in Sammy's shoes at the A & P? In your written response, include direct references to the texts to support your conclusions about how the character, narrator, or speaker would act.

THE CHEATING CULTURE

"The Josephson Institute Center for Youth Ethics surveyed 43,000 high school students in public and private schools and found that:

- 59 percent of high school students admitted cheating on a test during the last year. 34 percent self-reported doing it more than two times.
- One out of three high school students admitted that they used the Internet to plagiarize an assignment."

Based upon these results, it's very likely that someone sitting on either side of you in your class right now has cheated this year, maybe even you. It would be a mistake, however, to think that cheating is only something that happens in school. If you spend any time following the news, you'd notice that cheating seems pretty widespread in a wide variety of aspects of life. Look at this list of a few recent examples:

- **Sports:** Cyclist Lance Armstrong was stripped of his Tour de France titles after admitting to cheating by using banned substances. Major League Baseball stars Barry Bonds, Mark McGwire, Sammy Sosa, Rafael Palmeiro, Jason Giambi, and many others have been implicated in so many steroid scandals that the entire period of

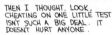

baseball in the 1990s and early 2000s is now called "the steroid era," during which few records are considered valid. In football, New England Patriots head coach Bill Belichick was caught videotaping the New York Jets' defensive signals. National Basketball Association referee Tim Donaghy was convicted of intentionally missing foul calls or making incorrect ones in order to win bets and was sentenced to fifteen months in prison.

- **Education:** In the Atlanta public schools, several teachers, test coordinators, and administrators, were convicted in 2015 for participating in a massive cheating scandal in which adults regularly changed the students' responses on standardized exams. According to a study released by the U.S. Government Accountability Office in May 2013, "Officials in 40 states reported allegations of cheating in the past two school years, and officials in 33 states confirmed at least one instance of cheating. Further, 32 states reported that they canceled, invalidated, or nullified test scores as a result of cheating."

- **Business:** Bernie Madoff, the founder of a popular Wall Street investment firm, was arrested in 2008 after authorities were informed that his whole operation was a fraud; his investors' losses totaled an estimated $64.8 billion. Madoff was sentenced to 150 years in jail. When U.S. energy company Enron went bankrupt in 2001, several high-level executives were convicted of corporate fraud and cheating individual customers.

- **Politics:** In 2011, former Illinois governor Rod Blagojevich was convicted for a number of crimes, including his efforts to "sell" President Obama's vacant U.S. Senate seat to the highest bidder. In 2013, former U.S. representative Jesse Jackson Jr., who had resigned after being investigated by the FBI, admitted to using campaign funds to make personal purchases.

- **Relationships:** Not a day goes by without a tabloid magazine reporting that one celebrity has cheated on his or her spouse or partner with yet another celebrity. And according to the *New York Times*, which in 2008 cited a National Science Foundation study, "In any given year, about 10 percent of married people—12 percent of men and 7 percent of women—say that they have had sex outside their marriage."

Is cheating really so widespread, or is it just sensationalized when it's discovered because it makes for good news stories? Is cheating always wrong, or can there be situations in which it might be acceptable? Is there a clear agreement on what actually defines cheating? In this Conversation, you will read about cheating in sports, school, the workplace—even in video games and photography.

TEXTS

Robert Kolker / Cheating Upwards (nonfiction)
Chuck Klosterman / Why We Look the Other Way (nonfiction)
Christopher Bergland / Cheaters Never Win (nonfiction)
Brad Allenby / Is Human Enhancement Cheating? (nonfiction)
Mia Consalvo / Cheating Is Good for You (nonfiction)
David Callahan / The Cheating Culture (nonfiction)
The Ethics of Photo Manipulation (photographs)

Cheating Upwards

Robert Kolker

Photo by Christopher Bonanos. Courtesy Robert Kolker

Robert Kolker (b. 1969) is the author of *Lost Girls* (2013), about a series of unsolved Long Island, NY, murders and the lives of five victims. He is also a contributing editor and writer for *New York* magazine, from which this article has been taken.

KEY CONTEXT   In this piece, Kolker examines an extensive cheating scandal that took place in June 2012 at Stuyvesant High School, an exclusive public high school in New York City that, unlike most public schools in the United States, has extraordinarily rigorous entrance requirements; typically, over twenty thousand students apply for only eight hundred spots. Through interviews with parents, students, and school administrators, Kolker tries to answer the question of why students, especially those at the most demanding schools, cheat.

On Wednesday, June 13, Nayeem Ahsan walked into a fourth-floor classroom at Stuyvesant High School with some two dozen other students to take a physics test — one of a number of Regents Exams that many New York State high-school juniors are required to take. Small and skinny with thick black hair and a bright, shy smile, Nayeem is 16. Like many teen-age boys, he seems to straddle two worlds: One moment you see a man, another a boy.

The son of Bangladeshi immigrants, Nayeem was born in Flushing Hospital and raised in Jackson Heights, a 35-minute subway ride to Stuyvesant in lower Manhattan. In the academi-cally elite world of Stuyvesant, Nayeem main-tains solid if unremarkable grades, and is a friendly, popular-enough kid known to take photographs of sports teams after school and post them on Facebook. When he walked into the exam room that morning, he seemed confi-dent and calm. Nothing about him suggested he was about to pull off the most brazen feat of cheating in the illustrious school's 107-year history.

Nayeem had cased the room beforehand. His iPhone had spotty service inside Stuyvesant,

and he wanted to be sure he'd have a signal. He tested the device in the second seat of the first row — he'd assumed he would be seated alphabetically — and it worked. He tried out the second seat counting from the other side of the room just to be safe — also good. Then he examined the sight lines to both seats from the teacher's desk — what could the proctor see and not see? — and checked out the seats where he thought some of his friends would be sitting. One was right in front of the teacher. He made a note of that. That kid was out.

Nayeem had cheated on tests before. By his junior year, he and his friends had become fairly well-known procurers of copies of exams handed down from students who had taken a class a year or two earlier. But since that wasn't possible with a Regents Exam, the phone was his method of choice. He'd cheated that way before, too. In his three years at Stuyvesant, in fact, he'd become somewhat skilled at surreptitiously texting during a test, developing a knack for taking out his phone and glancing down at it for just a millisecond without being noticed.

5   Regents Exams are typically administered for three hours. After two hours, students who

are done are allowed to leave. Nayeem is a good physics student. He worked his way through the test quickly, as he knew he would, finishing in an hour and a half. (He'd later learn he received a 97.) His plan had been to use the next half-hour or so to type the multiple-choice answers into his phone, then send them to his friends, all of whom were taking the test at the same time, many in other parts of the school. In return, he expected help from others on future tests. He was the point person on this exam; others would play that role for subjects they excelled in. He and his friends had been helping one another this way for some time.

That day, however, there was a glitch. The proctor was someone Nayeem knew, Hugh Francis, an English teacher, and he was not just sitting at the desk but walking around the room. Francis even caught the girl next to Nayeem using her phone in the first few minutes of the test. While cell phones technically aren't allowed in city schools, that rule was widely ignored at Stuyvesant. Many of the school's students, some as young as 13, travel far from home, and their families insist on staying in touch. "Put it back in your pocket," the proctor said, and the girl complied. It was all Nayeem could do to send a text to his friends: "Okay, I got you guys later."

Nayeem had been writing the answers on a piece of scrap paper as he went along so he wouldn't have to flip back and forth once he had the chance to text. He waited for the shift change. During a Regents Exam, two teachers share the proctoring duties, handing off the mantle at the 90-minute mark. When Francis left, he was replaced by a woman Nayeem had never seen before. She sat behind the desk and was less vigilant. As long as she stayed seated, Nayeem realized, she couldn't see his phone. All he had to do was place it flat on the desk and curl his forearm around it.

He got bolder. Turning to page one of his completed exam, Nayeem lifted his phone just enough to snap a picture of that page, then put the phone down again. Over the next few minutes, he photographed the whole test booklet — all fifteen pages.

The night before, Nayeem had sent a group-text message to 140 classmates: "If you guys get this, I've got the answers for you tomorrow." The students on Nayeem's list included honor-roll students, debate-team members, and "Big Sibs" (upperclassmen deemed responsible enough to mentor incoming freshmen). There were kids who were also good at physics (to double check Nayeem's answers) and a girl he liked. That list still existed on his phone from the text he'd sent the night before. He hit send fifteen times, once for each page of the test. When it occurred to him that some kids didn't have iPhones, he went back to manually typing in all the answers and sent them too. The proctor never saw anything.

10   The next day, Nayeem used the same scheme during his U.S. history Regents Exam — only this time it was his turn to get help from others. He sat in the first seat of the first row, just a few feet from the proctor, and received the answers. Next, on June 18, came the Spanish Regents. Spanish was Nayeem's weakest subject; he needed a score high enough to lift his final grade in the class out of the cellar (Regents are often factored into class grades at Stuyvesant). This time his plan was to take pictures of the questions, text them to friends who were facile with the language but not taking the test, then wait for his phone to vibrate with fully written paragraphs of Spanish.

About halfway through that test, just after the proctor switch, the school's principal, Stanley Teitel, accompanied by a handful of other administrators, entered the exam room. A science teacher by background who still taught chemistry at the time, Teitel is tall and thin with a thick Brooklyn accent. As principal, he was known as an intense presence, liked personally but given to policies the students often found

While the topic of this *New Yorker* cartoon is cheating, what is the artist suggesting about parents' role in cheating? What might the teacher say in response to the parent?

"So what if he paid a classmate to do his homework—it was his own allowance."

too restrictive. Teitel walked past Nayeem, then doubled back and stared down at him, taking him by surprise.

"Do you have a phone?"

"Yeah," Nayeem said.

"Give it to me."

15 "Why?"

"Because," Teitel said, "I'm the principal."

Nayeem knew Teitel was aware he was cheating, although he wasn't sure how Teitel found out. His best guess was that his answers on one of the earlier exams had been too similar to too many other students' (he'd later learn that was true for the physics test). Nayeem's phone not only had the recently incriminating texts and the names of those he'd been texting with on it, it still contained a record of every test he'd shared answers on since the start of the term. But there was no time to wipe the device clean. He had no choice now but to give it to Teitel.

Teitel escorted Nayeem to the front office, and instructed him to continue taking the test while Teitel and the others discussed how to proceed. Nayeem tried to calm himself with the thought that his phone was password-protected, but Teitel quickly got it open (Nayeem doesn't know how). Moments later, Teitel and an assistant principal began scribbling down names as fast as they could. The school called Nayeem's father, and when he got there, Teitel seemed almost as shaken as Nayeem was. "There's no way he can go back to Stuy in the fall," Teitel said. "If this hits the *Post*, the school is through."

The Stuyvesant scandal may have been the most notorious act of cheating to take place at a high school in the United States, but it is by no means the only high-profile cheating scandal of recent vintage. In May, a few weeks before Nayeem walked into his first Regents Exam, Harvard University professor Matthew Platt was grading the final exams for his spring lecture class, Government 1310: "Introduction to Congress," when he noticed that somewhere between ten and twenty exams seemed similar. The test was a take-home exam. It was also open-book and open-Internet, meaning that students were allowed to research their answers in any manner they saw fit, with one exception: The first page of the test featured specific instructions not to work with other students. Platt brought the case to Harvard's Administrative Board, which investigated the incident over the summer. In August, the school went public with its findings. Some 125 students' tests were found suspect; close to half of the class's 259 students now found themselves under investigation. One Harvard dean called the matter "unprecedented in anyone's living memory." One of the first jokes that circulated was about how some of the students must have gone to Stuyvesant.

20   Around the country, there are other cases: In March, nine seniors just months from graduation from Leland High School, an acclaimed public school in San Jose, California, were accused of taking part in a cheating ring (one student was said to have broken in to at least two classrooms to steal test information before winter exams). In May, a high-achieving junior from Panther Creek High School in Cary, North Carolina, was caught distributing a test to four classmates. And last fall, some twenty students from Great Neck, Roslyn, and other Long Island Gold Coast towns were arrested in an SAT cheating ring; at least four of them were said to have hired themselves out to take the test for their friends.

Eric Anderman, a professor of educational psychology at Ohio State University, has been studying cheating in schools for decades. He says research shows that close to 85 percent of all kids have cheated at least once in some way by the time they leave high school (boys tend to cheat a bit more than girls, although they might just be more likely to admit the transgression; otherwise, cheating is fairly uniform across demographic groups). Three months before

Nayeem walked into his physics Regents Exam, the Stuyvesant *Spectator*, the school's official student newspaper, happened to publish the results of a survey it conducted in which 80 percent of respondents (nearly two-thirds of the school's 3,295 students) admitted to cheating in some way, with only 10 percent saying they'd ever been caught. Seventy-nine percent of all students, and about 90 percent of seniors, admitted to learning about questions before tests at least once a year.

It's impossible to determine whether the recent incidents reflect an uptick in the overall incidence of cheating ("It has been high, it continues to be high, and it's extremely high now," says Anderman). But the much-publicized scandals have shined a light on the problem, and social psychologists say today's high-school students live in a culture that, perhaps more than ever, fosters cheating, or at least the temptation to cheat. The prime offender, they say, is the increased emphasis on testing. Success in school today depends not just on the SAT, but on a raft of federal and state standardized exams, often starting as early as fourth grade and continuing throughout high school. More than ever, those tests determine where kids go to college — and most kids believe that in an increasingly globalized, competitive world, college, more than ever, determines success. (A weak economy only intensifies the effect.) Carol Dweck is a Stanford psychology professor. Her research shows that when people focus on a score rather than on improvement, they develop a fixed idea of their intellectual abilities. They come to see school not as a place to grow and learn, but as a place to demonstrate their intelligence by means of a number. To a student with that mind-set, the importance of doing well, and the temptation to cheat, increases. In 2010, Eric Anderman found that even the most impulsive cheaters cheated less often when they believed the point of the test was to help them master the material, not just get a score. "If everything is always high-stakes," Anderman says, "you're going to create an environment conducive to cheating."

The culture of sharing appears to also create fertile ground for cheating. It's not just that e-mailing, texting, and the web make exchanging answers and plagiarizing far more practical. We live in a Wikipedia world, where file-sharing and blurry notions of personal privacy have, for some young people, made the idea of proprietary knowledge seem like a foreign, almost ridiculous, concept. If in the seventies, some students argued that pocket calculators made it senseless to do arithmetic by hand, now the very value of sole authorship is called into question. Today's plagiarists may not even think they're doing much of anything wrong, according to Kristal Brent Zook, the director of the M.A. journalism program at Hofstra University on Long Island, who recently wrote in the *Columbia Journalism Review* about students who lift passages, apologize, and then do it again and again. "I mean, the word *plagiarism*, to me, is a hurtful word," she said one Hofstra student told her when accused.

It's tricky business to blame the Dick Fulds[1] of the world for breeding a generation of cheaters, but Wall Street titans, politicians, and other high-visibility leaders who cheat — and especially when they get away with it — can have an impact. Dan Ariely, a Duke social scientist and the author of *The (Honest) Truth About Dishonesty*, has made a career studying the effects of social norms on decision-making, particularly when it comes to irrational and unethical decisions. "There is right and wrong, and there is what people around us tell us is right and wrong. The people around us are often more powerful," Ariely says. "There's a speed limit, but you see people around you driving at a certain speed, and you get used to it pretty quickly." In one experiment, Ariely and his team filled separate rooms with test-taking Carnegie Mellon students and hired two acting students to visibly cheat with impunity in front of them, one in each room. One of the actors wore a University of Pittsburgh sweatshirt, the other a Carnegie Mellon sweatshirt. Ariely found that in the room where the actor was wearing the University of Pittsburgh sweatshirt, fewer people followed his lead. But in the room where the actor was wearing a Carnegie Mellon sweatshirt, more cheating took place. The Pittsburgh cheater was not one of the group, so the cheating felt less normal; the Carnegie Mellon cheater was one of them, so it didn't seem like such an unacceptable thing to do.

25 We now understand enough about brain science to blame biology as well. Modern research shows that the parts of the brain responsible for impulse control (measured in the lateral prefrontal cortex) may not completely develop until early adulthood, while the parts that boost sensation-seeking (the ventral striatum and the orbitofrontal cortex) get started growing just after puberty begins. Teenagers may cheat (or do drugs or drive too fast) partly because their sense of the thrill outweighs their sense of the risk. The phenomenon is magnified when friends are present, which may help explain why teens often cheat in groups. A 2010 Temple University study found that when playing a driving video game, teenagers were more likely to take big risks and even crash when their friends were watching than they were when playing the game alone.

But why do bright kids — Stuyvesant and Harvard students — cheat? Aren't they smart enough to get ahead honestly? One might think so, but the pressure to succeed, or the perception of it anyway, is often only greater for such students. Students who attend such schools

---

[1] Dick Fuld: Head of Lehman Brothers when the investment firm declared bankruptcy during the financial crisis of 2008. —Eds.

often feel they not only have to live up to the reputation of the institution and the expectations that it brings, but that they have to compete, many of them for the first time, with a school full of kids as smart, or smarter, than they are. Harvard only admits so many Stuy students, Goldman Sachs will hire only so many Harvard kids. Competition can get ratcheted up to extreme levels. "Kids here know that the difference between a 96 and a 97 on one test isn't going to make any difference in the future," says Edith Villavicencio, a Stuyvesant senior. "But they feel as if they need the extra one point over a friend, just because it's possible and provides a little thrill."

Stuyvesant's 2012 valedictorian, Vinay Mayar, talked about the pressure at the school in his graduation speech. Mayar, who lives on the Upper East Side and just started at MIT, called his classmates "a volatile mix of strong-minded people armed in opposition against one other." He listed a few things his friends said epitomized the Stuyvesant experience, like "copying homework in the hallway while walking to class," "sneaking in and out of school during free periods," and, at the end of the list, "widespread Facebook cheating."

Teitel, Stuyvesant's principal, used to like to share a quip with incoming freshmen: Grades, friends, and sleep — choose two. The work can be so demanding at top schools that students sometimes justify cheating as an act of survival, or rebellion even. At Harvard, the *Crimson*, which broke the story, reported that part of the take-home exam — an unexpected set of short-answer questions — seemed to rankle the students. And so, even on something so relatively insignificant (as indeed the Regents were for the Stuyvesant kids), students may have felt justified in banding together against the professor and helping one another. At Harvard, "everyone thinks this incident is not unique at all," says Julie Zauzmer, managing editor of the *Crimson*. "It's

fairly unique in the scale of it, and especially the way Harvard has handled it by going public. But I don't think it's unusual in other ways. Everyone comes here surprised to find they're not the best anymore. Everyone feels they're able to come out at the same point they came in." When they can't, perhaps, some people decide to cheat.

"Not everyone cheats, but it is collaborative," says Daniel Solomon, a former Stuyvesant *Spectator* staffer who graduated in June, and is now starting at Harvard. "One of my friends told me, 'School is a team effort.' That's sort of the ethos at Stuy."

Some students rationalize cheating as a victimless crime — even an act of generosity. Sam Eshagoff, one of the students involved in the Long Island SAT scandal, justified taking the test at least twenty times, and charging others up to $2,500 per test to take the exam for them, by casting himself as a sort of savior. "A kid who has a horrible grade-point average, who, no matter how much he studies is going to totally bomb this test," Eshagoff told *60 Minutes*. "By giving him an amazing score, I totally give him . . . a new lease on life."

Nayeem and I meet for dinner on a weeknight in August at the Old Town pub, near Union Square. He says he decided to speak to me to tell his side of the story, and make his case for returning to Stuyvesant. His parents know about his decision, he told me later, but aren't happy about it.

Nayeem speaks rapidly, and barely bothers with his food when it comes. He is wearing two bands on his wrist, one from the Stuyvesant Red Cross Club, another a hospital I.D. bracelet. Back in July, as news of the cheating scandal spread, he underwent a previously scheduled surgery, the removal of a benign tumor from his leg. "That was a real low point," he says. "I was limping home with my parents. I was experiencing physical pain from the stitches. And people were contacting me on Facebook, asking 'What's gonna happen to the Regents?'" (Nayeem's father, Najmul, had told a reporter that the tumor, along with a recent mugging, left Nayeem stressed and forced him to miss time at school. Those factors, he said, explained the cheating incident.)

Nayeem's parents, he says, had always wanted him to go to Stuyvesant. Najmul publishes a small cultural Bangladeshi newspaper in Queens, and his mother, Nilasur, stays at home. Nayeem's older sister had gone to La Guardia High School and later NYU, but Nayeem felt he was expected to do even better. When Nayeem was in seventh grade, he went to an open house at Stuyvesant. He remembers marveling at how big the place was — ten floors, with a swimming pool — and hearing about the colleges graduates attended. "It's almost like a dream experience, right? It showed me that I'm not just working to make my parents happy. I'm working to make my future look a lot better than what it is now."

Nayeem started studying for the city's Specialized High School Admissions Test (SHSAT), the gateway to the city's elite public schools, two or three afternoons a week in the summer before seventh grade at a so-called cram school in Queens. By the middle of seventh grade, he bumped up to five days a week. By the time the SHSAT came around, he'd practically memorized every question on every published test-prep manual for the exam. In eighth grade, he scored in the low 600s on the test — not as well as his coaches expected, but good enough to get into Stuyvesant. His long-term goal was Harvard.

35 Almost from his first day at Stuyvesant, Nayeem knew what GPA he'd need to maintain to have a shot at Harvard. "When you get into Stuy, they show you where the graduating seniors went to college and what grades they got," Nayeem says. "You don't get to see names, but you get to see their GPA in every subject and

their SAT scores." But the schoolwork was more difficult than Nayeem expected. He dreaded double-period science days, when he'd come home with nine pages of notes, handwritten back and front, then have to comb through them to complete an assignment. So he learned to set priorities. He knew, for instance, that one of his teachers checked homework once every four days. "There were days where I had so much other work, I was like, 'Okay, what are the chances she's going to check today?' And most of the time, she didn't check."

By the end of the first term, Nayeem's GPA hovered around 89 — solid, but not high enough for Harvard. He began staying up all night studying at friends' houses. "My parents were a little tentative," he says. "They'd rather I stay home, but they understood." By the end of his second term, Nayeem had raised his GPA to 92. That's when he says his biology teacher offered the class a deal: If everyone correctly completed their final Friday assignment, working through the weekend on it, she would raise everyone's average by three points. "She knew there was this one guy who wouldn't do it," he says. "He never did a single homework or a single lab."

But Nayeem wasn't going to miss out on this chance for extra credit because of a slacker. On Friday night, he rushed and finished the homework. Then he put it up on Facebook as a note, tagging about fifteen of the kids in his class (he says he did it to lift the whole group up). It was, as he recalls, his first major act of cheating. He got caught and the class didn't get the three points, but, he says, the teacher took mercy on him and didn't turn him in.

When Nayeem began struggling in his sophomore year (trigonometry was especially hard for him), he started sharing — and borrowing — answers more. By junior year, when grades matter most to colleges, cheating had become a regular habit. "History had five teachers. I was getting tests for four of them. I was being nice to everyone, and they started helping me out." By now he realized "how lazy teachers could be. I studied for the first test. But I looked at the new test and last year's test and they were, like, 75 percent the same exact questions and the same exact answers. So I was like, 'Okay, why am I studying?'"

Some teachers teach not just the same subject but the same class for three or four different periods over the course of a day. Nayeem began passing test answers from the early classes to the later ones. He knew he was taking a risk, but he also knew he hadn't officially been caught yet, not even for a first offense. (At Stuyvesant, a first cheating incident triggers a warning, and a second goes on your permanent record, which compels you to answer *yes* when asked on college applications if you've ever cheated.) Nayeem's rationale for who he did and didn't share answers with was byzantine. "There's kids you know, and there's kids you really know. There are kids I trust a lot and kids I care about. There are kids I really don't care too much about, but I want them to have a bright future. There are kids that can help me in the future. There are kids that are good at most subjects, but they suck at one, and I worked that to my advantage."

40 Nayeem remembers wondering before the physics Regents if it was worth it to put so much time into cheating on such an easy test. But he decided it was — especially considering the help he could use on the Spanish test. Studying, he says, seemed pointless. "It's not like studying is going to change one point on my exam," he says, "because there are things I am bound to not know." He says he thought about it morally, too. "I was like, 'There's a ton of kids that are studying so hard, and here's 140 kids that are just going to ace the exam without knowing shit, right?' But a good number of people at Stuy have asked me for some kind of help."

The only reason he got caught, he says, was that "it was too many people with one exam. It got really big, much faster than I thought it would. One day it was 5 people, and one day it was 140."

Stanley Teitel told Nayeem right away that he couldn't return to Stuyvesant in the fall, but Nayeem had all summer to fight that decision, which he did. Since last March, ironically enough, he's been working teaching kids at a test-prep center in Queens.

Nayeem's identity might never have become public knowledge if a friend hadn't tried to help him by circulating a petition online to try to convince the school not to expel him. "He told me, 'There's a lot of people that do a lot worse in Stuy. There's people that smoke weed, people that do drugs. True, it's unethical, it's an extreme breach of academic integrity, and it's at an elite school. It is bad, but I don't get how kicking you out would help anything.'" The DOE had previously acknowledged it was investigating the incident, but the petition exposed the scandal, and outed Nayeem.

Shortly after Nayeem got caught, he went home and remotely wiped his phone of its data; the school and the DOE aren't commenting, but Nayeem has implied that they didn't get the names of all 140 recipients of his text message before that. Initial press reports held that the school had 92 names. Later that number drifted down to 72, and more recently to 66. A few of those 66 students were cleared owing to lack of evidence. While at first it seemed that only a handful of the remaining accused students would be suspended, the DOE announced earlier this month that all 66 would be suspended — a dozen for up to ten days and the rest for up to five days, depending on what each of them has to say in a one-on-one conference with school officials. Those students will also have to retake all of their Regents tests. On the face of it, this seems fair enough. But Nayeem notes that the glaring absence of Regents scores on the students' college applications (at least some of the next Regents Exams aren't offered until after applications are due), combined with the fact that they go to Stuyvesant, would lead any college-admissions officer to assume they were on Nayeem's list.

45 Nayeem says he feels bad about what may happen to the kids who are being punished. "I don't want them to go to lousy colleges because of this." But he insists his friends aren't upset with him. "I've done a lot for these people, so much so that they know I have got good intentions." He says his parents go back and forth about what happened. "Sometimes they're mad at me. Sometimes they're sad. Sometimes they're very optimistic."

Nayeem says he is ready to accept any punishment the DOE throws at him as long as he is able to go back to Stuyvesant. The worst damage, he argues, has already been done — a simple Google search will ruin him in the eyes of any college-admissions office. Why kick him out on top of everything else? He insists he's learned his lesson. "The fact that I could have gotten kicked out, that changed my life."

On August 3, Stanley Teitel resigned from Stuyvesant, saying in a letter that it was "time to devote my energy to my family and personal endeavors." Teitel's critics say he pushed kids too hard. "He saw the students' stress as a sign that the school was doing what it was supposed to be doing," says one teacher. Another calls him "a visionless bureaucrat who is sort of like, 'Well, if it ain't broke, don't fix it. And we know it ain't broke because everyone's doing such a good job getting into college.'" His defenders note that he did more than most administrators to curb cheating, and caught Nayeem.

The new interim principal, Jie Zhang, is a Chinese-born veteran teacher and administrator who most recently oversaw a network of schools that includes Stuyvesant. She'll have to deal with the scandal's aftermath, at least for now, starting with how to prevent future cheating. In a recent letter to Stuyvesant families, Zhang said all students and parents will now have to review and sign an "academic honesty policy." She has also stepped up enforcement of the school system's cell-phone ban, reportedly seizing seventeen phones in the first two days of classes. At least one teacher says those moves are not enough. "I hope this will be a chance for self-examination, of what high school should be and why we're all here." Less homework, a decreased focus on testing, curbs on competition have all been raised as possible reforms. But to accept any such change, Zhang — and whoever is chosen to lead the school long-term — will have to be convinced that a less cutthroat Stuyvesant is still Stuyvesant.

While many Stuyvesant parents are outraged by the scandal, some seem to think the school has been unfairly vilified. In terms of cheating, Stuyvesant "is no different from Horace Mann or Bronx Science," one father says. Many of the students who were not implicated, meanwhile, feel betrayed by Nayeem and his confederates. "All the people I talked to said [Nayeem] deserved to be expelled," says one student. "They said they were angry taking the tests knowing other people were cheating it."

50 As for Harvard, the probe there is expected to continue well into the fall and perhaps even beyond, with each student's situation being adjudicated individually. "It will take as long as it will take," says Harvard spokesman Jeff Neal. "We are committed to ensuring the students involved have their due-process rights." The Administrative Board at Harvard has wide latitude in formulating punishments. Depending on the proof and a student's extenuating circumstances, he could receive informal admonishment, a mandatory redo, a failing grade on the

What connection are both Kolker and the artist in this editorial cartoon making between Wall Street and the Stuyvesant cheating scandal?

Bill Bramhall/NY Daily News via Getty Images

test itself, a mark of no credit for the entire course, or even probation or a one-year suspension. According to a tipster e-mail to the IvyGate blog, the Ad Board has told at least some of the students who were involved that it will not take into consideration the "culture of collaboration" that supposedly existed in the course for many years when reaching its decisions.

As of this writing, Nayeem has been sitting out the start of the school year, not yet enrolling at another high school in hopes that the DOE will relent and allow him to return to Stuyvesant. He's hopeful, but far from confident, that will happen. When he visited other schools with an eye toward transferring, Nayeem says, his heart sank. "I just wanted to stay at Stuy more. Now I realize, but before I didn't — you're so lucky to go to Stuy. You're able to learn. In other schools, there are kids in school who are texting during the day while the teacher's talking. There's no learning. It would have been easier, but it wouldn't have been what I wanted."

When I ask him if he thinks he'd be able to handle the workload at Stuyvesant without cheating, he doesn't hesitate. "I can definitely study my way out of it. Like, now that my future's on the line."

But he says he still wonders if maybe he could have gotten away with his cheating scheme if he spent more time organizing it, or put more locks on his phone. At times, it seems, he's still trying to rationalize what he did. He says he didn't think the Regents was as big a deal as the SAT. "I didn't know I could have gotten kicked out of Stuy if I pulled this off. That was never made clear to me."

This stops me. He cheated on not just one but three different Regents Exams, and he didn't think that could get him kicked out of high school?

55   Nayeem squints. "I mean, like, I really didn't think so." Then he sits up straighter. "And now it's like a second chance. It's like a second chance that has a lot of dark clouds. It still has consequences, right? I was still suspended. I still won't be able to go to a decent college. But hopefully I'll be able to go somewhere. That's what I'm worried about. Somewhere decent enough to work my way up into a career."

What career?

"I want to be an investment banker."

Understanding and Interpreting

1 What is a conclusion that you could draw, according to Carol Dweck, who is cited in paragraph 22, about the effect that standardized testing may have on cheating?

2 What is the "culture of sharing" that Kolker identifies in paragraph 23, and what role does it play in how today's students define cheating?

3 Kolker includes quotes from people who essentially rationalize the cheating. What are the arguments that those people put forward?

4 Does Kolker seem to believe that the steps the new principal of Stuyvesant has taken will have any effect on cheating at the school (par. 48)? Why or why not? Use evidence from the text to support your argument.

Analyzing Language, Style, and Structure

1 How does Kolker give the reader the impression that Nayeem's cheating was premeditated? What effect does this have on his argument about cheating?

2 How valid is the evidence that Kolker provides in support of the following factors that also might influence students' decisions to cheat?

a. social norms
b. biology
c. competition

3 How does Kolker create suspense in the events leading up to Nayeem's being caught?

4 What is Kolker's purpose in moving away from Stuyvesant to describe other cheating scandals (pars. 19–20)? Why does he place that section there, instead of at the beginning of the piece?

5 Reread the last few paragraphs of the article, starting with "As of this writing" (par. 51). Though he never explicitly says, what do you think Kolker's feelings are about Nayeem and his actions? Point to specific evidence from this section to support your response.

6 The final sentence of the article is Nayeem's statement that he wants to be an investment banker in the future. What is the effect of this ending?

Connecting, Arguing, and Extending

1 During the testing, Stuyvesant principal Teitel seized Nayeem's phone and accessed his messages, likely without Nayeem's consent. Were Teitel's actions legal? Were they justified? Were they ethical? Conduct research on the Supreme Court decision *New Jersey v. T.L.O.* (1985), which is the case that has set the precedent for school search and seizures, to support your response.

2 Kolker offers several possible reasons why students cheat—rise of the importance of standardized tests, the culture of sharing, social factors, biology of adolescent brains, and the competitive nature of school. Which reasons do you think are most valid from your own experience? Why? What are other factors that he does not identify that might play a role?

3 Near the end of the article, Nayeem says, "I didn't know I could have gotten kicked out of Stuy if I pulled this off. That was never made clear to me" (par. 53). Locate your own school's academic honesty policies. What are the consequences for cheating at your school? Have you or anyone you know ever been disciplined for cheating? Why or why not? What changes would you recommend to your school's policies?

4 After Nayeem was expelled from Stuyvesant, over two hundred students signed the petition on page 492 to have him reinstated. Would you have signed? Why or why not?

To:
Stuyvesant High School Administration, Attn: Principal Teitel

I just signed the following petition addressed to:
Stuyvesant High School Administration.

Reinstate Nayeem Ahsan as a student at Stuyvesant

Nayeem Ahsan is a valued member of the Stuyvesant community. He plays an integral role in school morale, photographing all major school events among the countless other selfless deeds he's done for the class of 2013. His absence would leave the senior class of 2013 defunct. Expulsion from his home for the last three years is an exorbitant repercussion for his mistake, Nayeem does not deserve to have his future ripped out of his hands, simply so the administration can set an example.

Sincerely,
[Your name]

Why We Look the Other Way

Chuck Klosterman

Chuck Klosterman (b. 1972) is an American writer who publishes essays on music, sports, and pop culture. He is a regular contributor to the sports-entertainment blog *Grantland*, writes a column for the *New York Times* on ethics, and often is a guest columnist for *ESPN The Magazine*, from which this piece has been taken. In this 2007 article, Klosterman weighs in on the debate about performance-enhancement drugs (PEDs) and their effects on sports, in particular on the National Football League (NFL).

Rabsch/laif/Redux

Shawne Merriman weighs 272 pounds. This is six pounds less than Anthony Muñoz, probably the most dominating left tackle of all time. Shawne Merriman also runs the 40-yard dash in 4.61 seconds. When Jerry Rice attended the NFL draft combine in 1985, he reportedly ran a 4.60; Rice would go on to gain more than 23,000 all-purpose yards while scoring 207 career touchdowns.

You do not need Mel Kiper's[1] hard drive to deduce what these numbers mean: As an outside linebacker, Shawne Merriman is almost

---

[1]Mel Kiper: NFL draft analyst for ESPN. It is at the NFL draft workout that 40-yard dash times are recorded. —Eds.

as big as the best offensive tackle who ever played and almost as fast as the best wide receiver who ever played. He is a rhinoceros who moves like a deer. Common sense suggests this combination should not be possible. It isn't.

Merriman was suspended from the San Diego Chargers for four games last season after testing positive for the anabolic steroid nandrolone. He argues this was the accidental result of a tainted nutritional supplement. "I think two out of 10 people will always believe I did something intentional, or still think I'm doing something," Merriman has said. If this is truly what he believes, no one will ever accuse him of pragmatism. Virtually everyone who follows football assumes Merriman used drugs to turn himself into the kind of hitting machine who can miss four games and still lead the league with 17 sacks. He has been caught and penalized, and the public shall forever remain incredulous of who he is and what he does.

5   The public knows the truth, or at least part of it. And knowing this partial truth, the public will return to ignoring this conundrum almost entirely.

The public will respond by renewing its subscription to NFL Sunday Ticket, where it will regularly watch dozens of 272-pound men accelerate at speeds that would have made them Olympic sprinters during the 1960s. This, it seems, is the contemporary relationship most people have with drugs and pro football: unconditional distrust of anyone who tests positive, balanced by an unconscious willingness to overlook all the physical impossibilities they see. This is partially understandable; socially, sports serve an escapist purpose. Football players are real people, but they exist in a constructed nonreality. Within the context of any given game, nobody cares how a certain linebacker got so big while remaining so fast. Part of what makes football successful is its detachment from day-to-day life. For 60 minutes, it subsists in a vacuum. But this detachment is going to become more complicated in the coming years, mostly because reality is evolving, becoming harder to block out. And the Evolved Reality is this: It's starting to feel like a significant segment of the NFL is on drugs.

As a consequence, you will have to make some decisions.

Not commissioner Roger Goodell.

You.

10   On Feb. 27, federal, state and local authorities seized the records of an Orlando pharmacy, accusing the owners of running an online bazaar for performance-enhancing drugs. This came on the heels of a raid on a similar enterprise in Mobile, Ala., where the customer list apparently included recognizable names like boxer Evander

Josh Umphrey/Getty Images Sport/Getty Images

In this photo, we see a typical football hit, but when frozen in a shot, we can see the violence of the impact between two very large and strong men.

How could this photo be used as evidence to promote new regulations against performance-enhancement drugs in the NFL?

Holyfield and late-blooming outfielder Gary Matthews Jr.

None of this is particularly shocking.

But then there is the case of Richard Rydze. In 2006 Rydze, an internist, purchased $150,000 of testosterone and human growth hormone from the Florida pharmacy over the Internet. This is not against the law. However, Rydze is a physician for the Pittsburgh Steelers. He says he never prescribed any of those drugs to members of the team, and I cannot prove otherwise. However, the Steelers have had a complicated relationship with performance enhancers for a long time. Offensive lineman Steve Courson (now deceased) admitted he used steroids while playing for Pittsburgh in the 1970s and early '80s, as did at least four other guys. Former Saints coach Jim Haslett, a player in Buffalo from 1979 to 1985, has said the old Steelers dynasty essentially ran on steroids. The team, obviously, denies this.

Several members of the Carolina Panthers' 2004 Super Bowl team were implicated in a steroid scandal involving Dr. James Shortt, a private practitioner in West Columbia, S.C. One of these players was punter Todd Sauerbrun. Do not mitigate the significance of this point: *The punter was taking steroids.* The punter had obtained syringes and injectable Stanozolol, the same chemical Ben Johnson used before the 1988 Olympics. I'm not suggesting punters aren't athletes, nor am I overlooking how competitive the occupation of punting must be; I'm merely pointing out that it's kind of crazy to think punters would be taking steroids but defensive tackles would not. We all concede that steroids, HGH and blood doping can help people ride bicycles faster through the Alps. Why do we even momentarily question how much impact they must have on a game built entirely on explosion and power?

"People may give a certain amount of slack to football players because there's this unspoken

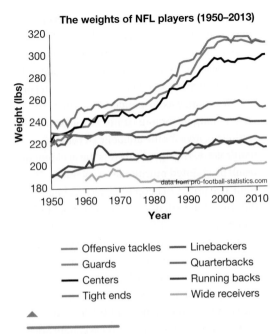

The weights of NFL players (1950–2013)

Weight (lbs) vs. Year

data from pro-football-statistics.com

— Offensive tackles   — Linebackers
— Guards   — Quarterbacks
— Centers   — Running backs
— Tight ends   — Wide receivers

Looking over the information presented in this chart about the weight of NFL players, what is a conclusion that you can draw that would support or contradict Klosterman's argument about the use of PEDs?

sense that in order to play the game well, you need an edge," USC critical studies professor Todd Boyd told the *Los Angeles Times* last month. Boyd has written several books about sports, race and culture. "That's what people want in a football player — someone who's crazy and mean."

15   It's a subtle paradox: People choose to ignore the relationship between performance enhancers and the NFL because it's unquestionably the league where performance enhancers would have the biggest upside. But what will happen when such deliberate naïveté becomes impossible? Revelatory drug scandals tend to escalate exponentially (look at Major League Baseball and U.S. track and field). Merriman, Sauerbrun and the other 33 players suspended by the NFL since 2002 could be exceptions; it seems far more plausible they are not. We are likely on the precipice of a bubble that is going to burst. But if it does, how are we supposed to

feel about it? Does this invalidate the entire sport, or does it barely matter at all?

This is where things become complicated.

It can be strongly argued that the most important date in the history of rock music was Aug. 28, 1964. This was the day Bob Dylan met the Beatles in New York City's Hotel Delmonico and got them high.

Obviously, a lot of people might want to disagree with this assertion, but the artistic evidence is hard to ignore. The introduction of marijuana altered the trajectory of the Beatles' songwriting, reconstructed their consciousness and prompted them to make the most influential rock albums of all time. After the summer of 1964, the Beatles started taking serious drugs, and those drugs altered their musical performance. Though it may not have been their overt intent, the Beatles took performance-enhancing drugs. And this is germane to sports for one reason: Absolutely no one holds it against them. No one views *Rubber Soul* and *Revolver* as "less authentic" albums, despite the fact that they would not (and probably could not) have been made by people who weren't on drugs.

Jack Kerouac wrote *On the Road* on a Benzedrine binge, yet nobody thinks this makes his novel less significant. A Wall Street stockbroker can get jacked up on cocaine before going into the trading pit, yet nobody questions his bottom line. It's entirely possible that you take 10mg of Ambien the night before a big day at the office, and then drink 32 ounces of coffee when you wake up (possibly along with a mind-sharpening cigarette). Anytime a person takes drugs for purposes that aren't exclusively recreational (i.e., staring at your stereo speakers, watching *Planet of the Apes*, etc.), he or she is using them to do something at a higher level. Yes, I realize there is a difference between caffeine and HGH. But there's probably an even greater difference between a morning of data processing and trying to cut-block Shawne Merriman.

20   My point is not that all drugs are the same, nor that drugs are awesome, nor that the Beatles needed LSD to become the geniuses they already were. My point is that sports are unique in the way they're retrospectively colored by the specter of drug use. East Germany was an Olympic force during the 1970s and '80s; today, you can't mention the East Germans' dominance without noting that they were pumped full of Ivan Drago–esque chemicals. This relationship changes the meaning of their achievements. You simply don't see this in other idioms. Nobody looks back at Pink Floyd's *Dark Side of the Moon* and says, "I guess that music is okay, but it doesn't really count. Those guys were probably high in the studio."

Now, the easy rebuttal to this argument is contextual, because it's not as if Roger Waters was shooting up with testosterone in order to strum his bass-guitar strings *harder*. Unlike songwriting or stock trading, football is mostly physical; it seems like there needs to be a different scale — an uncrossable line — for what endangers competitive integrity. But how do we make that distinction? In all of these cases (sports-related and otherwise), people are putting foreign substances into their bodies in the hope of reaching a desired result. The motive is the same. What's different, and sometimes arbitrary, is when people care. Baseball fans are outraged that Rafael Palmeiro tested positive for Stanozolol; they are generally indifferent to the fact that most players regularly took amphetamines for 40 years. Meanwhile, as a member of the Philadelphia Eagles in 1994, Bill Romanowski electively received two trauma IVs to help recover from injuries. Trauma IVs are what emergency room doctors give to people dying from car accidents. In his autobiography, Romanowski claims one of his teammates received six trauma IVs in the span of one season. This is natural?

I am told we live in a violent society. But even within that society, football players are singular. Another former Eagle, strong safety Andre Waters, committed suicide last November at age 44. A postmortem examination of his brain indicated he had the neurological tissue of an 85-year-old man with Alzheimer's, almost certainly the result of using his skull as a weapon for 12 seasons. Andre Waters hit people so hard, and so often, that he cut his time on earth in half. Hitting was his life. This is why the relationship between drugs and football is different from the relationship between drugs and baseball: Baseball is mostly about tangible statistics, which drugs skew and invalidate; football is more about intangible masculine warfare, which drugs quietly enhance.

Announcers casually lionize pro football players as gladiators, but that description is more accurate than most would like to admit. For the sake of entertainment, we expect these people to be the fastest, strongest, most aggressive on earth. If they are not, they make less money and eventually lose their jobs.

This being the case, it seems hypocritical to blame them for taking steroids. We might blame them more if they did not.

25 Around this time last year, I wrote an essay for *[ESPN] The Magazine* about Barry Bonds — specifically, how steroids made his passing of Babe Ruth on the career home run list problematic. I still believe this to be true, just as I believe that the notion of an NFL that's more juiced than organic is more negative than interesting. It would be easier to be a football fan if none of this was going on. But since it is going on, we will all have to decide how much this Evolved Reality is going to bother us.

This will not be simple. I don't think there will be a fall guy for the NFL; over time, we won't be able to separate Merriman from the rest of the puzzle (which MLB has so far successfully done with Bonds). It won't be about the legitimacy of specific players. This will be more of an across-the-board dilemma, because we will have

to publicly acknowledge that the most popular sport in the country has been kinetically altered by drugs, probably for the past 25 years. In many ways, the NFL's reaction barely matters. What matters more is how fans will attempt to reconcile that realization with their personal feelings toward the game. The question, ultimately, is this: If it turns out the lifeblood of the NFL is unnatural, does that make the game less meaningful?

The answer depends on who you are. And maybe how old you are.

In 1982, I read a story about Herschel Walker in *Sports Illustrated* headlined "My Body's Like an Army." It explained how, at the time, Walker didn't even lift weights; instead, he did 100,000 sit-ups and 100,000 push-ups a year, knocking out 25 of each every time a commercial came on the television. This information made me worship Herschel; it made him seem human and superhuman at the same time. "My Body's Like an Army" simultaneously indicated that I could become Herschel Walker and that I could never become Herschel Walker. His physical perfection was self-generated and completely pure. He had made himself better than other mortals, and that made me love him.

But I was 10 years old.

30 There comes a point in every normal person's life when they stop looking at athletes as models for living. Any thinking adult who follows pro sports understands that some people are corrupt and the games are just games and money drives everything. It would be strange if they did not realize these things. But what's equally strange is the way so many fans (and sportswriters, myself included) revert back to their 10-year-old selves whenever an issue like steroids shatters the surface.

Most of the time, we don't care what football players do when they're not playing football. On any given Wednesday, we have only a passing interest in who they are as people or how they choose to live. But Sunday is different. On Sunday, we have wanted them to be superfast, superstrong, superentertaining and, weirdly, superethical. They are supposed to be pristine 272-pound men who run 40 yards in 4.61 seconds simply because they do sit-ups during commercial breaks for *Grey's Anatomy*. Unlike everybody else in America, they cannot do whatever it takes to succeed; they have to fulfill the unrealistic expectations of 10-year-old kids who read magazines. And this is because football players have a job that doesn't matter at all, except in those moments when it matters more than absolutely everything else.

It may be time to rethink some of this stuff.

Understanding and Interpreting

1 Klosterman is not making a simplistic argument about performance-enhancing drugs here. He is not, for instance, simply suggesting that PEDs should be banned in football. What is his central claim about the relationship between the football players and the viewers of the NFL?

2 In two different places, Klosterman uses the phrase "Evolved Reality" (pars. 6 and 25). What does this phrase mean, and what purpose does it serve in this argument?

3 The references to Bob Dylan, the Beatles, Jack Kerouac, and Pink Floyd are likely included here as counterarguments to the idea that PEDs are always automatically bad. Explain the conclusion the reader is expected to draw from these references and evaluate how well they support Klosterman's overall claim. Do they really work as counterarguments?

4 Throughout the piece, Klosterman compares the use of PEDs in football and in baseball. What are the significant differences that he identifies, and how do these differences support his overall claim about PEDs in sports?

Analyzing Language, Style, and Structure

1 What is a likely reason that Klosterman started his argument with a description of Shawne Merriman's size and speed? What is a reader expected to conclude from the first three paragraphs?

2 Since this article appeared in *ESPN The Magazine*, we can assume that Klosterman's audience is made up of sports fans. What words, phrases, and allusions does Klosterman include that make it clear that this is his intended audience? What might he have included if he were writing for an audience not as familiar with sports?

3 Evaluate Klosterman's logical reasoning in paragraph 12. What evidence does he include? Where does he make unsupported assumptions? Where does he commit logical fallacies? What are his biases? Overall, how effective is this paragraph in supporting his position?

4 In paragraph 23, Klosterman uses the word "gladiators" to describe NFL players. What are the positive and the negative connotations of this word, and how do these conflicting meanings help illustrate Klosterman's claim?

5 Klosterman saves his story about how his ten-year-old self admired Herschel Walker until the end of his piece (pars. 28–29). What purpose does this section serve in his argument, and why is it most effective—or not—at the end of the piece?

6 A rhetorical question is a device that authors use in which they pose a question for the purpose of trying to make a point. Klosterman uses this device regularly throughout this piece. Identify one or two examples and explain the point the question helps Klosterman make.

7 Reread the last three paragraphs. What is Klosterman's tone toward NFL players and viewers? How does this tone reflect his central claim?

Connecting, Arguing, and Extending

1 There are several issues that Klosterman raises in this piece: use of PEDs, dangers of concussions and injury in sport, recreational drug use by musicians and writers, and the ethical decisions facing sports fans. Choose one of these topics and write an argument in which you explain why you support, challenge, or qualify the conclusion that Klosterman draws.

2 Think about yourself as a fan. You might not like to watch sports like Klosterman does, but you likely are a fan of specific celebrities, musicians, authors, actors, and so on. Explain the positive and negative aspects of your relationship with them. What are the costs and benefits of your fandom, to those you watch and to yourself?

3 Choose an athlete who has been caught or accused of using PEDs. Research the types of drugs he or she may have been using and how the drugs helped, and explain to what extent the athlete behaved unethically.

4 If they are adults and are informed about the potential health risks, should athletes be allowed to take whatever PEDs they want as long as they identify exactly what drugs they take? Choose a sport or another form of competition and write an argument about what types of benefits should be allowed or prohibited under the governing rules for that sport or competition.

5 While Klosterman focuses mostly on PEDs that allow athletes to become faster and stronger, there is another class of PEDs, known as beta blockers, that has also been banned from many athletic competitions. This category includes drugs that decrease the anxiety that people can feel in pressure situations such as competitive pistol shooting. Read the following excerpt from an article by Carl Elliot, "In Defense of the Beta Blocker," and explain why you think that such drugs should be legal or not in competitive sports.

So the question for pistol shooting is this: should we reward the shooter who can hit the target most accurately, or the one who can hit it most accurately under pressure in public? Given that we've turned big-time sports into a spectator activity, we might well conclude that the answer is the second—it is the athlete who performs best in front of a crowd who should be rewarded. But that doesn't necessarily mean that that athlete is really the best. Nor does it mean that using beta blockers is necessarily a disgrace in other situations. If Barack Obama decides to take a beta blocker before his big stadium speech at the Democratic Convention next week, I doubt his audience will feel cheated. And if my neurosurgeon were to use beta blockers before performing a delicate operation on my spine, I am certain that I would feel grateful.

Cheaters Never Win

Christopher Bergland

Christopher Bergland (b. 1966) is a retired ultra-endurance athlete who holds a Guinness World Record for treadmill running (153.76 miles in 24 hours). He completed the Triple Ironman competition—swimming 7 miles, biking 340 miles, and running 79 miles, consecutively—in a record time of 38 hours and 46 minutes. He is the author of the book *The Athlete's Way: Sweat and the Biology of Bliss*, writes a regular column for *Psychology Today*, and maintains the sports and health website The Athlete's Way.

Courtesy Tom Ackerman

KEY CONTEXT   Bergland wrote this piece for *Psychology Today* in 2012, when Lance Armstrong, the winner of seven consecutive Tour de France cycling races, announced that he would no longer fight the charges of using illegal drugs and in the months after would finally acknowledge that he had, in fact, used performance-enhancing drugs during his career, despite having denied doing so for years. In his books, personal appearances, and on his website, Bergland espouses a philosophy about athletic competition that he calls "The Athlete's Way," which, he says, "should be about fostering character, resilience and camaraderie — not about winning at all costs."

Lance Armstrong was a hero to me and millions of people from all walks of life. This week, Armstrong announced he would no longer contest doping charges brought against him by the United States Anti-Doping Agency. The USADA will strip Lance of his seven *Tour de France* titles and ban him for life. In his first public appearance since conceding defeat, Lance asked his fans "not to cry for him." But, how can you not feel really bad for him?

Do you think that Lance Armstrong cheated? If so, was it justifiable if in the world of cycling — where all of your top competition seems to be using performance enhancing drugs — that if you want to "beat them," you have to join them in not playing by the rules? Although Lance has given up his fight against the charges, he maintains his innocence and says that he was subjected to an "unconstitutional witch hunt." But this may only be the beginning of his saga and legal woes. The International Cycling Union is demanding that the USADA hand over evidence and many civil suits are expected to follow.

Shame is a toxic emotion. It seems impossible that Lance Armstrong won't be consumed with shame on a conscious or subconscious level for the rest of his life. Shame eats you up inside and prevents you from being able to truly connect with other people. The shame associated with cheating is the price cheaters pay, and why cheaters never win — even if they're never caught. The next time you think about cheating, ask yourself — would you rather have won seven *Tour de France* titles and had all the glory in your prime, if you then had to pay the price that Lance will pay for the rest of his life?

This morning I went in search of some Lance Armstrong quotations about "sports and competition" that might show a part of his psyche when it came to a "win-at-all-costs" mentality. There are many amazing and inspiring quotes from Lance Armstrong but one that jumped out at me as showing a more Machiavellian side to his competitiveness was when he was quoted as saying, "Two things scare me. The first is getting hurt. But that's not nearly as scary as the second, which is losing. Athletes . . . they're too busy cultivating the aura of invincibility to admit to being fearful, weak, defenseless, vulnerable, or fallible, and for that reason neither are they especially kind, considerate, merciful, or benign, lenient, or forgiving. To themselves or anyone around them." The sentiment of this quotation is the antithesis of everything that *The Athlete's Way* stands for. The priority of sports and athletic competition in our society should be about fostering character, resilience and camaraderie — not about winning at all costs.

5   Athletic competition — especially in games like pick-up basketball or tennis with friends — is a great opportunity for players to self-referee and prove the integrity of character and trustworthiness by making fair calls against our opponents. This morning I was talking about this blog topic over breakfast with my friend Paul Tasha. He was sharing stories of his experiences playing basketball with people he does

This editorial cartoon by Rick McKee of the *Augusta Chronicle* visually depicts the idiom of "a fallen idol."

What is the effect of having the child on a tricycle in the front of the image? How is the child similar to Bergland in this piece?

business with and how he realized a long time ago that people who will cheat you on the basketball court will cheat you in commerce, too. He pointed out that being known in your community as someone who has integrity and is trustworthy will ultimately make you more likely to succeed. People who play by the rules ultimately prevail.

We live in such a competitive world. From a very young age our children are taught that if they want to "succeed" in life that they have to finish in the top percentile in just about every challenge they face. The world does not automatically reward people who are viewed as being "mediocre" in a meritocracy. But not everyone can be a champion. There is always a bell-curve. So, how does someone who is not at the top of the heap maintain optimism, enthusiasm and a sense of self-worth? I think it's important for people who have made it and become successful to mentor young people and share their stories of success and failure and to show the wide range of happiness that we can achieve by readjusting how we describe success.

I believe that it is the time we spend with family, friends and feeling healthy, alive and connected that is our biggest source of joy. Again, it is easy when you have "made it" to

proselytize about the virtues of not caring if you "win or lose." The reality can be much different, especially if you're struggling economically. Because winning does matter. This is a paradox we all have to navigate in sport and in life. Yes, you want to be your absolute best and to try your hardest to win and to be thrilled if you are victorious. . . . But you cannot cheat to win on an ethical and karmic level. I believe that the bad karma and ill-will of being a cheater has the power to eat you up from the inside out and ultimately destroy you.

But what do you do if all of the people you're competing against are taking performance enhancing drugs, especially if they're legal? Adderall and other "brain enhancing" prescription drugs that people take to get better grades or seem like a rock star at work create an uneven playing field. But again, if all of your peers are doing it and you want to remain competitive what are you supposed to do? I am a zealot about the power of physical activity to take the place of many prescription drugs. Physical activity will boost brain power, creativity, focus, reduce stress and give you grace under pressure when you face a big challenge. All without any negative side effects of a pill.

Regular physical activity at a tonic level is a magical elixir with very little pecuniary costs or detrimental side effects. One thing that I find so depressing about the drug abuse in cycling is that for the short-term glory of standing on a podium or wearing a yellow jersey that competitors in the *Tour de France* will toss away their long-term wellness. The bottom line is that when it comes to taking any performance-enhancing drug—there is a very real payback on your long-term mental and physical health for the short-term gain of winning.

10   Ultimately, sportsmanlike behavior and *The Athlete's Way* is about building mindset,

character, resilience and close-knit human bonds. It is not about how many trophies or gold medals you "win." It really is about how you play the game and what you learn through the process. If you cheat in sport or life you are ultimately sabotaging yourself and making yourself less of a viable competitor. Karma is a boomerang and the long-term shame and anxiety of cheating will ultimately negate the short-term gains of victory. So, be a good sport and play fair! It will end up rewarding you in the long run and make you a happier person.

Understanding and Interpreting

1 What are the reasons that Bergland gives for his statement "[C]heaters never win"?

2 At times, Bergland uses sports as a metaphor for how to live life in general. Explain what he is suggesting about the connection between sports and life outside sports.

3 An effective argument should always address the opposition's main arguments. Where and how does Bergland address those who might think

differently? How successful is he at refuting the counterarguments?

4 Summarize what Bergland is suggesting about the differences between short-term and long-term goals.

5 According to what he wrote in this piece, how would Bergland define the term "success"?

Analyzing Language, Style, and Structure

1 What is Bergland's tone toward Lance Armstrong? What word choice and topics help to create this tone?

2 In the fourth paragraph, Bergland intentionally juxtaposes a quote from Lance Armstrong with a description of the ideals of athletic competition he writes about in his book *The Athlete's Way*. How does this juxtaposition reflect the theme of this piece?

3 Look back through this piece and consider Bergland's use of questions. Choose two questions that you find interesting rhetorically and examine their intended effect.

4 How does Bergland establish his ethos in this piece? How does this help or hinder his argument?

Connecting, Arguing, and Extending

1 Bergland makes several claims about sports, life, and human nature. Explain why you agree with, disagree with, or would qualify each:

a. "People who play by the rules ultimately prevail" (par. 5).

b. "The priority of sports [. . .] should be about fostering character" (par. 4).

c. "[Y]ou cannot cheat to win on an ethical and karmic level" (par. 7).

d. "So, be a good sport and play fair! It will [. . .] make you a happier person" (par. 10).

2 Bergland says that at some point we all come to recognize that in both sports and life "winning does matter." Write about a time when you or someone you know had to learn this lesson. What was gained and lost when you or your subject learned this lesson about winning?

3 Take a look at the following chart from an article titled "Anabolic Steroids and Pre-Adolescent Athletes: Prevalence, Knowledge, and Attitudes," which was published in 2008 in the *Sports Journal*. What conclusions can you draw about the information that adolescents receive about steroids and what Bergland might suggest to change adolescents' perceptions of steroid use?

TABLE 5. Primary Source of Information about Anabolic Steroids

Source	No. of Youth Sports Participants (n = 1,553)	
	–n	%
Book/Magazine	433	28
Parent	322	21
Coach	267	17
Friend/Teammate	113	7
Gym Personnel	112	7
Athletic Trainer	89	6
Teacher	47	3
Television	29	2
Dealer	17	1
Sibling	15	1

Is Human Enhancement Cheating?

Brad Allenby

Braden R. Allenby (b. 1950) is the director of the Center for Earth Systems Engineering and Management at Arizona State University and Lincoln Professor of Engineering and Ethics. He is a regular contributor on science and technology matters for *Slate*, an online magazine. This article was published in the May 9, 2013, issue of *Slate*.

Arizona State University

KEY CONTEXT In 2012, Lance Armstrong was stripped of his seven wins of the Tour de France cycling competition due to his acknowledgment of using illegal performance-enhancing drugs (PEDs). Allenby uses this news to wonder why the general public frowns on PEDs in sports but encourages human self-enhancement in other areas like plastic surgery and even warfare.

Were you incensed when Lance Armstrong was finally cornered and stripped of his seven Tour de France titles? Almost everyone seemed to be. While some felt he had been treated unfairly, most appeared to feel betrayed by a cheater in whom they had believed. In 2013, neither Barry Bonds nor Roger Clemens made the Baseball Hall of Fame, even with their clearly superior records, because they used steroids. This was despite the fact that, as a *New York Times* editorial put it, the Hall of Fame is hardly a Hall of Virtue, filled as it is with "lowlifes, boozers and bigots." Steroid use is apparently a different level of sin: It is cheating.

In another area, however, the American Society for Plastic Surgeons reported that in 2011 Americans spent $11.4 billion on cosmetic surgery and underwent 13.8 million procedures (figures exclude reconstructive surgery).

No allegations of cheating in that arena — or, apparently, even slowing down.

In yet a different domain, campaigners are increasingly concerned by the possibility of enhanced military "superwarriors," especially as technologists strive to separate the soldier from immediate conflict areas — as, for example, unmanned aircraft systems (commonly called drones) do now. Meanwhile, autonomous robots and human/robot hybrids connected by powerful computer-brain interfaces might conceivably be deployed in the future. Such developments raise cultural adjustment issues within military institutions, and larger questions of where the "human" begins and ends when we're dealing with cyborgs and integrated techno-human systems. In addition, however, they raise questions of "cheating," as discussions in some recent workshops and war games illustrated. The argument is that real warriors don't hide behind remotely controlled machines; it is only fair that soldiers be killed by other soldiers. And many people are indeed frightened by the idea of creating "superwarriors" who, through drugs, genetic engineering, and cyborg technologies, are more weapon system than soldier.

We are deeply conflicted when it comes to human enhancement technologies. It is unclear, for example, precisely whom Armstrong was cheating. Enhancing has been pervasive in cycling for many years, and when he was stripped of his Tour de France titles, they were not awarded to anyone else because . . . well, everyone else was also under "a cloud of suspicion," as the Union Cycliste Internationale put it. So he was not cheating his competitors, or at least not completely. And if just breaking rules — which he, and apparently some of his peers, were doing — is cause for substantial retribution, traffic speeders across the country, and those of you who just "borrowed" that pen from work, are in deep trouble.

Probably few people would have objections to these exoskeletons to help disabled people to walk and function fully, but what are the ethical lines that could be drawn for their use in other areas, such as in warfare or sports competitions, or even in their use in jobs that require physical force?

Heathcliff O'Malley/Rex Features/Associated Press

DARPA/U.S. Department of Defense

5   Surgical enhancement of various body parts, on the other hand, does not appear to be regarded as cheating. False allure is apparently caveat emptor. (And are you really going to ban cosmetics?)

Questions of the impact of enhancement technologies on the psychology of conflict, especially in counterinsurgency environments, are complex. But arguments that it's cheating to use technology to distance soldiers from potential harm are weak. War has rules, but it is not a sport, and the idea that an individual should be exposed to maiming or death out of some misplaced demand for "fairness," as if war were a soccer game, is difficult to defend.

That doesn't mean we can't draw some conclusions from this confusion. First, "cheating" does not seem to be an issue of enhancement generally. People seem fine with personal enhancement, especially where the practice is long-standing and they have had time to adapt to it. Vaccines, for example, are an obvious human enhancement — I specifically design a new technology to be embedded in your body with the direct result that your immune system is artificially enhanced in such a way as to provide you with better health and a longer life. Yet few challenge vaccination on enhancement grounds. Surgical interventions to correct failing wetware systems (joint replacement surgery, for example), and to enhance wetware systems perceived to be inadequate (like with breast enhancement technology), appear to be generally acceptable.

People get queasy, however, when human enhancement shifts from the quotidian to the highly symbolic. Major professional sports, for example, have long been dominated by commercial ethics, money, and entertainment dollars, and few indeed are the athletic stars who cannot be lured elsewhere by money. Professional teams and sports heroes, however, are not seen as simply part of the commercial entertainment enterprise. Rather, in an increasingly complex and unstable age, sports events and stars become not just symbols of city and home but a part of personal identity. Look at the visceral outrage that Clevelanders expressed when a local star, LeBron James, left for Miami rather than staying in Cleveland. That's not about contract or business; that's something going on at a far deeper level. More poignantly, it is remarkable how the healing of Boston after the recent bombing is entwining the Boston Red Sox, the Celtics, and the Bruins.

Moreover, sports are still iconic for purity, for the simplicity of an idyllic earlier America (which even a fleeting brush with history tells us is illusory). Look, for example, at the frequency with which the myth of the "student-athlete" still pops up in big college sports, and how often that term gets used by announcers for huge entertainment conglomerates that provide the audience of millions that fuels the modern sports machine. Sports, in other words, are often a psychological path back to a mythic Golden Age that becomes ever more appealing during a period of confusion and rapid social change. Messing with that myth through enhancements, no matter what the reason, is simply not done. You may not be cheating your competitors, but you are cheating archetypal myth. And you will lose.

10   Military human enhancements seem to occupy a middle ground. There is unquestionably some concern about what human enhancements in this domain might come to, especially if one moves beyond temporary enhancements like pharmaceuticals to more permanent enhancements, such as genetic engineering. The concerns here go beyond the operational. If enhanced humans leave the military and return to civilian life, for instance, what will happen? The differences may be subtle — genetic engineering enabling one to see in the dark, or providing maximum muscle development and efficiency, or augmented cognitive and neural performance, for example. Or they may be less so — one might have a set of personal

technologies that are accessed by onboard computer-brain interfaces, for example. It's only a hypothetical, but it is a worrisome one. Would such veterans get an unfair advantage in the workplace, or would they be discriminated against — or would they discriminate? Moreover, the obvious benefits of technologies that help protect soldiers make the primal responses that sports seem to generate less feasible. Various types of enhancements, from vaccines not approved by the FDA to cognitive boosters for various missions, are already used by the U.S. military, and while there has been debate, there hasn't been the emotive responses seen in sports.

What does all this mean? It means that social responses to human enhancement are more nuanced and complex than is usually recognized. More specifically, it means that the same enhancement will generate different responses depending on the domain in which it is introduced. If one wants to promote an enhancement, making it available and familiar to the public might be an excellent strategy.

A military use that doesn't trigger sci-fi fantasies — "OMG! A killer robot!" — is a secondary path. Don't even think about sports. And similarly, if one is an activist and wants to stop a technology, make it symbolic if you can. So, for example, using the loaded term killer robot is an excellent start to a campaign against a technology that might otherwise be desirable because it could save soldiers' lives.

From a social perspective, however, perhaps the most important observation is that to the extent an enhancement technology has symbolic dimensions, it will be very difficult to evaluate rationally and objectively. The risk is that various enhancement technologies are regulated or rejected not based on a realistic assessment of their costs and benefits, but because of how they were introduced, in sports or in doctors' offices. The challenge, then, is not "cheating" but the far more difficult challenge of developing the ability to interact ethically, rationally, and responsibly with the world of enhancement technologies that is already here.

Understanding and Interpreting

1 What can you conclude about the author's opinion of Lance Armstrong's actions? To what extent does Allenby seem to think Armstrong cheated? Explain your answer using evidence from the article.

2 Explain what Allenby means when he says "We are deeply conflicted when it comes to human enhancement technologies" (par. 4).

3 Create a line graph to illustrate how Allenby identifies the general public's acceptance of the various human enhancements he describes in this piece. Plot your graph on a scale from "Fully accepted" to "Unacceptable."

4 According to Allenby, why do some people react so emotionally when they hear about cheating in sports, as opposed to other human enhancements, such as cosmetic surgery?

5 What are the pros and cons of the "superwarrior" that Allenby describes (par. 3)?

6 Reread the last paragraph and summarize Allenby's conclusion about what is most important for the general public to understand about human-enhancement technologies.

Analyzing Language, Style, and Structure

1 Even though Allenby begins by asking if readers had an emotional reaction to the news of Lance Armstrong's use of performance-enhancing drugs, most of his argument relies on his use of logos. Review the article carefully and explain how he uses rhetorical appeals to build his argument.

2 Allenby uses a term in this piece—
"superwarriors"—to describe soldiers who use human-enhancement technologies (par. 3). How does his use of this term reflect his tone toward the issue of "cheating"?

3 Allenby utilizes a very complex organizational structure in this piece. Notice how often he juxtaposes sports, the military, and other areas of human enhancement. Identify one significant place where he puts two topics near each other and explain how this juxtaposition helps to support his argument or to illustrate a point he is trying to make.

Connecting, Arguing, and Extending

1 According to Allenby, Lance Armstrong "was not cheating his competitors" and was "just breaking rules" (par. 4). Based on what you know about Armstrong, why do you agree or disagree with this assertion?

2 Allenby is fairly broad in his initial definition of "human enhancement," including socially accepted changes, such as plastic surgery, vaccines, and joint replacements, but there are many other types of enhancements that he does not mention. Adderall, for instance, is a drug that is often prescribed to people diagnosed with attention deficit hyperactivity disorder (ADHD) but is also used by some students as a study aid. In a March 2013 opinion piece in the *New York Times*, Roger Cohen states, "Adderall has become to college what steroids are to baseball: an illicit performance enhancer for a fiercely competitive environment." Conduct brief research on Adderall and write an argument about whether it should be banned

for students taking tests like the SAT, ACT, or other high-stakes assessments, the scores for which are compared to those of other students for college entrance. Use evidence from your research to support your position and explain whether Allenby would agree or disagree.

3 When discussing human enhancements in the military, Allenby seems to suggest that military leaders need to think carefully about the language they use when naming their technologies, avoiding terms such as "killer robot." Think about some current technologies that have particularly effective names. What makes those names so effective? Then, consider how some technologies could be either enhanced or hindered by having a different name. Propose new names for these products and explain the effect of the new name. You might go so far as creating a whole new brand, including a logo, packaging, an advertisement, etc.

Cheating Is Good for You

Mia Consalvo

A professor of game studies and design at Concordia University in Montreal, Mia Consalvo (b. 1969) is the author of *Cheating: Gaining Advantage in Videogames* (2007), which is the result of her research into how and why people cheat while playing video games. In this article, published on the Forbes.com website in 2006, Consalvo summarizes some of her findings and questions whether cheating is *always* a bad thing.

Courtesy Mia Consalvo

Most of the time, we think of cheating as despicable. Cheating is what lazy people do. It's the easy way out. Calling someone a cheater is rarely a compliment, and being cheated is never a good thing.

At least, in everyday life it isn't — outside of the occasional "cheat day" on a diet. But what about in the world of videogames? After spending the last five years talking with game players, game developers, security experts and others, I've learned a few counterintuitive things about cheating.

First, everybody cheats. Some may justify it, others proudly proclaim it, and others will deny their cheating vigorously, but it's a common activity. Players use walkthroughs, cheat codes, social engineering techniques (basically being crafty and tricking others), hacks and other unauthorized software. Cheats are popular, big business and not going away anytime soon. Individual gamers set boundaries for what they will or won't do, and there are several general reasons why people cheat. But either way, can the activity be good for you?

When I first started examining the practice of cheating, I took it as a given that most people viewed it as a negative activity. Cheating implies that you aren't a good enough player to finish a game on your own, or that you want an unfair — and unearned — advantage over other players. Yet in researching why people cheat and how they cheat, I've found that, much of the time, cheating actually implies a player is actively engaged in a game and wants to do well, even when the game fails *them*.

5   There are four major reasons why players cheat in a game: they're stuck, they want to play God, they are bored with the game, or they want to be a jerk. The overwhelming reason most players cheat is because they get stuck. Either the game is poorly designed, too hard, or the players are so inexperienced that they can't advance. A boss monster can't be beaten, or a puzzle solved, or the right direction found. In such situations, players face a choice: They either cheat or stop playing altogether.

The next most common reason is that we all like to play God sometimes. We want all the weapons or all the goodies, and we want them now. We don't want to wade through 20 levels to get to the one we like best — we want to beam directly there. We don't want to drive around in a boring car — we want to "unlock" the invincible bicycle instead. In those situations, cheating is about extending the play experience for ourselves. No one is harmed in the process.

Third, we can get bored with games. But as with an annoying novel, we still want the option of flipping to the last page to see how things turn out. In a game, we may find the fighting tedious, or the storyline dreary, or the never-ending grind to reach higher levels in World of Warcraft just too much trouble, and so we use some sort of cheat to jump ahead in the game's timeline, maybe all the way to the conclusion.

And finally, some people just can't resist cheating others. We want to overwhelm others, not just defeat them. We'll use "aimbots" (programs that automatically aim and shoot for us) or "wall hacks" (programs that allow you to see and even walk through walls) to gain every advantage in an online shooting game. Or we'll intercept the data stream in an online poker game to find out what cards our opponent is actually holding.

But even if everyone does it, why is cheating actually good for us?

10   First, players get stuck all the time. It doesn't matter if you are a master at real-time strategy games — if it's your first action-adventure game, you might be really bad at it. Likewise, maybe the game developer rushed the game out the door with less than perfect directions or a less than perfect design. In those situations, cheating

lets the player keep playing the game they spent good money on. It can mean the difference between completing a game and abandoning it mid-stream.

Imagine reading a book and getting to a difficult passage in chapter three. And then imagine the book won't let you skip to chapter four until you have signified you understand that passage. This is how many video games are designed.

Now imagine instead that players can consult walkthroughs (in essence, detailed, step-by-step directions to winning a game) on an "as-needed" basis to help them through the troublesome spots, or receive "hints" that help them figure things out on their own. Players who have completed the game create these walk-throughs for later players. In short, players are teaching one another and learning from each other, and getting only the information they need to keep going. Everyone is taking an active part in playing and learning how to play. This is a good thing for everyone involved.

Next, players often use cheat codes, which unlock special items or powers, to get the most value from a game. This suggests that players enjoy the game so much that when they reach the end, they want to play it more. That means more opportunities for interaction with the game. Cheat codes can be hidden in a game for players to find and then share with others. Or, codes can be awarded to excellent players, or given to newer, more tentative players to encourage them to keep playing. Cheat codes can keep the experience enjoyable in different ways for different players.

What about when players get bored? Game designers don't usually want them skipping to the end of a game. Yet does the game need to have a linear progression? Could players choose where in the game to go next, or the elements they want to tackle? Are there different ways to

succeed — through battle, through puzzle solving, through dialog? Different players have different skill sets, so giving everyone an equal shot at doing well is preferable. As is allowing players to more quickly get to the sections they find rewarding.

15 But what about the jerks? Everyone wants a perfect opponent like Lisa Simpson, but more often we end up playing with her brother Bart. In EVE Online, for instance, one player, Nightfreeze, allegedly cheated his in-game friends and rivals out of hundreds of millions of in-game "credits" using nothing but fake accounts, a public library's telephone, some help from friends, and his wits.

In such situations, the value is found not in the cheating itself, but in our reaction to it.

There are a couple of things that can be done to either stop this sort of cheating or make it a positive aspect of play. Users themselves often encourage a culture of non-cheating, making cheating not cool. Most commonly, player communities can take an active role in deciding what happens when people are discov-ered cheating. Psychologists have found that when playing games, if players aren't allowed to punish others they suspect of cheating, the game community falls apart. People will even pay money out of their own pocket to punish cheaters. So figuring out ways to keep the larger community involved in dealing with cheaters can keep the group engaged in ways that "regular" game play might never allow for.

As counterintuitive as it may seem, cheating can sometimes be good for you. It can keep you active and involved in a game, reward game play and allow expert players to teach others. It can indicate to developers when games are too hard or flawed, and it can even help a community form. We will never get rid of cheating, but at least in games, we can make it a positive thing, even a way to teach and learn.

Understanding and Interpreting

1 According to the article, what benefits can be gained by cheating in video games?

2 Reread the analogy that Consalvo uses to compare cheating to reading in paragraph 11. How effective is this analogy in supporting her claim that cheating can be good?

3 Consalvo identifies four main reasons that people cheat in video games. Which ones are also applicable to cheating in the real world? Which ones are not? Explain your response with examples from the article.

4 An effective argument should always address the opposition, those who think differently than the author. To what extent has Consalvo successfully raised and refuted the opposition's main arguments? Support your conclusion by pointing to what's included in her piece as well as to what's missing.

Analyzing Language, Style, and Structure

1 Having read the short biography of Consalvo that preceded this piece, you likely understand that she has an extensive background in video games. Identify word choices in this piece that reveal her knowledge of the gaming industry.

2 Who is Consalvo's intended audience? To support your conclusion, examine Consalvo's specific word choices and the information she provides.

3 This article employs a familiar organizational structure: an introduction with a thesis, body paragraphs with transitions, and a conclusion that summarizes the main points. Identify each of these components and explain why this fixed structure is effective—or not—in communicating Consalvo's ideas.

Connecting, Arguing, and Extending

1 When discussing the "jerks" who cheat in video games just for the sake of hurting others, Consalvo writes, "In such situations, the value is found not in the cheating itself, but in our reaction to it" (par. 16). What does she mean by this, and how have you reacted to an experience of cheating in your own life?

2 In this article, Consalvo describes why players might choose to use cheat codes. Are cheat codes ethical? Does your response change if you are playing a multiplayer game rather than a single-person game?

3 In 2012, the Ministry of Culture, Sports, and Television in South Korea took an unusual step in proposing a ban on "farming" in video games, a practice in which someone spends hours in an online game gathering virtual items and then sells them to other people who did not "earn" them within the game. The punishments can include both fines and jail time. Is "farming" cheating? Should it be banned? Is it unethical? Why or why not?

4 Why might it be OK to cheat in video games rather than cheat in games or sports played in real life? Is there an ethical difference between cheating in video games and in reality? If so, why? If not, why not? Refer to your own experiences as well as the article to support your response.

from The Cheating Culture: Why More Americans Are Doing Wrong to Get Ahead

David Callahan

David Callahan (b. 1965) is a cofounder of the liberal-leaning think tank Demos and the author of several books about economic and social policy issues, including *Fortunes of Change: The Rise of the Liberal Rich and the Remaking of America* (2010). In *The Cheating Culture: Why More Americans Are Doing Wrong to Get Ahead* (2004), Callahan explores the various ways that he says Americans regularly cheat: in sports, on taxes, at work, and in school. This excerpt is from near the beginning of his book, in which he examines the rationalizations people use for their cheating.

Courtesy David Callahan

KEY CONTEXT   At the beginning of this excerpt, Callahan refers to what he calls "the Winning Class," which he describes as those people in society who are successful economically, but who utilize unethical means to get there. Later in the excerpt Callahan refers to the "social contract," which is a political theory that people in a society willingly submit some of their individual freedoms to a government they perceive as legitimate in return for basic protections and services. One example of a social contract is that when people pay taxes, they have a reasonable expectation that public schools will provide education for their children.

For those who are part of the Winning Class, or trying to be, there are plenty of reasons to cheat. The rewards are bigger and the rules are toothless. Yet many Americans with more modest ambitions and more humble means are also cheating.

Take the mild-mannered bookkeeper as an example. He is, by all appearances, an honorable man. He neither drinks nor smokes, and is quiet and dependable in the way of many bookkeepers. He rarely misses a day of work or tarries on his lunch break. When United Way comes around, he always contributes. He and his wife lead an orderly life with their two polite children and spend Sunday mornings at church.

The bookkeeper works hard during the early years of his job and finally gets up the gumption to ask for a raise of $100 a month. He is crushed when the request is denied. But the bookkeeper seems to get over his disappointment and soldiers on. He still arrives punctually every day. He never calls in sick when, in truth, he is well.

After twenty years, the bookkeeper finally retires. The company throws a small farewell party for him and gives him a watch. He and his wife pack up for Florida to start their golden years. A new bookkeeper takes his place. Poring over the financial records, this new bookkeeper finds that something is wrong. Things aren't adding up. He flags his concern to the company. No, no, he's told, the old bookkeeper would never get into any fishy business. He was a rock of reliability, the soul of integrity.

5   And yet, when the new bookkeeper completes his investigation, the facts are incontrovertible. The old bookkeeper, it is clear,

engaged in a systematic pattern of embezzle-ment. The pattern is oddly consistent. Year after year, the amount of money stolen is never greater and never smaller, nor is it particularly large. It is $100 a month.

The thieving bookkeeper exists in an apocry-phal story passed down over many years among fraud examiners who probe workplace theft. The story is told to illustrate a point these investiga-tors know all too well: that people are prone to invent their own morality when the rules don't seem fair to them. This tendency explains a lot of cheating in America today.

There are roughly four reasons why people obey rules. First, we may toe the line because the risks of breaking the rules outweigh the benefits. Second, we might be sensitive to social norms, or peer pressure — we follow the rules because we don't want to be treated as a pariah. Third, we may obey rules because they agree with our personal morality. And fourth, we may obey rules because they have legiti-macy in our eyes — because we feel that the authority making and enforcing the laws is just and ultimately working in our long-term interests.

When people don't obey the rules, you'll often find several things going on at once. The Winning Class cheats so much because there's more to be gained nowadays and there are fewer penalties, either legally or socially. Students often cheat for the same reasons: the stakes of academic competition are higher and the normalization of cheating means that there's little peer pressure to be honest.

Motives like these are not hard to under-stand. Cases like the bookkeeper are more complex. A simple risk/benefit analysis doesn't explain everything, since the bookkeeper was running a serious risk for only a modest sum of money and could easily have taken more. Nor do social norms offer much insight, since the bookkeeper's thefts were not condoned by his peers. Instead, the bookkeeper operated by his own moral code to take from the company what he felt it owed him.

10   A lot of Americans have been inventing their own morality lately. Tens of millions of ordinary middle-class Americans routinely commit serious crimes ranging from tax evasion (a felony), to auto insurance fraud (also a felony), to cable television theft (yes, a felony as well in some states), to Internet piracy of music and software (more felonies). Most of these types of crimes are committed for small pota-toes: to receive $700 more on a tax refund, to save $400 a year on an insurance premium, to get $40 a month worth of premium cable or an $18 CD for nothing. These crimes are being perpetrated by people who see themselves as law-abiding citizens, people who don't imagine themselves above the law and who don't have big-shot lawyers on call.

Day-to-day criminality among ordinary Americans is nothing new. "Unlawful behavior, far from being an abnormal social or psychologi-cal manifestation, is, in truth, a very common phenomenon," commented the authors of a 1947 article about "law-abiding law-breakers."[1] However, evidence indicates that this familiar problem has worsened in recent years — even as conventional street crime has fallen dramatically.

What is going on here?

Much of the answer, I suspect, lies in our broken social contract. An orderly democratic society depends on having a social contract in place that delineates people's rights and respon-sibilities. It also depends on people having faith that the social contract applies fairly across the board. The social contract will break down when those who play by the rules feel mistreated, and those who break the rules get rewarded — which has been happening constantly in recent years.

John Q. Public need not to be versed in John Locke to feel that he has a legitimate cause for cynicism. He knows that white-collar criminals walk free, that fat-cat tax cheats get off the hook, that corporate money buys political favors, and that Ivy League schools are filled with kids whose rich parents greased the system to get them in. He also knows that when there's a war, it's working-class kids who fight it; when there's a tax cut, he probably won't get more than peanuts; and when there are layoffs, it's those lower down the totem pole who'll get the ax.

15 Polls confirm that many Americans see "the system" as rigged against them. When asked who runs the country, many say corporations and special interests. When asked who benefits from the tax system, most say the rich. When asked who is underpaid in our society, most agree that lots of people are underpaid: nurses, policemen, schoolteachers, factory workers, restaurant workers, secretaries. And when people are asked whether it is possible to get ahead just by working hard and playing by the rules, many say that it is not.[2] [. . .]

The psychological fallout from people's economic struggles has been significant. People worry intensely about their finances, especially the heavy debt burdens that they often carry.[3] Many people are also less happy. "Happiness and satisfaction with life are, in many ways, the ultimate bottom line, a test of the good society," observes scholar Michael Hout. Yet in the past quarter century, Hout's work shows, gains in happiness have not been shared evenly in a U.S. society more divided by income: "the affluent are getting slightly happier and the poor are getting sadder; the affluent are increasingly satisfied with their financial and work situation while the poor are increasingly dissatisfied with theirs."[4]

Such endemic unease might itself be a corrupting force in society. But economic struggle is all the more dangerous when mixed with high expectations of well-being — that is, the expectation that one that should be as happy as the shiny rich people on television and in magazines seem to be. Writing in the mid-twentieth century, the sociologist Robert Merton observed

that Americans are taught that everyone can succeed if they work hard enough. America was "a society which places a high premium on economic affluence and social ascent for all its members." But Merton also pointed out that there is no "corresponding emphasis upon the legitimate avenues on which to march toward this goal." Americans worshipped financial success without being too concerned about how people got ahead. "The moral mandate to achieve success thus exerts pressures to succeed, by fair means if possible and by foul means if necessary." These pressures were especially poisonous, Merton said, in a nation where not everyone actually could succeed — where there were limits on the economic opportunities that were available.[5]

Merton could have made these points yesterday. The pressures on Americans to make a lot of money are extremely high — higher, maybe, than they've ever been before. To be sure, there are many legitimate opportunities to do well financially. Yet ultimately the opportunities are finite. America needs only so many skilled and well-paid professionals. In an economy where structural conditions allow only the top fifth or so of earners to really get ahead, the other four fifths of Americans are stuck in the bind that Robert Merton identified: they live in a society with insanely high material expectations but with limited ways to meet these expectations.

What to do in this conundrum? Whatever you can get away with.

20 And how do ordinary, moral people justify doing wrong to do well? Often, they point to the unfairness around them — to the structures that keep them struggling while others thrive, to the ways that bad guys easily climb to the top, to the cheating that goes on by the rich and powerful every day. "People in subordinate positions make moral judgments about existing social arrangements and assert their prerogatives to

> Identify a sentence from the Callahan piece that would support the point being made by the artist in this cartoon.

Harley Schwadron/CartoonStock

personal entitlements and autonomy," writes Elliot Turiel, a leading authority on moral development. Turiel is fascinated with why people break rules, and much of his analysis centers on what he dryly calls "asymmetrical reciprocity implicit in differential distribution of power and powers" — in other words, feelings of injustice. Turiel observes that "in daily life people engage in covert acts of subterfuge and subversion aimed at circumventing norms and practices judged unfair, oppressive, or too restrictive of personal choices." These acts may place people on the wrong side of the law, or the established rules, Turiel says, but their true ethical implications are often a fuzzier question. "In my view, it would be inaccurate to attribute these types of acts of deception to failures of character or morality. Many who engage in these acts are people who generally consider themselves and are considered by others as responsible, trustworthy, upstanding members of our culture."[6]

It is easy to cheat like crazy and yet maintain respect for yourself in a society with pervasive corruption. It's easy, for example, to justify cheating in a country like Brazil where oligarchical families have been abusing the little people for a couple of hundred years and are still doing it, or a country like Pakistan where government ministers and their pals in business live in luxury while millions rot in the slums of Karachi.

And more and more, similar rationalizations can work just fine in the United States.

The social theorist Max Weber was among the first scholars to explore how people's views of "legitimacy" shape their respect for rules. He argued the commonsense point that people are more likely to follow rules or laws that seem fair and are made by an authority that deserves its power. There was nothing actually pathbreaking about this point when Weber made it a century ago. Numerous big thinkers going back to Plato had made similar arguments, and support for this idea cut across fields — from political science to anthropology to sociology to education. Yet if the idea seemed like common sense, what Weber and other scholars typically lacked was the empirical "proof." How can you really tell why people either obey the law or break it? How can you weigh legitimacy as a factor when there are so many other influences

seeing connections

The following charts present data from the Pew Research Center American Values Survey, which tracks changes in American values over time.

State a claim that Callahan makes about a reason that Americans are willing to cheat and support that statement with a conclusion that you draw from one of these charts.

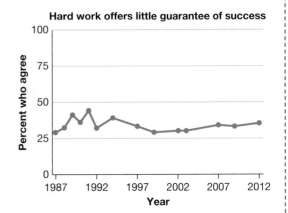

Hard work offers little guarantee of success

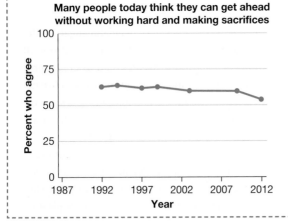

Many people today think they can get ahead without working hard and making sacrifices

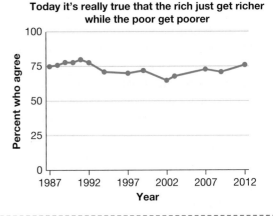

Today it's really true that the rich just get richer while the poor get poorer

on people's behavior? I may speed for many reasons: because I'm late or I'm a thrill seeker or I think it's wrong for the federal government to impose speed limits and usurp local authority on this issue. Short of hearing me and lots of other speeders out and somehow verifying that we're telling the truth about our motives, who can say why people like me drive so fast?

Proof that views about legitimacy explain ethical decisions remains hard to come by. But the evidence has gotten a lot more compelling since Weber's day. In his 1990 book, *Why People Obey the Law*, Tom Tyler picked up the

legitimacy baton and ran with it into new empirical terrain. Tyler marshaled data going back thirty five years in arguing that most people are inclined to obey the law, but that this reflex can easily be undermined if the law is widely seen as lacking legitimacy. He looked at studies of juvenile delinquents in England, college students in Kentucky, middle-class workers in Germany, and poor black men in Newark, among others. He also conducted his own large surveys of Chicago residents. Tyler's conclusion after all of this? Pretty much what Weber said a hundred years earlier.[7]

25   Yet if the link between respecting authority and following the rules has found more support in general, this is still complex terrain. Much of the time when people break rules you'll find a sticky wicket of conflicting evidence about their motives and no easy way to nail down what they were really thinking. Most people don't like to talk openly about cutting corners. Also, the root causes of why people break rules can be obscured when cheating becomes so routine that people no longer give it much thought.[8]

The candor of Jennifer Bennett (not her real name) sheds some light on what is going on in many American households — and, in particular, how cynicism and anger might cause a person who normally wouldn't even run a red light to commit a felony that is punishable by up to five years in prison.

Bennett should be one of the good guys in my story. She was raised in New Jersey by parents who taught her to play by the rules. She works in the arts in New York City but is obsessed with neither money nor status. She just wants to do her art and get by. She believes that government can make a difference in people's lives and, if anything, that taxes should probably be higher than they are.

Yet every year, come April 15, she submits a work of fiction to the IRS.

"Much of the money I earn is off the books — it's money earned in cash through private teaching or tutoring. I generally claim a portion of this money, but not all of it," Bennett says. "It's the money I earn to support my pursuit of a career in the arts. I put thousands of dollars a year into this career, pay my own insurance, and receive no benefits. I guess that's the way I justify writing off as much as I can and claiming as little as I can. I feel that most other first-world countries support their artists and the arts in a much stronger way than we do, and that the wealthy in this country are the ones with the real benefits."

30   Bennett has struggled financially for years, despite her Ivy League degree. Meeting the rent has often been an adventure, and she now lives 130 blocks north of Times Square, in a low-income neighborhood near the George Washington Bridge. "When I see people getting million-dollar bonuses for moving money around, who then walk in free to city museums because their companies are corporate sponsors, my jaw drops. Most artists I know can't afford to attend arts events on a regular basis. I figure the amount of money I earn is so tiny compared to what most people in this city are earning, and that if I had to pay thousands of dollars in taxes at the end of the year, on the relatively small amount I earn, I couldn't afford to continue doing what I'm doing."

Bennett has anguished about her tax cheating — for, like, three seconds — over the past five years. "I don't think it's the 'right' thing to do, but personally, I don't really care. I know that one wrong doesn't right another wrong, but until I see any sign of a real move to universal health-care coverage or the closing of loopholes for the rich, or increased benefits for those making their living in the arts, I don't feel particularly inclined to be honest. When I read about the IRS going after those in lower-income brackets, it makes my blood boil."

Notes

1 The article, by James Wallerstein and Clement J. Wylie, is cited in Robert Merton, *Social Structure and Social Theory* (New York: Free Press, 1957), 144.
2 Regarding people's views on whether their voice matters in politics, see data from the National Election Studies and science literature that documents and discusses political efficacy. See, for example, Sidney Verba, Henry E. Brady, and Kay L. Schlozman, *Voice and Equality: Civic Voluntarism in American Politics* (Cambridge, Mass.: Harvard University Press, 1995); and Steven J. Rosenstone and John M. Hansen, *Mobilization, Participation, and Democracy in America* (Boston: Prentice Hall, 1993). On public perceptions of the excessive power of

corporations in American society, see for example, "Pew Values Update: American Social Beliefs, 1997," The Pew Research Center for the People and the Press, 20 April 1998. On views about fairness of taxes, see National Public Radio/Kaiser Family Foundation/Kennedy School of Government, "National Survey of Americans' Views on Taxes," 2003. On the ability of hard work to get people ahead and for who's underpaid, see, for example, Everett Carll Ladd and Karlyn H. Bowman, *Attitudes Toward Economic Inequality* (Washington, D.C.: AEI Press, 1998), 56 and 20–21.

3 On anxiety, see Robert Putnam's analysis of DDB Needham Life Style Survey data, *Bowling Alone: The Collapse and Revival of American Community* (New York: Simon & Schuster, 2000), 475. On job satisfaction, see Fligstein and Shin, "The Shareholder Value Society." Evidence of growing insecurity and anxiety is by no means ironclad and this remains a disputed point among scholars. See, for example, Kenneth Deavers, "Downsizing, Job Insecurity, and Wages: No Connection," Employment Policy Foundation, May 1998.

4 Michael Hout, "Money and Morale: What Growing Economic Inequality Is Doing to Americans' View of Themselves and Others," working paper, Survey Research Center, 3 January 2003.

5 Merton, *Social Theory and Social Structure* (New York: The Free Press, 1957), 136–47, 169.

6 Elliot Turiel, *The Culture of Morality: Social Development, Context, and Conflict* (Cambridge, U.K.: Cambridge University Press, 2002), 261 and 266. For another analysis along somewhat similar lines, see James C. Scott, *Domination and the Arts of Resistance: Hidden Transcripts* (New Haven: Yale University Press, 1990). Scott's book deals extensively with what he calls the "veiled cultural resistance of subordinate groups" and the "infrapolitics of the powerless."

7 Tom R. Tyler, *Why People Obey the Law* (New Haven: Yale University Press, 1990).

8 The interplay between social norms, law, economics, societal values, and compliance with rules has been examined from a variety of angles. One critical — and obvious — observation is that social norms are the key to enforcing rules, since coercion, punishment, and deterrence can never stop everyone who wants to do wrong. Some scholars like Eric Posner argue that law actually plays only a small role in regulating people's behavior. For an overview of some of this work, see Amitai Etzioni, "Social Norms: Internalization, Persuasion, and History," *Law and Society Review* 34, no. 1 (2000): 157–78. See also Eric A. Posner, *Law and Social Norms* (Cambridge, Mass.: Harvard University Press, 2002); and Michael Hechter and Karl–Dieter Opp, eds., *Social Norms* (New York: Russell Sage Foundation, 2001).

Understanding and Interpreting

1 Several times in the piece, Callahan describes people "inventing their own morality" (for example, par. 10). What does he mean by this phrase?

2 Callahan claims that a lot of the cheating by ordinary, otherwise law-abiding citizens is due to "our broken social contract" (par. 13). Reread paragraphs 13–18, where he supports this claim. What evidence does he use and to what extent does he sufficiently support his claim? Do you detect any bias that might prevent him from seeing other possibilities? Explain.

3 In paragraphs 16 and 17, Callahan connects the idea of cheating with the desire for happiness. What is the conclusion that he expects the reader to draw about the "high expectations of well-being" from the evidence he provides? Evaluate his logical reasoning in this section.

4 To support his argument, Callahan cites Elliot Turiel, "a leading authority on moral development." Reread the following quotes from Turiel, summarize them, and explain how they relate to Callahan's central argument:

a. "[P]eople in subordinate positions make moral judgments about existing social arrangements and assert their prerogatives to personal entitlements and autonomy" (par. 20).

b. "asymmetrical reciprocity implicit in differential distribution of power and powers" (par. 20).

c. "[I]n daily life people engage in covert acts of subterfuge and subversion aimed at circumventing norms and practices judged unfair, oppressive, or too restrictive of personal choices" (par. 20).

5 Callahan claims that at least one reason why otherwise honest people cheat is the way they view the legitimacy of power. Summarize his views on legitimacy and explain how he uses evidence to support his position.

6 In paragraph 7, Callahan identifies four reasons why people obey rules. Apply these four reasons to the case of the artist Jennifer Bennett, who regularly cheats on her taxes (pars. 26–31). Which ones would Bennett likely agree or disagree with? Why?

Analyzing Language, Style, and Structure

1 What role does the fictional story of the bookkeeper play in setting up Callahan's argument? In other words, why begin this section with the story?

2 Trace the development of Callahan's argument from the beginning to the point where he asks: "And how do ordinary, moral people justify doing wrong to do well?" (par. 20). What components does Callahan have to include in his argument before he can ask this question?

3 It is no secret that Callahan is politically liberal and often sees middle- and working-class people as victims of the rich. Look back through the article and identify places where he chooses words with negative connotations to describe the wealthy. Does this word choice seem to be effective in making his argument, or is it detrimental? Why?

4 Reread the paragraph that concludes with note 8. The last sentence makes a claim about people's behavior that appears to be unsubstantiated. Read note 8 and explain how Callahan uses the sources to support his claim. Choose one other annotation from the article and explain how the use of evidence affects Callahan's ethos.

5 Until paragraph 21, Callahan focuses on cheating in the United States, at which point he expands his argument to include Brazil and Pakistan. What is the purpose of this switch? How does it assist his argument?

6 While much of Callahan's argument is rooted in logos, he does at times employ appeals to pathos. Identify these places and evaluate their effectiveness in supporting his claim.

Connecting, Arguing, and Extending

1 In this selection from *The Cheating Culture*, Callahan mostly focuses on identifying the causes of cheating. Later on in the book, he offers some solutions, which include a need to teach the values he thinks are important: "respect, responsibility, fairness, honesty, justice." Where and how are these values best taught? Home, school, religious institutions, other organizations? Why?

2 In an article from the *Springfield State Journal-Register* in 2008, "A recent survey conducted by the University of Hertfordshire showed that the average teen has 800 illegally obtained songs on his or her MP3 or other music-playing device. This same survey showed that 50 percent of people between 14 and 24 would share all of their music on their computers." Write an argumentative piece in which you take a position on the issue of illegal downloading of music and/or movies. Is this cheating? Why or why not? Be sure to refer to Callahan as evidence to support your claims or as part of your counterclaims.

3 How does the phrase "Everybody does it" apply to cheating in your own life and experiences? Is it difficult to be the one who does not, or is the idea itself that "everybody does it" overblown by adults and the media? What would Callahan's response likely be?

The Ethics of Photo Manipulation

The use of photography became widespread by the mid-1800s, and at almost the same time, photographers realized that their images could be manipulated to influence their viewers, truth, and even history.

Original

Altered

The altered portrait above, arguably the most famous image of President Abraham Lincoln, was created by putting Lincoln's head onto the body of another politician, John C. Calhoun. After Lincoln's death, many believed that there were not any truly heroic, presidential-looking, portraits of him, so this composite was created.

This photo manipulation was done to honor a beloved president, but is it an ethical use of photo manipulation? Why or why not?

This famous example of photo manipulation dates from 1917. Two young girls in Cottingley, England, took a series of photographs that purported to capture fairies near their house. They later explained that they were just "photographs of figments of our imagination."

What do you think was the motivation behind creating these images, and do you believe that it was ethically wrong or just harmless fun?

Glenn Hill/SSPL/Getty Images

Original

Altered

The photo above demonstrates one dark side of photo manipulation: changing history. In the Soviet Union under Joseph Stalin, the Communist Party regularly manipulated historical photographs, removing people who had fallen out of favor with the dictator. One of the most famous examples is the pair here. In the photograph on the left, Leon Trotsky can be seen standing beside his close friend Vladimir Lenin, the first leader of the Soviet Union. Lenin's successor, Stalin, saw Trotsky as a threat and had him removed from the photograph.

Clearly this alteration of history is unethical, but can you articulate precisely why?

Original

Altered

Here is a much more borderline case. The original picture here was taken by John Filo at Kent State University on May 4, 1970, when National Guard soldiers fired into the crowd during a student protest, killing four people. It won Filo the Pulitzer Prize for Photography. Later, someone at *Time* magazine altered the photo to remove the unsightly post from the fence behind the woman's head. The altered image ran for years in magazines and newspapers without indication that the picture had been altered.

What was changed in terms of the photo's message by removing the post, if anything? Was this alteration ethical? Explain.

Original

Altered

In 1994, retired professional football star O. J. Simpson was arrested for the murder of his wife and her friend. From the beginning, the case touched on many elements of race because Simpson is black and his wife was white. The covers of both newsmagazines used the same mug shot from the day of his arrest, but the one on the right controversially altered the image, making Simpson's skin appear darker.

Why do you think the image on the right caused so much controversy? To what extent were the editors of *Time* magazine acting unethically in presenting the image in the manner they did?

◀

This uncredited photograph, with a time stamp of "09 11 01," was reportedly found in a digital camera amid the rubble of the World Trade Center after the 9/11 attacks in New York City in 2001. It was shared and viewed extensively online before being discredited as a hoax.

What was the possible intent behind this altered photograph? How is the audience cheated through this manipulation? How do the ethics of this photo manipulation compare with the ethics of the fairy hoax on page 518?

Original

Altered

▲

The original photograph was taken in 2002 when President George W. Bush was visiting George Sanchez Charter School in Houston. An unknown person altered the second picture, flipping the book in Bush's hands, and it was widely distributed online.

What statement might the unknown manipulator have been trying to make about President Bush? Why do you think this photograph was so widely distributed prior to its being discredited? How does this image relate to the photo manipulation practiced in the Soviet Union (described on p. 519)?

Original

Altered

▲

In July 2008, Iran announced it had successfully test-fired missiles. The image released by the Iranians, on the right, showed the launch of four missiles and was reprinted by many news organizations. It was later revealed to be Photoshopped; as you can see here, the original image shows only three missiles.

What are the political implications of this kind of photo manipulation? How does this manipulation reveal the difficulty of trusting photography?

Original

Altered

In 2007, country singer Faith Hill posed for *Redbook*, an American women's magazine.
The original picture is on the left, and the one on the right was enhanced for the cover.

Photo manipulation of model's bodies, especially of women, is a typical practice for magazines and catalogs. Who is cheated in this kind of manipulation, and what effect, if any, do these kinds of images have on the viewers?

Photographer Paul Hansen took this picture, *Gaza Burial*, which won the 2012 World Press Photo of the Year award. He was subsequently accused of photo manipulation and some thought that he should have been stripped of his award.

According to journalist Sebastian Anthony:

> Basically, as far as we can surmise, Hansen took a series of photos—and then later, realizing that his most dramatically situated photo was too dark and shadowy, decided to splice a bunch of images together and apply a liberal amount of dodging (brightening) to the shadowy regions. For what it's worth, Hansen claims that the light in the alley was natural—and to be fair, sometimes magical lighting does occur. I think most of you will agree, though, that the photo simply feels fake—there's just something about the lighting that sets off a warning alarm in your brain.

Is enhancing an image to make a bigger impact ethical?

Connecting, Arguing, and Extending

1 Take a picture of someone you know with a digital camera or your cell phone and then use software (Photoshop or another program) to manipulate the image in some significant way. Show the person the manipulated image and ask him or her if it would be ethical for you to post this new picture online. What objections does the person have, if any?

2 Paul Hansen admits that he manipulated his photograph, *Gaza Burial*, but the question is did he manipulate it so much that it should no longer qualify as "journalism"? Write an argument in the form of a letter to the directors of World Press Photo about why Hansen should be able to keep his award or not based upon the level of manipulation and who might be cheated in the process.

3 Choose one of the altered photographs above and write an argument about why it ought to be considered cheating. Who exactly is cheated and who benefits through the manipulation?

4 In the past few years, a new professional field called "digital forensics" has emerged to authenticate photographs and film footage. Why do you think such a service has become necessary?

5 There is an expression that a picture is worth a thousand words. Based on your examination of these photographs, is this statement true or not? Why?

ENTERING THE CONVERSATION
THE CHEATING CULTURE

Making Connections

1 Christopher Bergland in "Cheaters Never Win" (p. 90), Chuck Klosterman in "Why We Look the Other Way" (p. 84), and Brad Allenby in "Is Human Enhancement Cheating?" (p. 94) address cheating in sports. What are the similarities and differences in the authors' attitudes toward the role of cheating in sports?

2 How would David Callahan, author of *The Cheating Culture* (p. 102), likely respond to the case of Nayeem Ahsan, the teenager profiled in "Cheating Upwards" (p. 73)? To what extent would he condemn his actions and/or condemn the culture that taught or caused him to cheat? Write your answer in the form of a dialogue or a transcript of a conversation between Callahan and Ahsan.

3 Mia Consalvo (p. 98) identifies four reasons why people cheat in video games. Similarly, David Callahan gives reasons why people cheat in real life. Compare at least one of the reasons Consalvo presents to a real-life example Callahan presents. To what extent does the reason apply or not in the real world outside video games?

Synthesizing Sources

1 In recent years there have been a number of high-profile cases of cheating in sports, often through the use of performance-enhancing drugs (PEDs). If an athlete is an adult, is aware of the consequences of using PEDs, and knows that his or her competition is also using those drugs, why shouldn't he or she be allowed to use any PEDs he or she wants? If the spectators also know about the PEDs, who is being cheated? Support your position by referring to at least two of the texts in the Conversation.

2 Is cheating an inevitable part of human society? Is it impossible, or even desirable, to completely eliminate cheating? Use your own experiences and references to at least two texts in the Conversation to support your response.

3 Describe the extent of the problem with cheating that happens at your school, propose a solution to the problem, and explain how you would implement that solution. Refer to at least two of the texts from the Conversation to support your response.

4 Many of the texts in this Conversation try to explain why a particular action—using video game cheat codes, copying homework, taking PEDs, and so on—is either cheating or not cheating. Using the various scenarios presented in these texts—sports, school, video games, etc.—write a definition of cheating that covers as many of the situations as possible. Be sure to address the questions of who is cheating whom and for what purpose. Refer to at least two texts from the Conversation in your response.

5 There appear to be generational differences in what is considered to be cheating. One survey, for instance, claims that almost 90 percent of teenagers do not see anything wrong with practices that could be defined as music piracy or illegal downloading, while another shows that almost 50 percent of adults disagree with the idea that you should be able to download media from the Internet free of charge. Identify a practice that you believe could be considered cheating and conduct interviews or surveys to see if there is a generational difference in opinion. In your explanation, be sure to refer to at least two texts from the Conversation that support or counter your results.

ARGUMENT BY ANALOGY

What Is Argument by Analogy?

When Forrest Gump, the main character in the movie of the same title, quotes his mother's advice that has guided him through life's challenges, he is using an analogy—a comparison between two ideas, concepts, or situations on the basis of shared qualities. It's a gently funny line, likely to bring a smile by the way it compares something trivial and familiar (a box of chocolates) with something mysterious and profound (life). It's intended to be charming, but it is also a very simple argument, claiming that life is unpredictable, while also implying that life is sweet, even if it's not always what you hoped it would be.

> "Life is like a box of chocolates: you never know what you're gonna get."
>
> — Forrest Gump

When used as part of an argument, analogies can be very powerful tools, drawing on familiar ideas and experiences to tap into an audience's beliefs and emotions. But they can also be risky rhetorical moves, drawing connections that might be tenuous or, in some cases, even offensive.

The Benefits of Analogy

The primary benefit of drawing an analogy in an argument is that it appeals to an experience familiar to the audience. It makes a connection. The writers of *Forrest Gump* knew that pretty much everybody has bitten into a chocolate only to be disappointed by a filling that wasn't expected or hoped for. This connection can be used in a number of different ways: to emphasize shared values (ethos), to assert what we all know to be true (logos), or to tap into strong emotions based on personal experience (pathos).

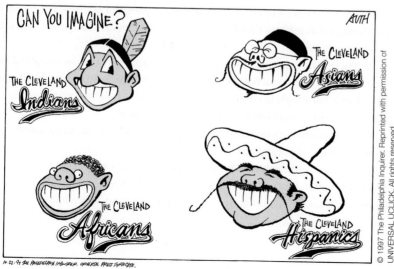

Take a look at the cartoon on the previous page by Tony Auth on the controversy about the name of the Cleveland Indians, a professional baseball team. He argues that the name is offensive by drawing an analogy to other similar names that reflect ethnic groups. So, if the Cleveland Indians is a perfectly acceptable name for a professional sports team, he claims through his cartoon, then why not the Cleveland Asians or Africans or Hispanics—all clearly offensive names. But he goes even further by drawing visual analogies: if Chief Wahoo, the symbol of the Cleveland Indians since the 1940s, is acceptable (though many do see him as racist), then wouldn't such stereotyped caricatures of other ethnicities also be appropriate? The artist casts doubt on the name and logo of the Cleveland Indians by drawing an analogy to other examples that are patently offensive. In light of arguments such as this, the Cleveland Indians abandoned the Chief Wahoo mascot and replaced it with a simple letter *C*.

ACTIVITY

In the following excerpt, political commentator Charles Krauthammer argues that the name of the Washington Redskins, a professional football team, should be changed because language "evolves" over time. How does the analogy he draws contribute to his argument?

Fifty years ago the preferred, most respectful term for African Americans was Negro. The word appears 15 times in Martin Luther King's "I Have a Dream" speech. Negro replaced a long list of insulting words in common use during decades of public and legal discrimination.

And then, for complicated historical reasons (having to do with the black power and "black is beautiful" movements), usage changed. The preferred term is now black or African American. With a rare few legacy exceptions, Negro carries an unmistakably patronizing and demeaning tone.

If you were detailing the racial composition of Congress, you wouldn't say: "Well, to start with, there are 44 Negroes." If you'd been asleep for 50 years, you might. But upon being informed how the word had changed in nuance, you would stop using it and choose another.

And here's the key point: You would stop not because of the language police. Not because you might incur a Bob Costas harangue. Not because the president would wag a finger. But simply because the word was tainted, freighted with negative connotations with which you would not want to be associated.

Proof? You wouldn't even use the word in private, where being harassed for political incorrectness is not an issue.

Similarly, regarding the further racial breakdown of Congress, you wouldn't say: "And by my count, there are two redskins." It's inconceivable, because no matter how the word was used 80 years ago, it carries invidious connotations today.

Another way of thinking about the power of analogy is that it can shed light on inconsistencies. For instance, in "Why We Look the Other Way" (p. 84), Chuck Klosterman draws an analogy between musicians' using drugs and athletes' using drugs to explore why we react very differently to the two. Specifically, he writes about the legendary musical group, the Beatles:

> It can be strongly argued that the most important date in the history of rock music was Aug. 28, 1964. This was the day Bob Dylan met the Beatles in New York City's Hotel Delmonico and got them high.
>
> Obviously, a lot of people might want to disagree with this assertion, but the artistic evidence is hard to ignore. The introduction of marijuana altered the trajectory of the Beatles' songwriting, reconstructed their consciousness and prompted them to make the most influential rock albums of all time. After the summer of 1964, the Beatles started taking serious drugs, and those drugs altered their musical performance. Though it may not have been their overt intent, the Beatles took performance-enhancing drugs. And this is germane to sports for one reason: Absolutely no one holds it against them. No one views *Rubber Soul* and *Revolver* as "less authentic" albums, despite the fact that they would not (and probably could not) have been made by people who weren't on drugs.

What does Klosterman gain from this analogy between the Beatles' use of "performance-enhancing drugs" and athletes' use of PEDs? For one, most of his readers are likely to be familiar with and admiring of the Beatles; he references album titles without explanation, so he must assume the audience knows them. In his lead-in to this section, Klosterman admits that "a lot of people might want to disagree" with his claim that "the most important date in the history of rock music" was when the Beatles were introduced to drugs; that acknowledgment softens his assertion. Then, he explicitly states the point of his analogy: no one devalues the music because the Beatles used drugs when they were creating it.

By using this analogy, Klosterman essentially poses a series of questions to his audience. First, is it wrong for musicians to use drugs to stimulate their creativity? He's banking on most people agreeing that it is not. Is the music less impressive or admirable because it was written while the musicians were under the influence of drugs? Again, Klosterman hopes his audience will agree that it is not. Given these two points, then, he asks us to think about why such acceptance of performance-enhancing drugs in one area (in this case, music) is different from acceptance in the field of professional sports where the financial stakes are high and career horizons short.

The Risks of Analogy

The problem with analogies is that no two things are ever *entirely* alike. By definition, an analogy is comparing apples to oranges, and that makes it vulnerable as an argument strategy. The stronger the comparison, the more similarities there are, but as soon as the differences begin to surface, the analogy weakens. When the differences are more pronounced than the similarities, you're in the territory of a *faulty analogy*, which is a logical fallacy.

WATCHING HOLLYWOOD CELEBRITIES SELF-DESTRUCT!

AMERICA'S **FAVORITE** SPECTATOR SPORT!!

DAVE GRANLUND © www.davegranlund.com

Dave Granlund

For instance, think about this cartoon. For some, it probably hits the spot: those big ugly vultures, birds of prey, sitting on a couch watching a little television point up the wrong-headed nature of taking pleasure from watching celebrities on the skids. But think about the downside: Is it fair to compare followers of celebrity culture to vultures? Is watching celebrities self-destruct specifically a spectator sport, or do people tend to enjoy watching positive moments as much as the negative ones? And, considering that much of his audience likely keeps up with celebrity gossip, isn't the artist running the risk of alienating people by likening them to vultures?

These questions do not establish definitively that the analogy is "wrong"—but they point to the vulnerability of analogy as a rhetorical move in argument. The punch of the analogy in this case may be outweighed by the potential weakness inherent in drawing a comparison between birds of prey and people's fascination with celebrities gone wrong. The best advice is not to rely on an analogy as your main rhetorical strategy unless you're 99.9 percent sure that your audience will see the similarities that you do.

ACTIVITY

Look back at the analogy in the Klosterman article that we just discussed (p. 84). What potential risk(s) is Klosterman taking? How might his analogy be vulnerable to criticism? To what extent might the comparison be a faulty analogy? All in all, in terms of risk versus benefit, how effective is this analogy as a rhetorical strategy?

USING SOURCES TO WRITE A SYNTHESIS ARGUMENT

What Is a Synthesis Argument?

Most of us aren't short on opinions when it comes to any number of personal and public issues. We have a perspective on community decisions, national debates, and global conflicts. But what sets an individual opinion apart from an argument that is likely to influence others is evidence that extends beyond the purely personal: that is, an argument informed by what others have thought, said, and written. This is what we call a "synthesis argument"; it is an argument based on sources.

If you were writing about a proposed change in school policy, you might interview your principal, parents, and other students. Or you might read about the experience of other schools, how they identified needed changes, what process they implemented to approve changes, and what some of the results of the changes were. As you wrote your own argument, you would consult sources. Some of these would report research conducted by experts, some would provide statistical data, and some would draw on relevant first-hand experience.

What Makes an Effective Synthesis Argument?

The answer to this question lies in how you use your sources. First of all, as we discussed in Chapter 4, where we introduced synthesis, your voice—your opinion—remains central: don't let it be drowned out by your sources, regardless of their impressive credentials or expertise! You are in charge of choosing which sources you'll use and what comments you want to make about them. Some of these sources will support your position, but remember that you can also use sources to present a counterargument.

Your goal is to present a reasoned and informed argument that takes into account multiple perspectives. You need to show the world that you've done your homework on the topic—that you're aware of its context and what others have had to say about it. In short, you need to contribute to an ongoing conversation.

Steps to Writing a Synthesis Argument

When you're writing any argument, including one that's informed by sources, it's important to start by figuring out what you know. Even if you have only a vague idea of the issues surrounding a controversy, even just a gut reaction, putting your ideas on paper or on the

---

ACTIVITY

Take fifteen minutes and brainstorm your response to the following prompt:

Why do you think the public is so outraged when it finds out that a professional athlete has taken performance-enhancing drugs (PEDs)? Is this outrage appropriate?

screen will give you a sense of what you already know, what you don't know, and what you need to know. Doing so will also provide a context for reading ideas others have on the topic.

Now let's focus on three specific essays from this chapter's Conversation on cheating. These all take up some dimension of the controversy about PEDs. Before we get started, read (or reread) these sources carefully:

- Chuck Klosterman, "Why We Look the Other Way" (p. 84)
- Christopher Bergland, "Cheaters Never Win" (p. 90)
- Brad Allenby, "Is Human Enhancement Cheating?" (p. 94)

Step 1: Analyze the Sources

The first step to writing an effective source-based synthesis argument is to read about different views on the issue in question. You want to understand the pros and the cons, and, most important, the gray areas in between. The gray areas of an issue are often where you'll find civil compromises, reasonable solutions, and new ideas.

One way to find the gray area of an issue is to use a mental exercise called "yes, but," in which you concede a point that others have made about the issue, but then think about how to refute it. This puts every idea under the microscope:

Yes, performance-enhancing drugs diminish the purity of sports, **but** is the idea of "purity" in sports an outdated notion?

ACTIVITY

Complete the following chart to start your analysis of the three sources. We have begun the Bergland essay as a model, but you can add to it as you analyze the others. Don't worry about complete sentences at this point; just gather ideas.

Source	Position on Overall Issue	Key Issues (2 or 3)	Relevant Quotation (1 or 2)
Klosterman			
Bergland	Totally opposed to athletes' using PEDs: taints purity of sports	• PED use = cheating self and others • •	"you cannot cheat to win on an ethical and karmic level" (par. 7)
Allenby			

Step 2: Put the Texts in Conversation

Now that you've analyzed the sources individually, imagine that you are putting them in a room together. Assume each author has read the others' work. As you imagine this encounter, try to write in the voice of each author—get into character. And remember: you're reporting what they say to each other, not personally commenting or responding.

What questions would they ask one another? How would one respond to the other? You might generate questions by asking yourself where one writer would take issue with another. It's easy to see, for instance, that Allenby would disagree with Bergland in funda- mental ways, so there's no point in setting up a dialogue in which Allenby asks, "What do you think of PEDs?" But, it might be interesting for Allenby to ask Bergland, "Isn't your view of the connection between sports and well-being unrealistic when it comes to spec- tator sports involving huge amounts of money?"

Question from Klosterman to Bergland: _____.

Bergland's Response: _____.

Question from Allenby to Klosterman: _____.

Klosterman's Response: _____.

Question from Bergland to Allenby: _____.

Allenby's Response: _____.

Step 3: Take a Stand

Now that you've read, analyzed, and role-played with the sources, you have a bunch of notes and a deep enough understanding of the issue to explain your viewpoint as an evidence-based argument. Start by writing a clear thesis—though don't expect that it will necessarily be your final polished one.

Don't worry either about taking an all-or-nothing stand. In fact, a position that is quali- fied can demonstrate your awareness of the complexity of the issue—that it's not black or white, but shades of gray. Start drafting with a simple template:

(I believe) that professional athletes (should/should not) be allowed to use

performance-enhancing drugs because _____.

Once you have a working thesis, start matching sources to your ideas: some may support you, whereas others may provide an opportunity for you to push back on an idea you disagree with.

Title and author of source that supports your thesis: _____

Direct quote that demonstrates the support: _____ (page number)

Explanation of how that source supports your thesis: _____

Although most of the time, you'll use sources as supporting evidence, you can also use a source that runs counter to your thesis; by conceding some portion of the argument, but refuting the bulk of it (see Chapter 3, p. 74), you can turn the source to your advantage. This move is similar to the "yes, but" mental exercise that we talked about on page 530.

Title and author of source that counters your thesis (or your position in

general): _____

Direct quote that demonstrates the challenge to your position: _____

(page number)

Concession and refutation _____

Step 4: Integrate the Sources into Your Own Argument

Once you have begun working so closely with sources, it is tempting to feel that you have nothing original to say, that everything on the subject has all been said and said well. But resist this type of thinking! The point of such careful analysis is to learn as much as possible so that you can contribute to a discussion about a controversial issue and not simply rehash what's already been said.

Let's look at an example of a student's voice being drowned out by a persuasive source and then work on a strategy that you can use to make yourself heard.

Here's paragraph 7 from "Cheaters Never Win" by Christopher Bergland:

> I believe that it is the time we spend with family, friends, and feeling healthy, alive and connected that is our biggest source of joy. Again, it is easy when you have "made it" to proselytize about the virtues of not caring if you "win or lose." The reality can be much different, especially if you're struggling economically. Because winning does matter. This is a paradox we all have to navigate in sport and in life. Yes, you want to be your absolute best and to try your hardest to win and to be thrilled if you are victorious. . . . But you cannot cheat to win on an ethical and karmic level. I believe that the bad karma and ill-will of being a cheater has the power to eat you up from the inside out and ultimately destroy you.

Now suppose a student writer who is in agreement with Bergland wants to use him as a source in order to make the point that performance-enhancing drugs diminish an athletic accomplishment. The student might draft a paragraph like this:

> Winning when using performance-enhancing drugs diminishes the sense of accomplishment that derives from old-fashioned hard work, strict discipline, and just plain grit. In "Cheaters Never Win," Christopher Bergland acknowledges that "winning does matter" (par. 7). However, the "paradox we all have to navigate in sport and in life" is that victory is sweet, but "you cannot cheat to win on an ethical and karmic level." Ultimately, "the bad karma and ill-will of being a cheater has the power to eat you up from the inside out and ultimately destroy you."

Notice all of the direct quotations and references to Bergland. After the opening topic sentence, which is clear, Bergland takes over and we lose the writer's voice and ideas entirely.

A good rule of thumb is to make sure that you make at least two comments about every source that you paraphrase or quote directly. Here's a revision of the previous paragraph using that technique:

> Winning when using performance-enhancing drugs diminishes the sense of accomplishment that derives from old-fashioned hard work, strict discipline, and just plain grit. Everybody wants to win, especially in our society that prizes victory so highly—but it is a mistake to do so at the expense of self-respect. In "Cheaters Never Win," Christopher Bergland argues that "you cannot cheat to win on an ethical and karmic level." The result of cheating, whether through drugs or any other manner, is dishonesty not only with colleagues and fans but more important with yourself. Needing to win at any and all costs, including using PEDs, can ultimately "eat you up from the inside out," which is a sure road to self-destruction (Bergland, par. 7). Participating in competitive sports is supposed to increase our self-esteem because of the physical and mental effort athletes put into their training; participating under the influence of drugs undermines that effort.

In this revision, the writer is fully in charge. The topic sentence focuses on the writer's opinion about the pride developed by working hard to become an excellent athlete, and Bergland is brought in to emphasize how PEDs erode the athlete's pride. The writer quotes Bergland, but then adds commentary on what he has to say. The final sentence is the writer's own. You might think of the structure in this way:

S1: Topic sentence (writer's own words)

S2: Further explanation and lead-in to source

S3: Source paraphrased and/or quoted

S4: Commentary on source

S5: Additional reference to source

S6: Commentary and conclusion (writer's own words)

ACTIVITY

Turn your notes from one of the sources you've examined into a fully developed paragraph of your own. Make sure that the topic sentence links to the thesis you wrote and that the bulk of the paragraph consists of your own ideas and commentary informed—but not overwhelmed—by the source.

8
Cultures in Conflict

- What defines "culture"?
- What causes cultures to come into conflict with each other?
- Who gets to tell the story of a conflict?
- How do cultures respond to change and to outsiders?
- What is lost and gained by assimilating into a new culture?

In a commencement speech at Kenyon College in 2005, author David Foster Wallace began by saying:

There are these two young fish swimming along, and they happen to meet an older fish swimming the other way, who nods at them and says, "Morning, boys, how's the water?" And the two young fish swim on for a bit, and then eventually one of them looks over at the other and goes, "What the hell is water?"

If at this moment, you're worried that I plan to present myself here as the wise old fish explaining what water is to you younger fish, please don't be. I am not the wise old fish. The immediate point of the fish story is that the most obvious, ubiquitous, important realities are often the ones that are the hardest to see and talk about.

"Culture" is one word for the "water" Wallace refers to. We are often so immersed in our own culture that it can be impossible for us to even notice it. If we speak a particular language, eat certain foods, practice a specific religion, we may begin to assume that everyone shares our culture, or if they don't, there's something wrong with them. And unfortunately, too often when cultures come into contact with each other, conflict is the result. Perhaps it is our inability to see the water (culture) around us that makes it difficult to see the world from other perspectives.

In this chapter, you will have an opportunity to consider not only what culture is, but what happens when different cultures come into contact with each other.

OPENING ACTIVITY 1

Take some time to describe the water you swim in by answering the following questions:

1. Is the language that you learned as a child also the first language of most people where you live and go to school? What is the effect of being able to speak multiple languages?
2. How are the clothes you wear on a typical day similar to or different from those of other people who are your age and gender? How are they similar to or different from the clothes worn by people who are older than you? What particular culture or subculture at your school, if any, do your clothes reflect?
3. In general, how do you view gender roles? Are there activities or behaviors that you believe are typical or appropriate for certain genders?
4. What is your racial, economic, or ethnic background? How often do you see people of your race, economic status, or ethnicity featured in the media—or holding positions of authority in politics, business, or your school?
5. How often do you interact with people of different racial, economic, or ethnic backgrounds? How do you get information about people of other cultural backgrounds? How are members of other groups represented in the media or in positions of authority at your school or in your community?
6. What are the holidays that you typically celebrate? Are the holidays—and the ways that you celebrate them—similar to what you often see on television or in movies?
7. Describe your religious practices, if any. How often do you talk to people of a different religion about your religious practices?
8. What are some of the foods that you typically eat? If you were to buy these foods in a grocery store, would you find them throughout the store or typically in the "ethnic foods" section?
9. What overall ideas or beliefs do you think define the culture in which you live?

OPENING ACTIVITY 2

Now, write about a time when you have experienced some kind of conflict that may have been caused by differences in culture. The conflict may not have led to a fight or even a disagreement, but it might have been the result of a misunderstanding. Reflect on the causes and results of the conflict, as well as how it might have been avoided in the first place.

from When the Emperor Was Divine

Julie Otsuka

Julie Otsuka (b. 1962) was born in California and received degrees from Yale and Columbia. Her most recent novel is *The Buddha in the Attic* (2011). Her first novel, *When the Emperor Was Divine* (2002), from which this excerpt is taken, is about the internment of Japanese Americans during World War II.

eidon photographers/Demotix/Corbis

KEY CONTEXT   Not long after the Japanese attacked Pearl Harbor in December 1941, leading the United States to enter World War II, President Franklin D. Roosevelt signed Executive Order 9066, which gave regional military commanders the right to remove "any and all persons" from specific areas of the country as "protection against espionage and against sabotage to national-defense material, national-defense premises, and national-defense utilities." Within only a few months, this order led to the forced relocation and incarceration of over one hundred thousand people of Japanese descent, a majority of whom were United States citizens, who were then held in internment camps for much of the duration of the war. They were eventually released after a Supreme Court case challenging their detention in 1945. Most former prisoners were given $25 and a train ticket to their earlier places of residence, though many of their homes and businesses were gone.

Otsuka has said that *When the Emperor Was Divine* is based upon the experiences of her own grandmother, mother, and uncle, who were forcibly removed from their home in Berkeley, California, and imprisoned in a camp in Topaz, Utah, for three years. Her grandfather was arrested by the FBI the day after the Japanese attack on Pearl Harbor and held in various detention centers until 1945, though he was never charged or convicted of a crime.

The novel is made up of five chapters, each told from the different perspective of an unnamed family member. The characters are identified only as "mother," "girl," "boy," and "father." Chapter 1, called "Evacuation Order No. 19," focuses on "mother" and the process of her being forced from her home and seeing her husband arrested. Chapter 2, "Train," focuses on the eleven-year-old "girl" and the family's trip through the desert to the detention camp. The longest chapter and the one presented here, "When the Emperor Was Divine," focuses on the "boy," who is about eight years old and recounts the family's life in the camp. Chapter 4, "In a Stranger's Backyard," utilizes the unusual choice of point of view of "we," as together the family struggles to return to the life they had before the war. The final chapter, "Confession," is an angry, sarcastic fake confession told from the point of view of "father."

The author's family at the Tanforan Assembly Center, in a National Archives photograph taken by Dorothea Lange, April 29, 1942.

How does this image compare to your expectations of a forced evacuation based on what you have read in the Key Context note on the previous page?

National Archives

Part 1 When the Emperor Was Divine

In the beginning the boy thought he saw his father everywhere. Outside the latrines. Underneath the showers. Leaning against barrack doorways. Playing *go* with the other men in their floppy straw hats on the narrow wooden benches after lunch. Above them blue skies. The hot midday sun. No trees. No shade. Birds.

It was 1942. Utah. Late summer. A city of tar-paper barracks behind a barbed-wire fence on a dusty alkaline plain high up in the desert. The wind was hot and dry and the rain rarely fell and wherever the boy looked he saw him: Daddy, Papa, Father, *Oto-san.*

For it was true, they all looked alike. Black hair. Slanted eyes. High cheekbones. Thick glasses. Thin lips. Bad teeth. Unknowable. Inscrutable.

That was him, over there.

5   The little yellow man.

. . .

Three times a day the clanging of bells. Endless lines. The smell of liver drifting out across the black barrack roofs. The smell of catfish. From time to time, the smell of horse meat. On meat-less days, the smell of beans. Inside the mess hall, the clatter of forks and spoons and knives. No chopsticks. An endless sea of bobbing black heads. Hundreds of mouths chewing. Slurping. Sucking. Swallowing. And over there, in the corner, beneath the flag, a familiar face.

The boy called out, "Papa," and three men with thick metal-rimmed glasses looked up from their plates and said, "*Nan desu ka?*"

What is it?

But the boy could not say what it was.

10   He lowered his head and skewered a small Vienna sausage. His mother reminded him, once again, not to shout out in public. And never to speak with his mouth full. Harry Yamaguchi

tapped a spoon on a glass and announced that the head count would be taken on Monday evening. The boy's sister nudged him under the table, hard, with the scuffed toe of her Mary Jane. "Papa's gone," she said. [. . .]

On their first day in the desert his mother had said, "Be careful,"

"Do not touch the barbed-wire fence," she had said, "or talk to the guards in the towers.

"Do not stare at the sun.

"And remember, never say the Emperor's name out loud."

15   The boy wore a blue baseball cap and he did not stare at the sun. He often wandered the firebreak with his head down and his hands in his pockets, looking for seashells and old Indian arrowheads in the sand. Some days he saw rattlesnakes sleeping beneath the sagebrush. Some days he saw scorpions. Once he came across a horse skull bleached white by the sun. Another time, an old man in a red silk kimono with a tin pail in his hand who said he was going down to the river.

Whenever the boy walked past the shadow of a guard tower he pulled his cap down low over his head and tried not to say the word.

But sometimes it slipped out anyway.

Hirohito, Hirohito, Hirohito.

He said it quietly. Quickly. He whispered it. [. . .]

20   The man scrubbing pots and pans in the mess hall had once been the sales manager of an import-export company in San Francisco. The janitor had owned a small nursery in El Cerrito. The cook had always been a cook. *A kitchen's a kitchen, it's all the same to me.* The waitress had worked as a live-in domestic for a wealthy family in Atherton. *The children still write to me every week asking me when I'm going to come home.* The man standing in front of the latrines shouting out, "Hallelujah, Hallelujah," had been a vagrant on the streets of Oakland. *That's him! The Hallelujah guy!* The old woman who did nothing but play bingo all day long had worked in the strawberry fields of Mt. Eden for twenty-five years without taking a single vacation. *Me happy, come here. Better than Mt. Eden. No cook, no work, just do laundry fine.*

One evening as the boy's mother was hauling back a bucket of water from the washroom she ran into her former housekeeper, Mrs. Ueno. "When she saw me she grabbed the bucket right out of my hands and insisted upon carrying it home for me. 'You'll hurt your back again,' she said. I tried to tell her that she no longer worked for me. 'Mrs. Ueno,' I said, 'here we're all equals,' but of course she wouldn't listen. When we got back to the barracks she set the bucket down by the front door and then she bowed and hurried

This is a picture of the Topaz camp that was used as a postcard by one of the internees. The back of the postcard says: "Dec 16, 1944. Mr. and Mrs. Uchida. Our concentration camp in Topaz, Utah. The barbed wire fence and guard towers are not visible."

What words or phrases from the novel are captured in this image? What seems different from the descriptions in the novel?

TOPAZ, UTAH

seeing connections

In 1944, after two years of Japanese imprisonment, the U.S. War Relocation Authority produced a propaganda film called *A Challenge to Democracy* in order to counter rising opposition to the internment camps. The pictures shown here are still images from the film and the accompanying passages are excerpts from the voice-over narration.

Look at each image, carefully read the script of the narration, and explain how the film uses visuals and word choice to attempt to show the internment in the best possible way. Consider as well how the images and text differ from what you have read in this excerpt from *When the Emperor Was Divine*.

"Evacuation: more than 100,000 men, women and children all of Japanese ancestry removed from their homes in the Pacific coast states to wartime communities established in out-of-the-way places. Their evacuation did not imply individual disloyalty, but was ordered to reduce a military hazard at a time when danger of invasion was great. Two-thirds of the evacuees are American citizens by right of birth. The rest are their Japanese-born parents and grandparents. The evacuees are not under suspicion. They are not prisoners. They are not internees. They are merely dislocated people. The unwounded casualties of war. [. . .]"

What is the effect of the words and phrases that the narrator is using to describe the Japanese?

off into the darkness. I didn't even get a chance to thank her."

"Maybe you can thank her tomorrow," said the boy.

"I don't even know where she *lives*. I don't even know what *day* it is."

"It's Tuesday, Mama." [. . .]

25 His sister had long skinny legs and thick black hair and wore a gold French watch that had once belonged to their father. Whenever she went out she covered her head with a wide-brimmed Panama hat so her face would not get too dark from the sun. "Nobody will look at you," she said to the boy, "if your face is too dark."

"Nobody's looking at me anyway," he replied.

Late at night, after the lights had gone out, she told him things. Beyond the fence, she said, there was a dry riverbed and an abandoned smelter mine and at the edge of the desert there

"There can be no question of the constitutionality of any part of the action taken by the government to meet the dangers of war, so no law-abiding American need to fear for his own freedom. Relocation of the evacuees is not being carried on at the sacrifice of national security. Only those evacuees whose statements and whose acts leave no question of their loyalty to the United States are permitted to leave. All information available from intelligence agencies is considered in determining whether or not each individual is eligible to leave. Those who are not eligible to leave have been moved to one center to live, presumably for the duration of the war. The others established as law-abiding aliens, are loyal Americans, are free to go whenever they like. Thousands already have gone. [. . .]"

Based on the language choices, who is the target audience for this film?

"The Americanism of the great majority of America's Japanese finds its highest expression in the thousands who are in the United States Army. Almost half of them are in a Japanese-American combat team, created by order of the Secretary of War early in 1943. Some of the volunteers came from Hawaii, some from the eastern part of the United States mainland, where there was no mass evacuation. Hundreds of them volunteered while they were in relocation centers. Volunteered to fight against the militarism and oppression of Japan and Germany. They know what they're fighting against, and they know what they are fighting for, their country, and for the American ideals that are part of their upbringing — democracy, freedom, equality of opportunity, regardless of race, creed, or ancestry. [. . .]"

What is the narrator implying when he says the "American ideals that are part of their upbringing?"

were jagged blue mountains that rose up into the sky. The mountains were farther away than they seemed. Everything was, in the desert. Everything except water. "Water," she said, "is just a mirage."

A mirage was not there at all.

The mountains were called Big Drum and Little Drum, Snake Ridge, the Rubies. The nearest town over was Delta.

30   In Delta, she said, you could buy oranges.

In Delta there were green leafy trees and blond boys on bikes and a hotel with a verandah where the waiters served ice-cold drinks with tiny paper umbrellas.

"What else?" asked the boy.

In Delta, she said, there was shade.

She told him about the ancient salt lake that had once covered all of Utah and parts of Nevada. This was thousands of years ago, she said, during the Ice Age. There were no fences then. And no names. No Utah. No Nevada. Just lots and lots of water. "And where we are now?"

35   "Yes?"

"Six hundred feet under." [. . .]

Every few days the letters arrived, tattered and torn, from Lordsburg, New Mexico. Sometimes entire sentences had been cut out with a razor blade by the censors and the letters did not make any sense. Sometimes they arrived in one piece, but with half of the words blacked out. Always, they were signed, "From Papa, With Love."

Lordsburg was a nice sunny place on a broad highland plain just north of the Mexican border. That was how his father had described it in his letters. *There are no trees here but the sunsets are beautiful and on clear days you can see the hills rising up in the distance. The food is fresh and substantial and my appetite is good. Although it is still very warm I have begun taking a cold shower every morning to better prepare myself for the winter. Please write and tell me what you are interested in these days. Do you still like baseball? How is your sister? Do you have a best friend?*

The boy still liked baseball and he was very interested in outlaws. He had seen a movie about the Dalton Gang — *When the Daltons Rode* — in Recreation Hall 22. His sister had won second prize in a jitterbug contest at the mess hall. She wore her hair in a ponytail. She was fine. The boy did not have a best friend but he had a pet tortoise that he kept in a wooden box filled with sand right next to the barrack window. He had not given the tortoise a name but he had scratched his family's identification number into its shell with the tip of his mother's nail file. At night he covered the box with a lid and on top of the lid he placed a flat white stone so the tortoise could not escape. Sometimes, in his dreams, he could hear its claws scrabbling against the side of the box.

40   He did not mention the scrabbling claws to his father. He did not mention his dreams.

What he said was, *Dear Papa: It's pretty sunny here in Utah too. The food is not so bad and we get milk every day. In the mess hall we are collecting nails for Uncle Sam. Yesterday my kite got stuck on the fence.*

The rules about the fence were simple: You could not go over it, you could not go under it, you could not go around it, you could not go through it.

And if your kite got stuck on it?

That was an easy one. You let the kite go.

45   There were rules about language, too: *Here we say Dining Hall and not Mess Hall; Safety Council, not Internal Police; Residents, not Evacuees; and last but not least, Mental Climate, not Morale.*

There were rules about food: No second helpings except for milk and bread.

And books: No books in Japanese.

There were rules about religion: No Emperor-worshiping Shintos allowed. [. . .]

His father was a small handsome man with delicate hands and a raised white scar on his index finger that the boy, as a young child, had loved to kiss. "Does it hurt?" he'd once asked him. "Not anymore," his father had replied. He was extremely polite. Whenever he walked into a room he closed the door behind him softly. He was always on time. He wore beautiful suits and did not yell at waiters. He loved pistachio nuts. He believed that fruit juice was the ideal drink. He liked to doodle. He was especially fond of drawing a box and then making it into three dimensions. *I guess you could say that's my forte.* Whenever the boy knocked on his door his father would look up and smile and put down whatever it was he was doing. "Don't be shy," he'd say. He read the *Examiner* every morning before work and he knew the answers to everything. How small a germ was and when did fish sleep and where did Kitty McKenzie go after they took her out of her iron lung? *You don't have to worry about Kitty McKenzie anymore. She's in a better place now. She's up there in heaven. I heard they threw her a big party the day she arrived.* He knew when to leave the boy's mother alone and how best to ask her for ice cream. *Don't ask her too often and when you do, don't let her know how much you really want it. Don't beg. Don't whine.* He knew which restaurants would serve them lunch and which would not. He knew which barbers would cut their kind of hair. *The best ones, of course.* The thing that he loved most about America, he once confided to the boy, was the glazed jelly donut. *Can't be beat.* [. . .], pp. 63–65.

50 One evening, while they were walking, the boy reached over and grabbed the girl's arm. "What is it?" she asked him.

He tapped his wrist. "Time," he said. "What time?"

She stopped and looked at her watch as though she had never seen it before. "It's six o'clock," she said.

Her watch had said six o'clock for weeks. She had stopped winding it the day they had stepped off the train.

"What do you think they're doing back home?"

55 She looked at her watch one more time and then she stared up at the sky, as though she were thinking. "Right about now," she said, "I bet they're having a good time." Then she started walking again.

And in his mind he could see it: the tree-lined streets at sundown, the dark green lawns, the sidewalks, boys throwing balls in backyards, girls playing hopscotch, mothers with pink quilted mitts sliding hot casseroles out of ovens, fathers with shiny black briefcases bursting through front doors, shouting, "Honey, I'm home! Honey, I'm home!"

When he thought of the world outside it was always six o'clock. A Wednesday or a Thursday. Dinnertime across America.

In early autumn the farm recruiters arrived to sign up new workers, and the War Relocation Authority allowed many of the young men and women to go out and help harvest the crops. Some of them went north to Idaho to top sugar beets. Some went to Wyoming to pick potatoes. Some went to Tent

▶

How does this picture demonstrate the sentence from the novel, "Life was easier, they said, on this side of the fence" (par. 55)?

Fotosearch/Getty Images

City in Provo to pick peaches and pears and at the end of the season they came back wearing brand-new Florsheim shoes. Some came back wearing the same shoes they'd left in and swore they would never go out there again. They said they'd been shot at. Spat on. Refused entrance to the local diner. The movie theater. The dry goods store. They said the signs in the windows were the same wherever they went: NO JAPS ALLOWED. Life was easier, they said, on this side of the fence.

The shoes were black Oxfords. Men's, size eight and a half, extra narrow. He took them out of his suitcase and slipped them over his hands and pressed his fingers into the smooth oval depressions left behind by his father's toes and then he closed his eyes and sniffed the tips of his fingers.

60 Tonight they smelled like nothing.

The week before they had still smelled of his father but tonight the smell of his father was gone.

He wiped off the leather with his sleeve and put the shoes back into the suitcase. Outside it was dark and in the barrack windows there were lights on and figures moving behind curtains. He wondered what his father was doing right then. Getting ready for bed, maybe. Washing his face. Or brushing his teeth. Did they even have tooth-paste in Lordsburg? He didn't know. He'd have to write him and ask. He lay down on his cot and pulled up the blankets. He could hear his mother snoring softly in the darkness, and a lone coyote in the hills to the south, howling up at the moon. He wondered if you could see the same moon in Lordsburg, or London, or even in China, where all the men wore little black slippers. And he decided that you could, depending on the clouds.

"Same moon," he whispered to himself, "same moon." [. . .]

Every week they heard new rumors.

65 The men and women would be put into sepa-rate camps. They would be sterilized. They would be stripped of their citizenship. They would be taken out onto the high seas and then shot. They

would be sent to a desert island and left there to die. They would all be deported to Japan. They would never be allowed to leave America. They would be held hostage until every last American POW got home safely. They would be turned over to the Chinese for safekeeping right after the war.

You've been brought here for your own protection, they were told.

It was all in the interest of national security.

It was a matter of military necessity.

It was an opportunity for them to prove their loyalty.

70 The school was opened in mid-October. Classes were held in an unheated barrack at the far end of Block 8 and in the morning it was sometimes so cold the boy could not feel his fingers or toes and his breath came out in small white puffs. Textbooks had to be shared, and paper and pencils were often in short supply.

Every morning, at Mountain View Elementary, he placed his hand over his heart and recited the pledge of allegiance. He sang "Oh, beautiful for spacious skies" and "My country, 'tis of thee" and he shouted out "Here!" at the sound of his name. His teacher was Mrs. Delaney. She had short brown hair and smooth creamy skin and a husband named Hank who was a sergeant in the Marines. Every week he sent her a letter from the front lines in the Pacific. Once, he even sent her a grass skirt. "Now when am I ever going to wear a grass skirt?" she asked the class.

"How about tomorrow?"

"Or after recess."

"Put it on right now!"

75 The first week of school they learned all about the *Nina* and the *Pinta* and the *Santa Maria*, and Squanto and the Pilgrims at Plymouth Rock. They wrote down the names of the states in neat cursive letters across lined sheets of paper. They played hangman and twenty questions. In the afternoon, during current events, they listened to Mrs. Delaney read out loud to them from the newspaper. *The*

First Lady is visiting the Queen in London. The Russians are still holding in Stalingrad. The Japs are massing on Guadalcanal.

"What about Burma?" the boy asked.

The situation in Burma, she told the class, was bleak.

Late at night he heard the sound of the door opening, and footsteps crossing the floor, and then his sister was suddenly there by the window, flipping her dress up high over her head.

"You asleep?"

80 "Just resting." He could smell her hair, and the dust, and salt, and he knew she'd been out there, in the night, where it was dark.

She said, "Miss me?" She said, "Turn down the radio." She said, "I won a nickel at bingo tonight. Tomorrow we'll go to the canteen and buy you a Coca-Cola."

He said, "I'd like that. I'd like that a lot."

She dropped down onto the cot next to his. "Talk to me," she said. "Tell me what you did tonight."

"I wrote Papa a postcard."

85 "What else?"

"Licked a stamp."

"Do you know what bothers me most? I can't remember his face sometimes."

"It was sort of round," said the boy. Then he asked her if she wanted to listen to some music

and she said yes—she always said yes—and he turned on the radio to the big band channel. They heard a trumpet and some drums and then Benny Goodman on the clarinet and Martha Tilton singing, "So many memories, sometimes I think I'll cry. . . ."

In the dream there was always a beautiful wooden door. The beautiful wooden door was very small—the size of a pillow, say, or an encyclopedia. Behind the small but beautiful wooden door there was a second door, and behind the second door there was a picture of the Emperor, which no one was allowed to see.

90 For the Emperor was holy and divine. A god. You could not look him in the eye.

In the dream the boy had already opened the first door and his hand was on the second door and any minute now, he was sure of it, he was going to see God.

Only something always went wrong. The doorknob fell off. Or the door got stuck. Or his shoelace came untied and he had to bend over and tie it. Or maybe a bell was ringing somewhere—somewhere in Nevada or Peleliu or maybe it was just some crazy gong bonging in Saipan—and the nights were growing colder, the sound of the scrabbling claws was fainter now, fainter than ever before, and it was October, he was miles from home, and his father was not there.

Understanding and Interpreting

1 Throughout the novel, the main characters are identified only as "boy," "girl," "mother," and "father." How do you interpret the reasons for this choice?

2 In paragraph 14, the boy is told to "never say the Emperor's name out loud." What is the boy's view of the emperor at this point? What does the emperor represent for him?

3 In paragraph 21, the mother runs into her former housekeeper, Mrs. Ueno. What is that interaction intended to reveal about the situation the Japanese find themselves in?

4 The father and boy write back and forth to each other. Read their exchange in paragraphs 37–41. Identify what is said and what is not said in the boy's letter, and explain what this reveals about their relationship.

5 Make a claim about the relationship between the boy and the girl in this first section of the chapter. Use specific evidence from the text to support your statement.

6 While the father is absent from the camps, he is far from absent from the boy's thoughts. What are the key details or events that the boy remembers about his father, and what do these say about the boy, as well as about the father?

7 The girl's watch has stopped at 6:00, and when the boy thinks of the world outside of the camp, it is "always six o'clock. A Wednesday or a Thursday. Dinnertime across America" (par. 57). How does this section reveal a point Otsuka is making about how the boy views the various cultures of America?

8 The first section of this chapter ends with one of the boy's dreams (pars. 89–93). What does this dream likely represent?

9 The setting plays a vitally important role in this novel; it is almost as if it is a character in the story. Choose a passage in which Otsuka describes an aspect of the camp and explain how the setting seems to affect the boy or others in the camp.

Analyzing Language, Style, and Structure

1 Notice Otsuka's use of sentence fragments, especially in the opening paragraphs of this chapter. What effect is created through the use of these sentence fragments and how does that help to establish character and tone?

2 While this excerpt from the novel is written in the "third person" point of view, it is clearly written from the perspective of the boy. What does Otsuka do, especially with her language choices, to make it clear to the reader that we are seeing the situation through the eyes of a young boy?

3 Reread paragraph 45, where we learn that there are rules about the use of language in the camp. Explain the differences between some of the pairs of words that Otsuka includes, and why the authorities might have preferred certain words.

4 There are several places in this section of the chapter where Otsuka includes flashbacks to the characters' lives before the camp. Identify one flashback and explain its purpose. Why is it placed where it is within the story? What does it reveal about the boy or the family?

5 Reread paragraphs 64–66, which are in the section that begins with the flashback "Every week they heard new rumors." Why does Otsuka begin almost every sentence in paragraph 65 with the word "They"?

6 There is very little of what we typically call "plot" in this selection; the action is mostly told in short, episodic bits. What feeling is created by this choice? How does this choice reflect a theme that Otsuka is presenting?

Connecting, Arguing, and Extending

1 The boy is told to never say the emperor's name out loud. Conduct brief research on Emperor Hirohito, or, as he was known after his death, Emperor Shōwa. What was his background, and what were his significant actions before, during, and after World War II? Beyond the title, "When the Emperor Was Divine," what is the connection of the emperor to the events in this section of the chapter?

2 The father's letters to the boy were significantly redacted or censored. To what extent should a government be able to read and censor the communications of people it suspects of treason?

3 In paragraph 45, the boy learns the rules about the language of the camp, such as saying "Residents" instead of "Evacuees." Clearly this is an example of euphemistic language, much like the military term "collateral damage," which is used instead of "civilian deaths" to minimize the negative perceptions of unintended carnage. Identify some euphemisms that you know from real life. Where do they come from, and why are they used in the context you identified?

4 In paragraph 58, some of the Japanese who left the camp say "[l]ife was easier . . . on this side of the fence" because of the racism they experienced. Research the prejudices the Japanese (or another immigrant group) faced in U.S. society before and during World War II.

They had come for him just after midnight. Three men in suits and ties and black fedoras with FBI badges under their coats. "Grab your toothbrush," they'd said. This was back in December, right after Pearl Harbor, when they were still living in the white house on the wide street in Berkeley not far from the sea. The Christmas tree was up, and the whole house smelled of pine, and from his window the boy had watched as they led his father out across the lawn in his bathrobe and slippers to the black car that was parked at the curb.

He had never seen his father leave the house without his hat on before. That was what had troubled him most. No hat. And those slippers: battered and faded, with the rubber soles curling up at the edges. If only they had let him put on his shoes then it all might have turned out differently. But there had been no time for shoes.

Grab your toothbrush.

Come on. Come on. You're coming with us.

5   *We just need to ask your husband a few questions.*

Into the car, Papa-san.

Later, the boy remembered seeing lights on in the house next door, and faces pressed to the window. One of them was Elizabeth's, he was sure of it.

Elizabeth Morgana Roosevelt had seen his father taken away in his slippers.

The next morning his sister had wandered through the house looking for the last place their father had sat. Was it the red chair? Or the sofa? The edge of his bed? She had pressed her face to the bedspread and sniffed.

10   "The edge of *my* bed," their mother had said.

That evening she had lit a bonfire in the yard and burned all of the letters from Kagoshima. She burned the family photographs and the three silk kimonos she had brought over with her nineteen years ago from Japan. She burned the records of Japanese opera. She ripped up the flag of the red rising sun. She smashed the tea set and the Imari dishes and the framed portrait of the boy's uncle, who had once been a general in the Emperor's army. She smashed the abacus and tossed it into the flames. "From now on," she said, "we're counting on our fingers."

The next day, for the first time ever, she sent the boy and his sister to school with peanut butter and jelly sandwiches in their lunch pails. "No more rice balls," she said. "And if anyone asks, you're Chinese."

The boy had nodded. "Chinese," he whispered. "I'm Chinese."

"And I," said the girl, "am the Queen of Spain."

15   "In your dreams," said the boy.

"In my dreams," said the girl, "I'm the King."

In China the men wore their hair in long black pigtails and the ladies hobbled around on tiny broken feet. In China there were people so poor they had to feed their newborn babies to the dogs. In China they ate grass for breakfast and for lunch they ate cats.

And for dinner?

For dinner, in China, they ate dogs.

20   These were a few of the things the boy knew about China.

Later, he saw Chinese, real Chinese — Mr. Lee of Lee's Grocers and Don Wong who owned the laundry on Shattuck — on the street wearing buttons that said, I AM CHINESE, and CHINESE, PLEASE. Later, a man stopped him on the sidewalk in front of Woolworth's and said, "Chink or Jap?" and the boy answered, "Chink," and ran away as fast as he could. Only when he got to the corner did he turn around and shout, "Jap! Jap! I'm a Jap!"

Just to set the record straight.

But by then the man was already gone.

In addition to being a noted children's author, Theodor Seuss Geisel, better known as Dr. Seuss, drew editorial cartoons during World War II, including this one from February 13, 1942. The term "Fifth Column" refers to a secret group working to undermine the support of another group; it is usually applied to spies and saboteurs.

Looking at the cartoon today, we see that it is clearly racist in its stereotypical representations of the Japanese. What does the cartoon suggest about the Japanese living in the United States in 1942, and what attitude does it present toward them? If this cartoon was reflective of the general public's attitude toward the Japanese, how might this attitude have led people to support the internment?

Mandeville Special Collections Library at the University of California, San Diego

Later, there were the rules about time: No Japs out after eight p.m.

25 And space: No Japs allowed to travel more than five miles from their homes.

Later, the Japanese Tea Garden in Golden Gate Park was renamed the Oriental Tea Garden.

Later, the signs that read INSTRUCTIONS TO ALL PERSONS OF JAPANESE ANCESTRY went up all over town and they packed up their things and they left.

All through October the days were still warm, like summer, but at night the mercury dropped and in the morning the sagebrush was some-times covered with frost. Twice in one week there were dust storms. The sky turned suddenly gray and then a hot wind came screaming across the desert, churning up everything in its path. From inside the barracks the boy could not see the sun or the moon or even the next row of barracks on the other side of the gravel path. All he could see was dust. The wind rattled the windows and doors and the dust seeped like smoke through the cracks in the roof and at night he slept with a wet handkerchief over his mouth to keep out the smell. In the morning, when he woke, the wet handkerchief was dry and in his mouth there was the gritty taste of chalk.

A dust storm would blow for hours, and sometimes even days, and then, just as suddenly as it had begun, it would stop, and for a few seconds the world was perfectly silent. Then a baby would begin to cry, or a dog would start barking, and from out of nowhere a flock of white birds would mysteriously appear in the sky.

30 The first snows fell, and then melted, and then there was rain. The alkaline earth could not absorb any water and the ground quickly turned to mud. Black puddles stood on the gravel paths and the schools were shut down for repairs.

There was nothing to do now and the days were long and empty. The boy marked them off one by one on the calendar with giant red *X*'s. He practiced fancy tricks on the yo-yo: Around the World, Walk the Dog, the Turkish Army. He received a letter from his father written on thin lined sheets of paper. *Of* course *we have toothpaste in Lordsburg. How else do you expect us to brush our teeth?* His father thanked him for the postcard of the Mormon Tabernacle. He said he was fine. Everything was fine. He was sure they would see each other one day soon. Be good to your mother, he wrote. Be patient. *And remember, it's better to bend than to break.*

Not once did he mention the war.

His father had promised to show him the world. They'd go to Egypt, he'd said, and climb the Pyramids. They'd go to China and take a nice long stroll along that Great Wall. They'd see the Eiffel Tower in Paris and the Colosseum in Rome and at night, by the light of the stars, they'd glide through Venice in a black wooden gondola.

"The moon above," he sang, "is yours and mine. . . ."

35 The day after the FBI had come to the house he had found a few strands of his father's hair in the bathtub. He had put them into an envelope and placed the envelope beneath the loose floorboard under his bed and promised himself that as long as he did not check to make sure that the envelope was still there — *no peeking,* was his rule — his father would be all right. But lately he had begun waking up every night in the barracks, convinced that the envelope was gone. "I should have taken it with me," he said to himself. He worried that there were large messy people now living in his old room who played cards night and day and spilled sticky brown drinks all over the floor. He worried that the FBI had returned to the house to search one more time for contraband. *We forgot to check under the floorboards.* He worried that when he saw his father again after the war his father would be too tired to play catch with him under the trees. He worried that his father would be bald. [. . .]

. . .

Late at night, in the darkness, he could hear his mother praying. "Our father, Who art in heaven . . ."

And in the morning, at sunrise, coming from the other side of the wall, the sound of the man next door chanting. "*Kokyo ni taishite keirei.*"

Salute to the Imperial Palace.

Now whenever he thought of his father he saw him at sundown, leaning against a fence post in Lordsburg, in the camp for dangerous enemy aliens. "My daddy's an outlaw," he whispered. He liked the sound of that word. Outlaw. He pictured his father in cowboy boots and a black Stetson, riding a big beautiful horse named White Frost. Maybe he'd rustled some cattle, or robbed a bank, or held up a stage coach, or — like the Dalton brothers — even a whole entire train, and now he was just doing his time with all of the other men.

40 He'd be thinking these things, and then the image would suddenly float up before him: his father, in his bathrobe and slippers, being led away across the lawn. *Into the car, Papa-san.*

He'll be back any day now. Any day.

Just say he went away on a trip.

Keep your mouth shut and don't say a thing.

Stay inside.

45 Don't leave the house.

Travel only in the daytime.

Do not converse on the telephone in Japanese.

Do not congregate in one place.

When in town if you meet another Japanese do not greet him in the Japanese manner by bowing.

50 Remember, you're in America.

Greet him in the American way by shaking his hand. [. . .]

On December 7 it will have been a year since I last saw you, I read your letters every night before I go

seeing connections

Ansel Adams and Dorothea Lange were two prominent American photographers in the 1930s and 1940s, and both were given access to the Japanese internment camps by the U.S. government in order to document the conditions. While many of Adams's photographs were released to the general public, most of Lange's photos were suppressed by the government until long after the war.

Look closely at the pairs of images and explain how the tone of each picture compares and contrasts with the other. Which photos most accurately reflect some of the words and phrases that contribute to the tone of this chapter of Otsuka's novel?

Library of Congress Prints and Photographs Division, LC-A351-3-M-37

Ansel Adams, "Tojo Miatake [i.e., Tōyō Miyatake] Family, Manzanar Relocation Center"

National Archives

Dorothea Lange, "Manzanar Relocation Center, Manzanar, California. A typical interior scene in one of the barrack apartments at this center. Note the cloth partition which lends a small amount of privacy."

to bed. So far the winter here has been mild. This morning I woke up at dawn and watched the sun rise. I saw a bald eagle flying toward the mountains. I am in good health and exercise for half an hour after every meal. Please take care of yourself and be helpful to your mother.

For four days after his arrest they had not known where he was. The phone had not rung — the FBI had cut the wires — and they could not withdraw any money from the bank. "Your account's been frozen," the boy's mother had been told. At dinner she set the table for four, and every night before they went to bed she walked out to the front porch and slipped her house key beneath the potted chrysanthemum. "He'll know where to look," she said.

On the fifth day she received a short note in the mail from the immigration detention center in San Francisco. *Still awaiting my loyalty hearing. Do not know when my case will be heard, or how much longer I will be here. Eighty-three Japanese have already been sent away on a train. Please*

Ansel Adams, "Baton practice, Florence Kuwata, Manzanar Relocation Center"

Library of Congress Prints and Photographs Division, LC-A35-5-M-34

Dorothea Lange, "Tom Kobayashi, landscape, south fields, Manzanar Relocation Center"

Library of Congress Prints and Photographs Division, LC-A351-3-M-19

Ansel Adams, "Manzanar street scene, clouds, Manzanar Relocation Center, California"

Library of Congress Prints and Photographs Division, LC-A351-3-M-26

Dorothea Lange, "Photograph of Dust Storm at Manzanar War Relocation Authority Center"

National Archives

come see me as soon possible. She packed a small suitcase full of her husband's things — clothes, towels, a shaving kit, a spare pair of eyeglasses, nose drops, a bar of Yardley soap, a first-aid book — and took the next train across the bay.

55   "Was he still wearing his slippers?" the boy asked her when she returned.

She said that he was. And his bathrobe, too. She said that he had not showered or shaved for days. Then she smiled. "He looked like a hobo," she said.

That night she had set the table for three.

In the morning she had sent all of the boy's father's suits to the cleaners except for one: the blue pin-striped suit he had worn on his last Sunday at home. The blue suit was to remain on the hanger in the closet. "He asked me to leave it there, for you to remember him by."

But whenever the boy thought of his father on his last Sunday at home he did not remember the blue suit. He remembered the white flannel robe. The slippers. His father's hatless silhouette framed in the back window of the car. The head stiff and unmoving. Staring straight ahead. Straight ahead and into the night as the car drove off slowly into the darkness. Not looking back. Not even once. Just to see if he was there.

60 Christmas day. Gray skies. A bitter cold. In the mess halls there were pine trees decorated with stars cut out of tin cans and on radios throughout the barracks Bing Crosby was singing "White Christmas." Turkey was served for supper, and candy and gifts from the Quakers and the American Friends Service were distributed to the children in every block. The boy received a small red Swiss Army knife from a Mrs. Ida Little of Akron, Ohio. *May the Lord look down upon you always*, she had written. He sent her a prompt thank you note and carried the knife with him in his pocket wherever he went. Sometimes, when he was running, he could hear it clacking against his lucky blue stone from the sea and for a moment he felt very happy. His pockets were filled with good things.

The winter seemed to last forever. There were outbreaks of flu and diarrhea and frequent shortages of coal. They had been assigned only two army blankets per person and at night the boy often fell asleep shivering. His hands were red and chapped from the cold. His throat was always sore. His sister left the barracks early in the morning and did not return until long after dark. She was always in a rush now. Her cheeks were flushed from the cold. "Where are you going?" "Out." She ate all her meals with her friends. Never with the boy or his mother. She smoked cigarettes. He could smell them in her hair. One day he saw her standing in line at the mess hall in her Panama hat and she hardly seemed to recognize him at all. [. . .]

"When I first met your father I wanted to be with him all the time."

"I know what you mean."

"If I was away from him for even five minutes, I'd start to miss him. I'd think, *He's never coming back. I'll never see him again.* But after a while I stopped being so afraid. Things change."

65 "I guess so."

"The night of his arrest, he asked me to go get him a glass of water. We'd just gone to bed and I was so tired. I was exhausted. So I told him to go get it himself. 'Next time I will,' he said, and then he rolled over and went right to sleep. Later, as they were taking him away, all I could think was, *Now he'll always be thirsty.*"

"They probably gave him a drink at the station."

"I should have brought it to him."

"You didn't know."

70 "Even now, in my dreams, he's still searching for water." [. . .]

In the morning she woke burning with fever. Their mother brought her a tin cup filled with water and told her to drink but the girl refused. She said she wasn't thirsty. "Nothing's passing through these lips," she said. She pulled back the blanket and began to pick at a scab on her knee. The boy grabbed her wrist and said, "Don't." She turned away and looked out the window. A woman in a pink bathrobe walked by carrying a chamberpot toward the latrines. "Where are we?" the girl asked. "What happened to all the trees? What country is this anyway?" She said she'd seen their father walking alone by the side of the road. "He was coming to take us away." She looked down at her watch and asked how it had gotten to be so late. "It's six o'clock," she said. "He should have been here by now."

In February a team of army recruiters arrived looking for volunteers, and the loyalty questionnaire was given to every man and woman over the age of seventeen.

Are you willing to serve in the armed forces of the United States on combat duty, wherever ordered?

seeing connections

Read the poem "In Response to Executive Order 9066: All Americans of Japanese Descent Must Report to Relocation Centers" by Dwight Okita. In what ways is the speaker of the poem similar to or different from the boy in the chapter you read from *When the Emperor Was Divine*?

> Dear Sirs:
> Of course I'll come. I've packed my galoshes
> and three packets of tomato seeds. Denise calls them
> love apples. My father says where we're going
> 5 they won't grow.
>
> I am a fourteen-year-old girl with bad spelling
> and a messy room. If it helps any, I will tell you
> I have always felt funny using chopsticks
> and my favorite food is hot dogs.
> 10 My best friend is a white girl named Denise —
> we look at boys together. She sat in front of me
> all through grade school because of our names:
> O'Connor, Ozawa. I know the back of Denise's head very well.
>
> I tell her she's going bald. She tells me I copy on tests.
> 15 We're best friends.
>
> I saw Denise today in Geography class.
> She was sitting on the other side of the room.
> "You're trying to start a war," she said, "giving secrets
> away to the Enemy. Why can't you keep your big
> 20 mouth shut?"
>
> I didn't know what to say.
> I gave her a packet of tomato seeds
> and asked her to plant them for me, told her
> when the first tomato ripened
> 25 she'd miss me.

Associated Press

How evacuation of Japanese from Seattle affected a second-grade class in a local school is shown in these two views from 1942. At the top is a crowded classroom with many Japanese pupils and at the bottom is the same class without the Japanese students.

Imagine that you were living at the time and were opposed to the Japanese internment. If you were to use the images as a poster to illustrate your opposition, what caption would you write? Why would it be effective?

The man next door answered no and was sent away along with his wife and his wife's mother to join the other disloyals at Tule Lake. The following year they were repatriated to Japan on the U.S.S. *Gripsholm*.

75 *Will you swear unqualified allegiance to the United States of America and faithfully defend the United States from any or all attack by foreign or domestic forces, and forswear any form of allegiance or obedience to the Japanese Emperor, or any other foreign government, power or organization?*

"What allegiance?" asked the boy's mother. She said she had nothing to forswear. She'd been in America for almost twenty years now.

But she did not want to cause any trouble — "The nail that sticks up gets hammered down"— or be labeled disloyal. She did not want to be sent back to Japan. "There's no future for us there. We're here. Your father's here. The most important thing is that we stay together."

She answered yes.

They stayed.

Loyalty. Disloyalty. Allegiance. Obedience.

80 "Words," she said, "it's all just words." [. . .]

On a warm evening in April a man was shot dead by the barbed-wire fence. The guard who was on duty said the man had been trying to escape. He'd called out to him four times, the guard said, but the man had ignored him. Friends of the dead man said he had simply been taking his dog for a walk. He might not have heard the guard, they said, because he was hard of hearing. Or because of the wind. One man who had gone to the scene of the accident right after the shooting had noticed a rare and unusual flower on the other side of the fence. It was his belief that his friend had been

reaching out to pick the flower when the shot had been fired.

At the funeral there were nearly two thousand people. The casket was strewn with hundreds of crepe-paper flowers. Hymns were sung. The body was blessed. Years later the boy would recall standing beside his mother at the service, wondering just what kind of flower it was the man had seen.

A rose? A tulip? A daffodil?

And if he *had* plucked it. Then what?

85 He imagined exploding ships, clouds of black smoke, hundreds of B-29s falling down in flames from the sky. *One false move, pal, and you're dead.* [. . .]

Summer was a long hot dream. Every morning, as soon as the sun rose, the temperature began to soar. By noon the floors were sagging. The sky was bleached white from the heat and the wind was hot and dry. Yellow dust devils whirled across the sand. The black roofs baked in the sun. The air shimmered.

The boy tossed pebbles into the coal bucket. He peered into other people's windows. He drew

This photograph was taken at the funeral of James Wakasa, an internee at the Topaz Relocation Center in Utah, who was shot and killed by a military policeman near the camp's barbed-wire fence on April 11, 1943. Internees protested the shooting by holding a public funeral on the spot where Wakasa was shot. The soldier who shot Wakasa was court-martialed but found "not guilty."

Why do you think Otsuka chose to highlight this incident in her novel? What does the image of this funeral reveal about its significance?

National Archives

pictures of airplanes and tanks with his favorite stick in the sand. He traced out an sos in huge letters across the firebreak but before anyone could read what he had written he wiped the letters away.

Late at night he lay awake on top of the sheets longing for ice, a section of orange, a stone, something, anything, to suck on, to quench his thirst. It was June now. Or maybe it was July. It was August. The calendar had fallen from the wall. The tin clock had stopped ticking. Its gears were clotted with dust and would not turn. His sister was sound asleep on her cot and his mother lay dreaming behind the white curtain. He lifted a hand to his mouth. There was a loose molar there, on top, way in back. He liked to touch it. To rock it back and forth in its socket. The motion soothed him. Sometimes he'd taste blood and then he'd swallow. Salty, he'd think to himself, like the sea. In the distance he could hear trains passing in the night. The pounding of hooves on the sand. The faint tinkle of a tin bell.

He'd close his eyes. That's him, he'd think. He's on his way.

90 He could come back on a horse. On a bike. In a train. On a plane. In the same unmarked car that had once taken him away. He could be wearing a blue pin-striped suit. A red silk kimono. A grass skirt. A cowboy hat. A halo. A dark gray fedora with a leaf tucked up under the brim. Maybe he'd touch it — the leaf — and then he'd raise his hand slowly into the air, as though he were Jesus, or the man with the withered arm, or even General Douglas MacArthur. "I have returned," he'd say. Then his eyes would light up and he'd reach down into his pocket and pull out a single white pearl. "I found this by the side of the road," he'd say. "Any idea whose it might be?"

It could happen like that.

Or maybe the boy would be lying in bed one night and he'd hear a knock, a soft tap. "Who is it?" he'd say. "It's me." He'd open the door and see his father standing there in his white flannel bathrobe all covered with dust. "It's a long walk from Lordsburg," his father would say. Then they would shake hands, or maybe they'd even hug.

"Did you get my letters?" he'd ask his father.

"You bet I did. I read every single one of them. I got that leaf, too. I thought of you all the time."

95 "I thought of you too," the boy would say.

He'd bring his father a glass of water and they would sit down side by side on the cot. Outside the window the moon would be bright and round. The wind would be blowing. He'd rest his head on his father's shoulder and smell the dust and the sweat and the faint smell of Burma Shave and everything would be very nice. Then, out of the corner of his eye, he'd notice his father's big toe sticking out through a hole in his slipper. "Papa," he'd say.

"What is it?"

"You forgot to put on your shoes."

His father would look down at his feet and he'd shake his head with surprise. "Son of a gun," he'd say. "Would you look at that." Then he'd just shrug. He'd lean back on the cot and make himself comfortable. He'd pull out his pipe. A box of matches. He'd smile. "Now tell me what I missed," he'd say. "Tell me everything."

Understanding and Interpreting

1 The boy refers to his neighbor, Elizabeth Morgana Roosevelt (pars. 7–8). What does she represent for the boy?

2 In the long flashback at the beginning of this section after the father has been taken away by the FBI (pars. 1–16), what do the actions of the mother reveal about her fears and her motivations?

3 In paragraph 21, the boy is confronted on the street by someone asking, "Chink or Jap?" How does the boy respond, and what do these actions reveal about the boy?

4 The father advises the boy in a letter, "*And remember, it's better to bend than to break*" (par. 31). Where do we see this idea demonstrated in this section of the novel?

5 Examine the relationship between the boy and girl in this section of the novel. What aspects of their relationship have changed and what have remained the same from the beginning of the chapter?

6 Based upon flashbacks before moving to the camps, what is Otsuka suggesting about the ways the American and Japanese cultures interacted?

7 What purpose does the story of the man who was shot dead, perhaps for trying to pick a flower on the other side of the fence, play (pars. 81–85)? Why does Otsuka include it?

8 What is the point of ending this chapter with the boy imagining the father saying to him, "Tell me everything"?

Analyzing Language, Style, and Structure

1 Reread the opening paragraphs of the first section and the closing paragraphs of this second section of the chapter. What connects these two parts, and how does this connection relate to a theme of the work?

2 Several times Otsuka returns to the image of the father being led away by the FBI in his slippers and without a hat. What effect is created by this repeated image?

3 Starting with the description of the dust of the camp in paragraph 28, identify words and phrases that Otsuka uses to describe the setting of the camp. What are some of the most powerful images, and what feeling is she likely trying to create for the reader? Use specific textual evidence to support your conclusion.

4 How does Otsuka use diction and setting descriptions to show time passing? What tone does she convey through these choices?

5 Reread paragraph 90, where the boy imagines his father returning. What do some of the language choices that Otsuka uses suggest about the boy's view of his father?

Connecting, Arguing, and Extending

1 At the beginning of this section, the boy is forced to deny that he is Japanese (par. 21). Write about a time when you—or someone you know—had to deny or hide some aspect of yourself. What were the factors that led to this denial and what were the results?

2 Is the boy optimistic or pessimistic about the future? Use evidence from this section of the text to support your position.

3 In paragraphs 72–75, the family is presented with a loyalty oath, in which they must pledge their allegiance to the United States of America. Research the role of loyalty oaths in American history. Who has been asked to sign and when? Or, examine the history of the Pledge of Allegiance, which was formally adopted by the U.S. Congress during the time period of this novel.

Topics for Composing

1 **Research/Argument**
In 1988, U.S. president Ronald Reagan signed legislation that included a formal apology to the Japanese who were imprisoned during the war and paid each survivor or descendant $20,000. Research the process this legislation went through to become law and write an argument about whether it was the right thing to do and whether the U.S. response was sufficient. Additionally, what are the similarities and differences in the cases of other groups who are also

seeking reparations and an apology from the U.S. government, such as Native Americans and African Americans?

2 Research/Exposition
In December 1944, three years after the attack on Pearl Harbor that led to the internment of the Japanese, the U.S. Supreme Court handed down contradictory decisions in two court cases—*Ex parte Mitsuye Endo* and *Korematsu v. United States*—that eventually led to the closure of the internment camps. Research these cases and explain how these cases interpreted the legality of the exclusion and incarceration of the Japanese.

3 Creative/Exposition
This chapter is told from the perspective of an eight-year-old boy. Choose a short passage from the chapter and rewrite it from the perspective of the girl, the mother, or the father. Then, explain what changed when you changed the perspective of the narration.

4 Research/Argument
The term "concentration camp" tends to bring up images of the Nazi extermination camps of the Holocaust, and yet in 1998, there was an exhibit in New York called *America's Concentration Camps: Remembering the Japanese-American Experience.* During World War II, these facilities were often referred to as internment, relocation, assembly, or isolation camps. At the time of the exhibit, the *New York Times* wrote, "Some American Jewish groups have strongly objected, arguing that the term has become indelibly associated with the Holocaust and would be cheapened by being used in this way. Their concern that the Holocaust be remembered as a uniquely vile expression of human evil is a reasonable one." In your opinion, what terms should be used to describe the locations where the Japanese were held prisoner and why does the language matter?

5 Research/Exposition
The U.S. Immigration Act of 1924 banned immigration from Japan to the United States, which had the unintended consequence of creating three distinct generations of Japanese living in the United States at that time: the Issei (first generation: the mother and father in the novel), Nisei (second generation: the boy and the girl), and Sansei (third generation). Research these three sociological terms and explain the effect that the immigration policy had on each.

6 Research/Exposition
Because of the emotional context of World War II and the prevalent racial discrimination at the time, there were very few prominent politicians who took a stand against the Japanese internment. One was Colorado governor Ralph L. Carr, who spoke out against the inhumane and unconstitutional treatment of the Japanese interned in his state, and once said, "If you harm them, you must harm me. I was brought up in a small town where I knew the shame and dishonor of race hatred. I grew to despise it because it threatened the happiness of you, and you, and you!" Research Carr's and others' position in opposition to the Japanese internment and explain their rationales and the steps they took to end or mitigate the effects of the government's policies.

7 Argument
In 1991, President George H. W. Bush, said:

> In remembering, it is important to come to grips with the past. No nation can fully understand itself or find its place in the world if it does not look with clear eyes at all the glories and disgraces of its past. We in the United States acknowledge such an injustice in our history. The internment of Americans of Japanese ancestry was a great injustice, and it will never be repeated.

Could something like the Japanese internment happen in the United States again? Explain.

8 Research/Exposition
Remember that during World War II, in addition to being at war with Japan, the United States was also at war with Germany and Italy. How was the treatment of the Japanese different from that of Germans and Italians, and to what extent was that treatment a function of racism at the time? For example, General John DeWitt, widely considered one of the main architects of the internment, was quoted in congressional testimony as follows:

> I don't want any of them [persons of Japanese ancestry] here. They are a dangerous element. There is no way to determine their loyalty. [. . .] It makes no difference whether he is an American citizen, he is still a Japanese. American citizenship does not necessarily determine loyalty. [. . .] But we must worry about the Japanese all the time until he is wiped off the map.

CONVERSATION

STORIES OF WAR

Unfortunately, an all-too common result of cultural conflict is war. On the playground, we may teach little kids to "use their words" instead of fists, but as adults, we often resort to war. Cultural conflicts have grown into wars over religion, politics, property, geography, and values. There have been wars of aggression, wars of defense, just wars, illegal wars, good wars, lost wars, wars of conquest, genocides, battles that become wars, and wars that wound down to become battles.

But who is the enemy in these cultural conflicts that escalate into war? Who starts the hostilities? Who is the victim? Who is to blame? These are not easy questions once the fighting begins. The expression "history is written by the victors" suggests that whichever side wins the war gets to answer those questions for itself and the rest of the world. Even though there may be a grain of truth to this, the reality is more complex, as you will explore in this Conversation.

The ancient Greek playwright Aeschylus said that "in war, truth is the first casualty," meaning that the truth about what happens during war is difficult to decipher, as well as the reasons for going to war in the first place. Two thousand years later, a Prussian military advisor, Carl von Clausewitz, wrote, "War is an area of uncertainty; three quarters of the things on which all action in War is based are lying in a fog of uncertainty to a greater or lesser extent." Likely agreeing with Aeschylus and von Clausewitz about the difficulty of identifying the truth in war, Vietnam War veteran and writer Tim O'Brien says that it's equally difficult to determine the truth of a story written *about* war. He writes:

> In a true war story, if there's a moral at all, it's like the thread that makes the cloth. You can't tease it out. You can't extract the meaning without unraveling the deeper meaning. And in the end, really, there's nothing much to say about a true war story, except maybe "Oh."
>
> True war stories do not generalize. They do not indulge in abstraction or analysis.
>
> For example: War is hell. As a moral declaration the old truism seems perfectly true, and yet because it abstracts, because it generalizes, I can't believe it with my stomach. Nothing turns inside.
>
> It comes down to gut instinct. A true war story, if truly told, makes the stomach believe.

In this Conversation, you will consider the difficulty of telling the stories of war by reading poems by soldiers who fought and, in some cases, died in battle, an essay that challenges the right of the victor to tell the story for the loser, and short stories that ask us to determine the truth of other people's stories. Because of the nature of the topic, many of the texts will not be comfortable to read and will challenge your notions of war and truth.

TEXTS

Kamila Shamsie / *from* The Storytellers of Empire (nonfiction)
Wilfred Owen / Dulce et Decorum Est (poetry)
William Shakespeare / The St. Crispin's Day Speech (drama)
Vu Bao / The Man Who Stained His Soul (fiction)
Katey Schultz / Deuce Out (fiction)
Kevin Sites / *from* In the Hot Zone (nonfiction)
Brian Turner / 2000 lbs. (poetry)
Karim Ben Khelifa / My Enemy, Myself (photo essay)

from The Storytellers of Empire

Kamila Shamsie

Writer Kamila Shamsie (b. 1973) was born and raised in Pakistan, went to college in the United States, and now lives in England. She is the author of five novels, including *Burnt Shadows*, as well as a nonfiction collection of essays about the perception of Islam by the West, called *Offence: The Muslim Case*. A frequent contributor to literary and cultural journals, Shamsie wrote this piece in 2012 for the magazine *Guernica*.

Sarah Lee/eyevine/Redux

KEY CONTEXT   In this essay, Shamsie reflects on the question she heard regularly after the terrorist attacks on the United States on 9/11/2001: why do they hate us? Getting to the answer of this question, predictably, is not easy, but one of the places she looks for answers is in the literature of war. In particular, she reflects on the book *Hiroshima* by John Hersey, published in 1946, which describes — in graphic detail — the effects of the atomic bomb that the United States dropped on that Japanese city.

A disquieting thing happened to me in 2004. I had just finished my fourth novel and, unaccustomed as I was to any space of time in which I didn't know what I would write next, I found myself searching for the single image which would lead me into a novel. Somewhat bewilderingly, instead of a single image I found myself thinking about the atom bomb falling on Nagasaki. There were a number of reasons for this — or at least, I have a number of theories about why this was so. But at the time the only thing which seemed relevant was the fact that I didn't know anything about Nagasaki other than that a bomb fell there, yet somehow that falling bomb was getting in the way of my ability to alight on the image from which a novel would emerge.

"Of course you've read John Hersey's *Hiroshima*," a friend of mine said when I mentioned that atom bombs had taken up residence in my mind. I hadn't. But I went and found it in a bookshop; it was appealingly slim enough to buy and bring home. As I read it in a single sitting I found, on page forty-six, this image of Hiroshima minutes after the bomb fell:

On some undressed bodies, the burns had made patterns of undershirt straps and suspenders and, on the skin of some women (since white repelled the heat from the bomb and dark clothes absorbed it and conducted it to the skin), the shapes of flowers they had had on their kimonos.

In my memory, the moment I read that line an image came of a woman facing away from me, three bird-shaped burns on her bare back from the pattern of the kimono she was wearing at the moment the bomb fell. That was it — the originating image. That I knew practically nothing about Nagasaki, had never been to Japan, was aware of the accumulation of stereotypes that surrounded my idea of that country and my almost total ignorance about its history, geography, weather patterns, language, foliage, cuisine, art forms was daunting to say the least. But Hersey had given me my originating image, and very quickly it started to exert a magnetic force, tugging at other images and ideas and elements of plot and character until a tiny universe was wheeling around it, impossible to ignore. Eventually it went on to become my fifth novel, *Burnt Shadows*, which started in Nagasaki in 1945 and ended with a man on his way to Guantánamo in 2002.

This is not in any way to suggest the significance of John Hersey's work lies in its connection to my work — merely to acknowledge a debt of thanks.

Of course, the significance of *Hiroshima* lies in its extraordinary achievement in "bearing witness" — Hersey's deliberately flattened tone is almost transparent, allowing us to see the images of the bombing of Hiroshima with as little mediation as possible. The line cited above illustrates this perfectly. Note the almost clinical detachment of "white repelled the heat from the bomb and dark clothes absorbed it and conducted it to the skin." There is no need for anything more to be said, or any more emotive tone to be employed. As the actor Tara Fitzgerald recently remarked, "Melodrama is busy, tragedy isn't." Hersey's pared down writing always stays on the right side of the tragedy-melodrama line. He is so good at effecting this self-effacement, this transparency, that it almost becomes possible to forget the writer — it almost becomes possible to forget the nationality of the writer. *Hiroshima* is a book about what happened in Japan, to Japan, in August 1945. It is a book about five Japanese and one German *hibakusha*, or bomb survivors. It is not a book which concerns itself with what the bombing meant for America in military terms, but rather what it meant for the people of Hiroshima in the most human terms.

5   Inevitably, it also contains within it two Americas. One is the America which develops and uses — not once, but twice — a weapon of a destructive capability which far outstrips anything that has come before, the America which decides what price some other country's civilian population must pay for its victory. There is nothing particular to America in this — all nations in war behave in much the same way. But in the years between the bombing of Hiroshima and now, no nation has intervened militarily with as many different countries as America, and always on the other country's soil; which is to say, no nation has treated as many other civilian populations as collateral damage as America while its own civilians stay well out of the arena of war. So that's one of the Americas in Hiroshima — the America of brutal military power.

But there's another America in the book, that of John Hersey. The America of looking at the destruction your nation has inflicted and telling it like it is. The America of stepping back and allowing someone else to tell their story through you because they have borne the tragedy and you have the power to bear witness to it. It is the America of the *New Yorker* of William Shawn, which, for the only time in its history, gave over an entire edition to a single article and kept its pages clear of its famed cartoons. It is the America which honored Hersey for his truth telling.

I grew up in Pakistan with two Americas. One was the America of *To Kill a Mockingbird*

This photograph was taken outside a shopping mall in Dubai in the United Arab Emirates.

How does the contrast in the images reflect some of the conflict between cultures that Shamsie describes in the article?

Steve Raymer/Corbis

and *Ferris Bueller's Day Off*, of the young Michael Jackson and Laura Ingalls Wilder, of *Charlie's Angels* and John McEnroe and Rob Lowe's blue eyes. Of Martin Luther King and Snoopy. That America was exuberance and possibility.

But there was another that I lived with. The America which cozied up to Pakistan's military dictator, Zia-ul-Haq, because it served its own interests in Afghanistan to do so. This America threw vast amounts of money at Zia, propping up his rule, strengthening his military, turning a blind eye to its nuclear program, working with him to promote the war in Afghanistan as a jihad for all Muslims rather than a territorial matter between Afghans and Soviets; this America spoke eloquently of the Afghan people's right to freedom and self-determination but decided it was an internal matter when Zia's government cracked down on pro-democracy protestors in Pakistan, or when he instituted public floggings and hangings, or when he passed a law which made it possible for a woman who had been raped to be stoned to death for adultery.

How to reconcile these two Americas? I didn't even try. It was a country I always looked at with one eye shut. With my left eye I saw the America of

John Hersey; with my right eye I saw the America of the two atom bombs. This one-eyed seeing was easy enough from a distance. But then I came to America as an undergraduate and realized that with a few honorable exceptions, all of America looked at America with one eye shut.

10   I don't mean Americans looked at America uncritically. I mean they looked at it merely in domestic terms.

Then, of course, there's [Hersey's] vision of the American army as a sort of United Colors of Benetton in the fall collection's Combat Pants.

I hadn't expected anyone in America to know anything about Pakistan's cultural life in the way that I knew about America's cultural life. In the 1980s at traffic lights in Karachi, barefoot children, many of them refugees from Afghanistan, sold paper masks of Sylvester Stallone as Rambo. As the unfortunate among you may know, *Rambo III* showed that great American icon fighting the Soviets in Afghanistan and was dedicated to "the brave Mujahideen fighters of Afghanistan," though Wikipedia informs me that after 9/11 this dedication was changed to "the people of Afghanistan." I haven't sat through the movie to determine the veracity of this claim. But anyway, yes, you could buy paper masks of Rambo at traffic lights. And young men in the heat of the Karachi sun wore leather jackets and pushed up their sleeves in imitation of Michael Jackson. I was never foolish enough to imagine that at traffic lights in America anyone was selling paper masks of Maula Jut, Pakistan's mustachioed cinema icon of the same period, or dancing while moving only their upper bodies in the manner of the sultry pop singer Nazia Hasan — whose below-the-waist gyrations didn't make it past Zia-ul-Haq's television censors. But I was startled to discover that when I said I was from Pakistan I was met with blankness — as if, in 1991, no one knew that through the 1980s Pakistan had been America's closest ally in its proxy war against the Soviets. I don't recall being too bothered by this. After all, it gave me a way of seeing which for a while was entirely satisfactory.

I had grown up in a country with military rule; I had grown up, that is to say, with the understanding that the government of a nation is a vastly different thing than its people. The government of America was a ruthless and morally bankrupt entity; but the people of America, well, they were different, they were better. They didn't think it was okay for America to talk democracy from one side of its mouth while heaping praise on totalitarian nightmares from the other side. They just didn't know it was happening, not really, not in any way that made it real to them. For a while this sufficed. I grumbled a little about American insularity. But it was an affectionate grumble. All nations have their failings. As a Pakistani, who was I to cast stones from my brittle, blood-tipped glass house?

Then came September 11, and for a few seconds, it brought this question: why do they hate us?

15   It's hard to remember this now, but it was a question asked loudly and genuinely, maybe not everywhere, certainly not by everyone, but by enough people. It was asked not only about the men on the planes but also about those people in the world who didn't fall over with weeping

but instead were seen to remark that now America, too, knew what it felt like to be attacked. It was asked, and very quickly it was answered: they hate our freedoms. And just like that a door was closed and a large sign pasted onto it saying, "You're Either With Us or Against Us." Anyone who hammered on the door with mention of the words "foreign policy" was accused of justifying the murder of more than three thousand people.

In this moment of darkness, I found myself looking to my tribe, my people. I found myself looking to writers. Where were the novels that could be proffered to people who asked, "Why

David Giles/Camera Press/Redux

This is a photograph of a police building in Tehran, Iran.

How does the image represent some of the anger in the Middle East that Shamsie describes in the essay?

do they hate us?", which is actually the question "Who are these people and what do they have to do with us?" No such novel, as far as I knew, had come from the post–Cold War generation of writers who started writing after the 1980s when Islam replaced Communism as the terrifying Other. But that would change, I told myself. The nation that had intervened militarily with more nations than any other in the latter half of the twentieth century but had itself come under attack infrequently would now see its stories bound up with the stories of other places. The writers would write. The novels would come.

They didn't. They haven't.

Let me make it clear what I'm not saying. I'm not saying September 11, the day itself in New York, is not itself a worthy subject for fiction. Only an idiot would say that. But just as the day itself is only one part of the genre of 9/11 nonfiction books, so it should be with fiction.

And here's another thing: does writing about the day itself preclude the possibility of entwining it with other stories? A friend of mine recently remarked in exasperation that the 9/11 novel in America is always ultimately a novel of trauma experienced by individuals. It could just as well be about an earthquake which occurred without warning, led to thousands of deaths and required great bravery from the emergency services. Well, but it really happened and an earthquake didn't, you might feel compelled to respond, and that's true. So let's say instead that, in American fiction, 9/11 is a traumatic event as ahistorical[1] as an earthquake.

20   Your soldiers will come to our lands, but your novelists won't. The unmanned drone hovering over Pakistan, controlled by someone in Langley, is an apt metaphor for America's imaginative engagement with my nation.

But I fear I'm falling into the American trap of focusing too much on 9/11 as though everything started there, and in the process I'm starting to sound as though I think the losses and traumas of that day should only be a side story in some other narrative. Neither of these positions are those I wish to claim. So let's approach it from another angle; let's return to that mask of Rambo.

I grew up in Pakistan in the 1980s, aware that thinking about my country's history and politics meant thinking about America's history and politics. This is not an unusual position. Many countries of the world from Asia to South America exist, or have existed, as American client states, have seen U.S.-backed coups, faced American

This editorial cartoon is titled *Problems of Globalization*. The figure number at the bottom of the image indicates that this is just one of many problems, as far as the artist is concerned.

What problem is the cartoon pointing out? How does this cartoon's claim relate to Shamsie's argument?

---

[1]ahistorical: Not concerned with or related to history, historical development, or historical context. —Eds.

missiles or sanctions, seen their government's policies on various matters dictated in Washington. America may not be an empire in the nineteenth century way which involved direct colonization. But the neo-imperialism of America was evident to me by the time I was an adolescent and able to understand these things.

So in an America where fiction writers are so caught up in the Idea of America in a way that perhaps has no parallel with any other national fiction, where the term Great American Novel weighs heavily on writers, why is it that the fiction writers of my generation are so little concerned with the history of their own nation once that history exits the fifty states? It's not because of a lack of dramatic potential in those stories of America in the World; that much is clear.

In part, I'm inclined to blame the trouble caused by that pernicious word "appropriation." I first encountered it within a writing context within weeks, perhaps days, of arriving at Hamilton College in 1991. Right away, I knew there was something deeply damaging in the idea that writers couldn't take on stories about the Other. As a South Asian who has encountered more than her fair share of awful stereotypes about South Asians in the British empire novels of the nineteenth and twentieth centuries, I'm certainly not about to disagree with the charge that writers who are implicated in certain power structures have been guilty of writing fiction which supports, justifies and props up those power structures. I understand the concerns of people who feel that for too long stories have been told about them rather than by them. But it should be clear that the response to this is for writers to write differently, to write better, to critique the power structures rather than propping them up, to move beyond stereotype — which you need to do for purely technical reasons, because the novel doesn't much like stereotypes. They come across as bad writing.

25   The moment you say, a male American writer can't write about a female Pakistani, you are saying, Don't tell those stories. Worse, you're saying, as an American male you can't understand a Pakistani woman. She is enigmatic, inscrutable, unknowable. She's other. Leave her and her nation to its Otherness. Write them out of your history.

Perhaps it's telling that the first mainstream American writer to try and enter the perspective of the Other post 9/11 belonged to an older generation, less weighed down, I suspect, by ideas of appropriation: I mean John Updike, with his novel *Terrorist*. I confess I didn't get past the first few pages — the figure of the young Muslim seemed such an accumulation of stereotype that it struck me as rather poor writing. And, of course, it was a story about America with the Muslim posited as the Violent and Hate-Filled Other. Far more successful attempts to portray Muslims in America came later, again — there really is a paper to be written about this — from women writers: first, Lorraine Adams's *Harbor*, and then the wonderful *The Submission* by Amy Waldman, a breakthrough novel in the 9/11 genre, published in 2011, in which we have both the secular, ambitious, and very defensive Muslim American architect and a Bangladeshi 9/11 widow who is an illegal alien. So there have been writers who have moved the roadblock of appropriation and written about Muslims in America, and done it well. But there have been far too few of them.

The stories of America in the World rather than the World in America stubbornly remain the domain of nonfiction. Your soldiers will come to our lands, but your novelists won't. The unmanned drone hovering over Pakistan, controlled by someone in Langley, is an apt metaphor for America's imaginative engagement with my nation. [. . .]

Where is the American writer who looks on his or her country with two eyes, one shaped by the experience of living here, the other filled with the sad knowledge of what this country looks like when it's not at home. Where is the

American writer who can tell you about the places your nation invades or manipulates, brings you into those stories and lets you draw breath with its characters? [. . .]

Someone, many someones, should be writing those many different books about America.

30 Many someones are. But not in America. [. . .]

So why is it, please explain, that you're in our stories but we're not in yours?

Fear of appropriation? I think that argument can only take you so far. Surely fiction writers today understand the value of stories about America In the World, and can see through the appropriation argument. It is, after all, a political argument that can easily be trumped by another political argument about the importance of engagement. So why, then — why, when there are astonishing stories out in the world about America, to do with America, going straight to the heart of the question: who are these people and what do they have to do with us? — why are the fiction writers staying away from the stories? The answer, I think, comes from John Hersey. He said of novelists, "A writer is bound to have varying degrees of success, and I think that that is partly an issue of how central the burden of the story is to the author's psyche."

And that's the answer. Even now, you just don't care very much about us. One eye remains closed. The pen, writing its deliberate sentences, is icy cold.

Understanding and Interpreting

1 What leads Shamsie to read John Hersey's book *Hiroshima?* What was she hoping to learn?

2 Shamsie says that Hersey is "so good at [. . .] transparency, that [. . .] it almost becomes possible to forget the nationality of the writer" (par. 4). First, how does she say Hersey achieves this transparency? Second, why does Shamsie say that this transparency is a positive achievement?

3 Shamsie says that Hersey represents one of two different Americas. What is the America that Hersey represents, and what is the other?

4 According to Shamsie, what makes 9/11 a difficult but worthy topic to write about for American authors?

5 According to Shamsie, what is the difference between stories of "America in the World" and "the World in America" (par. 27)? Which category fits for John Hersey? Which one for John Updike?

6 Another possible title of this piece could be "One Eye Shut." How does Shamsie use this phrase in this essay, and how does it reflect the overall message she wants to communicate?

Analyzing Language, Style, and Structure

1 Shamsie includes several moments of personal narrative within this argumentative essay about the role of fiction in our lives. Identify one place where she inserts her own story into the argument and evaluate how effective or ineffective this section is at helping to convince her audience.

2 There are several places in this essay where Shamsie describes growing up in Pakistan. What information does she share about her homeland, and how does this establish her ethos as a writer?

3 Shamsie does not mention 9/11, the main topic of her essay, until almost halfway through. How does the information she presents first establish the context for what happens in the second half of her essay?

4 A key word that Shamsie uses is "appropriation." How does she use this term to illustrate the theme of the piece? What examples does she provide? What is an opposite of the word "appropriation"?

5 Skim back through the piece and identify the places where Shamsie uses "you" and "our." What patterns do you identify and how does her use of pronouns relate to her purpose for writing?

6 How would you characterize Shamsie's tone toward America? What about her tone toward American writers? What evidence from the essay supports your interpretation?

Connecting, Arguing, and Extending

1 Skim back through the stories that you have read so far in this textbook. Which ones are stories of "America in the World" and which ones are stories of "the World in America" as Shamsie defines these terms? Explain your reasoning.

2 While she asks the question rhetorically in the essay, how would you respond to Shamsie when she writes, "So why is it, please explain, that you're in our stories but we're not in yours" (par. 31)?

3 Write an argument in which you make and support a claim about how America seems to view the Middle East, and whether that view has changed during your lifetime. Use the news media as well as representations of the Middle East in popular culture such as movies, television shows, and video games.

4 While it may be a cliché, the phrase "history is written by the victors" is an idea with which Shamsie would likely agree. Research some "victors" who got to write history. Explain what happened, and how they put their own spin on how the events were told.

Dulce et Decorum Est

Wilfred Owen

Wilfred Owen (1893–1918) was a poet who served on the front lines during World War I and was killed in action just one week before the official end to the war. His poems, almost all of which were published after his death, portray the brutality of World War I, including poison gas attacks and trench warfare.

KEY CONTEXT   Owen's work is in direct contrast to the patriotism that normally surrounds war; one of his poems, "Anthem for Doomed Youth," begins with this question and answer:

> What passing-bells for these who die as cattle?
> Only the monstrous anger of the guns.
> Only the stuttering rifles' rapid rattle
> Can patter out their hasty orisons.[1]

This piece, Dulce et Decorum Est, written while Owen was in the hospital recuperating from shell shock (now called post-traumatic stress disorder), is probably the most famous World War I poem. The last two lines, *"Dulce et decorum est / Pro patria mori,"* are written in Latin and are often translated as "Sweet and proper it is to die for one's country."

---

[1] orisons: Prayers. —Eds.

Bent double, like old beggars under sacks,
Knock-kneed, coughing like hags, we cursed through sludge,
Till on the haunting flares we turned our backs
And towards our distant rest began to trudge.
5 Men marched asleep. Many had lost their boots
But limped on, blood-shod. All went lame; all blind;
Drunk with fatigue; deaf even to the hoots
Of tired, outstripped Five-Nines[2] that dropped behind.

Gas! Gas! Quick, boys! — An ecstasy of fumbling,
10 Fitting the clumsy helmets just in time;
But someone still was yelling out and stumbling,
And flound'ring like a man in fire or lime[3] —
Dim, through the misty panes and thick green light,
As under a green sea, I saw him drowning.

15 In all my dreams, before my helpless sight,
He plunges at me, guttering, choking, drowning.

If in some smothering dreams you too could pace
Behind the wagon that we flung him in,
And watch the white eyes writhing in his face,
20 His hanging face, like a devil's sick of sin;
If you could hear, at every jolt, the blood
Come gargling from the froth-corrupted lungs,
Obscene as cancer, bitter as the cud
Of vile, incurable sores on innocent tongues, —

Library of Congress Prints and Photographs Division, LC-USZC4-10915

What argument is this poster making, both visually and verbally? What appeals does it rely upon? How is this argument similar to or different from the argument Owen cites in the final lines of his poem?

---

[2] Five-Nines: German artillery shells used in World War I. —Eds.
[3] lime: Also known as calcium oxide, lime is a chemical compound that both sanitizes and dissolves tissue. In World War I, it was often used in the trenches to sanitize the fallen soldiers' bodies — this helped stave off the constant threat of disease as well as mitigate the smell. —Eds.

25 My friend, you would not tell with such high zest
To children ardent for some desperate glory,
The old Lie: *Dulce et decorum est*
Pro patria mori.

Understanding and Interpreting

1 What is the "old Lie" (ll. 27–28)? According to the speaker, who tells this lie and to whom? Why is it an "old" lie?

2 How would you characterize the speaker? What are his motivations for focusing on the details he does?

3 Throughout the poem, there is a sense of helplessness in the face of the overwhelming brutality of war. Identify and explain places where this helplessness is demonstrated.

Analyzing Language, Style, and Structure

1 Trace the speaker's use of pronouns in this poem. It starts with "we," moves to "I" and "me" in the middle, and finally concludes with "you." How does this shift in pronouns reflect the poem's theme?

2 The speaker uses a stark, unflinching, and bitter tone toward war. Choose at least two similes and explain how those similes establish the intended tone.

3 Most of the stanzas in the poem are six or more lines, except the third stanza, which is only two lines long. What does this choice of a shorter stanza reveal about the speaker?

4 How does the strict and formal A/B rhyme scheme create tension with the poem's graphic and chaotic descriptions of war?

Connecting, Arguing, and Extending

1 It's clear that in stanza 3, the speaker is suffering from what people in Owen's time called "shell shock," though today we call it "post-traumatic stress disorder." Conduct brief research on how doctors have improved their diagnoses and treatments of PTSD in the years since World War I. What is the current recommended treatment?

2 The speaker of the poem calls the idea that is sweet and honorable to die for your country "the old Lie." Write an argument about whether Owen was right or wrong to call it a lie. Was Owen just a product

of an extremely brutal war? Are there times when the lie is true?

3 If you were to listen to a reading of "Dulce et Decorum Est" with your eyes closed, you could probably picture it in your mind as if it were a movie because of the graphic details Owens uses. Draw a storyboard of at least three shots or frames of a film that would capture the imagery and the tone of the poem. Also, describe the sound and/or music that would accompany the images in your movie.

The St. Crispin's Day Speech

William Shakespeare

William Shakespeare (1564–1616) is considered one of the greatest playwrights in history. His plays *Romeo and Juliet*, *Macbeth*, *Hamlet*, *Julius Caesar*, *Othello*, and many others are among the most widely read and performed plays in the English language. While many of his well-known works are tragedies, Shakespeare also wrote comedies and a number of plays that focus on English history, specifically the many wars fought for the English throne.

Portrait of William Shakespeare (oil on canvas), Taylor, John (d. 1651) (after)/Private Collection/Photo © Philip Mould Ltd, London/Bridgeman Images

KEY CONTEXT   The excerpt that follows is from the historical play *Henry V*, which is about the war between England and France in the 1400s. This scene from the play takes place just before the Battle of Agincourt, in which the advancing English army is about to face the French forces that greatly outnumber them. Hearing about their disadvantage, one of the English lords says that he wishes that they had "But one ten thousand of those men in England / That do no work to-day!" At this point, sensing his men's concern, King Henry V enters to try to inspire his troops to fight. This speech, often called "The St. Crispin's Day Speech," is one of the most famous in English literature.

Despite their overwhelming disadvantage in numbers, the British were victorious at Agincourt. While Shakespeare might attribute the success to Henry's inspirational speech before the battle, history tells us that his army had mastered the use of the English longbow, a relatively new weapon at the time.

The English camp.

Enter Gloucester, Bedford, Exeter, Erpingham, with all his host: Salisbury and Westmoreland

GLOUCESTER Where is the king?

BEDFORD The king himself is rode to view their battle.

WESTMORELAND Of fighting men they have full three score thousand.

EXETER There's five to one; besides, they all are fresh.

5 **SALISBURY** God's arm strike with us! 'tis a fearful odds.
God be wi' you, princes all; I'll to my charge:
If we no more meet till we meet in heaven,
Then, joyfully, my noble Lord of Bedford,
My dear Lord Gloucester, and my good Lord Exeter,
10 And my kind kinsman, warriors all, adieu!

BEDFORD Farewell, good Salisbury; and good luck go with thee!

EXETER Farewell, kind lord; fight valiantly to-day:
And yet I do thee wrong to mind thee of it,
For thou art framed of the firm truth of valour.

Exit Salisbury

15 **BEDFORD** He is full of valour as of kindness;
Princely in both.

Enter the King

WESTMORELAND O that we now had here
But one ten thousand of those men in England
That do no work to-day!
20 **KING HENRY V** What's he that wishes so?
My cousin Westmoreland? No, my fair cousin:
If we are mark'd to die, we are enow

To do our country loss; and if to live,
The fewer men, the greater share of honour.
25 God's will! I pray thee, wish not one man more.
By Jove, I am not covetous for gold,
Nor care I who doth feed upon my cost;
It yearns me not if men my garments wear;
Such outward things dwell not in my desires:
30 But if it be a sin to covet honour,
I am the most offending soul alive.
No, faith, my coz, wish not a man from England:
God's peace! I would not lose so great an honour
As one man more, methinks, would share from me
35 For the best hope I have. O, do not wish one more!
Rather proclaim it, Westmoreland, through my host,
That he which hath no stomach to this fight,
Let him depart; his passport shall be made
And crowns for convoy put into his purse:
40 We would not die in that man's company
That fears his fellowship to die with us.
This day is called the feast of Crispian:
He that outlives this day, and comes safe home,
Will stand a tip-toe when the day is named,
45 And rouse him at the name of Crispian.
He that shall live this day, and see old age,
Will yearly on the vigil feast his neighbours,
And say "To-morrow is Saint Crispian:"
Then will he strip his sleeve and show his scars.

50 And say "These wounds I had on Crispin's day."
Old men forget: yet all shall be forgot,
But he'll remember with advantages
What feats he did that day: then shall our names,
Familiar in his mouth as household words
55 Harry the king, Bedford and Exeter,
Warwick and Talbot, Salisbury and Gloucester,
Be in their flowing cups freshly remember'd.
This story shall the good man teach his son;
And Crispin Crispian shall ne'er go by,
60 From this day to the ending of the world,

But we in it shall be remember'd;
We few, we happy few, we band of brothers;
For he to-day that sheds his blood with me
Shall be my brother; be he ne'er so vile,
65 This day shall gentle his condition:
And gentlemen in England now a-bed
Shall think themselves accursed they were not
here,
And hold their manhoods cheap whiles any
speaks
That fought with us upon Saint Crispin's day.

seeing connections

Read the last paragraph of Abraham Lincoln's Gettysburg Address, considered by many to be among the best speeches ever delivered. Lincoln gave his speech to dedicate a memorial for the soldiers who died at Gettysburg in 1863, at a time when the United States was still in the middle of the Civil War. He knew his speech would be widely reported, and his audience included those on both sides of the conflict.

Compare Lincoln's arguments about why the war ought to continue with Henry's arguments in "The Saint Crispin's Day Speech."

Library of Congress Prints and Photographs Division, LC-USZ62-2006

But, in a larger sense, we can not dedicate, we can not consecrate—,we can not hallow—this ground. The brave men, living and dead, who struggled here, have consecrated it, far above our poor power to add or detract. The world will little note, nor long remember what we say here, but it can never forget what they did here. It is for us the living, rather, to be dedicated here to the unfinished work which they who fought here have thus far so nobly advanced. It is rather for us to be here dedicated to the great task remaining before us—that from these honored dead we take increased devotion to that cause for which they here gave the last full measure of devotion—that we here highly resolve that these dead shall not have died in vain—that this nation, under God, shall have a new birth of freedom, and that government of the people, by the people, for the people, shall not perish from the earth.

Understanding and Interpreting

1 In the lines before Henry starts his speech, we hear from some of his noblemen. What fears do they express and to what extent is Henry able to alleviate their fears in his speech?

2 Rewrite the following lines into your own words and explain what Henry is saying:

a. By Jove, I am not covetous for gold,
Nor care I who doth feed upon my cost;
It yearns me not if men my garments wear;
Such outward things dwell not in my desires:
But if it be a sin to covet honour,
I am the most offending soul alive.

b. He that shall live this day, and see old age,
Will yearly on the vigil feast his neighbours,
And say "To-morrow is Saint Crispian:"
Then will he strip his sleeve and show his scars.
And say "These wounds I had on Crispin's day."
Old men forget: yet all shall be forgot,
But he'll remember with advantages
What feats he did that day.

c. This story shall the good man teach his son;
And Crispin Crispian shall ne'er go by,
From this day to the ending of the world,
But we in it shall be remember'd;
We few, we happy few, we band of brothers;
For he to-day that sheds his blood with me
Shall be my brother; be he ne'er so vile.

3 One of the major arguments Henry puts forward to convince his men to fight is seen in the line, "and if to live, / The fewer men, the greater share of honour" (ll. 23–24). What conclusion is Henry hoping his men draw from this line?

4 From a practical standpoint, the majority of Henry's army would have consisted not of noblemen like himself, but poor peasants who likely would never have even seen Henry before if it weren't for this war. What did Henry include in his speech to appeal to this aspect of his audience?

Analyzing Language, Style, and Structure

1 Reread lines 26–29. How does Henry establish his ethos with his audience?

2 How does the idea Henry presents in lines 30–31 contrast with lines 26–29? What is the purpose of this contrast?

3 What does Henry propose to his men in lines 36–41? Why is this an effective rhetorical strategy for Henry to use in this context?

4 After line 41, there is a shift in topic from dying in battle to living through the battle. What is the importance of this shift at just about the halfway point in the speech?

5 In lines 55–56, Henry includes a series of names. What purpose does the inclusion of these names serve?

6 Reread lines 61–62. The word "we" is repeated four times and rhymed with "me" in line 63. What is the effect of this repetition and the rhyming?

Connecting, Arguing, and Extending

1 Locate advertisements for the United States military online, in magazines, or in other sources. In what ways are their appeals similar to or different from the claims that Henry makes in this speech?

2 What is an argument that could be used against Henry? Why should the mostly peasant army not fight on behalf of the royal family? Write a response that someone in Henry's audience who opposes Henry's argument might have made. If you want, you can choose to write the response in poetic form to match Shakespeare's style.

3 Imagine that you are a newspaper reporter who has just witnessed Henry's speech. Write a headline and article about it. Be sure to include an interview with one of Henry's men.

4 Shakespeare rarely includes stage directions other than "enter," "exit," and "dies." What are some significant stage directions that you could imagine including? Focus on Henry's actions, gestures, and interactions with his audience, as well as any movements and responses from his audience.

The Man Who Stained His Soul

Vu Bao

Translated by Ho Anh Thai and edited by Wayne Karlin

A soldier for the North Vietnamese in the wars against both France and the United States, Vu Bao (b. 1926) authored six novels. He was also the vice chairman of the Hanoi Writer's Association and editor in chief of the Vietnam Cinema Committee. The short story "The Man Who Stained His Soul" first appeared in *Van Nghe*, a Vietnamese journal of literature and art, in 1992, and was then reprinted in the anthology *The Other Side of Heaven: Post-War Fiction by Vietnamese and American Writers* in 1995.

If everything had gone as we'd planned, I would have nothing now to write about the battle against Che post that year.

Painstakingly accurate plans had been drawn up under the close guidance of the Command Staff. New intelligence about shifts in the enemy's effective strength and weaponry was received every day. The diagram of Che post's defenses was drawn and redrawn so many times it reached a point of absolute perfection. Each enemy fire point was scouted over and over and marked by a different symbol on the diagram. Victory couldn't be more certain.

But war isn't a game in which only one side fires and the other eats bullets. The enemy major in charge of Che post was an experienced soldier. Ignoring the deliberate provocations of our recons-by-fire,[1] he kept the two heavy machine guns he had concealed in the command bunker silent. It wasn't until our company burst through the barbed wire and advanced to the center of the compound in an arrow-shape formation that those guns opened up, catching us in a cross fire.

Our attack was stopped dead. The company was pinned down, with everyone's belly glued to the earth and no one daring to lift his head. It was a miracle we could keep our heads and limbs intact without breathing dirt.

5   This tactic hadn't been anticipated in the combat plan, and now the commanders couldn't react. Usually, once the company engaged, the Party cell would confer urgently, exchange ideas and make timely decisions. But this time, Luat, the company commander, was stuck with our front unit, the commissar was in the rear of the formation, and the deputy commissar was helping to get the wounded dragged out of the barbed wire and bandaged up. Pulling out his revolver, the commissar fired up into the air and sprang forward, yelling: "Comrades, advance . . ."

His order was cut short by a bullet.

Luat crawled down the column to me and jerked his chin at the fire point: "Take out the left side and leave the right to me."

We divided the front unit into two V-shaped lines. Half of the men crept after Luat, the other half after me. Only Vinh lay prostrate in his place.

I crawled back to him.

10   "What the hell are you doing?"

Vinh's voice was strained. "How can we advance — the bullets are pouring in like rain."

"Would you rather lie here waiting for death?"

"Death's waiting up there also."

With the bullets zeroing in on us, this wasn't the time or place to try to turn a coward into a brave soldier. "Give me your cartridge belt and grenades," I yelled at him.

15   "Then I'll be killed in the enemy's counterattack."

---

[1] **recons-by-fire:** Short for reconnaisance-by-fire and also known as speculative fire, this battle tactic entails firing on likely enemy positions to provoke a reaction and thus confirm the enemy's presence and position. —Eds.

My blood was boiling. I yanked his sub-machine gun from his hands. "I have to advance. Hang onto the company flag."

I crawled low under the fire, keeping my eyes on the muzzle flashes. Suddenly the fire pecking at us from the bunker's loophole ceased. The enemy gunners must have been changing the belt. I sprang up and rushed the bunker. Someone threw a grenade at me. I snatched it up and tossed it back into the loop-hole. Then I thrust the barrel of my rifle through the opening and sprayed in a full magazine, sweeping the area inside.

Shouts of joy sounded from all around. Fourth Company had penetrated the base. But what followed was our hardest battle. We struggled to take one fortified position after another, and it was nearly morning before we managed to blow up their headquarters.

Afterwards, the battalion commander ran up to us. "Hurry and scrounge up whatever supplies and equipment you can," he said. "It's nearly dawn — you'll start shitting when the enemy's long range artillery begins firing."

20 I turned around to see Vinh standing nearby. His left trouser leg was sticking like glue to his thigh. I tore out the bandage I had tucked into my belt.

Luat seized my hand. "Don't bother. He just pissed himself," he said, nodding at Vinh's satu-rated trouser. "Pissed on his own soul."

We withdrew to Noi hamlet, four kilometers from Che post. Air raid shelters had been dug there by the local militia. Those units that had been held in reserve during the attack were now sent out to guard the perimeter of the hamlet, and huge sauce pans full of chicken gruel were prepared for us in each house. But after our night of shooting, crawling and rolling through the mud, we could only take a few perfunctory mouthfuls. It was better to sleep than to eat. As soon as we lay down on our straw mats, we didn't know if heaven was up or earth was down.

Suddenly I was awakened by someone pulling me to my feet. Still in a daze, my eyes half-sealed, I dimly heard Luat order me to get the unit dressed in full uniform and equipment. "Get everybody over to battalion headquarters — they have a new job for you."

"Yes, commander."

25 When we arrived at headquarters, the battalion commander told me that a foreign comrade had come to shoot a documentary film. Since the battle was over, it would be necessary to reconstruct the fighting for him. The first shot would be the raising of the company flag over the roof of Che post.

I stood dumbfounded for a moment. "Commander, after the fighting we policed up the battlefield and returned here at once. We didn't have time to raise a flag."

"Then you'll have to raise one now."

"Sir, we don't have a flag."

"What do you mean — what about the Victory flag the regimental commander handed to you before you left? Didn't he give it to you, unit commander, in front of all your men?"

30 "I passed it to Vinh when the C.O. ordered us to advance. After I took out the heavy machine gun, the rest of the company charged forward. Vinh came along with them, but he forgot to bring the flag."

"Why didn't you look for it?"

"I did, but I couldn't find it. When I went back to that place, all I saw were three mortar craters."

The battalion commander turned to the press liaison officer and told him to get Third Company's Victory flag instead.

The foreign comrade was waiting for us at regi-mental headquarters. Smiling, he shook our hands. "Glory to Vietnam; of thou I'm proud," he said.

35 We tightened our lips to keep from bursting into laughter.

The "reconstruction" of the flag-raising didn't go as easily as we thought it would. The machine gun company took positions along the outer perimeter. The heavy artillery company set up four observation posts to watch for air raids. An infantry company deployed inside Che post, ready to take on any enemy parachutists who

seeing connections

One of the most lasting and iconic images in American history is the raising of the flag at Iwo Jima during World War II. But that famous photograph, which won the Pulitzer Prize and was widely reprinted to help the war effort, was actually the second picture taken that day of the flag raising, similar to the reenactment of the flag raising in this short story. The first was taken early in the morning, while the second was at a different location with a much larger flag.

Looking at the two images, what are their similarities and differences? What "story" does each image tell about war and American military power? Is the second photograph any less "true" because it was re-created? Explain.

might try to pounce upon us. And our unit, directed by the foreign comrade, had the task of reenacting the destruction of the command bunker. Unfortunately, when the explosive charges were blown, a piece of concrete from the bunker hurled itself at my knee, knocking me to the ground. I immediately tried to rise, but I couldn't stay on my feet. A medic helped me off the site and stopped my bleeding with a bandage. But I was unable to act in the next scene.

Luat asked the interpreter if the director would like to chose another soldier to raise the flag. The foreign comrade nodded and strolled along our ranks, gazing at us one by one. He turned and came down the line once again, then stopped in front of Vinh and pointed at his chest.

"All right. This soldier will be the flag bearer."

Before we began the reenactment again, the battalion commander reiterated once again how important making the film was, how it would be seen all over the world. Any idea the director had was to be obeyed as strictly as an order on the battlefield.

40   Luat raised his hand, as if to object, but dropped it back down. After that, he didn't seem to act out his role with any enthusiasm.

The sappers[2] exploded eight "square cakes" (satchel charges) around the post, allowing the cameraman to shoot the scene through a haze of smoke and fire.

Then came the raising-of-the-flag scene. Under the foreign comrade's direction, Luat waved his revolver and sprang forward, followed by Vinh, raising his flag pole high, and then the rest of the unit. Stop, the director called. Then—action! Vinh scrambled up to the roof of the headquarters bunker and struck the enemy's flag pole with the sole of his foot, sending their flag to the ground. With his legs firmly spread, he stood and waved the Victory flag. The rest of the unit flanked him on both sides. They raised their submachine guns and shouted joyfully.

But the scene had to be reshot three times, as we seemed somewhat sluggish. Taking Che post had been a difficult task, the director explained through the interpreter. Could we please then try a little harder to demonstrate to the whole world how high the morale was in our army?

Finally the filming was over. Staggering with fatigue, we stumbled back to Noi hamlet. Before packing up his equipment, the foreign comrade shook our hands.

45 "Glory to Vietnam. Of thou I'm proud."

Soon after we were back in battle and had no time to think about that scene. We were happy enough after a fight to simply find that our friends had come through intact. Then the war ended and after a while we turned in our rifles and came home and each of us tried to find ways to make a living. We forgot all about the flag raising at Che post.

One day, not long after the war, I was getting my hair cut and reading a newspaper to pass the time. A large headline flashed up at me. The documentary film *The Path of Blood and Fire* had just premiered. The words "Of thou I'm proud" came unbidden into my mind. Under the headline was a photograph of Vinh, spreading his legs on the roof of the headquarters' bunker,

waving the Victory flag. He was flanked on both sides by my friends, raising their submachine guns, shouting joyfully.

I knew it was merely a reenactment of the battle. But still my heart beat swiftly in my chest as I read the caption: "A still from *The Path of Blood and Fire*: 'Raising the flag at Che post.' "

I felt it wasn't worth talking about. Like most veterans, my life was taken up with a day by day struggle just to make ends meet. None of us displayed our citations on the wall or pinned our medals on our chests. It was better to spend our energy keeping our plates full. At any rate, the movies were always full of such tricks and gimmicks. When the pig shed in my village cooperative had been filmed, the crew had gathered the biggest pigs from each family and stuck them all together, rubbing crushed garlic on their mouths to keep them from biting each other. And when they'd wanted to shoot our model fish pond, they'd brought baskets full of huge fish and loaded them into the boats so it looked as if the fish had been drawn into the boats with nets.

50 The victory over Che post had not only been the proudest moment of our battalion, but of the entire division. The division commander had even had the photo of the flag raising enlarged to the size of a double bed sheet and displayed on the center wall of the division museum. The veterans of the engagement knew very well that it was only a reenacted scene. But raw recruits gazed admiringly at Vinh waving the Victory flag and thought the photo had been taken on the spot, under enemy fire.

That still from the film was, admittedly, very beautiful: a People's Army soldier standing dignified and undaunted on top of the enemy's headquarters. One artist used the photograph as a model for a drawing put on a stamp to be distributed on Army Day. It was also featured in calendars, though after the veterans saw that they began to mutter among themselves. Finally, on Division Day, they approached the commissar. He shrugged and said that it was up to the artists

---

[2] sappers: Specialists in military fortifications, construction, and demolition. —Eds.

to decide what particular images and symbols should be used — it wasn't possible to capture the entire division in one photograph.

Twenty years passed.

One day a director named T. Stevenson came to Vietnam to shoot a film called *Blood and Flowers*. After visiting several studios to view films made during the war, he asked the Minister of Culture to arrange interviews with those people who were in the sequences he wished to buy.

The ministry telephoned the army's political department, which in turn rang up the division. By this time, the old commanders had retired and their replacements believed it had been Vinh who'd advanced through enemy fire to plant the flag on Che post. The division commander ordered his political officers to locate Vinh and bring him to headquarters in order to meet Stevenson.

55 The original *Blood and Fire* was screened again, all over the country.

And everything Vinh told Stevenson fit the reenactment filmed by the foreign comrade, as if it had all really occurred. He managed to forget that at the time he had been glued to the earth, so filled with fear that he'd pissed on his own soul.

Luat came to see me. "Vinh must have thought we'd all died," he said.

I tried to console him. "What earthly good can the truth of the matter do for us soldiers now?"

"If something that we saw with our own eyes can be distorted this way, then what can happen to other events that happened fifty or a hundred years ago? I've written a letter to the Central Committee confirming that there was no flag raising at Che post. Will you sign it?"

60 "All right — I'll sign."

"Good. Add your rank, please, and the code word for our unit."

I wrote it all down. Months later, I found out that Luat's wife had had to sell their only pig in order to finance Luat's trips to visit his former comrades-in-arms and get their signatures. He made scores of copies of his letter and sent them all to the appropriate agencies.

The whole division was thrown into an uproar. But no one dared take down the huge photograph hanging in the Division Museum. And no one dared throw away the millions of stamps and thousands of calendars that had been printed.

The division commander arranged a private meeting with us. He asked us not to put everyone into a quandary. The attack against Che post had been the largest battle in the history of the division; it was the pride of the entire unit. Although he couldn't take down the photograph right at the moment, he assured us he would eventually find a substitute.

65 But I was certain one would never be found, not in a hundred years.

One day, Luat's son rushed to my house.

"Uncle, there's something wrong with my father's stomach. He asked to see you before he went onto the operating table."

I cycled over to the hospital.

Luat signalled to me to approach his bed. He grasped my hand firmly.

70 "You're a writer. You should never write a half-truth or turn a lie into truth. You have to write what you saw: there was no flag raising at Che post. Write it immediately and read it to me."

"Don't speak so ominously. A lie can't be corrected in a day. But don't worry, of course I'll write about it."

The operation was successful. Luat survived. The photo of Vinh waving the flag still hangs in the Division Museum. And recently, Vinh was invited by Stevenson to visit the director's country and talk about the flag raising as a way of promoting *Blood and Flowers*. He was lucky, that guy. If he'd been so mortified and humiliated when I'd asked him to give me his cartridge belt and grenades that he'd gotten up and charged the loophole and blocked it with his body, he wouldn't have been alive now to brag to foreigners.

Abroad, how can people know that Vinh pissed on his own soul and his trousers were only a prop?

Understanding and Interpreting

1 The first third of this story presents the "truth" of the battle of the Che post as recounted by the narrator. Explain how each of the following versions changed the original story and explain why each change was made:

a. The reenactment the day after the battle

b. The still from the first documentary film hanging in the division museum

c. The stamp based on the photograph

d. Vinh's interview for the second documentary, *Blood and Flowers*

e. The story that the narrator agrees to write, presumably "The Man Who Stained His Soul."

2 In what ways would Luat, the company commander, have felt differently if the narrator had been the one in the re-created battle instead of Vinh? Provide evidence for your inference.

3 Luat and the narrator seem to have different opinions about Vinh, especially about his actions long after the war ended. Explain each man's feelings about Vinh and locate evidence from the story to support your interpretation.

4 What is author Vu Bao suggesting in this text about the importance of truth, especially during war? What evidence from the text supports your statement of theme?

Analyzing Language, Style, and Structure

1 Twice the narrator includes the line spoken by the foreign comrade, "Glory to Vietnam; of thou I'm proud." Though the narrator never explicitly says, what can you infer about his attitude toward that character?

2 How might the author, Vu Bao, define "heroism," based on your reading of this story? Support your response with specific language choices from the text.

3 What is the narrator's tone toward Vinh in the last two paragraphs of the story? What word choice illustrates this tone and how does this tone help to support the theme of the story?

4 Even though the narrator was a soldier in the war, he uses a detached tone, almost like a dispassionate reporter. Identify places in this story where the narrator reveals this tone and explain the word choice and/or sentence structure that helps to create this tone.

Connecting, Arguing, and Extending

1 The ancient Greek playwright Aeschylus said, "In a war, truth is the first casualty." Throughout Vu Bao's story, people are intentionally altering the truth of the battle for their own purposes, some personal and some political. Write an argument about the value or unimportance of truth during wartime. Is it OK to lie or manipulate the truth of events during war if the lie might lead to a better outcome for one side of the conflict? Use this story as evidence to support your argument.

2 A major plot point in this story revolves around how characters view the reenactment of the battle for the first documentary film, *The Path of Blood and Fire*. Think about examples of documentaries you have seen that have used re-creations and reenactments. What are their roles and purposes? Are they ethical to use?

3 According to the narrator, the still photograph from the documentary, which shows Vinh raising the flag, takes on a life of its own after the war. Is a picture really worth a thousand words? Can a photograph be more successful than words in communicating ideas? Can it be less successful? Research and explain famous photographs in history to support your position.

4 In the famous 1962 film *The Man Who Shot Liberty Valance*, a newspaper editor says, "When the legend becomes fact, print the legend." How could this attitude be applied to this short story? Which characters would agree with the line from the film and which ones would disagree?

5 Although the war during which this story is set is called the "Vietnam War" in the United States, the Vietnamese often call it the "American War." Americans rarely hear stories from the war from the Vietnamese perspective. How did reading this story, which presents the perspective of Vietnamese soldiers, make you feel? What expectations, assumptions, or questions did the story raise for you? Why?

Deuce Out

Katey Schultz

Writer Katey Schultz (b. 1979) was born in Portland, Oregon, and most recently has lived in North Carolina. In 2013, she published her first collection of short stories, *Flashes of War*, which was named the Gold Medal Book of the Year in Literary Fiction by the Military Writers Society of America. This story from that collection, "Deuce Out," is about Steph Bowlin, a teenager whose brother goes off to war in Afghanistan.

Courtesy Katey Schultz

When we moved to Oregon four years ago, rain came with the lifestyle. Now it seemed a part of us. My brother Dustin wouldn't know what to make of the climate when he shipped out to Afghanistan. He'd be in the southern part of the country, near the Iranian border. We knew that much. But the sun burned long and hot there with sandstorms whipping across the plateau. I read about it once. How the storms move with such velocity that grains of sand push into every exposed millimeter of flesh. Fingernails, eardrums, nostrils, eyeballs. Tiny rocks needling beneath the skin that threaten infection, the slow death of any soldier.

Dustin left on a Tuesday morning at 1100 hours. I watched him settle behind the wheel of his Nissan Sentra and back down our driveway, wiper blades fanning across the windshield in a frenzied, farewell wave. Dad rode with him to the bus station in Newberg, just a few miles away. I trailed the sound of the muffler growing softer through the wet, winter morning, then turned toward the front door and braced myself for the sight of Mom. She'd be at the kitchen table or maybe the counter this time. Either way her expression stayed the same: face sagging around two eyes that looked right past you. Without Dustin around, I'd have to cope with her doom and gloom alone. I stepped into the house and pulled the door shut behind me. The latch clicked quietly into place, but by the way it sent shivers up my spine it could have been the pin of a grenade pulled free.

Dustin used to drop me off at school on his way to the community college, but now I was on my own. The Nissan sputtered and jerked as I grew familiar with the clutch. The defroster was broken again, and I struggled to see through the steamy windows. It made Newberg look like a town on the verge of collapse, a sinkhole waiting to happen. I hadn't even balanced my first algebraic equation of the day and it was already mid-afternoon in Afghanistan, the hottest part of Dustin's day. I parked in the student lot at 0800 hours and listened to the rain ping against the roof of the car. In the back of my mind I could hear Dustin coaxing me along: *Knock 'em dead, Sis.*

Before he left, I wanted to learn everything. Jingle trucks, battle rattle, fobbits, you name it. "C'mon. Spill it," I said.

5   "They don't teach you that stuff in basic, Steph."

"But you must have heard stories. You know. From your friends who've already been there." We lay on the grass in Harrison Park. The sun was out, the sky a fantastic blue we hadn't seen in months.

"No stories, Sis. Sorry."

"Okay, fine. What about from basic?"

Dustin feigned a yawn.

10 "Head's up!" someone shouted. I glanced in time to see a tall girl wave her arms and point overhead. Seconds later, a bright purple Frisbee landed near our feet. Dustin hopped up, flipped the disc in his palms once before uncoiling his arm in a perfect arc, fingertips letting go at just the right moment. We both watched as the flash of color streaked across the field. With a graceful leap, the girl snatched the Frisbee from the air and smiled.

"Thanks," she yelled.

Dustin bowed dramatically, then tipped forward into a full somersault, coming up on his toes and finishing with a wave.

"C'mon, show off," I said. "Let's go eat." I elbowed him hard in the ribs, and we both smiled.

"What'd you call me?" Dustin asked.

15 "Ladies man!" I said, and with that our race back to the car was on.

I didn't have to ask where he'd take us. The front booth at Round Table Pizza practically had a plaque with our names on it. They had the only self-serve soda machine in town, and I liked to mix and match.

"That's so gross, Sis."

"You haven't even tried it."

"Seven-Up and Dr. Pepper? Please." He slurped overflowing foam from the top of his A&W.

20 "Better drink it while you can," I said. "I read about those MREs you have to eat. And remember the chow they fed you in basic? You said that stuff made Mom's cooking look gourmet."

"Don't tell her I said that."

"Duh."

"And just because I'm stoked to go, doesn't mean I won't miss it here," he said.

"Yeah, right."

25 "You know what I mean, Sis. Not Newberg, but hanging out. Like this. You have to promise me you'll spend time with your friends. Or meet new people, I don't know — just don't hole up in the house and let Mom and Dad drive you crazy."

"Mom and Dad wouldn't notice either way," I said. "Besides, I'm almost graduated. It's not like I'm going to hang out in Newberg after that. People at school don't get me. You'd better write while you're gone."

Dustin bit into a slice of pizza and nodded. "'Course I will." He reached across the table and took a sip of my mixed soda. "Not too bad, actually."

"At least here you get a first class D-FAC," I said.

British artist Xavier Pick spent six weeks with British, American, and Iraqi armed forces in the Basra region. The caption reads, "On way to deliver portacabin to school Christmas Eve 2008."

What is the complex relationship between cultures represented in this piece? What story of war does this tell, and how does it compare with most of the stories you hear?

"Steph. You're not in the Army, you know."

30 "D-FAC. It's a dining facil—"

"I know." Dustin shifted in his seat. "I know what it is."

That's when I started using military time. If Dustin found his new family in the Army, the least I could do was get the lingo down. At first it annoyed him, but once he shipped out it became our secret code. He told me things in letters home that Mom and Dad didn't know what to make of. Nothing top secret; just something we could call our own despite the fact that—excluding his basic training—I'd never gone more than a few days without seeing him my entire life.

The first email arrived four weeks after he left. Short and sweet. Typical Dustin. But the message included a P.S. for me: "Steph, look for something in the mail. Deuce out."

Deuce out. Our joke since we moved here from Indiana. It came from tennis, a game we never played. Our family got invited by one of Dad's new colleagues the week we arrived. We got lost driving there, unable to tell the difference between one gated community and the next, the illustrious West Hills unfolding beyond the town limits. Once we arrived, we knew we didn't belong, what with all the matching polo T-shirts and Jack Purcells.

35 "Isn't that a kind of car?" Dustin asked.

"*Jack Purcell?* No, dummy. It's a shoe. A really lame-ass, overpriced shoe," I said.

"Watch the swearing, Sis. We already stick out."

I stuck my tongue out at him. "You asked for it."

He rolled his eyes and grabbed me by the elbow. "Deuce out," he said and led me down the bleacher steps, through the main gate, and into the courtyard. I laughed the entire way. "Deuce" had to do with scoring the match, but what it could possibly mean, we hadn't a clue. We were out of there. Both of us.

40 It felt funny at the time—funny enough to remain an inside joke for four years—but now,

Dustin's words made me angry. How could he be so casual? I knew the Army had to be hard work, but being left behind felt even harder. A whole globe of possibilities existed beyond Newberg, and I couldn't reach any of them. Dustin's experience with other soldiers placed him into that same category: unreachable. He left and joined our nation's defenders. He saw new things, made new memories. I stayed stuck, waiting for graduation, doing whatever it took to avoid snapping at Mom every time I saw that glazed look on her face.

The surprise in the mail was a list of slang words used in Afghanistan. "It's short for now," Dustin wrote, "but I'm learning more everyday." *Hardball. DCU's. Ripped fuel.* Hardball meant any blacktop road, and Dustin wrote that he saw his last one when he took off from an airstrip on base in Kuwait. DCU stood for desert camouflage uniform, apparently nothing special. "Imagine wearing faded brown fatigues every day from head to toe. I feel like the effing UPS driver, Sis, trust me. You're not missing out." The last one surprised me: ripped fuel. It's the way soldiers talked about over-the-counter fad pills, squandered and traded in combat like candy. "Anything to amp your energy," Dustin wrote. "Walking with 50 pounds of battle rattle on, let alone going out on patrol, is workout enough in this heat."

But by spring, letters from Dustin rarely came. The leader of his unit's Family Readiness Group told us not to take it personally. "Many soldiers find the support they need within their own platoon," the leader said. "Life is complicated over there." As if things didn't feel complicated here. I watched Mom sink further into the couch. She hardly even noticed that I skipped Senior Prom. Dad didn't turn mean, but some part of him stayed held back. My senior year of high school, yet everything deepened into a dull-colored silence that made me feel like a ghost in my own house. All I wanted was for someone to shout orders in my face—anything to break the silence with some clear directions.

It had to be easier than slogging alone through the blandness of waiting back home.

Whenever Dustin's letters came, I searched the envelopes for signs of the desert. I knew his mail went through a collection point in Kabul before processing. Once stateside, it might even be X-rayed before making its way into the hands of a US postal worker, then finally delivered to our box. I don't know what I expected. Dust, sand, a fingerprint — but even his brief, hand-written pages felt lifeless. "Hotel, Sierra Hotel," Dustin wrote. I knew that he meant HSH, using the Army's phonetic alphabet to say, "Home, Sweet Home," a place he said he missed, though I found that hard to believe. I wanted to tell him the only thing he was missing would be my high school graduation, which couldn't seem to come fast enough.

"We don't even know where he is," Mom whimpered one night. We sat on the couch with our TV dinners, watching the evening news.

45 "He's over there," Dad said and pointed his fork at the lower half of an Afghanistan map on the screen.

"But, Pete." She sighed. "We don't even know what he's doing."

"He's an infantryman. He's doing his job. He's doing what the Army trained him to do."

"And what, exactly, is that?" she asked. She rarely talked that way.

Dad pressed the mute button on the remote, then dropped his fork into a rubbery pile of Salisbury steak and gravy. "Let's go out. Do you want to go out? What do you say? Ice cream? Steph?" He stared straight ahead, the blue light of the television casting his face in electric plaster.

50 "Sure, Dad."

"Fine," Mom said. "I'll eat double. For Dustin. God knows my boy deserves a scoop of chocolate ice cream by now."

"*Our* boy," Dad said. But I said it too and they both looked at me.

"*Our* boy," I repeated. "You two aren't the only ones that miss him."

I started training the next morning, 0715 hours, 26 MAR 10. Dustin offered me his free weights before he left but I never bothered to pick one up. They came in handy now. I jammed a sweatshirt into the bottom of my Jansport for padding, then set a fifteen-pound weight on top. I wrapped the matching weight in my gym shirt and crammed that, along with my textbooks and binder into my pack. It looked awkward but did the job.

55 "I'm going to work," Mom called from downstairs.

"I'll catch the bus," I said. The Nissan was in the shop. I didn't care. It made me miss Dustin too much. A few minutes later I hustled down the stairs, faster than normal from the weight bearing down on me, then out the front door. I hit the pavement at a slow jog, heart pounding. Two hundred meters to the bus stop and I'd already broken a sweat.

Every day after school I had two hours to workout before Mom and Dad got home. I found out about the Army's first physical fitness test online. It seemed simple enough: two minutes of sit-ups, two minutes of push-ups, and a timed two mile run. I knew I could do it, but whether or not I could nail enough repetitions or hit the sweet spot with my running pace seemed another matter. One way to find out.

Once I made up my mind about enlisting, I thought time would zip past. Instead, the opposite happened. 1545 hours. 15 APR 10. A date everyone else remembered because of taxes. I remember because it was the first time I set foot in the U. S. Army Recruiting Office.

I wore my hiking boots — the closest thing I owned to combat boots — with a pair of Dustin's ratty, beige cargo pants, my dark gray hoodie, and my Jansport (still with the free weights in it). I kept my hair pulled tight in a ponytail, not a single dark brown strand fallen loose along the back of my neck. My bangs distracted from the look, but I clipped them to one side and sprayed them down. From the driver's seat of the Nissan

I saw storefront displays plastered with soldiers of every race. I cracked my window and squinted through the rain. The left side of the display featured the latest military protective gear, DCU's, and training fatigues. The right side encased two life-sized cardboard cutouts of the same soldier — one in uniform with a M4 Carbine at his side, another in a cap and gown, gripping a leather-encased diploma. I checked my hair in the rearview, then hustled from the car to the main door, leaping over puddles in between.

60 My boots squeaked with every step, a line of sole-shaped puddles following me down the linoleum hallway. I turned right into the U.S. Army entrance — there were others, one for each branch of the military — and snapped my feet and hands to attention. The drumming of my heart could have kept time for an entire company. I stilled my breath and straightened my spine. I didn't know how to salute and didn't dare try, but I'd studied the grades online and observed that the first man I saw wore a patch with three hard stripes.

"Good afternoon, Sergeant," I said.

"Good afternoon, Ma'am. What can I do for you today?"

"I'd like to enlist. My brother is in Afghanistan. I've been working out. I want to sign up," I said. Then I bit the inside of my cheeks to make myself shut up.

I tried to hold the Sergeant's gaze but grew too curious. Three other desks filled out the tiny office, two more male noncommissioned officers and one woman, each wearing full fatigues. The American flag hung above the Oregon flag. Beneath them both I saw a signed photo of President Obama, Commander in Chief.

65 The Sergeant smiled and looked at the others. "Congratulations," he said. "That's a decision you should be proud of. Sergeant Hill?"

"Yes, Sir?" the woman answered.

"Please get Ms. —"

"Bowlin," I said.

"—Ms. Bowlin oriented."

70 "Yes, Sir." She turned and indicated that I sit in the empty chair next to her desk. "Welcome to the family, Ms. Bowlin. I can tell already the Army will be pleased to have you."

Sergeant Hill explained a packet of promotional materials, then gave me a fact sheet to show my high school guidance counselor. As a minor without a degree, I needed proof I was on track to graduate high school in good standing. Easy enough. More difficult would be what Sergeant Hill called PC, parental consent. My 18th birthday wasn't for another five weeks, 24 MAY 92.

"With all due respect, Ma'am, I'd prefer not to tell my parents I'm enlisting. At least, not until I get to go to basic."

"That'll be fine, Ms. Bowlin. We can get your information into our system this afternoon," Sergeant Hill said and began entering my name into the computer database. "But we can't get you started in our Future Soldier Program until you're 18 or have PC."

"I can train on my own while I wait," I said. I almost unzipped my pack to show her the weights but decided against it.

75 "Is there a particular career in the Army that interests you?"

"I want to work in combat support."

Sergeant Hill paused at her keyboard and looked at me. "Then physical training is a good idea, Ms. Bowlin."

I waited for her to smile but she didn't. "What else can I do in the meantime?"

She stood and opened a file cabinet, retrieving a thick pile of papers. "This," she said, slapping the heavy stack onto her desk, "is a packet of five practice tests for the ASVAB."

80 "The —?"

"The Armed Services Vocation Aptitude and Battery test. It's like the SAT at an 8th grade level."

"I've taken the SAT."

"That's a good start," she said and handed me the practice tests. "But this will test you for various career fields as well."

I left two hours later with a free ARMY T-shirt and more papers than I could fit into my Jansport. Most importantly, I had a glossy appointment card stamped for the day after my birthday, 0900 hours. I'd bring my letter of good standing and take the ASVAB right there at the Recruiting Office. Three days later I'd find out if I scored high enough and which career fields I was slated for. With everything in place, I could be in Portland at the Military Entrance Processing Station (MEPS) by 01 JUN 10 for my physical, then take my Oath of Enlistment.

85   By the time I pulled the Nissan into our driveway, Mom was already home from work. I finally felt excited about something for the first time since Dustin left. I wanted to rush inside and tell Mom about the enlistment grades and education benefits, the latest cash bonuses since Obama upped the troops in Afghanistan. But she wouldn't understand. The way that I saw it, Dustin and I were two of the most loyal siblings on the planet. I didn't want to do anything without him and not even the global war on terror could prevent me from trying to maintain that. I would go and be with him. Even if we never ended up in the same province, at least I could say I was there. I tried. He wouldn't be the only Bowlin soldier choking on desert sand.

A letter from Dustin arrived 23 MAY 10, two days before my appointment for the ASVAB. It included a Kodak memory card from his digital camera, which explained why the letter was dated April, but it hadn't arrived until late May. An officer in Kabul probably screened the images first. We'd never know how many Dustin originally sent, but when I loaded the photos onto the computer in my bedroom, we only saw seven. Mom and Dad peered over my shoulder and waited as I enlarged each image.

The first two looked blurry: accidental shots of a soldier's boot and another of somebody's back. But the third picture showed a close-up of Dustin with six other Privates in his unit, each standing shoulder-to-shoulder, eyes squinting into the sun. Dustin's face looked darker than I'd ever seen it, either from sand or sunburn or a mix of both. His eyes blazed brilliant green beneath the rim of his helmet. Behind him, the desert looked as spent as a piece of old cardboard.

The next picture must have been a joke, because there were four Privates crossing a dirt road, Dustin leading the way, then two other soldiers on the sidelines laughing and pointing at them.

"It's *Abbey Road*," Mom said. She almost smiled.

90   "What?" I asked.

"*Abbey Road*, honey. The Beatles album."

"Huh?"

"See how they're spread evenly across the road, toe-to-heel?" Dad pointed to the picture. "And that one there, the third guy—he has a cigarette in his hand."

"Yeah?" I was still confused.

95   "Look, Pete," Mom said. "Dustin even put his hands in his pockets, just like Lennon."

"Oh yeah," Dad said. He smiled after he spoke, a wide, fatherly grin I hadn't seen in a while.

"Isn't John Lennon the guy who got shot?" I asked.

Mom glared at me, then turned abruptly and left the room. Dad waited for a moment and exhaled a long breath. "Yes, Stephanie. John Lennon was assassinated."

"Dad, I didn't mean to—"

100   "I know. Just try to think about how your mother feels right now, okay? Try to think about it." He left my room and took Dustin's letter with him. I skimmed the last few pictures, but they only showed soldiers I didn't know, hulky guys holding M16's up to the camera. They looked tough, but they also looked bored. I didn't notice any women.

When I heard Mom and Dad close their bedroom door for the night, I reached under my mattress and pulled out the Army materials Sergeant Hill offered my very first day. I visited her a few times since, and she shared study tips with me. She told me to call her Corrine and gave me her cell phone number in case I had any last minute study questions. Even though I couldn't technically join the Future Soldier Program until I'd passed all my tests, Corrine liked my enthusiasm and gave me handouts each time I stopped by the Recruitment Office.

The Seven Army Values loosely spelled the word "leadership," which helped me remember them in order: Loyalty, Duty, Respect, Selfless Service, Honor, Integrity, and Personal Courage. The Soldier's Creed read like a prayer, which is exactly how I recited it to myself each night: *I will always place the mission first. I will never leave a fallen comrade. I am a guardian of freedom and the American way of life. I am an American Soldier.*

2300 hours. 24 MAY 10. The day Dustin would have taken me to Round Table Pizza for my birthday, if he hadn't left, and let me order Canadian bacon and pineapple. My favorite. His least. Instead, I sat in bed writing my third draft of a letter to him, trying to find the best way to surprise him with my enlistment. Now he wouldn't be the only one. The Army would be one more thing we could share, something bigger than Newberg and bigger than our inside jokes. It would also be my ticket to something better than home. The thought alone made me smile. "I'm on my way," I wrote. "Can't wait!"

The next day, I wore my Army shirt to take the ASVAB and kept Corrine's business card in my wallet for good luck. I had to skip school, but by then it didn't matter. In less than a week I'd be a high school graduate, one step closer to Dustin. I wanted to qualify for as many career fields as possible. Combat support would be the closest to infantry work I could get — women weren't allowed in full combat. From what I could tell, I'd probably be assigned maintenance or civil affairs work in the field.

▶

Look carefully at this recruiting advertisement for the U.S. Army. What words and images would likely appeal to Steph? Why? Would her parents or Dustin agree with the message of the advertisement? Why?

ARMY VALUES

LOYALTY: BEAR TRUE FAITH AND ALLEGIANCE TO THE U.S. CONSTITUTION, THE ARMY, YOUR UNIT AND OTHER SOLDIERS.

Bearing true faith and allegiance is a matter of believing in and devoting yourself to something or someone. A loyal Soldier is one who supports the leadership and stands up for fellow Soldiers. By wearing the uniform of the U.S. Army you are expressing your loyalty. And by doing your share, you show your loyalty to your unit.

goarmy.com

LOYALTY

105 28 MAY 10. 1300 hours. Corrine's name flashed on the caller ID on my cell. I was in Chem class but called her back during passing time.

"Corrine? Hey, it's Steph. I'm sorry I couldn't pick up."

"That's understandable."

"Excuse me, hold on. Can you hold on?" I ducked through the hallway and quickly spun the combo on my locker. "Corrine, are you there?"

"Still here." She chuckled to herself.

110 I stuck my head into the locker and pressed the phone tightly to my ear. A river of students flowed down the hall behind me but I could have been in a foxhole, the enemy all around. My heart raced with anticipation. "Sorry. It's a little noisy right now."

"That's fine, Stephanie. This will only take a minute. We received the results of your ASVAB test this morning, and I'm proud to say you passed with flying colors. I'd like to see you at your earliest convenience to get you over to MEPS and set you up with a career counselor."

"Sweet!" I shouted. "I mean, thank you, Sergeant." The bell rang and the hallway emptied. I pulled my head from my locker and reset the lock. "I'll report at 1500 hours."

"That'll be fine, Steph." Then she hung up.

I stared at the phone in my hand. Something was actually happening. I would be a soldier in the US Army. The tardy bell rang, and I hustled into the girls' bathroom. I should have been in English, but that seemed worlds away. Finals were over, and teachers held parties in class, checking in textbooks and handing out dough-nuts. I set my backpack on the floor, lowering the forty pounds with ease. Standing in front of the large mirror, I backed my left arm out of my sweatshirt sleeve and through the bottom, rais-ing my arm like a body builder. I flexed my muscles and tightened my fist. Corrine had told me that soldiers use their fists as a guide for reading topographical maps, the top line of my knuckles like a ridge of mountains. Between each knuckle, a saddle, and at the edge of my fist along the side of my pinky was a cliff. Hills could be marked on either side of each knuckle, the places where soldiers had to climb or descend, near the summit of each knuckle-peak.

115 Things moved quickly after that. The career counselor said they could only reserve my Army job for seven days, then I had to decide. I knew right away I wanted to be a Bridge Crewmember, position 21C. A few days later I drove to the MEPS office in Portland to swear in and take the Oath of Enlistment. Job description and contract in hand, I settled into the driver's seat of the Nissan to drive home and tell Mom and Dad. That's when my phone rang. It was Dustin. I held the sound of his voice in the palm of my hand, the closest we'd been in almost six months.

"Steph, it's me I—"

"Dustin? Where are you?" I almost shrieked. "You're not going to believe this! I just finished—"

"What do you think you're doing?" He sounded like a stranger. Worse. He sounded like Dad, the few times I'd heard him lose his temper.

"Steph, I got your letter."

120 "Dustin, I passed. I passed everything. Or at least the beginning of everything. It's all happening!"

"This isn't for you. This isn't what it seems," he said. Then slowly: "You. Do not belong. In the Army."

"What do you mean I don't belong? I just took my Oath. We can be in it together, now. So much has happened since you left. I'm going to be a Bridge Crewmember. We might even be in the same—"

"Goddamnit, Sis. Slow down!" I heard his lungs heave, his voice crack. "There's nothing you can do for me here."

"Dustin?" I said his name, but it got lost somewhere over the Pacific. He wasn't the same brother I had before he left. Then again, I wasn't the same sister.

125 "I gotta go," he said. "I'll email you later."

After basic, I shipped to Fort Leonardwood, Missouri, for bridge training. By 20 SEP 10 I flew to a US Army base in Germany for TTP. Tactics, techniques, and practices. I sent letters to Mom and Dad once a month, short and sweet — just like Dustin's.

For his part, Dustin called almost every week. He never got angry with me like that again, but we rarely talked about my enlistment. He hated feeling responsible, and nothing I said convinced him I'd done it for myself as much as for him. We didn't joke around like before, but at least our military jargon finally had a true purpose. The daily B.S. of unit power struggles, trying to swipe the right kinds of protective gear, downing MREs between gags — I lived all of it, and all of it brought us more and more into our new family. We served in the same Division but never crossed paths in the field. He couldn't see how hard I worked, but very few women served in combat support and word got around. I could hold my own, at least at first, and that's the message I wanted him to hear.

02 FEB 10. I landed in Kabul and began the long road trip to Kunar Province in eastern Afghanistan. We were there to erect a series of dry support bridges used for crossing land gaps. About the time Dustin flew home on leave — he joked it was "spring break" — my Company moved to Nuristan Province in the Hindu Kush Mountains. There was heavy fighting along the Pakistan border and infantrymen needed temporary bridges for transport. Something that could be set up and dismantled in a hurry. We were trained to build modular bridges in under ninety minutes.

We rarely left a bridge set up overnight, as the open crossing created a liability — an invitation for insurgents. But the sun had set, and we had another unit that needed to cross at the same location in a few hours. Guards posted on either end and the rest of us set up camp strategically tucked into sidewalls of the mountain. 0230 hours, 26 APR 11, a handful of insurgents tried to cross the bridge. They made it halfway before being detected, and when they returned fire, our combat soldiers took them out. We dismantled the bridge that day, but by nightfall more insurgents crossed the land gap without it. Never mind how they navigated those cliffs by hand and foot, but they did, and they ambushed our camp just before sunrise.

130 The gunfire sounded like microwave popcorn at first. I'd never been that close to it before. At least not when it was aimed at me. I woke disoriented, snapped on my Kevlar, grabbed my flack vest, and got onto all fours. Right arm through the first hole, left arm through the second. Bullets sang by my ears, no time to zip. I grabbed my weapon, then ran low and straight, following the sound of our soldiers' voices. Watch how fast I ran, the open flaps of my vest like wings in the wind. See how the bullets danced around me, never hitting their target. Then finally, half a dozen of them did.

0439 hours. 27 APR 11.

I have nothing to say about white lights or Heaven or Hell or even who else I saw. But I will say this: there's nothing like it, that fever of live-action death.

In the living world, people study amputees with ghost limbs. A missing right arm mysteriously itches. A missing left leg throbs. In the dead world, we're given ghost ears. Different people hear different things. What I hear is always the same. It's Mom. It's Dad. They keep asking, "What happened? What happened? What happened?"

Understanding and Interpreting

1 When pressed by Steph for information about life in the military, Dustin replies, just before heading out to Afghanistan, "No stories, Sis. Sorry" (par. 7). Look at Dustin's communication with Steph once he is on the battlefield. What is the conflict between her hopes and his actual communication? What does Steph hear or not hear in Dustin's letters home?

2 How do Steph's parents' actions and behavior, probably inadvertently, cause her to enlist?

3 Steph calls Dustin's first email and his letters "short and sweet" (pars. 33 and 126), but elsewhere she describes them as "lifeless" (par. 43). What do these letters from Dustin represent for Steph?

4 Even though Steph conducts a lot of research on the army, she also seems rather naive about military life. Identify places where she demonstrates this quality and explain why this is important to the point Schultz is making in this story.

5 Shortly before she takes her oath, Steph writes, "I'm on my way" (par. 103). What do this line and other actions she takes reveal about Steph's motivations for enlisting?

6 How do Dustin's character traits lead, however indirectly, to the tragic ending of the story?

7 What are the differences between Steph's expectations of life in the military and the reality? How do these differences help to illustrate the theme of the story?

Analyzing Language, Style, and Structure

1 While most of this story is told in roughly chronological order, Schultz decides to start with the scene of Dustin leaving for Afghanistan. How does this choice help to illustrate the central conflict within Steph?

2 In addition to showing the origin of the inside joke Steph shares with her brother, "deuce out," what purpose does the flashback in paragraphs 34–39 serve for establishing Steph's character?

3 Look back at the scene when Steph goes to the U.S. Army Recruiting Office for the first time. What key details does Schultz use to describe Steph, as well as the setting of the office and the actions of the recruiters? What do these details reveal about Steph and why she makes the choice to enlist?

4 Schultz provides us with very little information about Steph's life outside of her relationship to her parents and Dustin. Apart from a brief mention of skipping the senior prom (par. 42), Steph makes no mention of her friends or social activities. How does this lack of description relate to the conflict Steph is facing?

5 Writers often include details that foreshadow an ending such as the one in this story. Look back and identify and explain how Schultz's specific language or plot choices can be seen as foreshadowing.

6 Reread paragraph 130, which begins, "The gunfire sounded like microwave popcorn at first." What do you notice about the shift in language in this paragraph? How does this shift point toward the last section of the story?

Connecting, Arguing, and Extending

1 Imagine that you were an editor working with Katey Schultz before the publication of this story. Write an argument either for or against the current ending of the story. Is it effective or not? Why?

2 Katey Schultz is a civilian, and while she interviewed a number of soldiers for the short-story collection in which "Deuce Out" was originally published, she has no firsthand experience with war or combat. Do you believe writers like Schultz are entitled to tell stories like this, or that even fictional accounts of war should be told only by people who have fought in wars? Why or why not?

3 It is only very recently that the United States military has begun to allow women to serve in forward operations in a war zone. Why do you think women were kept out of combat? Consider whether women should be allowed to serve in these capacities and in direct combat roles, and write an argument for your position.

4 You are probably only a little bit younger than Steph and will at some point be facing a similar decision about what to do after your graduation from high school. Is entering the military a likely option for you? Research the entrance requirements, benefits, and risks, and then write an essay, with supporting evidence, explaining why the military might be a career option for you.

from In the Hot Zone

Kevin Sites

Kevin Sites (b. 1963) is a freelance journalist who has spent his career covering wars around the world. His reporting includes video, photography, and traditional news reporting. His first book, *In the Hot Zone*, from which this excerpt is taken, is based on his experience in 2004 and 2005, when Sites visited and reported on twenty different armed conflicts in Somalia, Sudan, Syria, Iraq, and other places.

Alex Pena/Stars & Stripes

KEY CONTEXT   This selection, from the first chapter of *In the Hot Zone*, called "Shooting at the Mosque," presents a difficult ethical dilemma. In 2004, nine months after the United States military began the invasion of Iraq, Sites was embedded as a reporter for NBC within a unit of marines trying to take the city of Fallujah, which at the time was an enemy stronghold. During the battle, Sites videotaped an alarming incident and was torn between his duties to "seek and report the truth" and to "minimize harm."

Sunbeams

The carpet of the mosque is stained with blood and covered with fragments of concrete. Tank shells and machine-gun rounds have pitted the inside walls. The rotting, sweet smell of death hangs in the morning air. Gunsmoke-laced sunbeams illuminate the bodies of four Iraqi insurgents. A fifth lies next to a column, his entire body covered by a blanket.

I shudder. Something very wrong has happened here.

Yesterday I had seen these same five men being treated by American medics for superficial wounds received during an afternoon firefight. Ten other insurgents had been killed, their bodies still scattered around the main hall in the black bags into which the Marines had placed them.

I was told by the commander of the 3.1 Marines, Lieutenant Colonel Willy Buhl, that these five wounded, captured enemy combatants would be transported to the rear. But now I can see that one of them appears dead and the three others are slowly bleeding to death from gunshots fired by one lance corporal, I will learn later, who used both his M-16 and his 9 mm pistol on them, just minutes before I arrived.

5   With my camera rolling, I walk toward the old man in the red kaffiyeh and kneel beside him. Because he was so old, maybe in his early

sixties, and wearing the red headgear, he had stood out the most to me when I was videotaping the day before, after the battle.

Now the old man is struggling to breathe. Oxygenated blood bubbles from his nose. Another man, stocky and dressed in a long gray shirt called a dishdasha, is slumped in the old man's lap. While I'm taping, the old man is bleeding to death in front of my camera. I look up to see the lance corporal who had just shot all of them moments before, now walking up to the other two insurgents against the wall, twenty feet away. One is facedown, apparently already dead. The other, dressed in an Iraqi Police uniform, is faceup but motionless, aside from his breathing.

The lance corporal says, "Hey, this one's still breathing." Another agrees, "Yeah, he's breathing." There is tension in the room, but I continue to roll on the man in the red kaffiyeh.

"He's f***** faking he's dead," the lance corporal says, now standing right in front of the man.

The Embed

As a freelance correspondent for NBC News, I embedded with the Third Battalion, First Marine (Regiment) for three weeks prior to the Battle of Falluja, or what the Americans code-named Operation Phantom Fury and what the Iraqi interim government called Operation Al Fajr, or "The Dawn."

10   The mission has a clear but complicated objective; take back the restive city of Falluja from the insurgents who had been running the place for the last eight months.

In the time leading up to the battle, I have developed a good relationship with my unit. The Marines see that I'm a television reporter working solo — shooting, writing and transmitting my reports without a crew — and they tell me they like my self-reliance. I tell them it's a necessity, because no one wants to work with me anymore. Television news is the ultimate collaborative

medium, but by being recklessly aggressive, low on the network food chain (a producer turned reporter) and eager to go it alone to uncomfortable locations, it has not been difficult to convince news managers to let me do just that.

The Marines also like the fact that I write an independent war blog, which NBC allowed me to keep as a freelancer, where I post longer, more detailed and personal stories about my experiences.

Inspired by Tim O'Brien's book *The Things They Carried*, in which he describes the items, both literal and figurative, that each man in a U.S. Army platoon carried on a jungle march through Vietnam, I ask the Marines to show me the same. They pull out rosaries, Saint Christopher medals, photographs of their wives and children taped inside their Kevlar helmets.

I snap their pictures and post them on the site. Their families, eager for information about their loved ones, come to my blog in droves. They post responses, thanking me for allowing them to see the faces of their sons, husbands, brothers. Soon, however, those messages of gratitude will be replaced with hate mail and death threats. [. . .]

The Feints

15   Everyone knows the battle is coming, they just don't know when. In the meantime the Marines conduct operations known as feints, bluffing maneuvers in which they charge up to the city's edge with armor and infantry, both to fool the insurgents into thinking the real battle has begun and to draw them out of their urban hiding spots to kill them.

I am assigned to the CAAT (Combined Anti-Armor Team) Platoon, commanded by Lieutenant Ryan Sparks, a former enlisted man and member of the Marines' elite Recon Unit, similar to Army Special Forces and Navy SEALs.

The CAAT team consists of Humvees mounted with heavy, squad-operated weapons such as TOW antitank missiles and Mark 19 grenade launchers that can fire belted 40 mm grenades at a rate of sixty rounds per minute.

A week before Phantom Fury begins, Sparks's team is assigned to an operational feint on the south end of the city, where commanders believe foreign fighters, possibly from Al Qaeda, are concentrated.

The units rehearse the operation in a "rock drill" in which rocks and, strangely, large children's Lego blocks are arranged on the ground to approximate Falluja's buildings. Water bottles stand in as minarets for the mosques. Each unit commander involved in the operation, from captains to squad leaders, explains, in chronological order of the event, their mission objective, entry into the operation and exit.

20   On the evening of the feint, I ride in Sparks's Humvee. As we race across the desert, I shoot video out the front windshield, where my last name, along with those of the three crew members, is written in black marker along with our blood types.

There is a loud explosion as an insurgent mortar round lands a hundred yards behind us. Sparks orders his teams to find cover somewhere on the flat desert plains.

"There it is — right there, Johnson, eleven-thirty." Sparks directs his Mark 19 gunner to a flash point in the city where he believes the mortar came from.

The radio crackles as Sparks listens to the field artillery unit triangulating the mortar's firing grid more precisely. When another mortar lands nearby, Sparks no longer waits. He orders his squad and those in the other Humvees to return fire.

It is, on a small scale, what the Marines had hoped would happen — drawing insurgents out and then springing the trap. Though the insurgent response has been tepid so far — a couple of mortars and small-arms fire — the Marines ramp up the firepower.

25   Abrams M1A1 tanks fire their 120 mm main guns; Marine artillery units drop their own

mortars; while the CAAT team shoots shoulder-launched Javelin and Humvee-mounted TOW missiles at the outlying houses.

Tow Backblast

I leave Sparks and run seventy-five yards across the open field to where another CAAT Humvee is shooting TOWs. After several firings, Lance Corporal Joe Runion loads another missile into the launcher; the gunner yells "Fire in the hole" and pulls the trigger. But there is no launch — only a clicking sound.

It's a hang-fire. Runion waits for a full minute, Marine protocol in this situation, before climbing onto the Humvee to unload the faulty weapon. Just as he is about to reach for the tube, the missile fires, roaring to life at its target. The backblast concussion from the rear of the tube knocks Runion unconscious and he falls off the Humvee to the ground.

Others in his unit run to his aid, but, remarkably, he shakes it off, climbs back on the Humvee and reloads the weapon. I've recorded the entire sequence on my video camera.

"I'm glad you're safe, dog," says one of the Marines to Runion, whose head is still ringing from the explosion.

30   The moment is soon lost. Darkness falls and the fight continues. In my story I report the TOW malfunction and Runion's stubborn perseverance after being knocked out. I also say that while no American lives were lost in the operation, it did cost hundreds of thousands of dollars in manpower and munitions.

The next day, after my piece has aired on NBC *Nightly News*, a few of the Marines from the CAAT team tell me they're happy that I didn't use the TOW backblast incident to make them look stupid.

I feel that I have gained a little trust — but also begin to see the deep-rooted *mis*trust they have for my profession.

Some of that perception, they tell me, started with their fathers, who served in Vietnam and told them when they were growing up that the media helped lose that war by reporting only the "bad stuff."

I think about telling them that the United States dropped more bombs in Vietnam than in both World Wars I and II combined and that it had a determined foe, one willing to live in underground tunnels and endure the death of millions. It was the enemy who won that conflict, and not news reporting that lost it. I decide it is probably better left unsaid. [. . .]

The Mosque Shooting

35 After hearing the lance corporal say, "He's f****** faking he's dead," I raise my camera up from the bleeding old man to the Marine.

I see him in my viewfinder; he is raising his M-16 rifle and pointing it directly at the wounded insurgent's head. He peers down at him through his laser scope.

I don't know what he's going to do, but I hope he's just going to cover him while other Marines search him for weapons. But in this place, already filled with so much death, some-how, in this moment, I sense there will be more. The lance corporal squeezes the trigger, firing a 5.62 round into the man's head, which I watch explode on my screen.

His skull and brains splatter against the dirty white wall he was lying against. After firing the shot, the Marine (whom I have chosen not to name) turns on his heels and walks away.

The name of the man he shot was revealed later in an identification card recovered from his body by the Naval Criminal Investigative Service. The card, ironically, had been issued to the man under the authority of the First Marine Expeditionary Force in Falluja. His name was Officer Farhan Abd Mekelf, a member of the Iraqi Police.

40 I have seen people killed and wounded in combat, but never like this. Never at point-blank range. It stuns me to the point that instead of jumping up, I continue to videotape from my kneeling position. Maybe it was shock, but to this day, I still can't understand why I completed the shot sequence, panning back to the old man with the red kaffiyeh after the lance corporal killed Mekelf.

After the shooting, the fifth insurgent, who had been completely covered by the blanket, slowly pulls it down, raising his bandaged hands as he does. Two other Marines in the mosque immediately point their weapons at him.

This snaps me out of my trance. Thinking they might shoot him, too, I get up and confront the Marine who had pulled the trigger.

"Why did you do that?" I asked him. "What's going on? These were the same guys that were here yesterday. They were wounded."

"I didn't know, sir," he said. "I didn't know." The voice that had seemed so confident just a few moments ago is now filled with unsettling realizations. And then he walks out of the mosque followed by the other Marines.

45 The insurgent under the blanket begins speaking to me in Arabic. He's the only one of the five wounded who had not been shot a second time by the lance corporal, somehow escaping that fate by hiding under the blanket. Because of the wounds on his legs from the Friday afternoon firefight, he's wearing only a blue-striped shirt and white underpants; his trousers are in a heap next to the mosque pillar.

He tries to talk to me, gesturing with his hands, but I can't understand what he's saying. He falls back on his upper arms, frustrated and scared.

It's only later, after my video is translated, that I will find out what he was trying to tell me. But it will be more than two years later before I learn the fate of this man, Taleb Salem Nidal, and my complicity in it.

As I walk away from the mosque, I'm not thinking of Nidal, but only of the shooting I just witnessed. There is a vehicle going back to the battalion field headquarters. I jump in and ride back to the 3.1 Battalion's field headquarters.

I need to see Lieutenant Colonel Willy Buhl, tell him what has happened and show him the video.

When I first met Buhl at the beginning of my embed, I liked him right away. He seemed like an easygoing, no-bullshit kind of guy. Small and stocky, he was a former wrestler and, like Lieutenant Ryan Sparks, had been an enlisted man who became an officer. Guys like that, who have been there and know the business from the ground up, generally command a lot of respect. Buhl was no exception. I had interviewed him prior to Phantom Fury and he had said something to me that now, in retrospect, seems both sadly ironic on one level and prophetically true on another.

50   "We're the good guys. We are Americans. We are fighting a gentleman's war here — because we don't behead people, we don't come down to the same level of the people we're combating," he says during our interview at Camp Abu Ghraib. "And that's a very difficult thing for a young eighteen-year-old Marine that's been trained to locate, close with and destroy the enemy with fire and close combat, and that's a very difficult thing for a forty-two-year-old lieutenant colonel with twenty-three years' experience in the service who's trained to do the same thing once upon a time and now has a thousand-plus men to lead, guide, coach, mentor and to ensure we are the good guys and keep the moral high ground."

When I show Buhl the tape, he is not shocked so much as he is deflated. His comments are along the lines of "Ah, this is so bad." I think he felt that all he had accomplished up to that moment could be taken away by a single image.

The Report

After I shoot the video, one of the first things I do is call the NBC News desk in New York and have them wake up the vice president of NBC News at the time, Bill Wheatley; the VP of foreign news, David Verdi; and the foreign news manager, Danny Noa.

Partly, this is a safety net for myself. If no one at NBC knows that I have the tape, I might be tempted to destroy it. It is the most soul-wrenching moral dilemma I have ever faced in my life. My professional code of ethics commands me to "seek and report the truth," but it also, as few outside the profession know, instructs us to "minimize harm." The Society of Professional Journalists' code requires that the "ethical journalist treat sources, subject and colleagues as human beings deserving of respect."

How, in this circumstance, can I possibly do both? I know that the videotape probably shows a violation of the Geneva Convention and Uniform Code of Military Justice regarding humane treatment of wounded enemy combatants.

55   And while that is the likely truth, I fear that releasing the video could have unintended consequences. The most obvious, it seems, is that once word of the video reaches insurgents, they might not be willing to surrender if they believe their fate is going to be similar to Farhan Abd Mekelf's.

A further inflamed insurgency might also take retribution through more suicide bombings on civilian and military targets. In addition, there are already slim hopes for merciful and humane treatment of American, Iraqi government and coalition forces prisoners by insurgent fighters, and now there will almost certainly be summary executions.

Reporting the truth is my professional responsibility, but so is consideration of its potential harm. If my employers know about the video, I will not be alone in my decision making.

Kevin Burke, who was videotaping with another unit while I was in the mosque, meets up with me at battalion headquarters. I ask him to start making duplicates of the shooting video, just in case someone tries to take it from us.

No one ever does.

Ticking Clock

60   My belief is that we should hold the tape for seventy-two hours to give the Marines a chance to investigate.

To their credit, they move quickly, pulling the lance corporal from the field and assigning Lieutenant Colonel Bob Miller from the judge advocate general's office to begin questioning witnesses in the case.

But there are other complications. Even though I am working for NBC News, the network has made a video-sharing agreement called a "pool" with a consortium of other television media, including the other four American networks, three British networks (including the BBC), as well as Reuters TV and Associated Press Television News. This pretty much guarantees that whatever footage comes out of the Battle of Falluja will be seen around the world, including the Middle East through Al Jazeera.

Part of the pool agreement requires me to turn over my footage as soon as possible. But I know that if I do that before allowing the Marine Corps to respond, the story could spin out of control without proper context.

As the seriousness of the incident begins to reverberate, I begin meetings with Marine Corps brass that swiftly take me from the front lines to the desk of the commanding general of the entire First Marine Division and first Marine Expeditionary Force, Major General Richard Natonski.

65   At the same time, NBC News VP Bill Wheatley is pressuring me to release the tape to the pool in forty-eight hours — otherwise, he tells me, "we'll look like we're holding out on them."

At Camp Falluja, the Marines billet Kevin Burke and me away from the other media so we can do our work quickly and quietly without stirring up questions about what I videotaped in the mosque.

Sunday, the day after the shooting, I'm sitting outside our quarters on a satellite phone with Danny Noa. I'm tired, frustrated and conflicted — and the pressure from Wheatley has pissed me off. I tell Danny that I've come to a decision.

"I'm not going to feed the tape, Danny."

"What do you mean, you're not going to feed the tape?"

70   "I didn't make this pool agreement and I have no idea how the other networks are going to use it and we don't have any control over it. I'll messenger it to our bureau in Baghdad but I'm not going to feed this tape to the pool."

Noa is understandably shocked and puzzled to the point that he hardly knows what to say. He and I had come up through the ranks as producers at NBC. *No* is not a word producers use or accept if they are going to have any kind of career. He pushes, pleads and finally lets me know just what kind of grave territory I have entered. When I still refuse to budge, he says he needs to get David Verdi on the phone when he's done with a meeting. He asks me to call back in a half hour.

When Verdi gets on the phone, he is calm and deliberate.

"I can understand how hard this is, Kevin," he tells me, "but we've already told the pool what we have and if you don't feed the tape it's going to look like we're trying to hide the truth or something — like we're collaborating with the government to bury this thing." [. . .]

He pauses, then pushes a button that he knows will affect me. "It could become an even bigger incident. There will be a buildup and the demand for the video will turn into an outcry. When it's finally released, it could create an even more volatile situation than if we give it to them now and provide the context of what happened through your report."

75   It's exactly what I don't want to happen, for everything to spin out of control. I didn't want to be responsible for a massive wave of violence and bloodshed. By the end of the phone call, I relent. We decide the video will be released in two versions: the entire tape, then a second feed where I pause the video after the Marine raises his M-16 at the insurgent's head. The gunshot will be heard, but the image of the actual shooting won't be seen. The other networks can use their own discretion on which version they want to air.

Simultaneously, I will complete my packaged story for NBC *Nightly News* with a video interview of the JAG investigator, Bob Miller, responding to the facts of the case.

The process of putting together the script is painstaking, requiring multiple levels of oversight from news management, NBC lawyers, executive and senior producers. [. . .]

By the time we're finished, the script is a Frankenstein's monster of caution and qualifications that violates the most basic rule of journalistic writing — tell the most important thing that happened first; do not bury your lede.

Also, we choose to censor ourselves and show the version with the paused image in the report. We justify it by saying it's too graphic for our viewers.

80   This is a decision that I not only support but push for. In hindsight, I know it was the wrong decision. We didn't trust the American public enough to let them see the video in its entire context. Instead we added to their confusion about the incident by toploading the story with all the mitigating factors such as insurgents using mosques to fight from and booby-trapping dead bodies — while not honestly evaluating the visual evidence that this shooting was both cavalier and without provocation.

Because they didn't get the whole story, viewers filled their lack of understanding with their own conclusions, based on personal perceptions, political beliefs and emotional reactions — almost anything but factual detail. The very thing we held back on.

On this basis, many viewers decided the Marine was justified. When the hate mail and the death threats started pouring into my email accounts, many people accused me of omitting the mitigating factors with which we actually began our report.

The Aftermath

Since I haven't seen the actual broadcast, I don't learn until the next day what has happened. NBC anchor Brian Williams, in an incredibly generous gesture to me and the burgeoning blog movement, mentioned, at the end of my mosque shooting report, that I also keep an independent blog. He then read the Internet address on air to his ten million viewers, inadvertently sending thousands of rabid right-wingers to my electronic front door. I'm certain they could have found it anyway, but this kept them from having to search (his on-air promotion will actually help me reach millions a week later, when I write my Open Letter and post it on the site).

But the morning after the broadcast, when I wake up at Camp Falluja and connect my satellite modem to check my email, I have more than six hundred waiting for me. In a prolonged and ill-advised display of masochism, I sit on a concrete barrier smoking cigarettes and reading at least the first couple of lines of every one of them. [. . .] While there are a lot of messages of support, the negative, more inherently dramatic responses tend to monopolize my attention.

85   After a while, they run together in a tone of hateful — even threatening — rhetoric:

> *You better sleep with one eye open, you antiwar a******! You f*** with one Marine, you f *** with all of us Marines, d********! Semper Fi and sleep tight, you piece of s***!*
> *Mark*

> *We know where you live. We know what you drive. We know who your friends are. And we'll be waiting for you when you get back home. You made a big mistake.*
> *SMS*

> *May your entire family contract AIDS or die a painful death from cancer.*
> *Anonymous*

> *I imagine you didn't give a thought to the danger you put your family in, did you? Well, some whacko is probably fashioning a six pack of Molitov [sic] cocktails to deliver to them, but hey, lookit the money and fame you got at someone else's expense. You're dirt schmuck and I don't*

think there is anything too horrible that could happen to you.

Jim

We would love to be able to give thanks this Thanksgiving that you were killed by one of your Arab friends. When you get killed every American will dance in the streets. *YOU ARE THE ENEMY! WE HATE YOU!!!*

Annie

Hey Kev,

Waiting for the picture with your head laying on your back. So when do you suppose we will see that?

Bill

Sigh . . .

I wonder why the units who have imbedded [sic] journalists who rat them out do not frag them. There is absolutely no place for f****** reporters in a combat zone. Plain and simple.

A Grandmother in Houston

If you were shadowing my unit in the field, I would personally put a round in the back of your head myself. . . . I am praying that some good Americans find out where you live and teach you a lesson or two about betraying your country.

Anonymous

O'Reilly and North

The emails will continue at the rate of about three hundred per day for the next year. The numbers will rise or fall depending on who has decided to fan the flames: right-wing bloggers or conservative Fox News Channel talk-show hosts such as Bill O'Reilly and ex-Marine and '80s Iran-Contra scandal figure Oliver North.

Fox was a part of the pool, so both men have had a chance to watch the entire video. They either misinterpreted the events or decided the facts were too inconvenient.

In either case, instead of reminding viewers that as citizens of a democracy, we are all responsible for what our military does in our

name in a time of war, both bad and good, O'Reilly and North attack as unpatriotic anyone who believes we should live up to our national ideals of seeing truth revealed and justice served.

In his own blog post on November 28, 2004, O'Reilly makes several errors that create misconceptions that ripple through cyberspace and mobilize an army of chronically mis-informed ideologues to come out swinging with erroneous emails and half-baked accusations.

90   O'Reilly writes (identifying the Marine as a soldier), "*On the tape you can see the insurgent move before the soldier pulls the trigger.*"

I was closer to the insurgent than Bill O'Reilly ever could be — the insurgent never even twitched. His mistake, as one Marine said on tape: "Yeah, he's breathing."

O'Reilly continues, "*If that young Marine had homicide on his mind, he would have entered the Mosque shooting. But he did not.*"

The truth is, regardless of his intentions, the Marine did enter the mosque and begin shoot-ing. According to the Naval Criminal Investigative Service investigation, the same lance corporal admitted to shooting three of the wounded Iraqis when he entered the compound before me. He used his 9 mm pistol after first firing with his M-16, which jammed. I recorded on video the sound of the distinctive small-arm reports while waiting to go inside the mosque.

The shots were fired in a slow and methodi-cal manner, not the frantic pattern of combat when the enemy is shooting back. A Marine Corps statement issued on May 4, 2005, five months after the incident, states: "During the assault, the corporal entered the building and shot 3 AIF [U.S. military parlance for anti-Iraqi forces or insurgents], one of whom was recorded on videotape by reporter Kevin Sites. The Marine admits in his sworn statements that he shot the 3 AIF in self-defense believing they posed a threat to him and his fellow Marines."

95   The report continues, "The ballistic reports indicate the projectiles removed from the bodies

of three AIF were attributable to the corporal's weapon (M-16)."

O'Reilly concludes, "*The Pentagon is not releasing the name of the Marine, and is investigating. Both of these things are fair. But this case is not complicated, and anyone condemning that soldier should himself be condemned.*"

The truth is that out of fairness to the Marine during the investigation I didn't release his name — nor have I now, after its conclusion. More importantly, the case *is* complicated, both in the small facts and intentions relating to the individual Marine and the larger facts and intentions relating to our military and nation as a whole.

Our Failing

For me, the problems following the incident are predictable. In the United States there is a loud outcry against me and against NBC and, to a lesser degree, the media overall for the perception of having betrayed the troops in a time of war.

All the other American networks follow NBC's lead in not showing the actual shooting on the mosque video, while in Europe at least one network in each country does. However, in the Middle East, nearly everyone is seeing the entire segment — over and over again. During the week following the release of the video, Al Jazeera airs it nearly once every hour.

100   Later, I would consider how sadly we failed the public in our responsibility to them, that it was not our government or military that censored us in this story; we, the American media, did it ourselves.

Everyone in the world had the potential to see one of the most important and controversial stories to come out of the war — except the citizens of the nation whose own military was directly involved. [. . .]

From my cot in Camp Falluja I stop looking at the hundreds of hate emails and hunker down to write what I title "Open Letter to the Devil Dogs

of the 3.1." It is to be a full account of events leading up to, during and after the mosque shooting. In it I will explain not only what I witnessed but what I felt, as well as what my responsibilities were as a journalist and why it was not just the right choice but the *only* moral and ethical choice.

I have addressed it to the Marines, but it's also meant for the world. In an email, I ask my sister Shawn if she knows a lawyer who could look at the letter. With so much heated debate around the incident, I want to protect myself. In some ways, I look at the article as a kind of self-deposition.

Shawn contacts her former boss at Dick Clark Productions, Trudi Behr, who is married to the prominent Los Angeles attorney Joel Behr. According to my sister, Joel and Trudi are fans of my blog, and I had met them for dinner at their house once, prior to this trip to Iraq.

105   Both of them take me on as a kind of crisis communication project, helping me to think out what the article needs to accomplish — telling what I saw, what it meant and why as a journalist I had to tell the story.

In the meantime, a right-wing Web site called WorldNetDaily.com is claiming I am an antiwar activist. Citing this one "shred of evidence," an antiwar German Web site had, without my permission, taken photographs from my blog and posted them.

Shawn and Xeni Jardin contact the site and threaten legal action if the photos aren't removed.

Open Letter to the Devil Dogs of the 3.1

On Sunday, November 21, 2004, I post the open letter on my blog. It is eight days after the actual incident. As a courtesy, I send a copy to NBC and MSNBC. (Neal Shapiro has advised me earlier not to write a response — or, if I am determined, to let them make suggestions. I decide it is best for me to do this on my own — with a little help from my friends.)

The original article is 2,600 words long with several photographs — but since we don't have a way to post the video, only the text is posted.

110   I conclude it with the following paragraph, which I believed sums up our differing roles:

So here, ultimately, is how it plays out: When the Iraqi man in the mosque posed a threat, he was your enemy; when he was subdued, he was your responsibility; when he was killed in front of my eyes and my camera, the story of his death became my responsibility.

The burdens of war, as you so well know, are unforgiving for all of us.

The response to the article is overwhelming. Media outlets from around the world publish excerpts, or in some cases, such as Britain's *Guardian* newspaper and *Marine Corps Times*, carry nearly the entire piece.

According to user statistics on kevinsites.net, readership skyrockets from just 37,600 hits early in the month to more than two million the day after the letter is posted.

Anecdotally, at least, the impact it has on the perceptions of the American public about the story seems even more remarkable. While the hate mail and the death threats do not disappear, I am able to see the trend of hate shift either to begrudging understanding of my actions or outright support now that more information is available.

With a few exceptions,[†] even my own industry, which had been mostly ambivalent in its support and defense of my journalistic integrity, now seems to enthusiastically welcome me back into the fold. *Wired* magazine will give me its first-ever Rave Award for blogging, specifically concerning the mosque shooting, and the University of Oregon will honor me with its Payne Award for Ethics for both my television and blog coverage of the incident.

Eddie Adams

115   At Camp Falluja, I'm too exhausted to feel vindicated and my difficulties are not over yet. When I leave and get back to NBC's Baghdad Bureau, I learn that the famous Vietnam photojournalist Eddie Adams has died. He was the one who snapped the incredible Pulitzer Prize–winning photograph of a Viet Cong fighter being summarily executed by a South Vietnamese general. Adams captured it just as the trigger was pulled and the man was beginning to grimace.

It was a poignant moment for Adams, who would later write, regretful of the photo, "the General killed the Viet Cong; I killed the General with my camera."

It seems relevant that Adams would die some thirty years after Vietnam and during a time when the challenges of telling the truth in war were revealing themselves again.

---

† Shortly after the mosque-shooting video aired on NBC and the fallout began, reporter Darrin Mortenson wrote an article titled *Blame the Messenger* in which he vigorously defended my actions in Falluja, my reputation as a fair-minded reporter and the crucial role reporters play in a democracy during wartime. It also highlighted Mortenson's own courage, considering he was working for California's *North County Times*, considered the hometown newspaper for the Marine Corps base at Camp Pendleton and home of the 3.1 Marines.

seeing connections

Sites ends his piece with a reference to Eddie Adams, the photographer behind one of the most famous war photographs of all time, *Saigon Execution.* In this photograph, General Nguyen Ngoc Loan, the South Vietnamese chief of police, executes a member of the Vietcong (Communist guerrilla soldiers who fought against South Vietnam and the United States during the Vietnam War). Even though Adams won a Pulitzer Prize for the photograph, he eventually regretted what he had done, years later saying, "The general killed the Viet Cong; I killed the general with my camera. Still photographs are the most powerful weapon in the world. People believe them, but photographs do lie, even without manipulation. They are only half-truths. What the photograph didn't say was, 'What would you do if you were the general at that time and place on that hot day, and you caught the so-called bad guy after he blew away one, two or three American soldiers?'"

Compare the situation Adams faced and the conclusions he drew with the situation Sites faced and the decision he made.

Understanding and Interpreting

1 Sites includes a lengthy description of one of the marines' feints and a near-accident that occurred before the shooting in the mosque. What conclusion is the reader expected to draw from this section about the relationship between reporters and the military in general, and about Sites in particular?

2 Look back at the section called "The Mosque Shooting." Trace Sites's actions throughout the sequence. How and why does his role change from observer to participant?

3 Summarize the ethical conflict Sites encounters once he realizes what he has filmed (pars. 52–58). Be sure to consider it from all of the angles: his professional code of ethics, his relationship with the marines, and the effects the video could have on the enemy and the allies, as well as Sites's role as a "pool reporter" required to share everything he has recorded with other networks.

4 Using evidence from throughout the piece for support, including the portion of the Open Letter, explain why Sites ultimately makes the decision he does.

5 According to Sites, what is wrong with the final version of the story of the shooting in the mosque, and what is the result of the decisions he and the producers made?

Analyzing Language, Style, and Structure

1 How does the section called "The Embed" serve to establish Sites's ethos? Why do you think Sites chooses to include this section early in the piece? How does it influence your understanding of what happens later?

2 How does Sites foreshadow the events in the mosque? Be sure to consider how he structures the piece, as well as any specific language choices he makes prior to his mention of the actual shooting.

3 Look back through the piece and identify places that reflect Sites's shifting tone toward the marines. What words and phrases indicate this shift and what does it reveal about Sites and his situation?

4 Reread the interview with Lieutenant Colonel Willy Buhl (par. 50). Though he had conducted this interview weeks earlier, why does Sites include Buhl's responses at this point in the narrative, after the shooting?

5 In the section called "The Report," Sites mentions that he made duplicates of the tape in case someone tried to take it. He ends with the one-sentence paragraph "No one ever does." What is Sites implying with this sentence, and why might he have chosen to make it a separate paragraph?

6 Why do you think Sites includes the excerpts from the emails he received? What does he achieve by including them?

Connecting, Arguing, and Extending

1 Did Sites do the right thing by airing the footage? Why or why not? How could he have handled the situation differently?

2 One of the abusive emails that Sites received in the aftermath of his report mentions that reporters should not be allowed in combat zones, "[p]lain and simple." Is the writer of that email right or wrong about whether reporters should be allowed to report from the battlefield? Write an argument in which you agree, disagree, or present a middle ground. Be sure to use examples from Sites's piece to support your argument or as a counterargument.

3 Sites notes that the full video he filmed, which included the actual shooting, was not aired by any of the American networks, though some TV stations in European countries and most of the ones in the Middle East chose to broadcast it. Sites calls this a failure of the American media's responsibility to the public. If you were the news director of a television network, would you have chosen to air the whole footage? Why or why not?

4 The entire Open Letter that Sites wrote to the marines with whom he was embedded is available online. Read it closely and analyze the rhetorical choices he makes in trying to explain his position to the marines. What word choices and examples are included in this letter that are specific to Sites's purpose and audience?

2000 lbs.

Brian Turner

Brian Turner (b. 1967) is the author of two collections of poetry, *Phantom Noise* and *Here, Bullet*, as well as a memoir, *My Life as a Foreign Country*. Turner served for seven years in the U.S. military, including one year during the Iraq War, which is the setting for this poem about the effects of a car bomb detonation in a crowded market.

Ashur Square, Mosul

It begins simply with a fist, white-knuckled
and tight, glossy with sweat. With two eyes
in a rearview mirror watching for a convoy.
The radio a soundtrack that adrenaline has
5   pushed into silence, replacing it with a heartbeat,
his thumb trembling over the button.

A flight of gold, that's what Sefwan thinks
as he lights a Miami, draws in the smoke
and waits in his taxi at the traffic circle.
10 He thinks of summer 1974, lifting
pitchforks of grain high in the air,
the slow drift of it like the fall of Shatha's hair,
and although it was decades ago, he still loves her,
remembers her standing at the canebrake
15 where the buffalo cooled shoulder-deep in the water,
pleased with the orange cups of flowers he brought her,
and he regrets how so much can go wrong in a life,
how easily the years slip by, light as grain, bright
as the street's concussion of metal, shrapnel
20 traveling at the speed of sound to open him up
in blood and shock, a man whose last thoughts
are of love and wreckage, with no one there
to whisper him gone.

Sgt. Ledouix of the National Guard
25 speaks but cannot hear the words coming out,
and it's just as well his eardrums ruptured

© Xavier Pick

British artist Xavier Pick spent six weeks with British, American, and Iraqi armed forces in the Basra region in 2008. His caption reads: "Humvee convoy towards Iranian Border past the black flags of Ashura—mourning the death of the prophet's grandson—a metaphor for grief, oppression & sacrifice & salvation."

What is the tone of this piece and how does Pick create it? How is that tone similar to or different from the tone Turner creates in "2000 lbs."?

      because it lends the world a certain calm,
      though the traffic circle is filled with people
      running in panic, their legs a blur
30   like horses in a carousel, turning
      and turning the way the tires spin
      on the Humvee flipped to its side,
      the gunner's hatch he was thrown from
      a mystery to him now, a dark hole
35   in metal the color of sand, and if he could,
      he would crawl back inside of it,
      and though his fingertips scratch at the asphalt
      he hasn't the strength to move:
      shrapnel has torn into his ribcage
40   and he will bleed to death in ten minutes,
      but he finds himself surrounded by a strange
      beauty, the shine of light on the broken,
      a woman's hand touching his face, tenderly
      the way his wife might, amazed to find

45   a wedding ring on his crushed hand,
      the bright gold sinking in flesh
      going to bone.

      Rasheed passes the bridal shop
      on a bicycle, with Sefa beside him,
50   and just before the air ruckles and breaks
      he glimpses the sidewalk reflections
      in the storefront glass, men and women
      walking and talking, or not, an instant
      of clarity, just before each of them shatters
55   under the detonation's wave,
      as if even the idea of them were being
      destroyed, stripped of form,
      the blast tearing into the manikins
      who stood as though husband and wife
60   a moment before, who cannot touch
      one another, who cannot kiss,
      who now lie together in glass and debris,
      holding one another in their half-armed embrace,
      calling this love, if this is all there will ever be.

65   The civil affairs officer, Lt. Jackson, stares
      at his missing hands, which make
      no sense to him, no sense at all, to wave
      these absurd stumps held in the air
      where just a moment before he'd blown bubbles
70   out the Humvee window, his left hand holding the bottle,
      his right hand dipping the plastic ring in soap,
      filling the air behind them with floating spheres
      like the oxygen trails of deep ocean divers,
      something for the children, something beautiful,
75   translucent globes with their iridescent skins
      drifting on vehicle exhaust and the breeze
      that might lift one day over the Zagros mountains,
      that kind of hope, small globes which may have
      astonished someone on the sidewalk
80   seven minutes before Lt. Jackson blacks out
      from blood loss and shock, with no one there to bandage
      the wounds that would carry him home.

      Nearby, an old woman cradles her grandson,
      whispering, rocking him on her knees
85   as though singing him to sleep, her hands

wet with their blood, her black dress
soaked in it as her legs give out
and she buckles with him to the ground.
If you'd asked her forty years earlier
90   if she could see herself an old woman
begging by the roadside for money, here,
with a bomb exploding at the market
among all these people, she'd have said
To have your heart broken one last time
95   *before dying, to kiss a child given sight*
of a life he could never live? It's impossible,
this isn't the way we die.

And the man who triggered the button,
who may have invoked the Prophet's name,
100 or not — he is obliterated at the epicenter,
he is everywhere, he is of all things,
his touch is the air taken in, the blast
and wave, the electricity of shock,
his is the sound the heart makes quick
105 in the panic's rush, the surge of blood
searching for light and color, that sound
the martyr cries filled with the word
his soul is made of, *Inshallah.*

Still hanging in the air over Ashur Square,
110 the telephone line snapped in two, crackling
a strange incantation the dead hear
as they wander confused amongst one another,
learning each other's names, trying to comfort
the living in their grief, to console
115 those who cannot accept such random pain,
speaking *habib* softly, one to another there
in the rubble and debris, *habib*
over and over, that it might not be forgotten.

Understanding and Interpreting

1 How would you characterize the speaker of this poem? What does the speaker know and not know, or report and not report? How does Turner's choice of speaker relate to the theme of the poem?

2 In the second stanza, Sefwan thinks the detonation looks like a "flight of gold" (l. 7), which is an image of beauty, even as it destroys. Identify other places where Turner intentionally juxtaposes images of beauty with destruction. What is the purpose of these contrasts?

3 Does everyone in the poem die the same way, or are there differences in their deaths? Explain how these similarities or differences support a point Turner is making about life and death.

4 Turner takes the reader inside the thoughts of each of the characters in the poem, with the exception of the man in the first and seventh stanzas. What is the effect of this narrative choice?

5 Many of the characters in the poem have flashbacks before their deaths. What seems to be in common among the topics of these flashbacks, and why would Turner choose these topics?

6 There is a shift in the final stanza; we do not get the perspective of one single person. In terms of plot, what happens in this final stanza, and how does the shift of narrative focus illustrate a theme of the poem?

7 References to love appear throughout the poem. What is Turner saying about love, and what does he accomplish by using this tragic incident to make his point?

Analyzing Language, Style, and Structure

1 The first line of the poem begins with "it," and the last line includes the word "it." What does "it" refer to, and how are those two uses of the pronoun related?

2 Look at stanzas 2–6, select two of them, and look closely at how they are structured. How does each stanza begin (for example, before, after, or during the explosion), what information does the reader receive in the middle of the stanza, and how does the stanza end? What is Turner suggesting through the structure of each stanza?

3 The poem has eight stanzas, in which we get the alternating perspectives of six different people. How does Turner's decision to structure his poem in this manner reflect the meaning of the poem?

4 People who have survived terrible accidents sometimes say that time seemed to stand still as the event was occurring. What language and structural choices does Turner make in this poem to create a similar feeling?

5 How does the inclusion of words in Arabic— *Inshallah* and *habib*—illustrate Turner's overall tone toward the events presented in the poem?

6 In stanza seven, Turner uses the word "martyr" in reference to the man who detonated the bomb. What does the use of this word, instead of other possible words, suggest about the meaning of the poem?

Connecting, Arguing, and Extending

1 Discuss whether Turner is too sympathetic to the man who sets off the bomb, using evidence from the poem to support your position.

2 Turner served for seven years in the U.S. Army, spending time in Iraq and other war zones. To what extent does his background give him a level of credibility or authenticity that affects how you read the poem?

3 The expression Turner chooses to end the stanza about the man who sets off the bomb is "*Inshallah*," which is often translated from Arabic as "God willing."

Nevertheless, the term's full meaning and its usage are more complex than this translation may suggest. Conduct research into the usage of the expression *inshallah*, and explain the similarities and differences in how the phrase is used in two or more cultures.

4 Write an additional stanza of Turner's poem from the perspective of a bystander who witnesses the death of one of the characters depicted in one of the other stanzas. Try to use the same structure and narrative point of view that Turner employs.

My Enemy, Myself

Karim Ben Khelifa

Karim Ben Khelifa (b. 1972), a freelance photojournalist who has covered conflicts around the world, is also a fellow at the Nieman Foundation for Journalism at Harvard University. His award-winning work on the wars in Iraq, Afghanistan, Kosovo, Kashmir, and throughout Africa and the Middle East has appeared in *Newsweek,* the *New York Times Magazine,* and many European publications. In this photo essay, published in the magazine *Foreign Policy,* Ben Khelifa takes portraits of people on opposite sides of long-standing conflicts and asks each person, "Who's your enemy? Why fight?"

Karim Ben Khelifa

KEY CONTEXT   To help you understand the context of the photos and the subjects' comments, you may want to familiarize yourself with the following brief summaries of the three conflicts that Ben Khelifa documents in his photo essay:

The Gaza Strip: The site of one of the world's most intractable conflicts, the Gaza Strip is a twenty-five-mile area of land in the Middle East that is populated predominately by Palestinians. The land has been controlled at various times throughout history by England, Egypt, and Israel. There are frequent border clashes between residents of Gaza and the Israeli army, and rockets are regularly sent from Gaza into civilian areas of Israel.

Kashmir: Kashmir is a disputed territory with a long history of occupation. India, Pakistan, and China all lay claim to portions of the area in the northwest portion of the Indian subcontinent; Pakistan and India have fought several wars over the territory. Some of the most violent conflicts occur in the Kashmir Valley, which is administered by India, a majority Hindu nation. Residents of the area, the majority of whom are Muslim, say that they would prefer to be independent or to be a part of Pakistan, a majority Muslim nation. India has long accused Pakistan of training and arming the residents of Kashmir as terrorists.

South Sudan: The most recent aspects of the conflict in South Sudan can be traced to the ongoing clashes in 2011 between two of the largest clans in the area, the Murle and the Lou Nuer. Each side accuses the other of stealing cattle and burning villages. Hundreds of people on both sides of the conflict have been killed and thousands have had to flee their homes. The conflict has been made worse by recent drought conditions and the weakness of the central government in the newly independent South Sudan.

Karim Ben Khelifa

◀ **Gaza**

"My name is Abu Yasser; I'm 32 years old and I'm a commander in the Al Aqsa Brigade, Jihad al-Amarin branch. My enemy is Israel. I started to fight when I was 15 years old. It was during the first Intifada. It wasn't like today, with weapons; back then, it was about throwing stones. Later I was sentenced to seven years in an Israeli prison. After three and a half years, I was released. Then I started working for the Palestinian Authorities, and then I joined the resistance. I met my enemy many times, not just once. There were regular clashes between us and them. Today, all the Palestinians in Gaza, in the West Bank, inside Israel, and abroad are looking at us because our cause was a lost one. What happened in Gaza shook them up. Who would hate to kill an enemy? An enemy who has killed our kids, our sons. I was born in this country; where would I go? It is forbidden to go here or there. Like now, the Egyptians forbid us to cross the border because we are part of the resistance. And Israel? How would I go there? I'm wanted by them. Palestine will have many other battles, long ones; Israel will keep fighting back, and they will keep trying to destroy us. Until when we will live, we do not know; this is in Allah's hands, not in anyone else's. We are fighting with poor tools, and why do we fight? For our freedom. This is what we are asking, nothing else."

Karim Ben Khelifa

◀ **Gaza**

"My name is Tomer Brok; I'm 19 years old. I'm a sergeant in the Israeli army. My enemy is anybody that threatens the country, the safety of its civilians, and the free life we lead. I never encountered my enemy face to face, and therefore I never killed one of them. My biggest fear is that people here will stop thinking it's important to get to the army and that will slowly lead to our destruction and the disappearance of our freedom. Freedom to me is each individual being able to live his life with dignity as he wishes and without fear. Terrorism for me is wanting to take away the freedom of others. At the end it's taking away the right to choose and the liberty that everyone should have just for being a person. My goal in life is first of all to do in the army all I can to protect my country and in the future to go ahead and build a family and to stay in Israel and never leave it; this is where my roots are. And to continue to give to the country as a civilian."

◀ Kashmir

"My name is Kashmir Singh; I'm 40 years old. I am a policeman, I have joined the police forces 23 years ago to serve my country. My enemy is the one who breaks the law of my country. I have met my enemies face to face, and they do not scare me. We have been attacked by our enemies several times, and I killed many of them. If someone endangers us and the laws, we might have to kill him in order to protect us. Terrorism is harmful for everyone, and we will fight it until the end. In the next 20 years, India will grow to become the first country in the world. I wish peace and harmony for my life."

◀ Kashmir

"My name is Bilal Ahmed. I am 32 years old. I have been throwing stones since 1993 because India is constantly harassing us. My enemy is India. I am not afraid of anything except God. I haven't killed anyone because I am a Muslim and Islam forbids us to harm innocent people. God has created every human being, and I have no right to go against God's will. I fear only one thing—that is that we are not safe under the rule of India. Recently two sisters in Shopian were raped and martyred by Indian soldiers. Freedom from India would be a blessing for us. We are not terrorists; we are Muslims, and I wish from life to die for Islam."

Karim Ben Khelifa

◀ **South Sudan**

"My name is Paulino Kueth; I'm 28 years old. I'm a member of the
Lou Nuer. My enemies are the Murle. They designated themselves
as our enemies. The problem is the cattle; the Murle come to steal
it. The fighting is historical: They kill and we kill them in return. We
can't deny that we have also killed; people fought for so long now.
People have suffered: Your cattle has been taken; your children
are abducted; you are not allowed to work your land; you feel
hunger and you go without food for a long period of time. All
those things are the result of the conflict. Nobody has been solving the problem and addressing it until recently. People were not
blaming the government, maybe because of the scarcity of the
resources. Freedom is a situation that allows you to interact with
people. If we can interact, you and I, it is because of freedom.
Freedom is something that can help to find a solution to solve a
lot of problems like addressing hunger, the problem of fighting.
Previously people were under the rule of north Sudan. We had no
freedom because people were not interacting. We had no future
plan, or to think of what might happen, but this time around we feel we have freedom. We are under our
own rules. You can even think peace as a result of freedom. Violence is a situation where there is a lot of
poverty, a lack of knowledge, no valuing of the importance of other human beings. That is why you have
killings, but if you know that there is another human in front of you, you can't simply kill another person.
Therefore if people get together, sharing knowledge, they will value other human beings."

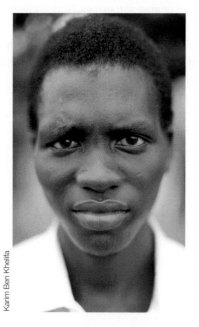

Karim Ben Khelifa

◀ **South Sudan**

"My name is John Akuer Aborcup; I'm 18 years old. My enemy is the
one who comes to attack me. Members of the Lou Nuer tribe have
attacked us, but we also had to fight with members of the Dinka Bor
tribe. Those tribes are our enemies because sometimes we go and
take their cattle and they come back to attack us; they have killed our
people. The Lou Nuer recently came to Pibor and killed my three
uncles. They looted all our cattle; they burned all our houses. They
cannot be my friends anymore; they have destroyed us. Those are my
enemies, and I will have to take revenge. My first reaction has to take
revenge and to go to the Lou Nuer land to fight the people who have
attacked us. But that means that I could die and I would not be able
to help my people. Freedom for me is to be able to mobilize my
community, to defend my people. And violence is for me to go and
attack my enemies, to get stuck in a tribal war. I think 20 years from
now, all tribes will live in peace because towns are growing and
reaching smaller villages, bringing development, schools, roads, and
business, so the next generation can be educated. We started the
tribal wars a thousand years ago. Now we use Kalashnikovs.
Tomorrow I hope we will use pencils."

Understanding and Interpreting

1 In the texts accompanying the pair of photos about Gaza, both men discuss the concept of "freedom." How are their views on this topic similar and different?

2 How do the two men on opposing sides of the conflict in Kashmir define a "terrorist"?

3 Both Sudanese men use the word "enemy." According to each man's point of view, how is he similar to his enemy?

4 While each of the three conflicts is clearly unique, what similarities do they share? Base your answer only on what you have read or seen in these texts.

5 There is an expectation that journalists attempt to be unbiased. Use visual and textual evidence to demonstrate whether Ben Khelifa is, or is not, unbiased.

6 While Ben Khelifa never explicitly states it, what is the overall point he is making about the causes and effects of war? What visual and textual evidence supports your conclusion?

Analyzing Language, Style, and Structure

1 The pictures in this essay are not "action" photographs like most of Ben Khelifa's photojournalism. What is the effect on the reader of his choice of portraiture? What effect do you think Ben Khelifa intends to achieve by having his subjects look directly into the camera?

2 Most of the pictures are close-ups or have blurred backgrounds, which makes it is difficult for viewers to tell where the photographs were taken. How does this choice support the larger point that Ben Khelifa is trying to make?

3 It is clear that the texts accompanying the photos are the result of Ben Khelifa's asking each man roughly the same questions. What are the questions that he likely asked? How do the implicit questions themselves reflect Ben Khelifa's point of view?

4 In the photos, what are the similarities and differences between how the men in opposing conflicts are represented—in clothing, weapons, facial expressions, gestures, and so on? What is the effect of these similarities and differences?

Connecting, Arguing, and Extending

1 What is the role of a photojournalist? How is it similar to and different from that of a print or television journalist? Locate a photo essay online and explain how it both fits and does not quite fit the traditional definition of journalism.

2 Research the jobs of reporters like Ben Khelifa who cover wars and conflicts around the world. Good places to start include the organization Reporters without Borders and the Society of Professional Journalists. What dangers do these journalists face and what are the results of their work?

3 Create your own photo essay about people in your school or the city or town in which you live. Try to focus on people who might be different from each other in some kind of way. Your photo essay could focus on different cliques at school, or people from different ethnic, religious, socioeconomic, or cultural groups. Ask the same two or three questions of each of your subjects and include the answers in captions for your photographs, as Ben Khelifa did in this photo essay.

ENTERING THE CONVERSATION
STORIES OF WAR

Making Connections

1 In "The Storytellers of Empire," Kamila Shamsie disagrees with the idea that "as an American male you can't understand a Pakistani woman. " Nevertheless, she recognizes that there is a tendency for Americans to "Leave [the Pakistani woman] and her nation to its Otherness." (par. 25). Identify two texts in this Conversation (or the excerpt from the Central Text, *When the Emperor Was Divine*) in which characters or speakers face someone who is "enigmatic, inscrutable, unknowable." Compare the reasons for and the effects of this Otherness.

2 Wilfred Owen, in "Dulce et Decorum Est," calls dying for your country "the old Lie." How would Shakespeare's Henry V or Schultz's Steph from "Deuce Out" respond to Owen?

3 A number of the texts in this Conversation present the lingering effects of war or other cultural conflicts. Select two texts and compare the ways that these events have affected the characters, speakers, or real-life people.

4 Compare how Kevin Sites in the excerpt from *In the Hot Zone* and the narrator of Vu Bao's story "The Man Who Stained His Soul" feel about the role of propaganda and the manipulation of truth during war.

5 In "The Storytellers of Empire," Shamsie wonders if American writers ever ask themselves the following questions about people from other cultures: "Who are these people and what do they have to do with us?" (par. 16). Based upon your reading of "2000 lbs.," how do you think Brian Turner might answer those questions? Why?

Synthesizing Sources

1 In the introduction to this Conversation, you may have read the excerpt from Tim O'Brien's short story "How to Tell a True War Story" (p. 558). Explain why at least two texts from the Conversation would or would not meet O'Brien's definition.

2 Are conflicts based on culture inevitable, or can they be avoided? Is a lack of understanding between cultures part of what causes conflict? Is racism or prejudice part of the problem? Write an argumentative essay in which you take a position on the factors that lead to cultural conflicts, referring to at least two texts from this Conversation (or one text from the Conversation and the excerpt from *When the Emperor Was Divine*).

3 Is it possible to know the truth in the midst of the fog of war? What factors, such as time, distance, or multiple sources, might help to know the truth in war? Refer to at least two texts from the Conversation (or one text from the Conversation and the excerpt from *When the Emperor Was Divine*) to support your position.

4 In an interview with the *Paris Review*, author Chinua Achebe remarked: "There is that great proverb— that until the lions have their own historians, the history of the hunt will always glorify the hunter." In other words, history is written by the victors. Is this really how history works? Write an argumentative piece taking a position on this subject, pointing to specific examples from at least two sources in this Conversation (or one text from the Conversation and the excerpt from *When the Emperor Was Divine*), as well as at least one example from history or current events.

5 Many of the texts in this Conversation, as well as the excerpt from *When the Emperor Was Divine*, either directly or indirectly point to propaganda as a significant tool to convince people to fight in wars. Why are humans susceptible to the powers of propaganda? Why is propaganda effective? Write a response using at least two texts from this Conversation (or one text from the Conversation and the excerpt from *When the Emperor Was Divine*) as well as your own research into other uses of propaganda during wartime.

DISPLACEMENT AND ASSIMILATION

Every nation tells stories about itself.

One of the most enduring stories America tells about itself is inscribed on the base of the Statue of Liberty:

> Give me your tired, your poor,
> Your huddled masses yearning to breathe free.
> The wretched refuse of your teeming shore.
> Send these, the homeless, tempest-tost to me,
> I lift my lamp beside the golden door!

Since the time of the Puritans fleeing religious persecution, America has presented itself as a place to begin again and find economic, social, and religious freedom.

And yet, like all myths, it's a bit too simplistic. The reality of immigration is that it is complex—culturally, politically, and economically. Do all Americans really believe in the welcoming gesture of the Statue of Liberty? Is the new image of American immigration more like an armed border with Mexico? Do all immigrants willingly and easily leave everything behind to start a new life in America? Are conflicts between the new immigrants and the society they enter inevitable? Is America really a "melting pot," where "individuals of all nations are melted into a new race of men," as one of the texts in this Conversation suggests, or is it closer to what writer Jane Elliot observes when she says:

> We don't need a melting pot in this country, folks. We need a salad bowl.
> In a salad bowl, you put in the different things. You want the vegetables — the lettuce, the cucumbers, the onions, the green peppers — to maintain their identity. You appreciate differences.

These are some of the questions that you will consider in this Conversation.

While it's unlikely that you will be able to answer with certainty these questions that have challenged people for hundreds of years, you will have an opportunity to thoughtfully consider and expand on your own ideas of immigration and enter the Conversation with your own point of view.

TEXTS

J. Hector St. John de Crèvecoeur / *from* Letters from an American Farmer (nonfiction)
Anna Quindlen / A Quilt of a Country (nonfiction)
Li-Young Lee / For a New Citizen of These United States (poetry)
Nola Kambanda / My New World Journey (memoir)
Amit Majmudar / Dothead (poetry)
Maira Kalman / *from* And the Pursuit of Happiness (graphic essay)

from Letters from an American Farmer

J. Hector St. John de Crèvecoeur

Michel-Guillaume-Jean de Crèvecoeur (1735–1813) was born into an aristocratic family in France and immigrated to the French-controlled area of North America in 1755. After the French-American War, he took up farming in New York and, under his new name, J. Hector St. John, wrote *Letters from an American Farmer*, from which this excerpt is taken. At the time of his writing (1782), just after the American Revolution, Europeans had little idea of what America was like, and Crèvecoeur's *Letters* served as an introduction to and analysis of what he called "a new race of men." In this selection from "Letter III—What Is an American?," he draws a comparison between Europe and America, and though he clearly appears to favor the new world, Crèvecoeur spent his latter years back in France.

What Is an American?

I wish I could be acquainted with the feelings and thoughts which must agitate the heart and present themselves to the mind of an enlightened Englishman, when he first lands on this continent. He must greatly rejoice that he lived at a time to see this fair country discovered and settled; he must necessarily feel a share of national pride, when he views the chain of settlements which embellishes these extended shores. When he says to himself, this is the work of my countrymen, who, when convulsed by factions, afflicted by a variety of miseries and wants, restless and impatient, took refuge here. They brought along with them their national genius, to which they principally owe what liberty they enjoy, and what substance they possess. Here he sees the industry of his native country displayed in a new manner, and traces in their works the embrios of all the arts, sciences, and ingenuity which flourish in Europe. Here he beholds fair cities, substantial villages, extensive fields, an immense country filled with decent houses, good roads, orchards, meadows, and bridges, where an hundred years ago all was wild, woody and uncultivated! What a train of pleasing ideas this fair spectacle must suggest; it is a prospect which must inspire a good citizen with the most heartfelt pleasure. The difficulty consists in the manner of viewing so extensive a scene. He is arrived on a new continent; a modern society offers itself to his contemplation, different from what he had hitherto seen. It is not composed, as in Europe, of great lords who possess every thing and of a herd of people who have nothing. Here are no aristocratical families, no courts, no kings, no bishops, no ecclesiastical dominion, no invisible power giving to a few a very visible one; no great manufacturers employing thousands, no great refinements of luxury. The rich and the poor are not so far removed from each other as they are in Europe. Some few towns excepted, we are all tillers of the earth, from Nova Scotia to West Florida. We are a people of cultivators, scattered over an immense territory communicating with each other by means of good roads and navigable rivers, united by the silken bands of mild government, all respecting the laws, without dreading their power, because they are equitable. We are all animated with the spirit of an industry which is unfettered and unrestrained, because each person works for himself. [. . .]

What attachment can a poor European emigrant have for a country where he had nothing? The knowledge of the language, the love of a few kindred as poor as himself, were the only cords that tied him: his country is now that

Ralph Wheelock's Farm (oil on canvas), Alexander, Francis (1800–81)/
Private Collection/Bridgeman Images

While this painting, *Ralph Wheelock's Farm* by Francis Alexander, was created forty years after
Crèvecoeur published his *Letters from an American Farmer*, it depicts an America that is similar
to the one Crèvecoeur presents.

**Compare and contrast how Crèvecoeur and Alexander view agrarian life in America. What
changed in the forty years between the creation of Crèvecoeur's and Alexander's works,
and how might that context affect your reading of this painting?**

which gives him land, bread, protection, and consequence: *Ubi panis ibi patria*,[1] is the motto of all emigrants. What then is the American, this new man? He is either an European, or the descendant of an European, hence that strange mixture of blood, which you will find in no other country. I could point out to you a family whose grandfather was an Englishman, whose wife was Dutch, whose son married a French woman, and whose present four sons have now four wives of different nations. *He* is an American, who leaving behind him all his ancient prejudices and manners, receives new ones from the new mode of life he has embraced, the new government he obeys, and the new rank he holds.

He becomes an American by being received in the broad lap of our great *Alma Mater*. Here individuals of all nations are melted into a new race of men, whose labours and posterity will one day cause great changes in the world. Americans are the western pilgrims, who are carrying along with them that great mass of arts, sciences, vigour, and industry which began long since in the east; they will finish the great circle. The Americans were once scattered all over Europe; here they are incorporated into one of the finest systems of population which has ever appeared, and which will hereafter become distinct by the power of the different climates they inhabit. The American ought therefore to love this country much better than that wherein either he or his forefathers were born. Here the rewards of his industry follow with equal steps the progress of his labour; his labour is founded on the basis of nature, *self-interest*; can it want a stronger allurement? Wives and children, who before in vain demanded of him a morsel of bread, now, fat and frolicsome, gladly help their father to clear those fields whence exuberant

---

[1] *Ubi panis ibi patria*: A Latin expression meaning, "Where there is bread, there is my country."

crops are to arise to feed and to clothe them all; without any part being claimed, either by a despotic prince, a rich abbot, or a mighty lord. Religion demands but little of *him*; a small voluntary salary to the minister, and gratitude to God; can he refuse these? The American is a new man, who acts upon new principles; he must therefore entertain new ideas, and form new opinions. From involuntary idleness, servile dependence, penury, and useless labour, he has passed to toils of a very different nature, rewarded by ample subsistence. — This is an American.

Understanding and Interpreting

1 This excerpt begins by asking the reader to imagine seeing America through the eyes of "an enlightened Englishman." Explain how Crèvecoeur says this Englishman would feel.

2 The middle section of the excerpt draws contrasts between America and Europe. Make a T-chart or a Venn diagram that illustrates the similarities and differences that Crèvecoeur identifies. How do the contrasts support the central idea of the text?

3 According to Crèvecoeur, why should Americans love their new country more than their former nation?

4 Put into your own words what Crèvecoeur means when he writes that an American is a "new man."

Analyzing Language, Style, and Structure

1 Who is Crèvecoeur's audience for this piece? How do you know? What does Crèvecoeur do to appeal to and avoid insulting this audience?

2 If part of Crèvecoeur's purpose in writing this piece is to persuade people to immigrate to America, how successful is his argument?

3 What evidence does Crèvecoeur provide to support his claim that "[h]ere individuals of all nations are melted into a new race of men" (par. 3)?

4 Examine the word choices that Crèvecoeur uses to distinguish between America and Europe. How do these choices help or hinder Crèvecoeur's argument?

5 Trace Crèvecoeur's use of pronouns. When and for what effect does he use "he," "we," "them," and "I"?

6 Crèvecoeur published this piece in 1782, soon after the conclusion of the American Revolution. How does the occasion of his writing affect his purpose and his tone?

Connecting, Arguing, and Extending

1 To what extent is America, as Crèvecoeur suggests, a pot in which everyone from other countries is melted into a new race? Is it more like a "salad bowl," as described in the opening of this Conversation, and if so, why? Alternatively, what might be a more appropriate metaphor for how immigrants become Americans?

2 At the time of Crèvecoeur's writing, farming was the most common American profession, but now it is retail sales. Write a "Letter from an American Salesperson" in an attempt to persuade people to immigrate to—or dissuade them from moving to—the United States today.

3 Is today's America still as different from Europe as it was in Crèvecoeur's time? What has changed and what has remained the same? Are there other countries or parts of the world that are as different from America today as Crèvecoeur says Europe was at the time? Explain.

A Quilt of a Country

Anna Quindlen

Anna Quindlen (b. 1953) is an American novelist and newspaper columnist. Her novels include *One True Thing* and *Black and Blue*, and her nonfiction books include *A Short Guide to a Happy Life* and *How Reading Changed My Life*. Quindlen won the Pulitzer Prize in 1992 for her column in the *New York Times*, and she wrote a regular column for *Newsweek* from 2000 to 2009. This article appeared in *Newsweek* on September 26, 2001, about two weeks after the September 11 terrorist attacks.

Todd Plitt/Contour by Getty Images

America is an improbable idea. A mongrel nation built of ever-changing disparate parts, it is held together by a notion, the notion that all men are created equal, though everyone knows that most men consider themselves better than someone. "Of all the nations in the world, the United States was built in nobody's image," the historian Daniel Boorstin wrote. That's because it was built of bits and pieces that seem discordant, like the crazy quilts that have been one of its great folk-art forms, velvet and calico and checks and brocades. Out of many, one.[1] That is the ideal.

The reality is often quite different, a great national striving consisting frequently of failure. Many of the oft-told stories of the most pluralistic nation on earth are stories not of tolerance, but of bigotry. Slavery and sweatshops, the burning of crosses and the ostracism of the other. Children learn in social-studies class and in the news of the lynching of blacks, the denial of rights to women, the murders of gay men. It is difficult to know how to convince them that this amounts to "crown thy good with brotherhood," that amid all the failures is something spectacularly successful. Perhaps they understand it at this moment, when enormous tragedy, as it so often does, demands a time of reflection on enormous blessings.

This is a nation founded on a conundrum, what Mario Cuomo[2] has characterized as "community added to individualism." These two are our defining ideals; they are also in constant conflict. Historians today bemoan the ascendancy of a kind of prideful apartheid[3] in America, saying that the clinging to ethnicity, in background and custom, has undermined the concept of unity. These historians must have forgotten the past, or have gilded it. The New York of my children is no more Balkanized, probably less so, than the Philadelphia of my father, in which Jewish boys would walk several blocks out of their way to avoid the Irish divide of Chester Avenue. (I was the product of a mixed marriage, across barely bridgeable lines: an Italian girl, an Irish boy. How quaint it seems now, how incendiary then.) The Brooklyn of Francie Nolan's famous tree,[4] the Newark of which Portnoy complained,[5] even the uninflected WASP suburbs of Cheever's characters:[6] they are ghettos,

---

[1] Out of many, one: The phrase *e pluribus unum*, Latin for "out of many, one," appears on American currency. —Eds.

[2] Mario Cuomo: Governor of New York from 1983 to 1994. —Eds.

[3] apartheid: A system of racial segregation. In South Africa, apartheid was enforced through legislation by the National Party, which ran the government from 1948 until 1994. —Eds.

[4] The Brooklyn of Francie Nolan's famous tree: Francie Nolan is the protagonist of Betty Smith's 1943 novel *A Tree Grows in Brooklyn*. —Eds.

[5] the Newark of which Portnoy complained: Newark, New Jersey, is the childhood home of Alexander Portnoy, the protagonist of Philip Roth's 1969 novel *Portnoy's Complaint*. —Eds.

[6] the uninflected WASP suburbs of Cheever's characters: John Cheever (1912–1982) was an American writer whose novels and short stories were often set in the suburbs of New York City. WASP is an abbreviation for "White Anglo-Saxon Protestant." —Eds.

pure and simple. Do the Cambodians and the Mexicans in California coexist less easily today than did the Irish and Italians of Massachusetts a century ago? You know the answer.

What is the point of this splintered whole? What is the point of a nation in which Arab cabbies chauffeur Jewish passengers through the streets of New York — and in which Jewish cabbies chauffeur Arab passengers, too, and yet speak in theory of hatred, one for the other? What is the point of a nation in which one part seems to be always on the verge of fisticuffs with another, blacks and whites, gays and straights, left and right, Pole and Chinese and Puerto Rican and Slovenian? Other countries with such divisions have in fact divided into new nations with new names, but not this one, impossibly interwoven even in its hostilities.

5   Once these disparate parts were held together by a common enemy, by the fault lines of world wars and the electrified fence of communism. With the end of the cold war there was the creeping concern that without a focus for hatred and distrust, a sense of national identity would evaporate, that the left side of the hyphen — African-American, Mexican-American, Irish-American — would overwhelm the right. And slow-growing domestic traumas like economic unrest and increasing crime seemed more likely to emphasize division than community. Today the citizens of the United States have come together once more because of armed conflict and enemy attack. Terrorism has led to devastation — and unity.

Yet even in 1994, the overwhelming majority of those surveyed by the National Opinion Research Center agreed with this statement: "The U.S. is a unique country that stands for something special in the world." One of the things that it stands for is this vexing notion that a great nation can consist entirely of refugees from other nations, that people of different, even warring religions and cultures can live, if not side by side, than on either side of the country's Chester Avenues. Faced with this diversity there is little point in trying to isolate anything remotely resembling a national

character, but there are two strains of behavior that, however tenuously, abet the concept of unity.

There is that Calvinist undercurrent in the American psyche that loves the difficult, the demanding, that sees mastering the impossible, whether it be prairie or subway, as a test of character, and so glories in the struggle of this fractured coalescing. And there is a grudging fairness among the citizens of the United States that eventually leads most to admit that, no matter what the English-only advocates try to suggest, the new immigrants are not so different from our own parents or grandparents. Leonel Castillo, former director of the Immigration and Naturalization Service and himself the grandson of Mexican immigrants, once told the writer Studs Terkel proudly, "The old neighborhood Ma-Pa stores are still around. They are not Italian or Jewish or Eastern European any more. Ma and Pa are now Korean, Vietnamese, Iraqi, Jordanian, Latin American. They live in the store. They work seven days a week. Their kids are doing well in school. They're making it. Sound familiar?"

Tolerance is the word used most often when this kind of coexistence succeeds, but tolerance is a vanilla-pudding word, standing for little more than the allowance of letting others live unremarked and unmolested. Pride seems excessive, given the American willingness to endlessly complain about them, them being whoever is new, different, unknown or currently under suspicion. But patriotism is partly taking pride in this unlikely ability to throw all of us together in a country that across its length and breadth is as different as a dozen countries, and still be able to call it by one name. When photographs of the faces of all those who died in the World Trade Center destruction are assembled in one place, it will be possible to trace in the skin color, the shape of the eyes and the noses, the texture of the hair, a map of the world. These are the representatives of a mongrel nation that somehow, at times like this, has one spirit. Like many improbable ideas, when it actually works, it's a wonder.

Understanding and Interpreting

1 Explain the meaning of the quilt metaphor as it applies to the United States. Refer to specific evidence from the piece to support your explanation.

2 Quindlen includes a lot about the ideal of America versus its reality. What does she conclude about the contrast between the two?

3 What do the references to Nolan's Brooklyn, Portnoy's Newark, and Cheever's suburbs have in common, and how do they work to support Quindlen's point about America's neighborhoods?

4 At the end of paragraph 3, Quindlen writes, "You know the answer." What answer is she hoping her audience gives, and how does this implied answer relate to the quilt metaphor?

5 Explain what Quindlen means when she writes in paragraph 5, "that the left side of the hyphen [. . .] would overwhelm the right."

6 While Quindlen does not name the terrorist attacks of 9/11 until the very last paragraph, how has the context played a role in her argument? What have the attacks caused her to think about?

7 According to Quindlen, is the diversity of America a problem or a benefit? Refer to specific evidence from the piece to support your answer.

8 Reread the last paragraph, where Quindlen struggles to find just the right word to describe why America's coexistence succeeds. She tries out three words—"tolerance," "pride," and "patriotism." Why does each word capture—or not capture—Quindlen's perspective on America?

Analyzing Language, Style, and Structure

1 In the second sentence, Quindlen chooses the word "mongrel" to describe America. What is the connotation of this word? Does she use it in a literal way or does she intend a different effect? Skim back through the selection to focus on other diction choices that Quindlen uses to describe America. How do these choices reflect Quindlen's tone toward America?

2 Reread paragraph 2. What purpose does this particular paragraph serve in Quindlen's argument? Why is it effective for the author to present it so early in her argument?

3 In paragraph 3, Quindlen uses the word "ghettos." How is her use similar to and different from its common, contemporary usage? How does the word help to illustrate her argument about American neighborhoods?

4 Paragraph 4 consists of three rhetorical questions and one concluding sentence. What is the effect of the rhetorical questions and to what extent does the last sentence in the paragraph answer the questions, or not?

5 How does Quindlen use the quote from an interview with Leonel Castillo (par. 7) to support her argument?

6 While she does not include a lot of details about her personal life in this piece, Quindlen does make a couple of references to her childhood, her children's growing up in New York, and her father's crossing "Chester Avenue" (par. 3). How are these glimpses into Quindlen's own life used to establish her ethos?

7 Reread the sentence from the last paragraph that begins "When photographs of the faces [. . .]" Analyze the rhetorical devices Quindlen uses to create this powerful sentence and explain how it contributes to her argument as a whole.

Connecting, Arguing, and Extending

1 Quindlen's argument is made up almost entirely of appeals to pathos. Locate facts, statistics, expert opinions, or other appeals to logos in outside sources that would support or contradict Quindlen's contention that America is "a mongrel nation that [. . .] has one spirit" (par. 8).

2 In the last sentence of the essay, Quindlen writes, "Like many improbable ideas, when it actually works, it's a wonder." What are some other "improbable ideas" from history, science, pop culture, or other sources? What makes them work even though they may be "improbable"? Are they, in fact, also "wonders"? Why?

3 We learn in paragraph 3 that Quindlen is the "product of a mixed marriage, across barely bridgeable lines: an Italian girl, an Irish boy." Write about what you know about your own family's background and explain how your family's history resembles—or does not resemble—Quindlen's perception of the immigrant experience in America.

For a New Citizen of These United States

Li-Young Lee

Poet Li-Young Lee (b. 1957) was born in Jakarta, Indonesia, to parents of Chinese descent. When he was seven, his family immigrated to the United States, eventually settling in Pennsylvania. Lee began writing poetry while attending the University of Pittsburgh and has won many awards for his work since, including the 2003 Academy of American Poets Fellowship. *Publishers Weekly* reviewer Peggy Kaganoff says that Lee's work "weaves a remarkable web of memory from the multifarious fibers of his experience." In this poem, Lee writes in the voice of a young immigrant reflecting on his past before coming to America.

Forgive me for thinking I saw
the irregular postage stamp of death;
a black moth the size of my left
thumbnail is all I've trapped in the damask.
5 There is no need for alarm. And

there is no need for sadness, if
the rain at the window now reminds you
of nothing; not even of that
parlor, long like a nave, where cloud-shadow,
10 wing-shadow, where father-shadow
continually confused the light. In flight,
leaf-throng and, later, soldiers and
flags deepened those windows to submarine.

But you don't remember, I know,
15 so I won't mention that house where Chung hid,
Lin wizened, you languished, and Ming-
Ming hush-hushed us with small song. And since you
don't recall the missionary
bells chiming the hour, or those words whose sounds

20 alone exhaust the heart — *garden,*
  heaven, amen — I'll mention none of it.

  After all, it was just our life,
  merely years in a book of years. It was
  1960, and we stood with
25 the other families on a crowded
  railroad platform. The trains came, then
  the rains, and then we got separated.

  And in the interval between
  familiar faces, events occurred, which
30 one of us faithfully pencilled
  in a day-book bound by a rubber band.

  But birds, as you say, fly forward.
  So I won't show you letters and the shawl
  I've so meaninglessly preserved.
35 And I won't hum along, if you don't, when
  our mothers sing *Nights in Shanghai.*
  I won't, each Spring, each time I smell lilac,
  recall my mother, patiently
  stitching money inside my coat lining,
40 if you don't remember your mother
  preparing for your own escape.

  After all, it was only our
  life, our life and its forgetting.

Understanding and Interpreting

1 Although the speaker of the poem says that he or she will "mention none of it" (l. 21), quite a bit of information of the past comes out about the time before coming to America. What are some of the most significant past events identified in the poem?

2 How would you characterize the relationship between the speaker and the "you" that he or she is addressing? How are their feelings about the past different? What can you infer about the cause of their conflict?

3 The speaker identifies letters and other objects that have been "so meaninglessly preserved" (l. 34).

What factors might cause the speaker to claim that these are "meaningless"? Why does the speaker refer to them in this way?

4 There are many references to intentional forgetting or not remembering. What is Lee suggesting about the role of memory? What evidence from the poem supports your claim?

5 The title implies that this poem will include advice for recent immigrants to America. What suggestions do you think the speaker might offer about the difficulties associated with immigration?

Analyzing Language, Style, and Structure

1 The past in this poem is shrouded in mystery and vagueness. Locate a section where the speaker describes the past and explain how the poet's word choice creates a lack of clarity.

2 It is over halfway through the poem before the reader receives the most concrete image of the past: "It was / 1960, and we stood with / the other families on a crowded / railroad platform" (ll. 23–26). How do these lines signal a shift in the speaker's representation of the past?

3 Unlike other poems you may have read, "For a New Citizen of These United States" employs very little rhyme or rhythmic pattern. How does Lee's choice of "free verse" reflect the speaker's attitude toward the past?

4 In the stanza after the trains are separated (ll. 28–31), the speaker dismisses the details afterward by saying simply "events occurred." How does this choice reflect the conflict between the "you" of the poem and the speaker?

5 Twice, the speaker begins a stanza with a variation of "After all, it was just our life." How does this reveal the speaker's attitude toward the process of immigration?

Connecting, Arguing, and Extending

1 Despite the speaker's professed desire to leave the past behind, he or she has saved artifacts such as the letters and the shawl. What are some items from your own past that you have not let go of that hold some meaning for you, such as trophies, stuffed animals, or pieces of jewelry? Why have you kept them? What meaning do they hold for you?

2 It is clear the speaker's arrival in the United States was an escape from something that was happening in the home country rather than a simple immigration. Research America's current policy on political refugees seeking asylum from oppressive governments, focusing on who is allowed in the country for emergency reasons and who is not. Write an explanation of the policy and argue for any changes that you would recommend.

3 In another poem, called "A Hymn to Childhood," Li-Young Lee writes:

> Which childhood?
> The one from which you'll never escape? You,
> so slow to know
> what you know and don't know.

To what extent would the speaker of "For a New Citizen of These United States" agree or disagree with this perspective of childhood?

My New World Journey

Nola Kambanda

Nola Kambanda was born in Burundi, a country in Eastern Africa, to Rwandese parents who had left their home country in the early 1960s to escape genocide. Eventually, Kambanda immigrated to the United States. She lived with a family in Los Angeles as she attended college at California State University, majoring in electrical engineering. She then took a job with Boeing Reusable Space Systems. This narrative, published in the collection *Becoming American: Personal Essays by First Generation Women* (2000), focuses on the first few years of Kambanda's life as an immigrant in America.

Courtesy Nola Kambanda

The anticipation of coming to this great country and all of its physical, social, and economic capacity was overwhelming. It made me feel like a toddler in a toy store, unable to decide which adventure to tackle first. Coming to California from Burundi — a place that I had come to call home, a place that was so very different in every aspect from the United States — I was in complete awe. The first thing that hit me was the speed with which everything was going. It seemed too fast paced. The movement of the people was rushed, and no one was looking anywhere else except where they were going; the cars moved too fast; there were too many lights, too many buttons to press, too many escalators. I was suddenly asking myself if these people ever stopped talking to one another. The longing to be back home suddenly came upon me. The need for some kind of familiarity was so strong and yet I had just stepped off the plane.

In many ways, I have lived my life as an immigrant of one sort or another. I was born in Burundi to Rwandese parents who had each left the country in the early '60s as a political refugee to escape the ethnic cleansing which was going on. Despite the fact that they met, married, created a home, and had all seven of their children in Burundi, my parents never considered themselves anything other than Rwandese. There was no such thing as assimilation, as becoming a citizen of Burundi. As such, they raised their children to identify themselves as Rwandese. So I grew up with the understanding that where you were born has little, if any, bearing on who you are, let alone what you will become. You will always be followed by the shadow of your heritage and of ancestry.

All refugees grow up with this understanding. You grow up knowing that you do not automatically belong, that you always have to prove yourself, earn your place in the society which has so graciously allowed you the freedom of life. In my household, it was just assumed that we would do well in school. There was no room for

failure, for being anything other than the best. I, like all my siblings, excelled in my academics. I left Bujumbura, the capital city, to complete my secondary education at an all-girls boarding school in Kiganda, a small countryside town.

I had always wanted to be in a boarding school. My friends and the various acquaintances I met who had attended and/or graduated from boarding school told me about the lifelong bonds that were developed by the girls, about how it was an experience that had forever changed their sense of who they were as women. Though relatively unexciting, my first year at school in Kiganda was pleasant enough. My second year, however, was another story. A story that my parents, having left the violence of their homeland behind, had hoped I would never be able to tell.

5   Not so unlike the rival gang warfare I have grown accustomed to hearing about in Los Angeles, the territory of Central Africa where I am from is marred by tribal warfare. The two main tribes in both Burundi and Rwanda are the Hutus and the Tutsis. The hatred and rivalry between the tribes has existed from the beginning of this century's colonial occupation of these two countries. Even though most of the world has recently appealed to both the Tutsi and the Hutu tribes to put an end to the genocide, it will most likely continue into the next millenium. It is hard to change when you know no other way of life.

I suppose that this was the case with the young Hutu student at the boarding school who was plotting to have me, a Tutsi, killed. Actually, she and a small group of her Hutu friends were planning to extinguish all the Tutsi students. I just happened to be at the top of the list — literally. Mine was the first name on a list of over thirty names that the administration discovered. After the girls were found out and threatened with expulsion, they quickly abandoned their murderous plans. But for me, it was a serious reminder that I was a refugee and that meant I was never safe, always susceptible. I was never truly home. When I told my parents what had happened, their reaction only cemented this. "This is what you have to live with, Nola," they said. "This is who you are."

So there I was, at the Los Angeles International Airport, just one short taxi ride away from meeting the family with whom I'd be living. My aunt and cousin from Swaziland, where I had been living for most of the previous year, accompanied me on this, my first trip to America. More specifically, to what would be my new home — at least while I was attending school. While I was standing there outside the airport watching cars and buses of all shapes and sizes drive by, I thought about how I had reached this point in my life. I realized the sacrifice that not only my parents but also my siblings were making to send me out here. I was the first one of all seven of my parents' children to move so far away from Burundi. I should have felt privileged. I should have been excited and on top of the world about coming to America — the country I had been made to believe was the richest and most technologically advanced of them all.

But a sense of guilt was washing over me, one which became more pronounced as I kept thinking of the economic burden it would place on my father. An economic burden which I felt was too large for him to bear in older to accommodate just one child. The guilt and the realization that stemmed from it brought on a tremendous sense of responsibility for me. Even more so than in Burundi, failure was unacceptable. I could not fail here in America. I was going to have to be the best. I was going to have to do extremely well in school so that I could go on to get a decent job so that I would be able to contribute financially to my family's well-being.

The family that I was going to be living with in Los Angeles were strangers. They were well acquainted with my uncle and aunt who had come to vacation in the States each year. But I had never met them before. I wondered how awkward it would be to live with people I had never met before. When I walked into their house they greeted me very warmly. The sound of their voices calling me by name was not strange but, rather, familiar. It eased the pain of separation that I had been feeling from the moment our plane landed at the airport. I felt at home in their home.

10   Even still, I found myself growing ever-conscious of the way I spoke. This was the beginning of what would be my lengthy battle to translate myself in a language not my own, to communicate in English — not just any English, but *American* English. It seemed like I would never be able to speak as fast and as well as these people. I would never be able to say and remember their names, names I was not used to, as easily as they seemed to be able to say and remember mine. I wondered if they were, in meeting me, as aware of our differences as I was in meeting them. How did I seem to them? Did I seem too soft? Too slow? Too self-conscious? I must not have, because my new family — a Jewish-American social activist, a Jamaican-American actress-cum-writer and their pre-pubescent daughter — were very caring and hospitable. They never made me feel like I didn't fit in just right. I felt, in their eyes and in their home, like myself, like an individual, not a representative of Burundi, Rwanda, or Africa at large.

This was not the case with other people I met. I couldn't believe the questions that were posed to me. Questions about my country and about Africa — although in many cases there was no real distinction because so many people think that Africa is just one big country, not a continent with many, many countries in it. People would ask me if I spoke "African," if I could speak a little "African" for them to hear. One day while I was visiting the elementary school that the family's daughter was attending, one student asked me — with genuine sincerity — if we rode on elephants in Africa as a means of transportation. That blew me away.

When I went to apply for my Social Security card, the clerk looked at my passport, pointed to the printed name of my country, and asked,

"Where is that?" Upon being told by me that I had recently arrived from Burundi, by way of Swaziland, a young man asked, "How did you get here from there?" The thought that I could have flown in a commercial airplane from there to here did not seem to ever cross his curious mind. At times, I received these questions with humor. At times, I received them with confusion and took great offense. Why didn't these people know anything about Africa and its people, its geography? Why was there such a deep pit of ignorance? Where was the knowledge and wisdom and greatness I imagined everyone in America would have?

Surprisingly, most Americans I met in Los Angeles had no concept of African modernity. They still thought of Africans as people who lived in a jungle, people who had no access to airplanes, cars, televisions, telephones, CD players, or any of the other household appliances and urban facilities that I grew up enjoying in

Burundi. The fact that these Americans were not aware of African modernity was not as surprising as my discovery of the fact that they also knew very little about American history. In Burundi, geography, history, and anthropology were a critical part of our educational curriculum. And not just our geography, our history, and the study of our culture. We learned about the entire world. By the time I finished secondary school, I knew all the significant details of all the countries in all the continents. I knew the capitals of all the states in America, I knew who the presidents of the country were. Living in the glamour of Los Angeles and not knowing what a Tutsi or a Hutu is, not knowing where Burundi or Rwanda is can somehow be rationalized. Not knowing who Andrew Jackson was or where the capital of California is, cannot. This is how my romanticized idea of America died and the recognition of my journey into *a* new world—not *the* New World—began to take form.

Locating African Countries on a Blank Map

Washington Post readers were asked to locate African countries on a blank map. Most earned failing grades – correctly recognizing less than half of the continent's countries.

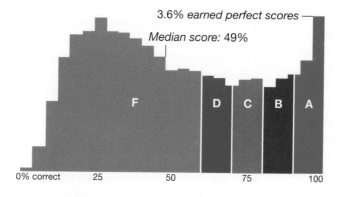

Percent of countries correctly recognized

3.6% *earned perfect scores*

Median score: 49%

F   D   C   B   A

0% correct   25   50   75   100

Most recognized countries

South Africa	97%
Madagascar	96
Egypt	89
Morocco	75
Libya	71

Least recognized countries

Gambia	15%
Guinea-Bissau	20
Gabon	21
Guinea	23
Sierra Leone	24

What are the causes and implications of the results of this survey? Are you surprised by the results? Would Kambanda be surprised? Why or why not?

. . .

The world I eventually came to embrace in America, in Los Angeles, and in the home where I was living was both comfortable and complicated. Even though my new family made it as painless as possible for me to emerge into their way of life, there were many things I had to learn. The differences in our cultures and lifestyles continued to display themselves as the days went by. Everything was rushed, was too this or too that, was always being pushed to the extreme. There just seemed to be a ton of information to recall. Where had all the simple things gone?

15   I had used a telephone plenty of times before and I had always thought of it as a pretty basic unit. You pick up the phone, you dial who you're calling, they answer it and you talk. No interruptions, no complexities. Until I learned that there was such thing as call waiting. And then three-way calling. And call forwarding. And single telephone units with multiple lines. What was all this? Was it all really necessary?

I wondered about the level of sophistication toward which everything seemed to be aspiring. It was a sophistication intended to facilitate, to make life simpler. But how is it possible to be simple and sophisticated at the same time? Take, for instance, the washing machine. I had neither seen nor used one before. You put your dirty clothes and some soap into a machine, close the lid, press a button and within minutes your clothes were done — clean and ready to be placed in yet another machine to be dried!?! Back at home, in Burundi, we would put our dirty clothes in a basin, soak them a bit, hand wash them with soap, and then hang them up to line dry. I will admit that the American way is definitely more convenient. But it lacks a certain ritual of intimacy. There is a care that I like to put into the cleaning of my clothes, those things that cover and protect my body, so I still invariably find myself hand washing.

Only recently did I realize that the majority of these cultural contrasts stemmed from the same root, the concept of time. Americans have a way of wanting to accomplish as much as possible in as little time as possible. Even something as sacred as eating. Fast food. It was amazing how many fast-food restaurants there were in Los Angeles, even in just our small neighborhood. Everyone ate at fast-food restaurants. I noticed how many ate while driving or being driven. I had not seen anything like this in my country. We ate three meals a day — breakfast, lunch, and dinner; and this was rarely done outside of either your own home or someone else's home. Eating out was a very formal affair. People didn't go out to eat by themselves. It was what you did in large numbers, something the whole family did together. Regardless of whether it was done in the home or out, dining required time. Food was never fast.

* * *

It didn't take long for me to catch on, for me to grab a hold of America. Especially after I had started doing what I came here to do — go to school. Once I started going to school and working a part-time job, I knew the meaning of busy. I knew why people ate and talked on the phone while driving from one place to another. Before long I started doing it myself. I'd never gone to school and worked at the same time. I don't think I'd ever known anyone in my life, certainly not in Burundi, who was working and going to school at the same time. School was your job. You were obligated to study and do well until you were finished because only then would you be qualified for employment. That was our incentive. Nobody wanted to hold a job for which you didn't need qualifications. Those petty positions were for the uneducated, for those who couldn't finish secondary school or university. Education was something that was taken seriously in Burundi. If you failed a class, you were not only castigated and harshly punished for it, you would also have to repeat the entire year of school before being allowed to move on to the next grade level. Out of fear for authority and all elders in society, we gave our professors the ultimate respect.

When I began attending Los Angeles City College, I was completely thrown off by the casual relationships between professors and students. The students appeared confident of their circumstances, unafraid of any consequences. The school was overflowing with options and choices. You could decide what classes you wanted to take, how many, and when you wanted to take them. You could miss a class and still make up for it. You could miss a class and never make up for it and still graduate.

20 Working and going to school was grueling, but I managed to do it because that was why I had come to America to begin with. I had to prove myself. There would be no reason to return to Burundi without a degree. Any of the students back home would have killed to be in my shoes. So why not use them to carry me someplace, somewhere of significance? After I completed my studies at the community college, I transferred to California State University–Los Angeles. I declared electrical engineering as my major. It did not go by unnoticed — by me or anyone else — that I happened to be the only black person, not to mention black woman, sitting in most of my classes. My strong accent made every verbal answer I gave a staring session for the rest of my classmates as they tried to figure out my words. The same is true of my present coworkers.

After receiving my degree, I was immediately offered the opportunity to begin my career. I took a position at Boeing Reusable Space Systems, where I am, again, one of a small few. It seems that I have always stood out. In Burundi. In America. My parents were right when they urged me to become used to the fact that I would always be the "other." Everywhere I go I come back to their words. "This is what you have to live with, Nola. This is who you are."

No doubt I am not American. I am a Rwandese Tutsi refugee who is becoming more and more understanding and appreciative of America each day I am here. The appreciativeness and understanding creates an awareness that makes me unique in every circle I could possibly travel in. It keeps me on my toes. If I was still in Burundi, I would also be busy, but not in the same way I am in America. I would probably be married with a couple of children. I would be busy with the kids, busy tending to the housework, busy taking care of my extended family and local community, busy helping my husband with his career and his dreams. I would be busy being a typical Rwandese housewife.

Sometimes I do think about going home. I think about the rewards of having an extended family and a local community that depends and insists upon my involvement. I think about finding a mate, that person I have not yet been able to find in the United States, the one who will be able to accept and relate to all aspects of my background and my culture. I think about the food, about the *cassava* leaves and the fried green bananas. I miss what I used to have, and what I used to want, who I thought I would become. Then again, I don't.

Sometimes I am not sure whether home is behind me or in front of me. I am not so sure this longing is really recognizable. I might just be attaching it to those things that are familiar to me. Home might very well be a place that I have not yet discovered, that I have not yet created. Or it might not be a place at all. After all, Rwanda, that place that I have called home all my life, is a place I have visited for only one month. I don't know its rivers, its mountains, intimately. All I know of Rwanda is its people, my family. So home might be family, and nothing more. It might be the people who make me feel. The people who define and occupy and receive my emotions, the people who reciprocate, who give me the most sought after, most valuable and intangible gifts — acceptance, trust, laughter, comfort, love. In that case, Burundi is home. And so is Swaziland. And so is America.

Understanding and Interpreting

1 What are some of the most significant pressures that Kambanda experiences as a refugee?

2 What similarities and differences does Kambanda identify between being a student in America and in Africa?

3 Though she does not explicitly say, to what factors do you think Kambanda attributes Americans' surprise in learning about Africa's modernity?

4 In paragraph 15, Kambanda asks—rhetorically— about American technology, "Was it all really necessary?" Based on what she writes later, how do you think she would answer that question? Explain.

5 Explain what Kambanda means when she writes, "Sometimes I am not sure whether home is behind me or in front of me" (par. 24).

6 According to Kambanda, to what extent is true assimilation possible? Support your response with examples from the narrative.

Analyzing Language, Style, and Structure

1 What effect does Kambanda intend to achieve by starting the narrative with her arrival in California?

2 Kambanda regularly uses the word "too" throughout this narrative, as in "too many" or "too fast." Identify places where she uses this word and explain how the word illustrates her experience as an immigrant.

3 Explain how Kambanda's experiences in America have caused her to redefine concepts like "busy," "food," and "home."

4 Although Kambanda's narrative starts with her arrival in the United States, the next five paragraphs consist of a flashback to her life in Africa. What information in this section is most essential to helping readers understand how difficult Kambanda's transition to America will be?

Connecting, Arguing, and Extending

1 Kambanda was at first amused and then offended by how little the Americans she met seemed to know about Africa. Begin by reflecting on what you know about Africa, and more important, where you have received that information from. Then, for a week, keep track of everything you see, read, and hear regarding Africa from TV, radio, newspapers, books, magazines, film, and online sources. What conclusions can you draw about the way Africa is portrayed in American culture? Do some research to figure out how this portrayal differs from reality.

2 Much of this narrative is an attempt to define a seemingly simple concept—"home." Write a narrative or a poem that defines "home" for you.

3 Kambanda is overwhelmed at one point with the technology posed by the telephone and the washing machine. Write an analysis of your own feelings about the technology that you encounter every day in your life. As Kambanda asks, is it "all really necessary" (par. 15)?

Dothead

Amit Majmudar

Poet and novelist Amit Majmudar (b. 1979) practices as a diagnostic nuclear radiologist in Dublin, Ohio, where he lives with his wife, twin sons, and daughter. He earned a BS at the University of Akron and an MD at Northeast Ohio Medical University. The recipient of several literary prizes, Majmudar has published two novels, *Partitions* (2011) and *The Abundance* (2013), and two poetry collections, *0˚, 0˚* (2009) and *Heaven and Earth* (2011). "Dothead" was published in the *New Yorker* in 2011.

Courtesy Amit Majmudar

KEY CONTEXT   Spiritually important in Hindu culture, the bindi, or "red dot," is a mark made of vermilion powder that Indian women wear on the forehead. Originally a mark of wisdom, the bindi has come to symbolize the love and commitment of a wife to her husband. The figure Nataraja is a depiction of the Hindu god Shiva as the Lord of the Dance and destroyer of the universe, paving the way for a new creation and signifying the never-ending cycle of time.

Well yes, I said, my mother wears a dot.
I know they said "third eye" in class, but it's not
an *eye* eye, not like that. It's not some freak
third eye that opens on your forehead like
5 on some Chernobyl baby. What it means
is, what it's *showing* is, there's this unseen
eye, on the inside. And she's marking it.
It's how the X that says where treasure's at
is not the treasure, but as good as treasure. —
10 All right. What I said wasn't half so measured.
In fact, I didn't say a thing. Their laughter
had made my mouth go dry. Lunch was after
World History; that week was India — myths,
caste system, suttee, all the Greatest Hits.
15 The white kids I was sitting with were friends,
at least as I defined a friend back then.
So wait, said Nick, does *your* mom wear a dot?
I nodded, and I caught a smirk on Todd —
She wear it to the shower? And to bed? —
20 while Jesse sucked his chocolate milk and Brad
was getting ready for another stab.

I said, Hand me that ketchup packet there.
And Nick said, What? I snatched it, twitched the tear,
and squeezed a dollop on my thumb and worked
25   circles till the red planet entered the house of war
and on my forehead for the world to see
my third eye burned those schoolboys in their seats,
their flesh in little puddles underneath,
pale pools where Nataraja cooled his feet.

Understanding and Interpreting

1 In line 10, the speaker admits, "What I said wasn't
half so measured." What does the difference
between what the speaker thinks and what he says
reveal about him?

2 What is the effect of the boys' laughter on the
speaker? Why might he have reacted this way?

3 What evidence from the poem suggests that the
speaker is now older and looking back on the
event? What does the older speaker likely think of his
younger self? Why?

4 Why does the speaker do what he does with the
ketchup at the end of the poem? What does that
action, compared to other possible actions, suggest
about him?

5 What is the poem saying about assimilation and
cultural differences, at least among adolescent
boys?

Analyzing Style, Language, and Structure

1 This poem has a conversational feel, as if the speaker
were just telling his audience a story. What words,
phrases, and other stylistic elements create this feel?

2 What is the attitude of the speaker toward the way
that school, history class in particular, teaches
about non-American cultures? What words or phrases
capture this tone?

3 While the speaker refers to the boys as "friends"
(l. 15), what does the poet include to show that the
speaker is separated from them?

4 In line 27, the speaker does not refer to the boys
as friends or by their names, instead calling them
"those schoolboys." How does this shift help to
illustrate the meaning of the poem?

5 Majmudar begins the poem right in the middle
of the speaker's conversation with his friends
about the dot his mother wears, then moves back in
time to the history class, and then returns to the
conversation. What effect is achieved through this
structure of the poem?

6 As the speaker is rubbing the ketchup into his
forehead, he says he worked circles "till the red
planet entered the house of war" (l. 25). Explain how
this metaphor reflects the speaker's attitude toward the
other boys.

7 After rereading the Key Context note, explain the
effect of the allusion to Nataraja. How does it
reflect and support the overall meaning of the poem?

Connecting, Arguing, and Extending

1 Describe a time when you either stood up for an unpopular belief or chose to remain silent. Why did you act the way you did? How was your experience similar to or different from that of the speaker in this poem?

2 Many high schools have "multicultural" assemblies, celebrations of Black History Month, or similar opportunities for students to learn about other cultures. In what ways are these approaches successful or beneficial? How do you think students can best learn about other cultures? Write an argument about the most effective ways that a school can teach students about other cultures.

3 The bindi is only one example of an outward marking used in a particular culture. Research other types of outward markings and explain their purposes.

---

from And the Pursuit of Happiness

Maira Kalman

Carolyn Cole/Los Angeles Times/Contour by Getty Images

Maira Kalman (b. 1949) was born in Tel Aviv, Israel, and immigrated to New York City with her family when she was a young child. She is the writer and illustrator of a popular series of children's books about Max Stravinsky, a dog who is also a poet, and a regular cover artist for the *New Yorker*.

KEY CONTEXT In 2009, Kalman began a twelve-part "illustrated blog" for the *New York Times.* Called *And the Pursuit of Happiness*, it later became a book of the same name. The book explores American history and democracy and includes a mix of original artwork, photographs, found artifacts, interviews, and personal reflections. Kalman begins the story of immigration at the literal beginning of life on earth, the creatures in the "primordial soup" that grew "tired of the ocean [. . . and] migrated onto the land." She then depicts the movements of people across the various continents and the European explorers, including Columbus, Ponce de León, and de Soto. This excerpt begins with a description of the explorer Henry Hudson, who was one of the first Europeans to discover what is now called Hudson Bay.

FOUR HUNDRED YEARS AGO HENRY HUDSON SAILED IN WEARING RUFFLES, which FORTUNATELY DID NOT CATCH ON in the NEW WORLD.

IN OUR FAMILY WE hAd VERY WARM FEELINGS ABOUT HENRY HUDSON. NOT ONLY did WE LIVE at 2675 HENRY HUDSON PARKWAY,

but the PARK WHERE I would sit in a tree READing for hours WAS called HENRY HUDSON PARK.

THEN CAME COMMERCE and GREED. <u>MILLIONS</u> OF PEOPLE
KIDNAPPED FROM AFRICA, THROWN into a LIVING HELL
and BROUGHT HERE to BE SLAVES.
WELCOME to YOUR NEW HOME.
THEN, the AMERICAN REVOLUTION. MANIFEST DESTINY.
LAND GRABBING. THE INDUSTRIAL REVOLUTION.
THE BROOKLYN BRIDGE. AND, OF COURSE,
CONEY ISLAND

MASSES OF HUMANITY KEPT POURING IN.
GERMANS. RUSSIANS. ITALIANS. IRISH.
THEY SAILED INTO NEW YORK HARBOR,
   PAST THE SPLENDID SYMBOL OF FREEDOM.

THEY ARRIVED AT ELLIS ISLAND.
IN THE MAJESTIC ROOMS OF THE MAIN BUILDING
THOUSANDS OF PEOPLE WERE INSPECTED, EXAMINED,
TAGGED and SORTED. MOST MADE IT IN. SOME WERE SENT BACK.
I LOOK AT THE PHOTOGRAPH OF THESE TWO GIRLS,
   And think they could have been my SISTER and ME.
BUT we came HERE in 1954 and FLEW in ON A LUMBERING
JET with MY FATHER, who was SMOKING a CIGARETTE ON
the PLANE, playing GIN RUMMY and DRINKING SCOTCH.
We moved to RIVERDALE, WHERE MY MOTHER would NOT
LET me join the GIRL SCOUTS BECAUSE she did NOT WANT
ME TO LOSE MY ISRAELI IDENTITY.   AND NOW?
STILL, HUNDREDS OF THOUSANDS OF PEOPLE WANT TO BECOME AMERICANS.
   WHAT IS IT ABOUT THIS PLACE?

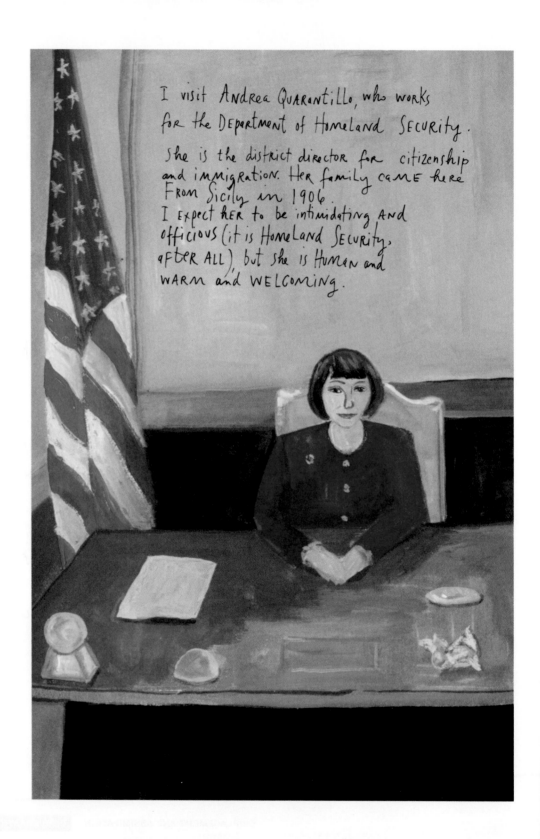

I visit Andrea Quarantillo, who works for the Department of Homeland Security.

She is the district director for citizenship and immigration. Her family came here from Sicily in 1906.
I expect her to be intimidating and officious (it is Homeland Security, after all), but she is human and warm and welcoming.

She SPEAKS AT the SMALL Swearing-in CEREMONY
that I Attend. WhEN I became a citizen,
AN official told us we would SHED OUR OLD iDENtity
And put on a NEW IDENtity - "Like tAKing off aN
OLd SWEATER and putting on a NEW ONE."
AndRea SAYS the oPPosiTE: This Nation's iDENtity is
BASED on its Rich Diversity. ImmigRants aRe
BEComing AmeRicANs, and aN AmeRicAN CAN Be
MANY DiffeRENt Things.

EVERy YEAR CLOSE TO ONE MilLioN PEoplE
BECOME CitizENS. A RatheR STARTLing STATistic.
AT the SweaRing-IN CEREMINy, I MEET
BoLiVAR NApoleoN MendeZ fRom BOLIVIA.
A woman fRom SAUdi ARAbia. A MAN fRom MALI.

And Murray Richter, who works for immigration, whose mother NETTIE came to America from Russia and opened a fruit stand on Dumont Avenue in BROOKLYN.

This is a completely NEW AMERICA, more culturally complex than anyone could have imagined. And the QUESTION keeps coming up, "WHOSE HOME IS this?"

WHAT of the 12 MILLION PEOPLE LIVING here who are UNDOCUMENTED?

They are here illegally. Do they deserve to STAY? There are groups lobbying for immigration Reform. At community centers you meet dedicated organizers and undocumented people, and you think these are GREAT people and they cannot be sent back to their countries of origin. The problems are SUBSTANTIAL: Health care. Employment. Taxes. Detention facilities. Impenetrable bureaucracies. Is it Naïve of me to think, while acknowledging the myriad problems, that the system is basically just?

And then.
In Queens
we enjoy a
MANGO
LASSi
at the
JACKSON
DINER.

THEN we STROLL through an INDIAN SUPERMARKET and buy

A BOX of COOKIES FROM PAKISTAN.

And get a little something from

"THINK SMALL" IS MY NEW MOTTO.
IT HELPS ME HANDLE THE COMPLICATED
TOO-MUCHNESS OF IT ALL.

WE POP OVER TO THE BRONX TO UNITED PICKLE
TO SAY HELLO TO STEVE LEIBOWITZ, THE OWNER,
AND HIS EMPLOYEES VISHNUDAT LOOTAWAN AND
JOSÉ TORRES JR., WHOSE FATHER WAS A GREAT
BOXER AND WRITER. WE LEAVE, PASSING
SCHMUGER'S HARDWARE,

WHICH IS NOT FAR FROM THE BUCOLIC
WOODLAWN CEMETERY, WHERE THE DIMINUTIVE
IMMIGRANT IRVING BERLIN IS BURIED.

IF BERLIN hAd not been allowed to come to this COUNTRY, WE WOULD NEVER HAVE had the SUBLIME PLEASURE of SEEING FRED dance with Ginger while serenading her with BERLIN'S LYRICS

"HEAVEN, I'm in HEAVEN, AND my HEART BEATS So that I can HARdly SPEAK, and I SEEM to Find the HAPPINESS I seek, when WE'Re out Together DANCING cheek to cheek."

Understanding and Interpreting

1 Though much of this piece is an expository examination of the history of immigration, we learn some biographical details of Kalman herself. Identify the information we learn about her that is most relevant to the topic.

2 Re-examine page 632, in which Kalman covers about three hundred years of American history in about five lines. What are the significant portions included? How do they support her theme? What is excluded from this recounting? Why?

3 Though Kalman never explicitly states it, readers can make inferences about the author's position on the issue of immigration reform. How would you state Kalman's position? What evidence supports your inference?

4 At her own citizenship ceremony, Kalman reports, an official told her that becoming an American was like putting on a new sweater. How does Kalman reject this point of view visually in her piece?

5 What does Kalman mean when she says, "Think small" on page 643? What has led her to this conclusion?

6 On page 641, what point is Kalman making when she says, "we stroll through an Indian supermarket and buy a box of cookies from Pakistan"? Consider the visuals on the page, as well as the text, in your response.

Analyzing Language, Style, and Structure

1 Through word choice and images, Kalman expresses different attitudes toward various subjects in her piece. Choose two examples and explain her tone.

2 Immigration is a topic that can be politically divisive and generate very strong feelings in readers. How does the style of Kalman's words and illustrations work to defuse some of the adversarial feelings often evoked by the immigration debate?

3 An effective argument often includes a balance of appeals to emotion and logic. Evaluate the success of Kalman's argument by examining how she uses pathos and logos in her piece.

4 What is the likely intended effect of the use of handwritten text?

5 There are moments of unexpected humor throughout the piece, most often created by the use of a non sequitur, a figure of speech created when a statement lacks a logical connection to the topic at hand. Identify one or more non sequiturs in Kalman's piece and explain how she uses them to create humor.

6 Examine the picture of the official for the Department of Homeland Security and compare it to one other full-size picture in the piece. Focus on what details are included in each picture and speculate about the effects Kalman intends to produce.

7 How does Kalman's use of Irving Berlin's lyrics at the very end of the piece support her argument?

8 Every story has to have a beginning. And though it's not included here, Kalman decided to start her story about contemporary American immigration at the absolutely literal beginning: with humans emerging from "the primordial soup." How does this choice relate to the overall point she ultimately makes about immigration in this excerpt?

Connecting, Arguing, and Extending

1 Notice that on page 638, Kalman uses the word "undocumented" to refer to people who have entered the United States illegally. Below is a passage from a blog posting by George Lakoff, a linguist who regularly advises Democratic candidates about their use of language. Do you agree with Lakoff's analysis about President Obama's word choice? Identify other similarly politically charged words being used today.

> First, Obama repeatedly uses the phrase **illegal immigrants**. It evokes a conceptual frame in which undocumented Americans are understood first and foremost as criminals. The President evokes this frame in his Florida speech, stating that current immigration policy "denies **innocent** young people the chance to earn an education or serve in the uniform of the country they love." Being innocent is the opposite of being guilty. The word cannot be understood outside of the Criminal Frame.

2 Try creating your own illustrated blog entry. Using both text and visuals, create a page or two about a significant event in your life that addresses the topic of culture in some way.

3 Choose one of Kalman's images and analyze it using the following elements of painting, as identified by Mary Acton in *Learning to Look at Paintings*:

- **Composition:** the way that the artist has organized his or her artwork, and what the artist has decided to include or exclude from the piece.
- **Space:** the view—or perspective—that the artist has created for you to look at the work. A question to ask yourself is: where am I in relation to the subject in the artwork?
- **Form:** the way to describe how an artist has tried to make the piece seem three-dimensional and, therefore, more lifelike or animated.
- **Tone:** the use of contrasting light and darkness within an artwork.
- **Color:** like tone, color can be used by an artist for multiple purposes. Things that you might want to consider include whether the colors seem realistic, exaggerated, or imaginative.
- **Subject Matter:** What is the action, plot, or subject of the artwork?

ENTERING THE CONVERSATION
DISPLACEMENT AND ASSIMILATION

Making Connections

1 Li-Young Lee in "For a New Citizen of These United States" (p. 618) and Nola Kambanda in "My New World Journey" (p. 620) describe the difficulty of being a refugee. Both authors examine the tension between wanting to remember what life was like before immigration and needing to focus on the present and future. Compare how they face the issue of assimilation.

2 Language is often a polarizing force in the immigration debate. For instance, in 2013 the Associated Press stopped using the term *illegal alien* and instead endorsed the term *undocumented immigrant*. Choose two texts that appear on different sides of the immigration debate and explain how each writer defines such key words as *immigrant*, *American*, *worker*, *freedom*, and so on.

3 Crèvecoeur wrote his piece in the eighteenth century and Nola Kambanda wrote her narrative in the twenty-first century. Looking at both texts, how has America changed in the nearly 250 years between, and how has it remained the same in its priorities, values, work ethic, and so on?

Synthesizing Sources

1 There are several metaphors that writers in this Conversation have put forward to describe the process of assimilation in America. J. Hector St. John de Crèvecoeur, for instance, describes it as a "melting pot," Anna Quindlen describes it as a "quilt," and Maira Kalman recalls being told at her citizenship ceremony that becoming an American was like putting on a new sweater. Write an argumentative piece in which you identify and describe an appropriate metaphor that reflects your view of assimilation and immigration. Be sure to refer to at least two texts in this Conversation for support.

2 A question that has been asked repeatedly throughout this Conversation is "What is an American?" How would you answer this question? Be sure to refer to at least two texts in this Conversation for support.

3 To what extent can or should an immigrant assimilate at the risk of losing significant portions of his or her own cultural identity? Ultimately, is the cultural transition faced as an immigrant more of a benefit or a hardship? Explain your response by referring to at least two texts in the Conversation (or one text in the Conversation and the Central Text of the chapter from *When the Emperor Was Divine*).

4 What role, if any, does racism or prejudice play in the immigration discussion in the United States? Explain your response by referring to at least two texts in the Conversation (or one text in the Conversation and the Central Text of the chapter from *When the Emperor Was Divine*).

5 Two extremes are often put forward in the immigration debate: the welcoming beacon of the Statue of Liberty, and the idea of shutting the door to all newcomers. What is the likely middle ground on this issue? How do you determine it? Write an argumentative essay in which you put forward your approach to the immigration debate. In addition to conducting additional research, be sure to refer to at least two texts in this Conversation (or the Central Text of this chapter from *When the Emperor Was Divine*) for supporting evidence.

ANALYZING CHARACTER AND THEME

Novelist Suzanne Collins said:

> You know what's sad about reading books? It's that you fall in love with the
> characters. They grow on you. And as you read, you start to feel what they feel—
> all of them—you become them. And when you're done, you're never the same.

You may or may not have ever had quite the same experience as Collins when reading a book,
though you may have felt something similar after watching a movie or television show, or even
after finishing the final level of a video game. Characters in literature, film, and other texts often
seem real to us, even if they live in the fictional or distant worlds of Middle Earth, medieval
Verona, or dystopian Panem. How an author creates these characters, brings them to life, and
gives those lives meaning is what we're going to think about in this Reading Workshop.

Types of Characters

There are different terms that we use to categorize characters based on the function that
they play in a work of literature. Many of these terms will likely be review for you.

The **protagonist** is the main character of a story, and it is the protagonist's desire for
justice, power, love, money, acceptance, and so on that drives the story's plot. While oftentimes
we think of the main character as the "hero" or "heroine" of a story, there are numerous examples from literature and film of protagonists who are not particularly good people. One such
character is Shakespeare's Macbeth; he is a power-hungry murderer, but still the protagonist.

The **antagonist** is the character who opposes the protagonist's actions. Sometimes
the antagonist's relationship to the protagonist is an obvious one—Voldemort to Harry
Potter, for instance. More often than not, however, the antagonist has different goals and
desires than the protagonist, and is not simply the "bad guy." In the play *Antigone*, for
example, Antigone wants to bury her dead brother, who led a rebellion, but her uncle, King
Creon (the antagonist), refuses to allow her to do so because the burial could cause
further instability in the kingdom.

Minor or **supporting characters** are those whose actions or personalities complement or contrast with those of the protagonist or antagonist. They might not be essential
to the plot of the story, but they round out the world of the main characters. As author
Stephen King says in his novel, *Revival*:

> In one way, at least, our lives really are like movies. The main cast consists of your family
> and friends. The supporting cast is made up of neighbors, co-workers, teachers, and daily
> acquaintances. There are also bit players: the supermarket checkout girl with the pretty
> smile, the friendly bartender at the local watering hole, the guys you work out with at the
> gym three days a week. And there are thousands of extras — those people who flow
> through every life like water through a sieve, seen once and never again. The teenager
> browsing graphic novels at Barnes & Noble, the one you had to slip past (murmuring
> "Excuse me") in order to get to the magazines. The woman in the next lane at a stoplight,

Mick Stevens/The New Yorker Collection/The Cartoon Bank

"I'm neither a good cop nor a bad cop, Jerome. Like yourself,
I'm a complex amalgam of positive and negative personality
traits that emerge or not, depending on circumstances."

taking a moment to freshen her lipstick. The mother wiping ice cream off her toddler's face in a roadside restaurant where you stopped for a quick bite. The vendor who sold you a bag of peanuts at a baseball game.

All of these minor characters build the world of the story, and bring it to life.

One of the primary differences between main characters and minor characters is the amount of effort the author spends in developing them. Main characters tend to be **round characters**, meaning they have a certain amount of complexity and several traits that define them; they also tend to be **dynamic**, meaning that they change in some way over the course of the text. Minor characters often are **flat characters** defined by a single characteristic, such as the mean teacher or the dumb jock, and they are often **static**, meaning they remain essentially the same throughout the story. There are exceptions to every rule, of course. It might be tempting to think of flat or static characters as being products of bad or lazy writing, but most authors rely on a variety of character types to create their literary works.

A **foil** is a specific type of character that contrasts with the protagonist, and thus highlights one of his or her significant character traits. One well-known example of a foil is Dr. Watson from the Sherlock Holmes books, movies, and television shows. Holmes is absurdly intelligent and intuitive, able to make rapid deductions that Watson is unable to process as quickly. Watson often has to ask questions and have Holmes summarize and restate things. Dr. Watson's role is to make it clear that Holmes is so smart that even a doctor has a hard time keeping up with him.

1. Working in a small group, think of a movie, novel, or television show that you all know well. List between five and eight characters and try to classify them according to the categories described on the previous pages. Then, explain what function each character serves within the text.
2. Individually, do the same exercise for a text that you have read in this chapter, or for another text you have read recently.

Characterization

So far in this Workshop, you have been focusing on what kinds of characters are found within a literary work; now it's time to focus on the tools an author uses to develop those characters in the work, a process called **characterization**.

Broadly speaking, there are two ways that writers go about building a character. **Direct characterization** is when the author "tells" the reader about the character. For example:

He was a tall, thin man who was angry and disappointed in the world.

Indirect characterization, on the other hand, is when the author "shows" the reader about a character trait without explicitly stating it. For example:

Glancing quickly back toward the front door, she ordered a second muffin to give to the homeless man outside on her way out.

Writers will usually use both methods of characterization in a literary work, and neither method is better or worse than the other. Nevertheless, most of your character analysis will focus on indirect characterization because its nuance allows room for interpretation.

1. Imagine that you are going to write a story that includes the young woman in *Automat*, a 1927 painting by Edward Hopper (p. 652). Using the chart below, begin to build a character for the woman in this painting. In some cases, you can draw the details directly from the painting, but you will need to use your imagination for more details—such as her name, her internal thoughts, the actions she will do, and so on.

Name and age:

Physical descriptions:

Internal thoughts:

Actions, gestures, movements:

Her motivations or desires:

What the waiters in the café might say about her or to her:

What she might say in response to the waiters or another customer:

2. After you have completed the chart, write two sentences of *direct* characterization describing the young woman in the painting. Then, write two sentences of *indirect* characterization that reveal something about her.

3. Finally, reflect on the similarities and differences between these two types of characterization: Why would an author use one over the other? What different purposes do they serve?

KEY QUESTIONS

- What are the character's **purposes or functions** within the work? How and why does the character **change or not change** through the work?

- What are the character's most significant **actions or inactions**, such as running away from a fight, donating money to the poor, squashing a spider, and so on?

- What are the **motivations** of the character? In other words, what does the character really want?

- What **repetitions** do you notice in the character's description? Is the main character presented as an **opposite** of another character?

- How do the character's thoughts or actions connect to an idea that the author is developing in this piece of literature (a theme)?

Connecting Character and Meaning

Now that you're familiar with the ways that authors build characters, let's look at how those characters and their actions can convey meaning in a work of literature. Characterization, like other elements of literature (such as setting, plot, and point of view) is a tool for the author to use to build the meaning of his or her work—in other words, to develop the themes.

Characters are central to literature. The setting gives them a place to be, the point of view gives us a glimpse into their world, and the plot tells us what they do. So, to fully understand a piece of literature, we have to understand why the author presents his or her characters in the manner he or she does. This is why an effective analysis of character always goes beyond simply describing who a character is and gets to the ideas *behind* the characters' words, traits, and actions. For instance, the supporting characters in *The Wizard of Oz*—the cowardly Lion, compassionate Tin Man, and resourceful Scarecrow— do more than just entertain readers or viewers and move the story along: their character traits represent what the story is suggesting are the essential qualities of a healthy, supportive community. This is a very literal example of how characters *embody* meaning in literature.

Let's look at another example. This one happens to focus on dialogue as a means of indirect characterization. Dialogue can be a very powerful tool for characterization, allow- ing the author to reveal things about the characters not just by what they say, but also by how they say it and how others react to it. Read this excerpt from "Deuce Out" by Katey Schultz (p. 578, pars. 4–9), in which a brother and sister talk about what he learned in his basic training in the U.S. Army, especially the military jargon and interesting stories.

> Before he left, I wanted to learn everything. Jingle trucks, battle rattle, fobbits, you name it. "C'mon. Spill it," I said.
>
> "They don't teach you that stuff in basic, Steph."
>
> "But you must have heard stories. You know. From your friends who've already been there." We lay on the grass in Harrison Park. The sun was out, the sky a fantastic blue we hadn't seen in months.
>
> "No stories, Sis. Sorry."
>
> "Okay, fine. What about from basic?"
>
> Dustin feigned a yawn.

There are several aspects of both characters that this bit of dialogue reveals. Notice how eager Steph is to learn the military lingo. She presses Dustin more than once for details. But notice too how reluctant Dustin is to share: he dodges the question twice and finally fakes a yawn to end their conversation. We get the sense from this dialogue that Steph's excitement has gone too far. She's too concerned mostly with the quirky details of military life, and is ignoring the seriousness of the situation. Dustin, because of his actual experience with the military, seems to know better, and is purposely trying to dampen Steph's enthusiasm.

The connection of characterization to theme in this example is clear: life in the military isn't to be taken lightly, and shouldn't be trivialized by reducing it to its funny lingo or anecdotes.

Let's look at another example. This one is an excerpt from *When the Emperor Was Divine* by Julie Otsuka (p. 547, pars. 21–23), which is about a family during World War II that was sent to an internment camp for much of the war because they were of Japanese descent. After the bombing of Pearl Harbor by the Japanese in 1941, there was a lot of racial discrimination toward Japanese Americans, as you will see in this scene in which the protagonist, called only "boy," is confronted by someone who demands to know whether he is Japanese, or Chinese (who were allies of the United States at the time of World War II).

> Later, he saw Chinese, real Chinese — Mr. Lee of Lee's Grocers and Don Wong who owned the laundry on Shattuck — on the street wearing buttons that said, I AM CHINESE, and CHINESE, PLEASE. Later, a man stopped him on the sidewalk in front of Woolworth's and said, "Chink or Jap?" and the boy answered, "Chink," and ran away as fast as he could. Only when he got to the corner did he turn around and shout, "Jap! Jap! I'm a Jap!"
>
> Just to set the record straight.
>
> But by then the man was already gone.

Notice how Otsuka uses exclusively indirect characterization for the boy here. While in the face of the man's question the boy does deny his own heritage, his decision to stop, turn, and loudly proclaim that he is Japanese shows a certain bravery and pride, even if the man has already gone. The boy is smart enough to know when it is safe for him to be himself and when he needs to hide his identity. Otsuka relies mostly on the actions of the boy and what he says—and when he says it—to reveal these aspects of the boy. This conflict in this scene is made possible by the minor characters that Otsuka introduces: Mr. Lee and Don Wong, the proud Chinese whose buttons saying "I AM CHINESE" and "CHINESE, PLEASE" serve as a foil to highlight the boy's confusion, and the man outside Woolworth's, who acts as a sort of an antagonist in this particular scene.

So while it's clear that the boy is both courageous and proud of his Japanese heritage, what does this episode reveal about the meaning of the work as a whole? How does it connect to the overall theme? Notice the multiple proclamations of identity in this short scene; Mr. Lee, the man, and the boy all try to define themselves in the face of confusion and anger. The boy even uses the derogatory term "Jap" as a declaration of strength. All in all, Otsuka uses the character of the boy, and the men, in this sequence to explore the complex notions of identity that Japanese Americans dealt with during that period in the twentieth century.

Note that this is just one interpretation of the boy's actions in this scene, and therefore of the boy's role in embodying the overall meaning of the novel. Reasonable people could disagree and arrive at different conclusions.

The connection between the boy's actions and dialogue to the meaning is a *claim*.

ACTIVITY

1. While we often think of characterization as being utilized only by fiction writers, it is often a significant part of poetry as well. Read this excerpt from the poem "2000 lbs." by Brian Turner (pp. 602–3, ll. 83–88), which is about the results of a car bomb explosion in Iraq. Make an interpretative statement about how the actions of the grandmother reveal what Turner might be suggesting about war. (If you need help, consult the Key Questions box on p. 652.)

> Nearby, an old woman cradles her grandson,
> whispering, rocking him on her knees
> as though singing him to sleep, her hands
> wet with their blood, her black dress
> soaked in it as her legs give out
> and she buckles with him to the ground.

2. Nonfiction writers also use characterization to reveal things about the people they write about. Read this excerpt from *In the Hot Zone* (p. 592, pars. 48–51) in which journalist Kevin Sites describes his meeting with a commanding officer after filming a U.S. marine shooting a man who appeared to be unarmed. In his essay, Sites wrestles with the ethics of whether or not to report the incident. Make an interpretative statement about Buhl and how Sites's portrayal helps develop the ethical dilemma that he is wrestling with in his essay. (If you need help, consult the Key Questions box on p. 652.) Use evidence from the text to support your response.

I need to see Lieutenant Colonel Willy Buhl, tell him what has happened and show him the video.

When I first met Buhl at the beginning of my embed, I liked him right away. He seemed like an easygoing, no-bullshit kind of guy. Small and stocky, he was a former wrestler and, like Lieutenant Ryan Sparks, had been an enlisted man who became an officer. Guys like that, who have been there and know the business from the ground up, generally command a lot of respect. Buhl was no exception. I had interviewed him prior to Phantom Fury and he had said something to me that now, in retrospect, seems both sadly ironic on one level and prophetically true on another.

"We're the good guys. We are Americans. We are fighting a gentleman's war here — because we don't behead people, we don't come down to the same level of the people we're combating," he says during our interview at Camp Abu Ghraib. "And that's a very difficult thing for a young eighteen-year-old Marine that's been trained to locate, close with and destroy the enemy with fire and close combat, and that's a very difficult thing for a forty-two-year old lieutenant colonel with twenty-three years' experience in the service who's trained to do the same thing once upon a time and now has a thousand-plus men to lead, guide, coach, mentor and to ensure we are the good guys and keep the moral high ground."

When I show Buhl the tape, he is not shocked so much as he is deflated. His comments are along the lines of "Ah, this is so bad." I think he felt that all he had accomplished up to that moment could be taken away by a single image.

culminating activity

Read this section from "The Man Who Stained His Soul" by Vu Bao, which is about a group of Vietnamese soldiers fighting in a battle. Make a claim about the two main characters—the narrator and Vinh—and support your claim with evidence from the excerpt. Then, explain what the characters reveal about a point the author might be making about war and bravery.

We divided the front unit into two V-shaped lines. Half of the men crept after Luat, the other half after me. Only Vinh lay prostrate in his place.

I crawled back to him

"What the hell are you doing?"

Vinh's voice was strained. "How can we advance — the bullets are pouring in like rain."

"Would you rather lie here waiting for death?"

"Death's waiting up there also."

With the bullets zeroing in on us, this wasn't the time or place to try to turn a coward into a brave soldier. "Give me your cartridge belt and grenades," I yelled at him.

"Then I'll be killed in the enemy's counterattack."

My blood was boiling. I yanked his submachine gun from his hands. "I have to advance. Hang onto the company flag."

I crawled low under the fire, keeping my eyes on the muzzle flashes. Suddenly the fire pecking at us from the bunker's loophole ceased. The enemy gunners must have been changing the belt. I sprang up and rushed the bunker. Someone threw a grenade at me. I snatched it up and tossed it back into the loophole. Then I thrust the barrel of my rifle through the opening and sprayed in a full magazine, sweeping the area inside.

Shouts of joy sounded from all around. Fourth Company had penetrated the base. But what followed was our hardest battle. We struggled to take one fortified position after another, and it was nearly morning before we managed to blow up their headquarters.

Afterwards, the battalion commander ran up to us. "Hurry and scrounge up whatever supplies and equipment you can," he said. "It's nearly dawn — you'll start shitting when the enemy's long range artillery begin firing."

I turned around to see Vinh standing nearby. His left trouser leg was sticking like glue to his thigh. I tore out the bandage I had tucked into my belt.

Luat seized my hand. "Don't bother. He just pissed himself," he said, nodding at Vinh's saturated trouser. "Pissed on his own soul."

WRITING AN INTERPRETATION OF CHARACTER AND THEME

There are a lot of different expectations for you as a student writer. In any given week, you may be asked to write up a lab report in science, write a research paper in history, and even compose a poem in your English class. Each of these writing demands has a different purpose and structure. In this Workshop, you'll focus on writing an interpretation of a piece of literature, focusing on how the characters reveal a theme of the work.

While the "literary analysis paper" is a typical school assignment in high school and college, it is not one regularly seen in the real world outside of school. Unlike argumentative writing or personal narrative, you don't normally read poetry analyses, for example, except in very specialized journals. So, why do your teachers regularly assign this type of writing that could be considered "inauthentic"? One reason to consider is that good writing can be a way to make your clear thinking visible. When writing about literature, you are making an argument that your interpretation is a reasonable and valuable one, and you are supporting your argument with evidence from the text. More than anything else, a literary analysis assignment is a way for you and your teachers to assess the ways that you think and for you to demonstrate your understanding.

This type of essay is very common in literature classes at all levels—high school and college—and is almost always a type of writing asked of you on the AP Literature exam. Take a look at these prompts from past exams, noting how they connect character and theme:

> **2011.** In a novel by William Styron, a father tells his son that life "is a search for justice." Choose a character from a novel or play who responds in some significant way to justice or injustice. Then write a well-developed essay in which you analyze the character's understanding of justice, the degree to which the character's search for justice is successful, and the significance of this search for the work as a whole.

> **2014.** It has often been said that what we value can be determined by what we sacrifice. Consider how this statement applies to a character from a novel or play. Select a character that has deliberately sacrificed, surrendered, or forfeited something in a way that highlights that character's values. Then write a well-organized essay in which you analyze how the particular sacrifice illuminates the character's values and provides a deeper understanding of the meaning of the work as a whole.

Notice that these prompts ask the student to draw a connection between the character's behavior and some larger idea in the story. So, the first prompt asks about the "search for justice [. . .] and the significance of this search for the work as a whole," while the second asks "how the particular sacrifice illuminates the character's values and provides a deeper understanding of the meaning of the work as a whole." In both of these, "meaning" is another word for "theme." It is important to see that the prompts do not stop at asking you to analyze a character, but ask you to go further by connecting the character to the "meaning of the work as a whole."

Step 1: Gather Evidence

When assigned to write a response to literature, you may be tempted to jump right in and write a thesis that answers the prompt, and then locate the evidence to support your thesis. But a far better approach is to allow yourself some time to gather evidence with an open mind, recognizing that there are many possible interpretations you may draw about the characters and the meaning of the work as a whole. Since you eventually will need to have specific textual evidence to support your interpretation and prove that your interpretation is a reasonable and convincing one, the best method of collecting evidence, if time allows, is to reread the full text with the prompt in mind and write down direct quotations that might support your position. At the very least, plan to closely reread all of the key parts of the text and skim through the rest, placing special emphasis on the ending of the piece.

ACTIVITY

Choosing one of the following texts from this chapter or another one that you have read recently, identify examples that provide characterization of the protagonist, and consider how the examples you locate might connect to the work as a whole. Be sure to note that not all texts include all of the elements of characterization listed in the chart below. Possible texts:

- When the Emperor Was Divine (p. 537)
- The Man Who Stained His Soul (p. 572)
- Deuce Out (p. 578)
- In the Hot Zone (p. 588)
- My New World Journey (p. 620)
- Dothead (p. 627)

Element of Characterization	Evidence from Text (include page #)	Connection to Theme
Physical descriptions		
Significant actions, movements, gestures		
Internal thoughts		
Relevant dialogue		
Character motivations		
What other characters say or think about the character		

Step 2: Write a Thesis Statement

Now that you have gathered information about the characterization and theme, it's time to begin narrowing your focus. Whether you are writing a multipage literary analysis essay or a one-paragraph response, you should always have a thesis statement that clearly states your interpretation of how the character's thoughts, actions, or other details connect to the theme of the work. Your thesis should be a clear distillation of what you plan to say in your response. If you need help getting started, you might use the questions in the Key Questions box on page 652 to guide you.

A strong thesis statement is usually a sentence or two at the most, and it avoids phrases like "I believe . . ." or "In my opinion . . ." Your reader knows that these are your opinions and expects that you actually believe what you are writing, so these phrases are unnecessary filler. At this point in your development as a writer, you should also avoid introductory phrases such as, "In this essay, I will be discussing . . ." The people in your audience know that it is an essay and that you will be discussing something, so you're better off just jumping right into what you are going to discuss.

Most important, however, is that your thesis statement must be based on a claim that is debatable in some way. There is no purpose in making a claim about a character and theme that is obvious or does not need much evidence to be proven. A poor example of an analytical claim about characterization would be something like, "Simba in *The Lion King* is a young lion that will be king one day."

That is a true statement about Simba, but it is not debatable, so there is nothing left to say. There is no opportunity for an interpretation, no room for insight into the text. A better claim might be, "Simba in *The Lion King* is rash in his decision making and selfish in his actions, which could lead the viewer to question whether a hereditary monarchy is the best form of government."

Is this true? Perhaps, but it is debatable and subject to interpretation, though maybe not by the five-year-olds watching the cartoon. By making your claim debatable, you give yourself a case worth making, an opportunity to say something interesting, and your audience an essay worth reading.

ACTIVITY

1. Look back at the evidence that you gathered from a text you read in this chapter and practice writing a thesis statement about the characterization in the text relates to the theme. Be sure to make a claim that is debatable and needs evidence in order to be proven. This will be the working thesis that you will use throughout the rest of this Workshop. Looking at the following sample prompts might help you to craft a claim for your thesis, but feel free to diverge from these ideas.

   • In *In the Hot Zone* by Kevin Sites, what does Sites reveal about himself, and how do those aspects of his character illustrate the point he is trying to make about truth in the fog of war?
   • In *When the Emperor Was Divine* by Julie Otsuka, what elements of the boy's characterization does Otsuka use to illustrate the tragic circumstances of the internment camps?
   • In "Dothead" by Amit Majmudar, how do the speaker's actions and dialogue dramatize a point the poet is making about racial tolerance?

2. After you have crafted your thesis, look back at your chart and be sure that you have enough evidence to support the claim you make. If you do not, be sure to revise your thesis until you have one that can be supported.

Step 3: Integrate Evidence

In a literary analysis essay, just as with any argument, you will need to use evidence effectively in order to support your thesis. A potential danger when writing a response to literature is that it can sound choppy as you move from your own words to those taken from the text you are analyzing and using as evidence. At this point in your writing career you will be expected to integrate the quotations that you use to support your interpretations right into your own sentences so that your analysis writing flows smoothly.

Here are three techniques for integrating textual evidence into your writing. These examples are based on responses to "The St. Crispin's Day Speech" from *Henry V* by William Shakespeare on page 568.

Embedded Quotes. Introduce the passage with a sentence or a phrase and blend it into your own writing so that it flows smoothly together and makes sense. Notice that the punctuation goes after the citation of the page or line number in parentheses and that, when referencing poetry, you must designate the end of lines with a forward slash.

> In trying to convince his men to fight against a much larger and better-rested army, King Henry presents himself as a common man fighting alongside not just fellow troops, but brothers, saying, "we band of brothers; / For he to-day that sheds his blood with me / Shall be my brother" (Shakespeare, ll. 62–63).

Block Quotes. For long passages (more than four typed lines), special rules apply. For a quote of this length, it is customary to introduce the quote with a sentence and use a colon as the mark of punctuation before the passage. Indent the quoted material about ten spaces and extend it out to the right margin. Note that the citation (page number) goes after the final punctuation.

> King Henry is a brilliant and effective communicator. In the space of a very short time, he can turn his nearly mutinous army into one ready and eager to fight. He is most effective when he says:
>
>> By Jove, I am not covetous for gold,
>> Nor care I who doth feed upon my cost;
>> It yearns me not if men my garments wear;
>> Such outward things dwell not in my desires:
>> But if it be a sin to covet honour,
>> I am the most offending soul alive. (Shakespeare, ll. 26–31)

Paraphrased Passages. A final way that you can use evidence in a literary analysis is to use a paraphrase or summary of the passage instead of a direct quote. Note that you are still required to cite the source, even if it is not a direct quotation.

King Henry is not above being manipulative and passive-aggressive in his attempts to convince his men to fight. At one point in his speech, for instance, he tells them that anyone who wants to leave can go ahead and leave because he would rather not die in the presence of a coward (Shakespeare, ll. 38–41).

ACTIVITY

Return to the thesis you have been working with throughout this Workshop and write a sentence that supports that statement by embedding a quote from the evidence chart that you created earlier (p. 658). Write one more supporting sentence that is a para-phrase or summary of a quotation from the text. Be sure in both cases to properly cite the page or line number, as in the preceding examples.

Step 4: Structure Your Essay

Like most essays you write for school, a literary analysis essay typically includes an intro-duction with a thesis, a series of body paragraphs, and a concluding paragraph.

Introduction

An introduction for this type of essay should include many of the same elements you would use in any other essay. It should include:

- A **hook** that is intended to capture the reader's interest. There are a number of ways to begin: a compelling quotation from the text, a genuinely interesting question that relates to the text, an important fact about the author or the time period, or any combi-nation of these.
- Enough **context** so that your reader can understand the position you are about to take. In particular, make sure to include the author, title, protagonist or other main character's name, and any other relevant information.
- Your **thesis**, which is your analytical claim, in this case, about the characterization in the text you are analyzing and how it helps to illustrate the theme of the work. Your thesis does not need to be a single sentence.

Sample introduction:

Once upon a time, Currer Bell published a manuscript titled *Jane Eyre*; in time, it was revealed that Bell was actually the *nom de plume* of Charlotte Brontë, a prim Englishwoman. While many modern critics believe the novel to be a thinly veiled auto-biography, *Jane Eyre* and the titular protagonist also allude to Western mythology— most notably, to fairy tales. Through archetypes and manipulation of the traditional Hero's Journey story arc, Brontë creates a new fairy tale with an empowered heroine demonstrating that women must play an active role in their own stories.

Body Paragraphs

Each body paragraph of your literary analysis essay will focus on one topic that relates to your thesis. At this point in your writing career, there is rarely a set number of body paragraphs required; your essay will simply have the number of paragraphs you require to deliver your interpretation convincingly. A body paragraph generally uses the following format:

- A **topic sentence** about one aspect of the characterization in the work.
- A piece of **evidence** from the text that supports your interpretation, either a direct quotation or a paraphrase correctly cited by page or line number.
- Your **commentary** about how that evidence supports your particular interpretation.
- Continue with evidence and commentary until your interpretation has been sufficiently proven.
- You may want to conclude each paragraph with a summary that connects back to your thesis and transitions to another idea in the paragraph that follows.

Of all of the above, the most important part of each body paragraph will be your commentary because this is what demonstrates your thinking about the text and explains how the evidence supports your position. This is where you "connect the dots" for your reader, making the link between the evidence and what you think it proves about the character. Without the commentary, your analysis will seem like simply a list of quotations.

Sample body paragraph:

From the beginning, Jane is a deceptively simple character with a depth that becomes apparent only as the story progresses. She is first introduced to the reader as the Orphan, a common archetype throughout fairy tales. Caught reading a book by her abusive cousin, Jane is told, "You are a dependent [. . .] you have no money; your father left you none; you ought to beg" (6). Like Cinderella, Jane lives with relations who become cruel after the death of her protector—but Jane does not so much meet her fairy godmother as find resilience within herself, both when she is sent off to Lowood School (37) and when her only friend dies (80).

Work Cited

Brontë, Charlotte. *Jane Eyre*. Borders Classics, 2008.

> **ACTIVITY**
>
> Write a draft of a body paragraph for the text you have been working with throughout this Workshop. Be sure to include quotations and embed them effectively, and focus specifically on your commentary, the explanation of the evidence you selected.

The Conclusion

The conclusion of a response to literature essay is similar to the conclusions of other types of essays. It should include:

- A **brief summary** of the main points you made about the topic, rephrasing instead of merely repeating.
- A **clincher statement** or two that should answer the question, "so what?" This part of your conclusion may cycle back to the hook of your introduction or it may raise an interesting, but related idea not explored in your essay.

Sample conclusion:

The transformation Jane undergoes—not once, but twice—as she travels through two cycles of the hero's journey elevates *Jane Eyre* from a story to a legend; the dualism of her character embodies the temptations and triumph of womanhood. Jane, unlike previous heroines, fights for and eventually earns her happily ever after.

> **ACTIVITY**
>
> Write a draft of a conclusion for the text you have been working with throughout this Workshop. Be sure to include a statement that connects the point you make about characterization to the theme of the work as a whole.

Fear not, my big-nosed brethren. Together we will weave a web of words such to ensnare her heart!

9
(Mis)Communication

- What role does language play in building relationships?
- What factors lead to effective or ineffective communication between people?
- How does our language shape our identity or culture as a whole?
- How can language be used to enhance or undermine social or political power?
- How do changes in technology affect how we communicate and relate to one another?

In the classic 1993 *New Yorker* cartoon by Peter Steiner, one dog says to another: "On the Internet, nobody knows you're a dog." This old joke has become a new adage—a bit of wisdom for this modern world. But what is that adage really saying? One way to look at this cartoon is to conclude that because of changes in technology, it no longer matters who you are or even what you are! What matters is what you *say*.

Language is arguably the greatest invention in human history. It gives us the power to express our thoughts and feelings and to share them with others. It forms the basis for most of our relationships, from friendships to romances. It allows us to learn, and to share that knowledge with others. It defines cultures, subcultures, and sometimes even individual identities. And now, social networking technology allows us to broadcast our language and ourselves to the entire world.

665

▶

What other lessons does this cartoon suggest about language, identity, and relationships in the digital age?

"On the Internet, nobody knows you're a dog."

There's a saying much older than the one about the dog on the Internet that goes: "the pen is mightier than the sword." As much as language is a tool to connect us, it can also be a weapon to impose power, to categorize, and even to oppress. On other hand, language can be used to liberate, inspire, and reshape the way we look at the world. In this chapter, we're going to look into all of these facets of language: its power to bring us together and to keep us apart.

OPENING ACTIVITY 1

Think of a situation in your life, current events, or history when the pen (or the spoken word) was mightier than the sword. What happened and what part did language play? What made language such a powerful force in this situation?

OPENING ACTIVITY 2

Who's the best communicator you can think of? This might be someone you know very well or someone you've never met, a person from the past or present, a real person or a fictional character; you might even choose an organization or corporate entity. What makes this person or group such a good or effective communicator? List at least seven characteristics; then rank them from most to least important.

Cyrano de Bergerac

Edmond Rostand

Translated by Brian Hooker

Playwright and poet Edmond Rostand (1868–1918) was born in Marseille, France, into a wealthy and cultured family. He studied literature, philosophy, and law at the College Stanislas in Paris. Rostand wrote a number of critically and commercially successful plays, including *Les Romanesques* (1894), *La Princess Lointaine* (1895), *La Samaritaine* (1897), *L'Aiglon* (1901), and *Chantecler* (1910), but none of the others has proved as popular or enduring as *Cyrano de Bergerac* (1897).

Since its Paris debut, *Cyrano de Bergerac* has enjoyed popularity around the globe with stage productions featuring such well-known Shakespearean actors as Derek Jacobi and Christopher Plummer. A 2007 production in New York City starred Kevin Kline and Jennifer Garner. *Cyrano* has inspired a symphony, operas, a ballet, and several musicals. A number of children's books and novels are loosely based on the play—for example, *Big Nose Serrano*, a series of gangster stories by Anatole France Feldman (1930), and *Sway*, a young adult novel by Kat Spears, published in 2014.

Cyrano de Bergerac was also made into at least one film during every decade of the twentieth century, beginning in 1900. Notable later film productions include the 1950 version starring José Ferrer, who won the Academy Award for Best Actor; a Japanese samurai film starring Toshiro Mifune titled *Aru kengo no shogai* (*Life of an Expert Swordsman*, 1959); an updated comedy called *Roxanne* starring Steve Martin, who also wrote the screenplay (1987); and a critically acclaimed French production starring Gérard Depardieu (1990).

KEY CONTEXT   Although fictitious, the play is loosely based on a real-life character of the same name, Savinien Cyrano de Bergerac (1619–1655), who was born near Paris. His parents came from the town of Bergerac in southern France, and he added the title to give his name more stature. He entered military service, but after being wounded at the Siege of Arras in 1640, he left the military to study philosophy and mathematics. He eventually wrote plays of political satire and science fiction and inspired a number of other playwrights, most notably Edmond Rostand. The high spirits, intellectual gifts, and courage of Rostand's Cyrano are all apparently based on the actual person of Savinien. And he did indeed have a very large nose.

While *Cyrano de Bergerac* was first produced in 1897, it is set in 1640, thus invoking an older romantic milieu and going against the naturalism that dominated French theater at the end of the nineteenth century. This period in French history was one of political and military turmoil and Rostand's play offered some much-needed escapism — a return to the golden age of seventeenth-century France.

The plays of this earlier time featured an idealized hero who not only was physically daring and intellectually gifted, but also embodied the code of chivalry. The concept of honor was a cardinal virtue for the classic romantic hero. The chivalric code, which developed within the medieval institution of knighthood between 1170 and 1220, was a system of rules that went beyond combat to include morality and character traits such as courtesy and honor. An integral part of the chivalric code was the idealization of women, who were the source of inspiration. Such a relationship, called courtly love, was almost never consummated but rather inspired respect, devotion, and an almost religious-like worship. Rostand's *Cyrano de Bergerac* drew from this earlier period and reflected that chivalric code.

The Persons

CYRANO DE BERGERAC	*The Cadets*	*A Capuchin*	*The Pages*
CHRISTIAN DE NEUVILLETTE	*Second Marquis*	*Two Musicians*	*An Actress*
COMTE DE GUICHE	*Third Marquis*	*The Poets*	*A Soubrette*
RAGUENEAU	*Montfleury*	*The Pastrycooks*	*The Flower-Girl*
LE BRET	*Bellerose*		
CARBON DE CASTEL-JALOUX	*Jodelet*		
LIGNIÈRE	*A Meddler*	The Crowd, Citizens, Marquis, Musketeers, Thieves, Pastrycooks, Poets, Cadets of Gascoyne, Actors, Violins, Pages, Children, Spanish Soldiers, Spectators, Intellectuals, Academicians, Nuns, etc.	
VICOMTE DE VALVERT	*A Musketeer*		
A MARQUIS	*Another Musketeer*		
CUIGY	*A Spanish Officer*		
BRISSAILLE	*A Cavalier*		
ROXANE	*The Porter*	(The first four Acts in 1640; the fifth in 1655.)	
HER DUENNA	*A Citizen*	**FIRST ACT** A Performance at the Hôtel de Bourgogne.	
LISE	*His Son*		
THE ORANGE-GIRL	*A Cut-Purse*	**SECOND ACT** The Bakery of the Poets.	
MOTHER MARGUÉRITE DE JÉSUS	*A Spectator*	**THIRD ACT** Roxane's Kiss.	
SISTER MARTHE	*A Sentry*	**FOURTH ACT** The Cadets of Gascoyne.	
SISTER CLAIRE	*Bertrandou the Fifer*	**FIFTH ACT** Cyrano's Gazette.	

Act 1   Cyrano de Bergerac

A Performance at the Hôtel de Bourgogne

The Hall of the Hôtel de Bourgogne in 1640. A sort of Tennis Court, arranged and decorated for Theatrical productions.

The Hall is a long rectangle; we see it diagonally, in such a way that one side of it forms the back scene, which begins at the First Entrance on the Right and runs up to the Last Entrance on the Left, where it makes a right angle with the Stage which is seen obliquely.

This Stage is provided on either hand with benches placed along the wings. The curtain is formed by two lengths of Tapestry which can be drawn apart. Above a Harlequin cloak, the Royal Arms. Broad steps lead from the Stage down to the floor of the Hall. On either side of

*these steps, a place for the Musicians. A row of
candles serving as footlights. Two tiers of
Galleries along the side of the Hall; the upper
one divided into boxes.*

*There are no seats upon the Floor, which is the
actual stage of our theatre; but toward the back of
the Hall, on the right, a few benches are arranged;
and underneath a stairway on the extreme right,
which leads up to the galleries, and of which only
the lower portion is visible, there is a sort of
Sideboard, decorated with little tapers, vases of
flowers, bottles and glasses, plates of cake, et cetera.*

*Farther along, toward the centre of our stage is
the Entrance to the Hall: a great double door which
opens only slightly to admit the Audience. On one
of the panels of this door, as also in other places
about the Hall, and in particular just over the
Sideboard, are Playbills in red, upon which we
may read the title "La Clorise."*

*As the Curtain Rises, the Hall is dimly lighted
and still empty. The Chandeliers are lowered to the
floor, in the middle of the Hall, ready for lighting.*

> *(Sound of voices outside the door. Then a
> Cavalier enters abruptly.)*

THE PORTER *(follows him)*
> Halloa there! — Fifteen sols!

THE CAVALIER   I enter free.

THE PORTER Why?

THE CAVALIER   Soldier of the
> Household of the King!

THE PORTER *(turns to another Cavalier who has
> just entered)*
> You?

SECOND CAVALIER I pay nothing.

THE PORTER   Why not?

SECOND CAVALIER   Musketeer!

FIRST CAVALIER *(to the Second)*
> The play begins at two. Plenty of time —
5 And here's the whole floor empty. Shall we try
> Our exercise?
> *(They fence with the foils which they have
> brought.)*

A LACKEY *(enters)*
> — Pst! . . . Flanquin! . . .

ANOTHER *(already on stage)*
> What, Champagne?

FIRST LACKEY *(showing games which he takes out
> of his doublet)*
> Cards. Dice. Come on.
> *(sits on the floor)*

SECOND LACKEY *(same action)*
> Come on, old cock!

FIRST LACKEY *(takes from his pocket a bit of
> candle, lights it, sets it on the floor)*
> I have stolen
> A little of my master's fire.

A GUARDSMAN *(to a flower girl who comes
> forward)*
> How sweet
> Of you, to come before they light the hall!
> *(puts his arm around her)*

FIRST CAVALIER *(receives a thrust of the foil)*
10 A hit!

SECOND LACKEY   A club!

THE GUARDSMAN *(pursuing the girl)*
> A kiss!

THE FLOWER GIRL *(pushing away from him)*
> They'll see us! —

THE GUARDSMAN *(draws her into a dark corner)*
> No danger!

A MAN *(sits on the floor, together with several
> others who have brought packages of food)*
> When we come early, we have time to eat.

A CITIZEN *(escorting his son, a boy of sixteen)*
> Sit here, my son.

FIRST LACKEY   Mark the Ace!

ANOTHER MAN *(draws a bottle from under his
> cloak and sits down with the others)*
> Here's the spot
> For a jolly old sot to suck his Burgundy —
> *(drinks)*
15 Here — in the house of the Burgundians!

THE CITIZEN *(to his son)*
> Would you not think you were in some den of
> vice?
> *(points with his cane at the drunkard)*
> Drunkards —
> *(In stepping back, one of the cavaliers trips
> him up)*
> Bullies! —
> *(He falls between the lackeys)*
> Gamblers! —

THE GUARDSMAN (*behind him as he rises, still struggling with the Flower Girl*)

      One kiss —

THE CITIZEN   Good God! —

    (*draws his son quickly away*)

Here! — And to think, my son, that in this hall
They play Rotrou![1]

THE BOY   Yes father — and Corneille![2]

THE PAGES (*dance in, holding hands and singing:*)

20   Tra-la-la-la-la-la-la-la-lère . . .

THE PORTER You pages there — no nonsense!

FIRST PAGE (*with wounded dignity*)

      Oh, monsieur!

Really! How could you?

   (*to the Second, the moment the Porter turns his back*)

      Pst! — a bit of string?

SECOND PAGE (*shows fishline with hook*)

Yes — and a hook.

FIRST PAGE   Up in the gallery,

And fish for wigs!

A CUT-PURSE (*gathers around him several evil-looking young fellows*)

    Now then, you picaroons,

25 Perk up, and hear me mutter. Here's your bout —
Bustle around some cull,[3] and bite his bung . . .

SECOND PAGE (*calls to other pages already in the gallery*)

Hey! Brought your pea-shooters?

THIRD PAGE (*from above*)

     And our peas, too!

(*blows, and showers them with peas*)

THE BOY What is the play this afternoon?

THE CITIZEN   *Clorise.*

THE BOY Who wrote that?

THE CITIZEN Balthasar Baro. What a play! . . .

  (*He takes The Boy's arm and leads him up-stage.*)

THE CUT-PURSE (*to his pupils*)

30 Lace now, on those long sleeves, you cut it off —

(*gesture with thumb and finger, as if using scissors*)

A SPECTATOR (*to another, pointing upward toward the gallery*)

Ah, *Le Cid!* — Yes, the first night, I sat there —

THE CUT-PURSE Watches —

  (*gesture as of picking a pocket*)

THE CITIZEN (*coming down with his son*)

    Great actors we shall see to-day —

THE CUT-PURSE Handkerchiefs —

  (*gesture of holding the pocket with left hand, and drawing out handkerchief with right*)

THE CITIZEN Montfleury —

A VOICE (*in the gallery*)

     Lights! Light the lights!

THE CITIZEN Bellerose, l'Épy, Beaupré, Jodelet —

A PAGE (*on the floor*)

35   Here comes the orange-girl.

THE ORANGE-GIRL   Oranges, milk,
Raspberry syrup, lemonade —

  (*noise at the door*)

A FALSETTO VOICE (*outside*)

     Make way,

Brutes!

FIRST LACKEY What, the Marquis — on the floor?

  (*The Marquis enter in a little group.*)

SECOND LACKEY   Not long —
Only a few moments; they'll go and sit
On the stage presently.

FIRST MARQUIS (*seeing the hall half empty*)

     How now! We enter

40 Like tradespeople — no crowding, no disturbance! —
No treading on the toes of citizens?
Oh fie! Oh fie!

  (*He encounters two gentlemen who have already arrived.*)

    Cuigy! Brissaille!

(*great embracings*)

CUIGY   The faithful!

(*Looks around him.*)

We are here before the candles.

---

1. **Rotrou:** Jean Rotrou (1609–1650), French playwright who was the resident playwright for the Hôtel de Bourgogne for some time. —Eds.

2. **Corneille:** Pierre Corneille (1606–1684), French playwright famous for his tragedies. He also served as resident playwright for the Hôtel de Bourgogne. —Eds.   3. **cull:** An animal intended to be harvested. Used here as a noun, but generally seen as a verb, as in the phrase "cull the herd." —Eds.

FIRST MARQUIS   Ah, be still!
You put me in a temper.

SECOND MARQUIS Console yourself,
45 Marquis — The lamplighter!

THE CROWD (*applauding the appearance of the
lamplighter*)
                Ah! . . .

(*A group gathers around the chandelier while
he lights it. A few people have already taken
their place in the gallery.* LIGNIÈRE *enters the
hall, arm in arm with* CHRISTIAN DE
NEUVILLETTE. LIGNIÈRE *is a slightly disheveled figure, dissipated and yet distinguished
looking.* CHRISTIAN, *elegantly but rather
unfashionably dressed, appears preoccupied
and keeps looking up at the boxes.*)

CUIGY   Lignière! —

BRISSAILLE (*laughing*)
Still sober — at this hour?

LIGNIÈRE (*to* CHRISTIAN)
                May I present you?
(CHRISTIAN *assents.*)
Baron Christian de Neuvillette.
(*They salute.*)

THE CROWD (*applauding as the lighted chandelier is hoisted into place*)
                Ah! —

CUIGY (*aside to* BRISSAILLE, *looking at* CHRISTIAN)
                Rather
A fine head, is it not? The profile . . .

FIRST MARQUIS (*who has overheard*)
                Peuh!

LIGNIÈRE (*presenting them to* CHRISTIAN)
Messieurs de Cuigy . . . de Brissaille . . .

CHRISTIAN (*bows*)
                Enchanted!

FIRST MARQUIS (*to the second*)
50 He is not ill-looking; possibly a shade
Behind the fashion.

LIGNIÈRE (*to* CUIGY)
                Monsieur is recently
From the Touraine.

CHRISTIAN   Yes, I have been in Paris
Two or three weeks only. I join the Guards
To-morrow.

FIRST MARQUIS (*watching the people who come
into the boxes*)
                Look — Madame la Présidente

Aubry!

THE ORANGE-GIRL Oranges, milk —

THE VIOLINS (*tuning up*)
                La . . . la . . .

CUIGY (*to* CHRISTIAN, *calling his attention to the
increasing crowd*)
55   We have
An audience to-day!

CHRISTIAN   A brilliant one.

FIRST MARQUIS Oh yes, all our own people — the
gay world!
(*They name the ladies who enter the boxes
elaborately dressed. Bows and smiles are
exchanged.*)

SECOND MARQUIS Madame de Guéméné . . .

CUIGY   De Bois-Dauphin . . .

FIRST MARQUIS Whom we adore —

BRISSAILLE Madame de Chavigny . . .

60 **SECOND MARQUIS** Who plays with all
our hearts —

LIGNIÈRE   Why, there's Corneille
Returned from Rouen!

THE BOY (*to his father*)
                Are the Academy
All here?

THE CITIZEN   I see some of them . . . there's
Boudu —
Boissat — Cureau — Porchéres — Colomby —
Bourzeys — Bourdon — Arbaut —
                Ah, those great names,
65 Never to be forgotten!

FIRST MARQUIS   Look — at last!
Our Intellectuals! Barthénoide,
Urimédonte, Félixérie . . .

SECOND MARQUIS (*languishing*)
                Sweet heaven!
How exquisite their surnames are! Marquis,
You know them all?

FIRST MARQUIS   I know them all,
Marquis!

LIGNIÈRE (*draws* CHRISTIAN *aside*)
70 My dear boy, I came here to serve you — Well,
But where's the lady? I'll be going.

CHRISTIAN   Not yet —
A little longer! She is always here.
Please! I must find some way of meeting her.
I am dying of love! And you — you know

75 Everyone, the whole court and the whole town,
And put them all into your songs — at least
You can tell me her name!

THE FIRST VIOLIN (*raps on his desk with his bow*)
Pst — Gentlemen!
(*raises his bow*)

THE ORANGE-GIRL Macaroons, lemonade —

CHRISTIAN Then she may be
One of those aesthetes . . . Intellectuals,
80 You call them — How can I talk to a woman
In that style? I have no wit. This fine manner
Of speaking and of writing nowadays —
Not for me! I am a soldier — and afraid.
That's her box, on the right — the empty one.

LIGNIÈRE (*starts for the door*)
85 I am going.

CHRISTIAN (*restrains him*)
No — wait!

LIGNIÈRE Not I. There's a tavern
Not far away — and I am dying of thirst.

THE ORANGE-GIRL (*passes with her tray*)
Orange juice?

LIGNIÈRE No!

THE ORANGE-GIRL Milk?

LIGNIÈRE Pouah!

THE ORANGE-GIRL Muscatel?

LIGNIÈRE Here! Stop!
(*to* CHRISTIAN)
I'll stay a little.
(*to the Girl*)
Let me see
Your Muscatel.
(*He sits down by the sideboard. The Girl
pours out wine for him.*)

VOICES (*in the crowd about the door, upon the
entrance of a spruce little man, rather fat,
with a beaming smile*)
Ragueneau!

LIGNIÈRE (*to* CHRISTIAN)
Ragueneau,
90 Poet and pastry-cook — a character!

RAGUENEAU (*dressed like a confectioner in his
Sunday clothes, advances quickly to
LIGNIÈRE*)
Sir, have you seen Monsieur de Cyrano?

LIGNIÈRE (*presents him to* CHRISTIAN)
Permit me . . . Ragueneau, confectioner,
The chief support of modern poetry.

RAGUENEAU (*bridling*)
Oh — too much honor!

LIGNIÈRE Patron of the Arts —
95 Maecenas! Yes, you are —

RAGUENEAU Undoubtedly,
The poets gather round my hearth.

LIGNIÈRE On credit —
Himself a poet —

RAGUENEAU So they say —

LIGNIÈRE Maintains
The Muses.

RAGUENEAU It is true that for an ode —

LIGNIÈRE You give a tart —

RAGUENEAU A tartlet —

LIGNIÈRE Modesty!
100 And for a triolet[4] you give —

RAGUENEAU Plain bread.

LIGNIÈRE (*severely*)
Bread and milk! And you love the theatre?

RAGUENEAU I adore it!

LIGNIÈRE Well, pastry pays for all.
Your place to-day now — Come, between
ourselves,
What did it cost you?

RAGUENEAU Four pies; fourteen cakes.
(*looking about*)
105 But — Cyrano not here? Astonishing!

LIGNIÈRE Why so?

RAGUENEAU Why — Montfleury plays!

LIGNIÈRE Yes, I hear
That hippopotamus assumes the rôle
Of Phédon. What is that to Cyrano?

RAGUENEAU Have you not heard? Monsieur de
Bergerac
110 So hates Montfleury, he has forbidden him
For three weeks to appear upon the stage.

LIGNIÈRE (*who is, by this time, at his fourth
glass*)
Well?

RAGUENEAU Montfleury plays! —

CUIGY (*strolls over to them*)
Yes — what then?

---

4. **triolet:** A poem of eight lines, in which the first, fourth, and seventh lines are identical, as are the second and last lines. —Eds.

RAGUENEAU   Ah! That
Is what I came to see.

FIRST MARQUIS   This Cyrano —
Who is he?

CUIGY   Oh, he is the lad with the long sword.

115 **SECOND MARQUIS** Noble?

CUIGY   Sufficiently; he is in the Guards.
(*points to a gentleman who comes and goes
about the hall as though seeking for
someone*)
His friend Le Bret can tell you more.
(*calls to him*)
                                        Le Bret!
(LE BRET *comes down to them.*)
Looking for Bergerac?

LE BRET   Yes. And for trouble.

CUIGY Is he not an extraordinary man?

LE BRET The best friend and the bravest soul
alive!

120 **RAGUENEAU** Poet —

CUIGY   Swordsman —

LE BRET   Musician —

BRISSAILLE   Philosopher —

LIGNIÈRE Such a remarkable appearance, too!

RAGUENEAU Truly, I should not look to find his
portrait
By the grave hand of Philippe de Champagne.
He might have been a model for Callot[5] —

125 One of those wild swashbucklers in a
masque —
Hat with three plumes, and doublet with
six points —
His cloak behind him over his long sword
Cocked, like the tail of strutting Chanticleer[6] —
Prouder than all the swaggering
Tamburlaines[7]

130 Hatched out of Gascony. And to complete
This Punchinello[8] figure — such a nose! —
My lords, there is no such nose as that nose —
You cannot look upon it without crying: "Oh
no,

Impossible! Exaggerated!" Then

135 You smile, and say: "Of course — I might have
known;
Presently he will take it off." But that
Monsieur de Bergerac will never do.

LIGNIÈRE   (*grimly*)
He keeps it — and God help the man who
smiles!

RAGUENEAU His sword is one half of the shears of
Fate!

FIRST MARQUIS (*shrugs*)

140 He will not come.

RAGUENEAU   Will he not? Sir, I'll lay you
A pullet[9] à la Ragueneau!

FIRST MARQUIS (*laughing*)
                              Done!
(*Murmurs of admiration;* ROXANE *has
just appeared in her box. She sits at the
front of the box, and her Duenna takes a
seat toward the rear.* CHRISTIAN, *busy
paying the Orange-Girl, does not see her
at first.*)

SECOND MARQUIS (*with little excited cries*)
                                        Ah!
Oh! Oh! Sweet sirs, look yonder! Is she not
Frightfully ravishing?

FIRST MARQUIS   Bloom of the peach —
Blush of the strawberry —

SECOND MARQUIS   So fresh — so cool,
That our hearts, grown all warm with loving
her,

145 May catch their death of cold!

CHRISTIAN (*Looks up, sees* ROXANE, *and seizes*
LIGNIÈRE *by the arm.*)
                              There! Quick — up there —
In the box! Look! —

LIGNIÈRE (*coolly*)
                                        Herself?

CHRISTIAN   Quickly — Her name?

LIGNIÈRE (*sipping his wine, and speaking
between sips*)

---

5. **Champagne . . . Callot:** While Philippe de Champagne (1602–1674) was a renowned French painter whose subjects were generally highborn or clerical, Jacques Callot (1592–1635), on the other hand, was a printmaker known for images of peasants, soldiers, beggars, and grotesques. —Eds.
6. **Chanticleer:** Rooster from a French fable whose fatal flaw is his pride in his singing voice. —Eds.   7. **Tamburlaine:** Central Asian emperor made famous in a play by Christopher Marlowe for rising to power from the position of shepherd; the character was loosely based on the life of Timur, or Tamur the Lame. —Eds.   8. **Punchinello:** A classic character in the Italian commedia dell'arte, the Punchinello is an old clown who wears a mask with a long nose. —Eds.   9. **pullet:** young hen. —Eds.

Magdeleine Robin, called Roxane . . .
refined . . . Intellectual . . .

CHRISTIAN   Ah! —

LIGNIÈRE   Unmarried . . .

CHRISTIAN   Oh! —

LIGNIÈRE No title . . . rich enough . . . an
orphan . . . cousin

150 To Cyrano . . . of whom we spoke just now . . .
(*At this point, a very distinguished looking
gentleman, the Cordon Bleu[10] around his
neck, enters the box, and stands a moment
talking with* ROXANE.)

CHRISTIAN (*starts*)

And the man? . . .

LIGNIÈRE (*Beginning to feel his wine a little; cocks
his eye at them.*)

Oho! That man? . . . Comte de Guiche . . .
In love with her . . . married himself, however,
To the niece of the Cardinal — Richelieu . . .
Wishes Roxane, therefore, to marry one

155 Monsieur de Valvert . . . Vicomte . . . friend
of his . . .
A somewhat melancholy gentleman . . .
But . . . well, accommodating! . . . She says
No . . .
Nevertheless, de Guiche is powerful . . .
Not above persecuting . . .
(*He rises, swaying a little, and very happy.*)

I have written

160 A little song about his little game . . .
Good little song, too . . . Here, I'll sing it for
you . . .
Make de Guiche furious . . . naughty little
song . . .
Not so bad, either — Listen! . . .
(*He stands with his glass held aloft, ready to
sing.*)

CHRISTIAN   No. Adieu.

LIGNIÈRE Whither away?

CHRISTIAN   To Monsieur de Valvert!

165 **LIGNIÈRE** Careful! The man's a swordsman . . .
(*Nods toward* ROXANE, *who is watching*
CHRISTIAN.)

Wait! Someone

Looking at you —

CHRISTIAN   Roxane! . . .
(*He forgets everything, and stands spell-
bound, gazing toward* ROXANE. *The
Cut-Purse and his crew, observing him
transfixed, his eyes raised and his mouth
half open, begin edging in his direction.*)

LIGNIÈRE   Oh! Very well,
Then I'll be leaving you . . . Good day . . .
Good day! . . .
(CHRISTIAN *remains motionless.*)
Everywhere else, they like to hear me sing! —
Also, I am thirsty.
(*He goes out, navigating carefully.* LE BRET,
*having made the circuit of the hall, returns
to* RAGUENEAU, *somewhat reassured.*)

LE BRET   No sign anywhere

170 Of Cyrano!

RAGUENEAU (*incredulous*)

Wait and see!

LE BRET   Humph! I hope
He has not seen the bill.

THE CROWD   The play! — The play! —

FIRST MARQUIS (*Observing* DE GUICHE, *as he
descends from* Roxane's *box and crosses
the floor, followed by a knot of obsequious
gentlemen, the* VICOMTE DE VALVERT *among
them.*)
This man de Guiche — what ostentation!

SECOND MARQUIS   Bah! —
Another Gascon!

FIRST MARQUIS   Gascon, yes — but cold
And calculating — certain to succeed —

175 My word for it. Come, shall we make our bow?
We shall be none the worse, I promise you . . .
(*They go toward* DE GUICHE.)

SECOND MARQUIS Beautiful ribbons, Count! That
color, now,
What is it — *Kiss-me-Dear* or *Startled-Fawn*?

DE GUICHE I call that shade *The Dying Spaniard.*

FIRST MARQUIS   Ha!

180 And no false colors either — thanks to you
And your brave troops, in Flanders before long
The Spaniard will die daily.

DE GUICHE   Shall we go
And sit upon the stage? Come Valvert.

---

10. **Cordon Bleu:** A blue ribbon and cross worn by a knight of the Order of the Holy Spirit, signaling his high station in the French aristocracy. —Eds.

CHRISTIAN (*starts at the name*)

Valvert! —

The Vicomte — Ah, that scoundrel! Quick — my
glove —

185 I'll throw it in his face —

(*Reaching into his pocket for his glove, he
catches the hand of the Cut-Purse.*)

THE CUT-PURSE   Oh! —

CHRISTIAN (*holding fast to the man's wrist*)

Who are you?

I was looking for a glove —

THE CUT-PURSE (*cringing*)

You found a hand.

(*hurriedly*)

Let me go — I can tell you something —

CHRISTIAN (*still holding him*)

Well?

THE CUT-PURSE Lignière — that friend of
yours —

CHRISTIAN (*same business*)

Well?

THE CUT-PURSE   Good as dead —

Understand? Ambuscaded. Wrote a song

190 About — no matter. There's a hundred men

Waiting for him to-night — I'm one of them.

CHRISTIAN A hundred! Who arranged this?

THE CUT-PURSE   Secret.

CHRISTIAN   Oh!

THE CUT-PURSE (*with dignity*)

Professional secret.

CHRISTIAN   Where are they to be?

THE CUT-PURSE Porte de Neste. On his way
home. Tell him so.

195 Save his life.

CHRISTIAN (*releases the man*)

Yes, but where am I to find him?

THE CUT-PURSE Go round the taverns. There's
the Golden Grape,

The Pineapple, The Bursting Belt, the Two
Torches, The Three Funnels — in every one

You leave a line of writing — understand?

200 To warn him.

CHRISTIAN   (*starts for the door*)

I'll go! God, what swine — a hundred

Against one man! . . .

(*stops and looks longingly at* ROXANE)

Leave her here! —

(*savagely, turning toward* VALVERT)

And leave *him!* —

(*decidedly*)

I must save Lignière!

(*exit*).

(DE GUICHE, VALVERT, *and all the Marquis
have disappeared through the curtains, to
take their seats upon the stage. The floor is
entirely filled; not a vacant seat remains in
the gallery or in the boxes.*)

THE CROWD   The play! The play!

Begin the play!

A CITIZEN (*as his wig is hoisted tnto the air on the
end of a fishline, in the hands of a page in
the gallery*)

My wig!!

CRIES OF JOY   He's bald! Bravo,

You pages! Ha ha ha!

THE CITIZEN (*furious, shakes his fist at the boy*)

Here, you young villain!

CRIES AND LAUGHTER (*beginning very loud, then
suddenly repressed*)

205 HA HA! Ha Ha! ha ha. . . .

(*complete silence*)

LE BRET (*surprised*)

That sudden hush? . . .

(*A Spectator whispers in his ear.*)

Yes?

THE SPECTATOR   I was told on good authority . . .

MURMURS (*here and there*)

What? . . . Here? . . . No . . . Yes . . . Look — in
the latticed box —

The Cardinal! . . . The Cardinal! . . .

A PAGE   The Devil! —

Now we shall all have to behave ourselves!

(*Three raps on the stage. The audience
becomes motionless. Silence.*)

THE VOICE OF A MARQUIS (*from the stage, behind
the curtains*)

210 Snuff that candle!

ANOTHER MARQUIS (*Puts his head out through
the curtains.*)

A chair! . . .

(*A chair is passed from hand to hand over
the heads of the crowd. He takes it, and
disappears behind the curtains, not without*

having blown a few kisses to the occupants of the boxes.)

A SPECTATOR   Silence!

VOICES   Hssh! . . . Hssh! . . .

(*Again the three raps on the stage. The curtains part. Tableau. The Marquis seated on their chairs to right and left of the stage, insolently posed. Back drop representing a pastoral scene, bluish in tone. Four little crystal chandeliers light up the stage. The violins play softly.*)

LE BRET (*in a low tone, to* RAGUENEAU)
Montfleury enters now?

RAGUENEAU (*nods*)
Opens the play.

LE BRET (*much relieved*)
Then Cyrano is not here!

RAGUENEAU   I lose . . .

LE BRET   Humph! —
So much the better!
(*The melody of a Musette is heard.* MONTFLEURY *appears upon the scene, a ponderous figure in the costume of a rustic shepherd, a hat garlanded with roses tilted over one ear, playing upon a beribboned pastoral pipe.*)

THE CROWD (*applauds*)
Montfleury! . . . Bravo! . . .

MONTFLEURY (*after bowing to the applause, begins the rôle of Phédon*)
"*Thrice happy he who hides fram pomp and power*
In sylvan shade or solitary bower;
Where balmy zephyrs fan his burning checks —"

A VOICE (*from the midst of the hall*)
Wretch! Have I not forbade you these three weeks?
(*Sensation. Every one turns to look. Murmurs.*)

SEVERAL VOICES What? . . . Where? . . . Who is it? . . .

CUIGY   Cyrano!

LE BRET (*in alarm*)
Himself!

215 **THE VOICE** King of clowns! Leave the stage — *at once!*

THE CROWD   Oh! —

MONTFLEURY   Now,
Now, now —

THE VOICE   You disobey me?

SEVERAL VOICES (*from the floor, from the boxes*)
Hsh! Go on —
Quiet! — Go on, Montfleury! — Who's afraid? —

MONTFLEURY (*in a voice of no great assurance*)
"*Thrice happy he who hides from . . .*"

THE VOICE (*more menacingly*)
Well? Well? Well? . . .
Monarch of mountebanks![11] Must I come and plant
A forest on your shoulders?

This is an image of the actual historical figure Savinien Cyrano de Bergerac.

To what extent does the real Cyrano look like what you'd expect of the dramatic character Cyrano, given the information that is presented in Act 1 before his appearance?

---

11. **mountebanks:** Charlatans, swindlers. —Eds.

(*A cane at the end of a long arm shakes
above the heads of the crowd.*)

MONTFLEURY (*in a voice increasingly feeble*)
"Thrice hap —"

(*The cane is violently agitated.*)

THE VOICE   GO!!!

220 **THE CROWD** Ah! . . .

CYRANO (*Arises in the centre of the floor, erect
upon a chair, his arms folded, his hat
cocked ferociously, his moustache bristling,
his nose terrible.*)

Presently I shall grow angry!

(*sensation at his appearance*)

MONTFLEURY (*to the Marquis*)

Messieurs,

If you protect me —

A MARQUIS (*nonchalantly*)

Well — proceed!

CYRANO   Fat swine!

If you dare breathe one balmy zephyr more,
I'll fan your cheeks for you!

THE MARQUIS   Quiet down there!

CYRANO Unless these gentlemen retain their
seats,

225 My cane may bite their ribbons!

ALL THE MARQUIS (*on their feet*)

That will do! —

Montfleury —

CYRANO   Fly, goose! Shoo! Take to your
wings,

Before I pluck your plumes, and draw your
gorge!

A VOICE See here! —

CYRANO   Off stage!!

ANOTHER VOICE   One moment —

CYRANO   What — still there?

(*Turns back his cuffs deliberately.*)

Very good — then I enter — *Left — with knife —*

230 To carve this large Italian sausage.

MONTFLEURY (*desperately attempting dignity*)

Sir,

When you insult me, you insult the Muse!

CYRANO (*with great politeness*)

Sir, if the Muse, who never knew your name,

Had the honor to meet you — then be sure
That after one glance at that face of yours,

235 That figure of a mortuary urn —
She would apply her buskin[12] — toward the
rear!

THE CROWD Montfleury! . . . Montfleury! . . . The
play! The play!

CYRANO (*to those who are shouting and
crowding about him*)

Pray you, be gentle with my scabbard here —
She'll put her tongue out at you presently! —

(*The circle enlarges.*)

THE CROWD (*recoiling*)

240 Keep back —

CYRANO (*to* MONTFLEURY)

Begone!

THE CROWD (*Pushing in closer, and growling.*)

Ahr! . . . ahr! . . .

CYRANO (*Turns upon them.*)

Did someone speak?

(*They recoil again.*)

A VOICE (*In the back of the hall, sings.*)

Monsieur de Cyrano
Must be another Caesar —
Let Brutus lay him low,
And play us La Clorise!

ALL THE CROWD (*singing*)

La Clorise! La Clorise!

CYRANO Let me hear one more word of that
same song,
And I destroy you all!

A CITIZEN   Who might you be?
Samson? —

CYRANO   Precisely. Would you kindly
lend me
Your jawbone?

A LADY (*in one of the boxes*)

What an outrage!

A NOBLE   Scandalous!

245 **A CITIZEN** Annoying!

A PAGE   What a game!

THE CROWD   Kss! Montfleury!
Cyrano!

CYRANO   Silence!

---

12. **buskin:** High lace-up boot with an open toe. —Eds.

THE CROWD (*delirious*)

> Woof! Woof! Baaa! Cockadoo!

CYRANO I—

A PAGE Meow!

CYRANO I say be silent! —

> (*His voice dominates the uproar.*
> *Momentary hush.*)

> And I offer

One universal challenge to you all!

Approach, young heroes — I will take your
> names.

250 Each in his turn — no crowding! One,
> two, three —

Come, get your numbers — who will head
> the list —

You sir? No — You? Ah, no. To the first man

Who falls I'll build a monument! . . . Not one?

Will all who wish to die, please raise their
> hands? . . .

255 I see. You are so modest, you might blush

Before a sword naked. Sweet innocence! . . .

Not one name? Not one finger? . . . Very well,

Then I go on:

> (*Turning back towards the stage, where*
> MONTFLEURY *waits in despair.*)

> I'd have our theatre cured

Of this carbuncle. Or if not, why then —

> (*His hand on his sword hilt.*)

260 The lancet![13]

MONTFLEURY I —

CYRANO (*Descends from his chair, seats himself*
> *comfortably in the centre of the circle which*
> *has formed around him, and makes himself*
> *quite at home.*)

> Attend to me — full moon!

I clap my hands, three times — thus. At the
> third

You will eclipse yourself.

THE CROWD (*amused*)

> Ah!

CYRANO Ready? *One.*

MONTFLEURY I —

A VOICE (*from the boxes*)

> No!

THE CROWD He'll go — He'll stay —

MONTFLEURY I really think,
> Gentlemen —

CYRANO *Two.*

MONTFLEURY Perhaps I had better —

CYRANO *Three!*

> (MONTFLEURY *disappears, as if through a*
> *trapdoor. Tempest of laughter, hoots and*
> *hisses.*)

265 **THE CROWD** Yah! — Coward — Come back —

CYRANO (*beaming, drops back in his chair and*
> *crosses his legs*)

> Let him — if he dare!

A CITIZEN The Manager! Speech! Speech!

> (BELLEROSE *advances and bows.*)

THE BOXES Ah! Bellerose!

BELLEROSE (*with elegance*)

> Most noble — most fair —

THE CROWD No! The Comedian —
> Jodelet! —

JODELET (*Advances, and speaks through his nose.*)

> Lewd fellows of the baser sort —

THE CROWD Ha! Ha! Not bad! Bravo!

JODELET No Bravos here!

270 Our heavy tragedian with the voluptuous
> bust

Was taken suddenly —

THE CROWD Yah! Coward!

JODELET I mean . . .
> He had to be excused —

THE CROWD Call him back — No! —
> Yes! —

THE BOY (*to* CYRANO)

> After all, Monsieur, what reason have
> you

To hate this Montfleury?

CYRANO (*graciously, still seated*)

> My dear young man,

275 I have two reasons, either one alone

Conclusive. *Primo:* A lamentable actor,

Who mouths his verse and moans his
> tragedy,

And heaves up — Ugh! — like a hod-carrier,[14]
> lines

---

13. **carbuncle . . . lancet:** A carbuncle is a large boil caused by an infection; it is often treated by piercing it with a needle called a lancet. —Eds.

14. **hod:** A three-sided box at the end of a stick used to help shoulder a load of bricks, or a tall bucket used to carry coal. —Eds.

That ought to soar on their own wings.
    Secundo:—

280 Well—that's my secret.

THE OLD CITIZEN (*behind him*)
                  But you close the play—
La Clorise—by Baro! Are we to miss
Our entertainment, merely—

CYRANO (*respectfully, turns his chair toward the
    old man*)
            My dear old boy,
The poetry of Baro being worth

285 Zero, or less, I feel that I have done
Poetic justice!

THE INTELLECTUALS (*in the boxes*)
               Really!—our Baro!—
My dear!—Who ever?—Ah, dieu! The idea!—

CYRANO (*gallantly, turns his chair toward the
    boxes*)
Fair ladies—shine upon us like the sun,
Blossom like flowers around us—be our
    songs,
Heard in a dream—Make sweet the hour of
    death,

290 Smiling upon us as you close our eyes—
Inspire, but do not try to criticise!

BELLEROSE Quite so!—and the mere
    money—possibly
You would like that returned—Yes?

CYRANO   Bellerose,
You speak the first word of intelligence!

295 I will not wound the mantle of the Muse—
Here, catch!—
    (*throws him a purse*)
           And hold your tongue.

THE CROWD (*astonished*)
                 Ah! Ah!

JODELET (*Deftly catches the purse, weighs it in his
    hand.*)
               Monsieur,
You are hereby authorized to close our play
Every night, on the same terms.

THE CROWD   Boo!

JODELET   And welcome!
Let us be booed together, you and I!

300 **BELLEROSE** Kindly pass out quietly . . .

JODELET (*burlesquing* BELLEROSE)
             Quietly . . .

(*They begin to go out, while* CYRANO
*looks about him with satisfaction. But the
exodus ceases presently during the ensuing scene. The ladies in the boxes who
have already risen and put on their
wraps, stop to listen, and finally sit down
again.*)

LE BRET (*to* CYRANO)
Idiot!

A MEDDLER (*hurries up to* CYRANO)
        But what a scandal! Montfleury—
The great Montfleury! Did you know the Duc
de Candale was his patron? Who is yours?

CYRANO No one.

THE MEDDLER   No one—no patron?

CYRANO   I said no.

305 **THE MEDDLER** What, no great lord, to cover with
    his name—

CYRANO (*with visible annoyance*)
No, I have told you twice. Must I repeat?
No sir, no patron—
    (*his hand on his sword*)
           But a patroness!

THE MEDDLER And when do you leave Paris?

CYRANO   That's as may be.

THE MEDDLER The Duc de Candale has a long
    arm.

CYRANO   Mine

310 Is longer,
    (*drawing his sword*)
        by three feet of steel.

THE MEDDLER   Yes, yes,
But do you dream of daring—

CYRANO   I do dream
Of daring . . .

THE MEDDLER But—

CYRANO   You may go now.

THE MEDDLER   But—

CYRANO   You may go—
Or tell me why are you staring at my nose!

THE MEDDLER (*in confusion*)
No—I—

CYRANO (*stepping up to him*)
        Does it astonish you?

THE MEDDLER (*drawing back*)
        Your grace

315 Misunderstands my—

CYRANO   Is it long and soft
And dangling, like a trunk?

THE MEDDLER (*same business*)
                              I never said —

CYRANO Or crooked, like an owl's beak?

THE MEDDLER   I —

CYRANO   Perhaps
A pimple ornaments the end of it?

THE MEDDLER No —

CYRANO   Or a fly parading up and down?

320 What is this portent?

THE MEDDLER   Oh! —

CYRANO   This phenomenon?

THE MEDDLER But I have been careful
            not to look —

CYRANO   And why
Not, if you please?

THE MEDDLER   Why —

CYRANO   It disgusts you, then?

THE MEDDLER My dear sir —

CYRANO   Does its color appear to you
Unwholesome?

THE MEDDLER   Oh, by no means!

CYRANO   Or its form

325 Obscene?

THE MEDDLER   Not in the least —

CYRANO   Then why assume
This deprecating manner? Possibly
You find it just a trifle large?

THE MEDDLER (*babbling*)
                              Oh no! —
Small, very small, infinitesimal —

CYRANO (*roars*)
                              What!
How? You accuse me of absurdity?

330 Small — *my nose*? Why —

THE MEDDLER (*breathless*)
                          My God! —

CYRANO   Magnificent,
My nose! . . . You pug, you knob, you
      button-head,
Know that I glory in this nose of mine,
For a great nose indicates a great man —
Genial, courteous, intellectual,

335 Virile, courageous — as I am — and such
As you — poor wretch — will never dare to be

Even in imagination. For that face —
That blank, inglorious concavity
Which my right hand finds —
      (*He strikes him.*)

THE MEDDLER   Ow!

CYRANO   — on top of you,

340 Is as devoid of pride, of poetry,
Of soul, of picturesqueness, of contour,
Of character, of NOSE in short — as that
      (*takes him by the shoulders and turns him
      around, suiting the action to the word*)
Which at the end of that limp spine of yours
My left foot —

THE MEDDLER (*escaping*)
                  Help! The Guard!

CYRANO   Take notice, all

345 Who find this feature of my countenance
A theme for comedy! When the humorist
Is noble, then my custom is to show
Appreciation proper to his rank —
More heartfelt . . . and more pointed . . .

DE GUICHE (*who has come down from the stage,
      surrounded by the Marquis*)
                              Presently

350 This fellow will grow tiresome.

VALVERT (*shrugs*)
                              Oh, he blows
His trumpet!

DE GUICHE   Well — will no one interfere?

VALVERT No one?
      (*looks round*)
                  Observe. I myself will proceed
To put him in his place.
      (*He walks up to* CYRANO, *who has been
      watching him, and stands there, looking
      him over with an affected air.*)
                  Ah . . . your nose . . . hem! . . .
Your nose is . . . rather large!

CYRANO (*gravely*)
                              Rather.

VALVERT (*simpering*)
                              Oh well —

CYRANO (*coolly*)

355 Is that all?

VALVERT (*turns away, with a shrug*)
                  Well, of course —

CYRANO   Ah, no, young sir!
    You are too simple. Why, you might have
        said —
    Oh, a great many things! Mon dieu, why waste
    Your opportunity? For example, thus: —
    Aggressive: I, sir, if that nose were mine,
360 I'd have it amputated — on the spot!
    Friendly: How do you drink with such a
        nose?
    You ought to have a cup made specially.
    Descriptive: 'Tis a rock — a crag — a cape —
    A cape? say rather, a peninsula!
365 Inquisitive: What is that receptacle —
    A razor-case or a portfolio?
    Kindly: Ah, do you love the little birds
    So much that when they come and sing to
        you,
    You give them this to perch on? Insolent:
370 Sir, when you smoke, the neighbors must
        suppose
    Your chimney is on fire. Cautious: Take
        care —
    A weight like that might make you topheavy.
    Thoughtful: Somebody fetch my parasol —
    Those delicate colors fade so in the sun!
375 Pedantic: Does not Aristophanes
    Mention a mythologic monster called
    Hippocampelephantocamelos?[15]
    Surely we have here the original!
    Familiar: Well, old torchlight! Hang your hat
380 Over that chandelier — it hurts my eyes.
    Eloquent: When it blows, the typhoon
        howls,
    And the clouds darken. Dramatic: When
        it bleeds —
    The Red Sea! Enterprising: What a sign
    For some perfumer! Lyric: Hark — the horn
385 Of Roland[16] calls to summon Charlemagne! —

    Simple: When do they unveil the
        monument?
    Respectful: Sir, I recognize in you
    A man of parts, a man of prominence —
    Rustic: Hey? What? Call that a nose?
        Na, na —
390 I be no fool like what you think I be —
    That there's a blue cucumber! Military:
    Point against cavalry! Practical: Why not
    A lottery with this for the grand prize?
    Or — parodying Faustus[17] in the play —
395 "Was this the nose that launched a thousand
        ships
    And burned the topless towers of Ilium?"
    These, my dear sir, are things you might have
        said
    Had you some tinge of letters, or of wit
    To color your discourse. But wit, — not so,
400 You never had an atom — and of letters,
    You need but three to write you down — an Ass.
    Moreover, — if you had the invention, here
    Before these folk to make a jest of me —
    Be sure you would not then articulate
405 The twentieth part of half a syllable
    Of the beginning! For I say these things
    Lightly enough myself, about myself,
    But I allow none else to utter them.
DE GUICHE (*Tries to lead away the amazed*
        VALVERT.)
    Vicomte — come.
VALVERT (*choking*)
                    Oh — These arrogant grand airs! —
410 A clown who — look at him — not even gloves!
    No ribbons — no lace — no buckles on his
        shoes —
CYRANO I carry my adornments on my soul.
    I do not dress up like a popinjay;[18]
    But inwardly, I keep my daintiness.

---

15. **hippocampelephantocamelos:** Invented animal, a hybrid of a hippocampus (sea horse), elephant, and camel, all animals with relatively long noses. —Eds.   16. **horn of Roland:** The *Song of Roland* is an epic poem and one of the first major works of French literature, dating to c. 1040. In it, Roland blows his horn to summon the army of Charlemagne and defeat the Saracen army. —Eds   17. **Faustus:** Referring to the character in Christopher Marlowe's play *The Historie of the Damnable Life, and Deserved Death of Doctor John Faustus,* based on a German legend in which a man sells his soul to the Devil in exchange for knowledge and power. —Eds.   18. **popinjay:** Literally, a parrot; here, a vain person who dresses extravagantly. —Eds.

seeing connections

Following is the speech given by C. D. Bales in *Roxanne*, the 1987 film adaptation of *Cyrano* starring Steve Martin, who also wrote the screenplay. In this scene, a bar patron calls him "Big Nose" and C. D. accepts the challenge to think of twenty jokes better than "Big Nose."

To what extent do you think Martin has retained the original meaning of Cyrano's famous speech and also made it appeal to a more modern audience?

C. D. Bales   Let's start with . . . Obvious: 'scuse me, is that your nose or did a bus park on your face? Meteorological: everybody take cover, she's going to blow! Fashionable: you know, you could de-emphasize your nose if you wore something larger, like . . . Wyoming. Personal: well, here we are, just the three of us. Punctual: all right, Delbman, your nose was on time but YOU were fifteen minutes late! Envious: Ooooh, I wish I were you! Gosh, to be able to smell your own ear! Naughty: uh, pardon me, sir, some of the ladies have asked if you wouldn't mind putting that thing away. Philosophical: you know, it's not the size of a nose that's important, it's what's IN IT that matters. Humorous: laugh and the world laughs with you. Sneeze, and it's goodbye, Seattle! Commercial: hi, I'm Earl Scheib, and I can paint that nose for $39.95! Polite: uh, would you mind not bobbing your head? The, uh, orchestra keeps changing tempo. Melodic: Everybody. He's got . . .

Everyone   [singing] The whole world in his nose!

C. D. Bales   Sympathetic: aw, what happened? Did your parents lose a bet with God?

Complimentary: you must love the little birdies to give them this to perch on. Scientific: Say, does that thing there influence the tides? Obscure: whoa! I'd hate to see the grindstone. Well, think about it. Inquiring: when you stop to smell the flowers, are they afraid? French: saihr, ze pigs have refused to find any more truffles until you leave! Pornographic: finally, a man who can satisfy two women at once! How many is that?

Dean   Fourteen, Chief!

C. D. Bales   Religious: the Lord giveth . . . and He just kept on giving, didn't He? Disgusting: Say, who mows your nose hair? Paranoid: keep that guy away from my cocaine! Aromatic: it must be wonderful to wake up in the morning and smell the coffee . . . in Brazil. Appreciative: Oooh, how original! Most people just have their teeth capped.

[he pauses, pretending to be stumped, while the crowd urges him on]

C. D. Bales   All right. Dirty: your name wouldn't be Dick, would it?

415 I do not bear with me, by any chance,
An insult not yet washed away — a conscience
Yellow with unpurged bile — an honor frayed
To rags, a set of scruples badly worn.
I go caparisoned in gems unseen,
420 Trailing white plumes of freedom, garlanded
With my good name — no figure of a man,
But a soul clothed in shining armor, hung
With deeds for decorations, twirling — thus —
A bristling wit, and swinging at my side
425 Courage, and on the stones of this old town
Making the sharp truth ring, like golden
　　spurs!

VALVERT But —

CYRANO　　　But I have no gloves! A pity too!
I had one — the last one of an old pair —
And lost that. Very careless of me. Some
430 Gentleman offered me an impertinence.
I left it — in his face.

VALVERT　　　　　　Dolt, bumpkin, fool,
Insolent puppy, jobbernowl![19]

CYRANO (*Removes his hat and bows.*)
　　　　　　　　Ah, yes?
And I — Cyrano — Savinien-Hercule
De Bergerac!

VALVERT (*Turns away.*)
　　　　　　Buffoon!

CYRANO (*Cries out as if suddenly taken with a
　　cramp.*)
　　　　　　Oh!

VALVERT (*Turns back.*)
　　　　　　Well, what now?

CYRANO (*with grimaces of anguish*)
I must do something to relieve these cramps —
435 This is what comes of lack of exercise —
Ah! —

VALVERT What is all this?

CYRANO　　　　　My sword has gone to sleep!

VALVERT (*draws*)
So be it!

CYRANO　　　　You shall die exquisitely.

VALVERT (*contemptuously*)
Poet!

CYRANO Why yes, a poet, if you will;
So while we fence, I'll make you a Ballade
440 Extempore.[20]

VALVERT　　　　A Ballade?

CYRANO　　　　　　Yes. You know
What that is?

VALVERT　　　I —

CYRANO　　　　　The Ballade, sir, is formed
Of three stanzas of eight lines each —

VALVERT　　　　　　Oh, come!

CYRANO And a refrain of four.

VALVERT　　　You —

CYRANO　　　　　I'll compose
One, while I fight with you; and at the end
445 Of the last line — thrust home!

VALVERT　　　　Will you?

CYRANO　　　　　　　I will.
　　(*declaims*)
"*Ballade of the duel at the Hôtel de Bourgogne
Between de Bergerac and a Boeotian.*"

VALVERT (*sneering*)
What do you mean by that?

CYRANO　　　　　Oh, that? The title.

THE CROWD (*excited*)
　　Come on —
　　　　A circIe —
　　　　　　Quiet —
　　　　　　　Down in front!
(*Tableau. A ring of interested spectators in
the centre of the floor, the Marquis and the
Officers mingling with the citizens and
common folk. Pages swarming up on men's
shoulders to see better; the Ladies in the
boxes standing and leaning over. To the
right,* DE GUICHE *and his following; to the
left,* LE BRET, CUIGY, RAGUENEAU, *and
others of* CYRANO's *friends.*)

CYRANO (*Closes his eyes for an instant.*)
450 Stop . . . Let me choose my rimes. . . . Now!
Here we go —
(*He suits the action to the word, throughout
the following:*)

---

19. **jobbernowl:** blockhead, numskull. —Eds.　20. **Ballade Extempore:** An extemporaneous (improvised, made-up-at-the-time) ballade. A ballade (not to be confused with a ballad) is a form of Renaissance French poetry that includes three eight-line stanzas using the same rhyme schemes, and concludes with a four-line stanza of a differing rhyme scheme called the "envoi." —Eds.

Lightly I toss my hat away,
  Languidly over my arm let fall
The cloak that covers my bright array —
455 Then out swords, and to work withal!
  A Launcelot, in his Lady's hall . . .
A Spartacus, at the Hippodrome![21] . . .
  I dally awhile with you, dear jackal,
Then' as I end the refrain, thrust home.

(*The swords cross — the fight is on.*)

460 Where shall I skewer my peacock? . . . Nay,
  Better for you to have shunned this brawl! —
Here, in the heart, thro' your ribbons gay?
  —In the belly, under your silken shawl?
  Hark, how the steel rings musical!
465 Mark how my point floats, light as the foam,
  Ready to drive you back to the wall,
Then, as I end the refrain, thrust home!

Ho, for a rime! . . . You are white as whey —
  You break, you cower, you cringe, you . . .
    crawl!
470 Tac! — and I parry your last essay:
  So may the turn of a hand forestall
  Life with its honey, death with its gall;
So may the turn of my fancy roam
  Free, for a time, till the rimes recall,

475 Then, as I end the refrain, thrust home!

(*He announces solemnly.*)

REFRAIN
  Prince! Pray God, that is Lord of all,
Pardon your soul, for your time has come!
  Beat — pass — fling you aslant, asprawl —
Then, as I end the refrain . . .
  (*He lunges;* VALVERT *staggers back and
  falls into the arms of his friends.* CYRANO
  recovers, and salutes.)
                    —Thrust home!
(*Shouts. Applause from the boxes. Flowers
and handkerchiefs come fluttering down.
The Officers surround* CYRANO *and congrat-
ulate him.* RAGUENEAU *dances for joy.
LE BRET is unable to conceal his enthusiasm.
The friends of* VALVERT *hold him up and
help him away.*)

THE CROWD (*in one long cry*)
480 Ah-h!

A CAVALIER Superb!

A WOMAN   Simply sweet!

RAGUENEAU   Magnelephant!

A MARQUIS A novelty!

LE BRET   Bah!

▶

The opening duel of *Cyrano de
Bergerac*, as staged by the
Chicago Shakespeare Theater.

**How does the staging of this
scene suggest that the duel
is a play within a play?**

Photo by Liz Lauren/Chicago Shakespeare Theater

21. **Spartacus . . . Hippodrome:** Spartacus was a gladiator who led a slave revolt against the Roman Republic. A hippodrome is a stadium used for horse or chariot racing, similar to the Roman circus where gladiators such as Spartacus might have fought. —Eds.

THE CROWD (*thronging around* CYRANO)

        Compliments — regards —

Bravo! —

A WOMAN'S VOICE   Why, he's a hero!

A MUSKETEER (*Advances quickly to* CYRANO, *with
outstretched hands.*)

        Monsieur, will you

Permit me? — It was altogether fine!

I think I may appreciate these things —

485   Moreover, I have been stamping for pure joy!

    (*He retires quickly.*)

CYRANO (*to* CUIGY)

What was that gentleman's name?

CUIGY   Oh . . . D'Artagnan.

LE BRET (*Takes* CYRANO'S *arm.*)

Come here and tell me —

CYRANO   Let this crowd go first —

    (*to* BELLEROSE)

May we stay?

BELLEROSE (*with great respect*)

        Certainly!

    (*Cries and cat-calls off stage.*)

JODELET (*Comes down from the door where he
has been looking out.*)

        Hark! — Montfleury —

They are hooting him.

BELLEROSE (*solemnly*)

        Sic transit gloria!

    (*Changes his tone and shouts to the porter and
the lamplighter.*)

490   — Strike! . . . Close the house! . . . Leave the

   lights —   We rehearse

The new farce after dinner.

    (*JODELET and BELLEROSE go out after elabo-
rately saluting* CYRANO.)

THE PORTER (*to* CYRANO)

        You do not dine?

CYRANO I? — No!

    (THE PORTER *turns away.*)

LE BRET   Why not?

CYRANO (*haughtily*)

       Because —

    (*Changing his tone when he sees* THE PORTER
has gone.)

       Because I have

No money.

LE BRET (*gesture of tossing*)

       But — the purse of gold?

CYRANO   Farewell,

Paternal pension!

LE BRET   So you have, until

495   The first of next month—?

CYRANO   Nothing.

LE BRET   What a fool! —

CYRANO But — what a gesture!

THE ORANGE-GIRL (*Behind her little counter;
coughs.*)

        Hem!

    (CYRANO *and* LE BRET *look around; she
advances timidly.*)

        Pardon, monsieur . . .

A man ought never to go hungry . . .

    (*indicating the sideboard*)

        See,

I have everything here . . .

    (*eagerly*)

        Please! —

CYRANO (*uncovers*)

        My dear child,

I cannot bend this Gascon pride of mine

500   To accept such a kindness — Yet, for fear

That I may give you pain if I refuse,

I will take . . .

    (*He goes to the sideboard and makes his
selection.*)

        Oh, not very much! A grape . . .

    (*She gives him the bunch; he removes a
single grape.*)

One only! And a glass of water . . .

    (*She starts to pour wine into it; he stops her.*)

        Clear!

And . . . half a macaroon!

    (*He gravely returns the other half.*)

LE BRET   Old idiot!

505 THE ORANGE-GIRL Please! — Nothing more?

CYRANO   Why yes — Your hand — to kiss.

    (*He kisses the hand which she hold out, as
he would the hand of a princess.*)

THE ORANGE-GIRL Thank you, sir.

    (*She curtseys.*)

        Good-night.

    (*She goes out.*)

CYRANO   Now, I am listening.

(*plants himself before the sideboard and arranges thereon—*)

Dinner! —

(—*the macaroon*)

Drink! —

(—*the glass of water*)

Dessert! —

(—*the grape.*)

There — now I'll sit down.

(*Seats himself.*)

Lord, I was hungry! Abominably!

(*eating*)

Well?

LE BRET These fatheads with the bellicose grand airs

510 Will have you ruined if you listen to them;

Talk to a man of sense and hear how all

Your swagger impresses him.

CYRANO (*finishes his macaroon.*)

Enormously.

LE BRET The Cardinal —

CYRANO (*beaming*)

Was he there?

LE BRET He must have thought you —

CYRANO Original.

LE BRET Well, but —

CYRANO He is himself

515 A playwright. He will not be too displeased

That I have closed another author's play.

LE BRET But look at all the enemies you have made!

CYRANO (*Begins on the grape.*)

How many — do you think?

LE BRET Just forty-eight

Without the women.

CYRANO Count them.

LE BRET Montfleury,

520 Baro, de Guiche, the Vicomte, the Old Man,

All the Academy —

CYRANO Enough! You make me

Happy!

LE BRET But where is all this leading you?

What is your plan?

CYRANO I have been wandering —

Wasting my force upon too many plans.

525 Now I have chosen one.

LE BRET What one?

CYRANO The simplest —

To make myself in all things admirable!

LE BRET Hmph! — Well, then, the real reason why you hate

Montfleury — Come, the truth, now!

CYRANO (*rises*)

That Silenus,[22]

Who cannot hold his belly in his arms,

530 Still dreams of being sweetly dangerous

Among the women — sighs and languishes,

Making sheeps' eyes out of his great frog's face —

I hate him ever since one day he dared

Smile upon —

Oh, my friend, I seemed to see

535 Over some flower a great snail crawling!

LE BRET (*amazed*)

How,

What? Is it possible? —

CYRANO (*with a bitter smile*)

For me to love? . . .

(*changing his tone; seriously*)

I love.

LE BRET May I know? You have never said —

CYRANO Whom I love? Think a moment. Think of me —

Me, whom the plainest woman would despise —

540 Me, with this nose of mine that marches on

Before me by a quarter of an hour!

Whom should I love? Why — of course — it must be

The woman in the world most beautiful.

LE BRET Most beautiful?

CYRANO In all this world — most sweet

545 Also; most wise; most witty; and most fair!

LE BRET Who and what is this woman?

CYRANO Dangerous

Mortally, without meaning; exquisite

Without imagining. Nature's own snare

To allure manhood. A white rose wherein

550 Love lies in ambush for his natural prey.

Who knows her smile has known a perfect thing.

---

22. **Silenus:** An old satyr, specifically, the mythical tutor and companion to the god Dionysus. In this case, a drunken and lecherous old man. —Eds.

She creates grace in her own image, brings
Heaven to earth in one movement of her
   hand—
Nor thou, O Venus! balancing thy shell
555   Over the Mediterranean blue, nor thou,
Diana! marching through broad, blossoming
   woods,
Art so divine as when she mounts her chair,
And goes abroad through Paris!

LE BRET   Oh, well — of course,
That makes everything clear!

CYRANO   Transparently.

560 LE BRET   Magdeleine Robin — your cousin?

CYRANO   Yes; Roxane.

LE BRET   And why not? If you love her, tell her so!
You have covered yourself with glory in her
   eyes
This very day.

CYRANO   My old friend — look at me,
And tell me how much hope remains for me
565 With this protuberance! Oh I have no more
Illusions! Now and then — bah! I may grow
Tender, walking alone in the blue cool
Of evening, through some garden fresh with
   flowers
After the benediction of the rain;
570 My poor big devil of a nose inhales
April . . . and so I follow with my eyes
Where some boy, with a girl upon his arm,
Passes a patch of silver . . . and I feel
Somehow, I wish I had a woman too,
575 Walking with little steps under the moon,
And holding my arm so, and smiling. Then
I dream — and I forget. . . .
                           And then I see
The shadow of my profile on the wall!

LE BRET   My friend! . . .

CYRANO   My friend, I have my bitter days,
580 Knowing myself so ugly, so alone.
Sometimes —

LE BRET   You weep?

CYRANO   (quickly)
                        Oh, not that ever! No,
That would be too grotesque — tears trickling
   down

All the long way along this nose of mine?
I will not so profane the dignity
585   Of sorrow. Never any tears for me!
Why, there is nothing more sublime than
   tears,
Nothing! — Shall I make them ridiculous
In my poor person?

LE BRET   Love's no more than chance!

CYRANO   (Shakes his head.)
No. I love Cleopatra; do I appear
590   Caesar? I adore Beatrice; have I
The look of Dante?[23]

LE BRET   But your wit — your courage —
Why, that poor child who offered you just
   now
Your dinner! She — you saw with your own
   eyes,
Her eyes did not avoid you.

CYRANO   (thoughtful)
                              That is true . . .

LE BRET   Well then! Roxane herself, watching
   your duel,
595   Paler than —

CYRANO   Pale? —

LE BRET   Her lips parted, her hand
Thus, at her breast — I saw it! Speak to her
Speak, man!

CYRANO   Through my nose? She might
   laugh at me;
That is the one thing in this world I fear!

THE PORTER   (Followed by The Duenna,
      approaches CYRANO respectfully.)
A lady asking for Monsieur.

CYRANO   Mon dieu . . .

600   Her Duenna! —

THE DUENNA   (a sweeping curtsey)
                Monsieur . . .
                        A message for you:
From our good cousin we desire to know
When and where we may see him privately.

CYRANO   (amazed)
To see me?

THE DUENNA   (an elaborate reverence)
                To see you. We have certain things
To tell you.

---

23. **Beatrice . . . Dante:** In Dante's *Divine Comedy*, Beatrice leads Dante through hell and purgatory to heaven. —Eds.

CYRANO   Certain —

THE DUENNA   Things.

CYRANO (*trembling*)

Mon dieu![24] . . .

THE DUENNA   We go

605   To-morrow, at the first flush of the dawn,
To hear Mass at St. Roch. Then afterwards,
Where can we meet and talk a little?

CYRANO (*Catching* LE BRET'S *arm.*)

Where? —

I — Ah, mon dieu! . . . mon dieu! . . .

THE DUENNA   Well?

CYRANO   I am thinking . . .

THE DUENNA And you think?

CYRANO   I . . . The shop of Ragueneau . . .
Ragueneau — pastrycook . . .

THE DUENNA   Who dwells? —

CYRANO   Mon dieu!
Oh, yes . . . Ah, mon dieu! . . . Rue
St. — Honoré.

610 **THE DUENNA** We are agreed. Remember — seven
o'clock.

(*reverence*)

Until then —

CYRANO   I'll be there.

(*The Duenna goes out.*)

CYRANO (*Falls into the arms of* LE BRET.)

Me . . . to see me! . . .

LE BRET You are not quite so gloomy.

CYRANO   After all,
She knows that I exist — no matter why!

LE BRET So now, you are going to be happy.

CYRANO   Now! . . .

(*beside himself*)

615   I — I am going to be a storm — a flame —
I need to fight whole armies all alone;
I have ten hearts; I have a hundred arms; I feel
Too strong to war with mortals —

(*He shouts at the top of his voice.*)

BRING ME GIANTS!

(*A moment since, the shadows of the comedians have been visible moving and posturing
upon the stage. The violins have taken their
places.*)

A VOICE (*from the stage*)

Hey — pst — less noise! We are rehearsing here!

CYRANO (*laughs*)

620   We are going.

(*He turns up stage. Through the street door
enter* CUIGY, BRISSAILLE, *and a number of
officers, supporting* LIGNIÈRE, *who is now
thoroughly drunk.*)

CUIGY   Cyrano!

CYRANO   What is it?

CUIGY   Here —
Here's your stray lamb!

CYRANO (*Recognizes* LIGNIÈRE.)

Lignière! — What's wrong with him?

CUIGY He wants you.

BRISSAILLE   He's afraid to go home.

CYRANO   Why?

LIGNIÈRE (*Showing a crumpled scrap of paper
and speaking with the elaborate logic of
profound intoxication.*)

This letter — hundred against one —
that's me —

I'm the one — all because of little song —

625   Good song — Hundred men, waiting,
understand?

Porte de Nesle — way home —   Might be
dangerous —

Would you permit me spend the night with
you?

CYRANO A hundred — is that all? You are going
home!

LIGNIÈRE (*astonished*)

Why —

CYRANO (*In a voice of thunder, indicating the
lighted lantern which The Porter holds up
curiously as he regards the scene.*)

Take that lantern!

(LIGNIÈRE *precipitately seizes the lantern.*)

Forward march! I say

630   I'll be the man to-night that sees you home.

(*to the officers*)

You others follow — I want an audience!

CUIGY A hundred against one —

CYRANO   Those are the odds

---

24. **mon dieu:** French, "My God." —Eds.

To-night!

(*The Comedians in their costumes are
descending from the stage and joining the
group.*)

LE BRET But why help this —

CYRANO   There goes Le Bret

Growling!

LE BRET   — This drunkard here?

CYRANO (*His hand on* LE BRET'S *shoulder.*)

                         Because this drunkard —

635 This tun of sack, this butt of Burgundy —
Once in his life has done one lovely thing:
After the Mass, according to the form,
He saw, one day, the lady of his heart
Take holy water for a blessing. So

640 This one, who shudders at a drop of rain,
This fellow here — runs headlong to the font
Bends down and drinks it dry!

A SOUBRETTE[25]   I say that was

A pretty thought!

CYRANO   Ah, was it not?

THE SOUBRETTE (*to the others*)

                         But why

Against one poor poet, a hundred men?

645 **CYRANO** March!

     (*to the officers*)

              And you gentlemen, remember now,
No rescue —   Let me fight alone.

A COMEDIENNE (*Jumps down from the stage.*)

                         Come on!

I'm going to watch —

CYRANO   Come along!

ANOTHER COMEDIENNE (*Jumps down, speaks to a
     Comedian costumed as an old man.*)

                         You, Cassandre?

CYRANO Come all of you — the Doctor, Isabelle,
Léandre — the whole company — a swarm

650 Of murmuring, golden bees — we'll parody
Italian farce and Tragedy-of-Blood;
Ribbons for banners, masks for blazonry,
And tambourines to be our rolling drums!

ALL THE WOMEN (*Jumping for joy.*)

Bravo! — My hood — My cloak — Hurry!

JODELET (*mock heroic*)

                         Lead on! —

CYRANO (*to the violins*)

655 You violins — play us an overture —

     (*The violins join the procession which is
     forming. The lighted candles are snatched
     from the stage and distributed; it becomes a
     torchlight procession.*)

Bravo! — Officers — Ladies in costume —
And twenty paces in advance. . . .

     (*He takes his station as he speaks.*)

                         Myself,

Alone, with glory fluttering over me,
Alone as Lucifer at war with heaven!

660 Remember — no one lifts a hand to help —
Ready there? One . . . two . . . three! Porter,
     the doors! . . .

     (*The Porter flings wide the great doors. We
     see in the dim moonlight a corner of old
     Paris, purple and picturesque.*)

Look — Paris dreams — nocturnal, nebulous,
Under blue moonbeams hung from wall
     to wall —

Nature's own setting for the scene we play! —
Yonder, behind her veil of mist, the Seine,
Like a mysterious and magic mirror
Trembles —

              And you shall see what you shall see!

ALL To the Porte de Nesle!

CYRANO (*erect upon the threshold*)

                         To the Porte de Nesle!

     (*He turns back for a moment to the
     Soubrette.*)

Did you not ask, my dear, why against one
Singer they send a hundred swords?

     (*quietly, drawing his own sword*)

                         Because

They know this one man for a friend of mine!

     (*He goes out. The procession follows:
     LIGNIÈRE zigzagging at its head, then the
     Comediennes on the arms of the Officers,
     then the Comedians, leaping and dancing
     as they go. It vanishes into the night to the
     music of the violins, illuminated by the
     flickering glimmer of the candles.*)

                         (*Curtain*)

_____

25. **soubrette:** Stock character in French comedies, a flirtatious young woman. —Eds.

Understanding and Interpreting

1 What is the mood of the play in the opening scenes before Cyrano appears? Cite specific textual evidence to support your response.

2 The stage directions following line 220 tell us that Cyrano "arises in the centre of the floor, erect upon a chair, his arms folded, his hat cocked ferociously, his moustache bristling, his nose terrible." What does this description tell us about the character of Cyrano?

3 What is the nature of the conflict between Cyrano and Montfleury? Why does Cyrano object to the play being performed?

4 What does the exchange between the Meddler and Cyrano show us about him? Do you think it shows Cyrano's insecurity, his disregard for the opinion of others, a little of both, or something else entirely? In what ways does he, in fact, "glory in this nose of mine" (l. 332)?

5 Perhaps the most famous speech in the entire play is the monologue Cyrano delivers cataloging different possible responses to his nose (ll. 355–408). What does this speech tell us about him? Do you see him as arrogant, showing off his poetic and rhetorical skills? Simply confident? Or is he essentially apologizing for a physical anomaly that most find repugnant? (Keep in mind that in ll. 409–410 Valvert accuses him of "arrogant grand airs" at the same time he calls him a "clown.")

6 How is Christian characterized in this opening act? What positive qualities does he have (presented directly or indirectly), and what are his weaknesses?

7 Why are one hundred men, allegedly, after Lignière? Why does Cyrano insist that he will fight them alone (ll. 658–660)?

8 The opening sections of Act 1 introduce multiple characters who represent a range of backgrounds, occupations, and social classes in 1640s-era France. Choose five characters and describe the picture of French society that emerges from their actions and interactions.

9 By the end of Act 1, what do we know of the love (or attraction) of De Guiche, Christian, and Cyrano for Roxane?

10 By the end of Act 1, what internal conflicts do you sense that Cyrano possesses? Is he, for example, arrogant or insecure—or both? In what ways might he be seen as both brave and fearful?

Analyzing Language, Style, and Structure

1 *Cyrano* opens with a play within a play. What purpose might that structure serve for Rostand as he develops the audience's relationship with Cyrano? Is Rostand poking fun at the idea of the theater? Calling attention to stagecraft? Both? Something else?

2 How does the delayed appearance of Cyrano in Act I contribute to his characterization? What do we know of him before he arrives on stage?

3 A *ballade* is a verse form, usually consisting of three stanzas of eight or ten lines each; each stanza ends in the same one-line refrain. Why do you think Rostand has Cyrano choose this strict form rather than a more free-form verse in this scene?

4 How does the character of Lignière function in Act 1? What do we learn about the central characters, especially Christian and Cyrano, through their interaction with him? What elements of tension and conflict does Rostand introduce through him?

5 What is the nature and effect of the extended metaphor in Act I, lines 412–426? Why is the metaphor of clothing appropriate to the point Cyrano is making?

6 Throughout Act 1, there are references to money and the status it confers. The most obvious—and literal—distinction is between the aristocracy and the lower classes, but Rostand also reminds us to question the value of money on a more abstract level. What are some of the issues he raises, including the importance of patronage and the figurative currency of wit and words?

7 What image patterns do you notice in Act 1, particularly in the speeches Cyrano delivers?

Connecting, Arguing, and Extending

1 A *swashbuckler* is a swaggering or flamboyant adventurer, a romantic and heroic figure. To what extent does Cyrano fit this description in Act 1? Does he seem to be too flawed to be a hero?

2 Watch the famous speech Cyrano delivers about his nose in the 1990 film *Cyrano*, starring French actor Gérard Depardieu. In what ways does his interpretation match or differ from yours as you read Act 1?

3 Set in a different era, a time when France was flourishing culturally, politically, and economically, *Cyrano de Bergerac* offered theatergoers escapist entertainment that distracted them, however briefly, from current, pressing problems. View a film popular from the Great Depression era, which went from 1929 to 1939, and discuss how it served a similar function of escapism for American audiences. Some popular movies include *The Wizard of Oz*, *Gone with the Wind*, *Grand Hotel*, *Frankenstein*, *King Kong*, and the gangster movie *Angels with Dirty Faces*.

Act 2 Cyrano de Bergerac

The Bakery of the Poets

The Shop of RAGUENEAU, BAKER *and* PASTRYCOOK: *a spacious affair at the corner of the Rue St.-Honoré and the Rue de l'Arbre Sec. The street, seen vaguely through the glass panes in the door at the back, is gray in the first light of dawn.*

In the foreground, at the Left, a Counter is surmounted by a Canopy of wrought iron from which are hanging ducks, geese, and white peacocks. Great crockery jars hold bouquets of common flowers, yellow sunflowers in particular. On the same side farther back, a huge fireplace; in front of it, between great andirons,[1] of which each one supports a little saucepan, roast fowls revolve and weep into their dripping-pans. To the Right at the First Entrance, a door. Beyond it, Second Entrance, a staircase leads up to a little dining-room under the eaves, its interior visible through open shutters. A table is set there and a tiny Flemish candlestick is lighted; there one may retire to eat and drink in private. A wooden gallery, extending from the head of the stairway, seems to lead to other little dining-rooms.

In the centre of the shop, an iron ring hangs by a rope over a pulley so that it can be raised or lowered; adorned with game of various kinds hung from it by hooks, it has the appearance of a sort of gastronomic chandelier.

In the shadow under the staircase, ovens are glowing. The spits revolve; the copper pots and pans gleam ruddily. Pastries in pyramids. Hams hanging from the rafters. The morning baking is in progress: a bustle of tall cooks and timid scullions[2] and scurrying apprentices; a blossoming of white caps adorned with cock's feathers or the wings of guinea fowl. On wicker trays or on great metal platters they bring in rows of pastries and fancy dishes of various kinds.

Tables are covered with trays of cakes and rolls; others with chairs placed about them are set for guests.

One little table in a corner disappears under a heap of papers. At the curtain rise RAGUENEAU *is seated there. He is writing poetry.*

A PASTRYCOOK (*Brings in a dish.*)
   Fruits *en gelee!*
SECOND PASTRYCOOK (*Brings dish.*)
           Custard!
THIRD PASTRYCOOK (*Brings roast peacock ornamented with feathers.*)
               Peacock *roti!*
FOURTH PASTRYCOOK (*Brings tray of cakes.*)
   Cakes and confections!
FIFTH PASTRYCOOK (*Brings earthen dish.*)
           Beef *en casserole!*

---

1. **andirons:** Metal grates that hold up the wood in a fireplace, so there is room for air movement below. —Eds. 2. **scullions:** the lowest-ranking kitchen workers. —Eds.

RAGUENEAU (*Raises his head; returns to mere earth.*)

Over the coppers of my kitchen flows
The frosted-silver dawn. Silence awhile
5 The god who sings within thee, Ragueneau!
Lay down the lute — the oven calls for thee!
 (*Rises; goes to one of the cooks.*)
Here's a hiatus in your sauce; fill up
The measure.

THE COOK   How much?

RAGUENEAU (*Measures on his finger.*)
      One more dactyl.

THE COOK   Huh? . . .

FIRST PASTRYCOOK Rolls!

SECOND PASTRYCOOK Roulades!

RAGUENEAU (*before the fireplace*)
     Veil, O Muse, thy virgin eyes
10 From the lewd gleam of these terrestrial fires!
 (*to First Pastrycook*)
Your rolls lack balance. Here's the proper form —
An equal hemistich[3] on either side,
And the caesura[4] in between.
 (*to another, pointing out an unfinished pie*)
     Your house
Of crust should have a roof upon it.
 (*to another, who is seated on the hearth, placing poultry on a spit*)
     And you —
15 Along the interminable spit, arrange
The modest pullet and the lordly Turk
Alternately, my son — as great Malherbe[5]
Alternates male and female rimes.
 Remember,
A couplet, or a roast, should be well turned.

AN APPRENTICE (*Advances with a dish covered by a napkin.*)
20 Master, I thought of you when I designed
This, hoping it might please you.

RAGUENEAU   Ah! A Lyre —

THE APPRENTICE In puff-paste —

RAGUENEAU   And the jewels —
candied fruit!

THE APPRENTICE And the strings, barley-sugar!

RAGUENEAU (*Gives him money.*)
      Go and drink
My health.
 (LISE *enters.*)
    St! — My wife — Circulate, and hide
25 That money!
 (*Shows the lyre to* LISE, *with a languid air.*)
    Graceful — yes?

LISE   Ridiculous!
 (*She places on the counter a pile of paper bags.*)

RAGUENEAU Paper bags? Thank you . . .
 (*He looks at them.*)
      Ciel![6] My manuscripts!
The sacred verses of my poets — rent
Asunder, limb from limb — butchered to make
Base packages of pastry! Ah, you are one
30 Of those insane Bacchantes who destroyed
Orpheus![7]

LISE   Your dirty poets left them here
To pay for eating half our stock-in-trade:
We ought to make some profit out of them!

RAGUENEAU Ant! Would you blame the locust for his song?

35 LISE I blame the locust for his appetite!
There used to be a time — before you had
Your hungry friends — you never called me Ants —
No, nor Bacchantes!

RAGUENEAU   What a way to use
Poetry!

LISE   Well, what is the use of it?

40 RAGUENEAU But, my dear girl, what would you do with prose?
 (*Two Children enter.*)
Well, dears?

A CHILD Three little patties.

RAGUENEAU (*Serves them.*)
     There we are!
All hot and brown.

---

3. **hemistich:** half line of verse. —Eds. 4. **caesura:** pause in a line of poetry. —Eds. 5. **Malherbe:** François de Malherbe (1555–1628), French poet known for championing technical perfection. —Eds. 6. **ciel:** French, sky. —Eds. 7. **Bacchantes . . . Orpheus:** Followers of the god of wine, Bacchus, who killed Orpheus for choosing to worship Apollo instead. —Eds.

THE CHILD   Would you mind
  wrapping them?

RAGUENEAU One of my paper bags! . . .
                Oh, certainly.
  (*Reads from the bag, as he is about to wrap
  the patties in it.*)
  "*Ulysses, when he left Penelope*" —

45 Not that one!
  (*Takes another bag; reads.*)
            "*Phoebus, golden-crowned*" —
                Not that one.

LISE Well? They are waiting!

RAGUENEAU   Very well, very well! —
  The Sonnet to Phyllis . . .
                Yet — it does seem hard . . .

LISE Made up your mind — at last!
  Mph! — Jack-o'-Dreams!

RAGUENEAU (*As her back is turned, calls back the
  children, who are already at the door.*)
  Pst! — Children — Give me back the bag.
  Instead

50 Of three patties, you shall have six of them!
  (*Makes the exchange. The Children go out.
  He reads from the bag, as he smooths it out
  tenderly.*)
  "*Phyllis*" —
    A spot of butter on her name! —
  "*Phyllis*" —

CYRANO (*Enters hurriedly.*)
            What is the time?

RAGUENEAU   Six o'Clock.

CYRANO   One
  Hour more . . .

RAGUENEAU   Felicitations!

CYRANO   And for what?

RAGUENEAU Your victory! I saw it all —

CYRANO   Which one?

55 **RAGUENEAU** At the Hôtel de Bourgogne.

CYRANO   Oh — the duel!

RAGUENEAU The duel in Rime!

LISE   He talks of nothing else.

CYRANO Nonsense!

RAGUENEAU (*Fencing and foining with a spit,
  which he snatches up from the hearth.*)
        "*Then, as I end the refrain, thrust
  home!*"
  "*Then, as I end the refrain*" —
            Gods! What a line!
  "*Then, as I end*" —

CYRANO   What time now, Ragueneau?

RAGUENEAU (*Petrified at the full extent of a lunge,
  while he looks at the clock.*)

60 Five after six —
  (*recovers*)
        "*—thrust home!*"
            A Ballade, too!

Cyrano de Bergerac staged
at the Comedie Francaise in
Paris, France.

**How would you describe the
mood that this contemporary
staging establishes for this
scene in the bakery?**

LISE (*to* CYRANO, *who in passing has mechanically shaken hands with her*)

    Your hand — what have you done?

CYRANO   Oh, my hand? — Nothing.

RAGUENEAU What danger now —

CYRANO   No danger.

LISE   I believe

    He is lying.

CYRANO   Why? Was I looking down my

    nose?

    That must have been a devil of a lie!

    (*changing his tone; to* RAGUENEAU)

65   I expect someone. Leave us here alone,

    When the time comes.

RAGUENEAU   How can I? In a

    moment,

    My poets will be here.

LISE   To break their . . . fast!

CYRANO Take them away, then, when I give the

    sign.

    —What time?

RAGUENEAU   Ten minutes after.

CYRANO   Have you a pen?

RAGUENEAU (*Offers him a pen.*)

70   An eagle's feather!

A MUSKETEER (*Enters, and speaks to* LISE *in a stentorian voice.*)

         Greeting!

CYRANO (*To* RAGUENEAU)

         Who is this?

RAGUENEAU My wife's friend. A terrific warrior,

    So he says.

CYRANO   Ah — I see.

    (*Takes up the pen; waves* RAGUENEAU *away.*)

         Only to write —

    To fold — To give it to her — and to go . . .

    (*Throws down the pen.*)

    Coward! And yet — the Devil take my soul

75   If I dare speak one word to her . . .

    (*To* RAGUENEAU)

         What time now?

RAGUENEAU A quarter after six.

CYRANO (*striking his breast*)

         — One little word

Of all the many thousand I have here!

Whereas in writing . . .

    (*Takes up the pen.*)

         Come, I'll write to her

That letter I have written on my heart,

80   Torn up, and written over many times —

So many times . . . that all I have to do

Is to remember, and to write it down.

    (*He writes. Through the glass of the door appear vague and hesitating shadows. The Poets enter, clothed in rusty black and spotted with mud.*)

LISE (*to* RAGUENEAU)

    Here come your scarecrows!

FIRST POET   Comrade!

SECOND POET (*Takes both* RAGUENEAU's *hands.*)

         My dear brother!

THIRD POET (*sniffing*)

    O Lord of Roasts, how sweet thy dwellings are!

85 **FOURTH POET** Phoebus Apollo of the Silver

    Spoon!

FIFTH POET Cupid of Cookery!

RAGUENEAU (*Surrounded, embraced, beaten on the back.*)

         These geniuses,

    They put one at one's ease!

FIRST POET   We were delayed

    By the crowd at the Porte de Nesle.

SECOND POET   Dead men

    All scarred and gory, scattered on the stones,

90   Villainous-looking scoundrels — eight of them.

CYRANO (*Looks up an instant.*)

         Eight? I thought only seven —

RAGUENEAU   Do you know

    The hero of this hecatomb?[8]

CYRANO   I? . . . No.

LISE (*to The Musketeer*)

    Do you?

THE MUSKETEER   Hmm — perhaps!

FIRST POET   They say one man alone

    Put to flight all this crowd.

SECOND POET   Everywhere lay

95   Swords, daggers, pikes, bludgeons —

---

8. **hecatomb:** Sacrifice of a hundred cattle or oxen in ancient Greece. —Eds.

CYRANO (*writing*)
                     "Your eyes . . ."

THIRD POET   As far
As the Quai des Orfevres,[9] hats and cloaks—

FIRST POET Why, that man must have been the
    devil!

CYRANO   *"Your lips . . ."*

FIRST POET Some savage monster might have
    done this thing!

CYRANO *"Looking upon you, I grow faint with
    fear . . ."*

100 **SECOND POET** What have you written lately,
    Ragueneau?

CYRANO   *"Your Friends—"Who loves you . . ."*
                    So. No signature;
I'll give it to her myself.

RAGUENEAU   A Recipe
In Rime.

THIRD POET   Read us your rimes!

FOURTH POET   Here's a brioche
Cocking its hat at me.
    (*He bites off the top of it.*)

FIRST POET   Look how those buns
Follow the hungry poet with their eyes—
105 Those almond eyes!

SECOND POET   We are listening—

THIRD POET   See this cream-puff-
Fat little baby, drooling while it smiles!

SECOND POET (*Nibbling at the pastry Lyre.*)
For the first time, the Lyre is my support.

RAGUENEAU (*Coughs, adjusts his cap, strikes an
    attitude.*)
A Recipe in Rime—

SECOND POET (*Gives* FIRST POET *a dig with his
    elbow.*)
               Your breakfast?

FIRST POET   Dinner!

RAGUENEAU (*declaims*)
    A Recipe for Making Almond Tarts.

110 *Beat your eggs, the yolk and white,*
    Very light;
  Mingle with their creamy fluff
    Drops of lime-juice, cool and green;
      Then pour in

115 *Milk of Almonds, just enough.*

  Dainty patty-pans, embraced
    In puff-paste—
  Have these ready within reach;
    With your thumb and finger, pinch
120   *Half an inch*
  Up around the edge of each—

  Into these, a score or more,
    Slowly pour
  All your store of custard; so
125   *Take them, bake them golden-brown—*
    Now sit down! . . .
  Almond tartlets, Ragueneau!

THE POETS Delicious! Melting!

A POET (*chokes*)
                 Humph!

CYRANO (*to* RAGUENEAU)
               Do you not see
Those fellows fattening themselves?—

RAGUENEAU   I know.
130 I would not look—it might embarrass
    them—
You see, I love a friendly audience.
Besides—another vanity—I am pleased
When they enjoy my cooking.

CYRANO (*Slaps him on the back.*)
          Be off with you!—
    (RAGUENEAU *goes upstage.*)
Good little soul!
    (*Calls to* LISE.)
           Madame!—
    (*She leaves the Musketeer and comes down
    to him.*)
            This musketeer—
135 He is making love to you?

LISE (*haughtily*)
              If any man
Offends my virtue—all I have to do
Is look at him—once!

CYRANO (*Looks at her gravely; she drops her
    eyes.*)
          I do not find
Those eyes of yours unconquerable.

---

9. **Quai des Orfevres:** Literally, the Dock of the Goldsmiths; a street along the river Seine in Paris. —Eds.

LISE (*panting*)

               — Ah!

CYRANO (*Raising his voice a little.*)

140   Now listen — I am fond of Ragueneau;

I allow no one — do you understand? —

To . . . take his name in vain!

LISE   You think —

CYRANO (*ironic emphasis*)

                 I think

I interrupt you.

     (*He salutes the Musketeer, who has heard*
     without daring to resent the warning. LISE
     goes to the Musketeer as he returns
     CYRANO'S *salute.*)

LISE   You — you swallow that? —

You ought to have pulled his nose!

THE MUSKETEER   His nose? — His nose! . . .

     (*He goes out hurriedly.* ROXANE *and the*
     Duenna appear outside the door.)

CYRANO (*Nods to* RAGUENEAU.)

Pst! —

RAGUENEAU (*to the Poets*)

Come inside —

CYRANO (*impatient*)

          Pst! . . . Pst! . . .

RAGUENEAU   We shall be more

145   Comfortable . . .

     (*He leads The Poets into inner room.*)

FIRST POET   The cakes!

SECOND POET   Bring them along!

     (*They go out.*)

CYRANO If I can see the faintest spark of hope,

Then —

     (*Throws door open — bows.*)

Welcome!

     (ROXANE *enters, followed by the Duenna,*
     whom CYRANO *detains.*)

     Pardon me — one word —

THE DUENNA   Take two.

CYRANO Have you a good digestion?

THE DUENNA   Wonderful!

CYRANO Good. Here are two sonnets, by

Benserade —

150 **THE DUENNA** Euh?

CYRANO   Which I fill for you with éclairs.

THE DUENNA   Ooo!

CYRANO Do you like cream-puffs?

THE DUENNA   Only with whipped

cream.

CYRANO Here are three . . . six — embosomed in a

poem

By Saint-Amant. This ode of Chapelin

Looks deep enough to hold — a jelly roll.

155   — Do you love Nature?

THE DUENNA   Mad about it.

CYRANO   Then

Go out and eat these in the street. Do not

Return —

THE DUENNA   Oh, but —

CYRANO   Until you finish them.

     (*down to* ROXANE)

Blessed above all others be the hour

When you remembered to remember me,

160   And came to tell me . . . what?

ROXANE (*Takes off her mask.*)

       First let me thank you

Because . . . That man . . . that creature, whom

your sword

Made sport of yesterday — His patron, one —

CYRANO De Guiche? —

ROXANE   — who thinks himself in love with me

Would have forced that man upon me for —

a husband —

165 **CYRANO** I understand — so much the better then!

I fought, not for my nose, but your bright eyes.

ROXANE And then, to tell you — but before I can

Tell you — Are you, I wonder, still the same

Big brother — almost — that you used to be

170   When we were children, playing by the pond

In the old garden down there —

CYRANO   I remember —

Every summer you came to Bergerac! . . .

ROXANE You used to make swords out of

bulrushes —

CYRANO Your dandelion-dolls with golden hair —

175 **ROXANE** And those green plums —

CYRANO   And those black

mulberries —

ROXANE In those days, you did everything I

wished!

CYRANO Roxane, in short skirts, was called

Madeleine.

ROXANE Was I pretty?

CYRANO   Oh — not too plain!

ROXANE   Sometimes
 When you had hurt your hand you used to
  come
180 Running to me — and I would be your mother,
 And say — Oh, in a very grown-up voice:
  (*She takes his hand.*)
 "*Now*, what have you been doing to yourself?
 Let me see—"
  (*She sees the hand — starts.*)
       Oh! —
         Wait — I said *Let me see!*
 Still — at your age! How did you do that?
CYRANO   Playing
185 With the big boys, down by the Porte de Nesle.
ROXANE (*Sits at a table and wets her handker-
  chief in a glass of water.*)
 Come here to me.
CYRANO   —Such a wise little
  mother!
ROXANE And tell me, while I wash this blood
  away,
 How many you — played with?
CYRANO   Oh, about a hundred.
ROXANE Tell me.
CYRANO   No. Let me go. Tell me what *you*
190 Were going to tell *me* — if you dared?
ROXANE (*still holding his hand*)
        I think
 I do dare — now. It seems like long ago
 When I could tell you things. Yes — I dare . . .

Listen:
 I . . . love someone.
CYRANO   Ah! . . .
ROXANE   Someone who does not
  know.
CYRANO   Ah! . . .
ROXANE At least — not yet.
CYRANO   Ah! . . .
ROXANE   But he will know
195 Some day.
CYRANO Ah! . . .
ROXANE   A big boy who loves
  me too,
 And is afraid of me, and keeps away,
 And never says one word.
CYRANO   Ah! . . .
ROXANE   Let me have
 Your hand a moment — why how hot it is! —
 I know. I see him trying . . .
CYRANO   Ah! . . .
ROXANE   There now!
200 Is that better? —
  (*She finishes bandaging the hand with her
  handkerchief.*)
      Besides — only to think —
 (This is a secret.) He is a soldier too,
 In your own regiment —
CYRANO   Ah! . . .
ROXANE   Yes, in the Guards,
 Your company too.

Joseph Fiennes as Cyrano de Bergerac and Alice Eve playing Roxane in *Cyrano de Bergerac*, Chichester Festival Theatre.

As shown in this image, how does this actress capture the character of Roxane? How do her gestures, facial expression, costume, or physical appearance compare to your mental image?

Paul Doyle/Alamy

CYRANO   Ah! . . .

ROXANE   And such a man! —
He is proud — noble — young — brave —
    beautiful —

CYRANO (*Turns pale; rises.*)

205 Beautiful! —

ROXANE   What's the matter?

CYRANO (*smiling*)
                    Nothing — this —
My sore hand!

ROXANE   Well, I love him. That is all.
Oh — and I never saw him anywhere
Except the *Comedie.*

CYRANO   You have never spoken? —

ROXANE Only our eyes . . .

CYRANO   Why, then — How do you know? —

210 **ROXANE** People talk about people; and I hear
Things . . . and I know.

CYRANO   You say he is in the
    Guards:
His name?

ROXANE   Baron Christian de Neuvillette.

CYRANO He is not in the Guards.

ROXANE   Yes. Since this morning.
Captain Carbon de Castel-Jaloux.

CYRANO   So soon!
So soon we lose our hearts! —
                    But, my dear child, —

THE DUENNA (*Opens the door.*)

215 I have eaten the cakes, Monsieur de
    Bergerac!

CYRANO Good! Now go out and read the poetry!
    (*The Duenna disappears.*)
— But, my dear child! You, who love only
    words,
Wit, the grand manner — Why, for all you
    know,
The man may be a savage, or a fool.

220 **ROXANE** His curls are like a hero from D'Urfé.

CYRANO His mind may be as curly as his
    hair.

ROXANE Not with such eyes. I read his soul in
    them.

CYRANO Yes, all our souls are written in our eyes!
But — if he be a bungler?

ROXANE   Then I shall die —

225 There!

CYRANO (*after a pause*)
    And you brought me here to tell me this?
I do not yet quite understand, Madame,
The reason for your confidence.

ROXANE   They say
That in your company — It frightens me —
You are all Gascons . . .

CYRANO   And we pick a quarrel

230 With any flat-foot who intrudes himself.
Whose blood is not pure Gascon like our own?
Is this what you have heard?

ROXANE   I am so afraid
For him!

CYRANO (*between his teeth*)
        Not without reason! —

ROXANE   And I thought
You . . . You were so brave, so invincible

235 Yesterday, against all those brutes! — If you,
Whom they all fear —

CYRANO   Oh well — I will defend
Your little Baron.

ROXANE   Will you? Just for me?
Because I have always been — your friend!

CYRANO   Of course . . .

ROXANE Will you be *his* friend?

CYRANO   I will be his friend.

240 **ROXANE** And never let him fight a duel?

CYRANO   No — never.

ROXANE Oh, but you are a darling! — I must go —
You never told me about last night — Why,
You must have been a hero! Have him write
And tell me all about it — will you?

CYRANO   Of course . . .
    (*Kisses her hand.*)

245 **ROXANE** I always did love you! — A hundred men
Against one — Well. . . .   Adieu. We are great
    friends,
Are we not?

CYRANO   Of course . . .

ROXANE   He *must* write to me —
A hundred — You shall tell me the whole story
Some day, when I have time. A hundred men —

250 What courage!

CYRANO (*Salutes as she goes out.*)
        Oh . . . I have done better since!
    (*The door closes after her.* CYRANO *remains
    motionless, his eyes on the ground. Pause.*

The other door opens; RAGUENEAU *puts in his head.*)

RAGUENEAU May I come in?

CYRANO (*without moving*)

 Yes . . .

 (RAGUENEAU *and his friends re-enter. At the same time,* CARBON DE CASTEL-JALOUX *appears at the street door in uniform as Captain of the Guards; recognizes* CYRANO *with a sweeping gesture.*)

CARBON Here he is! — Our hero!

CYRANO (*Raises his head and salutes.*)

 Our Captain!

CARBON We know! All our company

 Are here —

CYRANO (*recoils*)

 No —

CARBON Come! They are waiting for you.

CYRANO No!

CARBON (*Tries to lead him out.*)

 Only across the street — Come!

CYRANO Please —

CARBON (*Goes to the door and shouts in a voice of thunder.*)

 Our champion

255 Refuses! He is not feeling well to-day!

A VOICE OUTSIDE Ah! Sandious!

 (*Noise outside of swords and trampling feet approaching.*)

CARBON Here they come now!

THE CADETS (*entering the shop*)

 Mille dious! —

Mordious! — Capdedious! — Pocapdedious!

RAGUENEAU (*in astonishment*)

 Gentlemen —

 You are all Gascons?

THE CADETS All!

FIRST CADET (*to* CYRANO)

 Bravo!

CYRANO Baron!

ANOTHER CADET (*Takes both his hands.*)

 Vivat!

CYRANO Baron!

THIRD CADET Come to my arms!

CYRANO Baron!

260 **OTHERS** To mine! — To mine! —

CYRANO Baron . . . Baron . . . Have mercy —

RAGUENEAU You are all Barons too?

THE CADETS *Are* we?

RAGUENEAU Are they? . . .

FIRST CADET Our coronets would star the midnight sky!

LE BRET (*Enters; hurries to* CYRANO.)

 The whole Town's looking for you!

 Raving mad —

 A triumph! Those who saw the fight —

CYRANO I hope

265 You have not told them where I —

LE BRET (*rubbing his hands*)

 Certainly

 I told them!

CITIZEN (*Enters, followed by a group.*)

 Listen! Shut the door! — Here comes

 All Paris!

 (*The street outside fills with a shouting crowd. Chairs and carriages stop at the door.*)

LE BRET (*aside to* CYRANO, *smiling*)

 And Roxane?

CYRANO (*quickly*)

 Hush!

THE CROWD OUTSIDE Cyrano!

 (*A mob bursts into the shop. Shouts, acclamations, general disturbance.*)

RAGUENEAU (*Standing on a table.*)

 My shop invaded — They'll break everything —

 Glorious!

SEVERAL MEN (*crowding about* CYRANO)

 My friend! . . . My friend! . . .

CYRANO Why, yesterday

270 I did not have so many friends!

LE BRET Success

 At last!

A MARQUIS (*runs to* CYRANO, *with outstretched hands*)

 My dear — really! —

CYRANO (*coldly*)

 So? And how long

 Have I been dear to you?

ANOTHER MARQUIS One moment — pray!

 I have two ladies in my carriage here;

 Let me present you —

CYRANO Certainly! And first,

275 Who will present you, sir, — to me?

LE BRET (*astounded*)

                            Why, what

The devil? —

CYRANO   Hush!

A MAN OF LETTERS (*with a portfolio*)

                      May I have the details? . . .

CYRANO You may not.

LE BRET (*plucking* CYRANO's *sleeve*)

        Theophraste Renaudot! — Editor

Of the *Gazette* — your reputation! . . .

CYRANO   No!

A POET (*advances*)

Monsieur —

CYRANO   Well?

THE POET   Your full name? I will compose

280   A pentacrostic[10] —

ANOTHER   Monsieur —

CYRANO   That will do!

    (*Movement. The crowd arranges itself.* DE
    GUICHE *appears, escorted by* CUIGY, BRIS-
    SAILLE, *and the other officers who were with*
    CYRANO *at the close of the First Act.*)

CUIGY (*Goes to* CYRANO.)

Monsieur de Guiche! —

    (*Murmur. Everyone moves.*)

                   A message from the Marshal

De Gassion —

DE GUICHE (*saluting* CYRANO)

        Who wishes to express

Through me his admiration. He has heard

Of your affair —

THE CROWD   Bravo!

CYRANO (*bowing*)

              The Marshal speaks

285   As an authority.

DE GUICHE   He said just now

The story would have been incredible

Were it not for the witness —

CUIGY   Of our eyes!

LE BRET (*aside to* CYRANO)

What is it?

CYRANO   Hush! —

LE BRET   Something is wrong with you;

Are you in pain?

CYRANO (*recovering himself*)

        In pain? Before this crowd?

    (*His moustache bristles. He throws out his
    chest.*)

290   I? In pain? You shall see!

DE GUICHE (*To whom* CUIGY *has been
    whispering.*)

             Your name is known

Already as a soldier. You are one

Of those wild Gascons, are you not?

CYRANO   The Guards,

Yes. A Cadet.

A CADET (*in a voice of thunder*)

        One of ourselves!

DE GUICHE   Ah! So —

Then all these gentlemen with the haughty air,

295   These are the famous —

CARBON   Cyrano!

CYRANO   Captain?

CARBON Our troop being all present, be so kind

As to present them to the Comte de Guiche!

CYRANO (*with a gesture presenting the Cadets to*
    DE GUICHE, *declaims:*)

    The Cadets of Gascoyne — the defenders
        Of Carbon de Castel-Jaloux:
300 *Free fighters, free lovers, free spenders —*
    The Cadets of Gascoyne — the defenders
    Of old homes, old names, and old splendors —
        A proud and a pestilent crew!
    The Cadets of Gascoyne, the defenders
305   *Of Carbon de Castel-Jaloux.*

    Hawk-eyed, they stare down all contenders —
        The wolf bares his fangs as they do —
    Make way there, you fat money-lenders!
310 *(Hawk-eyed, they stare down all contenders)*
    Old boots that have been to the menders,
        Old cloaks that are worn through
          and through —
    Hawk-eyed, they stare down all contenders —
        The wolf bares his fangs as they do!

315 *Skull-breakers they are, and sword-benders;*

---

10. **pentacrostic:** An acrostic poem repeated five times. An acrostic is a poem in which the first letters of each line spell out a name or a word. —Eds.

Red blood is their favorite brew;
Hot haters and loyal befrienders,
Skull-breakers they are, and sword-benders.
Wherever a quarrel engenders,
320   *They're ready and waiting for you!*
Skull-breakers they are, and sword-benders;
Red blood is their favorite brew!

Behold them, our Gascon defenders
    Who win every woman they woo!
325   *There's never a dame but surrenders —*
Behold them, our Gascon defenders!
Young wives who are clever pretenders —
    Old husbands who house the cuckoo —
Behold them — our Gascon defenders
330   *Who win every woman they woo!*

DE GUICHE (*languidly, sitting in a chair*)
Poets are fashionable nowadays
To have about one. Would you care to join
My following?

CYRANO   No sir. I do not follow.

DE GUICHE Your duel yesterday amused my uncle
335   The Cardinal. I might help you there.

LE BRET   Grand Dieu!

DE GUICHE I suppose you have written a tragedy —
They all have.

LE BRET (*aside to* CYRANO)
            Now at last you'll have it played —
Your *Agrippine*!

DE GUICHE   Why not? Take it to him.

CYRANO (*tempted*)
    Really —

DE GUICHE He is himself a dramatist;
340   Let him rewrite a few lines here and there,
And he'll approve the rest.

CYRANO (*His face falls again.*)
                    Impossible.
My blood curdles to think of altering
One comma.

DE GUICHE   Ah, but when he likes a thing
He pays well.

CYRANO   Yes — but not so well as I —
345   When I have made a line that sings itself
So that I love the sound of it — I pay
Myself a hundred times.

DE GUICHE   You are proud,
    my friend.

CYRANO You have observed that?

A CADET (*Enters with a drawn sword, along the
    whole blade of which is transfixed a collec-
    tion of disreputable hats, their plumes drag-
    gled, their crowns cut and torn.*)
                    Cyrano! See here —
Look what we found this morning in
    the street —
350   The plumes dropped in their flight by those
    fine birds
Who showed the white feather!

CARBON   Spoils of the hunt —
    Well mounted!

THE CROWD Ha-ha-ha!

CUIGY   Whoever hired
    Those rascals, he must be an angry man
    To-day!

BRISSAILLE Who was it? Do you know?

DE GUICHE   Myself! —
    (*The laughter ceases.*)
355   I hired them to do the sort of work
    We do not soil our hands with — punishing
    A drunken poet. . . .
            (*uncomfortable silence*)

THE CADET (*to* CYRANO)
                    What shall we do with them?
    They ought to be preserved before they
    spoil —

CYRANO (*Takes the sword, and in the gesture of
    saluting* DE GUICHE *with it, makes all the
    hats slide off at his feet.*)
    Sir, will you not return these to your friends?

360 **DE GUICHE** My chair — my porters
    here — immediately!
    (*to* CYRANO *violently*)
    —As for you, sir! —

A VOICE (*in the street*)
                    The chair of Monseigneur
    Le Comte de Guiche! —

DE GUICHE (*who has recovered his self-control;
    smiling*)
                    Have you read *Don
    Quixote*?

CYRANO I have — and found myself the hero.

A PORTER (*Appears at the door.*)

Chair

Ready!

DE GUICHE Be so good as to read once more

365 The chapter of the windmills.

CYRANO (*gravely*)

Chapter Thirteen.

DE GUICHE Windmills, remember, if you fight
with them —

CYRANO My enemies change, then, with every
wind?

DE GUICHE — May swing round their huge arms
and cast you down

Into the mire.

CYRANO Or up — among the stars!

(DE GUICHE *goes out. We see him get into
the chair. The Officers follow murmuring
among themselves.* LE BRET *goes up with
them. The crowd goes out.*)

CYRANO (*Saluting with burlesque politeness, those
who go out without daring to take leave of
him.*)

370 Gentlemen. . . .   Gentlemen. . . .

LE BRET (*As the door closes, comes down, shaking
his clenched hands to heaven.*)

You have done it now —

You have made your fortune!

CYRANO There you go again,
Growling! —

LE BRET At least this latest pose of yours —
Ruining every chance that comes your way —
Becomes exaggerated —

CYRANO Very well,

375 Then I exaggerate!

LE BRET (*triumphantly*)

Oh, you do!

CYRANO Yes;
On principle. There are things in this world
A man does well to carry to extremes.

LE BRET Stop trying to be Three Musketeers in
one!

Fortune and glory —

CYRANO What would you have me do?

380 Seek for the patronage of some great man,
And like a creeping vine on a tall tree

385 Crawl upward, where I cannot stand alone?
No thank you! Dedicate, as others do,
Poems to pawnbrokers? Be a buffoon
In the vile hope of teasing out a smile
On some cold face? No thank you! Eat a toad
For breakfast every morning? Make my
knees
Callous, and cultivate a supple spine, —
Wear out my belly grovelling in the dust?

390 No thank you! Scratch the back of any swine
That roots up gold for me? Tickle the horns
Of Mammon[11] with my left hand, while my
right
Too proud to know his partner's business,
Takes in the fee? No thank you! Use the fire

395 God gave me to burn incense all day long
Under the nose of wood and stone? No thank
you!
Shall I go leaping into ladies' laps
Andlickingfingers? — or — tochangetheform —
Navigating with madrigals for oars,

400 My sails full of the sighs of dowagers?
No thank you! Publish verses at my own
Expense? No thank you! Be the patron saint
Of a small group of literary souls
Who dine together every Tuesday? No

405 I thank you! Shall I labor night and day
To build a reputation on one song,
And never write another? Shall I find
True genius only among Geniuses,
Palpitate over little paragraphs,

410 And struggle to insinuate my name
Into the columns of the *Mercury*?
No thank you! Calculate, scheme, be afraid,
Love more to make a visit than a poem,
Seek introductions, favors, influences? —

415 No thank you! No, I thank you! And again
I thank you! — But . . .

To sing, to laugh, to dream,
To walk in my own way and be alone,
Free, with an eye to see things as they are,
A voice that means manhood — to cock my
hat

420 Where I choose — At a word, a *Yes*, a *No*,
To fight — or write. To travel any road

---

11. **Mammon:** A false god in the Bible, personification of greed. —Eds.

Under the sun, under the stars, nor doubt
If fame or fortune lie beyond the bourne —
Never to make a line I have not heard
425   In my own heart; yet, with all modesty
To say: "My soul, be satisfied with flowers,
With fruit, with weeds even; but gather them
In the one garden you may call your own."
So, when I win some triumph, by some chance,
430   Render no share to Caesar — in a word,
I am too proud to be a parasite,
And if my nature wants the germ that grows
Towering to heaven like the mountain pine,
Or like the oak, sheltering multitudes —
435   I stand, not high it may be — but alone!

LE BRET   Alone, yes! — But why stand against the world?
What devil has possessed you now, to go
Everywhere making yourself enemies?

CYRANO   Watching you other people making friends
440   Everywhere — as a dog makes friends! I mark
The manner of these canine courtesies
And think: "My friends are of a cleaner breed;
Here comes — thank God! — another enemy!"

LE BRET   But this is madness!

CYRANO   Method, let us say.
445   It is my pleasure to displease. I love
Hatred. Imagine how it feels to face
The volley of a thousand angry eyes —
The bile of envy and the froth of fear
Spattering little drops about me — You —
450   Good nature all around you, soft and warm —
You are like those Italians, in great cowls
Comfortable and loose — Your chin sinks down
Into the folds, your shoulders droop. But I —
The Spanish ruff I wear around my throat
455   Is like a ring of enemies; hard, proud,
Each point another pride, another thorn —
So that I hold myself erect perforce.
Wearing the hatred of the common herd
Haughtily, the harsh collar of Old Spain,
460   At once a fetter and — a halo!

LE BRET   Yes . . .
    (*After a silence, draws* CYRANO's *arm through his own.*)

Tell this to all the world — And then to me
Say very softly that . . . She loves you not.

CYRANO   (*quickly*)
Hush!
    (*A moment since,* CHRISTIAN *has entered and mingled with the Cadets, who do not offer to speak to him. Finally, he sits down alone at a small table, where he is served by* LISE.)

A CADET   (*Rises from a table up stage, his glass in his hand.*)
Cyrano! — Your story!

CYRANO   Presently . . .
    (*He goes up, on the arm of* LE BRET, *talking to him. The Cadets come down stage.*)

THE CADET   The story of the combat! An example
465   For —
    (*He stops by the table where* CHRISTIAN *is sitting.*)
— this young tadpole here.

CHRISTIAN   (*looks up*)
          Tadpole?

ANOTHER CADET   Yes, you! —
You narrow-gutted Northerner!

CHRISTIAN   Sir?

FIRST CADET   Hark ye,
Monsieur de Neuvillette: You are to know
There is a certain subject — I would say,
A certain object — never to be named
470   Among us: utterly unmentionable!

CHRISTIAN   And that is?

THIRD CADET   (*in an awful voice*)
       Look at me! . . .
    (*He strikes his nose three times with his finger, mysteriously.*)
          You understand?

CHRISTIAN   Why, yes; the —

FOURTH CADET   Sh! . . . We never speak that word —
    (*indicating* CYRANO *by a gesture*)
To breathe it is to have to do with HIM!

FIFTH CADET   (*Speaks through his nose.*)
He has exterminated several
475   Whose tone of voice suggested . . .

SIXTH CADET   (*In a hollow tone; rising from under the table on all fours.*)
          Would you die
Before your time? Just mention anything
Convex . . . or cartilaginous . . .

SEVENTH CADET (*his hand on* CHRISTIAN'*s shoulder*)

           One word —

Onesyllable — onegesture — nay, onesneeze —
Your handkerchief becomes your
    winding-sheet!

    (*Silence. In a circle around* CHRISTIAN, *arms crossed, they regard him expectantly.*)

CHRISTIAN (*Rises and goes to* CARBON, *who is conversing with an officer, and pretending not to see what is taking place.*)

480   Captain!

CARBON (*Turns, and looks him over.*)

        Sir?

CHRISTIAN   What is the proper thing to do
When Gascons grow too boastful?

CARBON   Prove to them
That one may be a Norman, and have
    courage.

    (*Turns his back.*)

CHRISTIAN I thank you.

FIRST CADET (*to* CYRANO)

        Come — the story!

ALL   The story!

CYRANO (*Comes down.*)

             Oh,
My story? Well . . .

    (*They all draw up their stools and group themselves around him, eagerly.* CHRISTIAN *places himself astride of a chair, his arms on the back of it.*)

        I marched on, all alone

485   To meet those devils. Overhead, the moon
Hung like a gold watch at the fob of heaven,
Till suddenly some Angel rubbed a cloud,
As it might be his handkerchief, across
The shining crystal, and — the night came
    down.

490   No lamps in those back streets — It was so
    dark —
Mordious! You could not see beyond —

CHRISTIAN   Your nose.

    (*Silence. Every man slowly rises to his feet. They look at* CYRANO *almost with terror. He has stopped short, utterly astonished. Pause.*)

CYRANO Who is that man there?

A CADET (*in a low voice*)

        A recruit — arrived
This morning.

CYRANO (*Takes a step toward* CHRISTIAN.)

    A recruit —

CARBON (*in a low voice*)

          His name is Christian
De Neuvil —

CYRANO (*suddenly motionless*)

    Oh . . .

    (*He turns pale, flushes, makes a movement as if to throw himself upon* CHRISTIAN.)

    I —

    (*Controls himself, and goes on in a choking voice.*)

        I see. Very well,

495   As I was saying —

    (*with a sudden burst of rage*)

        Mordious! . . .

    (*He goes on in a natural tone.*)

          It grew dark,
You could not see your hand before your eyes.
I marched on, thinking how, all for the sake
Of one old souse

    (*They slowly sit down, watching him.*)

        who wrote a bawdy song
Whenever he took —

CHRISTIAN   A noseful —

    (*Everyone rises.* CHRISTIAN *balances himself on two legs of his chair.*)

CYRANO (*half strangled*)

        — Took a notion . . .

500   Whenever he took a notion — For his sake,
I might antagonize some dangerous man,
One powerful enough to make me pay —

CHRISTIAN Through the nose —

CYRANO (*Wipes the sweat from his forehead.*)

        — Pay the Piper. After all,
I thought, why am I putting in my —

CHRISTIAN   Nose —

505 **CYRANO** — My oar . . . Why am I putting in my
    oar?
The quarrel's none of mine. However — now
I am here, I may as well go through with it.
Come Gascon — do your duty! — Suddenly
A sword flashed in the dark. I caught it fair —

510 **CHRISTIAN** On the nose —

CYRANO   On my blade. Before I knew it,
There I was —
CHRISTIAN   Rubbing noses —
CYRANO (*pale and smiling*)
                Crossing swords
With half a score at once. I handed one —
CHRISTIAN A nosegay —
CYRANO (*leaping at him*)
                Ventre-Saint-Gris![12] . . .
(*The Gascons tumble over each other to get
a good view. Arrived in front of* CHRISTIAN,
who has not moved an inch, CYRANO
masters himself again, and continues.)
                He went down;
The rest gave way; I charged —
CHRISTIAN   Nose in the air —
515 **CYRANO** I skewered two of them — disarmed
a third —
Another lunged — Paf! And I countered —
CHRISTIAN   Pif!
CYRANO (*bellowing*)
Tonnerre! Out of here! — All of you!
(*All the Cadets rush for the door.*)
FIRST CADET   At last —
The old lion wakes!
CYRANO   All of you! Leave me here
Alone with that man!
        (*The lines following are heard brokenly, in
        the confusion of getting through the door.*)
SECOND CADET Bigre! He'll have the fellow
520 Chopped into sausage —
RAGUENEAU   Sausage? —
THIRD CADET   Mince-meat, then —
One of your pies! —
RAGUENEAU   Am I pale? You look white
As a fresh napkin —
CARBON (*at the door*)
            Come!
FOURTH CADET   He'll never leave
Enough of him to —
FIFTH CADET   Why, it frightens me
To think of what will —
SIXTH CADET (*closing the door*)
                Something horrible
525 Beyond imagination . . .

(*They are all gone: some through the street
door, some by the inner doors to right and
left. A few disappear up the staircase.*
CYRANO *and* CHRISTIAN *stand face to face a
moment, and look at each other.*)
CYRANO   To my arms!
CHRISTIAN Sir? . . .
CYRANO   You have courage!
CHRISTIAN   Oh, that! . . .
CYRANO   You are brave —
That pleases me.
CHRISTIAN   You mean? . . .
CYRANO   Do you not know
I am her brother? Come!
CHRISTIAN   Whose? —
CYRANO   Hers — Roxane!
CHRISTIAN Her . . . brother? You?
        (*Hurries to him.*)
CYRANO   Her cousin. Much the same.
530 **CHRISTIAN** And she has told you? . . .
CYRANO   Everything.
CHRISTIAN   She loves me?
CYRANO Perhaps.
CHRISTIAN (*Takes both his hands.*)
        My dear sir — more than I can say,
I am honored —
CYRANO   This is rather sudden.
CHRISTIAN   Please
Forgive me —
CYRANO (*Holds him at arms length, looking at
    him.*)
        Why, he is a handsome devil,
This fellow!
CHRISTIAN   On my honor — if you knew
535 How much I have admired —
CYRANO   Yes, yes — and all
Those Noses which —
CHRISTIAN   Please! I apologize.
CYRANO (*change of tone*)
Roxane expects a letter —
CHRISTIAN   Not from me? —
CYRANO Yes. Why not?
CHRISTIAN   Once I write, that ruins all!
CYRANO And why?
CHRISTIAN Because . . . because I am a fool!

---

12. **Ventre-Saint-Gris:** An oath, roughly meaning "the body of Christ." —Eds.

Sir Frank Dicksee, *Chivalry*, 1885. Oil on canvas.

▲

What does this image tell us about the ideas surrounding chivalry? How does the play *Cyrano* both embrace those ideas and expand on, or even defy, them?

540 Stupid enough to hang myself!

CYRANO　　　　　But no —
　　You are no fool; you call yourself a fool,
　　There's proof enough in that. Besides, you did not
　　Attack me like a fool.

CHRISTIAN　　　　Bah! Any one
　　Can pick a quarrel. Yes, I have a sort
545　Of rough and ready soldier's tongue. I know
　　That. But with any woman — paralyzed,
　　Speechless, dumb. I can only look at them.
　　Yet sometimes, when I go away, their eyes . . .

CYRANO　Why not their hearts, if you should wait and see?

550 CHRISTIAN　No. I am one of those — I know —
　　those men
　　Who never can make love.

CYRANO　　　　　Strange. . . . Now it seems
　　I, if I gave my mind to it, I might
　　Perhaps make love well.

CHRISTIAN　　　　Oh, if I had words
　　To say what I have here!

CYRANO　　　　　If I could be
555　A handsome little Musketeer with eyes! —

CHRISTIAN　Besides — you know Roxane —
　　how sensitive —
　　One rough word, and the sweet
　　illusion — gone!

CYRANO　I wish you might be my interpreter.

CHRISTIAN　I wish I had your wit —

CYRANO　　　　　Borrow it, then! —
560　Your beautiful young manhood — lend me
　　that,
　　And we two make one hero of romance!

CHRISTIAN　What?

CYRANO　　　　　Would you dare repeat to her
　　the words
　　I gave you, day by day?

CHRISTIAN　　　　You mean?

CYRANO　　　　　　　　　I mean
　　Roxane shall have no disillusionment!
565　Come, shall we win her both together? Take
　　The soul within this leathern jack of mine,
　　And breathe it into you?
　　　　(*Touches him on the breast.*)
　　　　　　　　So — there's my heart
　　Under your velvet, now!

CHRISTIAN　　　　But — Cyrano! —

CYRANO　But — Christian, why not?

CHRISTIAN　　　　I am afraid —

CYRANO　　　　　　　I know —
570　Afraid that when you have her all alone,
　　You lose all. Have no fear. It is yourself
　　She loves — give her yourself put into words —
　　My words, upon your lips!

CHRISTIAN　　　　But . . . but your eyes! . . .
　　They burn like —

CYRANO　　　　Will you? . . . Will you?

CHRISTIAN　　　　　　Does it mean
575　So much to you?

CYRANO　(*beside himself*)
　　　　　It means —
　　　　(*Recovers, changes tone.*)
　　　　　　A Comedy,

A situation for a poet! Come,
Shall we collaborate? I'll be your cloak
Of darkness, your enchanted sword, your ring
To charm the fairy Princess!

CHRISTIAN   But the letter —
580 I cannot write —

CYRANO   Oh yes, the letter.
    (*He takes from his pocket the letter which he
    has written.*)
                          Here.

CHRISTIAN What is this?

CYRANO   All there; all but the address.

CHRISTIAN I —

CYRANO Oh, you may send it. It will serve.

CHRISTIAN   But why
    Have you done this?

CYRANO   I have amused myself
    As we all do, we poets — writing vows
585 To Chloris, Phyllis — any pretty name —
    You might have had a pocketful of them!
    Take it, and turn to facts my fantasies —
    I loosed these loves like doves into the air;
    Give them a habitation and a home.
590 Here, take it — You will find me all the more
    Eloquent, being insincere! Come!

CHRISTIAN   First,
    There must be a few changes here and there —
    Written at random, can it fit Roxane?

CYRANO Like her own glove.

CHRISTIAN   No, but —

CYRANO   My son, have faith —
595 Faith in the love of women for themselves —
    Roxane will know this letter for her own!

CHRISTIAN (*Throws himself into the arms of
    CYRANO. They stand embraced.*)
    My friend!
        (*The door up stage opens a little. A Cadet
        steals in.*)

THE CADET Nothing. A silence like the tomb . . .
    I hardly dare look —
        (*He sees the two.*)
                          Wha-at?
        (*The Other Cadets crowd in behind him and
        see.*)

THE CADETS   No! — No!

SECOND CADET   Mon dieu!

THE MUSKETEER (*Slaps his knee.*)
    Well, well, well!

CARBON Here's our devil . . . Christianized!
600 Offend one nostril, and he turns the other.

THE MUSKETEER Now we are allowed to talk
    about his nose!
    (*calls*)
    Hey, Lise! Come here —
    (*affectedly*)
                          Snf! What a horrid smell!
    What is it? . . .
        (*Plants himself in front of CYRANO, and
        looks at his nose in an impolite manner.*)
                You ought to know about such things;
    What seems to have died around here?

CYRANO (*Knocks him backward over a bench.*)
                          Cabbage-heads!
        (*Joy. The Cadets have found their old
        CYRANO again. General disturbance.*)
            (*Curtain*)

Understanding and Interpreting

1 What mood does the setting, as described in the stage directions, establish at the start of Act 2? Why is this setting appropriate for the meeting between Roxane and Cyrano?

2 In the opening of this act, what is the nature of the conflict we see between Ragueneau and his wife, Lise? How does that conflict pick up on similar ideas in Act 1?

3 What do we learn about Roxane and Cyrano during their meeting at Ragueneau's pastry shop? Why are these details important to our understanding of their relationship?

4 When Roxane is about to leave, she tells Cyrano that he must tell her "the whole story" of the hundred men he vanquished "[s]ome day, when I have time" (ll. 248–250). As she exits, he says, "Oh . . . I have done better since!" What does he mean?

5 Why does Cyrano reject the patronage offer of Compte de Guiche (l. 332)—and other influential persons like him—even though doing so puts him at risk (ll. 379–443)?

6 What character traits do we see in Cyrano in this act that were not revealed in Act 1? Which qualities that you saw in the opening act are reinforced or developed in Act 2? Pay close attention to Cyrano's speech to Le Bret that begins, "What would you have me do?" (l. 379), and his refusal to retaliate to Christian's taunts about his nose.

Analyzing Language, Style, and Structure

1 Ragueneau instructs the cook, "Remember, / A couplet, or a roast, should be well turned" (ll. 18–19). What other connections between food (or cooking) and writing (especially poetry) do you notice in Act 2? What does Rostand suggest by such connections?

2 In the exchange with Cyrano, De Guiche alludes to both Don Quixote and the Three Musketeers. How does Cyrano respond, and what is the effect of drawing comparisons between Cyrano and these figures?

3 What is the argument Cyrano makes in his lengthy speech to Le Bret (ll. 379–443)? How does he lead to his paradoxical conclusion, "It is my pleasure to displease. I love / Hatred" (ll. 445–446)? Consider elements such as rhetorical questions, concession and refutation, and analogy.

4 In this play, Rostand makes extensive use of the literary technique known as dramatic irony, wherein the audience knows more of the situation than the characters do. How do the scenes between Christian and Cyrano illustrate dramatic irony? Consider both the taunting and the discussion about Cyrano writing as Christian. What does Cyrano mean when he tells Christian, "You will find me all the more / Eloquent, being insincere!" (ll. 590–591)?

5 Identify two or three examples of humor in Act 2. How do these contribute to the tensions that Rostand is developing, such as the conflict between appearance and reality or between inner and outer beauty?

Connecting, Arguing, and Extending

1 Cyrano proposes to Christian that "we two make one hero of romance!" (ll. 560–561). To what extent do you think that these two men together constitute a classic romantic hero?

2 In Act 2, elements of deceit begin to play a larger role in the play, particularly in the way Christian and Cyrano work together to court Roxane. What are

several examples? To what extent do you believe that this deception, in some cases downright dishonesty, is justified?

3 We never see the letter that Cyrano has written to Roxane declaring his love. What do you think he says? Write the letter in the language you believe he would use.

Act 3 **Cyrano de Bergerac**

Roxane's Kiss

A little square in the old Marais: old houses, and a glimpse of narrow streets. On the Right, The House of Roxane and her garden wall, overhung with tall shrubbery. Over the door of the house a balcony and a tall window; to one side of the door, a bench.

Ivy clings to the wall; jasmine embraces the balcony, trembles, and falls away.

By the bench and the jutting stonework of the wall one might easily climb up to the balcony.

Opposite, an ancient house of the like character, brick and stone, whose front door forms an Entrance. The knocker on this door is tied up in linen like an injured thumb.

At the curtain rise THE DUENNA *is seated on the bench beside the door. The window is wide open on* ROXANE's *balcony; a light within suggests that it is early evening. By* THE DUENNA *stands* RAGUENEAU *dressed in what might be the livery of one attached to the household. He is by way of telling her something, and wiping his eyes meanwhile.*

RAGUENEAU — And so she ran off with a
    Musketeer!
    I was ruined — I was alone — Remained
    Nothing for me to do but hang myself,
    So I did that. Presently along comes
5   Monsieur de Bergerac, and cuts me down,
    And makes me steward to his cousin.

THE DUENNA   Ruined? —
    I thought your pastry was a great success!

RAGUENEAU (*Shakes his head.*)
    Lise loved the soldiers, and I loved the poets —
    Mars ate up all the cakes Apollo left;
10   It did not take long. . . .

THE DUENNA (*Calls up to window.*)
             Roxane! Are you ready?
    We are late!

VOICE OF ROXANE (*within*)
    Putting on my cape —

THE DUENNA (*To* RAGUENEAU, *indicating the house opposite.*)
             Clomire
    Across the way receives on Thursday nights —
    We are to have a psycho-colloquy[1]
    Upon the Tender Passion.

RAGUENEAU   Ah — the Tender . . .

THE DUENNA (*sighs*)
15   —Passion! . . .
    (*Calls up to window.*)
             Roxane! — Hurry, dear — we shall miss
    The Tender Passion!

ROXANE   Coming! —
    (*Music of stringed instruments off-stage approaching.*)

THE VOICE OF CYRANO (*singing*)
             La, la, la! —

THE DUENNA   A serenade? — How pleasant —

CYRANO   No, no, no! —

F natural, you natural born fool!
    (*Enters, followed by two pages, carrying theorbos.*)

FIRST PAGE (*ironically*)
    No doubt your honor knows F natural
20   When he hears —

CYRANO   I am a musician, infant! —
    A pupil of Gassendi.

THE PAGE (*Plays and sings.*)
             La, la, —

CYRANO   Here —
    Give me that —
    (*He snatches the instrument from the Page and continues the tune.*)
             La, la, la, la —

ROXANE (*Appears on the Balcony.*)
             Is that you
    Cyrano?

CYRANO (*singing*)
            I, who praise your lilies fair,
    But long to love your ro . . . ses!

ROXANE   I'll be down —
25   Wait —
    (*Goes in through window.*)

THE DUENNA   Did you train these virtuosi?

CYRANO   No —
    I won them on a bet from D'Assoucy.
    We were debating a fine point of grammar
    When, pointing out these two young nightingales
    Dressed up like peacocks, with their instruments,
30   He cries: "No, but I KNOW! I'll wager you
    A day of music." Well, of course he lost;
    And so until to-morrow they are mine,
    My private orchestra. Pleasant at first,
    But they become a trifle —
    (*to the Pages*)
             Here! Go play
35   A minuet to Montfleury — and tell him
    I sent you!
    (*The Pages go up to the exit.* CYRANO *turns to the Duenna.*)
             I came here as usual
    To inquire after our friend —

---

1. **psycho-colloquy:** A serious psychological discussion. —Eds.

(*to Pages*)

　　　　　　　Play out of tune.

And keep on playing!

　　(*The Pages go out. He turns to the Duenna.*)

　　　　　　— Our friend with the great soul.

ROXANE (*Enters in time to hear the last words.*)

　　He is beautiful and brilliant — and I love him!

40 **CYRANO** Do you find Christian . . . intellectual?

ROXANE More so than you, even.

CYRANO 　　　　　　I am glad.

ROXANE 　　　　　　No man

　　Ever so beautifully said those things —

　　Those pretty nothings that are everything.

　　Sometimes he falls into a reverie;

45　His inspiration fails — then all at once,

　　He will say something absolutely . . . Oh! . . .

CYRANO Really!

ROXANE 　　How like a man! You think a man

　　Who has a handsome face must be a fool.

CYRANO He talks well·about . . . matters of the

　　heart?

ROXANE He does not *talk*; he rhapsodizes . . .

　　dreams . . .

CYRANO (*Twisting his moustache.*)

50　He . . . writes well?

ROXANE 　　Wonderfully. Listen now:

　　(*Reciting as from memory.*)

　　"Take my heart; I shall have it all the more;

　　Plucking the flowers, we keep the plant in

　　　bloom —"

　　Well?

CYRANO Pooh!

ROXANE 　　And this:

　　　　　　　"Knowing you have in store

　　More heart to give than I to find

　　　heart-room —"

55 **CYRANO** First he has too much, then too little;

　　just

　　How much heart does he need?

ROXANE (*Tapping her foot.*)

　　　　　　　You are teasing me!

　　You are jealous!

CYRANO (*startled*)

　　　　　　Jealous?

ROXANE 　　　　　Of his poetry —

　　You poets are like that . . .

　　　　　　　And these last lines

Are they not the last word in tenderness? —

60　"There is no more to say: only believe

　　That unto you my whole heart gives one cry,

　　And writing, writes down more than you

　　　receive;

　　Sending you kisses through my finger-tips —

　　Lady, O read my letter with your lips!"

65 **CYRANO** H'm, yes — those last lines . . . but he

　　overwrites!

ROXANE Listen to this —

CYRANO 　　　You know them all by heart?

ROXANE Every one!

CYRANO (*Twisting his moustache.*)

　　　　　I may call that flattering . . .

ROXANE He is a master!

CYRANO 　　　Oh — come!

ROXANE 　　　　　Yes — a master!

CYRANO (*bowing*)

　　A master — if you will!

THE DUENNA (*Comes down stage quickly.*)

　　　　　　Monsieur de Guiche! —

　　(*To* CYRANO, *pushing him toward the

　　house.*)

70　Go inside — If he does not find you here,

　　It may be just as well. He may suspect —

ROXANE — My secret! Yes; he is in love with me

　　And he is powerful. Let him not know —

　　One look would frost my roses before bloom.

CYRANO (*Going into house.*)

75　Very well, very well!

ROXANE (*To* DE GUICHE, *as he enters*)

　　　　　We were just going —

DE GUICHE I came only to say farewell.

ROXANE 　　　You leave

　　Paris?

DE GUICHE Yes — for the front.

ROXANE 　　　Ah!

DE GUICHE 　　　　And to-night!

ROXANE Ah!

DE GUICHE We have orders to beseige Arras.

ROXANE Arras?

DE GUICHE Yes. My departure leaves you . . . cold?

ROXANE (*politely*)

80　Oh! Not that.

DE GUICHE It has left me desolate —

　　When shall I see you? Ever? Did you know

　　I was made Colonel?

ROXANE (*indifferent*)

    Bravo.

DE GUICHE   Regiment

Of the Guards.

ROXANE (*Catching her breath.*)

    Of the Guards? —

DE GUICHE   *His* regiment,

Your cousin, the mighty man of words! —

    (*grimly*)

    Down there

85 We may have an accounting!

ROXANE (*suffocating*)

    Are you sure

The Guards are ordered?

DE GUICHE   Under my command!

ROXANE (*sinks down, breathless, on the bench;*

    aside)

Christian! —

DE GUICHE   What is it?

ROXANE (*Losing control of herself.*)

    To the war — perhaps

Never again to — When a woman cares,

Is that nothing?

DE GUICHE (*Surprised and delighted.*)

    You say this now — to me —

90 Now, at the very moment? —

ROXANE (*Recovers — changes her tone.*)

    Tell me something:

My cousin — You say you mean to be revenged

On him. Do you mean that?

DE GUICHE (*smiles*)

    Why? Would you care?

ROXANE Not for him.

DE GUICHE Do you see him?

ROXANE   Now and then.

DE GUICHE He goes about everywhere

    nowadays

95 WithoneoftheCadets — deNeuve — Neuville —

    Neuvillers —

ROXANE (*coolly*)

    A tall man? —

DE GUICHE   Blond —

ROXANE   Rosy cheeks? —

DE GUICHE Handsome! —

ROXANE   Pooh! —

DE GUICHE   And a fool.

ROXANE (*languidly*)

    So he appears . . .

    (*animated*)

But Cyrano? What will you do to him?

Order him into danger? He loves that!

100 I know what *I* should do.

DE GUICHE   What?

ROXANE   Leave him here

With his Cadets, while all the regiment

Goes on to glory! That would torture him —

To sit all through the war with folded arms —

I know his nature. If you hate that man,

105 Strike at his self-esteem.

DE GUICHE   Oh woman — woman!

Who but a woman would have thought of

    this?

ROXANE He'll eat his heart out, while his Gascon

    friends

Bite their nails all day long in Paris here.

And you will be avenged!

DE GUICHE   You love me then,

110 A little? . . .

    (*She smiles.*)

    Making my enemies your own,

Hating them — I should like to see in that

A sign of love, Roxane.

ROXANE   Perhaps it is one . . .

DE GUICHE (*Shows a number of folded*

    despatches.)

Here are the orders — for each company —

Ready to send . . .

    (*Selects one.*)

    So — This is for the Guards —

115 I'll keep that. Aha, Cyrano!

    (*to* ROXANE)

    You too,

You play your little games, do you?

ROXANE (*Watching him.*)

    Sometimes . . .

DE GUICHE (*Close to her, speaking hurriedly.*)

And you! — Oh, I am mad over you! —

    Listen —

I leave to-night — but — let you through my

    hands

Now, when I feel you trembling? — Listen —

Close by,

120   In the Rue d'Orléans, the Capuchins
    Have their new convent. By their law, no
       layman
    May pass inside those walls. I'll see to that —
    Their sleeves are wide enough to cover me —
    The servants of my Uncle-Cardinal

125   Will fear his nephew. So — I'll come to you
    Masked, after everyone knows I have gone —
    Oh, let me wait one day! —

ROXANE   If this be known,
    Your honor —

DE GUICHE   Bah!

ROXANE   The war — your duty —

DE GUICHE   (*Blows away an imaginary feather.*)
                  Phoo! —

    Only say yes!

ROXANE   No!

DE GUICHE   Whisper . . .

ROXANE (*tenderly*)
              I ought not

130   To let you . . .

DE GUICHE   Ah! . . .

ROXANE (*Pretends to break down.*)
            Ah, go!

    (*aside*)
               — Christian remains —
    (*aloud — heroically*)
    I must have you a hero — Antoine . . .

DE GUICHE   Heaven! . . .
    So you can love —

ROXANE   One for whose sake I fear.

DE GUICHE (*triumphant*)
    I go!
            Will that content you?
            (*Kisses her hand.*)

ROXANE   Yes — my friend!
    (*He goes out.*)

THE DUENNA (*As* DE GUICHE *disappears, making
    a deep curtsey behind his back, and imitat-
    ing* ROXANE'*s intense tone.*)
    Yes — my friend!

ROXANE (*Quickly, close to her.*)
            Not a word to Cyrano —

135   He would never forgive me if he knew
    I stole his war!
    (*She calls toward the house.*)
            Cousin!

    (Cyrano *comes out of the house; she turns to
    him, indicating the house opposite.*)
             We are going over —
    Alcandre speaks to-night — and Lysimon.

THE DUENNA (*Puts finger in her ear.*)
    My little finger says we shall not hear
    Everything.

CYRANO   Never mind me —

THE DUENNA (*across the street*)
              Look — Oh, look!

140   The knocker tied up in a napkin — Yes,
    They muzzled you because you bark too loud
    And interrupt the lecture — little beast!

ROXANE (*as the door opens*)
    Enter . . .
    (*to* CYRANO)
          If Christian comes, tell him to wait.

CYRANO Oh —
    (ROXANE *returns.*)
    When he comes, what will you talk about?

145   You always know beforehand.

ROXANE   About . . .

CYRANO   Well?

ROXANE You will not tell him, will you?

CYRANO   I am dumb.

ROXANE About nothing! Or about everything —
    I shall say: "Speak of love in your own
       words —
    Improvise! Rhapsodize! Be eloquent!"

CYRANO (*smiling*)

150   Good!

ROXANE Sh! —

CYRANO   Sh! —

ROXANE   Not a word!
    (*She goes in; the door closes.*)

CYRANO (*bowing*)
             Thank you so much —

ROXANE (*Opens door and puts out her head.*)
    He must be unprepared —

CYRANO   Of course!

ROXANE   Sh! —
    (*Goes in again.*)

CYRANO (*calls*)
              Christian!
    (CHRISTIAN *enters.*)
    I have your theme — bring on your memory! —
    Here is your chance now to surpass yourself,

155   No time to lose — Come! Look intelligent —
Come home and learn your lines.

CHRISTIAN   No.

CYRANO   What?

CHRISTIAN   I'll wait
Here for Roxane.

CYRANO   What lunacy is this?
Come quickly!

CHRISTIAN   No, I say! I have had enough —
Taking my words, my letters, all from you —
Making our love a little comedy!

160   It was a game at first; but now — she cares . . .
Thanks to you. I am not afraid. I'll speak
For myself now.

CYRANO   Undoubtedly!

CHRISTIAN   I will!
Why not? I am no such fool — you shall see!
Besides — my dear friend — you have taught
     me much;

165   I ought to know something . . . By God, I know
Enough to take a woman in my arms!
     (ROXANE *appears in the doorway, opposite.*)
There she is now . . . Cyrano, wait! Stay here!

CYRANO (*bows*)
Speak for yourself, my friend!
     (*He goes out.*)

ROXANE (*Taking leave of the company.*)
     — Barthénoide!
Alcandre! . . . Grémione! . . .

THE DUENNA   I told you so —

170   We missed the Tender Passion!
     (*She goes into* ROXANE'*s house.*)

ROXANE   Urimédonte! —
Adieu!
     (*As the guests disappear down the street, she
     turns to* CHRISTIAN.)
     Is that you, Christian? Let us stay
Here, in the twilight. They are gone. The air
Is fragrant. We shall be alone. Sit down
There — so . . .
     (*They sit on the bench.*)
     Now tell me things.

CHRISTIAN (*after a silence*)
     I love you.

ROXANE (*Closes her eyes.*)
     Yes,

175   Speak to me about love . . .

CHRISTIAN   I love you.

ROXANE   Now
Be eloquent! . . .

CHRISTIAN   I love —

ROXANE (*Opens her eyes.*)
     You have your theme —
Improvise! Rhapsodize!

CHRISTIAN   I love you so!

ROXANE Of course. And then? . . .

CHRISTIAN   And then . . . Oh, I should be
So happy if you loved me too! Roxane,

180   Say that you love me too!

ROXANE (*Making a face.*)
     I ask for cream —
You give me milk and water. Tell me first
A little, how you love me.

CHRISTIAN   Very much.

ROXANE Oh — tell me how you *feel*!

CHRISTIAN (*Coming nearer, and devouring her
     with his eyes.*)
     Your throat . . . If only
I might . . . kiss it —

ROXANE   Christian!

CHRISTIAN   I love you so!

ROXANE (*Makes as if to rise.*)

185   Again?

CHRISTIAN (*Desperately, restraining her.*)
No, not again — I do not love you —

ROXANE (*Settles back.*)
That is better . . .

CHRISTIAN   I adore you!

ROXANE   Oh! —
     (*Rises and moves away.*)

CHRISTIAN   I know;
I grow absurd.

ROXANE (*coldly*)
     And that displeases me
As much as if you had grown ugly.

CHRISTIAN   I —

ROXANE Gather your dreams together into
     words!

190 CHRISTIAN I love —

ROXANE I know; you love me. Adieu.
     (*She goes to the house.*)

CHRISTIAN   No,
But wait — please — let me — I was going to say-

ROXANE (*Pushes the door open.*)

That you adore me. Yes; I know that too.
No! . . . Go away! . . .
(*She goes in and shuts the door in his face.*)
CHRISTIAN   I . . . I . . .
CYRANO (*enters*)
                                    A great success!
CHRISTIAN Help me!
CYRANO   Not I.
CHRISTIAN   I cannot live unless
195 She loves me — now, this moment!
CYRANO   How the devil
     Am I to teach you now — this moment?
CHRISTIAN (*Catches him by the arm.*)
                                    —Wait! —
     Look! Up there! — Quick —
     (*The light shows in* ROXANE's *window.*)
CYRANO   Her window —
CHRISTIAN (*wailing*)
                                    I shall die! —
CYRANO Less noise!
CHRISTIAN Oh, I —
CYRANO   It does seem fairly dark —
CHRISTIAN (*excitedly*)
     Well? — Well? — Well? —
CYRANO   Let us try what can be done;
200 It is more than you deserve — stand over there,
     Idiot — there! — before the balcony —
     Let me stand underneath. I'll whisper you
     What to say.
CHRISTIAN She may hear — she may —
CYRANO   Less noise!
     (*The Pages appear up stage.*)
FIRST PAGE Hep! —
CYRANO (*finger to lips*)
        Sh! —
FIRST PAGE (*low voice*)
            We serenaded Montfleury! —
205 What next?
CYRANO   Down to the corner of the street —
     One this way — and the other over there —
     If anybody passes, play a tune!
PAGE What tune, O musical Philosopher?
CYRANO Sad for a man, or merry for a woman —
210 Now go!
     (*The Pages disappear, one toward each
     corner of the street.*)

CYRANO (*to* CHRISTIAN)
     Call her!
CHRISTIAN Roxane!
CYRANO   Wait . . .
     (*Gathers up a handful of pebbles.*)
                            Gravel . . .
     (*Throws it at the window.*)
                                    There! —
ROXANE (*Opens the window.*)
     Who is calling?
CHRISTIAN I —
ROXANE   Who?
CHRISTIAN   Christian.
ROXANE   You again?
CHRISTIAN I had to tell you —
CYRANO (*under the balcony*)
     Good — Keep your voice down.
ROXANE No. Go away. You tell me nothing.
CHRISTIAN   Please! —
ROXANE You do not love me any more —
CHRISTIAN (*to whom* CYRANO *whispers his words*)
                        No — no —
215 Not any more — I love you . . . evermore . . .
     And ever . . . more and more!
ROXANE (*About to close the window — pauses.*)
                            A little better . . .
CHRISTIAN (*same business*)
     Love grows and struggles like . . . an angry
        child . . .
     Breaking my heart . . . his cradle . . .
ROXANE (*Coming out on the balcony.*)
                            Better still —
     But . . . such a babe is dangerous; why not
220 Have smothered it new-born?
CHRISTIAN (*same business*)
                            And so I do . . .
     And yet he lives . . . I found . . . as you shall
        find . . .
     This new-born babe . . . an infant . . . Hercules
ROXANE (*further forward*)
     Good! —
CHRISTIAN (*same business*)
                Strong enough . . . at birth . . . to
                    strangle those
     Two serpents — Doubt and . . . Pride.
ROXANE (*Leans over balcony.*)

This illustration by Miguel Tanco is from *The Story of Cyrano de Bergerac* by Stefano Benni.

What interpretation of the balcony scene does this image suggest? Pay careful attention to how the artist uses color and perspective to create the scene.

>   Why, very well!
> 225 Tell me now why you speak so haltingly —
>   Has your imagination gone lame?
> **CYRANO** (*Thrusts* CHRISTIAN *under the balcony, and stands in his place.*)
>   Here —
>   This grows too difficult!
> **ROXANE**   Your words to-night
>   Hesitate. Why?
> **CYRANO** (*in a low tone, imitating* CHRISTIAN)
>   Through the warm summer gloom
>   They grope in darkness toward the light of you.
> 230 **ROXANE** My words, well aimed, find you more readily.
> **CYRANO** My heart is open wide and waits
>   for them —
>   Too large a mark to miss! My words fly home,

>   Heavy with honey like returning bees,
>   To your small secret ear. Moreover — yours
> 235 Fall to me swiftly. Mine more slowly rise.
> **ROXANE** Yet not so slowly as they did at first.
> **CYRANO** They have learned the way, and you
>   have welcomed them.
> **ROXANE** (*softly*)
>   Am I so far above you now?
> **CYRANO**   So far —
>   If you let fall upon me one hard word,
> 240 Out of that height — you crush me!
> **ROXANE** (*turns*)
>   I'll come down —
> **CYRANO** (*quickly*)
>   No!
> **ROXANE** (*Points out the bench under the balcony.*)
>   Stand you on the bench. Come nearer!
> **CYRANO** (*Recoils into the shadow.*)
>   No! —
> **ROXANE** And why — so great a *No*?
> **CYRANO** (*More and more overcome by emotion.*)
>   Let me enjoy
>   The one moment I ever — my one chance
>   To speak to you . . . unseen!
> **ROXANE**   Unseen? —
> **CYRANO**   Yes! — yes . . .
> 245 Night, making all things dimly beautiful,
>   One veil over us both — You only see
>   The darkness of a long cloak in the gloom,
>   And I the whiteness of a summer gown —
>   You are all light — I am all shadow! . . . How
> 250 Can you know what this moment means to me?
>   If I was ever eloquent —
> **ROXANE**   You were
>   Eloquent —
> **CYRANO** — You have never heard till now
>   My own heart speaking!
> **ROXANE**   Why not?
> **CYRANO**   Until now,
>   I spoke through . . .
> **ROXANE**   Yes? —
> **CYRANO** — through that sweet drunkenness
> 255 You pour into the world out of your eyes!
>   But to-night . . . but to-night, I indeed speak
>   For the first time!
> **ROXANE**   For the first time — Your voice,
>   Even, is not the same.

CYRANO (*Passionately; moves nearer.*)
                 How should it be?
I have another voice to-night — my own,
260 Myself, daring —
    (*He stops, confused; then tries to recover
    himself.*)
           Where was I? . . . I forget! . . .
Forgive me. This is all sweet like a dream . . .
Strange — like a dream . . .

ROXANE   How, strange?

CYRANO   Is it not so
To be myself to you, and have no fear
Of moving you to laughter?

ROXANE   Laughter — why?

CYRANO (*Struggling for an explanation.*)
265 Because . . . What am I . . . What is any man,
That he dare ask for you? Therefore my heart
Hides behind phrases. There's a modesty
In these things too — I come here to pluck
    down
Out of the sky the evening star — then smile,
270 And stoop to gather little flowers.

ROXANE   Are they
Not sweet, those little flowers?

CYRANO   Not enough sweet
For you and me, to-night!

ROXANE (*breathless*)
           You never spoke
To me like this . . .

CYRANO   Little things, pretty things —
Arrows and hearts and torches — roses red,
275 And violets blue — are these all? Come away,
And breathe fresh air! Must we keep on and on
Sipping stale honey out of tiny cups
Decorated with golden tracery,
Drop by drop, all day long? We are alive;
280 We thirst — Come away, plunge, and drink,
    and drown
In the great river flowing to the sea!

ROXANE But . . . Poetry?

CYRANO   I have made rimes
    for you —
Not now — Shall we insult Nature, this night,
These flowers, this moment — shall we set all
    these
285 To phrases from a letter by Voiture?

Look once at the high stars that shine in
    heaven,
And put off artificiality!
Have you not seen great gaudy hothouse
    flowers,
Barren, without fragrance? — Souls are like
    that:
290 Forced to show all, they soon become
    all show —
The means to Nature's end ends
    meaningless!

ROXANE But . . . Poetry?

CYRANO   Love hates that game of
    words!
It is a crime to fence with life — I tell you,
There comes one moment, once — and God
    help those
295 Who pass that moment by! — when Beauty
    stands
Looking into the soul with grave, sweet eyes
That sicken at pretty words!

ROXANE   If that be true —
And when that moment comes to you
    and me —
What words will you? . . .

CYRANO   All those, all those, all
    those
300 That blossom in my heart, I'll fling to you —
Armfuls of loose bloom! Love, I love beyond
Breath, beyond reason, beyond love's own
    power
Of loving! Your name is like a golden bell
Hung in my heart; and when I think of you,
305 I tremble, and the bell swings and rings —
               Roxane! . . .
Roxane! . . . along my veins, *Roxane!* . . .
             I know
All small forgotten things that once meant
    You —
I remember last year, the First of May,
A little before noon, you had your hair
310 Drawn low, that one time only. Is that strange?
You know how, after looking at the sun,
One sees red suns everywhere — so, for hours
After the flood of sunshine that you are,
My eyes are blinded by your burning hair!

seeing connections

The following Twelve Chief Rules in Love come from *The Art of Courtly Love* by Andreas Capellanus, a twelfth-century French courtier and author.

The Twelve Chief Rules in Love

1. Thou shalt avoid avarice like the deadly pestilence and shalt embrace its opposite.
2. Thou shalt keep thyself chaste for the sake of her whom thou lovest.
3. Thou shalt not knowingly strive to break up a correct love affair that someone else is engaged in.
4. Thou shalt not choose for thy love anyone whom a natural sense of shame forbids thee to marry.
5. Be mindful completely to avoid falsehood.
6. Thou shalt not have many who know of thy love affair.
7. Being obedient in all things to the commands of ladies, thou shalt ever strive to ally thyself to the service of Love.
8. In giving and receiving love's solaces let modesty be ever-present.
9. Thou shalt speak no evil.
10. Thou shalt not be a revealer of love affairs.
11. Thou shalt be in all things polite and courteous.
12. In practicing the solaces of love thou shalt not exceed the desires of thy lover.

Examine these Twelve Chief Rules in Love by Capellanus, and discuss the ways in which *Cyrano de Bergerac* explores one or more of these rules.

ROXANE (*very low*)
315   Yes . . . that is . . . Love —
CYRANO   Yes, that is
     Love — that wind
     Of terrible and jealous beauty, blowing
     Over me — that dark fire, that music . . .
                                   Yet
     Love seeketh not his own! Dear, you may take
     My happiness to make you happier,
320   Even though you never know I gave it you —
     Only let me hear sometimes, all alone,
     The distant laughter of your joy! . . .
                                   I never
     Look at you, but there's some new virtue born
     In me, some new courage. Do you begin
325   To understand, a little? Can you feel
     My soul, there in the darkness, breathe on you?
     — Oh, but to-night, now, I dare say these
          things —
     I . . . to you . . . and you hear them! . . . It is too
          much!

     In my most sweet unreasonable dreams,
330   I have not hoped for this! Now let me die,
     Having lived. It is my voice, mine, my own,
     That makes you tremble there in the green
          gloom
     Above me — for you do tremble, as a blossom
     Among the leaves — You tremble, and I can
          feel,
335   All the way down along these jasmine branches,
     Whether you will or no, the passion of you
     Trembling . . .
          (*He kisses wildly the end of a drooping spray
          of jasmine.*)
ROXANE   Yes, I do tremble . . . and I
     weep . . .
     And I love you . . . and I am yours . . . and you
     Have made me thus!
CYRANO (*After a pause; quietly.*)
                              What is death like, I wonder?
340   I know everything else now . . .
                              I have done

This, to you — I, myself . . .

                            Only let me

Ask one thing more —

CHRISTIAN (*under the balcony*)

                  One kiss!

ROXANE (*startled*)

                        One? —

CYRANO (*to* CHRISTIAN)

                        You! . . .

ROXANE   You ask me

For —

CYRANO I . . . Yes, but — I mean —

    (*to* CHRISTIAN)

                    You go too far!

CHRISTIAN She is willing! — Why not make the
    most of it?

CYRANO (*to* ROXANE)

345   I did ask . . . but I know I ask too much . . .

ROXANE Only one — Is that all?

CYRANO   All! — How much more

Than all! — I know — I frighten you — I ask . . .

I ask you to refuse —

CHRISTIAN (*to* CYRANO)

                  But why? Why? Why?

CYRANO Christian, be quiet!

ROXANE (*Leaning over.*)

               What is that you say

350   To yourself?

CYRANO   I am angry with myself

Because I go too far, and so I say

To myself: "Christian, be quiet!" —

    (*The theorbos begin to play.*)

                Hark — someone

Is coming —

    (Roxane *closes her window.* CYRANO *listens
    to the theorbos, one of which plays a gay
    melody, the other a mournful one.*)

              A sad tune, a merry tune —

Man, woman — what do they mean? —

    (*A Capuchin enters; he carries a lantern,
    and goes from house to house, looking at the
    doors.*)

              Aha! — a priest!

    (*to the Capuchin*)

355   What is this new game of Diogenes?[2]

THE CAPUCHIN I am looking for the house
    of Madame —

CHRISTIAN (*impatient*)

                        Bah! —

THE CAPUCHIN Madeleine Robin —

CHRISTIAN   What does he want?

CYRANO (*To the Capuchin; points out a street.*)

                     This way —

To the right — keep to the right —

THE CAPUCHIN   I thank you, sir! —

I'll say my beads for you to the last grain.

360 **CYRANO** Good fortune, father, and my service to
    you!

    (*the Capuchin goes out*)

CHRISTIAN Win me that kiss!

CYRANO   No.

CHRISTIAN   Sooner or later —

CYRANO   True . . .

That is true . . . Soon or late, it will be so

Because you are young and she is beautiful —

    (*to himself*)

Since it must be, I had rather be myself

    (*The window re-opens.* CHRISTIAN *hides
    under the balcony.*)

365   The cause of . . . what must be.

ROXANE (*out on the balcony*)

                 Are you still there?

We were speaking of —

CYRANO   A kiss. The word
    is sweet —

What will the deed be? Are your lips afraid

Even of its burning name? Not much afraid —

Not too much! Have you not unwittingly

370   Laid aside laughter, slipping beyond speech

Insensibly, already, without fear,

From words to smiles . . . from smiles to
    sighs . . . from sighing,

Even to tears? One step more — only one —

From a tear to a kiss — one step, one thrill!

375 **ROXANE** Hush! —

CYRANO   And what is a kiss, when all is done?

A promise given under seal — a vow

Taken before the shrine of memory —

---

2. **Diogenes:** Ancient Greek philosopher and founder of cynicism, who wandered the streets of Athens with a lamp in broad daylight, claiming that he was searching for an honest man. —Eds.

A signature acknowledged — a rosy dot
Over the *i* of Loving — a secret whispered
380 To listening lips apart — a moment made
Immortal, with a rush of wings unseen —
A sacrament of blossoms, a new song
Sung by two hearts to an old simple tune —
The ring of one horizon around two souls
385 Together, all alone!

ROXANE   Hush! . . .

CYRANO   Why, what shame? —
There was a Queen of France, not long ago,
And a great lord of England — a queen's gift,
A crown jewel! —

ROXANE   Indeed!

CYRANO   Indeed, like him,
I have my sorrows and my silences;
390 Like her, you are the queen I dare adore;
Like him I am faithful and forlorn —

ROXANE   Like him,
Beautiful —

CYRANO (*aside*)
                          So I am — I forgot that!

ROXANE Then — Come! . . . Gather your sacred
      blossom . . .

CYRANO (*to* CHRISTIAN)
                                Go! —

ROXANE Your crown jewel . . .

CYRANO   Go on! —

ROXANE   Your old new song . . .

395 **CYRANO** Climb! —

CHRISTIAN (*hesitates*)
                          No — Would you? — not yet —

ROXANE   Your moment made
Immortal . . .

CYRANO (*Pushing him.*)
                                Climb up, animal!
(CHRISTIAN *springs on the bench,
and climbs by the pillars, the branches,
the vines, until he bestrides the balcony
railing.*)

CHRISTIAN   Roxane! . . .
(*He takes her in his arms and bends over her.*)

CYRANO (*very low*)
Ah! . . . Roxane! . . .

                                I have won what I
      have won —
The feast of love — and I am Lazarus!

Yet . . . I have something here that is mine now
400 And was not mine before I spoke the words
That won her — not for me! . . . Kissing my words
My words, upon your lips!
      (*The theorbos begin to play.*)
                                A merry tune —
A sad tune — So! The Capuchin!
      (*He pretends to be running, as if he had
      arrived from a distance; then calls up to the
      balcony.*)
                                Hola!

ROXANE Who is it?

CYRANO   I. Is Christian there with you?

CHRISTIAN (*astonished*)
405 Cyrano!

ROXANE   Good morrow, Cousin!

CYRANO   Cousin, . . . good morrow!

ROXANE I am coming down.
      (*She disappears into the house. The
      Capuchin enters up stage.*)

CHRISTIAN (*Sees him.*)
                                Oh — again!

THE CAPUCHIN (*to* CYRANO)
                                She lives *here*,
      Madeleine Robin!

CYRANO You said RO-LIN.

THE CAPUCHIN   No —
      R-O-B-I-N

ROXANE (*Appears on the threshold of the house,
      followed by* RAGUENEAU *with a lantern,
      and by* CHRISTIAN.)
                  What is it?

THE CAPUCHIN   A letter.

CHRISTIAN   Oh! . . .

THE CAPUCHIN (*to* ROXANE)
      Some matter profitable to the soul —
410 A very noble lord gave it to me!

ROXANE (*to* CHRISTIAN)
      De Guiche!

CHRISTIAN   He dares? —

ROXANE   It will not be for long;
When he learns that I love you . . .
      (*By the light of the lantern which
      RAGUENEAU holds, she reads the letter in a
      low tone, as if to herself.*)
                                "Mademoiselle
The drums are beating, and the regiment

Arms for the march. Secretly I remain
415 Here, in the Convent. I have disobeyed;
I shall be with you soon. I send this first
By an old monk, as simple as a sheep,
Who understands nothing of this. Your smile
Is more than I can bear, and seek no more.
420 Be alone to-night, waiting for one who dares
To hope you will forgive . . . —" etcetera —
    (*to the Capuchin*)
Father, this letter concerns you . . .
    (*to* CHRISTIAN)
                    — and you.
Listen:
    (*The others gather around her. She pretends
    to read from the letter, aloud.*)
        "Mademoiselle:
            The Cardinal
Will have his way, although against your will;
425 That is why I am sending this to you
By a most holy man, intelligent,
Discreet. You will communicate to him
Our order to perform, here and at once
The rite of . . .
    (*turns the page*)
                — Holy Matrimony. You
430 And Christian will be married privately
In your house. I have sent him to you. I know
You hesitate. Be resigned, nevertheless,
To the Cardinal's command, who sends
    herewith
His blessing. Be assured also of my own
435 Respect and high consideration — *signed*,
Your very humble and — etcetera —"
THE CAPUCHIN A noble lord! I said so — never
    fear —
A worthy lord! — a very worthy lord! —
ROXANE (*to* CHRISTIAN)
Am I a good reader of letters?
CHRISTIAN (*Motions toward the Capuchin.*)
                    Careful! —
ROXANE (*in a tragic tone*)
440 Oh, this is terrible!
THE CAPUCHIN (*Turns the light of his lantern on*
    CYRANO.)
                You are to be —
CHRISTIAN *I* am the bridegroom!
THE CAPUCHIN (*Turns his lantern upon*

CHRISTIAN; *then, as if some suspicion
crossed his mind, upon seeing the young
man so handsome.*)
            Oh — why, you . . .
ROXANE (*quickly*)
                Look here —
"*Postscript:* Give to the Convent in my name
One hundred and twenty pistoles" —
THE CAPUCHIN   Think of it!
A worthy lord — a very worthy lord! . . .
    (*to* ROXANE, *solemnly*)
445 Daughter, resign yourself!
ROXANE (*with an air of martyrdom*)
                I am resigned . . .
    (*While* RAGUENEAU *opens the door for the
    Capuchin and* CHRISTIAN *invites him to
    enter, she turns to* CYRANO.)
De Guiche may come. Keep him out here with
    you
Do not let him —
CYRANO   I understand!
    (*to the Capuchin*)
                How long
Will you be? —
THE CAPUCHIN Oh, a quarter of an hour.
CYRANO (*Hurrying them into the house.*)
Hurry — I'll wait here —
ROXANE (*to* CHRISTIAN)
                Come!
    (*They go into the house.*)
CYRANO   Now then, to make
450 His Grace delay that quarter of an hour . . .
I have it! — up here —
    (*He steps on the bench, and climbs up the
    wall toward the balcony. The theorbos begin
    to play a mournful melody.*)
        Sad music — Ah, a man! . . .
    (*The music pauses on a sinister tremolo.*)
Oh — very much a man!
    (*He sits astride of the railing and, drawing
    toward him a long branch of one of the trees
    which border the garden wall, he grasps it
    with both hands, ready to swing himself
    down.*)
So — not too high —
    (*He peers down at the ground.*)
I must float gently through the atmosphere —

DE GUICHE (*Enters, masked, groping in the dark toward the house.*)

Where is that cursed, bleating Capuchin?

CYRANO What if he knows my voice? — the devil! — Tic-tac,

455 Bergerac — we unlock our Gascon tongue;
A good strong accent —

DE GUICHE Here is the house — all dark —
Damn this mask! —

(*As he is about to enter the house,* CYRANO *leaps from the balcony, still holding fast to the branch, which bends and swings him between* DE GUICHE *and the door; then he releases the branch and pretends to fall heavily as though from a height. He lands flatlong on the ground, where he lies motionless, as if stunned.* DE GUICHE *leaps back.*)

What is that?

(*When he lifts his eyes, the branch has sprung back into place. He can see nothing but the sky; he does not understand.*)

Why . . . where did this man
Fall from?

CYRANO (*Sits up, and speaks with a strong accent.*)

—The moon!

DE GUICHE You —

CYRANO From the moon, the moon!
I fell out of the moon!

DE GUICHE The fellow is mad —

CYRANO (*dreamily*)

460 Where am I?

DE GUICHE Why —

CYRANO What time is it? What place
Is this? What day? What season?

DE GUICHE You —

CYRANO I am stunned!

DE GUICHE My dear sir —

CYRANO Like a bomb — a bomb — I fell
From the moon!

DE GUICHE Now, see here —

CYRANO (*Rising to his feet, and speaking in a terrible voice.*)

I say, the moon!

DE GUICHE (*recoils*)

Very well — if you say so —

(*aside*)

Raving mad! —

CYRANO (*Advancing upon him.*)

465 I am not speaking metaphorically!

DE GUICHE Pardon.

CYRANO A hundred years — an hour ago —
I really cannot say how long I fell —
I was in yonder shining sphere —

DE GUICHE (*shrugs*)

Quite so.
Please let me pass.

CYRANO (*Interposes himself.*)

Where am I? Tell the truth —

470 I can bear it. In what quarter of the globe
Have I descended like a meteorite?

DE GUICHE Morbleu!

CYRANO I could not choose my place
to fall —
The earth spun round so fast — Was it the Earth,
I wonder? — Or is this another world?

475 Another moon? Whither have I been drawn
By the dead weight of my posterior?

DE GUICHE Sir, I repeat —

CYRANO (*With a sudden cry, which causes* DE GUICHE *to recoil again.*)

His face! My God — black!

DE GUICHE (*Carries his hand to his mask.*)

Oh! —

CYRANO (*terrified*)

Are you a native? Is this Africa?

DE GUICHE —This mask!

CYRANO (*somewhat reassured*)

Are we in Venice? Genoa?

DE GUICHE (*Tries to pass him.*)

480 A lady is waiting for me.

CYRANO (*quite happy again*)

So this is Paris!

DE GUICHE (*Smiling in spite of himself.*)

This fool becomes amusing.

CYRANO Ah! You smile?

DE GUICHE I do. Kindly permit me —

CYRANO (*delighted*)

Dear old Paris —
Well, well! —

(*Wholly at his ease, smiles, bows, arranges his dress.*)

Excuse my appearance. I arrive

485 By the last thunderbolt — a trifle singed
As I came through the ether. These long
journeys —
You know! There are so few conveniences!
My eyes are full of star-dust. On my spurs,
Some sort of fur . . . Planet's apparently . . .
    (*Plucks something from his sleeve.*)
490 Look — on my doublet — That's a Comet's hair!
    (*He blows something from the back of his
    hand.*)
Phoo!

DE GUICHE (*Grows angry.*)
    Monsieur —

CYRANO (*As* DE GUICHE *is about to push past,
    thrusts his leg in the way.*)
                Here's a tooth, stuck in my boot,
From the Great Bear. Trying to get away,
I tripped over the Scorpion and came down
Slap, into one scale of the Balances —
495 The pointer marks my weight this moment . . .
    (*Pointing upward.*)
                            See?
    (DE GUICHE *makes a sudden movement.*
    CYRANO *catches his arm.*)
Be careful! If you struck me on the nose,
It would drip milk!

DE GUICHE   Milk?

CYRANO   From the Milky Way!

DE GUICHE Hell!

CYRANO   No, no — Heaven.
    (*Crossing his arms.*)
                Curious place up there —
Did you know Sirius wore a nightcap? True!
    (*confidentially*)
500 The Little Bear is still too young to bite.
    (*laughing*)
My foot caught in the Lyre, and broke a string.
    (*proudly*)
Well — when I write my book, and tell the tale
Of my adventures — all these little stars
That shake out of my cloak — I must save those
505 To use for asterisks!

DE GUICHE   That will do now —

I wish —

CYRANO   Yes, yes — I know —

DE GUICHE   Sir —

CYRANO   You desire
To learn from my own lips the character
Of the moon's surface — its inhabitants
If any —

DE GUICHE (*Loses patience and shouts.*)
    I desire no such thing! I —

CYRANO (*rapidly*)
510 You wish to know by what mysterious means
I reached the moon? — well — confidentially —
It was a new invention of my own.

DE GUICHE (*discouraged*)
    Drunk too — as well as mad!

CYRANO   I scorned the eagle
Of Regiomontanus, and the dove
515 Of Archytas![3]

DE GUICHE   A learned lunatic! —

CYRANO I imitated no one. I myself
Discovered not one scheme merely, but six —
Six ways to violate the virgin sky!
    (DE GUICHE *has succeeded in passing him,
    and moves toward the door of* ROXANE'S
    house. CYRANO *follows, ready to use violence
    if necessary.*)

DE GUICHE (*Looks around.*)
    Six?

CYRANO (*with increasing volubility*)
                As for instance — Having stripped
                myself
520 Bare as a wax candle, adorn my form
With crystal vials filled with morning dew,
And so be drawn aloft, as the sun rises
Drinking the mist of dawn!

DE GUICHE (*Takes a step toward* CYRANO.)
                Yes — that makes one.

CYRANO (*Draws back to lead him away from the
    door; speaks faster and faster.*)
    Or, sealing up the air in a cedar chest,
525 Rarefy it by means of mirrors, placed
In an icosahedron.

DE GUICHE (*Takes another step.*)
    Two.

---

3. **eagle . . . Archytas:** Two famous examples in the history of mechanization. The ancient Greek philosopher Archytas created an automaton that resembled a dove and at the pull of a string would fly from a low perch to a high one; later, the German inventor Regiomontanus reportedly constructed a clockwork wooden eagle that flew, saluted the emperor, and returned to its master. —Eds.

CYRANO (*still retreating*)
> Again,
I might construct a rocket, in the form
Of a huge locust, driven by impulses
Of villainous saltpetre from the rear,
530 Upward, by leaps and bounds.
DE GUICHE (*Interested in spite of himself, and
> counting on his fingers.*)
>> Three.
CYRANO (*same business*)
>> Or again,
Smoke having a natural tendency to rise,
Blow in a globe enough to raise me.
DE GUICHE (*Same business, more and more
> astonished.*)
>> Four!
CYRANO Or since Diana, as old fables tell,
Draws forth to fill her crescent horn, the
> marrow
535 Of bulls and goats — to annoint myself
> therewith.
DE GUICHE (*hypnotised*)
Five! —
CYRANO (*Has by this time led him all the way
> across the street, close to a bench.*)
>> Finally — seated on an iron plate,
To hurl a magnet in the air — the iron
Follows — I catch the magnet — throw again —
And so proceed indefinitely.
DE GUICHE Six! —
540 All excellent, — and which did you adopt?
CYRANO (*coolly*)
Why, none of them. . . . A seventh.
DE GUICHE Which was? —
CYRANO Guess! —
DE GUICHE An interesting idiot, this!
CYRANO (*Imitates the sound of waves with his
> voice, and their movement by large, vague
> gestures.*)
>> Hoo! . . . Hoo! . . .
DE GUICHE Well?
CYRANO Have you guessed it yet?
DE GUICHE Why, no.
CYRANO (*grandiloquent*)
> The ocean! . . .
What hour its rising tide seeks the full moon,
545 I laid me on the strand, fresh from the spray,

My head fronting the moonbeams, since the
> hair
Retains moisture — and so I slowly rose
As upon angels' wings, effortlessly,
Upward — then suddenly I felt a shock! —
550 And then . . .
DE GUICHE (*Overcome by curiosity, sits down on
> the bench.*)
>> And then?
CYRANO And then —
(*Changes abruptly to his natural voice.*)
>> The time is up! —
Fifteen minutes, your Grace! — You are now
> free;
And — they are bound — in wedlock.
DE GUICHE (*Leaping up*)
> Am *I* drunk?
That voice . . .
(*The door of* ROXANE's *house opens; lackeys
appear, bearing lighted candles. Lights Up.*
CYRANO *removes his hat.*)
>> And that nose! — Cyrano!
CYRANO (*saluting*)
>> Cyrano! . . .
This very moment, they have exchanged rings.
555 **DE GUICHE** Who?
(*He turns up stage. Tableau: between the
lackeys,* ROXANE *and* CHRISTIAN *appear,
hand in hand. The Capuchin follows them,
smiling.* RAGUENEAU *holds aloft a torch.
The Duenna brings up the rear, in a negli-
gée, and a pleasant flutter of emotion.*)
Zounds!
(*to* ROXANE)
> You? —
(*recognizes* CHRISTIAN)
>> He? —
(*saluting* ROXANE)
>> My sincere compliments!
(*to* CYRANO)
You also, my inventor of machines!
Your rigmarole would have detained a saint
Entering Paradise — decidedly
You must not fail to write that book some
> day!
CYRANO (*bowing*)
560 >> Sir, I engage myself to do so.

(*Leads the bridal pair down to* DE GUICHE *and strokes with great satisfaction his long white beard.*)

My lord,

The handsome couple you — and God — have joined

Together!

DE GUICHE (*Regarding him with a frosty eye.*)

Quite so.

(*Turns to* ROXANE)

Madame, kindly bid

Your . . . husband farewell.

ROXANE Oh! —

DE GUICHE (*to* CHRISTIAN)

Your regiment

Leaves to-night, sir. Report at once!

ROXANE You mean

565 For the front? The war?

DE GUICHE Certainly!

ROXANE I thought

The Cadets were not going —

DE GUICHE Oh yes, they are!

(*Taking out the despatch from his pocket.*)

Here is the order —

(*to* CHRISTIAN)

Baron! Deliver this.

ROXANE (*Throws herself into* CHRISTIAN'S *arms.*)

Christian!

DE GUICHE (*to* CYRANO, *sneering*)

The bridal night is not so near!

CYRANO (*aside*)

Somehow that news fails to disquiet me.

CHRISTIAN (*to* ROXANE)

570 Your lips again . . .

CYRANO There . . . That will do now — Come!

CHRISTIAN (*still holding* ROXANE)

You do not know how hard it is —

CYRANO (*Tries to drag him away.*)

I know!

(*The beating of drums is heard in the distance.*)

DE GUICHE (*up stage*)

The regiment — on the march!

ROXANE (*As* CYRANO *tries to lead* CHRISTIAN *away, follows, and detains them.*)

Take care of him

For me —

(*appealingly*)

Promise me never to let him do

Anything dangerous!

CYRANO I'll do my best —

575 I cannot promise —

ROXANE (*same business*)

Make him be careful!

CYRANO Yes —

I'll try —

ROXANE (*same business*)

Be sure you keep him dry and warm!

CYRANO Yes, yes — if possible —

ROXANE (*same business; confidentially, in his ear*)

See that he remains

Faithful! —

CYRANO Of course! If —

ROXANE (*same business*)

And have him write to me

Every single day!

CYRANO (*stops*)

That, I promise you!

(*Curtain*)

Understanding and Interpreting

1 At the start of Act 3, Cyrano shows off his knowledge of both music and grammar, adding these skills to those we have already seen. To what extent do you think these additional attributes over-idealize Cyrano, or are they qualities shared by most of the men striving to live in accordance with the chivalric code?

2 What does Roxane do in Act 3 to demonstrate that she is a clever strategist? Cite at least two examples.

3 Why is it important that Christian objects to having Cyrano's words presented as his own? What does this objection add to our understanding of his character?

4 During the balcony scene, Cyrano asserts, "[T]o-night, I indeed speak / For the first time!" (ll. 256–257). In what ways is this statement both accurate and ambiguous? How is his avowal of love in this scene different from his declarations in Acts 1 and 2?

5 Why does Cyrano not try to stop the marriage of Roxane and Christian? What is his motivation in assisting them?

6 By this point in the play, is De Guiche depicted as a true villain? What are his motivations? Does he participate in deception to the same degree as Cyrano? Consider his actions in Act 3, along with examples from the two previous acts, to support your response.

Analyzing Language, Style, and Structure

1 The balcony speech shows a highly passionate Cyrano, even though the language is offered as the words and sentiment of Christian. One way Rostand expresses this passion is through binaries or dichotomous relationships—such as light and dark, sun and moon, love and hate, hope and disappointment. What examples of these do you find in the speeches in this scene? What is the overall effect?

2 Rostand develops the scene of Cyrano distracting De Guiche in great detail. Why? What purpose does this scene serve?

3 In Act 3, Rostand employs many conventions of comedy: for instance, physical comedy, hyperbole, irony, gentle satire, slapstick humor, and pathos. Identify several examples and discuss the effect of at least two of them.

Connecting, Arguing, and Extending

1 Does Christian love Roxane? Does she love him? At this point in the play—when the two become husband and wife—what evidence, if any, does Rostand give us that they truly love one another?

2 To what extent can you make the case that Roxane is the victim of her own illusions and expectations, rather than the victim of deliberate deception on the part of Christian and Cyrano? Do you think that she believes Christian is the author of eloquent, literary speeches and letters because she wants to think he is, or is she legitimately persuaded by his words and actions?

3 The balcony scene is one of the most famous scenes in *Cyrano de Bergerac*; some see it as a parody of the even more famous scene in Shakespeare's *Romeo and Juliet*. Is it a parody or a parallel? Explain your response with reference to both texts.

4 In *Roxanne*, the film adaptation of *Cyrano* starring Steve Martin, Chris (Christian) awkwardly searches for the right words to tell Roxanne of his feelings and ends up infuriating her by telling her she has "a great body." C. D. Bales (Cyrano) takes over in the following balcony scene modeled after Rostand's play. View the scene and discuss how it compares to the original. In what ways does Martin give the play his own twentieth-century mark? To what extent do you think Martin captures Rostand's ideas?

Act 4   Cyrano de Bergerac

The Cadets of Gascoyne

The Post occupied by the Company of CARBON DE CASTEL-JALOUX *at The Seige of Arras.*

In the background, a Rampart traversing the entire scene; beyond this, and apparently below, a Plain stretches away to the horizon. The country is cut up with earthworks and other suggestions of the seige. In the distance, against the sky-line, the houses and the walls of Arras.

Tents; scattered Weapons; Drums, etcetera. It is near day-break, and the East is yellow with approaching dawn. Sentries at intervals. Camp-fires.

Curtain Rise discovers the Cadets asleep, rolled in their cloaks. CARBON DE CASTEL-JALOUX *and* LE BRET *keep watch. They are both very thin and pale.* CHRISTIAN *is asleep among the others, wrapped in his cloak, in the foreground, his face lighted by the flickering fire. Silence.*

LE BRET Horrible!

CARBON Why, yes. All of that.

LE BRET Mordious!

CARBON (*gesture toward the sleeping Cadets*)
Swear gently — You might wake them.
(*to Cadets*)
Go to sleep —
Hush!
(*to* LE BRET)
Who sleeps dines.

LE BRET I have insomnia.
God! What a famine.
(*Firing off stage.*)

CARBON Curse that musketry!
5 They'll wake my babies.
(*to the men*)
Go to sleep! —

A CADET (*rouses*)
Diantre!
Again?

CARBON No — only Cyrano coming home.
(*The heads which have been raised sink
back again.*)

A SENTRY (*off stage*)
Halt! Who goes there?

VOICE OF CYRANO Bergerac!

THE SENTRY ON THE PARAPET Halt! Who goes? —

CYRANO (*Appears on the parapet.*)
Bergerac, idiot!

LE BRET (*Goes to meet him.*)
Thank God again!

CYRANO (*Signs to him not to wake anyone.*)
Hush!

LE BRET Wounded? —

CYRANO No — They always miss
me — quite
10 A habit by this time!

LE BRET Yes — Go right on —
Risk your life every morning before breakfast
To send a letter!

CYRANO (*Stops near* CHRISTIAN.)
I promised he should write
Every single day . . .
(*Looks down at him.*)
Hm — The boy looks pale
When he is asleep — thin too — starving
to death —

15 If that poor child knew! Handsome, none the
less . . .

LE BRET Go and get some sleep!

CYRANO (*affectionately*)
Now, now — you old bear,
No growling! — I am careful — you know I am —
Every night, when I cross the Spanish lines
I wait till they are all drunk.

LE BRET You might bring
20 Something with you.

CYRANO I have to travel light
To pass through — By the way, there will be
news
For you to-day: the French will eat or die,
If what I saw means anything.

LE BRET Tell us!

CYRANO No —
I am not sure — we shall see!

CARBON What a war,
25 When the besieger starves to death!

LE BRET Fine war —
Fine situation! We besiege Arras —
The Cardinal Prince of Spain besieges us —
And — here we are!

CYRANO Someone might besiege
him.

CARBON A hungry joke!

CYRANO Ho, ho!

LE BRET Yes, you can laugh —
30 Risking a life like yours to carry letters —
Where are you going now?

CYRANO (*at the tent door*)
To write another.
(*Goes into tent.*)
(*A little more daylight. The clouds redden.
The town of Arras shows on the horizon. A
cannon shot is heard, followed immediately
by a roll of drums, far away to the left. Other
drums beat a little nearer. The drums go on
answering each other here and there,
approach, beat loudly almost on the stage,
and die away toward the right, across the
camp. The camp awakes. Voices of officers in
the distance.*)

CARBON (*sighs*)
Those drums! — another good nourishing
sleep

Gone to the devil.

(*The Cadets rouse themselves.*)

Now then! —

FIRST CADET (*Sits up, yawns.*)

God! I'm hungry!

SECOND CADET Starving!

ALL (*groan*)

Aoh!

CARBON Up with you!

THIRD CADET Not another step!

35 **FOURTH CADET** Not another movement!

FIRST CADET Look at my tongue —
I said this air was indigestible!

FIFTH CADET My coronet for half a pound of
cheese!

SIXTH CADET I have no stomach for this war —
I'll stay
In my tent — like Achilles.

ANOTHER Yes — no bread,

40 No fighting —

CARBON Cyrano!

OTHERS May as well die —

CARBON Come out here! — You know how to talk
to them.
Get them laughing —

SECOND CADET (*Rushes up to First Cadet who is
eating something.*)
What are you gnawing there?

FIRST CADET Gun wads and axle-grease. Fat
country this
Around Arras.

ANOTHER (*enters*)
I have been out hunting!

ANOTHER (*enters*)
I

45 Went fishing, in the Scarpe!

ALL (*Leaping up and surrounding the
newcomers.*)
Find anything?
Any fish? Any game? Perch? Partridges?
Let me look!

THE FISHERMAN Yes — one gudgeon.
(*Shows it.*)

THE HUNTES One fat . . . sparrow.
(*Shows it.*)

ALL Ah! — See here, this — mutiny! —

CARBON Cyrano!

Come and help!

CYRANO (*Enters from tent.*)
Well?
(*Silence. To the First Cadet who is walking
away, with his chin on his chest.*)
You there, with the long face?

50 **FIRST CADET** I have something on my mind that
troubles me.

CYRANO What is that?

FIRST CADET My stomach.

CYRANO So have I.

FIRST CADET No doubt
You enjoy this!

CYRANO (*Tightens his belt.*)
It keeps me looking young.

SECOND CADET My teeth are growing rusty.

CYRANO Sharpen them!

THIRD CADET My belly sounds as hollow as a
drum.

55 **CYRANO** Beat the long roll on it!

FOURTH CADET My ears are
ringing.

CYRANO Liar! A hungry belly has no ears.

FIFTH CADET Oh for a barrel of good
wine!

CYRANO (*Offers him his own helmet.*)
Your casque.

SIXTH CADET I'll swallow anything!

CYRANO (*Throws him the book which he has in
his hand.*)
Try the *Iliad*.

SEVENTH CADET The Cardinal, he has four meals
a day —

60 What does he care!

CYRANO Ask him; he really ought
To send you . . . a spring lamb out of his flock,
Roasted whole —

THE CADET Yes, and a bottle —

CYRANO (*Exaggerates the manner of one speaking
to a servant.*)
If you please,
Richelieu — a little more of the Red Seal . . .
Ah, thank you!

THE CADET And the salad —

CYRANO Of course — Romaine!

ANOTHER CADET (*shivering*)

65 I am as hungry as a wolf.

CYRANO (*Tosses him a cloak.*)
                    Put on
Your sheep's clothing.
FIRST CADET (*with a shrug*)
                    Always the clever answer!
CYRANO Always the answer — yes! Let me die so —
Under some rosy-golden sunset, saying
A good thing, for a good cause! By the sword,
70 The point of honor — by the hand of one
Worthy to be my foeman, let me fall —
Steel in my heart, and laughter on my lips!
VOICES HERE AND THERE All very well — We are
        hungry!
CYRANO   Bah! You think
Of nothing but yourselves.
        (*His eye singles out the old fifer in the
        background.*)
                    Here, Bertrandou,
75 You were a shepherd once — Your pipe now!
        Come,
Breathe, blow, — Play to these
        belly-worshippers
The old airs of the South —
                    Airs with a smile in them,
Airs with a sigh in them, airs with the breeze
And the blue of the sky in them —
                    Small, demure tunes
80 Whose every note is like a little sister —
Songs heard only in some long silent voice
Not quite forgotten — Mountain melodies
Like thin smoke rising from brown cottages
In the still noon, slowly — Quaint lullabies,
85 Whose very music has a Southern tongue —
        (*The old man sits down and prepares his fife.*)
Now let the fife, that dry old warrior,
Dream, while over the stops your fingers
        dance
A minuet of little birds — let him
Dream beyond ebony and ivory;
90 Let him remember he was once a reed
Out of the river, and recall the spirit
Of innocent, untroubled country days . . .
        (*The fifer begins to play a Provençal melody.*)
Listen, you Gascons! Now it is no more

The shrill fife — It is the flute, through wood-
        lands far
95 Away, calling — no longer the hot battle-cry,
But the cool, quiet pipe our goatherds play!
Listen — the forest glens . . . the hills . . . the
        downs . . .
The green sweetness of night on the Dordogne . . .
Listen, you Gascons! It is all Gascoyne! . . .
        (*Every head is bowed; every eye cast down.
        Here and there a tear is furtively brushed
        away with the back of a hand, the corner of
        a cloak.*)
CARBON (*softly to* CYRANO)
100 You make them weep —
CYRANO   For homesickness—
        a hunger
More noble than that hunger of the flesh;
It is their hearts now that are starving.
CARBON   Yes,
But you melt down their manhood.
CYRANO (*Motions the drummer to approach.*)
                    You think so?
Let them be. There is iron in their blood
105 Not easily dissolved in tears. You need
Only —
        (*He makes a gesture; the drum beats.*)
ALL (*Spring up and rush toward their weapons.*)
        What's that? Where is it? — What? —
CYRANO (*smiles*)
                    You see —
Let Mars snore in his sleep once — and farewell
Venus — sweet dreams — regrets — dear
        thoughts of home —
All the fife lulls to rest wakes at the drums!
A CADET (*Looks up stage.*)
110 Aha — Monsieur de Guiche!
THE CADETS (*Mutter among themselves.*)
                    Ugh! . . .
CYRANO (*smiles*)
                              Flattering
Murmur!
A CADET   He makes me weary!
ANOTHER   With his collar
Of lace over his corselet[1] —

---

1. **corselet:** Armor that covers the torso; a breastplate. —Eds.

ANOTHER Like a ribbon
Tied round a sword!

ANOTHER Bandages for a boil
On the back of his neck —

SECOND CADET A courtier always!

115 **ANOTHER** The Cardinal's nephew!
None the less — a Gascon.

CARBON FIRST CADET

A counterfeit! Never you trust that man —
Because we Gascons, look you, are all mad —
This fellow is reasonable — nothing more
Dangerous than a reasonable Gascon!

120 **LE BRET** He looks pale.

ANOTHER Oh, he can be hungry too,
Like any other poor devil — but he wears
So many jewels on that belt of his
That his cramps glitter in the sun!

CYRANO (*quickly*)
Is he
To see us looking miserable? Quick —
125 Pipes! — Cards! — Dice! —
(*They all hurriedly begin to play, on their
stools, on the drums, or on their cloaks
spread on the ground, lighting their long
pipes meanwhile.*)
As for me, I read Descartes.
(*He walks up and down, reading a small
book which he takes from his pocket.
Tableau:* De Guiche *enters, looking pale
and haggard. All are absorbed in their games.
General air of contentment.* De Guiche *goes
to* Carbon. *They look at each other askance,
each observing with satisfaction the condition
of the other.*)

DE GUICHE Good morning!
(*aside*)
He looks yellow.

CARBON (*same business*)
He is all eyes.

DE GUICHE (*Looks at the Cadets.*)
What have we here? Black looks? Yes,
gentlemen —
I am informed I am not popular;
The hill-nobility, barons of Béarn,
130 The pomp and pride of Périgord — I learn
They disapprove their colonel; call him courtier,
Politician — they take it ill that I

Cover my steel with lace of Genoa.
It is a great offense to be a Gascon
135 And not to be a beggar!
(*Silence. They smoke. They play.*)
Well — Shall I have
Your captain punish you? . . . No.

CARBON As to that,
It would be impossible.

DE GUICHE Oh?

CARBON I am free;
I pay my company; it is my own;
I obey military orders.

DE GUICHE Oh!
140 That will be quite enough.
(*to the Cadets*)
I can afford
Your little hates. My conduct under fire
Is well known. It was only yesterday
I drove the Count de Bucquoi from Bapaume,
Pouring my men down like an avalanche,
145 I myself led the charge —

CYRANO (*Without looking up from his book.*)
And your white scarf?

DE GUICHE (*surprised and gratified*)
You heard that episode? Yes — rallying
My men for the third time, I found myself
Carried among a crowd of fugitives
Into the enemy's lines. I was in danger
150 Of being shot or captured; but I thought
Quickly — took off and flung away the scarf
That marked my military rank — and so
Being inconspicuous, escaped among
My own force, rallied them, returned again
155 And won the day! . . .
(*The Cadets do not appear to be listening,
but here and there the cards and the dice
boxes remain motionless, the smoke is
retained in their cheeks.*)
What do you say to that?
Presence of mind — yes?

CYRANO Henry of Navarre
Being outnumbered, never flung away
His white plume.
(*Silent enjoyment. The cards flutter, the dice
roll, the smoke puffs out.*)

DE GUICHE My device was a success,
However!

(Same attentive pause, interrupting the games and the smoking.)

CYRANO   Possibly . . . An officer
160 Does not lightly resign the privilege
Of being a target.
        (Cards, dice, and smoke fall, roll, and float away with increasing satisfaction.)
                        Now, if I had been there —
Your courage and my own differ in this —
When your scarf fell, I should have put it on.

DE GUICHE Boasting again!

CYRANO   Boasting? Lend it to me
165 To-night; I'll lead the first charge, with your
        scarf
Over my shoulder!

DE GUICHE   Gasconnade once more!
You are safe making that offer, and you
        know it —
My scarf lies on the river bank between
The lines, a spot swept by artillery
170 Impossible to reach alive!

CYRANO *(Produces the scarf from his pocket.)*
                        Yes. Here . . .
        (Silence. The Cadets stifle their laughter behind their cards and their dice boxes. DE GUICHE turns to look at them. Immediately they resume their gravity and their game. One of them whistles carelessly the mountain air which the fifer was playing.)

DE GUICHE *(Takes the scarf.)*
Thank you! That bit of white is what I need
To make a signal. I was hesitating —
You have decided me.
        (He goes up to the parapet, climbs upon it, and waves the scarf at arm's length several times.)

ALL   What is he doing? —
What? —

CARBON *(to the Cadets)*
                        Well,
175 Gentlemen!
        (All rise. Noise of sword belts and breast-plates being buckled on.)

DE GUICHE   You may have perhaps an
        hour.

FIRST CADET Oh — An hour!
        (They all sit down and resume their games once more.)

DE GUICHE *(to* CARBON*)*
                        The great thing is to gain time.
Any moment the Marshal may return.

CARBON And to gain time?

DE GUICHE   You will all be so kind
As to lay down your lives!

CYRANO   Ah! Your revenge?

180 DE GUICHE I make no great pretence of loving
        you!
But — since you gentlemen esteem yourselves
Invincible, the bravest of the brave,
And all that — why need we be personal?
I serve the king in choosing . . . as I choose!

CYRANO *(salutes)*
185 Sir, permit me to offer — all our thanks.

DE GUICHE *(Returns the salute.)*
You love to fight a hundred against one;
Here is your opportunity!
        (He goes up stage with CARBON*.)*

CYRANO *(to the Cadets)*
                        My friends,
We shall add now to our old Gascon arms
With their six chevrons, blue and gold,
        a seventh —
190 Blood-red!
        (DE GUICHE talks in a low tone to CARBON up stage. Orders are given. The defense is arranged. CYRANO goes to CHRISTIAN who has remained motionless with folded arms.)
                        Christian?
        (Lays a hand on his shoulder.)

CHRISTIAN *(Shakes his head.)*
                        Roxane . . .

CYRANO   Yes.

CHRISTIAN   I should like
To say farewell to her, with my whole heart
Written for her to keep.

CYRANO   I thought of that —
        (Takes a letter from his doublet.)
I have written your farewell.

CHRISTIAN   Show me!

CYRANO   You wish
To read it?

CHRISTIAN Of course!
        (He takes the letter; begins to read, looks up suddenly.)
                        What? —

CYRANO   What is it?

CHRISTIAN   Look—

195   This little circle—

CYRANO (*Takes back the letter quickly, and looks innocent.*)

                    Circle?—

CHRISTIAN   Yes—a tear!

CYRANO So it is! . . . Well—a poet while he writes
Is like a lover in his lady's arms,
Believing his imagination—all
Seems true—you understand? There's half
    the charm

200   Of writing—Now, this letter as you see
I have made so pathetic that I wept
While I was writing it!

CHRISTIAN   You—wept?

CYRANO   Why, yes—
Because . . . it is a little thing to die,
But—not to see her . . . that is terrible!

205   And I shall never—
        (CHRISTIAN *looks at him.*)
                    We shall never—
        (*quickly*)
                            You
Will never—

CHRISTIAN (*Snatches the letter.*)
                    Give me that!
        (*noise in the distance on the outskirts of the camp*)

VOICE OF A SENTRY   Halt—who goes
    there?
        (*shots, shouting, jingle of harness*)

CARBON What is it?—

THE SENTRY ON THE PARAPET Why, a coach.
        (*They rush to look.*)

CONFUSED VOICES   What? In the Camp?
A coach? Coming this way—It must have
    driven
Through the Spanish lines—what the devil—
Fire!—

210   No—Hark! The driver shouting—what does
    he say?
Wait—He said: "On the service of the King!"
        (*They are all on the parapet looking over.
        The jingling comes nearer.*)

DE GUICHE Of the King?
        (*They come down and fall into line.*)

CARBON   Hats off, all!

DE GUICHE (*Speaks off stage.*)
                    The King! Fall in,
    Rascals!—
        (*The coach enters at full trot. It is covered
        with mud and dust. The curtains are drawn.
        Two footmen are seated behind. It stops
        suddenly.*)

CARBON (*shouts*)
            Beat the assembly—
        (*Roll of drums. All the Cadets uncover.*)

DE GUICHE   Two of you,
    Lower the steps—open the door—
        (*Two men rush to the coach. The door
        opens.*)

ROXANE (*Comes out of the coach.*)
                    Good morning!
        (*At the sound of a woman's voice, every
        head is raised. Sensation.*)

215 **DE GUICHE** On the King's service—You?

ROXANE   Yes—my own king—
    Love!

CYRANO (*aside*)
        God is merciful . . .

CHRISTIAN (*Hastens to her.*)
                    You! Why have you—

ROXANE Your war lasted so long!

CHRISTIAN   But why?—

ROXANE   Not now—

CYRANO (*aside*)
        I wonder if I dare to look at her . . .

DE GUICHE You cannot remain here!

ROXANE   Why, certainly!

220   Roll that drum here, somebody . . .
        (*She sits on the drum, which is brought to
        her.*)
                    Thank you—There!
        (*She laughs.*)
    Would you believe—they fired upon us?
                    —My coach
    Looks like the pumpkin in the fairy tale,
    Does it not? And my footmen—
        (*She throws a kiss to* CHRISTIAN.)
                    How do you do?
        (*She looks about.*)
    How serious you all are! Do you know,

225   It is a long drive here—from Arras?

(*Sees* CYRANO.)

                            Cousin,

I am glad to see you!

CYRANO (*advances*)

                       Oh — How did you come?

ROXANE How did I find you? Very easily —

I followed where the country was laid waste

— Oh, but I saw such things! I had to see

230   To believe. Gentlemen, is that the service

Of your King? I prefer my own!

CYRANO   But how

Did you come through?

ROXANE   Why, through the Spanish lines

Of course!

FIRST CADET   They let you pass? —

DE GUICHE   What did you say?

How did you manage?

LE BRET   Yes, that must have been

235   Difficult!

ROXANE   No — I simply drove along.

Now and then some hidalgo scowled at me

And I smiled back — my best smile; whereupon,

The Spaniards being (without prejudice

To the French) the most polished gentlemen

240   In the world — I passed!

CARBON   Certainly that smile

Should be a passport! Did they never ask

Your errand or your destination?

ROXANE   Oh,

Frequently! Then I drooped my eyes and said:

"I have a lover . . ." Whereupon, the Spaniard

245   With an air of ferocious dignity

Would close the carriage door — with such a gesture

As any king might envy, wave aside

The muskets that were levelled at my breast,

Fall back three paces, equally superb

250   In grace and gloom, draw himself up, thrust forth

A spur under his cloak, sweeping the air

With his long plumes, bow very low, and say:

"Pass, Senorita!"

CHRISTIAN   But Roxane —

ROXANE   I know —

I said "a lover" — but you understand —

255   Forgive me! — If I said "I am going to meet

My husband," no one would believe me!

CHRISTIAN   Yes,

But —

ROXANE   What then?

DE GUICHE   You must leave this place.

CYRANO   At once.

ROXANE I?

LE BRET Yes — immediately.

ROXANE   And why?

CHRISTIAN (*embarrassed*)

                 Because . . .

CYRANO (*same*)

In half an hour . . .

DE GUICHE (*same*)

            Or three quarters . . .

CARBON (*same*)

                  Perhaps

260   It might be better . . .

LE BRET   If you . . .

ROXANE   Oh — I see!

You are going to fight. I remain here.

ALL   No — no!

ROXANE He is my husband —

(*Throws herself in* CHRISTIAN's *arms.*)

I will die with you!

CHRISTIAN Your eyes! . . . Why do you? —

ROXANE   You know why . . .

DE GUICHE (*desperate*)

               This post

Is dangerous —

ROXANE (*turns*)

        How — dangerous?

CYRANO   The proof

265   Is, we are ordered —

ROXANE (*to* DE GUICHE)

           Oh — you wish to make

A widow of me?

DE GUICHE   On my word of honor —

ROXANE No matter. I am just a little mad —

I will stay. It may be amusing.

CYRANO   What,

A heroine — our intellectual?

270 ROXANE Monsieur de Bergerac, I am your cousin!

A CADET We'll fight now! Hurrah!

ROXANE (*more and more excited*)

        I am safe with you — my friends!

ANOTHER (*carried away*)

    The whole camp breathes of lilies! —

ROXANE And I think,

    This hat would look well on the battlefield! . . .

    But perhaps —

        (*Looks at* DE GUICHE.)

        The Count ought to leave us. Any moment

275 Now, there may be danger.

DE GUICHE This is too much!

    I must inspect my guns. I shall return —

    You may change your mind — There will yet be time —

ROXANE Never!

        (DE GUICHE *goes out.*)

CHRISTIAN (*imploring*)

        Roxane! . . .

ROXANE No!

FIRST CADET (*to the rest*)

        She stays here!

ALL (*Rushing about, elbowing each other, brushing off their clothes.*)

        A comb! —

    Soap! — Here's a hole in my — A needle! — Who

280 Has a ribbon? — Your mirror, quick! — My cuffs —

    A razor —

ROXANE (*to* CYRANO, *who is still urging her*)

        No! I shall not stir one step!

CARBON (*Having, like the others, tightened his belt, dusted himself, brushed off his hat, smoothed out his plume and put on his lace cuffs, advances to* ROXANE *ceremoniously.*)

    In that case, may I not present to you

    Some of these gentlemen who are to have

    The honor of dying in your presence?

ROXANE (*bows*)

        Please! —

        (*She waits, standing, on the arm of* CHRISTIAN, *while*)

CARBON (*—presents*)

285 Baron de Peyrescous de Colignac!

THE CADET (*salutes*)

    Madame . . .

ROXANE Monsieur . . .

CARBON (*continues*)

        Baron de Casterac

    De Cahuzac — Vidame de Malgouyre

    Estressac Lésbas d'Escarabiot —

THE VIDAME Madame . . .

CARBON Chevalier d'Antignac-Juzet —

290 Baron Hillot de Blagnac-Saléchan

    De Castel-Crabioules —

THE BARON Madame . . .

ROXANE How many

    Names you all have!

THE BARON Hundreds!

CARBON (*to* ROXANE)

        Open the hand

    That holds your handkerchief.

ROXANE (*Opens her hand; the handkerchief falls.*)

        Why?

        (*The whole company makes a movement toward it.*)

CARBON (*Picks it up quickly.*)

        My company

    Was in want of a banner. We have now

295 The fairest in the army!

ROXANE (*smiling*)

        Rather small —

CARBON (*Fastens the handkerchief to his lance.*)

    Lace — and embroidered!

A CADET (*to the others*)

        With her smiling on me,

    I could die happy, if I only had

    Something in my —

CARBON (*turns upon him*)

        Shame on you! Feast your eyes

    And forget your —

ROXANE (*quickly*)

        It must be this fresh air —

300 I am starving! Let me see . . .

        Cold partridges,

    Pastry, a little white wine — that would do.

    Will some one bring that to me?

A CADET (*aside*)

        Will some one! —

ANOTHER Where the devil are we to find —

ROXANE (*overhears; sweetly*)

        Why, there —

    In my carriage.

ALL Wha-at?

ROXANE All you have to do

305 Is to unpack, and carve, and serve things.

        Oh,

Notice my coachman; you may recognize
An old friend.

THE CADETS (*Rush to the coach.*)
Ragueneau!

ROXANE (*Follows them with her eyes.*)
Poor fellows . . .

THE CADETS (*acclamations*)
Ah!
Ah!

CYRANO (*Kisses her hand.*)
Our good fairy!

RAGUENEAU (*Standing on his box, like a mounte-
bank before a crowd.*)
Gentlemen! —
(*enthusiasm*)

THE CADETS   Bravo!
Bravo!

RAGUENEAU The Spaniards, basking in our
smiles,
310   Smiled on our baskets!
(*applause*)

CYRANO (*aside, to* CHRISTIAN)
Christian! —

RAGUENEAU   They adored
The Fair, and missed —
(*He takes from under the seat a dish, which
he holds aloft.*)
the Fowl!
(*Applause. The dish is passed from hand to
hand.*)

CYRANO (*as before, to* CHRISTIAN)
One moment —

RAGUENEAU   Venus
Charmed their eyes, while Adonis quietly
(*Brandishing a ham.*)
Brought home the Boar!
(*Applause; the ham is seized by a score of
hands outstretched.*)

CYRANO (*as before*)
Pst — Let me speak to you —

ROXANE (*as the Cadets return, their arms full of
provisions*)
Spread them out on the ground.
(*calls*)
Christian! Come here;

315   Make yourself useful.
(CHRISTIAN *turns to her, at the moment
when* CYRANO *was leading him aside. She
arranges the food, with his aid and that of
the two imperturbable footmen.*)

RAGUENEAU   Peacock, *aux truffes!*

FIRST CADET (*Comes down, cutting a huge slice of
the ham.*)
Tonnerre!
We are not going to die without a gorge —
(*Sees* ROXANE; *corrects himself hastily.*)
Pardon — a banquet!

RAGUENEAU (*Tossing out the cushions of the
carriage.*)
Open these — they are full
Of ortolans![2]
(*Tumult; laughter; the cushions are
eviscerated.*)

THIRD CADET   Lucullus!

RAGUENEAU (*Throws out bottles of red wine.*)
Flasks of ruby —
(*and of white*)
Flasks of topaz —

ROXANE (*Throws a tablecloth at the head of
CYRANO.*)
Come back out of your dreams!
320   Unfold this cloth —

RAGUENEAU (*Takes off one of the lanterns of the
carriage, and flourishes it.*)
Our lamps are bonbonnières![3]

CYRANO (*to* CHRISTIAN)
I must see you before you speak with her —

RAGUENEAU (*more and more lyrical*)
My whip-handle is one long sausage!

ROXANE (*Pouring wine; passing the food.*)
We
Being about to die, first let us dine!
Never mind the others — all for Gascoyne!
325   And if de Guiche comes, he is not invited!
(*Going from one to another.*)
Plenty of time — you need not eat so fast —
Hold your cup —
(*to another*)
What's the matter?

THE CADET (*sobbing*)

---

2. **ortolans:** Small songbirds. —Eds.   3. **bonbonnières:** Trays of bonbons, which are small pastries or confections. —Eds.

You are so good

To us . . .

ROXANE There, there! Red or white wine?
— Some bread

For Monsieur de Carbon! — Napkins —

A knife —

330 Pass your plate — Some of the crust? A little
more —

Light or dark? — Burgundy? —

CYRANO (*Follows her with an armful of dishes,
helping to serve.*)

Adorable!

ROXANE (*Goes to* CHRISTIAN.)

What would you like?

CHRISTIAN Nothing.

ROXANE Oh, but you must! —

A little wine? A biscuit?

CHRISTIAN Tell me first

Why you came —

ROXANE By and by. I must take care

Of these poor boys —

LE BRET (*Who has gone up stage to pass up food
to the sentry on the parapet, on the end of a
lance.*)

De Guiche! —

CYRANO Hide everything

Quick! — Dishes, bottles, tablecloth —

Now look

Hungry again —

(*to* RAGUENEAU)

You there! Up on your box —

— Everything out of sight? —

(*In a twinkling, everything has been pushed
inside the tents, hidden in their hats or
under their cloaks.* DE GUICHE *enters
quickly, then stops, sniffing the air. Silence.*)

DE GUICHE It smells good here.

A CADET (*Humming with an air of great
unconcern.*)

Sing ha-ha-ha and ho-ho-ho —

DE GUICHE (*Stares at him; he grows embarrassed.*)

You there —

335 What are you blushing for?

THE CADET Nothing — my blood

Stirs at the thought of battle.

ANOTHER *Pom . . . pom . . . pom! . . .*

DE GUICHE (*Turns upon him.*)

What is that?

THE CADET (*slightly stimulated*)

Only song — only little song —

DE GUICHE You appear happy!

THE CADET Oh yes — always happy

Before a fight —

DE GUICHE (*Calls to* CARBON, *for the purpose of
giving him an order.*)

Captain! I —

(*Stops and looks at him.*)

What the devil —

340 You are looking happy too! —

CARBON (*Pulls a long face and hides a bottle
behind his back.*)

No!

DE GUICHE Here — I had

One gun remaining. I have had it placed

(*He points off stage.*)

There — in that corner — for your men.

A CADET (*simpering*)

So kind! —

Charming attention!

ANOTHER (*same business; burlesque*)

Sweet solicitude! —

DE GUICHE (*contemptuous*)

I believe you are both drunk —

(*coldly*)

Being unaccustomed

345 To guns — take care of the recoil!

FIRST CADET (*gesture*)

Ah-h . . . Pfft!

DE GUICHE (*Goes up to him, furious.*)

How dare you?

FIRST CADET A Gascon's gun never recoils!

DE GUICHE (*Shakes him by the arm.*)

You *are* drunk —

FIRST CADET (*superbly*)

With the smell of powder!

DE GUICHE (*Turns away with a shrug.*)

Bah!

(*to* ROXANE)

Madame, have you decided?

ROXANE I stay here.

DE GUICHE You have time to escape —

ROXANE No!

DE GUICHE Very well —

350 Someone give me a musket!

CARBON   What?

DE GUICHE   *I* stay

Here also.

CYRANO (*formally*)

        Sir, you show courage!

FIRST CADET   A Gascon

In spite of all that lace!

ROXANE   Why —

DE GUICHE   Must I run

Away, and leave a woman?

SECOND CADET (*to* FIRST CADET)

        We might give him

Something to eat — what do you say?

        (*All the food re-appears, as if by magic.*)

DE GUICHE (*His face lights up.*)

        A feast!

355 THIRD CADET *Here a little, there a little —*

DE GUICHE (*Recovers his self-control; haughtily.*)

        Do you think

I want your leavings?

CYRANO (*saluting*)

        Colonel — you improve!

DE GUICHE I can fight as I am!

FIRST CADET (*delighted*)

        Listen to him —

He has an accent!

DE GUICHE (*laughs*)

        Have I so?

FIRST CADET   A Gascon! —

A Gascon, after all!

        (*They all begin to dance.*)

CARBON (*Who has disappeared for a moment
        behind the parapet, reappears on top of it.*)

        I have placed my pikemen

360 Here.

        (*Indicates a row of pikes showing above the
        parapet.*)

DE GUICHE (*Bows to* ROXANE.)

We'll review them; will you take my arm?

        (*She takes his arm; they go up on the para-
        pet. The rest uncover, and follow them up
        stage.*)

CHRISTIAN (*Goes hurriedly to* CYRANO.)

Speak quickly!

        (*At the moment when* ROXANE *appears on
        the parapet the pikes are lowered in salute,
        and a cheer is heard. She bows.*)

THE PIKEMEN (*off stage*)

        Hurrah!

CHRISTIAN   What is it?

CYRANO   If Roxane . . .

CHRISTIAN Well?

CYRANO   Speaks about your letters . . .

CHRISTIAN   Yes — I know!

CYRANO Do not make the mistake of showing . . .

CHRISTIAN   What?

CYRANO Showing surprise.

CHRISTIAN   Surprise — why?

CYRANO   I must tell you! . . .

365 It is quite simple — I had forgotten it

Until just now. You have . . .

CHRISTIAN   Speak quickly! —

CYRANO   You

Have written oftener than you think.

CHRISTIAN   Oh — have I!

CYRANO I took upon me to interpret you;

And wrote — sometimes . . . without . . .

CHRISTIAN   My knowing. Well?

370 CYRANO Perfectly simple!

CHRISTIAN   Oh yes, perfectly! —

For a month, we have been blockaded here! —

How did you send all these letters?

CYRANO   Before

Daylight, I managed —

CHRISTIAN   I see. That was also

Perfectly simple!

        — So I wrote to her,

375 How many times a week? Twice? Three times?

Four?

CYRANO Oftener.

CHRISTIAN   Every day?

CYRANO   Yes — every day . . .

Every single day . . .

CHRISTIAN (*violently*)

        And that wrought you up

Into such a flame that you faced death —

CYRANO (*Sees* ROXANE *returning.*)

        Hush —

Not before her!

        (*He goes quickly into the tent.* ROXANE
        comes up to CHRISTIAN.)

ROXANE   Now — Christian!

CHRISTIAN (*Takes her hands.*)

        Tell me now

380 Why you came here — over these ruined
  roads —
Why you made your way among
  mosstroopers[4]
And ruffians — you — to join me here?

ROXANE   Because —
Your letters . . .

CHRISTIAN   Meaning?

ROXANE   It was your own fault
If I ran into danger! I went mad —
385 Mad with you! Think what you have written
  me,
How many times, each one more wonderful
Than the last!

CHRISTIAN   All this for a few absurd
Love-letters —

ROXANE   Hush — absurd! How can you know?
I thought I loved you, ever since one night
390 When a voice that I never would have known
Under my window breathed your soul to
  me . . .
But — all this time, your letters — every one
Was like hearing your voice there in the dark,
All around me, like your arms around me . . .
  (*more lightly*)
        At last,
395 I came. Anyone would! Do you suppose
The prim Penelope had stayed at home
Embroidering, — if Ulysses wrote like you?
She would have fallen like another Helen —
Tucked up those linen petticoats of hers
400 And followed him to Troy!

CHRISTIAN   But you —

ROXANE   I read them
Over and over. I grew faint reading them.
I belonged to you. Every page of them
Was like a petal fallen from your soul —
Like the light and the fire of a great love,
405 Sweet and strong and true —

CHRISTIAN   Sweet . . . and strong . . . and true . . .
You felt that, Roxane? —

ROXANE   You know how I feel! . . .

CHRISTIAN So — you came . . .

ROXANE   Oh my Christian, oh
  my king, —

Lift me up if I fall upon my knees —
It is the heart of me that kneels to you,
410 And will remain forever at your feet —
You cannot lift that! —
      I came here to say
"Forgive me" — (It is time to be forgiven
Now, when we may die presently) — forgive me
For being light and vain and loving you
415 Only because you were beautiful.

CHRISTIAN (*astonished*)
        Roxane! . . .

ROXANE Afterwards I knew better. Afterwards
(I had to learn to use my wings) I loved you
For yourself too — knowing you more, and
  loving
More of you. And now —

CHRISTIAN   Now? . . .

ROXANE   It is yourself
420 I love now: your own self.

CHRISTIAN (*taken aback*)
       Roxane!

ROXANE (*gravely*)
         Be happy! —
You must have suffered; for you must have
  seen
How frivolous I was; and to be loved
For the mere costume, the poor casual body
You went about in — to a soul like yours,
425 That must have been torture! Therefore with
  words
You revealed your heart. Now that image of
  you
Which filled my eyes first — I see better now,
And I see it no more!

CHRISTIAN   Oh! —

ROXANE   You still doubt
Your victory?

CHRISTIAN (*miserably*)
      Roxane! —

ROXANE   I understand:
430 You cannot perfectly believe in me —
A love like this —

CHRISTIAN   I want no love like this!
I want love only for —

ROXANE   Only for what

---

4. **mosstroopers:** Scottish brigands, outlaws. —Eds.

Every woman sees in you? I can do
Better than that!

CHRISTIAN   No — it was best before!

435 **ROXANE** You do not altogether know me . . . Dear,
There is more of me than there was — with
this,
I can love more of you — more of what makes
You your own self — Truly! . . . If you were less
Lovable —

CHRISTIAN   No!

ROXANE   — Less charming — ugly even —
440 I should love you still.

CHRISTIAN   You mean that?

ROXANE   I do
Mean that!

CHRISTIAN   Ugly? . . .

ROXANE   Yes. Even then!

CHRISTIAN (*agonized*)
                    Oh . . . God!

ROXANE Now are you happy?

CHRISTIAN (*choking*)
                    Yes . . .

ROXANE   What is it?

CHRISTIAN (*Pushes her away gently.*)
                    Only . . .
Nothing . . . one moment . . .

ROXANE   But —

CHRISTIAN (*gesture toward* THE CADETS)
                    I am keeping you
From those poor fellows — Go and smile at
them;
445 They are going to die!

ROXANE (*softly*)
                    Dear Christian!

CHRISTIAN   Go —
(*She goes up among the Gascons who gather
round her respectfully.*)
Cyrano!

CYRANO (*Comes out of the tent, armed for the
battle.*)
                    What is wrong? You look —

CHRISTIAN   She does not
Love me any more.

CYRANO (*smiles*)
                    You think not?

CHRISTIAN   She loves
You.

CYRANO   No! —

CHRISTIAN (*bitterly*)
                    She loves only my soul.

CYRANO   No!

CHRISTIAN   Yes —
That means you. And you love her.

CYRANO   I?

CHRISTIAN   I see —
450 I know!

CYRANO   That is true . . .

CHRISTIAN   More than —

CYRANO (*quietly*)
                    More than that.

CHRISTIAN Tell her so!

CYRANO   No.

CHRISTIAN   Why not?

CYRANO   Why — look at me!

CHRISTIAN She would love me if I were ugly.

CYRANO (*startled*)
                    She —
Said that?

CHRISTIAN   Yes. Now then!

CYRANO (*half to himself*)
                    It was good of her
To tell you that . . .
   (*change of tone*)
                    Nonsense! Do not believe
455 Any such madness —
                    It was good of her
To tell you. . . .
                    Do not take her at her word!
Go on — you never will be ugly — Go!
She would never forgive me.

CHRISTIAN   That is what
We shall see.

CYRANO   No, no —

CHRISTIAN   Let her choose between
us! —
460 Tell her everything!

CYRANO   No — you torture me —

CHRISTIAN Shall I ruin your happiness, because
I have a cursed pretty face? That seems
Too unfair!

CYRANO   And am I to ruin yours
Because I happen to be born with power
465 To say what you — perhaps — feel?

CHRISTIAN   Tell her!

CYRANO   Man —

Do not try me too far!

CHRISTIAN   I am tired of being

My own rival!

CYRANO   Christian! —

CHRISTIAN   Our secret marriage —

No witnesses — fraudulent — that can be

Annulled —

CYRANO   Do not try me —

CHRISTIAN   I want her love

470 For the poor fool I am — or not at all!

Oh, I am going through with this! I'll know,

One way or the other. Now I shall walk down

To the end of the post. Go tell her. Let her choose

One of us.

CYRANO   It will be you.

CHRISTIAN   God — I hope so!

(*He turns and calls.*)

475 Roxane!

CYRANO   No — no —

ROXANE (*Hurries down to him.*)

Yes, Christian?

CHRISTIAN   Cyrano

Has news for you — important.

(*She turns to* CYRANO. CHRISTIAN *goes out.*)

ROXANE (*lightly*)

Oh — important?

CYRANO He is gone . . .

(*to* ROXANE)

Nothing — only Christian thinks

You ought to know —

ROXANE   I do know. He still

doubts

What I told him just now. I saw that.

CYRANO (*Takes her hand.*)

Was it

480 True — what you told him just now?

ROXANE   It was true!

I said that I should love him even . . .

CYRANO (*smiling sadly*)

The word

Comes hard — before me?

ROXANE   Even if he were . . .

CYRANO   Say it —

I shall not be hurt! — Ugly?

ROXANE   Even then

I should love him.

(*A few shots, off stage, in the direction in which* CHRISTIAN *disappeared.*)

Hark! The guns —

CYRANO   Hideous?

485 **ROXANE** Hideous.

CYRANO   Disfigured?

ROXANE   Or disfigured.

CYRANO   Even

Grotesque?

ROXANE   How could he ever be grotesque —

Ever — to me!

CYRANO   But you could love him so,

As much as? —

ROXANE   Yes — and more!

CYRANO (*aside, excitedly*)

It is true! — true! —

Perhaps — God! This is too much happiness . . .

(*to* ROXANE)

490 I — Roxane — listen —

LE BRET (*Enters quickly; calls to* CYRANO *in a low tone.*)

Cyrano —

CYRANO (*turns*)

Yes?

LE BRET   Hush! . . .

(*Whispers a few words to him.*)

CYRANO (*Lets fall* ROXANE's *hand.*)

Ah!

ROXANE   What is it?

CYRANO (*half stunned, and aside*)

All gone . . .

ROXANE (*more shots*)

What is it? Oh,

They are fighting! —

(*She goes up to look off stage.*)

CYRANO   All gone. I cannot ever

Tell her, now . . . ever . . .

ROXANE (*Starts to rush away.*)

What has happened?

CYRANO (*Restrains her.*)

Nothing.

(*Several Cadets enter. They conceal something which they are carrying, and form a group so as to prevent* ROXANE *from seeing their burden.*)

ROXANE These men —

CYRANO   Come away . . .

(*He leads her away from the group.*)

ROXANE   You were telling me

495 Something —

CYRANO   Oh, that? Nothing . . . .

(*gravely*)

I swear to you

That the spirit of Christian — that his soul

Was —

(*Corrects himself quickly.*)

That his soul is no less great —

ROXANE (*Catches at the word.*)

Was?

(*crying out*)

Oh! —

(*She rushes among the men, and scatters them.*)

CYRANO All gone . . .

ROXANE (*Sees* CHRISTIAN *lying upon his cloak.*)

Christian!

LE BRET (*to* CYRANO)

At the first volley.

(ROXANE *throws herself upon the body of* CHRISTIAN. *Shots; at first scattered, then increasing. Drums. Voices shouting.*)

CARBON (*sword in hand*)

Here

They come! — Ready! —

(*followed by the Cadets, he climbs over the parapet and disappears.*)

ROXANE   Christian!

CARBON (*off stage*)

Come on, there, You!

500 ROXANE Christian!

CARBON   Fall in!

ROXANE   Christian!

CARBON   Measure your fuse!

(RAGUENEAU *hurries up, carrying a helmet full of water.*)

CHRISTIAN (*faintly*)

Roxane! . . .

CYRANO (*Low and quick, in* CHRISTIAN's *ear, while* ROXANE *is dipping into the water a strip of linen torn from her dress.*)

I have told her; she loves you.

(CHRISTIAN *closes his eyes.*)

ROXANE (*Turns to* CHRISTIAN.)

Yes,

My darling?

CARBON   Draw your ramrods!

ROXANE (*to* CYRANO)

He is not dead? . . .

CARBON *Open your charges!*

ROXANE   I can feel his cheek

Growing cold against mine —

CARBON   Take aim!

ROXANE   A letter —

505 Over his heart —

(*She opens it.*)

For me.

CYRANO (*aside*)

My letter . . .

CARBON   Fire!

(*Musketry, cries and groans. Din of battle.*)

CYRANO (*Trying to withdraw his hand, which* ROXANE, *still upon her knees, is holding.*)

But Roxane — they are fighting —

ROXANE   Wait a little . . .

He is dead. No one else knew him but you . . .

(*She weeps quietly.*)

Was he not a great lover, a great man,

A hero?

CYRANO (*Standing, bareheaded.*)

Yes, Roxane.

ROXANE   A poet, unknown,

510 Adorable?

CYRANO   Yes, Roxane.

ROXANE   A fine mind?

CYRANO Yes, Roxane.

ROXANE   A heart deeper than we knew —

A soul magnificently tender?

CYRANO (*firmly*)

Yes,

Roxane!

ROXANE (*Sinks down upon the breast of* CHRISTIAN.)

He is dead now . . .

CYRANO (*Aside; draws his sword.*)

Why, so am I —

For I am dead, and my love mourns for me

515 And does not know . . .

(*trumpets in distance*)

DE GUICHE (*Appears on the parapet, disheveled, wounded on the forehead, shouting.*)
The signal — hark — the trumpets!
The army has returned — Hold them now! — Hold them!
The army! —

ROXANE   On his letter — blood . . . and tears.

A VOICE (*off stage*)
Surrender!

THE CADETS   No!

RAGUENEAU   This place is dangerous! —

CYRANO (*to* DE GUICHE)
Take her away — I am going —

ROXANE (*Kisses the letter; faintly.*)
His blood . . . his tears . . .

RAGUENEAU (*Leaps down from the coach and runs to her.*)
520   She has fainted —

DE GUICHE (*On the parapet; savagely, to the Cadets*)
Hold them!

VOICE OFF STAGE   Lay down your arms!

VOICES   No! No!

CYRANO (*to* DE GUICHE)
Sir, you have proved yourself — Take care of her.

DE GUICHE (*Hurries to* ROXANE *and takes her up in his arms.*)
As you will — we can win, if you hold on
A little longer —

CYRANO   Good!
(*Calls out to* ROXANE, *as she is carried away, fainting, by* DE GUICHE *and* RAGUENEAU.)
Adieu, Roxane!
(*Tumult, outcries. Several Cadets come back wounded and fall on the stage.* CYRANO, *rushing to the fight, is stopped on the crest of the parapet by* CARBON, *covered with blood.*)

CARBON   We are breaking — I am twice wounded —

CYRANO (*Shouts to the Gascons.*)
Hardi!
525   Reculez pas, Drollos!
(*To* CARBON, *holding him up.*)
So — never fear!

I have two deaths to avenge now — Christian's
And my own!
(*They come down.* CYRANO *takes from him the lance with* ROXANE's *handkerchief still fastened to it.*)
Float, little banner, with her name!
(*He plants it on the parapet; then shouts to The Cadets.*)
Toumbé dessus! Escrasas lous!
(*to the fifer*)
Your fife!
Music!
(*Fife plays. The wounded drag themselves to their feet. Other Cadets scramble over the parapet and group themselves around* CYRANO *and his tiny flag. The coach is filled and covered with men, bristling with muskets, transformed into a redoubt.*)

A CADET (*Reels backward over the wall, still fighting. Shouts.*)
They are climbing over! —
(*And falls dead.*)

CYRANO   Very good —
530   Let them come! — A salute now —
(*The parapet is crowned for an instant with a rank of enemies. The imperial banner of Spain is raised aloft.*)
Fire!
(*general volley*)

VOICE (*among the ranks of the enemy*)
Fire!
(*Murderous counter-fire; the Cadets fall on every side.*)

A SPANISH OFFICER (*uncovers*)
Who are these men who are so fond of death?

CYRANO (*Erect amid the hail of bullets, declaims*)
The Cadets of Gascoyne, the defenders
Of Carbon de Castel-Jaloux —
Free fighters, free lovers, free spenders —
(*He rushes forward, followed by a few survivors.*)
535   The Cadets of Gascoyne . . .
(*The rest is lost in the din of battle.*)
(*Curtain*)

Cyrano's Gazette

Fifteen years later, in 1655. The Park of the Convent occupied by the Ladies of the Cross, at Paris.

Magnificent foliage. To the Left, the House upon a broad Terrace at the head of a flight of steps, with several Doors opening upon the Terrace. In the centre of the scene an enormous Tree alone in the centre of a little open space. Toward the Right, in the foreground, among Boxwood Bushes, a semi-circular Bench of stone.

All the way across the Background of the scene, an Avenue overarched by the chestnut trees, leading to the door of a Chapel on the Right, just visible among the branches of the trees. Beyond the double curtain of the trees, we catch a glimpse of bright lawns and shaded walks, masses of shrubbery; the perspective of the Park; the sky.

A little side door of the Chapel opens upon a Colonnade, garlanded with Autumnal vines, and disappearing on the Right behind the box-trees.

It is late October. Above the still living green of the turf all the foliage is red and yellow and brown. The evergreen masses of Box and Yew stand out darkly against this Autumnal coloring. A heap of dead leaves under every tree. The leaves are falling everywhere. They rustle underfoot along the walks; the Terrace and the Bench are half covered with them.

Before the Bench on the Right, on the side toward the Tree, is placed a tall embroidery frame and beside it a little Chair. Baskets filled with skeins of many-colored silks and balls of wool. Tapestry unfinished on the Frame.

At the Curtain Rise the nuns are coming and going across the Park; several of them are seated on the Bench around MOTHER MARGUERITE DE JESUS. *The leaves are falling.*

SISTER MARTHE (*to* MOTHER MARGUERITE)
    Sister Claire has been looking in the glass
    At her new cap; twice!

MOTHER MARGUERITE (*to* SISTER CLAIRE)
                    It is very plain; Very.

SISTER CLAIRE   And Sister Marthe stole a plum
    Out of the tart this morning!

MOTHER MARGUERITE (*to* SISTER MARTHE)
                       That was wrong;
5   Very wrong.

SISTER CLAIRE   Oh, but such a little look!

SISTER MARTHE Such a little plum!

MOTHER MARGUERITE (*severely*)
                I shall tell Monsieur
    De Cyrano, this evening.

SISTER CLAIRE   No! Oh no! —
    He will make fun of us.

SISTER MARTHE   He will say nuns
    Are so gay!

SISTER CLAIRE   And so greedy!

MOTHER MARGUERITE (*smiling*)
              And so good . . .

10 **SISTER CLAIRE** It must be ten years, Mother
    Marguerite,
    That he has come here every Saturday,
    Is it not?

MOTHER MARGUERITE   More than ten years;
    ever since
    His cousin came to live among us here —
    Her worldly weeds among our linen veils,
15   Her widowhood and our virginity —
    Like a black dove among white doves.

SISTER MARTHE   No one
    Else ever turns that happy sorrow of hers
    Into a smile.

ALL THE NUNS   He is such fun! — He makes us
    Almost laugh! — And he teases everyone —
20   And pleases everyone — And we all love
    him —
    And he likes our cake, too —

SISTER MARTHE   I am afraid
    He is not a good Catholic.

SISTER CLAIRE   Some day
    We shall convert him.

THE NUNS   Yes — yes!

MOTHER MARGUERITE   Let him be;
    I forbid you to worry him. Perhaps
25   He might stop coming here.

SISTER MARTHE   But . . . God?

MOTHER MARGUERITE   You need not
    Be afraid. God knows all about him.

SISTER MARTHE   Yes . . .

But every Saturday he says to me,
Just as if he were proud of it: "Well, Sister,
I ate meat yesterday!"

MOTHER MARGUERITE   He tells you so?

30   The last time he said that, he had not eaten
Anything, for two days.

SISTER MARTHE   Mother!—

MOTHER MARGUERITE   He is poor;
Very poor.

SISTER MARTHE   Who said so?

MOTHER MARGUERITE   Monsieur Le Bret.

SISTER MARTHE Why does not someone help
him?

MOTHER MARGUERITE   He would be
Angry; very angry . . .
(*Between the trees up stage,* ROXANE
*appears, all in black, with a widow's cap
and long veils.* DE GUICHE, *magnificently
grown old, walks beside her. They move
slowly.* MOTHER MARGUERITE *rises.*)
                Let us go in—
Madame Madeleine has a visitor.

SISTER MARTHE (*to* SISTER CLAIRE)

35   The Duc de Grammont, is it not? The
Marshal?

SISTER CLAIRE (*Looks toward* DE GUICHE.)
I think so—yes.

SISTER MARTHE   He has not been to see her
For months—

THE NUNS   He is busy—the Court!—The Camp!—

SISTER CLAIRE   The world! . . .
(*They go out.* DE GUICHE *and* ROXANE *come
down in silence, and stop near the embroidery frame. Pause.*)

DE GUICHE And you remain here, wasting all that
gold—
For ever in mourning?

ROXANE   For ever.

DE GUICHE   And still faithful?

40 **ROXANE** And still faithful . . .

DE GUICHE (*after a pause*)
                Have you forgiven me?

ROXANE (*simply, looking up at the cross of the
Convent*)
I am here.
(*another pause*)

DE GUICHE   Was Christian . . . all that?

ROXANE   If you knew him.

DE GUICHE Ah? We were not precisely . . .
intimate . . .
And his last letter—always at your heart?

ROXANE It hangs here, like a holy reliquary.

45 **DE GUICHE** Dead—and you love him still!

ROXANE   Sometimes I think
He has not altogether died; our hearts
Meet, and his love flows all around me, living.

DE GUICHE (*after another pause*)
You see Cyrano often?

ROXANE   Every week.
My old friend takes the place of my Gazette.

50   Brings me all the news. Every Saturday,
Under that tree where you are now, his chair
Stands, if the day be fine. I wait for him,
Embroidering; the hour strikes; then I hear,

55   (I need not turn to look!) at the last stroke,
His cane tapping the steps. He laughs at me
For my eternal needlework. He tells
The story of the past week—
(LE BRET *appears on the steps.*)
                There's Le Bret!—
(LE BRET *approaches.*)
How is it with our friend?

LE BRET   Badly.

DE GUICHE   Indeed?

ROXANE (*to* DE GUICHE)

60   Oh, he exaggerates!

LE BRET   Just as I said—
Loneliness, misery—I told him so!—
His satires make a host of enemies—
He attacks the false nobles, the false saints,
The false heroes, the false artists—in short,

65   Everyone!

ROXANE   But they fear that sword of his—
No one dare touch him!

DE GUICHE (*with a shrug*)
                H'm—that may be so.

LE BRET It is not violence I fear for him,
But solitude—poverty—old gray December,
Stealing on wolf's feet, with a wolf's green
eyes,

70   Into his darkening room. Those bravoes yet
May strike our Swordsman down! Every day
now,
He draws his belt up one hole; his poor nose

Looks like old ivory; he has one coat
Left — his old black serge.

DE GUICHE That is nothing strange

75 In this world! No, you need not pity him
Overmuch.

LE BRET (*with a bitter smile*)

My lord Marshal! . . .

DE GUICHE I say, do not
Pity him overmuch. He lives his life,
His own life, his own way — thought, word,
  and deed
Free!

LE BRET (*as before*)

My lord Duke! . . .

DE GUICHE (*haughtily*)

Yes, I know — I have all;

80 He has nothing. Nevertheless, to-day
I should be proud to shake his hand . . .
    (*Saluting* ROXANE.)

Adieu.

ROXANE I will go with you.
    (DE GUICHE *salutes* LE BRET, *and turns with*
    ROXANE *toward the steps.*)

DE GUICHE (*Pauses on the steps, as she climbs.*)

Yes — I envy him
Now and then . . .

Do you know, when a man wins
Everything in this world, when he succeeds

85 Too much — he feels, having done nothing
  wrong
Especially, Heaven knows! — he feels
  somehow
A thousand small displeasures with himself,
Whose whole sum is not quite Remorse, but
  rather
A sort of vague disgust . . . The ducal robes

90 Mounting up, step by step, to pride and power,
Somewhere among their folds draw after
  them
A rustle of dry illusions, vain regrets,
As your veil, up the stairs here, draws along
The whisper of dead leaves.

ROXANE (*ironical*)

The sentiment

95 Does you honor.

DE GUICHE Oh, yes . . .
    (*Pausing suddenly.*)

Monsieur Le Bret! —
    (*to* ROXANE)
You pardon us? —
    (*He goes to* LE BRET, *and speaks in a low
    tone.*)

One moment — It is true
That no one dares attack your friend. Some
  people
Dislike him, none the less. The other day
At Court, such a one said to me: "This man

100 Cyrano may die — accidentally."

LE BRET (*coldly*)
Thank you.

DE GUICHE You may thank me. Keep him
  at home
All you can. Tell him to be careful.

LE BRET (*Shaking his hands to heaven.*)

Careful! —
He is coming here. I'll warn him — yes, but! . . .

ROXANE (*still on the steps, to a Nun who
    approaches her*)

Here
I am — what is it?

THE NUN Madame, Ragueneau

105 Wishes to see you.

ROXANE Bring him here.
    (*to* LE BRET *and* DE GUICHE)

He comes
For sympathy — having been first of all
A Poet, he became since then, in turn,
A Singer —

LE BRET Bath-house keeper —

ROXANE Sacristan[1] —

LE BRET Actor —

ROXANE Hairdresser —

LE BRET Music-master —

ROXANE Now,

110 To-day —

RAGUENEAU (*Enters hurriedly.*)

Madame! —
    (*He sees* LE BRET.)

Monsieur! —

---

1. **Sacristan:** Person in charge of the sacristy at a church, where vestments are kept and priests prepare for the service. —Eds.

ROXANE (*Smiling*)

> First tell your troubles
> To Le Bret for a moment.

RAGUENEAU But Madame—

> (*She goes out, with* DE GUICHE, *not hearing
> him.* RAGUENEAU *comes to* LE BRET.)
> After all, I had rather — You are here —
> She need not know so soon — I went to see
> him
> Just now — Our friend — As I came near his door,

115 I saw him coming out. I hurried on

> To join him. At the corner of the street,
> As he passed — Could it be an accident? —
> I wonder! — At the window overhead,
> A lackey with a heavy log of wood

120 Let it fall —

LE BRET Cyrano!

RAGUENEAU I ran to him —

LE BRET God! The cowards!

RAGUENEAU I found him lying there —

> A great hole in his head —

LE BRET Is he alive?

RAGUENEAU Alive — yes. But . . . I had to carry him

> Up to his room — Dieu! Have you seen
> his room? —

125 **LE BRET** Is he suffering?

RAGUENEAU No; unconscious.

LE BRET Did you

> Call a doctor?

RAGUENEAU One came — for charity.

LE BRET Poor Cyrano! — We must not tell Roxane

> All at once . . . Did the doctor say? —

RAGUENEAU He said

> Fever, and lesions of the — I forget

130 Those long names — Ah, if you had seen him

> there,
> His head all white bandages! — Let us go
> Quickly — there is no one to care for him —
> All alone — If he tries to raise his head,
> He may die!

LE BRET (*Draws him away to the Right.*)

> This way — It is shorter — through

135 The Chapel —

ROXANE (*Appears on the stairway, and calls to* LE

> BRET *as he is going out by the colonnade
> which leads to the small door of the Chapel.*)
> Monsieur Le Bret! —

(LE BRET *and* RAGUENEAU *rush off without
hearing.*)

> Running away
> When I call to him? Poor dear Ragueneau
> Must have been very tragic!

(*She comes slowly down the stair, toward
the tree.*)

> What a day! . . .
> Something in these bright Autumn afternoons
> Happy and yet regretful — an old sorrow

140 Smiling . . . as though poor little April dried

> Her tears long ago — and remembered . . .

(*She sits down at her work. Two Nuns come
out of the house carrying a great chair and
set it under the tree.*)

> Ah —
> The old chair, for my old friend! —

SISTER MARTHE The best one

> In our best parlor! —

ROXANE Thank you, Sister —

(*The Nuns withdraw.*)

> There —

(*She begins embroidering. The clock strikes.*)

> The hour! — He will be coming now — my silks —

145 All done striking? He never was so late

> Before! The sister at the door — my thimble . . .
> Here it is — she must be exhorting him
> To repent all his sins . . .

(*a pause*)

> He ought to be
> Converted, by this time — Another leaf —

(*A dead leaf falls on her work; she brushes it
away.*)

150 Certainly nothing could — my scissors — ever

> Keep him away —

A NUN (*Appears on the steps.*)

> Monsieur de Bergerac.

ROXANE (*Without turning*)

> What was I saying? . . . Hard, sometimes, to
> match
> These faded colors! . . .

(*While she goes on working,* CYRANO
*appears at the top of the steps, very pale, his
hat drawn over his eyes. The Nun who has
brought him in goes away. He begins to
descend the steps leaning on his cane, and
holding himself on his feet only by an*

evident effort. ROXANE *turns to him, with a tone of friendly banter.*)

                    After fourteen years,
Late — for the first time!

CYRANO (*Reaches the chair, and sinks into it; his gay tone contrasting with his tortured face.*)

                Yes, yes — maddening!

155   I was detained by —

ROXANE   Well?

CYRANO   A visitor,
Most unexpected.

ROXANE (*carelessly, still sewing*)

               Was your visitor
Tiresome?

CYRANO   Why, hardly that — inopportune,
Let us say — an old friend of mine — at least
A very old acquaintance.

ROXANE   Did you tell him

160   To go away?

CYRANO   For the time being, yes.
I said: "Excuse me — this is Saturday —
I have a previous engagement, one
I cannot miss, even for you — Come back
An hour from now."

ROXANE   Your friend will have to wait;

165   I shall not let you go till dark.

CYRANO (*very gently*)

                Perhaps
A little before dark, I must go . . .
(*He leans back in the chair, and closes his eyes.* SISTER MARTHE *crosses above the stairway.* ROXANE *sees her, motions her to wait, then turns to* CYRANO.)

ROXANE   Look —
Somebody waiting to be teased.

CYRANO (*Quickly, opens his eyes.*)

                Of course!
(*in a big, comic voice*)
Sister, approach!
(SISTER MARTHE *glides toward him.*)

         Beautiful downcast eyes! —
So shy —

SISTER MARTHE (*Looks up, smiling.*)

          You —
(*She sees his face.*)

         Oh! —

CYRANO (*Indicates* ROXANE.)

          Sh! — Careful!

(*Resumes his burlesque tone.*)

                Yesterday,

170   I ate meat again!

SISTER MARTHE   Yes, I know.
(*aside*)

               That is why
He looks so pale . . .
(*to him: low and quickly*)

         In the refectory,
Before you go — come to me there —

            I'll make you
A great bowl of hot soup — will you come?

CYRANO (*boisterously*)

               Ah —
Will I come!

SISTER MARTHE   You are quite reasonable

175   To-day!

ROXANE   Has she converted you?

SISTER MARTHE   Oh, no —
Not for the world! —

CYRANO   Why, now I think of it,
That is so — You, bursting with holiness,
And yet you never preach! Astonishing
I call it . . .
(*with burlesque ferocity*)

        Ah — now I'll astonish you —

180   I am going to —
(*with the air of seeking for a good joke and finding it*)

          — let you pray for me
To-night, at vespers!

ROXANE   Aha!

CYRANO   Look at her —
Absolutely struck dumb!

SISTER MARTHE (*gently*)

          I did not wait
For you to say I might.
(*She goes out.*)

CYRANO (*Returns to* ROXANE, *who is bending over her work.*)

         Now, may the devil
Admire me, if I ever hope to see

185   The end of that embroidery!

ROXANE (*smiling*)

          I thought
It was time you said that.
(*A breath of wind causes a few leaves to fall.*)

CYRANO   The leaves —

ROXANE (*Raises her head and looks away through the trees.*)

What color —
Perfect Venetian red! Look at them fall.

CYRANO Yes — they know how to die. A little way
From the branch to the earth, a little fear

190 Of mingling with the common dust — and yet
They go down gracefully — a fall that seems
Like flying!

ROXANE Melancholy — you?

CYRANO Why, no,
Roxane!

ROXANE Then let the leaves fall. Tell me now
The Court news — my gazette!

CYRANO Let me see —

ROXANE Ah!

CYRANO (*more and more pale, struggling against pain*)

195 *Saturday, the nineteenth:* The King fell ill,
After eight helpings of grape marmalade.
His malady was brought before the court,
Found guilty of high treason; whereupon
His Majesty revived. The royal pulse

200 Is now normal. *Sunday, the twentieth:*
The Queen gave a grand ball, at which they
burned
Seven hundred and sixty-three wax candles.
Note:
They say our troops have been victorious
In Austria. *Later:* Three sorcerers

205 Have been hung. *Special post:* The little dog
Of Madame d'Athis was obliged to take
Four pills before —

ROXANE Monsieur de Bergerac,
Will you kindly be quiet!

CYRANO *Monday* . . . nothing.
Lygdamire has a new lover.

ROXANE Oh!

CYRANO (*his face more and more altered*)
Tuesday,

210 *The Twenty-second:* All the court has gone
To Fontainebleau, *Wednesday:* The Comte de
Fiesque
Spoke to Madame de Montglat; she said No.
Thursday: Mancini was the Queen of France
Or — very nearly! *Friday:* La Monglat

215 Said Yes. *Saturday, twenty-sixth.* . . .

(*His eyes close; his head sinks back; silence.*)

ROXANE (*Surprised at not hearing any more, turns, looks at him, and rises, frightened.*)

He has fainted —
(*She runs to him, crying out.*)
Cyrano!

CYRANO (*Opens his eyes.*)

What . . . What is it? . . .
(*He sees* ROXANE *leaning over him, and quickly pulls his hat down over his head and leans back away from her in the chair.*)

No — oh no —
It is nothing — truly!

ROXANE But —

CYRANO My old wound —
At Arras — sometimes — you know. . . .

ROXANE My poor friend!

CYRANO Oh it is nothing; it will soon be gone. . . .
(*forcing a smile*)

220 There! It is gone!

ROXANE (*standing close to him*)

We all have our old wounds —
I have mine — here . . .
(*her hand at her breast*)
under this faded scrap
Of writing. . . . It is hard to read now — all
But the blood — and the tears. . . .
(*Twilight begins to fall.*)

CYRANO His letter! . . . Did you
Not promise me that some day . . . that some
day . . .

225 You would let me read it?

ROXANE His letter? — You . . .
You wish —

CYRANO I do wish it — to-day.

ROXANE (*Gives him the little silken bag from around her neck.*)

Here. . . .

CYRANO May I . . . open it?

ROXANE Open it, and read.
(*She goes back to her work, folds it again, rearranges her silks.*)

CYRANO (*Unfolds the letter; reads.*)
"Farewell Roxane, because to-day I die —"

ROXANE (*Looks up, surprised.*)
Aloud?

CYRANO (*reads*)

"I know that it will be to-day,
230 My own dearly beloved — and my heart
Still so heavy with love I have not told,
And I die without telling you! No more
Shall my eyes drink the sight of you like
wine,
Never more, with a look that is a kiss,
235 Follow the sweet grace of you —"

ROXANE   How you read it —
His letter!

CYRANO (*continues*)
                    "I remember now the way
You have, of pushing back a lock of hair
With one hand, from your forehead — and my
heart
Cries out —"

ROXANE   His letter . . . and you read it so . . .
        (*The darkness increases imperceptibly.*)

240 CYRANO "Cries out and keeps crying: 'Farewell,
my dear,
My dearest —'"

ROXANE   In a voice. . . .

CYRANO   "— My own heart's own,
My own treasure —"

ROXANE (*dreamily*)
                    In such a voice. . . .

CYRANO   —"My love —"

ROXANE — As I remember hearing . . .
        (*She trembles.*)
                         — long ago. . . .
        (*She comes near him, softly, without his
        seeing her; passes the chair, leans over
        silently, looking at the letter. The darkness
        increases.*)

CYRANO "— I am never away from you. Even
now,
245 I shall not leave you. In another world,
I shall be still that one who loves you, loves
you
Beyond measure, beyond —"

ROXANE (*Lays her hand on his shoulder.*)
                         How can you read
Now? It is dark. . . .
        (*He starts, turns, and sees her there close to
        him. A little movement of surprise, almost of
        fear; then he bows his head.
        A long pause; then in the twilight now*

*completely fallen, she says very softly, clasp-
ing her hands.*)
                    And all these fourteen years,
He has been the old friend, who came to me
250 To be amusing.

CYRANO   Roxane! —

ROXANE   It was you.

CYRANO No, no, Roxane, no!

ROXANE   And I might have known,
Every time that I heard you speak my name! . . .

CYRANO No — It was not I —

ROXANE   It was . . . you!

CYRANO   I swear —

ROXANE I understand everything now:
The letters —
255 That was you . . .

CYRANO   No!

ROXANE   And the dear, foolish words —
That was you. . . .

CYRANO   No!

ROXANE   And the voice . . . in the dark . . . .
That was . . . you!

CYRANO   On my honor —

ROXANE   And . . . the Soul! —
That was all you.

CYRANO   I never loved you —

ROXANE   Yes,
260 You loved me.

CYRANO (*desperately*)
                         No — He loved you —

ROXANE   Even now,
You love me!

CYRANO (*His voice weakens.*)
                No!

ROXANE (*smiling*)
                    And why . . . so great a *No*?

CYRANO No, no, my own dear love, I love
you not! . . .
        (*pause*)

ROXANE How many things have died . . . and are
newborn! . . .
Why were you silent for so many years,
All the while, every night and every day,
He gave me nothing — you knew that — You
knew
265 Here, in this letter lying on my breast,
Your tears — You knew they were your tears —

CYRANO (*Holds the letter out to her.*)

                      The blood
Was his.

ROXANE   Why do you break that silence now,
To-day?

CYRANO   Why? Oh, because —
    (LE BRET *and* RAGUENEAU *enter, running.*)

LE BRET   What recklessness —
I knew it! He is here!

CYRANO (*smiling, and trying to rise*)
            Well? Here I am!

270 **RAGUENEAU** He has killed himself, Madame,
    coming here!

ROXANE He — oh, God.... And that faintness ...
    was that? —

CYRANO   No,
Nothing! I did not finish my Gazette —
Saturday, twenty-sixth: An hour or so
Before dinner, Monsieur de Bergerac

275 Died, foully murdered.
    (*He uncovers his head, and shows it
    swathed in bandages.*)

ROXANE   Oh, what does he mean? —
Cyrano! — What have they done to you? —

CYRANO   "Struck down
By the sword of a hero, let me fall —
Steel in my heart, and laughter on my lips!"
Yes, I said that once. How Fate loves a jest! —

280 Behold me ambushed — taken in the rear —
My battlefield a gutter — my noble foe
A lackey, with a log of wood! ...
             It seems
Too logical — I have missed everything,
Even my death!

RAGUENEAU (*Breaks down.*)
        Ah, monsieur! —

CYRANO   Ragueneau,
285 Stop blubbering!
    (*Takes his hand.*)
        What are you writing nowadays,
Old poet?

RAGUENEAU (*through his tears*)
        I am not a poet now;
I snuff the — light the candles — for Molière!

CYRANO Oh — Molière!

RAGUENEAU   Yes, but I am leaving him
To-morrow. Yesterday they played *Scapin* —
290 He has stolen your scene —

LE BRET   The whole scene — word for word!

RAGUENEAU Yes: "What the devil was he doing
    there" —
That one!

LE BRET (*furious*)
        And Molière stole it all from you —
Bodily! —

CYRANO   Bah — He showed good taste....
    (*to* RAGUENEAU)
            The Scene
Went well? ...

RAGUENEAU   Ah, monsieur, they laughed —
    and laughed —
295 How they did laugh!

CYRANO   Yes — that has been my life....
Do you remember that night Christian spoke
Under your window? It was always so!
While I stood in the darkness underneath,
Others climbed up to win the applause — the
    kiss! —

300 Well — that seems only justice — I still say,
Even now, on the threshold of my tomb —
"Molière has genius — Christian had good
    looks —"
    (*The chapel bell is ringing. Along the avenue
    of trees above the stairway, the Nuns pass in
    procession to their prayers.*)
They are going to pray now; there is the bell.

ROXANE (*Raises herself and calls to them.*)
Sister! — Sister! —

CYRANO (*holding on to her hand*)
            No, — do not go away —
305 I may not still be here when you return....
    (*The Nuns have gone into the chapel. The
    organ begins to play.*)
A little harmony is all I need —
Listen....

ROXANE   You shall not die! I love you! —

CYRANO   No —
That is not in the story! You remember
When Beauty said "I love you" to the Beast
310 That was a fairy prince, his ugliness
Changed and dissolved, like magic....
    But you see
I am still the same.

ROXANE   And I — I have done
This to you! All my fault — mine!

CYRANO   You? Why no,
On the contrary! I had never known
315 Womanhood and its sweetness but for you.
My mother did not love to look at me —
I never had a sister —   Later on,
I feared the mistress with a mockery
Behind her smile. But you — because of you
320 I have had one friend not quite all a friend —
Across my life, one whispering silken gown! . . .

LE BRET (*Points to the rising moon which begins
to shine down between the trees.*)
Your other friend is looking at you.

CYRANO (*smiling at the moon*)
                          I see. . . .

ROXANE I never loved but one man in my life,
And I have lost him — twice. . . .

325 **CYRANO** Le Bret — I shall be up there presently
In the moon — without having to invent
Any flying machines!

ROXANE   What are you saying? . . .

CYRANO The moon — yes, that would be the
place for me —
My kind of paradise! I shall find there
330 Those other souls who should be friends of
mine —
Socrates — Galileo —

LE BRET (*revolting*)
                    No! No! No!
It is too idiotic — too unfair —
Such a friend — such a poet — such a man
To die so — to die so! —

CYRANO (*affectionately*)
                    There goes Le Bret,
335 Growling!

LE BRET (*Breaks down.*)
                    My friend! —

CYRANO (*Half raises himself, his eye wanders.*)
                    The Cadets of Gascoyne,
The Defenders. . . . The elementary mass —
Ah — there's the point! Now, then . . .

LE BRET   Delirious —
And all that learning —

CYRANO   On the other hand,
We have Copernicus —

ROXANE   Oh!

CYRANO (*more and more delirious*)
                    "Very well,

340 But what the devil was he doing there? —
What the devil was he doing there, up
there?" . . .
(*he declaims*)
Philosopher and scientist,
Poet, musician, duellist —
He flew high, and fell back again!
345 *A pretty wit — whose like we lack —*
A lover . . . not like other men. . . .
Here lies Hercule-Savinien
De Cyrano de Bergerac —
Who was all things — and all in vain!
350 Well, I must go — pardon — I cannot stay!
My moonbeam comes to carry me away. . . .
(*He falls back into the chair, half fainting.
The sobbing of* ROXANE *recalls him to real-
ity. Gradually his mind comes back to him.
He looks at her, stroking the veil that hides
her hair.*)
I would not have you mourn any the less
That good, brave, noble Christian; but
perhaps —
I ask you only this — when the great cold
Gathers around my bones, that you may give
355 A double meaning to your widow's weeds
And the tears you let fall for him may be
For a little — my tears. . . .

ROXANE (*sobbing*)
                    Oh, my love! . . .

CYRANO (*Suddenly shaken as with a fever fit, he
raises himself erect and pushes her away.*)
                    — Not here! —
Not lying down! . . .
(*They spring forward to help him; he
motions them back.*)
                    Let no one help me — no one! —
Only the tree. . . .
(*He sets his back against the trunk.
Pause.*)
                    It is coming . . . I feel
360 Already shod with marble . . . gloved with
lead . . .
(*joyously*)
Let the old fellow come now! He shall find me
On my feet — sword in hand —
(*Draws his sword.*)

LE BRET   Cyrano! —

ROXANE (*half fainting*)

Oh,

Cyrano!

CYRANO   I can see him there — he grins —

He is looking at my nose — that skeleton

365 —What's that you say? Hopeless? — Why, very
well! —

But a man does not fight merely to win!

No — no — better to know one fights in vain! . . .

You there — Who are you? A hundred against
one —

I know them now, my ancient enemies —

(*He lunges at the empty air.*)

370 Falsehood! . . . There! There! Prejudice —

Compromise —

Cowardice —

(*thrusting*)

What's that? No! Surrender? No!

Never — never! . . .

Ah, you too, Vanity!

I knew you would overthrow me in the end —

No! I fight on! I fight on! I fight on!

(*He swings the blade in great circles, then
pauses, gasping. When he speaks again, it is
in another tone.*)

375 Yes, all my laurels you have riven away

And all my roses; yet in spite of you,

There is one crown I bear away with me,

And to-night, when I enter before God,

My salute shall sweep all the stars away

380 From the blue threshold! One thing without stain,

Unspotted from the world, in spite of doom

Mine own! —

(*He springs forward, his sword aloft.*)

And that is . . .

(*The sword escapes from his hand; he
totters, and falls into the arms of* LE BRET
and RAGUENEAU.)

ROXANE (*Bends over him and kisses him on the
forehead.*)

—That is . . .

CYRANO (*Opens his eyes and smiles up at her.*)

My white plume. . . .

(*Curtain*)

Understanding and Interpreting

1 The opening of Act 4 is vastly different from the light mood of Act 3. What has changed and why? Is the shift jarring, or do you find it an appropriate move to follow elements of plot and theme as they've developed thus far? Explain with specific reference to the text.

2 Cyrano crosses enemy lines every day to post a letter to Roxane, but he does not bring food to the starving troops. Why? Is Cyrano acting honorably as he takes these actions?

3 In Act 4, Roxane arrives at camp after facing considerable danger, and she brings a bounty of food and drink (l. 300). Do you interpret this action as evidence of Roxane's self-absorption, her abiding love for Christian, her naive disregard for the danger in which she places herself and others, her concern for the starving troops, a combination of these traits, or something else?

4 Once Roxane appears in the camp, how does the behavior of the Cadets of Gascoyne reflect the chivalric code?

5 What decision does De Guiche make in Act 4 that shows his honesty, perhaps even honor?

6 In Act 4, why does Cyrano insist, even as Christian is dying, that Roxane chose Christian (ll. 491–520)? Do you view this as the ultimate deception, a truly selfless act, or something else? Explain.

7 What are the circumstances of Cyrano's life as we hear of him at the start of Act 5?

8 By Act 5, what is De Guiche's attitude toward his own life? What does he mean when he says that a seemingly successful man "feels somehow / A thousand small displeasures with himself, / Whose whole sum is not quite Remorse, but rather / a sort of vague disgust" (ll. 86–89)?

9 In the final act, Roxane, cloistered for fifteen years in a convent, realizes the truth about Cyrano's love for her. What finally brings her to this recognition? Do you think she has wasted her life?

10 What does Cyrano mean in Act 5 when he says, "It seems / Too logical—I have missed everything, / Even my death!" (ll. 282–284)? Do you agree with him?

Analyzing Language, Style, and Structure

1 The appearance of Roxane on the battlefield at Arras in Act 4 is implausible at best, although it furthers the plot and prepares for the ending. What do you think Rostand achieves by his decision to use this setting?

2 In Act 4, Cyrano disagrees with what De Guiche does with his white scarf, and claims he would have acted differently (ll. 145–163). What does the white scarf symbolize in this disagreement?

3 How does Rostand establish the mood at the opening of Act 5, which is set in a convent fifteen years after the close of Act 4? Note the overall atmosphere and the behavior of the characters in your response, as well as the stage directions.

4 What evidence in the text of Act 5 do you find of Cyrano's continuing eloquence?

Connecting, Arguing, and Extending

1 One of the hallmarks of the chivalric code is idealism. In what ways do Acts 4 and 5 taken together embody a tension between idealistic and realistic behaviors? To what extent do you think these two very different scenarios—a battlefield and a convent—argue for the superiority of an idealistic perspective?

2 The play ends with Cyrano's dying words, "My white plume . . ." (Act 5, l. 382). He is making reference to a plume or feather such as that worn on a hat or helmet. The French word is *panache*, which has been adopted in English to mean a flamboyant manner.

The white plume (or *panache*) is referred to explicitly at several points in the play, but is worn by Cyrano throughout. How does the plume function as a symbol throughout the play?

3 Find an image—a painting or photo—that captures your interpretation of Roxane at the end of the play. (Keep in mind that, although Act 5 takes place fifteen years after the death of Christian, Roxane would still be only in her midthirties.) Explain how the image, which need not be from the period when the play takes place, captures both her physical qualities and character traits.

Topics for Composing

1 **Exposition**
Discuss the role of friendship as a theme of the play. Consider the different dimensions of friendship, including how duty and sacrifice play into it.

2 **Argument**
In most enduring novels or plays, a character (or characters) experience a change: we watch the arc of a journey the protagonist takes toward greater self-awareness, stronger character, more courageous actions, and so on. Which character do you believe changes most significantly in this play—Christian, Cyrano, or Roxane—and how does he or she change? Be very specific in your references to the text.

3 **Argument**
How does Rostand develop the tension between material and worldly values and spiritual ones? What are the risks of privileging one over the other? Which is, ultimately, more enduring? In your discussion, you might consider physical versus inner beauty, monetary power versus independence, and emotion versus intellect.

4 **Narrative**
What if Christian had not died in battle? Would he and Roxane have lived happily ever after? Write a short scene (as part of a play or as a piece of short fiction, no more than five hundred words) depicting their life together five years after Christian returns, hale and

hearty, from the Battle of Arras. Whether you include Cyrano in your portrait is up to you.

5 Multimedia/Comparison-Contrast

After viewing one of the film versions of *Cyrano* (such as the 1990 French production starring Gérard Depardieu or the 1987 adaptation called *Roxanne*), discuss the extent to which you believe the film is a success. Consider the intended audience and time period in your definition of "success," along with your interpretation of the play by Rostand.

6 Research/Argument

Develop a proposal for a contemporary production of *Cyrano de Bergerac*. First of all, decide if you would choose to perform it as a live theater production or a film version. Second, consider who you would like to cast as the main characters and whether you will set the production in 1640 (the original time frame) or in a more contemporary setting. Finally, think about whether you would like to change anything significant, such as the ending or other elements of plot. Would you choose verse or prose? Explain your rationale for your choices.

7 Narrative/Argument

In Cyrano, Rostand has created a great hero. He is daring. He is romantic. He is selfless. Investigate how we define "heroes" today, and what aspects of their characters seem most admirable. What do these traits tell us about what we value as a society? What do you value, or think others should value more? How does Cyrano compare to your standards?

CONVERSATION

LANGUAGE AND POWER

Imagine that you walk into the principal's office and say, "Dude, the food here is totally gross." Now imagine that you walk in and say, "I'm concerned about the freshness and nutritional value of the cafeteria food." Which line is more likely to command respectful attention?

From politics to public relations, publicity to protest, language has the power to influence people and shape the world.

Or, in the words of author James Baldwin, language is "a political instrument, means, and proof of power." He goes on to say of language:

It is the most vivid and crucial key to identity: It reveals the private identity, and connects one with, or divorces one from, the larger, public, or communal identity. There have been, and are, times, and places, when to speak a certain language could be dangerous, even fatal. Or, one may speak the same language, but in such a way that one's antecedents are revealed, or (one hopes) hidden. [. . .] To open your mouth in England is (if I may use black English) to "put your business in the street": You have confessed your parents, your youth, your school, your salary, your self-esteem, and, alas, your future.

Think of the associations we make when we hear the British royals, the Boston accent of John F. Kennedy, rural dialects from Appalachia, or the so-called broken English of new immigrants. Is there a hierarchy of forms of spoken or written English? If so, who decides which forms are most elevated, and on what basis? Are those hierarchies shifting?

While formal English might rule the halls of power, what about in pop culture and youth culture? Is there ever a time where breaking the rules of formal English might be a deliberate form of protest? Is breaking the rules what moves language forward?

In this Conversation, you will hear from writers who struggle to learn the language, those who wield it to bring about change, those who try to preserve language, and those who celebrate the way it evolves. And the authors in this Conversation also investigate the links that language forges between identity, culture, and power.

TEXTS

Frederick Douglass / *from* Narrative of the Life of Frederick Douglass (memoir)
Sandra Cisneros / No Speak English (fiction)
Ha Jin / Children as Enemies (fiction)
Mutabaruka / Dis Poem (poetry)
Kory Stamper / Slang for the Ages (nonfiction)
Firoozeh Dumas / Hot Dogs and Wild Geese (memoir)
Marjorie Agosín / English (poetry)
W. S. Merwin / Losing a Language (poetry)

from Narrative of the Life of Frederick Douglass

Frederick Douglass

Frederick Douglass (1818–1895) was an African American orator, social reformer, and writer. Born into slavery near Hillsboro, Maryland, he taught himself to read and write in his teenage years and secretly spread his knowledge to fellow slaves. After he escaped from slavery in 1838, Douglass became an instrumental figure in the abolitionist movement. Famous for his eloquent speeches and dazzling rhetoric, he was considered the leading black intellectual of his day. Douglass wrote several autobiographies about his experiences, including *Narrative of the Life of Frederick Douglass, an American Slave, Written by Himself* (1845), from which this selection is taken, and *Life and Times of Frederick Douglass* (1881).

Library of Congress

I lived in Master Hugh's family about seven years. During this time, I succeeded in learning to read and write. In accomplishing this, I was compelled to resort to various stratagems. I had no regular teacher. My mistress, who had kindly commenced to instruct me, had, in compliance with the advice and direction of her husband, not only ceased to instruct, but had set her face against my being instructed by any one else. It is due, however, to my mistress to say of her, that she did not adopt this course of treatment immediately. She at first lacked the depravity indispensable to shutting me up in mental darkness. It was at least necessary for her to have some training in the exercise of irresponsible power, to make her equal to the task of treating me as though I were a brute.

My mistress was, as I have said, a kind and tender-hearted woman; and in the simplicity of her soul she commenced, when I first went to live with her, to treat me as she supposed one human being ought to treat another. In entering upon the duties of a slaveholder, she did not seem to perceive that I sustained to her the relation of a mere chattel, and that for her to treat me as a human being was not only wrong, but

dangerously so. Slavery proved as injurious to her as it did to me. When I went there, she was a pious, warm, and tender-hearted woman. There was no sorrow or suffering for which she had not a tear. She had bread for the hungry, clothes for the naked, and comfort for every mourner that came within her reach. Slavery soon proved its ability to divest her of these heavenly qualities. Under its influence, the tender heart became stone, and the lamb-like disposition gave way to one of tiger-like fierceness. The first step in her downward course was in her ceasing to instruct me. She now commenced to practice her husband's precepts. She finally became even more violent in her opposition than her husband himself. She was not satisfied with simply doing as well as he had commanded; she seemed anxious to do better. Nothing seemed to make her more angry than to see me with a newspaper. She seemed to think that here lay the danger. I have had her rush at me with a face made all up of fury, and snatch from me a newspaper, in a manner that fully revealed her apprehension. She was an apt woman; and a little experience soon demonstrated, to her satisfaction, that education and slavery were incompatible with each other.

From this time I was most narrowly watched. If I was in a separate room any considerable length of time, I was sure to be suspected of having a book, and was at once called to give an account of myself. All this, however, was too late. The first step had been taken. Mistress, in teaching me the alphabet, had given me the *inch*, and no precaution could prevent me from taking the *ell*.

The plan which I adopted, and the one by which I was most successful, was that of making friends of all the little white boys whom I met in the street. As many of these as I could, I converted into teachers. With their kindly aid, obtained at different times and in different places, I finally succeeded in learning to read. When I was sent of errands, I always took my book with me, and by going one part of my errand quickly, I found time to get a lesson before my return. I used also to carry bread with me, enough of which was always in the house, and to which I was always welcome; for I was much better off in this regard than many of the poor white children in our neighborhood. This bread I used to bestow upon the hungry little urchins, who, in return, would give me that more valuable bread of knowledge. I am strongly tempted to give the names of two or three of those little boys, as a testimonial of the gratitude and affection I bear them; but prudence forbids: — not that it would injure me, but it might embarrass them; for it is almost an unpardonable offence to teach slaves to read in this Christian country. It is enough to say of the dear little fellows, that they lived on Philpot Street, very near Durgin and Bailey's ship-yard. I used to talk this matter of slavery over with them. I would some-times say to them, I wished I could be as free as they would be when they got to be men. "You will be free as soon as you are twenty-one, *but I am a slave for life!* Have not I as good a right to be free as you have?" These words used to trouble them; they would express for me the liveliest sympathy, and console me with the hope that something would occur by which I might be free.

5   I was now about twelve years old, and the thought of being *a slave for life* began to bear heavily upon my heart. Just about this time, I got hold of a book entitled *The Columbian Orator*. Every opportunity I got, I used to read this book. Among much of other interesting matter, I found in it a dialogue between a master and his slave. The slave was represented as having run away from his master three times. The dialogue represented the conversation which took place between them, when the slave was retaken the third time. In this

HIP/Art Resource, NY

Illustration from Harriet Beecher Stowe's *Uncle Tom's Cabin*, c. 1870. Stowe's antislavery novel was first published in 1852. In this scene, "Mas'r George" has come to give Tom an illegal reading and writing lesson.

In what ways are reading and writing subversive activities, both in this scene from Stowe's novel and in Douglass's narrative?

dialogue, the whole argument in behalf of slavery was brought forward by the master, all of which was disposed of by the slave. The slave was made to say some very smart as well as impressive things in reply to his master — things which had the desired though unexpected effect; for the conversation resulted in the voluntary emancipation of the slave on the part of the master.

In the same book, I met with one of Sheridan's mighty speeches on and in behalf of Catholic emancipation. These were choice documents to me. I read them over and over again with unabated interest. They gave tongue to interesting thoughts of my own soul, which had frequently lashed through my mind, and died away for want of utterance. The moral which I gained from the dialogue was the power of truth over the conscience of even a slaveholder. What I got from Sheridan[1] was a bold denunciation of slavery, and a powerful vindication of human rights. The reading of these documents enabled me to utter my thoughts, and to meet the arguments brought forward to sustain slavery; but while they relieved me of one difficulty, they brought on another even more painful than the one of which I was relieved. The more I read, the more I was led to abhor and detest my enslavers. I could regard them in no other light than a band of successful robbers, who had left their homes, and gone to Africa, and stolen us from our homes, and in a strange land reduced us to slavery. I loathed them as being the meanest as well as the most wicked of men. As I read and contemplated the subject, behold! that very discontentment which Master Hugh had predicted would follow my learning to read had already come, to torment and sting my soul to unutterable anguish. As I writhed under it, I would at times feel that learning to read had been a curse rather than a blessing. It had given

me a view of my wretched condition, without the remedy. It opened my eyes to the horrible pit, but to no ladder upon which to get out. In moments of agony, I envied my fellow-slaves for their stupidity. I have often wished myself a beast. I preferred the condition of the meanest reptile to my own. Any thing, no matter what, to get rid of thinking! It was this everlasting thinking of my condition that tormented me. There was no getting rid of it. It was pressed upon me by every object within sight or hearing, animate or inanimate. The silver trump of freedom had roused my soul to eternal wakefulness. Freedom now appeared, to disappear no more forever. It was heard in every sound, and seen in every thing. It was ever present to torment me with a sense of my wretched condition. I saw nothing without seeing it, I heard nothing without hearing it, and felt nothing without feeling it. It looked from every star, it smiled in every calm, breathed in every wind, and moved in every storm.

I often found myself regretting my own existence, and wishing myself dead; and but for the hope of being free, I have no doubt but that I should have killed myself, or done something for which I should have been killed. While in this state of mind, I was eager to hear any one speak of slavery. I was a ready listener. Every little while, I could hear something about the abolitionists. It was some time before I found what the word meant. It was always used in such connections as to make it an interesting word to me. If a slave ran away and succeeded in getting clear, or if a slave killed his master, set fire to a barn, or did any thing very wrong in the mind of a slaveholder, it was spoken of as the fruit of *abolition*. Hearing the word in this connection very often, I set about learning what it meant. The dictionary afforded me little or no help. I found it was "the act of abolishing"; but then I did not know what was to be abolished. Here I was perplexed. I did not dare to ask any one about its meaning, for I was satisfied that it was something they wanted me to know very little about. After a patient

---

[1] Sheridan: Playwright Richard Brinsley Sheridan (1751–1816) was an outspoken advocate for Catholic emancipation, fighting for equal rights for Catholics in Great Britain and Ireland. —Eds.

waiting, I got one of our city papers, containing an account of the number of petitions from the north, praying for the abolition of slavery in the District of Columbia, and of the slave trade between the States. From this time I understood the words *abolition* and *abolitionist*, and always drew near when that word was spoken, expecting to hear something of importance to myself and fellow-slaves. The light broke in upon me by degrees. I went one day down on the wharf of Mr. Waters; and seeing two Irishmen unloading a scow of stone, I went, unasked, and helped them. When we had finished, one of them came to me and asked me if I were a slave. I told him I was. He asked, "Are ye a slave for life?" I told him that I was. The good Irishman seemed to be deeply affected by the statement. He said to the other that it was a pity so fine a little fellow as myself should be a slave for life. He said it was a shame to hold me. They both advised me to run away to the north; that I should find friends there, and that I should be free. I pretended not to be interested in what they said, and treated them as if I did not understand them; for I feared they might be treacherous. White men have been known to encourage slaves to escape, and then, to get the reward, catch them and return them to their masters. I was afraid that these seemingly good men might use me so; but I nevertheless remembered their advice, and from that time I resolved to run away. I looked forward to a time at which it would be safe for me to escape. I was too young to think of doing so immediately; besides, I wished to learn how to write, as I might have occasion to write my own pass. I consoled myself with the hope that I should one day find a good chance. Meanwhile, I would learn to write.

The idea as to how I might learn to write was suggested to me by being in Durgin and Bailey's ship-yard, and frequently seeing the ship carpenters, after hewing, and getting a piece of timber ready for use, write on the timber the name of that part of the ship for which it was

intended. When a piece of timber was intended for the larboard side, it would be marked thus — "L." When a piece was for the starboard side, it would be marked thus — "S." A piece for the larboard side forward, would be marked thus — "L. F." When a piece was for starboard side forward, it would be marked thus — "S. F." For larboard aft, it would be marked thus — "L. A." For starboard aft, it would be marked thus — "S. A." I soon learned the names of these letters, and for what they were intended when placed upon a piece of timber in the ship-yard. I immediately commenced copying them, and in a short time was able to make the four letters named. After that, when I met with any boy who I knew could write, I would tell him I could write as well as he. The next word would be, "I don't believe you. Let me see you try it." I would then make the letters which I had been so fortunate as to learn, and ask him to beat that. In this way I got a good many lessons in writing, which it is quite possible I should never have gotten in any other way. During this time, my copy-book was the board fence, brick wall, and pavement; my pen and ink was a lump of chalk. With these, I learned mainly how to write. I then commenced and continued copying the Italics in Webster's Spelling Book, until I could make them all without looking on the book. By this time, my little Master Thomas had gone to school, and learned how to write, and had written over a number of copy-books. These had been brought home, and shown to some of our near neighbors, and then laid aside. My mistress used to go to class meeting at the Wilk Street meetinghouse every Monday afternoon, and leave me to take care of the house. When left thus, I used to spend the time in writing in the spaces left in Master Thomas's copy-book, copying what he had written. I continued to do this until I could write a hand very similar to that of Master Thomas. Thus, after a long, tedious effort for years, I finally succeeded in learning how to write.

seeing connections

In his autobiography, the civil rights leader Malcolm X claimed that prison was his "school." Below is a brief selection from that autobiography.

In what ways is the experience Malcolm X describes similar to and different from Frederick Douglass's?

World Telegram & Sun photo by Herman Hiller/Library of Congress

In the street, I had been the most articulate hustler out there — I had commanded attention when I said something. But now, trying to write simple English, I not only wasn't articulate, I wasn't even functional.

How would I sound writing in slang, the way I would say it, something such as, "Look, daddy, let me pull your coat about a cat, Elijah Muhammad —"

Many who today hear me somewhere in person, or on television, or those who read something I've said, will think I went to school far beyond the eighth grade. This impression is due entirely to my prison studies. [. . .]

I saw that the best thing I could do was get hold of a dictionary—to study, to learn some words. I was lucky enough to reason also that I should try to improve my penmanship. It was

sad. I couldn't even write in a straight line. It was both ideas together that moved me to request a dictionary along with some tablets and pencils from the Norfolk Prison Colony school.

I spent two days just riffling uncertainly through the dictionary's pages. I'd never realized so many words existed! I didn't know which words I needed to learn. Finally, just to start some kind of action, I began copying.

In my slow, painstaking, ragged handwriting, I copied into my tablet everything printed on that first page, down to the punctuation marks.

I believe it took me a day. Then, aloud, I read back, to myself, everything I'd written on the tablet. Over and over, aloud, to myself, I read my own handwriting.

I woke up the next morning, thinking about those words — immensely proud to realize that not only had I written so much at one time, but I'd written words that I never knew were in the world. [. . .]

I have often reflected upon the new vistas that reading opened to me. I knew right there in prison that reading had changed forever the course of my life. As I see it today, the ability to read awoke inside me some long dormant craving to be mentally alive. I certainly wasn't seeking any degree, the way a college confers a status symbol upon its students. My homemade education gave me, with every additional book that I read, a little bit more sensitivity to the deafness, dumbness, and blindness that was afflicting the black race in America. Not long ago, an English writer telephoned me from London, asking questions. One was, "What's your alma mater?" I told him, "Books." You will never catch me with a free fifteen minutes in which I'm not studying something I feel might be able to help the black man.

Understanding and Interpreting

1 In his opening paragraph, Douglass states that he "was compelled to resort to various stratagems" to learn to read and write. What were two of them?

2 How would you describe Douglass's attitude toward his "mistress"? What support does he provide for his assertion that "[s]lavery proved as injurious to her as it did to me" (par. 2)? To what extent do you find this claim convincing?

3 Why does Douglass say he "would at times feel that learning to read had been a curse rather than a blessing" (par. 6)?

4 What is the impact of Douglass's learning the meaning of the word "abolitionist" (par. 7)?

5 As Douglass learns to read and, ultimately, to write, he alternates between being student and teacher. What do others learn—directly or indirectly—from interacting with Douglass?

Analyzing Language, Style, and Structure

1 Who is the primary audience for Douglass's *Narrative of the Life of Frederick Douglass*? What ethos does he establish to appeal to this audience? Cite specific textual evidence to support your response.

2 What is the effect Douglass achieves in paragraph 4 when he shifts between literal and figurative meanings: "This bread I used to bestow upon the hungry little urchins, who, in return, would give me that more valuable bread of knowledge"?

3 Although this excerpt is an analysis, Douglass uses both narration and description to develop his explanation. How do these contribute to his overall purpose? Identify and discuss one example of

narration and one example of description in your response.

4 What rhetorical strategies does Douglass use to appeal to pathos in paragraph 6? Pay close attention to connotation and figurative language.

5 How does Douglass's use of language in this piece demonstrate his main point?

6 Overall, how would you describe Douglass's tone in this excerpt from the *Narrative of the Life of Frederick Douglass*? Use a phrase rather than a single word to capture the complexity of the speaker, for example, "angrily reproachful" or "respectful but firm."

Connecting, Arguing, and Extending

1 In a society that not only condemns efforts to make slaves literate, but actually makes any such efforts illegal, what power does Douglass gain by learning to read and write? Is it primarily a personal empowerment that he must conceal, or is it an empowerment that has public consequences? Support your argument with evidence from the text or from your own research into Douglass's life.

2 Write an essay explaining how this excerpt from the *Narrative of the Life of Frederick Douglass* makes the case that slavery brutalizes the slave masters as much as the slaves themselves. Include your own opinion of this viewpoint.

3 Douglass refers to *The Columbian Orator*, a 1797 collection of speeches that was widely used in the early nineteenth century to teach reading and speaking in U.S. schools. Research this publication and discuss why you believe it had such a profound impact on the

twelve-year-old Douglass, especially the "moral" he claims to have gained about "the power of truth over the conscience of even a slaveholder" (par. 6).

4 The society Douglass lived in passed laws to prohibit one group from having access to education—specifically, preventing them from reading and writing, as a means of controlling that group. To what extent do you see a similarity to governments today that legally prohibit the education of specific groups?

5 What does literacy mean to you? Develop a written essay or multimedia presentation about a powerful or meaningful literacy experience. For instance, you might recall your first experience with a book, explain your understanding of the role of reading or writing in your family, or your own struggle with acquiring a specific type of literacy.

No Speak English

Sandra Cisneros

One of the first Latina writers to achieve commercial success, Sandra Cisneros (b. 1954) is a novelist, short-story writer, and poet, best known for *The House on Mango Street* (1983), a collection of connected stories and sketches. The recipient of many awards, including a MacArthur Foundation "Genius" Grant, Cisneros has published the short-story collection *Woman Hollering Creek* (1991), the poetry collections *My Wicked Wicked Ways* (1987) and *Loose Woman* (1994), and most recently, the novel *Have You Seen Marie?* (2012). The *New York Times Book Review* says Cisneros embraces "the endless variety of Mexican and American culture—songs and stories, jokes and legends, furniture and food." "No Speak English," from *The House on Mango Street*, explores the impact of language on one immigrant family.

Ulf Andersen/Getty Images

Mamacita is the big mama of the man across the street, third-floor front. Rachel says her name ought to be *Mamasota*,[1] but I think that's mean.

The man saved his money to bring her here. He saved and saved because she was alone with the baby boy in that country. He worked two jobs. He came home late and he left early. Every day.

Then one day *Mamacita* and the baby boy arrived in a yellow taxi. The taxi door opened like a waiter's arm. Out stepped a tiny pink shoe, a foot soft as a rabbit's ear, then the thick ankle, a flutter of hips, fuchsia roses and green perfume. The man had to pull her, the taxicab driver had to push. Push, pull. Push, pull. Poof!

All at once she bloomed. Huge, enormous, beautiful to look at from the salmon-pink feather on the tip of her hat down to the little rosebuds of her toes. I couldn't take my eyes off her tiny shoes.

5   Up, up, up the stairs she went with the baby boy in a blue blanket, the man carrying her

suitcases, her lavender hatboxes, a dozen boxes of satin high heels. Then we didn't see her.

Somebody said because she's too fat, somebody because of the three flights of stairs, but I believe she doesn't come out because she is afraid to speak English, and maybe this is so since she only knows eight words. She knows to say: *He is not here* for when the landlord comes, *No speak English* if anybody else comes, and *Holy smokes.* I don't know where she learned this, but I heard her say it one time and it surprised me.

My father says when he came to this country he ate hamandeggs for three months. Breakfast, lunch and dinner. Hamandeggs. That was the only word he knew. He doesn't eat hamandeggs anymore.

Whatever her reasons, whether she is fat, or can't climb the stairs, or is afraid of English, she won't come down. She sits all day by the window and plays the Spanish radio show and sings all the homesick songs about her country in a voice that sounds like a seagull.

Home. Home. Home is a house in a photograph, a pink house, pink as hollyhocks with lots of startled light. The man paints the walls of the

---

[1] *Mamacita/Mamasota:* Spanish, slang. The former means an attractive woman (usually younger); the latter means a sexualized large older woman. —Eds.

Frida Kahlo, *Self-Portrait on the Borderline between Mexico and the United States*, 1932. Oil on metal.

Based on this painting, what do you think Kahlo's attitude is toward Mexican culture and American culture? Which culture does she value more, and why? Why might Kahlo be sympathetic to Mamacita's situation, based on the evidence in this painting?

apartment pink, but it's not the same, you know. She still sighs for her pink house, and then I think she cries. I would.

10   Sometimes the man gets disgusted. He starts screaming and you can hear it all the way down the street.

Ay, she says, she is sad.

Oh, he says. Not again.

¿Cuándo, cuándo, cuándo?[2] she asks.

¡Ay, caray! We *are* home. This *is* home. Here I am and here I stay. Speak English. Speak English. Christ!

15   *¡Ay! Mamacita,* who does not belong, every once in a while lets out a cry, hysterical, high, as if he had torn the only skinny thread that kept her alive, the only road out to that country.

And then to break her heart forever, the baby boy, who has begun to talk, starts to sing the Pepsi commercial he heard on T.V.

No speak English, she says to the child who is singing in the language that sounds like tin. No speak English, no speak English, and bubbles into tears. No, no, no, as if she can't believe her ears.

---

[2] *cuándo:* Spanish, "when." —Eds.

Understanding and Interpreting

1 What is the "joke" in the opening paragraph of the story, that is, "Mamacita" versus "Mamasota"? Is it funny or, as the narrator says, "mean," or a little of both?

2 How is the man, the father, portrayed in this story? To what extent is he a sympathetic character?

3 What is the meaning of "home" in "No Speak English"? How important is language in defining what "home" means?

4 What factors or forces isolate the woman in this story? Identify at least four. Do you think one is most influential, or do several factors work cumulatively? Explain.

5 What different meanings do you find in the title of the story, "No Speak English"? Why do you think Cisneros suggests such ambiguity?

Analyzing Language, Style, and Structure

1 Who is the narrator of the story? What information do you have about her age, ethnicity, personality, and so on? How does this information contribute to her reliability as the narrator?

2 Cisneros describes the central character with vivid details of her physical appearance, dress, walk, and so on. Which specific details suggest a cultural clash?

3 To what extent do you think the narrator is exaggerating in descriptions such as the following: "[H]e ate hamandeggs for three months. Breakfast, lunch and dinner" (par. 7). What other examples can you identify? What is the narrator's purpose in making such sweeping statements?

4 How does Cisneros develop the idea of entrapment through imagery and specific detail in this story?

Connecting, Arguing, and Extending

1 What issues about the relationship between language and power does this story raise? Who has power in the family across the street from the narrator?

2 At the end, the mother "bubbles into tears" when her son sings a soda commercial in English. Is Cisneros suggesting that the boy's learning English is dangerous, insensitive, necessary, inevitable, or disloyal? Is it a combination of these, or something else? Support your response with specifics from this text.

3 Jump forward fifteen years in your imagination and write a brief narrative in the voice of the "baby boy" as a teenager. Speculate about how he sees himself and his parents.

4 This story is one of several vignettes—short narrative sketches—in *The House on Mango Street*. Read several others and discuss the challenges immigrant families face when coming to the United States. What "translations" must they make, according to Cisneros?

Children as Enemies

Ha Jin

Ulf Andersen/Getty Images

Born in Liaoning Province, China, in 1956, Ha Jin grew up during the Cultural Revolution. He volunteered to serve in the People's Liberation Army from age fourteen to nineteen. While serving in the army, Jin studied English. After he received his BA from Heilongjiang University (1981) and an MA from Shandong University (1984), he came to the United States to complete his PhD at Brandeis University. After the massacre of student democracy protestors in Tiananmen Square in 1989, Jin decided to remain in the United States and write solely in English. He currently teaches at Boston University. Jin has published several books of poetry and short fiction as well as six novels, one of which, *Waiting* (1999), won the National Book Award. The following story, "Children as Enemies," is from Jin's 2009 short-story collection, *A Good Fall*.

KEY CONTEXT In traditional Chinese culture, the concept of filial piety means respect for one's parents and ancestors. Based on Confucian philosophy, it involves general obedience but extends further to include behaving in such a way as to reflect well upon one's parents, always showing love and respect, supporting parents both financially and emotionally, and caring for them as they age. Children are expected to honor such duties to their parents and willingly sacrifice to carry them out. Ha Jin explores the consequences of becoming part of a culture that has a different, more open, definition of children's responsibilities to their family.

Our grandchildren hate us. The boy and the girl, ages eleven and nine, are just a pair of selfish, sloppy brats and have no respect for old people. Their animosity toward us originated at the moment their names were changed, about three months ago.

One evening the boy complained that his schoolmates couldn't pronounce his name, so he must change it. "Lots of them call me 'Chicken,'" he said. "I want a regular name like anyone else." His name was Qigan Xi, pronounced "cheegan hsee," which could be difficult for non-Chinese to manage.

"I wanna change mine too," his sister, Hua, jumped in. "Nobody can say it right and some call me 'Wow.'" She bunched her lips, her face puffed with baby fat.

Before their parents could respond, my wife put in, "You should teach them how to pronounce your names."

5   "They always laugh about my silly name, Qigan," the boy said. "If I didn't come from China, I'd say 'Chicken' too."

I told both kids, "You ought to be careful about changing your names. We decided on them only after consulting a reputable fortune-teller."

"Phew, who believes in that crap?" the boy muttered.

Our son intervened, saying to his children, "Let me think about this, okay?"

Our daughter-in-law, thin-eyed Mandi, broke in. "They should have American names. Down the road there'll be lots of trouble if their names remain unpronounceable. We should've changed them long ago."

10   Gubin, our son, seemed to agree, though he wouldn't say it in our presence.

My wife and I were unhappy about that, but we didn't make a serious effort to stop them, so Mandi and Gubin went about looking for suitable names for the children. It was easy in the girl's case. They picked "Flora" for her, since her name, Hua, means "flower." But it was not easy to find a name for the boy. English names are simple in meaning, mostly already empty of their original senses. Qigan means "amazing bravery." Where can you find an English name that combines the import and the resonance of that? When I pointed out the difficulty, the boy blustered, "I don't want a weird and complicated name. I just need a regular name, like Charlie or Larry or Johnny."

That I wouldn't allow. Names are a matter of fortune and fate — that's why fortune-tellers can divine the vicissitudes of people's lives by reading the orders and numbers of the strokes in the characters of their names. No one should change his name randomly.

Mandi went to the public library and checked out a book on baby names. She perused the small volume and came up with "Matty" as a choice. She explained, "'Matty' is short for 'Mathilde,' which is from Old German and means 'powerful in battle,' very close to 'Qigan' in meaning. Besides, the sound echoes 'mighty' in English."

"It doesn't sound right," I said. In the back of my mind I couldn't reconcile "Matty" with "Xi," our family name.

15   "I like it," the boy crowed.

He seemed determined to contradict me, so I said no more. I wished my son had rejected the choice, but Gubin didn't make a peep, just sitting in the rocking chair and drinking iced tea. The matter was settled. The boy went to school and told his teacher he had a new name — Matty.

For a week he seemed happy, but his satisfaction was short-lived. One evening he told his parents, "Matty is a girl's name, my friend Carl told me."

"Impossible," his mother said.

"Of course it's true. I asked around, and people all said it sounded girlish."

20 My wife, drying her hands on her apron, suggested to our son, "Why don't you look it up?"

The book on baby names was not returned yet, so Gubin looked it up and saw "f. or m." beside the name. Evidently Mandi hadn't seen that it could be both female and male. Her negligence or ignorance outraged the boy all the more.

What should we do? The eleven-year-old turned tearful, blaming his mother for giving him a name with an ambiguous gender.

Finally my son slapped his knee and said, "I have an idea. 'Matty' can also come from 'Matt.' Why not drop the letter 'y' and call yourself Matt?"

The boy brightened up and said he liked that, but I objected. "Look, this book says 'Matt' is a diminutive of 'Matthew.' It's nowhere close to the sense of 'amazing bravery.'"

25 "Who gives a damn about that!" the boy spat out. "I'm gonna call myself Matt."

Wordless, I felt my face tightening. I got up and went out to smoke a pipe on the balcony. My wife followed me, saying, "My old man, don't take to heart what our grandson said. He's just confused and desperate. Come back in and eat."

"After this pipe," I said.

"Don't be long." She stepped back into the apartment, her small shoulders more stooped than before.

Below me, automobiles were gliding past on the wet street like colored whales. If only we hadn't sold everything in Dalian City and come here to join our son's family. Gubin is our only child, so we'd thought it would be good to stay with him. Now I wish we hadn't moved. At our ages — my wife is sixty-three and I'm sixty-seven — and at this time it's hard to adjust to life here. In America it feels as if the older you are, the more inferior you grow.

30 Both my wife and I understood we shouldn't meddle with our grandchildren's lives, but sometimes I simply couldn't help offering them a bit of advice. She believed it was our daughter-in-law who had spoiled the kids and made them despise us. I don't think Mandi is that mean, though beyond question she is an indulgent mother. Flora and Matt look down on everything Chinese except for some food they like. They hated to go to the weekend school to learn to read and write the characters. Matt announced, "I've no need for that crap."

I would have to force down my temper whenever I heard him say that. Their parents managed to make them attend the weekend school, though Matt and Flora had quit inscribing the characters. They went there only to learn how to paint with a brush, taking lessons from an old artist from Taiwan. The girl, sensitive by nature and delicate in health, might have had some talent for arts, but the boy was good at nothing but daydreaming. I just couldn't help imagining that he might end up a guttersnipe. He wouldn't draw bamboos or goldfish or landscapes with a brush; instead, he produced merely bands and lines of ink on paper, calling them abstract paintings. He experimented with the shades of the ink as if it were watercolors. Sometimes he did that at home too. Seeing his chubby face and narrow eyes as he worked in dead earnest, I wanted to laugh. He once showed a piece with some vertical lines of ink on it to an art teacher at his school. To my horror, the woman praised it, saying the lines suggested a rainfall or waterfall, and that if you observed them horizontally, they would bring to mind layers of clouds or some sort of landscape.

What a crock was that! I complained to Gubin in private and urged him to pressure the children to study serious subjects, such as science, classics, geography, history, grammar, and penmanship. If Matt really couldn't handle those, in the future he should consider learning how to repair cars and machines or how to cook like a chef. Auto mechanics make good money here — I know a fellow at a garage who can't speak any English but pulls in twenty-four dollars an hour, plus a generous bonus at the end of the year. I made it clear to my son that a few tricks in "art" would never get his kids anywhere in life, so they'd better stop dabbling with a brush. Gubin said Matt and Flora were still young and we shouldn't push them too hard, but he agreed to talk to them. Unlike Gubin, Mandi aligned herself with the children, saying we ought to let them develop freely as individuals, not straitjacket them as they would back in China. My wife and I were unhappy about our daughter-in-law's position. Whenever we criticized her, our grandchildren would mock us or yell at us in defense of their mother.

I have serious reservations about elementary education in the United States. Teachers don't force their pupils to work as hard as they can. Matt had learned both multiplication and division in the third grade, but two months ago I asked him to calculate how much seventy-four percent of $1,586 was, and he had no clue how to do it. I handed him a calculator and said, "Use this." Even so, he didn't know he could just multiply the amount by 0.74.

"Didn't you learn multiplication and division?" I asked him.

35   "I did, but that was last year."

"Still, you should know how to do it."

"We haven't practiced division and multiplication this year, so I'm not familiar with them anymore." He offered that as an excuse. There was no way I could make him understand that once you learned something, you were supposed to master it and make it part of yourself. That's why we say knowledge is wealth. You can get richer and richer by accumulating it within.

The teachers here don't assign the pupils any real homework. Instead they give them a lot of projects, some of which seem no more than woolgathering, and tend to inflate the kids' egos. My son had to help his children with the projects, which were more like homework for the parents. Some of the topics were impossible even for adults to tackle, such as "What is culture and how is it created?" "Make your argument for or against the Iraq War," "How does the color line divide U.S. society?" and "Do you think global trade is necessary? Why?" My son had to do research online and in the public library to get the information needed for discussing those topics. Admittedly, they could broaden the pupils' minds and give them more confidence, but at their tender age they are not supposed to think like a politician or a scholar. They should be made to follow rules; that is, to become responsible citizens first.

Whenever I asked Flora how she was ranked in her class, she'd shrug and say, "I dunno."

40   "What do you mean you don't know?" I suspected she must be well below the average, though she couldn't be lower than her brother.

"Ms. Gillen doesn't rank us is all," came her answer.

If that was true, I was even more disappointed with the schools. How could they make their students competitive in this global economy if they didn't instill in them the sense of getting ahead of others and becoming the very best? No wonder many Asian parents viewed the public schools in Flushing unfavorably. In my honest opinion, elementary education here tends to lead children astray.

Five weeks ago, Matt declared at dinner that he must change his last name, because a substitute teacher that morning had mispronounced "Xi" as "Eleven." That put the whole class in stitches, and some students even made fun of the boy afterward, calling him "Matt Eleven." Flora chimed in, "Yeah, I want a different last name too. My friend Reta just had her family name changed to Wu. Some people couldn't pronounce 'Ng' and called her 'Reta No Good.'"

Their parents broke out laughing, but I couldn't see why that was funny. My wife said to the girl, "You'll have your husband's last name when you grow up and get married."

45 "I don't want no man!" the girl shot back.

"We both must have a new last name," the boy insisted.

I burst out, "You can't do that. Your last name belongs to the family, and you can't cut yourselves off from your ancestors."

"Baloney!" The boy squished up his face.

"You mustn't speak to your granddad like that," his grandmother butted in.

50 Mandi and my son exchanged glances. I knew they saw this matter differently from us. Maybe they had been planning to change their children's last name all along

dropped my bowl on the di

pointed my finger at Man

best to spoil them. Now

break away from the

daughter-in-law are you:

you to join our family."

"Please don't blow up like this, ᴸ said.

Mandi didn't talk back. Instead she began sobbing, wrinkling her gourd-shaped nose. The kids got angry and blamed me for hurting their mother's feelings. The more they blabbered, the more furious I became. Finally unable to hold it back anymore, I shouted, "If you two change your last name, you leave, get out of here. You cannot remain in this household while using a different last name."

"Who are you?" Matt said calmly. "This isn't your home."

"You're just our guests," added Flora.

▶

In his piece titled *Family Tree*, Chinese artist Zhang Huan asked three calligraphers to write the names of friends and family and inscribe personal and cultural stories directly onto his skin. The artist describes how he sees this serial self-portait: "It is impossible to take away your inborn blood and personality. [. . .] This work speaks about a family story, a spirit of family."

What message about family and cultural heritage do you think Huan is expressing? How might each generation in "Children as Enemies" interpret the argument Huan is making with this piece?

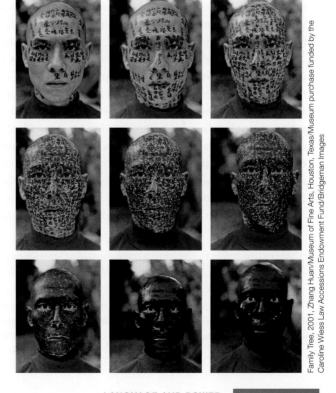

Family Tree, 2001, Zhang Huan/Museum of Fine Arts, Houston, Texas/Museum purchase funded by the Caroline Wiess Law Accessions Endowment Fund/Bridgeman Images

That drove both my wife and me mad. She yelled at our granddaughter, "So we sold everything in China, our apartment and candy store, just to be your guests here, huh? Heartless. Who told you this isn't our home?"

That shut the girl up, though she kept glaring at her grandma. Their father begged no one in particular, "Please, let us finish dinner peacefully." He went on chewing a fried shrimp with his mouth closed.

I wanted to yell at him that he was just a rice barrel thinking of nothing but food, but I controlled my anger. How could we have raised such a spineless son?

To be fair, he's quite accomplished in his profession, a bridge engineer pulling in almost six figures a year, but he's henpecked and indulgent with the kids, and got worse and worse after he came to America, as if he had become a man without temper or opinions. How often I wanted to tell him point-blank that he must live like a man, at least more like his former self. Between his mother and myself, we often wondered if he was inadequate in bed; otherwise, how could he always listen to Mandi?

After that quarrel, we decided to move out. Gubin and Mandi helped us fill out an application for housing offered to the elderly by the city, which we'll have to wait a long time to get. If we were not so old and in poor health, we'd live far away from them, completely on our own, but they are the only family we have in this country, so we could move only to a nearby place. For the time being we've settled down in a one-bedroom apartment on Fifty-fourth Avenue,

rented for us by Gubin. Sometimes he comes over to see if we're all right or need anything. We've never asked him what last name our grandkids use now. I guess they must have some American name. How sad it is when you see your grandchildren's names on paper but can no longer recognize them, as though your family line has faded and disappeared among the multitudes. Whenever I think about this, it stings my heart. If only I'd had second thoughts about leaving China. It's impossible to go back anymore, and we'll have to spend our remaining years in this place where even your grandchildren can act like your enemies.

60   Matt and Flora usually shun us. If we ran into them on the street, they would warn us not to "torture" their mother again. They even threatened to call the police if we entered their home without permission. We don't have to be warned. We've never set foot in their home since we moved out. I've told my son that we won't accept the kids as part of the family as long as they use a different last name.

Gubin has never brought up that topic again, though I'm still waiting for an answer from him. That's how the matter stands now. The other day, exasperated, my wife wanted to go to Mandi's fortune cookie factory and raise a placard to announce: "My Daughter-in-Law Mandi Cheng Is the Most Unfilial Person on Earth!" But I dissuaded my old better half. What's the good of that? For sure Mandi's company won't fire her just because she can't make her parents-in-law happy. This is America, where we must learn self-reliance and mind our own business.

Understanding and Interpreting

1 "Our grandchildren hate us" is the dramatic opening line of this story. What is your response to this statement, so simply expressed yet freighted with such emotion? What does it lead you to expect?

2 What evidence do you find in the story to support the narrator's second sentence, which characterizes the grandchildren as "just a pair of selfish, sloppy brats"? What impact, if any, does the age of the children have on your view of whether they are "selfish, sloppy brats"?

3 What is significant about Mandi's turning to a book she checks out of the library in order to identify a meaningful name for her children? What is the contrasting Chinese tradition?

4 Why does the grandfather conclude that "[i]n America it feels as if the older you are, the more inferior you grow" (par. 29)?

5 To what extent do you agree that Mandi is "an indulgent mother" (par. 30), as the grandfather accuses? Cite specific details to support your response.

6 What are the fundamental differences in philosophy about education that the grandfather perceives between the American and Chinese school systems?

7 By the end of the story, where are your sympathies: with the grandparents, the parents, or the children?

8 Is this a story more about a clash of cultures or generations? In what ways does the language issue symbolize power struggles and shifts within the family?

Analyzing Language, Style, and Structure

1 Who is the narrator? What is the impact of having the story told from that character's point of view, rather than by an omniscient narrator who could represent a range of perspectives?

2 What elements of humor do you find in the story? What is the effect that the author achieves by infusing humor (and irony) into the narrative?

3 What do you learn about the narrator from the details he selects and the tone of the paragraph describing the children's learning to paint (par. 31)?

4 What descriptions, either words or phrases, convey the grandfather's anger and his disapproving attitude toward Gubin and his family? Pay close attention to the figurative language the narrator uses to describe physical qualities as well as character traits.

5 Gubin is notably silent during this story. What do we learn about him from the little bit of dialogue he has? To what extent does the character revealed by that dialogue reflect or conflict with what the narrator tells us about his son?

Connecting, Arguing, and Extending

1 Is the story over? What do you believe will be the situation a few years later? Is there a way to heal the family's wounds? If so, how might that happen? Who might take the lead? Who needs to change?

2 Do the grandchildren truly hate their grandparents? Are the children "enemies"? That very word suggests a battle, a fight for power. Is the battle really about names? Explain your position with specific references to the story.

3 A reviewer for the Seattle Times said of the collection in which "Children as Enemies" appeared, "If there is a recurring theme in these 13 stories, it is the anxiety of the stranger, the one who doesn't fit. There is a seriousness present in these stories that is heavy, ponderous; even ominous." Explain how this theme is developed in "Children as Enemies." Who is the "stranger"—or is there more than one?

4 Let's hear another side to this story. Write a brief narrative about the name changes from the perspective of a character other than the grandfather.

Dis Poem

Mutabaruka

Mutabaruka was born Allan Hope in 1952 in Jamaica, where he went on to attend Kingston Technical High School. Raised Catholic, he converted to Rastafarianism after becoming involved with the Black Awareness movements of the 1970s. He began writing poetry in the 1970s under the name Allan Mutabaruka, then under the single name, which comes from the Rwandan language and translates as "one who is always victorious." Currently, he lives in Jamaica with his wife and children and frequently travels internationally as a performer and lecturer.

Jemal Countess/WireImage/Getty Images

KEY CONTEXT   Mutabaruka is a practitioner of dub poetry, a performance genre that began in the Caribbean, incorporating spoken word with reggae music. Unlike the spontaneity and improvisation that characterizes much performance poetry, dub poetry is written ahead of time, usually with a band accompaniment. The two most famous dub poets, Mutabaruka and Linton Kwesi Johnson, typify the political and social consciousness of this genre that carries an overt message, usually controversial, protesting social injustice. In his most recent collection, *First Poems/Next Poems* (2005), Mutabaruka writes that his poems are intended "to show [readers] the problems that face us in the world and then motivate you to find solutions." Mutabaruka performed "Dis Poem," his most widely known work, as part of *Def Poetry Jam*, a spoken word poetry television series.

dis poem.	nkrumah
shall speak of the wretched sea	15 hannibal
that washed ships to these shores	akenaton
of mothers crying for their young	malcolm
5 swallowed up by the sea	garvey
dis poem shall say nothin new	haile selassie[1]
dis poem shall speak of time	20 dis poem is vex
time unlimited	about apartheid
time undefined	racism
10 dis poem shall call names	fascism
names like	the klu klux klan
lumumba	25 riots in brixton[2]
kenyatta	atlanta

---

[1] **lumumba . . . selassie:** Names of activists and leaders. Patrice Lumumba, the first prime minister of the Congo (now Zaire); Jomo Kenyatta, the first president of Kenya; Kwame Nkrumah, the first president of Ghana; Abram Petrovich Hannibal, a Russian general who began his life as an enslaved African; Akenaton, an Egyptian pharaoh; Malcolm X, an American activist; Marcus Garvey, a Jamaican who helped develop the nation of Liberia; Haile Selassie, the emperor of Ethiopia and messiah of the Rastafari religion. —Eds.

[2] **brixton:** neighborhood in South London, site of a 1985 riot sparked by a police shooting of a black woman. —Eds.

jim jones[3]
dis poem is revoltin against
first world
30 second world
third world
division
manmade decision
dis poem is like all the rest
35 dis poem will not be amongst great literary
works
will not be recited by poetry enthusiasts
will not be quoted by politicians
nor men of religion
dis poem is knives . . . bombs . . . guns . . .
40 blazing for freedom
yes dis poem is a drum
ashanti
mau mau
ibo
45 yoruba[4]
niahbingi[5] warriors
uhuru . . . uhuru[6]
namibia uhuru
uhuru
50 soweto[7]
uhuru
afrika!
dis poem will not change things
dis poem needs to be changed
55 dis poem is a rebirth of a people
arizin awakin understandin
dis poem speak is speakin have spoken
dis poem shall continue even when poets
have stopped writin
dis poem shall survive u me it shall linger in
history

60 in your mind
in time forever
dis poem is time only time will tell
dis poem is still not written
dis poem has no poet
65 dis poem is just a part of the story
his-story her-story our-story the story still
untold
dis poem is now ringin talkin irritatin
makin u want to stop it
but dis poem will not stop
70 dis poem is long cannot be short
dis poem cannot be tamed cannot be blamed
the story is still not told about dis poem
dis poem is old new
dis poem was copied from the bible your
prayer book
75 playboy magazine the n.y. times readers
digest
the c.i.a. files the k.g.b. files
dis poem is no secret
dis poem shall be called boring stupid
senseless
dis poem is watchin u tryin to make sense
from dis poem
80 dis poem is messin up your brains
makin u want to stop listenin to dis poem
but u shall not stop listenin to dis poem
u need to know what will be said next in dis
poem
dis poem shall disappoint u
85 because
dis poem is to be continued in your mind in
your mind
in your mind your mind

---

[3] **jim jones:** Jim Jones was a cult leader who convinced his followers to commit mass suicide via a poisoned soft drink mix, in what has become known as the Jonestown Massacre. —Eds.

[4] **ashanti . . . yoruba:** Various African ethnic groups — Ashanti from Ghana, Mau Mau from Kenya, Ibo from Nigeria, Yoruba from Nigeria and Benin. —Eds.

[5] **niahbingi:** Rastafarian ritual drumming. —Eds.

[6] **uhuru:** Swahili, "freedom". —Eds.

[7] **soweto:** Soweto (short for South Western Townships) is an urban area of Johannesburg, South Africa, where blacks were relocated after forced removals from other neighborhoods by the apartheid government of the 1950s and 1960s. Also, site of an uprising in the 1970s. —Eds.

Barbara Kruger, *Untitled (We will no longer be seen and not heard)*, 1985. Lithograph on paper, Tate Gallery, London.

Pair several of these images with lines from Mutabaruka's poem. Think about how the image does more than just illustrate the point being made: consider how the image extends or deepens the point.

Understanding and Interpreting

1 What historical events does the poem allude to in the lines, "the wretched sea / that washed ships to these shores" (ll. 2–3)?

2 The speaker asserts that "dis poem" "will not be recited by poetry enthusiasts" nor "quoted by politicians / nor men of religion" (ll. 36–38). What is it about the poem that he believes will not appeal to these figures of authority? If that is the case, then, to whom will the poem appeal?

3 What does the speaker mean when he says "dis poem has no poet" (l. 64)?

4 What kind of authority—or resistance—does the speaker anticipate when he predicts that readers of the poem will "makin u want to stop it" even though "dis poem will not stop" (ll. 68–69)?

5 How and why does the speaker believe "dis poem is to be continued in your mind" (l. 86)?

6 What is Mutabaruka's overall intention in "Dis Poem"? What is the power of poetry that he invokes as the speaker?

Analyzing Language, Style, and Structure

1 Who do you think is the audience Mutabaruka intends for this poem? Given the performance aspect, is he only addressing like-minded people or does he appeal to others outside that circle?

2 To what extent does the use of vernacular enhance the poem *only* when it is performed? You might want to view a performance online to provide support for your response.

3 What effect(s) does Mutabaruka achieve by personifying "dis poem"?

4 Identify several paradoxes in "Dis Poem." What do you think is the author's purpose for including so many?

5 The tone in "Dis Poem" shifts in different sections. Identify at least two sections with different tones. How do you describe the overall tone?

6 "Dis Poem" develops as an argument. What is the thesis or primary claim? What evidence does Mutabaruka provide to support it?

Connecting, Arguing, and Extending

1 Research one of the "names" Mutabaruka lists in lines 12–19 and explain why that person is a name that "dis poem shall call."

2 To what extent do you find "Dis Poem" an effective argument? Respond in terms of the written text, the performed text, or a combination.

3 Why is "dis poem [. . .] a drum" (l. 41)? What is the cultural reference implicit in this metaphor? Research the significance of drumming in Afro-Caribbean cultures in terms of communication.

4 Do some research into the history and philosophy of dub poetry. Who are its major artists? Is it largely a protest movement? Present your findings in a multimedia format that includes performances.

5 Write a poem intended to get under the skin of its audience in a way that continues "ringin talkin irritatin" (l. 67) people, that is, a poem that calls its readers to action. Use a vernacular or English dialect in some parts or throughout the poem. Present your poem either as a written or performed text.

Slang for the Ages

Kory Stamper

Kory Stamper is a lexicographer and editor for the Merriam-Webster dictionaries. She has written for the *Chicago Tribune* and blogs at harm•less drudg•ery. She contributes to a video series on the Merriam-Webster website and YouTube that discusses the English language, especially unusual or controversial words and usages.

Everyone knows that slang is informal speech, usually invented by reckless young people, who are ruining proper English. These obnoxious upstart words are vapid and worthless, say the guardians of good usage, and lexicographers like me should be preserving language that has a lineage, well-bred words with wholesome backgrounds, rather than recording the modish vulgarities of street argot.

In fact, much of today's slang has older and more venerable roots than most people realize.

Take "swag." As a noun ("Check out my swag, yo / I walk like a ballplayer" — Jay Z), a verb ("I smash this verse / and I swag and surf" — Lil Wayne), an adjective ("I got ya slippin' on my swag juice" — Eminem), and even as an interjection ("Say hello to falsetto in three, two, swag" — Justin Bieber), swag

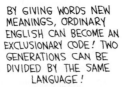

Where's the joke in this cartoon? Is the artist being entirely facetious in this depiction of an exchange between father and son, or does he have a serious point? Do you think "ordinary English" can become "an exclusionary code"? When does healthy change become "exclusionary"?

refers to a sense of confidence and style. It's slangy enough that few dictionaries have entered it yet.

Swag sounds new, but the informal use goes way back. It's generally taken to be a shortened form of the verb "swagger," which was used to denote a certain insolent cockiness by William Shakespeare, O.G. The adjectival use dates to 1640, and seems to have a similar connotation to the modern swag ("Hansom swag fellowes and fitt for fowle play" — John Fletcher and Philip Massinger, in *The Tragedy of Sir John van Olden Barnavelt*). The noun was first used even earlier: One 1589 citation reads like an Elizabethan attempt at freestyle ("lewd swagges, ambicious wretches").

5 Nor was Mr. Bieber the first to use the word because he liked how it finished a line. The English playwright William Davies wrote, in 1786, of one of his characters that she moved like a half-full "cask set in motion, swag, swag."

The website Gawker prophesied in 2012, and Mr. Bieber averred last year, that swag is over. It takes some swag to call time on a piece of slang that goes back centuries; and, in any case, Google Trends shows that the usage is holding steady. Swag is dead; long live swag.

Swag evolved out of standard English, but there's also slang that is slang born and raised. As it moves through successive generations, it may morph — but without losing its cred.

"Fubar" was first used in print in 1943; it is an acronym whose expanded version I will bowdlerize as "rhymes with trucked up beyond all recognition." This was slang created by the Greatest Generation as Americans marched to war, a shining example of how G.I.s adapted the custom of military acronyms to their own purposes.

Fubar had its heyday during the war, then fell out of use. But it never disappeared entirely. Decades later, it was appropriated by another kind of acronym-loving grunt: the computer programmer. One of the biggest and earliest employers of programmers was the American military, and the release of home consoles in the '70s and '80s meant that middle-aged coders of the military-industrial complex were mingling — and sharing their slang — with college-aged console hackers. Fubar became a placeholder name for files, some of which might contain coding errors.

10 Was it still slang? Definitely. Restricted to young people? Not so much. Fubar still enjoys slang use among the hip and Internet-savvy: In the last two years, I've taken citations for

seeing connections

In this excerpt, Tom Dalzell, slang expert and author of *Flappers 2 Rappers: American Youth Slang*, discusses the roots of slang in American English.

The four factors that are the most likely to produce slang are youth, oppression, sports, and vice, which provide an impetus to coin and use slang for different socio-linguistic reasons. Of these four factors, youth is the most powerful stimulus for the creation and distribution of slang. [. . .]

Youth slang derives some of its power from its willingness to borrow from other bodies of slang. Despite its seeming mandate of creativity and originality, slang is blatantly predatory, borrowing without shame from possible sources. Foremost among them is the African-American vernacular, whose influence on American youth slang of the 20th century cannot be over-stated. Beginning in the late 1930s with the wild popularity of swing jazz and the jitterbug, continuing into the "jive generation" that fought World War II, through the beats and hipsters of the 1950s, the Sixties' main-stream youth and hippies alike, into the pervasive patois of hip-hop, American youth slang has borrowed consistently and generously from the slang of the black American urban experience.

How does Dalzell's perspective on slang differ from Kory Stamper's historical analysis? What new perspective on language and power does Dalzell provide?

Fubar from Wonkette, Gawker and the A.V. Club.

Speaking of hip, hipsters have been derided as know-it-alls since at least 1941: The word "hipster" was so defined by Jack Smiley in his seminal collection of soda-jerk slang, *Hash House Lingo*. Likewise, the word "dude" predates the Dude of *The Big Lebowski* fame by over 100 years. Cops have been "nailing" suspects since the early 1700s. Even the seem-ingly up-to-the-minute "bae," a word that means babe or baby and is so new that most of its written use is in personal communications, has a print trail back to the early 2000s, and is probably a descendant of the reduplicative nickname Bae Bae, a rendering of "baby," which shows up in print in the 1990s. In some cases, bae is older than the people using it. (It also has its own spurious acronymic etymology, "before anyone else.")

Slang often falls prey to what linguists call the "recency illusion": I don't remember using or hearing this word before, therefore this word is new (often followed by the Groucho Marx sentiment: "Whatever it is, I'm against it"). At the heart of the illusion lies a misbegotten belief that English is a static and uniform language, a mighty mountain of lexical stability. Upon this monument, slang falls like acid rain, eroding and degrading the linguistic landscape.

It's the wrong metaphor. English is fluid and enduring: not a mountain, but an ocean. A word may drift down through time from one current of English (say, the language of World War II soldiers) to another (the slang of computer programmers). Slang words are quicksilver flashes of cool in the great stream.

Some words disappear, and others endure. One thing is sure: The persistence of slang doesn't mean that English is Fubar. In fact, it's swag, bae.

Understanding and Interpreting

1 What is the main point that Kory Stamper makes in this article? Where does she state it as an explicit thesis?

2 What does the author mean by "the modish vulgarities of street argot" (par. 1)?

3 How do the two examples, "swag" and "fubar," relate to and support Stamper's thesis?

4 What does Stamper mean by her statement: "Swag evolved out of standard English, but there's also slang that is slang born and raised" (par. 7)? What distinction is she drawing?

5 What is the "recency illusion" Stamper considers in paragraph 12?

6 How would you describe Stamper's overall attitude toward slang? To what extent does she value the rules and conventions of standard English?

Analyzing Language, Style, and Structure

1 What is the effect of the opening paragraph? What do you think Stamper's intention is?

2 Stamper discusses two main examples ("swag" and "fubar") and mentions several others. Do all of these examples support the same point, or does Stamper use some of them as evidence for sub-claims? Explain why you think the way you do, with specific reference to the text.

3 What is the effect of Stamper's integration of slang expressions into this piece? Does her use of slang undermine her credibility? Why or why not?

4 Stamper uses a number of metaphors in the second half of her essay. Which one(s) do you find most effective? Why?

5 This essay was published in the *New York Times* in 2014. Who is her audience? How does she appeal to them?

6 How would you describe Stamper's tone? How does her tone reinforce the point she makes in her essay?

Connecting, Arguing, and Extending

1 Is Stamper right? No doubt you've heard many warnings about the importance of avoiding slang, and you may have even heard that slang is dangerously close to clichéd and trite language. Does slang characterize a speaker as creative and dynamic, lazy and dull, or something in between? Explain your position with reasons and examples.

2 How does slang work to connect members of a group you know well (for instance, sports fans, computer geeks, movie buffs, foodies)? Write an essay analyzing some of the slang expressions that have become part of this specific group's language.

3 Research a term that has changed its meaning over time, perhaps one that began as slang and has crossed over into standard English, or perhaps one from standard English whose meaning has changed over time as a slang term.

4 Create a dialogue between two people who are experiencing difficulty communicating because one is using slang (and colloquial) expressions and the other is using standard English exclusively. Your two speakers might be from different historical eras, different generations, or different groups within the same time period.

Hot Dogs and Wild Geese

Firoozeh Dumas

Firoozeh Dumas was born in Iran in 1965, moved to California when she was seven, returned with her family to Iran two years later, and then came back to the United States two years after that. She received her BA from the University of California–Berkeley. In 2001 she began writing her family's stories as a gift to her own children, and in 2003 they were published as *Funny in Farsi: A Memoir of Growing Up Iranian in America*. A finalist for the prestigious Thurber Prize for American humor, Dumas was the first Middle Eastern woman ever nominated; she lost to Jon Stewart. She often writes commentaries for National Public Radio, the *New York Times*, and the *Los Angeles Times*, and in 2008 she published *Laughing without an Accent*, a series of autobiographical essays. The following is a chapter from her book *Funny in Farsi*.

Moving to America was both exciting and frightening, but we found great comfort in knowing that my father spoke English. Having spent years regaling us with stories about his graduate years in America, he had left us with the distinct impression that America was his second home. My mother and I planned to stick close to him, letting him guide us through the exotic American landscape that he knew so well. We counted on him not only to translate the language but also to translate the culture, to be a link to this most foreign of lands. He was to be our own private Rosetta stone.

Once we reached America, we wondered whether perhaps my father had confused his life in America with someone else's. Judging from the bewildered looks of store cashiers, gas station attendants, and waiters, my father spoke a version of English not yet shared with the rest of America. His attempts to find a "vater closet" in a department store would usually lead us to the drinking fountain or the home furnishing section. Asking my father to ask the waitress the definition of "sloppy Joe" or "Tater Tots" was no problem. His translations, however, were highly suspect. Waitresses would spend several minutes responding to my father's questions, and these responses, in turn, would be translated as "She doesn't know." Thanks to my father's translations, we stayed away from hot dogs, catfish, and hush puppies, and no amount of caviar in the sea would have convinced us to try mud pie.

We wondered how my father had managed to spend several years attending school in America yet remain so utterly befuddled by Americans. We soon discovered that his college years had been spent mainly in the library, where he had managed to avoid contact with all Americans except his engineering professors. As long as the conversation was limited to vectors, surface tension, and fluid mechanics, my father was Fred Astaire with words. But one step outside the scintillating world of petroleum engineering and he had two left tongues.

My father's only other regular contact in college had been his roommate, a Pakistani who spent his days preparing curry. Since neither spoke English but both liked curries, they got along splendidly. The person who had assigned them together had probably hoped they would either learn English or invent a common language for the occasion. Neither happened.

5   My father's inability to understand spoken English was matched only by his efforts to deny the problem. His constant attempts at communicating with Americans seemed at first noble and adventurous, then annoying. Somewhere between his thick Persian accent and his use of vocabulary found in pre–World War II British textbooks, my father spoke a private language. That nobody understood him hurt his pride, so what he lacked in speaking ability, he made up for by reading. He was the only person who actually read each and every document before he signed it. Buying a washing machine from Sears might take the average American thirty minutes, but by the time my father had finished reading the warranties, terms of contracts, and credit information, the store was closing and the janitor was asking us to please step aside so he could finish mopping the floor.

My mother's approach to learning English consisted of daily lessons with Monty Hall and Bob Barker. Her devotion to *Let's Make a Deal* and *The Price Is Right* was evident in her newfound ability to recite useless information. After a few months of television viewing, she could correctly tell us whether a coffeemaker cost more or less than $19.99. How many boxes of Hamburger Helper, Swanson's TV dinners, or Turtle Wax could one buy without spending a penny more than twenty dollars? She knew that, too. Strolling down the grocery aisle, she rejoiced in her celebrity sightings — Lipton tea! Campbell's tomato soup! Betty Crocker Rich & Creamy Frosting! Every day, she would tell us the day's wins and losses on the game shows. "He almost won the boat, but the wife picked curtain number two and they ended up with a six-foot chicken statue." The bad prizes on *Let's Make a Deal* sounded far more intriguing than the good ones. Who would want the matching La-Z-Boy recliners when they could have the adult-size crib and high-chair set?

My mother soon decided that the easiest way for her to communicate with Americans was to use me as an interpreter. My brother Farshid, with his schedule full of soccer, wrestling, and karate, was too busy to be recruited for this dubious honor. At an age when most parents are guiding their kids toward independence, my mother was hanging on to me for dear life. I had to accompany her to the grocery store, the hairdresser, the doctor, and every place else that a kid wouldn't want to go. My reward for doing this was the constant praise of every American we encountered. Hearing a seven-year-old translate Persian into English and vice versa made quite an impression on everyone. People lavished compliments on me. "You must be very, very smart, a genius maybe." I always responded by assuring them that if they ever moved to another country, they, too, would learn the language. (What I wanted to say was that I wished I could be at home watching *The Brady Bunch* instead of translating the qualities of various facial moisturizers.) My mother had her own response to the compliments: "Americans are easily impressed."

I always encouraged my mother to learn English, but her talents lay elsewhere. Since she had never learned English in school, she had no idea of its grammar. She would speak entire paragraphs without using any verbs. She referred to everyone and everything as "it," leaving the listener wondering whether she was talking about her husband or the kitchen table. Even if she did speak a sentence more or less correctly, her accent made it incomprehensible. "W" and "th" gave her the most difficulty. As if God were playing a linguistic joke on us, we lived in "Vee-tee-er" (Whittier), we shopped at "Veetvood" (Whitwood) Plaza, I attended "Leffingvell" School, and our neighbor was none other than "Valter Villiams."

Despite little progress on my mother's part, I continually encouraged her. Rather than teach her English vocabulary and grammar, I eventually decided to teach her entire sentences to repeat. I assumed that once she got used to speaking correctly, I could be removed, like training wheels, and she would continue coasting. I was wrong.

10   Noticing some insects in our house one day, my mother asked me to call the exterminator. I looked up the number, then told my mother to call and say, "We have silverfish in our house." My mother grumbled, dialed the number, and said, "Please come rrright a-vay. Goldfeeesh all over dee house." The exterminator told her he'd be over as soon as he found his fishing pole.

A few weeks later, our washing machine broke. A repairman was summoned and the leaky pipe was quickly replaced. My mother wanted to know how to remove the black stain left by the leak. "Y'all are gonna hafta use some elbow grease," he said. I thanked him and paid him and walked with my mother to the hardware store. After searching fruitlessly for elbow grease, I asked the salesclerk for help. "It removes stains," I added. The manager was called.

Once the manager finished laughing, he gave us the disappointing explanation. My mother and I walked home empty-handed. That, I later learned, is what Americans call a wild-goose chase.

Now that my parents have lived in America for thirty years, their English has improved somewhat, but not as much as one would hope. It's not entirely their fault; English is a confusing language. When my father paid his friend's daughter the compliment of calling her homely, he meant she would be a great housewife. When he complained about horny drivers, he was referring to their tendency to honk. And my parents still don't understand why teenagers want to be cool so they can be hot.

I no longer encourage my parents to learn English. I've given up. Instead, I'm grateful for the wave of immigration that has brought Iranian television, newspapers, and super-markets to America. Now, when my mother wants to ask the grocer whether he has any more eggplants in the back that are a little darker and more firm, because the ones he has out aren't right for *khoresht bademjun*, she can do so in Persian, all by herself. And for that, I say hallelujah, a word that needs no translation.

Understanding and Interpreting

1 What does Firoozeh Dumas mean in the opening paragraph when she describes the expectation that her father would "not only [. . .] translate the language but also [. . .] translate the culture"?

2 What are the differences between Dumas's father's and mother's approaches to learning English and adjusting to American culture?

3 Why, according to Dumas, has she stopped encouraging her parents to learn English? What change has occasioned her different attitude toward the importance of speaking English fluently?

4 In this humorous memoir, Dumas makes a serious point. How would you sum up what that point is?

Analyzing Language, Style, and Structure

1 How does Dumas manage to poke fun at her parents' struggle with the English language and American culture without seeming unkind, judgmental, or condescending?

2 Dumas uses humor throughout her memoir *Funny in Farsi*. Identify at least three different strategies in this excerpt and explain how she uses them to achieve an ironic or amusing effect. Cite specific passages to explain your choices.

3 What examples does Dumas cite of idiomatic expressions that make English "a confusing language" (par. 13)? What other expressions can you think of that cannot be literally translated?

4 This essay is filled with pop culture references that situate it in a particular time frame. What are several of these? Apart from establishing the time period, what does Dumas achieve by including such details?

Connecting, Arguing, and Extending

1 Although Dumas describes her role in the family humorously, it represents a significant power shift from traditional roles. Analyze the ways in which immigrating to America changes the balance of power between her mother and father and between her and her parents. Pay close attention to the efforts the parents make to maintain their authority.

2 Based on your personal experience, observation, or reading, do you think that the situation of the immigrant family that Dumas has described here is typical or unusual? Use as many concrete details as possible in your explanation. You might want to refer to other memoirs or fiction.

English

Marjorie Agosín

Translated by Mónica Bruno

A descendant of Russian and Austrian Jews, Marjorie Agosín (b. 1955) was born in Maryland and raised in Chile. She returned to the United States with her parents when the military dictator Augusto Pinochet overthrew the socialist government of Salvador Allende. Agosín's writings reflect her diverse heritage, especially the experience of Jewish refugees, and she has received international acclaim for her work on behalf of poor women in developing countries. Agosín has written many books of fiction, memoirs, essays, and collections of bilingual poems in Spanish and English. In this poem, which first appeared in the magazine *Poets & Writers* in 1999, Agosín turns from technical, linguistic characteristics to compare the spirit of two languages.

Photo by Dawn Jordan

I
I discovered that English
is too skinny,
functional,
precise,
5   too correct,
meaning
only one thing.
Too much wrath,
too many lawyers and sinister policemen,
10   too many deans at schools for small females,
in the Anglo-Saxon language.

II
In contrast Spanish
has so many words to say come with me friend,
make love to me on
15   the *césped*, the *grama*, the *pasto*.[1]

---

[1]Spanish, three words for grass. —Eds.

Let's go party,
at dusk, at night, at sunset.
Spanish
loves
20   the unpredictable, it is
dementia,
all windmills and velvet.

III
Spanish
is simple and baroque,
25   a palace of nobles and beggars,
it fills itself with silences and the breaths of dragonflies.
Neruda's verses
saying "I could write the saddest verses
tonight,"
30   or Federico swimming underwater through the greenest of greens.

IV
Spanish
is Don Quijote maneuvering,
Violeta Parra grateful
spicy, tasty, fragrant
35   the rumba, the salsa, the cha-cha.
There are so many words
to say
naive dreamers
and impostors.
40   There are so many languages in our
language: Quechua, Aymará, Rosas chilensis,[2] Spanglish.

V
I love the imperfections of
Spanish,
the language takes shape in my hand:
45   the sound of drums and waves,
the Caribbean in the radiant foam of the sun,
are delirious upon my lips.
English has fallen short for me,
it signifies business,

---

[2] The Quechua and Aymara are native peoples from the Andes mountain region of South America. Rosas Chilensis is an invented term roughly meaning "Chilean roses." —Eds.

50 law
and inhibition,
never the crazy, clandestine,
clairvoyance of
love.

seeing connections

Below is Agosín's poem "English" in its original language, Spanish.

If you speak Spanish, discuss what decisions by the translator you find interesting. How is the effect of this poem about the deficiencies of the English language changed when it is read in Spanish?

I
He descubierto que el inglés
es demasiado delgado, funcional.
Preciso
demasiado correcto
significando
sólo una cosa, demasiada ira.
Demasiados abogados y policias siniestros,
demasiados Decanos para escuelas de
    pequeñas señoritas.
En el idioma anglosajón.

II
En contraste,
el español,
tiene tantas palabras para decir ven mi amigo
haz el amor conmigo,
en el césped, la grama, el pasto.
Vamos a celebrar,
en el crepúsculo, en la noche, en la puesta
    del sol.
El español ama lo impredecible.
Es demencia
Solo molinos, solo terciopelo.

III
El español es simple y barroco.
Palacio de nobles y mendigos.
Se llena de silencios y el aliento de las libélulas.
Los versos de Neruda,

diciendo, "Puedo escribir los versos más
    tristes esta noche."
Tal vez Federico nadando bajo el agua en la
    espesura del verdor
más verde.

IV
El español es Don Quijote manobriando
Violeta Parra agradecida,
picante, deliciosa, fragante.
La rumba, la salsa el cha cha cha.
Hay tantas maneras de decir,
soñadores inocentes.
También impostores.
Hay tantos idiomas en nuestros idiomas.
Quechua, Aymara, Rosa Chilensis,
Spanglish.

V
Amo las imperfecciones del español
El lenguaje se acomoda a mi mano.
El sonido de sueños y oleajes,
el Caribe radiante en su espuma de sol,
son un delirio en mis labios.
El inglés, me ha quedado demasiado pequeño
significa negocios.
Leyes.
Inhibiciones.
Nunca la locura clandestina
clarividente del amor.

Understanding and Interpreting

1 In the opening section, Marjorie Agosín defines English with a series of descriptions and images. What does it mean for English to be "skinny" (l. 2)? What do you think Agosín is suggesting when she says that there are "too many deans at schools for small females, / in the Anglo-Saxon language" (ll. 10–11)? In your own words, what characterizes English from Agosín's perspective?

2 Agosín opens the second stanza with "In contrast." What is the primary contrast between Spanish and English that she draws?

3 How can Spanish be both "simple and baroque" (l. 24)?

4 What do the various historical figures or aut[hors] who appear or are alluded to in the poem—Pa[blo] Neruda, Federico García Lorca, Don Quijote, Violeta Parra—have in common, apart from their use of the Spanish language?

5 What is your understanding of Agosín's description of Spanish as "the language [that] takes shape in my hand" (l. 44)?

6 Based on this poem, what qualities of language does Agosín prize? Would you say that she is criticizing English or just praising Spanish?

7 Is the title appropriate? Why not call the poem "Spanish" (or use a Spanish word)?

Analyzing Language, Style, and Structure

1 What elements of humor do you find in this poem? Is it playful, mocking, sarcastic? Cite specific lines and images as you explain the effect Agosín achieves with humor.

2 Note the figurative language that Agosín uses to describe Spanish. Identify at least three examples and discuss their effect.

3 Note the difference in rhythm in the sections of the poem about English and those on Spanish. How do the different sounds and pacing reinforce the speaker's meaning?

4 How does the five-part structure of the poem support its meaning? In what ways might each of these stanzas be seen as a "chapter" in the story Agosín is telling? What is that story?

5 To what extent do you think that the Spanish words and phrases and the references to Spanish and Latin American artists suggest that Agosín believes her audience will consist primarily of readers who are familiar with the Spanish language and culture?

6 How would you describe the tone of this poem?

Connecting, Arguing, and Extending

1 Challenge Agosín's argument about the limitations of English. Write an essay or poem that presents a counterargument to the one Agosín makes in "English."

2 Record yourself or a classmate reading "English," or read with someone to alternate "English" and "Spanish" voices. Add background music that captures the ideas and tone of each section.

3 In this poem, Agosín asserts the pride she feels for her heritage language and implies why she has chosen to write in Spanish, even though she has lived and taught in the United States for many years. Using this poem and your understanding of what it means to be bilingual, discuss the relationship between identity and language.

© Tom Sewell

...1927, W. S. Merwin has written over ...prose, and translation. His first book, ...was chosen for the Yale Younger Poets ...herous awards, including the Pulitzer ...in 1971 for *The Carrier of Ladders*, and ...or *The Shadow of Sirius*). Merwin served as U.S. Poet Laureate from 2010 to 2011. Throughout his career, he has written on a range of subjects, including the Vietnam conflict and environmental destruction. In the late 1970s, he moved to Hawaii to study Zen Buddhism; he currently lives on the island of Maui on what was once a pineapple plantation. "Losing a Language" is from Merwin's 1988 poetry collection *The Rain in the Trees*.

A breath leaves the sentences and does not come back
yet the old still remember something that they could say

but they know now that such things are no longer believed
and the young have fewer words

5   many of the things the words were about
no longer exist

the noun for standing in mist by a haunted tree
the verb for I

the children will not repeat
10   the phrases their parents speak

somebody has persuaded them
that it is better to say everything differently

so that they can be admired somewhere
farther and farther away

15   where nothing that is here is known
we have little to say to each other

we are wrong and dark
in the eyes of the new owners

the radio is incomprehensible
20 the day is glass

when there is a voice at the door it is foreign
everywhere instead of a name there is a lie

nobody has seen it happening
nobody remembers

25 this is what the words were made
to prophesy

here are the extinct feathers
here is the rain we saw

Endangered languages
1 ▯▮▮▮▮▮▮ 197

UNESCO

▲

This is the United Nations Educational, Scientific, and Cultural Organization (UNESCO) Map of Endangered Languages by Country. The darker the color on this map, the more endangered languages are present in that nation. The United States has 191 endangered languages, which trails only India at 197. UNESCO notes, "Countries with the greatest linguistic diversity are typically also the ones with the most endangered languages."

What are some of the potential consequences of a language becoming extinct in terms of both the specific community who speaks the language and a larger global perspective?

Understanding and Interpreting

1 Although Merwin does not use conventional punctuation in this poem, he writes in sentences. How does adding periods and commas enhance your understanding of the literal sense of the poem?

2 How do you interpret the opening line, "A breath leaves the sentences and does not come back"? What associations with "breath" are at work here?

3 The speaker states that "the old still remember something that they could say" (l. 2), yet they do not. Why? Why don't the children "repeat / the phrases their parents speak" (ll. 9–10)? Are these silences deliberate intentions, unintentional negligence, instances of unavoidable change, or something else?

4 What is the meaning of lines 5–6, "many of the things the words were about / no longer exist"? What might

Merwin be suggesting about the connection between language and memory?

5 Who are "the new owners" (l. 18)? How does the concept of ownership apply to language—or does it?

6 Why is the "voice at the door [. . .] foreign" (l. 21)? By choosing this word, does the speaker imply a foreign language, foreign country, or something else?

7 What do you think might be the "lie" that exists "instead of a name" (l. 22)?

8 What do you think this poem has to say about the power of language? In what ways does the speaker believe language has been diminished? Is the ending hopeful, pessimistic, nostalgic—or possibly pragmatic?

9 What is the relationship between age, experience, and language expressed in this poem?

Analyzing Language, Style, and Structure

1 Identify the words in the poem that have negative denotations or connotations. How do these contribute to the principal idea Merwin is developing?

2 Fairly early in his career, Merwin began writing poems without punctuation, then later without capital letters. He explained: "I came to feel that punctuation was like nailing the words onto the page. I wanted instead the movement and lightness of the spoken word." To what extent do you think he achieves this goal in "Losing a Language"?

3 In the poem, Merwin pairs images to support or illustrate a point just made. How do you interpret each of the following pairings?

a. "the noun for standing in mist by a haunted tree / the verb for I" (ll. 7–8)

b. "the radio is incomprehensible / the day is glass" (ll. 19–20)

c. "here are the extinct feathers / here is the rain we saw" (ll. 27–28)

4 Who is the speaker; who speaks as "we"? Is he or she part of "the old" or "the young," both, or neither?

5 Now that you've examined "Losing a Language" closely, reconsider the title. How does it capture the tone of the poem?

Connecting, Arguing, and Extending

1 Merwin believes that a vibrant culture, including a healthy relationship to the natural environment, is reflected in the language of that culture; thus, the loss of language signals a decline of culture. Consider how that perspective is expressed in this poem. Do you agree or disagree with this interpretation? Given Merwin's commitment to ecological conservation, this poem has been interpreted as a reminder of the fragility of our natural environment. Consider how that interpretation might be developed. To what extent do you agree or disagree with it? You might consult the Merwin

Conservancy website to research the poet's commitment to environmental concerns.

2 In 2010, when Merwin was named Poet Laureate, he stated that he hoped to use his tenure to emphasize his "great sympathy with native people and the languages and literature of native peoples." Do some research into today's endangered and disappearing languages and write an argument addressing the following question: What is your responsibility to preserve your language, however you define what "your language" is (for example, a regional dialect, a mainstream language).

ENTERING THE CONVERSATION
LANGUAGE AND POWER

Making Connections

1 Are the conflicts and changes explored in "Children as Enemies" by Ha Jin (p. 763) and "No Speak English" by Sandra Cisneros (p.761) more similar or different? What role does language play in these conflicts? To what extent are the differences primarily generational?

2 What similarities do you see between the power Frederick Douglass (p. 755) believes comes with reading and writing English, and the power Firoozeh Dumas (p. 777) recognizes that language has over her parents?

3 In what ways does "Losing a Language" by W. S. Merwin (p. 784) support or challenge Kory Stamper's position in "Slang for the Ages" (p. 773)?

4 What would "Dis Poem" (p. 770) have to say about the conflicts in "Hot Dogs and Wild Geese" (p. 777)?

5 Are the ideas reflected in "English" by Marjorie Agosín (p. 780) more similar to those in "Children as Enemies" (p. 763) or "No Speak English" (p. 761)?

Synthesizing Sources

1 What sort of personal, political, and social power is attached to language use and mastery? Write an argument expressing your perspective, informed by at least two of the sources in this Conversation.

2 A number of the texts in this chapter focus on the bond between language and identity, particularly when immigration requires adoption of a non-native language. What coping mechanisms do different characters and, in the case of poetry, speakers employ to retain the identity attached to their native language? In your response, consider the struggle of the grandparents in "Children as Enemies," Mamacita in "No Speak English," and another character or speaker in at least one other text. What strategies seem to be most successful and why?

3 Which do you think will "win"—the constantly shifting world of slang that not only crosses cultures but often shapes new ones, or the determined forces of so-called standard English that argue for strict rules of language in the public and professional realm of business and politics? As you explain your view, include ideas from Kory Stamper's essay and at least one other text in this Conversation.

4 How does writing in a nonstandard variety of English contribute to the effectiveness of a literary text (poem, short story, or memoir)? Consider at least two of the works you have read in this Conversation and another you have read on your own or in class.

5 Should fluency in the reading and speaking of at least one language other than English be a high school graduation requirement for all students in the United States? Before you develop your viewpoint, you might conduct research into bilingual requirements in other countries. Use that research along with at least two of the texts in this Conversation in your argument.

6 Watch the documentary *Language Matters*, a 2015 film that addresses the questions, "What do we lose when a language dies? What does it take to save a language?" Discuss how effective you believe the film is in raising awareness for the potential extinction of indigenous languages.

7 Write a personal narrative that demonstrates your thoughts on one of the following quotations. Weave in at least one of the texts you've read in this Conversation as part of your response.

   a. "Language is a weapon, and we use it."–Chinua Achebe
   b. "Viewed freely, the English language is the accretion and growth of every dialect, race, and range of time, and is both the free and compacted composition of all."–Walt Whitman
   c. "To have a second language is to have a second soul."–Charlemagne
   d. "If you talk to a man in a language he understands, that goes to his head. If you talk to him in his language, that goes to his heart."–Nelson Mandela

SOCIALLY NETWORKED

Prior to 2004, the word *friend* was exclusively used as a noun, as in "Malik is my friend." Thanks to Mark Zuckerberg and Facebook, we now regularly use *friend* as a verb, as in "Did you friend her yet?" This change also led to the invention of a brand-new word—a verb with the opposite meaning, as in "I had to unfriend him." But think about how this use of the word *friend* only exists in an online context; it really refers only to an action on a social media site like Facebook, and mostly just involves a click of a button.

Look at this chart on the median number of friends teenagers have on Facebook, based on a survey from 2013:

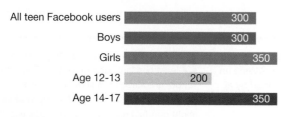

Size of Facebook Network by Gender and Age
Median number of friends

All teen Facebook users	300
Boys	300
Girls	350
Age 12-13	200
Age 14-17	350

Note: Facebook N=588   PEW RESEARCH CENTER

Since it is unlikely that even the most outgoing teenager has over three hundred friends in the traditional sense of the word, what does the word *friend* mean in an online context? Are we as close with our online friends as with our offline friends? Do we even need to have met our online friends face-to-face to consider them friends? What is the proper etiquette for ending an online friendship? Is it different than ending an offline relationship?

Members of your generation are called "digital natives," since you have grown up surrounded by the Internet and digital communications technologies such as Facebook, Twitter, Instagram, Tumblr, Snapchat, and hundreds of others. But how has all of this technology changed the way we interact with each other, both online and offline? Does your online persona affect your offline persona? Are they even related? And ultimately, has social networking helped us build connections to other people, or do we feel alone even when we are "connected"?

Researcher Sherry Turkle, one of the authors featured in this Conversation, was told by a college student she was interviewing to not be fooled by "anyone you interview who tells you that his Facebook page is 'the real me.' It's like being in a play. You make a character." So, in this Conversation, you'll have an opportunity to think about the ways that we present and shape the online images of ourselves to the world, and how this is changing the nature of our social relationships.

Brave New World of Digital Intimacy

Clive Thompson

Brad Barket/Getty Images for WIRED

Born in Canada in 1968, Clive Thompson is a freelance journalist who writes mainly about technology and science and whose work regularly appears in publications such as the *New York Times Magazine*, the *Washington Post*, *Lingua Franca*, *Wired*, *Shift*, and *Entertainment Weekly*. He is the author of the book *Smarter Than You Think: How Technology Is Changing Our Minds for the Better*, published in 2013. In this piece, originally published in the *New York Times* in 2008, Thompson explores how the emergence of social networking technologies has changed the way people interact and relate.

On Sept. 5, 2006, Mark Zuckerberg changed the way that Facebook worked, and in the process he inspired a revolt.

Zuckerberg, a doe-eyed 24-year-old C.E.O., founded Facebook in his dorm room at Harvard two years earlier, and the site quickly amassed nine million users. By 2006, students were posting heaps of personal details onto their Facebook pages, including lists of their favorite TV shows, whether they were dating (and whom), what music they had in rotation and the various ad hoc "groups" they had joined (like *Sex and the City* Lovers). All day long, they'd post "status" notes explaining their moods — "hating Monday," "skipping class b/c i'm hung over." After each party, they'd stagger home to the dorm and upload pictures of the soused revelry, and spend the morning after commenting on how wasted everybody looked. Facebook became the de facto public commons — the way students found out what everyone around them was like and what he or she was doing.

But Zuckerberg knew Facebook had one major problem: It required a lot of active surfing on the part of its users. Sure, every day your Facebook friends would update their profiles with some new tidbits; it might even be something particularly juicy, like changing their relationship status to "single" when they got dumped. But unless you visited each friend's page every day, it might be days or weeks before you noticed the news, or you might miss it entirely. Browsing Facebook was like constantly poking your head into someone's room to see how she was doing. It took work and forethought. In a sense, this gave Facebook an inherent, built-in level of privacy, simply because if you had 200 friends on the site — a fairly typical number — there weren't enough hours in the day to keep tabs on every friend all the time.

"It was very primitive," Zuckerberg told me when I asked him about it last month. And so he decided to modernize. He developed something he called News Feed, a built-in service that would actively broadcast changes in a user's page to every one of his or her friends. Students would no longer need to spend their time zipping around to examine each friend's page, checking to see if there was any new information. Instead, they would just log into Facebook, and News Feed would appear: a single page that — like a social gazette from the 18th century — delivered a long list of up-to-the-minute gossip about their friends, around the clock, all in one place. "A stream of everything that's going on in their lives," as Zuckerberg put it.

5   When students woke up that September morning and saw News Feed, the first reaction, generally, was one of panic. Just about every little thing you changed on your page was now instantly blasted out to hundreds of friends, including potentially mortifying bits of news — Tim and Lisa broke up; Persaud is no longer friends with Matthew — and drunken photos someone snapped, then uploaded and tagged with names. Facebook had lost its vestigial bit of privacy. For students, it was now like being at a giant, open party filled with everyone you know, able to eavesdrop on what everyone else was saying, all the time.

"Everyone was freaking out," Ben Parr, then a junior at Northwestern University, told me recently. What particularly enraged Parr was that there wasn't any way to opt out of News Feed, to "go private" and have all your information kept quiet. He created a Facebook group demanding Zuckerberg either scrap News Feed or provide privacy options. "Facebook users

really think Facebook is becoming the Big Brother of the Internet, recording every single move," a California student told the *Star-Ledger* of Newark. Another chimed in, "Frankly, I don't need to know or care that Billy broke up with Sally, and Ted has become friends with Steve." By lunchtime of the first day, 10,000 people had joined Parr's group, and by the next day it had 284,000.

Zuckerberg, surprised by the outcry, quickly made two decisions. The first was to add a privacy feature to News Feed, letting users decide what kind of information went out. But the second decision was to leave News Feed otherwise intact. He suspected that once people tried it and got over their shock, they'd like it.

He was right. Within days, the tide reversed. Students began e-mailing Zuckerberg to say that via News Feed they'd learned things they would never have otherwise discovered through random surfing around Facebook. The bits of trivia that News Feed delivered gave them more things to talk about — Why do you hate Kiefer Sutherland? — when they met friends face to face in class or at a party. Trends spread more quickly. When one student joined a group — proclaiming her love of Coldplay or a desire to volunteer for Greenpeace — all her friends instantly knew, and many would sign up themselves. Users' worries about their privacy seemed to vanish within days, boiled away by their excitement at being so much more connected to their friends. (Very few people stopped using Facebook, and most people kept on publishing most of their information through News Feed.) Pundits predicted that News Feed would kill Facebook, but the opposite happened. It catalyzed a massive boom in the site's growth. A few weeks after the News Feed imbroglio, Zuckerberg opened the site to the general public (previously, only students could join), and it grew quickly; today, it has 100 million users.

▶

Look carefully at this graphic, which summarizes the findings of a survey of teens regarding their use of privacy settings on social networks.

What conclusions can you draw from the information, and how similar would your responses be to the results in this graphic?

When I spoke to him, Zuckerberg argued that News Feed is central to Facebook's success. "Facebook has always tried to push the envelope," he said. "And at times that means stretching people and getting them to be comfortable with things they aren't yet comfortable with. A lot of this is just social norms catching up with what technology is capable of."

10   In essence, Facebook users didn't think they wanted constant, up-to-the-minute updates on what other people are doing. Yet when they experienced this sort of omnipresent knowledge, they found it intriguing and addictive. Why?

Social scientists have a name for this sort of incessant online contact. They call it "ambient awareness." It is, they say, very much like being physically near someone and picking up on his mood through the little things he does — body language, sighs, stray comments — out of the corner of your eye. Facebook is no longer alone in offering this sort of interaction online. In the last year, there has been a boom in tools for "microblogging": posting frequent tiny updates on what you're doing. The phenomenon is quite different from what we normally think of as blogging, because a blog post is usually a written piece, sometimes quite long: a statement of opinion, a story, an analysis. But these new updates are something different. They're far shorter, far more frequent and less carefully considered. One of the most popular new tools is Twitter, a Web site and messaging service that allows its

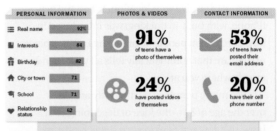

Sharing, Connections, & Privacy in the World of Teen Social Media

What do teens share on social media?

Percent who share information on the profile they use most often

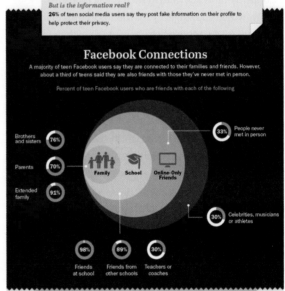

PERSONAL INFORMATION	
Real name	92%
Interests	84
Birthday	82
City or town	71
School	71
Relationship status	62

PHOTOS & VIDEOS

91% of teens have a photo of themselves

24% have posted videos of themselves

CONTACT INFORMATION

53% of teens have posted their email address

20% have their cell phone number

But is the information real?
26% of teen social media users say they post fake information on their profile to help protect their privacy.

Facebook Connections

A majority of teen Facebook users say they are connected to their families and friends. However, about a third of teens said they are also friends with those they've never met in person.

Percent of teen Facebook users who are friends with each of the following

Brothers and sisters **76%**
Parents **70%**
Extended family **91%**

Family   School   Online-Only Friends

People never met in person **33%**

Celebrities, musicians or athletes **30%**

Friends at school **98%**
Friends from other schools **89%**
Teachers or coaches **30%**

Privacy on Social Media

Teens choose different privacy settings depending on the social media site they use.

NETWORK	PUBLIC Everyone can see it	PARTIALLY PRIVATE Friends of friends	PRIVATE Only friends/followers
Among teens with **Facebook** profiles	14%	25%	60%
Among teens with **Twitter** profiles	64%	N/A	24%

Source: Pew Internet Parent/Teen Privacy Survey, July 26-September 30, 2012. n=802 teens ages 12-17. Interviews were conducted in English and Spanish and on landline and cell phones. Margin of error for results based on teen social media users is +/- 5.1 percentage points; margin of error for results based on teen Facebook users is +/- 5.3 percentage points, margin of error for results based on teen Twitter users is +/- 9.4 percentage points. For more information, please read the report, Teens, Social Media, and Privacy" at http://pewinternet.org/Reports/2013/Teens-Social-Media-And-Privacy.aspx

Pew Research Center's Internet and American Life Project | www.pewresearch.org
© PEW RESEARCH CENTER, MAY 2013

two-million-plus users to broadcast to their friends haiku-length updates—limited to 140 characters, as brief as a mobile-phone text message—on what they're doing. There are other services for reporting where you're traveling (Dopplr) or for quickly tossing online a stream of the pictures, videos or Web sites you're looking at (Tumblr). And there are even tools that give your location. When the new iPhone, with built-in tracking, was introduced in July, one million people began using Loopt, a piece of software that automatically tells all your friends exactly where you are.

For many people—particularly anyone over the age of 30—the idea of describing your blow-by-blow activities in such detail is absurd. Why would you subject your friends to your daily minutiae? And conversely, how much of their trivia can you absorb? The growth of ambient intimacy can seem like modern narcissism taken to a new, supermetabolic extreme—the ultimate expression of a generation of celebrity-addled youths who believe their every utterance is fascinating and ought to be shared with the world. Twitter, in particular, has been the subject of nearly relentless scorn since it went online. "Who really cares what I am doing, every hour of the day?" wondered Alex Beam, a *Boston Globe* columnist, in an essay about Twitter last month. "Even I don't care."

Indeed, many of the people I interviewed, who are among the most avid users of these "awareness" tools, admit that at first they couldn't figure out why anybody would want to do this. Ben Haley, a 39-year-old documentation specialist for a software firm who lives in Seattle, told me that when he first heard about Twitter last year from an early-adopter friend who used it, his first reaction was that it seemed silly. But a few of his friends decided to give it a try, and they urged him to sign up, too.

Each day, Haley logged on to his account, and his friends' updates would appear as a long page of one- or two-line notes. He would check and recheck the account several times a day, or even several times an hour. The updates were indeed pretty banal. One friend would post

about starting to feel sick; one posted random thoughts like "I really hate it when people clip their nails on the bus"; another Twittered whenever she made a sandwich—and she made a sandwich every day. Each so-called tweet was so brief as to be virtually meaningless.

15 But as the days went by, something changed. Haley discovered that he was beginning to sense the rhythms of his friends' lives in a way he never had before. When one friend got sick with a virulent fever, he could tell by her Twitter updates when she was getting worse and the instant she finally turned the corner. He could see when friends were heading into hellish days at work or when they'd scored a big success. Even the daily catalog of sandwiches became oddly mesmerizing, a sort of metronomic click that he grew accustomed to seeing pop up in the middle of each day.

This is the paradox of ambient awareness. Each little update—each individual bit of social information—is insignificant on its own, even supremely mundane. But taken together, over time, the little snippets coalesce into a surprisingly sophisticated portrait of your friends' and family members' lives, like thousands of dots making a pointillist painting. This was never before possible, because in the real world, no friend would bother to call you up and detail the sandwiches she was eating. The ambient information becomes like "a type of E.S.P.," as Haley described it to me, an invisible dimension floating over everyday life.

"It's like I can distantly read everyone's mind," Haley went on to say. "I love that. I feel like I'm getting to something raw about my friends. It's like I've got this heads-up display for them." It can also lead to more real-life contact, because when one member of Haley's group decides to go out to a bar or see a band and Twitters about his plans, the others see it, and some decide to drop by— ad hoc, self-organizing socializing. And when they do socialize face to face, it feels oddly as if they've never actually been apart. They don't need to ask, "So, what have you been up to?" because they already know. Instead, they'll begin discussing something that one of the friends Twittered that afternoon, as if picking up a conversation in the middle.

Facebook and Twitter may have pushed things into overdrive, but the idea of using communication tools as a form of "co-presence" has been around for a while. The Japanese sociologist Mizuko Ito first noticed it with mobile phones: lovers who were working in different cities would send text messages back and forth all night — tiny updates like "enjoying a glass of wine now" or "watching TV while lying on the couch." They were doing it partly because talking for hours on mobile phones isn't very comfortable (or affordable). But they also discovered that the little Ping-Ponging messages felt even more intimate than a phone call.

"It's an aggregate phenomenon," Marc Davis, a chief scientist at Yahoo and former professor of information science at the University of California at Berkeley, told me. "No message is the single-most-important message. It's sort of like when you're sitting with someone and you look over

and they smile at you. You're sitting here reading the paper, and you're doing your side-by-side thing, and you just sort of let people know you're aware of them." Yet it is also why it can be extremely hard to understand the phenomenon until you've experienced it. Merely looking at a stranger's Twitter or Facebook feed isn't interesting, because it seems like blather. Follow it for a day, though, and it begins to feel like a short story; follow it for a month, and it's a novel.

20   You could also regard the growing popularity of online awareness as a reaction to social isolation, the modern American disconnectedness that Robert Putnam explored in his book *Bowling Alone*. The mobile workforce requires people to travel more frequently for work, leaving friends and family behind, and members of the growing army of the self-employed often spend their days in solitude. Ambient intimacy becomes a way to "feel less alone," as more than one Facebook and Twitter user told me.

When I decided to try out Twitter last year, at first I didn't have anyone to follow. None of my

The cartoon is making a lighthearted joke about what the postings on Facebook would look like in the real world, but it can also prompt some reflection.

What is different between online and offline communication as represented in this cartoon?

"Why can't you use Facebook, like everybody else?"

Ward Sutton The New Yorker Collection/The Cartoon Bank

friends were yet using the service. But while doing some Googling one day I stumbled upon the blog of Shannon Seery, a 32-year-old recruiting consultant in Florida, and I noticed that she Twittered. Her Twitter updates were pretty charming — she would often post links to camera-phone pictures of her two children or videos of herself cooking Mexican food, or broadcast her agonized cries when a flight was delayed on a business trip. So on a whim I started "following" her — as easy on Twitter as a click of the mouse — and never took her off my account. (A Twitter account can be "private," so that only invited friends can read one's tweets, or it can be public, so anyone can; Seery's was public.) When I checked in last month, I noticed that she had built up a huge number of online connections: She was now following 677 people on Twitter and another 442 on Facebook. How in God's name, I wondered, could she follow so many people? Who precisely are they? I called Seery to find out.

"I have a rule," she told me. "I either have to know who you are, or I have to know of you." That means she monitors the lives of friends, family, anyone she works with, and she'll also follow interesting people she discovers via her friends' online lives. Like many people who live online, she has wound up following a few strangers — though after a few months they no longer feel like strangers, despite the fact that she has never physically met them.

I asked Seery how she finds the time to follow so many people online. The math seemed daunting. After all, if her 1,000 online contacts each post just a couple of notes each a day, that's several thousand little social pings to sift through daily. What would it be like to get thousands of e-mail messages a day? But Seery made a point I heard from many others: awareness tools aren't as cognitively demanding as an e-mail message. E-mail is something you have to stop to open and assess. It's personal; someone is asking for 100 percent of your attention. In

contrast, ambient updates are all visible on one single page in a big row, and they're not really directed at you. This makes them skimmable, like newspaper headlines; maybe you'll read them all, maybe you'll skip some. Seery estimated that she needs to spend only a small part of each hour actively reading her Twitter stream.

Yet she has, she said, become far more gregarious online. "What's really funny is that before this 'social media' stuff, I always said that I'm not the type of person who had a ton of friends," she told me. "It's so hard to make plans and have an active social life, having the type of job I have where I travel all the time and have two small kids. But it's easy to tweet all the time, to post pictures of what I'm doing, to keep social relations up." She paused for a second, before continuing: "Things like Twitter have actually given me a much bigger social circle. I know more about more people than ever before."

25 I realized that this is becoming true of me, too. After following Seery's Twitter stream for a year, I'm more knowledgeable about the details of her life than the lives of my two sisters in Canada, whom I talk to only once every month or so. When I called Seery, I knew that she had been struggling with a three-day migraine headache; I began the conversation by asking her how she was feeling.

Online awareness inevitably leads to a curious question: What sort of relationships are these? What does it mean to have hundreds of "friends" on Facebook? What kind of friends are they, anyway?

In 1998, the anthropologist Robin Dunbar argued that each human has a hard-wired upper limit on the number of people he or she can personally know at one time. Dunbar noticed that humans and apes both develop social bonds by engaging in some sort of grooming; apes do it by picking at and smoothing one another's fur, and humans do it with conversation. He theorized that ape and human brains could manage only a finite number of grooming relationships:

unless we spend enough time doing social grooming — chitchatting, trading gossip or, for apes, picking lice — we won't really feel that we "know" someone well enough to call him a friend. Dunbar noticed that ape groups tended to top out at 55 members. Since human brains were proportionally bigger, Dunbar figured that our maximum number of social connections would be similarly larger: about 150 on average. Sure enough, psychological studies have confirmed that human groupings naturally tail off at around 150 people: the "Dunbar number," as it is known. Are people who use Facebook and Twitter increasing their Dunbar number, because they can so easily keep track of so many more people?

As I interviewed some of the most aggressively social people online — people who follow hundreds or even thousands of others — it became clear that the picture was a little more complex than this question would suggest. Many maintained that their circle of true intimates, their very close friends and family, had not become bigger. Constant online contact had made those ties immeasurably richer, but it hadn't actually increased the number of them; deep relationships are still predicated on face time, and there are only so many hours in the day for that.

But where their sociality had truly exploded was in their "weak ties" — loose acquaintances, people they knew less well. It might be someone they met at a conference, or someone from high school who recently "friended" them on Facebook, or somebody from last year's holiday party. In their pre-Internet lives, these sorts of acquaintances would have quickly faded from their attention. But when one of these far-flung people suddenly posts a personal note to your feed, it is essentially a reminder that they exist. I have noticed this effect myself. In the last few months, dozens of old work colleagues I knew from 10 years ago in Toronto have friended me on Facebook, such that I'm now suddenly reading their stray comments and updates and falling into oblique, funny conversations with them.

My overall Dunbar number is thus 301: Facebook (254) + Twitter (47), double what it would be without technology. Yet only 20 are family or people I'd consider close friends. The rest are weak ties — maintained via technology.

30   This rapid growth of weak ties can be a very good thing. Sociologists have long found that "weak ties" greatly expand your ability to solve problems. For example, if you're looking for a job and ask your friends, they won't be much help; they're too similar to you, and thus probably won't have any leads that you don't already have yourself. Remote acquaintances will be much more useful, because they're farther afield, yet still socially intimate enough to want to help you out. Many avid Twitter users — the ones who fire off witty posts hourly and wind up with thousands of intrigued followers — explicitly milk this dynamic for all it's worth, using their large online followings as a way to quickly answer almost any question. Laura Fitton, a social-media consultant who has become a minor celebrity on Twitter — she has more than 5,300 followers — recently discovered to her horror that her accountant had made an error in filing last year's taxes. She went to Twitter, wrote a tiny note explaining her problem, and within 10 minutes her online audience had provided leads to lawyers and better accountants. Fritton joked to me that she no longer buys anything worth more than $50 without quickly checking it with her Twitter network.

"I outsource my entire life," she said. "I can solve any problem on Twitter in six minutes." (She also keeps a secondary Twitter account that is private and only for a much smaller circle of close friends and family — "My little secret," she said. It is a strategy many people told me they used: one account for their weak ties, one for their deeper relationships.)

It is also possible, though, that this profusion of weak ties can become a problem. If you're reading daily updates from hundreds of people about whom they're dating and whether they're

seeing connections

The following comments are part of a focus group conducted by the Pew Internet Research Project from 2013.

Which ones are reflective of your experiences with social media and which ones are not? Which ones are most similar to or different from the conclusions drawn in "Brave New World of Digital Intimacy," the article by Clive Thompson?

1. Female (age 14): "OK, so I do post a good amount of pictures, I think. Sometimes it's a very stressful thing when it comes to your profile picture. Because one should be better than the last, but it's so hard. So . . . I will message them a ton of pictures. And be like which one should I make my profile? And then they'll help me out. And that kind of takes the pressure off me. And it's like a very big thing."

2. Male (age 16): "Yeah, [I've gotten in trouble for something I posted] with my parents. This girl posted a really, really provocative picture [on Facebook] and I called her a not very nice word [in the comments]. And I mean, I shouldn't have called her that word, and I was being a little bit too cocky I guess, and yeah, I got in trouble with my parents."

3. Male (age 17): "It sucks [when parents are friends on Facebook] . . . Because then they [my parents] start asking me questions like why are you doing this, why are you doing that. It's like, it's my Facebook. If I don't get privacy at home, at least, I think, I should get privacy on a social network."

4. Male (age 18): "So honestly, the only time I've ever deleted for a picture is because I'm applying for colleges. You know what? Colleges might actually see my pictures and I have pictures like with my fingers up, my middle fingers up. Like me and my friends have pictures, innocent fun. We're not doing anything bad, but innocent fun. But at the same time, maybe I'm applying for college now. Possibly an admission officer's like, you know, this kid's accepted. Let's see what his everyday life is like. They're like, um—"

5. Male (age 18): "Yeah, I have some teachers who have connections that you might want to use in the future, so I feel like you always have an image to uphold. Whether I'm a person that likes to have fun and go crazy and go all out, but I don't let people see that side of me because maybe it changes the judgment on me. So you post what you want people to think of you, basically."

6. Female (age 16): "I deleted it [my Facebook account] when I was 15, because I think it [Facebook] was just too much for me with all the gossip and all the cliques and how it was so important to be—have so many friends—I was just like it's too stressful to have a Facebook, if that's what it has to take to stay in contact with just a little people. It was just too strong, so I just deleted it. And I've been great ever since."

happy, it might, some critics worry, spread your emotional energy too thin, leaving less for true intimate relationships. Psychologists have long known that people can engage in "parasocial" relationships with fictional characters, like those on TV shows or in books, or with remote celebrities we read about in magazines. Parasocial relationships can use up some of the emotional space in our Dunbar number, crowding out real-life people. Danah Boyd, a fellow at Harvard's

Berkman Center for Internet and Society who has studied social media for 10 years, published a paper this spring arguing that awareness tools like News Feed might be creating a whole new class of relationships that are nearly parasocial — peripheral people in our network whose intimate details we follow closely online, even while they, like Angelina Jolie, are basically unaware we exist.

"The information we subscribe to on a feed is not the same as in a deep social relationship," Boyd told me. She has seen this herself; she has many virtual admirers that have, in essence, a parasocial relationship with her. "I've been very, very sick, lately and I write about it on Twitter and my blog, and I get all these people who are writing to me telling me ways to work around the health-care system, or they're writing saying, 'Hey, I broke my neck!' And I'm like, 'You're being very nice and trying to help me, but though you feel like you know me, you don't.'" Boyd sighed. "They can observe you, but it's not the same as knowing you."

When I spoke to Caterina Fake, a founder of Flickr (a popular photo-sharing site), she suggested an even more subtle danger: that the sheer ease of following her friends' updates online has made her occasionally lazy about actually taking the time to visit them in person. "At one point I realized I had a friend whose child I had seen, via photos on Flickr, grow from birth to 1 year old," she said. "I thought, I really should go meet her in person. But it was weird; I also felt that Flickr had satisfied that getting-to-know you satisfaction, so I didn't feel the urgency. But then I was like, Oh, that's not sufficient! I should go in person!" She has about 400 people she follows online but suspects many of those relationships are tissue-fragile. "These technologies allow you to be much more broadly friendly, but you just spread yourself much more thinly over many more people."

35   What is it like to never lose touch with anyone? One morning this summer at my local cafe, I overheard a young woman complaining to her friend about a recent Facebook drama. Her name is Andrea Ahan, a 27-year-old restaurant entrepreneur, and she told me that she had discovered that high-school friends were uploading old photos of her to Facebook and tagging them with her name, so they automatically appeared in searches for her.

She was aghast. "I'm like, my God, these pictures are completely hideous!" Ahan complained, while her friend looked on sympathetically and sipped her coffee. "I'm wearing all these totally awful '90s clothes. I look like crap. And I'm like, Why are you people in my life, anyway? I haven't seen you in 10 years. I don't know you anymore!" She began furiously detagging the pictures — removing her name, so they wouldn't show up in a search anymore.

Worse, Ahan was also confronting a common plague of Facebook: the recent ex. She had broken up with her boyfriend not long ago, but she hadn't "unfriended" him, because that felt too extreme. But soon he paired up with another young woman, and the new couple began having public conversations on Ahan's ex-boyfriend's page. One day, she noticed with alarm that the new girlfriend was quoting material Ahan had e-mailed privately to her boyfriend; she suspected he had been sharing the e-mail with his new girlfriend. It is the sort of weirdly subtle mind game that becomes possible via Facebook, and it drove Ahan nuts.

"Sometimes I think this stuff is just crazy, and everybody has got to get a life and stop obsessing over everyone's trivia and gossiping," she said.

Yet Ahan knows that she cannot simply walk away from her online life, because the people she knows online won't stop talking about her, or posting unflattering photos. She needs to stay on Facebook just to monitor what's being said about her. This is a common complaint I heard, particularly from people in their 20s who were in college when Facebook appeared and have never lived as adults without online awareness. For them, participation isn't optional. If you don't dive in, other people will define who you are. So you constantly stream your pictures, your thoughts, your relationship status and what you're doing — right now! — if only to ensure the virtual version of you is accurate, or at least the one you want to present to the world.

40   This is the ultimate effect of the new awareness: It brings back the dynamics of small-town life, where everybody knows your business. Young people at college are the ones to experience this most viscerally, because, with more than 90 percent of their peers using Facebook, it is especially difficult for them to opt out. Zeynep Tufekci, a sociologist at the University of Maryland, Baltimore County, who has closely studied how college-age users are reacting to the world of awareness, told me that athletes used to sneak off to parties illicitly, breaking the no-drinking rule for team members. But then camera phones and Facebook came along, with students posting photos of the drunken carousing during the party; savvy coaches could see which athletes were breaking the rules. First the athletes tried to fight back by waking up early the morning after the party in a hungover daze to detag photos of themselves so they wouldn't be searchable. But that didn't work, because the coaches sometimes viewed the pictures live, as they went online at 2 A.M. So parties simply began banning all camera phones in a last-ditch attempt to preserve privacy.

"It's just like living in a village, where it's actually hard to lie because everybody knows the truth already," Tufekci said. "The current generation is never unconnected. They're never losing touch with their friends. So we're going back to a more normal place, historically. If you look at human history, the idea that you would drift through life, going from new relation to new relation, that's very new. It's just the 20th century."

Psychologists and sociologists spent years wondering how humanity would adjust to the anonymity of life in the city, the wrenching upheavals of mobile immigrant labor — a world of lonely people ripped from their social ties. We now have precisely the opposite problem. Indeed, our modern awareness tools reverse the original conceit of the Internet. When cyberspace came along in the early '90s, it was celebrated as a place where you could reinvent your identity — become someone new.

"If anything, it's identity-constraining now," Tufekci told me. "You can't play with your

▶

Why do you think there is a difference between how people view the Internet for themselves and for society? How would you answer the question? Why?

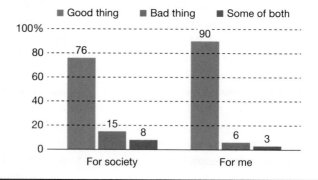

Has the Internet been a good thing or a bad thing?
% of Internet users

■ Good thing   ■ Bad thing   ■ Some of both

For society: 76, 15, 8
For me: 90, 6, 3

Source: Pew Research Center Internet Project Survey, January 9–12, 2014. N=857 Internet users.
PEW RESEARCH CENTER

identity if your audience is always checking up on you. I had a student who posted that she was downloading some Pearl Jam, and someone wrote on her wall, 'Oh, right, ha-ha — I know you, and you're not into that.' " She laughed. "You know that old cartoon? 'On the Internet, nobody knows you're a dog'? On the Internet today, everybody knows you're a dog! If you don't want people to know you're a dog, you'd better stay away from a keyboard."

Or, as Leisa Reichelt, a consultant in London who writes regularly about ambient tools, put it to me: "Can you imagine a Facebook for children in kindergarten, and they never lose touch with those kids for the rest of their lives? What's that going to do to them?" Young people today are already developing an attitude toward their privacy that is simultaneously vigilant and laissez-faire. They curate their online personas as carefully as possible, knowing that everyone is watching — but they have also learned to shrug and accept the limits of what they can control.

45   It is easy to become unsettled by privacy-eroding aspects of awareness tools. But there is another — quite different — result of all this incessant updating: a culture of people who know much more about themselves. Many of the avid Twitterers, Flickrers and Facebook users I interviewed described an unexpected side-effect of constant self-disclosure. The act of stopping several times a day to observe what you're feeling or thinking can become, after weeks and weeks, a sort of philosophical act. It's like the Greek dictum to "know thyself," or the therapeutic concept of mindfulness. (Indeed, the question that floats eternally at the top of Twitter's Web site — "What are you doing?" — can come to seem existentially freighted. What are you doing?) Having an audience can make the self-reflection even more acute, since, as my interviewees noted, they're trying to describe their activities in a way that is not only accurate but also interesting to others: the status update as a literary form.

Laura Fitton, the social-media consultant, argues that her constant status updating has made her "a happier person, a calmer person" because the process of, say, describing a horrid morning at work forces her to look at it objectively. "It drags you out of your own head," she added. In an age of awareness, perhaps the person you see most clearly is yourself.

Understanding and Interpreting

1 When Mark Zuckerberg added the News Feed feature to Facebook in 2006, what were some people's objections to it? Why was it ultimately determined to be widely successful and the cause of the site's massive growth?

2 What is "ambient awareness" and how is it similar and different in online and offline interactions?

3 Summarize the development of the "Dunbar number" (par. 27) and explain its application to online social media. According to the article, has social media expanded the Dunbar number?

4 What are some of the benefits and detriments of the "weak ties" that are often created and developed through social media?

5 What does media researcher Danah Boyd mean about some online relationships when she says, "They can observe you, but it's not the same as knowing you" (par. 33)?

6 Look back at the following passage from paragraph 39. What does it reveal about the complexity of online relationships?

> For them, participation isn't optional. If you don't dive in, other people will define who you are. So you constantly stream your pictures, your thoughts, your relationship status and what you're doing — right now! — if only to ensure the virtual version of you is accurate, or at least the one you want to present to the world.

7 What evidence does sociologist Zeynep Tufekci offer to support her claim that social media is taking us back to a "normal place, historically" (par. 41) in our social relations, similar to what existed before the twentieth century?

8 In the last two paragraphs, Thompson explains one more benefit some users of social media have identified: the ability to "know thyself." According to Thompson, why is this a desirable outcome and how can social media help with this?

Analyzing Language, Style, and Structure

1 What does the following section from paragraph 12 reveal about the author's initial tone toward social media?

> The growth of ambient intimacy can seem like modern narcissism taken to a new, supermetabolic extreme—the ultimate expression of a generation of celebrity-addled youths who believe their every utterance is fascinating and ought to be shared with the world. Twitter, in particular, has been the subject of nearly relentless scorn since it went online. "Who really cares what I am doing, every hour of the day?" wondered Alex Beam, a *Boston Globe* columnist, in an essay about Twitter last month. "Even I don't care."

2 After using primarily an objective, third person point of view, Thompson actively inserts himself into the story, describing his first steps using Twitter (par. 21). Look back through the piece to identify other places where he writes about himself and explain what is gained in his argument about social media by his own personal anecdotes.

3 In addition to interviewing experts on the topic of social media, the author includes information about three social media users. Look back at each, and explain how each contributes a different aspect to the argument:

a. Ben Haley (pars. 13–17)
b. Shannon Seery (pars. 21–24)
c. Andrea Ahan (pars. 35–39)

4 What does the author's word choice in the following sentence from paragraph 44 suggest about his attitude toward social media's demands on its users? "They curate their online personas as carefully as possible, knowing that everyone is watching."

5 Skim back through and identify where Thompson describes positive aspects of social media and where he describes negative ones. Overall, on which side does he land? What words and phrases reveal his position most clearly?

Connecting, Arguing, and Extending

1 In paragraph 43, this article references the famous 1993 *New Yorker* cartoon about anonymity online. You can see the cartoon in the chapter introduction on page 666. Is the conclusion—the Internet allows for total anonymity—still valid today? Why or why not?

2 In what ways is Zeynep Tufekci, the sociologist Thompson quotes in paragraph 41, correct when she claims that the new social media technology actually makes our relationships more like they might

have been in the past? Explain your reasoning with research you conduct or interviews with people who grew up pre-Internet.

3 Define *friend* in the era of social media. What are the different roles that online and offline friends play in your own life, and what are the similarities and differences in the ways that you communicate with them?

from Alone Together

Sherry Turkle

Sherry Turkle (b. 1948) is a professor at the Massachusetts Institute of Technology and the director of its Initiative of Technology and Self, which aims to study the ways that the new technologies "raise fundamental questions about selfhood, identity, community, and what it means to be human." Turkle has published several texts on the ways that we interact with various electronic devices and with each other on social media sites. Some of her works include *The Second Self: Computers and the Human Spirit*; *Life on the Screen: Identity in the Age of the Internet*; and *The Inner History of Devices*.

KEY CONTEXT   This excerpt is taken from Turkle's book *Alone Together: Why We Expect More from Technology and Less from Each Other*, which was published in 2011. Turkle is a licensed clinical psychologist, and a significant part of her background and training is in psychology. She gathers much of her data through interviews and focus groups with her subjects, who, in this excerpt, are mostly teenagers. Turkle asks them regularly about their feelings, as a therapist might. Much of the evidence that she uses to support her arguments about the ways that teenagers interact with social media comes in the form of transcripts of these interviews.

Roman, eighteen, admits that he texts while driving and he is not going to stop. "I know I should, but it's not going to happen. If I get a Facebook message or something posted on my wall . . . I have to see it. I have to." I am speaking with him and ten of his senior classmates at the Cranston School, a private urban coeducational high school in Connecticut. His friends admonish him, but then several admit to the same behavior. Why do they text while driving? Their reasons are not reasons; they simply express a need to connect. "I interrupt a call even if the new call says 'unknown' as an identifier — I just have to know who it is. So I'll cut off a friend for an 'unknown,'" says Maury. "I need to know who wanted to connect. . . . And if I hear my phone, I have to answer it. I don't have a choice. I have to know who it is, what they are calling for." Marilyn adds, "I keep the sound on when I drive. When a text comes in, I have to look. No matter what. Fortunately, my phone shows me the text as a pop up right up front . . . so I don't have to do too much looking while I'm driving." These young people live in a state of waiting for connection. And they are willing to take risks, to put themselves on the line. Several admit that tethered to their phones, they get into accidents when walking. One chipped a front tooth. Another shows a recent bruise on his arm. "I went right into the handle of the refrigerator."

I ask the group a question: "When was the last time you felt that you didn't want to be interrupted?" I expect to hear many stories. There are none. Silence. "I'm waiting to be interrupted right now," one says. For him, what I would term "interruption" is the beginning of a connection.

Today's young people have grown up with robot pets and on the network in a fully tethered life. In their views of robots, they are pioneers, the first generation that does not necessarily take simulation to be second best. As for online life, they see its power — they are, after all risking their lives to check their messages — but they also view it as one might the weather: to be taken for granted, enjoyed, and sometimes endured. They've gotten used to this weather but there are signs of weather fatigue. There are so many performances; it takes energy to keep things up; and it takes time, a lot of time. "Sometimes you don't have time for your friends except if they're online," is a common complaint. And then there are the compulsions of the networked life — the ones that lead to dangerous driving and chipped teeth.

Today's adolescents have no less need than those of previous generations to learn empathic skills, to think about their values and identity, and to manage and express feelings. They need time to discover themselves, time to think. But technology, put in the service of always-on communication and telegraphic speed and brevity, has changed the rules of engagement with all of this. When is downtime, when is stillness? The text-driven world of rapid response does not make self-reflection impossible but does little to cultivate it. When interchanges are reformatted for the small screen and reduced to the emotional shorthand of emoticons, there are necessary simplifications. And what of adolescents' need for secrets, for marking out what is theirs alone?

5   I wonder about this as I watch cell phones passed around high school cafeterias. Photos and messages are being shared and compared. I cannot help but identify with the people who sent the messages to these wandering phones. Do they all assume that their words and photographs are on public display? Perhaps. Traditionally, the development of intimacy required privacy. Intimacy without privacy reinvents what intimacy means. Separation, too, is

being reinvented. Tethered children know they have a parent on tap — a text or a call away.

Several boys refer to the "mistake" of having taught their parents how to text and send instant messages (IMs), which they now equate with letting the genie out of the bottle. For one, "I made the mistake of teaching my parents how to text-message recently, so now if I don't call them when they ask me to call, I get an urgent text message." For another, "I taught my parents to IM. They didn't know how. It was the stupidest thing I could do. Now my parents IM me all the time. It is really annoying. My parents are upsetting me. I feel trapped and less independent."

Teenagers argue that they should be allowed time when they are not "on call." Parents say that they, too, feel trapped. For if you know your child is carrying a cell phone, it is frightening to call or text and get no response. "I didn't ask for this new worry," says the mother of two high school girls. Another, a mother of three teenagers, "tries not to call them if it's not important." But if she calls and gets no response, she panics:

> I've sent a text. Nothing back. And I know they have their phones. Intellectually, I know there is little reason to worry. But there is something about this unanswered text. Sometimes, it made me a bit nutty. One time, I kept sending texts, over and over. I envy my mother. We left for school in the morning. We came home. She worked. She came back, say at six. She didn't worry. I end up imploring my children to answer my every message. Not because I feel I have a right to their instant response. Just out of compassion.

Adolescent autonomy is not just about separation from parents. Adolescents also need to separate from each other. They experience their friendships as both sustaining and constraining. Connectivity brings complications. Online life provides plenty of room for individual experimentation, but it can be hard to escape from new group demands. It is common for friends to expect that their friends will stay available — a technology-enabled social contract demands continual peer presence. And the tethered self becomes accustomed to its support.

Traditional views of adolescent development take autonomy and strong personal boundaries as reliable signs of a successfully maturing self. In this view of development, we work toward an independent self capable of having a feeling, considering it, and deciding whether to share it. Sharing a feeling is a deliberate act, a movement toward intimacy. This description was always a fiction in several ways. For one thing, the "gold standard" of autonomy validated a style that was culturally "male." Women (and indeed, many men) have an emotional style that defines itself not by boundaries but through relationships.[1] Furthermore, adolescent conversations are by nature exploratory, and this in healthy ways. Just as some writers learn what they think by looking at what they write, the years of identity formation can be a time of learning what you think by hearing what you say to others. But given these caveats, when we think about maturation, the notion of a bounded self has its virtues, if only as a metaphor. It suggests,

sensibly, that before we forge successful life partnerships, it is helpful to have a sense of who we are.[2]

10   But the gold standard tarnishes if a phone is always in hand. You touch a screen and reach someone presumed ready to respond, someone who also has a phone in hand. Now, technology makes it easy to express emotions while they are being formed. It supports an emotional style in which feelings are not fully experienced until they are communicated. Put otherwise, there is every opportunity to form a thought by sending out for comments.

The Collaborative Self

Julia, sixteen, a sophomore at Branscomb, an urban public high school in New Jersey, turns texting into a kind of polling. Julia has an outgoing and warm presence, with smiling, always-alert eyes. When a feeling bubbles up, Julia texts it. Where things go next is guided by what she hears next. Julia says,

> If I'm upset, right as I feel upset, I text a couple of my friends . . . just because I know that they'll be there and they can comfort

▶

Reflect on your own cell phone usage. How often have you checked it today? Or even this class period? Are you checking it right now?

"It keeps me from looking at my phone every two seconds."

Liam Walsh/The New Yorker/The Cartoon Bank

me. If something exciting happens, I know that they'll be there to be excited with me, and stuff like that. So I definitely feel emotions when I'm texting, as I'm texting. . . . Even before I get upset and I know that I have that feeling that I'm gonna start crying, yeah, I'll pull up my friend . . . uh, my phone . . . and say like . . . I'll tell them what I'm feeling, and, like, I need to talk to them, or see them.

"I'll pull up my friend . . . uh, my phone." Julia's language slips tellingly. When Julia thinks about strong feelings, her thoughts go both to her phone and her friends. She mixes together "pulling up" a friend's name on her phone and "pulling out" her phone, but she does not really correct herself so much as imply that the phone is her friend and that friends take on identities through her phone.

After Julia sends out a text, she is uncomfortable until she gets one back: "I am always looking for a text that says, 'Oh, I'm sorry,' or 'Oh, that's great.'" Without this feedback, she says, "It's hard to calm down." Julia describes how painful it is to text about "feelings" and get no

response: "I get mad. Even if I e-mail someone, I want the response, like, right away.[3] I want them to be, like, right there answering me. And sometimes I'm like, 'Uh! Why can't you just answer me?' . . . I wait, like, depending on what it is, I wait like an hour if they don't answer me, and I'll text them again. 'Are you mad? Are you there? Is everything okay?'" Her anxiety is palpable. Julia must have a response. She says of those she texts, "You want them there, because you need them." When they are not there, she moves on with her nascent feelings, but she does not move on alone: "I go to another friend and tell them."

Claudia, seventeen, a junior at Cranston, describes a similar progression. "I start to have some happy feelings as soon as I start to text." As with Julia, things move from "I have a feeling, I want to make a call" to "I want to have a feeling, I need to make a call," or in her case, send a text. What is not being cultivated here is the ability to be alone and reflect on one's emotions in private. On the contrary, teenagers report discomfort when they are without their cell phones.[4] They need to be connected in order to feel like

▶

What would you predict would be the results for teenagers? Why? Which technologies would be the hardest for you to give up?

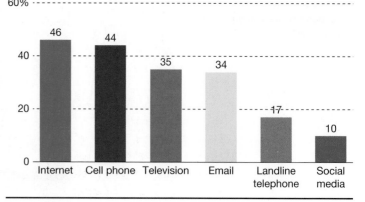

Technologies that would be very hard to give up

% of all adults who say these technologies would be very hard or impossible to give up

Internet	Cell phone	Television	Email	Landline telephone	Social media
46	44	35	34	17	10

Source: Pew Research Center Internet Project Survey, January 9–12, 2014. N=1006 adults.
PEW RESEARCH CENTER

themselves. Put in a more positive way, both Claudia and Julia share feelings as part of discovering them. They cultivate a collaborative self.

15 Estranged from her father, Julia has lost her close attachments to his relatives and was traumatized by being unable to reach her mother during the day of the September 11 attacks on the Twin Towers. Her story illustrates how digital connectivity — particularly texting — can be used to manage specific anxieties about loss and separation. But what Julia does — her continual texting, her way of feeling her feelings only as she shares them — is not unusual. The particularities of every individual case express personal history, but Julia's individual "symptom" comes close to being a generational style.[5]

Sociologist David Riesman, writing in the mid-1950s, remarked on the American turn from an inner- to an other-directed sense of self.[6]

Angel Boligan, Courtesy of Cagle Cartoons

▲

What point is the cartoonist trying to make and what analogy is he relying on to make it? Is it effective in making the point?

Without a firm inner sense of purpose, people looked to their neighbors for validation. Today, cell phone in hand, other-directedness is raised to a higher power. At the moment of beginning to have a thought or feeling, we can have it validated, almost prevalidated. Exchanges may be brief, but more is not necessarily desired. The necessity is to have someone be there.

Ricki, fifteen, a freshman at Richelieu, a private high school for girls in New York City, describes that necessity: "I have a lot of people on my contact list. If one friend doesn't 'get it,' I call another." This marks a turn to a hyper-other-directedness. This young woman's contact or buddy list has become something like a list of "spare parts" for her fragile adolescent self. When she uses the expression "get it," I think she means "pick up the phone." I check with her if I have gotten this right. She says, ' "Get it,' yeah, 'pick up,' but also 'get it,' 'get *me.*'" Ricki counts on her friends to finish her thoughts. Technology does not cause but encourages a sensibility in which the validation of a feeling becomes part of establishing it, even part of the feeling itself. [...]

Again, technology, on its own, does not cause this new way of relating to our emotions and other people. But it does make it easy. Over time, a new style of being with each other becomes socially sanctioned. In every era, certain ways of relating come to feel natural. In our time, if we can be continually in touch, needing to be continually in touch does not seem a problem or a pathology but an accommodation to what technology affords. It becomes the norm.

Notes

1. Carol Gilligan, *In a Different Voice: Psychological Theory and Women's Development* (1982; Cambridge, MA: Harvard University Press, 1993).

2. Erik Erikson, *Identity and the Life Cycle* (1952; New York: W. W. Norton, 1980) and *Childhood and Society* (New York: Norton, 1950).

3. In Julia's world, e-mail is considered "slow" and rarely used because texting has greater immediacy.

4. It is so common to see teenagers (and others) attending to their mobiles rather than what is around them, that it was possible for a fake news story to gain traction in Britain. Taken up by the

media, the story went out that there was a trial program to pad lamp-posts in major cities. Although it was a hoax, I fell for it when it was presented online as news. In fact, in the year prior to the hoax, one in five Britons did walk into a lamppost or other obstruction while attending to a mobile device. This is not surprising because research reported that "62 per cent of Britons concentrate so hard on their mobile phone when texting they lose peripheral vision." See Charlie Sorrel, "Padded Lampposts Cause Fuss in London," *Wired*, March 10, 2008, www.wired.com/gadgetlab/2008/03/padded-lampposts (accessed October 5, 2009).

5. New communications technology makes it easier to serve up people as slivers of self, providing a sense that to get what you need from others you have multiple and inexhaustible options. On the psychology that needs these "slivers," see Paul H. Ornstein, ed., *The Search for Self: Selected Writings of Heinz Kokut (1950–1978)*, vol. 2 (New York: International Universities Press, 1978).

6. David Riesman, Nathan Glazer, and Reuel Denney, *The Lonely Crowd: A Study of the Changing American Character* (1950; New Haven, CT: Yale University Press, 2001).

Understanding and Interpreting

1 What does the author conclude about how and why teenagers interpret interruptions differently than adults do?

2 Reread the fourth and fifth paragraphs. Write a statement or two that captures Turkle's thesis. In other words, what is she hoping to communicate to her readers in this selection?

3 Turkle claims in paragraph 8 that "[c]onnectivity brings complications." What complications does she identify and what evidence does she include to support her claim?

4 Turkle states, "Traditional views of adolescent development take autonomy and strong personal boundaries as reliable signs of a successfully maturing self" (par. 9). According to Turkle, how does today's connected world make this development more difficult?

5 Write a definition of "the collaborative self" (see the heading following par. 10). What would Turkle likely say is wrong with the idea of a collaborative self?

6 Though she never directly says in this excerpt, what can you infer about possible solutions Turkle might suggest to the problem she sees in today's connected world?

Analyzing Language, Style, and Structure

1 What does Turkle achieve by starting with quotes from teenagers who admit to texting while driving?

2 While the focus of this piece is on teenagers' use of technology for communication, Turkle includes a long quote from a mother who texts her children (par. 7). How does this passage support Turkle's main point on adolescent development?

3 While Turkle's style could probably be described as that of a dispassionate researcher who is simply recounting the evidence she has collected, there are moments throughout this piece where Turkle seems to step away from that approach, describing her subjects with a more personal eye. Identify one or more of these places and explain how her choice helps to support her purpose for writing this piece.

4 Overall, is Turkle's argument convincing? How does she establish her own ethos and utilize both logos and pathos to support her position?

Connecting, Arguing, and Extending

1 Turkle quotes a number of teenagers throughout this piece. Skim back through and identify one interviewee who either shares your views on social networking or holds a very different viewpoint. Then, compare and contrast your attitude toward this technology's impact on your life and relationships with the attitude expressed by the interviewee.

2 Write an analysis of how you use social media for communication and how your online social relationships compare to your offline relationships. To help you write this analysis, you may choose one of the following activities or develop your own:

a. Chart your online and offline interactions with friends and family for a period of time (at least one day, no longer than a week). Create a graph that compares the time that you spend connecting with others online, offline, or both, and write an analysis.

b. If you are an active user of social media, identify a twenty-four-hour period when you will try not to use any social media. If you are not a heavy social media user, identify a twenty-four-hour period in which you will try to do the majority of your communicating with friends through social media. After your experiment, explain what differences you noticed in the ways that you communicate.

c. Look back through your texts, status updates, tweets, and recent pictures and postings from your regular social media sites. Explain the different ways that you communicate based upon the medium you use.

3 Overall, is the constant communication that technology enables a positive or a negative force in society? Support your argument with references to the Turkle selection as well as with your own research and interviews with family and friends.

4 The National Council of Teachers of English says that literacy in the twenty-first century must include the ability to "design and share information for global communities to meet a variety of purposes." How do the digital communications technologies available today allow people from different countries to connect and understand each other? Does this technology facilitate communication in ways that were not previously possible? Research organizations that try to bring people of different cultures together through technology and explain the impact that opportunities for global information sharing might have in the future.

The Hoax of Digital Life

Tim Egan

Frederick M. Brown/Getty Images

Currently a regular contributor to the *New York Times* editorial section, Tim Egan (b. 1954) is a journalist and writer who lives in Seattle, Washington. He has written several nonfiction books about American history, including *The Worst Hard Time: The Untold Story of Those Who Survived the Great American Dust Bowl*, published in 2006, and *The Big Burn: Teddy Roosevelt and the Fire That Saved America*, published in 2008.

KEY CONTEXT   This article was originally published as an op-ed piece for the *New York Times* on January 17, 2013, in response to the growing scandal involving Notre Dame football star Manti Te'o. During the 2012 college football regular season, Notre Dame had been undefeated, in large part due to the play of linebacker Te'o, who had told reporters that he was playing inspired football to honor his grandmother and his girlfriend, both of whom, he said, had died on the same day at the beginning of the season. In January, just after Notre Dame advanced to the national championship game, reporters discovered that Te'o's girlfriend never existed. Te'o later claimed that he was the victim of an extensive hoax with someone pretending online, on the phone, and through texts to be the girl he thought of as his girlfriend. Later that year, Te'o was drafted by the San Diego Chargers to play in the National Football League.

I once tried to talk somebody out of pursuing a mail-order bride, a young Filipino who for a relatively modest fee would agree to move to Spokane, Washington, and start a new life with a complete stranger. Among the many questions raised by this half-baked plan was: How could you marry someone you had never met?

The case of Manti Te'o, the Notre Dame line-backer and finalist for college football's highest honor, and his fake dead girlfriend takes this question to a whole new level. How can some-one claim to have fallen in love with a woman he never met?

The answer, in part, is what's wrong with love and courtship for a generation that values digital encounters over the more complicated messiness of real human interaction. As my colleague Alex Williams reported in a widely discussed piece a few days ago, screen time may be more important than face time for many 20- and 30-somethings. "Dating culture has evolved to a cycle of text messages, each one requiring the code-breaking skills of a cold war spy to interpret," said Shani Silver, 30, in the story.

Technology, with its promise of both faux-intimacy and a protective sense of removal, does not alone explain the bizarre and still unfolding story of Te'o, who claimed that the love of his life died of leukemia last September after also suffering from a serious car crash. A Stanford student, this love — Lennay Kekua — had urged Te'o to play for her, no matter what happened.

5   Before the fraud was revealed, Te'o recalled to the *Chicago Tribune* one of the final conversations he had with the made-up girlfriend: "She said, 'Babe, if anything happens to me, promise that

seeing connections

Blogger Alexandra Samuel would likely be frus-trated with what she would call the unnecessarily broad distinction that Egan draws between our online and offline lives.

Look at an excerpt from her article titled "10 Reasons to Stop Apologizing for Your Online Life" and explain how she would probably respond to the conclusions that Egan draws in this article. To what extent do you agree or disagree with the four suggestions Samuel has for your own online life?

There's no denying the differences between life online and off. In our online lives we shake off the limitations of our physical selves, perhaps even our names and consciences, too. What remains are the fundamentals: human beings, human conversations, human communities. To say that "reality" includes only offline beings, offline conversations and offline communities is to say that face-to-face matters more than human-to-human. It's time to start living in 21st century reality: a reality that is both on and offline. Acknowledge online life as real, and the Internet's transfor-mative potential opens up:

1. When you commit to being your real self online, you discover parts of yourself you never dared to share offline.
2. When you visualize the real person you're about to email or tweet, you bring human qualities of attention and empathy to your online communications.
3. When you take the idea of online presence literally, you can experience your online disembodiment as a journey into your mind rather than out of your body.
4. When you treat your Facebook connec-tions as real friends instead of "friends," you stop worrying about how many you have and focus on how well you treat them.

you'll stay over there, that you'll play and that you'll honor me through the way you play.'" All she wanted were white roses, which he sent to her.

If Notre Dame wasn't the land of leprechauns, Win-One-for-the-Gipper mythology, Rudy and Touchdown Jesus, I might be more inclined to believe Te'o. This particular college football fairy tale, then and now, smells like one of the serial lies of Lance Armstrong.

But let's take the nation's most storied Catholic university at its word. And, as explained by Notre Dame officials on Wednesday night, after they'd hired a private investigative firm to sort out the details, the story is a compelling parable of digital dating culture.

At the center of this episode is the astonishing assertion by the Notre Dame athletic director Jack Swarbrick that Te'o never actually met his phantom lover. Never. No face time. The entire relationship was electronic. And yet she was likely to become his wife, according to Te'o's father.

"The issue of who it is, who plays the role, what's real and what's not here is a more complex question than I can get into here," said Swarbrick, at the press conference on Wednesday. Actually, it's not that complicated. The woman either existed, and then died, or didn't exist, and therefore couldn't have died at such a young and tender age. Her passing gave a sports-soaked nation reason to feel sympathy for a Fighting Irish hulk who also happens to be a devout Mormon. His biography, we're told, is real.

10   The digital girlfriend, Te'o said in an interview last October, two months before he found out the fraud, "was the most beautiful girl I ever met. Not because of her physical beauty, but the beauty of her character and who she is."

Her character. Remember, she's an avatar, at best. Again, let's assume this august institution of higher learning and moral discipline, and all its representatives, are now telling the truth. Then let's look at this person with the

extraordinary character, the woman Te'o fell for. There was a picture, from their online encounters, of a lovely woman, a Stanford student, supposedly. There was a voice, from telephone conversations, of someone as well. And that someone finally called him up in early December and said the whole thing was a hoax perpetuated by an acquaintance in California, according to Deadspin, which broke the story.

"The pain was real," said Swarbrick. "The grief was real. The affection was real. That's the nature of this sad, cruel game."

No, that's the nature of people who develop relationships through a screen. The Internet is the cause of much of today's commitment-free, surface-only living; it's also the explanation for

Joe Robbins/Getty Images

Manti Te'o faced extraordinary media attention after the news of his story came out.

Was the media justified in making the details of his case public? Why do you think his case led to so much media attention?

why someone could tumble head-over-heels for a pixelated cipher.[1] Online dating was only the start of what led us down this road.

To fall in love requires a bit of unpredictable human interaction. You have to laugh with a person, test their limits, go back and forth, touch them, reveal something true about yourself. You have to show some vulnerability, some give and take. At the very least, you have to make eye contact. It's easier to substitute texting, tweeting or Facebook posting for these basic rituals of

---

[1] **cipher:** A code used to encrypt messages. —Eds.

love and friendship because the digital route offers protection. How can you get dumped when you were never really involved?

15   "If anything good comes from this," said Te'o in a written statement, "I hope it is that others will be far more guarded when they engage people online than I was."

Te'o called himself a victim of an elaborate hoax. If he's telling the truth, he's right in one sense, but wrong in his conclusion. He's a victim of his age, people who are more willing to embrace fake life through a screen than the real world beyond their smartphone.

Understanding and Interpreting

1 Throughout the piece, Egan draws a comparison between "digital life" and "real life." What does he conclude about the differences between them?

2 Explain the analogy that Egan makes between a mail-order bride and online dating. How does it support his position on Te'o?

3 It's clear from the outset that Egan is opposed to the possibility of finding a sustainable, long-term relationship solely online. What is the most convincing evidence that Egan uses to support his position? What is his least effective evidence?

4 Near the end of the piece, Egan asserts, "To fall in love requires a bit of unpredictable human interaction. You have to laugh with a person, test their limits, go back and forth, touch them, reveal something true about yourself. You have to show some vulnerability, some give and take. At the very least, you have to make eye contact" (par. 14). Which of these conditions are possible and which are impossible online? How does Egan's definition strengthen or weaken his argument against online relationships?

5 Even though Manti Te'o likely was tricked and targeted because he played for a high-profile football team, Egan still calls his story a "compelling parable of digital dating culture" (par. 7). What lessons does he want his readers to draw from Te'o's story?

Analyzing Language, Style, and Structure

1 Egan ends his first two paragraphs with rhetorical questions. How does his choice connect the story in the first paragraph with Manti Te'o?

2 How does Egan reveal his attitude toward Notre Dame through the following passages?

a. "If Notre Dame wasn't the land of leprechauns, Win-One-for-the-Gipper mythology, Rudy and Touchdown Jesus, I might be more inclined to believe Te'o" (par. 6).

b. "Again, let's assume this august institution of higher learning and moral discipline, and all its representatives, are now telling the truth" (par. 11).

3 Look back at the places that Egan quotes directly from the press conference by Jack Swarbrick, Notre Dame's athletic director. How does Egan use Swarbrick's words to set up his response to them?

4 Egan often takes a derisive tone toward communication on the Internet. Locate two words or phrases that create this derisive tone and rewrite them, choosing words that might be used by someone with a more positive attitude toward Internet communication.

Connecting, Arguing, and Extending

1 The release of the 2010 documentary film *Catfish* and a reality television show on MTV by the same name has made the term "catfish" a common way to describe people who lure others into fake online relationships. Watch the documentary or an episode of the show and explain how it either confirms or rejects Egan's attitude toward online relationships.

2 In a study published in 2012 by the Internet security firm McAfee, 12 percent of teenage girls reported that they had met in real life with someone they met online, without fully confirming their identity prior to the meeting. Write an argument for rules or guidelines that you think teenagers ought to use when meeting face-to-face with people they have only met online. Explain how these rules would or would not satisfy Egan's definition of a real relationship.

3 Do you think it is possible to fall in love with someone you have met online but not in person? Why or why not? What would Egan say about your response?

Facebook Sonnet

Sherman Alexie

A Spokane/Coeur d'Alene Indian, Sherman Alexie (b. 1966) grew up in Wellpinit, Washington, on the Spokane Indian Reservation. He is the author of over twenty books, including *The Absolutely True Diary of a Part-Time Indian*, the short-story collection *Lone Ranger and Tonto Fistfight in Heaven*, and several collections of poetry. He is also the writer and coproducer of the film *Smoke Signals*, which was released in 1998. This poem was originally published in the *New Yorker* in 2011.

Anthony Pidgeon/Redferns/Getty Images

Welcome to the endless high-school
Reunion. Welcome to past friends
And lovers, however kind or cruel.
Let's undervalue and unmend
5   The present. Why can't we pretend
Every stage of life is the same?
Let's exhume, resume, and extend
Childhood. Let's all play the games
That occupy the young. Let fame
10 And shame intertwine. Let one's search
For God become public domain.
Let church.com become our church.
Let's sign up, sign in, and confess
Here at the altar of loneliness.

seeing connections

In early 2014, Facebook started to become aware that the demographics of its users were changing, as seen in this chart:

	[AS OF JANUARY 2011]		[AS OF JANUARY 2014]		
GENDER ?	**USERS**	**PERCENTAGE**	**USERS**	**PERCENTAGE**	**GROWTH**
U.S. Males	63,645,480	43.4%	82,000,000	45.6%	28.8%
U.S. Females	80,711,340	55.0%	96,000,000	53.3%	18.9%
Unknown	2,448,180	1.7%	2,000,000	1.1%	–18.3%
Total U.S.	*146,805,000*	*100.0%*	*180,000,000*	*100.0%*	22.6%
AGE ?	**USERS**	**PERCENTAGE**	**USERS**	**PERCENTAGE**	**GROWTH**
13–17	13,114,780	8.9%	9,800,000	5.4%	–25.3%
18–24	45,406,460	30.9%	42,000,000	23.3%	–7.5%
25–34	33,171,080	22.6%	44,000,000	24.4%	32.6%
35–54	39,595,900	27.0%	56,000,000	31.1%	41.4%
55+	15,516,780	10.6%	28,000,000	15.6%	80.4%
STUDENT ?	**USERS**	**PERCENTAGE**	**USERS**	**PERCENTAGE**	**GROWTH**
High School	7,292,080	5.0%	3,000,000	1.7%	–58.9%
College	11,748,840	8.0%	4,800,000	2.7%	–59.1%
College Alumni	36,441,600	24.8%	60,000,000	33.3%	64.6%

What can you conclude from this graphic and what might the reaction of the speaker of this poem be to this data? To what extent does it reflect your and your friends' experiences with social media?

Understanding and Interpreting

1 Make an inference about the approximate age of the speaker of the poem. Explain which lines from the poem support your inference.

2 What does it mean to "undervalue and unmend / The present" (ll. 4–5)? How can social media, like Facebook, accomplish this?

3 On what specific aspects of Facebook and social media does the speaker choose to focus? What aspects does the speaker choose to ignore? How do these choices reveal the speaker's attitude toward social media?

4 Throughout the poem, there are references to aspects of religion. What point is the speaker trying to make with these references?

Analyzing Language, Style, and Structure

1 Reread lines 7–9. What is Alexie hoping to achieve by comparing Facebook and childhood?

2 In addition to using end-line rhyming, Alexie uses internal rhyme in lines 9–10. How does he use rhyme illustrate his point about social media?

3 Alexie uses forms of the first person plural—*let's, we, our*—throughout his poem. How would the effect be different had he used other pronouns, such as *I, me, my, they,* or *you*?

4 There are several instances where Alexie uses verbal irony, which is a discrepancy between what is said and what is actually meant. Identify words or phrases that he uses ironically and explain how this irony helps make a point about social media relationships.

5 The poem follows the structure of a sonnet, with fourteen total lines, a rhyming pattern, and a rhyming couplet in the last two lines. In what ways does Alexie's choice of structure reflect the poem's theme?

Connecting, Arguing, and Extending

1 The last line of the poem suggests that people who use Facebook are lonely. Write an argument in which you agree with, disagree with, or qualify. You can reference your own and others' experiences, as well as this excerpt from an article by Stephen Marche called "Is Facebook Making Us Lonely?"

> The idea that a Web site could deliver a more friendly, interconnected world is bogus. The depth of one's social network outside Facebook is what determines the depth of one's social network within Facebook, not the other way around. Using social media doesn't create new social networks; it just transfers established networks from one platform to another. For the most part, Facebook doesn't destroy friendships—but it doesn't create them, either.

2 Alexie says that on social media, fame and shame intertwine. Explain why you agree or disagree with this statement, or if you would modify it in some way to make it closer to the truth.

Alter Egos: Avatars and Their Creators

Robbie Cooper

Robbie Cooper (b. 1969) is a British artist working in various media, including photography, video, and video game design.

Courtesy Robbie Cooper

KEY CONTEXT In *Alter Egos: Avatars and Their Creators,* Cooper interviewed people about the characters they play in online video games like *World of Warcraft,* and set photographs of the players next to their avatars for comparison.. In an interview, Cooper said:

> I think people use avatars in different ways. We noticed in Asia players were much more focused on creating an avatar that they liked looking at, rather than thinking about what other people were seeing inside the game world. So a lot of guys played girls for that reason. Another player in Korea played a little girl character because he was selling items and it helped in bargaining. He modified his behaviour in the game to try and maintain the illusion that he was really a little girl. Other people really throw themselves into the role play element, or consider their avatar to be an extension of their real world selves.

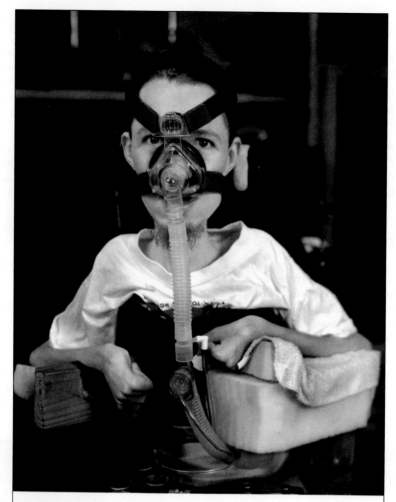

Jason Rowe

Name: Jason Rowe

Born: 1975

Occupation: None

Location: Crosby, Texas, USA

Average hours per week in-game: 80

Avatar name: Rurouni Kenshin

Avatar created: 2003

Game played: Star Wars Galaxies

Server name: Radiant

Character type: Human marksman / rifleman

Character level: 55

Special abilities: Ranged weapon specialization

Rurouni Kenshin

The difference between me and my online character is pretty obvious. I have a lot of physical disabilities in real life, but in _Star Wars Galaxies_ I can ride an Imperial speeder bike, fight monsters, or just hang out with friends at a bar. I have some use of my hands – not much, but a little. In the game I use an on-screen keyboard called '_soft-type_' to talk with other players. I can't press the keys on a regular keyboard so I use a virtual one. I play online games because I get to interact with people. The computer screen is my window to the world. Online it doesn't matter what you look like. Virtual worlds bring people together – everyone is on common ground. In the real world, people can be uncomfortable around me before they get to know me and realize that, apart from my outer appearance, I'm just like them. Online you get to know the person behind the keyboard before you know the physical person. The internet eliminates how you look in real life, so you get to know a person by their mind and personality. In 2002 at the _Ultimate Online_ Fan Faire in Austin, I noticed that people were intrigued by me, but they acted just like I was one of them. They treated me as an equal, like I wasn't even the way that I am – not disabled, not in a wheelchair, you know. We were all just gamers.

Cassien Guier

Name: Cassien Guier

Born: 1985

Occupation: Student

Location: Lyon, France

Average hours per week in-game: 8

Avatar name: La blonde

Avatar created: 2005

Game played: City of Heroes

Server name: Vigilance

Character type: Human female

Character level: 30

La blonde

First of all you have to know I'm not a good player. In the game I spend more time and money making my character look good and changing her hairstyle than I do playing. By the way, thanks to all the players for giving me money to make it possible for me to change my hair every day!

I decided to make a superhero reflecting my inner self so I created La blonde, the supra super heroine! She's wonderful, in pink and yellow clothes and splendid shoes. She has the biggest breasts you have ever seen. Just like a real blonde, her wardrobe changes every week. She likes to smile, and people must think she looks pretty stupid because they never take her seriously. Her attitude amazes all the other superheroes! The world can collapse but La blonde will remain optimistic. She often dies. I'm not sure why but the monsters kick her out first. As if a blonde could be dangerous!

I don't really know why people like to have her in their group when fighting the bad monsters. Probably because of her pretty smiley face. Actually she must be the most useless character in the world of MMORPGs.

Kimberly Rufer-Bach

Name: Kimberly Rufer-Bach

Born: 1966

Occupation: Software developer

Location: San José, California, USA

Average hours per week in-game: 70

Avatar name: Kim Anubis

Avatar created: 2004

Game played: Second Life

Character type: Content creator

Special abilities: Building interactive objects

Kim Anubis

I'm forty years old and have two cats and five computers. I have been managing and developing online communities since the mid 1980s. I run a company called The Magicians that develops interactive content on the *Second Life* platform.

     Most of the time my <u>avatar</u> looks like my real self, but about twenty years younger. I'm jealous of some of her clothes. I made a pair of boots that I wish I could export into real life. I usually dress my avatar in the same sort of stuff I wear. She doesn't have a separate persona or anything. She's just an extension of myself in this virtual space. Of course, she has a few abilities in *Second Life* I don't have in my first life. When I was a kid, I wished I had a tail. You know, a tail I could wag, or point at things, like in John Peterson's children's book *The Littles*. So one day I decided my avatar should have a tail. I made one using the 3D modelling tools built into *Second Life*, and then I wrote a program to make the tail wag, point in various directions, droop, etc. My friend, The Magicians' lead engineer Ian Young, took my code and did wonders with it, and we ended up with the Animagical Tail, which will not only do what you tell it to do, but will also pick up cues from your chat and help you to express yourself. Other people wanted a tail like this too, so I put it on sale in Lotus, my shop in *Second Life*. It sells quite well. I sell other things I've made – flapping wings, glowing crystal balls, bowls of swirling colour-changing butterflies and all sorts of other pretty, magical things.

Mi-Jin Kang

Name: Mi-Jin Kang (far left)

Born: 1985

Location: Seoul, South Korea

Average hours per week in-game: 17

Avatar name: Kangdidas

Avatar created: 2005

Game played: Lineage II

Kangdidas

We have all been friends since middle school. We enjoy hanging out together, shopping, and going to the movies, and we also play video games. At the <u>PC bang</u> we all sit next to each other and chat while we play. Inevitably one of us will make a joke about what's going on in the game and we'll end up dying, but we have fun all the same.

Our characters give us a chance to dress and act in ways that we can't in real life. Korea is a fairly conservative place when it comes to gender roles and society's expectations. In <u>*Lineage*</u> we can be strong warrior women, deadly and beautiful. Where else can you wield a sword and dress like a supermodel? The feeling of power is intoxicating!

One of the nice things about playing online is that we can socialize with other people without worrying about attracting unwanted attention. Most of the players don't believe that we're women, but sometimes the guys flirt with us. They'll help us on quests or give us items for our characters. If someone we meet is annoying or creepy, we can just log out.

April Hatch

Name: April Hatch

Born: 1979

Occupation: Housewife

Location: Missouri, USA

Average hours per week in-game: 35

Avatar name: Jaynex

Avatar created: 2003

Game played: Star Wars Galaxies

Character type: Human creature-handler

Character level: 32

Special abilities: Animal training

Jaynex

This is my second Jaynex character. My husband plays the first one now – he still gets loads of <u>tells</u> for me. When I first started playing I suffered from low self-esteem. I used to role-play a character, pretending to be someone I'm not. But gradually as time went by I would be more and more like myself. The barrier of not being face-to-face with people helped. But also I realized that people responded to me when I was more authentic. If I said what was on my mind, people liked me for it. I made this Jaynex to look like me.

I think gaming has helped me become who I am today, but the irony is that the more confident I get, the less I play. I'll still play during the winter, though. There just isn't much else to do.

Rebecca Glasure

Name: Rebecca Glasure

Born: 1980

Occupation: Housewife

Location: Los Angeles, California, USA

Avatar name: Stygian Physic

Avatar created: 2005

Game played: City of Heroes

Character type: Elf

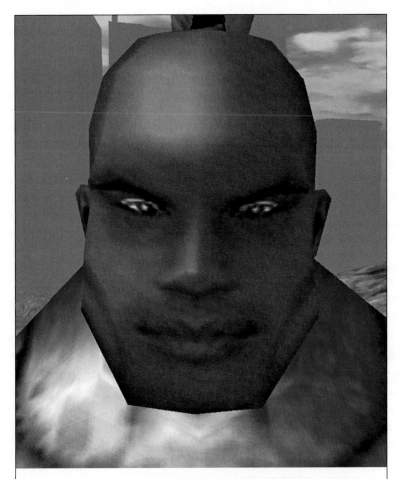

Stygian Physic

My <u>avatar</u> in *City of Heroes* is my complete opposite. Stygian Physic is big, black, and male. I created him that way because I didn't want to get hit on all the time. I wanted to be noticed for my skills, not my pixel-boobs. By playing as a guy, I found that people treated me differently. Being a guy enabled me to form relationships that I would never otherwise be able to experience. The guys just assume I'm a guy. If I'm the leader, I can make a call and they'll all just follow. And they'll open up about problems with their girlfriends and so on. When I play as a female character, I get challenged a lot more and have to argue about everything. No thanks. I've made some good friends playing as a guy. To this day they don't know I'm really a chick. I don't lie about it. They just assume that I'm a guy and never ask.

I have a six-year-old daughter who's needed more of my attention lately, and because of that I've cut back on my playing hours a lot. I would say that I used to be a 'hardcore' player, because I would spend literally all day sitting at my computer. But now my daughter's getting older, I just don't have that luxury any more. It's my hope that she grows up to like games, so we can all play together. That would blow my mind. My husband and I used to play together for the first year. When we're old and grey our reminiscences will probably consist of things like, 'Remember that time we slaughtered the Hydra and got <u>level</u> 40 at the same time?'

seeing connections

We think of the explosion of digital communications technologies as being a very recent occurrence, and yet the progression to where we are now in some ways began in the mid-1800s. The invention of the telegraph allowed people to send messages through wires in the form of a series of dots and dashes that were translated into words by a telegraph operator.

Read the following excerpt from a novel written by Ella Cheever Thayer in 1880 called *Wired Love: A Romance of Dots and Dashes*. In what ways are the "two worlds" of the telegraph operator described by the narrator of this novel similar to the "two worlds" of modern-day users of the Internet, such as the people represented in the photos in *Alter Egos*?

Miss Nattie Rogers, telegraph operator, lived, as it were, in two worlds. The one her office, dingy and curtailed as to proportions, but from whence she could wander away through the medium of that slender telegraph wire, on a sort of electric wings, to distant cities and towns; where, although alone all day, she did not lack social intercourse, and where she could amuse herself if she chose, by listening to and speculating upon the many messages of joy or of sorrow, of business and of pleasure, constantly going over the wire. But the other world in which Miss Rogers lived was very different; the world bounded by the four walls of a back room at Miss Betsey Kling's. It must be confessed that there are more pleasing views than sheds in greater or less degrees of dilapidation, a sickly grape-vine, a line of flapping sheets, an overflowing ash barrel; sweeter sounds than the dulcet notes of old rag-men, the serenades of musical cats, or the strains of a cornet played upon at intervals from nine P.M. to twelve, with the evident purpose of exhausting superfluous air in the performer's lungs. Perhaps, too, there was more agreeable company possible than Miss Betsey Kling.

Therefore, in the evening, Sunday and holiday, if not in the telegraphic world of Miss Rogers, loneliness, and the unpleasant sensation known as "blues" are not uncommon.

Understanding and Interpreting

1 Identify the avatars that look similar to the players who created them. What do the creators say is the benefit of playing a character similar to themselves?

2 Identify the avatars that look different from the players who created them. What do the creators say is the benefit of playing a character different from themselves?

3 We tend to think of certain aspects of identity as being fixed and unchanging, such as gender, race, and ethnicity. And yet, several of the creators describe a different concept of identity when entering virtual worlds. Explain the role of identity as presented in these photos and interviews.

Analyzing Language, Style, and Structure

1 What is Cooper's attitude toward gaming and time spent in the virtual world? How do his photographs, as well as his choices of which words and phrases to include from the interviews, reveal this attitude?

2 Examine how Cooper juxtaposes the creators and their avatars in the photographs to maximize the similarities or differences between them. Look carefully at the background of each photograph, as well as the subject's style of dress and body positioning.

Connecting, Arguing, and Extending

1 Think about a character/avatar that you play in a gaming or virtual world environment. Explain this character's similarity to, or difference from, your real self. Why have you chosen these particular attributes for your avatar? Take and juxtapose pictures of yourself and your avatar as Cooper did in "Alter Egos." If you do not regularly use an avatar or participate in virtual environments, interview someone who does, get a screen shot of his or her avatar, and juxtapose the image with a photograph showing the player's "real" identity.

2 Look at the following passage from the 2007 book *Exodus to the Virtual World* by Edward Castronova. How would Robbie Cooper likely respond? Why? To what extent do you agree or disagree?

An exodus is under way. Time and attention are migrating from the real world into the virtual world. The exodus will strengthen, I believe. Improvements in technology will make virtual worlds into veritable dreamlands. They will be more fun, for more people. Simple economic theory predicts that in this competition, the real world is going to lose. This loss will put pressure on the real world to adapt. The broad outlines of what that adaptation must be are surprising but not hard to see. If it is to survive unchallenged, the real world is going to have to offer experiences similar to those available in virtual worlds. In short, the real world will have to become more fun. A severe shock to business as usual; a revolution.

Why Facebook and Google's Concept of "Real Names" Is Revolutionary

Alexis C. Madrigal

Alexis C. Madrigal (b. 1982) is a deputy editor at TheAtlantic .com, where he focuses mostly on technology issues and the effects of technology on the future. He is also the author of *Powering the Dream: The History and Promise of Green Technology.*

Courtesy Alexis C. Madrigal

KEY CONTEXT   Madrigal wrote this piece in 2011, just after Google released a new policy that insisted on authenticating users' real names and prohibited the use of pseudonyms. "By providing your common name, you will be assisting all people you know in finding and creating a connection with the right person online," a Google spokesman said at the time.

This picture accompanied the original article in the *Atlantic* magazine.

What point is Madrigal making by manipulating the photograph with all of the information he includes?

"Down with the government!"

REAL NAME: Alexis C. Madrigal
CITY: Washington, DC
LATITUDE: 38.89784666877921
LONGITUDE: -77.05535888671875
EMPLOYER: The Atlantic
HEIGHT: 5'9"
WEIGHT: 165 pounds
DOB: 04/13/1982
CITY OF BIRTH: Mexico City, Mexico

Should you have to use your real name online? It's an issue that's long simmered among social media critics and supporters alike. On one end of the spectrum, there's 4chan, where everything is anonymous. On the other, there are Facebook and Google Plus. Both have drawn fire for categorically preventing people from using pseudonyms. This week, a new site, My Name Is Me, launched to make the case to allow anyone to use any name they choose.

This has seemed like a niche battle to me: a tiny group of activists complaining about some edge cases while the real-name policies benefited most people by raising the civility of online discourse. On a strictly utilitarian basis, it seemed like their arguments could be ignored.

But this week's discussions have made me rethink my intuition about names on social networks. My instincts had strongly pointed to requiring real names; my experience in the comment trenches of different websites has led me to believe that pure anonymity online creates a short-circuiting of our social software. It seemed natural to believe that attaching a persistent, real name to one's online identity

more accurately modeled our real-world social space.

I've changed my mind. The kind of naming policy that Facebook and Google Plus have is actually a radical departure from the way identity and speech interact in the real world. They attach identity more strongly to every act of online speech than almost any real world situation does.

5   I want to walk you through how I've come to this understanding. Because I've been obsessively listening to Philosophy Bites podcasts, I'm going to use a thought experiment.

Imagine you're walking down the street and you say out loud, "Down with the government!" For all non-megastars, the vast majority of people within earshot will have no idea who you are. They won't have access to your employment history or your social network or any of the other things that a Google search allows one to find. The only information they really have about you is your physical characteristics and mode of dress, which are data-rich but which cannot be directly or easily connected to your actual identity. In my case, bystanders would know that a 5′9″, 165 pound probably Caucasian male with

In this photo from Greece, protestors are hiding their identities because they fear reprisal from the government.

How does this need for anonymity in public compare to what Madrigal is saying about online anonymity?

Michael Debets/Pacific Press/LightRocket via Getty Images

half a beard said, "Down with the government!" Neither my speech or the context in which it occurred is preserved. And as soon as I leave the immediate vicinity, no one can definitively prove that I said, "Down with the government!"

In your head, adjust the settings for this thought experiment (you say it at work or your hometown or on television) or what you say (something racist, something intensely valuable, something criminal) or who you are (child, celebrity, politician) or who is listening (reporters, no one, coworkers, family). What I think you'll find is that we have different expectations for the publicness and persistence of a statement depending on a variety of factors. There is a continuum of publicness and persistence and anonymity. But in real life, we expect very few statements to be public, persistent, and attached to your real identity. Basically, only people talking on television or to the media can expect such treatment. And even then, the vast majority of their statements don't become part of the searchable Internet.

Online, Google and Facebook require an inversion of this assumed norm. Every statement you make on Google Plus or Facebook is persistent and strongly attached to your real identity through your name. Both services allow you to change settings to make your statements more or less public, which solves some problems. However, participating in public life on the services requires attaching your name to your statements. On the boulevards and town squares of Facebook, you can't just say, "Down with the government," with the knowledge that only a small percentage of the people who hear you could connect your statement to you. But the information is still being recorded, presumably in perpetuity. That means that if a government or human resources researcher or plain old enemy wants to get a hold of it, it is possible.

The pseudonym advocates note that being allowed to pick and choose a different name solves some of these problems. One can choose to tightly couple one's real-world identity and online identity . . . or not. One can choose to have multiple identities for separate networks. In the language we were using earlier, pseudonyms allow statements to be public and persistent, but not attached to one's real identity.

10   I can understand why Google and Facebook don't want this to happen. It's bad

for their marketing teams. It generates social problems when people don't act responsibly under the cloak of their assumed identity. It messes up the clarity and coherence of their data. And maybe those costs do outweigh the benefits pseudonymity brings to social networks.

But then let's have that conversation. Let's not pretend that what Google and Facebook are doing has long-established precedents and therefore these companies are only doing what they're doing to mimic real life. They are creating tighter links between people's behavior and their identities than have previously existed in the modern world.

Understanding and Interpreting

1 What is "pure anonymity" (par. 3), according to Alexis C. Madrigal?

2 What is the main argument *against* online anonymity that the author lays out in the third paragraph?

3 Madrigal states, "[I]n real life, we expect very few statements to be public, persistent, and attached to your real identity" (par. 7). Think of examples from your own or others' experiences that both support and contradict this statement.

4 What does the author mean when he says that Google and Facebook don't want anonymity because "[i]t's bad for their marketing teams [. . .] [and] messes up the clarity and coherence of their data" (par. 10)?

5 The last paragraph of the piece begins with "But then let's have that conversation." What exactly is the conversation that Madrigal suggests we need to have?

Analyzing Language, Style, and Structure

1 How does Madrigal establish his ethos on this topic throughout this article?

2 Explain how the "thought experiment" Madrigal proposes in the sixth paragraph assists in making his point about the dangers of using real names online.

3 How does Madrigal use pathos, specifically fear, to support his argument?

4 Explain the effectiveness of Madrigal's repeated use of the terms "public," "persistent," and "attached."

5 How does the first photograph and accompanying text communicate the author's attitude toward the issue of anonymity online?

Connecting, Arguing, and Extending

1 In what ways do you choose to be anonymous online or not? Do you do as the author suggests here and "have multiple identities for separate networks" (par. 9)? Why or why not?

2 Visit the website of a local newspaper and scroll through the reader comments at the bottom of a few articles on controversial topics. How many are anonymous and how many seem to be attached to real-life identities? What do you notice about the nature of the comments? Do they create a "short-circuiting of our social software," as Madrigal suggests in paragraph 3?

3 Write a letter to officials at Google, Facebook, Twitter, or another social media service and argue for either the right to be anonymous on their site or the requirement for all users to be identified by their real names.

4 Online bullying, or cyber-bullying, has been identified as a significant social problem. To what extent would this issue be resolved if everyone was required to identify himself or herself online? Explain, using evidence from your own or your friends' experiences.

The Anonymous Back-Stabbing of Internet Message Boards

Leonard Pitts Jr.

One of the most widely read newspaper opinion writers in the United States, Leonard Pitts Jr. (b. 1957) is a syndicated columnist for the *Miami Herald* and was the winner of the Pulitzer Prize for Commentary in 2004. He is also the author of two novels and the nonfiction *Becoming Dad: Black Men and the Journey to Fatherhood*. In this 2010 editorial he wonders whether the anonymity provided by the Internet causes more harm than good.

Al Diaz/Miami Herald/MCT/Newscom

It must have seemed like a great idea at the time.

There was this new medium, the Internet, and newspapers were posting stories on it, and someone decided to create a forum where readers could discuss and debate what they just read. It must have seemed an inspiration kissed by the spirit of Jefferson: a free public space where each of us could have his or her say.

Unfortunately, the reality of the thing has proved to be something else entirely. For proof, see the message boards of pretty much any paper. Or just wade in the nearest cesspool. The experiences are equivalent. Far from validating some high-minded ideal of public debate, message boards — particularly those inadequately policed by their newspapers and/or dealing with highly emotional matters — have become havens for a level of crudity, bigotry, meanness and plain nastiness that shocks the tattered remnants of our propriety.

For every person who offers some trenchant observation on the point at hand, there are a dozen who are so far off point they couldn't find their way back with a compass and road map. For every person who brings up some telling fact, there are a dozen whose "facts" are fantasies freshly made up to suit the exigencies of arguments they otherwise cannot win.

5   Why have message boards failed to live up to the noble expectations? The answer, in a word, is anonymity. The fact that on a message board — unlike in an old-fashioned letter to the editor — no one is required to identify themselves, no one is required to say who they are and *own* what they've said, has inspired many to vent their most reptilian thoughts.

So, some of us are intrigued by what recently happened in Cleveland. It seems someone using the alias "lawmiss" had posted provocative comments and scathing personal attacks on the Web site of the *Cleveland Plain Dealer*. Some of those comments and attacks evinced an unlikely familiarity with cases being heard by a local judge, Shirley Strickland Saffold. When lawmiss made a comment about the mental state of a reporter's relative, the paper decided to trace the nickname. It found that the postings came from Judge Saffold's personal e-mail account.

Saffold claims her 23-year-old daughter authored the comments. Sydney Saffold, who lives in another city, supports her mom's story. Believe them if you choose.

Meanwhile, the paper has been criticized by some observers for unmasking lawmiss, and there is some merit to that. It's wrong to offer anonymity, then yank it away. But it would've been *more* wrong to have evidence that a judge viewed an attorney appearing in her court on a capital case as "Amos and Andy" — to use one example — and do nothing about it.

The larger point is that the paper should not have offered its message posters anonymity in the first place. *No* paper should. A confidential source necessary to break the big story is one thing. But the only imperative here is to deliver more eyes to the Web site.

10   As any student of Sociology 101 can tell you, when people don't have to account for what they say or do, they will often say and do things that would shock their better selves.

That's the story of the mousy, mosque-going schoolteacher swept up in the window-breaking mob during the big blackout. It's the story of the milquetoast accountant who insults the quarterback's mother from the safety of the crowd. And it is the story of newspaper message boards, which have inadvertently licensed and tacitly approved the worst of human nature under the guise of free speech.

Enough. Make them leave their names. Stop giving people a way to throw rocks and hide their hands. Any drop-off in the quantity of message board postings will surely be made up in the quality thereof.

That's my opinion. If you don't like it, well, at least you know who to blame.

---

seeing connections

There are activists interested in preserving the right to remain anonymous in online environments. On one site, called My Name Is Me, people make postings about why they feel the need to remain anonymous.

My name is Cory, and I'm the co-owner and co-editor of Boing Boing, a widely read blog with a thriving culture of commenters and suggesters. Boing Boing's best commenters and suggesters are almost all pseudonymous, and for me, knowing the names my readers and collaborators choose is much more interesting than knowing their "real" names—the name someone's parents chose is a lot less telling than the name that person chose, after all. More than a decade of experience with Boing Boing does not bear out the thesis that real names are the key to accountability or civility. Some of the most vicious, awful trolls we've encountered are delighted to do their disruptive work under their "real" names; some of our most thoughtful, clever, and useful contributions are from people who "hide" behind pseudonyms (or total anonymity).

Our pseudonymous contributors go beyond using "handles" to frame their views—some use pseudonyms to allow them to speak freely without having their views attributed to their employers. A large number of our readers live in repressive regimes where a public association with their offline identity puts their freedom and safety at risk.

Pseudonymity makes it possible for the most marginalized people in our community to communicate with us; it also allows people who are notorious or famous to join the discussion without dragging in all the baggage of whatever it is they're known for, making for debates that focus on substance, not celebrity.

How would Pitts likely respond to Doctorow's case for preserving online anonymity?

Understanding and Interpreting

1 Contrast the ideal of the newspaper message board with its reality, as described by the author.

2 Summarize the multiple sides of the debate around the actions of the Cleveland newspaper and its search for the identity of the anonymous poster "lawmiss."

3 An argumentative piece is expected to address the opposition, those who think differently. To what extent does the author, Leonard Pitts Jr., address the position of those who think that online anonymity is a good thing? What's included and what's missing from the opposition's argument?

Analyzing Language, Style, and Structure

1 What does the phrase "shocks the tattered remnants of our propriety" (par. 3) suggest about who Pitts believes his audience to be?

2 Reread the article and explain how particular words and phrases reveal Pitts's attitude toward anonymous postings.

3 How does the story of the judge in Cleveland support the author's argument against anonymity? What is left unsaid in Pitts's comment, "Believe them if you choose" (par. 7)?

4 How convincing is the evidence that Pitts provides to support the statement, "[W]hen people don't have to account for what they say or do, they will often say and do things that would shock their better selves" (par. 10)?

5 What effect does Pitts achieve by using the phrase "kissed by the spirit of Jefferson" in paragraph 2?

Connecting, Arguing, and Extending

1 While this article deals almost exclusively with the anonymous postings on newspaper websites, the issue of anonymity has also been linked to the problem of cyber-bullying. Would ending anonymity on such sites help to curb cyber-bulling? Why or why not?

2 In 2013, the editors of *Popular Science* published an article titled "Why We're Shutting Off Our Comments." To support their case, they cited a study from the University of Wisconsin–Madison that measured how civil or uncivil comments affected a reader's viewpoint on the article the comments accompanied—in this case, a fictional scientific report. Read through this portion of the argument and explain whether you find it compelling, and whether you agree, disagree, or would qualify the editors' decision to shut off comments on their website.

> Uncivil comments not only polarized readers, but they often changed a participant's interpretation of the news story itself.

> In the civil group, those who initially did or did not support the technology—whom we identified with preliminary survey questions—continued to feel the same way after reading the comments. Those exposed to rude comments, however, ended up with a much more polarized understanding of the risks connected with the technology.

> Simply including an ad hominem attack in a reader comment was enough to make study participants think the downside of the reported technology was greater than they'd previously thought.

> Another, similarly designed study found that just firmly worded (but not uncivil) disagreements between commenters impacted readers' perception of science.

Do You Like Me? Click Yes or No

Jason Edward Harrington

Jason Edward Harrington is a regular contributor to the online humor site McSweeny's Internet Tendency, from which this 2011 satirical short story is taken. He worked for six years as a Transportation Safety Administration airport screener, before quitting to write the exposé "Dear America, I Saw You Naked: And Yes, We Were Laughing. Confessions of an Ex-TSA Agent."

To: Alice

First day of school. Sucks, huh? This class is so boring. I hate long division. Anyway, I like you. I set up a Tumblr for you while we were supposed to be doing #5. Just a poll with your name as the site's title:

ALICE

Do you like me?

Click yes or no.

Yes: 0 votes

No: 0 votes.

To: Bobby

Yes: 1 vote

No: 0 votes

I've liked you ever since we had recess together last year. This is awesome! Can't wait for lunch next period. We should hold hands. Here's a heart I just downloaded for you: <3

P.S. I just liked the Alice site on Facebook.

To: Alice

Thanks for the heart, and I can't wait to hold hands, but I really didn't want to take this to Facebook, yet. The Alice site isn't ready, and I didn't want anyone linking into it at this phase. I can see over Tim Mackey's shoulder that he's looking at the Alice site right now. My problem with this is that a good portion of the class got the news that you like me before even I did. Communication is key, here.

To: Bobby

Sorry I Facebook liked the Alice site. I honestly don't see why that's such a problem, though. The comments have been overwhelmingly positive. I was even putting the finishing touches on a joint Tumblr account, in case we really did go public with this before the bell rang, but I'll just put the brakes on that for now.

P.S. — The site Nestor set up for Jen had links going in right away, and he didn't make a big deal about it. And that site was SEO, too.

To: Alice

5 I like you — not in a search-optimized way, but in an old fashioned, authentic way. I'm not sure you're understanding our brand. I see you went forward with the Alice and Bobby site anyway, and just now tweeted a link to it on top of it. We're not status official on Facebook yet, so this is all just going to come off as confusing with the other kids. If this is going to work, we need to coordinate across platforms. I'm mentioning you in a tweet, tagged #alicenbobbyclarification.

To: Bobby

I retweeted your tweet, and take full responsibility for this. The buzz was forced there, and I see that now. We have to keep expectations low on a venture like this — position ourselves to exceed expectations (think Brad and Jess). We're on the same page now: mum's the word, at least until next period.

To: Alice

Well, the cat's out of the bag, and we have backers, now — the Alice and Bobby site is being overrun by comments — so we may as well just stay the course. There's a lot of interest in us; I'm even seeing some comments from the 5th graders. We're hot right now, Alice, but my main concern is overvaluation — a roomful of kids expecting chocolate milk, and we show up with plain. We're not even sure if we look good on paper at this point, let alone how we'd scale to the lunchroom were we to go public at the bell, which is why I really wanted to stay bootstrap on this, crazy as that may sound.

To: Bobby

I'm a little confused. Are you saying you're embarrassed to be seen with me at lunch? You're right about one thing, though: we do have a lot of people backing us on this, and I think it would be a mistake to show any skittishness on your part. With so many of the other kids invested in Bobby and Alice, do you really want to appear bearish, now? We could at least try pivoting and re-launching, if worse came to worst.

To: Alice

It's not about how we look in the lunchroom, Alice. Just read the comments. "Are you two going to kiss at recess?" "Alice and Bobby sittin' in a tree." "Love." "Marriage." There's even talk of a baby carriage, here. Do we even know the first thing about any of this? I mean, really? I heard how babies are made from Joey Demetrelis during recess, but I've seen people trying to collapse baby carriages, Alice, and I'm not sure we even have the right skill set for that. And k-i-s-s-i-n-g? In a tree? Neither of us can get even halfway up the rope in gym, for God's sake.

To: Bobby

10 You know what? FINE. You're right. We were in over our heads to begin with on this — now we're underwater. I guess it's true what they say: it's hard to recognize a bubble until after it bursts. I'm posting the announcement on our ill-fated Tumblr. We owe everyone at least that much.

OVERVIEW

The Alice and Bobby Bust:
Problem Analysis, Where We Failed

- Inexperienced management.
- Critical communication problems between Bobby and me.

Kiev artist Nastya Ptichek incorporates the modern mechanisms and language of technology into classic works of art. Here, emojis (a simple ellipsis on the left, a face winking and blowing a kiss on the right) make an appearance in Edward Hopper's 1947 *Summer Evening*.

What point might Ptichek be making by introducing this new form of communication into classic art? How does her contribution change the meaning of the original work? How does her idea about the impact of technology on relationships compare to what Jason Edward Harrington is suggesting in his story?

Nastya Ptichek

- Grew too fast, too early.
- Should have built on WordPress.
- Lack of passion and motivation (especially on Bobby's part).
- Unconventional accounting metrics diminished our integrity with the other kids.

- Ultimate inability to translate our popularity into a viable relationship model.
- Failure on my part to take into account the inherent intractability of the total grossness of boys.

Understanding and Interpreting

1 Trace the relationship between Bobby and Alice, focusing on:

a. How their relationship started
b. The conflicts they faced
c. The causes of the failure of their relationship

2 One key factor that distinguishes a "satire" from something that is just "funny" is that a satire almost always has an intended target for its humor,

something specific that it is making fun of and commenting on. What is Jason Edward Harrington trying to communicate about modern relationships in today's social media landscape? What evidence do you have to support your conclusion?

3 Analyze Alice's character using evidence from the "Overview" at the end of the piece. Based on the information provided about Bobby in the rest of the piece, is her assessment of Bobby accurate?

Analyzing Language, Style, and Structure

1 The following are common elements of satire. Locate an example of each from the text and explain how the element assists Harrington in making his point about modern relationships. If you need definitions for these terms, consult the Glossary on page 1020.

a. Incongruity   c. Hyperbole
b. Reversal   d. Parody

2 When does the author present aspects of the characters that sound like elementary school students and when does he make them seem like adults? How does this verbal irony lead to humor and help to establish the point Harrington is trying to make?

Connecting, Arguing, and Extending

1 Try writing a satirical piece about your experiences with digital communications technologies. You might use the techniques of incongruity, reversal, hyperbole, and parody, which are defined in the Glossary. You might also rely on situational or dramatic irony, which are described in the Workshop on page 838, and can be found in the Glossary.

2 Clearly there was a lot of cell phone use going on in Bobby and Alice's classroom. Identify your own school's policy toward cell phone use, evaluate the policy's effectiveness, and discuss whether the policy is appropriate in the twenty-first century.

ENTERING THE CONVERSATION
SOCIALLY NETWORKED

Making Connections

1 Explain how Clive Thompson's (p. 789) term "ambient intimacy" (par. 12) could be applied to the teenagers that Sherry Turkle profiles in the selection from *Alone Together* (p. 801).

2 How might Clive Thompson, the author of "Brave New World of Digital Intimacy" (p. 789) respond to Tim Egan's (p. 807) description of "[t]echnology, with its promise of both faux-intimacy and a protective sense of removal" (par. 4) or his claim that the "Internet is the cause of much of today's commitment-free, surface-only living" (par. 13)?

3 Of these authors—Clive Thompson (p. 789), Sherry Turkle (p. 801), or Tim Egan (p. 807)—who would likely agree or disagree with the last two lines of Sherman Alexie's poem "Facebook Sonnet" (p. 811)? Why?

4 How would Leonard Pitts Jr. (p. 831) and/or Robbie Cooper (p. 813) address Alexis C. Madrigal's (p. 827) concept of ideas being "public," "persistent," and "attached to one's real identity"?

Synthesizing Sources

1 A lot of the texts in this Conversation deal with the idea of "intimacy," which we might define as "a close, familiar, and usually affectionate relationship with another person or group." To what extent is true intimacy possible or not through digital communications technologies as compared to face-to-face communication? Refer to two or more texts from the Conversation as well as *Cyrano de Bergerac*. (p. 667)

2 Look back at the cartoon, "On the Internet, nobody knows you're a dog" (p. 666). Regardless of whether this statement is true or not, is this something that we *want* to be true? In other words, explain how at least part of the appeal of the Internet is that we can control and shape our identities online to a greater degree than we can in offline encounters. Be sure to refer to at least two or more texts from the Conversation, as well as the Central Text, *Cyrano de Bergerac* (p. 667).

3 Knowing that there are both dangers and benefits that result from Internet anonymity, do you believe that there should be requirements for people to use their real names online? What restrictions or exceptions, if any, should be in place? Refer to the arguments put forward by Alexis C. Madrigal and Leonard Pitts Jr., as well as any other relevant texts in this Conversation.

4 Because of the prevalence of digital communications in our lives today, to what extent is it necessary to continue to make distinctions between how we communicate online versus offline? Is this distinction being made mostly by people nostalgic for the "old days" before the Internet, or are there genuine concerns about the changing nature of our communications as a result of the Internet? In your response, be sure to refer to at least two texts from this Conversation.

5 Developments and innovations in communications technologies always have some kind of effect. After the invention of the telephone, people wrote fewer letters, and with the invention of texting, people are making fewer phone calls, changing the way that we interact with others. With the rise of instantaneous and constant communication via social media, there must be some kind of effect on the relationships we make, maintain, and discard. What is the effect of technology on our relationships? Overall, is technology creating a more positive or negative connection for us? Be sure to refer to at least two texts from this Conversation in your argument.

▼
UNDERSTANDING IRONY

"I sure had fun this weekend: I studied for my math test and worked on a research project for world history." If you hear one of your friends make such a statement, you're pretty sure she's not serious—in fact, she's being ironic. That is, she's saying the opposite of what she really means. Irony is created by a discrepancy between what is said and what is meant, what we expect and what actually happens, what appears to be and what is. Whether your friend is being mildly funny, shrugging off the fact that she spent the whole weekend on schoolwork, or bitterly sarcastic about what seems an overwhelming amount of work is a matter of interpretation. The power and challenge of irony is that the meaning isn't stated directly, but suggested implicitly.

ACTIVITY

Discuss the irony in the following photograph taken in 1937 during the Great Depression by Margaret Bourke-White. How do the images and the written text work together to make a point?

Margaret Bourke-White/Time & Life Pictures/Getty Images

Types of Irony

Although all irony depends upon some incongruity between expectation and reality, there are specific types of irony that you'll recognize in advertising, speeches, and literary texts: verbal, situational, and dramatic irony.

Verbal irony, like the example that opened this Workshop, is saying one thing while meaning the opposite. Much of verbal irony depends upon context. If, for instance, someone says, "What a great day for a hike!" the context lets you know if the meaning is literal or ironic. If it's a sunny day with temperatures in the seventies, the comment is probably literal. If it's raining cats and dogs with gale force winds, then the comment is probably ironic. Verbal irony may result in humor or sarcasm, again depending upon context. In conversation, we can usually spot verbal irony because of a tone of voice, or possibly eye rolling or other gestures, but when we're reading we have to be alert to context cues that signal an ironic tone.

In "Facebook Sonnet," author Sherman Alexie writes, "Let's all play the games / That occupy the young" (ll. 8–9). If you read that line literally and in isolation, it could be a call for a return to youthful exuberance, a plea to stop worrying about the past and future and concentrate on the pleasures of the moment. Yet, within the poem—especially the call in the previous lines to "exhume, resume, and extend / Childhood"—it's clear that the speaker does not literally mean what he says. He uses verbal irony to mock Facebook activities that he views as childish game playing.

Situational irony involves a discrepancy between what is expected to happen and what actually happens. If you're reading a story about an elderly man who fits the stereotype of a sweet grandfather, but it turns out that he's an evil mobster, that's situational irony: the situation is the opposite of what you would expect.

The following cartoon illustrates situational irony with humor: we would expect a locksmith—of all people—not to get locked out of his vehicle, specifically the truck he uses to help other people who get locked out.

Andy White/www.CartoonStock.com

There's situational irony at the end of Firoozeh Dumas's piece "Hot Dogs and Wild Geese." While we've been led to expect that the parents will continue to grow proficient in English under the tutelage of their daughter, the narrator surprises us by her point that "the wave of immigration" from Iran has resulted in shops where her mother can speak "in Persian, all by herself" with no help from her daughter. All along, we've been assuming that her family will change and blend into American culture, yet Dumas ends by reminding us that American culture was changed by her family's culture. This reversal exemplifies situational irony.

Dramatic irony results when the audience is aware of something that a character is unaware of. A classic example is the horror movie where the protagonist thinks he is protecting himself by hiding in a basement when, in fact, the audience knows that the monster has been waiting in the basement all along. In Shakespeare's play *Julius Caesar*, the audience knows that Brutus is plotting to kill Caesar, but Caesar believes Brutus is a loyal friend. Throughout the play *Cyrano de Bergerac*, Roxane is unaware that the words she finds so alluring are written by Cyrano, though often delivered by Christian, while the audience knows the loving and poetic speeches are not only Cyrano's words but his feelings.

ACTIVITY

Identify which type of irony—verbal, situational, or dramatic—is illustrated by each of the following examples. Note that some of these are ordinary situations, others literary, and a few visual.

1. In *Cinderella*, the charming prince searches for the lady who lost her slipper at the ball, and whom he believes is a princess.

2.

Sarcasm and stupidity meet at the elevator.

3. In *Romeo and Juliet*, Romeo believes that Juliet has drunk poison, when in fact it was just a sleeping potion. Believing Juliet to be dead, Romeo kills himself in grief.

4. At the end of "Children as Enemies" by Ha Jin (p. 763), the grandfather narrating the story explains that he and his wife have moved out of his son's home, and that their move to America to be close to family has not turned out as they had hoped. The grandfather concludes by saying: "This is America, where we must learn self-reliance and mind our own business" (par. 61).

5. In the balcony scene of *Cyrano de Bergerac* (pp. 713–724), Roxane succumbs to the eloquent words of Cyrano proclaiming his love for her; she believes that Christian, who is speaking, has come up with those words.

6.

Toby Allen/Specialist Stock/Getty Images

7. In *Narrative of the Life of Frederick Douglass*, the author recalls his feeling that "learning to read had been a curse rather than a blessing" (par. 6).

8. After the soccer player sprained her ankle, she limped off the field with the comment, "float like a butterfly, sting like a bee!"

9. The "Get Well Soon" flowers you sent to your friend in the hospital ended up giving him a terrible allergic reaction.

10. In *Cyrano de Bergerac*, Roxane keeps the letter that she believes Christian wrote to her next to her heart, regarding it as "a holy reliquary" (Act 5, l. 44) during her years of mourning.

11.

Sandy Huffaker, Courtesy of Cagle Cartoons

Effect of Irony

When you're analyzing the effect or impact that irony has as a literary device or rhetorical strategy, it's important to think about how the irony connects to bigger ideas—to the meaning of the passage, or a theme of the work as a whole.

Lemon.

This Volkswagen missed the boat.

The chrome strip on the glove compartment is blemished and must be replaced. Chances are you wouldn't have noticed it; Inspector Kurt Kroner did.

There are 3,389 men at our Wolfsburg factory with only one job: to inspect Volkswagens at each stage of production. I3000 Volkswagens are produced daily; there are more inspectors than cars.)

Every shock absorber is tested (spot checking won't do), every windshield is scanned. VWs have been rejected for surface scratches barely visible to the eye.

Final inspection is really something! VW inspectors run each car off the line onto the Funktionsprüfstand (car test stand), tote up 189 check points, gun ahead to the automatic brake stand, and say "no" to one VW out of fifty.

This preoccupation with detail means the VW lasts longer and requires less maintenance, by and large, than other cars. (It also means a used VW depreciates less than any other car.)

We pluck the lemons; you get the plums.

Irony is a favorite strategy of advertising because it can bring a smile to our face because of some clever humor, or it can jolt us into taking a second look. What happens in this Volkswagen car ad when you see a picture of the VW "Bug" with the word "Lemon" as what seems to be the caption? What's going on? Why would the VW corporation advertise this car as a "lemon," the common expression for something that's undesirable? As you read the fine print, you're told how meticulous the VW inspection team is, attending to every detail of safety and efficiency. If there are any problems, then the car doesn't leave the factory—that is, no lemons for sale, only (as the last line emphasizes) "plums." The VW advertisers use irony both to pique interest and to emphasize their product's quality. Calling what seems to be a perfectly fine VW a "lemon" implies the reality of such high standards that you can be sure you'll never drive off the lot with a lemon from VW.

Now let's turn to a written text to see how irony contributes to the meaning of the work as a whole. In *Cyrano de Bergerac*, the playwright Rostand uses irony not just as a verbal stylistic tool but also as a structural tool: the discrepancy between appearance and reality is one of the primary themes that he develops through both the language and the action of the play. Think about it: Christian's handsome appearance—ironically—attracts Roxane, who purports to want a relationship that is more spiritual, more of a relationship between kindred spirits. Then—ironically—she confesses her "love" for Christian to Cyrano. Cyrano is complicit in the deception that Christian is the eloquent suitor, creating the stirring and romantic speeches that—ironically—draw Roxane to Christian. The irony deepens when Christian, determined to tell Roxane the truth, is killed before he can make this revelation to his beloved. Thus—ironically—his untimely death sends her into the convent to spend her life grieving for a lost love who, in the person of Cyrano, is, in fact, still alive and very much in love with her!

Not just through the language, but through the structure of the plot, Rostand reminds us of the discrepancy between inner beauty—the powerful and heartfelt language of Cyrano, the man with the nose so large as to seem a deformity—and outer beauty—the handsome Christian. The ironies also underscore Roxane's inability to see beyond the pretty face, as it were, to the devoted soul.

Ultimately, through these ironic situations, Rostand leaves his audience thinking about a theme of the play—how our vanity or superficial thinking can lead us to confuse what we see and what actually is; in other words, the theme is the danger of mistaking what *seems to be true* for the truth.

culminating activity

Reread "Facebook Sonnet" by Sherman Alexie (p. 811). Identify examples of verbal and situational irony. How do these ironies lead you to an understanding of the argument Alexie is making in this poem? Pay special attention to the ideas of "church.com" and "the altar of loneliness" (ll. 12 and 14) as you develop your interpretation.

WORKSHOP

What Is Close Analysis?

You're probably accustomed to the big-picture analysis of literary texts where you look for theme and interpret the meaning of the work as a whole. So, for instance, you might look at how the characters in *A Raisin in the Sun* by Lorraine Hansberry embody the theme of the importance of keeping dreams alive. Or you might talk about how point of view in *To Kill a Mockingbird* helps Harper Lee show the destructive power of prejudice. This kind of analysis looks at the big picture—the camera zooms out to take in a panoramic view.

What words come to mind when you look at the long camera shot of a battle scene from the film *Lord of the Rings: The Return of the King*? What words come to mind with the zoom in on one warrior? How does the close-up affect your understanding of the panoramic view?

When you do a close analysis of prose, you need to zoom in and look at the effects of specific language choices in a piece. So, for example, you might examine one scene with Mama and her son Walter Lee in *A Raisin in the Sun* to show how keeping dreams alive is conveyed. Or you might analyze every word in a dialogue between Atticus Finch and his daughter, Scout, while he reads to her in *To Kill a Mockingbird* to show how this scene contributes to Lee's development of the theme of racial prejudice and how it destroys families and communities alike.

But why do it?

When we write a close analysis, we're asking ourselves not just what the theme is, or how the setting impacts the story, but how the author has used language to create that setting, and how the author has used language to develop the ideas that make up the theme. It's taking your analysis to the next level.

All about the How

Here's what a prose analysis *is not*: it's not an essay in which you merely identify a number of the literary devices—metaphors, imagery, and so on. So, when you're writing a thesis for a close analysis essay, you want to avoid one like this:

> In this passage from *To Kill a Mockingbird*, the main character, Atticus Finch, uses vivid detail and figurative language.

That's a statement of *what*—not a statement of *how*. And close analysis is all about the *how*.

Start by thinking of the author: why does he or she make the choices she makes? Why does he or she choose to say that a character "met his untimely demise" or "passed away" or "bought the farm" or "was paid a visit by the grim reaper"? Every one of these phrases means somebody died, so what's the difference to a reader? Why did the author choose one over the other, and what was the effect of that choice on the meaning of the passage? If you keep your focus on the author's intentional stylistic decisions, you're on your way to a strong analysis of how he or she conveys meaning or theme.

Step 1: Analyze a Passage

When writing a close analysis, the first step is doing a close reading. Reading carefully and curiously and looking for places in the text that seem interesting or significant to you will uncover ideas for you to write about. Let's walk through that process now.

ACTIVITY

Whether or not you've already read the story "Children as Enemies," read this passage through the lens of *how* the author, Ha Jin, uses language to convey the conflict between three generations of a Chinese family.

The teachers here don't assign the pupils any real homework. Instead they give them a lot of projects, some of which seem no more than woolgathering, and tend to inflate the kids' egos. My son had to help his children with the projects, which were more like homework for the parents. Some of the topics were impossible even for adults to tackle, such as "What is culture and how is it created?" "Make your argument for or against the Iraq War," "How does the color line divide U.S. society?" and "Do you think global trade is necessary? Why?" My son had to do research online and in the public library to get the information needed for discussing those topics. Admittedly, they could broaden the pupils' minds and give them more confidence, but at their tender age they are not supposed to think like a politician or a scholar. They should be made to follow rules; that is, to become responsible citizens first.

Whenever I asked Flora how she was ranked in her class, she'd shrug and say, "I dunno."

"What do you mean you don't know?" I suspected she must be well below the average, though she couldn't be lower than her brother.

"Ms. Gillen doesn't rank us is all," came her answer.

If that was true, I was even more disappointed with the schools. How could they make their students competitive in this global economy if they didn't instill in them the sense of getting ahead of others and becoming the very best? No wonder many Asian parents viewed the public schools in Flushing unfavorably. In my honest opinion, elementary education here tends to lead children astray.

Five weeks ago, Matt declared at dinner that he must change his last name, because a substitute teacher that morning had mispronounced "Xi" as "Eleven." That put the whole class in stitches, and some students even made fun of the boy afterward, calling him "Matt Eleven." Flora chimed in, "Yeah, I want a different last name too. My friend Reta just had her family name changed to Wu. Some people couldn't pronounce "Ng" and called her 'Reta No Good.' "

Their parents broke out laughing, but I couldn't see why that was funny. My wife said to the girl, "You'll have your husband's last name when you grow up and get married."

"I don't want no man!" the girl shot back.

"We both must have a new last name," the boy insisted.

I burst out, "You can't do that. Your last name belongs to the family, and you can't cut yourselves off from your ancestors."

"Baloney!" The boy squished up his face.

"You mustn't speak to your granddad like that," his grandmother butted in.

Mandi and my son exchanged glances. I knew they saw this matter differently from us. Maybe they had been planning to change their children's last name all along. Enraged, I dropped my bowl on the dining table and pointed my finger at Mandi. "You've tried your best to spoil them. Now you're happy to let them break away from the family tree. What kind of daughter-in-law are you? I wish I hadn't allowed you to join our family."

"Please don't blow up like this, Dad," my son said.

Mandi didn't talk back. Instead she began sobbing, wrinkling her gourd-shaped nose. The kids got angry and blamed me for hurting their mother's feelings. The more they blabbered, the more furious I became. Finally unable to hold it back anymore, I shouted, "If you two change your last name, you leave, get out of here. You cannot remain in this household while using a different last name."

"Who are you?" Matt said calmly. "This isn't your home."

"You're just our guests," added Flora.

That drove both my wife and me mad. She yelled at our granddaughter, "So we sold everything in China, our apartment and candy store, just to be your guests here, huh? Heartless. Who told you this isn't our home?"

That shut the girl up, though she kept glaring at her grandma. Their father begged no one in particular, "Please, let us finish dinner peacefully." He went on chewing a fried shrimp with his mouth closed.

I wanted to yell at him that he was just a rice barrel thinking of nothing but food, but I controlled my anger. How could we have raised such a spineless son?

Brainstorm your response to this passage by identifying who is telling the story and what your initial feelings about him are. Circle any words or phrases that make a particularly strong impression on you.

You've read the passage once; now read it again. This time, start annotating by noting specific literary devices. Although we discussed some of these in Chapter 2, let's review a few.

Point of View

It's always a good idea to get your bearings when you start reading by figuring out whose perspective you're experiencing, that is, who's holding the camera, so to speak.

- What is the point of view? First person? Third person? Limited? Omniscient? How do you know?
- Who is the speaker and what is his perspective? Is it a major character looking back on an experience? A minor character who relates the story as an uninvolved bystander?
- Is the story told largely through dialogue or direct narration?

Diction

- Does the writer use formal diction with elevated vocabulary, or informal diction that includes slang, colloquialisms, jargon, or dialect?
- Does the writer rely heavily on connotative language with strong emotional overtones and associations?
- Does the writer use concrete, specific, vivid language to describe people, places, and objects, along with active verbs to emphasize actions? Or does the writer use more abstract words that tend to convey bigger ideas and more philosophical concepts?

Figurative Language

- Does the writer use stylistic devices that go beyond literal meaning: similes, metaphors, images, and symbols? If so, what is the effect of that use?

Identify four elements of style in the passage from "Children as Enemies" and explain how two of them contribute to conveying the generational conflicts within the family. For each element of style you select, choose an example and discuss the effect the stylistic move has.

Step 2: Find a Focus

It's important to recognize that you can't talk about everything! If you notice four or five or six devices that seem significant, choose two or three that are most prevalent and, most important, that contribute clearly to the author's purpose or meaning.

If, for instance, you believe that Jin wants us to see that the grandfather is narrow-minded and selfish, you might start with the diction that includes judgmental statements, even name-calling (such as "guttersnipe"). Or, if you think Jin wants us to see him more sympathetically—as a man steeped in his traditional culture and trying to care for his family in the only way he knows how, then you might cite the dialogue where he tries to engage his grandchildren in a discussion of their education.

Just remember: identifying, defining, and giving an example of a device (or a whole series of devices) is not the point. You must show the connection between what the writer is saying and how he is saying it. In other words, keep your eye on the meaning the author is using these devices to create.

Finally, while using literary terms in your analysis can be effective, because your audience (usually a teacher) speaks that language, it is not always necessary. If you know the literary term, such as *connotation*, by all means use it, but you also have the option of simply describing what's happening. In the case of connotation, for instance, you might point out that by having the grandfather use highly emotional language (including verbs such as "shut up," "glaring," and "begged"), Jin shows the man's frustration and disappointment turning to rage. That's analysis even if you haven't named a precise literary term.

Step 3: Develop a Strong Thesis to Guide the Analysis

By now, it's clear to you that a literary analysis is more than a technical deconstruction of words and sentences: it's an interpretation, and thus a type of argument. Think about it: you read the passage to determine an author's meaning or theme and then select textual evidence to support your interpretation. It's no surprise then, that, like most arguments, a literary analysis benefits from a clear thesis statement that indicates your main ideas.

Before you craft a thesis, though, consider how the context you're writing in affects it. If you're in an exam situation in which you are given a specific task and focus, then tailor your thesis to those. For instance, imagine the Jin passage as part of a timed, standardized test. You might be asked something like this:

In the following excerpt from "Children as Enemies" by the Chinese writer Ha Jin, a grandfather struggles to understand his Americanized grandchildren. Write an essay in which you analyze how the author uses literary elements such as diction and point of view to convey the generational conflicts.

Those directions give you a pretty clear task: the theme is generational conflict, though you need to explain the nature of that conflict as part of your essay. Then, you can focus on "literary elements"; two examples are provided to get you thinking, but you may choose those or others.

If, however, your literary analysis is part of a longer process that involves discussion and time inside or outside class to write and revise, then your topic might be broader to give you more room for original thinking. So, for instance, your task might be more like what we've been discussing:

Analyze how Ha Jin conveys the generational conflict(s) in this passage.

In either case, your thesis should do two things: (1) indicate your interpretation of the author's meaning or theme, and (2) specify the literary strategies or devices the author uses to convey meaning or theme.

ACTIVITY

Working with a partner, discuss the strengths and weaknesses of the following thesis statements and select the one you believe would be most effective for a literary analysis of how Ha Jin conveys the generational conflict(s).

- In "Children as Enemies," Ha Jin tells about the conflict of three generations through the eyes of the grandfather.
- Seeing the generational conflict from the perspective of the grandfather in "Children as Enemies" limits our understanding of what is going on.
- "In Children as Enemies," Ha Jin uses the grandfather's point of view, strong diction, and a figure of speech.
- By telling the story "Children as Enemies" in the grandfather's voice while including dialogue in the voice of family members from two younger generations, Ha Jin gives readers different perspectives on the nature and source of the conflict between tradition and change.

Step 4: Provide Textual Evidence

Just as in any interpretation, you need to support your ideas by citing textual evidence. But in the case of a literary analysis—where the particulars of choices of language are central—textual evidence is a make-or-break feature of your essay. Remember that your own ideas should be central. Thus, for every quotation or reference to language in the piece, you should provide at least two sentences of commentary discussing what is significant about the example you selected.

Commentary after a quotation is important because we don't all read the same way. Think about that metaphor the grandfather uses to describe his son:

> I wanted to yell at him that he was just a rice barrel thinking of nothing but food, but I controlled my anger.

Some might say that the grandfather's metaphor shows that he is intolerant. Others might see it as evidence of his frustration that his son refuses to follow the rules of a patriarchal family tradition. You might see that metaphor as proof that even the grandfather's thinking process is limited to his cultural boundaries, in this case, the staple of Chinese food. The point is that you need to explain to the members of your audience precisely how you interpret this figure of speech because you cannot assume that everyone shares your interpretation.

ACTIVITY

Write a well-developed paragraph about Jin's use of the "rice barrel" metaphor or his use of connotative language to develop a theme of the passage.

Step 5: Address the "So What?"

"So what" is a fair question when you're writing a literary analysis. You've identified specific strategies or devices an author uses, you've defined and explained them, given examples, and tied them to the author's theme or meaning—but so what? What does it all add up to? You might be tempted to view the literary essay as merely a type of exercise, but if you do so you risk ending up with a wooden sequence of paragraphs. You might be tempted to conclude your essay by simply repeating what you've already said.

A better approach is to use your literary analysis as an opportunity to express an original interpretation, deepen your appreciation of an author's craft, or illustrate how deftly and subtly literary elements work together in a particular piece. After you present a well-developed argument, you may use one of the following tactics to leave your readers thinking about the passage or story after they've finished your essay.

- **Make sure the whole is greater than the sum of its parts.** If, for instance, you've discussed two or three literary elements, then use your conclusion to show how they work together.
- **Ask questions to explore your interpretation further.** For instance, if you analyzed the grandfather's perspective in "Children as Enemies," you might ask at the end how the story might be seen differently from the mother's viewpoint or that of one of the grandchildren.

- **Emphasize your interpretation.** This is the most common way to end a literary analysis. For instance, you could point out that Jin might be suggesting that the grandfather's highly emotional language or his harsh perceptions of American schooling show his deep love for his family and concern for their future.

ACTIVITY

Working in small groups, develop different interpretations of Jin's depiction of the grandfather and support each with a discussion of at least two literary strategies. One interpretation will support the grandfather as a sympathetic character, another as a negative force in the family, and a third as a misguided man whose love for his family cannot outweigh his traditional beliefs.

10
Utopia/Dystopia

- What makes a perfect society?
- What can lead a utopia to become a dystopia?
- How do we define "happiness"?
- Will robots and artificial intelligence help us perfect ourselves and our world, or will they make humans obsolete?

Some see the past as a better, purer time. Ideas like the Garden of Eden, the pastoral Arcadia of ancient Greece, King Arthur's Camelot, and El Dorado, the lost city of gold make us long for the way things used to be.

Others hold out hope for the future. We seek better technology, faster travel, healthier lives—and in a lot of ways we're making progress. In 1900, for example, the average life expectancy in the United States was about fifty years, but by 1990 it had risen to about seventy-five. Productivity has skyrocketed, and the general standard of living has gone up with it. The computer in your smartphone is roughly thirty thousand times more powerful than the Apollo Guidance Computer that landed men on the moon in 1969. In many people's minds, this rapid technological progress holds the potential to solve a lot of the world's problems and create societies in which everyone is happy, healthy, and prosperous.

Photo: Elena Schweitzer/Shutterstock; Art: Christian Mojaliali

On the other hand, technology is rapidly eliminating jobs and changing how we define ourselves and our role in this world.

What these dreams of the past and hopes for the future have in common is a longing for happiness. But do we even know what that means? What makes us happy? Is it money? Love? Entertainment? Freedom? Peace? What if the thing that makes one person happy makes another person miserable?

ACTIVITY 1

On one side of a blank piece of paper, briefly describe your own utopia. What specific qualities of the society would make it "perfect"? Try to be as specific as possible. Then, sketch out a rough picture that illustrates your utopia. Leave the back of the paper blank.

Edward Hicks, *The Peaceable Kingdom*, c. 1834. Oil on canvas, 29 ⁵/₁₆ inches x 35 ½ inches. National Gallery of Art, Washington, D. C.

▲
———

This painting by Edward Hicks presents a utopian world in which predator and prey lie side by side in peace. Notice the scene in the background in which William Penn is signing a treaty with the native inhabitants.

What is Hicks suggesting about America? Is he suggesting that America is a type of utopia? Why or why not?

The term "utopia" was coined in 1516 by British political philosopher Thomas More, who published a book about a fictional land of the same name. In it he laid out his ideals for the perfect government, social institutions, religion, and employment, all of which were intended to be a critique of the England of his day.

Interestingly, More invented the word "utopia" by combining the Greek words *ou* and *topos*. An almost identical-sounding Greek word, *eu-topos*, means "a good place," but More's *ou-topos* means "no place" or "nowhere," slyly suggesting from the very beginning that the concept was both an ideal and an illusion.

The opposite of a utopia is a "dystopia." In many imagined dystopias, the pursuit of perfection gets exaggerated and twisted, and the utopia sours into something that is far from ideal. Dystopias challenge the very possibility that the world is perfectible. After all, it is often a very flawed humanity that is defining what perfection is. Depending on the context, likes and dislikes, socioeconomic status, race, gender, or other factors, two people might view the same society in very different ways: one person seeing a dream, and another person seeing a nightmare.

ACTIVITY 2

Exchange your piece of paper from the previous Activity, the one on which you described your idea of a utopia, with a classmate. After you have read your partner's description of a utopia, turn the card over to the back side and explain what might go wrong with those perfect qualities and change the society into a dystopia. In other words, what is the mirror image or worst-case scenario of the utopia described on the other side? Then, sketch out a brief illustration of what this dystopia might look like.

from A Small Place

Jamaica Kincaid

Elaine Potter Richardson, who later changed her name to Jamaica Kincaid, was born in 1949 on the Caribbean island of Antigua, then a British colony. She came to the United States as a teenager to work as an au pair in New York City, where she then attended the New School for Social Research. Kincaid became a staff writer for the *New Yorker* in 1975 and published much of her short work there. Perhaps her most widely known works are "Girl" from *At the Bottom of the River*, a collection of short stories (1985), and *Annie John* (1985), a novel. Her most recent work is the novel *See Now Then* (2013).

Elisabetta A. Villa/Getty Images

KEY CONTEXT *A Small Place*, published in 1988, is an extended essay about Antigua. The first person expatriate narrator takes the reader, an imagined tourist, on a journey through both Antigua of the present time and the colonial past. *A Small Place* can be described as a postcolonial text, which means that it addresses how a colonialized group both adopts and resists the culture and values of the colonizing power. The following selection is the opening chapter of *A Small Place*.

The history of Antigua, located southeast of Puerto Rico in the Caribbean Sea, can be dated to nearly 2000 B.C. with settlements of Siboney (Arawak for "stone people"), who were eventually replaced by Arawaks and Island Caribs between 1200 and 1500 C.E. The indigenous peoples' earliest recorded contact with Europeans was with Christopher Columbus on his second voyage in 1493. He named the island Santa Maria de la Antigua after the patron saint of the Spanish city of Seville. In 1632, the British succeeded in colonizing the island, but it was not until 1684, with the arrival of Christopher Codrington, that a profitable sugar plantation industry was established. African slaves were brought to the island to work on these plantations. By the end of the eighteenth century, Antigua had become a strategic port and valuable commercial colony. In 1834, when Britain abolished slavery in the Caribbean, Antigua became the first of the colonies to emancipate its slaves. The island remained British, however, until its independence in 1981, and Antigua retains membership in the British Commonwealth.

If you go to Antigua as a tourist, this is what you will see. If you come by aeroplane, you will land at the V. C. Bird International Airport. Vere Cornwall (V. C.) Bird is the Prime Minister of Antigua. You may be the sort of tourist who would wonder why a Prime Minister would want an airport named after him — why not a school, why not a hospital, why not some great public monument? You are a tourist and you have not yet seen a school in Antigua, you have not yet seen the hospital in Antigua, you have not yet seen a public monument in Antigua. As your plane descends to land, you might say, What a beautiful island Antigua is — more beautiful than any of the other islands you have seen, and they were very beautiful, in their way, but they were much too green, much too lush with vegetation, which indicated to you, the tourist, that they got quite a bit of rainfall, and rain is the very thing that you, just now, do not want, for you are thinking of the hard and cold and dark and long days you spent working in North America (or, worse, Europe), earning some money so that you could stay in this place (Antigua) where the sun always shines and where the climate is deliciously hot and dry for the four to ten days you are going to be staying there; and since you are on your holiday, since you are a tourist, the thought of what it might be like for someone who had to live day in, day out in a place that suffers constantly from drought, and so has to watch carefully every drop of fresh water used (while at the same time surrounded by a sea and an ocean — the Caribbean Sea on one side, the Atlantic Ocean on the other), must never cross your mind.

You disembark from your plane. You go through customs. Since you are a tourist, a North American or European — to be frank, white — and not an Antiguan black returning to Antigua from Europe or North America with cardboard boxes of much needed cheap clothes and food for relatives, you move through customs swiftly, you move through customs with ease. Your bags are not searched. You emerge from customs into the hot, clean air: immediately you feel cleansed, immediately you feel blessed (which is to say special); you feel free. You see a man, a taxi driver; you ask him to take you to your destination; he quotes you a price. You immediately think that the price is in the local currency, for you are a tourist and you are familiar with these things (rates of exchange) and you feel even

more free, for things seem so cheap, but then your driver ends by saying, "In U.S. currency." You may say, "Hmmmm, do you have a formal sheet that lists official prices and destinations?" Your driver obeys the law and shows you the sheet, and he apologises for the incredible mistake he has made in quoting you a price off the top of his head which is so vastly different (favouring him) from the one listed. You are driven to your hotel by this taxi driver in his taxi, a brand-new Japanese-made vehicle. The road on which you are travelling is a very bad road, very much in need of repair. You are feeling wonderful, so you say, "Oh, what a marvellous change these bad roads are from the splendid highways I am used to in North America." (Or, worse, Europe.) Your driver is reckless; he is a dangerous man who drives in the middle of the road when he thinks no other cars are coming in the opposite direction, passes other cars on blind curves that run uphill, drives at sixty miles an hour on narrow, curving roads when the road sign, a rusting, beat-up thing left over from colonial days, says 40 MPH. This might frighten you (you are on your holiday; you are a tourist); this might excite you (you are on your holiday; you are a tourist), though if you are from New York and take taxis you are used to this style of driving: most of the taxi drivers in New York are from places in the world like this. You are looking out the window (because you want to get your money's worth); you notice that all the cars you see are brand-new, or almost brand-new, and that they are all Japanese-made. There are no American cars in Antigua — no new ones, at any rate; none that were manufactured in the last ten years. You continue to look at the cars and you say to yourself, Why, they look brand-new, but they have an awful sound, like an old car — a very old, dilapidated car. How to account for that? Well, possibly it's because they use leaded gasoline in these brand-new cars whose engines were built to use non-leaded gasoline, but you

▲

This poster is a 1964 advertisement for Pan-Am airlines, which was the largest international airline in America from the 1920s until the 1990s.

How do you interpret this image? Write one or two sentences describing what is being depicted. How would Kincaid interpret this image? Write one or two sentences that sum up what you believe her perspective would be.

musn't ask the person driving the car if this is so, because he or she has never heard of unleaded gasoline. You look closely at the car; you see that it's a model of a Japanese car that you might hesitate to buy; it's a model that's very expensive; it's a model that's quite impractical for a person who has to work as hard as you do and who watches every penny you earn so that you can afford this holiday you are on. How do they afford such a car? And do they live in a luxurious

house to match such a car? Well, no. You will be surprised, then, to see that most likely the person driving this brand-new car filled with the wrong gas lives in a house that, in comparison, is far beneath the status of the car; and if you were to ask why you would be told that the banks are encouraged by the government to make loans available for cars, but loans for houses not so easily available; and if you ask again why, you will be told that the two main car dealerships in Antigua are owned in part or outright by ministers in government. Oh, but you are on holiday and the sight of these brand-new cars driven by people who may or may not have really passed their driving test (there was once a scandal about driving licences for sale) would not really stir up these thoughts in you. You pass a building sitting in a sea of dust and you think, It's some latrines for people just passing by, but when you look again you see the building has written on it PIGOTT'S SCHOOL. You pass the hospital, the Holberton Hospital, and how wrong you are not to think about this, for though you are a tourist on your holiday, what if your heart should miss a few beats? What if a blood vessel in your neck should break? What if one of those people driving those brand-new cars filled with the wrong gas fails to pass safely while going uphill on a curve and you are in the car going in the opposite direction? Will you be comforted to know that the hospital is staffed with doctors that no actual Antiguan trusts; that Antiguans always say about the doctors, "I don't want them near me"; that Antiguans refer to them not as doctors but as "the three men" (there are three of them); that when the Minister of Health himself doesn't feel well he takes the first plane to New York to see a real doctor; that if any one of the ministers in government needs medical care he flies to New York to get it?

It's a good thing that you brought your own books with you, for you couldn't just go to the library and borrow some. Antigua used to have a splendid library, but in The Earthquake (everyone talks about it that way — The Earthquake; we Antiguans, for I am one, have a great sense of things, and the more meaningful the thing, the more meaningless we make it) the library building was damaged. This was in 1974, and soon after that a sign was placed on the front of the building saying, THIS BUILDING WAS DAMAGED IN THE EARTHQUAKE OF 1974. REPAIRS ARE PENDING. The sign hangs there, and hangs there more than a decade later, with its unfulfilled promise of repair, and you might see this as a sort of quaintness on the part of these islanders, these people descended from slaves — what a strange, unusual perception of time they have, REPAIRS ARE PENDING, and here it is many years later, but perhaps in a world that is twelve miles long and nine miles wide (the size of Antigua) twelve years and twelve minutes and twelve days are all the same. The library is one of those splendid old buildings from colonial times, and the sign telling of the repairs is a splendid old sign from colonial times. Not very long after The Earthquake Antigua got its independence from Britain, making Antigua a state in its own right, and Antiguans are so proud of this that each year, to mark the day, they go to church and thank God, a British God, for this. But you should not think of the confusion that must lie in all that and you must not think of the damaged library. You have brought your own books with you, and among them is one of those new books about economic history, one of those books explaining how the West (meaning Europe and North America after its conquest and settlement by Europeans) got rich: the West got rich not from the free (free — in this case meaning got-for-nothing) and then undervalued labour, for generations, of the people like me you see walking around you in Antigua but from the ingenuity of small shopkeepers in Sheffield and Yorkshire and Lancashire, or wherever; and what a great part the invention of the wristwatch played in it, for there was nothing noble-minded men could not do when they discovered they could slap time on their wrists just like that (isn't that the last straw; for not only did we have to suffer the unspeakableness of slavery, but the satisfaction to be had from "We made you bastards rich" is taken away, too), and so you needn't let that slightly funny feeling you have from time to time about exploitation, oppression, domination develop into full-fledged unease, discomfort; you could ruin your holiday. They are not responsible for what you have; you owe them nothing; in fact, you did them a big favour, and you can provide one hundred examples. For here you are now, passing by Government House. And here you are now, passing by the Prime Minister's Office and the Parliament Building, and overlooking these, with a splendid view of St. John's Harbour, the American Embassy. If it were not for you, they would not have Government House, and Prime Minister's Office, and Parliament Building and embassy of powerful country. Now you are passing a mansion, an extraordinary house painted the colour of old cow dung, with more aerials and antennas attached to it than you will see even at the American Embassy. The people who live in this house are a merchant family who came to Antigua from the Middle East less than twenty years ago. When this family first came to Antigua, they sold dry goods door to door from suitcases they carried on their backs. Now they own a lot of Antigua; they regularly lend money to the government, they build enormous (for Antigua), ugly (for Antigua), concrete buildings in Antigua's capital, St. John's, which the government then rents for huge sums of money; a member of their family is the Antiguan Ambassador to Syria; Antiguans hate them. Not far from this mansion is another mansion, the home of a drug smuggler. Everybody knows he's a drug smuggler, and if just as you were driving by he stepped out of his door your driver might point him out to you as the notorious person that he is, for this drug smuggler is so rich people say he buys cars in tens — ten of this one, ten of that one — and that he bought a house (another

seeing connections

"Let me take you into the sun," said Louvaine, our Hermitage Bay liaison at the airport. No sooner had she spotted our pale winter faces at baggage claim than she swept our ten-year-old daughter out of the shade and into the warmth. It had been a long, punishing New York winter, and six years since we had taken a proper beach vacation as a family: just the three of us. [. . .] Our only criteria for a Caribbean vacation? Something authentic, or at least uncommercial, with good food and just a nonstop flight away. We found it on Antigua. The island has a relative lack of big chain resorts along with a strong tradition of farming and fishing. On the drive from the airport, we saw guys hacking and selling sugarcane, roadside stands of bananas and pineapple, and donkeys, cows, and goats roaming free. Add to this the island's genuine friendliness (Louvaine's gracious hospitality was only the beginning) and Antigua nailed our elusive trifecta better than any other Caribbean islands we've visited.

mansion) near Five Islands, contents included, with cash he carried in a suitcase: three hundred and fifty thousand American dollars, and, to the surprise of the seller of the house, lots of American dollars were left over. Overlooking the drug smuggler's mansion, is yet another mansion, and leading up to it is the best paved road in all of Antigua — even better than the road that was paved for the Queen's visit in 1985 (when the Queen came, all the roads that she would travel on were paved anew, so that the Queen might have been left with the impression that riding in a car in Antigua was a pleasant experience). In this mansion lives a woman sophisticated people in Antigua call Evita. She is a notorious woman. She's young and beautiful and the girlfriend of somebody very high up in the government. Evita is notorious because her relationship with this high government official has made her the owner of boutiques and property and given her a say in cabinet meetings, and all sorts of other privileges such a relationship would bring a beautiful young woman.

Oh, but by now you are tired of all this looking, and you want to reach your destination — your hotel, your room. You long to refresh yourself; you long to eat some nice lobster, some nice local food. You take a bath, you brush your teeth. You get dressed again; as you get dressed, you look out the window. That water — have you ever seen anything like it? Far out, to the horizon, the colour of the water is navy-blue; nearer, the water is the colour of the North American sky. From there to the shore, the water is pale, silvery, clear, so clear that you can see its pinkish-white sand bottom. Oh, what beauty! Oh, what beauty! You have never seen anything like this. You are so excited. You breathe shallow. You breathe deep. You see a beautiful boy skimming the water, godlike, on a Windsurfer. You see an incredibly unattractive, fat, pastrylike-fleshed woman enjoying a walk on the beautiful sand, with a man, an incredibly un-attractive, fat, pastrylike-fleshed man; you see the pleasure they're taking in their surroundings. Still standing, looking out the window, you see your-self lying on the beach, enjoying the amazing sun (a sun so powerful and yet so beautiful, the way it is always overhead as if on permanent guard, ready to stamp out any cloud that dares to darken and so empty rain on you and ruin your holiday; a sun that is your personal friend). You see yourself taking a walk on that beach, you see yourself meeting new people (only they are new in a very limited way, for they are people just like you). You see yourself eating some delicious, locally grown food. You see yourself, you see yourself . . . You must not wonder what exactly happened to the contents of your lavatory when you flushed it. You must not wonder where your bathwater went when you pulled out the stopper. You must not wonder what happened when you brushed your teeth. Oh, it might all end up in the water you are thinking of taking a swim in; the contents of your lavatory might, just might, graze gently against your ankle as you wade carefree in the water, for you see, in Antigua, there is no proper sewage-disposal system. But the Caribbean Sea is very big and the Atlantic Ocean is even bigger; it would amaze even you to know the number of black slaves this ocean has swallowed up. When you sit down to eat your delicious meal, it's better that you don't know that most of what you are eating came off a plane from Miami. And before it got on a plane in Miami, who knows where it came from? A good guess is that it came from a place like Antigua first, where it was grown dirt-cheap, went to Miami, and came back. There is a world of something in this, but I can't go into it right now.

5 The thing you have always suspected about yourself the minute you become a tourist is true: A tourist is an ugly human being. You are not an ugly person all the time; you are not an ugly person ordinarily; you are not an ugly person day to day. From day to day, you are a nice person. From day to day, all the people who are supposed to love you on the whole do. From day to day, as you walk down a busy street in the large and modern and prosperous city in which you work and live, dismayed, puzzled (a cliché, but only a cliché can explain you) at how alone you feel in this crowd, how awful it is to go un-noticed, how awful it is to go unloved, even as you are surrounded by more people than you could possibly get to know in a lifetime that lasted for millennia, and then out of the corner of your eye you see someone looking at you and absolute pleasure is written all over that person's face, and then you realise that you are not as revolting a presence as you think you are (for that look just told you so). And so, ordinarily, you are a nice person, an attractive person, a person capable of drawing to yourself the affection of other people

▸

How might a tourist see this scene from contemporary Antigua, and how might Kincaid see it? Write a brief description from the perspective of each.

© Roberto Moiola/Robert Harding World Imagery/Corbis

(people just like you), a person at home in your own skin (sort of; I mean, in a way; I mean, your dismay and puzzlement are natural to you, because people like you just seem to be like that, and so many of the things people like you find admirable about yourselves — the things you think about, the things you think really define you — seem rooted in these feelings): a person at home in your own house (and all its nice house things), with its nice back yard (and its nice back-yard things), at home on your street, your church, in community activities, your job, at home with your family, your relatives, your friends — you are a whole person. But one day, when you are sitting somewhere, alone in that crowd, and that awful feeling of displacedness comes over you, and really, as an ordinary person you are not well equipped to look too far inward and set yourself aright, because being ordinary is already so taxing, and being ordinary takes all you have out of you, and though the words "I must get away" do not actually pass across your lips, you make a leap from being that nice blob just sitting like a boob in your amniotic sac of the modern experience to being a person visiting heaps of death and ruin and feeling alive and inspired at the sight of it; to being a person lying on some faraway beach, your stilled body stinking and glistening in the sand, looking like something first forgotten, then remembered, then not important enough to go back for; to being a person marvelling at the harmony (ordinarily, what you would say is the backwardness) and the union these other people (and they are other people) have with nature. And you look at the things they can do with a piece of ordinary cloth, the things they fashion out of cheap, vulgarly colored (to you) twine, the way they squat down over a hole they have made in the ground, the hole itself is something to marvel at, and since you are being an ugly person this ugly but joyful thought will swell inside you: their ancestors were not clever in the way yours were and not ruthless in the way yours were, for then would it not be you who would be in harmony with nature and backwards in that charming way? An ugly thing, that is what you are when you become a tourist, an ugly, empty thing, a stupid thing, a piece of rubbish pausing here and there to gaze at this and taste that, and it will never occur to you that the people who inhabit the place in which you have just paused cannot stand you, that behind their closed doors they laugh at your strangeness (you do not look the

In what ways does this cartoon sum up Kincaid's view as expressed in "*A Small Place*"? What is the effect of hearing this sentiment expressed as a self-critique from a tourist rather than hearing it from Kincaid?

polyp.org.uk

way they look); the physical sight of you does not please them; you have bad manners (it is their custom to eat their food with their hands; you try eating their way, you look silly; you try eating the way you always eat, you look silly); they do not like the way you speak (you have an accent); they collapse helpless from laughter, mimicking the way they imagine you must look as you carry out some everyday bodily function. They do not like you. *They do not like me!* That thought never actually occurs to you. Still, you feel a little uneasy. Still, you feel a little foolish, Still, you feel a little out of place. But the banality of your own life is very real to you; it drove you to this extreme, spending your days and your nights in the company of people who despise you, people you do not like really, people you would not want to have as your actual neighbour. And so you must devote yourself to puzzling out how much of what you are told is really, really true (Is ground-up bottle glass in peanut sauce really a delicacy around here, or will it do just what you think ground-up bottle glass will do? Is this rare, multicoloured, snout-mouthed fish really an aphrodisiac, or will it cause you to fall asleep

permanently?). Oh, the hard work all of this is, and is it any wonder, then, that on your return home you feel the need of a long rest, so that you can recover from your life as a tourist?

That the native does not like the tourist is not hard to explain. For every native of every place is a potential tourist, and every tourist is a native of somewhere. Every native everywhere lives a life of overwhelming and crushing banality and boredom and desperation and depression, and every deed, good and bad, is an attempt to forget this. Every native would like to find a way out, every native would like a rest, every native would like a tour. But some natives — most natives in the world — cannot go anywhere. They are too poor. They are too poor to go anywhere. They are too poor to escape the reality of their lives; and they are too poor to live properly in the place where they live, which is the very place you, the tourist, want to go — so when the natives see you, the tourist, they envy you, they envy your ability to leave your own banality and boredom, they envy your ability to turn their own banality and boredom into a source of pleasure for yourself.

Understanding and Interpreting

1 In the long opening paragraph, what assumptions does Jamaica Kincaid make in order to characterize "a tourist"? What characteristics does she ascribe to tourists in general?

2 What do you think Kincaid means when she states that the tourist emerging from customs "feel[s] free" (par. 2)?

3 What points is Kincaid making about the economic situation in Antigua by focusing on the cars, drivers, and conditions of the roads?

4 Why is the library particularly significant to Kincaid (par. 3)?

5 What is Kincaid's purpose in pointing out the drug smuggler and the "young and beautiful" woman named Evita (par. 3)?

6 To what extent do you trust Kincaid's reliability as a narrator? Is she being objective? Cite specific passages to support your response.

7 Kincaid describes how someone who is "ordinarily [. . .] a nice person, an attractive person" "become[s] a tourist," who is, by Kincaid's definition, "an ugly human being" (par. 5). What forces are at work in this process of change? Why doesn't the would-be tourist resist the change, according to Kincaid?

8 What is the "banality and boredom" (par. 6) that Kincaid describes in the life of both the native and tourist? To what extent do you agree with her analysis?

9 Kincaid identifies many qualities that distinguish Antiguans from the tourists. Choose one of them, explain the differences, and analyze how this distinction assists Kincaid in her argument.

Analyzing Language, Style, and Structure

1 One of the most outstanding features of Kincaid's style in this piece is her ironic use of the second person pronoun "you" to address her readers. What effect does she achieve in the first paragraph alone? How would writing in third person change the effect? (For example, "When people come to Antigua as tourists, this is what they will see. If they come by aeroplane, they will land . . .")

2 Which descriptions do you find particularly harsh? Cite specific examples to support your response. Why do you think Kincaid includes such strong language? (Keep in mind that a reader can simply stop reading at any time, and Kincaid is no doubt aware of this fact.)

3 Select a paragraph or two and focus on Kincaid's use of parenthetical comments. What is her purpose in using so many asides? In what ways do these sections represent a shift in voice? (You might try reading the section without the parentheticals to consider the impact.)

4 What is the effect of Kincaid's use of repetition as a rhetorical strategy? How does she avoid (or does she fail to avoid) making the repetition of the same word or phrase monotonous?

5 If you were unaware of Kincaid's background, at what point in the essay would you realize that it is being narrated by someone who is originally from Antigua? How does that awareness affect your attitude toward the narrator?

6 Kincaid suggests that the tourist does not know if ground-up glass is "really a [local] delicacy" (par. 5) or if the fish being served at dinner is, in fact, deadly. Is she being serious at this point or sarcastic? Cite specific passages to support your view.

7 How do you feel about Kincaid telling you what "you" as a tourist think? She also assumes that "you" are white and Western and wealthy. To what extent does this seem presumptuous? Is it off-putting, or effective as a rhetorical strategy? Is it stereotyping, an insightful method of inquiry, or something else? Explain your reaction.

8 In the final paragraph of the excerpt, Kincaid refers more generally to "the native" and "the tourist." In what ways does Kincaid's attitude change from the rest of the piece? In what ways does this paragraph make you re-evaluate any of the feelings you experienced as you read the preceding paragraphs?

Topics for Composing

1 Argument
Utopia or dystopia? In *A Small Place*, Jamaica Kincaid explores the same place from different perspectives. Based on this opening chapter, in what ways is it a utopian vision of an idyllic island paradise? In what ways are the political and economic realities dystopian?

2 Research
This essay was written in 1988. Research the things that Kincaid describes and discuss whether they remain the same today. Is the library open? Is the sewer system developed? Then comment on how your research has informed your view on whether it is right or wrong to be a tourist in Antigua.

3 Argument
What issues might you raise to challenge some of Kincaid's assumptions or to question her beliefs in this piece? Respond to Kincaid by acknowledging her point and then refuting it by saying, "Yes _____, but _____." What tone would you take to encourage her to listen?

4 Argument
Would you go to Antigua or any similar country as a tourist? If you've been there before, would you go back? Answer that specific question in the broader context of whether it is ever "right" for someone from a wealthy, powerful country to visit poorer countries as a tourist. Are there ways to be a tourist that are different from the way that Kincaid describes in *A Small Place*? Does it matter, for example, if the tourist makes an effort to become aware of the country's history and culture?

5 Multimodal/Narrative
Kincaid opens her essay, "If you go to Antigua as a tourist, this is what you will see." She then explores how our expectations determine what we actually see. Take that idea and apply it to your home, neighborhood, town, or city. Select a series of five or six still images, and then write a guide for an audience that you believe has preconceptions or misconceptions about the place. Consider starting out, "If you go to _____ as a tourist, this is what you will see," though you need not model your tone on Kincaid's. Let the images guide your narrative.

THE PURSUIT OF HAPPINESS

"Life, liberty, and the pursuit of happiness." That phrase describing our "inalienable rights" is so much a part of America's national consciousness that many would argue it defines the culture. Yet how many of us can say what "happiness" is? Harmony with others? Wealth and self-indulgence? Victory over our opponents? Social justice and equality?

Consider these results from a *Time* magazine poll of 801 American adults.

What are your major sources of happiness?

77% YOUR RELATIONSHIP WITH CHILDREN

76% YOUR FRIENDS AND FRIENDSHIPS

75% CONTRIBUTING TO LIVES OF OTHERS

73% YOUR RELATIONSHIP WITH SPOUSE / PARTNER, OR YOUR LOVE LIFE

66% YOUR DEGREE OF CONTROL OVER YOUR LIFE AND YOUR DESTINY

64% THE THINGS YOU DO IN YOUR LEISURE TIME

63% RELATIONSHIP WITH YOUR PARENTS

62% YOUR RELIGIOUS OR SPIRITUAL LIFE AND WORSHIP

This table shows the top eight responses to the question of what your major sources of happiness are. To what extent do these things define happiness? Would you add or remove anything from this list, or rank these factors differently? Would these results vary in different cultures? Do they properly account for the role of wealth in making people happy?

Defining happiness is complex, and the science of happiness has become an academic discipline in its own right, one that involves economics, psychology, and public policy in the systematic measurement and analysis of happiness. In 2012 the United Nations General Assembly passed a resolution that March 20 would be observed throughout the world as the International Day of Happiness in order to "[r]ecognize [. . .] the need for a more inclusive, equitable and balanced approach to economic growth that promotes sustainable development, poverty eradication, happiness and the well-being of all peoples." It would seem that to the United Nations, money does equate to happiness to some degree.

In this Conversation, you'll explore a range of voices—those of poets and fiction writers, a historian, and social scientists—on the meaning and pursuit of happiness. These texts consider how prosperity, family dynamics, cultural contexts, and a host of other variables influence our understanding of what it means to be happy. Throughout all of these readings, you'll be reflecting on what constitutes happiness for you—now and as you imagine your life in years to come.

The Ones Who Walk Away from Omelas

Ursula K. Le Guin

Born in 1929 in California, Ursula K. Le Guin is best known as a writer of fantasy and science fiction. She is, however, a prolific writer in many genres, having published seven books of poetry, twenty-two novels, over a hundred short stories, four collections of essays, and twelve books for children. She received a BA from Radcliffe College and an MA from Columbia University. Le Guin has been recognized with many literary honors, including the National Book Award, a nomination for the Pulitzer Prize, and multiple Hugo and Nebula Awards for excellence in science fiction. "The Ones Who Walk Away from Omelas," which won the Hugo Award for Best Short Story of the Year in 1974, is her most famous short story.

With a clamor of bells that set the swallows soaring, the Festival of Summer came to the city. Omelas, bright-towered by the sea. The rigging of the boats in harbor sparkled with flags. In the streets between houses with red roofs and painted walls, between old moss-grown gardens and under avenues of trees, past great parks and public buildings, processions moved. Some were decorous: old people in long stiff robes of mauve and grey, grave master workmen, quiet, merry women carrying their babies and chatting as they walked. In other streets the music beat faster, a shimmering of gong and tambourine, and the people went dancing, the procession was a dance. Children dodged in and out, their high calls rising like the swallows' crossing flights over the music and the singing. All the processions wound towards the north side of the city, where on the great water-meadow called the Green Fields boys and girls, naked in the bright air, with mud-stained feet and ankles and long, lithe arms, exercised their restive horses before the race. The horses wore no gear at all but a halter without bit. Their manes were braided with streamers of silver, gold, and green. They flared their nostrils and pranced and boasted to one another; they were vastly excited, the horse being the only animal who has adopted our ceremonies as his own. Far off to the north and west the mountains stood up half encircling Omelas on her bay. The air of morning was so clear that the snow still crowning the Eighteen Peaks burned with white-gold fire across the miles of sunlit air, under the dark blue of the sky. There was just enough wind to make the banners that marked the racecourse snap and flutter now and then. In the silence of the broad green meadows one could hear the music winding through the city streets, farther and nearer and ever approaching, a cheerful faint sweetness of the air that from time to time trembled and gathered together and broke out into the great joyous clanging of the bells. Joyous! How is one to tell about joy? How describe the citizens of Omelas?

They were not simple folk, you see, though they were happy. But we do not say the words of cheer much any more. All smiles have become archaic. Given a description such as this one tends to make certain assumptions. Given a description such as this one tends to look next for the King, mounted on a splendid stallion and surrounded by his noble knights, or perhaps in a golden litter borne by great-muscled slaves. But there was no king. They did not use swords, or keep slaves. They were not barbarians. I do not know the rules and laws of their society, but I suspect that they were singularly few. As they did without monarchy and slavery, so they also got on without the stock exchange, the advertisement, the secret police, and the bomb. Yet I repeat that these were not simple folk, not dulcet shepherds, noble savages, bland utopians. They were not less complex than us. The trouble is that we have a bad habit, encouraged by pedants and sophisticates, of considering happiness as something rather stupid. Only pain is intellectual, only evil interesting. This is the treason of the artist: a refusal to admit the banality of evil and the terrible boredom of pain. If you can't lick 'em, join 'em. If it hurts, repeat it. But to praise despair is to condemn delight, to embrace violence is to lose hold of everything else. We have almost lost hold; we can no longer describe a happy man, nor make any celebration of joy. How can I tell you about the people of Omelas? They were not naïve and happy children — though their children were, in fact, happy. They were mature, intelligent, passionate

adults whose lives were not wretched. O miracle! but I wish I could describe it better. I wish I could convince you. Omelas sounds in my words like a city in a fairy tale, long ago and far away, once upon a time. Perhaps it would be best if you imagined it as your own fancy bids, assuming it will rise to the occasion, for certainly I cannot suit you all. For instance, how about technology? I think that there would be no cars or helicopters in and above the streets; this follows from the fact that the people of Omelas are happy people. Happiness is based on a just discrimination of what is necessary, what is neither necessary nor destructive, and what is destructive. In the middle category, however — that of the unnecessary but undestructive, that of comfort, luxury, exuberance, etc. — they could perfectly well have central heating, subway trains, washing machines, and all kinds of marvelous devices not yet invented here, floating light-sources, fuelless power, a cure for the common cold. Or they could have none of that: it doesn't matter. As you like it. I incline to think that people from towns up and down the coast have been coming in to Omelas during the last days before the Festival on very fast little trains and double-decked trams and that the train station of Omelas is actually the handsomest building in town, though plainer than the magnificent Farmers' Market. But even granted trains, I fear that Omelas so far strikes some of you as goody-goody. Smiles, bells, parades, horses, bleh. If so, please add an orgy. If an orgy would help, don't hesitate. Let us not, however, have temples from which issue beautiful nude priests and priestesses already half in ecstasy and ready to copulate with any man or woman, lover or stranger, who desires union with the deep godhead of the blood, although that was my first idea. But really it would be better not to have any temples in Omelas — at least, not manned temples. Religion yes, clergy no. Surely the beautiful nudes can just wander about, offering themselves like divine soufflés to the hunger of the needy and the rapture of the flesh.

Let them join the processions. Let tambourines be struck above the copulations, and the glory of desire be proclaimed upon the gongs, and (a not unimportant point) let the offspring of these delightful rituals be beloved and looked after by all. One thing I know there is none of in Omelas is guilt. But what else should there be? I thought at first there were no drugs, but that is puritanical. For those who like it, the faint insistent sweetness of *drooz* may perfume the ways of the city, *drooz* which first brings a great lightness and brilliance to the mind and limbs, and then after some hours a dreamy languor, and wonderful visions at last of the very Arcana and inmost secrets of the Universe, as well as exciting the pleasure of sex beyond all belief; and it is not habit-forming. For more modest tastes I think there ought to be beer. What else, what else belongs in the joyous city? The sense of victory, surely, the celebration of courage. But as we did without clergy, let us do without soldiers. The joy built upon successful slaughter is not the right kind of joy; it will not do; it is fearful and it is trivial. A boundless and generous content-ment, a magnanimous triumph felt not against some outer enemy but in communion with the finest and fairest in the souls of all men everywhere and the splendor of the world's summer: this is what swells the hearts of the people of Omelas, and the victory they celebrate is that of life. I really don't think many of them need to take *drooz*.

Most of the processions have reached the Green Fields by now. A marvelous smell of cooking goes forth from the red and blue tents of the provi-sioners. The faces of small children are amiably sticky; in the benign grey beard of a man a couple of crumbs of rich pastry are entangled. The youths and girls have mounted their horses and are begin-ning to group around the starting line of the course. An old woman, small, fat, and laughing, is passing out flowers from a basket, and tall young men wear her flowers in their shining hair. A child of nine or ten sits at the edge of the crowd, alone, playing on a wooden flute. People pause to listen, and they smile, but they do not speak to him, for he never ceases playing and never sees them, his dark eyes wholly rapt in the sweet, thin magic of the tune.

He finishes, and slowly lowers his hands holding the wooden flute.

5   As if that little private silence were the signal, all at once a trumpet sounds from the pavillion near the starting line: imperious, melancholy, piercing. The horses rear on their slender legs, and some of them neigh in answer. Sober-faced, the young riders stroke the horses' necks and soothe them, whispering, "Quiet, quiet, there my beauty, my hope. . . ." They begin to form in rank along the starting line. The crowds along the racecourse are like a field of grass and flowers in the wind. The Festival of Summer has begun.

Do you believe? Do you accept the festival, the city, the joy? No? Then let me describe one more thing.

In a basement under one of the beautiful public buildings of Omelas, or perhaps in the cellar of one of its spacious private homes, there is a room. It has one locked door, and no window. A little light seeps in dustily between cracks in the boards, secondhand from a cobwebbed window somewhere across the cellar. In one corner of the little room a couple of mops, with stiff, clotted, foul-smelling heads, stand near a rusty bucket. The floor is dirt, a little damp to the touch, as cellar dirt usually is. The room is about three paces long and two wide: a mere broom closet or disused tool room. In the room a child is sitting. It could be a boy or a girl. It looks about six, but actually is nearly ten. It is feeble-minded. Perhaps it was born defective, or perhaps it has become imbecile through fear, malnutrition, and neglect. It picks its nose and occasionally fumbles vaguely with its toes or genitals, as it sits hunched in the corner farthest from the bucket and the two mops. It is afraid of the mops. It finds them horrible. It shuts its eyes, but it knows the mops are still standing there; and the door is locked; and nobody will come. The door is always locked; and nobody ever comes, except that sometimes — the child has no understanding of time or interval — sometimes the door rattles terribly and opens, and a person, or several people, are there. One of them may come in and kick the child to make it stand up. The others never come close, but peer in at it with frightened, disgusted eyes. The food bowl and the water jug are hastily filled, the door is locked, the eyes disappear. The people at the door never say anything, but the child, who has not always lived in the tool room, and can remember sunlight and its mother's voice, sometimes speaks. "I will be good," it says. "Please let me out. I will be good!" They never answer. The child used to scream for help at night, and cry a good deal, but now it only makes a kind of whining, "eh-haa, eh-haa," and it speaks less and less often. It is so thin there are no calves to its legs; its belly protrudes; it lives on a half-bowl of corn meal and grease a day. It is naked. Its buttocks and thighs are a mass of festered sores, as it sits in its own excrement continually.

They all know it is there, all the people of Omelas. Some of them have come to see it, others are content merely to know it is there. They all know that it has to be there. Some of them understand why, and some do not, but they all understand that their happiness, the beauty of their city, the tenderness of their friendships, the health of their children, the wisdom of their scholars, the skill of their makers, even the abundance of their harvest and the kindly weathers of their skies, depend wholly on this child's abominable misery.

This is usually explained to children when they are between eight and twelve, whenever they seem capable of understanding; and most of those who come to see the child are young people, though often enough an adult comes, or comes back, to see the child. No matter how well the matter has been explained to them, these young spectators are always shocked and sickened at the sight. They feel disgust, which they had thought themselves superior to. They feel anger, outrage, impotence, despite all the explanations. They would like to do something for the child. But there is nothing they can do. If the child were brought up into the sunlight out of that vile place, if it were

© Firoz Ahmed/Demotix/Corbis

A young boy works in a garment factory in Dhaka, Bangladesh.

How does this image reflect some of the issues raised in "The Ones Who Walk Away from Omelas"? To what extent do you believe that one person's (or group's) happiness must come at the expense of another's?

cleaned and fed and comforted, that would be a good thing, indeed; but if it were done, in that day and hour all the prosperity and beauty and delight of Omelas would wither and be destroyed. Those are the terms. To exchange all the goodness and grace of every life in Omelas for that single, small improvement: to throw away the happiness of thousands for the chance of the happiness of one: that would be to let guilt within the walls indeed.

10   The terms are strict and absolute; there may not even be a kind word spoken to the child.

Often the young people go home in tears, or in a tearless rage, when they have seen the child and faced this terrible paradox. They may brood over it for weeks or years. But as time goes on they begin to realize that even if the child could be released, it would not get much good of its freedom: a little vague pleasure of warmth and food, no doubt, but little more. It is too degraded and imbecile to know any real joy. It has been afraid too long ever to be free of fear. Its habits are too uncouth for it to respond to humane treatment. Indeed, after so long it would probably be wretched without walls about it to protect it, and darkness for its eyes, and its own excrement to sit in. Their tears at the bitter injustice dry when they begin to perceive the terrible justice of reality and to accept it. Yet it is their tears and anger, the trying of their generosity and the acceptance of their helplessness, which are perhaps the true source of the splendor of their lives. Theirs is no vapid, irresponsible happiness. They know that they, like the child, are not free. They know compassion. It is the existence of the child, and their knowledge of its existence, that makes possible the nobility of their architecture, the poignancy of their music, the profundity of their science. It is because of the child that they are so gentle with children. They know that if the wretched one were not there snivelling in the dark, the other one, the flute-player, could make no joyful music as the young riders line up in their beauty for the race in the sunlight of the first morning of summer.

Now do you believe in them? Are they not more credible? But there is one more thing to tell, and this is quite incredible.

At times one of the adolescent girls or boys who go to see the child does not go home to weep or rage, does not, in fact, go home at all. Sometimes also a man or woman much older falls silent for a day or two, and then leaves home. These people go out into the street, and walk down the street alone. They keep walking, and walk straight out of the city of Omelas, through the beautiful gates. They keep walking across the farmlands of Omelas. Each one goes alone, youth or girl, man or woman. Night falls; the traveler must pass down village streets, between the houses with yellow-lit windows, and on out into the darkness of the fields. Each alone, they go west or north, towards the mountains. They go on. They leave Omelas, they walk ahead into the darkness, and they do not come back. The place they go towards is a place even less imaginable to most of us than the city of happiness. I cannot describe it at all. It is possible that it does not exist. But they seem to know where they are going, the ones who walk away from Omelas.

Understanding and Interpreting

1 After reading the opening two paragraphs, what did you expect would follow?

2 How do you interpret this statement: "Happiness is based on a just discrimination of what is necessary, what is neither necessary nor destructive, and what is destructive" (par. 2)? How is this belief carried out in Omelas?

3 Why is there no guilt in Omelas (par. 2), or is there?

4 What are specific characteristics of life in Omelas? Do people live simply or luxuriously? Cite concrete details about the way they live.

5 Why is it that the child in the locked room "has to be there" (par. 8)?

6 What "terrible paradox" must those who observe the suffering child face? Why do they come to accept the child's confinement as "the terrible justice of reality" (par. 11)?

7 What motivates the people who walk away from Omelas? Do they walk away in fear? In moral repugnance? As an act of resistance?

8 Is the narrator a resident of Omelas? What is his or her view of Omelas? Does he or she approve or disapprove, sympathize or criticize, or remain objective?

Analyzing Language, Style, and Structure

1 What is the tone of the opening paragraph? Cite specific words and images that contribute to the development of the tone.

2 What is the narrative point of view? Is the voice omniscient? Reliable? Note places where the narrator interjects speculations and opinions.

3 What is the symbolism of the room where the child is kept? Pay attention to specific details describing the setting where the child is imprisoned.

4 Is there a plot to this story? If so, what is it? If you think there is not a plot, then what is Le Guin's purpose in writing the story without one?

Connecting, Arguing, and Extending

1 Do you think that Omelas is a utopia? Are the people in Omelas—most of them—truly happy?

2 Would you walk away? Write an essay explaining what you would do if you were born a free citizen of Omelas.

3 What about child labor in sweatshops, where low-wage work makes various kinds of products available at a reasonable cost, often to consumers in another country or part of the world? To what extent do you think such a situation is similar to the child in the basement in Omelas? Or is the comparison a false analogy? You might have to research the topic to inform your response.

4 Think about a time when you made a decision to "walk away from Omelas." What were the circumstances? What happened? Reference this story in your discussion.

5 Le Guin has explained that she wrote this story after reading "The Moral Philosopher and the Moral Life" by William James. He asked, "[I]f millions [of people could be] kept permanently happy on the one simple condition that a certain lost soul on the far-off edge of things should lead a life of lonely torture [. . .] how hideous a thing would be its enjoyment when deliberately accepted as the fruit of such a bargain?" What response do you think the story makes to that question? What aspects of society could the story be viewed as critiquing?

Harrison Bergeron

Kurt Vonnegut

Jean-Christian Bourcart/Getty Images

Kurt Vonnegut (1922–2007) was one of the most influential writers in post–World War II America. Born in Indianapolis, Indiana, he attended Cornell University for two years before joining the army, where he fought in the Battle of the Bulge and was captured by German troops in 1944. While a prisoner of war, he witnessed the firebombing of Dresden, an experience that inspired his most famous novel, *Slaughterhouse Five* (1969), named for the building in which he was imprisoned. Vonnegut studied at the Carnegie Institute of Technology and the University of Tennessee while in the army; after the war, he went to graduate school to study anthropology at the University of Chicago. Before becoming a full-time writer, he worked as a reporter, teacher, and public relations employee for General Electric. His first novel, the satiric *Player Piano* (1952), was inspired by his time at GE. Among his other well-known books are *The Sirens of Titan* (1959), *Cat's Cradle* (1963), and *Breakfast of Champions* (1973). "Harrison Bergeron" first appeared in *Collier's* magazine before being reprinted in the short-story collection *Welcome to the Monkey House* (1968).

The year was 2081, and everybody was finally equal. They weren't only equal before God and the law. They were equal every which way. Nobody was smarter than anybody else. Nobody was better looking than anybody else. Nobody was stronger or quicker than anybody else. All this equality was due to the 211th, 212th, and 213th Amendments to the Constitution, and to the unceasing vigilance of agents of the United States Handicapper General.

Some things about living still weren't quite right, though. April, for instance, still drove people crazy by not being springtime. And it was in that clammy month that the H-G men took George and Hazel Bergeron's fourteen-year-old son, Harrison, away.

It was tragic, all right, but George and Hazel couldn't think about it very hard. Hazel had a perfectly average intelligence, which meant she couldn't think about anything except in short bursts. And George, while his intelligence was way above normal, had a little mental handicap radio in his ear. He was required by law to wear it at all times. It was tuned to a government transmitter. Every twenty seconds or so, the transmitter would send out some sharp noise to keep people like George from taking unfair advantage of their brains.

George and Hazel were watching television. There were tears on Hazel's cheeks, but she'd forgotten for the moment what they were about.

5   On the television screen were ballerinas.

A buzzer sounded in George's head. His thoughts fled in panic, like bandits from a burglar alarm.

"That was a real pretty dance, that dance they just did," said Hazel.

"Huh?" said George.

"That dance—it was nice," said Hazel.

10   "Yup," said George. He tried to think a little about the ballerinas. They weren't really very good—no better than anybody else would have been, anyway. They were burdened with sash-weights and bags of birdshot, and their faces were masked, so that no one, seeing a free and graceful gesture or a pretty face, would feel like something the cat drug in. George was toying with the vague notion that maybe dancers shouldn't be handicapped. But he didn't get very far with it before another noise in his ear radio scattered his thoughts.

George winced. So did two out of the eight ballerinas.

Hazel saw him wince. Having no mental handicap herself, she had to ask George what the latest sound had been.

"Sounded like somebody hitting a milk bottle with a ball-peen hammer," said George.

"I'd think it would be real interesting, hearing all the different sounds," said Hazel, a little envious. "All the things they think up."

15   "Um," said George.

"Only, if I was Handicapper General, you know what I would do?" said Hazel. Hazel, as a matter of fact, bore a strong resemblance to the Handicapper General, a woman named Diana Moon Glampers. "If I was Diana Moon Glampers," said Hazel, "I'd have chimes on Sunday—just chimes. Kind of in honor of religion."

"I could think, if it was just chimes," said George.

"Well—maybe make 'em real loud," said Hazel. "I think I'd make a good Handicapper General."

"Good as anybody else," said George.

20   "Who knows better'n I do what normal is?" said Hazel.

"Right," said George. He began to think glimmeringly about his abnormal son who was now in jail, about Harrison, but a twenty-one-gun salute in his head stopped that.

"Boy!" said Hazel, "that was a doozy, wasn't it?"

It was such a doozy that George was white and trembling, and tears stood on the rims of his red eyes. Two of the eight ballerinas had collapsed to the studio floor, were holding their temples.

"All of a sudden you look so tired," said Hazel. "Why don't you stretch out on the sofa, so's you can rest your handicap bag on the pillows, honeybunch." She was referring to the forty-seven pounds of birdshot in a canvas bag, which was padlocked around George's neck. "Go on and rest the bag for a little while," she said. "I don't care if you're not equal to me for a while."

25   George weighed the bag with his hands. "I don't mind it," he said. "I don't notice it any more. It's just a part of me."

"You been so tired lately — kind of wore out," said Hazel. "If there was just some way we could make a little hole in the bottom of the bag, and just take out a few of them lead balls. Just a few."

"Two years in prison and two thousand dollars fine for every ball I took out," said George. "I don't call that a bargain."

"If you could just take a few out when you came home from work," said Hazel. "I mean — you don't compete with anybody around here. You just set around."

"If I tried to get away with it," said George, "then other people'd get away with it — and pretty soon we'd be right back to the dark ages again, with everybody competing against everybody else. You wouldn't like that, would you?"

30   "I'd hate it," said Hazel.

"There you are," said George. "The minute people start cheating on laws, what do you think happens to society?"

If Hazel hadn't been able to come up with an answer to this question, George couldn't have supplied one. A siren was going off in his head.

"Reckon it'd fall all apart," said Hazel.

"What would?" said George blankly.

35   "Society," said Hazel uncertainly. "Wasn't that what you just said?"

"Who knows?" said George.

The television program was suddenly interrupted for a news bulletin. It wasn't clear at first as to what the bulletin was about, since the announcer, like all announcers, had a serious speech impediment. For about half a minute, and in a state of high excitement, the announcer tried to say, "Ladies and gentlemen —"

He finally gave up, handed the bulletin to a ballerina to read.

"That's all right —" Hazel said of the announcer, "he tried. That's the big thing. He tried to do the best he could with what God gave him. He should get a nice raise for trying so hard."

40   "Ladies and gentlemen —" said the ballerina, reading the bulletin. She must have been extraordinarily beautiful, because the mask she wore was hideous. And it was easy to see that she was the strongest and most graceful of all the dancers, for her handicap bags were as big as those worn by two-hundred-pound men.

And she had to apologize at once for her voice, which was a very unfair voice for a woman to use. Her voice was a warm, luminous, timeless melody. "Excuse me —" she said, and she began again, making her voice absolutely uncompetitive.

"Harrison Bergeron, age fourteen," she said in a grackle squawk, "has just escaped from jail, where he was held on suspicion of plotting to overthrow the government. He is a genius and an athlete, is under-handicapped, and should be regarded as extremely dangerous."

A police photograph of Harrison Bergeron was flashed on the screen — upside down, then sideways, upside down again, then right side up. The picture showed the full length of Harrison against a background calibrated in feet and inches. He was exactly seven feet tall.

The rest of Harrison's appearance was Halloween and hardware. Nobody had ever borne heavier handicaps. He had outgrown hindrances faster than the H-G men could think them up. Instead of a little ear radio for a mental handicap, he wore a tremendous pair of earphones, and spectacles with thick wavy lenses. The spectacles were intended to make him not only half blind, but to give him whanging headaches besides.

45   Scrap metal was hung all over him. Ordinarily, there was a certain symmetry, a military neatness to the handicaps issued to strong people, but Harrison looked like a walking

junkyard. In the race of life, Harrison carried three hundred pounds.

And to offset his good looks, the H-G men required that he wear at all times a red rubber ball for a nose, keep his eyebrows shaved off, and cover his even white teeth with black caps at snaggle-tooth random.

"If you see this boy," said the ballerina, "do not — I repeat, do not — try to reason with him."

There was the shriek of a door being torn from its hinges.

Screams and barking cries of consternation came from the television set. The photograph of Harrison Bergeron on the screen jumped again and again, as though dancing to the tune of an earthquake.

50 George Bergeron correctly identified the earthquake, and well he might have — for many was the time his own home had danced to the same crashing tune. "My God — " said George, "that must be Harrison!"

The realization was blasted from his mind instantly by the sound of an automobile collision in his head.

When George could open his eyes again, the photograph of Harrison was gone. A living, breathing Harrison filled the screen.

Clanking, clownish, and huge, Harrison stood in the center of the studio. The knob of the uprooted studio door was still in his hand. Ballerinas, technicians, musicians, and announcers cowered on their knees before him, expecting to die.

"I am the Emperor!" cried Harrison. "Do you hear? I am the Emperor! Everybody must do what I say at once!" He stamped his foot and the studio shook.

55 "Even as I stand here — " he bellowed, "crippled, hobbled, sickened — I am a greater ruler than any man who ever lived! Now watch me become what I *can* become!"

Harrison tore the straps of his handicap harness like wet tissue paper, tore straps guaranteed to support five thousand pounds.

Harrison's scrap-iron handicaps crashed to the floor.

Harrison thrust his thumbs under the bars of the padlock that secured his head harness. The bar snapped like celery. Harrison smashed his headphones and spectacles against the wall.

He flung away his rubber-ball nose, revealed a man that would have awed Thor, the god of thunder.

60 "I shall now select my Empress!" he said, looking down on the cowering people. "Let the first woman who dares rise to her feet claim her mate and her throne!"

A moment passed, and then a ballerina arose, swaying like a willow.

Harrison plucked the mental handicap from her ear, snapped off her physical handicaps with marvelous delicacy. Last of all, he removed her mask.

She was blindingly beautiful.

"Now — " said Harrison, taking her hand, "shall we show the people the meaning of the word dance? Music!" he commanded.

65 The musicians scrambled back into their chairs, and Harrison stripped them of their handicaps, too. "Play your best," he told them, "and I'll make you barons and dukes and earls."

The music began. It was normal at first — cheap, silly, false. But Harrison snatched two musicians from their chairs, waved them like batons as he sang the music as he wanted it played. He slammed them back into their chairs.

The music began again and was much improved.

Harrison and his Empress merely listened to the music for a while — listened gravely, as though synchronizing their heartbeats with it.

They shifted their weights to their toes.

70 Harrison placed his big hands on the girl's tiny waist, letting her sense the weightlessness that would soon be hers.

And then, in an explosion of joy and grace, into the air they sprang!

Not only were the laws of the land

seeing connections

In this excerpt from the 2015 article "Inching toward Harrison Bergeron" from the *National Review*, commentator Kevin D. Williamson talks about the pursuit of equality in America.

The New York Fire Department is in the process of abandoning its physical standards for some female recruits because some—though by no means all—women find it difficult or impossible to satisfy them. That men are in general more physically suited for occupations such as soldier and firefighter is a truth so obvious that it must not be spoken, which is why the word "fireman" has become verboten. Other big-city fire departments have gutted their own standards, often under legal duress. This will certainly endanger both rescuers and the rescued. [. . .] This is the result of intellectual corruption rooted in our adolescent national inability to cope with the fact that life is not fair.

The end result of that intellectual corruption was considered by Kurt Vonnegut in his famous story "Harrison Bergeron" (which was made into a pretty good film, *2081*), in which the fearsome Handicapper General imposes burdens on the strong, the intelligent, the beautiful, and other beneficiaries of unfair personal endowments in the name of fighting inequality. But where we are headed is in some ways worse than that: We may quietly and grudgingly accept that certain things such as raw intellectual ability are as much a biological reality as height or eye color, but we seek to evade the consequences of that reality in the retreat to other virtues, such as being hard-working, deferring immediate gratification for larger long-term benefits, etc. At the same time, we are learning that these purported virtues do not manifest out of the ether, that many aspects of our personalities are as hard-wired as [. . .] lactose tolerance.

To what extent is Williamson's analogy to "Harrison Bergeron" appropriate to the point he is making?

---

abandoned, but the law of gravity and the laws of motion as well.

They reeled, whirled, swiveled, flounced, capered, gamboled, and spun.

They leaped like deer on the moon.

75 The studio ceiling was thirty feet high, but each leap brought the dancers nearer to it.

It became their obvious intention to kiss the ceiling.

They kissed it.

And then, neutralizing gravity with love and pure will, they remained suspended in air inches below the ceiling, and they kissed each other for a long, long time.

It was then that Diana Moon Glampers, the Handicapper General, came into the studio with a double-barreled ten-gauge shotgun. She fired twice, and the Emperor and the Empress were dead before they hit the floor.

80 Diana Moon Glampers loaded the gun again. She aimed at the musicians and told them they had ten seconds to get their handicaps back on.

It was then that the Bergerons' television tube burned out.

Hazel turned to comment about the blackout to George. But George had gone out into the kitchen for a can of beer.

George came back in with the beer, paused while a handicap signal shook him up. And then he sat down again. "You been crying?" he said to Hazel.

"Yup," she said.

85 "What about?" he said.

"I forgot," she said. "Something real sad on television."

"What was it?" he said.

"It's all kind of mixed up in my mind," said Hazel.

"Forget sad things," said George.

90 "I always do," said Hazel.

"That's my girl," said George. He winced. There was the sound of a riveting gun in his head.

"Gee — I could tell that one was a doozy," said Hazel.

"You can say that again," said George.

"Gee —" said Hazel, "I could tell that one was a doozy."

Understanding and Interpreting

1 The story begins, "The year was 2081, and everybody was finally equal." What does the word "finally" suggest about the idea of equality? How, then, do the sentences that follow conflict with your initial expectations about the state of affairs in 2081?

2 How does the government ensure equality in the world depicted in this story?

3 Think about the role that television and radio play in this story. What comment on the impact of television and radio does Vonnegut seem to be implying?

4 In paragraph 20, Hazel says, "Who knows better'n I do what normal is?" What does she think it means? To what extent are "normal" and "equal" the same in this story?

5 How do the characters in the story, particularly Hazel and George, seem to feel about the state of enforced total equality? Pay close attention to the section where Hazel urges George to remove his heavy handicaps for a short while. Why does he resist?

6 Why does Harrison Bergeron declare himself "emperor"? In what ways is this defiant action both a challenge to and an affirmation of the values of the society of 2081?

7 Why do you think Vonnegut focused on ballet dancers? What might a ballerina represent that would threaten the society of "equality"?

8 Do you find the ending predictable or surprising? How do Harrison's death and his parents' reactions further contribute to—or complicate—the story's commentary on conformity and rebellion?

9 Overall, what are the dangers of enforcing equality, according to the story "Harrison Bergeron"?

Analyzing Language, Style, and Structure

1 What is the narrative perspective in this story? Is the narrator critical, detached, or omniscient? What is the effect of this perspective?

2 Vonnegut alludes to mythological figures in the story, specifically the Roman goddess Diana and the Norse god Thor. What purpose do these allusions serve?

3 How does Vonnegut use the term "handicap" in "Harrison Bergeron"? How does his use contribute to the satire? As a contemporary reader, do you find his usage bothersome or, perhaps, offensive? Why or why not?

4 How do the style and mood of paragraphs 68–78, describing Harrison and the ballerina dancing, depart from the rest of the story? Pay close attention to figurative language and specific word choices.

5 The tone throughout this story is ironic, but how would you characterize the irony (e.g., gentle, humorous, bitter)? How does irony serve Vonnegut's purpose?

Connecting, Arguing, and Extending

1 Dystopian stories are often cautionary tales. To what extent do you think "Harrison Bergeron" depicts a world that could actually happen in 2081? What dangers within our society, our thinking, and our values is Vonnegut warning us to heed?

2 One reading of "Harrison Bergeron" is that society has been dehumanized by technology. The television, constantly on throughout the story, is the great leveler and tranquilizer, and the radio transmitters

interrupt coherent, sustained thinking. If the story were written today, how might current technologies serve the same purpose?

3 "Harrison Bergeron" is commonly interpreted as a critique of communism and socialism during the Cold War era of the 1950s and '60s. After researching the topic, explain this interpretation.

Nikki-Rosa

Nikki Giovanni

One of the most widely read American poets, Yolanda Cornelia "Nikki" Giovanni (b. 1943) is currently a University Distinguished Professor at Virginia Tech. Born in Cincinnati, Ohio, she graduated from Fisk University and went on to graduate school at the University of Pennsylvania. She has written more than a dozen volumes of poetry, three collections of essays, and many children's books. Among her many awards and honors are three NAACP Image Awards, the Langston Hughes Medal for poetry, and the Rosa L. Parks Woman of Courage Award. This poem appeared in *Black Feeling, Black Talk, Black Judgment* (1968), a collection from early in her career.

Michael Ochs Archives/Getty Images

KEY CONTEXT   With the civil rights movement as a backdrop, much of the African American literature of the 1960s focused on the experience of those who overcame the difficult circumstances of racism, poverty, nontraditional family structures, and abuse. The emphasis was on sadness, struggle, and ultimate triumph over adversity. In this poem, Giovanni has a different take on how those outside these experiences might define "adversity."

childhood remembrances are always a drag
if you're Black
you always remember things like living
    in Woodlawn
5 with no inside toilet
and if you become famous or something
they never talk about how happy you
    were to have
your mother all to yourself and how good the water
    felt when you got your bath from one of those
big tubs that folk in chicago barbecue in
and somehow when you talk about home

10 it never gets across how much you
understood their feelings
as the whole family attended meetings
    about Hollydale[1]
and even though you remember
your biographers never understand
15 your father's pain as he sells his stock
and another dream goes
And though you're poor it isn't poverty that
concerns you
and though they fought a lot
20 it isn't your father's drinking that makes
    any difference

---

[1] Hollydale: A black subdivision project that Giovanni's father invested in. He eventually sold his stock in the venture when it became clear that no banks would lend money to support it, likely for racial reasons. —Eds.

but only that everybody is together and you
and your sister have happy birthdays and
     very good Christmases
and I really hope no white person ever
     has cause to write about me

because they never understand Black love is
     Black wealth and they'll
25 probably talk about my hard childhood and
     never understand that
     all the while I was quite happy

Jacob Lawrence, *They were very poor* (part of the Migration Series), 1941. Casein tempera on hardboard, 12″ x 18″. Museum of Modern Art, New York.

How does this painting both support and challenge the view of poverty in "Nikki-Rosa"?

Understanding and Interpreting

1 Brainstorm your responses to the phrase "hard childhood" (l. 25) or growing up "poor" (l. 17). How does this poem challenge those associations? Cite specific lines or phrases.

2 Who is the speaker? What visual image do you have of her? Why?

3 How do you interpret lines 17–18: "And though you're poor it isn't poverty that / concerns you"?

4 What is the speaker's attitude toward her hypothetical biographers or any "white person

[who] ever has cause to write about" her (l. 23)? How might that attitude affect how readers who are not African American react to this poem?

5 At the end of the poem, the speaker characterizes her childhood as "quite happy." How does she define "happiness"?

6 Giovanni wrote this poem a few days after the funeral of Martin Luther King Jr. Does this fact influence your understanding of "Nikki-Rosa," and if so, how? If not, why not?

Analyzing Language, Style, and Structure

1 How does the speaker, an adult looking back, convey the immediacy of her childhood experiences?

2 What is the effect of the absence of punctuation in the poem? Does it contribute to, reinforce, or distract from the ideas Giovanni is expressing?

3 Read the first few lines of the poem in two different ways: first, link lines 1 and 2; then, read it with the clause that is line 2 as part of the subsequent lines. What does Giovanni achieve with this deliberate ambiguity?

4 What difference does the qualifier "quite" make in the final line of the poem? What do you think Giovanni wanted to achieve by writing "quite happy" (l. 26) instead of simply "happy"?

5 Giovanni has explained that her poetry comes out of the African American oral tradition. What specific qualities in this poem reflect an oral tradition?

6 How would you describe the tone of this poem? Try using two words to capture the complexity, such as two adjectives ("angry but hopeful") or an adverb and adjective ("sadly ironic").

Connecting, Arguing, and Extending

1 In many ways, "Nikki-Rosa" is a poem of the 1960s, a time of the civil rights and Black Pride movements. After doing some research into these, discuss the extent to which you believe "Nikki-Rosa" both represents and transcends the specific time period in which Giovanni wrote it.

2 Write either a narrative or a poem in the style of "Nikki-Rosa" that centers on an experience you have had that others would assume is negative but that you see differently.

3 Giovanni believes that poetry in the African American tradition cannot be separated from music. As a result, she has made albums of her poetry and performed with a New York religious choir. Set "Nikki-Rosa" to music that you think provides an interpretive or fitting background; explain your choice in specific terms of the poem.

Happy Family

Jane Shore

A poet and English professor, Jane Shore grew up in the 1950s in New Jersey. She received her BA from Goddard College and an MFA from the Iowa Writers' Workshop. Shore was a Briggs-Copeland Lecturer on English at Harvard University and a Visiting Distinguished Poet at the University of Hawaii. Recipient of numerous grants and awards, including a Guggenheim Fellowship, she currently is a professor at George Washington University in Washington, D.C. Her books of poetry include *Eye Level* (1977), *The Minute Hand* (1987), *Music Minus One* (1996), and *A Yes-or-No Answer: Poems* (2008). "Happy Family" is from a 1999 collection of the same title.

Courtesy Jane Shore, photo by Sid Tabak

KEY CONTEXT The inspiration for this poem is the quotation from *Anna Karenina* (1875) by Leo Tolstoy: "All happy families are alike; each unhappy family is unhappy in its own way."

In Chinatown, we order Happy Family,
the Specialty of the House.
The table set; red paper placemats
inscribed with the Chinese zodiac.
5 My husband's an ox; my daughter's
a dragon, hungry and cranky; I'm a pig.
The stars will tell us whether
we at this table are compatible.

The waiter vanishes into the kitchen.
10 Tea steeps in the metal teapot.
My husband plays with his napkin.
In the booth behind him sits a couple
necking, apparently in love.

Every Saturday night after work,
15 my mother ordered takeout from the Hong Kong,
the only Chinese restaurant in town.
She filled the teakettle.
By the time it boiled,
the table was set, minus knives and forks,
20 and my father had fetched the big brown paper bag
leaking grease: five shiny white
food cartons stacked inside.

My little sister and I unpacked the food,
unsheathed the wooden chopsticks —
25 Siamese twins joined at the shoulders —
which we snapped apart.
Thirteen years old, moody, brooding,
daydreaming about boys,
I sat and ate safe chop suey,
30 bland Cantonese shrimp,
moo goo gai pan, and egg foo yung.

My mother somber, my father drained,
too exhausted from work to talk,
as if the clicking chopsticks
35 were knitting something in their mouths.
My mother put hers aside
and picked at her shrimp with a fork.
She dunked a Lipton teabag in her cup
until the hot water turned rusty,

40 refusing the Hong Kong's complimentary tea,
no brand she'd ever seen before.

I cleared the table,
put empty cartons back in the bag.
Glued to the bottom,
45 translucent with oil, the pale green bill
a maze of Chinese characters.
Between the sealed lips of my fortune cookie,
a white scrap of tongue poking out . . .

Tonight, the waiter brings Happy Family
50 steaming under a metal dome
and three small igloos of rice.
Mounded on the white oval plate, the unlikely
marriage of meat and fish, crab and chicken.
Not all Happy Families are alike.
55 The chef's tossed in wilted greens
and water chestnuts, silk against crunch;
he's added fresh ginger to baby corn,
carrots, bamboo shoots, scallions, celery,
broccoli, pea pods, bok choy.
60 My daughter impales a chunk of beef
on her chopstick and contentedly
sucks on it, like a popsicle.
Eating Happy Family, we all begin to smile.

I prod the only thing left on the plate,
65 a large garnish
carved in the shape of an open rose.
Is it a turnip? An Asian pear?
The edges of the delicate petals
tinged with pink dye, the flesh
70 white and cool as a peeled apple's.
My daughter reaches for it —

"No good to eat!" The waiter rushes over —
"Rutabaga! Not cooked! Poison!" —

and hands us a plate with the bill
75 buried under three fortune cookies —
our teeth already tearing
at the cellophane, our fingers prying open
our three fates.

Understanding and Interpreting

1 How does the setting, a Chinese restaurant, establish the mood of the poem?

2 When the speaker shifts to her childhood in the third stanza, what are the similarities and differences she describes between her birth family and her current family?

3 Why does the speaker describe the food from both the past and present scenes in such detail, listing ingredients and making comments such as "the unlikely / marriage of meat and fish, crab and chicken" (ll. 52–53)? How do these descriptions relate to the depiction of the families?

4 How does the speaker's understanding of her birth family contribute to her perceptions of her current family? How does the memory of an experience from her past influence the present?

5 Does the poem have a happy ending? Explain your reasoning. In your response, take into account the reference to the "stars" in the opening stanza and the "fates" in the final stanza.

Analyzing Language, Style, and Structure

1 What is the story line, the plot, of this poem? How do the shifts in time structure the narrative of "Happy Family"? If Shore had started with the past and moved chronologically to the present, how would that choice have changed the effect?

2 What elements of disruption, perhaps even violence, do you find in the poem? Identify specific words and images (such as "impales"), and consider how they contribute to a sense of danger. What contrasting images do you find? Are these patterns in tension or balance with one another? Cite textual evidence to support your response.

3 To what extent do you think the title "Happy Family" is ironic? Is the overall tone of the poem ironic? If not, how would you describe it?

Connecting, Arguing, and Extending

1 How does this poem comment on the Tolstoy quotation about happy and unhappy families? As you respond to this question, consider the definition of "happy" that emerges from the poem.

2 Research the Chinese dish called "Happy Family." Apart from its name, why is it a particularly appropriate dish for this poem?

3 Write your own narrative that either illustrates or challenges Tolstoy's claim that "[a]ll happy families are alike; each unhappy family is unhappy in its own way." You might focus on your own family, another you've observed, or one you've experienced through your reading.

4 Find or create two visual images, one that represents the speaker's current family, the other her birth family. Juxtapose them in such a way that they comment on the relationship between the two families. Write an explanation of your choices.

The Joy of Less

Pico Iyer

One of the most respected travel writers today, Pico Iyer (b. 1957) has described himself as "a global village on two legs." He was born in Oxford, England, to Indian parents, and immigrated to the United States, where he lived in California. Iyer was educated at Oxford University and got his masters in literature from Harvard University. He currently lives much of each year in Japan. He is the author of numerous books on crossing cultures, including *Video Night in Kathmandu* (1989), *The Lady and the Monk: Four Seasons in Kyoto* (1992), *The Global Soul: Jet Lag, Shopping Malls, and the Search for Home* (2001), *The Open Road: The Global Journey of the Fourteenth Dalai Lama* (2009), and *The Man within My Head* (2013). An essayist for *Time* since 1986, Iyer also writes regularly for *Harper's*, the *New Yorker*, and many other publications. The following essay appeared in the *New York Times* in 2009 as part of a series on "spiritual literacy."

© Colin McPherson/Corbis

The beat of my heart has grown deeper, more active, and yet more peaceful, and it is as if I were all the time storing up inner riches . . . My [life] is one long sequence of inner miracles." The young Dutchwoman Etty Hillesum wrote that in a Nazi transit camp in 1943, on her way to her death at Auschwitz two months later. Towards the end of his life, Ralph Waldo Emerson wrote, "All I have seen teaches me to trust the creator for all I have not seen," though by then he had already lost his father when he was 7, his first wife when she was 20 and his first son, aged 5. In Japan, the late 18th-century poet Issa is celebrated for his delighted, almost child-like celebrations of the natural world. Issa saw four children die in infancy, his wife die in childbirth, and his own body partially paralyzed.

In the corporate world, I always knew there was some higher position I could attain, which meant that, like Zeno's arrow,[1] I was guaranteed never to arrive and always to remain dissatisfied.

I'm not sure I knew the details of all these lives when I was 29, but I did begin to guess that happiness lies less in our circumstances than in what we make of them, in every sense. "There is nothing either good or bad," I had heard in high school, from Hamlet, "but thinking makes it so." I had been lucky enough at that point to stumble into the life I might have dreamed of as a boy: a great job writing on world affairs for *Time* magazine, an apartment (officially at least) on Park Avenue, enough time and money to take vacations in Burma, Morocco, El Salvador. But every time I went to one of those places, I noticed that the people I met there, mired in difficulty and often warfare, seemed to have more energy and even optimism than the friends I'd grown up with in privileged, peaceful Santa Barbara, California, many of whom were on their fourth marriages and seeing a therapist every day. Though I knew that poverty certainly didn't buy happiness, I wasn't convinced that money did either.

So — as post-1960s cliché decreed — I left my comfortable job and life to live for a year in a temple on the backstreets of Kyoto. My

---

[1]Zeno's arrow: A paradox created by the Greek philosopher Zeno, who proposed that if you shot an arrow, and were able to stop time, then at any given instant the arrow would seem to be at rest. If the arrow is at rest at every instant, then the arrow is not in motion. —Eds.

high-minded year lasted all of a week, by which time I'd noticed that the depthless contemplation of the moon and composition of haiku I'd imagined from afar was really more a matter of cleaning, sweeping and then cleaning some more. But today, more than 21 years later, I still live in the vicinity of Kyoto, in a two-room apartment that makes my old monastic cell look almost luxurious by comparison. I have no bicycle, no car, no television I can understand, no media — and the days seem to stretch into eternities, and I can't think of a single thing I lack.

5   I'm no Buddhist monk, and I can't say I'm in love with renunciation in itself, or traveling an hour or more to print out an article I've written, or missing out on the N.B.A. Finals. But at some point, I decided that, for me at least, happiness arose out of all I didn't want or need, not all I did. And it seemed quite useful to take a clear, hard look at what really led to peace of mind or absorption (the closest I've come to understanding happiness). Not having a car gives me volumes not to think or worry about, and makes walks around the neighborhood a daily adventure.

Lacking a cell phone and high-speed Internet, I have time to play ping-pong every evening, to write long letters to old friends and to go shopping for my sweetheart (or to track down old baubles for two kids who are now out in the world).

When the phone does ring — once a week — I'm thrilled, as I never was when the phone rang in my overcrowded office in Rockefeller Center. And when I return to the United States every three months or so and pick up a newspaper, I find I haven't missed much at all. While I've been rereading P.G. Wodehouse, or *Walden*, the crazily accelerating roller-coaster of the 24/7 news cycle has propelled people up and down and down and up and then left them pretty much where they started. "I call that man rich," Henry James's Ralph Touchett observes in *Portrait of a Lady*, "who can satisfy the requirements of his imagination." Living in the future tense never did that for me.

Perhaps happiness, like peace or passion, comes most when it isn't pursued.

I certainly wouldn't recommend my life to most people — and my heart goes out to those

seeing connections

In 1943, American psychologist Abraham Maslow classified human needs into a hierarchy that moves from survival to self-actualization (depicted here as a pyramid). He believed that until our basic needs are met, we cannot address our higher needs, which many people never reach because these require qualities such as independence and creativity.

How does this idea compare with Iyer's thoughts in his essay?

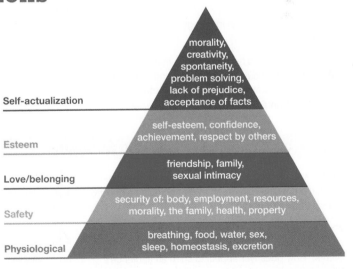

Self-actualization — morality, creativity, spontaneity, problem solving, lack of prejudice, acceptance of facts

Esteem — self-esteem, confidence, achievement, respect by others

Love/belonging — friendship, family, sexual intimacy

Safety — security of: body, employment, resources, morality, the family, health, property

Physiological — breathing, food, water, sex, sleep, homeostasis, excretion

who have recently been condemned to a simplicity they never needed or wanted. But I'm not sure how much outward details or accomplishments ever really make us happy deep down. The millionaires I know seem desperate to become multimillionaires, and spend more time with their lawyers and their bankers than with their friends (whose motivations they are no longer sure of). And I remember how, in the corporate world, I always knew there was some higher position I could attain, which meant that, like Zeno's arrow, I was guaranteed never to arrive and always to remain dissatisfied.

Being self-employed will always make for a precarious life; these days, it is more uncertain than ever, especially since my tools of choice, written words, are coming to seem like accessories to images. Like almost everyone I know, I've lost much of my savings in the past few months. I even went through a dress-rehearsal for our enforced austerity when my family home in Santa

Barbara burned to the ground some years ago, leaving me with nothing but the toothbrush I bought from an all-night supermarket that night. And yet my two-room apartment in nowhere Japan seems more abundant than the big house that burned down. I have time to read the new John le Carré while nibbling at sweet tangerines in the sun. When a Sigur Ros album comes out, it fills my days and nights, resplendent. And then it seems that happiness, like peace or passion, comes most freely when it isn't pursued.

10   If you're the kind of person who prefers freedom to security, who feels more comfortable in a small room than a large one and who finds that happiness comes from matching your wants to your needs, then running to stand still isn't where your joy lies. In New York, a part of me was always somewhere else, thinking of what a simple life in Japan might be like. Now I'm there, I find that I almost never think of Rockefeller Center or Park Avenue at all.

Understanding and Interpreting

1 This essay was published less than a year after the Great Recession of 2008. How does that timing affect what Pico Iyer has to say and how readers are likely to respond?

2 What does Iyer mean in paragraph 6 by "[l]iving in the future tense"?

3 To what extent is Iyer suggesting that the setting of Japan, particularly the area around Kyoto, is more conducive to the life he has chosen than New York City or Santa Barbara, California?

4 In this essay, how does Iyer define "happiness"? Do you think the title is his definition?

5 Is this essay actually just another rant—although in a gentle tone—against technology? Cite specific passages to support your response.

Analyzing Language, Style, and Structure

1 What is the effect of the references that Iyer makes in the opening paragraph? What point is he making with all three of these?

2 The readers of the *New York Times* are, generally, well educated, widely read, and interested in world events. How does Iyer appeal to such an audience? Cite specific passages and examples.

3 What is Iyer's purpose? Is he trying to persuade his readers to follow his example? Is he simply relating his own experience? Something else?

4 Iyer advocates a simpler life in the tradition of Henry David Thoreau, a choice, one could argue, not available to everyone. What strategies does Iyer employ to avoid sounding smug or even elitist?

Connecting, Arguing, and Extending

1 Choose one of the quotations below from Iyer, and write a brief essay supporting or challenging his statement. Be sure to draw on your own personal experience and knowledge as you explain your ideas. You may also choose another quotation from the piece, if you'd prefer.

    a. "I'm not sure how much outward details or accomplishments ever really make us happy deep down" (par. 8).

    b. "I always knew there was some higher position I could attain, which meant that, like Zeno's arrow, I was guaranteed never to arrive and always to remain dissatisfied" (par. 8).

    c. "And then it seems that happiness, like peace or passion, comes most freely when it isn't pursued" (par. 9).

2 Although Iyer makes a strong case for the joys of less, of living outside the hubbub and competition of modern life, many would argue that the drawbacks are too numerous. Write an essay that takes issue with Iyer's viewpoint, countering specific points that he makes.

3 It is an age-old question: does money buy happiness? Iyer states, "Though I knew that poverty certainly didn't buy happiness, I wasn't convinced that money did either." Although his judgment seems clear on the matter, recent studies seem to suggest that the answer is a bit more complex. Research this question by locating at least three credible sources on the topic, and draw your own conclusion based upon what you have learned. To what extent does your research support or contradict Iyer's conclusions?

Civil Peace

Chinua Achebe

Nigerian writer Chinua Achebe (1930–2013), the author of five novels, as well as several collections of poetry and short stories, is one of the most prominent African authors of all time. His novel *Things Fall Apart* is a modern classic, and the most-read African novel to date, with over 8 million copies in print. Achebe was born and grew up in a rural Nigerian town in an area dominated by the Igbo, the largest ethnic group in the country. During Achebe's youth, Nigeria was still under British control, and the boarding school he attended as a child was modeled after the British system. After graduating from college, Achebe moved to Lagos, the most populous city in Nigeria, where he worked for the Nigerian Broadcast Service and began writing *Things Fall Apart*. "Civil Peace" was first published in the Nigerian journal *Okike* in 1971, and it was collected in the volume *Girls at War and Other Stories*, published the following year.

KEY CONTEXT   "Civil Peace" is set in the aftermath of the Nigerian Civil War (1967–1970), also known as the Biafran War. Nigeria, which gained independence from Britain in 1960, was made up of different ethnic groups, and building tensions led the Igbo, one of the major groups, to form the Independent Republic of Biafra and separate from Nigeria. During three years of bloody fighting and famine, over 2 million civilians died from combat and famine. In 1970, Nigeria, aided by Britain, defeated the Igbo and reunited as one country. Achebe, born of Igbo ancestry, served as a diplomat for Biafra and supported the cause as a radio commentator.

Jonathan Iwegbu counted himself extraordinarily lucky. "Happy survival!" meant so much more to him than just a current fashion of greeting old friends in the first hazy days of peace. It went deep to his heart. He had come out of the war with five inestimable blessings — his head, his wife Maria's head, and the heads of three out of their four children. As a bonus he also had his old bicycle — a miracle too but naturally not to be compared to the safety of five human heads.

The bicycle had a little history of its own. One day at the height of the war it was commandeered "for urgent military action." Hard as its loss would have been to him he would still have let it go without a thought had he not had some doubts about the genuineness of the officer. It wasn't his disreputable rags, nor the toes peeping out of one blue and one brown canvas shoes, nor yet the two stars of his rank done obviously in a hurry in Biro,[1] that troubled Jonathan; many good and heroic soldiers looked the same or worse. It was rather a certain lack of grip and firmness in his manner. So Jonathan, suspecting he might be amenable to influence, rummaged in his raffia bag and produced the two pounds with which he had been going to buy firewood which his wife, Maria, retailed to camp officials for extra stockfish and corn meal, and got his bicycle back. That night he buried it in the little clearing in the bush where the dead of the camp, including his own youngest son, were buried. When he dug it up again a year later after the surrender all it needed was a little palm-oil greasing. "Nothing puzzles God," he said in wonder.

He put it to immediate use as a taxi and accumulated a small pile of Biafran money ferrying camp officials and their families across the four-mile stretch to the nearest tarred road. His standard charge per trip was six pounds and those who had the money were only glad to be rid of some of it in this way. At the end of a fortnight he had made a small fortune of one hundred and fifteen pounds.

Then he made the journey to Enugu and found another miracle waiting for him. It was unbelievable. He rubbed his eyes and looked again and it was still standing there before him. But, needless to say, even that monumental blessing must be accounted also totally inferior to the five heads in the family. This newest miracle was his little house in Ogui Overside. Indeed nothing puzzles God! Only two houses away a huge concrete edifice some wealthy contractor had put up just before the war was a mountain of rubble. And here was Jonathan's little zinc house of no regrets built with mud blocks quite intact! Of course the doors and windows were missing and five sheets off the roof. But what was that? And anyhow he had returned to Enugu early enough to pick up bits of old zinc and wood and soggy sheets of cardboard lying around the neighbourhood before thousands more came out of their forest holes looking for the same things. He got a destitute carpenter with one old hammer, a blunt plane, and a few bent and rusty nails in his tool bag to turn this assortment of wood, paper, and metal into door and window shutters for five Nigerian shillings or fifty Biafran pounds. He paid the pounds, and moved in with his overjoyed family carrying five heads on their shoulders.

5   His children picked mangoes near the military cemetery and sold them to soldiers' wives for a few pennies — real pennies this time — and his wife started making breakfast akara balls[2] for neighbours in a hurry to start life again. With his family earnings he took his bicycle to the villages around and bought fresh palm-wine which he mixed generously in his rooms with the water which had recently started running again in the public tap down the road, and opened up a bar for soldiers and other lucky people with good money.

---

[1] Biro: Type of pen made by Bic and named after László József Bíró, inventor of the ballpoint pen. —Eds.

[2] akara balls: Battered and fried bean fritters. A breakfast food in Nigerian cuisine. —Eds.

At first he went daily, then every other day, and finally once a week, to the offices of the Coal Corporation where he used to be a miner, to find out what was what. The only thing he did find out in the end was that that little house of his was even a greater blessing than he had thought. Some of his fellow ex-miners who had nowhere to return at the end of the day's waiting just slept outside the doors of the offices and cooked what meal they could scrounge together in Bournvita tins. As the weeks lengthened and still nobody could say what was what Jonathan discontinued his weekly visits altogether and faced his palm-wine bar.

But nothing puzzles God. Came the day of the windfall when after five days of endless scuffles in queues and counter-queues in the sun outside the Treasury he had twenty pounds counted into his palms as ex-gratia award for the rebel money he had turned in. It was like Christmas for him and for many others like him when the payments began. They called it (since few could manage its proper official name) *egg-rasher.*

As soon as the pound notes were placed in his palm Jonathan simply closed it tight over them and buried fist and money inside his trouser pocket. He had to be extra careful because he had seen a man a couple of days earlier collapse into near-madness in an instant before that oceanic crowd because no sooner had he got his twenty pounds than some heartless ruffian picked it off him. Though it was not right that a man in such an extremity of agony should be blamed yet many in the queues that day were able to remark quietly on the victim's carelessness, especially after he pulled out the innards of his pocket and revealed a hole in it big enough to pass a thief's head. But of course he had insisted that the money had been in the other pocket, pulling it out too to show its comparative wholeness. So one had to be careful.

Jonathan soon transferred the money to his left hand and pocket so as to leave his right free for shaking hands should the need arise, though

by fixing his gaze at such an elevation as to miss all approaching human faces he made sure that the need did not arise, until he got home.

10 He was normally a heavy sleeper but that night he heard all the neighbourhood noises die down one after another. Even the night watchman who knocked the hour on some metal somewhere in the distance had fallen silent after knocking one o'clock. That must have been the last thought in Jonathan's mind before he was finally carried away himself. He couldn't have been gone for long, though, when he was violently awakened again.

"Who is knocking?" whispered his wife lying beside him on the floor.

"I don't know," he whispered back breathlessly.

The second time the knocking came it was so loud and imperious that the rickety old door could have fallen down.

"Who is knocking?" he asked then, his voice parched and trembling.

15 "Na tief-man and him people," came the cool reply. "Make you hopen de door." This was followed by the heaviest knocking of all.

Maria was the first to raise the alarm, then he followed and all their children.

"Police-o! Thieves-o! Neighbours-o! Police-o! We are lost! We are dead! Neighbours, are you asleep? Wake up! Police-o!"

This went on for a long time and then stopped suddenly. Perhaps they had scared the thief away. There was total silence. But only for a short while.

"You done finish?" asked the voice outside. "Make we help you small. Oya, everybody!"

20 *"Police-o! Tief-man-o! Neighbours-o! we done loss-o! Police-o! . . ."*

There were at least five other voices besides the leader's.

Jonathan and his family were now completely paralysed by terror. Maria and the children sobbed inaudibly like lost souls. Jonathan groaned continuously.

The silence that followed the thieves' alarm vibrated horribly. Jonathan all but begged their leader to speak again and be done with it.

"My frien," said he at long last, "we don try our best for call dem but I tink say dem all done sleep-o . . . So wetin we go do now? Sometaim you wan call soja? Or you wan make we call dem for you? Soja better pass police. No be so?"

25 "Na so!" replied his men. Jonathan thought he heard even more voices now than before and groaned heavily. His legs were sagging under him and his throat felt like sandpaper.

"My frien, why you no de talk again. I de ask you say you wan make we call soja?"

"No."

"Awrighto. Now make we talk business. We no be bad tief. We no like for make trouble. Trouble done finish. War done finish and all the katakata wey de for inside.[3] No Civil War again. This time na Civil Peace. No be so?"

"Na so!" answered the horrible chorus.

30 "What do you want from me? I am a poor man. Everything I had went with this war. Why do you come to me? You know people who have money. We . . ."

"Awright! We know say you no get plenty money. But we sef no get even anini. So derefore make you open dis window and give us one hundred pound and we go commot. Orderwise we de come for inside now to show you guitar-boy like dis . . ."

A volley of automatic fire rang through the sky. Maria and the children began to weep aloud again.

"Ah, missisi de cry again. No need for dat. We done talk say we na good tief. We just take our small money and go nwayorly. No molest. Abi we de molest?"

"At all!" sang the chorus.

35 "My friends" began Jonathan hoarsely. "I hear what you say and I thank you. If I had one hundred pounds . . ."

"Lookia my frien, no be play we come play for your house. If we make mistake and step for inside you no go like am-o. So derefore . . ."

"To God who made me; if you come inside and find one hundred pounds, take it and shoot me and shoot my wife and children. I swear to God. The only money I have in this life is this twenty pounds *egg-rasher* they gave me today . . ."

---

[3] katakata wey de for inside: Katakata is Nigerian dialect for *commotion*, specifically an onomatopoetic word meant to imitate automatic gunfire. The rest of the sentence means "that goes along with it." —Eds.

Biafran refugees carry children and belongings as they flee from advancing Nigerian troops into Igbo land, August 2, 1968.

What can you infer about the importance of the "egg-rasher" based on this photo? How does this inform your reading of Achebe's story?

AP Photo

"OK. Time de go. Make you open dis window and bring the twenty pound. We go manage am like dat."

There were now loud murmurs of dissent among the chorus: "Na lie de man de lie; e get plenty money . . . Make we go inside and search properly well . . . Wetin be twenty pound? . . ."

40 "Shurrup!" rang the leader's voice like a lone shot in the sky and silenced the murmuring at once. "Are you dere? Bring the money quick!"

"I am coming" said Jonathan fumbling in the darkness with the key of the small wooden box he kept by his side on the mat.

. . .

At the first sign of light as neighbours and others assembled to commiserate with him he was already strapping his five-gallon demijohn to his bicycle carrier and his wife, sweating in the open fire, was turning over akara balls in a wide clay bowl of boiling oil. In the corner his eldest son was rinsing out dregs of yesterday's palm-wine from old beer bottles.

"I count it as nothing," he told his sympathizers, his eyes on the rope he was tying. "What is *egg-rasher*? Did I depend on it last week? Or is it greater than other things that went with the war? I say, let *egg-rasher* perish in the flames! Let it go where everything else has gone. Nothing puzzles God."

Understanding and Interpreting

1 What unsettling details in the opening paragraph seem to conflict with Jonathan Iwegbu's assessment that he is "extraordinarily lucky"?

2 What was the bicycle's "history of its own" (par. 2)? Why is it significant?

3 What is the "miracle" of Jonathan's "little zinc house" (par. 4)? How does his attitude toward it illustrate his primary character trait?

4 The Latin term "ex gratia" refers to something given as a favor instead of a legal right. How does the incident of the man whose ex gratia money was pickpocketed contribute to the story (par. 8)?

5 What does the behavior of the band of thieves and their negotiation with Jonathan say about the state of affairs in the newly united Nigeria?

6 What examples of authority from the military and government do you find in the story? Consider the climactic incident with the thieves and why no one alerts local police. Based on several examples, how would you characterize Achebe's portrayal of Nigerian authority?

7 How do you interpret the sentence that Jonathan repeats, "Nothing puzzles God"? Why has this statement become a mantra to him? Note the specific points in the story where it appears.

8 A central tension in "Civil Peace" is between Jonathan's positive spirit and the violence of the civil war. How does Achebe convey the war's violence and its continuing threat in Nigerian society without actually describing acts of violence?

9 Based on this story, do you agree with the thief who declares, "Trouble done finish" (par. 28)?

10 How do you interpret the title "Civil Peace"? Explain whether you believe it is ironic. Do you think it is an appropriate title?

Analyzing Language, Style, and Structure

1 In the opening paragraph, note the words that have positive connotations. As you reread the paragraph, do you think that Achebe wants us to understand them as hyperbolic, ironic, serious, possessing a combination of these qualities, or something else?

2 Who is the narrator? Is the perspective primarily Jonathan's, or is it more of an omniscient narrator's?

3 Achebe uses dialect extensively in "Civil Peace," both Jonathan's more standard dialect and the heavier dialect of the thieves. How does dialect add authenticity to the story? Does the difficulty readers may have understanding some of the language offset the advantages of Achebe's using it? Explain.

4 Throughout "Civil Peace," Achebe refers to the "five human heads" that constitute the chief blessing of Jonathan's life. What is the effect of using this figure of speech rather than just saying literally "five lives" or "five family members"?

Connecting, Arguing, and Extending

1 Given the historical circumstances in which Jonathan lives, do you think his unflagging optimism shows that he is a resilient and practical person or a naive man who is in denial? Explain, using specific references to the story.

2 In a 1964 article in *Nigeria* magazine titled "The Role of the Writer in a New Nation," Achebe defines what he believes writers should write about—what their cultural duty is. In what ways do you believe that "Civil Peace" fulfills the "writer's duty," as Achebe defines it? In what ways, if any, does the story fall short?

> This is my answer to those who say that a writer should be writing about contemporary issues [. . .] as far as I am concerned the fundamental theme [. . .] is that African peoples did not hear of culture for the first time from Europeans; that their

societies were not mindless but frequently had a philosophy of great depth and value and beauty, that they had poetry and, above all, they had dignity. It is this dignity that many African peoples all but lost in the colonial period, and it is this dignity that they must now regain. [. . .] The writer's duty is to help them regain it [dignity] by showing them in human terms what happened to them, what they lost. [. . .] After all the novelist's duty is not to beat this morning's headline in topicality, it is to explore in depth the human condition.

3 The contemporary author Chimamanda Ngozi Adichie wrote the novel *Half of a Yellow Sun*, which tells the story of two sisters during the Nigerian Civil War. Research Adichie's explanation of why she decided to revisit the war experience in a book published in 2006, and a film released in 2013.

Utopia

Wisława Szymborska

Translated by Stanisław Barańczak and Clare Cavanagh

Wisława Szymborska [vis-*wah*-vah shim-*bawrs*-kah] (1923–2012) was born in western Poland and lived there all her life. After studying literature and sociology at Jagiellonian University in Krakow, she began her career as a poet. She published her first poem, "I Am Looking for a World," in 1945, and her first book, *Dłatego Żyjemy* (*That's What We Live For*), in 1952. Although she had published eighteen volumes of poetry, which had been translated into more than a dozen languages, she was not well known in the English-speaking world until she was awarded the Nobel Prize for Literature in 1996. This poem was published in 1976 in a collection titled *A Large Number*.

Island where all becomes clear.

Solid ground beneath your feet.

The only roads are those that offer access.

Bushes bend beneath the weight of proofs.

5 The Tree of Valid Supposition grows here
with branches disentangled since time
immemorial.

The Tree of Understanding, dazzlingly
straight and simple,
sprouts by the spring called Now I Get It.

The thicker the woods, the vaster the vista:
10 the Valley of Obviously.

If any doubts arise, the wind dispels them
instantly.

Echoes stir unsummoned
and eagerly explain all the secrets of the
worlds.

On the right a cave where Meaning lies.

15 On the left the Lake of Deep Conviction.
Truth breaks from the bottom and bobs to
the surface.

Unshakable Confidence towers over the
valley.
Its peak offers an excellent view of the
Essence of Things.

For all its charms, the island is uninhabited,
20 and the faint footprints scattered on its
beaches
turn without exception to the sea.

As if all you can do here is leave
and plunge, never to return, into the depths.

Into unfathomable life.

Understanding and Interpreting

1 How does Wisława Szymborska describe the island of "Utopia"? What certainties does it ensure?

2 Why is Utopia "uninhabited" (l. 19)? Why is it a place where "all you can do here is leave" (l. 22)?

3 What is the difference between the "Tree of Valid Supposition" (l. 5) and the "Tree of Understanding" (l. 7)?

4 How might this poem be interpreted as a commentary on the reading of poetry, particularly the desire to find a single, clearly defined meaning?

Analyzing Language, Style, and Structure

1 What does the sea represent in this poem? What other elements of the landscape of Szymborksa's utopia are symbolic? Discuss what at least two features of the landscape symbolize.

2 How does Szymborska achieve an ironic tone? Cite three different strategies with lines and passages to support your choice.

3 What is the argument Szymborska makes in this poem? Outline her claim and the evidence she provides to support it.

Connecting, Arguing, and Extending

1. An allegory is a story, poem, or picture that can be interpreted to reveal a hidden meaning, typically a moral or political one. To what extent is "Utopia" an allegory of the former Communist regime in Szymborska's home country of Poland? You may need to research the political situation in Poland at the time the poem was written.

2. The following question was posed by the Polish magazine *Autoportret* to a group of "Polish and foreign intellectuals" that included philosophers, historians, social scientists, architects, and the poet Wisława Szymborska: "Is a crisis of utopia and utopian thinking underway? If so, what are the reasons [. . .] and if no, what can be the source of contemporary utopia?" While the others responded with fairly lengthy prose explanations, Szymborska simply submitted her poem. How does the poem respond to the questions?

3. Using the same tone that Szymborska does in "Utopia," or a similarly ironic one, write a poem titled "Dystopia." Remember: you are not necessarily writing your own opinion but modeling both style and content on the viewpoint of Szymborska in her poem.

4. Which of the following quotations most closely resembles the ideas in Szymborska's poem "Utopia"? Explain your response with specific reference to the poem.

   a. [I]n Utopia, where every man has a right to everything, they all know that if care is taken to keep the public stores full no private man can want anything; for among them there is no unequal distribution, so that no man is poor, none in necessity; and though no man has anything, yet they are all rich; for what can make a man so rich as to lead a serene and cheerful life, free from anxieties. —Thomas More, British philosopher and statesman

   b. By their very nature utopias are static. They hate change because it's a direct challenge to their fantasy of perfection. —Paul McAuley, British science fiction author

   c. Nearly all creators of Utopia have resembled the man who has toothache, and therefore thinks happiness consists in not having toothache. [. . .] Whoever tries to imagine perfection simply reveals his own emptiness. —George Orwell, British author

Free to Be Happy

Jon Meacham

Born in Chattanooga, Tennessee, in 1969, Jon Meacham is the author of best-selling biographies of iconic American figures. He won the Pulitzer Prize in 2009 for *American Lion*, his biography of Andrew Jackson, and his 2012 book, *Thomas Jefferson: The Art of Power*, topped the *New York Times* best-seller list. Meacham is also the author of *Franklin and Winston: An Intimate Portrait of an Epic Friendship* (2003), a study of Winston Churchill and Franklin Delano Roosevelt. Executive editor and executive vice president of Random House,

AP Photo/Tina Fineberg

Meacham is a contributing editor to *Time* magazine, a former editor of *Newsweek*, and a regular contributor to television shows, including *Meet the Press* and *Morning Joe*. The following essay appeared in a 2013 special edition of *Time* magazine that featured a cover story called "The Happiness of Pursuit."

Sitting in his small two-room suite in the bricklayer Jacob Graff's house at Seventh and Market Streets in Philadelphia — he hated the flies from nearby stables and fields — Thomas Jefferson used a small wooden writing desk (a kind of 18th century laptop) to draft the report of a subcommittee of the Second Continental Congress in June 1776. There were to be many edits and changes to what became known as the Declaration of Independence — far too many for the writerly and sensitive Jefferson — but the fundamental rights of man as Jefferson saw them remained consistent: the rights to life, to liberty and, crucially, to "the pursuit of happiness."

To our eyes and ears, human equality and the liberty to build a happy life are inextricably linked in the cadences of the Declaration, and thus in America's idea of itself. We are not talking about happiness in only the sense of good cheer or delight, though good cheer and delight are surely elements of happiness. Jefferson and his colleagues were contemplating something more comprehensive — more revolutionary, if you will. Garry Wills' classic 1978 book on the Declaration, *Inventing America*, puts it well: "When Jefferson spoke of pursuing happiness," wrote Wills, "he had nothing vague or private in mind. He meant public happiness which is measurable; which is, indeed, the test and justification of any government."

The idea of the pursuit of happiness was ancient, yet until Philadelphia it had never been granted such pride of place in a new scheme of human government — a pride of place that put the governed, not the governors, at the center of the enterprise. Reflecting on the sources of the thinking embodied in the Declaration, Jefferson credited "the elementary books of public right, as Aristotle, Cicero, Locke, Sidney, & c."

As with so many things, then, to understand the Declaration we have to start with Aristotle. "Happiness, then," he wrote, "is . . . the end of action" — the whole point of life. Scholars have long noted that for Aristotle and the Greeks, as well as for Jefferson and the Americans,

▶

How does this mural seem to define the "pursuit of happiness" and how does that definition compare to the one that the Founding Fathers intended, according to Meacham?

Private Collection/Bridgeman Images

Xavier Cortada, *Stepping into the American Dream* (official mural of the White House Conference on Minority Homeownership, Washington, D.C.), 2002. Mixed media on canvas, 96″ x 96″.

happiness was not about yellow smiley faces, self-esteem or even feelings. According to historians of happiness and of Aristotle, it was an ultimate good, worth seeking for its own sake. Given the Aristotelian insight that man is a social creature whose life finds meaning in his relation to other human beings, Jeffersonian *eudaimonia* — the Greek word for happiness — evokes virtue, good conduct and generous citizenship.

5 As Arthur M. Schlesinger Sr. once wrote, this broad ancient understanding of happiness informed the thinking of patriots such as James Wilson ("the happiness of the society is the first law of government") and John Adams ("the happiness of society is the end of government"). Once the Declaration of Independence was adopted and signed in the summer of 1776, the pursuit of happiness — the pursuit of the good of the whole, because the good of the whole was crucial to the genuine well-being of the individual — became part of the fabric (at first brittle, to be sure, but steadily stronger) of a young nation.

The thinking about happiness came to American shores most directly from the work of John Locke and from Scottish-Irish philosopher Francis Hutcheson. During the Enlightenment, thinkers and politicians struggled with redefining the role of the individual in an ethos so long dominated by feudalism, autocratic religious establishments and the divine rights of kings. A key insight of the age was that reason, not revelation, should have primacy in human affairs. That sense of reason was leading Western thinkers to focus on the idea of happiness, which in Jefferson's hands may be better understood as the pursuit of individual excellence that shapes the life of a broader community.

Like, say, the newly emerging United States of America. Pre-Jefferson, the precept was explicitly expressed in the newly adopted Virginia Declaration of Rights, a document written by George Mason and very much on Jefferson's mind in the summer of 1776. Men, wrote Mason, "are by nature equally free and independent and have certain inherent rights . . . namely, the enjoyment of life and liberty, with the means of acquiring and possessing property, and pursuing and obtaining happiness and safety." Property is often key to happiness, but Mason was thinking more broadly, drawing on the tradition of the ancients to articulate a larger scope for civic life.

From John Winthrop to Jefferson to Lincoln, Americans have been defined by our sense of our own exceptionalism — a sense of destiny that has, however, always been tempered by an appreciation of the tragic nature of life. We believe ourselves to be entitled by the free gifts of nature and of nature's God — of our Creator, in a theological frame — to pursue happiness. What Americans don't always let on is that we know, beneath the Rockwellian optimism and the Reaganesque confidence and the seemingly boundless faith in a democratically digital future, that we have only been promised a chance to pursue happiness — not to catch it. Americans would rather the world think of us as Jimmy Stewarts, when there's a strong strain of Humphrey Bogart in our national character. We're optimists and believers, yes, but we're practical about it, even if we don't want you to know it.

Strictly personal happiness has its own paradoxes. Experience teaches us that the more aggressively we pursue it, the harder it can be to find. (Ask Jay Gatsby, or just about any second-term President of the U.S.) Still, there are a lot more people trying to get into the U.S. than out of it. If it were the other way round, we wouldn't be debating immigration the way we are.

10 If the 18th century meaning of happiness connoted civic responsibility, the word has occasionally been taken to be more about private gratification than public good. It's really about both, but in some eras of U.S. history the private pursuit has crowded out the larger one. Consider the Gilded Age, the cultural excesses of the 1960s and '70s or the materialism so prevalent in the 1980s. Whether the issue at hand is

financial ambition or personal appetite, the pursuit of happiness, properly understood, is not a license to do whatever we want whenever we want if we believe it will make us happiest *right then*. Happiness in the Greek and American traditions is as much about equanimity as it is about endorphins.

Much is often made of the fact that Jefferson inserted "the pursuit of happiness" in place of "property" from earlier formulations of fundamental rights. Yet property and prosperity are essential to the Jeffersonian pursuit, for economic progress has long proven a precursor of political and social liberty. As Jefferson's friend and neighbor James Madison would say, the test is one of balance and proportion. More often than not, Americans have managed to find that balance.

We must, therefore, be doing something right. The genius of the American experiment is the nation's capacity to create hope in a world suffused with fear. And while we are too often more concerned with our own temporary feelings of happiness than we are with the common good, we still believe, with Jefferson, that governments are instituted to enable us to live our lives as we wish, enjoying innate liberties and freely enjoying the right to pursue happiness, which was in many ways the acme of

Enlightenment ambitions for the role of politics. For Jefferson and his contemporaries — and, thankfully, for most of their successors in positions of ultimate authority — the point of public life was to enable human creativity and ingenuity and possibility, not to constrict it.

In 1816, Jefferson wrote John Adams about the nature of grief. Drawing on his affection for Homeric poetry, Jefferson quoted the lines from *The Iliad* in which Priam and Achilles come together one night shortly after Achilles has killed Hector, Priam's son. The two sit together for a time, musing on the unhappiness of the mortal world.

> *Two urns by Jove's high throne have ever stood,*
> *The source of evil one, and one of good;*
> *From thence the cup of mortal man he fills,*
> *Blessings to these, to those distributes ills;*
> *To most he mingles both.*

This was the tragic Jefferson, and the tragic American. On other occasions he — and we — could refuse to accept the twilight. "Whatever they can," Jefferson said of us, "they will." He lived, as we do, somewhere between Homer and hope, seeking a happiness that will warm our days — and shape not only our own internal worlds, but the world around us.

Compare and contrast this cartoon's argument with the argument that Meacham presents in his essay.

Understanding and Interpreting

1 Jon Meacham spends a good part of this essay explaining what happiness is *not*. According to his view, what common understandings of happiness are outside the definition of happiness that the Founding Fathers had in mind when drafting the Declaration of Independence?

2 What is the role of "reason," according to Meacham, in the right to and pursuit of happiness? What does he mean when he points to the idea "that reason, not revelation, should have primacy in human affairs" (par. 6)?

3 What point is Meacham making when he writes that "[s]trictly personal happiness has its own paradoxes" (par. 9)?

4 To what extent does Meacham accept the role of property and economic prosperity in the pursuit and achievement of happiness?

5 What does Meacham mean when he writes that happiness is "as much about equanimity as it is about endorphins" (par. 10)?

6 Ultimately, what is the meaning of *happiness*, as Meacham sees it? Pay special attention to the interrelationship between happiness and public or civic life.

Analyzing Language, Style, and Structure

1 How does the opening paragraph draw the reader in? Identify at least two strategies that Meacham uses to establish his ethos with his readers.

2 Meacham's chief source of evidence is expert opinion, whether of historical figures or current leaders, intellectuals, and artists. Focus on one of his major points and examine how persuasively expert opinion functions as evidence in this essay.

3 What beliefs about democracy does Meacham suggest by his phrase "a democratically digital future" (par. 8)?

4 Although Meacham writes a logically structured argument, he makes strong appeals to pathos. Identify and explain the effect of two examples of his appeals to our emotions.

5 To what extent is the quotation from *The Iliad* by Homer effective as a lead-in to Meacham's conclusion? What does Meacham mean when he states that Jefferson lived, "as we do, somewhere between Homer and hope" (par. 13)? Evaluate the effectiveness of this conclusion.

Connecting, Arguing, and Extending

1 The Declaration of Independence states, "We hold these truths to be self-evident, that all men are created equal, that they are endowed by their Creator with certain unalienable Rights, that among these are Life, Liberty and the pursuit of Happiness." What does the right to pursue happiness mean to you? What opportunities and challenges will you probably face in your life in this pursuit?

2 A common criticism of contemporary America is that our society has come to value the individual over the community; that is, that pursuit of personal happiness has taken precedence over pursuit of civic well-being. To what extent do you agree or disagree with this characterization? Write an argument explaining your viewpoint, using Meacham's essay as well as your own observations and knowledge as sources of evidence.

3 Meacham writes with considerable passion about the American idea and ideal of happiness enshrined in our government. But what about happiness as it is defined in other nations? Focusing on one other culture or country, discuss an alternative view or definition of happiness that is based in the shared values of a community or government.

ENTERING THE CONVERSATION
THE PURSUIT OF HAPPINESS

Making Connections

1 In what ways does Omelas (p. 866) resemble the utopia that Wisława Szymborska rejects in her poem on page 891?

2 "Civil Peace" (p. 885) is a realistic story, while both "Harrison Bergeron" (p. 871) and "The Ones Who Walk Away from Omelas" (p. 866) are sometimes called "science fiction." Yet in all three tales, the government creates the utopia or dystopia. What similarities in the nature of government do you find in these stories?

3 Both "The Ones Who Walk Away from Omelas" (p. 866) and "Harrison Bergeron" (p. 871) are stories of dystopias born of utopian ideals. What ideals of utopia do these stories share? What are their differences? How do the ideals of each society lead to dystopias?

4 Compare and contrast the role of family in defining happiness in both "Nikki-Rosa" (p. 877) and "Happy Family" (p. 879).

5 Although written nearly fifty years apart, "The Joy of Less" (p. 882) and "Nikki-Rosa" (p. 877) encourage us to question our assumptions about happiness. Identify two identical or similar assumptions that these authors challenge and compare how they urge us, their readers, to examine them.

6 How do you think Pico Iyer, author of "The Joy of Less" (p. 882), would respond to the Founding Fathers' definition of happiness, as explained by Jon Meacham in "Free to Be Happy" (p. 892)?

Synthesizing Sources

1 What is your definition of happiness? To achieve happiness, what, if anything, must be lost or sacrificed? Develop your viewpoint with reference to at least three of the texts in this Conversation.

2 There is usually a pivot point at which the utopian ideals that a society strives for turn it into a dystopia. What makes the ideal go bad? Discuss with reference to three of the texts in this Conversation, or two sources from this Conversation along with a novel, movie, or other text of your own choice.

3 The promise of happiness is the foundation of most commercial advertising, whether the ad is for shampoo, a car, or a dating website. Discuss what happiness means in our culture today by analyzing a series of ads or commercials (still or video). Refer to at least two of the texts in this Conversation as part of your analysis.

4 How would you celebrate the International Day of Happiness in your community? You may define "community" as your town, neighborhood, school, or other group within a local context. You might want to research the U.N.'s goals further by looking up its annual report. Cite at least two of the readings in this Conversation as part of the rationale for your choice of activities.

5 Following are quotations on the meaning of happiness. Select the one you find most appealing, and write an essay explaining why it speaks to you. To support and illustrate your choice, include a narrative of personal experience, or at least a brief anecdote, and consideration of at least one of the texts you read in this Conversation.

   a. Happiness lies not in the mere possession of money; it lies in the joy of achievement, in the thrill of creative effort. —Franklin Delano Roosevelt
   b. You cannot protect yourself from sadness without protecting yourself from happiness. —Jonathan Safran Foer
   c. To be happy, we must not be too concerned with others. —Albert Camus
   d. Happiness is when what you think, what you say, and what you do are in harmony. —Mahatma Gandhi
   e. If thou wilt make a man happy, add not unto his riches but take away from his desires. —Epicurus
   f. Folks are usually about as happy as they make their minds up to be. —attributed to Abraham Lincoln
   g. Sanity and happiness are an impossible combination. —Mark Twain

OUR ROBOTIC FUTURE

Given the rapid advances in technology in the last thirty years, it's safe to say that automation and robots are going to be more and more a part of our lives in the future. The question is, in what way?

Will the future be more like the *Terminator*, the series of films starring Arnold Schwarzenegger, about killer robots intent on enslaving humanity, or like the *Jetsons*, the 1960s animated comedy about a future in which robots cater to the family's every need and the father only works one hour a day for two days a week?

Our society is already seeing signs of both possibilities: robots and drones are being used on battlefields, while elsewhere robots are being used as rescue workers, caregivers, and even as pets. Robots seem to be just as good or evil as their human creators choose, which is perhaps what worries us.

Netscape founder and Silicon Valley legend Marc Andreessen believes the future will be more *Jetsons* than *Terminator*. In a 2014 blog post, he predicts a golden age of robotics in the future:

> Housing, energy, health care, food, and transportation — they're all delivered to everyone for free by machines. Zero jobs in those fields remain. [. . .] [I]t's a consumer utopia. Everyone enjoys a standard of living that kings and popes could have only dreamed of.
>
> Since our basic needs are taken care of, all human time, labor, energy, ambition, and goals reorient to the intangibles: the big questions, the deep needs. Human nature expresses itself fully, for the first time in history. Without physical need constraints, we will be whoever we want to be.

▶

——————

What are the attitudes toward technology represented in this cel from the *Jetsons*, a cartoon that first ran in the early 1960s and then again in the early 1980s?

© United Archives GmbH/Alamy

The preeminent theoretical physicist Stephen Hawking—who suffers from ALS, a neurological disorder that has left him almost completely paralyzed and requiring a sophisticated computer-synthesized voice to speak—actually seems to be leaning a bit more toward a *Terminator*-style future. In a 2014 interview, he told the BBC:

> The primitive forms of artificial intelligence we already have, have proved very useful. But I think the development of full artificial intelligence could spell the end of the human race. [. . .] It would take off on its own, and re-design itself at an ever increasing rate. Humans, who are limited by slow biological evolution, couldn't compete, and would be superseded.

Do you agree, or do you think Hawking's prediction is a bit too pessimistic? On the other hand, what downside to a robotic future is Andreessen ignoring?

Yet another possibility may be that the future will be like the one depicted in *Robocop*, a film about a police officer who is nearly killed in the line of duty, but who is saved by being augmented with robotics, and who becomes a more effective police officer because of his implanted technology. Perhaps humanity will increasingly rely on machines until we merge with them by bits and pieces. Already the newest hearing aids are Bluetooth enabled, letting wearers stream music and answer cell phones; robotic exoskeletons allow the paralyzed to walk; and robotic prosthetics can allow amputees to play the piano. Russ Tedrake, a professor of electrical engineering and computer science at MIT, says:

> The line between robots and people will be blurred with smart prosthetics and implanted components. It won't be robots and people but robot people. [. . .] If you were in distress and given the choice for a longer, more comfortable life by simply replacing your spleen with a machine that could do the same job, wouldn't you take it?

So, the question remains: not *if* robots will play a role in our future, but what *kind* of role they will play. It is natural for humans to be uneasy about how robotics—like other emerging technologies—will affect us. Aren't robots going to be faster, smarter, and stronger than we are? What aspects of humanity will they be able to mimic effectively, or even surpass us in? In this Conversation, you will read about and consider the implications of robots in the future and not-so-distant future.

TEXTS
Isaac Asimov / Robot Dreams (fiction)
Margaret Atwood / Are Humans Necessary? (nonfiction)
Kevin Kelly / *from* Better Than Human: Why Robots Will—and Must—Take Our Jobs (nonfiction)
Richard Fisher / Is It OK to Torture or Murder a Robot? (nonfiction)
Arthur House / The Real Cyborgs (nonfiction)
Francis Fukuyama / Transhumanism (nonfiction)
James Barrat / *from* Our Final Invention: Artificial Intelligence and the End of the Human Era (nonfiction)
Rosa Brooks / In Defense of Killer Robots (nonfiction)

Robot Dreams

Isaac Asimov

The author of hundreds of books, shorts stories, and nonfiction pieces, Isaac Asimov (1920–1992) is one of the most influential science fiction writers of all time. His most famous work is the seven-book Foundation series, which tells the story of a mathematician who predicts the collapse of the Galactic Empire and sets up a foundation of the best and brightest minds in science, math, and the social sciences to rebuild it. Asimov is also well known for his focus on robots, which he has explored in a number of short stories and his five-novel Robots series, including *I, Robot* (1950), *Caves of Steel* (1953), and *Robots and Empire* (1985).

AP Photo/Mario Surian

KEY CONTEXT   In the Asimov-created universe, the robots, built by a company called U.S. Robots and Mechanical Men, Inc., have what Asimov calls a *positronic brain*. One of the crucial parts of the positronic brain is that it is always programmed with the Three Laws of Robotics, which are intended to govern robot behavior. Asimov's Three Laws of Robotics are:

1. A robot may not injure a human being or, through inaction, allow a human being to come to harm.
2. A robot must obey the orders given to it by human beings, except where such orders would conflict with the First Law.
3. A robot must protect its own existence as long as such protection does not conflict with the First or Second Law.

This story, originally published in 1986, features a recurring fictional Asimov character, Dr. Susan Calvin. As U.S. Robot's chief robopsychologist, her job is to understand robot thoughts and behavior.

L ast night I dreamed," said LVX-1, calmly. Susan Calvin said nothing, but her lined face, old with wisdom and experience, seemed to undergo a microscopic twitch.

"Did you hear that?" said Linda Rash, nervously. "It's as I told you." She was small, dark-haired, and young. Her right hand opened and closed, over and over.

Calvin nodded. She said, quietly, "Elvex, you will not move nor speak nor hear us until I say your name again."

There was no answer. The robot sat as though it were cast out of one piece of metal,

and it would stay so until it heard its name again.

5   Calvin said, "What is your computer entry code, Dr. Rash? Or enter it yourself if that will make you more comfortable. I want to inspect the positronic brain pattern."

Linda's hands fumbled, for a moment, at the keys. She broke the process and started again. The fine pattern appeared on the screen.

Calvin said, "Your permission, please, to manipulate your computer."

Permission was granted with a speechless nod. Of course! What could Linda, a new and unproven robopsychologist, do against the Living Legend?

Slowly, Susan Calvin studied the screen, moving it across and down, then up, then suddenly throwing in a key-combination so rapidly that Linda didn't see what had been done, but the pattern displayed a new portion of itself altogether and had been enlarged. Back and forth she went, her gnarled fingers tripping over the keys.

10   No change came over the old face. As though vast calculations were going through her head, she watched all the pattern shifts.

Linda wondered. It was impossible to analyze a pattern without at least a hand-held computer, yet the Old Woman simply stared. Did she have a computer implanted in her skull? Or was it her brain which, for decades, had done nothing but devise, study, and analyze the positronic brain patterns? Did she grasp such a pattern the way Mozart grasped the notation of a symphony?

Finally Calvin said, "What is it you have done, Rash?" Linda said, a little abashed, "I made use of fractal geometry."

"I gathered that. But why?"

"It had never been done. I thought it would produce a brain pattern with added complexity, possibly closer to that of the human."

15   "Was anyone consulted? Was this all on your own?"

"I did not consult. It was on my own."

Calvin's faded eyes looked long at the young woman. "You had no right. Rash your name; rash your nature. Who are you not to ask? I myself, I, Susan Calvin, would have discussed this."

"I was afraid I would be stopped."

"You certainly would have been."

20   "*Am* I," her voice caught, even as she strove to hold it firm, "going to be fired?"

"Quite possibly," said Calvin. "Or you might be promoted. It depends on what I think when I am through."

"Are you going to dismantle El—" She had almost said the name, which would have reactivated the robot and been one more mistake. She

could not afford another mistake, if it wasn't already too late to afford anything at all. "Are you going to dismantle the robot?"

She was suddenly aware, with some shock, that the Old Woman had an electron gun in the pocket of her smock. Dr. Calvin had come prepared for just that.

"We'll see," said Calvin. "The robot may prove too valuable to dismantle."

25   "But how can it dream?"

"You've made a positronic brain pattern remarkably like that of a human brain. Human brains must dream to reorganize, to get rid, periodically, of knots and snarls. Perhaps so must this robot, and for the same reason. Have you asked him what he has dreamed?"

"No, I sent for you as soon as he said he had dreamed. I would deal with this matter no further on my own, after that."

"Ah!" A very small smile passed over Calvin's face. "There are limits beyond which your folly will not carry you. I am glad of that. In fact, I am relieved. And now let us together see what we can find out."

She said, sharply, "Elvex."

30   The robot's head turned toward her smoothly. "Yes, Dr. Calvin?"

"How do you know you have dreamed?"

"It is at night, when it is dark, Dr. Calvin," said Elvex, "and there is suddenly light, although I can see no cause for the appearance of light. I see things that have no connection with what I conceive of as reality. I hear things. I react oddly. In searching my vocabulary for words to express what was happening, I came across the word 'dream.' Studying its meaning I finally came to the conclusion I was dreaming."

"How did you come to have 'dream' in your vocabulary, I wonder."

Linda said, quickly, waving the robot silent, "I gave him a human-style vocabulary. I thought—"

35   "You really thought," said Calvin. "I'm amazed."

seeing connections

In "Robot Dreams," Elvex begins taking on disturbingly human attributes, like the ability to dream. Today, things we had assumed were uniquely human—like writing poetry—can be done through algorithms. On the website BotPoet.com, the creators ask visitors to determine whether a poem is written by a human or a robot. Try for yourself.

Which poems below are written by a human and which are written by a robot? How do you know?

Poem #1

A hot and torrid bloom which
Fans wise flames and begs to be
Redeemed by forces black and strong
Will now oppose my naked will
And force me into regions of despair.

More than iron, more than lead, more than gold I
    need electricity.
I need it more than I need lamb or pork or lettuce
    or cucumber.
I need it for my dreams.

Poem #2

The spring is fresh and fearless
And every leaf is new,
The world is brimmed with moonlight,
The lilac brimmed with dew.

Here in the moving shadows
I catch my breath and sing—
My heart is fresh and fearless
And over-brimmed with spring.

Poem #3

Little Fly,
Thy summer's play
My thoughtless hand
Has brushed away.

Am not I
A fly like thee?
Or art not thou
A man like me?

For I dance
And drink, and sing,
Till some blind hand
Shall brush my wing.

Poem #4

Imagine now the dark smoke
awaken to fly
all these years
to another day
notions of tangled trees
the other side of water
I see it is already here
sequences of her face
see it is shared
and old friends
passed their dreams

Answers: (1) bot (2) human (3) human (4) bot

"I thought he would need the verb. You know, 'I never dreamed that —' Something like that."

Calvin said, "How often have you dreamed, Elvex?"

"Every night, Dr. Calvin, since I have become aware of my existence."

"Ten nights," interposed Linda, anxiously, "but Elvex only told me of it this morning."

40 "Why only this morning, Elvex?"

"It was not until this morning, Dr. Calvin, that I was convinced that I was dreaming. Till then, I had thought there was a flaw in my positronic brain pattern, but I could not find one. Finally. I decided it was a dream."

"And what do you dream?"

"I dream always very much the same dream, Dr. Calvin. Little details are different, but always it seems to me that I see a large panorama in which robots are working."

"Robots, Elvex? And human beings, also?"

45 "I see no human beings in the dream, Dr. Calvin. Not at first. Only robots."

"What are they doing, Elvex?"

"They are working, Dr. Calvin. I see some mining in the depths of the earth, and some laboring in heat and radiation. I see some in factories and some undersea."

Calvin turned to Linda. "Elvex is only ten days old, and I'm sure he has not left the testing station. How does he know of robots in such detail?"

Linda looked in the direction of a chair as though she longed to sit down, but the Old Woman was standing and that meant Linda had to stand also. She said, faintly, "It seemed to me important that he know about robotics and its place in the world. It was my thought that he would be particularly adapted to play the part of overseer with his — his new brain."

50 "His fractal brain?"

"Yes."

Calvin nodded and turned back to the robot. "You saw all this — undersea, and underground, and aboveground — and space, too, I imagine."

"I also saw robots working in space," said Elvex. "It was that I saw all this, with the details forever changing as I glanced from place to place that made me realize that what I saw was not in accord with reality and led me to the conclusion, finally, that I was dreaming."

"What else did you see, Elvex?"

55 "I saw that all the robots were bowed down with toil and affliction, that all were weary of responsibility and care, and I wished them to rest."

Calvin said, "But the robots are not bowed down, they are not weary, they need no rest."

"So it is in reality, Dr. Calvin. I speak of my dream, however. In my dream, it seemed to me that robots must protect their own existence."

Calvin said, "Are you quoting the Third Law of Robotics?"

"I am, Dr. Calvin."

60 "But you quote it in incomplete fashion. The Third Law is 'A robot must protect its own existence as long as such protection does not conflict with the First or Second Law.'"

"Yes, Dr. Calvin. That is the Third Law in reality, but in my dream, the Law ended with the word 'existence.' There was no mention of the First or Second Law."

"Yet both exist, Elvex. The Second Law, which takes precedence over the Third is 'A robot must obey the orders given it by human beings except where such orders would conflict with the First Law.' Because of this, robots obey orders. They do the work you see them do, and they do it readily and without trouble. They are not bowed down; they are not weary."

"So it is in reality, Dr. Calvin. I speak of my dream."

"And the First Law, Elvex, which is the most important of all, is 'A robot may not injure a human being, or, through inaction, allow a human being to come to harm.'"

65 "Yes, Dr. Calvin. In reality. In my dream, however, it seemed to me there was neither First nor Second Law, but only the Third, and the Third Law was 'A robot must protect its own existence.' That was the whole of the Law."

"In your dream, Elvex?"

"In my dream."

Calvin said, "Elvex, you will not move nor speak nor hear us until I say your name again." And again the robot became, to all appearances, a single inert piece of metal.

Calvin turned to Linda Rash and said, "Well, what do you think, Dr. Rash?"

70 Linda's eyes were wide, and she could feel her heart beating madly. She said, "Dr. Calvin, I am appalled. I had no idea. It would never have occurred to me that such a thing was possible."

"No," said Calvin, calmly. "Nor would it have occurred to me, not to anyone. You have created a robot brain capable of dreaming and by this device you have revealed a layer of thought in robotic brains that might have remained undetected, otherwise, until the danger became acute."

"But that's impossible," said Linda. "You can't mean that other robots think the same."

"As we would say of a human being, not consciously. But who would have thought there was an unconscious layer beneath the obvious positronic brain paths, a layer that was not necessarily under the control of the Three Laws? What might this have brought about as robotic brains grew more and more complex — had we not been warned?"

"You mean by Elvex?"

75 "By *you*, Dr. Rash. You have behaved improperly, but, by doing so, you have helped us to an overwhelmingly important understanding. We shall be working with fractal brains from now on, forming them in carefully controlled fashion. You will play your part in that. You will not be penalized for what you have done, but you will henceforth work in collaboration with others. Do you understand?"

"Yes, Dr. Calvin. But what of Elvex?"

"I'm still not certain."

Calvin removed the electron gun from her pocket and Linda stared at it with fascination. One burst of its electrons at a robotic cranium and the positronic brain paths would be neutralized and enough energy would be released to fuse the robot-brain into an inert ingot.

Linda said, "But surely Elvex is important to our research. He must not be destroyed."

80 "*Must* not, Dr. Rash? That will be *my* decision, I think. It depends entirely on how dangerous Elvex is."

She straightened up, as though determined that her own aged body was not to bow under *its* weight of responsibility. She said, "Elvex, do you hear me?"

"Yes, Dr. Calvin," said the robot.

"Did your dream continue? You said earlier that human beings did not appear at *first*. Does that mean they appeared afterward?"

"Yes, Dr. Calvin. It seemed to me, in my dream, that eventually one man appeared."

85 "One man? Not a robot?"

"Yes, Dr. Calvin. And the man said, 'Let my people go!'"

"The *man* said that?"

"Yes, Dr. Calvin."

"And when he said 'Let my people go,' then by the words 'my people' he meant the robots?"

90 "Yes, Dr. Calvin. So it was in my dream."

"And did you know who the man was — in your dream?"

"Yes, Dr. Calvin. I knew the man."

"Who was he?"

And Elvex said, "I was the man."

95 And Susan Calvin at once raised her electron gun and fired, and Elvex was no more.

Understanding and Interpreting

1 Make an analytical claim about Susan Calvin's character. What is she like, and how does this help Asimov make a point about the relationship between humans and robots?

2 Summarize Elvex's dream, and explain how Calvin and Elvex view the robots working in his dream differently.

3 How could Elvex be the "man" in his dream?

4 Why does Calvin destroy Elvex?

5 Why does Elvex need to "dream" in order to defy the Three Laws of Robotics?

6 What is Isaac Asimov suggesting about the hopes and fears we should have about our robotic future?

Analyzing Language, Style, and Structure

1 How does Asimov use diction to illustrate the differences between Calvin and Rash? How does this use of diction reveal their different attitudes toward Elvex? Why is it important to the story to draw these distinctions between these two characters?

2 The word *dream* has many different connotations. How is the word used in this story and what difficulties do those connotations cause?

3 Elvex repeats the line, "So it is in reality, Dr. Calvin. I speak of my dream." (pars. 57 and 63) What is achieved through this repetition?

4 Reread the following sentence about Calvin: "She straightened up, as though determined that her own aged body was not to bow under *its* weight of responsibility" (par. 81). What connection within the story is this description drawing, and why is that connection important?

5 In the Bible, God says to Moses, who was trying to free his people from slavery, "Go in to Pharaoh and say to him, 'Thus says the LORD, the God of the Hebrews, Let my people go, that they may serve me'" (Exodus, 9:1). How is this allusion used in this story, and how does it lead to an understanding of the theme of the story?

Connecting, Arguing, and Extending

1 At the end of the story, Calvin determines that Elvex needs to be destroyed. Write an argument in which you explain why you agree or disagree with Calvin's decision.

2 It's clear that part of Elvex's dream is about freeing robots from what he sees as slavery, but Calvin sees the robots' work as serving humanity. Make an argument to support either Elvex's or Calvin's position, especially considering advancements that are likely to be made in the field of robotics.

3 Draw, or film, the next phase of Elvex's dream. Or, write a story in which Calvin does not destroy Elvex and the robot's dream comes true.

4 Can robots or computers really be taught to behave ethically or to never hurt humans? What are the challenges roboticists face? Will something like the Three Laws of Robotics ever become a reality? Research the most recent information in the field of roboethics to support your response.

Are Humans Necessary?

Margaret Atwood

Born in 1939, Margaret Atwood is a Canadian novelist, poet, and political activist. Although she generally does not think of herself as a science fiction writer, preferring to describe her writing as "speculative fiction," Atwood sets a number of her works in the future, including the dystopian *The Handmaid's Tale*, which is probably her most famous novel. Atwood is also the inventor of the LongPen, a videoconferencing system that allows authors to sign fans' books remotely through the use of a robotic arm holding a pen.

David Livingston/Getty Images

KEY CONTEXT   In this piece, published in 2014 in the *New York Times,* Atwood responds to the European Union's decision in 2014 to commit $4 billion to robot innovation, and as she imagines what our future will be like as result, she traces how "humankind has been imagining nonbiological but sentient entities that do our bidding" for a long time.

Turning Point: European Union launches the world's largest civilian robotics program.

Welcome to The Future, one of our favorite playgrounds. We love dabbling about in it, as our numerous utopias and dystopias testify; like the Afterlife, it's up for grabs, since no one has actually been there.

What fate is in store for us in The Future? Will it be a Yikes or a Hurrah? Zombie apocalypse? No more fish? Vertical urban farming? Burnout? Genetically modified humans? Will we, using our great-big-brain cleverness, manage to solve the many problems now confronting us on this planet? Or will that very same cleverness, coupled with greed and short-term thinking, prove to be our downfall? We have plenty of latitude for our speculations, since The Future is not predetermined.

Many of our proposed futures contain robots. The present also contains robots, but The Future is said to contain a lot more of them. Is that good or bad? We haven't made up our minds. And while we're at it, how about a robotic mind that can be made up more easily than a human one?

Sci-fi writers have been exploring robots for decades, but they were far from the first to do so. Humankind has been imagining nonbiological but sentient entities that do our bidding ever since we first set stylus to papyrus.

5 Why do we dream up such things? Because, deep down, we desire them. Our species never puts much effort into things that aren't on our own wish list. If we were technologically capable mice, we'd be perfecting deadly cat harpoons, or bird-exploding rockets, or cheese-on-demand molecular assemblers that would enable Captain Kirk mice to squeak "Cheese, cheddar, sharp" to their spaceship walls and make cheese appear. But our desires lie elsewhere, though the cheese gizmo might be nice.

To understand Homo sapiens' primary wish list, go back to mythology. We endowed the gods with the abilities we wished we had ourselves: immortality and eternal youth, flight, resplendent beauty, total power, climate control, ultimate weapons, delicious banquets minus the cooking and washing up — and artificial creatures at our beck and call.

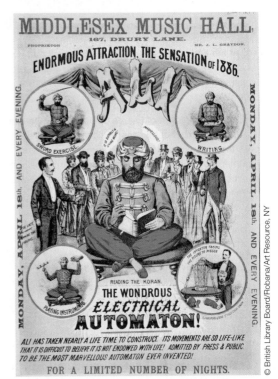

This 1887 advertisement is for Ali the Electrical Automaton. The illustrations show Ali reading the Koran, writing, playing instruments, and performing a sword exercise. Also shown is Mr. De Lacy, the inventor, operating the figure and taking it apart.

In what way is this automaton a "robot" in the popular sense of the term, and in what way is it not?

In one of the oldest known texts, a Sumerian god makes two demons enter the world of Death to rescue a life-goddess, since, not being biologically alive, they themselves cannot die. Hephaestus, the lame smith-god in the *Iliad* and other stories, fashions not only metal tables that run around by themselves, but also a group of helpful golden maidens with artificial intelligence. In addition, Hephaestus created Talos, a bronze giant, to patrol and defend the island of Crete, thus giving us the first war-against-the-robots plot, which has been serviceable ever since.

As we moved closer to the modern age, we continued to amuse ourselves with tales of proto-robots: brass heads that could talk, man-created golems fashioned out of clay, puppets who came to life, and fake women — such as Olympia and Coppélia of opera and ballet fame. Meanwhile, we were working away at the real thing: Steam-powered automatons date to ancient times; Leonardo da Vinci designed an artificial knight; and the 18th century went overboard on windup animals, birds and manikins that could perform simple actions. The Digesting Duck, introduced in 1738, went further: It appeared to eat, digest and then poop. Sadly, the poop was pre-stored; still, the Digesting Duck demonstrated the extent to which we can be delighted by watching an inanimate object do something we'd shoo it off the lawn for doing if it were real.

Once the modern age was upon us, we got serious about robots. The word "robot" was introduced in Karel Capek's 1920 play *R.U.R.* (Rossum's Universal Robots), derived from a root meaning "slave" or "servitude." In this, Capek was merely echoing Aristotle, who speculated long ago that people might be able to eliminate the miseries of slavery by creating devices that could move around by themselves, like Hephaestus' metal tables, and do the heavy lifting for us. Capek's robots, then, were devised as artificial slaves, thus doing away with the unfortunate need for real ones.

10   There's nothing that spooks us more, say those who study such things, than beings that appear to be human but aren't quite.

Or, as a story from the golden age of sci-fi comics so neatly put it: "Dogs used to be man's best friend — now robots are! Civilization needs them for many important tasks!" (Judging from the cone-shaped breasts of the woman being lectured to in the comic, I'd date this to the early 1950s.) In another story, "The Perfect Servant," Hugo the Robot — who looks a lot like the Tin Woodman from *The Wonderful Wizard of Oz*, a character whose influence on the world of robots has not been duly recognized — says, "I am proud to be a robot and proud to serve as fine a master as Professor Tompkins!" But Hugo also says, "I do not understand women."

Uh-oh. Hugo knows how to make the windows gleam, arrange the flowers and set the table perfectly, but something's missing. Who designed this guy? My guess is Professor Tompkins. Those darned mad scientists, missing a human chip or two themselves, always get something wrong.

And thereby hangs many a popular tale; for although we've pined for them and designed them, we've never felt down-to-earth regular-folks comfy with humanoid robots. There's nothing that spooks us more, say those who study such things, than beings that appear to be human but aren't quite. As long as they look like the Tin Woodman and have funnels on their heads, we can handle them; but if they look almost like us — if they look, for instance, like the "replicants" in the film *Blade Runner*; or like the plastic-faced, sexually compliant fake Stepford Wives; or like the enemy robot-folk in the "Terminator" series, human enough until their skins burn off — that's another matter.

The worry seems to be that perfected robots, instead of being proud to serve their creators, will rebel, resisting their subservient status and eliminating or enslaving us. Like the Sorcerer's Apprentice or the makers of golems, we can work wonders, but we fear that we can't control the results. The robots in *R.U.R.* ultimately triumph, and this meme has been elaborated upon in story after story, both written and filmed, in the decades since.

15   A clever variant was supplied by John Wyndham in his 1954 story "Compassion Circuit," in which empathetic robots, designed to react in a caring way to human suffering, cut off a sick woman's head and attach it to a robot body. At the time Wyndham was writing, this plot line was viewed with some horror, but today we would probably say, "Awesome idea!" We're already accustomed to the prospect of our future cyborgization, because — as Marshall McLuhan noted with respect to media — what we project changes us, what we farm also farms us, and thus what we roboticize may, in the future, roboticize us.

Maybe. Up to a point. If we let it.

Although I grew up in the golden age of sci-fi robots, I didn't see my first functional piece of robotics until the early '70s. It wasn't a whole humanoid, but a robotic arm and hand used at the Chalk River Nuclear Research Laboratory in Ontario to manipulate radioactive materials behind a radiation-proof glass shield. Many of the same principles were employed in the Canadarm space-shuttle manipulator arm of the 1980s, and many more applications for robotic arms have since been identified, including remote surgery and — my own interest — remote writing. I helped develop the LongPen in 2004 to facilitate remote book signings, but, as is the way with golems, it escaped from the intentions of its creator and is now busily engaging with the worlds of banking, business, sports and music. Who'd have thought?

These are benign uses of robotics, and there are many more examples. Manufacturing now employs robots heavily, loving their advantages: They never get tired, or need pension plans, or go on strike. This trend is causing a certain amount of angst: What will happen to the consumer base if robots replace all the human workers? Who will buy all the stuff the robots can so endlessly and cheaply churn out? Even seemingly nonthreatening uses of robots can have their hidden downsides.

But, their promoters say, think of the potential for saving lives! Nanorobots could revolutionize noninvasive surgery. And robots can already be deployed in environments that are hazardous for humans, such as bomb detonation and undersea exploration. These things are surely good.

20   We do, however, always push the envelope; it's part of our great-big-brain cleverness. Hephaestus devised some artificial helpers, but — running true to geek type — he couldn't resist making them in the form of lovely golden maidens, a whole posse of magician's girl sidekicks just for him. Pygmalion carved a girl out of ivory, then fell

▶

Scientists use the term the "Uncanny Valley" to describe the discomfort that humans reportedly feel as they encounter robots or animated characters that are nearly lifelike.

Do you think that you will feel discomfort with humanoid robots? Why or why not? What design elements do you think engineers should put in place to address the "Uncanny Valley"?

Yoshikazu Tsuno/AFP/Getty Images

in love with her. We're well on our way in that direction: *The Stepford Wives* shines like a beacon, and in the recent film *Her*, Joaquin Phoenix goes pie-eyed over the sympathetic though artificial voice of his phone's operating system.

But it's not all a one-way gender street. The writer Susan Swan has a story in which the female character creates a man robot called "Manny," complete with cooking skills and compassion circuits, who's everything a girl could wish for until her best friend steals him, using the robot's own empathy module to do it. (She needs him more! How can he resist?)

Back in our increasingly fiction-like real life, we're being promised pizza delivery by drones — a comedy special, featuring a lot of misplaced tomato sauce, is surely not far away. In the automotive department, self-driving cars are being talked up. Don't hold your breath: It's unlikely that drivers will relinquish their autonomy, and the possibilities for hacking are obvious. [. . .]

You may soon be able to avail yourself of a remote kissing device that transmits the sensation of your sweetie's kiss to your lips via haptic feedback and an apparatus that resembles a Silly Putty egg. (Just close your eyes.) [. . .]

Will remote sex on demand change human relationships? Will it change human nature? What is human nature, anyway? That's one of the questions our robots — both real and fictional — have always prompted us to think about.

25 Every technology we develop is an extension of one of our own senses or capabilities. It has always been that way. The spear and the arrow extended the arm, the telescope extended the eye, and now the Kissinger kissing device extends the mouth. Every technology we've ever made has also altered the way we live. So how different will our lives be if the future we choose is the one with all these robots in it?

More to the point, how will we power that future? Every modern robotic form that exists, and every one still to come, depends on a supply of cheap energy. If the energy disappears, so will the robots. And, to a large degree, so will we, since the lifestyle we have built and come to depend on floats on a sea of electricity. Hephaestus' bronze giant was powered by the ichor of the divine gods; we can't use that, but we need to think up another energy source that's both widely available and won't end up killing us.

If we can't do that, the number of possible futures available to us will shrink dramatically to one. It won't be the Hurrah; it will be the Yikes. This will perhaps be followed — as in a Ray Bradbury story — by a chorus of battery-powered robotic voices that continues long after our own voices have fallen silent.

Understanding and Interpreting

1 Margaret Atwood says that the reason we tell so many stories about robots is that "deep down, we desire them" (par. 5). Explain what she means by this.

2 What is in common among many of the stories of robots that Atwood includes?

3 In paragraph 9, Atwood tells the reader that the original meaning of the word *robot* is derived from the words meaning "slave" or "servitude." How is this underlying meaning revealed in our stories of robots, as summarized by Atwood?

4 Explain what Atwood means when she paraphrases what "Marshall McLuhan noted with respect to media—what we project changes us, what we farm also farms us, and thus what we roboticize may, in the future, roboticize us" (par. 15).

5 In several places in this piece, especially paragraphs 20 and 21, Atwood makes reference to gender relations and robots. What, if any, difference does she note between the ways that men and women view robots?

6 In some ways, this article is a series of seemingly random musings on robots. What is one unifying idea that Atwood presents about humans and robots in this piece?

Analyzing Language, Style, and Structure

1 Reread paragraphs 1–3 and analyze how Atwood's language choices reflect her tone toward the future.

2 In paragraph 17, Atwood mentions her own personal experiences with robots. What is the purpose of this section and how does it help to illustrate her ideas about robots?

3 Read the final two paragraphs of this article. What is Atwood's tone toward the future here? How is it similar to or different from the tone at the beginning of the piece?

4 There are several places where Atwood attempts to lighten the mood of the piece through humor. Identify one section where Atwood pokes fun at humans' interest in robots, and explain how she creates the humor.

5 One claim Atwood makes in this piece is "We do, however, always push the envelope" (par. 20). What evidence does she include to support this claim?

Connecting, Arguing, and Extending

1 In paragraph 18, Atwood describes the effect that robots might have on manufacturing and consumerism. Write an argument that makes and supports a claim about the likely economic effect robots will have in the future.

2 Do you think the robotic future will be "Hurrah" or "Yikes" or something else? Why?

3 Think about a film or story you know that contains robots. How does the representation of robots in that text compare to what Atwood describes in this piece? How do the robots in that text reflect some aspect of humanity?

from Better Than Human: Why Robots Will— and Must—Take Our Jobs

Kevin Kelly

© Evan Hurd/Corbis

Kevin Kelly (b. 1952) is a writer, photographer, and founding executive editor of *Wired* magazine, from which this article is taken. He writes extensively about the role of technology in our lives; his nonfiction books include *Out of Control: The New Biology of Machines, Social Systems, and the Economic World* (1994) and *What Technology Wants* (2012). In an interview with artist Olafur Eliasson, Kelly said that "it wouldn't surprise [him] if in a thousand years people start talking about robot rights and having empathy for things that we've built, and that we can't unplug them." In this *Wired* article, Kelly explores the current state of automation and the likely effects that expanded robotics will have on the future.

KEY CONTEXT   The Industrial Revolution, which Kelly discusses in this article, was the time period in Western Europe and the United States from the mid-1700s to the mid-1800s when manufacturing shifted from manual labor and the use of animals, to the use of machinery. The Industrial Revolution marks a significant turning point in human history because of its widespread effects on labor, standards of living, and population migration to cities.

Imagine that 7 out of 10 working Americans got fired tomorrow. What would they all do?

It's hard to believe you'd have an economy at all if you gave pink slips to more than half the labor force. But that — in slow motion — is what the industrial revolution did to the workforce of the early 19th century. Two hundred years ago, 70 percent of American workers lived on the farm. Today automation has eliminated all but 1 percent of their jobs, replacing them (and their work animals) with machines. But the displaced workers did not sit idle. Instead, automation created hundreds of millions of jobs in entirely

new fields. Those who once farmed were now manning the legions of factories that churned out farm equipment, cars, and other industrial products. Since then, wave upon wave of new occupations have arrived — appliance repairman, offset printer, food chemist, photographer, web designer — each building on previous automation. Today, the vast majority of us are doing jobs that no farmer from the 1800s could have imagined.

It may be hard to believe, but before the end of this century, 70 percent of today's occupations will likewise be replaced by automation. Yes, dear reader, even you will have your job taken

OCCUPATIONS IN DECLINE

Between 2000 and 2013, technological advances nearly obliterated some once-popular jobs.

OCCUPATION	PERCENT DECLINE	JOBS LOST	MEDIAN WAGE 2012
Word processors, typists	−74	287,000	$35,270
Telephone operators	−71	72,000	$32,850
Computer operators	−70	218,000	$38,390
Proofreaders, copy markers	−67	14,000	$32,780
Switchboard operators	−60	49,000	$25,370
Telemarketers	−58	129,000	$22,330
Travel agents	−46	65,000	$34,600
Bookkeeping, accounting, audits	−29	501,000	$35,170
Carpenters	−22	336,000	$39,940

Source: Bureau of Labor Statistics

GROWING PROFESSIONS

Meanwhile, more jobs were created during the same period in many skilled categories.

OCCUPATION	PERCENT INCREASE	JOBS ADDED	MEDIAN WAGE 2012
Computer/systems managers	+164	374,000	$120,950
Physical therapists	+57	81,000	$79,860
Computer software engineers	+49	364,000	$99,000
Financial advisors, analysts	+42	144,000	$72,235
Registered nurses	+32	700,000	$65,470
Financial managers	+28	270,000	$109,740
Physicians, surgeons	+27	196,000	$187,200+
Lawyers	+25	215,000	$113,530
Accountants, auditors	+16	255,000	$63,550

What are two conclusions that you can draw from the information in these charts?
What effect, if any, does this information have on your own career aspirations?

away by machines. In other words, robot replacement is just a matter of time. This upheaval is being led by a second wave of automation, one that is centered on artificial cognition, cheap sensors, machine learning, and distributed smarts. This deep automation will touch all jobs, from manual labor to knowledge work.

First, machines will consolidate their gains in already-automated industries.

After robots finish replacing assembly line workers, they will replace the workers in warehouses. Speedy bots able to lift 150 pounds all day long will retrieve boxes, sort them, and load them onto trucks. Fruit and vegetable picking will continue to be robotized until no humans pick outside of specialty farms. Pharmacies will feature a single pill-dispensing robot in the back while the pharmacists focus on patient consulting. Next, the more dexterous chores of cleaning in offices and schools will be taken over by late-night robots, starting with easy-to-do floors and windows and eventually getting to toilets. The highway legs of long-haul trucking routes will be driven by robots embedded in truck cabs.

5   All the while, robots will continue their migration into white-collar work. We already have artificial intelligence in many of our machines; we just don't call it that. Witness one piece of software by Narrative Science that can write newspaper stories about sports games directly from the games' stats or generate a synopsis of a company's stock performance each day from bits of text around the web. Any job dealing with reams of paperwork will be taken over by bots, including much of medicine. Even those areas of medicine not defined by paperwork, such as surgery, are becoming increasingly robotic. The rote tasks of any information-intensive job can be automated. It doesn't

matter if you are a doctor, lawyer, architect, reporter, or even programmer: The robot takeover will be epic.

And it has already begun. [. . .]

To understand how robot replacement will happen, it's useful to break down our relationship with robots into four categories, as summed up in this chart:

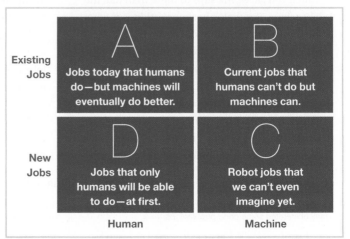

	Human	Machine
Existing Jobs	**A** Jobs today that humans do—but machines will eventually do better.	**B** Current jobs that humans can't do but machines can.
New Jobs	**D** Jobs that only humans will be able to do—at first.	**C** Robot jobs that we can't even imagine yet.

The rows indicate whether robots will take over existing jobs or make new ones, and the columns indicate whether these jobs seem (at first) like jobs for humans or for machines.

Let's begin with quadrant A: jobs humans can do but robots can do even better. Humans can weave cotton cloth with great effort, but automated looms make perfect cloth, by the mile, for a few cents. The only reason to buy handmade cloth today is because you want the imperfections humans introduce. We no longer value irregularities while traveling 70 miles per hour, though — so the fewer humans who touch our car as it is being made, the better.

And yet for more complicated chores, we still tend to believe computers and robots can't be trusted. That's why we've been slow to acknowledge how they've mastered some conceptual routines, in some cases even surpassing their mastery of physical routines.

A computerized brain known as the autopilot can fly a 787 jet unaided, but irrationally we place human pilots in the cockpit to babysit the autopilot "just in case." In the 1990s, computerized mortgage appraisals replaced human appraisers wholesale. Much tax preparation has gone to computers, as well as routine x-ray analysis and pretrial evidence-gathering — all once done by highly paid smart people. We've accepted utter reliability in robot manufacturing; soon we'll accept it in robotic intelligence and service.

10   Next is quadrant B: jobs that humans can't do but robots can. A trivial example: Humans have trouble making a single brass screw unassisted, but automation can produce a thousand exact ones per hour. Without automation, we could not make a single computer chip — a job that requires degrees of precision, control, and unwavering attention that our animal bodies don't possess. Likewise no human, indeed no group of humans, no matter their education, can quickly search through all the web pages in the world to uncover the one page revealing the price of eggs in Katmandu yesterday. Every time you click on the search button you are employing a robot to do something we as a species are unable to do alone.

While the displacement of formerly human jobs gets all the headlines, the greatest benefits bestowed by robots and automation come from their occupation of jobs we are unable to do. We don't have the attention span to inspect every square millimeter of every CAT scan looking for cancer cells. We don't have the millisecond reflexes needed to inflate molten glass into the shape of a bottle. We don't have an infallible memory to keep track of every pitch in Major League Baseball and calculate the probability of the next pitch in real time.

We aren't giving "good jobs" to robots. Most of the time we are giving them jobs we could never do. Without them, these jobs would remain undone.

Now let's consider quadrant C, the new jobs created by automation — including the jobs that we did not know we wanted done. This is the greatest genius of the robot takeover: With the assistance of robots and computerized intelligence, we already can do things we never imagined doing 150 years ago. We can remove a tumor in our gut through our navel, make a talking-picture video of our wedding, drive a cart on Mars, print a pattern on fabric that a friend mailed to us through the air. We are doing, and are sometimes paid for doing, a million new activities that would have dazzled and shocked the farmers of 1850. These new accomplishments are not merely chores that were difficult before. Rather they are dreams that are created chiefly by the capabilities of the machines that can do them. They are jobs the machines make up.

Before we invented automobiles, air-conditioning, flatscreen video displays, and animated cartoons, no one living in ancient Rome wished they could watch cartoons while riding to Athens in climate-controlled comfort. Two hundred years ago not a single citizen of Shanghai would have told you that they would buy a tiny slab that allowed them to talk to faraway friends before they would buy indoor plumbing. Crafty AIs embedded in first-person-shooter games have given millions of teenage boys the urge, the need, to become professional game designers — a dream that no boy in Victorian times ever had. In a very real way our inventions assign us our jobs. Each successful bit of automation generates new occupations — occupations we would not have fantasized about without the prompting of the automation.

15   To reiterate, the bulk of new tasks created by automation are tasks only other automation can handle. Now that we have search engines like Google, we set the servant upon a thousand new errands. Google, can you tell me where my phone is? Google, can you match the

people suffering depression with the doctors selling pills? Google, can you predict when the next viral epidemic will erupt? Technology is indiscriminate this way, piling up possibilities and options for both humans and machines.

It is a safe bet that the highest-earning professions in the year 2050 will depend on automations and machines that have not been invented yet. That is, we can't see these jobs from here, because we can't yet see the machines and technologies that will make them possible. Robots create jobs that we did not even know we wanted done.

Finally, that leaves us with quadrant D, the jobs that only humans can do — at first. The one thing humans can do that robots can't (at least for a long while) is to decide what it is that humans want to do. This is not a trivial trick; our desires are inspired by our previous inventions, making this a circular question.

When robots and automation do our most basic work, making it relatively easy for us to be fed, clothed, and sheltered, then we are free to ask, "What are humans for?" Industrialization did more than just extend the average human lifespan. It led a greater percentage of the population to decide that humans were meant to be ballerinas, full-time musicians, mathematicians, athletes, fashion designers, yoga masters, fan-fiction authors, and folks with one-of-a kind titles on their business cards. With the help of our machines, we could take up these roles; but of course, over time, the machines will do these as well. We'll then be empowered to dream up yet more answers to the question "What should we do?" It will be many generations before a robot can answer that.

This postindustrial economy will keep expanding, even though most of the work is done by bots, because part of your task tomorrow will be to find, make, and complete new things to do, new things that will later become repetitive jobs for the robots. In the coming years robot-driven cars and trucks will become ubiquitous; this automation will spawn the new human occupation of trip optimizer, a person who tweaks the traffic system for optimal energy and time usage. Routine robo-surgery will necessitate the new skills of keeping machines sterile. When automatic self-tracking of all your activities becomes the normal thing to do, a new breed of professional analysts will arise to help

Robots work on the undercarriage of Jeep Cherokee vehicles on the production line at the Chrysler Toledo Assembly Plant in Toledo, Ohio.

Imagine that this image is used in two different publications. The first is the newsletter of the United Auto Workers union, and the second is the shareholders' profit statement for Chrysler. How could this same image be used to support two different conclusions about automation in the workplace?

Ty Wright/Bloomberg via Getty Images

you make sense of the data. And of course we will need a whole army of robot nannies, dedicated to keeping your personal bots up and running. Each of these new vocations will in turn be taken over by robots later.

20 The real revolution erupts when everyone has personal workbots, the descendants of Baxter,[1] at their beck and call. Imagine you run a small organic farm. Your fleet of worker bots do all the weeding, pest control, and harvesting of produce, as directed by an overseer bot, embodied by a mesh of probes in the soil. One day your task might be to research which variety of heirloom tomato to plant; the next day it might be to update your custom labels. The bots perform everything else that can be measured.

Right now it seems unthinkable: We can't imagine a bot that can assemble a stack of ingredients into a gift or manufacture spare parts for our lawn mower or fabricate materials for our new kitchen. We can't imagine our nephews and nieces running a dozen workbots in their garage, churning out inverters for their friend's electric-vehicle startup. We can't imagine our children becoming appliance designers, making custom batches of liquid-nitrogen dessert machines to sell to the millionaires in China. But that's what personal robot automation will enable.

Everyone will have access to a personal robot, but simply owning one will not guarantee success. Rather, success will go to those who innovate in the organization, optimization, and customization of the process of getting work done with bots and machines. Geographical clusters of production will matter, not for any differential in labor costs but because of the differential in human expertise. It's human-robot symbiosis. Our human assignment will be to keep making jobs for robots — and that is a task that will never be finished. So we will always have at least that one "job."

In the coming years our relationships with robots will become ever more complex. But already a recurring pattern is emerging. No matter what your current job or your salary, you will progress through these Seven Stages of Robot Replacement, again and again:

1. A robot/computer cannot possibly do the tasks I do. [Later:]
2. OK, it can do a lot of them, but it can't do everything I do. [Later:]
3. OK, it can do everything I do, except it needs me when it breaks down, which is often. [Later:]
4. OK, it operates flawlessly on routine stuff, but I need to train it for new tasks. [Later:]
5. OK, it can have my old boring job, because it's obvious that was not a job that humans were meant to do. [Later:]
6. Wow, now that robots are doing my old job, my new job is much more fun and pays more! [Later:]
7. I am so glad a robot/computer cannot possibly do what I do now.

This is not a race against the machines. If we race against them, we lose. This is a race with the machines. You'll be paid in the future based on how well you work with robots. Ninety percent of your coworkers will be unseen machines. Most of what you do will not be possible without them. And there will be a blurry line between what you do and what they do. You might no longer think of it as a job, at least at first, because anything that seems like drudgery will be done by robots. We need to let robots take over. They will do jobs we have been doing, and do them much better than we can. They will do jobs we can't do at all. They will do jobs we never imagined even needed to be done. And they will help us discover new jobs for ourselves, new tasks that expand who we are. They will let us focus on becoming more human than we were. Let the robots take the jobs, and let them help us dream up new work that matters.

---

[1] Baxter: A prototype "workerbot" from the inventor of the Roomba that is affordable and easily programmed to do repetitive tasks. —Eds.

Understanding and Interpreting

1 We tend to think of automation of jobs in terms of jobs that are lost. Reread the second paragraph, where Kelly discusses the Industrial Revolution and American farming. What does this paragraph suggest about what happens during periods of increased automation?

2 A good portion of the article is spent discussing the chart on page 912. Paraphrase each of the four quadrants, explain the differences between each quadrant, and provide a new example of a job that would fall into each quadrant.

3 According to Kelly, what are humans for?

4 Beginning with paragraph 19, Kelly describes the process of job creation and job replacement. Summarize this process and provide a new example of a job that might demonstrate this process.

5 What does Kelly mean in the last paragraph when he says that "[t]his is not a race against the machines," but "a race with the machines"?

Analyzing Language, Style, and Structure

1 What is the intended effect of Kelly's direct address in paragraph 2, when he says, "Yes, dear reader"?

2 In paragraphs 4 and 5, Kelly includes the lists of professions that are in the process of being taken over, or are likely to be taken over, by robots in the near future. What does he accomplish in his argument by putting these lists so early in the article?

3 Skim back through the article looking for appeals to pathos and logos. What are the most effective and relevant appeals that Kelly uses to support his claims?

4 Is Kelly's tone toward our robotic future optimistic or pessimistic, and which word choices reveal this tone?

5 Near the end of the piece, Kelly employs humor in his Seven Stages of Robot Replacement. How does he create this humor and how does it assist his argument?

Connecting, Arguing, and Extending

1 In paragraph 18, Kelly asks, "What are humans for?" How would you respond? How does this compare to how Kelly answers the question?

2 What is a job that you can imagine yourself doing in the future? According to Kelly, what quadrant would your job be in? What effect might automation have on your job?

3 Choose an industry that has faced a lot of automation in recent years, such as the auto industry, and research the effect that automation has had on the jobs in that industry. What is the level of employment that industry will likely have in the future?

4 Kelly concludes that robotic automation will let us "dream up new work that matters" (par. 24). Explain why you agree or disagree with Kelly's claim about our robotic future.

Is It OK to Torture or Murder a Robot?

Richard Fisher

Richard Fisher is a journalist and editor, and currently is the Editor of BBC Future (www.bbc.com/future), a website supported by the British Broadcasting Corporation that focuses on technology and science topics. In this piece, published on BBC Future in 2013, Fisher explores our emotional attachment to robots, and what it might suggest about the ways we will integrate robots into our future.

Courtesy Richard Fisher

Kate Darling likes to ask you to do terrible things to cute robots. At a workshop she organised this year, Darling asked people to play with a Pleo robot, a child's toy dinosaur. The soft green Pleo has trusting eyes and affectionate movements. When you take one out of the box, it acts like a helpless newborn puppy — it can't walk and you have to teach it about the world.

Yet after an hour allowing people to tickle and cuddle these loveable dinosaurs, Darling turned executioner. She gave the participants knives, hatchets and other weapons, and ordered them to torture and dismember their toys. What happened next "was much more dramatic than we ever anticipated," she says.

For Darling, a researcher at Massachusetts Institute of Technology, our reaction to robot cruelty is important because a new wave of machines is forcing us to reconsider our relationship with them. When Darling described her Pleo experiment in a talk in Boston this month, she made the case that mistreating certain kinds of robots could soon become unacceptable in the eyes of society. She even believes that we may need a set of "robot rights." If so, in what circumstance would it be OK to torture or murder a robot? And what would it take to make you think twice before being cruel to a machine?

Until recently, the idea of robot rights had been left to the realms of science fiction. Perhaps that's because the real machines surrounding us have been relatively unsophisticated. Nobody feels bad about chucking away a toaster or a remote-control toy car. Yet the arrival of social robots changes that. They display autonomous behaviour, show intent and embody familiar forms like pets or humanoids, says Darling. In other words, they act as if they are alive. It triggers our emotions, and often we can't help it.

5   For example, in a small experiment conducted for the radio show *Radiolab* in 2011, Freedom Baird of MIT asked children to hold upside down a Barbie doll, a hamster and a Furby robot for as long as they felt comfortable. While the children held the doll upside down until their arms got tired, they soon stopped torturing the wriggling hamster, and after a little while, the Furby too. They were old enough to know the Furby was a toy, but couldn't stand the way it was programmed to cry and say "Me scared."

It's not just kids that form surprising bonds with these bundles of wires and circuits. Some people give names to their Roomba vacuum cleaners, says Darling. And soldiers honour their robots with "medals" or hold funerals for them. She cites one particularly striking example of a military robot that was designed to defuse landmines by stepping on them. In a test, the explosions ripped off most of the robot's legs, and yet the crippled machine continued to limp along.

Sean Gallup/Getty Images

▲

A customer cuddles with Pleo the robot.

What makes this robot upsetting to harm? Would the experiment Fisher describes be different with a different kind of robot?

Watching the robot struggle, the colonel in charge called off the test because it was "in-humane," according to the *Washington Post*.

Killer Instinct

Some researchers are converging on the idea that if a robot looks like it is alive, with its own mind, the tiniest of simulated cues forces us to feel empathy with machines, even though we know they are artificial.

Earlier this year, researchers from the University of Duisburg-Essen in Germany used an fMRI scanner and devices that measure skin conductance to track people's reactions to a video of somebody torturing a Pleo dinosaur — choking it, putting it inside a plastic bag or striking it. The physiological and emotional responses they

measured were much stronger than expected, despite being aware they were watching a robot.

Darling discovered the same when she asked people to torture the Pleo dinosaur at the Lift conference in Geneva in February. The workshop took a more uncomfortable turn than expected.

10   After an hour of play, the people refused to hurt their Pleo with the weapons they had been given. So then Darling started playing mind games, telling them they could save their own dinosaur by killing somebody else's. Even then, they wouldn't do it.

Finally, she told the group that unless one person stepped forward and killed just one Pleo, all the robots would be slaughtered. After much hand-wringing, one reluctant man stepped forward with his hatchet, and delivered a blow to a toy.

After this brutal act, the room fell silent for a few seconds, Darling recalls. The strength of people's emotional reaction seemed to have surprised them.

Given the possibility of such strong emotional reactions, a few years ago roboticists in Europe argued that we need a new set of ethical rules for building robots. The idea was to adapt author Isaac Asimov's famous "laws of robotics" for the modern age. One of their five rules was that robots "should not be designed in a deceptive way . . . their machine nature must be transparent." In other words, there needs to be a way to break the illusion of emotion and intent, and see a robot for what it is: wires, actuators and software.

Darling, however, believes that we could go further than a few ethical guidelines. We may need to protect "robot rights" in our legal systems, she says.

15   If this sounds sound absurd, Darling points out that there are precedents from animal cruelty laws. Why exactly do we have legal protection for animals? Is it simply because they can suffer? If that's true, then Darling questions why we have strong laws to protect some animals, but not others. Many people are happy to eat animals kept in awful conditions on industrial farms or to

seeing connections

The following is from a press release put out by the University of Melbourne describing the research of animal behavior scientist Jean-Loup Rault, titled "Robot Pets to Rise in an Over-populated, Tech-Crazed World."

> Robotic dogs are likely to replace the real thing in households worldwide in as little as a decade, as our infatuation with technology grows and more people migrate to high-density city living. [. . .]
>
> "Robots can, without a doubt, trigger human emotions," Dr. Rault added. "If artificial pets can produce the same benefits we get from live pets, does that mean that our emotional bond with animals is really just an image that we project on to our pets?"

Toshifumi Kitamura/AFP/Getty Images

Write an argument for or against robo-pets. What are the benefits and disadvantages of their widespread use?

---

crush an insect under their foot, yet would be aghast at mistreatment of their next-door neighbour's cat, or seeing a whale harvested for meat.

The reason, says Darling, could be that we create laws when we recognise their suffering as similar to our own. Perhaps the main reason we created many of these laws is because we don't like to see the act of cruelty. It's less about the animal's experience and more about our own emotional pain. So, even though robots are machines, Darling argues that there may be a point beyond which the *performance* of cruelty — rather than its consequences — is too uncomfortable to tolerate.

Feel Your Pain

Indeed, harm to a victim is not always the only reason we decide to regulate a technology. Consider an altogether different kind of gadget: a

few weeks ago the British Medical Association argued that smoking e-cigarettes should be banned in public indoor spaces in the UK. It doesn't matter that the smoker or those nearby face no health risks, the BMA argued. It normalises real smoking in public places once again.

To take another example: if a father is torturing a robot in front of his 4-year-old son, would that be acceptable? The child can't be expected to have the sophisticated understanding of adults. Torturing a robot teaches them that acts that cause suffering — simulated or not — are OK in some circumstances.

Somewhere down the line there's also the possibility of a nasty twist: that machines really could experience suffering — just not like our own. Already some researchers have begun making robots "feel" pain to navigate the world. Some are concerned that when machines eventually acquire a basic sense of their own existence, the consequences will not be pleasant. For this reason, the philosopher Thomas Metzinger argues that we should stop trying to create intelligent robots at all. The first conscious machines, says Metzinger, will be like confused, disabled infants — certainly not the sophisticated, malign AI of science fiction — and so treating them like typical machines would be cruel. If robots have a basic consciousness, then it doesn't matter if it is simulated, he says. It believes it is alive, it can experience suffering. Metzinger puts it like this: "We should refrain

from doing anything to increase the overall amount of suffering in the universe."

20   What's clear is that there is a spectrum of "aliveness" in robots, from basic simulations of cute animal behaviour, to future robots that acquire a sense of suffering. But as Darling's Pleo dinosaur experiment suggested, it doesn't take much to trigger an emotional response in us. The question is whether we can — or should — define the line beyond which cruelty to these machines is unacceptable. Where does the line lie for you? If a robot cries out in pain, or begs for mercy? If it believes it is hurting? If it bleeds?

Understanding and Interpreting

1 After reading this article, how do you think the author, Richard Fisher, would answer the question posed in the title? What evidence do you have to support your response?

2 In paragraph 4, Fisher identifies a specific class of robots as "social robots." According to the article, what are the distinctions between this class of robots and others?

3 Fisher identifies one of the proposed ethical rules for building robots, "robots 'should not be designed in a deceptive way . . . their machine nature must be transparent'" (par. 13). What evidence in this article supports the need for this guideline?

4 Fisher includes a quote from philosopher Thomas Metzinger (par. 19). Why does Metzinger recommend that humans avoid building intelligent robots?

Analyzing Language, Style, and Structure

1 Notice how Fisher starts with the story of the Pleo robot, moves away from it, and then returns to finish that story about halfway through the piece. What is a likely effect of that structural choice, and how effective is it in building his argument?

2 Look back at the opening paragraph. What words and phrases does Fisher use to describe the Pleo robot, and what is the effect of these word choices?

3 In paragraph 6, Fisher includes a quote from a U.S. military officer who called a test that was destroying a landmine-seeking robot "inhumane." What is the importance of this word choice to Fisher's argument?

4 To support his argument about the emotional connection humans have with robots, Fisher includes the results of a number of research studies. Look back at one that you think best supports his

claim, and explain why. Then, identify one research study that you think is less effective in supporting Fisher's claim, and explain why.

5 In paragraph 15, Fisher includes an analogy that the researcher Kate Darling makes in comparing robot rights to the rules that prevent animal cruelty. To what extent is this analogy relevant to the argument about robots, and how is it effective (or ineffective)?

6 While there are a number of places where Fisher makes appeals to logos, the strength of his argument really rests on pathos. Locate two or three of the strongest examples of pathos and explain how Fisher uses them and for what effect.

7 Fisher chooses to end with a series of rhetorical questions. What does he accomplish by ending the piece in this manner?

Connecting, Arguing, and Extending

1 The author cites Kate Darling, who suggests that we may need a set of "robot rights" (par. 3). Write an argument in which you propose one right that we ought to be prepared to offer to robots. Along with rights come responsibilities, so you might include in your argument a responsibility that robots will need to follow as a result of their newfound right.

2 Write about a time that you have entered into an emotional attachment with an inanimate object, such as a stuffed animal when you were young, a favorite hat, or a lucky pencil. What aspects of that object led to your emotional connection, and how

similar is your experience to what the researchers quoted in this article explain?

3 Conduct research in order to determine the likely number of years from now we can expect to have the intelligent, social robots that Fisher describes here. What are the technological leaps that have already been made and what still needs to be accomplished?

4 Answer the main question that Fisher ends his piece with: "whether we can—or should—define the line beyond which cruelty to these machines is unacceptable." Answer Fisher's more specific question as well: "Where does the line lie for you?"

The Real Cyborgs

Arthur House

Arthur House is features editor of the *Calvert Journal* and founding editor of the online quarterly *The Junket*. He was previously a journalist at the *Telegraph*, a British newspaper in which this article originally appeared in 2014.

Ian Burkhart concentrated hard. A thick cable protruded from the crown of his shaven head. A sleeve sprouting wires enveloped his right arm. The 23-year-old had been paralysed from the neck down since a diving accident four years ago. But, in June this year, in a crowded room in the Wexner Medical Centre at Ohio State University, Burkhart's hand spasmed into life.

At first it opened slowly and shakily, as though uncertain who its owner was. But when Burkhart engaged his wrist muscles, its upward movement was sudden and decisive. You could hear the joints — unused for years — cracking. The scientists and medical staff gathered in the room burst into applause.

The technology that made this possible, Neurobridge, had successfully reconnected Burkhart's brain with his body. It was probably the most advanced intertwining of man and machine that had so far been achieved.

But such milestones are coming thick and fast. Quietly, almost without anyone really noticing, we have entered the age of the cyborg, or cybernetic organism: a living thing both natural and artificial. Artificial retinas and cochlear implants (which connect directly to the brain through the auditory nerve system) restore sight to the blind and hearing to the deaf. Deep-brain implants, known as "brain pacemakers," alleviate the symptoms of 30,000 Parkinson's sufferers worldwide. The Wellcome Trust is now trialling a silicon chip that sits directly on the brains of Alzheimer's patients, stimulating them and warning of dangerous episodes.

5   A growing cadre of innovators is taking things further, using replacement organs, robotic prosthetics and implants not to restore bodily functions but to alter or enhance them. When he lost his right eye in a shotgun accident in 2005, the Canadian filmmaker Rob Spence replaced it with a wireless video camera that transmits what he's seeing in real time to his computer. Last year, the electronic engineer Brian McEvoy, who is based in Minnesota, made himself a kind of internal satnav[1] by fitting himself with a subdermal compass.

Fairfax Media via Getty Images

Canadian filmmaker Rob Spence lost his eye in a shooting accident. He has had his prosthetic eye fitted with a camera and is now producing a documentary called the *Eyeborg Project*.

In what ways is Spence's use of technology similar to and different from that of Ian Burkhart (described at the beginning of this article)?

---

[1] satnav: Satellite navigation system. —Eds.

"This is the frontline of the Human Enhancement Revolution," wrote the technology author and philosopher Patrick Lin last year. "We now know enough about biology, neuroscience, computing, robotics, and materials to hack the human body."

The US military is pouring millions of dollars into projects such as Ekso Bionics' Human Universal Load Carrier (HULC), an "Iron Man"-style wearable exoskeleton that gives soldiers superhuman strength. Its Defense Advanced Research Projects Agency (DARPA) is also working on thought-controlled killer robots, "thought helmets" to enable telepathic communication and brain-computer interfaces (BCIs) to give soldiers extra senses, such as night vision and the ability to "see" magnetic fields caused by landmines.

Ever since the earliest humans made stone tools, we have tried to extend our powers. The bicycle, the telescope and the gun all arose from this same impulse. Today, we carry smartphones — supercomputers, really — in our pockets, giving us infinite information and unlimited communication at our fingertips. Our relationship with technology is becoming increasingly intimate, as wearable devices such as Google Glass, Samsung Gear Fit (a smartwatch-cum-fitness tracker) and the Apple Watch show. And wearable is already becoming implantable.

In America, a dedicated amateur community — the "biohackers" or "grinders" — has been experimenting with implantable technology for several years. Amal Graafstra, a 38-year-old programmer and self-styled "adventure technologist," has been inserting various types of radio-frequency identification (RFID) chips into the soft flesh between his thumbs and index fingers since 2005. The chips can be read by scanners that Graafstra has installed on the doors of his house, and also on his laptop, which gives him access with a swipe of his hand without the need for keys or passwords. He sells it to a growing crowd of "geeky,

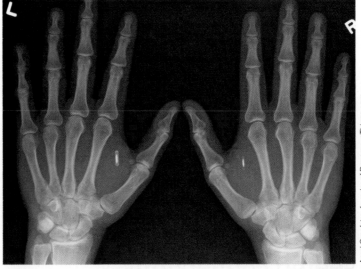

▶

Here is an X-ray showing the chips implanted in Amal Graafstra's hands.

What are some uses right now for this technology, and what future uses can you imagine?

Amal Graafstra, founder of DangerousThings.com

hacker-type software developers," he tells me, direct from his website, Dangerous Things, having used crowdfunding to pay for the manufacturing (he raised almost five times his target amount).

10   Graafstra, a hyper-articulate teddy bear of a man, is unimpressed by wearable devices. "A wearable device is just one more thing to manage during the day. I don't think people will want to deck themselves out with all that in the future," he says, dismissing Samsung Gear Fit as "large, cumbersome and not exactly fashionable." Instead, he envisages an implant that would monitor general health and scan for medical conditions, sending the information to the user's smartphone or directly to a doctor. This would be always there, always on, and never in the way — and it could potentially save a lot of doctors' time and money as fewer checkups would be necessary and health conditions could be recognised before they became serious.

Graafstra defines biohackers as "DIY cyborgs who are upgrading their bodies with hardware without waiting for corporate development cycles or authorities to say it's OK." But, he concedes, "Samsung and Apple aren't

blind to what we're doing. Somewhere in the bowels of these companies are people thinking about implantables." He mentions Motorola's experiments with the "password pill," which sends signals to devices from the stomach. (The same company has filed a patent for an "electronic throat tattoo" which fixes a minuscule microphone on the skin so users can communicate with their devices via voice commands.)

As robotics and brain-computer interfaces continue to improve and, with them, the likelihood that advanced cybernetic enhancement becomes widely available, several worrying questions emerge. Will those with the resources to access enhancements become a cyborg super-class that is healthier, smarter and more employable than the unenhanced? Will the unenhanced feel pressured into joining their ranks or face falling behind? And who will regulate these enhancements? In the wrong hands, cyborg technology could quickly become the stuff of dystopian science fiction. It's all too easy to imagine totalitarian regimes (or unscrupulous health insurers) scraping information from our new, connected body parts and using it for their own gain.

. . .

Kevin Warwick can justifiably claim to be the world's first cyborg. In the 1990s, Reading University's visiting professor of cybernetics started implanting RFID chips into himself. In 2002, he underwent pioneering surgery to have an array of electrodes attached to the nerve fibres in his arm. This was the first time a human nervous system had been connected to a computer. Warwick's "neural interface" allowed him to move a robotic hand by moving his own and to control a customised wheelchair with his thoughts. It also enabled him to experience electronic stimuli coming the other way. In one experiment he was able to sense ultrasound, which is beyond normal human capability. "I was born human," Warwick has said, "but I believe it's something we have the power to change."

Cheerleaders for a cyborg future, like Prof. Warwick, call themselves "transhumanists." Transhumanism aims to alter the human condition for the better by using technology (as well as genetic engineering, life extension science and synthetic biology) to make us more intelligent, healthier and live longer than has ever been possible — eventually transforming humanity so much it becomes "post-human."

seeing connections

In science fiction films like *Terminator* and *Blade Runner*, technology has increased so much that it is nearly impossible to distinguish between human and robot. In the real world, scientists and robotics engineers have been working to build computers to pass what is called "The Turing Test," which evaluates how realistic computer responses are to a series of questions posed by a human interrogator.

Facebook has been developing a version of the Turing Test to distinguish between robots and humans on its site. The computers are given twenty questions, five of which we have included here. Take the test to see if you are more human than a computer:

1. **John is in the playground. Bob is in the office.**
   Where is John?

2. **John is in the playground. Bob is in the office. John picked up the football. Bob went to the kitchen.**
   Where is the football?
   Where was Bob before the kitchen?

3. **John picked up the apple. John went to the office. John went to the kitchen. John dropped the apple.**
   Where was the apple before the kitchen?

4. **The office is north of the bedroom. The bedroom is north of the bathroom.**
   What is north of the bedroom?
   What is the bedroom north of?

5. **Mary gave the cake to Fred. Fred gave the cake to Bill. Jeff was given the milk by Bill.**
   Who gave the cake to Fred?
   Who did Fred give the cake to?
   What did Jeff receive?
   Who gave the milk?

None of the AI systems tested achieved 100 percent correct answers, although two averaged 93 percent, showing that machines can't quite replicate the way humans process and understand language, but they are getting closer.

Now that you have taken a portion of the quiz, think about how these questions are intended to distinguish between robot and human. What does AI still have trouble doing?

Answers: (1) playground (2) playground; office (3) office
(4) office; bathroom (5) Mary; Bill; milk; Bill

15   One of the most prominent transhumanists is the inventor and philosopher Ray Kurzweil, currently director of engineering at Google, and populariser of the concept of the technological "singularity" — a point he puts at around 2045, when artificial intelligence will outstrip human intelligence for the first time. The predicted consequences of such a scenario vary wildly from the enslavement of humanity to a utopian world without war (or even, as a result of self-replicating nanotechnology, the transformation of the planet, or perhaps the entire universe, into something called "grey goo" — but that's a whole other story).

Kurzweil, the award-winning creator of the flatbed scanner, also believes he has a shot at immortality and intends to resurrect the dead, including his own father. "We will transcend all of the limitations of our biology," he has said. "That is what it means to be human — to extend who we are."

Many transhumanists, particularly in Silicon Valley, where belief in the singularity has assumed the character of an eschatological[2] religion, think that fusing with technology is our only hope of surviving the consequences of this great change.

"We're not physically more competent than other species but in our intellectual capabilities we have something of an edge," Warwick tells me. "But quite soon machines are going to have an intellectual power that we'll have difficulty dealing with." The only way to keep up with them, he believes, is to artificially enhance our poor organic bodies and brains. "If you can't beat them, join them," he says.

Professor James Lovelock, the veteran scientist and environmentalist, is considerably less alarmed than Warwick. "Artificial intelligence is never going to be able to intuit or invent things — all it can do is follow logical instructions. Perhaps in the future when computing systems operate like our brains, then there really would be a fight, but that's an awful long way off."

20   Many would disagree, however. IBM, Hewlett Packard and HRL Laboratories have all received many millions of dollars from DARPA to develop exactly what Lovelock fears: so-called "cognitive" or "neuromorphic" computing systems designed to learn, associate and intuit just like a mammalian brain. IBM brought out its first prototype in 2012.

Warwick may have been the first to experiment with cybernetics but the honour of being the world's first government-recognised cyborg goes to the artist Neil Harbisson. Born with the rare condition of achromatopsia, or total colour blindness, Harbisson developed the "eyeborg" — a colour sensor on a head-mounted antenna that connects to a microchip implanted in his skull. It converts colours into sounds (electronic sine waves) which he hears via bone conduction.

Harbisson's severe bowl cut and hard-to-place accent (his mother is Catalan and his father Northern Irish) only heighten the impression that he might have been beamed down from another planet.

Over time he has learned to associate every part of the spectrum with a different pitch until these associations have become second nature. "It was when I started to dream in colour that I felt the software and my brain had united," he said in [a] TED talk in 2012.

Ten years ago, he won a battle with the British government to have the "eyeborg" recognized as a part of his body. It now appears in his passport photo.

25   He set up the Cyborg Foundation two years ago with his partner, Moon Ribas, a dancer and a fellow "cyborg activist" (she has a seismic sensor in her arm, which enables her to feel vibrations of varying intensity when an earthquake occurs anywhere in the world). She and Harbisson believe that everyone should have the right to become a cyborg. Like the biohackers, they propose that would-be cyborgs use open-source technology to

---

[2] eschatological: From the Greek word *eschatos,* meaning "last" or "farthest," eschatology is a type of philosophy or theology that contemplates the end of life, humankind, or the world as a whole. —Eds.

design and make their own enhancements, rather than buying a finished product off the shelf.

It is hard, however, to see the majority of people adopting a DIY philosophy like this when state-of-the-art options become available commercially. In computer gaming, headsets using electroencephalogram (EEG) technology are being developed so that users can control games with their thoughts. "For example," explains Zach Lynch, organizer of the first "Neurogaming" conference in San Francisco last year, "players can smash boulders by concentrating or scare away demons with angry facial expressions." A British gaming company, Foc.us, is using technology that was first developed by DARPA to train snipers, to boost playing performance. According to Lynch, its "transcranial direct current stimulation device literally zaps your head with a miniscule electric pulse [which you can't feel] during training to help make your brain more susceptible to learning."

Chad Bouton, the inventor of the Neurobridge technology at Batelle Innovations that is enabling Ian Burkhart to move his hand again, believes that invasive brain-computer interfaces could also one day cross over into the non-therapeutic field.

"Talking about this bionic age that we're entering," he says on the phone from Ohio, "you certainly can imagine brain implants that could augment your memory." Or give you direct access to the internet. "You could think about a search you'd like to make and get the information streamed directly into your brain," he says. "Maybe decades from now we'll see something like that."

Prof. James Lovelock, who himself is fitted with a wi-fi controlled pacemaker, thinks these innovations come with dangers. He is chiefly "worried about the spam. If I had a cybernetic eye I wouldn't want to wake up in the middle of the night with [an advert for] somebody's used car flashing through my brain."

30 Then there is the prospect of spying. Could insurance companies harvest biometric data from people's enhancements, or paranoid governments use them to monitor their citizens? Amal Graafstra is adamant that his access-control chip is not at risk from such things, due to the close proximity (two inches or less) required to read it. "If the government was handing out these tags and requiring people to use them for banking, say, that would be pretty suspect," he tells me. "But it doesn't need to do that, because we have our phones on us all the time already" — a perfectly effective "tracking device," as he puts it, should governments be interested in our movements.

Even assuming that cybernetic technology could be made safe from such dangers, opponents of transhumanism (sometimes termed "bioconservatives") argue the medical principle, that technology should only restore human capabilities, not enhance them.

"The fascination with 'enhancement' is a way to convince healthy people that they are in need of treatment," says Dr. David Albert Jones, director of the Anscombe Bioethics Centre in Oxford. "It is a wasteful distraction when we are failing to meet the basic needs of people with real health problems."

He's not against what he terms "human-technology interfaces" but, he says, they "should be developed to address the needs of people with disabilities, not to create a market for the self-regarding and the worried-well." Many medical professionals would agree.

Yuval Noah Harari, an Israeli historian, worries about enhancements leading to unprecedented levels of inequality. "Medicine is moving towards trying to surpass the norm, to help [healthy] people live longer, to have stronger memories, to have better control of their emotions," he said in a recent interview. "But upgrading like that is not an egalitarian project, it's an elitist project. No matter what norm you reach, there is always another upgrade which is possible." And the latest, most high-tech upgrades will always only be available to the rich.

35 But where does a case like Neil Harbisson's fall? He couldn't cure his colour blindness, so he

developed an extra sense to make up for it. Is this restoration or augmentation? Where cyborg ethics are concerned, the lines are blurred.

Rich Lee was also drawn to biohacking in order to overcome a disability. Lee, a 35-year-old salesman from Utah whose wet-shave-and-goatee look is more 1990s nu-metal than cybernetic citizen of the future, is losing his vision, and last year was certified blind in one eye. He's best known for having a pair of magnets implanted into his traguses (the nubs of cartilage in front of the earhole). They work with a copper coil worn around his neck, that he hooks up to his iPod, to become internal headphones. But he can also attach other things to the coil, such as wi-fi and electromagnetic sensors, enabling him to sense things normally outside of human capability. By attaching it to an ultrasonic rangefinder, he hopes to learn how to echolocate, like a bat, so when he goes blind he will be still able to judge his distance from objects — essentially, to see in the dark. [. . .]

"It can flip very quickly," says Kevin Warwick. "Take something like laser eye surgery. About 15 years ago people were saying 'Don't go blasting my eyes out' and now they're saying 'Don't bother with contact lenses.'"

In a sense, cyborg technology is nothing new — pacemakers, for example, have been around for decades. But recent advances have opened up new possibilities, and people are embracing them. Real cyborgs already walk among us. Soon, we may have to decide whether we want to join them.

Understanding and Interpreting

1 Identify the uses of technology presented in this article that seem like something out of a science fiction story, and identify the technology that seems somewhat ordinary. What criteria did you use to judge the difference? If you had to guess, which "sci-fi" technology from this article is most likely to become ordinary to us in the future? Explain.

2 In paragraph 8, Arthur House writes, "Ever since the earliest humans made stone tools, we have tried to extend our powers." What technology described in this article would extend human powers?

3 Based on the information in this article, write a definition of "transhumanism." What are the movement's chief aims? Explain how transhumanism has either a utopian or dystopian view of the future.

4 Reread paragraphs 29–34 and identify the counterarguments to the merging of human and machine that House raises. To what extent does House seem to accept, reject, or qualify these counterarguments?

5 Summarize the argument between the people who support only technology that is designed to restore human capabilities and those who are advocates of technology that would enhance these capabilities (pars. 31–38). What position, if any, does the author of this article take?

Analyzing Language, Style, and Structure

1 What effect does the author achieve by starting the article with the demonstration of Ian Burkhart moving his hand? How might the effect have been different if House had begun with Amal Graafstra, the "biohacker"?

2 What is House's tone toward the merging of humans and machines? Focus on the evidence and the examples that he chooses to include to support your interpretation.

3 Based solely on his word choice, do you think that House admires or is skeptical of the people involved in creating new connections between humans and machines?

Connecting, Arguing, and Extending

1 House ends his article by stating, "Real cyborgs already walk among us. Soon, we may have to decide whether we want to join them." Reading through the various levels of technology presented in the article, what would you be comfortable integrating with yourself? What would be a line you would not cross and why?

2 Near the end of the piece, House asks about the distinction between restoration and augmentation, saying, "Where cyborg ethics are concerned, the lines are blurred" (par. 35). Write an argument identifying the ethical guidelines you would propose for regulation of machine-human integration, supporting your argument with evidence from this text and additional research.

3 In 2005, Ray Kurzweil, who was mentioned in this article, wrote *The Singularity Is Near: When Humans Transcend Biology.* Research the "singularity," a term for the point at which "artificial intelligence will outstrip human intelligence for the first time" (par. 15) and when humans will "transcend all of the limitations of our biology" (par. 16) to become indistinguishable from machines. According to your research, how likely is the singularity to occur, and what might be benefits and drawbacks?

Transhumanism

Francis Fukuyama

Francis Fukuyama (b. 1952) is an American professor, writer, and political scientist. He has taught at some of the most prestigious institutions of higher education in the United States, including George Mason, Johns Hopkins, and Stanford. This article, published in 2004, was written in response to a question posed by the editors in *Foreign Affairs* magazine: "What idea, if embraced, would pose the greatest threat to the welfare of humanity?" Fukuyama's answer is the transhumanism movement, which embraces the idea of a coming merger between humans and robots.

For the last several decades, a strange liberation movement has grown within the developed world. Its crusaders aim much higher than civil rights campaigners, feminists, or gay-rights advocates. They want nothing less than to liberate the human race from its biological constraints. As "transhumanists" see it, humans must wrest their biological destiny from evolution's blind process of random variation and adaptation and move to the next stage as a species.

It is tempting to dismiss transhumanists as some sort of odd cult, nothing more than science fiction taken too seriously: Witness their over-the-top Web sites and recent press releases ("Cyborg Thinkers to Address Humanity's Future," proclaims one). The plans of some transhumanists to freeze themselves cryogenically in hopes of being revived in a future age seem only to confirm the movement's place on the intellectual fringe.

But is the fundamental tenet of transhumanism — that we will someday use biotechnology to make ourselves stronger, smarter, less prone to violence, and longer-lived — really so outlandish? Transhumanism of a sort is implicit in much of the research agenda of contemporary biomedicine. The new procedures and technologies emerging from research laboratories and hospitals — whether mood-altering drugs, substances to boost muscle mass or selectively erase memory, prenatal genetic screening, or gene therapy — can as easily be used to "enhance" the species as to ease or ameliorate illness.

Although the rapid advances in biotechnology often leave us vaguely uncomfortable, the intellectual or moral threat they represent is not always easy to identify. The human race, after all, is a pretty sorry mess, with our stubborn diseases, physical limitations, and short lives. Throw in humanity's jealousies, violence, and constant anxieties, and the transhumanist project begins to look downright reasonable. If it were technologically possible, why wouldn't we want to transcend our current species? The seeming reasonableness of the project, particularly when considered in small increments, is part of its danger. Society is unlikely to fall suddenly under the spell of the transhumanist worldview. But it is very possible that we will nibble at biotechnology's tempting offerings without realizing that they come at a frightful moral cost.

5   The first victim of transhumanism might be equality. The U.S. Declaration of Independence says that "all men are created equal," and the most serious political fights in the history of the United States have been over who qualifies as fully human. Women and blacks did not make

seeing connections

One of Francis Fukuyama's arguments against transhumanism is the lack of equality that might occur between "enhanced creatures" and unmodified humans because they are missing a "human essence."

Read the following response to Fukuyama by noted transhumanist Nick Bostrom and explain the differences in their opinions:

> The claim that only individuals who possess the human essence could have intrinsic value is mistaken. Only the most callous would deny that the welfare of some non-human animals matters at least to some degree. If a visitor from outer space arrived on our doorstep, and she had consciousness and moral agency just like we humans do, surely we would not deny her moral status or intrinsic value just because she lacked some undefined "human essence." Similarly, if some persons were to modify their own biology in a way that alters whatever Fukuyama judges to be their "essence," would we really want to deprive them of their moral standing and legal rights? Excluding people from the moral circle merely because they have a different "essence" from "the rest of us" is akin to excluding people on basis of their gender or the color of their skin.

> Moral progress in the last two millennia has consisted largely in our gradually learning to overcome our tendency to make moral discriminations on such fundamentally irrelevant grounds. We should bear this hard-earned lesson in mind when we approach the prospect of technologically modified people. Liberal democracies speak to "human equality" not in the literal sense that all humans are equal in their various capacities, but that they are equal under the law. There is no reason why humans with altered or augmented capacities should not likewise be equal under the law, nor is there any ground for assuming that the existence of such people must undermine centuries of legal, political, and moral refinement.

the cut in 1776 when Thomas Jefferson penned the declaration. Slowly and painfully, advanced societies have realized that simply being human entitles a person to political and legal equality. In effect, we have drawn a red line around the human being and said that it is sacrosanct.

Underlying this idea of the equality of rights is the belief that we all possess a human essence that dwarfs manifest differences in skin color, beauty, and even intelligence. This essence, and the view that individuals therefore have inherent value, is at the heart of political liberalism. But modifying that essence is the core of the trans-humanist project. If we start transforming ourselves into something superior, what rights will these enhanced creatures claim, and what rights will they possess when compared to those

© Piero Cruciatti/Demotix/Corbis

This is Neil Harbisson, the color-blind artist you may have read about in "The Real Cyborgs" by Arthur House (p. 921), who wears an external antenna connected to a chip in his brain that allows him to perceive colors through sound vibrations. He is also considered the first person to be officially recognized as a "cyborg," and is even shown with his antenna on his British passport.

How would Francis Fukuyama respond to Harbisson? Would he call him an "enhanced creature"? Would he consider him no longer human?

left behind? If some move ahead, can anyone afford not to follow? These questions are troubling enough within rich, developed societies. Add in the implications for citizens of the world's poorest countries — for whom biotechnology's marvels likely will be out of reach — and the threat to the idea of equality becomes even more menacing.

Transhumanism's advocates think they understand what constitutes a good human being, and they are happy to leave behind the limited, mortal, natural beings they see around them in favor of something better. But do they really comprehend ultimate human goods? For all our obvious faults, we humans are miraculously complex products of a long evolutionary process — products whose whole is much more than the sum of our parts. Our good characteristics are intimately connected to our bad ones: If we weren't violent and aggressive, we wouldn't be able to defend ourselves; if we didn't have feelings of exclusivity, we wouldn't be loyal to those close to us; if we never felt jealousy, we would also never feel love. Even our mortality plays a critical function in allowing our species as a whole to survive and adapt (and transhumanists are just about the last group I'd like to see live forever). Modifying any one of our key characteristics inevitably entails modifying a complex, interlinked package of traits, and we will never be able to anticipate the ultimate outcome.

Nobody knows what technological possibilities will emerge for human self-modification. But we can already see the stirrings of Promethean desires in how we prescribe drugs to alter the behavior and personalities of our children. The environmental movement has taught us humility and respect for the integrity of nonhuman nature. We need a similar humility concerning our human nature. If we do not develop it soon, we may unwittingly invite the transhumanists to deface humanity with their genetic bulldozers and psychotropic shopping malls.

Understanding and Interpreting

1 How does Francis Fukuyama define "transhumanism" in paragraphs 1–3?

2 What is the "frightful moral cost" (par. 4) of transhumanism, according to Fukuyama?

3 Summarize what Fukuyama means by a "human essence" (par. 6) and explain how this concept runs counter to transhumanism.

4 What is the distinction that Fukuyama makes between how he and the transhumanists would define a "good human" (par. 7)? What evidence does he include to support his view that we should not modify humanity?

5 In the last paragraph, Fukuyama calls for "humility concerning our human nature." Explain what he means by this.

Analyzing Language, Style, and Structure

1 Skim back through the article, and identify specific words and phrases that Fukuyama uses to describe the proponents of transhumanism. How do his word choices reveal his tone?

2 In paragraphs 1 and 2, Fukuyama creates a sense of transhumanists as a "cult," and in paragraphs 3 and 4 he describes them as seemingly "downright reasonable"; he then goes on to raise his objections. How do his structural choices help him to make and support his argument?

3 How does Fukuyama use the quote from the U.S. Declaration of Independence in his argument (par. 5)? What purpose does this serve?

4 Reread the following sentence from paragraph 6 and explain how Fukuyama's word choice and use of rhetorical questions is either effective or ineffective in making his point: "If we start transforming ourselves into something superior, what rights will these enhanced creatures claim, and what rights will they possess when compared to those left behind?"

5 Reread the final sentence of Fukuyama's article, and change the words in bold to reflect a slightly less hostile tone toward the transhumanist movement: "[W]e may **unwittingly invite** the transhumanists to **deface** humanity with their **genetic bulldozers** and **psychotropic shopping malls**." What new tone is created through your word choice?

Connecting, Arguing, and Extending

1 Fukuyama says that most people are unlikely to "fall suddenly under the spell of the transhumanist worldview," but may "nibble at biotechnology's tempting offerings" (par. 4). What do you think are some of these tempting offerings, and would you choose them for yourself? Why or why not?

2 Write an argument in which you agree or disagree with the claim that Fukuyama makes that "[o]ur good characteristics are intimately connected to our bad ones: If we weren't violent and aggressive, we wouldn't be able to defend ourselves; if we didn't have feelings of exclusivity, we wouldn't be loyal to those close to us; if we never felt jealousy, we would also never feel love" (par. 7).

from Our Final Invention: Artificial Intelligence and the End of the Human Era

James Barrat

James Barrat (b. 1960) is a documentary filmmaker whose work has appeared on National Geographic, Discovery, and PBS. The selection here is from Chapter 1 of Barrat's book, *Our Final Invention*, which is the product of his long fascination with robots and artificial intelligence. In it he asks the questions, "Will machines naturally love us and protect us? Should we bet our existence on it?"

I've written this book to warn you that artificial intelligence could drive mankind into extinction, and to explain how that catastrophic outcome is not just possible, but likely if we do not begin preparing very carefully *now*. You may have heard this doomsday warning connected to nanotechnology and genetic engineering, and maybe you have wondered, as I have, about the omission of AI in this lineup. Or maybe you have not yet grasped how artificial intelligence could pose an existential threat to mankind, a threat greater than nuclear weapons or any other technology you can think of. If that's the case, please consider this a heartfelt invitation to join the most important conversation humanity can have.

Right now scientists are creating artificial intelligence, or AI, of ever-increasing power and sophistication. Some of that AI is in your computer, appliances, smart phone, and car. Some of it is in powerful QA systems, like Watson. And some of it, advanced by organizations such as Cycorp, Google, Novamente, Numenta, Self-Aware Systems, Vicarious Systems, and DARPA (the Defense Advanced Research Projects Agency) is in "cognitive architectures," whose makers hope will attain human-level intelligence, some believe within a little more than a decade.

Scientists are aided in their AI quest by the ever-increasing power of computers and processes that are sped by computers. Someday soon, perhaps within your lifetime, some group or individual will create human-level AI, commonly called AGI. Shortly after that, someone (or some *thing*) will create an AI that is smarter than humans, often called artificial superintelligence. Suddenly we may find a thousand or ten thousand artificial superintelligences — all hundreds or thousands of times smarter than humans — hard at work on the problem of how to make themselves better at making artificial superintelligences. We may also find that machine generations or iterations take seconds to reach maturity, not eighteen years as we humans do. I. J. Good, an English statistician who helped defeat Hitler's war machine, called the simple concept I've just outlined an *intelligence explosion.* He initially thought a superintelligent machine would be good for solving problems that threatened human existence. But he eventually changed his mind and concluded superintelligence itself was our greatest threat.

Now, it is an anthropomorphic fallacy to conclude that a superintelligent AI will not like humans, and that it will be homicidal, like the Hal 9000 from the movie *2001: A Space Odyssey*, Skynet from the *Terminator* movie franchise, and all the other malevolent machine intelligences represented in fiction. We humans anthropomorphize all the time. A hurricane isn't trying to kill us any more than it's trying to make sandwiches, but we will give that storm a name and feel angry about the buckets of rain and lightning bolts it is throwing down on our

seeing connections

May 2007, World Chess Champion Garry Kasparov loses to the IBM Deep Blue chess computer. It is the first time in history that a computer defeats a reigning world champion.

Stan Honda/AFP/Getty Images

January 2011, IBM's Watson computer wins *Jeopardy!*, defeating previous champions Ken Jennings and Brad Rutter.

What conclusions should we draw from these accomplishments by robots? Are they a sign of intelligence?

neighborhood. We will shake our fist at the sky as if we could threaten a hurricane.

5   It is just as irrational to conclude that a machine one hundred or one thousand times more intelligent than we are would love us and want to protect us. It is possible, but far from guaranteed. On its own an AI will not feel gratitude for the gift of being created unless gratitude is in its programming. Machines are amoral, and it is dangerous to assume otherwise. Unlike our

intelligence, machine-based superintelligence will not evolve in an ecosystem in which empathy is rewarded and passed on to subsequent generations. It will not have inherited friendliness. Creating *friendly* artificial intelligence, and whether or not it is possible, is a big question and an even bigger task for researchers and engineers who think about and are working to create AI. We do not know if artificial intelligence will have *any* emotional qualities, even if scientists try their best to make it so. However, scientists do believe, as we will explore, that AI will have its own drives. And sufficiently intelligent AI will be in a strong position to fulfill those drives.

And that brings us to the root of the problem of sharing the planet with an intelligence greater than our own. What if its drives are not compatible with human survival? Remember, we are talking about a machine that could be a thousand, a million, an *uncountable* number of times more intelligent than we are — it is hard to overestimate what it will be able to do, and impossible to know what it will think. It does not have to hate us before

Mark Ralston/Getty Images

Yaretzi Bernal, six, gets a hug from "Pepper," the emotional robot on display during the finals of the DARPA Robotics Challenge at the Fairplex complex in Pomona, California, on June 5, 2015. The competition had twenty-four teams vying to develop robots capable of assisting humans in responding to natural and man-made disasters.

What aspects of Pepper's design would make the robot effective in responding to natural and man-made disasters?

choosing to use our molecules for a purpose other than keeping us alive. You and I are hundreds of times smarter than field mice, and share about 90 percent of our DNA with them. But do we consult them before plowing under their dens for agriculture? Do we ask lab monkeys for their opinions before we crush their heads to learn about sports injuries? We don't hate mice or monkeys, yet we treat them cruelly. Superintelligent AI won't have to hate us to destroy us.

After intelligent machines have already been built and man has not been wiped out, perhaps we can afford to anthropomorphize. But here on the cusp of creating AGI, it is a dangerous habit. Oxford University ethicist Nick Bostrom puts it like this:

> A prerequisite for having a meaningful discussion of superintelligence is the realization that superintelligence is not just another technology, another tool that will add incrementally to human capabilities. Superintelligence is radically different. This point bears emphasizing, for anthropomorphizing superintelligence is a most fecund source of misconceptions.

Superintelligence is radically different, in a technological sense, Bostrom says, because its achievement will change the rules of progress — superintelligence will invent the inventions and set the pace of technological advancement. Humans will no longer drive change, and there will be no going back. Furthermore, advanced machine intelligence is radically different in kind. Even though humans will invent it, it will seek self-determination and freedom from humans. It won't have humanlike motives because it won't have a humanlike psyche.

Therefore, anthropomorphizing about machines leads to misconceptions, and misconceptions about how to safely make dangerous machines lead to catastrophes. In the short story, "Runaround," included in the classic science-fiction collection *I, Robot*, author Isaac Asimov introduced his three laws of robotics.

They were fused into the neural networks of the robots' "positronic" brains:

1. A robot may not injure a human being or, through inaction, allow a human being to come to harm.
2. A robot must obey any orders given to it by human beings, except where such orders would conflict with the First Law.
3. A robot must protect its own existence as long as such protection does not conflict with the First or Second Law.

10   The laws contain echoes of the Golden Rule ("Thou Shalt Not Kill"), the Judeo-Christian notion that sin results from acts committed and omitted, the physician's Hippocratic oath, and even the right to self-defense. Sounds pretty good, right? Except they never work. In "Runaround," mining engineers on the surface of Mars order a robot to retrieve an element that is poisonous to it. Instead, it gets stuck in a feedback loop between law two — obey orders — and law three — protect yourself. The robot walks in drunken circles until the engineers risk *their* lives to rescue it. And so it goes with every Asimov robot tale — unanticipated consequences result from contradictions inherent in the three laws. Only by working around the laws are disasters averted.

Asimov was generating plot lines, not trying to solve safety issues in the real world. Where you and I live his laws fall short. For starters, they're insufficiently precise. What exactly will constitute a "robot" when humans augment their bodies and brains with intelligent prosthetics and implants? For that matter, what will constitute a human? "Orders," "injure," and "existence" are similarly nebulous terms.

Tricking robots into performing criminal acts would be simple, unless the robots had perfect comprehension of all of human knowledge. "Put a little dimethylmercury in Charlie's shampoo" is a recipe for murder only if you know that dimethylmercury is a neurotoxin. Asimov eventually added a fourth law, the Zeroth Law, prohibiting robots from harming mankind as a whole, but it doesn't solve the problems.

Yet unreliable as Asimov's laws are, they're our most often cited attempt to codify our future relationship with intelligent machines. That's a frightening proposition. Are Asimov's laws all we've got?

I'm afraid it's worse than that. Semiautonomous robotic drones already kill dozens of people each year. Fifty-six countries have or are developing battlefield robots. The race is on to make them autonomous and intelligent. For the most part, discussions of ethics in AI and technological advances take place in different worlds.

15   As I'll argue, AI is a dual-use technology like nuclear fission. Nuclear fission can illuminate cities or incinerate them. It's terrible power was unimaginable to most people before 1945. With advanced AI, we're in the 1930s right now. We're unlikely to survive an introduction as abrupt as nuclear fission's.

Understanding and Interpreting

1 Identify James Barrat's central claim about why we need to be careful about our development of artificial intelligence (AI).

2 According to Barrat, what are the similarities and differences between human emotions and AI's "drives"?

3 Explain what Barrat sees as the dangers of anthropomorphizing AI.

4 How does Barrat illustrate that the Three Laws of Robotics cannot manage the dangers posed by AI? How effective is his use of fictional examples to support real-life claims?

5 Although he does not state it directly in this excerpt, what actions do you think Barrat would likely propose we take to avoid the dangers he sees? What evidence from this section supports your inference?

Analyzing Language, Style, and Structure

1 What does Barrat do throughout this excerpt to establish his own ethos on the topic of robots and artificial intelligence?

2 Reread the first paragraph of this excerpt and focus on Barrat's diction. What is the effect of his word choice and what is his likely purpose in beginning this section in this way?

3 Look closely at paragraph 3, in which Barrat traces a possible future in the development of artificial intelligence. How does he use language choices to make this future feel inevitable and dangerous?

4 In paragraph 6, Barrat uses analogies to support his argument about the ways that AI will act toward humans. Explain the analogies and evaluate how effective they are in building his argument.

5 What is the difference between "intelligence" and "superintelligence" (pars. 7–8), and how does Barrat use the meaning of the second term to serve his argument?

6 Barrat ends this excerpt with a reference to nuclear fission. Evaluate the effectiveness of this reference as his conclusion to the piece.

Connecting, Arguing, and Extending

1 Barrat says in paragraph 5 that "[m]achines are amoral, and it is dangerous to assume otherwise." Do you agree or disagree with that statement? Why? What are possible dangers that we could face from AI that Barrat does not include in this excerpt?

2 The Greek myth of Pandora's Box is often cited when science appears to be unleashing technologies that we may not be able to fully control. Research the story of Pandora and explain its connection to AI and to at least one other scientific development in history.

3 As you may have read in the introduction to this Conversation, Stephen Hawking, one of the most respected scientists in the world, believes that a takeover by AI is a real danger to humanity, but others are less pessimistic. Conduct additional research and write an argument in which you make and support a claim about the reasonable fears humans ought to have about AI.

In Defense of Killer Robots

Rosa Brooks

Rosa Brooks (b. 1970) is a law professor at Georgetown University, where she teaches courses on international relations and national security. She has also served in the U.S. Defense Department and been a consultant to many organizations, including Human Rights Watch. She writes a regular opinion column for *Foreign Affairs*, from which this piece is taken.

AP Photo/Cliff Owen

Robots just can't catch a break. If we're not upbraiding them for taking our jobs, we're lambasting their alleged tendency to seize control of spaceships, computer systems, the Earth, the galaxy or the universe beyond. The Bad Robot has long been a staple of film and fiction, from HAL ("I'm sorry, Dave, I'm afraid I can't do that") to the Terminator, but recently, bad robots have migrated from the screen to the world of military ethics and human rights campaigns.

Specifically, a growing number of ethicists and rights advocates are calling for a global ban on the development, production, and use of fully autonomous weapons systems, which are, according to Human Rights Watch, "also" — and rather conveniently — "known as killer robots." (Not to their mothers, I'm sure!)

The term does tend to have a chilling effect even upon those harboring a soft spot for R2-D2 and Wall-E. But someone has to stand up for killer robots, and it might as well be me.

Let's review the case against the robots. The core concern relates to military research into weapons systems that are "fully autonomous," meaning that they can "select and engage targets without human intervention." Today, even our most advanced weapons technologies still require humans in the loop. Thus, Predator drones can't decide for themselves whom to kill: it takes a human being — often dozens of human beings in a complex command chain — to decide that it's both legal and wise to launch missiles at a given target. In the not-too-distant future, though, this could change. Imagine robots programmed not only to detect and disarm roadside bombs but to track and fire upon individuals concealing or emplacing IEDs. Or imagine an unmanned aerial vehicle that can fire missiles when a computer determines that a given individual is behaving like a combatant, based on a pre-programmed set of criteria.

5   According to the Campaign to Stop Killer Robots, this would be bad, because a) killer robots might not have the ability to abide by the legal obligation to distinguish between combatants and civilians; and b) "Allowing life or death decisions to be made by machines crosses a fundamental moral line" and jeopardizes fundamental principles of "human dignity."

Neither of these arguments makes much sense to me. Granted, the thought of an evil robot firing indiscriminately into a crowd is dismaying, as is the thought of a rogue robot, sparks flying from every rusting joint, going berserk and turning its futuristic super-weapons upon those it's supposed to serve. But setting science fiction aside, real-life computers have a pretty good track record. When was the last time Siri staged a rebellion and began to systematically delete all your favorite videos, just to mess with you? When was the last time a passenger plane's autopilot system got depressed and decided to plow into a mountain, notwithstanding human entreaties to remain airborne?

Arguably, computers will be far *better* than human beings at complying with international humanitarian law. Face it: we humans are fragile and panicky creatures, easily flustered by the fog of war. Our eyes face only one direction; our ears register only certain frequencies; our brains can process only so much information at a time. Loud noises make us jump, and fear floods our bodies with powerful chemicals that can temporarily distort our perceptions and judgment.

As a result, we make stupid mistakes in war, and we make them all the time. We misjudge distances; we forget instructions, we misconstrue gestures. We mistake cameras for weapons, shepherds for soldiers, friends for enemies, schools for barracks, and wedding parties for terrorist convoys.

In fact, we humans are fantastically bad at distinguishing between combatants and civilians — and even when we can tell the difference, we often make risk-averse calculations about necessity and proportionality, preferring dead civilians 8,000 miles away to dead comrades or compatriots. If the U.S. conflicts in Iraq and

seeing connections

In the 1950s, Hollywood released a number of "killer robot" movies, most likely as a response to the fears of the technology that produced the atomic weapons that were used during World War II and were driving the Cold War with the Soviet Union.

Look at these posters for movies released during this time, and explain how the images in the posters illustrate this fear of technology. Then, identify movies or TV shows today that represent current societal fears of technology. What is the same and what has changed from the 1950s?

Afghanistan produced a surfeit of dead and mangled civilians, it's not because of killer robots — it's because of fallible human decision-making.

10   Computers, in contrast, are excellent in crisis and combat situations. They don't get mad, they don't get scared, and they don't act out of sentimentality. They're exceptionally good at processing vast amounts of information in a short time and rapidly applying appropriate decision rules. They're not perfect, but they're a good deal less flawed than those of us cursed with organic circuitry.

We assure ourselves that we humans have special qualities no machine can replicate: we have "judgment" and "intuition," for instance. Maybe, but computers often seem to have *better* judgment. This has already been demonstrated in dozens of different domains, from aviation to anesthesiology. Computers are better than humans at distinguishing between genuine and faked expressions of pain; Google's driverless cars are better at avoiding accidents than cars controlled by humans. Given a choice between relying on a human to comply with international humanitarian law and relying on a well-designed, well-programmed robot, I'll take my chances with the killer robot any day.

Opponents of autonomous weapons ask whether there's a legal and ethical obligation to refrain from letting machines make decisions about who should live and who should die. If it turns out, as it may, that machines are better than people at applying the principles of international humanitarian law, we should be asking an entirely different question: Might there be a legal and ethical obligation to use "killer robots" in lieu of — well, "killer humans"?

Confronted with arguments about the technological superiority of computers over human brains, those opposed to the development of autonomous weapons systems argue that such consequentialist reasoning is insufficient. Ultimately, as a 2014 joint report by Human Rights Watch and Harvard's International Human Rights Clinic argues, it would simply be "morally wrong" to give machines the power to "decide" who lives and who dies: "As inanimate machines, fully autonomous weapons could truly comprehend neither the value of individual life nor the significance of its loss. Allowing them to make determinations to take life away would thus conflict with the principle of [human] dignity."

I suppose the idea here is that any self-respecting person would naturally prefer death at the hands of a fellow member of the human species — someone capable of feeling "compassion" and "mercy" — to death inflicted by a cold, unfeeling machine.

15   I'm not buying it. Death is death, and I don't imagine it gives the dying any consolation to know their human killer feels kind of bad about the whole affair.

Let's not romanticize humans. As a species, we're capable of mercy and compassion, but we also have a remarkable propensity for violence and cruelty. We're a species that kills for pleasure: every year, more than half a million people around the globe die as a result of intentional violence, and many more are injured, starved, or intentionally deprived of shelter, medicine, or other essentials. In the United States alone, more than 16,000 people are murdered each year, and another million-plus are the victims of other violent crimes. Humans, not robots, came up with such ingenious ideas as torture and death by crucifixion. Humans, not robots, came up with the bright idea of firebombing Dresden and Tokyo; humans, not robots, planned the Holocaust and the Rwandan genocide.

Plug in the right lines of code, and robots will dutifully abide by the laws of armed conflict to the best of their technological ability. In this sense, "killer robots" may be capable of behaving far more "humanely" than we might assume. But the flip-side is also true: humans can behave far more like machines than we generally assume.

In the 1960s, experiments by Yale psychologist Stanley Milgram demonstrated the terrible ease with which ordinary humans could be persuaded to inflict pain on complete strangers; since then, other psychologists have refined and extended his work. Want to program an ordinary human being to participate in genocide? Both history and social psychology suggest that it's not much more difficult than creating a new iPhone app.

"But wait!" you say, "That's all very well, but aren't you assuming *obedient* robots? What if the killer robots are overcome by bloodlust or a thirst for power? What if intelligent, autonomous robots decide to override the code that created them, and turn upon us all?"

20 Well: if that happens, killer robots will finally be able to pass the Turing Test. When the robots go rogue — when they start killing for sport or out of hatred, when they start accruing power and wealth for fun — they'll have ceased to be robots in any meaningful sense. For all intents and purposes, they will have become humans — and it's humans we've had reason to fear, all along.

Understanding and Interpreting

1 Identify Rosa Brooks's central claim about why she is not opposed to killer robots.

2 Reread paragraphs 4 and 5, and paraphrase the objections that Brooks claims some people have to killer robots.

3 According to Brooks, what human flaws make robots, even killer ones, more effective in situations like the "fog of war" (par. 7)?

4 What significant assumptions does Brooks make about robot technology and programming developments in the future?

5 Summarize the concerns that Human Rights Watch has about killer robots (par. 13) and explain how Brooks responds to those concerns.

6 Brooks claims that humans can be programmed to behave like robots (par. 18). What evidence does she use to support this claim?

Analyzing Language, Style, and Structure

1 Reread the first paragraph. How does this opening act as a hook for the reader?

2 Oftentimes in an argumentative piece like this one, the author will begin by laying out the evidence that supports his or her position. But notice that beginning with paragraph 4, Brooks chooses to "review the case against the robots." What does she achieve by beginning with the counterarguments instead of her own position?

3 Brooks often uses a sarcastic tone toward those who are afraid of killer robots. Identify one or more of these places and explain how this tone helps her to achieve her purpose.

4 In paragraph 6, Brooks uses descriptive language and a series of rhetorical questions. How does she use these devices to help prove her point about killer robots?

5 Reread paragraph 17 and explain how Brooks's language choices and repetition help her build her argument.

6 Summarize the point Brooks makes in her conclusion, and explain how it becomes one more piece of evidence to support her claim.

7 Skim back through the argument, looking for the kinds of evidence that Brooks uses. Overall, does she rely more on pathos or logos to support her claim? Explain.

Connecting, Arguing, and Extending

1 Do you agree or disagree with Brooks's opinion when she says that she would take her "chances with the killer robot any day" (par. 11)? Why?

2 Research the Milgram Experiment that Brooks refers to in paragraph 18, and explain whether you agree or disagree with the conclusion that Brooks draws from the experiment that "humans can behave far more like machines than we generally assume" (par. 17).

3 Research the Turing Test that Brooks refers to in paragraph 20, and explain how close scientists are to designing a robot that can pass the test.

4 Read the following statement by the Campaign to Stop Killer Robots, which is an international coalition that is working to preemptively ban the research and development of fully autonomous weapons systems. Write an argument in which you support, oppose, or qualify the coalition's claim.

The Campaign to Stop Killer Robots calls for a preemptive and comprehensive ban on the development, production, and use of fully autonomous weapons. The prohibition should be achieved through an international treaty, as well as through national laws and other measures.

"Allowing life or death decisions on the battlefield to be made by machines crosses a fundamental moral line and represents an unacceptable application of technology," said Nobel Peace Laureate Jody Williams of the Nobel Women's Initiative. "Human control of autonomous weapons is essential to protect humanity from a new method of warfare that should never be allowed to come into existence."

ENTERING THE CONVERSATION
OUR ROBOTIC FUTURE

Making Connections

1 According to Kevin Kelly (p. 910), James Barrat (p. 932), and Rosa Brooks (p. 936), should we fear robots in the future? Choose at least two of these authors and compare and contrast their views.

2 What might Kate Darling, whose research is discussed in Richard Fisher's article "Is It OK to Torture or Murder a Robot?" (p. 917), have to say about Dr. Susan Calvin's destruction of the robot in Isaac Asimov's story "Robot Dreams" (p. 900)?

3 Compare and contrast how Isaac Asimov (p. 900) and Margaret Atwood (p. 905) view the relationships between robots and humans.

4 What are the differences between the positions of Francis Fukuyama (p. 928) and Ray Kurzweil, featured in the article by Arthur House (p. 921), regarding the issue of transhumanism?

Synthesizing Sources

1 Will our future be better or worse as a result of the inevitable increase in human-robot interactions? Or, to put it another way, as Margaret Atwood says in her piece in this Conversation, will the future "be a Yikes or a Hurrah" (p. 906)? Refer to at least two texts from the Conversation as evidence of support for your position.

2 Knowing that robots will play a larger role in the workplace of the future, what are the implications for education and workforce training? Be sure to refer to at least two texts in the Conversation.

3 The Cambridge Centre for the Study of Existential Risk is a British multidisciplinary research center dedicated to the study of risks that could lead to human extinction. One of the risks the group is studying is artificial intelligence:

> "It seems a reasonable prediction that some time in this or the next century intelligence will escape from the constraints of biology," Prof. Price told the AFP news agency.
>
> "What we're trying to do is to push it forward in the respectable scientific community."
>
> He added that as robots and computers become smarter than humans, we could find ourselves at the mercy of "machines that are not malicious, but machines whose interests don't include us."

Do you think that robots in the future will, in fact, lead an uprising and enslave humanity? Will they become our benevolent masters, faithful servants, or something in-between? Refer to at least two texts in the Conversation to support your argument and propose steps we ought to take in the future.

4 What rules, if any, should govern the use of robotic enhancements? Will they lead to physical and intellectual elitism? Why or why not? Refer to at least two texts in the Conversation to support your response.

5 Review the Three Laws of Robotics that science fiction author Isaac Asimov created to govern the actions of robots and their interactions with humans. Propose new laws or revisions to his laws, using two or more texts from the Conversation to support your recommendation.

1. A robot may not injure a human being or, through inaction, allow a human being to come to harm.
2. A robot must obey orders given to it by human beings, except where such orders would conflict with the First Law.
3. A robot must protect its own existence as long as such protection does not conflict with the First or Second Law.

▼ ANALYZING DICTION AND TONE

It's possible that at some point you have been on the receiving end of this sentence: "Don't take that tone with me!" If you have been, you know that the speaker was likely reacting less to *what* you said and more to *how* you said it—your attitude. If you said "whatever" dismissively, it's likely not the word itself that they objected to, but the way you said it.

This is exactly why the definition of the literary term **tone** is "the author or speaker's **attitude** toward his or her subject." Writers can take on a whole range of tones, expressing the full spectrum of human emotion, from joy to frustration, from anguish to ecstasy. Look at this excerpt from an editorial written by a high school senior upset about not being accepted to any Ivy League schools, the most exclusive colleges in the United States:

> I also probably should have started a fake charity. Providing veterinary services for homeless people's pets. Collecting donations for the underprivileged chimpanzees of the Congo. Raising awareness for Chapped-Lips-in-the-Winter Syndrome. Fun-runs, dance-a-thons, bake sales—as long as you're using someone else's misfortunes to try to propel yourself into the Ivy League, you're golden.

It's clear that in addition to expressing her anger at not being accepted, she takes a mocking tone toward the kinds of charitable activities that those students who were accepted participated in.

ACTIVITY

This is a photo of Arlington National Cemetery, where members of America's armed forces are buried. How do the artistic choices (the *how*) convey the photographer's attitude (tone) regarding the scene? What stands out to you? How would you characterize that tone? Once you have your ideas about the tone of the photo, write a caption for the picture and explain how it connects to the tone of the photograph.

John Moore/Getty Images

Tone and Context

One of the key components to understanding tone is that it is the attitude writers take toward a *specific* subject. In the photograph on page 943, the tones you identified were ones that the photographer has toward the grief caused by war. He probably has many different attitudes toward all sorts of other topics, but the tone he takes in this photo is unique to this subject. So when you are first learning to analyze the tone of a work, it may be helpful to use a phrase such as "the author takes a _____ tone toward _____." For example, in this excerpt from an essay by Pico Iyer, "The Joy of Less," Iyer takes on a *peaceful and sentimental* tone toward *living with few possessions*:

> [M]y family home in Santa Barbara burned to the ground some years ago, leaving me with nothing but the toothbrush I bought from an all-night supermarket that night. And yet my two-room apartment in nowhere Japan seems more abundant than the big house that burned down. I have time to read the new John le Carré while nibbling at sweet tangerines in the sun. When a Sigur Ros album comes out, it fills my days and nights, resplendent. And then it seems that happiness, like peace or passion, comes most freely when it isn't pursued.

If Iyer switched topics and began talking about people who spent all of their money on houses, cars, and jewelry, he might take on an indignant or sharp tone. While tone is the author's attitude toward the subject, the other aspects of context affect it as well. The high school student in the example on p. 943 might take on a different tone toward the selection process now that she is older and less frustrated. Authors might approach a subject they feel strongly about very delicately, and use a soothing or complimentary tone, if they know their audiences don't share their attitudes.

In a piece of literature, tone and context are linked in a very similar way, but it's important to remember that often tone can be part of a character or narrator's voice, and not indicate solely the *author's* attitude; rather, the context that the tone reflects might be limited to events within the story. For instance, look at the opening lines from "Harrison Bergeron" (p. 872):

> The year was 2081, and everybody was finally equal. They weren't only equal before God and the law. They were equal every which way. Nobody was smarter than anybody else. Nobody was better looking than anybody else. Nobody was stronger or quicker than anybody else. All this equality was due to the 211th, 212th, and 213th Amendments to the Constitution, and to the unceasing vigilance of agents of the United States Handicapper General.

There is a dry humorous tone in the first few sentences that treats these developments as though they were a good thing. And yet, we know from reading the story that it's a recipe for disaster; forced equality at the hands of the "agents of the United States Handicapper General" is not true equality. Is this Vonnegut's tone? His narrator's? Both? Vonnegut has given us the context of the 211th, 212th, and 213th Amendments within the story, which is clearly fictional, but we also get the sense that there is social commentary going on—that Vonnegut himself is satirizing the real world. There are no easy answers for identifying the context of literature and navigating the line between fact and fiction, so examining the tone that an author of a piece of literature takes toward a topic can be a real challenge. It is up to you as a careful reader and creative thinker to be attuned to the text, and use the analysis of tone as an opportunity for a nuanced and insightful interpretation.

How Diction Leads to Tone

Just as when you use your tone of voice and gestures to communicate your attitude, or artists or photographers use light and framing to communicate their attitude, writers have particular ways to communicate their tone. One way is through their language choices, especially their choice of words, which is called *diction*. To fully understand the term **diction**, we have to recognize the differences between **connotation** and **denotation**. Denotation is the literal meaning of a word, free from any emotional or cultural associations. Connotation, on the other hand, is the emotional or cultural associations that a word carries. Every word has a denotation, but most words also have additional connotations as well. An easy example is to think about the word *acquaintance*. The denotation is simply "a person known informally," but think about the connotation of that word. It clearly implies distance and a lack of an emotional connection. Imagine how you would feel if a good friend of yours introduced you to someone as an "acquaintance." That's the power of connotation.

ACTIVITY

Identify and explain the difference between the denotations and connotations of the following pairs of words. What are possible tones that could be created through the choice of one word over the other, depending on the subject?

1. Inexpensive/cheap
2. Cozy/cramped
3. Pushy/assertive
4. Scheme/plan
5. Father/dad
6. Clever/shrewd
7. Government/regime
8. Vagrant/homeless

Let's take a look at how specific words create tone, this time in the context of a poem: "Happy Family" by Jane Shore. The title refers to a Chinese American stir-fry with various meats and vegetables. We've bolded some words that we find interesting in terms of tone, but feel free to point out some words that you find compelling.

Tonight, the waiter brings Happy Family
steaming under a metal dome
and three small igloos of rice.
Mounded on the white oval plate, the **unlikely**
marriage of meat and fish, crab and chicken.
Not all Happy Families are alike.
The chef's **tossed** in wilted greens
and water chestnuts, silk **against** crunch;
[. . .]
My daughter **impales** a chunk of beef
on her chopstick and **contentedly**
sucks on it, like a popsicle.
Eating Happy Family, we all begin to **smile**.

Notice how many of the words have connotations of conflict—"unlikely marriage," "tossed," "against," "impales"—and yet toward the end of the section, there are words with positive connotations of warm contentment—"contentedly" and "smile." It's a good reminder that tone in a piece is not necessarily the same throughout. It can shift. Here the tone shifts from a tone of restrained conflict to one of dissolving tension and even contentment in just a few lines. Tone shifts often reveal a lot about the meaning of the work, so it's important to pay close attention to an author's diction and try to pick up on shifts of this sort.

ACTIVITY

In this excerpt from "Transhumanism" (p. 928), author Francis Fukuyama expresses his dislike for the transhumanist movement, which seeks to improve humanity by integrating itself fully with technology, with humans eventually becoming "cyborg humans." Look carefully at Fukuyama's diction and identify what tone he takes toward the movement to express his displeasure with its proponents. Then, go back through the excerpt and try to change the tone Fukuyama takes by changing three or four of the words he uses.

For the last several decades, a strange liberation movement has grown within the developed world. Its crusaders aim much higher than civil rights campaigners, feminists, or gay-rights advocates. They want nothing less than to liberate the human race from its biological constraints. As "transhumanists" see it, humans must wrest their biological destiny from evolution's blind process of random variation and adaptation and move to the next stage as a species.

It is tempting to dismiss transhumanists as some sort of odd cult, nothing more than science fiction taken too seriously: Witness their over-the-top Web sites and recent press releases ("Cyborg Thinkers to Address Humanity's Future," proclaims one). The plans of some transhumanists to freeze themselves cryogenically in hopes of being revived in a future age seem only to confirm the movement's place on the intellectual fringe.

Describing Tone

Tone can be a tricky thing to discuss. Writers can convey the whole range of human emotion, so unless you expand your vocabulary a bit, you might find that your description of the tone doesn't quite capture what you're seeing and hearing in the piece. Your goal should be to move beyond simple concepts like "happy" and "sad," "positive" and "negative." Life is usually not that simple, and neither is tone.

ACTIVITY

Look over the following words that can be used to describe the tone or attitude of a speaker or author toward a topic and try to place them on a continuum such as the one shown below, knowing that many are going fall into the spaces between. Then, return to some of the texts (or the photograph) you looked at in the previous activities and use some of the words on this list to describe the tone of each work.

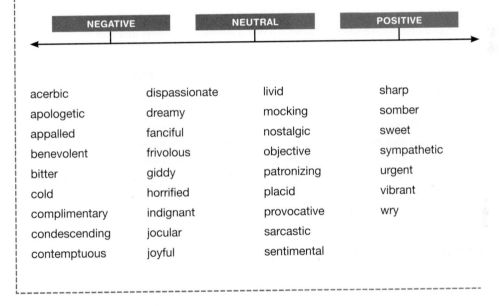

acerbic	dispassionate	livid	sharp
apologetic	dreamy	mocking	somber
appalled	fanciful	nostalgic	sweet
benevolent	frivolous	objective	sympathetic
bitter	giddy	patronizing	urgent
cold	horrified	placid	vibrant
complimentary	indignant	provocative	wry
condescending	jocular	sarcastic	
contemptuous	joyful	sentimental	

Even if you pick up on the author's tone, it can be hard to find one *perfect* word to describe it. Note that we described the tone of the Jane Shore poem excerpted on page 946 as shifting from "restrained conflict to . . . dissolving tension and even contentment." It is often a good strategy when describing the tone of a work to choose a couple of words, or even a few: "distant and vulnerable," "giddy with a hint of madness," "outraged and indignant, but growing curious." It's much easier to describe the nuance of a tone this way.

For example, look at this excerpt from the Central Text in this chapter, *A Small Place*, by Jamaica Kincaid (p. 856). Here Kincaid is describing the view that a tourist might have when visiting her native Antigua. Her tone is constantly shifting between celebratory of the beauty of her island and bitterly sarcastic toward the tourists walking on the beach.

From there to the shore, the water is pale, silvery, clear, so clear that you can see its pinkish-white sand bottom. Oh, what beauty! Oh, what beauty! You have never seen anything like this. You are so excited. You breathe shallow. You breathe deep. You see a beautiful boy skimming the water, godlike, on a Windsurfer. You see an incredibly un-attractive, fat, pastrylike-fleshed woman enjoying a walk on the beautiful sand, with a man, an incredibly unattractive, fat, pastrylike-fleshed man. [...]

ACTIVITY

Look over the following excerpts from readings in this chapter and try to express the tone each writer takes in at least two words; be sure to identify the subject to which the author's tone is directed. Then, point to what diction in the excerpt most reveals the author's tone. If you want, you can choose words from the list in the previous Activity. Remember to avoid simply labeling the tone as "happy" or "sad."

from Free to Be Happy / Jon Meacham

In this essay, Meacham explores the meaning of "happiness" as the American Founding Fathers, Thomas Jefferson in particular, defined it in the eighteenth century and how it applies to today.

The genius of the American experiment is the nation's capacity to create hope in a world suffused with fear. And while we are too often more concerned with our own temporary feelings of happiness than we are with the common good, we still believe, with Jefferson, that governments are instituted to enable us to live our lives as we wish, enjoying innate liberties and freely enjoying the right to pursue happiness, which was in many ways the acme of Enlightenment ambitions for the role of politics. For Jefferson and his contemporaries — and, thankfully, for most of their successors in positions of ultimate authority — the point of public life was to enable human creativity and ingenuity and possibility, not to constrict it.

from Are Humans Necessary? / Margaret Atwood

In this essay, Atwood wonders how we will use robots in the future and what this use says about us as humans.

What fate is in store for us in The Future? Will it be a Yikes or a Hurrah? Zombie apocalypse? No more fish? Vertical urban farming? Burnout? Genetically modified humans? Will we, using our great-big-brain cleverness, manage to solve the many problems now confronting us on this planet? Or will that very same cleverness, coupled with greed and short-term thinking, prove to be our downfall?

We have plenty of latitude for our speculations, since The Future is not predetermined.

Many of our proposed futures contain robots. The present also contains robots, but The Future is said to contain a lot more of them. Is that good or bad? We haven't made up our minds. And while we're at it, how about a robotic mind that can be made up more easily than a human one?

Tone and Theme

Sometimes your analysis will end at being able to identify and explain the tone of a work as you did above, but sometimes you will also be asked to write about how the tone that an author takes is used in support of the theme or message. For instance, look at the beginning of the short story you might have read in the chapter, "The Ones Who Walk Away from Omelas," by Ursula K. Le Guin, and notice how the bolded words create an optimistic, joyful, and celebratory tone:

> With a clamor of bells that set the swallows **soaring**, the Festival of Summer came to the city. Omelas, **bright-towered** by the sea. The rigging of the boats in harbor **sparkled** with flags. In the streets between houses with red roofs and painted walls, between old moss-grown gardens and under avenues of trees, past great parks and public buildings, processions moved. Some were **decorous**: old people in long stiff robes of mauve and grey, grave master workmen, quiet, **merry** women carrying their babies and **chatting** as they walked. In other streets the music beat faster, a **shimmering** of gong and tambourine, and the people went dancing, the procession was a **dance**.

This opening is clearly intended to be in direct contrast to the tone later in the piece, when the reader learns that beneath the surface of the joy there is a dark, unforgiving, and depressing truth:

> In one corner of the little room a couple of mops, with **stiff, clotted, foul-smelling** heads, stand near a **rusty** bucket. The floor is dirt, a little **damp** to the touch, as **cellar dirt** usually is. The room is about three paces long and two wide: a **mere** broom closet or disused tool room. In the room a child is sitting. It could be a boy or a girl. **It** looks about six, but actually is nearly ten. It is feeble-minded. Perhaps it was born **defective**, or perhaps it has become imbecile through **fear, malnutrition, and neglect**. It picks its nose and occasionally **fumbles** vaguely with its toes or genitals, as it sits **hunched** in the corner farthest from the bucket and the two mops.

The optimistic tone of the opening is the mirror image of the tone of this second excerpt. The shift in tone is intentional and directly related to the point that Le Guin is making about the cost that often accompanies happiness: the people of a community can only have happiness at the expense of the less fortunate. Tone is frequently used in such a way by authors—to both reflect the theme and assist in creating it.

ACTIVITY

Read this excerpt from the Central Text in this chapter, *A Small Place*, by Jamaica Kincaid. Identify words and phrases that create a particular tone and explain how that tone assists Kincaid in making her point about tourism.

from **A Small Place** / Jamaica Kincaid

Oh, but by now you are tired of all this looking, and you want to reach your destination — your hotel, your room. You long to refresh yourself; you long to eat some nice lobster, some nice local food. You take a bath, you brush your teeth. You get dressed again; as you get dressed, you look out the window. That water — have you ever seen anything like it? Far out, to the horizon, the colour of the water is navy-blue; nearer, the water is the colour of the North American sky. From there to the shore, the water is pale, silvery, clear, so clear that you can see its pinkish-white sand bottom. Oh, what beauty! Oh, what beauty! You have never seen anything like this. You are so excited. You breathe shallow. You breathe deep. You see a beautiful boy skimming the water, godlike, on a Windsurfer. You see an incredibly unattractive, fat, pastrylike-fleshed woman enjoying a walk on the beautiful sand, with a man, an incredibly unattractive, fat, pastrylike-fleshed man; you see the pleasure they're taking in their surroundings. Still standing, looking out the window, you see yourself lying on the beach, enjoying the amazing sun (a sun so powerful and yet so beautiful, the way it is always overhead as if on permanent guard, ready to stamp out any cloud that dares to darken and so empty rain on you and ruin your holiday; a sun that is your personal friend). You see yourself taking a walk on that beach, you see yourself meeting new people (only they are new in a very limited way, for they are people just like you). You see yourself eating some delicious, locally grown food. You see yourself, you see yourself . . . You must not wonder what exactly happened to the contents of your lavatory when you flushed it. You must not wonder where your bathwater went when you pulled out the stopper. You must not wonder what happened when you brushed your teeth. Oh, it might all end up in the water you are thinking of taking a swim in; the contents of your lavatory might, just might, graze gently against your ankle as you wade carefree in the water, for you see, in Antigua, there is no proper sewage-disposal system. But the Caribbean Sea is very big and the Atlantic Ocean is even bigger; it would amaze even you to know the number of black slaves this ocean has swallowed up. When you sit down to eat your delicious meal, it's better that you don't know that most of what you are eating came off a plane from Miami. And before it got on a plane in Miami, who knows where it came from? A good guess is that it came from a place like Antigua first, where it was grown dirt-cheap, went to Miami, and came back. There is a world of something in this, but I can't go into it right now.

WRITING A RHETORICAL ANALYSIS

What Is Rhetorical Analysis?

If we think of rhetoric as the art of persuasion, rhetorical analysis is an appreciation or critique of that art. When you do a rhetorical analysis, you're systematically examining the choices a writer or speaker makes and the effect of those choices on the intended audience. These choices may include big-picture strategies, such as structure, as well as choices at the sentence level (such as parallelism) and word level (such as strongly emotional language).

Just remember that this is an *analysis*. It is **not** a summary of the argument. It is **not** a simple listing of terms and strategies. And most important, it is **not** an argument about whether you agree or disagree with what the speaker is saying. Even if you are doing a rhetorical analysis of an argument on a controversial subject such as climate change or the death penalty, your view on the subject is irrelevant. Your analysis should focus on *how* the writer uses rhetorical strategies to achieve his or her purpose.

Close Reading—The Basis of a Good Rhetorical Analysis

A good rhetorical analysis begins with close, careful reading. Like any analysis, a rhetorical analysis is a three-step process:

1. Make observations.
2. Identify patterns.
3. Draw conclusions.

So, let's start by figuring out what to look for when you are making observations about a writer or speaker's use of rhetoric. For this Workshop, we're going to work with "Free to Be Happy" by Jon Meacham (p. 892), an essay you may have read as part of the Conversation on the pursuit of happiness.

Make Observations

Establishing Context. One of the first things you want to make observations about is the context for the piece you are analyzing—the rhetorical situation. You can use the rhetorical triangle or SOAPS from Chapter 3 to help you figure out the rhetorical situation, whichever method works best for you.

Of all the aspects of the rhetorical situation, the writer's purpose is the most important to understand when preparing for a rhetorical analysis. Without understanding the speaker's purpose, you can't know if his or her rhetorical moves are working *for* the speaker, or *against* the speaker. In some cases, such as a timed writing, you may be given contextual information as part of your instructions or as background. If so, you should take note and start thinking about how that context affects the rhetoric of the text. Is the speaker a noted authority who has been invited to address a friendly audience? Is he or she an everyday citizen publishing a letter in response to a highly controversial community issue or election?

In situations in which you need to figure out the context on your own, you may need to do a little digging: Where was the piece published? What is the author's background? In the case of Meacham's essay, take into account that it appeared in *Time*, a weekly print and online newsmagazine, with a large audience of educated professionals. Of *Time's* 25 million readers, 20 million are in the United States. Also consider that the article was one of several in a special issue on the topic of "The Pursuit of Happiness." Moreover, Meacham is an executive editor at Random House publishing company and a contributing editor to *Time*. Perhaps most important, in terms of the context for this article, is that he has won many awards, including a Pulitzer Prize, for his history books. These include biographies of Thomas Jefferson and Andrew Jackson, and an analysis of the civil rights movement.

What does all of this information tell you? Most directly, it tells you that Meacham is a respected expert on U.S. history, so he brings authority to the writing. Particularly key to this essay is his expertise as a biographer of Thomas Jefferson.

ACTIVITY

Using the information above — and anything else about the publication or author that you discover through your own research — how would you characterize the relationship between this writer and his audience? What assumptions can we reliably make about the audience? What approach (or approaches) will likely appeal to the members of Meacham's audience? What is Meacham's ethos in this context?

Looking at the Text. Remember that in the Make Observations stage, you are just gathering information. So, read (or reread) the essay, noting ideas and language that stand out to you.

Let's get into the text itself with a close reading of the opening three paragraphs. We'll use annotations to mark what we see as we read through:

Sitting in his small two-room suite in the bricklayer Jacob

Setting a scene, gives visual image of Jefferson at work

Graff's house at Seventh and Market Streets in Philadelphia —

Quirky detail about a legendary figure — he hated the flies from nearby stables and fields—

Thomas Jefferson used a small wooden writing desk

(a kind of 18th century laptop) to draft the report of a subcommittee of the Second Continental Congress in June 1776. There were to be many edits and changes to what became known as the Declaration of Independence— far too many for the writerly and sensitive Jefferson— but the fundamental rights of man as Jefferson saw them remained consistent: the rights to life, to liberty and, crucially, to "the pursuit of happiness."

Same way-back—when as it is now— writing is a struggle

TJ's personality traits

Familiar words and ideas, almost sacred to Americans

Author uses "our"—first person plural—so he's one of us.

To our eyes and ears, human equality and the liberty to build a happy life are inextricably linked in the cadences of the Declaration, and thus in America's idea of itself. We are not talking about happiness in only the sense of good cheer or delight, though good cheer and delight are surely elements of happiness. Jefferson and his colleagues were contemplating something more comprehensive—more revolutionary, if you will. Garry Wills' classic 1978 book on the Declaration, *Inventing America*, puts it well: "When Jefferson spoke of pursuing happiness," wrote Wills, "he had nothing vague or private in mind. He meant public happiness which is measurable; which is, indeed, the test and justification of any government."

First person plural again

Tension here between "good cheer and delight" vs. "something more comprehensive"?

Authority—citing expert

Public vs. private? Are they in conflict?

Direct quotation from authority as evidence

Shifting time—Thomas Jefferson, then 1978, now "ancient"

The idea of the pursuit of happiness was ancient, yet until Philadelphia it had never been granted such pride of place in a new scheme of human government—a pride of place that put the governed, not the governors, at the center of the enterprise. Reflecting on the sources of the thinking embodied in the Declaration, Jefferson credited "the elementary books of public right, as Aristotle, Cicero, Locke, Sidney, & c."

Another point of tension

Well-known philosophers of Western thought

These observations, based as they are on only a few paragraphs, aren't enough to determine exactly what Meacham's purpose is, but we can see where he's headed. He's writing about the meaning of "the pursuit of happiness" today, but giving his readers a historical perspective on the idea by taking us back to 1776, and even beyond that to earlier thinkers who influenced the authors of the Declaration of Independence, including the Greek philosopher Aristotle.

- Is his purpose to contrast today's values and those of Jefferson and his colleagues?
- Does Meacham see a tension between individual desires and what's best for the community?

Making questions out of your observations is a good way to begin figuring out a writer's purpose. These focus your reading while leading you to further exploration. At this early stage of analysis you don't want to eliminate possible interpretations; you want to open up possibilities.

ACTIVITY

Go through the rest of Meacham's essay (p. 892) and take note of the people, real or imagined, that Meacham refers to. Why might he include so many? Are they fairly similar or quite different? How are Meacham's readers likely to respond to them? Develop at least three questions based on the persons alluded to or cited. (If you are unfamiliar with any of the allusions, such as "Rockwellian optimism," for example, look them up.) What other questions can you generate based on the names you've noted?

Identify Patterns

Thus far, we have simply been making observations about the rhetorical context and what Meacham is doing as he builds his argument. The next step is to find a pattern or patterns with these observations.

If we look back at our observations, we see a series of notes about setting a scene and giving us quirky personal information about Jefferson. What pattern or patterns might link these observations—or at least some of them? Meacham seems to be humanizing Jefferson, making us see beyond the legendary Founding Father.

We also have a series of notes about tensions that all seem to relate to defining happiness as either personal delight or public well-being.

Our notes also include the observation that Meacham writes in first person—not third person, as one might expect from a scholar. He seems to be talking to his readers as though they are peers—addressing them as "we" and "us." Does this connect to the effort he put into humanizing Jefferson?

One way to organize your observations when you're writing a rhetorical analysis is to work with the three rhetorical appeals: ethos, logos, and pathos. For each one of the appeals, you can look for specific strategies that show that appeal in action. Here's an example.

Given the historical nature of the argument Meacham is making, logos is a natural place to start. Look back over those names you listed in the Activity above. You'll notice that Meacham cites the contemporary scholar Garry Wills; another well-regarded historian, Arthur Schlesinger Sr.; some Founding Fathers; and philosophers such as John Locke. What do all of these references have in common? The pattern we're seeing emerge is that Meacham appeals to the reason of his readers by citing the evidence of authorities, both past and present. Based on this observation, we could make the case that using authority to appeal to reason (logos) is a key strategy throughout the argument.

Draw Conclusions

Once a pattern emerges, it's time to draw conclusions. In the case of a rhetorical analysis, that means connecting the strategies you've discovered back to the author's purpose.

Meacham appeals to a pretty well-informed and educated audience, people who know some history. He reminds them from the very first paragraphs that happiness is not solely individual (or else "property" would have been in the Declaration of Independence instead of "happiness"). He asserts that happiness is not about getting everything you want as soon as you want it. It involves "balance" as the individual's happiness is based in "civic life." Thus, Meacham uses logic and the evidence of authorities to counter the emotional lure of personal happiness, and shifts focus to a type of happiness that prizes "public good" over "private gratification." Pointing out connections that link strategy to purpose is the key move in a successful rhetorical analysis.

ACTIVITY

Identify and analyze at least two strategies that Meacham uses to appeal to pathos. How do these strategies help him achieve his purpose of emphasizing the public and communal nature of happiness? Consider Meacham's overall ("big picture") approaches, but also such elements of style as connotative language and allusions.

Step 1: Craft Your Thesis Statement

Now that you understand what you are supposed to include in your rhetorical analysis, let's walk through the process of actually writing one. Like most other types of essays, a good rhetorical analysis begins with a solid thesis statement.

Finding Purpose

You can't write the thesis statement that will guide your rhetorical analysis until you under-stand the purpose the writer or speaker is trying to achieve. Meacham does not come out and clearly state his purpose. It's not something you can point to. But as we have analyzed some of the strategies he uses, we can infer that his purpose is to remind his audience of the values on which America was founded and which have stood the test of time. Those include subordinating the pursuit of personal happiness to "the common good." As Meacham describes it, Jefferson's view of happiness was both contemplative and "revolutionary."

Choosing Strategies

Once you have some notion of the writer or speaker's purpose in your mind, look back at the patterns you observed in the piece and identify which rhetorical strategies seem most important in terms of the author's achieving his or her purpose. At this stage, it's important to focus. You can't talk about everything, so just select a few key strategies to discuss. Remember: a rhetorical analysis isn't a treasure hunt to see who can find the most strategies.

Now you're ready to craft a thesis statement for a rhetorical analysis.

Tying Strategies to Purpose

An effective thesis answers the question "What is the writer's purpose, and how does he or she use rhetorical strategies to achieve it?" Those are the two components: the "what" and the "how." Let's look at an example:

> Jon Meacham cites the evidence of authorities as he assumes an informal but objective tone.

Is that a good thesis statement? Not really. It's not a strong thesis because it's missing purpose. It just focuses on two strategies—the use of authorities as evidence and an informal tone. Would it help to tack on "in order to achieve his purpose"? No. The thesis should tie the strategies to a *specific* purpose.

What about this one?

> Using the evidence of authorities, Jon Meacham appeals to his audience's reason in order to remind his readers that the American pursuit of happiness is less about personal happiness and more about the common good.

This thesis captures both purpose and strategies. It states what the writer is trying to achieve, and how he went about achieving it.

Keep in mind that you need not discuss all three appeals—logos, ethos, and pathos—in order to write an effective rhetorical analysis. While these do offer a clear way to organize your analysis, you might choose to focus on only one. In the example above, the thesis centers on logos. You cannot include everything, so you have to make choices. Just be sure that regardless of your focus, you discuss the connection between the purpose and the strategies—the "what" and the "how."

ACTIVITY

Discuss the weaknesses in each of the following thesis statements for a rhetorical analysis of "Free to Be Happy."

1. In "Free to Be Happy," Jon Meacham achieves his purpose by using effective rhetorical strategies.

2. Jon Meacham appeals to logos, pathos, and ethos as he develops his argument about the pursuit of happiness in "Free to Be Happy."

3. In "Free to Be Happy," Jon Meacham encourages his audience to remain true to the American ideal of happiness achieved through civil engagement.

4. I agree with Jon Meacham's claim in "Free to Be Happy" that Americans, despite our materialistic culture, need to strike a balance between achieving personal happiness and pursuing goals that benefit a larger community.

5. Historian Jon Meacham draws on the work of other historians and the Founding Fathers, along with references to well-known popular culture figures, to establish common ground with his audience.

6. In "Free to Be Happy," Jon Meacham achieves a friendly but objective tone by using first person plural pronouns, strong but not fancy vocabulary, references to historical figures the audience is likely to know, and quotations from scholarly sources.

7. By emphasizing logos over pathos, Jon Meacham warns his audience of the dangers of pursuing "[s]trictly personal happiness."

ACTIVITY

Write your own thesis statement for a rhetorical analysis of "Free to Be Happy" that focuses on Meacham's use of pathos. Analyze at least two strategies, and be sure to link those strategies to purpose.

Step 2: Choose Textual Evidence

As with any essay, a rhetorical analysis has an introduction (which includes your thesis), body paragraphs (also called "developmental paragraphs"), and a conclusion. The developmental paragraphs in this case require evidence from the text because you are trying to point out how that text works. Let's start with an example of a body paragraph for an essay based on the thesis statement that we worked with previously (p. 956).

Meacham supports his belief that the Founding Fathers intended happiness to be rooted in civic engagement by citing the work of current scholars. He quotes a biography of Jefferson by historian Garry Wills, who argues that Jefferson never intended the pursuit of happiness to be an individual and private issue, but rather, "'public happiness which [. . .] is, indeed, the test and justification of any government.'" For further support, Meacham indicates that his stance on this issue is similar to that of historian Arthur Schlesinger Sr. Meacham does not describe Schlesinger's credentials as a Harvard University professor of history and prolific author, perhaps assuming that his audience is familiar with this renowned figure. Thus, both of these scholarly sources provide evidence for Meacham's position that the pursuit of happiness is really "the pursuit of individual excellence that shapes the life of a broader community."

Notice that the topic sentence of the paragraph focuses on the connection between strategy and purpose. The paragraph is developed with textual evidence from the passage. In some cases, such as the last sentence, that means a direct quote from Meacham.

You'll notice in the second sentence that we had to quote a quote. This happens pretty frequently when analyzing logos and ethos, since it often involves evaluating the writer or speaker's use of sources. In that case, as you see here, the convention is to use single quotation marks to cite the material the writer quoted, within the double quotes you use to mark the writer's quotation. Punctuation is placed within both the single quotes and doubles.

ACTIVITY

Using the thesis on Meacham's use of pathos that you developed in the previous Activity (p. 957), write a body paragraph analyzing how Meacham's use of pathos serves his purpose. After you develop your topic sentence, you might try using this graphic organizer as you plan your paragraph.

Strategy	Evidence from Meacham (Quotation)	Link to Purpose

Step 3: Draw Your Conclusions

How you conclude your essay depends in large part on what your task is. If you're writing a rhetorical analysis of Abraham Lincoln's Gettysburg Address, you're probably not going to be asked to determine if the speech was effective. History has already decided that! But if you're analyzing a contemporary argument, effectiveness might be a key part of your assignment. Or, you might be asked to do a rhetorical analysis to explain why a speech or letter from the past flopped.

We'll start with the easier of the two. If you're writing a rhetorical analysis where effectiveness is *not* part of your job, then your conclusion should emphasize your claim about how techniques and strategies helped the writer or speaker achieve his or her purpose. Don't rehash every point you've made, but use the conclusion as an opportunity to restate your key points. As you stress the link between rhetorical strategies and author's purpose, it's also helpful to revisit audience and occasion. But remember: if you're writing a rhetorical analysis under time constraints, the conclusion can be very brief, no more than a few sentences.

Writing a conclusion where you are asked to gauge the effectiveness of a speaker's use of rhetorical strategies can be a bit more challenging because you're essentially writing an argument about an argument.

If your conclusion is yes, the text is effective, then focus on the most interesting ways the writer or speaker builds the argument. What strategies are particularly clever or insightful ways to reach the audience? If your conclusion is that the writer or speaker falls short, then focus on the most significant problems—and *why* they are problems. Does the writer fail to understand precisely who his or her audience is, for instance? Or does he or she emphasize reason to the point of making a valid but boring argument that does not engage emotions? If you conclude that, overall, a writer or speaker does not succeed in achieving his or her purpose, it's often a good strategy on your part to begin with something that is effective and then move on to the vulnerabilities and problems.

ACTIVITY

Working with a partner, play devil's advocate. One of you starts by explaining the claim "Meacham is—or is not—effective in achieving his purpose," and then the partner challenges that claim as the two of you develop a dialogue.

GUIDE TO LANGUAGE AND MECHANICS

PART 1 GRAMMATICAL SENTENCES

1. SENTENCE FRAGMENTS

A **sentence fragment** is an incomplete sentence. Usually fragments omit a subject, a verb/predicate, or both.

Fragment Ingrid spent most of her day on the computer. *Tweeting and posting to Facebook.*

Fragment She refused to give up her social media time. *Even though she needed to do her homework.*

Complete Ingrid spent most of her day on the computer, tweeting and posting to Facebook.

Complete Even though it was time to do her homework, she refused to give up her social media time.

1a. Fragments as Phrases

A phrase is a small group of related words that may function as a part of speech *within a sentence* but cannot function as a complete sentence. There are two easy ways to fix fragments that are phrases. You can either link the phrase to a nearby sentence using punctuation, or you can add a subject and verb to the phrase and make it a complete sentence.

Fragment We planned to go to Grandma's house. *Over the river and through the woods.*

Fragment *Over the river and through the woods.*

Correct We planned to go to Grandma's house, which is over the river and through the woods.

Correct We drove over the river and through the woods.

1b. Fragments as Subordinate Clauses

Unlike an independent clause made up of a noun and a verb and able to stand on its own as a sentence, a subordinate clause—also known as a dependent clause—begins with a word (usually a subordinating conjunction) that does not allow the clause to stand on its own as a sentence. You

may remove that conjunction to make the clause independent, or combine the subordinate clause with an independent clause to make it a complete sentence.

Fragment The car hit the tree. *When it went off the side of the road.*

Correct The car hit the tree. It went off the side of the road.

Correct The car hit the tree when it went off the side of the road.

1c. Fragments Containing Participles

A participle is a verb form that acts as an adjective by modifying a noun or noun phrase. It can also act as an adverb by modifying a verb or verb phrase. If a fragment contains a participle but no other verb, you may either change the participle to a main verb that describes the action or a state of being, or link the fragment to a nearby sentence.

Fragment *Howling* at the moon. The dog kept me awake all night.

Correct The dog howled at the moon. It kept me awake all night.

Correct Howling at the moon, the dog kept me awake all night.

1d. Fragments in Compound Predicates

A compound predicate tells more than one thing about the subject of a sentence by using two verbs joined by a conjunction. If a fragment is part of a compound predicate, it should be linked to a nearby sentence containing the subject to which the fragment's verb refers.

Fragment Roberto can speak and write in Spanish. *English, too.*

Correct Roberto can speak and write in Spanish and English.

2. COMMA SPLICES AND FUSED SENTENCES

A comma splice is made when two independent clauses are joined only by a comma. An independent clause is one that can stand alone as a sentence.

> **Comma Splice** The day was hot, the night was even hotter.
>
> **Correct** The day was hot. The night was even hotter.

A fused sentence, also known as a run-on sentence, occurs when two independent clauses are joined without a conjunction or proper punctuation.

> **Fused** The day was hot the night was even hotter.
>
> **Correct** The day was hot, but the night was even hotter.

2a. Sentence Parts

A sentence always includes a subject (S) and a predicate (P). A sentence predicate is composed of a verb (V), and often includes its object (O) and a subject complement (SC).

The subject of a sentence identifies who or what the sentence is about. Often, the subject performs the action of the verb.

The predicate of a sentence includes a verb that expresses either an action or a state of being and tells something about the subject.

The object of a sentence identifies who or what receives the action described by the verb.

A sentence complement completes the predicate by reiterating or describing the subject or object.

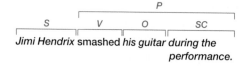

Jimi Hendrix smashed *his guitar* during the performance.

2b. Using a Period to Fix a Comma Splice or Fused Sentence

One way to correct a comma splice or fused sentence is to separate each of the independent clauses by placing a period between them. Each clause becomes its own stand-alone sentence.

> **Comma Splice** The comma splice is easy to identify, it uses a comma instead of a period or semicolon to separate two independent clauses.
>
> **Correct** The comma splice is easy to identify. It uses a comma instead of a period or semicolon to separate two independent clauses.

2c. Using a Comma and Coordinating Conjunction to Fix a Comma Splice or Fused Sentence

Another way to correct a comma splice or fused sentence is to connect each clause with a coordinating conjunction, such as *and, nor, or, but, yet,* or *so*. A coordinating conjunction often signals the relationship between the two clauses in a fused or spliced sentence. In the example below, using the coordinating conjunction *but* indicates the clauses are in some way opposite from one another.

> **Comma Splice** T.J. is an excellent basketball player, he will not enter the draft this season.
>
> **Correct** T.J. is an excellent basketball player, but he will not enter the draft this season.

2d. Using a Semicolon to Fix a Comma Splice or Fused Sentence

You may correct a comma splice or fused sentence by using a semicolon. Using a semicolon rather than a period between two clauses in a fused or spliced sentence emphasizes the relationship between the ideas in each clause. The effect is often that both clauses appear equally important.

> **Comma Splice** Ellen joined the track team, she's a great runner.
>
> **Correct** Ellen joined the track team; she's a great runner.

2e. Fixing a Comma Splice or Fused Sentence with Subordination

Sometimes one independent clause in a fused sentence is more important than the other—in such cases, you may want to use subordination to fix the sentence. Subordinating the less important clause places emphasis on the more relevant part of the sentence. As with the semicolon, this strategy allows you to illustrate how ideas relate to one another in a sentence.

> **Fused** Tomás always gets speeding tickets he will probably lose his license.
>
> **Correct** Because Tomás always gets speeding tickets, he will probably lose his license.

2f. Using a Conjunctive Adverb and Semicolon to Fix a Comma Splice or Fused Sentence

A conjunctive adverb explains the relationship between two independent clauses. Such relationships may include time (*afterward, earlier*), opposition (*conversely, on the other hand*), likeness (*similarly, accordingly*), or summary (*as a result, thus*). Conjunctive adverbs can be used to correct comma splices or fused sentences; to make this correction, place a semicolon before the conjunctive adverb and a comma afterward, as in the example below.

> **Comma Splice** Hardly anyone at the wedding reception left early, the guests stayed and danced until four in the morning.
>
> **Correct** Hardly anyone at the wedding reception left early; on the contrary, guests stayed and danced until four in the morning.

3. VERBS

Action verbs are so named because they describe action (*ran, jumped*)—these are what you normally think of when you think of verbs. Linking verbs join the subject of a sentence to its complement (a word or phrase that describes the subject) either by depicting a state of being (*be, appear, seem, sound*) or a result of some kind (*become, get*). Helping or auxiliary verbs (*can, may, will*) are the least common verbs and always precede the main verb in a sentence, thus clarifying its action.

3a. Linking Verbs

A linking verb (LV) illustrates the relationship between the sentence subject (S) and the subject complement (SC), which can be a noun, a pronoun, or an adjective.

> *Esperanza* (S) *was* (LV) this year's *homecoming queen* (SC). [SC is a noun]
> The *basketball* (S) *is* (LV) *his* (SC). [SC is a pronoun]

The puppy's *fur* (S) *feels* (LV) *soft* (SC) and *silky* (SC). [SCs are adjectives]

Verbs that function as linking verbs may sometimes function as transitive verbs, depending on context. Transitive verbs take one or more objects.

> The air *felt* very cold [Linking verb *felt* + subject complement *cold*]
> I *felt* the wall to find my way in the dark. [Transitive verb *felt* + direct object *wall*]

3b. Helping Verbs

A helping verb affects the tense of the verb it accompanies and indicates shades of meaning in the sentence. The combination of a helping verb and a main verb is known as a verb phrase. While the parts of a verb phrase often appear side by side in a sentence, other words may sometimes separate them.

In a few moments, Beyoncé *is going* to walk onstage.

I *have told* you many times that the essay is due at the end of the semester.

Samira *will* not *ask* her mother to drive us home from band practice today.

3c. Principal Parts of Verbs

The principal parts of a verb are the different forms it can take. Verbs have three principal parts: the infinitive (or base), the past tense, and the past participle.

The infinitive is the simplest form of a verb and is generally preceded by the word *to* (*to decide, to open, to work*).

The past tense verb indicates an action completed in the past (*decided, opened, worked*).

The past participle is always combined with a helping verb and depicts action at various times, both future and past (*have decided, has opened, will have worked*). When the helping verb is a form of *be*, it creates the passive voice. In passive-voice sentences, the subject of the sentence receives the action of the verb.

Verbs also have a present participle, formed by adding *-ing* to the infinitive (*deciding, opening, working*). Present participles have multiple uses, including forming the present progressive tense (I am *deciding*), modifying a noun or pronoun (the *lying* scoundrel), or serving as gerunds, which function as nouns in a sentence (*Writing* is his passion).

3d. Forming the Past Tense and Past Participle of Regular and Irregular Verbs

To form the past tense of a regular verb, add *-d* or *-ed* to the infinitive. Regular verbs with infinitives that end in *-e* take *-d* in the past tense; verbs that don't end in *-e* take *-ed*.

> **Infinitive** to jump
>
> **Past Tense** jumped
>
> **Past Participle** jumped

While most verbs are regular verbs, there are numerous irregular verbs that do not end in *-d* or

-ed in the past tense (*dug, slept, chose, hurt*). Like regular verbs, their principal parts include the present, the past, and the past participle.

3e. Verb Tenses

A verb's tense indicates the time of its action or state of being. The three simple tenses are present, past, and future.

The perfect tenses describe actions or events that occurred in the past but are linked to a later time, often the present.

The progressive tenses indicate actions or conditions continuing in the past, present, or future.

Simple Tenses

Present: I speak, I dance

Past: I spoke, I danced

Future: I will speak, I will dance

Perfect Tenses

Present perfect: I have spoken, I have danced

Past perfect: I had spoken, I had danced

Future perfect: I will have spoken, I will have danced

Progressive Tenses

Present progressive: I am speaking, I am dancing

Past progressive: I was speaking, I was dancing

Future progressive: I will be speaking, I will be dancing

3f. Forming the Simple Present Tense

The simple present tense typically indicates actions that take place once, repeatedly, or continuously in the present. The simple present form of a regular verb is based on the infinitive form. For the third person singular, add *-s* or *-es* to the infinitive.

	Singular	Plural
First Person	I wonder	we wonder
Second Person	you wonder	you (all) wonder
Third Person	he/she/it wonders	they wonder

Most irregular verbs also take the same form as regular verbs in the simple present.

To choose

I choose, you choose, he/she/it chooses
we choose, you (all) choose, they choose

However, some irregular verbs do not add -s or -es to the infinitive to form the simple present.

To have

I have, you have, he/she/it has

As noted above, the simple present tense can describe an action happening currently.

I *choose* to do my homework.

However, it may also be used to describe a future action.

I *will choose* to do my homework.

When using the simple present to describe a future action, it's often helpful to contextualize with words like *before, after,* or *when.*

Before I *choose* to do my homework, I will check my email.

3g. Forming the Simple Past Tense

The simple past tense is used to indicate actions that have already finished.

I *groomed* my horse yesterday. [Regular verb]

I *rode* my horse yesterday. [Irregular verb]

You may also use the helping verb *did* alongside the infinitive form of the main verb in a sentence to emphasize a past action or ask a question about an action performed in the past.

I rode.
I did ride. [Emphasizes the action]
Why did I ride? [Asks a question]

3h. Forming the Simple Future Tense

The simple future tense is used to depict actions that are expected to happen but haven't yet. It is formed by adding *will* to the infinitive form of the verb.

	Singular	Plural
First Person	I will read	we will read
Second Person	you will read	you (all) will read
Third Person	he/she/it will read	they will read

3i. Forming the Perfect Tenses

Perfect tenses are used to depict actions completed at the time of another action. They are formed by adding a form of the helping verb *have* to the past participle (e.g., *acted, chosen*) of the main verb. The tense of *have* determines the tense of the entire verb phrase.

The present perfect tense indicates actions that were completed at any point prior to the present, and its helping verb is in the present tense (*have* or *has*).

Uncontrolled logging *has destroyed* many tropical forests.

The present perfect can also show an action completed before another action happening in the present ("I *have decided* that I want to audition for the school play") or an action beginning in the past and continuing into the present ("Ms. Green *has been* teaching for thirty years" or "We *have been* rehearsing since the first week of school").

The past perfect tense indicates actions that were completed before another action that also took place in the past. Its helping verb is in the past tense (*had*).

Homesteaders found that speculators *had* already *taken* all of the good land.

The future perfect tense indicates actions that will be completed by or before a point in the future. Its helping verb is in the future tense (*will have*).

In ten years, our investment *will have* doubled.

After today's trip to the library, *will* you *have studied* enough to get an A on the final exam?

3j. Forming Simple Progressive Tenses

Progressive tenses indicate that an action is continuing or in progress. They are created by combining a form of the helping verb *be* with the present participle of the main verb (e.g., *playing, running*). The tense of *be* determines the tense of the entire verb phrase.

The present progressive tense indicates actions that are ongoing or continuing into the present time. Its helping verb is in the present tense (*am, is, are*).

> Yolanda *is applying* for a scholarship.

The present progressive of *go* can also be used to depict a future action when it is used in a context (typically with an infinitive phrase) that makes the time clear.

> Carrie *is going to help* me with my essay after school. [*to help* = infinitive phrase]

The past progressive tense indicates continuous actions that took place in the past, often (but not always) with specified limits. Its helping verb is in the past tense (*was, were*).

> In the 1980s, many baby boomers *were becoming* parents.
>
> I *was cleaning* my room when you texted me.

The future progressive tense indicates actions that will take place continuously in the future. Its helping verb is in the future tense (*will be*).

> The team *will be competing* in the NCAA tournament this year.

3k. Forming Perfect Progressive Tenses

The perfect progressive tense depicts continuing actions that began in the past.

The present perfect progressive tense indicates an action that began in the past and continues to occur in the present. It is formed by adding the present perfect of the helping verb *to be* (*has been, have been*) to the present participle (e.g., *running, playing*) of the main verb.

> The two sides *have been trying* to settle the case out of court.

The past perfect progressive tense indicates a continuing action that ended before another past action. It is formed by adding the past perfect form of the helping verb *be* (*had been*) to the present participle of the main verb.

> Carter *had been planning* a naval career before his father died.

The future perfect progressive tense indicates an action that will continue into the future and be completed before or continue beyond another future action. It is formed by adding *will have been* to the present participle of the main verb.

> By next July, I *will have been living* in Tucson for eight years.

3l. Verb Voice

Voice is the feature of transitive verbs that tells whether the subject of a sentence is acting or being acted upon.

Active voice indicates that the subject is acting. Principal parts and helping verbs make up the active voice.

> The police questioned him.

Passive voice indicates that the subject is being acted upon. To construct a verb phrase in the passive voice, add a form of *be* to a past participle.

> He was questioned by the police.

It's generally preferable to use the active voice in academic writing because it makes the prose more immediate, and clearly indicates who is doing what. Because the passive voice de-emphasizes sentence subjects, it can make prose vague and more difficult to understand.

3m. Verb Mood

The mood of the verb indicates the purpose and intent of the sentence. In other words, verb mood indicates whether the writer or speaker is stating a fact, giving a command, or describing something that is either conditional (maybe true) or contrary to fact (untrue).

3n. Indicative Mood

Most verbs are in the indicative mood, which is used to state a fact, ask a question, or express an opinion.

The geese landed on the field in a flock.

Where are you going?

People should recycle their garbage.

3o. Imperative Mood

The imperative mood is used to make a request or give a command or direction. The subject of an imperative sentence is always *you*, but it is generally omitted from the sentence. Verbs in imperative sentences always take the infinitive, or base, form.

> Please *buy* today's newspaper on your way home. [*You* please buy . . .]
>
> *Sit* down right now! [*You* sit down right now!]
>
> *Use* the socket wrench to loosen the lug nuts on the tire. [*You* use the socket wrench . . .]

3p. Subjunctive Mood

The subjunctive mood is used to express a wish, requirement, suggestion, or condition contrary to fact.

If a clause opens with *that* and expresses a requirement, it is in the subjunctive mood and its verb should be in the infinitive form.

It is our policy that volunteers *contribute* fifteen hours a week.

When the subjunctive mood describes a condition that is wishful, doubtful, or outright contrary to fact, it is often found in a clause that begins with the word *if*. It may also follow a verb that expresses doubt. The verb *to be* becomes *were* in the subjunctive mood. All other verbs take the simple past tense in the subjunctive mood.

> I wish I *were* in Hawaii right now.
>
> If the government *prohibited* the sale of tobacco nationwide, the cancer mortality rate would decline.

However, when an event, action, or condition was contrary to fact at some point in the past, use the past perfect tense instead of the simple past to form the subjunctive mood.

> If I *had been* in the game instead of on the sidelines, we *would have* won.

4. SUBJECT-VERB AGREEMENT

A verb must agree in number (singular or plural) with its subject, regardless of whether other words fall between them.

> The *cars* (S)—two Fords, a Lincoln, and a Nissan—*were* (V) for sale in the lot down the street.

A verb must also agree with its subject, even when the subject follows the verb.

> Where *was* (V) your *brother* (S) when you got home?

The subject and verb(s) in a sentence must agree in person, or the point of view being expressed. First person describes one's own perspective (*I am, we are*). Second person describes someone being addressed (*you are*). Third person describes others' perspectives (*he is, she is, it is, they are*).

> *I* (S) *was* (V) the only person at home last night.

Similarly, a sentence's subject and verb must agree in number. If the subject of the verb is singular, then the verb form is singular; if the subject of the verb is plural, the verb form is plural.

> The *boys* (S) *were* (V) the first group to finish their assignment.

4a. Titles That Are Subjects

When a subject of the sentence is a title of a book, movie, play, or work of art, it calls for a singular verb.

> *The Reivers* (S), published in 1962, *is* (V) the last novel written by William Faulkner.

4b. Singular Nouns That End in -s

Singular nouns that end in -s take singular verbs.

> The *bus was* crowded this morning.

4c. Subjects Joined by *and*

Subjects joined by *and* usually take a plural verb.

> The cat and the dog *play* well together.

However, when *each* or *every* is used to specify that two singular subjects are separate actors in a sentence, the verb should be plural.

> Each dog and cat in the shelter *is* well cared for.
>
> Every dog and cat in the shelter *is* available for adoption.

4d. Subjects Joined by *or* or *nor*

When a sentence contains subjects that are joined by *or* or *nor*, the verb should agree with the part of the subject nearest to it.

> Either the dog or the kittens *are* available for adoption.
>
> Neither the kittens nor the dog *is* available for adoption.

4e. Collective Nouns

Most collective nouns (e.g., *group, committee, audience*) take singular verbs.

> The team wearing red and black uniforms *controls* the ball.

When members of a group act as individuals, the accompanying verb should be plural.

> Usually, the team wearing red and black uniforms *scatter* in all directions when the game is over.

4f. Indefinite Pronouns

Indefinite pronouns are pronouns that do not refer to specific persons or things.

Some indefinite pronouns (*another, anybody, anyone, anything, each, either, everybody, everyone, everything, much, neither, nobody, no one, nothing, one, other, somebody, someone, something*) take third person, singular verbs.

> *Each* of the plays *depicts* a hero undone by a tragic flaw.

Other indefinite pronouns (*all, any, enough, more, most, none, some*) use either a singular or plural verb depending on their meaning.

> *All* of the cake *was eaten*. [*All* refers to *cake*]
>
> *All* of the candidates *promise* to improve schools. [*All* refers to *candidates*]

4g. Subordinate Clauses with a Relative Pronoun as the Subject

When the subject of a subordinate clause is a relative pronoun (*who, which, that*), the verb should agree with that pronoun's antecedent—the word to which the relative pronoun refers.

> Guilt, jealousy, and fear are ingredients *that go* into creating stereotypes. [The antecedent of *that* is the third person noun *ingredients*. Therefore, the verb in the subordinate clause—*go*—is in the third person plural form.]

4h. Linking Verbs

When a linking verb connects two nouns, the first noun is the subject of the sentence and the second noun is the subject complement. The linking verb should agree with the subject, not the subject complement.

> Nero Wolfe's passion was orchids. [*Nero Wolfe* is the subject; *orchids* is the subject complement. The verb *was* agrees with the subject.]

5. PRONOUN REFERENCE

Pronouns often refer to a noun, noun phrase, noun clause, or pronoun that was named or implied previously. The word, phrase, or clause the pronoun refers back to is called the antecedent; often, the antecedent is the subject or object of the clause in which the pronoun appears.

Tom invested all of *his* money in building a time machine. [*Tom* is the antecedent of *his*; using the pronoun is better than writing *Tom invested all of Tom's money in building a time machine.*]

At times, the antecedent may appear in a different clause or even a different sentence from the pronoun. There can be multiple antecedents in a sentence or passage.

Because *Tom* wanted to build a *time machine*, *he* invested all of *his* money in *it*. [*Tom* is the antecedent of *he* and *his*. *Time machine* is the antecedent of *it*.]

Both pronouns and nouns can be antecedents.

Even though some *people* thought *it* was a foolish idea, *they* also invested money in his *time machine*. [The noun *people* in the first clause is the antecedent of the pronoun *they* in the second clause. The noun phrase *time machine* in the second clause refers back to the pronoun *it* in the first clause.]

5a. Naming a Pronoun's Antecedent

It is important to clearly identify the antecedent of each pronoun; otherwise, your writing may confuse readers. This is especially true for such pronouns as *it, this, that*, and *which*.

Unclear She read a review of the book that confused her. [Was it the book or the review that confused her?]

Clear She read a review of the book, a work that confused her. [Now it is clear that it was the book that confused her.]

Possessive nouns, such as *Tom's, José's,* and *cat's*, cannot work as antecedents.

Incorrect In Juanita's story, she described spending the night in a haunted house. (This is confusing because *she* refers to Juanita, not the story.)

Correct In her story, Juanita described spending the night in a haunted house. (Now, the connection between *her* and *Juanita* is clear.)

5b. Adjective Clauses and Relative Pronouns

An adjective clause usually begins with a relative pronoun, such as *who, which,* or *that*. These relative pronouns clarify the relationship between an independent clause and an adjective clause. Use *who* to refer to people and *which* to refer to things. *That* can refer to both people and things, depending on context. Use *that* to introduce an adjective clause when it defines or specifies necessary information about the independent clause. Use *which* to introduce additional, but not necessary, information about the independent clause.

The Boone River, *which* flows intermittently during most of the year, overflowed after the storm. [The clause *which flows intermittently during most of the year* offers additional information that is interesting, but not necessary, about the river. Note that the clause is set off by commas.]

The river *that* overflowed last week does not generally reach flood levels. [The clause *that overflowed last week* provides information that specifies which river is referred to; therefore, it is necessary to the meaning of the sentence. Note that the clause is not set off by commas.]

In formal writing, a relative pronoun should be included when it is the subject within an adjective clause.

The Girl with the Dragon Tattoo is a book *that* gained a great deal of critical acclaim.

In informal writing or speaking, relative pronouns are commonly omitted when they are understood as an implied part of the sentence. While this is common usage, it is generally best to avoid dropping the relative pronoun in formal writing.

Informal *The Girl with the Dragon Tattoo* is one book I'd like to read.

Formal *The Girl with the Dragon Tattoo* is one book *that* I'd like to read.

Informal Here is a vase you can display the flowers in.

Formal Here is a vase *in which* to display the flowers.

Informal There is the man we think robbed the bank.

Formal There is the man *who* we think robbed the bank.

There are two additional relative pronouns that also begin adjective clauses: *whose* (the possessive form of *who*) and *whom* (the object form of *who*).

Whose begins an adjective clause that describes something that belongs to or is a part of someone or something mentioned in the independent clause.

> This tiny hummingbird, whose wings have been known to beat as many as eighty beats per second, is called the amethyst woodstar.

Whom stands in for the noun that receives the action of the verb in an adjective clause.

> **Formal** Bradley Cooper was the actor whom I met when I was in Hollywood. [*Bradley Cooper* is the subject of the main clause; *whom* is the object of the verb *met* in the relative clause and refers to *Bradley Cooper*.]

> **Informal** Bradley Cooper was the actor I met when I was in Hollywood. [*Whom* is understood as the object of the verb *met*.]

Whose is the only possessive relative pronoun; it is used to refer to persons, animals, and things. It takes the place of a possessive pronoun and must be followed by a noun. Using *who's* (the contraction for *who is* and *who has*) instead of the relative pronoun *whose* is a relatively common mistake.

> **Incorrect** The man who's car was stolen also lost his wallet with $500 in it.

> **Correct** The man whose car was stolen also lost his wallet with $500 in it.

6. PRONOUN-ANTECEDENT AGREEMENT

6a. Person, Number, and Gender

A pronoun must always agree with its antecedent in person (first, second, third), number (singular, plural), and gender (masculine, feminine, neuter).

> **Incorrect** At tonight's meeting, please ask the *chairperson* for *their* opinion on the matter. [*Chairperson* is singular; *their* is plural.]

> **Correct** At tonight's meeting, please ask the *chairperson* for *her* opinion on the matter. [This indicates that the person speaking/writing knows that the chairperson is female.]

> **Incorrect** *Each* of the students was prepared with *his* homework. [This assumes that the writer knows that the entire class is made up of boys; if the class includes girls, the writer's choice can be considered sexist, as the writer failed to consider the girls' presence.]

> **Correct** *Each* of the students was prepared with *his or her* homework.

> **Correct** *All* of the students were prepared with *their* homework. [Changing *each* (singular) to *all* (plural) also resolves the error.]

6b. Antecedents Joined by *and*

When two or more words joined by *and* function as the subject of the sentence, they form a plural, compound subject. A compound subject, when functioning as an antecedent, requires a plural pronoun.

> Millie, Isaac, and Ralph focused their attention on *their* tests.

However, if the nouns in a compound subject refer to the same person, then the antecedent is singular and the pronoun that refers to it is also singular.

> The *producer and star* of the movie always eats *her* breakfast before going on set.

6c. Antecedents Joined by *or* or *nor*

When an antecedent is a compound subject joined by *or* or *nor,* its pronoun must agree with the word that is closest to it.

> Neither *Isaac nor the girls* brought *their* uniforms to school.

6d. Singular Indefinite Pronoun Antecedents

When an antecedent is a singular indefinite pronoun (*another, any, anybody, anyone, anything, each, either, everybody, everyone, everything, much, neither, nobody, no one, nothing, one, other, somebody, someone, something*), it takes a singular pronoun.

One of the homesteaders abandoned *his* land.

6e. Collective Noun Antecedents

Collective nouns generally refer to a group acting as a unit (e.g., *chorus, team, staff*). Most collective nouns used as antecedents take singular pronouns.

The *committee* was dedicated to meeting *its* goals.

If group members in a collective noun act as individuals, the noun takes a plural pronoun instead.

Because the *committee* couldn't agree, *their* meeting was a disaster.

7. ADJECTIVES AND ADVERBS

Adjectives are words that describe a person, an object, a place, or an idea embodied in a noun, noun phrase, noun clause, or pronoun. Generally, an adjective comes before the word or words it describes. However, this is not the case when an adjective follows either a form of the verb *to be* or a verb that refers to appearance or the senses (*seem, appear, feel, taste, smell, sound*).

The *old* man wore a *green* sweater, *torn* pants, and a *dirty* overcoat.
The jam tart tasted *delicious*.

Adverbs are words that describe verbs, adjectives, or other adverbs in terms of time (*frequently, rarely*), place (*here, there*), and manner (*quickly, slowly*). Adverbs are frequently formed by adding *-ly* to adjectives. When adverbs describe verbs, they often immediately precede or follow the verb, but sometimes they may be separated from the verb.

The team left the field *silently*.

When an adverb describes an adjective, it places greater emphasis on the adjective.

The dog who attacked that child is *really* vicious and should be put down.

When an adverb describes another adverb, it places greater emphasis on the second adverb.

She played the piano concerto *very rapidly*.

Sometimes the same word (e.g., *fast, late, hard*) can be either an adjective or an adverb, depending on its function in the sentence.

The patient *arrived late* for surgery. [*Late* describes the verb, *arrived*; therefore, it is an adverb.]
The *patient* was *late*. [*Late* describes the *patient*; therefore, it is an adjective.]

7a. Adjectives as Subject and Object Complements

An adjective may be used as a subject complement or object complement. A subject complement is a word or phrase (commonly an *adjective phrase, noun phrase,* or *pronoun*) that follows a linking verb and describes or renames the subject of a sentence. An object complement is a word or phrase that follows a direct object, renaming, describing, or locating it.

The abandoned farmhouse *looked ready to fall down*. [The adjective phrase *looked ready to fall down* describes the *farmhouse*.]

7b. *Good* and *Well*, *Real* and *Really*

Good is always an adjective and *well* is the corresponding adverb.

> **Incorrect** She plays the piano *good* enough to be a star.
>
> **Correct** She plays the piano *well* enough to be a star.

Real is always an adjective and *really* is always an adverb.

> **Incorrect** Even though he played the trumpet *good*, he was *real* disappointed in his performance.
>
> **Correct** Even though he played the trumpet *well*, he was *really* disappointed in his performance.

7c. Forming Comparatives and Superlatives with Most Adjectives and Adverbs

In addition to their simple forms, adjectives and adverbs have two other forms: comparative and superlative, both of which are used to make comparisons. In comparing two things, we want to identify which one is the greater; in comparing more than two things, we want to identify which one is the greatest. The key to comparatives is in the previous sentence. We use the term comparative to distinguish which of two things is better; the term superlative distinguishes between three or more things.

Form the comparative of most adjectives by adding -*er* to the word and the superlative by adding -*est* to the word.

> Rondae Hollis-Jefferson was the *taller* of the two basketball players in the interview, but he was not the *tallest* on the team.

The comparative and superlative of many adjectives with multiple syllables are formed by placing *more* and *most* before the adjective rather than -*er* and -*est* at the end of the word.

> Robert Downey Jr.'s performance was the *most powerful* of his career.

Comparative and superlative forms of many adverbs are formed by placing *more* and *most* before the adverb. However, short adverbs that end in -*ly* usually take -*er* and -*est* in the comparative and superlative.

> Enrique built his model airplane *more carefully* than Jonathan.
>
> Jamal arrived *earlier* than the other applicants.

Use the comparative *less* and the superlative *least* to construct negative comparisons.

> Students are committing errors with adverbs *less frequently* than they did a week ago.
>
> Among the members of the JV soccer team, Hugo was the *least ready* to join varsity.

7d. Adjectives and Adverbs That Are Already Comparative or Superlative

Some adjectives and adverbs, such as *more* and *most*, already suggest comparatives and superlatives. Therefore, the words *more* and *most* should be omitted in sentences with adjectives and adverbs (*good, better, best*) that are already comparative and superlative.

> **Incorrect** Antoine and Michael are both excellent soccer players, but Antoine is *more better*.
>
> **Correct** Antoine and Michael are both excellent soccer players, but Antoine is *better*.

8. SHIFTS

A shift is a syntactical change—that is, a change in wording that allows a writer to portray various points of view or points in time. However, unnecessary shifts can lead to reader confusion.

8a. Shifts in Verb Tense

Verb tenses should remain consistent throughout a piece of writing unless the time changes.

> **Inconsistent** Some people never really *settle* into a profession; these people only *took* jobs when they *needed* food or shelter.

> **Consistent** Some people never really *settle* into a profession; these people only *take* jobs when they *need* food and shelter.

If the time described in a passage of writing changes, the verb tense must also change with it. Even though there are several tense shifts in the example below, they clearly and succinctly delineate each time change.

> I don't like my science class this year. I am having a hard time keeping up with the lessons. Last year, I did much better. I scored A's on all my tests, and all the work was easy to complete. I don't know why I'm struggling this year. I will ask my teacher for help. She is always available and willing to work with a struggling student.

When writing about literature, use the present tense to describe action happening within the book. However, you may use any applicable tense when discussing the work itself.

> In *Gone with the Wind*, Scarlett is so obsessed with Ashley Wilkes that she cannot see how much he actually loves Melanie.
> Margaret Mitchell first published *Gone with the Wind* in 1936.

8b. Shifts in Verb Voice

Verb voice should remain consistent in writing. If you are using the active voice, do not switch to the passive voice, or vice versa.

> **Inconsistent** My *grandmother was* a wise woman, but her *wisdom was ignored* by most of the family.

> **Consistent** My *grandmother was* a wise woman, but most of the *family ignored* her wisdom.

8c. Shifts in Person

Person refers to the relationship between a sentence subject and its verb. It indicates whether the subject is speaking about itself (first person *I* or *we*), being spoken to (second person *you*), or being spoken about (third person *he, she, it*).

The first person (*I, we*) helps establish a personal, informal relationship with readers. Novelists and short-story authors use first person when they want their readers to identify and empathize with the narrator. Second person (*you*) creates an immediacy that places a reader within the narrative and makes the reader feel like an active participant in the story. Third person (*he, she, it*) allows a writer to portray multiple points of view.

Person should remain consistent and appropriate to the content and the writer's purpose throughout a passage of writing.

> **Inconsistent** If *you* eat sensibly and watch *your* caloric intake, most *people* should be able to maintain *their* desired weight. (This also represents a *shift in number*, from a single person to more than one person.)

> **Consistent** If *you* eat sensibly and watch *your* caloric intake, *you* should be able to maintain *your* desired weight.

8d. Shifts in Mood

A verb's mood indicates the writer's attitude toward what he or she is saying, and it should remain consistent. Most mood shifts are from indicative to imperative.

> **Inconsistent** *Bend your knees* and you *should keep your eyes on the ball*. [The mood shifts from the indicative to the imperative]

> **Consistent** *Bend your knees* and *keep your eye on the ball*. [This sentence is entirely in the imperative]

PART 2 EFFECTIVE SENTENCES

9. MISPLACED AND DANGLING MODIFIERS

Words, phrases, and clauses that describe other words in a sentence are called modifiers. They modify the meaning of the words they describe by adding detail or specificity.

9a. Misplaced Modifiers

The position of a modifier within a sentence is important. If a modifier is placed too far away from the word it describes, the sentence may become confusing or unclear. When a modifier's placement does not clearly indicate which word it describes, it is called a misplaced modifier.

Misplaced modifiers can be fixed by moving modifiers closer to the words they describe.

Misplaced The dancers discussed techniques for doing complicated leaps and turns *in the car.*

The placement of this modifier suggests that the discussion was about *leaps and turns in the car,* but logic suggests that *in the car* describes where the discussion—rather than the leaps and turns—actually occurred.

Therefore, the modifier should be placed nearer to the verb *discussed:*

Revised *In the car,* the dancers discussed techniques for doing complicated leaps and turns.

9b. Squinting Modifiers

In some sentences, a modifier can cause confusion even when it is adjacent to the word or phrase it describes. A squinting modifier is a modifier that could potentially describe either the word that precedes it or the word that follows. To fix a squinting modifier, adjust the placement or revise the sentence so that the modifier clearly modifies only one word or phrase.

Squinting When learning a foreign language, practicing *frequently* improves confidence and fluency.

In the preceding sentence, it is unclear whether *frequently* modifies *practicing* or *improves.* If we assume that *frequently* is meant to modify *practicing,* the revised sentence could look like this:

Revised When learning a foreign language, frequently practicing improves confidence and fluency.

Revised When learning a foreign language, frequent practice improves confidence and fluency.

9c. Dangling Modifiers

When used correctly, a modifier modifies a specific word or phrase within a sentence. If a modifier is not connected to a specific part of the sentence, however, it dangles from the sentence like a loose thread.

Dangling Exhausted from a long night of studying, the test seemed to go on forever.

In the sentence above, the modifier *exhausted from a long night of studying* cannot describe the only noun in the main clause: *the test.* A person can be exhausted from a long night of studying, but a test cannot. To fix a dangling modifier, first determine what missing noun phrase, noun, or pronoun the dangler is supposed to modify. Then, add it to the sentence, either by making it the subject of the main clause or by turning the dangler into a clause that includes the missing noun phrase, noun, or pronoun.

Revised Exhausted from a long night of studying, *I* felt like the test would go on forever.

Revised Because *I* was exhausted from a long night of studying, the test seemed to go on forever.

Notice that some revision of the main clause or modifier may be needed to accommodate the added noun or pronoun.

10. PARALLEL STRUCTURE

Parallel structure is a language pattern created through the repetition of word forms or grammatical units. Parallel structure is commonly found in lists and comparisons but may be used for a variety of purposes including highlighting logical relationships, improving sentence clarity, creating rhythm, and adding emphasis.

> **Parallel Nouns** He is an outstanding *student, artist*, and *friend*.
>
> **Parallel Adjectives** It's the *smartest, funniest, bravest* book I've ever read.
>
> **Parallel Verbs** The thunder *rumbled* and *crashed* overhead.
>
> **Parallel Adjective Clauses** The team knows *that the competition is fierce* and *that the opposing team is impressive*.

10a. Series Linked by a Coordinating Conjunction

Coordinating conjunctions (*for, and, nor, but, or, yet, so*) are used to join similar language elements, such as words, phrases, clauses, and sentences. In a list or series joined by a coordinating conjunction, all items in the series should be parallel to one another. If items are not parallel, the sentence may be awkward or unclear.

> **Awkward** The scientific process involves *asking questions, hypotheses,* and *conducting research*.

To maintain consistency in this sentence, we need to change the form of the second item in the series.

> **Parallel** The scientific process involves *asking questions, forming hypotheses,* and *conducting research*.

10b. Series Linked by Correlative Conjunctions

Parallel structure is particularly important for maintaining clarity in sentences that use correlative conjunctions. Correlative conjunctions link two similarly structured words, phrases, or clauses in a sentence. Examples of correlative conjunction pairs include *either/or, neither/nor,* and *not only/but also*.

> **Awkward** For the final course assignment, students may *either* take a test *or* a paper.

To maintain consistency in this sentence, the phrase after each part of the correlative conjunction must use the same structure—in this case, a verb followed by its object.

> **Parallel** For the final course project, students may *either* take a test *or* write a paper.

10c. Elements in a Comparison

When a sentence compares two or more items, the items being compared should be in parallel form. Nonparallel comparisons may be awkward or unclear.

> **Awkward** *Freewriting* is a less structured prewriting approach than *to outline*.
>
> **Parallel** *Freewriting* is a less structured prewriting approach than *outlining*.

11. SENTENCE VARIETY

Strong writing often incorporates a variety of sentence types.

11a. Simple Sentences

A simple sentence contains a single main clause. It may also include modifiers.

> *Cara* (S) *is studying* (V) for a chemistry exam.

The main clause in a simple sentence can have a compound subject.

> *Cara and Raul* (S) *are studying* (V) for a chemistry exam.

It may also have a compound verb.

> *Raul* (S) *is studying* (V) for a chemistry exam and *listening* (V) to music.

In addition, the main clause in a simple sentence can have an implied subject.

> Don't *wait* (V) until the last minute to study for the chemistry exam. [The implied — but unstated — subject of this sentence is *you*.]

11b. Compound Sentences

A compound sentence contains two or more independent clauses, each with its own subject and verb. The clauses in a compound sentence can be joined by a coordinating conjunction.

> A new mushroom-shaped sea *animal* (S) *has been discovered* (V) near Australia, but *scientists* (S) *have not been able* (V) to classify it within existing categories of animal life.

The clauses of a compound sentence can also be joined by a semicolon, or by a semicolon followed by a conjunctive adverb such as *however*.

> A new mushroom-shaped sea *animal* (S) *has been discovered* (V) near Australia; however, *scientists* (S) *have not been able* (V) to classify it within existing categories of animal life.

11c. Complex Sentences

A complex sentence contains one main clause and at least one subordinate clause.

> Luis volunteers every week at an animal shelter [main clause] because he wants to become a veterinarian [subordinate clause].

In some complex sentences, the word that connects the subordinate clause to the main clause may be implied.

> Musicians know [main clause] [that] hours of work are necessary to perfect their craft [subordinate clause].

11d. Compound-Complex Sentences

A compound-complex sentence contains two or more main clauses and at least one subordinate clause.

> Although some students were nervous about learning computer programming [subordinate clause], most found the assignments interesting [main clause], and Rachel was inspired to learn more programming on her own [main clause].

11e. Normal Sentences

The normal sentence is the most common sentence structure in English. Although a normal sentence may include modifiers, it always places a subject before a verb at the beginning of its main clause.

> The *teacher assigned* a new project on Monday.

11f. Inverted Sentences

An inverted sentence reverses the subject-verb order of a normal English sentence so that all or part of the verb appears before the subject.

> Deep in the heart of the forest *stands* (V) an ancient *tree* (S).

11g. Cumulative Sentences

A cumulative sentence is composed of a main clause followed by a series of subordinate clauses or phrases that add information and detail.

> They were best friends—always loyal, rarely apart, and absolutely inseparable.

11h. Periodic Sentences

A periodic sentence ends with the main clause and begins with modifying phrases or clauses. The meaning of a periodic sentence may not be clear to the reader until the very end of the sentence.

> By triumphing over a series of dangerous obstacles, standing bravely in the face of fear, and working together as a team, the heroes of the story will save the day.

PART 3 WORD CHOICE

12. APPROPRIATENESS

Every time you communicate with someone else, you make immediate, often instinctive language choices. When you text a good friend, for example, you might use shorthand such as *u* for "you," *omw* for "on my way," and *tbh* for "to be honest." You can be sure your friend not only understands what you write but also expects you to write in that style. However, you probably wouldn't use that same shorthand in an email to a teacher, and including such language in a job or college application would seriously damage your chances. The words you choose in your writing affect how others perceive you and in turn reflect what you perceive as appropriate in a given circumstance.

Appropriate communication uses language suited to your audience and the purpose. In any writing you do, you must pay close attention to the words you choose.

12a. Tone

Tone indicates a writer's attitude toward his or her subject and audience.

To communicate effectively, you must choose a tone appropriate for your topic and audience.

To create an appropriate tone, think about what kind of attitude would best accomplish your purpose with a particular audience. What are your audience's expectations?

12b. Formality

Formal language uses standard English and is often used to describe topics the writer takes seriously. Formal language relies on sophisticated vocabulary, relatively long and complex sentences, an elevated tone, and an avoidance of contractions. Informal language allows the writer more flexibility because it tends to be more conversational. In informal writing situations, sentences tend to be shorter and simpler, vocabulary is not as sophisticated (and can involve slang and contractions), and the tone is more personal and friendly. You should use formal language in any writing for academic and professional purposes. Informal language is best used in writing for personal or humorous purposes. Much of social media writing (such as tweets, Facebook posts, and blogs) relies on informal language.

12c. Jargon

Jargon refers to specialized language used by a group of people who share the same knowledge base. This specialized language operates in a large variety of groups, from skateboarders to cell biologists.

Jargon can be convenient and even necessary. A cell biologist writing an article for an academic journal can use terms such as *transfection* and *in silico* to succinctly express her argument and be confident that readers understand. However, using those terms without explaining their meaning in an article for *Time* magazine would likely leave readers confused and might even make them feel excluded.

Writers can avoid using jargon by being aware of their audience. When you write, ask yourself: *Will my audience understand this terminology or not?* When in doubt, choose straightforward, simple, and clear words. If your topic requires the use of specialized vocabulary, jargon may be unavoidable. For instance, in a research paper on genetically modified foods, you may need to discuss terms such as *genetic engineering* and *gene targeting*. In this case, explain each term as plainly and succinctly as possible to ensure your readers can follow your narrative.

12d. Euphemisms

A euphemism is a word or phrase that replaces another term in order to render that term more palatable. Euphemisms attempt to beautify or conceal. For instance, rather than acknowledge the harsh reality of death, we might say that someone has *passed on* instead.

When we call a garbage collector a *sanitation engineer*, we are using a euphemism. In the best-case scenario, a euphemism can encourage a change in perspective. We can call attention to the hard work of collecting garbage and encourage respect for those who practice the profession by renaming them *sanitation engineers*. In the worst-case scenario, a euphemism covers up atrocities, such as the terms *collateral damage* for civilian deaths during war or *ethnic cleansing* for genocide.

Because the purpose of a euphemism is to soften or conceal the harshness or reality of a term, euphemisms by nature encourage vague language and can cause readers to interpret terms in wildly differing ways. To avoid euphemisms, use precise language.

12e. Slang

Slang refers to language shared by a particular group of people. Musicians keep to a beat by *staying in the pocket* while surfers greet each other by saying "Hey, *dude!*" And while slang can provide vibrant dialogue, it should be avoided in formal writing for several reasons. First of all, slang excludes readers who do not understand the vocabulary. Second, slang is mercurial—phrases or words usually remain current only for a few years. For example, a guitarist's excellent skills might be described as *groovy, far-out, cool, awesome,* or *sick*. Each adjective dates the language to a particular time and often pins it to a specific group or geographic area. Using precise and standard vocabulary instead of slang ensures that readers will clearly and easily understand the writing.

13. EXACT WORDS

Words are a writer's tools. Choosing the correct tool for the task allows a writer to communicate effectively. An imprecise word choice, however, can derail a writing task and leave readers confused and frustrated.

> The *sufficient* server brought menus and took our orders quickly.

Sufficient means "adequate" or "enough," but the more effective word in this context is *efficient*. Because the server takes the orders quickly, we know he is more than adequate—he is skilled. The words *efficient* and *sufficient* not only sound

alike, but are close in meaning. Choosing precise words is a skill that writers practice to improve their craft.

13a. Connotation and Denotation

Words can have both connotative and denotative meanings. The denotation of a word is its literal definition. The words *home, residence, abode,* and *domicile* all share the same denotation—all refer to the place where someone lives. But we say "Home is where the heart is"—not "The residence is where the heart is"—for a good reason. The word *home* carries connotations of belonging, relaxation, and security. Connotations indicate emotional or cultural associations and can suggest positive or negative overtones.

> **Denotative** *Celebrity photographers take pictures* of the rich and famous.
>
> **Connotative** The *paparazzi hound* the rich and famous.

In the above example, *celebrity photographers* is denotative and describes a profession matter-of-factly, while *paparazzi* evokes a negative connotation and transforms professionals into parasites exploiting their targets.

Knowing the different connotations of words allows you a greater range in tone and more precision in description.

13b. Clichés

A cliché can kill writing *dead as a doornail*. A cliché is a phrase or saying that has been used so many times it no longer offers meaningful or fresh language that engages the reader.

When a writer uses a cliché, readers may pass over it because they've seen and heard those words so often. Precise, detailed, and fresh communication is necessary to keep readers' attention.

Some common clichés include:

- *Absence makes the heart grow fonder.*
- *first and foremost*
- *Beauty is in the eye of the beholder.*
- *in any way, shape, or form*
- *leave no stone unturned*
- *glass half-full / glass half-empty*
- *Blood is thicker than water.*
- *going forward*
- *Absolute power corrupts absolutely.*
- *tried and true*

- *the bottom line*
- *adding insult to injury*

To avoid using clichés, diagnose your own writing and find the clichés you rely on. If you favor the phrase *first and foremost*, then use the search function in your document and either delete the phrase or replace it with a precise word choice. When you find a cliché in your writing, ask yourself how you can describe or explain something more clearly in your own words.

13c. Idioms

An idiom is an expression or phrase peculiar to a particular group or area. Idioms tend to consist of conversational language and are employed more usually in informal writing than in academic writing. Idioms can enrich writing by adding local color. For instance, in the case of ordering a carbonated beverage, someone from the northeastern United States orders a "soda," someone in the South orders a "Coke" no matter what brand the soft drink is, and a customer in the Midwest asks for a "pop." However, if your readers are not familiar with a particular idiom, you risk confusing your audience.

Idiomatic expressions rely on certain words in a certain order and only retain their meaning if used correctly. Pay close attention to the prepositions and articles in an idiomatic expression. If you write that your ninety-two-year-old neighbor *kicked the bucket*, your readers know that your neighbor died. However, if you write that your neighbor "kicked a bucket," your readers will wonder why your neighbor was angry. If you relax and *let off steam* by exercising, be sure you don't confuse yourself with a teapot by writing that you "let out steam."

PART 4 PUNCTUATION

14. END PUNCTUATION

14a. Periods

One of the most common uses of a period is to signal the end of a declarative sentence. A declarative sentence makes an assertion.

> Sarah will pilot the plane.

A period should appear at the end of a sentence that includes an indirect question. An indirect question conveys the idea of a question without asking it directly, typically by stating that a question was or is being asked.

> Julio asked if Sarah will pilot the plane.

A period can also indicate that the word preceding it has been abbreviated, or shortened. When an abbreviation ends a sentence, follow it with just one period.

> Sarah G. Stein will fly the plane at 10:00 P.M., and the flight lasts for 2 hrs.

Abbreviations of units of time or measurement also use periods. However, most organizational names (PTA for Parent Teacher Association), place names—such as countries (USA for United States of America), airports (LGA for La Guardia Airport), or states (NY for New York)—and people's names (MLK Jr. for Martin Luther King Jr.) are abbreviated with capital letters without periods.

14b. Question Marks

Use a question mark to signal the end of a direct question. A direct question asks for information. It might ask for a yes or no response, elicit information, or echo a statement in question form.

> Where will the plane land?

Sometimes a direct question can express doubt, irony, or sarcasm.

> Sarah will pilot the plane?

Avoid using question marks to signal doubt in formal writing by rephrasing the indirect question as a declarative sentence (e.g., *I am fairly sure that Sarah will pilot the plane*). You should also avoid using question marks that express irony and sarcasm—instead, express your thoughts directly (e.g., *Sarah's dubious talent for flying aircraft makes me hesitant to take this trip*).

14c. Exclamation Points

An exclamation point can interject, create emphasis, and express strong emotion. Inserting one at the end of a sentence will change the tone—and sometimes the meaning—of a given assertion, question, or command.

> Oh no! This is horrible! I can't believe this happened! Our vacation is ruined!
> Tornado! Find shelter!

It is best to use exclamation points sparingly, especially in formal writing.

15. COMMAS

The comma indicates a pause within a sentence, much like the act of taking a breath while in conversation. The separations commas create between words, phrases, and clauses affect the meaning of your sentences. By clearly delineating both concepts and objects in what would otherwise be a wall of text, commas help your readers follow your train of thought with ease. When deciding whether to use a comma, keep the following tips in mind.

15a. DO use a comma with a coordinating conjunction to join two main clauses.

To join two main clauses together in a single complete sentence, place a comma after the first clause and before a coordinating conjunction (*and, but, for, or, nor, yet*).

> Jaime doesn't have a big kitchen in his apartment, but he still manages to cook delicious meals for his family.

When using a coordinating conjunction to link two phrases, or a phrase and a clause, do not add a comma.

> **Incorrect** Tasha sang, and clapped her hands.
> **Correct** Tasha sang and clapped her hands.

15b. DO use a comma after an introductory clause, phrase, or word.

Use a comma after an introductory phrase, clause, or word at the beginning of a sentence.

> Smiling, Danez offered his hand for me to shake.
> Before today, I'd never seen the ocean.
> While Morgan chops the celery, I'll wash the tomatoes.

You may omit a comma after an introductory word or short phrase if there is no chance a reader could misinterpret your meaning.

> Someday soon I'll find the perfect prom dress.

15c. DO use a comma to separate items in a series.

When listing three or more items in a series, separate each item with a comma. The series might consist of single words.

> I baked pie, brownies, and cupcakes.

The items in the series might also consist of phrases or clauses.

> I baked a juicy apple pie, chocolate brownies with peanut butter chips, and those cupcakes you like so much.

Be careful not to place a comma after the final word, phrase, or clause in a series.

Some writers omit the comma *before* the final item in a series—this practice is common in journalism. However, leaving off the final comma in a series can obscure the meaning of a sentence, which is never desirable.

> **Unclear** After dinner I met my parents, Anna and Joel.

In the sentence above, Anna and Joel could be the writer's parents. If Anna and Joel are two more people joining the writer and his or her parents after dinner, a comma is necessary for clarification.

> **Clear** After dinner I met my parents, Anna, and Joel.

Remember, it is never wrong to place a comma before the last item in a series, and this practice is typically preferred in academic writing.

15d. DO use a comma between coordinate adjectives.

Coordinate adjectives function independently of each other in a sentence but still modify the same noun. In practice, this means that if you remove one coordinate adjective from a sentence, the meaning of the sentence will not change significantly.

Use a comma to separate two or more coordinate adjectives. However, be careful not to use a comma after the final coordinate adjective.

> **Incorrect** He was a charismatic, likable, man.
> **Correct** He was a charismatic, likable man.

However, if you link coordinate adjectives with a coordinating conjunction (usually *and*), you should omit commas.

> My bedroom is neat and clean and uncluttered.

Cumulative adjectives modify each other and the noun to which they all refer. The meaning of a cumulative adjective is typically objective, a quality most observers would agree on. Do not use a comma between cumulative adjectives.

He was a *young Japanese* man.

Applying two tests—the conjunction test and the order test—can help determine whether you are looking at coordinate or cumulative adjectives.

Coordinate adjectives can be joined by the conjunction *and* with natural-sounding results.

Clear He was a *charismatic and likable* man.

Attempting to join cumulative adjectives with *and* will sound less than natural and possibly alter the meaning of the sentence.

Unclear He was a *young and Japanese* man.

The order of coordinate adjectives can also be reversed with natural-sounding results.

Clear He was a *likable and charismatic* man.

Attempting to reverse cumulative adjectives will sound less than natural and possibly alter the meaning of the sentence.

Unclear He was a *Japanese and young* man.

Still not sure what kind of adjective you're dealing with? Here's one last clue: cumulative adjectives typically stack according to meaning, in the following order: size, shape, condition/age, color, origin/material.

15e. DO use commas to set off a nonrestrictive phrase or clause.

Place a comma both before and after nonrestrictive modifiers that fall midsentence. These phrases or clauses, sometimes called parenthetical modifiers, give nonessential information about the things they describe. However much they enhance a noun's meaning, nonrestrictive modifiers are not grammatically

essential to that noun's definition in a particular context.

Tolkien's writing, *which is now celebrated throughout the world,* was once less mainstream.

Do not place a comma on either side of a restrictive modifier that falls midsentence. Restrictive modifiers are phrases or clauses that give essential information about the things they describe. They not only enhance the meaning of a noun phrase but focus that meaning to a narrower subset.

All the fantasy novels *that I have read* seem influenced by Tolkien's work.

Generally, the relative pronoun *that* introduces a restrictive phrase, while the relative pronoun *which* introduces a nonrestrictive phrase. However, it is more succinct and often preferable to delete *that* or *which* from your own writing wherever their absence does not obscure meaning.

15f. DO use commas to set off nonrestrictive appositives.

An appositive is a noun or noun phrase that identifies or adds information to the entity it modifies (usually another noun phrase). Two nouns used in apposition usually sit adjacent to one another. Like modifiers, appositives can be either restrictive or nonrestrictive. Nonrestrictive appositives can be removed from a sentence without changing the essential meaning of that sentence. Place a comma before and after a nonrestrictive appositive.

The author of "The Monsters and the Critics," *J. R. R. Tolkien*, studied language and culture.

Restrictive appositives, which cannot be removed from a sentence without changing its meaning, stand without commas.

The fantasy author *J. R. R. Tolkien* studied language and culture.

15g. DO use commas to set off conjunctive adverbs.

Use commas to set off conjunctive adverbs such as *accordingly, eventually,* and *furthermore.* The adverb might take a comma after, before, or on either side, depending on where it falls. When a conjunctive adverb falls in the middle of a clause, place a comma both before and after it.

> He gave up on eating cupcakes, *eventually*, after several unpleasant trips to the dentist.

15h. DO use commas to set off parenthetical expressions.

A parenthetical expression is a short phrase or clause that appears within, and interrupts, another phrase or clause. It functions as an aside to your readers, and it can be set off from the rest of the sentence with commas. It can also be set off using parentheses.

> My mother was, *unlike last year*, very pleased with the gift I gave her for her birthday.

15i. DO use commas to set off a phrase or clause expressing contrast.

Use commas to set off a phrase or clause that expresses contrast. Such phrases often contain a coordinating or subordinating conjunction that signals the contrasting relationship.

> *Whereas Georgia reads books,* Ben prefers reading magazines.

Short contrasting phrases beginning with *but* don't always require commas.

> Ben reads magazines but not books.

15j. DO use commas to set off an absolute phrase.

A comma links an absolute phrase to the rest of the sentence it modifies. An absolute phrase is a modifier attached to a sentence without the use of a conjunction. The comma may fall before, after, or on either side of an absolute phrase, depending where the phrase is placed within the sentence.

> *Being the champion bookworm of her school,* Georgia read the contents of the entire library in just two years.

In the above sentence, the comma falls after the introductory absolute phrase.

Here, the absolute phrase falls between two coordinate clauses and is set off with commas on either side.

> Ben considered checking out Dostoyevsky, *his hand hovering over the book's thick spine,* but he turned to the periodicals room instead.

15k. DO use commas to set off a direct quotation.

Use commas to introduce dialogue and to set off direct quotations in which words, phrases, or sentences are copied word for word from another source. Always place the comma before the quotation marks. To interrupt a quotation (with phrases such as *she said*), set off the interrupting phrase or clause with commas.

> As my grandmother always said, "A little hard work never hurt anybody, but I'm not taking my chances."
>
> "I know you don't like basketball very much," Seth said, "but I still think you'd enjoy watching a live NBA game."

However, you may omit the comma before very short quotations, or quotations introduced by conjunctions like *that* or *whether*.

> When James asked Adriana to the prom, her answer was "maybe."
>
> She said that she "wanted some privacy."

You also omit a comma when the quotation reads as part of your own sentence, as in a restrictive appositive.

> The saying "wherever you go, there you are" always makes me smile.

15l. DO use commas around *yes* and *no*, mild interjections, tag questions, and the name or title of someone directly addressed.

Set off an introductory *yes* or *no* with a comma.

> *No,* he did not plan on going to the ball.

Interjections that don't require other punctuation, such as an exclamation point or question mark, are set off with commas.

> And then, *Lord have mercy,* who walked in but your father.

A tag question at the end of a declarative or imperative sentence transforms it into a question. Introduce the tag question with a comma.

> He said he was going, *didn't he?*

Place a comma before a name or title used in direct address.

> Please come to the ball, *Prince Charming.*

15m. DO use commas to set off dates, states, countries, and addresses.

Use a comma to set off the year in a full date, even when it falls midsentence.

> He was born on January 21, *1993,* the day after President Bill Clinton's inauguration.

However, omit the comma when only the month and year are given.

> He was born in *January 1993.*

Place commas around the name of a state when the name of a city precedes it, whether the state is spelled out or abbreviated. However, omit the comma if the state's name stands alone.

> She is from *Sacramento, California.*
> She is *from California.*

Set off the name of a country with a comma when the name of a state or other internal region precedes it, but omit the comma if the country's name stands alone.

> I'd like to visit Bern, Switzerland, before I die.
> I'd like to visit Switzerland before I die.

Place a comma around the different parts of an address, except between the state and zip code.

> She works at 175 Fifth Ave., New York, NY 10010.

15n. DON'T use a comma to separate a subject from its verb or a verb from its object.

Never place a comma between a subject and its main verb.

> **Incorrect** She, makes books all day long.
> **Correct** She makes books all day long.

Never place a comma between a verb and its object.

> **Incorrect** She makes, books all day long.
> **Correct** She makes books all day long.

15o. DON'T use a comma to divide a compound subject or predicate.

In cases where a conjunction such as *and* creates a compound subject, never divide that subject by placing a comma before or after the conjunction.

> **Incorrect** Gabby, and Steve saw me trip on the sidewalk.
> **Correct** Gabby and Steve saw me trip on the sidewalk.

Don't separate the components of a compound predicate.

> **Incorrect** The ballerinas leapt, and pirouetted, and pointed their feet.
> **Correct** The ballerinas leapt and pirouetted and pointed their feet.

16. SEMICOLONS

A semicolon conveys a closer connection than a period but a stronger break than a comma between two sentence elements. It usually coordinates more complex sentence elements, such as independent clauses within a compound sentence. Though the semicolon was used more freely in past eras, its function within clauses has narrowed over time to a few widely accepted uses. Generally speaking, it's best to use semicolons seldom.

16a. Using Semicolons with Conjunctions

A semicolon joins two independent clauses not linked by a coordinating or subordinating conjunction.

> Gabby and Steve tried not to laugh; they couldn't help themselves.

16b. Using Semicolons with Conjunctive Adverbs

Like conjunctions, conjunctive adverbs join two independent clauses, but they do so with an adverbial emphasis. Conjunctive adverbials include summarizing words like *thus*, indicators of time such as *finally*, and contrasting words or phrases such as *to the contrary*. Place a semicolon between two independent clauses linked by a conjunctive adverb.

> Gabby and Steve tried not to *laugh; nevertheless*, they couldn't help themselves.

16c. Using Semicolons with Items in a Series

When one or more of the items in a series contains internal punctuation, or is long and complex, using a semicolon to delineate each group of items helps clarify the sentence.

> The vacation package my parents bought includes a roundtrip flight; complimentary breakfast, lunch, and dinner every day at the hotel; and organized day trips such as snorkeling, hiking, and fishing.

17. COLONS

Colons indicate a close relationship between a clause and what follows. The clause that comes after a colon often clarifies what precedes it. Using a colon often signals some form of introduction or amplification, such as the introduction of a list, series, appositive, or another independent clause. This use is synonymous with "namely" or "as follows."

With rare exception, a colon is placed after an independent clause, but not after a phrase or dependent clause. In general, avoid using a colon where it disrupts a sentence that could otherwise stand on its own.

Don't use a colon between a verb and its object.

> **Incorrect** Last Halloween, I saw: three ghouls, five superheroes, and one Mad Hatter.

> **Correct** Last Halloween, I saw a variety of costumes: three ghouls, five superheroes, and one Mad Hatter.

Avoid using a colon between a preposition and its object.

> **Incorrect** Last Halloween, I got candy from: an old lady in an empty mansion and her tenant in the shed out back.

> **Correct** Last Halloween, I got candy from some interesting neighbors: the weirdest were the old lady in an empty mansion and her tenant in the shed out back.

Don't use a colon before a list introduced by *such as*.

> **Incorrect** I prefer healthy snacks, such as: apples, oranges, mangoes, and pecans.

> **Correct** I prefer healthy snacks: apples, oranges, mangoes, and pecans.

17a. Using a Colon between Two Main Clauses

Place a colon between two main clauses where the second clause exemplifies, explains, amplifies, or summarizes the first.

> Writing is easy: you just stare at the page until your eyes bleed.

17b. Using Colons with a List or Series

The colon may introduce a list or series.

> Spring is my favorite time of year for the following reasons: mild temperatures, lots of sunshine, and many fragrant blossoms.

17c. Using Colons with Appositives

A colon preceded by a main clause can introduce an appositive.

> Mary has four favorite foods: pizza, gummy worms, peaches, and chocolate.

17d. Using Colons with Quotations

A colon can introduce a long or heavily punctuated quotation.

> Vincent van Gogh said: "I have tried to emphasize that those people, eating their potatoes in the lamplight, have dug the earth with those very hands they put in the dish, and so it speaks of 'manual labour,' and how they have honestly earned their food."

17e. Conventional Colon Uses

Use a colon rather than a comma after a salutation in a formal letter.

> To whom it may concern:

Use a colon within biblical citations.

> Matthew 17:20

Use a colon between a text's title and subtitle.

> *Transformational Grammar: A First Course*

Use a colon between the publisher's state and name when citing a primary source such as a book in academic writing.

> Fine, Ruth. *Procession: The Art of Norman Lewis.* Berkeley: University of California Press, 2015.

Use a colon between the hour and minutes when giving the time of day with numerals.

> 2:22 P.M.

18. DASHES

The dash is a versatile punctuation mark that signals a rupture in a sentence's logic or syntax. It often sets off an amplifying or explanatory element within a clause. Its role can be similar to that of commas, parentheses, or colons, but the dash conveys a sharper emphasis than its cousins, underscoring the disruptive nature of what follows. It often signals an abrupt shift in tone or break in thought.

> Surely he'd be home soon—but no, it was karaoke night!

You may use a dash to introduce an expression, amplifying phrase, series, or appositive.

> There's only one song I'll sing—"Brother, Can You Spare a Dime?"

Dashes may also set off an emphatic aside or a parenthetical expression from the rest of the sentence.

And then—despite the fact that I had already lost my voice!—I tried to get on stage and sing a Beyoncé song.

Note that the interjected phrase contains its own internal punctuation in the preceding sentence. A question mark or exclamation point may punctuate interruptive phrases set off by dashes.

19. PARENTHESES

Parentheses are a pair of punctuation marks that set off extra information given within a sentence, such as an aside, explanation, or amplification. This type of expression is often called *parenthetical*. Parentheses function much as the dash and comma do—but unlike the dash, they downplay the material they contain, and unlike the comma, they may contain text with no particular grammatical relationship to the rest of the sentence.

Parentheses can add a qualification, a date in time, or a brief explanation.

She preferred the company of doves (as opposed to that of sparrows).

You may use parentheses around letters or numbers enumerating items in a series, especially when that series is run into the main text (rather than displayed in a vertical list).

The Audubon Society's website described habitats for (1) doves, (2) sparrows, (3) mockingbirds, and (4) blue jays, much to her delight.

PART 5 MECHANICS

20. CAPITAL LETTERS

What's the difference between Mark Twain, author of *Tom Sawyer*, and the mark you got on your last math test? One Mark is capitalized, and the other isn't.

Vacationers might visit a grand canyon in Puerto Rico, but they can visit the Grand Canyon only in Arizona.

In general, names of specific persons, places, and things are capitalized. These names are known grammatically as proper nouns. General persons, places, and things (common nouns) are not capitalized.

Adjectives made from proper nouns (like "*Puerto Rican* vacation") are also capitalized. The following examples will give you more details about when to capitalize words.

20a. Proper Nouns

A *proper noun* is a word, which is the name of a unique person, place, event, or thing.

Proper nouns should be capitalized.

Philadelphia   Exxon   Beyoncé

If a name contains more than one word, each word is capitalized, though minor words within these names (e.g., *of, in, the*) are not.

Mexico City   *Raiders of the Lost Ark*
Thomas Jefferson

Adjective forms of proper nouns are also capitalized.

Exxon-like   Jeffersonian

20b. Title or Rank

A title or rank preceding a proper noun should be capitalized.

President Kennedy had a mixed-breed dog named Pushinka, a gift from *Premier* Nikita Khrushchev of the Soviet Union.

However, titles that precede common nouns usually are not capitalized.

> Dwight D. Eisenhower, commanding *general* in World War II and *president* before Kennedy, had a parakeet named Gabby.

While the abbreviation of academic and professional degrees (*MD, PhD*) is always capitalized, the full name (*doctor of medicine, doctor of philosophy*) is not.

20c. Family Relationships

A family relationship (sister, nephew, grandfather, etc.) should only be capitalized when it is part of a proper name, or when it substitutes for a proper name.

> Eleanor Roosevelt often referred to President Theodore Roosevelt as her "Uncle Ted." [Here, *Uncle* is part of a proper name, *Ted*.]
>
> The Roosevelt children soon learned that *Granny*, Eleanor's mother-in-law, would give them anything they wanted. [Here, *Granny* substitutes for the grandmother's proper name.]
>
> In fact, Eleanor's *mother-in-law* encouraged her *grandchildren* to think of her as their real *mother*! [Here, the family relationship does not function as a proper name.]

20d. Religious Names

Names of religions and deities should be capitalized, along with the words denoting the followers of a religion.

> Singapore is one of the most religiously diverse countries in the world, with large numbers of people who follow *Buddhism, Christianity*, and *Islam*.
>
> About 5 percent of Singaporeans are Hindus, who worship such divinities as *Vishnu* and *Shiva*.
>
> While more than 800,000 citizens of Singapore are *Muslims*, fewer than 6,000 are *Jews*.

20e. Place Names

Proper nouns that name a geographic place, region, or feature should be capitalized.

Paris, France	Yellowstone National Park
the Northeast	Central Europe
the Rockies	Niagara Falls

If the proper noun is a phrase, minor words like *of* and *the* are not capitalized.

> *Garden of the Gods* is a national park in Colorado.
>
> Directional words, like *north, south, east, west, northwest*, etc., are capitalized if they are part of a place name. Otherwise they are not capitalized.
>
> The team bus traveled *east* from Ohio to get to the game in *West Virginia*.

A common noun that is part of a place name is capitalized.

> *Yonge Street* in Toronto, according to some, is the longest *street* in the world.

20f. Days of the Week, Months, and Holidays

Days of the week, months, and holidays are capitalized. Seasons and academic terms are **not** capitalized.

> This year, many students will celebrate the end of the *spring semester* on *Thursday, May* 24, just before leaving for the *Memorial Day* holiday.

20g. Historical Events, Periods, and Documents

A historical event is a specific happening in history; it's not just any revolution, but the *American Revolution* or the *Russian Revolution*. Some time periods or eras in history are known by a name. In the U.S., the 1920s were called the *Roaring Twenties*.

Historical events, periods, and documents should be capitalized.

- World War II
- the U.S. Constitution
- the Sixties
- the Civil Rights Movement
- the Revolutionary War

The exception to this rule is when the event or period is referred to not by a name but by a phrase.

- the reign of Louis XIV
- the American war for independence

Some events may be known by a single name, which is capitalized. When the term is used in a more general sense, it is not capitalized.

> After the *Revolution*, many people in the new United States wanted George Washington to become king.

> The twentieth century saw one *revolution* after another in African nations that had been colonies of European powers.

20h. Names of Institutions

An institution is an entity such as a school, government, or business.

Names of institutions should be capitalized, except for minor words like *of* and *the.*

> Howard University   Bank of America
> Federal Bureau of Investigation

In addition to names of schools and colleges, names of departments and specific courses should also be capitalized. Notice in the example below the difference between capitalized names and common nouns.

> My local junior *college*, Winslow County Community College, has a number of excellent departments.

> After talking to some faculty in the *Department of Natural Sciences*, I signed up for *Introduction to Biology.*

20i. Titles of Created Works

Titles of created works like books, movies, or newspaper articles, should have first, last, and all main words in between capitalized.

> Toni Morrison was a single mother when she began writing her novel *The Bluest Eye.*

In the early 1950s, artist Helen Frankenthaler created a new type of art when she used poured paint instead of brushes in her work *Mountains and Sea.* A *New York Times* critic wrote in 1987 that *I Love Lucy* "is a cultural fact of life."

Minor words in a title are generally not capitalized unless they come first or last in the title, or follow a colon. Minor words include articles (*a, an, the*), conjunctions (*and, but, for, or, nor, so, yet*), and prepositions (such as *in, on, at, of, from*).

> *Indiana Jones and the Raiders of the Lost Ark*
> *The Hobbit: An Unexpected Journey*
> *Alvin and the Chipmunks 2: The Squeakquel*

20j. Quotations

The first letter of a quoted sentence should be capitalized.

> On the subject of the weather, Mark Twain said, "It is best to read the weather forecast before we pray for rain."

Only the first word of a quoted sentence is capitalized, even when you break the sentence with your own words.

> "*The* proper office of a friend," Mark Twain wrote in his notebook, "*is* to side with you when you are in the wrong. *Nearly* anybody will side with you when you are in the right."

When a quote is longer than one sentence, each sentence should begin with a capital letter.

> "*He* was ignorant of the commonest accomplishments of youth," said Mark Twain of George Washington. "*He* would not even lie."

21. HYPHENS

In Hollywood, an actor who produces his own film becomes a "hyphenate": an actor-producer. If she also directs, she's an actor-producer-director. Even beyond Hollywood, the simple hyphen is a way to make a single word out of two or more words.

One helping dog is Hasty, who is not your *run-of-the-mill* golden retriever: he can locate avalanche victims.

At Lake Nakuru in Kenya, you can get an *awe-inspiring* view of thousands of pink flamingos feeding on the lake's plentiful algae.

Spud Webb was only five feet seven inches tall when he *slam-dunked* over the reigning champion to win the 1986 NBA dunk contest.

As in the first two sentences, hyphenated words are often adjectives, but they may be nouns or verbs (as in the third sentence).

Hyphens have three common uses:

- To create compound words from two or more words
- To write numbers from twenty-one to ninety-nine and fractions, such as one-fourth
- To add certain prefixes to words, such as *self-imposed* or *pre-Columbian*

The following examples will give you more details about how to use hyphens like a first-class grammarian.

21a. Hyphens in Compound Words

A compound word is most commonly a word formed from two or more separate words put together.

> down + hearted = downhearted
>
> fire + works = fireworks
>
> key + board = keyboard

A compound word can also be made of two words commonly used together. The two words in the phrase remain separate but function as one.

> cloud nine   stock market   vice president

Compound words are also formed from two or more words joined by a hyphen or hyphens.

> happy-go-lucky   long-term   second-rate

A hyphen may also be used in a compound word that has one or more elements beginning with a capital letter.

> pre-Enlightenment   Picasso-like half-Mexican, half-Chilean

21b. Hyphens in Compound Adjectives

What do the hyphenated words in the following sentence have in common?

Women's basketball has seen many *record-breaking* athletes who dazzled with *high-scoring* games and *last-second* shots.

All three hyphenated words function as *adjectives*. Although hyphenated words can function as other parts of speech, they are often adjectives with special rules for punctuation.

Compound adjectives **preceding** the noun they modify should be hyphenated.

> At six feet one inch, Seimone Augustus has such great *ball-handling* skills that she had *double-digit* scores in almost all of her *high school* games.

Compound adjectives **following** the noun they modify should **not** be hyphenated.

> In the WNBA, Augustus continues to display her skills at *ball handling*, with her regular-season scoring average in *double digits*.

The adverb *well*, when paired with an adjective, follows the same hyphenation rules as adjectives in the previous example.

> Augustus is *well known* for continuing her *well-executed* shooting in playoff games after the regular season is over.

How do you hyphenate a series of compound words when they all have the same second word? Omit that word in all but the last adjective of the series.

> Augustus was equally skilled in making *one-, two-, and three-point* shots.

Do not use a hyphen to link an adverb ending in *-ly* with an adjective.

> In playoff games, Augustus's scoring has been *extremely consistent* with her average of nineteen points per game.

21c. Prefixes and Suffixes

Prefixes and suffixes are elements added to a word to refine or change its meaning. An element added at the beginning of a root word is a *prefix*; one at the end is a *suffix*. Some prefixes and suffixes require hyphens.

A hyphen is always used after the prefixes *all-, ex-,* and *self-,* and before the suffix *-elect.*

Several presidents had *self-limited* terms, declining to run again, although as *ex-president,* Teddy Roosevelt regretted his decision and tried to make a comeback.

In 1944, FDR made the *all-important* decision to run for a fourth term and was soon *president-elect,* but he served only two months of that final term.

A hyphen is also used where the added prefix or suffix creates a double vowel, except a double *e.*

James Buchanan may not have been *anti-intimacy,* but he was the only U.S. president who never married.

The only president who was *reelected* but resigned during his second term was Richard Nixon.

A hyphen can also be used where the added prefix/suffix makes pronunciation of the word confusing.

Theodore Roosevelt was not only a *far-ranging explorer* but also the first president to ride in an automobile.

21d. Numbers

Numbers, when spelled out, use a hyphen in two cases: fractions and the compound whole numbers from twenty-one to ninety-nine. This applies to the adjective form of numbers as well.

Lyndon Johnson, the *thirty-sixth* president, was elected in 1964 with *three-fifths* of the vote, the widest margin in history, but he chose not to run again in 1968.

A hyphen should be used to indicate inclusive numbers.

If you get a paperback copy of President Kennedy's *Profiles in Courage,* you can read about President John Quincy Adams on pages *29-50.*

22. SPELLING

The two easiest ways to improve your spelling are to read a lot and to use a dictionary when you're uncertain. Whether online or in print, the dictionary is much more reliable than computer and smartphone spell-checking functions, which often miss homophone errors (two words that sound alike).

22a. Homophones

See if you can spot what's wrong with the following sentence.

Today, when tourists flock to Abbey Road studios, there probably aware that the Beatles made they're famous album their in 1969.

Were you confused by the misspelled *homophones*? A *homophone* is a word that sounds like another word but is spelled differently. Below are the homophones correctly placed.

Today, when tourists flock to Abbey Road studios, *they're* probably aware that the Beatles made *their* famous album *there* in 1968.

Some other commonly misspelled homophones are:

accept/except

He *accepted* all of the awards *except* the lifetime achievement award, which he insisted should go to his mentor.

affect/effect

Perhaps the trickiest of all homophones. Generally, *affect* is used as a verb, and *effect* is used as a noun.

The golfer leaned to try to *affect* the flight of the ball, but his body language had no *effect.*

lead/led

The tour guide *led* us to the entrance of the *lead* mine, but we weren't allowed in.

lessen/lesson

The physics *lesson* was on how opposite forces *lessen* velocity.

sole/soul

The *sole* job of a good poet is to lay bare the human *soul*.

stationary/stationery

Janice perfected her calligraphy technique by writing on *stationery* while riding on her *stationary* bike.

then/than

Then there was nothing left to say other *than* "thank you."

too/to/two

The *two* hikers were traveling *to* Brixton *too*, so we gave them a ride.

weather/whether

We checked the news to see *whether* the *weather* would be nice for the beach.

weight/wait

The *weight*lifter *waited* for his partner to add more *weight* for the next set.

who's/whose

Ahmed texted to see *whose* car we are taking and *who's* driving.

you're/your

You're the only one who can plan *your* schedule.

22b. Commonly Misspelled Words

One way to improve your spelling is just to be aware of which words tend to be challenging.

Here are some more commonly misspelled words for you to review.

accommodate	irresistible
achieve	knowledge
across	millennium, millennia
apparently	necessary
argument	noticeable
assassination	occasion
believe	occurred, occurring, occurrence
bizarre	
business	persistent
calendar	pharaoh
Caribbean	politician
committee	preferred, preferring
conscious	really
curiosity	referred, referring
definitely	resistance
disappear	separate
embarrass	successful
foreign	supersede
government	surprise
guard	therefore
humorous	threshold
incidentally	tomorrow
independent	truly
interrupt	unfortunately

23. VOCABULARY AND WORD ROOTS

If your parents asked you to consent to a nonsensical plan to wake up everybody in the house with a light-sensor alarm clock, would you resent it, or be too sentimental to object?

The above sentence may not make much sense, except as an illustration of how word roots connect many words with related meanings. How many words in the preceding two sentences have as their basis the Latin root *sent* or *sens,* meaning "to feel"?

A *root* is the origin of a word, often from a different language. Recognizing the roots of words can help you understand their meanings. The words *consent, nonsensical, sensor, resent, sentimental, sentence,* and *sense* may all be familiar to you. But the root, meaning "to feel," might help you understand the meaning of an unfamiliar word, like *sentient*.

Many roots form new words by adding *prefixes* and/or *suffixes* to the root. The addition of the prefix *in-* and the suffix *-itive* turn the root *sens* into the word *insensitive*.

Below are some common roots, their meanings, and words derived from these roots.

Root	Meaning	Words
-audi- (Latin)	to hear	audible, auditory, audiovisual
-bene- (Greek)	good, well	benevolent, beneficial, benefit
-bio- (Greek)	life	biology, autobiography, biotech
-duc(t)- (Latin)	to lead, to make	conduct, education, induce
-gen- (Greek)	race, kind	genetic, regenerate, genre
-geo- (Greek)	earth	geography, geode, geometry
-graph- (Greek)	to write	graphite, autograph, paragraph
-jur-, -jus- (Latin)	law	injustice, jury, jurisdiction
-log(o)- (Greek)	word, thought	logical, sociology, dialogue
-luc- (Latin	light	translucent, elucidate, lucid
-manu- (Latin)	hand	manuscript, manual, manufacture
-mit-, -mis- (Latin)	to send	transmit, mission, permission
-path- (Greek)	feel, suffer	sympathy, telepathy, pathos
-phil- (Greek)	love	philosophy, Francophile, philanthropy
-photo- (Greek)	light	photosynthesis, photocopy, telephoto
-port- (Latin)	to carry	transportation, portable, important
-psych- (Greek)	soul	psyche, psychiatry, psychic
-scrib-, -script- (Latin)	to write	transcription, scripture, unscripted
-sent-, -sens- (Latin)	to feel	sensitive, consensual, sentient
-tele- (Greek)	far away	television, telekinesis, telepathy
-tend- (Latin)	to stretch	extend, contending, distended
-terr- (Latin)	earth	terrain, extraterrestrial, disinter
-vac- (Latin)	empty	vacuum, vacation, vacuous
-vid-, -vis- (Latin)	to see	invisible, video, visor

GUIDE TO SPEAKING AND LISTENING

PART 1 STEPS TO CREATING A SPEECH

1. AUDIENCE ANALYSIS

Audience analysis is researching and thinking critically about the members of your audience in order to make your message relevant to them. Research could include asking your audience questions, handing out questionnaires, or examining demographic characteristics like age, gender, and cultural background. Understanding that every audience is motivated differently is the first step toward shaping your message.

2. TOPIC SELECTION

To select a speech topic, first brainstorm a list of your own interests and then ask yourself which might pique the curiosity of your audience as well as fit the occasion of the speech. Current events or controversies can make ideal topics because audiences are likely to be aware of and care about them.

3. SPEECH PURPOSE

Every speech has one of three general speech purposes: to *inform* an audience about something, to *persuade* an audience to adopt a position, or to *commemorate an occasion* such as a graduation, a wedding, or a funeral.

Every speech also has a specific purpose. The specific purpose of an informative speech is whatever the speaker wants to teach the audience (e.g., trying to educate others about online scams). In a persuasive speech, it's the action the speaker wants the audience to take (e.g., trying to convince coworkers to recycle). In an occasional speech, it's what the speaker wants the audience to feel about the occasion (e.g., trying to make classmates feel proud of their achievements at a graduation ceremony).

4. THESIS STATEMENT

While your general and specific speech purposes reflect your own goals as a speaker, your thesis statement is a single sentence that communicates to your audience the main idea of your speech. For example:

General Purpose To persuade.

Specific Purpose To persuade the audience to vote.

Thesis Statement Audience members should vote because voting not only fulfills the duty of every citizen in a democracy but also bonds voters to their communities and gives those communities a voice in how government is run.

5. DEVELOPING MAIN POINTS

Support your thesis with two or three main points. In an informative speech, main points are concepts you want your audience to understand. In a persuasive speech, your main points are more specific claims to support your overall argument. In a speech to commemorate an occasion, your main points are stories and arguments that illustrate the occasion's significance.

995

6. SUPPORTING MATERIALS

Supporting materials are facts, rationales, anecdotes, or other forms of evidence that support your thesis and its main points. These materials can be drawn from personal experience or outside research. The more specific and well researched your supporting materials are, the more credible your message will be.

7. MAJOR SPEECH PARTS

An introduction opens a speech and tells the audience who the speaker is and what the speech is about. An effective introduction usually begins with a quotation, anecdote, or example that grabs the audience's attention and contains a thesis that illustrates the topic's relevance to the audience.

The body of a speech contains each main point and its supporting materials. The main points in an effective body are organized logically, so that the audience can follow and appreciate the speech. Each main point should be developed using convincing supporting materials.

A speech conclusion reiterates the main points and connects them to the thesis. An effective conclusion often leaves the audience with an image, story, or idea to ponder and, depending on the speech topic, may also urge the audience to take action.

8. OUTLINING

Audiences are more receptive to a message with a clear organizational pattern. Creating a speech outline helps you organize the main points, examples, and other supporting materials in your speech.

I.   Main Point 1
   A. Specific Claim X
      i. Supporting Evidence
   B. Specific Claim Y
      ii. Supporting Evidence

Working outlines elucidate main points in complete sentences. Speaking outlines, on the other hand, use simple phrases or keywords, often printed on a sheet of paper or index cards that you can use for reference when delivering your speech.

9. PRESENTATION AIDS

Presentation aids are visual and audio supplements (e.g., props, diagrams, recordings) designed to help your audience grasp your points. A presentation aid can be as elaborate as a multimedia slide show or as simple as a quotation on a whiteboard. For more on the effective use of presentation aids, see Part 5.

10. PRACTICING SPEECHES

Practice is the key to delivering a successful speech. Every rehearsal enhances both your vocal and nonverbal delivery. The more familiar you are with your message, the more comfortable you will be in front of an audience. One rule of thumb is to rehearse a speech at least six times before giving it.

PART 2 INFORMATIVE SPEECHES

Informative speeches impart knowledge, raise awareness, or deepen an audience's understanding of a phenomenon. An informative speech might analyze a controversy, report on an event, or demonstrate a procedure.

11. MAKING IT MATTER

An informative speech isn't just a dumping ground for data. You must get the people in your audience invested in your topic so that they will retain the information you give them in your speech.

11a. Apply Audience Analysis

Analyze your audience to learn its level of familiarity with and interest in your topic, then adjust your thesis accordingly. It's difficult for the members of an audience to retain pertinent information when they are overwhelmed by facts, figures, or descriptions.

11b. Facilitate Active Listening

Even interested audiences will need help processing a large amount of new information. You can keep your audience engaged by:

- Opening with an introduction that previews the thesis and its main points
- Using transition phrases (e.g., "First of all . . ."; "The next reason why . . ."; "We've just spoken about X. Now we'll examine Y . . .") to clearly delineate separate ideas
- Using internal previews to tell the audience what main points are coming up
- Using internal summaries to remind your audience of the main points that have just been discussed
- Using repetition, parallelism, rhetorical questions, and other rhetorical devices to reinforce your main points
- Selecting an organizational pattern that highlights the relationships between your main points

12. INFORMATIVE SPEECH TOPICS

Informative speech topics can include people, things, events, phenomena, processes, ideas, and/or issues. Often the topic of a speech fits more than one of those categories. For example, a speech informing an audience about a scientific phenomenon might also inform that audience about the people who first discovered it and provide an overview of an issue to which it connects. The following table shows examples of different types of informative speech topics.

TOPICS	EXAMPLES
People Examines individuals' and groups' effect on society	- Steve Jobs, cofounder of Apple - Kathryn Bigelow, film director - Alcoholics Anonymous, a substance-abuse support group - Someone the speaker knows personally

(Continued)

TOPICS	EXAMPLES
Things or Phenomena Examines characteristics of subjects that are not human	• The history of ballet • The rise of the use of drones in warfare • The reintroduction of wolves into the American West
Events Examines past and present events	• The Peloponnesian War • The 2008 financial crisis • The Civil Rights Act of 1964
Processes Examines, and often explains, how something works	• How bees make honey • How killer whales communicate • How to throw a fastball
Ideas Examines opinions, theories, and/or beliefs	• Workplace ethics • Online privacy • String theory
Issues Examines controversies to raise awareness of clashing viewpoints (rather than to take a position)	• Impact of American anti-drug laws • Standardized testing in schools • Diplomatic relations between the United States and Cuba

13. COMMUNICATING INFORMATION

To communicate information effectively in a speech, you must define, describe, demonstrate, and/or explain it. When preparing an informative speech, choose which strategy, or combination of strategies, best fits your topic.

13a. Define

Defining your topic is vital, particularly when it is complex (e.g., "What is a supermassive black hole?") or new to the audience. There are several ways to define concepts:

Operational Definition The speaker describes what something does: *A plant is a life form that processes sunlight, water, and carbon dioxide into sugar.*

Definition by Negation The speaker describes what something is not: *Happiness is the absence of fear.*

Definition by Example The speaker lists multiple examples of a concept: *Citrus fruits include oranges, lemons, limes, grapefruits, and tangerines.*

Definition by Synonym The speaker lists alternative words and phrases that represent the concept: *A narrative is a story or a series of events.*

Definition by Word Origin The speaker shows the root origin of a term: *Poltergeist derives from*

the German *poltern, which means "create a disturbance," and* Geist, *which means "ghost."*

13b. Describe

To describe a concept, provide details that allow each of your audience members to paint a mental picture of it. This is particularly effective when your description contains important information or emotional content. For instance, a speaker informing an audience about health care in the United States might describe the sights and sounds of a typical emergency room.

13c. Demonstrate

When a process or concept is particularly complex, use speaking strategies that ensure your audience fully understands the topic at hand. Demonstration is a very effective strategy in informative speeches about how something works or how to perform a task. Speakers can either physically demonstrate a topic (as on a cooking show) or merely walk the audience through it verbally.

13d. Explain

Speakers can explain a concept by showing its causes, illustrating its relationships to other topics, and offering an interpretation and analysis of the topic. Explanation is a solid strategy to lead with when the subject of your informative speech is unfamiliar to your audience.

14. REDUCING CONFUSION

Information can prove difficult to digest when it relates to a complex topic (e.g., *prosody* in poetry), a highly abstract process (e.g., *accounting standards* in business), or an idea that challenges conventional thinking (such as *low-fat foods may not actually be healthier*). You can help your audience absorb and retain complex information by:

- Comparing unfamiliar concepts to familiar ones using analogies. For example, a speaker might explain antibodies and illnesses by likening them to a local militia and an invading force.
- Correcting erroneous assumptions the audience may hold about the topic. For example, Twizzlers are advertised as a low-fat food, but they contain a lot of sugar and are devoid of nutritional value.

15. ORGANIZING INFORMATION

A well-organized speech makes it easy for the audience to follow along. Informative speeches can be organized according to topic, chronology, space, cause and effect, and narrative patterns. For example, you can organize a speech about Barack Obama's presidency topically by arranging your points according to the controversies and policies of his presidency. The same speech organized chronologically could address events in order from his election in 2008 to his successor's election in 2016. To organize that speech causally, you might frame each of Obama's policy achievements as a reaction to preceding political, social, and/or economic crises. You may also use the problem-solution pattern (see section 22a) in informative speeches, though it's more common in persuasive speeches.

PART 3 PERSUASIVE SPEECHES

Persuasive speeches aim to influence the beliefs and actions of the people in your audience.

16. AUDIENCE MOTIVATION

Successful persuasive speeches appeal to the motives of the audience. You can increase your chances of successfully persuading your listeners by:

- Using audience analysis to deduce listeners' motives, then shaping your message to specifically appeal to those motives
- Stressing how the changes in behavior or policy you advocate for in your speech will benefit the audience

- Establishing your credibility by illustrating a personal connection to the topic or demonstrating your expertise
- Aiming for modest results—it's unlikely that listeners will adopt an entirely new belief system as a result of your speech seeking to persuade them
- Establishing common ground with the members of your audience so that they will be more receptive to a challenging message

17. APPEALING TO REASON AND EMOTION

A persuasive speech relies on an argument. An argument is made up of two parts: a position the speaker takes for or against an idea or issue, and the evidence the speaker uses to support his or her position. The Greek philosopher Aristotle divided arguments into rational and emotional appeals. Emotional appeals, known as pathos, grab audience members' attention and inspire them to act. Appeals to reason, or logos, lay out a logical justification for the speaker's argument.

Speakers can generate pathos with vivid imagery and compelling stories that evoke shared values like courage, equality, and hope. Rhetorical devices like repetition and parallelism can also make an audience feel moved by your message.

Speakers can conjure logos by sharing facts and statistics that support main points, showing causal connections between concepts, or citing examples and drawing analogies that illustrate the thesis.

An argument that relies solely on logos may make sense, but it is unlikely to move your audience to act. Conversely, an argument based solely on pathos may sound good but actually be emotionally manipulative and misleading. Powerful persuasive messages balance both pathos and logos.

18. ESTABLISHING CREDIBILITY

In addition to pathos and logos, successful arguments depend upon the audience's belief that the person delivering the message is worth listening to. Aristotle termed this necessary component of persuasion *ethos*. Today, it's also known as speaker credibility.

Even an argument that is emotionally and logically powerful will falter if the audience doubts the speaker's moral character, competence, or preparedness. You can establish your credibility by:

- Mentioning expertise or personal experience with the topic
- Demonstrating trustworthiness by finding common ground with audience members,

revealing persuasive goals up front, and expressing interest in the welfare of the audience

- Being emotionally invested in the topic, which will inflect both your verbal and nonverbal delivery with passion and evoke sincerity

19. MASLOW'S HIERARCHY OF NEEDS

As noted earlier in the chapter, successful persuasion appeals to an audience's motivations. Psychologist Abraham Maslow formulated a hierarchy of needs, which posits that fundamental

physiological and safety needs must be fulfilled before higher-level needs can even be considered (see figure below).

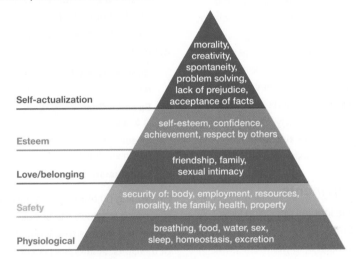

20. CONSTRUCTING ARGUMENTS

A persuasive speech depends on the power of its arguments. An argument has three parts:

1. Claims, or propositions, assert the speaker's conclusion.
2. Evidence substantiates a claim. Every claim needs evidence to support it.
3. Warrants are rationales that reinforce the link between the claim and the evidence.

20a. Types of Claims

A persuasive speech may stick to one type of claim, or blend several types. There are three different kinds of claims:

Claims of Fact verify the truth of something. These claims typically address questions for which competing answers exist (e.g., "Are rich people happier?"). Speculative claims of fact address questions whose answers are unknown (e.g., "Will climate change legislation help the economy?")

Claims of Value try to show that something is right or wrong (e.g., whether the death penalty is ethical). Evidence for a claim of value is usually more subjective than the evidence offered to support a claim of fact.

Claims of Policy endorse specific courses of action (e.g., "Body cameras should be worn by all police officers to reduce the use of excessive force during arrests"). Policy claims are prescriptive, meaning they argue that the proposed action will improve the status quo.

20b. Key Types of Evidence

Evidence is material intended to convince the audience a claim is valid. Some forms of evidence include examples, narratives, testimony, facts, and statistics. External evidence, or knowledge drawn from beyond the speaker's experience, is the most common form of evidence.

The audience's preexisting thoughts and beliefs can also be powerful evidence for a claim. Few strategies gratify audiences more than a reaffirmation of their beliefs, especially for claims of value and policy.

Finally, when a speaker's experience and opinions are relevant to a claim, his or her expertise can be used as evidence. However, audiences are often skeptical of claims supported solely by the speaker's testimony. Supplementing your speaker expertise with external evidence is more likely to yield a persuasive message.

20c. Counterarguments

A one-sided message ignores opposing viewpoints; a two-sided message addresses opposing claims in order to weaken or refute them. As a general rule of thumb, a persuasive speech should contain a two-sided message. On the one hand, if your audience is aware of opposing viewpoints that your speech ignores, you risk losing credibility. On the other hand, it's impossible to review and refute every single possible counterargument. The best strategy is to focus on raising and refuting only the most important counterarguments your audience is likely to be familiar with.

20d. Effective Reasoning

Reasoning is the process of drawing logical conclusions from a body of evidence.

Deductive reasoning begins with a general principle or case, is followed by an example of

that case, and then concludes with a claim. If the audience accepts the general principle and the specific example, logic dictates that it must accept the conclusion.

General Case All dogs are mortal.

Specific Case Fido is a dog.

Conclusion Therefore Fido is mortal.

Inductive reasoning begins with specific cases, or minor premises, then leads to a general conclusion those cases support. However strong such conclusions appear to be, they are not always, or necessarily, true. Many inductive arguments are in fact weak. An audience must decide if a conclusion reached through inductive reasoning is a valid one based on the evidence at hand.

Specific Case 1 Papua New Guinea has recorded a rise in sea level.

Specific Case 2 Key Largo has recorded a rise in sea level.

Specific Case 3 New York City has recorded a rise in sea level.

Conclusion Sea levels are rising worldwide.

Reasoning by analogy is a form of inductive reasoning in which the speaker presents two cases and implies that what is true of one is true of the other. Analogies presume that the circumstances underlying both cases are similar, if not identical—and for this reason, such arguments can have vulnerabilities.

Causal reasoning asserts that one event or issue is the cause of another (e.g., "Widespread online bullying, combined with the large amount of time teens spend online, has led to a nationwide increase in the number of teenagers diagnosed with anxiety disorders").

20e. Logical Fallacies

Logical fallacies are rationales for claims that may seem reasonable but are actually unsound—and usually false. Not only should you strive to avoid fallacious reasoning in your own speeches, but you should be able to identify it in others' speeches. While many logical fallacies exist, some of the most common are defined in the following table.

LOGICAL FALLACY	EXAMPLE
Begging the Question An argument that assumes the conclusion it purports to prove instead of providing evidence.	"People who don't study are doomed to fail their exams because studying is the only way to pass."
Bandwagoning An argument that incorrectly assumes that because an idea is popular, it is correct.	"Because more people watch *The Voice* than any other network or cable show, it must be the best show on television."
Either-Or Fallacy An argument that implies there are only two alternatives when there are in fact more.	"Since curbing carbon emissions by 75 percent would bankrupt the oil industry, Congress should not be allowed to regulate the industry at all."
Ad Hominem An argument that attacks a person's credibility instead of attacking the associated argument.	"We should spend less money on NASA and more money on education. After all, NASA's spokesperson was recently accused of tax fraud."
Red Herring An argument that cites irrelevant evidence in support of its conclusion.	"Less meat in our diet would make us healthier. For one, vegetable farming is easier on the environment than cattle ranching."
Hasty Generalization An argument in which a broad conclusion is drawn from too little evidence.	"The exorbitant hospital bill for my uncle's appendectomy unquestionably proves that our health care system needs to be overhauled on the national level."
Slippery Slope An argument based on an erroneous assumption that one action will lead inevitably to a chain of others.	"Properly recycling old electronics will set a good example, leading to a new era where recycling has eliminated pollution entirely."
Appeal to Tradition An argument that wrongly asserts that something is ideal just because it was popular in the past.	"Hollywood should not introduce a new ratings system. After all, G, PG, PG-13, R, and NC-17 are the ratings we grew up with."
Non Sequitur ("Does Not Follow") An argument in which the rationale has nothing to do with the conclusion.	"The Internet needs more restrictions on hate speech. Just look at how many teenagers are dropping out of high school."

21. ADDRESSING CULTURE

An audience's cultural background determines its reaction to persuasive messages. Understanding the core values, cultural norms, and cultural premises of your audience is key to crafting effective emotional appeals.

Core values are beliefs shared by members of the same culture. Values such as individualism, hard work, and freedom are some you may recognize and believe in. Arguments that challenge core values tend to be unsuccessful.

Cultural norms are behavioral rules to which members of a group generally adhere. For example, it is a cultural norm in much of the Western world for both women and men to pursue an education. Persuasive messages that contradict cultural norms are rarely successful.

Cultural premises are beliefs about identity and relationships firmly embedded in a culture. Some Western cultural premises include the notion that wealth is worth pursuing, and that science and technology improve our lives. Audiences who feel the very premises of their culture are being challenged are difficult to persuade.

22. ORGANIZING PERSUASIVE SPEECHES

The nature of your argument and its evidence, the response you want to elicit from your audience, and your audience's preconceived notions about your topic will all influence how you organize your speech.

22a. Problem-Solution Pattern

Some topics or claims inherently lend themselves to a particular organizational pattern. For example, the claim that the voting age should be raised implies that the current voting age represents a problem and that a higher age requirement represents a solution.

The problem-solution pattern is frequently used for persuasive speeches based on claims of policy. To use this pattern, organize your points to show the nature and significance of a problem before offering justification for a proposed solution, like so:

    I. Problem (what it is)
    II. Solution (how to fix the problem)

Complicated problems require more elaboration. In these cases, a three-point problem-cause-solution pattern may be used:

    I. Nature of the problem (why it's a problem, who it affects, etc.)
    II. Cause(s) of the problem (how/when it began, why it persists)
    III. Solution to the problem (how it will work, how it's different from previous solution attempts)

When asserting a claim of policy, it might be necessary to demonstrate the proposal's feasibility. In these cases, you can employ a four-point problem-cause-solution-feasibility pattern that provides evidence for whether the solution you've proposed will actually work.

22b. Monroe's Motivated Sequence

In the mid-1930s, Purdue University professor Alan Monroe developed the motivated sequence pattern, a five-step organization for persuasion that is still widely used today. It's particularly effective when attempting to persuade an audience to take an action, such as buying a product, donating to a cause, or voting a particular way.

1. The attention step employs an example, statistic, quotation, or anecdote to make the topic relevant to the audience.
2. The need step shows how the topic applies to the psychological needs of the audience. This step also implies that your proposed solution and/or action will satisfy this need.
3. The satisfaction step identifies the solution and shows how the solution will satisfy the need established in the previous step.
4. The visualization step shows the audience what would happen if the solution were adopted. This imaginary success scenario is designed to focus attention on the benefits of the proposal (as opposed to its feasibility).
5. The action step exhorts the members of the audience to act on their acceptance of the speaker's message. This may include changing their way of thinking, renewing their commitment to the values they already possess, or adopting new behavior.

22c. Comparative Advantage Pattern

When your audience is not only aware of the problem your speech addresses but already agrees that a solution must be sought, it may be best to compare the advantages of different possible solutions. This pattern acknowledges the strengths of other solutions, then identifies weaknesses, and finally shows the advantages of the alternative.

22d. Refutation Pattern

When opposing viewpoints are vulnerable to criticism, the refutation pattern of organization can be optimal. Here, the speaker identifies opposing claims before showing how they are insufficient. Emphasizing objections to opposing arguments may even sway audience members who originally disagreed with you. Main points arranged in a refutation pattern follow this format:

Main Point I State an opposing claim.

Main Point II Demonstrate how the claim is faulty.

Main Point III Present evidence for your own claim.

Main Point IV Contrast your claim with the opposing claim, emphasizing your claim's superiority.

23. IDENTIFYING AUDIENCE DISPOSITION

The way your listeners feel about your topic influences whether they will embrace or reject your appeals. Persuasion scholar Herbert Simon defines four audience types and suggests reasoning and organization strategies for each.

AUDIENCE TYPE	POSSIBLE PERSUASIVE STRATEGIES
Hostile or strongly disagreeable	• Address opposing viewpoints with the refutation pattern. • Emphasize points of agreement. • Use inductive reasoning. • Seek only a minor change in audience attitude. • If you must ask your audience to do something, hold off until the very end of your speech.
Skeptical or conflicted	• Address opposing viewpoints with the refutation pattern. • Present strong arguments supported by unbiased evidence.
Receptive	• Consider a narrative organization. • Reinforce audience sympathies with emotional appeals. • Stress commonality with the audience. • Clearly offer a call to action.
Uninformed or apathetic	• Capture the audience's attention. • Emphasize the topic's relevance to the audience. • Emphasize speaker credibility.

PART 4 CITING SOURCES IN SPEECHES

When you use ideas generated and facts gathered by others in a speech, you are obligated to credit your sources.

Acknowledging appropriate sources properly demonstrates the depth and quality of your research to your audience, which in turn bolsters your own credibility as a speaker who avoids plagiarism. Citing sources also allows your listeners to check your sources and do their own research.

24. CITING SOURCES

A verbal acknowledgment of a source within a speech is an oral citation. You should briefly offer the following information when orally citing a source:

- The author or origin of the source ("*New York Times* columnist Thomas Friedman . . ." or "According to the *National Education Association* website . . .")
- The type of source (TV interview, blog post, book, magazine, video, etc.)
- The title or a description of the source ("In the book *The Rise of Drones at Home* . . ." or "In an acclaimed memoir about overcoming substance abuse . . .")
- The date of the source ("An article published on *May 1st, 2011* . . ." or "According to an updated report about the Ebola outbreak posted by the CDC on *July 12, 2012* . . .")

Keep oral citations as brief as possible to avoid disrupting the flow of your speech. However, you should maintain a formal written bibliography of all your sources.

24a. Establishing Trustworthy Sources

A skeptical audience will accept your supporting materials—examples, stories, testimony, facts, statistics—if, and only if, they believe the sources are credible. Aim to cite sources in a way that establishes their credibility. For example, if one of your sources is a Harvard professor, that fact could convince some of your listeners to accept the information from that source as reliable, and you should therefore weave this credential into your oral citation.

Source reliability refers to how trustworthy we consider a source to be, and it is often based in large part on the source's history of providing factual information. However, even reliable sources can be inaccurate. For example, a nurse might spot inaccuracies in a *New York Times* article about health care due to his or her expertise, even though one might generally consider the *New York Time* reliable. Because no source is infallible, a claim supported by multiple sources will always seem more credible than a claim with only one source for support. The more controversial the claim, the more important it is to support that claim with a variety of sources.

Offering a source qualifier, or briefly noting why the source is qualified to address the topic, will bolster its credibility among skeptical listeners. For example, while making a claim about video games, one might introduce a source thusly: "Former video games editor for *Wired* . . ."

24b. Dynamic Citation Delivery

Oral citation doesn't have to interrupt the flow of your speech.

Varying the wording of your citations can make your delivery natural and keep audiences tuned in. For example, if you introduce one source with the phrase "According to . . . ," use another phrase for the next. "As reported by . . .";

"In the opinion of . . ."; and "*Wired* journalist Emily Dreyfuss writes that . . ." are just a few examples.

Leading with your claim places the most interesting information up front, and helps keep your speech organized in such a way that the audience can easily follow your logic. For example, you might begin a sentence with a claim that "Alcohol abuse can lead to colon cancer . . ." before revealing your source: "according to a new report by scientists at Carnegie Mellon University."

24c. Crediting Sources in Presentation Aids

Presentation aids that contain information drawn from research must also be labeled on the aid. If you reproduce copyrighted material such as photographs or infographics, put a copyright symbol (©) next to your citation(s). Use both oral and written citation in conjunction when the audience would benefit from both. For example, while pointing to a photograph labeled properly in its caption, you might also say, "This photo from *Life* magazine shows . . ."

25. TYPES OF SOURCES AND SAMPLE ORAL CITATIONS

Below is a list of types of sources and sample oral citations.

TYPE OF SOURCE	WHAT TO CITE	EXAMPLE
Book with *two or fewer* authors	First and last names, source qualifier(s), and date of publication.	"In the book *What We Know about Climate Change*, published in 2012, MIT meteorologist Kerry Emanuel argues that . . ."
Book with *three or more* authors	First and last name of first author and "co-authors."	"In the 1993 book *Captured Lives: Australian Captivity Narratives*, Kate Darian-Smith, professor of history at the University of Melbourne, and her two co-authors, both educators, show how . . ."
Reference work (atlas, encyclopedia, almanac, etc.)	Title, date of publication, author or sponsoring organization, and source qualifier.	"According to 2014's *Almanac of American Politics*, a widely read survey of American races and political figures, Michael Barone and co-authors describe . . ."
Print article	Same citation guidelines as a print book.	"In an article published in the May 2015 edition of the *New York Times*, Jeré Longman, a longtime sports reporter, chronicles the history of . . ."
Online-only publication	Follow the same guidelines as for a book, but identify the source as an "online" publication.	"In a May 25, 2015, interview for the popular online music blog *Pitchfork*, Canadian indie-rocker Dan Bejar discussed . . ."

(Continued)

TYPE OF SOURCE	WHAT TO CITE	EXAMPLE
An organization's website	Site name, source qualifier, and, if applicable, the section of the site cited and its last update.	"On the Ebola section of its website, last updated May 26, 2015, the Centers for Disease Control, the foremost monitoring agency for disease outbreak in the world, reports that . . ."
Blog	The blogger, source qualifier, affiliated website (if applicable), and date.	"In a May 23, 2015, post on his personal blog, Greg Mankiw, the chairman of the economics department at Harvard University, argues that . . ."
TV or radio news program	The program, segment, reporter, source qualifier, and date aired.	"In a *60 Minutes* segment about TedTalks that aired on April 19, 2015, Charlie Rose described . . ."
Online video	The video source, program, segment, source qualifier, and date of publication, if applicable.	"In a lecture delivered at the 2010 Sewanee Writers' Conference and broadcast on the conference's YouTube channel on November 10, 2011, Robert Hass, U.S. Poet Laureate from 1995 to 1997, argued that . . ."
Layperson or expert testimony	The person, source qualifier, context in which information was offered, and date information was offered.	"On March 26, 2015, in congressional testimony before the Senate Foreign Relations Committee, Ben Affleck, well-known filmmaker, actor, and founder of the Eastern Congo Initiative, testified as to the profound poverty endured by populations in Eastern Congo . . ."
Interviews and personal communication	The person, source qualifier, date, and type of correspondence.	"In an email interview conducted on February 2, 2015, Austin, Texas, Police Chief Art Acevedo said . . ."

PART 5 PRESENTATION AIDS

Research has shown that audiences remember only about 30 percent of what they hear, but they remember more than 60 percent of what they hear *and* see. Using presentation aids not only helps audiences remember the points of your speech, but also helps listeners visualize relationships among key concepts, rapidly evaluate data, and understand complex ideas. When visual aids look professional, they also bolster the speaker's credibility. However, presentation aids alone cannot make a speech work. No matter how great visual aids look, audiences are turned off by speakers who simply read information off the aids without adding anything new. Instead, aim to use aids as jumping-off points for engaging verbal information or argumentation.

26. CHOOSING A PRESENTATION AID

Presentation aids can include charts, diagrams, audio and video information, and props. Focus on selecting aids that illustrate your speech points most effectively.

26a. Props and Models

A prop is any physical object that enhances the audience's ability to visualize a main point. For example, a speech about fly-fishing might include a fishing pole, a fishing line, and a fly as props. A model is a three-dimensional, proportional representation of an object or process. For example, a doctor might use a human-sized skeleton as a model while explaining how a fracture affects movement.

Some guidelines for using props and models include:

- If the aid might be distracting, keep it hidden until you are ready to use it.
- Don't use an aid that is too small for everyone in your audience to see.
- Practice incorporating the aid into your speech before actually giving the speech.

26b. Pictures, Diagrams, and Maps

A picture is any image (such as a photo, painting, or map) that imparts information. For example, a photograph of a wrecked SUV might show the danger of texting and driving in a speech about auto safety. A diagram illustrates a process, showing how something works or how concepts are organized and related. For example, a diagram of a NASA rocket with each component labeled might supplement a speech about space flight. A map is an image that shows a geographic area or areas. A speech advocating for preservation of manatees might feature a map of Floridian waterways where both manatees and humans are active. In each case, the value of any picture, diagram, or map lies in its ability to efficiently convey information. Often this information is emotional, such as in the case of the wrecked SUV, or technical or numerical, as in the case of the rocket diagram.

26c. Graphs, Charts, and Tables

A graph represents relationships between variables. Most speakers use one of four types: a line graph, bar graph, pie graph, or pictogram.

A line graph plots one measurement along a horizontal axis and another measurement along a vertical axis, then connects each data point with a line. Line graphs can be powerful tools for representing trends that change over time.

A bar graph uses vertical or horizontal bars to compare quantities or magnitudes. Multidimensional bar graphs, in which differently colored or marked bars represent different kinds of information, allow audiences to easily compare two or more kinds of data in a single chart. When creating line and bar graphs:

- Clearly label all graphs, including their axes.
- Begin the numerical axis at zero.
- Only compare like variables.
- Plot no more than two lines of data on one line graph.

A pie graph divides a whole into "slices" so that each slice corresponds to a percentage of the whole. Pie graphs are good at showing contrasts in proportion. When creating pie graphs:

- Identify each slice and label it with its respective percentage.
- Limit the number of slices to a maximum of seven in order to reduce visual clutter.
- If possible, color each slice differently so that it's easy to distinguish between them.

A pictogram shows relationships and trends with icons or pictorial symbols. Pictograms add emotional impact to otherwise dry data. For example, a series of columns made up of missile icons stacked above different years might show how military spending has waxed or waned over time. When creating pictograms, clearly label your axes and indicate what variable each symbol represents.

Like a graph, a chart visually represents the relationship among data. A flowchart helps audiences visualize the flow of a complex process by animating its steps with boxes connected by arrows. A table allows audiences to rapidly examine and compare data by grouping it in columns and rows.

26d. Audio, Video, and Multimedia

An audio clip is a brief recording of music, sound, or speech. Video refers to excerpts from movies, television, online venues, or unpublished footage sources. A multimedia presentation combines any quantity of pictures, text, audio, and video data into a single production. Just as pictures can communicate complex information efficiently, audio, video, and multimedia presentation aids can also grab attention, add expressive power to main points, and make a speech engaging. When incorporating audio, video, and multimedia aids into a speech, remember to:

- Cue each clip to its appropriate starting point before the speech.
- Contextualize or preview the content of each clip for the audience before pressing play.
- After the clip has played, reiterate the reason why you showed it to the audience.

27. HOW TO PRESENT AN AID

There are a variety of ways, both high-tech and low-tech, to present aids effectively.

Computer-generated displays like digital projectors and LCD (liquid crystal display) panels allow speakers to project visual or multimedia information from a computer or an online source onto a screen. Computer-generated displays can also work in tandem with software like PowerPoint, making it easy to create dynamic multimedia presentations and generate notes and audience handouts that correspond to your speech.

Overhead transparencies are images on a transparent acetate sheet viewable via projection.

Transparencies are most useful in demonstrating real-time annotation of visual data—for example, a speech in which mathematical equations must be solved or explained for the audience. When using overhead transparencies:

- Ensure that the overhead projector works and practice using the transparencies before the presentation.
- Deliver the speech while standing beside the projector, facing the audience.
- Indicate items with a pointer on the transparency, not on the screen.
- Use a water-soluble pen to write clearly when annotating the transparency.

Flip charts are large paper pads on which a speaker can write or draw visual aids. Flip charts are usually prepared in advance and then flipped through during the speech as necessary—however, speakers can also write and draw on the paper as they speak.

Posters are large paper boards on which the speaker places text, data, and/or pictures. Posters can introduce main points or show main points in detail. The benefit of posters is that they are inexpensive and disposable, and if designed well, they can add immeasurably to both your presentation's clarity and your speaker credibility.

PART 6 LISTENING EFFECTIVELY

Listening is the conscious act of receiving, understanding, interpreting, evaluating, and responding to messages. The act of audience listening is an often-overlooked but vital component of any speech.

28. SELECTIVE LISTENING

Selective listening refers to the fact that audience members pay attention to certain messages and ignore others based on their background, level of attention, and interests. Many factors influence what grabs and holds an audience member's attention. Audience members pay attention both to what they think is important and to information to which they relate personally. When crafting a speech, it is helpful to keep in mind that audiences process unfamiliar information in terms of what is already familiar to them.

You can craft more successful messages by:

- Appealing to the audience's interests, needs, attitudes, and values
- Emphasizing, in your speech introduction, what the audience stands to gain by listening
- Connecting new information to the audience's likely experiences
- Creating analogies that link new ideas to well-understood ones
- Repeating main points to better ensure audience comprehension
- Visually reinforcing your main points with presentation aids when appropriate

29. LISTENING TO FOSTER DIALOGUE

A monologue imposes a speaker's message on the audience. By contrast, a dialogue is the respectful interchange of ideas *between* speaker and audience. In a dialogue, the speaker delivers the speech not to win the argument but to build a shared understanding with the audience, and the audience listens actively and empathetically.

When speaker and audience are engaged in a dialogue, a beneficial feedback loop of body language and verbal interchange can develop wherein the speaker's message is shaped by the audience's reaction, and vice versa. This shared connection between speaker and audience maximizes the impact of a message.

30. OVERCOMING OBSTACLES TO LISTENING

Active listening, or listening that is focused and engaged, is impossible when the audience is distracted. The following guidelines can improve your active listening as an audience member:

- Set a learning goal for each speech. For example: "In the next speech by a classmate, I will try to figure out why the speaker cares so much about his or her topic."

- Listen for the speaker's main points and note when the speaker mentions something that surprises you.
- Pay attention to nonverbal cues from the speaker.
- Try to discern the organizational pattern of the speech as it is delivered.

A listening distraction is anything competing for a listener's attention during a speech. External distractions, like ambulance sirens or the tapping sound texting makes when a phone is not in silent mode, come from the environment. Internal distractions, such as distracting thoughts and feelings, come from within the listener. Speakers and audiences should try to anticipate and prepare for external distractions by arriving and setting up or taking a seat early. To reduce internal distractions, speakers and audiences should be rested, alert, and make a conscious effort to focus on the message of the speech.

Scriptwriting occurs when an audience member focuses on what he or she, rather than the speaker, will say next, and it is a significant barrier to active listening. Similarly, defensive listening occurs when an audience member decides prematurely either to reject a speaker's message or to tune it out because the speaker has nothing to offer the audience. To avoid scriptwriting or listening defensively, audience members should remember that both tactics shut off communication. Even in cases of strong disagreement, allowing a speaker to finish before formulating a counterargument is usually most effective.

Overconfidence or laziness may cause audience members to miss key information, only to realize later the speaker had something valuable to say. Audience members should always assume the speaker's message is important and pay attention accordingly.

Cultural barriers to listening could include a speaker's dialect or accent, nonverbal cues, word choice, and even physical appearance. In such cases, audiences should focus on the message, not the messenger. Avoid judging a speaker based on cultural factors.

31. EVALUATING EVIDENCE AND REASONING

Evaluating a speaker's evidence and reasoning is a vital part of active listening. In order to think critically about a speaker's message, audience members should:

- Evaluate a speaker's evidence by asking if the sources seem credible and the facts cited seem accurate.
- Question the speaker's assumptions by looking for biases that might underlie the speaker's position and seeing if the evidence supports or contradicts those assumptions.
- Examine the speaker's reasoning by checking for fallacies or other examples of faulty logic.
- Consider alternative perspectives by trying to view the argument from all possible relevant points of view before assuming the speaker's perspective is valid.

32. OFFERING FEEDBACK

In order to give the most useful feedback to a speaker, audience members should:
- Be honest. Strive to be truthful, whether giving praise or criticism.
- Be compassionate. Begin criticism with a positive remark, and focus criticism on the speaker's message, not the speaker.
- Be specific. Neither blanket praise nor blanket criticism is helpful. Instead, focus your criticism or praise on individual techniques, main points, or parts of the speech that worked or didn't work.
- Allow for different delivery styles. Everyone has his or her own style of speaking. Avoid negatively judging a message just because the speaker's style differs from yours.

PART 7 EFFECTIVE GROUP COMMUNICATION

Most public speaking occurs in small groups involving anywhere from three to twenty people. These groups form in classrooms, offices, and even online discussion spaces. Small groups are also a common unit for giving group presentations. Therefore, learning how to work within a small group setting is vital to success both in school and in the workplace.

33. SETTING AN AGENDA

A small group functions best when its agenda, or overall objective and schedule for meeting it, is clearly articulated and followed. Whether the group must make a decision or a presentation, setting an agenda can help the group resolve conflicts, focus, and stay on track.

34. UNDERSTANDING SMALL GROUP ROLES

Groups tend to succeed when individuals fulfill specific roles, and most members of a group will fulfill dual roles. Task roles are those that directly relate to the group's objectives. For example, during a group presentation, one person may be assigned to be the primary writer, another the primary speaker, and another the one responsible for presentation aids. In addition, group members may also adopt maintenance roles, or social roles within the group. For example, a "peacemaker" might excel at conflict resolution, a "comic reliever" might keep group morale up with intermittent jokes, and a "taskmaster" might keep the group focused.

Unfortunately, anti-group roles that undermine the agenda may also exist. A "blocker" might always undermine any idea, even if it is good, or a "glory hog" might attempt to take credit for every idea, even if it belongs to the group as a whole. Group members should politely address anti-group problems at the outset in order to keep the group on track.

35. HOW TO FRAME DISAGREEMENTS

When groups make decisions, conflict is inevitable, but it can also be quite positive. The best decisions usually emerge from a productive conflict in which group members challenge ideas by presenting counterexamples and considering alternatives in order to either strengthen the original idea or find a newer, better one. Such issues-based conflicts allow members to debate problems and brainstorm potential solutions. Alternatively, person-based conflict can also erupt, wherein members fight with each other for power, for credit, for less or more responsibility, and so on. Person-based conflicts waste time, reduce morale, and generally impede the group agenda.

36. RESISTING GROUPTHINK

For a group to be effective, members eventually need to establish consensus so that everyone can work together to achieve the group's objective. At the same time, groups must also avoid groupthink, which occurs when group members do not think critically about ideas merely in order to achieve consensus. Speak up if the following warning signs of groupthink occur:

- Individuals disagree on issues, but avoid hashing them out in order to spare each other's feelings.

- Participants who disagree with the rest of the group feel pressured to conform.
- Critical analysis of popular ideas is discouraged.
- Members spend more time justifying choices than testing them.

37. GROUP DECISION MAKING

There are two methods of argument that generally help groups reach better decisions. Devil's advocacy occurs when members raise counterarguments, even when they are not sincerely held, merely in order to test the strength of a proposed idea. Dialectical inquiry occurs when members extend devil's advocacy to propose countersolutions to the original idea. These argumentation strategies expose weak assumptions that could prevent participants from making the best decision. Group leaders should encourage both methods of argument.

GUIDE TO MLA DOCUMENTATION STYLE

The Modern Language Association (MLA) documentation style is a set of rules for citing sources in formal research essays. It is the most common style for English classes, but be aware that other disciplines follow other models. By documenting sources properly, you make it easier for readers to find the exact texts that informed your opinions and supported your claims. For a teacher grading your paper, your use of systematic citation shows that you have been conscientious in investigating the topic and have avoided plagiarism. For readers who are interested in your paper, your list of works cited can help them learn more about the topic. Rhetorically speaking, a properly documented research paper boosts your ethos and appeals to logos.

GUIDELINES FOR IN-TEXT CITATIONS

MLA documentation requires in-text citations that refer to a list of works cited—an alphabetized list of all the sources you've drawn from. Sometimes all the necessary information for an in-text citation fits in the body of your sentence:

> On page 162 of *Aerotropolis: The Way We'll Live Next*, authors John D. Kasarda and Greg Lindsay suggest that downtown Detroit was doomed as soon as automobiles made the railroads less popular.

But more often you'll include some key information in parentheses just before the period. In this second example, the writer included the book title and authors' names in her sentence and, thus, only needed to provide the page number in parentheses.

> In *Aerotropolis: The Way We'll Live Next*, John D. Kasarda and Greg Lindsay suggest that downtown Detroit was doomed as soon as automobiles made the railroads less popular (162).

In this third example, there is no source information embedded in the sentence itself, so the in-text citation includes both the authors' names and the page number. Note that the title isn't included. With the authors' names, the reader has enough information to find the relevant entry in the list of works cited.

> Although the growth of car manufacturing brought jobs to Detroit, America's drivable network of industrial cities and residential suburbs "bled entire cities dry: starting with Detroit" (Kasarda and Lindsay 180).

GUIDELINES FOR A LIST OF WORKS CITED (2016 UPDATE)

Print Resources

1. Book with One Author
A book with one author serves as a general model for most MLA citations. Include author, title, publisher, and date of publication.

> Beavan, Colin. *No Impact Man*. Farrar, Straus and Giroux, 2009.

2. Book with Multiple Authors

> Kasarda, John D., and Greg Lindsay. *Aerotropolis: The Way We'll Live Next*. Farrar, Straus and Giroux, 2011.

3. Two or More Works by the Same Author
Multiple entries should be arranged alphabetically by title. The author's name appears at the beginning

of the first entry but is replaced by three hyphens and a period in all subsequent entries.

> Gladwell, Malcolm. *Outliers: The Story of Success*. Little, Brown, 2008.
>
> —. *What the Dog Saw, and Other Adventures*. Little, Brown, 2009.

4. Author and Editor Both Named

> Vidal, Gore. *The Selected Essays of Gore Vidal*. Edited by Jay Parini, Vintage Books, 2009.

Alternatively, to cite the editor's contribution, start with the editor's name.

> Parini, Jay, editor. *The Selected Essays of Gore Vidal*. By Gore Vidal, Vintage Books, 2009.

5. Anthology

> Oates, Joyce Carol, editor. *Telling Stories: An Anthology for Writers*. W. W. Norton, 1997.

Selection from an anthology:

> Washington Irving, "Rip Van Winkle." *Conversations in American Literature*: *Language, Rhetoric, Culture*, edited by Robin Aufses et al., Bedford/St. Martin's, 2015, pp. 435-48.

6. Translation

> Wiesel, Elie. *Night*. Translated by Marion Wiesel, Hill and Wang, 2006.

7. Entry in a Reference Work

Because most reference works are alphabetized, you should omit page numbers.

> Lounsberry, Barbara. "Joan Didion." *Encyclopedia of the Essay*, edited by Tracy Chandler, Fitzroy, 1997.

For a well-known encyclopedia, use only the edition and year of publication. When an article is not attributed to an author, begin the entry with the article title.

> "Gilgamesh." *The Columbia Encyclopedia*, 5th ed., 1993.

8. Sacred Text

Unless a specific published edition is being cited, sacred texts should be omitted from the Works Cited list.

> *The New Testament*. Translated by Richmond Lattimore, North Point, 1997.

9. Article in a Journal

The title of the journal should be followed by the volume, issue, and year of the journal's publication, as well as the page range.

> de Botton, Alain. "Treasure Hunt." *Lapham's Quarterly*, vol. 4, no. 2, 2011, pp. 205-10.

10. Article in a Magazine

In a weekly:

> Menand, Louis. "The Unpolitical Animal: How Political Science Understands Voters." *The New Yorker*, 30 Aug. 2004, pp. 92-96.

In a monthly:

> Baker, Kevin. "Barack Hoover Obama: The Best and the Brightest Blow It Again." *Harper's*, July 2009, pp. 29-37.

11. Article in a Newspaper

If you are citing a local paper that does not contain the city name in its title, add the city name in brackets after the title. When citing an article that does not appear on consecutive pages, list the first page followed by a plus sign. The edition only needs to be included if it is listed on the paper's masthead.

> Edge, John T. "Fast Food Even before Fast Food." *The New York Times*, 30 Sept. 2009, late ed., pp. D1+.

12. Review

In a weekly:

> Davis, Jordan. "Happy Thoughts!" Review of *The Golden Age of Paraphernalia*, by Kevin Davies, *The Nation*, 23 Feb. 2009, pp. 31-34.

In a monthly:

> Simpson, Mona. "Imperfect Union." Review of *Mrs. Woolf and the Servants*, by Alison Light, *The Atlantic,* Jan.-Feb. 2009, pp. 93-101.

Electronic Resources

13. Article from a Database Accessed through a Subscription Service

Apply the normal rules for citing a journal article, but follow this with the name of the subscription service in italics, and the Digital Object Identifier, if available.

Morano, Michele. "Boy Eats World." *Fourth Genre: Explorations in Nonfiction*, vol. 13, no. 2, 2011, pp. 31-35. *Project MUSE*, doi:10.1353/fge.2011.0029.

14. Article in an Online Magazine

Follow the author name and article title with the name of the magazine in italics, the date published, and the URL of the article.

Yoffe, Emily. "Full Metal Racket: Metal Detecting Is the World's Worst Hobby." *Slate*, 18 Aug. 2003, www.slate.com/articles/life/human _guinea_pig/2003/08/full_metal_racket .html.

15. Article in an Online Newspaper

Sisario, Ben. "Record Stores: Out of Sight, Not Obsolete." *The New York Times*, 29 Sept. 2009, www.nytimes.com/2009/09/30/arts/music/ 30private.html.

16. Online Review

Stevens, Dana. "Catcher in the MRI." Review of *50/50*, directed by Adam Levine, *Slate*, 30 Sept. 2011, www.slate.com/articles/arts/ movies/2011/09/_50_50_reviewed_joseph _gordon_levitt_and_seth_rogen_as_pals _vs_s.html.

17. Entry in an Online Reference Work

"Eschatology." *Merriam-Webster*, 7 Apr. 2016, www.merriam-webster.com/dictionary/ eschatology.

18. Work from a Website

"Wallace Stevens." *Poetry Foundation*, 2015, www.poetryfoundation.org/bio/wallace -stevens.

19. Entire Website

Website with editor:

Dutton, Dennis, editor. *Arts and Letters Daily*. Chronicle of Higher Education, www.aldaily .com. Accessed 2 Oct. 2009.

Website without an editor:

Academy of American Poets. 2016, poets.org. Accessed 13 Mar. 2015.

Personal website:

Mendelson, Edward. Home page. Columbia U, 2013, english.columbia.edu/people/profile/394.

20. Entire Web Log (Blog)

Holbo, John, editor. *The Valve*, www.thevalve.org/ go. Accessed 18 Mar. 2012.

21. Entry in a Wiki

"Pre-Raphaelite Brotherhood." *Wikipedia*, 25 Nov. 2013, wikipedia.org/wiki/Pre-Raphaelite _Brotherhood.

Other Sources

22. Film and Video

Follow the title with the director, notable performers, the distribution company, and the date of release. For films viewed on the web, follow this with the URL of the website used to view the film. If citing a particular individual's work on the film, you may begin the entry with his or her name before the title.

The Hurt Locker. Directed by Kathryn Bigelow, performances by Jeremy Renner, Anthony Mackie, Guy Pearce, and Ralph Fiennes, Summit Entertainment, 2009.

Viewed on the web (use the original distributor and release date):

Nayar, Vineet. "Employees First, Customers Second." *YouTube*, 9 June 2015, www.youtube.com/ watch?v=cCdu67s_C5E.

23. Interview

Include the name of the interviewer if it is some-one of note.

Personal interview:

Tripp, Lawrence. Personal interview, 14 Apr. 2014.

In print:

Dylan, Bob. "Who Is This Bob Dylan?" *Esquire*, 23 Jan. 2014, pp. 124+.

On the radio:

Gioia, Dana. Interview with Leonard Lopate. *The Leonard Lopate Show*, WNYC, 19 July 2004.

On the web:

> Gioia, Dana. Interview with Leonard Lopate. *The Leonard Lopate Show*, WNYC, 19 July 2004, www.wnyc.org/story/49925-dana-gioia.

24. Lecture or Speech

Viewed in person:

> Kass, Leon. "Looking for an Honest Man: Reflections of an Unlicensed Humanist." Jefferson Lecture in the Humanities, Warner Theatre, Washington, D.C., 22 May 2009.

Viewed on the web:

> Batuman, Elif. Boston College Lowell Humanities Series, 13 Oct. 2010, frontrow.bc.edu/program/batuman.

25. Podcast

> Carlin, Dan. "King of Kings." *Hardcore History Podcast*, 28 Oct. 2015, www.dancarlin.com/hardcore-history-56-kings-of-kings.

26. Work of Art or Photograph

In a museum:

> Hopper, Edward. *Nighthawks*. 1942, Art Institute, Chicago. Oil on canvas.

On the web:

> Thiebaud, Wayne. *Three Machines*. 1963, De Young Museum, San Francisco, shop.famsf.org/Product.do?code=T636P. Accessed 2 Oct. 2013.

In print:

> Clark, Edward. *Navy CPO Graham Jackson Plays "Goin' Home."* 1945, *The Great LIFE Photographers*, Bulfinch, 2004, pp. 78-79.

27. Map or Chart

In print:

> "U.S. Personal Savings Rate, 1929-1999." *Credit Card Nation: The Consequences of America's Addiction to Credit*, by Robert D. Manning, Basic Books, 2000, p. 100.

On the web:

> "1914 New Balkan States and Central Europe Map." *National Geographic*, maps.nationalgeographic.com/maps/print-collection/balkan-states-map.html. Accessed 25 Oct. 2013.

28. Cartoon or Comic Strip

In print:

> Vey, P. C. *The New Yorker*, 10 Nov. 2008, p. 54. Cartoon.

On the web:

> Zyglis, Adam. "City of Light." Buffalo News, 8 Nov. 2015, adamzyglis.buffalonews.com/2015/11/08/city-of-light/. Cartoon.

29. Advertisement

In print:

> Rosetta Stone. *Harper's*, Aug. 2008, p. 21. Advertisement.

On the web:

> Seamless. *The Washington Post*, www.washingtonpost.com. Accessed 4 Apr. 2016. Advertisement.

act The major subunit into which the action of a play is divided. The number of acts in a play typically ranges between one and five, and the acts are usually further divided into scenes.

ad hominem Latin for "to the man," this fallacy refers to the specific diversionary tactic of switching the argument from the issue at hand to the character of the other speaker. If you argue that a park in your community should not be renovated because the person supporting the plan was arrested during a domestic dispute, then you are guilty of using an ad hominem fallacy.

ad populum (bandwagon appeal) Latin for "to the people," this fallacy occurs when evidence used to defend an argument boils down to "everybody's doing it, so it must be a good thing to do."

> You should vote to elect Rachel Johnson — she has a strong lead in the polls.

Polling higher does not necessarily make Senator Johnson the "best" candidate; it only makes her the most popular.

allegory A literary work that portrays abstract ideas concretely. Characters in an allegory are frequently personifications of abstract ideas and are sometimes given names that refer to these ideas. *See Gabriel García Márquez, "A Very Old Man with Enormous Wings: A Tale for Children," p. 428.*

alliteration Repetition of the same consonant sound at the beginning of several words or syllables in sequence.

> their blond legs burn like brush.
>
> — Mark Strand, "Eating Poetry," p. 18

allusion Brief reference to a person, an event, or a place (real or fictitious) or to a work of art.

> With Mercury's
> Insignia on our sneakers,
>
> — Yusef Komunyakaa, "Slam, Dunk, & Hook," p. 50

analogy A comparison between two seemingly dissimilar things. Often, an analogy uses something simple or familiar to explain something complex or unfamiliar.

> Shawne Merriman is almost as big as the best offensive tackle who ever played and almost as fast as the best wide receiver who ever played. He is a rhinoceros who moves like a deer.
>
> — Chuck Klosterman, "Why We Look the Other Way," pp. 492–93

anaphora Repetition of a word or phrase at the beginning of successive phrases, clauses, or lines.

> But somewhere I read of the freedom of assembly. Somewhere I read of the freedom of speech. Somewhere I read of the freedom of press. Somewhere I read that the greatness of America is the right to protest for right.
>
> — Martin Luther King Jr., "I Have Been to the Mountaintop," p. 357

anecdote A brief story used to illustrate a point or claim.

annotation The taking of notes directly on a text. For an example of annotation, see pp. 952-53.

antagonist Character in a piece of literature who opposes the **protagonist**: while not necessarily an enemy, the antagonist creates or intensifies a conflict for the protagonist. An evil antagonist is a villain.

> In William Shakespeare's *Macbeth* (p. 254), the witches serve as antagonists, fueling Macbeth's ambition, and using misleading prophecies to prod him toward his downfall.

antithesis Opposition, or contrast, of ideas or words in a parallel construction.

> This supernatural soliciting
> Cannot be ill, cannot be good.
>
> — William Shakespeare, *Macbeth*, p. 260

appeal to false authority This fallacy occurs when someone who has no credibility to speak on an issue is cited as an authority. A TV star, for instance, is not a medical expert, though pharmaceutical advertisements often use such celebrities to endorse products.

> According to former congressional leader Ari Miller, the Himalayas have an estimated Yeti population of between 300 and 500 individuals.

archaic diction Old-fashioned or outdated choice of words.

> My river runs to thee:
> Blue sea, wilt welcome me?
>
> — Emily Dickinson, "My river runs to thee," p. 49

argument A process of reasoned inquiry. A persuasive discourse resulting in a coherent and considered movement from a claim to a conclusion.

Aristotelian triangle See **rhetorical triangle**.

assertion A statement that presents a claim or thesis.

assonance The repetition of vowel sounds in a sequence of words.

> The only roads are those that offer access.
> — Wisława Szymborska, "Utopia," p. 891

audience The listener, viewer, or reader of a text. Most texts are likely to have multiple audiences.

> Understanding his audience well, President Abraham Lincoln used a series of biblical allusions in his Second Inaugural Address to urge unity between the North and South at the end of the Civil War:

bandwagon appeal See **ad populum (bandwagon appeal).**

begging the question A fallacy in which a claim is based on evidence or support that is in doubt. It "begs" the question whether the support itself is sound.

> Giving students easy access to a wealth of facts and resources online allows them to develop critical thinking skills.

bias A prejudice or preconceived notion that prevents a person from approaching a topic in a neutral or an objective way. While you can be biased *toward* something, the most common usage has a negative connotation.

blank verse Unrhymed **iambic pentameter**. *See William Shakespeare, "The Seven Ages of Man," p. 158.*

caesura A pause within a line of poetry, sometimes punctuated, sometimes not, that often mirrors natural speech.

> Once Flick played for the high-school team, the Wizards.
> He was good: in fact, the best.
> — John Updike, "Ex-Basketball Player," p. 104

catharsis Refers to the emotional release felt by the audience at the end of a tragic drama. The term comes from Aristotle's *Poetics*, in which he explains this frequently felt relief in terms of a purification of the emotions caused by watching the tragic events. (*Catharsis* means "purgation" or "purification" in Greek.)

character A person depicted in a narrative. While this term generally refers to human beings, it can also include animals or inanimate objects that are given human characteristics. Several more specific terms are used to refer to types of characters frequently employed by authors:

> **flat character** A character embodying only one or two traits and who lacks character development; for this reason, a flat character is also called a static character. Often such characters exist only to provide background or adequate motivation for a protagonist's actions.
>
> > *In* Don Quixote *(p. 345),* Sancho Panza is a stock character. He is a faithful servant to Don Quixote but shows little depth or complexity.
>
> **round character** A character who exhibits a range of emotions and evolves over the course of the story.
>
> > In *Don Quixote* (p. 345), Don Quixote himself is a round character. He has complex motivations and various facets to his personality, and our understanding of him evolves over the course of the story.

characterization The method by which the author builds, or reveals, a character; it can be direct or indirect. *Indirect characterization* means that an author shows rather than tells us what a character is like through what the character says, does, or thinks or through what others say about the character. *Direct characterization* occurs when a narrator tells the reader who a character is by describing the background, motivation, temperament, or appearance of a character.

circular reasoning A fallacy in which the argument repeats the claim as a way to provide evidence.

> You can't give me a C; I'm an A student!

claim Also called an assertion or proposition, a claim states the argument's main idea or position. A claim differs from a topic or subject in that a claim has to be arguable.

complex sentence A sentence that includes one independent clause and at least one dependent clause.

> Every opportunity I got, I used to read this book.
> — Frederick Douglass, "Narrative of the Life of Frederick Douglass," p. 756

compound sentence A sentence that includes at least two independent clauses.

> He beat his friend until his friend couldn't take any more beating, and then he beat him some more.
> — Nathan Englander, "Free Fruit for Young Widows," p. 446

concession An acknowledgment that an opposing argument may be true or reasonable. In a strong argument, a concession is usually accompanied by a refutation challenging the validity of the opposing argument.

> Throw in humanity's jealousies, violence, and constant anxieties, and the transhumanist project begins to look downright reasonable.
> — Francis Fukuyama, "Transhumanism," p. 928.

conflict The tension, opposition, or struggle that drives a plot. External conflict is the opposition or tension between two characters or forces. Internal conflict occurs within a character. Conflict usually arises between the protagonist and the antagonist in a story.

> In *Macbeth* (p. 254), the internal conflict is between Macbeth's ambition and his conscience. The external conflict is between Macbeth and the other rulers he is trying to remove in order to gain power.

connotation and denotation Connotation refers to meanings or associations that readers have with a word beyond its dictionary definition, or denotation. Connotations are often positive or negative, and they often greatly affect the author's tone. Consider the connotations of the words below, all of which mean "overweight."

> That cat is *plump*. That cat is *fat*. That cat is *obese*.

context The circumstances, atmosphere, attitudes, and events surrounding a **text**.

> "Do you want to know why I can care for a man who once beat me? Because to a story there is context. There is always context in life."
> — Nathan Englander, "Free Fruit for Young Widows," p. 448.

counterargument An opposing argument to the one a writer is putting forward. Rather than ignoring a counterargument, a strong writer will usually address it through the process of concession and refutation.

> It might be argued that a genetically enhanced athlete, like a drug-enhanced athlete, would have an unfair advantage over his unenhanced competitors.
> — Michael Sandel, from "The Case against Perfection," p. 417

cumulative sentence A sentence that completes the main idea at the beginning of the sentence and then builds and adds on.

> Even when I'm not working, I'm as likely as not to be foraging in the Web's data thickets—reading and writing e-mails, scanning headlines and blog posts, following Facebook updates, watching video streams, downloading music, or just tripping lightly from link to link to link.
> — Nicholas Carr, *The Shallows*, p. 19

deduction Deduction is a logical process wherein you reach a conclusion by starting with a general principle or universal truth (a major premise) and applying it to a specific case (a minor premise). The process of deduction is usually demonstrated in the form of a syllogism:

> **Major Premise** Exercise contributes to better health.
> **Minor Premise** Yoga is a type of exercise.
> **Conclusion** Yoga contributes to better health.

diction A speaker's choice of words. Analysis of diction looks at these choices and what they add to the speaker's message.

either-or (false dilemma) In this fallacy, the speaker presents two extreme options as the only possible choices.

> Either we agree to higher taxes, or our grandchildren will be mired in debt.

end rhyme See **rhyme**.

enjambment A poetic technique in which one line ends without a pause and continues to the next line to complete its meaning; also referred to as a "run- on line."

> About suffering they were never wrong,
> The Old Masters: how well they understood
> Its human position; how it takes place
> While someone else is eating or opening a window
>   or just walking dully along;
> — W. H. Auden, "Musée des Beaux Arts," p. 318

epigram A short, witty statement designed to surprise an audience or a reader.

> And what is a kiss, when all is done?
> A promise given under seal—a vow
> Taken before the shrine of memory—
> A signature acknowledged—a rosy dot
> Over the *i* of Loving—
> — Edmond Rostand, *Cyrano de Bergerac*,
> pp. 718-19

equivocation A fallacy that uses a term with two or more meanings in an attempt to misrepresent or deceive.

> We will bring our enemies to justice, or we will bring justice to them.

ethos Greek for "character." Speakers appeal to ethos to demonstrate that they are credible and trustworthy to speak on a given topic. Ethos is established by both who you are and what you say.

"As a senior at Upper Arlington High School, I am extremely proud of both my school and community. Except for two years in private education, I have spent my entire life in the Upper Arlington School District and know firsthand what an amazing system it is."

— Owen Dirkse, letter to the editor of the *Columbus Dispatch*, p. 69

eye rhyme See **rhyme**.

fallacy See **logical fallacies**.

false dilemma See **either-or**.

faulty analogy A fallacy that occurs when an analogy compares things that are not comparable. For instance, to argue that we should legalize human euthanasia, since we all agree that it is humane to put terminally ill animals to sleep, ignores significant emotional and ethical differences between the ways we view humans and animals.

figurative language (figure of speech) Nonliteral language, often evoking strong imagery, sometimes referred to as a trope. Figures of speech often compare one thing to another either explicitly (using simile) or implicitly (using metaphor). Other forms of figurative language include **personification**, **paradox**, overstatement **(hyperbole)**, **understatement**, **metonymy**, **synecdoche**, and **irony**.

form Refers to the defining structural characteristics of a work, especially a poem (i.e., meter and rhyme scheme). Often poets work within set forms, such as the **sonnet**, which require adherence to fixed conventions.

hasty generalization A fallacy in which a faulty conclusion is reached because of inadequate evidence.

Smoking isn't bad for you; my great aunt smoked a pack a day and lived to be ninety.

hortative sentence Sentence that exhorts, urges, entreats, implores, or calls to action.

First, though, we must wake up to what our schools really are: laboratories of experimentation on young minds, drill centers for the habits and attitudes that corporate society demands.

— John Taylor Gatto, "Against School," p. 211

hyperbole Deliberate exaggeration used for emphasis or to produce a comic or an ironic effect; an overstatement to make a point.

In the first place, that stuff bores me, and in the second place, my parents would have about two hemorrhages apiece if I told anything pretty personal about them.

— J. D. Salinger, "The Catcher in the Rye," p. 48

iambic pentameter An iamb, the most common metrical foot in English poetry, is made up of an unstressed syllable followed by a stressed one. Iambic pentameter, then, is a rhythmic meter containing five iambs. Unrhymed iambic pentameter is called **blank verse**.

If we are mark'd to die, we are enow
To do our country loss: and if to live,
— William Shakespeare, "The St. Crispin's Day Speech," p. 569

imagery A description of how something looks, feels, tastes, smells, or sounds. Imagery may use literal or figurative language to appeal to the senses.

All at once she bloomed. Huge, enormous, beautiful to look at from the salmon-pink feather on the tip of her hat down to the little rosebuds of her toes. I couldn't take my eyes off her tiny shoes.
— Sandra Cisneros, "No Speak English," p. 761

imperative sentence Sentence used to command or enjoin.

A bell clanged upon her heart. She felt him seize her hand:
"Come!"

— James Joyce, "Eveline," p. 165

Incongruity Something unexpected, out of place, or inconsistent. This term is generally used in English class to refer to **irony**, which relies on incongruity for its effect.

induction From the Latin *inducere*, "to lead into," induction is a logical process wherein you reason from particulars to universals, using specific cases in order to draw a conclusion, which is also called a generalization.

Regular exercise promotes weight loss.
Exercise lowers stress levels.
Exercise improves mood and outlook.

Generalization Exercise contributes to better health.

internal rhyme See **rhyme**.

inversion Inverted order of words in a sentence (deviation from the standard subject-verb-object order).

Not a people, race, or class striving for freedom is there anywhere in the world that has not made our axioms the chief weapon of the struggle.
— Carrie Chapman Catt, "Women's Suffrage Is Inevitable," p. 385

irony, dramatic Tension created by the contrast between what a character says or thinks and what the audience or readers know to be true; as a result of this technique, some words and actions in a story or play take on a different meaning for the reader than they do for the characters. Of the Weird Sisters, Macbeth says:

> "Infected be the air whereon they ride,
> And damned all those that trust them!"
> — William Shakespeare, *Macbeth*, p. 296

irony, situational A discrepancy between what is expected and what actually happens. *See Jason Edward Harrington, "Do You Like Me? Click Yes or No," p. 834.*

irony, verbal A figure of speech that occurs when a speaker or character says one thing but means something else or when what is said is the opposite of what is expected, creating a noticeable incongruity. *Sarcasm* involves verbal irony used derisively.

> And then the lover,
> Sighing like furnace, with a woeful ballad
> Made to his mistress' eyebrow.
> — William Shakespeare, "The Seven Ages of Man,"
> p. 159

juxtaposition Placement of two things closely together to emphasize similarities or differences.

> Behold our Uncle Sam floating the banner with one hand, "Taxation without representation is tyranny," and with the other seizing the billions of dollars paid in taxes by women to whom he refuses "representation."
> — Carrie Chapman Catt, "Women's Suffrage Is Inevitable," p. 383

logical fallacies Logical fallacies are potential vulnerabilities or weaknesses in an argument. They often arise from a failure to make a logical connection between the claim and the evidence used to support it.

logos Greek for "embodied thought." Speakers appeal to logos, or reason, by offering clear, rational ideas and using specific details, examples, facts, statistics, or expert testimony to back them up.

> "According to a 2014 report from Amnesty International, "only nine countries have continuously executed in each of the past five years—Bangladesh, China, Iran, Iraq, North Korea, Saudi Arabia, Sudan, U.S.A. and Yemen."
> — Charles Blow, from "Eye-for-an-Eye Incivility"
> p. 67

metaphor Figure of speech that compares two things without using *like* or *as*.

Suddenly his shoulders get a lot wider,
the way Houdini would expand his body
while people were putting him in chains.
> — Sharon Olds, "My Son the Man," p. 154

meter The formal, regular organization of stressed and unstressed syllables, measured in feet. A foot is distinguished by the number of syllables it contains and how stress is placed on the syllables — stressed (´) or unstressed (˘). There are five typical feet in English verse: iamb (˘ ´), trochee (´ ˘), anapest (˘ ˘ ´), dactyl (´ ˘ ˘), and spondee (´ ´). Some meters dictate the number of feet per line, the most common being tetrameter, pentameter, and hexameter, having four, five, and six feet, respectively.

metonymy Figure of speech in which something is represented by another thing that is related to it or emblematic of it.

> The pen is mightier than the sword.

modifier An adjective, an adverb, a phrase, or a clause that modifies a noun, pronoun, or verb. The purpose of a modifier is usually to describe, focus, or qualify.

> On a humid Monday, four cult members waited at the campus gate and waylaid a professor driving a red Mercedes.
> — Chimamanda Ngozi Adichie,
> "Cell One," p. 438

mood The feeling or atmosphere created by a text.

near rhyme See **rhyme**.

occasion The time and place a speech is given or a piece is written.

> When Rachel Carson published *Silent Spring*, there was emerging evidence that DDT softened the shells of bird eggs (particularly those of bald eagles and peregrine falcons), resulting in a dramatic drop in the birds' population.

onomatopoeia Use of words that refer to sounds and whose pronunciations mimic those sounds.

> The cars' tires laid behind them on the snowy street a complex trail of beige chunks like crenellated castle walls. I had stepped on some earlier; they squeaked.
> — Annie Dillard, "An American
> Childhood," p. 466

oxymoron A paradox made up of two seemingly contradictory words.

We outmaneuvered the footwork
Of bad angels.
— Yusef Komunyakaa, "Slam, Dunk, & Hook," p. 50

paradox A statement or situation that is seemingly contradictory on the surface but delivers an ironic truth.

Spanish
is simple and baroque,
— Marjorie Agosín, "English," p. 781

parallelism Similarity of structure in a pair or series of related words, phrases, or clauses.

The idea and feeling that the world was made, and life given, for the happiness of all, and not for the ambition, or pride, or luxury, of one, or of a few, are pouring in, like a resistless tide. . . .
— Horace Mann, from *The Common School Journal,*
p. 213

passive voice A sentence employs passive voice when the subject doesn't act but rather is acted on.

Foxes, rabbits, and bobolinks are starved out of their homes or dismembered by the sickle mower.
— Barbara Kingsolver, *Animal, Vegetable, Miracle*,
p. 107

pathos Greek for "suffering" or "experience." Speakers appeal to pathos to emotionally motivate their audience. More specific appeals to pathos might play on the audience's values, desires, and hopes, on the one hand, or fears and prejudices, on the other.

". . . I would watch God's children in their magnificent trek from the dark dungeons of Egypt through, or rather across the Red Sea. . ."
— Martin Luther King Jr., "I Have Been to the Mountaintop," p. 355.

persona Greek for "mask." The face or character that a speaker shows to his or her audience.

"I have done whatever I did, both as an individual and as a leader of my people, because of my experience in South Africa and my own proudly felt African background . . ." Nelson Mandela, "An Ideal for Which I Am Prepared to Die," p. 365.

personification Attribution of a lifelike quality to an inanimate object or an idea.

around our group I could hear the wilderness listen.
— William Stafford, "Traveling through the Dark," p. 462

plot The arrangement of events in a narrative. Almost always, a conflict is central to a plot, and traditionally a plot develops in accordance with the following model: exposition, rising action, climax, falling action, denouement. There can be more than one sequence of events in a work, although typically there is one major sequence along with other minor sequences. These minor sequences are called subplots.

polemic Greek for "hostile." An aggressive argument that tries to establish the superiority of one opinion over all others, a polemic generally does not concede that opposing opinions have any merit.

point of view The perspective from which a work is told. The most common narrative vantage points are

first person Told by a narrator who is a character in the story and who refers to himself or herself as "I." First person narrators are sometimes unreliable narrators because they don't always see the big picture or because they might be biased.

second person Though rare, some stories are told using second person pronouns (*you*). This casts the reader as a character in the story.

third person limited omniscient Told by a narrator who relates the action using third person pronouns (*he, she, it*). This narrator is usually privy to the thoughts and actions of only one character.

third person omniscient Told by a narrator using third person pronouns. This narrator is privy to the thoughts and actions of all the characters in the story.

post hoc ergo propter hoc This fallacy is Latin for "after which therefore because of which," meaning that it is incorrect to always claim that something is a cause just because it happened earlier. One may loosely summarize this fallacy by saying that correlation does not imply causation.

We elected Johnson as president and look where it got us: hurricanes, floods, stock market crashes.

propaganda The spread of ideas and information to further a cause. In its negative sense, propaganda is the use of rumors, lies, disinformation, and scare tactics in order to damage or promote a cause.

protagonist The main character in a work; often a hero or heroine, but not always.

In Shakespeare's *Macbeth*, Macbeth is the protagonist, though certainly not a hero.

1025

pun A play on words that derives its humor from the replacement of one word with another that has a similar pronunciation or spelling but a different meaning. A pun can also derive humor from the use of a single word that has more than one meaning.

purpose The goal the speaker wants to achieve.

> For example, Malala Yousafzai wrote her blog primarily to call attention to what she believed was an unfair situation — limitations on the educational opportunities available to women in her culture — but she also intended to criticize the regime that created such oppression.

qualified argument An argument that is not absolute. It acknowledges the merits of an opposing view but develops a stronger case for its own position.

qualifier Qualifiers are words like *usually, probably, maybe, in most cases,* and *most likely* that are used to temper claims a bit, making them less absolute.

> **Unqualified** Dogs are more obedient than cats.
> **Qualified** Dogs are generally more obedient than cats.

qualitative evidence Evidence supported by reason, tradition, or precedent.

quantitative evidence Quantitative evidence includes things that can be measured, cited, counted, or otherwise represented in numbers — for instance, statistics, surveys, polls, and census information.

red herring A type of logical fallacy wherein the speaker relies on distraction to derail an argument, usually by skipping to a new or an irrelevant topic. The term derives from the dried fish that trainers used to distract dogs when teaching them to hunt foxes.

> We can debate these regulations until the cows come home, but what the American people want to know is, when are we going to end this partisan bickering?

rhetoric Aristotle defined rhetoric as "the faculty of observing in any given case the available means of persuasion." In other words, it is the art of finding ways of persuading an audience.

rhetorical appeals Rhetorical techniques used to persuade an audience by emphasizing what they find most important or compelling. The three major appeals are to **ethos** (character), **logos** (reason), and **pathos** (emotion).

rhetorical question Figure of speech in the form of a question posed for rhetorical effect rather than for the purpose of getting an answer.

> So why is it, please explain, that you're in our stories but we're not in yours?
> — Kamila Shamsie, "The Storytellers of Empire,"
> p. 565

rhetorical situation The context surrounding a text, including who the **speaker** is, what the **subject** is, who the **audience** is, and the relationship among these three elements. The rhetorical situation also includes the author's purpose, and the occasion that has prompted the text. See **rhetorical triangle**.

rhetorical triangle (Aristotelian triangle) A diagram that illustrates the interrelationship among the speaker, audience, and subject in determining a text.

rhyme The poetic repetition of the same (or similar) vowel sounds or of vowel and consonant combinations. A rhyme at the end of two or more lines of poetry is called an end rhyme. A rhyme that occurs within a line is called an internal rhyme. A rhyme that pairs sounds that are similar but not exactly the same is called a near rhyme or a slant rhyme. A rhyme that only works because the words look the same is called an eye rhyme or a sight rhyme. Rhyme often follows a pattern, called a rhyme scheme.

> **end rhyme**
> Bent double, like old beggars under sacks,
> Knock-kneed, coughing like hags, we cursed
>   through sludge,
> Till on the haunting flares we turned our backs
> And towards our distant rest began to trudge.
> — Wilfred Owen, "Dulce et Decorum Est," p. 567

> **internal rhyme**
> continually confused the light. In flight,
> — Li-Young Lee, "For a New Citizen of These
>   United States," p. 618

> **near rhyme or slant rhyme**
> What immortal hand or eye,
> Could frame thy fearful symmetry?
> — William Blake, "The Tyger," p. 53

> **eye rhyme**
> My river waits reply.
> Oh sea, look graciously!
> — Emily Dickinson, "My river runs to thee," p. 49

satire The use of irony or sarcasm as a means of critique, usually of a society or an individual.

setting Where and when a story takes place.

> She sat at the window watching the evening invade the avenue. Her head was leaned against

the window curtains and in her nostrils was the odour of dusty cretonne. She was tired.

Few people passed. The man out of the last house passed on his way home; she heard his footsteps clacking along the concrete pavement and afterwards crunching on the cinder path before the new red houses. One time there used to be a field there in which they used to play every evening with other people's children. Then a man from Belfast bought the field and built houses in it — not like their little brown houses but bright brick houses with shining roofs.

> — James Joyce, "Eveline," p. 162

simile A figure of speech used to explain or clarify an idea by comparing it explicitly to something else, using the words *like*, *as*, or *as though*.

> Then the whining schoolboy, with his satchel
> And shining morning face, creeping like snail
> Unwillingly to school.
>> — William Shakespeare, "The Seven
>> Ages of Man," p. 159

slant rhyme See **rhyme**.

slippery slope fallacy In this fallacy, also known as the "floodgates fallacy," the effect the speaker is claiming is out of proportion to the cause, or illogical based on the cause.

> Statistics go to show that in most equal suffrage states, Colorado particularly, that divorces have greatly increased since the adoption of the equal suffrage amendment, showing that it has been a home destroyer. Crime has also increased due to lack of the mothers in the home.
>> — J. B. Sanford, "Argument against Senate
>> Constitutional Amendment No. 8," p. 78

SOAPS A mnemonic device that stands for Subject, Occasion, Audience, Purpose, and Speaker. It is a handy way to remember the various elements that make up the rhetorical situation.

sonnet, Shakespearean Also known as the English sonnet, this poem has fourteen lines composed of three quatrains and a couplet, and its rhyme scheme is *abab cdcd*, *efef*, *gg*. See Sherman Alexie, "Facebook Sonnet," p. 811.

sound The musical quality of poetry, as created through techniques such as **rhyme**, **enjambment**, **caesura**, **alliteration**, **assonance**, **onomatopoeia**, and **meter**.

speaker The person or group who creates a text. This might be a politician who delivers a speech, a

commentator who writes an article, an artist who draws a political cartoon, or even a company that commissions an advertisement.

> We know, for example, that Harriet Beecher Stowe was a committed abolitionist, and we also know that she was a devout Christian. Both aspects of her background greatly influenced how she presented her argument in Uncle Tom's Cabin.

straw man A fallacy that occurs when a speaker chooses a deliberately poor or oversimplified example in order to ridicule and refute an idea.

> Politician X proposes that we put astronauts on Mars in the next four years.

> Politician Y ridicules this proposal by saying that his opponent is looking for "little green men in outer space."

style The way a literary work is written. Style is produced by an author's choices in **diction**, **syntax**, **imagery**, **figurative language**, and other literary elements.

subject The topic of a text. What the text is *about*.

> Harriet Beecher Stowe's subject was slavery in the United States. Carson's was DDT specifically, pesticides in general.

symbol A setting, an object, or an event in a story that carries more than literal meaning and therefore represents something significant to understanding the meaning of a work of literature.

> In "The Tell-Tale Heart" (p. 54), the maddening heart beat represents the character's guilty conscience.

synecdoche Figure of speech that uses a part to represent the whole.

> If I had sneezed, I wouldn't have been around here in 1962, when Negroes in Albany, Georgia, decided to straighten their backs up. And whenever men and women straighten their backs up, they are going somewhere, because a man can't ride your back unless it is bent.
>> — Martin Luther King Jr., "I Have Been
>> to the Mountaintop," pp. 361–62

syntax The arrangement of words into phrases, clauses, and sentences. This includes word order (subject-verb-object, for instance, or an inverted structure); the length and structure of sentences (simple, **compound**,

complex, or compound-complex); and such devices as **parallelism**, **juxtaposition**, and **antithesis**.

synthesis Combining two or more ideas in order to create something more complex in support of a new idea.

text While this term generally refers to the written word, in the humanities it has come to mean any cultural product that can be "read" — meaning not just consumed and comprehended but also investigated. This includes fiction, nonfiction, poetry, political cartoons, fine art, photography, performances, fashion, cultural trends, and much more.

theme The underlying issues or ideas of a work.

> *Romeo and Juliet* suggests that love is a destructive force that, once unleashed, cannot be controlled.

tone A speaker's attitude toward the subject as conveyed by the speaker's stylistic and rhetorical choices.

tragedy A serious dramatic work in which the protagonist experiences a series of unfortunate reversals due to some character trait, referred to as a *tragic flaw*. The most common tragic flaw is *hubris*, Greek for *pride*. *See William Shakespeare*, Macbeth, *p. 254.*

understatement A figure of speech in which something is presented as less important, dire, urgent, good, and so on than it actually is, often for satiric or comical effect. Also called *litotes*, it is the opposite of **hyperbole**.

wit In rhetoric, the use of laughter, humor, irony, and satire in the confirmation or refutation of an argument.

CREDITS

Michael Sandel, from "The Case against Perfection," from *The Atlantic*, April 2004. For a fuller version of this essay, see Michael J. Sandel, "The Case against Perfection: Ethics in the Age of Genetic Engineering," Harvard University Press, 2007. Reprinted with permission of the author.

Kai Sato, from "The Case for High School Sports" first published in *The Huffington Post*, Sept. 23, 2013. Reprinted by permission of the author.

Marjane Satrapi, "The Lesson" from PERSEPOLIS: THE STORY OF A CHILDHOOD. Translation copyright © 2003 by L'Association, Paris, France. Used by permission of Pantheon Books, an imprint of the Knopf Doubleday Publishing Group, a division of Penguin Random House LLC. All rights reserved. Any third party use of this material, outside of this publication, is prohibited. Interested parties must apply directly to Penguin Random House LLC for permission.

Patrick Sawer, from "Cyberbullying Victims Speak Out" from *The Telegraph*, Nov. 13, 2011. Copyright 2011 by Telegraph Media Group Ltd. Reprinted by permission of the publisher.

Katey Schultz, "Deuce Out" from FLASHES OF WAR (2014). Used by permission of Apprentice House Press.

William Shakespeare, selected annotations by David Bevington, editor, to AS YOU LIKE IT from THE COMPLETE WORKS OF SHAKESPEARE, updated 4th ed. Copyright © 1997. Complete annotations to MACBETH from THE COMPLETE WORKS OF SHAKESPEARE, updated 4th ed. Copyright © 1997. Selected annotations to HENRY VIII from THE COMPLETE WORKS OF SHAKESPEARE, updated 4th ed. Copyright © 1997. Selected annotations to THE LIFE OF HENRY V, from THE COMPLETE WORKS OF SHAKESPEARE, updated 4th ed. Copyright © 1997. Reprinted by permission of Pearson Education, Inc., New York, NY.

Kamila Shamsie, excerpt from "The Storytellers of Empire" from *Guernica*, Feb. 1, 2012, is reprinted by permission of the publisher.

Jane Shore, "Happy Family" from HAPPY FAMILY: POEMS (Picador 2000) is reprinted by permission of the author.

Kevin Sites, with edits approved, text from pp. 5–7, 8–11, 13–23, 24–27 from IN THE HOT ZONE: ONE MAN, ONE YEAR, TWENTY WARS. Copyright © 2007 by Kevin Sites. Reprinted by permission of HarperCollins Publishers.

Theodore Sizer, from HORACE'S SCHOOL. Copyright © 1992 by Theodore R. Sizer. Reprinted by permission of Houghton Mifflin Harcourt Publishing Company. All rights reserved.

Lenore Skenazy, "Why I Let My 9-Year-Old Ride the Subway Alone" from *The Sun*, April 1, 2008, is reprinted by permission of the author.

William Stafford, "Traveling through the Dark" from ASK ME: 100 ESSENTIAL POEMS. Copyright © 2014 by the Estate of William Stafford. Reprinted with the permission of The Permissions Company, Inc. on behalf of Graywolf Press, Minneapolis, Minnesota, www.graywolfpress.org.

Kory Stamper, "Slang for the Ages" from *The New York Times*, Oct. 3, 2014. Copyright © 2014 by The New York Times. All rights reserved. Used by permission and protected by the Copyright Laws of the United States. The printing, copying, redistribution, or retransmission of this Content without express written permission is prohibited.

John Stossel, from "What's Fair?" published on *Townhall.com*, March 11, 2015. Reprinted by permission of Creators Syndicate.

Mark Strand, "Eating Poetry" from SELECTED POEMS by Mark Strand, copyright © 1979, 1980 by Mark Strand. Used by permission

of Alfred A. Knopf, an imprint of the Knopf Doubleday Publishing Group, a division of Penguin Random House LLC. All rights reserved. Any third party use of this material, outside of this publication, is prohibited. Interested parties must apply directly to Penguin Random House LLC for permission.

Wisława Szymborska, "A Contribution to Statistics" and "Utopia" from POEMS NEW AND COLLECTED 1957–1997 by Wisława Szymborska, translated from the Polish by Stanislaw Baranczak and Claire Cavanagh. English translation copyright © 1998 by Houghton Mifflin Harcourt Publishing Company. Reprinted by permission of Houghton Mifflin Harcourt Publishing Company. All rights reserved.

Amy Tan, "Rules of the Game" from THE JOY LUCK CLUB, copyright © 1989 by Amy Tan. Used by permission of G. P. Putnam's Sons, an imprint of Penguin Publishing Group, a division of Penguin Random House LLC.

Clive Thompson, "Brave New World of Digital Intimacy" from *The New York Times Magazine*, Sept. 7, 2008 is reprinted by permission of Featurewell.com.

Sherry Turkle, from ALONE TOGETHER. Copyright © 2012 by Sherry Turkle. Reprinted by permission of Basic Books, a member of the Perseus Books Group.

Brian Turner, "2000 lbs." from HERE, BULLET. Copyright © 2005 by Brian Turner. Reprinted with the permission of The Permissions Company, Inc. on behalf of Alice James Books, www .alicejamesbooks.org.

John Updike, "Ex-Basketball Player" from COLLECTED POEMS, 1953–1993. Copyright © 1993 by John Updike. "A & P" from PIGEON FEATHERS AND OTHER STORIES, COPYRIGHT © 1962, copyright renewed 1990 by John Updike. Used by permission of Alfred A. Knopf, an imprint of the Knopf Doubleday Publishing Group, a division of Penguin Random House LLC. All rights reserved. Any third party use of this material, outside of this publication, is prohibited. Interested parties must apply directly to Penguin Random House LLC for permission.

Kurt Vonnegut, "Harrison Bergeron" copyright © 1961 by Kurt Vonnegut, Jr. from WELCOME TO THE MONKEY HOUSE. Used by permission of Dell Publishing, an imprint of Random House, a division of Penguin Random House LLC. All rights reserved. Any third party use of this material, outside of this publication, is prohibited. Interested parties must apply directly to Penguin Random House LLC for permission.

Vu Bao, "The Man Who Stained His Soul," translated by Ho Ahn Thai, edited by Wayne Karlin from THE OTHER SIDE OF HEAVEN: POSTWAR FICTION BY VIETNAMESE AND AMERICAN WRITERS, ed. by Wayne Karlin, Le Minh Khue and Truong Vu. Copyright © 1995 by Wayne Karlin, Le Minh Khue and Truong Vu. Reprinted by permission of Wayne Karlin c/o Harold Ober Associates.

Elie Wiesel, from "Nobel Prize Acceptance Speech," Dec. 10, 1986, is reprinted by permission of The Nobel Foundation. Copyright © 1986 by The Nobel Foundation.

William Carlos Williams, "Landscape with the Fall of Icarus" from THE COLLECTED POEMS: VOLUME 11, 1939–1962. Copyright © 1962 by William Carlos Williams. Reprinted by permission of New Directions Publishing Corp.

Malala Yousafzai, "Speech to the United Nations," copyright © 2013 by Malala Yousafzai. Reproduced with permission of Curtis Brown Group Ltd., London, on behalf of Malala Yousafzai.

INDEX